P9-CAZ-618

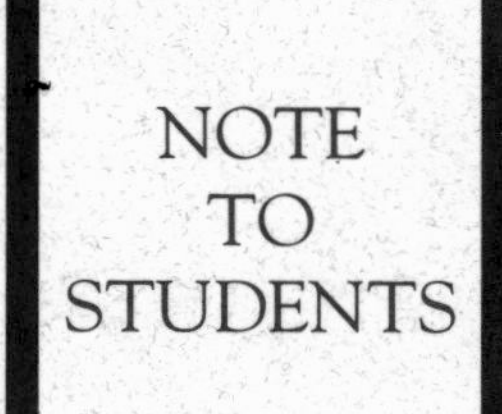

NOTE TO STUDENTS

Accounting is a stimulating, rewarding field of study. To be effective, professionals in all areas of business, such as finance, production, marketing, personnel, and general management, must have a good understanding of accounting. In addition, women and men whose careers are in nonbusiness areas can use a knowledge of accounting to perform more effectively in society. This text was written to provide the basic knowledge of accounting so essential for your future career.

As you begin your study of accounting, you may find the following suggestions helpful:

- Read each chapter objective before you begin studying a chapter.
- Take a few minutes and scan the chapter to get a flavor of the material before you begin a detailed reading of the chapter.
- As you read each chapter, you may wish to underline points that you feel are especially important. Also, you should give special attention to key terms which are identified in color when they first appear in the chapter.
- After reading the text of the chapter, carefully study the Chapter Review, giving special attention to the following items:

Key Points. You should thoroughly understand each of the key points presented in the chapter. If you have difficulty understanding any of the key points, review the section of the chapter where the key point is discussed and illustrated. The key points are organized according to the chapter objectives.

Key Terms. You should be able to define each key term. If you cannot, refer to the page of the chapter where the key term is first presented and discussed. You may also refer to the Glossary at the end of the text, where all of the key terms are listed in alphabetical order and defined.

Self-Examination Questions. Answer each of the self-examination questions and check your answers by referring to the explanation of the correct response, which is presented at the end of the chapter.

Illustrative Problem. Study the illustrative problem and its suggested solution. Each illustrative problem applies the concepts and principles discussed in the chapter to a problem situation. If you have difficulty understanding the illustrative problem, refer to the section of the chapter where the applicable concepts and principles are discussed and illustrated.

- Work all assigned homework. In many cases, the homework is related to specific chapter illustrations, and you may find it helpful to review the relevant chapter sections before you begin a homework assignment.
- Take notes during class lectures and discussions and give attention to the topics covered by your instructor.
- In reviewing for examinations, keep in mind those topics that your instructor has emphasized, and review your class notes and the text.
- If you feel you need additional aid, you may find the Study Guide that accompany this textbook helpful. The Study Guide can be ordered from South-Western Publishing Co. by your college or university bookstore.

PRINCIPLES OF

FINANCIAL & MANAGERIAL ACCOUNTING

THIRD EDITION

CARL S. WARREN, PhD, CPA, CMA, CIA

PROFESSOR OF ACCOUNTING
UNIVERSITY OF GEORGIA, ATHENS

&

PHILIP E. FESS, PhD, CPA

PROFESSOR EMERITUS OF ACCOUNTANCY
UNIVERSITY OF ILLINOIS, CHAMPAIGN-URBANA

COLLEGE DIVISION South-Western Publishing Co.

Cincinnati Ohio

Acquisitions Editor: Mark Hubble
Developmental Editor: Ken Martin
Production Editor: Nancy J. Ahr
Associate Editor: Robin Ruggles Schuster
Cover Design: Siebert Design
Cover Photograph: Laurie Rubin
Marketing Manager: Randy Haubner

AB60CA

Copyright © 1992
by SOUTH-WESTERN PUBLISHING CO.
Cincinnati, Ohio

ALL RIGHTS RESERVED

The text of this publication, or any part thereof, may not be reproduceır transmitted in any form or by any means, electronic or mechanical, includinghotocopying, recording, storage in an information retrieval system, or otherwise, wout the prior written permission of the publisher.

4 5 6 7 8 9 Ki 9 8 7 6 5 4 3

Printed in the United States of America

Library of Congress Cataloging-in-Publication Data

Warren, Carl S.
Principles of financial and managerial accounting / Carl S. Warren, Philip E. Fess. -- 3rd ed.
p. cm.
Includes index.
ISBN 0-538-81407-1
1. Accounting. 2. Managerial accounting. I. Fess, Philip E. II. Title
HF5635.W27 1992
657--dc20

91-648
CIP

PREFACE

The third edition of PRINCIPLES OF FINANCIAL AND MANAGERIAL ACCOUNTING is a student-oriented text. It presents the fundamental accounting concepts and principles in a business setting in a logical, concise, and clear manner. The text allows instructors to focus on clarifying issues and increasing students' understanding of accounting as it is applied in serving not only the business world but all of society. Such an approach meets the needs of students planning careers in accounting as well as in business administration, in liberal arts areas, in law, or in other disciplines.

IMPORTANT FEATURES OF THE THIRD EDITION

The basic foundation that made the first two editions of this text successful has been significantly enhanced in the third edition. In giving equal emphasis to financial accounting and managerial accounting, the text provides the most comprehensive and up-to-date coverage of any accounting principles text. New managerial chapters have been added and new material has been integrated in existing managerial chapters. In addition, many new features in both the text and its ancillaries make this complete package a superb choice for students of principles of accounting.

Financial Accounting

Financial accounting topics in Chapters 1-14 have been significantly reorganized or expanded.

The Accounting Cycle. The accounting cycle for a business enterprise is presented in the first four chapters. In Chapter 1, the basic accounting concepts and principles and the effect of business transactions on the accounting equation of a service enterprise are discussed and illustrated. To slow the pace of the presentation of the accounting cycle, accounts and journal entries for a service enterprise have been moved from Chapter 1 to Chapter 2, and the basic concepts of accounting for merchandising transactions have been moved from Chapter 2 to Chapter 4. The accounting cycle for service enterprises is continued in Chapter 3, where the concepts for adjusting the accounting records and for periodic reporting are presented, along with an in-depth discussion of the basic financial statements. The discussion of reversing entries has been moved to an appendix at the end of Chapter 3, since instructors may choose not to cover this topic. In Chapter 4, the discussion of accounting for a merchandising enterprise includes the basic concepts of the periodic and perpetual inventory systems and the closing method of handling merchandise inventory in a periodic system. Because perpetual inventories are increasingly being used in the business world, the use of the perpetual inventory system in the periodic reporting process is discussed in an appendix to Chapter 4.

Forms of Business Organization. The corporate form of business organization is used in the text, beginning with simple equity structures in Chapter 1. This form is dominant in today's business world and is therefore the one to which students are more likely to be exposed. (The concepts and principles applicable to the sole proprietorship and partnership are presented in Chapter 10.)

Statement of Cash Flows. The third edition introduces in Chapter 1 the statement of cash flows as one of the four basic financial statements. Using the direct method, a simple statement of cash flows for a service enterprise is described and illustrated. Several exercises and problems at the end of Chapter 1 require students to prepare simple statements of cash flows.

An in-depth discussion of the statement of cash flows is presented in Chapter 14. Early in Chapter 14 an illustration of the statement of cash flows, using both the direct method and the indirect method, is presented as a basis for discussion.

Two appendixes are included at the end of Chapter 14. The first appendix further describes and illustrates the direct method of preparing the statement of cash flows. The second appendix describes and illustrates a work sheet approach to preparing the statement of cash flows. The work sheet approach has been revised completely.

Alternate Methods of Recording Prepaid Expenses and Unearned Revenues. The discussion of recording prepaid expenses initially as expenses and unearned revenues initially as revenues is presented in Appendixes C and D. These appendixes include exercises.

Internal Control Structure. The discussion of internal controls has been revised to incorporate *Statements on Auditing Standards, No. 55.*Accordingly, the discussion of internal controls describes the importance of the control environment, the control procedures, and the accounting system.

Income Taxes. The effect of income taxes on accounting has been incorporated throughout the text. For example, Chapter 23 describes and illustrates the effect of the Modified Accelerated Cost Recovery Systems (MACRS) on capital investment decisions. In addition, a brief coverage of income taxes is presented in Appendix G. This appendix, which incorporates the 1990 changes in the tax law, provides students with an understanding of the basic nature of the federal income tax system and its effects on personal and business income. The appendix includes discussion questions and exercises.

Managerial Accounting

The coverage of managerial accounting has been expanded and reorganized in Chapters 15-28 to include the effects of the new manufacturing environment as well as the more traditional manufacturing operations.

Cost Concepts and Terminology. In the reorganized Chapter 15, the common cost concepts and terminology are discussed in depth. Included is a discussion of trends in manufacturing, such as just-in-time manufacturing, computer-integrated manufacturing, and total quality control, and the increased use of managerial accounting by service enterprises.

Cost Allocation. Chapter 18 is a new chapter that focuses on cost allocation, including traditional methods and activity-based costing. The potential for cost allocations to distort product costs and cost allocation in just-in-time manufacturing systems are also discussed.

Cost-Volume-Profit Analysis. Chapter 20 has been extensively revised to apply the contribution margin concept to cost-volume-profit analysis.

Product Pricing. A discussion of the "target cost" concept of product pricing was added to Chapter 22, "Differential Analysis and Product Pricing."

Capital Investment Analysis. A discussion of qualitative considerations in capital investment analysis was added to Chapter 23.

The New Manufacturing Environment. Chapter 24, "The New Manufacturing Environment, Inventory Management, and Decision Making," is a new chapter. This chapter presents an in-depth discussion of just-in-time manufacturing systems and the management of inventory costs in such systems as well as in more traditional systems. The implications of the new manufacturing environment on cost-volume-profit analysis, variable costing, differential analysis, and capital investment analysis are also discussed.

Quality Control. An appendix on quality control, its costs, and the role of managerial accounting in quality control is included at the end of Chapter 24.

Accounting for Decentralized Operations; Transfer Pricing. The two chapters on responsibility accounting were combined into one chapter in this edition of the text.

Managerial Accounting for Service Enterprises and Activities. The managerial accounting concepts and procedures that are relevant for service enterprises have been integrated throughout the text. These concepts relate to job order cost accounting, cost allocation, budgeting, responsibility accounting, standard costs, and setting fees.

End-of-Chapter Materials

Chapter Reviews. The chapter review at the end of each chapter is designed to increase and enhance student retention of important chapter concepts and principles. Each review includes key points, key terms, self-examination questions, and an illustrative problem and solution.

- The **key points,** organized by chapter objective, summarize the major concepts presented in a chapter. By studying the key points, students can quickly review the major concepts and principles of each chapter.

- Each **key term** listed in the chapter review is followed by the page number indicating where the term was first discussed in the chapter. Students may also refer to the Glossary at the end of the text, where all the key terms, with page references, are listed alphabetically and defined.
- Five **self-examination questions** are provided for each chapter. After studying the chapter, students can answer these questions and compare their answers with the correct ones. Explanations of both the correct and incorrect answers for each question, provided at the end of the chapter, increase students' understanding and enhance the learning process.
- The **illustrative problem** with suggested solution focuses on the concepts and principles discussed in the chapter. Students can use these problems as a means of building confidence in their ability to apply a chapter's concepts and principles to a problem situation. Each illustrative problem is similar to one or more end-of-chapter problems.

Exercises, Problems, and Mini-Cases. The exercises and problems have been carefully written and revised to be both practical and comprehensive. The variety and volume of the assignment materials presented at the end of each chapter provide a wide choice of subject matter and range of difficulty. In addition, selected problems may be solved using general ledger and spreadsheet software that is available from South-Western Publishing Co. As in previous editions, each chapter contains a mini-case for stimulating student interest. Each case, which presents situations with which students can easily identify, emphasizes important chapter concepts and principles.

Ethics Discussion Cases. An ethics discussion case has been added to the discussion questions for each chapter of the third edition, in response to the business world's increasing emphasis on ethical conduct. As a basis for discussion, the American Institute of Certified Public Accountants' *Code of Professional Conduct* and the Institute of Management Accountants' *Standards of Ethical Conduct for Management Accountants* are included in Appendix B. These codes of professional conduct supplement the presentation of professional ethics in Chapter 1 and Chapter 15.

Real World Focus Questions, Exercises, and Problems. At least one discussion question that requires students to interpret and respond to a real-world business situation is contained in each chapter. In some chapters, a real-world exercise or problem is also included. These questions, which are labeled "Real World Focus," are based on actual business data.

Comprehensive Problems. Four comprehensive problems are included--at the end of Chapters 3, 4, 9, and 12. These problems integrate and summarize the concepts and principles of several chapters. They may be assigned as mini practice sets to be worked manually or with the Solutions software that can be purchased with the text.

Alternate Problems. An alternate problem is presented for each problem in order to facilitate student and instructor usage.

Check Figures. Check figures are presented at the end of the textbook for student use in solving end-of-chapter problems. Agreement with the check figures is an indication that a significant portion of the solution is basically correct.

Other Significant Features

Chapter Objectives. The chapter objectives have been integrated with the text presentation and the instructor's materials as follows:

- Each chapter begins with a listing of the chapter objectives. This listing provides a framework for the presentation of the chapter material.
- Each chapter objective is repeated in the margin next to the discussion to which the objective relates.
- The key points in each chapter review are organized by chapter objective.
- All end-of-chapter exercises and problems are identified by chapter objective.
- The teaching outlines provided in the *Instructor's Manual* are organized by chapter objective.
- All questions and problems in the test bank are identified by chapter objective.

Illustrations. Additional charts, graphs, and diagrams are included throughout the text to enable students to visualize important concepts and principles. These charts, graphs, and diagrams are highlighted with color to enhance the learning process.

Real-World Examples. Many real-world business examples have been integrated throughout the text to provide students with a flavor of the real-world impact of accounting. These examples add concrete meaning to concepts and principles that might otherwise appear abstract. Many of these examples were taken directly from the latest annual reports of companies such as PepsiCo and General Motors. The American Institute of Certified Public Accountants' publication, *Accounting Trends & Techniques,* is cited where appropriate to indicate the frequency with which alternative accounting presentations and methods are used in the real world. Examples from such publications as *The Wall Street Journal* and *Fortune* were also cited.

Enrichment Material. Excerpts from well-known business periodicals, such as the *Journal of Accountancy, Management Accounting, The Wall Street Journal,* and *Forbes,* have been included in each chapter of the text. Each excerpt is designed to stir the students' interest and enrich their learning experiences by providing real-world information relevant to the topics that are discussed in the chapter.

Specimen Financial Statements. Appendix H includes a variety of examples of financial statements of large, publicly held corporations. These financial statements provide insight into the financial reporting of real companies.

Classification of Accounts. A classification of the accounts on the financial statement(s), including the normal account balance, is presented on the inside back cover for students' use when reading the text and in solving the end-of-chapter materials.

SUPPLEMENTARY MATERIALS

PRINCIPLES OF FINANCIAL AND MANAGERIAL ACCOUNTING is part of a well-integrated educational package that includes materials designed for use by both the student and the instructor. These materials are carefully prepared and reviewed to maintain consistency and high quality throughout.

Available to Instructors

Solutions Manuals. These manuals contain solutions to all end-of-chapter materials, including the discussion questions, ethics cases, exercises, problems, mini-cases, and comprehensive problems.

Instructor's Manual. This manual contains a summary of the chapter objectives, terminology, and concepts. In a section organized according to chapter objectives, a basis for developing class lectures and assigning homework is provided. In addition, exercise and problem descriptions, estimated time requirements for the problems, and suggestions for use of the appendixes and other supplementary items are included.

Spreadsheet Applications. These template diskettes are used with Lotus® 1-2-3®[1] for solving selected end-of-chapter exercises and problems that are identified with the symbol at the right. These diskettes, which also provide a Lotus 1-2-3 tutorial and "what if" analysis, are provided free of charge to instructors at educational institutions that adopt this text.

Solutions Transparencies and Teaching Transparencies. Transparencies of solutions to all exercises and the regular problems, including the comprehensive problems, are available. The teaching transparencies are designed to aid the instructor's focus on key concepts and principles discussed in the text. The transparencies are packaged in two boxes, one for Chapters 1-14 and Appendixes C, D, F, and G, and one for Chapters 15-28

Videos. Two videotapes for classroom use are available. **Setting the Stage** includes 19 brief role-play segments that bring the world of financial accounting to life. **Luca Pacioli: Unsung Hero of the Renaissance** is a 25-minute documentary of the life of the father of accounting.

---

[1] Lotus and 1-2-3 are registered trademarks of the Lotus Development Corporation. Any reference to Lotus or 1-2-3 refers to this footnote.

Test Bank. A collection of more than 2,500 examination problems, multiple-choice questions, and true or false questions, accompanied by solutions, is available in both printed and microcomputer **(MicroSWAT III)** versions. These items are identified by chapter objective and by level of difficulty. The Test Bank is designed to save time in preparing and grading periodic and final examinations. Individual items may also be selected for use as short quizzes. The number of questions and problems is sufficient to provide variety from year to year and from class section to class section. The printed version of the Test Bank also contains illustrative achievement tests and solutions.

Available to Students

Solutions: Applications Software, prepared by Warren W. Allen and Dale H. Klooster of Educational Technical Systems. This software is a general ledger program tailored specifically to PRINCIPLES OF FINANCIAL AND MANAGERIAL ACCOUNTING. It may be used with the IBM® PC, IBM PS/2[2], and the Tandy® 1000[3] microcomputers to solve selected end-of-chapter problems and the comprehensive problems, which are identified with the symbol at the right. It may also be used to solve most problems that require journal entries and a general ledger, as well as a manual practice set that in effect becomes a computerized practice set.

SOLUTIONS SOFTWARE

Working Papers. Appropriate printed forms on which to work end-of-chapter problems and mini-cases are available in two bound volumes. The first volume is for use with Chapters 1-14, and the second volume is for use with Chapters 15-28.

Study Guide, prepared by Carl S. Warren. The Study Guide is designed to assist in comprehending the concepts and principles presented in the text. This publication includes an outline and a glossary for each chapter as well as brief objective questions and problems. Solutions to these questions and problems are presented at the back of the Study Guide.

Financial Accounting Tutor and Managerial Accounting Tutor, prepared by Thomas P. Lawler of Marist College. These interactive computerized tutorials provide step-by-step explanations and examples for students' review of accounting principles.

Practice Sets. ***Campus Collections Inc. II,*** **prepared by Herman R. Andress of Santa Fe Community College.** This short practice set requires the recording, analysis, interpretation, and reporting of accounting data for a corporation. It is available in either a manual or computerized version. ***SEMO Sporting Goods Supply Inc.,*** **prepared by Deborah F. Beard, Stephen C. DelVecchio, and John A. Elfrink of Southeast Missouri State University.** This set requires the preparation of correcting entries and financial statements for a wholesaling corporation. ***Synertech Inc.,*** **prepared by Dieter H. Weiss of Ferris State College.** This short practice set is a budgeting set that emphasizes decision making rather than forms and procedures. The set is available in either a manual version or a computerized version based on Lotus 1-2-3.

Electronic Spreadsheet Applications for Accounting Principles, Financial Accounting, and Managerial Accounting, prepared by Gaylord N. Smith of Albion College. These supplemental text-workbooks with template diskettes include accounting applications and a Lotus 1-2-3 tutorial. Each text-workbook requires approximately 20-25 hours for completion.

ORGANIZATION OF THE THIRD EDITION

PRINCIPLES OF FINANCIAL AND MANAGERIAL ACCOUNTING is organized to facilitate the learning of accounting and the overall educational process. Concepts and principles are introduced in a logical, step-by-step way and are reinforced by applications from the business world.

---

[2]IBM is a registered trademark of International Business Machines Corpor
the IBM Personal Computer or the IBM Personal System/2 refers to this fo
[3]Tandy® 1000 is a registered trademark of the Radio Shack Division of T
reference to the Tandy 1000 microcomputer refers to this footnote.

Each chapter builds on the terminology, concepts, and principles introduced in previous chapters. The chapter objectives provide students with a basis for beginning their study of each chapter. In turn, each chapter is organized around the chapter objectives in aneducationally sound approach. The chapter reviews provide students with a means for review and a basis for assessing their knowledge of each chapter. The end-of-chapter discussion questions, ethics cases, exercises, problems, and mini-cases provide a vehicle for the instructor to assess the students' knowledge of each chapter's concepts and principles. Periodic assigning of comprehensive problems and the giving of examinations provide instructors with a means for assessing students' cumulative knowledge.

Introduction: Evolution of Accounting

The introduction presents a summary of the beginnings of accounting with Luca Pacioli in 1494 and its development to the present. Emphasis is given to the present-day profession of accountancy and its future. This overview provides students of all backgrounds an excellent perspective on the importance and influence of accounting on all phases of society.

Part 1—Fundamentals of Financial Accounting

- Chapters 1-4 focus on the basic concepts and principles of accounting, including accounting for both service enterprises and merchandise enterprises. These chapters are presented without the complexities of special journals and subsidiary ledgers.

Part 2—Financial Accounting Systems

- Chapters 5 through 9 begin with a brief discussion of the basic concepts of accounting systems design. Financial accounting principles for cash, receivables and temporary investments, inventories, plant and intangible assets, and payroll and other current liabilities are then discussed in depth in balance sheet order.

Part 3—Accounting for Equity Rights

- Chapters 10 and 11 briefly discuss alternative forms of business organization--sole proprietorships and partnerships--and complex business transactions affecting stockholders' equity. An in-depth discussion of the accounting for partnerships is presented as an appendix to Chapter 10.
- Chapter 12 discusses long-term liabilities and investments in bonds. Present value concepts are integrated throughout this chapter.
- Chapter 13 discusses principles and concepts involving long-term investments in stocks, consolidations, and accounting for international operations.

Part 4—Reporting Changes in Cash Flows

- Chapter 14 emphasizes the principles and conceptual logic of the statement of cash flows. Appendixes are provided for those instructors who wish to use a work sheet for preparing the statement of cash flows and who wish to emphasize the direct method of reporting cash flows from operations.

Part 5—Managerial Accounting Concepts and Systems

- Chapter 15 serves as the transition from financial accounting to managerial accounting. It provides students with an overview of the nature of the management process and the essential role of managerial accounting in this process. After completing Chapter 15, students will have been exposed to the majority of the cost concepts and terminology they will need in completing the remainder of the chapters on managerial accounting. This allows instructors flexibility in the order in which they assign subsequent chapters.
- Chapters 16 and 17 provide illustrations of the application of managerial accounting concepts to a manufacturing environment. Chapter 16 discusses job order cost accounting systems, and Chapter 17 discusses process cost accounting systems.
- Chapter 18 discusses cost allocation.
- Chapter 19 presents the concepts of cost behavior and cost estimation, including the common classifications of costs by behavior and the common methods of estimating costs.

Part 6—Analyses for Management Decision Making

- Chapter 20 discusses cost-volume-profit analysis.
- Chapter 21 discusses profit reporting for management analysis, including absorption costing and variable costing.
- Chapter 22 discusses the use of differential analysis in decision making. Also included in Chapter 22 is a discussion of pricing, including short-term special pricing situations and the setting of long-term prices. Integrated into this discussion is the economic approach to pricing and the impact of a product's life cycle on setting prices.
- Chapter 23 describes and illustrates capital investment analysis, including the average rate of return, cash payback, net present value, and internal rate of return methods of evaluating capital investments. Capital rationing and factors complicating capital investment analysis and are also discussed.
- Chapter 24 discusses inventory management and analyses for managerial decision making in the new manufacturing environment.

Part 7—Planning and Control

- Chapter 25 discusses budgeting, including an integrated example of the preparation of the master budget.
- Chapter 26 discusses standard cost systems.
- Chapter 27 discusses responsibility accounting for decentralized operations. The chapter concludes with a discussion of transfer pricing.

Part 8—Financial Analysis for Management Use

- Chapter 28 discusses the usefulness of financial statement analysis to management. Chapter 28 also includes a description of the essential elements and content of corporate annual reports.

Appendixes

- Appendix A presents complete present value and future value tables.
- Appendix B contains the professional codes of ethics for the American Institute of Certified Public Accountants and the Institute of Management Accountants.
- Appendix C presents the alternate method of recording prepaid expenses that were initially recorded as expenses. Exercise materials are included with the appendix.
- Appendix D presents the alternate method of recording unearned revenues that were initially recorded as revenues. Exercise materials are included with the appendix.
- Appendix E presents an alternative method of recording merchandise inventory at the end of an accounting period. This method is sometimes referred to as the adjusting method. Solutions to problems using this method are presented in the Solutions Manual.
- Appendix F discusses special journals and subsidiary ledgers. Problem materials are included with the appendix.
- Appendix G discusses income taxes for individuals and business enterprises. Question and exercise materials are included with the appendix.
- Appendix H contains selected financial statements for real companies.

ACKNOWLEDGMENTS

Throughout the textbook, relevant professional statements of the Financial Accounting Standards Board, the Institute of Management Accountants, and other authoritative publications are discussed, quoted, paraphrased, or footnoted. We are indebted to the American Accounting Association, the American Institute of Certified Public Accountants, the Financial Accounting Standards Board, and the Institute of Management Accountants for material from their publications.

Many of the changes in the third edition were based on extensive feedback from current users of the text and on independent manuscript reviews by scholars and educators. W especially thank C. J. McNair of Babson College for her contributions to the mana chapters of the text.

The following faculty provided helpful comments on the financial accounting chapters:

Mary Beth Caldwell
University of Arkansas

Keith Lantz
California State University—Fullerton

Grace Goodrich
Riverside Community College

J. Larry Hagler
East Carolina University

Mike Lawrence
Portland Community College

Steven C. Reimer
University of Iowa

Rebecca Phillips
University of Lousiville

R. K. McCabe
California State University—Fullerton

Charles A. Konkol
University of Wisconsin—Milwaukee

Hobart W. Adams
University of Akron

Patrick M. Premo
Saint Bonaventure University

The following faculty provided helpful comments on the managerial accounting chapters:

C. J. McNair
Babson College

Linda Bamber
University of Georgia

Mark Frigo
DePaul University

Earl Kay Stice
Rice University

Shrirish B. Seth
California State University - Fullerton

Don W. Finn
Texas Tech University

James Reeve
University of Tennessee

David Keys
Northern Illinois University

Frank W. Selto
University of Colorado

Jane Reimers
Florida State University

George J. Chorba
Villanova University

Timothy A. Farmer
Unversity of Missouri - St. Louis

We also thank Alice B. Sineath of Forsyth Technical College for her valuable comments in reviewing the Study Guide and the Test Bank.

We continue to welcome your comments and suggestions.

Carl S. Warren
Philip E. Fess

ABOUT THE AUTHORS

Professor Carl S. Warren is the Arthur Andersen & Co. Alumni Professor of Accounting at the J.M. Tull School of Accounting at the University of Georgia, Athens. Professor Warren received his PhD from Michigan State University in 1973 and has taught accounting at the University of Iowa, Michigan State University, the University of Chicago, and the University of Georgia. He has received teaching awards from three different student organizations at the University of Georgia.

Professor Warren is a CMA and a CPA. He was awarded a Certificate of Distinguished Performance for his scores on the CMA examination and a Certificate of Honorable Mention for his scores on the CPA examination. He is a member of the National Association of Accountants, the American Institute of CPAs, the Georgia Society of CPAs, the American Accounting Association, the Georgia Association of Accounting Educators, and the Financial Executives Institute. Professor Warren has served on numerous professional committees and editorial boards, including a term as editor of the American Accounting Association publication *Auditing: A Journal of Practice and Theory.* He has written ten textbooks and numerous articles in such journals as the *Journal of Accountancy,* the *Accounting Review,* the *Journal of Accounting Research,* the *CPA Journal, Corporate Accounting, Cost and Management,* and *Managerial Planning.*

Professor Warren resides in Athens, Georgia with his wife, Sharon, and two children, Stephanie (age 18), and Jeffrey (age 16). Professor Warren's hobbies include coaching Little League Baseball, golf, tennis, and fishing.

Professor Philip E. Fess is the Arthur Andersen & Co. Alumni Professor of Accountancy Emeritus at the University of Illinois, Champaign-Urbana. Professor Fess received his PhD from the University of Illinois and has been involved in textbook writing for over twenty-five years. In addition to having more than 30 years of teaching experience, he has won numerous teaching awards, including the University of Illinois, College of Commerce Alumni Association Excellence in Teaching Award and the Illinois CPA Society Educator of the Year Award.

Professor Fess is a CPA and a member of the American Institute of CPAs, the Illinois Society of CPAs, and the American Accounting Association. He has served many professional associations in a variety of ways, including a term as a member of the Auditing Standards Board, editorial advisor to the *Journal of Accountancy,* and chairperson of the American Accounting Association Committee on CPA Examinations. Professor Fess has written more than 100 books and articles, which have appeared in such journals as the *Journal of Accountancy,* the *Accounting Review,* the *CPA Journal,* and *Management Accounting.* He has also served as an expert witnesses before the U.S. Tax Court and as a member of the Cost Advisory Panel for the Secretary of the Air Force.

Professor Fess and his wife, Suzanne, have three daughters: Linda, who is an Assistant Professor of Accountancy at Northern Illinois University; Ginny, who is a CPA and is employed by Solar Turbine Co.; and Martha, who is also a CPA and is attending law school at the University of San Diego. Professor Fess' hobby is tennis, and he has represented the United States in international tennis competition.

CONTENTS IN BRIEF

INTRODUCTION: EVOLUTION OF ACCOUNTING 1

1 FUNDAMENTALS OF FINANCIAL ACCOUNTING 9
1 Accounting Concepts and Principles 10
2 The Accounting Cycle 52
3 Completion of the Accounting Cycle 98
4 Accounting for a Merchandising Enterprise 147

2 FINANCIAL ACCOUNTING SYSTEMS 215
5 Accounting Systems and Cash 216
6 Receivables and Temporary Investments 253
7 Inventories 288
8 Plant Assets and Intangible Assets 329
9 Payroll, Notes Payable, and Other Current Liabilities 373

3 ACCOUNTING FOR EQUITY RIGHTS 415
10 Forms of Business Organization 416
11 Stockholders' Equity, Earnings, and Dividends 458
12 Long-Term Liabilities and Investments in Bonds 502
13 Investments in Stocks; Consolidations; International Operations 540

4 REPORTING CHANGES IN CASH FLOWS 589
14 Statement of Cash Flows 590

5 MANAGERIAL ACCOUNTING CONCEPTS AND SYSTEMS 645
15 Nature of Managerial Accounting; Cost Concepts and Terminology 646
16 Job Order Cost Systems 691
17 Process Cost Systems 729
18 Cost Allocation and Activity-Based Costing 768

6 ANALYSES FOR MANAGERIAL DECISION MAKING 811
19 Cost Behavior and Cost Estimation 812
20 Cost-Volume-Profit Analysis 856
21 Profit Reporting for Management Analysis 892
22 Differential Analysis and Product Pricing 926
23 Capital Investment Analysis 961
24 The New Manufacturing Environment, Inventory Management, and Decision Making 998

7 PLANNING AND CONTROL 1047
25 Budgeting 1048
26 Standard Cost Systems 1084
27 Accounting for Decentralized Operations; Transfer Pricing 1113
28 Financial Statement Analysis and Annual Reports 1162

TABLE OF CONTENTS

INTRODUCTION: EVOLUTION OF ACCOUNTING 1
- Primitive Accounting 1
- Double-Entry System 1
- Industrial Revolution 2
- Corporate Organization 3
- Public Accounting 3
- Income Tax 4
- Government Influence 4
- Current Accounting Practice 5
  - Private Accounting 5
  - Public Accounting 6
- Accounting's Future 7
  - Computerized Accounting Systems 7
  - International Accounting 7
  - Socioeconomic Accounting 7

1 FUNDAMENTALS OF FINANCIAL ACCOUNTING 9

1 ACCOUNTING CONCEPTS AND PRINCIPLES 10
- Accounting as an Information System 12
- Financial and Managerial Accounting 12
- Development of Financial Accounting Concepts
- Concepts and Principles 14
  - Financial Accounting Standards Board 15
  - Governmental Accounting Standards Board 15
  - Accounting Organizations 15
  - Government Organizations 15
  - Other Influential Organizations 16
- Professional Ethics for Accountants 16
- Financial Accounting Concepts and Principles 17
  - Business Entity Concept 17
  - The Cost Principle 18
  - Business Transactions 19
  - Unit of Measurement 19
- Assets, Liabilities, and Owner's Equity 20
- Transactions and the Accounting Equation 20
- Financial Statements 24
  - Income Statement 25
  - Retained Earnings Statement 27
  - Balance Sheet 27
  - Statement of Cash Flows 28

2 THE ACCOUNTING CYCLE 52
- Chart of Accounts 53
  - Balance Sheet Accounts 55
  - Income Statement Accounts 58
  - Normal Balances of Accounts 59
- Flow of Business Transaction Data 59
  - Ledger Accounts 60
  - The Journal 60
  - Posting 61
  - Illustration of Journalizing and Posting 61
- Trial Balance 67
- Discovery and Correction of Errors 67
  - Discovery of Errors 67
  - Correction of Errors 68
- Materiality 69

3 COMPLETION OF THE ACCOUNTING CYCLE 98
- Accounting Period 99
  - Going Concern 99
  - Fiscal Year 100
- Matching Principle 101
- Nature of the Adjusting Process 102
- Illustrations of Adjusting Entries 103
  - Prepaid Expenses 103
  - Plant Assets 105
  - Accrued Expenses (Accrued Liabilities) 106
- Work Sheet for Financial Statements 107
  - Trial Balance Columns 107
  - Adjustment Columns 108
  - Income Statement and Balance Sheet Columns 110
- Financial Statements 113
  - Income Statement 115
  - Retained Earnings Statement 115
  - Balance Sheet 115
- Journalizing and Posting Adjusting Entries 116
- Nature of the Adjusting Process 117
  - Journalizing and Posting Closing Entries 117
  - Post-Closing Trial Balance 122
  - Accounting Cycle 122
- **APPENDIX Reversing Entries** 123

4 ACCOUNTING FOR A MERCHANDISING ENTERPRISE 147
- Accounting for Purchases 148
  - Purchases Discounts 148
  - Purchases Returns and Allowances 150
- Accounting for Sales 151
  - Sales Taxes 153
  - Sales Discounts 153
  - Sales Returns and Allowances 153
- Transportation Costs 154
- Merchandise Inventory Systems 156
- Cost of Merchandise Sold 156
- Periodic Reporting for Merchandising Enterprises 157
  - Work Sheet for Merchandising Enterprises 158

Completing the Work Sheet 162
Retained Earnings Statement 166
Balance Sheet 167
Adjusting and Closing Entries 167
Adjusting Entries 167
Closing Entries 168
APPENDIX The Perpetual Inventory System 170

2 FINANCIAL ACCOUNTING SYSTEMS 215

5 ACCOUNTING SYSTEMS AND CASH 216
Principles of Accounting Systems 217
Cost-Effectiveness Balance 218
Flexibility to Meet Future Needs 218
Adequate Internal Controls 218
Effective Reporting 219
Adaptation to Organizational Structure 219
Accounting System Installation and Revision 219
Systems Analysis 219
Systems Design 219
Systems Implementation 220
Internal Control Structure 220
The Control Environment 221
The Control Procedures 221
The Accounting System 223
Control Over Cash 223
The Bank Account as a Tool for Controlling Cash 223
Bank Statement 225
Bank Reconciliation 225
Internal Control of Cash Receipts 229
Cash Short and Over 229
Cash Change Funds 230
Internal Control of Cash Payments 230
The Voucher System 230
Purchases Discounts 233
Petty Cash 233
Other Cash Funds 235
Cash Transactions and Electronic Funds Transfer 235

6 RECEIVABLES AND TEMPORARY INVESTMENTS 253
Classification of Receivables 254
Control Over Receivables 255
Characteristics of Notes Receivable 256
Due Date 256
Interest-Bearing Notes and Non-Interest-Bearing Notes 257
Interest 257
Maturity Value 258
Accounting for Notes Receivable 258
Interest-Bearing Notes Receivable 259
Discounting Notes Receivable 259
Dishonored Notes Receivable 261
Uncollectible Receivables 261
Allowance Method of Accounting for Uncollectibles 262
Write-Offs to the Allowance Account 264
Estimating Uncollectibles 264
Direct Write-Off Method of Accounting for Uncollectibles 267
Receivables from Installment Sales 267
Temporary Investments 268
Temporary Investments and Receivables in the Balance Sheet 270

7 INVENTORIES 288
Importance of Inventories 289
The Effect of Inventory on the Current Period's Statements 289
The Effect of Inventory on the Following Period's Statements 291
Inventory Systems 292
Determining Actual Quantities in the Inventory 292
Determining the Cost of Inventory 293
Inventory Costing Methods Under a Periodic System 294
First-In, First-Out Method 295
Last-In, First-Out Method 296
Average Cost Method 297
Comparison of Inventory Costing Methods 297
Accounting for and Reporting Inventory Under a Perpetual System 300
Inventory Costing Methods Under a Perpetual System 302
Internal Control and Perpetual Inventory Systems 304
Automated Perpetual Inventory Records 304
Valuation of Inventory at Other than Cost 305
Valuation at Lower of Cost or Market 305
Valuation at Net Realizable Value 307
Presentation of Merchandise Inventory on the Balance Sheet 307
Estimated Inventory Cost 307
Retail Method of Inventory Costing 308
Gross Profit Method of Estimating Inventories 309
Inventories of Manufacturing Enterprises 309
Long-Term Construction Contracts 310

8 PLANT ASSETS AND INTANGIBLE ASSETS 329
Acquisition of Plant Assets 330
Nature of Depreciation 331
Accounting for Depreciation 332
Straight-Line Method 334
Units-of-Production Method 334
Declining-Balance Method 334
Sum-of-the-Years-Digits Method 335
Comparison of Depreciation Methods 336
Depreciation for Federal Income Tax 336
Revision of Periodic Depreciation 338
Recording Depreciation 339
Subsidiary Ledgers for Plant Assets 339
Depreciation of Plant Assets of Low Unit Cost 341
Composite-Rate Depreciation Method 341

Capital and Revenue Expenditures 342
Capital Expenditures 342
Revenue Expenditures 343
Summary of Capital and Revenue Expenditures 344
Disposal of Plant Assets 344
Discarding Plant Assets 344
Sale of Plant Assets 345
Exchange of Plant Assets 346
Acquisition of Plant Assets Through Leasing 347
Depletion 348
Intangible Assets 349
Patents 349
Copyrights 350
Goodwill 350
Reporting Depreciation Expense, Plant Assets, and Intangible Assets in the Financial Statements 351
Replacement Cost of Plant Assets 351

9 **PAYROLL, NOTES PAYABLE, AND OTHER CURRENT LIABILITIES** 373
Payroll and Payroll Taxes 374
Liability for Employee Earnings 375
Deductions from Employee Earnings 377
Computation of Employee Net Pay 378
Liability for Employer's Payroll Taxes 379
Accounting Systems for Payroll and Payroll Taxes 380
Payroll Register 380
Employee's Earnings Record 382
Payroll Checks 382
Payroll System Diagram 383
Internal Controls for Payroll Systems 384
Liability for Employees' Fringe Benefits 385
Liability for Vacation Pay 385
Liability for Pensions 386
Employee Stock Options 387
Short-Term Notes Payable 387
Product Warranty Liability 388
Contingent Liabilities 389
Litigation 389
Guarantees 390
Discounted Receivables 390
APPENDIX Payroll Register and Employee's Earnings Record 390

3 ACCOUNTING FOR EQUITY RIGHTS **415**

10 **FORMS OF BUSINESS ORGANIZATION** 416
Characteristics of Sole Proprietorships 417
Accounting for Sole Proprietorships 418
Characteristics of Partnerships 418
Accounting for Partnerships 420
Characteristics of a Corporation 420
Accounting for Corporations 422
Stockholders' Equity 422
Characteristics of Capital Stock 423
Issuing Capital Stock 426
Treasury Stock 429
Equity Per Share 431
Organization Costs 432
APPENDIX Partnership Accounting 433

11 **STOCKHOLDERS' EQUITY, EARNINGS, AND DIVIDENDS** 458
Paid-In Capital 459
Corporate Earnings and Income Taxes 460
Allocation of Income Tax Between Periods 461
Reporting Unusual Items in the Financial Statements 465
Unusual Items that Affect the Income Statement 465
Unusual Items that Affect the Retained Earnings Statement 467
Earnings Per Common Share 469
Appropriation of Retained Earnings 471
Nature of Dividends 473
Cash Dividends 474
Stock Dividends 475
Liquidating Dividends 477
Stock Splits 477
Dividends and Stock Splits for Treasury Stock 478

12 **LONG-TERM LIABILITIES AND INVESTMENTS IN BONDS** 502
Financing Corporations 503
Characteristics of Bonds 505
Present Value Concepts 506
Present Value Concepts for Bonds Payable 506
Present Value of $1 507
Present Value of Annuity of $1 508
Accounting for Bonds Payable 508
Bonds Issued at Face Amount 509
Bonds Issued at a Discount 510
Bonds Issued at a Premium 512
Zero-Coupon Bonds 514
Bond Sinking Fund 514
Future Value Concepts 514
Accounting for Bond Sinking Fund 516
Appropriation for Bonded Indebtedness 518
Bond Redemption 518
Balance Sheet Presentation of Bonds Payable 519
Investments in Bonds 519
Accounting for Bond Investments—Purchase, Interest, and Amortization 520
Accounting for Bond Investments—Sale 521

13 **INVESTMENTS IN STOCKS; CONSOLIDATIONS; IINTERNATIONAL OPERATIONS** 540
Investments in Stocks 541
Accounting for Long-Term Investments in Stock 542
Cost Method 542

Equity Method 543
Sale of Long-Term Investments in Stocks 544
Business Combinations 544
Mergers and Consolidations 545
Parent and Subsidiary Corporations 545
Accounting for Parent-Subsidiary Affiliations 546
Basic Principles of Consolidation of Financial Statements 547
Purchase Method 547
Pooling of Interests Method 555
Consolidated Income Statement and Other Statements 558
Corporation Financial Statements 559
Accounting for International Operations 559
Accounting for Transactions with Foreign Companies 559
Consolidated Financial Statements with Foreign Subsidiaries 563

4 REPORTING CHANGES IN CASH FLOWS 589

14 STATEMENT OF CASH FLOWS 590
Nature of the Statement of Cash Flows 591
Reporting Cash Flows 593
Cash Flows from Operating Activities 593
Cash Flows from Investing Activities 594
Cash Flows from Financing Activities 594
Illustrations of the Statement of Cash Flows 594
Noncash Investing and Financing Activities 596
Cash Flow per Share 596
Assembling Data and Preparing the Statement of Cash Flows 596
Retained Earnings 598
Common Stock 602
Preferred STock 603
Bonds Payable 603
Equipment 604
Building 604
Land 605
Investments 605
Preparing the Statement of Cash Flows 606
APPENDIX The Direct Method of Reporting Cash Flows from Operating Activities 607

5 MANAGERIAL ACCOUNTING CONCEPTS AND SYSTEMS 645

15 NATURE OF MANAGERIAL ACCOUNTING; COST CONCEPTS AND TERMINOLOGY 646
The Management Process 647
Planning 648
Organizing and Directing 649
Controlling 650
Decision Making 650
Role of Managerial Accounting in the Management Process 650
Organization of the Managerial Accounting Function 651
Managerial Accounting as a Profession 653
Characteristics of Managerial Accounting Reports 654
Relevance 654
Timeliness 655
Accuracy 655
Clarity 656
Conciseness 656
Costs vs. Benefits of Managerial Accounting Reports 656
Cost Concepts and Terminology 656
Direct and Indirect Costs 657
Differential Costs 658
Sunk Costs 658
Controllable and Noncontrollable Costs 658
Discretionary Costs 659
Variable Costs and Fixed Costs 659
Opportunity Costs 660
Classification of Costs 660
Manufacturing Operations: Costs and Terminology 660
Manufacturing Costs 661
Product Costs and Period Costs 663
Trends in Manufacturing and Service Enterprises 664
Just-in-Time Manufacturing 664
Total Quality Control 665
Computer-Integrated Manufacturing 665
Service Industry Awareness 666
APPENDIX Financial Statements for Manufacturing Enterprises 666

16 JOB ORDER COST SYSTEMS 691
Usefulness of Product Costs 692
Types of Accounting Systems 693
Types of Cost Accounting Systems 693
Perpetual Inventory Procedures 694
Job Order Cost Systems for Manufacturing Enterprises 695
Materials 695
Factory Labor 697
Factory Overhead 697
Work in Process 700
Finished Goods and Cost of Goods Sold 703
Sales 703
Illustration of Job Order Cost Accounting 704
Job Order Cost Systems for Service Enterprises 708

17 PROCESS COST SYSTEMS 729
Job Order Costing and Process Costing Compared 730
Flow of Costs in a Process Cost System 731
Inventories of Partially Processed Units 732
Flow of Materials 732
Equivalent Units of Production 733
Cost of Production Report 735

Service Departments and Process Costs 736
Joint Products and By-Products 737
Accounting for Joint Products 737
Accounting for By-Products 738
Illustration of Process Cost Accounting 739
Cost of Production Reports 742
Financial Statements 743
Inventory Costing Methods 745
First-In, First-Out (Fifo) Cost Method 745
Average Cost Method 746
Inventory Costing Methods and Just-in-Time Manufacturing 747
Hybrid Cost Accounting Systems 748

18 COST ALLOCATION AND ACTIVITY-BASED COSTING 768
Objectives of Cost Allocation 769
Evaluating Manufacturing Processes 770
Costing Products 770
Motivating Managers 771
Valuing Inventories 771
Principles of Cost Allocation 771
Cost Drivers 771
Budgeted Costs and Actual Costs 772
Fixed Costs and Variable Costs 772
Service Department Cost Allocation 774
Direct Method 774
Step Method 775
Predetermined Overhead Rates and Product Costing 777
Manufacturing Overhead in Product Costing 777
Plant-Wide Overhead Rate 777
Departmental Overhead Rates 778
Distortions of Product Costs 780
Activity-Based Costing 782
Cost Allocation in Just-in-Time Manufacturing Systems 786
APPENDIX The Reciprocal Method of Allocating Service Department Costs 787

6 ANALYSES FOR MANAGERIAL DECISION MAKING 811

19 COST BEHAVIOR AND COST ESTIMATION 812
Cost Behavior 813
Variable Costs 814
Fixed Costs 818
Mixed Costs 821
Summary of Cost Behavior Concepts 823
Cost Estimation 824
High-Low Method 824
Scattergraph Method 827
Least Squares Method 830
Comparison of Cost Estimation Methods 832
Other Methods of Cost Estimation 833
Judgmental Method 833
Engineering Method 834

20 COST-VOLUME-PROFIT ANALYSIS 856
Cost-Volume-Profit Relationships 857
Contribution Margin Concept 858
Contribution Margin Ratio 858
Unit Contribution Margin 859
Mathematical Approach to Cost-Volume-Profit Analysis 860
Break-Even Point 860
Desired Profit 864
Graphic Approach to Cost-Volume-Profit Analysis 864
Cost-Volume-Profit (Break-Even Chart) Chart 865
Profit-Volume Chart 866
Use of Computers in Cost-Volume-Profit Analysis 870
Sales Mix Considerations 871
Sales Mix and the Break-Even Point 871
Sales Mix and Desired Profit 872
Special Cost-Volume-Profit Relationships 873
Margin of Safety 873
Operating Leverage 874
Limitations of Cost-Volume-Profit Analysis 875

21 PROFIT REPORTING FOR MANAGEMENT ANALYSIS 892
Absorption Costing and Variable Costing 893
The Income Statement Under Variable Costing and Absorption Costing 894
Income Reported when Units Manufactured Equal Units Sold 896
Income Reported when Units Manufactured Exceed Units Sold 896
Income Reported when Units Manufactured are Less than Units Sold 897
Comparison of Income Reported Under the Two Concepts 898
Income Analysis Under Variable Costing and Absorption Costing 898
Management's Use of Variable Costing and Absorption Costing 901
Cost Control 901
Product Pricing 902
Production Planning 903
Sales Analysis 903
Contribution Margin Analysis 906

22 DIFFERENTIAL ANALYSIS AND PRODUCT PRICING 926
Differential Analysis 927
Lease or Sell 928
Discontinuance of a Segment of Product 929
Make or Buy 931
Equipment Replacement 932
Process or Sell 933
Acceptance or Business at a Special Price 934
Setting Normal Product Selling Prices 934
Total Cost Concept 935
Product Cost Concept 937

Variable Cost Concept 937
Choosing a Cost-Plus Approach Cost Concept 939
Economic Theory of Product Pricing 940
Maximization of Profits 940
Revenues 940
Costs 940
Product Price Determination 941
Pricing Strategies 942

23 **CAPITAL INVESTMENT ANALYSIS** 961
Nature of Capital Investment Analysis 962
Methods of Evaluating Capital Investment Proposals 963
Methods that Ignore Present Value 963
Present Value Methods 966
Qualitative Considerations in Capital Investment Analysis 971
Factors that Complicate Capital Investment Analysis 973
Income Tax 973
Unequal Proposal Lives 973
Lease Versus Capital Investment 975
Uncertainty 975
Changes in Price Levels 975
Capital Rationing 975
Planning and Controlling Capital Investment Expenditures 976
APPENDIX Impact of Income Taxes on Capital Investment Analysis 978

24 **THE NEW MANUFACTURING ENVIRONMENT, INVENTORY MANAGEMENT, AND DECISION MAKING** 998
Characteristics of the New Manufacturing Environment 999
Automated Manufacturing Processes 1000
Cost Allocation in the New Manufacturing Environment 1000
Just-in-Time Manufacturing Systems 1001
Costs of Investing in Inventory 1003
Opportunity Costs 1003
Ordering Costs 1004
Purchase Cost 1004
Storage Costs 1004
Costs of Interrupting Production 1004
Inventory Management in a Just-in-Time Manufacturing System 1005
Inventory Management in a Traditional Manufacturing System 1006
Economic Order Quantity 1006
Inventory Reorder Point 1007
Linear Programming for Purchasing Decisions 1009
Implications of the New Manufacturing Environment for Analyses 1013
Cost-Volume-Profit Analysis 1014
Variable Costing 1014
Differential Analysis 1016
Capital Investment Analysis 1017

APPENDIX 1 Quality Control 1019
APPENDIX 2 Decision Making Under Uncertainty 1023

7 **PLANNING AND CONTROL** 1047

25 **BUDGETING** 1048
Nature and Objectives of Budgeting 1049
Budgeting Systems 1050
Sales Budget 1051
Production Budget 1052
Direct Materials Purchases Budget 1053
Direct Labot Cost Budget 1053
Factory Overhead Cost Budget 1054
Cost of Goods Sold Budget 1054
Operating Expenses Budget 1055
Budgeted Income Statement 1056
Capital Expenditures Budget 1057
Cash Budget 1057
Budgeted Balance Sheet 1059
Budget Performance Reports 1060
Flexible Budgets 1060
Computerized Budgeting Systems 1062
Budgeting and Human Behavior 1062

26 **STANDARD COST SYSTEMS** 1084
The Nature and Objectives of Standards 1085
Setting Standards 1086
Types of Standards 1087
Variances from Standards 1087
Direct Materials Cost Variance 1088
Direct Labor Cost Variance 1089
Factory Overhead Cost Variance 1091
Standards in the Accounts 1094
Revision of Standards 1097
Standards for Nonmanufacturing Expenses 1097

27 **ACCOUNTING FOR DECENTRALIZED OPERATIONS; TRANSFER PRICING** 1113
Centralized and Decentralized Operations 1114
Advantages of Decentralization 1115
Disadvantages of Decentralization 1116
Types of Responsibility Centers 1116
Cost Centers 1117
Profit Centers 1117
Investment Centers 1118
Responsibility Accounting for Cost Centers 1119
Responsibility Accounting for Profit Centers 1121
Departmental Margin 1121
Gross Profit by Departments 1123
Operating Income by Departments 1123
Responsibility Accounting for Investment Centers 1128
Operating Income 1129
Rate of Return on Investment 1130
Residual Income 1133

	Transfer Pricing	1134
	Market Price Approach	1135
	Negotiated Price Approach	1135
	Cost Price Approach	1136
28	**FINANCIAL STATEMENT ANALYSIS AND ANNUAL REPORTS**	1162
	Basic Analytical Procedures	1163
	Horizontal Analysis	1164
	Vertical Analysis	1167
	Common-Size Statements	1169
	Other Analytical Measures	1170
	Focus of Financial Statement Analyses	1170
	Solvency Analysis	1170
	Current Position Analysis	1170
	Accounts Receivable Analysis	1172
	Inventory Analysis	1173
	Ratio of Plant Assets to Long-Term Liabilities	1174
	Ratio of Stockholders' Equity to Liabilities	1175
	Number of Times Interest Charges Earned	1175
	Profitability Analysis	1176
	Ratio of Net Sales to Assets	1176
	Rate Earned on Total Assets	1177
	Rate Earned on Stockholders' Equity	1177
	Rate Earned on Common Stockholders' Equity	1178
	Earnings Per Share on Common Stock	1179
	Price-Earnings Ratio	1180
	Dividend Yield	1180
	Summary of Analytical Measures	1181
	Corporate Annual Reports	1183
	Financial Highlights	1183
	President's Letter	1184
	Independent Auditor's Report	1184
	Management Report	1187
	Historical Summary	1188
	Segment of a Business	1188
	Supplemental Data on the Effects of Price-Level Changes	1189
	Other Information	1190
	Interim Financial Reports	1191

APPENDIXES

A	**INTEREST TABLES**	A-1
B	**CODES OF PROFESSIONAL ETHICS FOR ACCOUNTANTS**	B-1
C	**ALTERNATIVE METHOD OF RECORDING PREPAID EXPENSES**	C-1
D	**ALTERNATIVE METHOD OF RECORDING UNEARNED REVENUES**	D-1
E	**ALTERNATIVE METHOD OF RECORDING MERCHANDISE INVENTORIES**	E-1
F	**SPECIAL JOURNALS AND SUBSIDIARY LEDGERS**	F-1
G	**INCOME TAXES**	G-1
H	**SPECIMEN FINANCIAL STATEMENTS**	H-1

GLOSSARY GLOSSARY-1

INDEX INDEX-1

CHECK FIGURES CHECK FIGURES -1

TEXT OBJECTIVES

1 Describe the evolution of accounting.

2 Describe the basic structure of the accounting profession.

3 Describe and illustrate the basic financial accounting concepts and principles.

4 Describe and illustrate accounting systems for service and merchandising enterprises.

5 Describe and illustrate accounting concepts and principles for sole proprietorships, partnerships, and corporations.

6 Describe the basic nature and structure of managerial accounting.

7 Describe and illustrate the accounting systems for manufacturing operations.

8 Describe and illustrate managerial accounting concepts for planning and controlling operations and decision making.

9 Describe and illustrate financial analyses for management use.

INTRODUCTION

Accounting has evolved, as have medicine, law, and most other fields of human activity, in response to the social and economic needs of society. As business and society have become more complex over the years, accounting has developed new concepts and techniques to meet the ever increasing needs for financial information. Without such information, many complex economic developments and social programs might never have been undertaken. This introduction briefly describes the evolution of accounting.

PRIMITIVE ACCOUNTING

People in all civilizations have maintained various types of records of business activities. The oldest known are clay tablet records of the payment of wages in Babylonia around 3600 B.C. There are numerous evidences of record keeping and systems of accounting control in ancient Egypt and in the Greek city-states. The earliest known English records were compiled at the direction of William the Conqueror in the eleventh century to ascertain the financial resources of the kingdom.

For the most part, early accounting dealt only with limited aspects of the financial operations of private or governmental enterprises. There was no systematic accounting for all transactions of a particular unit, only for specific types or portions of transactions. Complete accounting for an enterprise developed somewhat later in response to the needs of the commercial republics of Italy.

DOUBLE-ENTRY SYSTEM

The evolution of the system of record keeping which came to be called "double entry" was strongly influenced by Venetian merchants. The first known description of the system was published in Italy in 1494. The author, a Franciscan monk by the name of Luca Pacioli, was a mathematician who taught in various universities in Perugia, Naples, Pisa, and Florence. Evidence of the position that Pacioli occupied among the intellectuals of his day was his close friendship with Leonardo da Vinci, with whom he collaborated on a mathematics book. Pacioli wrote the text and da Vinci developed the illustrations.[1]

Goethe, the German poet, novelist, scientist, and universal genius, wrote about double entry as follows: "It is one of the most beautiful inventions of the human spirit, and every good businessman should use it in his economic undertakings."[2] Double entry provides for recording both aspects of a transaction in such a manner as to establish an equilibrium. For example, if an individual borrows $1,000 from a bank, the amount of the loan is recorded both as cash of $1,000 and as an obligation to repay $1,000. Either of the $1,000 amounts is balanced by the other $1,000 amount. As the basic principles are developed further in the early chapters of this book, it will become evident that "double entry" provides for the recording of all business transactions in a systematic manner. It also provides for a set of integrated financial statements reporting in monetary terms the amount of (1) the profit (net income) for a single venture or for a specified period, (2) the properties (assets) owned by the enterprise and the ownership rights (equities) to the properties, and (3) the flow of cash into and out of the enterprise.

Historically, when the resources of a number of people were pooled to finance a single venture, such as a voyage of a merchant ship, the double-entry system provided records and reports of the income of the venture and the equity of the various participants. As single ventures were replaced by more permanent business organizations, the double-entry system was easily adapted to meet their needs. In spite of the tremendous development of business operations since 1494, and the ever increasing complexities of business and governmental organizations, the basic elements of the double-entry system have continued virtually unchanged.

INDUSTRIAL REVOLUTION

The Industrial Revolution, which occurred in England from the mid-eighteenth to the mid-nineteenth century, brought many social and economic changes, notably a change from the handicraft method of producing marketable goods to the factory system. The use of machinery gave rise to the need to determine the cost of a large volume of identical, machine-made products instead of the cost of a relatively small number of individually handcrafted products. The specialized field of cost accounting emerged to meet this need for the analysis of various costs and for recording techniques.

In the early days of manufacturing operations, when business enterprises were relatively small and often isolated geographically, competition frequently was not very keen. Cost accounting was primitive and focused primarily on providing management with records and reports on past operations. Most business decisions were made on the basis of this historical financial information combined with intuition or hunches about the potential success of proposed courses of action.

As manufacturing enterprises became larger and more complex and as competition among manufacturers increased, the "scientific management concept" evolved. This concept emphasized a systematic approach to the so-

[1]A video on the life and work of Luca Pacioli is available from South-Western Publishing Co.

[2]Goethe, Johann Wolfgang von, *Samtliche Werke,* edited by Edward von der Hellen (Stuttgart and Berlin: J. G. Cotta, 1902–07), Vol. XVII, p. 37.

lution of management problems. Paralleling this trend was the development of more sophisticated cost accounting concepts to supply management with analytical techniques for measuring the efficiency of current operations and in planning for future operations. This trend was accelerated in the twentieth century by the advent of the electronic computer with its capacity for manipulating large masses of data and its ability to determine the potential effect of alternative courses of action.

CORPORATE ORGANIZATION

The expanded business operations initiated by the Industrial Revolution required increasingly larger amounts of money to build factories and purchase machinery. This need for large amounts of capital resulted in the development of the corporate form of organization, which was first legally established in England in 1845. The Industrial Revolution spread rapidly to the United States, which became one of the world's leading industrial nations shortly after the Civil War. The accumulation of large amounts of capital was essential for establishment of new businesses in industries such as manufacturing, transportation, mining, electric power, and communications. In the United States, as in England, the corporation was the form of organization that facilitated the accumulation of the substantial amounts of capital needed.

Almost all large American business enterprises, and many small ones, are organized as corporations largely because ownership is evidenced by readily transferable shares of stock. The shareholders of a corporation control the management of corporate affairs only indirectly. They elect a board of directors, which establishes general policies and selects officers who actively manage the corporation. The development of a class of owners far removed from active participation in the management of the business created an additional dimension for accounting. Accounting information was needed not only by management in directing the affairs of the corporation but also by the shareholders, who required periodic financial statements in order to appraise management's performance.

As corporations became larger, an increasing number of individuals and institutions looked to accountants to provide economic information about these enterprises. Prospective shareholders and creditors sought information about a corporation's financial status and its prospects for the future. Governmental agencies required financial information for purposes of taxation and regulation. Employees, union representatives, and customers demanded information upon which to judge the stability and profitability of corporate enterprises. Thus accounting began to expand its function of meeting the needs of a relatively few owners to a public role of meeting the needs of a variety of interested parties.

PUBLIC ACCOUNTING

The development of the corporation also created a new social need—the need for an independent audit to provide some assurance that management's financial representations were reliable. This audit function, often referred to as the "attest function," was chiefly responsible for the creation and growth of the public accounting profession. Unlike private accountants, public accountants are independent of the enterprises for which they perform services.

Recognizing the need for accounting services of professional caliber, all of the states provide for the licensing of certified public accountants (*CPAs*). In 1944, fifty years after the enactment of the first CPA law, there were approximately 25,000 CPAs in the United States. Currently the number exceeds 400,000.

Auditing is still a major service offered by CPAs, but presently they also devote much of their time to assisting their clients with problems related to planning, controlling, and decision making. Such consulting services, commonly known as management advisory services, have increased in volume over the years until today they comprise a significant part of the practice of most public accounting firms.

INCOME TAX

Enactment of the federal income tax law in 1913 resulted in a tremendous stimulus to accounting activity. All business enterprises organized as corporations or partnerships, as well as many individuals, were required to maintain sufficient records to enable them to file accurate tax returns. Since that time the income tax laws and regulations have become increasingly complex. As a consequence businesses have depended upon both private and public accountants for advice on legal methods of tax minimization, for preparing tax returns, and for representing them in tax disputes with governmental agencies.

It should also be noted that accounting has influenced the development of income tax law to a great degree. Had accounting not progressed to a point where periodic net income could be determined, the enactment and enforcement of any tax law undoubtedly would have been extremely difficult, if not impossible.

GOVERNMENT INFLUENCE

Over the years government at various levels has intervened to an increasing extent in economic and social matters affecting ever greater numbers of people. Accounting has played an important role by providing the financial information needed to achieve the desired goals.

As the number and size of corporate enterprises grew and an ever increasing number of shares of stock were traded in the market place, laws regulating the activities of stock exchanges, stockbrokers, and investment companies were enacted for the protection of investors. These regulations involve accounting requirements. To protect the public from excessive charges by railroads and other monopolies, commissions were established to limit their rates to levels yielding net income considered to be a "fair return" on invested capital. This rate-making process required extensive accounting information. Regulated banks and savings and loan associations also had to meet record-keeping and reporting requirements and permit periodic examination of their records by governmental agencies. As labor unions became larger and more powerful, regulatory laws were enacted requiring them to submit periodic financial reports. With the enactment of social security and medicare legislation came record-keeping and reporting requirements for almost all businesses and many individuals.

As the federal government exercised increasing control over economic activities, accounting information became more essential as a basis for formulating legislation. One of the areas in which the government has influenced economic and social behavior has been through the income tax. For example, contributions to charitable organizations have been encouraged by permitting their deduction in determining taxable income. Controls over wages and prices have also been enacted at various times in attempts to control the economy by reducing the rate of inflation. An enormous volume of accounting data must be reported, summarized, and studied before proceeding with the evaluation of various governmental proposals such as the foregoing.

CURRENT ACCOUNTING PRACTICE

Accounting can be characterized as a profession that has experienced rapid development during the current century. This has been accompanied by an expansion of the career opportunities in accounting and an increasing number of professionally trained accountants. During the period 1960–1988, the profession of accountancy more than doubled in size. Among the factors contributing to this growth have been the increase in number, size, and complexity of business corporations; the frequent changes in the tax laws; and other governmental restrictions on business operations. As the complexity of the business and social environment continues to increase, employment and advancement opportunities in the profession of accountancy are expected to continue to grow and expand.

As professionals, accountants are typically engaged in either (1) private accounting or (2) public accounting. Accountants employed by a particular business firm or not-for-profit organization, perhaps as chief accountant, controller, or financial vice-president, are said to be engaged in **private accounting**. Accountants who render accounting services on a fee basis, and staff accountants employed by them, are said to be engaged in **public accounting**.

Both private and public accounting have long been recognized as excellent training for top managerial responsibilities. Many executive positions in government and in industry are held by men and women with education and experience in accounting. For example, in its 1990 Special Bonus Issue on "The Corporate Elite," *Business Week* reported that 31% of the chief executives of the 1,000 largest public corporations followed the career path of finance-accounting. Merchandising-marketing and engineering-technical were the career paths for 27% and 22% of the chief executives, respectively.

Private Accounting

The scope of activities and responsibilities of private accountants varies widely. They are frequently referred to as managerial accountants, or, if they are employed by a manufacturing concern, as industrial or cost accountants. Various governmental units and other not-for-profit organizations also employ accountants.

The Institute of Certified Management Accountants, which is an affiliate of the Institute of Management Accountants, grants the Certified Management Accountant (CMA) designation as evidence of professional competence in that field. Requirements for the CMA designation include the baccalaureate degree or equivalent, two years of experience in management accounting, and successful completion of examinations occupying two days. Participation in a program of continuing professional education is also required for renewal of the certificate. The Institute of Management Accountants has also set forth standards of ethical conduct for managerial accountants. These standards recognize the obligation of managerial accountants to maintain the highest standards of ethical conduct in serving their employers, their profession, and the public.[3]

The Institute of Internal Auditors administers a program of education, experience, and examination for internal auditors — accountants who review the accounting and operating procedures prescribed by their firms. Accountants qualifying under this program are entitled to use the designation Certified Internal Auditor (CIA).

Public Accounting

In public accounting, an accountant may practice as an individual or as a member of a public accounting firm. Public accountants who have met a state's education, experience, and examination requirements may become **certified public accountants**, commonly called **CPAs**.

Qualifications of CPAs. The qualifications required for the CPA certificate differ among the various states. A specified level of education is required, often the completion of a collegiate course of study in accounting. All states require that a candidate pass an examination prepared by the **American Institute of Certified Public Accountants (AICPA)**. The examination is administered twice a year, in May and November. Many states permit candidates to take the examination upon graduation from college or during the term in which they will complete the educational requirements. The examination, which occupies one afternoon and two all-day sessions, is divided into four parts: Accounting Theory, Accounting Practice, Auditing, and Business Law. Some states also require an examination in an additional subject, such as Rules of Professional Conduct. Most states do not permit successful candidates to practice as independent CPAs until they have had from one to three years' experience in public accounting or in employment considered equivalent. Details regarding the requirements in any particular state can be obtained from the respective State Board of Accountancy.

In recent years a majority of the states have enacted laws requiring public practitioners to participate in a program of continuing professional education or forfeit their right to continue in public practice. According to the statutes of one of the states, the continuing education must be a "formal program of learning which contributes directly to the professional competence of an individual after he or she has been licensed to practice public accounting." The states differ as to some of the details of the requirement, such as the number of hours of formal education required for renewal of the permit to practice. The rules adopted by a number of State Boards of Accountancy require forty hours per year (a fifty-minute class period counts as one hour). The AICPA and most state societies of CPAs also have established continuing professional education requirements for their members. For example, the AICPA requires its members in public practice to complete 120 hours of education every three years, including at least 20 hours each year.

---

[3]The text of *Standards of Ethical Conduct for Management Accountants*, Institute of Management Accountants (Montvale, New Jersey, 1983), is reproduced in Appendix B.

Professional Ethics for CPAs. CPAs have a duty not only to their clients but to their colleagues and the public to perform services competently and with integrity. However, many clients and much of the public do not have the capability of evaluating a CPA's performance. Therefore, standards of conduct have been established to guide CPAs in the conduct of their practices.[4]

ACCOUNTING'S FUTURE

Accounting is capable of supplying financial information that is essential for the efficient operation and for the evaluation of performance of any economic unit in society. Changes in the environment in which such organizations operate will inevitably be accompanied by alterations in accounting concepts and techniques. Although long-range predictions as to environmental changes are risky and of doubtful value, there are three areas that promise to receive increased attention in the immediate future— computerized accounting systems, international accounting, and socioeconomic accounting.

Computerized Accounting Systems

Since the electronic computer was first used to process business data in the middle of the twentieth century, it has played an ever increasing role in the design of accounting systems and the processing of economic data. It has generally enabled interested users of accounting information to receive relevant economic data on a more timely basis at a lower cost.

The integration of the electronic computer into accounting systems has created both opportunities and challenges for accountants. The computer provides opportunities for accountants to analyze efficiently a greater quantity of economic data for reporting to users. As the use of computers in business continues to accelerate, there will be an increasing demand for accountants to aid in the analysis, design, and implementation of these systems. This responsibility, in turn, will create ever greater challenges for accountants to obtain a complete understanding of business operations and the principles of designing systems that will gather all accurate, relevant data on a timely basis.

International Accounting

The rapid growth of multinational firms in recent years has had a significant impact on accounting because of the different environments existing in the various countries in which such firms operate. Currently, a major problem is the need to develop more uniform accounting standards among countries. Working toward this end are such international organizations as the International Accounting Standards Committee and the International Federation of Accountants.

Socioeconomic Accounting

The term socioeconomic accounting refers to the measurement and communication of information about the impact of various organizations on society. Three major areas of social measurement can be identified. First, at

---

[4]*The Code of Professional Conduct,* American Institute of Certified Public Accountants (New York, 1988). The text of this code is reproduced in Appendix B.

the societal level the interest is on the total impact of all institutions on matters that affect the quality of life. The second area is concerned with the programs undertaken by the government and socially oriented not-for-profit organizations to accomplish specific social objectives. The third area, sometimes referred to as corporate social responsibility, focuses on the public interest in corporate social performance in such areas as reduction of water and air pollution, conservation of natural resources, improvement in quality of product and customer service, and employment practices regarding minority groups and females. The concept of social measurement is relatively simple as a theory, but much additional study and research will be needed before measurement can be expressed in terms of monetary costs and benefits.

PART 1

FUNDAMENTALS OF FINANCIAL ACCOUNTING

CHAPTER 1

CHAPTER OBJECTIVES

1 Describe accounting as an information system for business enterprises.

2 Describe financial accounting and managerial accounting.

3 Describe the development of financial accounting concepts and principles.

4 Describe the codes of professional conduct for accountants.

5 Identify and illustrate the application of the following basic financial accounting concepts and principles:
   - Business entity
   - Cost principle
   - Business transactions
   - Unit of measurement

6 Identify the accounting equation and its basic elements.

7 Describe and illustrate how all business transactions can be stated in terms of the resulting changes in the three basic elements of the accounting equation.

8 Identify and describe the following financial statements:
   - Income statement
   - Retained earnings statement
   - Balance sheet
   - Statement of cash flows

ACCOUNTING CONCEPTS & PRINCIPLES

Accounting plays an important role in our economic and social system. Sound decisions made by individuals, businesses, governments, and other entities are essential for the efficient distribution and use of the nation's scarce resources. To make such decisions, these groups must have reliable information provided by the accounting system. The objective of accounting, therefore, is to record, summarize, report, and interpret economic data for use by many groups within our economic and social system.

Everyone engaged in business activity, from the youngest employee to the manager and owner, comes into contact with accounting. Individuals engaged in such areas of business as finance, production, marketing, personnel, and general management need not be expert accountants, but they are more effective if they have a good understanding of accounting principles. The higher the level of authority and responsibility, the greater is the need for an understanding of accounting concepts and terminology.

A study of U.S. corporations revealed that finance and accounting were the most common backgrounds of chief executive officers. Interviews with corporate executives produced the following comments.[1]

> *". . . it's vital that the chief executive officer know the corporation and . . . have an understanding of accounting."*
>
> *". . . my training in accounting and auditing practice has been extremely valuable to me throughout."*
>
> *"A knowledge of accounting carries with it an understanding of the establishment and the maintenance of sound financial controls—an area which is absolutely essential to a chief executive officer."*
>
> *"I try to have my entire staff understand the financial function and how to use financial data."*

The importance of understanding accounting is not limited to the business world. Many employees with specialized training in nonbusiness areas

[1] John R. Linden, "Rising Corporate Stars: The Accountant as Chief Executive Officer," *The Journal of Accountancy* (September, 1978), pp. 64–71.

also make use of accounting data and need to understand accounting principles and terminology. For example, an engineer responsible for selecting the most desirable solution to a technical manufacturing problem may consider cost accounting data to be the deciding factor. Lawyers use accounting data in tax cases and in lawsuits involving property ownership and damages from breach of contract. Governmental agencies rely on accounting data in evaluating the efficiency of government operations and for appraising the feasibility of proposed taxation and spending programs. Finally, every adult engages in business transactions and must necessarily be concerned with the economic aspects of life.

ACCOUNTING AS AN INFORMATION SYSTEM

OBJECTIVE 1
Describe accounting as an information system for business enterprises.

Accounting[2] is often called the "language of business." This language can be viewed as an information system that provides essential information about the financial activities of an entity to various individuals or groups for their use in making informed judgments and decisions. As such, accounting information is composed principally of economic data about business transactions, expressed in terms of money.

Accounting provides the conceptual framework for gathering economic data and the language for communicating these data to different individuals and institutions. Investors in a business enterprise need information about its financial status and its future prospects. Bankers and suppliers appraise the financial soundness of a business organization and assess the risks involved before making loans or granting credit. Government agencies are concerned with the financial activities of business organizations for purposes of taxation and regulation. Employees and their union representatives are also vitally interested in the stability and the profitability of the organization that hires them. The management of an enterprise, who is responsible for directing the operations of that enterprise, depends upon and makes the most use of many types of accounting data.

The process of using accounting to provide information to users is illustrated in the diagram at the top of page 13. First, user groups are identified and their information needs determined. These needs determine which economic data are gathered and processed by the accounting system. Finally, the accounting system generates reports that communicate essential information to users for decision making.

FINANCIAL AND MANAGERIAL ACCOUNTING

OBJECTIVE 2
Describe financial accounting and managerial accounting.

As a result of rapid technological advances and accelerated economic growth, a number of specialized fields in accounting have evolved. The two most important accounting fields, financial and managerial accounting, are briefly described in the following paragraphs.

Financial accounting is concerned with the measuring and recording of transactions for a business enterprise or other economic unit and the periodic preparation of various reports from such records. The reports, which may be for general purposes or for a special purpose, provide useful information for managers, owners, creditors, governmental agencies, and the general public. Of particular importance to financial accountants are the principles of accounting, termed **generally accepted accounting principles (GAAP).** Corporate en-

---

[2] A glossary of terms appears at the end of the text. The terms included in the glossary are printed in color the first time they appear in the text.

Accounting as a Provider of Information to Users

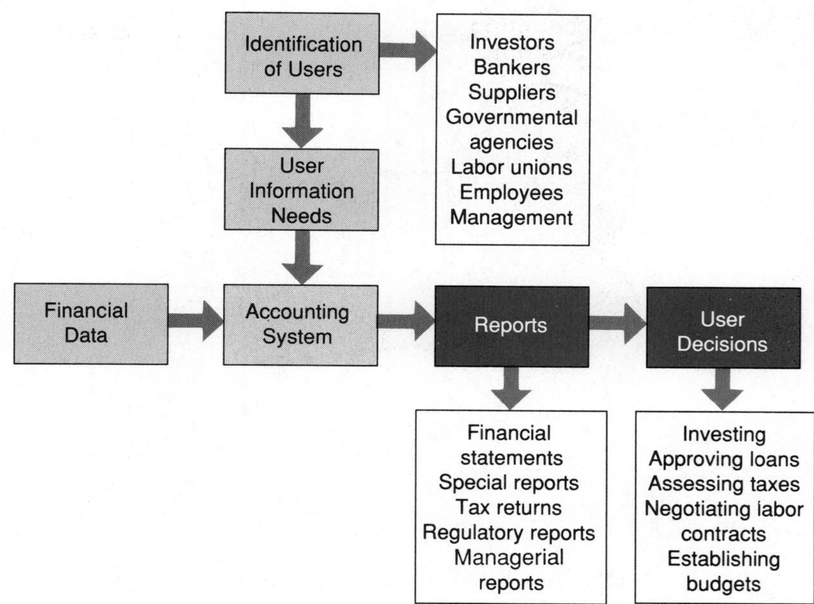

terprises must use these principles in preparing their annual reports on profitability and financial status for their stockholders and the investing public. The use of generally accepted accounting principles assures the comparability of financial statements between enterprises. This comparability of financial reports is essential if the nation's resources are to be divided among business organizations in a socially desirable manner.

Managerial accounting employs both historical and estimated data, which management uses in conducting and evaluating current operations, and in planning future operations. For example, in directing day-to-day operations, management relies upon accounting to provide information concerning the amount owed to each creditor, the amount owed by each customer and the date each amount is due. The treasurer uses these data and other data in the managment of cash. Accounting data may be used by top management in determining the selling price of a new product. Production managers, by comparing past performances with planned objectives, can take steps to accelerate favorable trends and reduce those trends that are unfavorable.

As indicated in the diagram at the top of page 14, managerial accounting overlaps financial accounting to the extent that management uses the financial statements or reports in directing current operations and planning future operations. However, managerial accounting extends beyond financial accounting by providing additional information and reports for management's use. In providing this additional information, the managerial accountant is *not* governed by generally accepted accounting principles. Since these data are used only by management, the accountant provides the data in the format that is most useful for management. The principle of "usefulness," then, is dominant in guiding the accountant in preparing management reports.

The first fourteen chapters of this text focus on financial accounting and the concepts and principles underlying the preparation and use of financial statements. Managerial accounting and the principles and concepts underlying the preparation of managerial accounting reports are presented in Chapters 15–28.

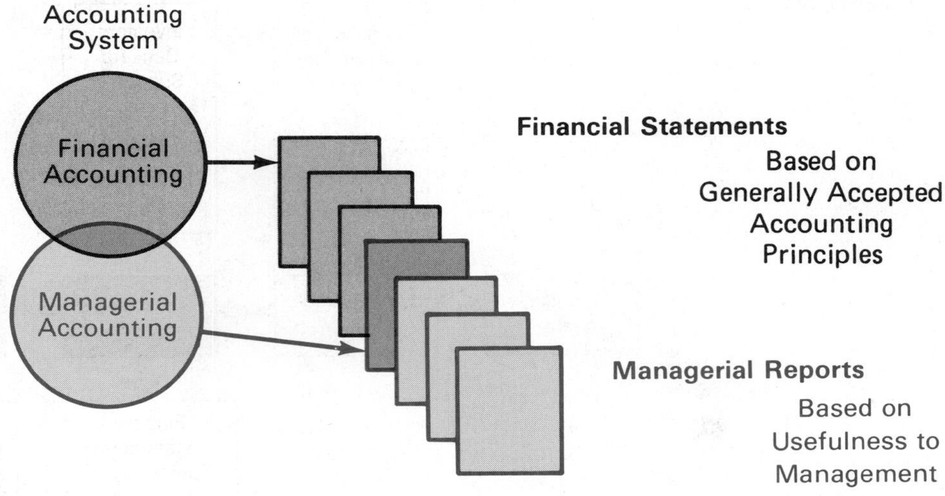

DEVELOPMENT OF FINANCIAL ACCOUNTING CONCEPTS AND PRINCIPLES

OBJECTIVE 3
Describe the development of financial accounting concepts and principles.

The historical development of the practice of accounting has been closely related to the economic development of the country. In the earlier stages of the American economy, a business enterprise was very often managed by its owner, and the accounting records and reports were used mainly by the owner-manager in conducting the business. Bankers and other lenders often relied on their personal relationship with the owner rather than on financial statements as the basis for making loans for business purposes. If a large amount was owed to a bank or supplier, the creditor often participated in management decisions.

As business organizations grew in size and complexity, "management" and "outsiders" became more clearly differentiated. Outsiders demanded accurate financial information. In addition, as the size and complexity of the business unit increased, the accounting problems involved in the issuance of financial statements became more and more complex. With these developments came an awareness of the need for a framework of concepts and generally accepted accounting principles to serve as guidelines for the preparation of the basic financial statements.

The word "principle" as used in the context of generally accepted accounting principles does not have the same authoritativeness as universal principles or natural laws relating to the study of astronomy, physics, or other physical sciences. Accounting principles have been developed by individuals to help make accounting data more useful in an ever-changing society. They represent guides for the achievement of the desired results, based on reason, observation, and experimentation. The selection of the best method from among many alternatives has come about gradually, and in some areas a clear consensus is still lacking. These principles are continually reexamined and revised to keep pace with the increasing complexity of business operations. General acceptance among the members of the accounting profession is the criterion for determining an accounting principle.

Responsibility for the development of accounting principles has rested primarily on practicing accountants and accounting educators, working both independently and under the sponsorship of various accounting organizations. These principles are also influenced by business practices and customs, ideas and beliefs of the users of the financial statements, governmental agencies, stock exchanges, and other business groups.

Financial Accounting Standards Board

The **Financial Accounting Standards Board (FASB)** is an independent board that was created in 1973. The FASB, which is presently the dominant body in the development of generally accepted accounting principles, is composed of seven members, four of whom must be CPAs drawn from public practice. The FASB employs a full-time research staff and administrative staff as well as task forces to study specific matters from time to time.

As problems in financial reporting are identified, the FASB conducts extensive research to identify the principal issues involved and the possible solutions. Generally, after issuing discussion memoranda and preliminary proposals and evaluating comments from interested parties, the Board issues *Statements of Financial Accounting Standards*, which become part of generally accepted accounting principles. To explain, clarify, or elaborate on existing pronouncements, the Board issues *Interpretations*, which have the same authority as the standards. The Board is also developing a broad conceptual framework for financial accounting, which is being published as *Statements of Financial Accounting Concepts*.

Governmental Accounting Standards Board

The **Governmental Accounting Standards Board (GASB)** was formed in 1984. It has a full-time chairperson, four part-time members, and a full-time research and administrative staff. The GASB has the responsibility for issuing *Statements of Governmental Accounting Standards*, which are to be followed by state and municipal governments.

Accounting Organizations

Among the oldest and most influential organizations of accountants are the **American Institute of Certified Public Accountants (AICPA)** and the **American Accounting Association (AAA)**. Each organization publishes a monthly or quarterly periodical and, from time to time, issues other publications in the form of research studies, technical opinions, and monographs. There are also other national accounting organizations as well as many state societies and local chapters of the national and state organizations. These groups provide forums for the interchange of ideas and discussion of accounting principles.

Government Organizations

Of the various governmental agencies with an interest in the development of accounting principles, the **Securities and Exchange Commission (SEC)** has been the most influential. Established by an act of Congress in 1934, the SEC issues regulations that must be observed in the preparation of financial statements and other reports filed with the Commission.

The **Internal Revenue Service (IRS)** issues regulations that govern the determination of income for purposes of federal income taxation. Because these regulations sometimes conflict with financial accounting principles, many enterprises maintain two sets of records to satisfy both reporting requirements. To avoid this increased record keeping, there have been times when firms have adopted practices that are acceptable both for tax purposes and for generally accepted accounting principles. A discussion of the nature of the income tax is presented in more detail in Appendix G.

Other regulatory agencies exercise a dominant influence on the accounting principles of the industries under their jurisdiction. In rare situations, Congress may also enact legislation that dictates accounting principles. These situations usually involve controversial issues on which no clear consensus has been reached within the profession.

Other Influential Organizations

The **Financial Executives Institute (FEI)** has influenced the development of accounting principles by encouraging and sponsoring accounting research. The FEI also comments on proposed pronouncements of the FASB, the SEC and other organizations.

The **Institute of Management Accountants (IMA)** is one of the largest organizations of accountants. It is primarily concerned with management's use of accounting information in directing business operations. Also, since management is responsible for the preparation of the basic financial statements, the IMA communicates its recommendations on generally accepted accounting principles to appropriate organizations.

PROFESSIONAL ETHICS FOR ACCOUNTANTS

OBJECTIVE 4
Describe the codes of professional conduct for accountants.

In addition to the financial accounting concepts and principles that guide public accountants, the AICPA has established standards to guide CPAs in the conduct of their practices. The purpose of these standards, called **codes of professional conduct** or **codes of professional ethics**, is to instill confidence in the quality of services rendered by public accountants by requiring them to commit to honorable behavior, even at the sacrifice of personal advantage. For example, under the current AICPA code of professional conduct, CPAs must act in a way that will serve the public interest, honor the public trust, and demonstrate commitment to professionalism.[3]

A CPA who violates the code of professional conduct is subject to disciplinary proceedings. The AICPA and state societies of CPAs have authority to revoke a CPA's membership in their organizations. If the violation also involves a regulatory agency, such as a State Board of Accountancy or the Securities and Exchange Commission, the CPA's ability to practice within the agency's jurisdiction may be revoked or otherwise limited. The combination of professional organization and regulatory agency sanctions guards against unethical behavior by the public accounting profession.

The IMA has set forth standards to guide managerial accountants in performing their duties. The purpose of these standards, called **standards of ethical conduct**, is to recognize the obligation of managerial accountants to

---

[3]The text of *The Code of Professional Conduct* of the American Institute of Certified Public Accountants (New York, 1988) is reproduced in Appendix B.

maintain the highest standards in serving their employers, their profession, and the public. For example, under current IMA ethics standards, managerial accountants have a responsibility to refuse any gift, favor, or hospitality that would influence or would appear to influence their actions.[4]

To meet the public's expectations of the role and responsibilities of accountants, codes of professional conduct change as society changes. However, ethical conduct is more than simply conforming to written standards of professional behavior. In a true sense, ethical conduct requires a personal commitment to honorable behavior. This thought was best expressed by Marcus Aurelius, who said, "A man should *be* upright; not be *kept* upright."

ETHICS

James K. Baker, chairman and CEO of Arvin Industries, Inc. and chairman of the United States Chamber of Commerce, often speaks out on ethics, an issue that has interested him all his working life. Baker is concerned about the lowering of ethical standards by both society and business. In addition to speaking out on the promotion of high standards of ethics, he tries to set a good example, as related in the following article that appeared in *The Christian Science Monitor*:

. . . He [Baker] recalls an early encounter with ethical issues when, at age 37, he had just been made executive vice president of Arvin. Reporting to him was a man 20 years his senior, for whom Baker had once worked. "He came to me and said, 'Would it be alright if we sent airline tickets to this purchasing agent in Philadelphia who works for the government? He and his wife want to go to his daughter's college graduation in California.' " . . . [Baker felt] that future government orders of Arvin products would be dependent upon his answer.

The law at the time made it illegal for the agent to accept the gift but did not make it illegal for Arvin to make the offer.

"My response was one of great impatience," says Baker. "I went to my boss within one or two hours and said that I felt that this was cause for dismissal: If he [Baker's employee] even considered that there was a likelihood for approval, there was something wrong, and his standards were not like the rest of ours. He was fired the next day."

The point, says Baker, is that ethical behavior in business includes "everything you do . . . The guy who goes for that extra hundred miles on the expense report—20 years later he may go for something that's really bad."

Source: Rushworth M. Kidder, "A Yardstick for Business Ethics," *Christian Science Monitor* (February 26, 1990), p. 14.

FINANCIAL ACCOUNTING CONCEPTS AND PRINCIPLES

OBJECTIVE 5
Identify and illustrate the application of basic accounting concepts and principles.

The remainder of this chapter is devoted to the underlying assumptions, concepts, and principles of the greatest importance and widest applicability. Attention will also be directed toward applications of financial accounting concepts and principles to specific situations and the reporting of the recorded data in the financial statements.

Business Entity Concept

The **business entity concept** is based on the applicability of accounting to individual economic units in society. These individual economic units include all business enterprises organized for profit; numerous governmental units,

[4]The text of *Standards of Ethical Conduct for Management Accountants*, Institute of Management Accountants (Montvale, New Jersey, 1983) is reproduced in Appendix B.

such as states, cities, and school districts; other not-for-profit units, such as charities, churches, hospitals, and social clubs; and individual persons and family units. The basic economic data for a unit must first be recorded, followed by analysis and summarization, and finally by periodic reporting. Thus, accounting applies to each separate economic unit.

This textbook is concerned primarily with the accounting principles and techniques applicable to profit-making businesses. Such businesses are customarily organized as sole proprietorships, partnerships, or corporations. A **sole proprietorship** is owned by one individual. A **partnership** is owned by two or more individuals in accordance with a contractual agreement. A **corporation,** organized in accordance with state or federal statutes, is a separate legal entity in which ownership is divided into shares of stock. The owners of a corporation are called **stockholders** or **shareholders.** Although the sole proprietorship is the most common business form, the corporation is the dominant form in terms of dollars of business activity, as indicated in the following charts:

Profit-Making Businesses

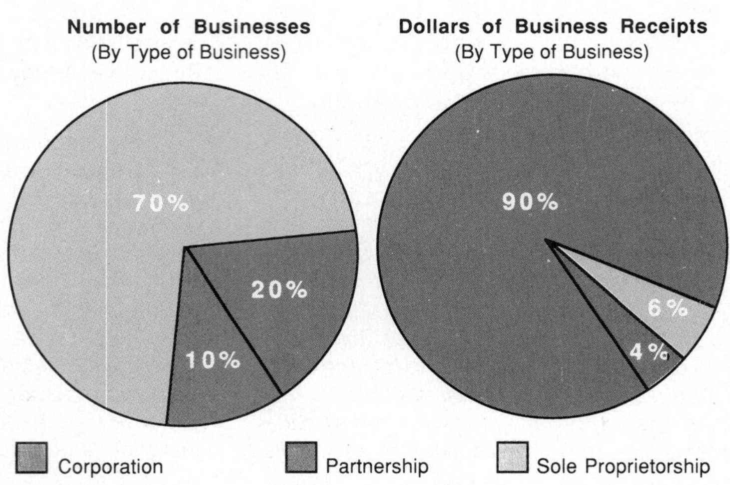

Source: U.S. Bureau of the Census, *Statistical Abstract of the United States*: 1990 (110th edition; Washington: U.S. Government Printing Office, 1990).

The Cost Principle

The records of properties and services purchased by a business are maintained in accordance with the **cost principle,** which requires that the monetary record be in terms of *cost*. For example, if a building is purchased at a cost of $150,000, that is the amount used in the buyer's accounting record. The seller may have been asking $170,000 for the building up to the time of the sale; the buyer initially may have offered $130,000 for it; the building may have been assessed at $125,000 for property tax purposes and insured for $135,000; and the buyer may have received an offer of $175,000 for the building the day after it was acquired. These latter amounts have no effect on the accounting records because they do not originate from an exchange. The exchange price, or cost, of $150,000 determines the monetary amount used in the records for the building.

Continuing the illustration, the $175,000 offer received by the buyer is an indication that the building was a bargain purchase at $150,000. To use $175,000 in the accounting records, however, would give recognition to an illusory or unrealized profit. If, after purchasing the building, the buyer should accept the offer and sell the building for $175,000, a profit of $25,000 would be realized, and the new owner would use $175,000 as the cost of the building.

The determination of costs incurred and revenues earned is fundamental to accounting. In exchanges between buyer and seller, both attempt to get the best price. Only the amount agreed upon is objective enough for accounting purposes. If the monetary amounts at which the accounting records for properties are maintained were constantly revised upward and downward on the basis of mere offers, appraisals, and opinions, accounting reports soon would become unstable and thus unreliable.

Business Transactions

A **business transaction** is the occurrence of an event or of a condition that must be recorded. For example, the payment of a monthly telephone bill of $68, the purchase of $1,750 of merchandise on credit, and the acquisition of land and a building for $210,000 are illustrative of the variety of business transactions.

The first two transactions are relatively simple: a payment of money in exchange for a service, and a promise to pay within a short time in exchange for goods. The purchase of a building and the land on which it is situated is usually a more complex transaction. The total price agreed upon must be divided between the land and the building, and the agreement usually provides for spreading the payment of a large part of the price over a period of years and for the payment of interest on the unpaid balance.

Unit of Measurement

All business transactions are recorded in terms of money. Other pertinent information of a nonfinancial nature also may be recorded, such as the terms of purchase and sale contracts, and the purpose, amount, and term of insurance policies. But it is only through the record of dollar amounts that the transactions and activities of a business may be measured, reported, and periodically compared. Money is both the common factor of all business transactions and the only feasible unit of measurement that can be used to achieve uniform financial data.

As a unit of measurement, the dollar differs from such quantitative standards as the kilogram, liter, or meter, which have not changed for centuries. The instability of the purchasing power of the dollar is well known, and the disruptive effect of the changing value of the dollar is acknowledged by accountants. However, the use of a monetary unit that is assumed to be stable insures **objectivity**. In spite of the inflationary trend in the United States, historical-dollar financial statements are considered to be better than statements based on movements of the general price level. Although the changing value of the dollar generally is not given recognition in the financial statements, supplemental statements are sometimes used to indicate the effect of changing prices.

ASSETS, LIABILITIES, AND OWNER'S EQUITY

OBJECTIVE 6
Identify the accounting equation and its basic elements.

The properties owned by a business enterprise are referred to as **assets** and the rights or claims to the properties are referred to as **equities.** If the assets owned by the business amount to $100,000, the equities in the assets must also amount to $100,000. The relationship between the two may be stated in the form of an equation, as follows:

Assets = Equities

Equities may be subdivided into two principal types: the rights of creditors and the rights of owners. The rights of creditors represent *debts* of the business and are called **liabilities.** The rights of owners are called **owner's equity**. Expansion of the equation to give recognition to the two basic types of equities yields the following, which is known as the **accounting equation:**

Assets = Liabilities + Owner's Equity

It is customary to place "Liabilities" before "Owner's Equity" in the accounting equation because creditors have preferential rights to the assets. The residual claim of the owners is sometimes given greater emphasis by transposing liabilities to the other side of the equation, yielding:

Assets − Liabilities = Owner's Equity

TRANSACTIONS AND THE ACCOUNTING EQUATION

OBJECTIVE 7
Describe and illustrate how all business transactions can be stated in terms of the resulting changes in the three basic elements of the accounting equation.

All business transactions, from the simplest to the most complex, can be stated in terms of the resulting change in the three basic elements of the accounting equation. The effect of these changes on the acounting equation can be demonstrated by studying some typical transacations. As the basis of the illustration, assume that Gramm Corporation is organized on January 2, 1992. Each transaction or group of similar transactions during the first month of operations is described, followed by an illustration of the effect on the accounting equation.

Transaction (a)

Gramm Corporation sells $60,000 of capital stock.

Direct investments by owners (stockholders) in a corporation are generally referred to as **capital stock.** The effect of the sale of $60,000 of capital stock to stockholders is to increase the asset (cash), on the left side of the equation, by $60,000 and to increase the owner's equity, on the other side of the equation, by the same amount. The effect of this transaction on the accounting equation is illustrated as follows:

	Assets		**Owner's Equity**	
	Cash	=	**Capital Stock**	
(a)	60,000		60,000	**Investment by stockholders**

Transaction (b)

For $40,000 in cash, Gramm Corporation purchases land as a future building site.

This transaction changes the composition of the assets but does not change the total amount. The items in the equation prior to this transaction, the effects of the transaction, and the new balances after the transaction are as follows:

	Assets				**Owner's Equity**
	Cash	**+**	**Land**		**Capital Stock**
Bal.	60,000			=	60,000
(b)	−40,000		+40,000		
Bal.	20,000		40,000		60,000

Transaction (c)

During the month, Gramm Corporation purchases $12,000 of supplies from various suppliers, agreeing to pay in the near future.

This type of transaction is called a purchase *on account*, and the liability created is termed an **account payable.** Liabilities of various types are commonly described as **payables**. Consumable goods purchased, such as supplies, and advance payments of expenses, such as insurance, are considered to be **prepaid expenses,** or assets. In actual practice, each purchase would be recorded as it occurred, and a separate record would be kept for each creditor. The effect of this transaction is to increase both assets and liabilities by $12,000, as follows:

	Assets						**Liabilities**	**+**	**Owner's Equity**
	Cash	**+**	**Supplies**	**+**	**Land**		**Accounts Payable**	**+**	**Capital Stock**
Bal.	20,000				40,000	=			60,000
(c)			+12,000				+12,000		
Bal.	20,000		12,000		40,000		12,000		60,000

Transaction (d)

During the month, Gramm Corporation pays $8,000 to the creditors on account.

The effect of this transaction is to decrease both the assets and the liabilities of the enterprise. The effect on the equation is as follows:

	Assets						**Liabilities**	**+**	**Owner's Equity**
	Cash	**+**	**Supplies**	**+**	**Land**		**Accounts Payable**	**+**	**Capital Stock**
Bal.	20,000		12,000		40,000	=	12,000		60,000
(d)	−8,000						−8,000		
Bal.	12,000		12,000		40,000		4,000		60,000

Transaction (e)

During the first month of operations, Gramm Corporation earned fees of $62,000, receiving the amount in cash.

The principal objective of a business enterprise is to increase owner's equity through earnings. For Gramm Corporation, this objective means that the cash and other assets acquired through the rendering of services must be greater than the cost of the supplies used, the wages of employees, the rent, and all the other expenses of operating the business.

In general, the amount charged to customers for goods or services is called **revenue.** Other terms may be used for certain kinds of revenue, such as *sales* for the sale of merchandise or services, *fares earned* for an enterprise that provides transportation services, *rent earned* for the use of real estate or other property, and *fees earned* for charges by a professional, such as an accountant or physician, to clients.

The effect of transaction (e) on the equation can be described as an increase in both the assets and the owner's equity of the enterprise and is illustrated as follows:

	Assets				=	Liabilities + Owner's Equity					
	Cash	+ **Supplies**	+	**Land**	=	**Accounts Payable**	+	**Capital Stock**	+	**Retained Earnings**	
Bal.	12,000	12,000		40,000		4,000		60,000			
(e)	+62,000									+62,000	**Fees earned**
Bal.	74,000	12,000		40,000		4,000		60,000		62,000	

Note that the increase in owner's equity resulting from revenue is listed in the equation under "Retained Earnings." **Retained earnings** is the owner's equity arising from the business' earnings (revenue less the expenses of operating the business). Transactions affecting earnings are kept separate from transactions related to the owner's investment (sale of capital stock). This separation is useful in preparing financial statements, in satisfying legal requirements, and for other reasons that will be discussed later in the text.

Instead of requiring the payment of cash at the time goods or services are sold, a business may make sales *on account,* allowing the customer to pay later. In such cases the firm acquires an **account receivable,** which is a claim against the customer. An account receivable is as much an asset as cash, and the revenue is realized in exactly the same manner as if cash had been immediately received. At a later date, when the money is collected, there is only an exchange of one asset for another, with cash increasing and accounts receivable decreasing.

Transaction (f)

Various business expenses incurred and paid during the month were as follows: wages, $25,000; rent, $10,000; utilities, $6,000; miscellaneous, $2,500.

In a broad sense, the amount of assets consumed or services used in the process of earning revenue is called **expense.** Expenses would include supplies used, wages of employees, and other assets and services used in operating the business. The effect of this group of transactions is to reduce cash and to reduce owner's equity, as follows:

	Assets				Liabilities + Owner's Equity			
	Cash	+ Supplies	+ Land		Accounts Payable	+ Capital Stock	+ Retained Earnings	
Bal.	74,000	12,000	40,000	=	4,000	60,000	62,000	
(f)	−43,500						−25,000	Wages exp.
							−10,000	Rent expense
							−6,000	Utilities exp.
							−2,500	Misc. expense
Bal.	30,500	12,000	40,000		4,000	60,000	18,500	

Note that the decrease in owner's equity resulting from expenses is listed in the equation under the "Retained Earnings" heading. As explained previously, such a procedure distinguishes the investments of owners (sale of capital stock) from owner's equity interests arising from earnings (revenue less the expenses of operating the business).

Transaction (g)

At the end of the month, it is determined that the cost of the supplies on hand is $4,500. The remainder of the supplies purchased in transaction (c), $7,500 ($12,000 − $4,500), were used in the operations of the business. This reduction of $7,500 in supplies and owner's equity may be shown as follows:

	Assets				Liabilities + Owner's Equity			
	Cash	+ Supplies	+ Land		Accounts Payable	+ Capital Stock	+ Retained Earnings	
Bal.	30,500	12,000	40,000	=	4,000	60,000	18,500	
(g)		−7,500					−7,500	Supplies exp.
Bal.	30,500	4,500	40,000		4,000	60,000	11,000	

Transaction (h)

At the end of the month, Gramm Corporation pays $5,000 of dividends.

The distributions of earnings to stockholders, called **dividends,** reduces both cash and owner's equity. The effect of this transaction is illustrated as follows:

	Assets				Liabilities + Owner's Equity			
	Cash	+ Supplies	+ Land		Accounts Payable	+ Capital Stock	+ Retained Earnings	
Bal.	30,500	4,500	40,000	=	4,000	60,000	11,000	
(h)	−5,000						−5,000	Dividends
Bal.	25,500	4,500	40,000		4,000	60,000	6,000	

Note that dividends are not an expense. They do not represent assets consumed or services used in the process of earning revenue. However, the decrease in owner's equity resulting from dividends is listed in the equation under the "Retained Earnings" heading because the dividends are a distribution of earnings.

Summary

The business transactions of Gramm Corporation are summarized in tabular form, as follows. The transactions are identified by letter, and the balance of each item is shown after each transaction.

	Assets					=	Liabilities + Owner's Equity					
	Cash	+	Supplies	+	Land	=	Accounts Payable	+	Capital Stock	+	Retained Earnings	
(a)	60,000								60,000			Investment by stockholders
(b)	−40,000				+40,000							
	20,000				40,000				60,000			
(c)			+12,000				+12,000					
	20,000		12,000		40,000		12,000		60,000			
(d)	−8,000						−8,000					
	12,000		12,000		40,000		4,000		60,000			
(e)	+62,000										+62,000	Fees earned
	74,000		12,000		40,000		4,000		60,000		62,000	
(f)	−43,500										−25,000	Wages exp.
											−10,000	Rent expense
											−6,000	Utilities expense
											−2,500	Misc. expense
	30,500		12,000		40,000		4,000		60,000		18,500	
(g)			−7,500								−7,500	Supplies expense
	30,500		4,500		40,000		4,000		60,000		11,000	
(h)	−5,000										−5,000	Dividends
	25,500		4,500		40,000		4,000		60,000		6,000	

The following observations, which apply to all types of businesses, should be noted:

1. The effect of every transaction can be stated in terms of increases and/or decreases in one or more of the accounting equation elements.
2. The equality of the two sides of the accounting equation is always maintained.
3. The owner's equity is increased by revenues and decreased by expenses. In addition, owner's equity is increased by amounts invested by stockholders and decreased by dividends distributed to stockholders. The effect of these four types of transactions on owner's equity is illustrated at the top of page 25.

FINANCIAL STATEMENTS

OBJECTIVE 8
Identify and describe the following financial statements:
Income statement
Retained earnings statement
Balance sheet
Statement of cash flows

After the effect of the individual transactions has been determined, the essential information is communicated to users. The accounting statements that communicate this information are called **financial statements**. The principal financial statements of a corporation are the income statement, the retained earnings statement, the balance sheet, and the statement of cash flows.

In preparing the financial statements of a business enterprise, the income statement is usually prepared first because the net income for the period is needed in order to prepare the retained earnings statement. The retained earnings statement is prepared next because the ending balance of retained earnings for the period is needed for the preparation of the balance sheet.

Effect of Transactions on Owner's Equity

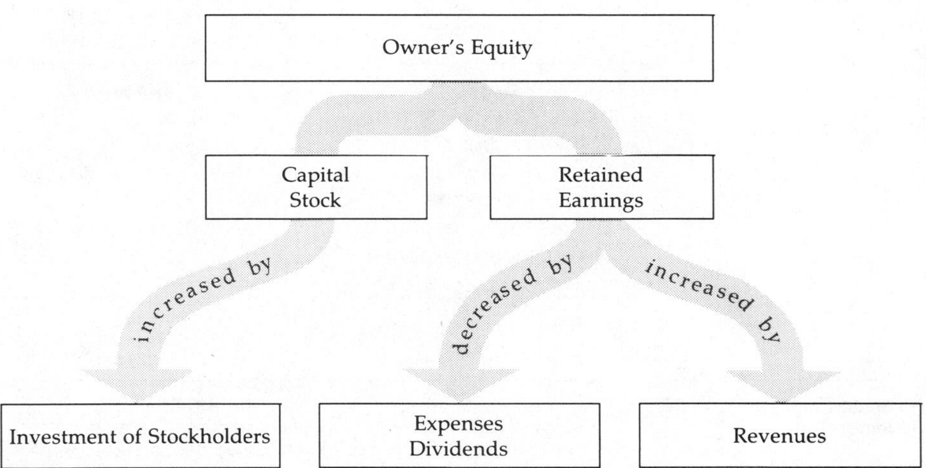

Then the balance sheet is prepared, and finally, the statement of cash flows is prepared. The basic features of the four statements and their interrelationships are illustrated on the following page. The data for the statements were taken from the summary of transactions of Gramm Corporation on page 24. The nature of the data presented in each statement, in general terms, is as follows:

Income statement

A summary of the revenue and the expenses of a business entity for a specific period of time, such as a month or a year.

Retained earnings statement

A summary of the changes in the earnings retained in the business entity for a specific period of time, such as a month or a year.

Balance sheet

A list of the assets, liabilities, and owner's equity of a business entity as of a specific date, usually at the close of the last day of a month or a year.

Statement of cash flows

A summary of the cash receipts and cash payments of a business entity for a specific period of time, such as a month or a year.

All financial statements should be identified by the name of the business, the title of the statement, and the date or period of time. The data presented in the income statement, the retained earnings statement and the statement of cash flows are for a period of time. The data presented in the balance sheet are for a specific date.

Income Statement

The excess of the revenue over the expenses incurred in earning the revenue is called **net income** or **net profit.** If the expenses of the enterprise exceed the revenue, the excess is a **net loss.** It is ordinarily impossible to determine the exact amount of expense incurred in connection with each revenue transaction. Therefore, it is considered satisfactory to determine the net income or the net loss for a stated period of time, such as a month or a year, rather than for each transaction or small group of transactions.

Income Statement

Gramm Corporation
Income Statement
For Month Ended January 31, 1992

Fees earned		$62,000
Operating expenses:		
Wages expense	$25,000	
Rent expense	10,000	
Supplies expense	7,500	
Utilities expense	6,000	
Miscellaneous expense	2,500	
Total operating expenses		51,000
Net income		$11,000

Retained Earnings Statement

Gramm Corporation
Retained Earnings Statement
For Month Ended January 31, 1992

Net income for the month	$11,000
Less dividends	5,000
Retained earnings, January 31, 1992	$6,000

Balance Sheet

Gramm Corporation
Balance Sheet
January 31, 1992

Assets		
Cash		$25,500
Supplies		4,500
Land		40,000
Total assets		$70,000
Liabilities		
Accounts payable		$ 4,000
Stockholders' Equity		
Capital stock	$60,000	
Retained earnings	6,000	
Total stockholders' equity		66,000
Total liabilities and stockholders' equity		$70,000

Statement of Cash Flows

Gramm Corporation
Statement of Cash Flows
For Month Ended January 31, 1992

Cash flows from operating activities:		
Cash received from customers	$62,000	
Deduct cash payments for expenses and payments to creditors	51,500	
Net cash flow from operating activities		$10,500
Cash flows from investing activities:		
Cash payments for acquisition of land		(40,000)
Cash flows from financing activities:		
Cash received from sale of capital stock	$60,000	
Deduct cash dividends	5,000	
Net cash flow from financing activities		55,000
Net cash flow and January 31, 1992 cash balance		$25,500

The determination of the periodic net income (or net loss) is a **matching** process involving two steps. First, revenues are recognized during the period. Second, the assets consumed in generating the revenues must be **matched** against the revenues in order to determine the net income or the net loss. Generally, the revenue for the rendering of a service is recognized after the service has been rendered to the customer. The assets consumed in generating revenue during a period must be recognized as expenses. In this way, the expenses are properly **matched** against the revenues generated. The details of this matching for Gramm Corporation, together with the net income in the amount of $11,000, are reported in the income statement on page 26.

The order in which the operating expenses are presented in the income statement varies among businesses. One of the arrangements commonly followed is a listing of expenses in the order of size, beginning with the larger items. Miscellaneous expense usually is shown as the last item, regardless of the amount.

Retained Earnings Statement

The primary focus for analyzing changes in the owners' equity of a corporation is often the retained earnings statement, which serves as a link between the income statement and the balance sheet. The retained earnings statement for Gramm Corporation, which appears on page 26, shows that two types of transactions affected the retained earnings during the month: (1) the revenues and expenses that resulted in net income of $11,000 for the month and (2) dividends of $5,000 paid to stockholders.

Since January was the first month of operations, Gramm Corporation had no retained earnings at the beginning of January. Changes in Gramm Corporation's retained earnings in future months may result from (1) additional net income (or net loss) and (2) dividends to stockholders. To illustrate, assume that Gramm Corporation earned net income of $20,000 and paid dividends of $15,000 during February. The retained earnings statement for Gramm Corporation for February would appear as follows:

Gramm Corporation
Retained Earnings Statement
For Month Ended February 29, 1992

Retained earnings, February 1, 1992		$ 6,000
Net income for the month	$20,000	
Less dividends	15,000	
Increase in retained earnings		5,000
Retained earnings, February 29, 1992		$11,000

Balance Sheet

The amounts of Gramm Corporation's assets, liabilities, and owner's equity at the end of January, the first month of operations, appear on the last line of the summary on page 24. Minor rearrangements of these data and the addition of a heading yield the balance sheet illustrated on page 26. This form of balance sheet, with the liability and owner's equity sections presented below the asset section, is called the **report form**. Another arrangement in common use lists the assets on the left and the liabilities and owner's equity on the right. Because of its similarity to the account, a basic accounting device described in the next chapter, it is referred to as the **account form of balance sheet.**

It is customary to begin the asset section with cash. This item is followed by receivables, supplies, and other assets that will be converted into cash or used up in the near future. Assets with a relatively long life, such as land, buildings, and equipment, are then listed in that order.

In the liabilities and owner's equity section of the balance sheet, it is customary to present the liabilities first, followed by owner's equity. In the illustration on page 26, liabilities are composed entirely of accounts payable. When there are two or more categories of liabilities, each should be listed and the total amount of liabilities presented in the following manner:

Liabilities		
Accounts payable	$1,100	
Salaries payable	300	
Total liabilities		$1,400

It is also customary on corporation balance sheets to refer to the owner's equity as **stockholders' equity.** For Gramm Corporation, the January 31, 1992 stockholders' equity consists of $60,000 of capital stock and retained earnings of $6,000. The retained earnings amount of $6,000 is taken from the retained earnings statement.

Statement of Cash Flows

It is customary to report cash flows (cash receipts and cash payments) in three sections: (1) operating activities, (2) investing activities, and (3) financing activities. Data for the preparation of these d three sections of the statement of cash flows for Gramm Corporation were included in the cash column of the summary on page 24.[5]

The cash flows from operating activities section includes cash transactions that enter into the determination of net income. For Gramm Corporation, the cash received from customers was $62,000. The cash payments totaled $51,500, which consisted of $8,000 paid to creditors for supplies purchased and $43,500 paid for wages, rent, utilities, and miscellaneous expense. The net cash flow from operating activities is $10,500 ($62,000 − $51,500).

The net cash flow from operating activities normally will differ from the amount of net income for the period. For Gramm Corporation, the net cash flow from operating activities ($10,500) differs from the net income ($11,000) by $500. This difference arises because supplies worth $7,500 were used but $8,000 was paid to creditors on account. Thus, while the income statement reports supplies expense of $7,500, the statement of cash flows includes $8,000 as cash payments for supplies.

The cash flows from investing activities section reports the cash transactions for the acquisition and sale of relatively long-term or permanent-type assets. Gramm Corporation's only cash flow related to investing activities was the acquisition of land for $40,000.

[5]In practice, an alternative means may be used to accumulate the data needed to prepare the statement of cash flows. The discussion of this method and additional complexities are reserved until Chapter 14, after various necessary concepts and principles have been explained and illustrated.

The cash flows from financing activities section reports the cash transactions related to the sale of capital stock and borrowings and cash dividends paid to shareholders. For Gramm Corporation, the cash flows from financing activities were $60,000 from the sale of capital stock less $5,000 of cash dividends distributed to shareholders. The amount of the dividends ($5,000) are subtracted from the cash received from the sale of capital stock ($60,000) in determining the net cash flow from financing activities ($55,000).

Since January was Gramm Corporation's first month of operations, the increase in cash flows for January is the January 31, 1992 cash balance. In future statements, the cash balance at the beginning of the period is added to the increase (or decrease) in cash for the period to indicate the cash balance at the end of the period. To illustrate, assume that Gramm Corporation's net cash flows for February increased by $2,500. The increase resulted from the following cash transactions:

Cash received from customers	$87,500
Cash payments for expenses and payments to creditors	70,000
Cash dividends paid	15,000

The statement of cash flows for Gramm Corporation for February would be as follows:

Gramm Corporation
Statement of Cash Flows
For Month Ended February 29, 1992

Cash flows from operating activities:		
Cash received from customers	$87,500	
Deduct cash payments for expenses and payments to creditors	70,000	
Net cash flow from operating activities		$ 17,500
Cash flows from financing activities:		
Cash dividends		(15,000)
Increase in cash		$ 2,500
Cash balance, February 1, 1992		25,500
Cash balance, February 29, 1992		$ 28,000

CHAPTER REVIEW

KEY POINTS

OBJECTIVE 1

Accounting as an Information System

The objective of accounting is to record, summarize, report, and interpret financial data for use by many groups within our economic and social system. In this sense, accounting is often called the "language of business." This language can be viewed as an information system that provides essential information about the financial activities of an entity to various individuals or groups for their use in making informed judgments and decisions. Examples of users of accounting information include investors, bankers, suppliers, government agencies, employees, and managers of the entity.

OBJECTIVE 2

Financial and Managerial Accounting

Financial accounting is concerned with the measuring and recording of transactions for a business enterprise and the periodic preparation of various reports from such records. Corporate enterprises must use generally accepted accounting principles in preparing their annual financial statements. Managerial accounting uses both historical and estimated data to assist management in conducting and evaluating current operations and in planning future operations. The principle of "usefulness" is dominant in guiding the accountant in preparing management reports.

OBJECTIVE 3

Development of Financial Accounting Concepts and Principles

As the American economy developed and as business organizations grew in size and complexity, there came an awareness of the need for a framework of concepts and generally accepted accounting principles to serve as guidelines for the preparation of the basic financial statements. These principles represent the best possible guides, based on reason, observation, and experimentation, to help make accounting data more useful in an ever-changing society.

Currently, the Financial Accounting Standards Board establishes accounting standards for business enterprises. The Governmental Accounting Standards Board has responsibility for establishing accounting standards to be followed by state and municipal governments.

Among the other organizations which have had an effect on the development of accounting principles are the American Institute of Certified Public Accountants, the American Accounting Association, the Securities and Exchange Commission, the Internal Revenue Service, the Financial Executives Institute, and the National Association of Accountants.

OBJECTIVE 4

Professional Ethics for Accountants

The AICPA has established codes of professional conduct to guide CPAs in public practice. The IMA has established standards of ethical conduct for managerial accountants. These ethics standards instill confidence in the quality of services rendered to the public, employers, and the accounting profession.

OBJECTIVE 5

Financial Accounting Concepts and Principles

Four of the most important accounting concepts relate to the business entity, the cost of properties and services, business transactions, and the unit of measurement.

The business entity concept is based on the applicability of accounting to individual economic units in society. Profit-making businesses are customarily organized as sole proprietorships, partnerships, or corporations.

The cost principle requires that properties and services purchased by a business be recorded in terms of cost.

A business transaction is the occurrence of an event or a condition that must be recorded. Business transactions may be either simple or complex and may lead to an event or a condition that results in yet another transaction.

All business transactions are recorded in terms of money. The use of the monetary unit in accounting for and reporting the activities of an enterprise assumes stability of the measurement unit.

OBJECTIVE 6

Assets, Liabilities, and Owner's Equity

The properties owned by a business and the rights or claims to properties may be stated in the form of an equation as follows: Assets = Equities. The expansion of the equation to give recognition to two basic types of equities yields the following, which is known as the accounting equation: Assets = Liabilities + Owner's Equity.

OBJECTIVE 7 Transactions and the Accounting Equation

All transactions, from the simplest to the most complex, can be stated in terms of the resulting change in the three basic elements of the accounting equation. That is, the effect of every transaction can be stated in terms of increases and/or decreases in one or more of the accounting equation elements such that the equality of the two sides of the accounting equation is always maintained.

OBJECTIVE 8 Financial Statements

After the effects of individual transactions have been determined and recorded, reports (financial statements) summarizing these effects are prepared and communicated to users. The principal accounting statements of a corporation are the income statement, the retained earnings statement, the balance sheet, and the statement of cash flows.

KEY TERMS

accounting 12
financial accounting 12
generally accepted accounting principles (GAAP) 12
managerial accounting 13
Financial Accounting Standards Board (FASB) 15
Governmental Accounting Standards Board (GASB) 15
business entity concept 17
sole proprietorship 18
partnership 18
corporation 18
stockholders 18
cost principle 18
business transaction 19
assets 20
equities 20
liabilities 20
owner's equity 20
accounting equation 20
capital stock 20
account payable 21
prepaid expenses 21
revenue 22
retained earnings 22
account receivable 22
expense 22
dividends 23
income statement 25
retained earnings statement 25
balance sheet 25
statement of cash flows 25
net income 25
net loss 25
matching 27
report form of balance sheet 27
account form of balance sheet 28
stockholders' equity 28

SELF-EXAMINATION QUESTIONS

Answers at end of chapter.

1. A profit-making business that is a separate legal entity and in which ownership is divided into shares of stock is known as a:
   A. sole proprietorship
   B. single proprietorship
   C. partnership
   D. corporation

2. The properties owned by a business enterprise are called:
   A. assets
   B. liabilities
   C. capital stock
   D. owner's equity

3. A list of assets, liabilities, and owner's equity of a business entity as of a specific date is:
   A. a balance sheet
   B. an income statement
   C. a statement of cash flows
   D. a retained earnings statement

4. If total assets increased $20,000 during a period of time and total liabilities increased by $12,000 during the same period, the amount and direction (increase or decrease) of the period's change in owner's equity is:
   A. $32,000 increase
   B. $32,000 decrease
   C. $8,000 increase
   D. $8,000 decrease

5. If revenue was $45,000, expenses were $37,500, and dividends were $10,000, the amount of net income or net loss was:
   A. $45,000 net income
   B. $7,500 net income
   C. $37,500 net loss
   D. $2,500 net loss

ILLUSTRATIVE PROBLEM

Acme Cleaners Inc. is a corporation that was organized recently. Currently, a building and equipment are being rented pending completion of construction of new facilities. The actual work of dry cleaning is done by another company at wholesale rates. The assets, liabilities, and owner's equity of the business on May 1 of the current year are as follows: Cash, $5,400; Accounts Receivable, $3,700; Supplies, $410; Land, $9,500; Accounts Payable, $2,380; Capital Stock, $10,000; Retained Earnings, $6,630. Business transactions during May are summarized as follows:

(a) Paid rent for the month, $850.
(b) Charged customers for dry cleaning sales on account, $5,646.
(c) Paid creditors on account, $1,730.
(d) Purchased supplies on account, $254.
(e) Received cash from cash customers for dry cleaning sales, $2,894.
(f) Received cash from customers on account, $2,750.
(g) Paid dividends of $760.
(h) Received monthly invoice for dry cleaning expense for May (to be paid on June 10), $3,416.
(i) Paid the following: wages expense, $675; truck expense, $310; utilities expense, $260; miscellaneous expense, $89.
(j) Determined the cost of supplies used during the month, $328.

Instructions:

1. State the assets, liabilities, and owner's equity as of May 1 in equation form similar to that shown in this chapter. In tabular form below the equation, indicate the increases and decreases resulting from each transaction and the new balances after each transaction. Explain the nature of each increase and decrease in retained earnings by an appropriate notation at the right of the amount.
2. Prepare an income statement and retained earnings statement for May.
3. Prepare a balance sheet as of May 31, 19—.
4. Prepare a statement of cash flows for May.

SOLUTION

(1)

	Assets				= Liabilities +	Owner's Equity		
	Cash +	Accounts Receivable +	Supplies +	Land =	Accounts Payable +	Capital Stock +	Retained Earnings	
Bal.	5,400	3,700	410	9,500	2,380	10,000	6,630	
(a)	−850						−850	Rent expense
Bal.	4,550	3,700	410	9,500	2,380	10,000	5,780	
(b)		+5,646					+5,646	Dry cleaning sales
Bal.	4,550	9,346	410	9,500	2,380	10,000	11,426	
(c)	−1,730				−1,730			
Bal.	2,820	9,346	410	9,500	650	10,000	11,426	
(d)			+254		+254			
Bal.	2,820	9,346	664	9,550	904	10,000	11,426	
(e)	+2,894						+2,894	Dry cleaning sales
Bal.	5,714	9,346	664	9,500	904	10,000	14,320	
(f)	+2,750	−2,750						
Bal.	8,464	6,596	664	9,500	904	10,000	14,320	
(g)	−760						−760	Dividends
Bal.	7,704	6,596	664	9,500	904	10,000	13,560	
(h)					+3,416		−3,416	Dry cleaning exp.
Bal.	7,704	6,596	664	9,500	4,320	10,000	10,144	
(i)	−1,334						−675	Wages expense
							−310	Truck expense
							−260	Utilities expense
							−89	Misc. expense
Bal.	6,370	6,596	664	9,500	4,320	10,000	8,810	
(j)			−328				−328	Supplies expense
Bal.	6,370	6,596	336	9,500	4,320	10,000	8,482	

(2)

Acme Cleaners Inc.
Income Statement
For Month Ended May 31, 19—

Dry cleaning sales		$8,540
Operating expenses:		
Dry cleaning expense	$3,416	
Rent expense	850	
Wages expense	675	
Supplies expense	328	
Truck expense	310	
Utilities expense	260	
Miscellaneous expense	89	
Total operating expenses		5,928
Net income		$2,612

Acme Cleaners Inc.
Retained Earnings Statement
For Month Ended May 31, 19—

Retained earnings, May 1, 19—		$6,630
Net income for the month	$2,612	
Less dividends	760	
Increase in retained earnings		1,852
Retained earnings, May 31, 19—		$8,482

(3)

Acme Cleaners Inc.
Balance Sheet
May 31, 19—

Assets

Cash		$ 6,370
Accounts receivable		6,596
Supplies		336
Land		9,500
Total assets		$22,802

Liabilities

Accounts payable		$ 4,320

Stockholders' Equity

Capital stock	$10,000	
Retained earnings	8,482	
Total stockholders' equity		18,482
Total liabilities and stockholders' equity		$22,802

(4)

Acme Cleaners Inc.
Statement of Cash Flows
For Month Ended May 31, 19—

Cash flows from operating activities:		
Cash received from customers	$5,644*	
Deduct cash payments for expenses and payments to creditors	3,914**	
Net cash flow from operating activities		$1,730
Cash flows from financing activities:		
Cash dividends		(760)
Increase in cash		$ 970
Cash balance, May 1, 19—		5,400
Cash balance, May 31, 19—		$6,370

*$2,894 (transaction e) + $2,750 (transaction f) = $5,644
**$850 (transaction a) + $1,730 (transaction c) + $1,334 (transaction i) = $3,914

DISCUSSION QUESTIONS

1–1. What is the objective of accounting?

1–2. Name some of the categories of individuals and institutions who use accounting information.

1–3. Distinguish between financial accounting and managerial accounting.

1–4. Accounting principles are broad guides to accounting practice. (a) How do these principles differ from the principles relating to the physical sciences? (b) Of what significance is acceptability in the development of accounting principles? (c) Why must accounting principles be continually reexamined and revised?

1–5. What body is currently dominant in the development of (a) generally accepted accounting principles for business enterprises and (b) principles for state and municipal governments?

1–6. What organization has established a code of professional ethics for (a) certified public accountants (CPAs); (b) managerial accountants?

1–7. (a) Name the three principal forms of profit-making business organizations. (b) Which of these forms is identified with the greatest number of businesses?

1–8. Ed Jones, president of Pronto Delivery Inc., purchased a new Dodge truck for the delivery service. Pronto Delivery Inc. is organized as a corporation, with Martha Richards as the sole stockholder. The truck was purchased for $22,300 cash from Evans Chrysler & Dodge Inc. of Hammond, Illinois. According to the business entity concept, which of the entities (Ed Jones, Pronto Delivery Inc., Martha Richards, Evans Chrysler & Dodge Inc.) should record this transaction in their records?

1–9. What is meant by the cost principle?

1–10. (a) Land with an assessed value of $100,000 for property tax purposes is acquired by a business enterprise for $175,000. At what amount should the land be recorded by the purchaser?
(b) Five years later the plot of land in (a) has an assessed value of $140,000 and the business enterprise receives an offer of $250,000 for it. Should the monetary amount assigned to the land in the business records now be increased and, if so, by what amount?
(c) Assuming that the land acquired in part (a) was sold for $275,000, (1) how much would the owner's equity increase, and (2) at what amount would the purchaser record the land?

1–11. Conventional financial statements do not give recognition to the instability of the purchasing power of the dollar. How can the effect of the fluctuating dollar on business operations be presented to the users of the financial statements?

1–12. (a) If the assets owned by a business enterprise total $450,000, what is the amount of the equities of the enterprise? (b) What are the two principal types of equities?

1–13. Name the three elements of the accounting equation.

1–14. (a) An enterprise has assets of $250,000 and liabilities of $175,000. What is the amount of its owner's equity?
(b) An enterprise has assets of $480,000 and owner's equity of $200,000. What is the total amount of its liabilities?
(c) A corporation has assets of $995,000, liabilities of $590,000, and capital stock of $250,000. What is the amount of its retained earnings?
(d) An enterprise has liabilities of $500,000 and owner's equity of $300,000. What is the total amount of its assets?

1–15. Describe how the following business transactions affect the three elements of the accounting equation:
(a) Issued capital stock for cash:
(b) Purchased supplies for cash.
(c) Purchased supplies on account.
(d) Received cash for services performed.
(e) Paid for utilities used in the business.

1–16. (a) A vacant lot acquired for $75,000, on which there is a balance owed of $45,000, is sold for $90,000 in cash. What is the effect of the sale on the total amount of the seller's (1) assets, (2) liabilities, and (3) owner's equity?
(b) After receiving the $90,000 cash in (a), the seller pays the $45,000 owed. What is the effect of the payment on the total amount of the seller's (1) assets, (2) liabilities, and (3) owner's equity?

1–17. During the month, a business corporation received $910,000 in cash and paid out $860,000 in cash. Do the data indicate that the corporation earned $50,000 during the month? Explain.

1–18. Operations of a service enterprise for a particular month are summarized as follows:
Service sales: on account, $24,000; for cash, $70,000
Expenses incurred: on account, $36,000; for cash, $45,000
What was the amount of the enterprise's (a) revenue, (b) expenses, and (c) net income?

1–19. A business enterprise had revenues of $85,000 and operating expenses of $92,750. Did the enterprise (a) incur a net loss or (b) realize a net income?

1–20. A business enterprise had revenues of $92,500 and operating expenses of $85,000. Did the enterprise (a) incur a net loss or (b) realize a net income?

1–21. Indicate whether each of the following types of transactions will (a) increase owner's equity or (b) decrease owner's equity:
(1) issuance of capital stock
(2) dividends
(3) expenses
(4) revenues

1–22. If total assets have increased by $19,000 during a specific period of time and owner's equity has decreased by $10,000 during the same period, what was the amount and direction (increase or decrease) of the period's change in total liabilities?

1–23. During the month, a business corporation received $925,000 in cash and paid out $790,000 in cash. Do the data indicate that the corporation earned $135,000 during the month? Explain.

1–24. Give the titles of the four major financial statements illustrated in this chapter, and briefly describe the nature of the information provided by each.

1–25. Indicate whether the data in each of the following financial statements (a) covers a period of time or (b) is for a specific date:
(1) income statement
(2) balance sheet
(3) retained earnings statement
(4) statement of cash flows

1–26. Name the three types of activities reported in the statement of cash flows.

1–27. What particular item of financial or operating data for a service enterprise, organized as a corporation, appears on (a) both the income statement and the retained earnings statement, and (b) both the balance sheet and the retained earnings statement?

1–28. House of High Fidelity had an owner's equity balance of $180,000 at the beginning of the period. At the end of the period, the company had total assets of $245,000 and total liabilities of $75,000. (a) What was the net income or net loss for the period, assuming no additional sale of capital stock and no dividends? (b) What was the net income or net loss for the period, assuming $25,000 of dividends had been paid during the period?

1–29. Indicate whether each of the following activities would be reported on the statement of cash flows as (a) operating activity, (b) investing activity, or (c) financing activity:
(1) cash received from sale of capital stock
(2) cash paid for land
(3) cash received from fees earned
(4) cash paid for expenses

Real World Focus

1–30. Based upon the annual report of Coca-Cola Enterprises Inc. presented in Appendix H, what are (a) the total assets at December 30, 1988, (b) the total liabilities and shareholders' equity at December 30, 1988, (c) the net operating revenues for the year ended December 30, 1988, (d) the net income for the year ended December 30, 1988, and (e) the ratio of the net income to the net operating revenues for the year ended December 30, 1988?

Ethics Discussion Case

1–31. Miller Enterprises Inc. applied for a $500,000 loan from First National Bank. The bank requested a set of financial statements as a basis for granting the loan. John Miller, President, has told his accountant to provide the bank with a balance sheet, an income statement, and a retained earnings statement. John Miller has decided to omit the statement of cash flows, since there was a net decrease in cash during the past year.

Discuss whether John Miller is behaving in an ethical manner by omitting the statement of cash flows.

EXERCISES

Ex. 1–32.
Business entity concept.
OBJ. 5

Splash Advertisers Inc., owned by Janet Smith and Beverly Farmer, specializes in media advertising for small business enterprises. Janet Smith serves as president and Beverly Farmer serves as the sales representative and aids in advertising design and art work. One of Splash's primary customers is Dr. Edward Hill, III, a local physician who places several promotional ads each week in the Gorman Banner Herald, a daily newspaper.

The following transactions were completed during a period:

(a) Beverly Farmer purchased $15,000 additional stock from Splash Advertisers Inc.
(b) Dr. Edward Hill, III rendered services to Janet Smith's daughter, who had been complaining of a sore throat. Janet Smith paid Dr. Hill $50 for an office visit.
(c) Beverly Farmer purchased art supplies for use in developing the week's advertisements, $120.
(d) Beverly Farmer purchased a business suit to wear to a hospital awards dinner that is being held in honor of Dr. Hill. Beverly charged the $450 suit to her personal credit card.
(e) Gorman Banner Herald purchased $3,000 of ink and paper supplies for the month's printing needs.

(f) Dr. Hill placed a "Help Wanted" advertisement for a receptionist in the Gorman Banner Herald.
(g) Janet Smith paid a $120 monthly fee for child care services for her daughter.
(h) Gorman Banner Herald billed Splash Advertisers Inc. $1,500 for last month's advertisements placed by Splash.
(i) Splash Advertisers Inc. paid $600 to Dr. Hill for physicals for life insurance policies on Janet Smith and Beverly Farmer. The insurance policies name Splash Advertisers Inc. as beneficiary.

Indicate which of the above transactions should be recorded by Splash Advertisers Inc. in its accounting records.

Ex. 1–33.
Transactions and the accounting equation.
OBJ. 7

The following selected transactions were completed by Lopez Delivery Company during June:

(1) Received cash from sale of capital stock, $20,000.
(2) Purchased supplies of gas and oil for cash, $850.
(3) Billed customers for delivery services on account, $900.
(4) Received cash from cash customers, $1,750.
(5) Paid advertising expense, $750.
(6) Paid rent for June, $1,500.
(7) Paid creditors on account, $350.
(8) Received cash from customers on account, $700.
(9) Paid cash dividends, $1,000.
(10) Determined by taking an inventory that $575 of supplies of gas and oil had been used during the month.

Indicate the effect of each transaction on the accounting equation by listing the numbers identifying the transactions, (1) through (10), in a vertical column, and inserting at the right of each number the appropriate letter from the following list:

(a) Increase in one asset, decrease in another asset.
(b) Increase in an asset, increase in a liability.
(c) Increase in an asset, increase in owner's equity.
(d) Decrease in an asset, decrease in a liability.
(e) Decrease in an asset, decrease in owner's equity.

Ex. 1–34.
Transactions and the accounting equation.
OBJ. 7

Matlock Corporation, engaged in a service business, completed the following selected transactions during the period:

(1) Issued additional capital stock, receiving cash.
(2) Purchased supplies on account.
(3) Charged customers for services sold on account.
(4) Returned defective supplies purchased on account for which payment has not yet been made.
(5) Paid a creditor on account.
(6) Received cash from customers on account.
(7) Paid utilities expense.
(8) Received cash as a refund from the erroneous overpayment of an expense.
(9) Determined the amount of supplies used during the month.
(10) Paid cash dividends to stockholders.

Using a tabular form with four column headings entitled Transaction, Assets, Liabilities, and Owner's Equity, respectively, indicate the effect of each transaction. Use + for increase and − for decrease.

Ex. 1–35.
Nature of transactions.
OBJ. 7

Ruth Tavel is engaged in a service business. Summary financial data for January are presented in equation form as follows. Each line designated by a number indicates the effect of a transaction on the equation. Each increase and decrease in retained earnings, except transaction (5), affects net income.

	Cash	+	Supplies	+	Land	=	Liabilities	+	Capital Stock	+	Retained Earnings
Bal.	7,500		750		10,000		3,750		10,000		4,500
(1)	+9,000										+9,000
(2)	−2,750						−2,750				
(3)	−3,300										−3,300
(4)			+900				+900				
(5)	−950										−950
(6)	−5,000				+5,000						
(7)			−980								−980
Bal.	4,500		670		15,000		1,900		10,000		8,270

(a) Describe each transaction.
(b) What is the amount of net decrease in cash during the month?
(c) What is the amount of net increase in retained earnings during the month?
(d) What is the amount of the net income for the month?
(e) How much of the net income of the month was retained in the business?

Ex. 1–36.
Net income for four corporations.
OBJ. 8

Four different corporations, A, B, C, and D, show the same balance sheet data at the beginning and end of a year. These data, exclusive of the amount of owner's equity, are summarized as follows:

	Total Assets	Total Liabilities
Beginning of the year	$410,000	$180,000
End of the year	505,000	250,000

On the basis of the above data and the following additional information for the year, determine the net income (or loss) of each company for the year. (*Suggestion:* First determine the amount of increase or decrease in owner's equity during the year.)

Company A: No additional capital stock was issued and no dividends were paid.
Company B: No additional capital stock was issued and dividends paid were $30,000.
Company C: Capital stock of $35,000 was issued and no dividends were paid.
Company D: Capital stock of $35,000 was issued and $30,000 of dividends were paid.

Ex. 1–37.
Balance sheet items.
OBJ. 8

From the following list of selected items taken from the records of J.A. Buck Corporation as of a specific date, identify those that would appear on the balance sheet:

(1) Retained Earnings
(2) Cash
(3) Salaries Expense
(4) Land
(5) Accounts Payable
(6) Capital Stock
(7) Fees Earned
(8) Salaries Payable
(9) Supplies
(10) Utilities Expense

Ex. 1–38.
Missing amounts from balance sheet and income statement data.
OBJ. 8

One item is omitted in each of the following summaries of balance sheet and income statement data for four different corporations, A, B, C, and D.

	A	B	C	D
Beginning of the year:				
Assets	$250,000	$70,000	$99,000	(d)
Liabilities	140,000	30,000	76,000	$27,100
End of the year:				
Assets	290,000	95,000	96,000	73,000
Liabilities	160,000	20,000	77,000	42,000
During the year:				
Additional issuance of capital stock	(a)	9,000	10,000	25,000
Dividends	20,000	12,000	(c)	21,000
Revenue	95,000	(b)	88,100	99,000
Expenses	80,000	35,000	89,600	78,000

Determine the amounts of the missing items, identifying them by letter. (*Suggestion*: First determine the amount of increase or decrease in owner's equity during the year.)

Ex. 1–39.
Income statement and statement of cash flows.
OBJ. 8

Barr Services was organized on June 1 by sale of capital stock for $5,000. A summary of the transactions for the remainder of June are as follows:

Fees earned	$4,900
Cash received from customers	4,900
Wages expense	1,200
Rent expense	900
Supplies expense	250
Miscellaneous expense	50
Cash payments for expenses and payments to creditors	2,300
Cash dividends	1,750

(a) Prepare an income statement for the month ended June 30.
(b) Prepare a statement of cash flows for the month ended June 30.
(c) What is the reason that the net income for June was less than the net cash flow from operating activities for June?

Ex. 1–40.
Balance sheet.
OBJ. 8

Financial information related to George Belmont Interiors as of June 30 of the current year is as follows:

Accounts Payable	$6,520
Accounts Receivable	9,900
Capital Stock	10,000
Cash	9,500
Retained Earnings	?
Supplies	975

Prepare a balance sheet for George Belmont Interiors as of June 30 of the current year.

PROBLEMS

Pb. 1–41.
Transactions.
OBJ. 7

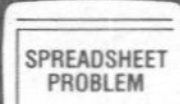

John Allen established John Allen Company on October 1 of the current year and completed the following transactions during October.

(a) Received cash from sale of capital stock, $5,000.
(b) Received cash from fees earned, $6,750.

(c) Purchased supplies on account, $925.
(d) Paid creditors on account, $625.
(e) Paid rent on office and equipment for the month, $3,000.
(f) Paid automobile expenses for month, $780, and miscellaneous expenses, $250.
(g) Paid salaries, $1,500.
(h) Determined that the cost of supplies on hand was $275; therefore, the cost of supplies used was $650.
(i) Billed customers for fees earned, $2,350.
(j) Paid dividends, $1,000.

Instructions:

Indicate the effect of each transaction and the balances after each transaction, using the following tabular headings:

Assets				Liabilities		Owner's Equity		
Cash +	Accounts Receivable	+ Supplies	=	Accounts Payable	+	Capital Stock	+	Retained Earnings

By appropriate notations at the right of each change, indicate the nature of each increase and decrease in retained earnings.

Pb. 1–42. Financial statements. OBJ. 8

Joan Bowan established Bowan Services Inc. on July 1 of the current year. The effect of each transaction and the balances after each transaction for July are as follows:

	Assets			= Liabilities +	Owner's Equity		
	Cash +	Accounts Receivable +	Supplies =	Accounts Payable +	Capital Stock +	Retained Earnings	
(a)	+5,000				+5,000		
(b)	+4,500					+4,500	Fees earned
Bal.	9,500				5,000	4,500	
(c)			+550	+550			
Bal.	9,500		550	550	5,000	4,500	
(d)	−2,000					−2,000	Rent expense
Bal.	7,500		550	550	5,000	2,500	
(e)	− 250			−250			
Bal.	7,250		550	300	5,000	2,500	
(f)		+1,250				+1,250	Fees earned
Bal.	7,250	1,250	550	300	5,000	3,750	
(g)	− 655					− 380	Auto expense
						− 275	Misc. expense
Bal.	6,595	1,250	550	300	5,000	3,095	
(h)	−1,000					−1,000	Salaries expense
Bal.	5,595	1,250	550	300	5,000	2,095	
(i)			−125			− 125	Supplies expense
Bal.	5,595	1,250	425	300	5,000	1,970	
(j)	−1,200					−1,200	Dividend
Bal.	4,395	1,250	425	300	5,000	770	

Instructions:

(1) Prepare an income statement for the month ended July 31.
(2) Prepare a retained earnings statement for the month ended July 31.
(3) Prepare a balance sheet as of July 31.
(4) Prepare a statement of cash flows for the month ended July 31.

Pb. 1–43.
Transactions; financial statements.
OBJ. 7, 8

On July 1 of the current year, Jill Hill established a business under the name Hill Realty Inc. The following transactions were completed during the month of July:

(a) Received cash from issuance of capital stock, $5,000.
(b) Paid rent on office and equipment for the month, $3,600.
(c) Purchased supplies (stationery, stamps, pencils, etc.) on account, $750.
(d) Paid creditor on account, $500.
(e) Earned sales commissions, receiving cash, $11,100.
(f) Paid office salaries, $3,150.
(g) Paid automobile expenses (including rental charge) for month, $900, and miscellaneous expenses, $550.
(h) Paid cash for dividends, $2,000.
(i) Determined that the cost of supplies used was $425.

Instructions:

(1) Indicate the effect of each transaction and the balances after each transaction, using the following tabular headings:

Assets				Liabilities		Owner's Equity		
Cash	+	Supplies	=	Accounts Payable	+	Capital Stock	+	Retained Earnings

By appropriate notations at the right of each change, indicate the nature of each increase and decrease in retained earnings.

(2) Prepare an income statement for July, a retained earnings statement for July, a balance sheet as of July 31, and a statement of cash flows for July.

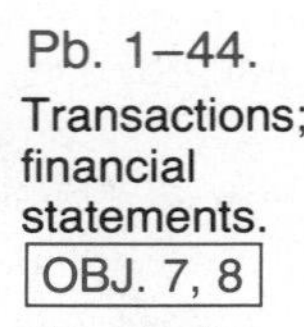

Pb. 1–44.
Transactions; financial statements.
OBJ. 7, 8

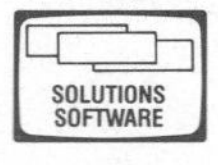

Moore Dry Cleaners Inc. is a corporation operated by Betty Moore. Currently, a building and equipment are being rented, pending expansion to new facilities. The actual work of dry cleaning is done by another company at wholesale rates. The assets and the liabilities of the business on June 1 of the current year are as follows: Cash, $9,400; Accounts Receivable, $4,750; Supplies, $560; Land, $15,000; Accounts Payable, $3,880; Capital Stock, $20,000; Retained Earnings, $5,830. Business transactions during June are summarized as follows:

(a) Paid rent for the month, $1,250.
(b) Charged customers for dry cleaning sales on account, $6,450.
(c) Paid creditors on account, $1,680.
(d) Purchased supplies on account, $310.
(e) Received cash from cash customers for dry cleaning sales, $3,600.
(f) Received cash from customers on account, $3,750.
(g) Received monthly invoice for dry cleaning expense for June (to be paid on July 10), $3,400.
(h) Paid the following: wages expense, $1,300; truck expense, $725; utilities expense, $510; miscellaneous expense, $190.
(i) Determined the cost of supplies used during the month, $570.

Instructions:

(1) State the assets, liabilities, and owner's equity as of June 1 in equation form similar to that shown in this chapter. In tabular form below the equation, indicate the increases and decreases resulting from each transaction and the new balances after each transaction. Explain the nature of each increase and decrease in retained earnings by an appropriate notation at the right of the amount.
(2) Prepare (a) an income statement for June, (b) a retained earnings statement for June, (c) a balance sheet as of June 30, and (d) a statement of cash flows for June.

Pb. 1–45.
Financial statements.
OBJ. 8

Following are the amounts of the assets and liabilities of Cole Company at June 30, the *end* of the current year, and its revenue and expenses for the year ended on that date. The capital stock was $50,000 throughout the year, retained earnings was $26,350 at July 1, *the beginning of the year,* and dividends of $40,000 were paid during the current year. Cash received from customers was $454,500 and cash paid for expenses and to creditors was $400,500.

Cash	$ 56,125
Accounts receivable	77,600
Supplies	6,675
Prepaid insurance	6,650
Accounts payable	31,100
Salaries payable	5,300
Fees earned	468,775
Salary expense	228,900
Rent expense	59,000
Advertising expense	45,950
Utilities expense	24,500
Supplies expense	12,600
Taxes expense	7,800
Insurance expense	6,900
Miscellaneous expense	8,825

Instructions:

(1) Prepare an income statement for the current year ended June 30.
(2) Prepare a retained earnings statement for the current year ended June 30.
(3) Prepare a balance sheet as of June 30 of the current year.
(4) Prepare a statement of cash flows for the current year ended June 30. The cash balance on July 1, beginning of the current year, was $42,125.

Pb. 1–46.
Financial statements.
OBJ. 8

Following are the amounts of ACJ Corporation's assets and liabilities at October 31, the end of the current year, and its revenue and expenses for the year ended on that date, listed in alphabetical order. ACJ Corporation had capital stock of $50,000 and retained earnings of $16,765 on November 1, the beginning of the current year. During the current year, the corporation paid cash dividends of $15,000 and received cash from the sale of capital stock of $20,000. Cash received from customers was $189,500 and cash paid for expenses and to creditors was $185,500.

Accounts payable	$ 12,100
Accounts receivable	21,250
Advertising expense	5,500
Cash	16,500
Insurance expense	1,900
Land	80,000
Miscellaneous expense	1,750
Prepaid insurance	950
Rent expense	42,000
Salaries payable	2,250
Salary expense	85,500
Fees earned	206,500
Supplies	865
Supplies expense	6,125
Taxes expense	5,775
Utilities expense	24,500

Instructions:

(1) Prepare an income statement for the current year ended October 31.
(2) Prepare a retained earnings statement for the current year ended October 31.

(Continued)

(3) Prepare a balance sheet as of October 31 of the current year.
(4) Prepare a statement of cash flows for the current year ended October 31. The cash balance on November 1, the beginning of the current year, was $7,500.

Pb. 1–47.
Transactions; financial statements.
OBJ. 7, 8

On July 1 of the current year, Shriver Delivery Inc. was organized as a corporation. The summarized transactions of the business for its first two months of operations, ending on August 31, are as follows:

(a) Received cash from stockholders for capital stock		$75,000
(b) Purchased a portion of a delivery service that had been operating as a sole proprietorship in accordance with the following details:		
Assets acquired by the corporation:		
Accounts receivable	$15,600	
Truck supplies	7,500	
Office supplies	900	$24,000
Liabilities assumed by the corporation:		
Accounts payable		9,000
Payment to be made as follows:		
Cash	$7,500	
Three notes payable of $2,500 each, due at two-month intervals	7,500	$15,000

(c) Purchased truck supplies on account	$ 1,750
(d) Purchased office supplies for cash	250
(e) Paid creditors on account	5,000
(f) Received cash from customers on account	12,000
(g) Paid insurance premiums in advance	2,400
(h) Paid advertising expense	1,100
(i) Charged delivery service sales to customers on account	40,500
(j) Paid rent expense on office and trucks	4,100
(k) Paid utilities expense	925
(l) Paid first of the three notes payable	2,500
(m) Paid miscellaneous expenses	1,475
(n) Paid taxes expense	275
(o) Paid wages expense	19,200
(p) Truck supplies used	2,800
(q) Office supplies used	325
(r) Insurance premiums that expired and became an expense	500
(s) Purchased land as future building site, paying $25,000 cash and giving a note payable due in 5 years for the balance of $25,000	50,000
(t) Paid cash dividends to stockholders	2,000

Instructions:

(1) List the following captions in a single line at the top of a sheet turned sideways.

Cash + Accounts Receivable + Truck Supplies + Office Supplies + Prepaid Insurance + Land =

Notes Payable + Accounts Payable + Capital Stock + Retained Earnings   Retained Earnings Notations

(2) In the appropriate columns, indicate the effect of the original investment and the remaining transactions, identifying each by letter. Indicate increases by + and decreases by −. *Do not determine the new balances of the items after each transaction.* In the space for retained earnings notations, identify each revenue and expense item and dividends paid to stockholders.
(3) Insert the final balances in each column and determine that the equation is in balance at August 31, the end of the period.
(4) Prepare the following: (a) income statement for the two months, (b) retained earnings statement for the two months, and (c) balance sheet as of August 31.

ALTERNATE PROBLEMS

Pb. 1–41A.
Transactions.
OBJ. 7

John Herr established John Herr Company on July 1 of the current year and completed the following transactions during July:

(a) Received cash from issuance of capital stock, $5,000.
(b) Paid rent for the month, $3,000.
(c) Purchased supplies (stationery, stamps, pencils, etc.) on account, $950.
(d) Received cash from fees earned, $6,500.
(e) Paid creditors on account, $650.
(f) Billed customers for fees earned, $1,250.
(g) Paid automobile expenses (including rental charges) for month, $480, and miscellaneous expenses, $275.
(h) Paid salaries, $1,500.
(i) Determined that the cost of supplies on hand was $425; therefore, the cost of supplies used was $525.
(j) Paid dividends, $1,200.

Instructions:

Indicate the effect of each transaction and the balances after each transaction, using the following tabular headings:

Assets						=	Liabilities	+	Owner's Equity		
Cash	+	Accounts Receivable	+	Supplies		=	Accounts Payable	+	Capital Stock	+	Retained Earnings

By appropriate notations at the right of each change, indicate the nature of each increase and decrease in retained earnings.

Pb. 1–42A.
Financial statements.
OBJ. 8

Robert May established May Services Inc. on May 1 of the current year. The effect of each transaction and the balances after each transaction for May are as follows:

	Assets			=	Liabilities	+	Owner's Equity		
	Cash	+ Accounts Receivable	+ Supplies	=	Accounts Payable	+	Capital Stock	+ Retained Earnings	
(a)	+4,000						+4,000		
(b)	+3,750							+3,750	Fees earned
Bal.	7,750						4,000	3,750	
(c)			+425		+425				
Bal.	7,750		425		425		4,000	3,750	
(d)	− 225				−225				
Bal.	7,525		425		200		4,000	3,750	
(e)	−1,800							−1,800	Rent expense
Bal.	5,725		425		200		4,000	1,950	
(f)	− 600							− 350	Auto expense
								− 250	Misc. expense
Bal.	5,125		425		200		4,000	1,350	

(continued)

	Cash	+ Accounts Receivable	+ Supplies	= Accounts Payable	+ Capital Stock	+ Retained Earnings	
	Assets			**= Liabilities +**	**Owner's Equity**		
Bal.	5,125		425	200	4,000	1,350	
(g)	− 900					− 900	Salaries expense
Bal.	4,225		425	200	4,000	450	
(h)			− 250			− 250	Supplies expense
Bal.	4,225		175	200	4,000	200	
(i)		+ 1,350				+ 1,350	Fees earned
Bal.	4,225	1,350	175	200	4,000	1,550	
(j)	− 1,500					− 1,500	Dividends
Bal.	2,725	1,350	175	200	4,000	50	

Instructions:

(1) Prepare an income statement for the month ended May 31.
(2) Prepare a retained earnings statement for the month ended May 31.
(3) Prepare a balance sheet as of May 31.
(4) Prepare a statement of cash flows for the month ended May 31.

Pb. 1–43A.
Transactions; financial statements.
OBJ. 7, 8

On July 1 of the current year, John Clark established a business under the name JC Realty Inc. The following transactions were completed during the month of July:

(a) Received cash from issuance of capital stock, $10,000.
(b) Paid rent on office and equipment for the month, $6,000.
(c) Purchased supplies (stationery, stamps, pencils, etc.) on account, $750.
(d) Paid creditor on account, $500.
(e) Earned sales commissions, receiving cash, $15,500.
(f) Paid office salaries, $4,000.
(g) Paid automobile expenses (including rental charge) for month, $900, and miscellaneous expenses, $550.
(h) Paid cash for dividends, $2,000.
(i) Determined that the cost of supplies used was $425.

Instructions:

(1) Indicate the effect of each transaction and the balances after each transaction, using the following tabular headings.

Assets		=	Liabilities	+	Owner's Equity		
Cash	+ Supplies	=	Accounts Payable	+	Capital Stock	+	Retained Earnings

By appropriate notations at the right of each change, indicate the nature of each increase and decrease in retained earnings.

(2) Prepare an income statement for July, a retained earnings statement for July, a balance sheet as of July 31, and a statement of cash flows for July.

Pb. 1–44A.
Transactions; financial statements.
OBJ. 7, 8

Moore Dry Cleaners Inc. is a corporation operated by Betty Moore. Currently, a building and equipment are being rented, pending expansion to new facilities. The actual work of dry cleaning is done by another company at wholesale rates. The assets and the liabilities of the business on May 1 of the current year are as follows: Cash, $9,250; Accounts Receivable, $14,100; Supplies, $900; Land, $25,000; Accounts Payable, $9,800; Capital Stock, $25,000; Retained Earnings, $14,450. Business transactions during May are summarized as follows:

(a) Received cash from cash customers for dry cleaning sales, $7,650.
(b) Paid rent for the month, $1,200.

(c) Purchased supplies on account, $320.
(d) Paid creditors on account, $7,700.
(e) Charged customers for dry cleaning sales on account, $5,020.
(f) Received monthly invoice for dry cleaning expense for May (to be paid on June 8), $6,500.
(g) Paid the following: wages expense, $1,400; truck expense, $580; utilities expense, $460; miscellaneous expense, $130.
(h) Received cash from customers on account, $8,100.
(i) Determined the cost of supplies used during the month, $470.

Instructions:

(1) State the assets, liabilities, and owner's equity as of May 1 in equation form similar to that shown in this chapter. In tabular form below the equation, indicate increases and decreases resulting from each transaction and the new balances after each transaction. Explain the nature of each increase and decrease in retained earnings by an appropriate notation at the right of the amount.
(2) Prepare (a) an income statement for May, (b) a retained earnings statement for May, (c) a balance sheet as of May 31, and (d) a statement of cash flows for May.

Pb. 1–45A. Financial statements. OBJ. 8

Following are the amounts of the assets and liabilities of Conrad Corporation at December 31, the *end* of the current year, and its revenue and expenses for the year ended on that date. The capital stock was $50,000 throughout the year, retained earnings was $16,765 at January 1, the *beginning of the year,* and dividends of $15,000 were paid during the year. Cash received from customers was $207,000 and cash paid for expenses and to creditors was $190,000.

Cash	$ 16,500
Accounts receivable	19,750
Supplies	865
Prepaid insurance	950
Land	60,000
Accounts payable	5,600
Notes payable	7,250
Sales	205,500
Salary expense	90,500
Rent expense	42,000
Utilities expense	19,500
Supplies expense	6,125
Taxes expense	5,775
Advertising expense	5,000
Insurance expense	1,900
Miscellaneous expense	1,250

Instructions:

(1) Prepare an income statement for the current year ended December 31.
(2) Prepare a retained earnings statement for the current year ended December 31.
(3) Prepare a balance sheet as of December 31 of the current year.
(4) Prepare a statement of cash flows for the current year ended December 31. The cash balance on January 1, beginning of the current year, was $14,500.

Pb. 1–46A. Financial statements. OBJ. 8

Following are the amounts of Borg Corporation's assets and liabilities at July 31, the end of the current year, and its revenue and expenses for the year ended on that date, listed in alphabetical order. Borg Corporation had capital stock of $50,000 and retained earnings of $97,890 on August 1, the beginning of the current year. During the current year, the corporation paid cash dividends of $40,000 and received cash from sale of capital stock of $50,000. Cash received from customers was $840,000 and cash paid for expenses and to creditors was $815,000.

1-48

Accounts payable	$ 84,000
Accounts receivable	69,750
Advertising expense	30,000
Cash	64,515
Insurance expense	22,500
Land	200,000
Miscellaneous expense	8,125
Prepaid insurance	6,000
Rent expense	165,000
Salaries payable	11,250
Salary expense	412,000
Fees earned	850,000
Supplies	6,250
Supplies expense	19,750
Taxes expense	33,500
Utilities expense	65,750

Instructions:

(1) Prepare an income statement for the current year ended July 31.
(2) Prepare a retained earnings statement for the current year ended July 31.
(3) Prepare a balance sheet as of July 31 of the current year.
(4) Prepare a statement of cash flows for the current year ended July 31. The cash balance on August 1, the beginning of the current year, was $29,515.

Pb. 1–47A.
Transactions; financial statements.
OBJ. 7, 8

On July 1 of the current year, Brown Delivery Inc. was organized as a corporation. The summarized transactions of the business for its first two months of operations, ending on August 31, are as follows:

(a)	Received cash from stockholders for capital stock		$50,000
(b)	Purchased a portion of a delivery service that had been operating as a sole proprietorship in accordance with the following details:		
	Assets acquired by the corporation:		
	Accounts receivable	$15,000	
	Truck supplies	4,550	
	Office supplies	900	$20,450
	Liabilities assumed by the corporation:		
	Accounts payable		10,450
	Payment to be made as follows:		
	Cash	$2,500	
	Three non-interest-bearing notes payable of $2,500 each, due at two-month intervals	7,500	$10,000
(c)	Purchased truck supplies on account		$ 950
(d)	Purchased office supplies for cash		250
(e)	Paid creditors on account		5,000
(f)	Received cash from customers on account		12,000
(g)	Paid insurance premiums in advance		1,800
(h)	Paid advertising expense		1,100
(i)	Charged delivery service sales to customers on account		39,250
(j)	Paid rent expense on office and trucks		4,100
(k)	Paid utilities expense		925
(l)	Paid first of the three notes payable		2,500
(m)	Paid miscellaneous expenses		1,475
(n)	Paid taxes expense		275

(o)	Paid wages expense	$17,100
(p)	Truck supplies used	2,720
(q)	Office supplies used	325
(r)	Insurance premiums that expired and became an expense	300
(s)	Purchased land as future building site, paying $15,000 cash and giving a note payable due in 5 years for the balance of $25,000	40,000
(t)	Paid cash dividends to stockholders	5,000

Instructions:

(1) List the following captions in a single line at the top of a sheet turned sideways.

Cash + Accounts Receivable + Truck Supplies + Office Supplies + Prepaid Insurance + Land =

Notes Payable + Accounts Payable + Capital Stock + Retained Earnings   Retained Earnings Notations

(2) In the appropriate columns, indicate the effect of the original investment and the remaining transactions, identifying each by letter. Indicate increases by + and decreases by −. *Do not determine the new balances of the items after each transaction.* In the space for retained earnings notations, identify each revenue and expense item and dividends paid to stockholders.

(3) Insert the final balances in each column and determine that the equation is in balance at August 31, the end of the period.

(4) Prepare the following: (a) income statement for the two months, (b) retained earnings statement for the two months, and (c) balance sheet as of August 31.

MINI-CASE 1

Chris Dunn, a junior in college, has been seeking ways to earn extra spending money. As an active sports enthusiast, Chris plays tennis regularly at the Vineyards Golf and Tennis Club, where her family has a membership. The president of the club recently approached Chris with the proposal that she manage the club's tennis courts on weekends. Chris's primary duty would be to supervise the operation of the club's two indoor and six outdoor courts, including court reservations. In return for her services, the club would pay Chris $50 per weekend, plus Chris could keep whatever she earned from lessons and the fees from the use of the ball machine. The club and Chris agreed to a one-month trial, after which both would consider an arrangement for the remaining two years of Chris's college career. On this basis, Chris organized Tennis Services Unlimited. During September, Chris managed the tennis courts and entered into the following transactions:

(a) Opened a business account by depositing $450.
(b) Paid $200 for tennis supplies (practice tennis balls, etc.).
(c) Paid $150 for the rental of video tape equipment to be used in offering lessons during September.
(d) Arranged for the rental of two ball machines during September for $100. Paid $50 in advance, with the remaining $50 due October 1.
(e) Received $950 for lessons given during September.
(f) Received $140 in fees from the use of the ball machines during September.
(g) Paid $250 for salaries of part-time employees who answered the telephone and took reservations while Chris was giving lessons.
(h) Paid $75 for miscellaneous expenses.
(i) Received $200 from the club for managing the tennis courts during September.
(j) Supplies on hand at the end of the month totaled $75.
(k) Chris withdrew $500 for personal use on September 30.

As a friend and accounting student, Chris has asked you to aid her in assessing the venture.

Instructions:

(1) Small business enterprises such as Tennis Services Unlimited are often organized as sole proprietorships. The accounting for sole proprietorships is similar to that for a corporation, except for owner's equity. Specifically, instead of Capital Stock and Retained Earnings, an item entitled Chris Dunn, Capital can be used to indicate owner's equity in the accounting equation. Indicate the effect of each transaction and the balances after each transaction, using the following tabular headings:

Assets		Liabilities		Owner's Equity
Cash + Supplies	=	Accounts Payable	+	C. Dunn, Capital

Explain the nature of each increase and decrease in owner's equity by an appropriate notation at the right of the amount.

(2) Prepare an income statement for September.

(3) (a) Assume that Chris Dunn could earn $6 per hour working 20 hours per weekend as a waitress. Evaluate which of the two alternatives, working as a waitress or operating Tennis Services Unlimited, would provide Chris with the most income per month.

(b) Discuss any other factors that you believe Chris should consider before discussing a long-term arrangement with Vineyards Golf and Tennis Club.

ANSWERS TO SELF-EXAMINATION QUESTIONS

1. D A corporation, organized in accordance with state or federal statutes, is a separate legal entity in which ownership is divided into shares of stock (answer D). A sole proprietorship, sometimes referred to as a single proprietorship (answers A and B), is a business enterprise owned by one individual. A partnership (answer C) is a business enterprise owned by two or more individuals.
2. A The properties owned by a business enterprise are referred to as assets (answer A). The debts of the business are called liabilities (answer B), and the equity of the owners is represented by capital stock or owner's equity (answers C and D).

3. A The balance sheet is a listing of the assets, liabilities, and owner's equity of a business entity at a specific date (answer A). The income statement (answer B) is a summary of the revenue and expenses of a business entity for a specific period of time. The statement of cash flows (answer C) summarizes the changes in cash during a specific period of time. The retained earnings statement (answer D) summarizes the changes in retained earnings for a corporation during a specific period of time.
4. C The accounting equation is:

   Assets = Liabilities + Owner's Equity

   Therefore, if assets increased by $20,000 and liabilities increased by $12,000, owner's equity must have increased by $8,000 (answer C) as indicated in the following computation:

   Assets = Liabilities + Owner's Equity
   $20,000 = $12,000 + Owner's Equity
   $20,000 – $12,000 = Owner's Equity
   $ 8,000 = Owner's Equity

5. B Net income is the excess of revenue over expenses, or $7,500 (answer B). If expenses exceed revenue, the difference is a net loss. Dividends do not affect the amount of net income or net loss but are distributions of net income.

CHAPTER 2

CHAPTER OBJECTIVES

1 Describe the nature of a chart of accounts and illustrate a chart of accounts for a service enterprise.

2 Describe the nature of an account and the general rules of debit and credit and normal balances of accounts.

3 Describe and illustrate the flow of business transaction data in an accounting system for a service enterprise.

4 Describe and illustrate the preparation and use of a trial balance.

5 Describe and illustrate procedures for the discovery and correction of errors.

6 Describe and illustrate the application of the materiality concept.

THE ACCOUNTING CYCLE

The transactions completed by an enterprise during a specific period may cause increases and decreases in many different asset, liability, and owner's equity items. To have the details of these transactions readily available and to prepare periodic financial statements, the effects of the transactions must be recorded in a systematic manner.

The nature of transactions and their effect on business enterprises were described and recorded in Chapter 1 by the use of the accounting equation, Assets = Liabilities + Owner's Equity. Although transactions can be analyzed and recorded in terms of their effect on the equation, such a format is not practical as a design for actual accounting systems.

Accountants must provide information on business transactions for use in directing operations and for the preparation of timely periodic financial statements. These goals are met by keeping a separate record for each item that appears on the financial statements. The individual records are then summarized at periodic intervals and the data thus obtained are presented in the financial statements or other reports. For example, a record would be used only for recording increases and decreases in cash, another record would be used only for recording increases and decreases in supplies, another for land, etc. Likewise, a separate record would be kept for fees earned, another record would be kept for salary expense, another for rent expense, etc. The type of record traditionally used for the purpose of recording individual transactions is called an **account.** A group of related accounts that comprise a complete unit, such as all of the accounts of a specific business enterprise, is called a **ledger.**

CHART OF ACCOUNTS

OBJECTIVE 1
Describe the nature of a chart of accounts and illustrate a chart of accounts for a service enterprise.

The number of accounts maintained by a specific enterprise is affected by the nature of its operations, its volume of business, and the extent to which details are needed for taxing authorities, managerial decisions, credit purposes, etc. For example, one enterprise may have separate accounts for executive salaries, office salaries, and sales salaries, while another may find it satisfactory to record all types of salaries in a single salary expense account.

The listing of accounts in a ledger is called a **chart of accounts.** Generally, the accounts in the chart of accounts should appear in the same order in which the accounts are presented on the balance sheet and income statement. The accounts are numbered to permit indexing and for use as references.

Although accounts in the ledger may be numbered consecutively as in the pages of a book, a flexible system of indexing is preferable. In the following chart of accounts for a service business, Hill Photographic Studio Inc., each account number has two digits. The first digit indicates the major division of the ledger in which the account is placed. Accounts beginning with 1 represent assets; 2, liabilities; 3, owner's equity; 4, revenue; and 5, expenses. The second digit indicates the position of the account within its division. A numbering system of this type has the advantage of permitting the later insertion of new accounts in their proper sequence without disturbing the other account numbers. For a large enterprise with a number of departments or branches, it is not unusual for each account number to have four or more digits.

Chart of Accounts for Hill Photographic Studio Inc.

Balance Sheet Accounts	Income Statement Accounts
1. Assets	4. Revenue
11 Cash	41 Sales
12 Accounts Receivable	5. Expenses
14 Supplies	51 Supplies Expense
15 Prepaid Rent	52 Salary Expense
18 Photographic Equipment	53 Rent Expense
19 Accumulated Depreciation[1]	54 Depreciation Expense[1]
2. Liabilities	59 Miscellaneous Expense
21 Accounts Payable	
22 Salaries Payable	
23 Notes Payable	
3. Owner's Equity	
31 Capital Stock	
32 Retained Earnings	
33 Dividends	
34 Income Summary[1]	

NATURE OF AN ACCOUNT

OBJECTIVE 2
Describe the nature of an account and the general rules of debit and credit and normal balances of accounts.

The simplest form of an account has three parts: (1) a title, which is the name of the item recorded in the account; (2) a space for recording increases in the amount of the item, in terms of money; and (3) a space for recording decreases in the amount of the item, also in monetary terms. This form of an account, illustrated below, is known as a **T account** because of its similarity to the letter T.

T Account

Left side debit	Right side credit

[1]The accumulated depreciation, depreciation expense, and income summary accounts are discussed in Chapter 3, when the process of preparing financial statements for Hill Photographic Studio Inc. is discussed.

The left side of the account is called the **debit** side and the right side is called the **credit** side.[2] Amounts entered on the left side of an account, regardless of the account title, are called **debits** to the account, and the account is said to be **debited**. Amounts entered on the right side of an account are called **credits**, and the account is said to be **credited.**

In the following illustration, receipts of cash during a period of time have been listed vertically on the debit side of the cash account. The cash payments for the same period have been listed in similar fashion on the credit side of the account. A memorandum total of the cash receipts for the period to date, $10,950 in the illustration, may be inserted below the last debit at any time the information is desired. This figure should be identified in such a way that it is not mistaken for an additional debit. The total of the cash payments, $6,850 in the illustration, may be inserted on the credit side in a similar manner. Subtraction of the smaller sum from the larger, $10,950 – $6,850, yields the amount of cash on hand, $4,100, which is called the **balance of the account.** This amount is inserted on the debit side of the account, next to the total of the debits, thus identifying the balance of the account as a **debit balance**. If financial statements were to be prepared at this time, the amount of cash reported thereon would be $4,100.

Cash		
	3,750	850
	4,300	1,400
	2,900	700
4,100	*10,950*	2,900
		1,000
		6,850

Balance Sheet Accounts

The manner of recording data in the accounts and the relationship of accounts to the balance sheet are presented in the two illustrations that follow. For the first illustration, assume that Davis Corporation is organized and capital stock is sold for $35,000. Immediately after the transaction, the balance sheet for the business, in account form, would contain the following information:

Assets		Stockholders' Equity	
Cash	$35,000	Capital stock	$35,000

Every business transaction affects a minimum of two accounts. The effect of the above transaction on accounts in the ledger can be described as a $35,000 debit to Cash and a $35,000 credit to Capital Stock. This information is initially entered in a record called a **journal.** In the journal, the information is stated in a formalized manner by listing the title of the account and the amount to be debited, followed by a similar listing, below and to the right of the debit, of the title of the account and the amount to be credited. The process of recording a

[2] Often abbreviated as *Dr.* for "debit" and *Cr.* for "credit," derived from the Latin *debere* and *credere*.

transaction in the journal is called **journalizing.** The form of presentation is called a **journal entry**, and is illustrated as follows:

Cash	35,000	
Capital Stock		35,000

The data in the journal entry are transferred to the appropriate accounts by a process known as **posting.** The accounts after posting the journal entry appear as follows:

Cash	
35,000	

Capital Stock	
	35,000

Note that the amount of the asset, which is reported on the left side of the account form of balance sheet, is posted to the left (debit) side of Cash. The owner's equity in the business, which is reported on the right side of the balance sheet, is posted to the right (credit) side of Capital Stock. When other assets are acquired, the increases will be recorded as debits to the appropriate accounts. As owner's equity is increased or liabilities are incurred, the increases will be recorded as credits.

For the second illustration, assume that Davis Corporation purchased equipment at a cost of $20,000, paying $5,000 in cash and giving a note payable for the remaining $15,000. A **note payable** is a liability similar to an account payable, except that it is a written promise to pay a sum of money at a definite time. After this transaction, the data reported in the balance sheet would be as follows:

Assets		Liabilities	
Cash	$30,000	Notes payable	$15,000
Equipment	20,000		
		Stockholders' Equity	
		Capital stock	35,000
Total assets	$50,000	Total liabilities and stockholders' equity	$50,000

The effect of the transaction can be described as a $20,000 debit (increase) to Equipment, a $5,000 credit (decrease) to Cash, and a $15,000 credit (increase) to Notes Payable. The same information can be presented in the form of the following journal entry. (An entry composed of two or more debits or of two or more credits is called a **compound journal entry**.)

Equipment	20,000	
Cash		5,000
Notes Payable		15,000

After the journal entry for the second transaction has been posted, the accounts of Davis Corporation appear as follows:

Cash	
35,000	5,000

Equipment	
20,000	

Notes Payable	
	15,000

Capital Stock	
	35,000

Note that the effect of the transaction was to increase one asset account, decrease another asset account, and increase a liability account. Note also that although the amounts, $20,000, $5,000, and $15,000, are different, the equality of debits and credits was maintained. Regardless of the complexity of a transaction or the number of accounts affected, the sum of the debits is always equal to the sum of the credits. This equality of debit and credit for each transaction is inherent in the equation A = L + OE. It is also because of this duality that the system is known as **double-entry accounting.**

TAKING THE HUMAN SPIRIT INTO ACCOUNT

Double-entry bookkeeping is one of the most beautiful discoveries of the human spirit. . . . It came from the same spirit which produced the systems of Galileo and Newton and the subject matter of modern physics and chemistry. By the same means, it organizes perceptions into a system, and one can characterize it as the first Cosmos constructed purely on the basis of mechanistic thought. . . . Without too much difficulty, we can recognize in double-entry bookkeeping the ideas of gravitation, of the circulation of the blood and of the conservation of matter.

Source: From the novel, *Wilhelm Meister's Lehrjahre* (Apprenticeship), written in 1795–6 by the German poet Johann Wolfgang von Goethe, translated by the German political economist Werner Sombart (1863–1941).

In the preceding paragraphs, it was observed that the left side of asset accounts is used for recording increases and the right side is used for recording decreases. It was also observed that the right side of liability and owner's equity accounts is used to record increases. It naturally follows that the left side of such accounts is used to record decreases. The left side of all accounts, whether asset, liability, or owner's equity, is the debit side and the right side is the credit side. Consequently, a debit may be either an increase or a decrease, depending on the nature of the account affected. A credit may likewise be either an increase or a decrease, depending on the nature of the account. The rules of debit and credit may therefore be stated as follows:

General Rules of Debit and Credit

Debit may signify:	*Credit* may signify:
Increase in asset accounts	Decrease in asset accounts
Decrease in liability accounts	Increase in liability accounts
Decrease in owner's equity accounts	Increase in owner's equity accounts

The rules of debit and credit may also be stated in relationship to the accounting equation and the account form of balance sheet, as in the diagram at the top of page 58.

Distributions of earnings to shareholders have the effect of decreasing owner's equity, and just as decreases in owner's equity are recorded as debits, dividends are recorded as debits. The balance in the dividends account is

Expanded Rules of Debit and Credit—Balance Sheet Accounts

Balance Sheet Accounts

ASSETS		LIABILITIES	
Asset Accounts		Liability Accounts	
Debit for increases	Credit for decreases	Debit for decreases	Credit for increases
		OWNER'S EQUITY	
		Owner's Equity Accounts	
		Debit for decreases	Credit for increases

periodically transferred to the retained earnings account. Debits to the dividends account have the effect of decreasing owner's equity (negative sense) or increasing dividends (positive sense).

Income Statement Accounts

The theory of debit and credit in its application to revenue and expense accounts is based on the relationship of these accounts to owner's equity. The net income or the net loss for a period, as reported on the income statement, is the net increase or the net decrease in owner's equity as a result of operations.

Revenue increases owner's equity. Just as increases in owner's equity are recorded as credits, increases in revenues during an accounting period are recorded as credits.

Expenses have the effect of decreasing owner's equity, and just as decreases in owner's equity are recorded as debits, increases in expense accounts are recorded as debits. Debits to expense accounts are usually referred to in the positive sense (as increases in expense) rather than in the negative sense (as decreases in owner's equity). The rules of debit and credit as applied to revenue and expense accounts are shown in the following diagram:

Expanded Rules of Debit and Credit—Income Statement Accounts

Income Statement Accounts

Debit for decreases in owner's equity		*Credit for increases in owner's equity*	
Expense Accounts		Revenue Accounts	
Debit for increases	Credit for decreases	Debit for decreases	Credit for increases

At the end of an accounting period, the revenue and expense account balances are reported in the income statement. Periodically, usually at the end of the accounting year, all revenue and expense account balances are transferred to a summarizing account and the accounts are then said to be *closed*. The balance in the summarizing account, which is the net income or net loss for the period, is then transferred to the retained earnings account and the summarizing account is also closed. Because revenue and expense accounts are periodically closed, they are sometimes called **temporary accounts** or **nominal accounts.** The balances of the accounts reported in the balance sheet are carried forward from year to year and because of their permanence are sometimes referred to as **real accounts.**

Normal Balances of Accounts

The sum of the increases recorded in an account is usually equal to or greater than the sum of the decreases recorded in the account. For this reason, the normal balances of all accounts are positive rather than negative. For example, the total debits (increases) in an asset account will ordinarily be greater than the total credits (decreases). Thus, asset accounts normally have debit balances.

The rules of debit and credit and the normal balances of the various types of accounts are summarized as follows. Note that the dividends and expense accounts are considered in the positive sense. Increases in these accounts, which represent decreases in owner's equity, are recorded as debits.

Normal Account Balances

	Increase	Decrease	Normal Balance
Balance sheet accounts:			
Asset	Debit	Credit	Debit
Liability	Credit	Debit	Credit
Owner's Equity *or* Stockholders' Equity			
Capital Stock	Credit	Debit	Credit
Retained Earnings	Credit	Debit	Credit
Dividends	Debit	Credit	Debit
Income statement accounts:			
Revenue	Credit	Debit	Credit
Expense	Debit	Credit	Debit

When an account that normally has a debit balance actually has a credit balance, or vice versa, it is an indication of an accounting error or of an unusual situation. For example, a credit balance in the office equipment account could result only from an accounting error. On the other hand, a debit balance in an account payable account could result from an overpayment.

FLOW OF BUSINESS TRANSACTION DATA

OBJECTIVE 3
Describe and illustrate the flow of business transaction data in an accounting system for a service enterprise.

The flow of business transaction data from the time a transaction occurs to its recording in the ledger may be diagrammed as follows:

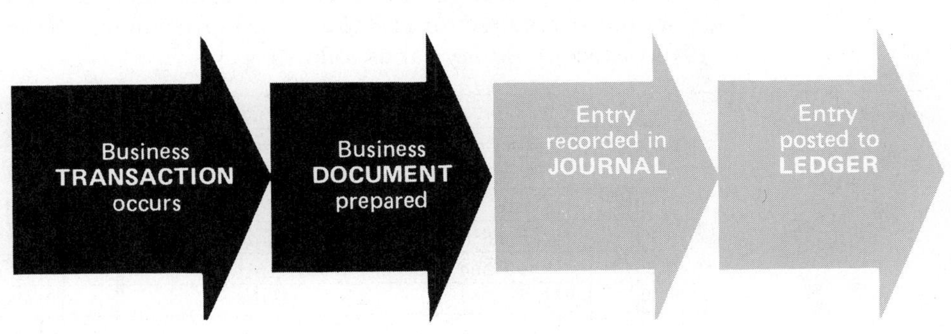

The initial record of each transaction, or of a group of similar transactions, is evidenced by a business document, such as a sales ticket, a bill, or a cash register tape. On the basis of the evidence provided by the business documents, the transactions are entered in the journal. The amounts of the debits and the credits in the journal are then posted to the accounts in the ledger.

Ledger Accounts

Accounts in the simple T form were used for illustrative purposes earlier in the chapter. A more formal form is the **standard account form**, sometimes called the **four-column account form**, which includes balance columns. The primary advantage of the standard account form is that the account balance is readily available, as shown in the following illustration:

Standard Account Form

ACCOUNT Cash ACCOUNT NO. 11

DATE		ITEM	POST. REF.	DEBIT	CREDIT	BALANCE	
						DEBIT	CREDIT
1992 May	1	Balance	✓			5245 00	
	1		17	1822 25		7067 25	
	1		17		350 00	6717 25	
	1		17		995 50	5721 75	
	3		17	960 40		6682 15	
	3		17		192 00	6490 15	
	3		17		1882 25	4607 90	

The Journal

The basic features of a journal entry were illustrated earlier in the chapter when the use of accounts and debits and credits were introduced. The **journal** is the formalized device used for recording business transactions in chronological order. Before a transaction is entered in the journal, it should be analyzed according to the following sequence of steps:

1. Determine whether an asset, a liability, owner's equity, revenue, or expense is affected.
2. Determine whether the affected asset, liability, owner's equity, revenue, or expense increases or decreases.
3. Determine whether the effect of the transaction should be recorded as a debit or as a credit in an asset, liability, owner's equity, revenue, or expense account.

To illustrate the results of such analyses, assume that $1,822.25 is received from cash sales for May 1. The asset Cash increases and therefore should be debited for $1,822.25. The revenue account Sales also increases and therefore should be credited for $1,822.25. The journal in which the transaction has been recorded would appear as follows:

Journal

JOURNAL PAGE 17

	DATE		DESCRIPTION	POST. REF.	DEBIT	CREDIT	
1	1992 May	1	Cash		1822 25		1
2			Sales			1822 25	2
3			Cash sales for the day.				3
4							4

In the journal, the transaction information is recorded by entering the date followed by the title of the account and the amount to be debited. The title of the account and the amount to be credited are entered below and to the right of the debit data. A brief explanation may be written below each entry, moderately indented.

Posting

The posting of a debit journal entry or a credit journal entry to an account in the ledger is performed in the following manner:

1. Record the date and the amount of the entry in the account.
2. Insert the number of the journal page in the Posting Reference column of the account.
3. Insert the ledger account number in the Posting Reference column of the journal.

These procedures are illustrated as follows by the posting of a debit to the cash account. The posting of a credit uses the same sequence of procedures.

Diagram of the Posting of a Debit

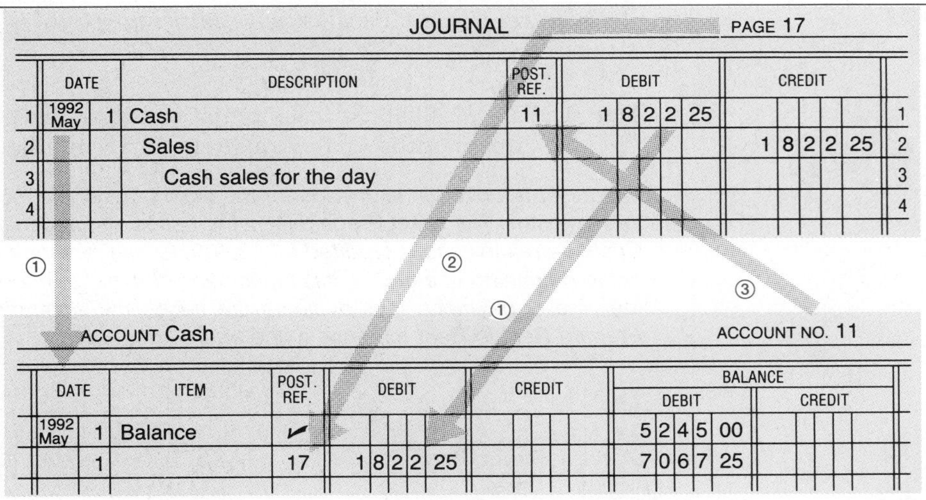

JOURNAL — PAGE 17

	DATE		DESCRIPTION	POST. REF.	DEBIT	CREDIT	
1	1992 May	1	Cash	11	1 8 2 2 25		1
2			Sales			1 8 2 2 25	2
3			Cash sales for the day				3
4							4

ACCOUNT Cash — ACCOUNT NO. 11

DATE		ITEM	POST. REF.	DEBIT	CREDIT	BALANCE DEBIT	BALANCE CREDIT
1992 May	1	Balance	✓			5 2 4 5 00	
	1		17	1 8 2 2 25		7 0 6 7 25	

Illustration of Journalizing and Posting

To illustrate the journalizing and posting process, a month's transactions for Hill Photographic Studio Inc. are used. Hill Photographic Studio Inc. is the service business whose chart of accounts was presented on page 54.

To reduce repetition, some of the following transactions are stated as a summary. For example, sales of services for cash are ordinarily recorded on a daily basis, but in the illustration, summary totals are given only at the middle and end of the month. Similarly, all sales of services on account during the month are summarized as a single transaction. In practice, each sale would be recorded separately.

Mar. 1. Ann and John Hill operated a photographic business in their home on a part-time basis. They decided to incorporate, to devote full time to the business, which was to be known as Hill Photographic Studio Inc., and to move to rented quarters as of March 1. The following assets were invested in the enterprise: cash, $3,500; accounts receivable, $950; supplies, $1,200; and photographic equipment, $15,000. There were no liabilities transferred to the business. Capital stock of $20,650 was issued in exchange for the assets.

The four asset accounts, Cash, Accounts Receivable, Supplies, and Photographic Equipment, increase and are debited for $3,500, $950, $1,200, and $15,000, respectively. The owner's equity in these assets is equal to the sum of the assets, or $20,650; hence, $20,650 of capital stock is issued and Capital Stock is credited for that amount. (The use of individual accounts receivable from customers is described in a later chapter.)

JOURNAL — PAGE 1

	DATE		DESCRIPTION	POST. REF.	DEBIT	CREDIT	
1	1992 Mar.	1	Cash	11	3 500 00		1
2			Accounts Receivable	12	950 00		2
3			Supplies	14	1 200 00		3
4			Photographic Equipment	18	15 000 00		4
5			Capital Stock	31		20 650 00	5

(The ledger to which the illustrative entries are posted is presented on pages 65-67.)

Mar. 1. Paid $2,400 on a lease rental contract, the payment representing three months' rent of quarters for the studio.

The asset acquired in exchange for the cash payment is the use of the property for three months. The asset Prepaid Rent increases and is debited for $2,400; the asset Cash decreases and is credited for $2,400. (When rent for a single month is prepaid at the beginning of a month, it is customarily debited to the rent expense account at the time of payment, thus avoiding the necessity of transferring the amount from Prepaid Rent to Rent Expense at the end of the month.)

	DATE		DESCRIPTION	POST. REF.	DEBIT	CREDIT	
6							6
7		1	Prepaid Rent	15	2 400 00		7
8			Cash	11		2 400 00	8

Mar. 4. Purchased additional photographic equipment on account from Palmer Photographic Equipment Inc. for $2,500.

The asset Photographic Equipment increases and is therefore debited for $2,500. The liability Accounts Payable increases and is credited for $2,500. (The use of individual accounts payable to creditors is described in a later chapter.)

	DATE		DESCRIPTION	POST. REF.	DEBIT	CREDIT	
9							9
10		4	Photographic Equipment	18	2 500 00		10
11			Accounts Payable	21		2 500 00	11

Mar. 5. Received $850 from customers in payment of their accounts.

The asset Cash increases and is debited for $850; the asset Accounts Receivable decreases and is credited for $850.

Date	Description	Post. Ref.	Debit	Credit
5	Cash	11	850 00	
	Accounts Receivable	12		850 00

Mar. 6. Paid $125 for a newspaper advertisement.

Expense accounts are subdivisions of owner's equity. Increases in expense are decreases in owner's equity; hence, an expense account is debited for $125. The asset Cash was decreased by the transaction; therefore that account is credited for $125. (Miscellaneous Expense is debited because total expenditures for advertising during an accounting period are expected to be relatively minor.)

Date	Description	Post. Ref.	Debit	Credit
6	Miscellaneous Expense	59	125 00	
	Cash	11		125 00

Mar. 10. Paid $500 to Palmer Photographic Equipment Inc. to apply on the $2,500 debt owed them.

This payment decreases the liability Accounts Payable, so that account is debited for $500. It also decreases the asset Cash, which is credited for $500.

Date	Description	Post. Ref.	Debit	Credit
10	Accounts Payable	21	500 00	
	Cash	11		500 00

Mar. 13. Paid receptionist $575 for two weeks' salary.

Similar to transaction of March 6.

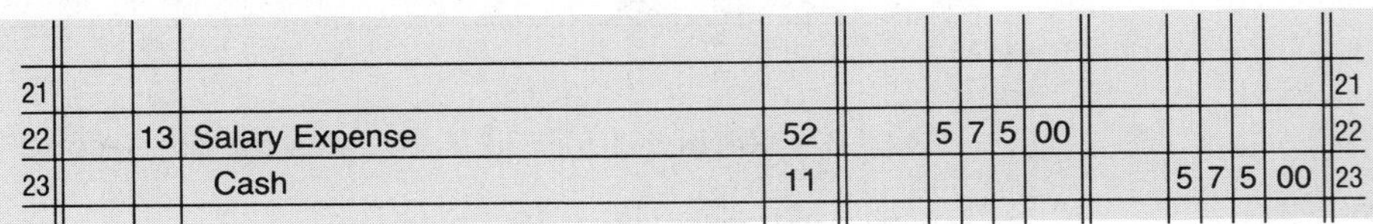

Date	Description	Post. Ref.	Debit	Credit
13	Salary Expense	52	575 00	
	Cash	11		575 00

Mar. 16. Received $1,980 from sales for the first half of March.

Cash increases and is debited for $1,980. The revenue account Sales, which is a subdivision of owner's equity, increases and is credited for $1,980.

Date	Description	Post. Ref.	Debit	Credit
16	Cash	11	1980 00	
	Sales	41		1980 00

Mar. 20. Paid $650 for supplies.

The asset Supplies increases and is debited for $650; the asset Cash decreases and is credited for $650.

27							27
28		20	Supplies	14	650 00		28
29			Cash	11		650 00	29

Mar. 27. Paid receptionist $575 for two weeks' salary.

Similar to transaction of March 6.

30							30
31		27	Salary Expense	52	575 00		31
32			Cash	11		575 00	32

Mar. 31. Paid $69 for telephone bill for the month.

Similar to transaction of March 6.

33							33
34		31	Miscellaneous Expense	59	69 00		34
35			Cash	11		69 00	35

Mar. 31. Paid $175 for electric bill for the month.

Similar to transaction of March 6.

36							36
37		31	Miscellaneous Expense	59	175 00		37
38			Cash	11		175 00	38

Mar. 31. Received $1,870 from sales for the second half of March.

Similar to transaction of March 16.

JOURNAL PAGE 2

	DATE		DESCRIPTION	POST. REF.	DEBIT	CREDIT	
1	1992 Mar.	31	Cash	11	1 870 00		1
2			Sales	41		1 870 00	2

Mar. 31. Sales on account totaled $1,675 for the month.

The asset Accounts Receivable increases and is debited for $1,675. The revenue account Sales increases and is credited for $1,675. (Note that the revenue is earned even though no cash is received; the claim against the customers is as much an asset as cash. As customers pay their accounts later, Cash will be debited and Accounts Receivable will be credited.)

Date	Description	Post. Ref.	Debit	Credit
31	Accounts Receivable	12	1 675 00	
	Sales	41		1 675 00

Mar. 31. Paid $1,500 cash dividends.

The transaction resulted in a decrease in the amount of owner's equity and is recorded by a $1,500 debit to Dividends; the decrease in business cash is recorded by a $1,500 credit to Cash.

Date	Description	Post. Ref.	Debit	Credit
31	Dividends	33	1 500 00	
	Cash	11		1 500 00

After all the entries for the month have been posted, the ledger will appear as shown below and on pages 66–67. In practice, each account would appear on a separate page in the ledger. Tracing each entry from the journal to the accounts in the ledger will give a clear understanding of the posting process.

The accounts are numbered in accordance with the chart shown on page 54. However, some of the accounts listed in the chart are not shown in the illustrative ledger. The additional accounts will be used later when the illustration for Hill Photographic Studio Inc. is completed in Chapter 3.

Ledger—Hill Photographic Studio Inc.

ACCOUNT Cash — ACCOUNT NO. 11

Date	Item	Post. Ref.	Debit	Credit	Balance Debit	Balance Credit
1992 Mar. 1		1	3 500 00		3 500 00	
1		1		2 400 00	1 100 00	
5		1	850 00		1 950 00	
6		1		125 00	1 825 00	
10		1		500 00	1 325 00	
13		1		575 00	750 00	
16		1	1 980 00		2 730 00	
20		1		650 00	2 080 00	
27		1		575 00	1 505 00	
31		1		69 00	1 436 00	
31		1		175 00	1 261 00	
31		2	1 870 00		3 131 00	
31		2		1 500 00	1 631 00	

ACCOUNT Accounts Receivable — ACCOUNT NO. 12

Date	Item	Post. Ref.	Debit	Credit	Balance Debit	Balance Credit
1992 Mar. 1		1	950 00		950 00	
5		1		850 00	100 00	
31		2	1 675 00		1 775 00	

Ledger—Hill Photographic Studio Inc. (continued)

ACCOUNT Supplies — ACCOUNT NO. 14

Date		Item	Post. Ref.	Debit	Credit	Balance Debit	Balance Credit
1992 Mar.	1		1	1200 00		1200 00	
	20		1	650 00		1850 00	

ACCOUNT Prepaid Rent — ACCOUNT NO. 15

Date		Item	Post. Ref.	Debit	Credit	Balance Debit	Balance Credit
1992 Mar.	1		1	2400 00		2400 00	

ACCOUNT Photographic Equipment — ACCOUNT NO. 18

Date		Item	Post. Ref.	Debit	Credit	Balance Debit	Balance Credit
1992 Mar.	1		1	15000 00		15000 00	
	4		1	2500 00		17500 00	

ACCOUNT Accounts Payable — ACCOUNT NO. 21

Date		Item	Post. Ref.	Debit	Credit	Balance Debit	Balance Credit
1992 Mar.	4		1		2500 00		2500 00
	10		1	500 00			2000 00

ACCOUNT Capital Stock — ACCOUNT NO. 31

Date		Item	Post. Ref.	Debit	Credit	Balance Debit	Balance Credit
1992 Mar.	1		1		20650 00		20650 00

ACCOUNT Dividends — ACCOUNT NO. 33

Date		Item	Post. Ref.	Debit	Credit	Balance Debit	Balance Credit
1992 Mar.	31		2	1500 00		1500 00	

ACCOUNT Sales — ACCOUNT NO. 41

Date		Item	Post. Ref.	Debit	Credit	Balance Debit	Balance Credit
1992 Mar.	16		1		1980 00		1980 00
	31		2		1870 00		3850 00
	31		2		1675 00		5525 00

ACCOUNT Salary Expense — ACCOUNT NO. 52

Date		Item	Post. Ref.	Debit	Credit	Balance Debit	Balance Credit
1992 Mar.	13		1	575 00		575 00	
	27		1	575 00		1150 00	

Ledger—Hill Photographic Studio Inc. (concluded)

ACCOUNT Miscellaneous Expense ACCOUNT NO. 59

DATE		ITEM	POST. REF.	DEBIT	CREDIT	BALANCE DEBIT	BALANCE CREDIT
1992 Mar.	6		1	125 00		125 00	
	31		1	69 00		194 00	
	31		1	175 00		369 00	

TRIAL BALANCE

OBJECTIVE 4
Describe and illustrate the preparation and use of a trial balance.

The equality of debits and credits in the ledger should be verified at the end of each accounting period, if not more often. Such a verification, which is called a **trial balance,** may be in the form of a calculator tape or in the form illustrated as follows. The summary listing of both the balances and the titles of the accounts is also useful in preparing the financial statements.

Hill Photographic Studio Inc.
Trial Balance
March 31, 1992

Cash	1,631.00	
Accounts Receivable	1,775.00	
Supplies	1,850.00	
Prepaid Rent	2,400.00	
Photographic Equipment	17,500.00	
Accounts Payable		2,000.00
Capital Stock		20,650.00
Dividends	1,500.00	
Sales		5,525.00
Salary Expense	1,150.00	
Miscellaneous Expense	369.00	
	28,175.00	28,175.00

DISCOVERY AND CORRECTION OF ERRORS

OBJECTIVE 5
Describe and illustrate procedures for the discovery and correction of errors.

Occasional errors in journalizing and posting transactions are unavoidable. The following paragraphs describe and illustrate how errors may be discovered and corrected.

Discovery of Errors

The trial balance is one of the principal means for discovering errors in the ledger. However, it indicates only that the *debits* and *credits* are *equal.* Among the types of errors that will not cause an inequality in the trial balance totals are the following:

1. Failure to record a transaction or to post a transaction.
2. Recording the same erroneous amount for both the debit and the credit parts of a transaction.
3. Recording the same transaction more than once.
4. Posting a part of a transaction correctly as a debit or credit but to the wrong account.

The preparation of the trial balance is of value because errors frequently affect the equality of debits and credits. If the two totals of a trial balance are not equal, it is probably due to one or more of the following types of errors:

1. Error in preparing the trial balance, such as:
   a. One of the columns of the trial balance was incorrectly added.
   b. The amount of an account balance was incorrectly recorded on the trial balance.
   c. A debit balance was recorded on the trial balance as a credit, or vice versa, or a balance was omitted entirely.
2. Error in determining the account balances, such as:
   a. A balance was incorrectly computed.
   b. A balance was entered in the wrong balance column.
3. Error in recording a transaction in the ledger, such as:
   a. An erroneous amount was posted to the account.
   b. A debit entry was posted as a credit, or vice versa.
   c. A debit or a credit posting was omitted.

If the two trial balance totals are not equal, the amount of the difference between them sometimes gives a clue as to the nature of the error or where it occurred. For example, a difference of 10, 100, or 1,000 between two totals can also be due to the omission of a debit or a credit posting or, if it is divisible evenly by 2, to the posting of a debit as a credit, or vice versa. For example, if the debit and the credit totals of a trial balance are $20,640 and $20,236 respectively, the difference of $404 may indicate that a credit posting of that amount was omitted or that a credit of $202 was erroneously posted as a debit.

Two other common types of errors are known as **transpositions** and **slides.** A transposition is the erroneous rearrangement of digits, such as writing $542 as $452 or $524. In a slide, the entire number is erroneously moved one or more spaces to the right or the left, such as writing $542.00 as $54.20 or $5,420.00. If an error of either type has occurred and there are no other errors, the discrepancy between the two trial balance totals will be evenly divisible by 9.

A preliminary examination along the lines suggested by the preceding paragraphs will frequently disclose the error. If it does not, the general procedure is to retrace the various steps in the accounting process, beginning with the last step and working back to the original entries in the journal. Ordinarily, errors that have caused the trial balance totals to be unequal will be discovered before all of the steps are retraced. While there are no rigid rules governing the procedures, the following plan is suggested:

1. Verify the accuracy of the trial balance totals by re-adding the columns.
2. Compare the listings in the trial balance with the balances shown in the ledger, making certain that no accounts have been omitted.
3. Recompute the balance of each account in the ledger.
4. Trace the postings in the ledger back to the journal, placing a small check mark by the item in the ledger and also in the journal. If the error is not found, examine each account to see if there is an entry without a check mark. Do the same with the entries in the journal.
5. Verify the equality of the debits and the credits in the journal.

Correction of Errors

When errors in journalizing and posting transactions are discovered, the procedures used to correct them vary according to the nature of the error and when the error is discovered. When an error in an account title or amount in the journal or ledger accounts is discovered before posting is completed, the correction may be made by drawing a line through the error and inserting the correct title or amount immediately above. If there is any likelihood of questions arising later, the person responsible may initial the correction.

When an erroneous account title appears in a journal entry and the error is not discovered until after posting is completed, the preferable procedure is to journalize and post a correcting entry. To illustrate, assume that a purchase of office equipment, which was paid in cash, was erroneously journalized and posted as a $500 debit to Office Supplies but correctly journalized and posted as a $500 credit to Cash. Before a correcting entry is made, it is advisable to establish clearly both (1) the debit(s) and credit(s) of the entry in which the error occurred and (2) the debit(s) and credit(s) that should have been recorded. T accounts may be helpful in making this analysis, as in the following example:

Entry in which error occurred:

Office Supplies	
500	

Cash	
	500

Entry that should have been recorded:

Office Equipment	
500	

Cash	
	500

Comparison of the two sets of T accounts shows that the erroneous debit of $500 to Office Supplies may be corrected by a $500 credit to that account and that Office Equipment should be debited for $500. The following correcting entry is then journalized and posted:

Correcting Entry

JOURNAL PAGE 22

	DATE		DESCRIPTION	POST. REF.	DEBIT	CREDIT	
1	1992 Oct.	31	Office Equipment	18	500 00		1
2			Office Supplies	15		500 00	2

MATERIALITY

OBJECTIVE 6
Describe and illustrate the application of the materiality concept

In the preceding section, the discovery and correction of errors was discussed. Although accurate accounting records and reports are essential, absolute accuracy is not an end in itself. There is no need to exceed the limits of practicality in correcting errors and following generally accepted accounting principles. The determination of what is significant (material) and what is not requires the exercise of judgment. Precise criteria cannot be formulated.

To determine **materiality** the size of an item and its nature must be considered in relationship to the size and the nature of other items. The erroneous recording of the purchase of $1,000 of equipment as utilities expense for an enterprise with total assets of $10,000,000 and annual net income of $1,000,000 would probably be immaterial. In such a case it may not be necessary to correct the error and thus strictly adhere to generally accepted accounting principles. If the assets totaled only $25,000 and annual net income was $2,500, however, it would certainly be material. In this latter case, the error should be corrected using the procedures described and illustrated in the preceding section.

Custom and practicality also influence criteria of materiality. Corporate financial statements seldom report the cents amounts or even the hundreds of dollars. A common practice is to round to the nearest thousand. For large corporations, there is an increasing tendency to report the financial data in terms of millions, carrying figures to one decimal. For example, the 1990 edition of *Accounting Trends & Techniques* indicated that 56 of 600 companies reported amounts to the nearest dollar, 404 to the nearest thousand dollars, and 140 to the nearest million dollars.

A technique known as "whole-dollar" accounting, which is used by some businesses, eliminates the cents amounts from accounting entries at the earliest possible point in the accounting sequence. There are some accounts, such as those with customers and creditors, in which it is not feasible to round to the nearest dollar. Nevertheless, the technique yields savings in office costs and improved productivity. The errors introduced into other accounts by rounding the amounts of individual entries at the time of recording tend to be compensating in nature, and the amount of the final error is not material.

It should not be inferred from the foregoing that whole-dollar accounting encourages or condones errors. The unrecorded cents are not lost; they are merely reported in a manner that reduces recording costs without materially affecting the accuracy of accounting data.

CONCERNING THE GNAT AND THE CAMEL

This is the story as it comes to us: An accountant . . . was [asked] to check the cash of a concern . . . where goods of small value were sold in fairly large quantities. When the cash . . . was counted it was found that the amount on hand was, let us say, $2.04—a fictitious amount greater than the actual sum—more than it should have been. . . . [The accountant] set to work to trace the mistake and to expose the guilty person. Here was a chance for him to demonstrate his incalculable value to his firm. . . . After two or three days of earnest effort, during which he had interrupted the work of the entire . . . office and had . . . considerable . . . time expended, he was compelled to admit that he could not . . . account for the surplus cash. . . . At last he regretfully reported the matter to his superior and confessed himself defeated. What the superior had to say about the matter is not recorded, but one can imagine the attitude of the [superior] and can form a reasonably accurate notion of the comments which were made. . . .

This little story bears a moral which every accountant may well take to heart. It might be unwise to say that errors should be overlooked or that carelessness should be condoned. But surely there is no sense whatever in a ridiculous adherence to meticulous detail when the sole purpose is to trace something which is not worth tracing. . . . What the [accountant] should have done in the present case is clear. He should have made a note of the excess, and, after spending a few minutes in trying to trace it to its source, he should have gone on to weightier things.

Source: A. P. Richardson, *The Journal of Accountancy* (October, 1936), pp. 233–235.

CHAPTER REVIEW

KEY POINTS

OBJECTIVE 1

Chart of Accounts

The record traditionally kept for each item that appears on the financial statements is the account. A group of related accounts that comprise a complete unit, such as all the accounts of a specific business enterprise, is called the ledger. Accounts in the ledger are numbered consecutively so as to permit easy indexing and for use in posting. A listing of the accounts used by a specific enterprise in its ledger is referred to as a chart of accounts.

OBJECTIVE 2

Nature of an Account

The simplest form of an account is the T account. Increases and decreases in an account are recorded as debits (entries on the left side of the account) and credits (entries on the right side of the account). Periodically, the debits and the credits in an account are summed and the difference between the two sums is determined. This difference is called the balance of the account. General rules of debit and credit have been established for recording increases or decreases to asset, liability, owner's equity, revenue and expense accounts. Regardless of the complexity of a transaction or the number of accounts affected, each transaction is recorded in a manner so that the sum of the debits is always equal to the sum of the credits.

The effects of transactions are initially entered in a record called a journal. Periodically, transactions that have been journalized are transferred to the accounts by a process known as posting.

The sum of the increases recorded in an account is usually equal to or greater than the sum of the decreases recorded in the account. For this reason, the normal balance of an account is indicated by the side of the account (debit or credit) that receives the increases.

The rules of debit and credit and normal account balances are summarized in the following table:

	Increase	Decrease	Normal Balance
Balance sheet accounts:			
Asset	Debit	Credit	Debit
Liability	Credit	Debit	Credit
Owner's Equity *or* Stockholders' Equity			
Capital Stock	Credit	Debit	Credit
Retained Earnings	Credit	Debit	Credit
Dividends	Debit	Credit	Debit
Income statement accounts:			
Revenue	Credit	Debit	Credit
Expense	Debit	Credit	Debit

OBJECTIVE 3

Flow of Business Transaction Data

The flow of business transaction data from the time a transaction occurs to its recording in the ledger is diagrammed as follows:

Business *TRANSACTION* occurs → Business *DOCUMENT* prepared → Entry recorded in *JOURNAL* → Entry posted to *LEDGER*

Before a transaction is entered in a journal, it should be analyzed according to the following sequence of steps:

1. Determine whether an asset, a liability, owner's equity, revenue, or expense is affected.
2. Determine whether the affected asset, liability, owner's equity, revenue, or expense increases or decreases.
3. Determine whether the effect of the transaction should be recorded as a debit or as a credit in an asset, liability, owner's equity, revenue, or expense account.

OBJECTIVE 4 Trial Balance

The equality of the debits and credits in a ledger is verified periodically by the preparation of a trial balance. The trial balance does not provide complete proof of accuracy of the ledger, but only indicates that the debits and credits are equal.

OBJECTIVE 5 Discovery and Correction of Errors

Occasional errors in journalizing and posting transactions are unavoidable. The trial balance is one of the principal means for discovering such errors. However, the trial balance indicates only that the debits and credits are equal.

A journal entry that is incorrect but not posted may be corrected by drawing a line through the error and inserting the correct item. Likewise, if the journal entry is correct but the posting is incorrect, a line may be drawn through the error and the correct posting inserted. If the journal entry is incorrect and posted, the error may be correct by journalizing and posting a correcting entry.

OBJECTIVE 6 Materiality

In following generally accepted accounting principles, the accountant must consider the relative importance of any event, accounting procedure, or change in procedure that affects items on the financial statements. The concept of materiality implies that accountants need not strictly adhere to generally accepted accounting principles if the amounts involved are not significant.

KEY TERMS

account 53
ledger 53
chart of accounts 54
T account 54
debit 55
credit 55
balance of the account 55
journal 55
journalizing 56
posting 56
note payable 56
double-entry accounting 57
temporary accounts 59
nominal accounts 59
real accounts 59
standard account form 60
trial balance 67
transpositions 68
slides 68
materiality 69

SELF-EXAMINATION QUESTIONS

Answers at end of chapter.

1. The separate record maintained for each item that appears on the financial statements is the:
   A. ledger
   B. account
   C. chart of accounts
   D. none of the above

2. A debit may signify:
   A. an increase in an asset account
   B. a decrease in an asset account
   C. an increase in a liability account
   D. an increase in the capital stock account

3. The type of account with a normal credit balance is:
   A. an asset
   B. a dividend
   C. a revenue
   D. an expense

4. The receipt of cash from customers in payment of their accounts would be recorded by a:
   A. debit to Cash; credit to Accounts Receivable
   B. debit to Accounts Receivable; credit to Cash
   C. debit to Cash; credit to Accounts Payable
   D. debit to Accounts Payable; credit to Cash

5. The form listing the balances and the titles of the accounts in the ledger on a given date is the:
   A. income statement
   B. balance sheet
   C. retained earnings statement
   D. trial balance

ILLUSTRATIVE PROBLEM

Midtown Laboratories Inc. completed the following transactions during June:

June 1. Paid office rent for June, $600.
2. Purchased equipment on account, $2,100.
5. Received cash on account from customers, $4,150.
8. Purchased X-ray film and other supplies on account, $145.
9. One of the items of equipment purchased on June 2 was defective. It was returned with the permission of the supplier, who agreed to reduce the account for the amount charged for the item, $125.
12. Paid cash to creditors on account, $1,250.
16. Sold X-ray film to another laboratory at cost, as an accommodation, receiving cash, $63.
17. Paid cash for renewal of a 2-year property insurance policy, $370.
20. Discovered that the balance of the cash account and of the accounts payable account as of June 1 were overstated by $50. A payment of that amount to a creditor in May had not been recorded. Journalize the $50 payment as of June 20.
23. Paid cash for laboratory expenses, $245.
27. Paid cash dividends, $1,250.
30. Recorded the cash sales during June, $1,720.
30. Paid salaries, $1,725.
30. Paid gas and electricity expense, $157.
30. Paid water expense, $29.
30. Recorded sales charged to customers on account for services performed in June, $4,145.
30. Paid telephone expense, $74.
30. Paid miscellaneous expenses, $132.

Midtown Laboratories Inc.'s account titles, numbers, and balances as of June 1 (all normal balances) are listed as follows: Cash, 11, $3,123; Accounts Receivable, 12, $6,725; Supplies, 13, $290; Prepaid Insurance, 14, $365; Equipment, 18, $19,745; Accounts Payable, 22, $765; Capital Stock, 31, $20,000; Retained Earnings, 32, $9,483; Dividends, 33; Sales, 41; Salary Expense, 51; Rent Expense, 53; Laboratory Expense, 55; Utilities Expense, 56; Miscellaneous Expense, 59.

Instructions:

1. Open a ledger for Midtown Laboratories Inc. as of June 1 of the current year. Enter the balances in the appropriate balance columns and place a check mark (✔) in the posting reference column. (It is advisable to verify the equality of the debit and credit balances in the ledger before proceeding with the next instruction.)
2. Record each transaction in a journal.
3. Post the journal to the ledger, extending the month-end balances to the appropriate balance columns after all posting is completed.
4. Prepare a trial balance as of June 30.

SOLUTION

(2) and (3) JOURNAL PAGE 27

DATE		DESCRIPTION	POST. REF.	DEBIT	CREDIT
19-- June	1	Rent Expense	53	600 00	
		Cash	11		600 00
	2	Equipment	18	2100 00	
		Accounts Payable	22		2100 00
	5	Cash	11	4150 00	
		Accounts Receivable	12		4150 00
	8	Supplies	13	145 00	
		Accounts Payable	22		145 00
	9	Accounts Payable	22	125 00	
		Equipment	18		125 00
	12	Accounts Payable	22	1250 00	
		Cash	11		1250 00
	16	Cash	11	63 00	
		Supplies	13		63 00
	17	Prepaid Insurance	14	370 00	
		Cash	11		370 00
	20	Accounts Payable	22	50 00	
		Cash	11		50 00
	23	Laboratory Expense	55	245 00	
		Cash	11		245 00
	27	Dividends	33	1250 00	
		Cash	11		1250 00
	30	Cash	11	1720 00	
		Sales	41		1720 00

JOURNAL PAGE 28

DATE		DESCRIPTION	POST. REF.	DEBIT	CREDIT
19-- June	30	Salary Expense	51	1725 00	
		Cash	11		1725 00
	30	Utilities Expense	56	157 00	
		Cash	11		157 00
	30	Utilities Expense	56	29 00	
		Cash	11		29 00
	30	Accounts Receivable	12	4145 00	
		Sales	41		4145 00
	30	Utilities Expense	56	74 00	
		Cash	11		74 00
	30	Miscellaneous Expense	59	132 00	
		Cash	11		132 00

(1) and (3)

ACCOUNT Cash ACCOUNT NO. 11

DATE		ITEM	POST. REF.	DEBIT	CREDIT	BALANCE DEBIT	BALANCE CREDIT
19-- June	1	Balance	✓			3123 00	
	1		27		600 00		
	5		27	4150 00			
	12		27		1250 00		
	16		27	63 00			
	17		27		370 00		
	20		27		50 00		
	23		27		245 00		
	27		27		1250 00		
	30		27	1720 00			
	30		28		1725 00		
	30		28		157 00		
	30		28		29 00		
	30		28		74 00		
	30		28		132 00	3174 00	

ACCOUNT Accounts Receivable ACCOUNT NO. 12

DATE		ITEM	POST. REF.	DEBIT	CREDIT	BALANCE DEBIT	BALANCE CREDIT
19-- June	1	Balance	✓			6725 00	
	5		27		4150 00		
	30		28	4145 00		6720 00	

ACCOUNT Supplies — ACCOUNT NO. 13

DATE		ITEM	POST. REF.	DEBIT	CREDIT	BALANCE DEBIT	BALANCE CREDIT
19-- June	1	Balance	✓			290 00	
	8		27	145 00			
	16		27		63 00	372 00	

ACCOUNT Prepaid Insurance — ACCOUNT NO. 14

DATE		ITEM	POST. REF.	DEBIT	CREDIT	BALANCE DEBIT	BALANCE CREDIT
19-- June	1	Balance	✓			365 00	
	17		27	370 00		735 00	

ACCOUNT Equipment — ACCOUNT NO. 18

DATE		ITEM	POST. REF.	DEBIT	CREDIT	BALANCE DEBIT	BALANCE CREDIT
19-- June	1	Balance	✓			19745 00	
	2		27	2100 00			
	9		27		125 00	21720 00	

ACCOUNT Accounts Payable — ACCOUNT NO. 22

DATE		ITEM	POST. REF.	DEBIT	CREDIT	BALANCE DEBIT	BALANCE CREDIT
19-- June	1	Balance	✓				765 00
	2		27		2100 00		
	8		27		145 00		
	9		27	125 00			
	12		27	1250 00			
	20		27	50 00			1585 00

ACCOUNT Capital Stock — ACCOUNT NO. 31

DATE		ITEM	POST. REF.	DEBIT	CREDIT	BALANCE DEBIT	BALANCE CREDIT
19-- June	1	Balance	✓				20000 00

ACCOUNT Retained Earnings — ACCOUNT NO. 32

DATE		ITEM	POST. REF.	DEBIT	CREDIT	BALANCE DEBIT	BALANCE CREDIT
19-- June	1	Balance	✓				9483 00

ACCOUNT Dividends — ACCOUNT NO. 33

DATE		ITEM	POST. REF.	DEBIT	CREDIT	BALANCE DEBIT	BALANCE CREDIT
19-- June	27		27	1250 00		1250 00	

ACCOUNT Sales — ACCOUNT NO. 41

DATE		ITEM	POST. REF.	DEBIT	CREDIT	BALANCE DEBIT	BALANCE CREDIT
19-- June	30		27		1,720.00		
	30		28		4,145.00		5,865.00

ACCOUNT Salary Expense — ACCOUNT NO. 51

DATE		ITEM	POST. REF.	DEBIT	CREDIT	BALANCE DEBIT	BALANCE CREDIT
19-- June	30		28	1,725.00		1,725.00	

ACCOUNT Rent Expense — ACCOUNT NO. 53

DATE		ITEM	POST. REF.	DEBIT	CREDIT	BALANCE DEBIT	BALANCE CREDIT
19-- June	1		27	600.00		600.00	

ACCOUNT Laboratory Expense — ACCOUNT NO. 55

DATE		ITEM	POST. REF.	DEBIT	CREDIT	BALANCE DEBIT	BALANCE CREDIT
19-- June	23		27	245.00		245.00	

ACCOUNT Utilities Expense — ACCOUNT NO. 56

DATE		ITEM	POST. REF.	DEBIT	CREDIT	BALANCE DEBIT	BALANCE CREDIT
19-- June	30		28	157.00			
	30		28	29.00			
	30		28	74.00		260.00	

ACCOUNT Miscellaneous Expense — ACCOUNT NO. 59

DATE		ITEM	POST. REF.	DEBIT	CREDIT	BALANCE DEBIT	BALANCE CREDIT
19-- June	30		28	132.00		132.00	

(4)

Midtown Laboratories Inc.
Trial Balance
June 30, 19--

Account	Debit	Credit
Cash	3,174.00	
Accounts Receivable	6,720.00	
Supplies	372.00	
Prepaid Insurance	735.00	
Equipment	21,720.00	
Accounts Payable		1,585.00
Capital Stock		20,000.00
Retained Earnings		9,483.00
Dividends	1,250.00	
Sales		5,865.00
Salary Expense	1,725.00	
Rent Expense	600.00	
Laboratory Expense	245.00	
Utilities Expense	260.00	
Miscellaneous Expense	132.00	
	36,933.00	36,933.00

DISCUSSION QUESTIONS

2–1. What is an account?

2–2. Differentiate between an account and a ledger.

2–3. Describe in general terms the sequence of accounts in the ledger.

2–4. What is the name of the record in which a transaction is initially recorded?

2–5. Define posting.

2–6. Do the terms *debit* and *credit* signify increase or decrease, or may they signify either? Explain.

2–7. Indicate whether each of the following is recorded by a debit or by a credit: (a) increase in an asset account, (b) decrease in a liability account, (c) increase in a revenue account.

2–8. What is the effect (increase or decrease) of debits to expense accounts (a) in terms of owner's equity and (b) in terms of expense?

2–9. What is the effect (increase or decrease) of credits to revenue accounts (a) in terms of owner's equity and (b) in terms of revenue?

2–10. John Collins Company adheres to a policy of depositing all cash receipts in a bank account and making all payments by check. The cash account as of March 31 has a credit balance of $925 and there is no undeposited cash on hand. (a) Assuming that there were no errors in journalizing or posting, what is the explanation of this unusual balance? (b) Is the $925 credit balance in the cash account an asset, a liability, owner's equity, a revenue, or an expense?

2–11. During the month, a business enterprise has a substantial number of transactions affecting each of the following accounts. State for each account whether it is likely to have (a) debit entries only, (b) credit entries only, or (c) both debit and credit entries.

(1) Rent Expense
(2) Sales
(3) Miscellaneous Expense
(4) Accounts Payable
(5) Dividends
(6) Accounts Receivable
(7) Notes Payable
(8) Cash

2–12. Rearrange the following in proper sequence: (a) entry posted to ledger, (b) business transaction occurs, (c) entry recorded in journal, (d) business document prepared.

2–13. Describe the three procedures required to post the credit portion of the following journal entry (Sales is account no. 41):

JOURNAL — PAGE 29

19-- May	30	Accounts Receivable ...... Sales....................	12	1,200	 1,200

2–14. Boswell Company performed services in May for a specific customer and the fee was $12,500. Payment was received in the following June. (a) Was the revenue earned in May or June? (b) What accounts should be debited and credited in (1) May and (2) June?

2–15. As of April 1, Retained Earnings had a credit balance of $15,000. During the year, the dividends totaled $12,000 and the business incurred a net loss of

$6,000. Assuming that there have been no recording errors, will the balance sheet prepared at March 31 balance? Explain.

2–16. During the month, a business corporation received $925,000 in cash and paid out $790,000 in cash. Do the data indicate that the corporation earned $135,000 during the month? Explain.

2–17. (a) Describe the form known as a trial balance. (b) What proof is provided by a trial balance?

2–18. When a trial balance is prepared, an account balance of $36,750 is listed as $63,750, and an account balance of $54,000 is listed as $5,400. Identify the transposition and the slide.

2–19. When a purchase of supplies of $950 for cash was recorded, both the debit and the credit were journalized and posted as $590. (a) Would this error cause the trial balance to be out of balance? (b) Would the answer be the same if the $950 entry had been journalized correctly, but the credit to Cash had been posted as $590?

2–20. Indicate which of the following errors, each considered individually, would cause the trial balance totals to be unequal:
(a) A payment of $25,000 for equipment purchased was posted as a debit of $25,000 to Equipment and a credit of $52,000 to Cash.
(b) A payment of $1,000 for supplies was journalized and posted as a debit of $100 to Salary Expense and a credit of $100 to Cash.
(c) A payment of $750 to a creditor was posted as a credit of $750 to Accounts Payable and a credit of $750 to Cash.
(d) A receipt of $950 from an account receivable was journalized and posted as a debit of $950 to Cash and a credit of $950 to Sales.
(e) A fee of $7,500 earned and due from a client was not debited to Accounts Receivable or credited to a revenue account, because the cash had not been received.

2–21. How is a correction made when an error is an account title or amount in the journal is discovered before the entry is posted?

2–22. In preparing and posting the journal entry to record the purchase of land by issuing a note payable, the capital stock account was erroneously credited. What is the preferred procedure to correct the error?

2–23. The acquisition of a $2,500 piece of equipment was recorded as an expense. Would this error be material (a) if total assets were $50,000 and annual net income was $5,000, (b) if total assets were $5,000,000 and annual net income was $500,000?

Real World Focus

2–24. The net income for Tandy Corporation for the year ended June 30, 1990, was $290,347,000. In the income statement, the amounts were reported "In thousands" and the net income was reported as $290,347. Which accounting concept supports the practice of rounding dollar amounts to the nearest thousand?

Ethics Discussion Case

2–25. At the end of the current month, Fran Briscoe prepared a trial balance for Witt Company. The debit side of the trial balance exceeds the credit side by a significant amount. Fran has decided to subtract the difference from the balance of the miscellaneous expense account in order to complete the preparation of the current month's financial statements by a 5 o'clock deadline. Fran will look for the difference next week when there is more time.

Discuss whether Fran Briscoe is behaving in an ethical manner.

EXERCISES

Ex. 2–26.
Chart of accounts.
OBJ. 1

Wilson Co. is a newly organized enterprise. The list of accounts to be opened in the general ledger is as follows:

Accounts Payable	Prepaid Rent
Accounts Receivable	Rent Expense
Accumulated Depreciation	Retained Earnings
Capital Stock	Salaries Payable
Cash	Salary Expense
Depreciation Expense	Sales
Dividends	Supplies
Equipment	Supplies Expense
Land	Utilities Expense
Miscellaneous Expense	

List the accounts in the order in which they should appear in the ledger of Wilson Co. and assign account numbers. Each account number is to have two digits: the first digit is to indicate the major classification ("1" for assets, etc.), and the second digit is to identify the specific account within each major classification ("11" for Cash, etc.)

Ex. 2–27.
Identify transactions.
OBJ. 2

Eight transactions are recorded in the following T accounts:

Cash	
(1) 25,000	(2) 2,500
(7) 12,500	(3) 950
	(4) 1,225
	(6) 5,000
	(8) 2,500

Accounts Receivable	
(5) 17,500	(7) 12,500

Supplies	
(3) 950	

Equipment	
(2) 10,000	

Capital Stock	
	(1) 25,000

Service Revenue	
	(5) 17,500

Accounts Payable	
(6) 5,000	(2) 7,500

Dividends	
(8) 2,500	

Operating Expenses	
(4) 1,225	

Indicate for each debit and each credit: (a) whether an asset, liability, owner's equity, dividends, revenue, or expense account was affected and (b) whether the account was increased (+) or decreased (−). Answers should be presented in the following form (transaction (1) is given as an example):

	Account Debited		Account Credited	
Transaction	Type	Effect	Type	Effect
(1)	asset	+	owner's equity	+

Ex. 2–28.
Transactions.
OBJ. 3

Dunston Company has the following accounts in its ledger: Cash; Accounts Receivable; Supplies; Office Equipment; Accounts Payable; Capital Stock; Retained Earnings; Dividends; Fees Earned; Rent Expense; Advertising Expense; Utilities Expense; Miscellaneous Expense.

Record the following selected transactions, completed during July of the current year, in a journal:

July 1. Paid rent for the month, $1,000.
2. Paid advertising expense, $350.
5. Paid cash for supplies, $125.
7. Purchased office equipment on account, $3,750.
10. Received cash from customers on account, $5,600.
12. Paid creditor on account, $2,150.
14. Paid cash dividends, $1,200.
15. Paid cash for repairs to office equipment, $75.
27. Paid telephone bill for the month, $195.
29. Fees earned and billed to customers for the month, $9,150.
31. Paid electricity bill for the month, $430.

Ex. 2–29.
Transactions.
OBJ. 3

Snyder Inc. has the following accounts in its ledger: Cash; Accounts Receivable; Supplies; Office Equipment; Accounts Payable; Capital Stock; Retained Earnings; Dividends; Fees Earned; Salary Expense; Rent Expense; Advertising Expense; Utilities Expense; Miscellaneous Expense.

Record the following selected transactions, completed during February of the current year, in a journal:

Feb. 1. Paid advertising expense, $1,500.
2. Paid rent for the month, $2,750.
5. Paid cash for supplies, $275.
7. Purchased office equipment on account, $10,500.
10. Received cash from customers on account, $9,700.
11. Paid cash for repairs to office equipment, $175.
12. Paid creditor on account, $7,150.
14. Paid cash dividend, $2,000.
24. Paid telephone bill for the month, $475.
27. Fees billed to customers for the month, $17,200.
28. Paid electricity bill for the month, $950.
28. Paid salaries, $4,900.

Ex. 2–30.
Trial balance.
OBJ. 4

The accounts in the ledger of Dobbs Realty Company as of June 30 of the current year are listed in alphabetical order as follows. All accounts have normal balances. The balance of the cash account has been intentionally omitted.

Accounts Payable	$ 21,910
Accounts Receivable	28,500
Cash	?
Capital Stock	100,000
Dividends	28,000
Fees Earned	350,000
Insurance Expense	5,000
Land	125,000
Miscellaneous Expense	9,900
Notes Payable	25,000
Prepaid Insurance	3,150
Rent Expense	48,000
Retained Earnings	50,000
Salary Expense	215,000
Supplies	3,900
Supplies Expense	6,100
Utilities Expense	41,500

Prepare a trial balance, listing the accounts in their proper order and inserting the missing figure for cash.

Ex. 2–31. Errors in trial balance. OBJ. 4

The following preliminary trial balance of King Carpet Company does not balance:

King Carpet Company
Trial Balance
December 31, 19--

Cash	67,500	
Accounts Receivable	17,000	
Prepaid Insurance		3,300
Equipment	4,500	
Accounts Payable		9,850
Salaries Payable		590
Capital Stock	40,000	
Retained Earnings	21,250	
Dividends		24,000
Service Revenue		64,940
Salary Expense		33,400
Advertising Expense	5,200	
Miscellaneous Expense		1,490
	155,450	137,570

When the ledger and other records are reviewed, you discover the following: (1) the debits and credits in the cash account total $67,500 and $62,300, respectively; (2) a sale of $500 to a customer on account was not posted to the accounts receivable account; (3) a payment of $1,900 made to a creditor on account was not posted to the accounts payable account; (4) the balance of the salaries payable account is $950; (5) the correct balance of the equipment account is $45,000; and (6) each account has a normal balance. Prepare a corrected trial balance.

Ex. 2–32. Effect of errors on trial balance. OBJ. 4

The following errors occurred in posting from a journal:

(1) A debit of $7,500 to Equipment was posted twice.
(2) A credit of $200 to Cash was posted as $2,000.
(3) A debit of $1,000 to Cash was posted to Salary Expense.
(4) A credit of $400 to Accounts Payable was posted as a debit.
(5) An entry debiting Cash and crediting Fees Earned for $2,250 was not posted.
(6) A debit of $810 to Supplies was posted as $180.
(7) A credit of $725 to Accounts Receivable was not posted.

Considering each case individually (i.e., assuming that no other errors had occurred), indicate: (a) by "yes" or "no" whether the trial balance would be out of balance; (b) if answer to (a) is "yes," the amount by which the trial balance totals would differ; and (c) the column of the trial balance that would have the larger total. Answers should be presented in the following form (error (1) is given as an example):

Error	(a) Out of Balance	(b) Difference	(c) Larger Total
(1)	yes	$7,500	debit

PROBLEMS

Pb. 2–33. Entries into T accounts; trial balance. OBJ. 2, 4

AIA Company was organized on May 1 of the current year. During May the following transactions were completed:

(a) Received cash from issuance of capital stock, $7,500.
(b) Purchased used automobile for $6,800, paying $1,400 cash and giving a non-interest-bearing note for the remainder.
(c) Paid May rent for office, $800.

(d) Paid cash for supplies, $225.
(e) Purchased equipment on account, $4,200.
(f) Paid cash for insurance policies on automobile and equipment, $392.
(g) Received cash from a client for plans delivered, $1,725.
(h) Paid cash to creditors on account, $2,100.
(i) Paid cash for miscellaneous expenses, $40.
(j) Received invoice for blueprint expense, due in following month, $75.
(k) Recorded fee earned on plans delivered, payment to be made in following month, $2,500.
(l) Paid salary of assistant, $1,000.
(m) Paid cash for miscellaneous expenses, $68.
(n) Paid installment due on note payable, $150.
(o) Paid gas, oil, and repairs on automobile for May, $70.

Instructions:

(1) Record the foregoing transactions in the following T accounts: Cash; Accounts Receivable; Supplies; Prepaid Insurance; Automobiles; Equipment; Notes Payable; Accounts Payable; Capital Stock; Professional Fees; Salary Expense; Rent Expense; Automobile Expense; Blueprint Expense; Miscellaneous Expense. To the left of each amount entered in the accounts, place the appropriate letter to identify the transactions.
(2) Determine the balances of the accounts in the ledger, pencil footing all accounts having two or more debits or credits. A memorandum balance should also be inserted in accounts having both debits and credits, in the manner illustrated on page 55. For accounts with entries on one side only (such as Professional Fees), there is no need to insert the memorandum balance in the item column. Accounts containing only a single debit and a single credit (such as Notes Payable) need no pencil footings; the memorandum balance should be inserted in the appropriate item column. Accounts containing a single entry only (such as Prepaid Insurance) need neither a pencil footing nor a memorandum balance.
(3) Prepare a trial balance as of May 31 of the current year.

Pb. 2–34.
Journal entries and trial balance.
OBJ. 2, 3, 4

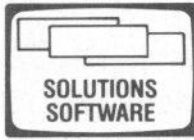

On July 1 of the current year, Janet Lopes established a corporation under the name of Lopes Realty Inc. During the month, Lopes Realty Inc. completed the following transactions:

(a) Issued capital stock for $25,000.
(b) Paid rent on office and equipment for the month, $15,000.
(c) Purchased supplies (stationery, stamps, pencils, ink, etc.) on account, $4,500.
(d) Paid creditor on account, $2,900.
(e) Earned sales commissions, receiving cash, $39,750.
(f) Paid automobile expenses (including rental charge) for month, $2,900, and miscellaneous expenses, $1,950.
(g) Paid office salaries, $8,000.
(h) Determined that the cost of supplies used was $1,325.
(i) Paid dividends, $5,000.

Instructions:

(1) Prepare a ledger of T accounts for the following accounts: Cash; Supplies; Accounts Payable; Capital Stock; Dividends; Sales Commissions; Rent Expense; Office Salaries Expense; Automobile Expense; Supplies Expense; Miscellaneous Expense.
(2) Prepare journal entries for transactions (a) through (i).
(3) Post the journal to the ledger, placing the appropriate letter to the left of each amount to identify the transactions. Determine the account balances after all posting is complete, pencil footing all accounts having two or more debits or credits. A

memorandum balance should also be inserted in accounts having both debits and credits, in the manner illustrated on page 55. For accounts with entries on one side only, there is no need to insert a pencil footing or a memorandum balance in the item column. Accounts containing only a single debit and a single credit also need no pencil footings, but the memorandum balance should be inserted in the appropriate item column.

(4) Prepare a trial balance as of July 31, 19--.
(5) Determine the following:
  (a) Amount of total revenue recorded in the ledger.
  (b) Amount of total expenses recorded in the ledger.
  (c) Amount of net income for July.

Pb. 2–35.
Journal entries and trial balance.
OBJ. 2, 3, 4

Conrad Decorators Inc. was established on March 10 of the current year. During the remainder of the month, the following business transactions were completed:

Mar. 10. Received cash from issuance of capital stock, $10,000.
10. Paid rent for period of March 10 to end of month, $800.
11. Purchased a truck for $10,000, paying $2,000 cash and giving a note payable for the remainder.
12. Purchased equipment on account, $1,700.
14. Paid premiums on property and casualty insurance, $510.
14. Purchased supplies for cash, $925.
15. Received cash for job completed, $850.
16. Purchased supplies on account, $240.
17. Paid wages of enployees, $650.
21. Paid creditor for equipment purchased on March 12, $1,700.
24. Recorded sales on account and sent invoices to customers, $1,900.
26. Received an invoice for truck expenses, to be paid in April, $225.
28. Received cash for job completed, $1,050. This sale had not been recorded previously.
29. Paid utilities expense, $205.
29. Paid miscellaneous expenses, $80.
29. Received cash from customers on account, $1,420.
31. Paid wages of employees, $1,350.
31. Paid cash dividends, $1,500.

Instructions:

(1) Open a ledger of standard accounts for Conrad Decorators Inc., using the following titles and account numbers: Cash, 11; Accounts Receivable, 12; Supplies, 13; Prepaid Insurance, 14; Equipment, 16; Truck, 18; Notes Payable, 21; Accounts Payable 22; Capital Stock, 31; Dividends, 33; Sales, 41; Wages Expense, 51; Rent Expense, 53; Utilities Expense, 54; Truck Expense, 55; Miscellaneous Expense, 59.
(2) Record each transaction in a journal, referring to the above list of accounts or to the ledger in selecting appropriate account titles to be debited and credited. (Do not insert the account numbers in the journal at this time.)
(3) Post the journal to the ledger, inserting appropriate posting references as each item is posted. Extend the month-end balances to the appropriate balance column after all posting is completed.
(4) Prepare a trial balance for Conrad Decorators Inc. as of March 31.

Pb. 2–36.
Journal entries and trial balance.
OBJ. 2, 3, 4

Kane Company completed the following transactions during May of the current year:

May 1. Paid office rent for May, $1,900.
2. Purchased equipment on account, $9,000.
5. Purchased supplies on account, $850.

May 6. Received cash on account from customers, $9,125.
7. Paid cash to creditors on account, $6,120.
10. Sold supplies at cost as an accommodation to another business, receiving cash, $75.
10. Paid cash for renewal of property insurance policy, $545.
15. Paid cash for laboratory expenses, $345.
20. Discovered that the balance of the cash account was understated and the accounts receivable account was overstated as of May 1 by $100. A cash receipt of that amount on account from a customer in April had not been recorded. Journalized the $100 receipt as of May 20.
24. One of the items of equipment purchased on May 2 was defective. It was returned with the permission of the supplier, who agreed to reduce the account for the amount charged for the item, $250.
26. Paid cash dividends, $2,200.
28. Paid miscellaneous expenses, $420.
30. Paid gas and electricity expense, $510.
30. Paid water expense, $130.
30. Paid telephone expense, $225.
31. Recorded fees charged to customers on account for services performed in May, $8,200.
31. Recorded the cash received in payment of services (on a cash basis) to customers during May, $9,910.
31. Paid salaries, $4,750.

Kane Company's account titles, numbers, and balances as of May 1 (all normal balances) are listed as follows: Cash, 11, $6,125; Accounts Receivable, 12, $14,960; Supplies, 13, $1,240; Prepaid Insurance, 14, $3,500; Equipment, 18, $55,600; Accounts Payable, 22, $9,850; Capital Stock, 31, $50,000; Retained Earnings, 32, $21,575; Dividends, 33; Fees Earned, 41; Salary Expense, 51; Rent Expense, 53; Utilities Expense, 55; Laboratory Expense, 56; Miscellaneous Expense, 59.

Instructions:

(1) Open a ledger of standard accounts as of May 1 of the current year. Enter the balances in the appropriate balance columns and place a check mark (✔) in the posting reference column. (It is advisable to verify the equality of the debit and credit balances in the ledger before proceeding with the next instruction.)
(2) Record each transaction in a journal.
(3) Post the journal to the ledger, extending the month-end balances to the appropriate balance columns after all posting is completed.
(4) Prepare a trial balance as of May 31.
(5) Assuming that the expenses which have not been recorded (such as supplies expense and insurance expense) amount to a total of $1,950 for the month, determine the following amounts:
 (a) Net income for the month of May.
 (b) Increase or decrease in owner's equity during May.
 (c) Owner's equity as of May 31.

Pb. 2–37.
Journal entries and trial balance.
OBJ. 2, 3, 4

The following business transactions were completed by Kim Theatre Corporation during May of the current year:

May 1. Received and deposited in a bank account $50,000 cash for capital stock.
2. Purchased the Coastland Drive-In Theatre for $150,000, divided as follows: land, $60,000; buildings, $60,000; equipment, $30,000. Paid $45,000 in cash and gave a note payable for the remainder.

May 4. Entered into a contract for the operation of the refreshment stand concession at a rental of 20% of the concessionaire's sales, with a guaranteed minimum of $750 a month, payable in advance. Received cash of $750 as the advance payment for the month of May.
6. Purchased supplies, $450, and equipment, $4,800, on account.
7. Paid premiums for property and casualty insurance policies, $2,250.
8. Paid for May billboard and newspaper advertising, $750.
10. Cash received from admissions for the week, $3,100.
12. Paid miscellaneous expense, $265.
17. Paid semimonthly wages, $1,450.
17. Cash received from admissions for the week, $2,980.
19. Paid miscellaneous expenses, $310.
20. Returned a portion of the supplies purchased on May 6 to the supplier, receiving full credit for the cost, $75.
23. Paid cash to creditors on account, $2,250.
24. Cash received from admissions for the week, $3,420.
26. Purchased supplies for cash, $210.
26. Paid for advertising leaflets for special promotion during last week in May, $375.
28. Recorded invoice of $5,400 for rental of film for May. Payment is due on June 7.
29. Paid electricity and water bills, $890.
31. Paid semimonthly wages, $1,610.
31. Cash received from admissions for remainder of the month, $3,600.
31. Recorded additional amount owed by the concessionaire for the month of May; sales for the month totaled $4,500. Rental charges in excess of the advance payment of $750 are not due and payable until June 10.

Instructions:

(1) Open a ledger of standard accounts for Kim Theatre Corporation, using the following account titles and numbers: Cash, 11; Accounts Receivable, 12; Prepaid Insurance, 13; Supplies, 14; Land, 17; Buildings, 18; Equipment, 19; Accounts Payable, 21; Note Payable, 24; Capital Stock, 31; Admissions Income, 41; Concession Income, 42; Wages Expense, 51; Film Rental Expense, 52; Advertising Expense, 53; Electricity and Water Expense, 54; Miscellaneous Expense, 59.
(2) Record the transactions in a journal.
(3) Post the journal to the ledger, extending the month-end balances to the appropriate balance columns after all posting is completed.
(4) Prepare a trial balance as of May 31.
(5) Determine the following:
  (a) Amount of total revenue recorded in the ledger.
  (b) Amount of total expenses recorded in the ledger.
  (c) Amount of net income for May, assuming that additional unrecorded expenses (including supplies used, insurance expired, etc.) totaled $950.
  (d) The understatement or overstatement of net income for May that would have resulted from failure to record the invoice for film rental until it was paid in June. (See transaction of May 28.)
  (e) The understatement or overstatement of liabilities as of May 31 that would have resulted from failure to record the invoice for film rental in May. (See transaction of May 28.)

Pb. 2–38.
Journal entries and trial balance.
OBJ. 2, 3, 4

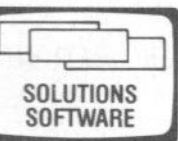

Park Realty Inc. acts as an agent in buying, selling, renting, and managing real estate. The account balances at the end of April of the current year are as follows:

11	Cash	44,500	
12	Accounts Receivable	31,600	
13	Prepaid Insurance	750	
14	Office Supplies	625	
16	Land	—0—	
21	Accounts Payable		5,250
22	Notes Payable		—0—
31	Capital Stock		50,000
32	Retained Earnings		22,025
33	Dividends	20,000	
41	Fees Earned		157,750
51	Salary and Commission Expense	122,100	
52	Rent Expense	6,000	
53	Advertising Expense	4,900	
54	Automobile Expense	3,950	
59	Miscellaneous Expense	600	
		235,025	235,025

2-87

The following business transactions were completed by Park Realty Inc. during May of the current year:

May 1. Paid rent on office for month, $1,500.
2. Purchased office supplies on account, $425.
3. Paid insurance premiums, $1,925.
9. Received cash from clients on account, $21,000.
15. Paid salaries and commissions, $19,650.
15. Purchased land for a future building site for $50,000, paying $10,000 in cash and giving a note payable for the remainder.
15. Recorded revenue earned and billed to clients during first half of month, $20,900.
18. Paid creditors on account, $4,150.
20. Returned a portion of the office supplies purchased on May 2, receiving full credit for their cost, $50.
29. Received cash from clients on account, $16,700.
29. Paid advertising expense, $2,150.
29. Discovered an error in computing a commission; received cash from the salesperson for the overpayment, $500.
30. Paid automobile expense (including rental charges for an automobile), $850.
30. Paid miscellaneous expenses, $215.
31. Recorded revenue earned and billed to clients during second half of month, $19,300.
31. Paid salaries and commissions, $19,850.
31. Paid dividends, $10,000.

Instructions:

(1) Open a ledger of standard accounts for the accounts listed. Record the balances in the appropriate balance columns as of May 1, write "Balance" in the item section, and place a check mark (✓) in the posting reference column.
(2) Record the transactions for May in a journal.
(3) Post to the ledger, extending the month-end balances to the appropriate balance columns after all posting is completed.
(4) Prepare a trial balance of the ledger as of May 31.

If the working papers correlating with the textbook are not used, omit Problem 2–39.

Pb. 2–39.
Errors in trial balance.
OBJ. 4

The following records of Evans TV Repair Inc. are presented in the working papers:
Journal containing entries for the period July 1–31.
Ledger to which the July entries have been posted.
Preliminary trial balance as of July 31, which does not balance.

Locate the errors, supply the information requested, and prepare a corrected trial balance, proceeding in accordance with the following detailed instructions. The balances recorded in the accounts as of July 1 and the entries in the journal are correctly stated. If it is necessary to correct any posted amounts in the ledger, a line should be drawn through the erroneous figure and the correct amount inserted above. Corrections or notations may be inserted on the preliminary trial balance in any manner desired. It is not necessary to complete all of the instructions if equal trial balance totals can be obtained earlier. However, the requirements of instructions (6) and (7) should be completed in any event.

Instructions:

(1) Verify the totals of the preliminary trial balance, inserting the correct amounts in the schedule provided in the working papers.
(2) Compute the difference between the trial balance totals.
(3) Compare the listings in the trial balance with the balances appearing in the ledger and list the errors found in the space provided in the working papers.
(4) Verify the accuracy of the balance of each account in the ledger and list the errors found in the space provided in the working papers.
(5) Trace the postings in the ledger back to the journal, using small check marks to identify items traced. Correct any amounts in the ledger that may be necessitated by errors in posting and list the errors in the space provided in the working papers.
(6) Journalize as of July 31 the payment of $210 for advertising expense. The bill had been paid on July 31 but was inadvertently omitted from the journal. Post to the ledger. (Revise any amounts necessitated by posting this entry.)
(7) Prepare a new trial balance.

Pb. 2–40.
Corrected trial balance.
OBJ. 4

Lakeview Carpet Cleaning prepared the following trial balance as of September 30 of the current year:

Cash	8,820	
Accounts Receivable	17,825	
Supplies	1,800	
Prepaid Insurance	400	
Equipment	22,500	
Notes Payable		25,000
Accounts Payable		5,000
Capital Stock		25,000
Retained Earnings		11,720
Dividends	8,000	
Sales		59,750
Wages Expense	31,500	
Rent Expense	1,800	
Advertising Expense	5,700	
Gas, Electricity, and Water Expense	5,650	
	103,995	126,470

The debit and credit totals are not equal as a result of the following errors:

(a) The balance of cash was understated by $700.
(b) A cash receipt of $470 was posted as a debit to Cash of $740.
(c) A credit of $325 to Accounts Receivable was not posted.

(d) A return of $245 of defective supplies was erroneously posted as a $425 credit to Supplies.
(e) An insurance policy acquired at a cost of $400 was posted as a credit to Prepaid Insurance.
(f) The balance of Notes Payable was overstated by $5,000.
(g) A credit of $910 in Accounts Payable was overlooked when determining the balance of the account.
(h) A debit of $1,000 for water expense was posted as a debit to Wages Expense.
(i) The balance of $18,000 in Rent Expense was entered as $1,800 in the trial balance.
(j) Miscellaneous Expense, with a balance of $1,100, was omitted from the trial balance.

Instructions:

Prepare a corrected trial balance as of September 30 of the current year.

ALTERNATE PROBLEMS

Pb. 2–33A.
Entries into T accounts; trial balance.
OBJ. 2, 4

Ace Draftsman Inc. was organized on July 1 of the current year. During the month the following transactions were completed:

(a) Received cash from issuance of capital stock, $10,000.
(b) Paid July rent for office, $1,250.
(c) Purchased used automobile for $7,500, paying $2,250 cash and giving a non-interest-bearing note for the remainder.
(d) Purchased equipment on account, $6,000.
(e) Paid cash for supplies, $900.
(f) Paid cash for insurance policies, $850.
(g) Received cash from client for plans delivered, $1,600.
(h) Paid cash for miscellaneous services, $75.
(i) Paid cash to creditors on account, $3,000.
(j) Paid installment due on note payable, $500.
(k) Received invoice for blueprint expenses due in August, $110.
(l) Recorded fee earned on plans delivered, payment to be made in August, $3,750.
(m) Paid salary of assistant, $1,250.
(n) Paid gas, oil, and repairs on automobile for July, $95.

Instructions:

(1) Record the foregoing transactions in the following T accounts: Cash; Accounts Receivable; Supplies; Prepaid Insurance; Automobiles; Equipment; Notes Payable; Accounts Payable; Capital Stock; Professional Fees; Salary Expense; Rent Expense; Automobile Expense; Blueprint Expense; Miscellaneous Expense. To the left of each amount entered in the accounts, place the appropriate letter to identify the transaction.
(2) Determine the balances of the accounts in the ledger, pencil footing all accounts having two or more debits or credits. A memorandum balance should also be inserted in accounts having both debits and credits, in the manner illustrated on page 55. For accounts with entries on one side only (such as Professional Fees), there is no need to insert the memorandum balance in the item column. Accounts containing only a single debit and a single credit (such as Notes Payable) need no pencil footings; the memorandum balance should be inserted in the appropriate item column. Accounts containing a single entry only (such as Prepaid Insurance) need neither a pencil footing nor a memorandum balance.
(3) Prepare a trial balance as of July 31 of the current year.

Pb. 2–34A.
Journal entries and trial balance.
OBJ. 2, 3, 4

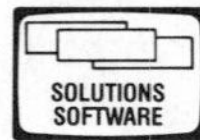

On July 1 of the current year, Rob Petrie established a corporation under the name of Midstate Realty Inc., which completed the following transactions during the month:

(a) Issued capital stock for $20,000.
(b) Paid rent on office and equipment for the month, $12,000.
(c) Purchased supplies (stationery, stamps, pencils, ink, etc.) on account, $5,900.
(d) Paid creditor on account, $4,000.
(e) Earned sales commissions, receiving cash, $41,500.
(f) Paid dividends, $5,000.
(g) Paid automobile expenses (including rental charge) for month, $3,900, and miscellaneous expenses, $1,950.
(h) Paid office salaries, $10,000.
(i) Determined that the cost of supplies used was $2,250.

Instructions:

(1) Prepare a ledger of T accounts for the following accounts: Cash; Supplies; Accounts Payable; Capital Stock; Dividends; Sales Commissions; Rent Expense; Office Salaries Expense; Automobile Expense; Supplies Expense; Miscellaneous Expense.
(2) Prepare journal entries for transactions (a) through (i).
(3) Post the journal to the ledger, placing the appropriate letter to the left of each amount to identify the transaction. Determine the account balances after all posting is complete, pencil footing all accounts having two or more debits or credits. A memorandum balance should also be inserted in accounts having both debits and credits, in the manner illustrated on page 55. For accounts with entries on one side only, there is no need to insert a pencil footing or a memorandum balance in the item column. Accounts containing only a single debit and a single credit also need no pencil footings, but the memorandum balance should be inserted in the appropriate item column.
(4) Prepare a trial balance as of July 31, 19--.
(5) Determine the following:
    (a) Amount of total revenue recorded in the ledger.
    (b) Amount of total expenses recorded in the ledger.
    (c) Amount of net income for July.

Pb. 2–35A.
Journal entries and trial balance.
OBJ. 2, 3, 4

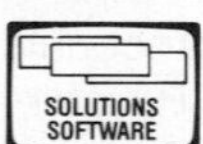

Mead Decorators Inc. was established on June 10 of the current year. During the remainder of the month, the following business transactions were completed:

June 10. Received cash from issuance of capital stock, $15,000.
10. Paid rent for period of June 10 to end of month, $800.
12. Purchased office equipment on account, $5,500.
14. Purchased a used truck for $15,000, paying $7,500 cash and giving a note payable for the remainder.
15. Purchased supplies for cash, $525.
16. Received cash for job completed, $500.
16. Paid wages of employees, $600.
20. Paid premiums on property and casualty insurance, $725.
22. Recorded sales on account and sent invoices to customers, $1,950.
24. Received an invoice for truck expenses, to be paid in July, $310.
26. Received cash for job completed, $650. This sale had not been recorded previously.
28. Purchased supplies on account, $190.
29. Paid utilities expense, $390.
29. Paid miscellaneous expenses, $95.
30. Received cash from customers on account, $1,300.
30. Paid wages of employees, $1,250.

June 30. Paid creditor a portion of the amount owed for equipment purchased on June 12, $2,500.
30. Paid cash dividends, $2,000.

Instructions:

(1) Open a ledger of standard accounts for Mead Decorators Inc., using the following titles and account numbers: Cash, 11; Accounts Receivable, 12; Supplies, 13; Prepaid Insurance, 14; Equipment, 16; Truck, 18; Notes Payable, 21; Accounts Payable, 22; Capital Stock, 31; Dividends, 33; Sales, 41; Wages Expense, 51; Rent Expense, 53; Utilities Expense, 54; Truck Expense, 55; Miscellaneous Expense, 59.
(2) Record each transaction in a journal, referring to the above list of accounts or to the ledger in selecting appropriate account titles to be debited and credited. (Do not insert the account numbers in the journal at this time.)
(3) Post the journal to the ledger, inserting appropriate posting references as each item is posted. Extend the month-end balances to the appropriate balance columns after all posting is completed.
(4) Prepare a trial balance for Mead Decorators Inc. as of June 30.

Pb. 2–36A.
Journal entries and trial balance.
OBJ. 2, 3, 4

Perez Company completed the following transactions during May of the current year:

May 1. Paid office rent for May, $2,100.
2. Purchased equipment on account, $9,000.
5. Purchased supplies on account, $900.
6. Received cash on account from customers, $8,500.
7. Paid cash to creditors on account, $5,920.
10. Sold supplies at cost as an accommodation to another business, receiving cash, $125.
10. Paid cash for renewal of property insurance policy, $545.
15. Paid cash for laboratory expenses, $345.
20. Discovered that the balance of the cash account was understated and the accounts receivable account was overstated as of May 1 by $100. A cash receipt of that amount on account from a customer in April had not been recorded. Journalized the $100 receipt as of May 20.
24. One of the items of equipment purchased on May 2 was defective. It was returned with the permission of the supplier, who agreed to reduce the account for the amount charged for the item, $250.
26. Paid cash dividends, $2,000.
28. Paid miscellaneous expenses, $420.
30. Paid gas and electricity expense, $490.
30. Paid water expense, $110.
30. Paid telephone expense, $265.
31. Recorded fees charged to customers on account for services performed in May, $7,575.
31. Recorded the cash received in payment of services (on a cash basis) to customers during May, $10,535.
31. Paid salaries, $4,750.

Perez Company's account titles, numbers, and balances as of May 1 (all normal balances) are listed as follows: Cash, 11, $6,125; Accounts Receivable, 12, $14,960; Supplies, 13, $1,240; Prepaid Insurance, 14, $3,500; Equipment, 18, $55,600; Accounts Payable, 22, $9,850; Capital Stock, 31, $40,000; Retained Earnings, 32, $31,575; Dividends, 33; Fees Earned, 41; Salary Expense, 51; Rent Expense, 53; Utilities Expense, 55; Laboratory Expense, 56; Miscellaneous Expense, 59.

Instructions:

(1) Open a ledger of standard accounts as of May 1 of the current year. Enter the balances in the appropriate balance columns and place a check mark (✔) in the posting reference column. (It is advisable to verify the equality of the debit and credit balances in the ledger before proceeding with the next instruction.)
(2) Record each transaction in a journal.
(3) Post the journal to the ledger, extending the month-end balances to the appropriate balance columns after all posting is completed.
(4) Prepare a trial balance as of May 31.
(5) Assuming that the expenses which have not been recorded (such as supplies expense and insurance expense) amount to a total of $1,750 for the month, determine the following amounts:
    (a) Net income for the month of May.
    (b) Increase or decrease in owner's equity during May.
    (c) Owner's equity as of May 31.

Pb. 2–37A.
Journal entries and trial balance.
OBJ. 2, 3, 4

The following business transactions were completed by Midway Theatre Corporation during June of the current year:

June 1. Deposited in a bank account $75,000 cash received for capital stock.
3. Purchased the Lakeview Drive-In Theatre for $250,000, divided as follows: land, $125,000; buildings, $75,000; equipment, $50,000. Paid $60,000 in cash and gave a note payable for the remainder.
4. Entered into a contract for the operation of the refreshment stand concession at a rental of 25% of the concessionaire's sales, with a guaranteed minimum of $1,000 a month, payable in advance. Received cash of $1,000 as the advance payment for the month of June.
5. Paid for advertising leaflets for June, $250.
6. Paid premiums for property and casualty insurance policies, $3,500.
8. Purchased supplies, $750, and equipment, $4,150, on account.
8. Paid for June billboard and newspaper advertising, $1,500.
10. Paid miscellaneous expense, $250.
12. Cash received from admissions for the week, $5,600.
15. Paid semimonthly wages, $2,950.
19. Cash received from admissions for the week, $5,900.
19. Paid miscellaneous expenses, $210.
19. Returned a portion of the supplies purchased on June 8 to the supplier, receiving full credit for the cost, $90.
21. Paid cash to creditors on account, $2,950.
26. Cash received from admissions for the week, $4,910.
26. Purchased supplies for cash, $300.
29. Recorded invoice of $5,800 for rental of film for June. Payment is due on July 9.
30. Paid electricity and water bills, $625.
30. Paid semimonthly wages, $3,450.
30. Cash received from admissions for remainder of the month, $3,100.
30. Recorded additional amount owed by the concessionaire for the month of June; sales for the month totaled $6,000. Rental charges in excess of the advance payment of $1,000 are not due and payable until July 10.

Instructions:

(1) Open a ledger of standard accounts for Midway Theatre Corporation, using the following account titles and numbers: Cash, 11; Accounts Receivable, 12; Prepaid Insurance, 13; Supplies, 14; Land, 17; Buildings, 18; Equipment, 19; Accounts Payable, 21; Note Payable, 24; Capital Stock, 31; Admissions Income, 41; Concession Income, 42; Wages Expense, 51; Film Rental Expense, 52; Advertising Expense, 53; Electricity and Water Expense, 54; Miscellaneous Expense, 59.

(2) Record the transactions in a journal.
(3) Post the journal to the ledger, extending the month-end balances to the appropriate balance columns after all posting is completed.
(4) Prepare a trial balance as of June 30.
(5) Determine the following:
   (a) Amount of total revenue recorded in the ledger.
   (b) Amount of total expenses recorded in the ledger.
   (c) Amount of net income for June, assuming that additional unrecorded expenses (including supplies used, insurance expired, etc.) totaled $2,750.
   (d) The understatement or overstatement of net income for June that would have resulted from failure to record the additional amount owed by the concessionaire for the month of June until it was paid in July. (See transaction of June 30.)
   (e) The understatement or overstatement of assets as of June 30 that would have resulted from failure to record the additional amount owed by the concessionaire in June. (See transaction of June 30.)

Pb. 2–38A.
Journal entries and trial balance.
OBJ. 2, 3, 4

Wood Realty Inc. acts as an agent in buying, selling, renting, and managing real estate. The account balances at the end of April of the current year are as follows:

11	Cash	36,000	
12	Accounts Receivable	32,100	
13	Prepaid Insurance	750	
14	Office Supplies	625	
16	Land	—0—	
21	Accounts Payable		6,500
22	Notes Payable		—0—
31	Capital Stock		50,000
32	Retained Earnings		22,025
33	Dividends	20,000	
41	Fees Earned		156,400
51	Salary and Commission Expense	130,600	
52	Rent Expense	6,000	
53	Advertising Expense	4,400	
54	Automobile Expense	3,950	
59	Miscellaneous Expense	500	
		234,925	234,925

The following business transactions were completed by Wood Realty Inc. during May of the current year:

May 1. Paid rent on office for month, $1,500.
2. Purchased office supplies on account, $675.
3. Paid insurance premiums, $1,875.
9. Received cash from clients on account, $20,500.
15. Paid salaries and commissions, $19,700.
15. Purchased land for a future building site for $50,000, paying $10,000 in cash and giving a note payable for the remainder.
15. Recorded revenue earned and billed to clients during first half of month, $20,900.
18. Paid creditors on account, $4,400.
20. Returned a portion of the office supplies purchased on May 2, receiving full credit for their cost, $50.
29. Received cash from clients on account, $16,700.
29. Paid advertising expense, $2,650.
29. Discovered an error in computing a commission; received cash from the salesperson for the overpayment, $500.

May 30. Paid automobile expense (including rental charges for an automobile), $850.
30. Paid miscellaneous expenses, $215.
31. Recorded revenue earned and billed to clients during second half of month, $19,300.
31. Paid salaries and commissions, $19,000.
31. Paid dividends, $10,000.

Instructions:

(1) Open a ledger of standard accounts for the accounts listed. Record the balances in the appropriate balance columns as of May 1, write "Balance" in the item section, and place a check mark (✓) in the posting reference column.
(2) Record the transactions for May in a journal.
(3) Post to the ledger, extending the month-end balances to the appropriate balance columns after all posting is completed.
(4) Prepare a trial balance of the ledger as of May 31.

If the working papers correlating with the textbook are not used, omit Problem 2–39A.

Pb. 2–39A.
Errors in trial balance.
OBJ. 4

The following records of Evans TV Repair Inc. are presented in the working papers:
Journal containing entries for the period July 1–31.
Ledger to which the July entries have been posted.
Preliminary trial balance as of July 31, which does not balance.

Locate the errors, supply the information requested, and prepare a corrected trial balance, proceeding in accordance with the following detailed instructions. The balances recorded in the accounts as of July 1 and the entries in the journal are correctly stated. If it is necessary to correct any posted amounts in the ledger, a line should be drawn through the erroneous figure and the correct amount inserted above. Corrections or notations may be inserted on the preliminary trial balance in any manner desired. It is not necessary to complete all of the instructions if equal trial balance totals can be obtained earlier. However, the requirements of instructions (6) and (7) should be completed in any event.

Instructions:

(1) Verify the totals of the preliminary trial balance, inserting the correct amounts in the schedule provided in the working papers.
(2) Compute the difference between the trial balance totals.
(3) Compare the listings in the trial balance with the balances appearing in the ledger and list the errors found in the space provided in the working papers.
(4) Verify the accuracy of the balance of each account in the ledger and list the errors found in the space provided in the working papers.
(5) Trace the postings in the ledger back to the journal, using small check marks to identify items traced. Correct any amounts in the ledger that may be necessitated by errors in posting and list the errors in the space provided in the working papers.
(6) Journalize as of July 31 the payment of $250 for gas and electricity. The bill had been paid on July 31 but was inadvertently omitted from the journal. Post to the ledger. (Revise any amounts necessitated by posting this entry.)
(7) Prepare a new trial balance.

Pb. 2–40A.
Corrected trial balance.
OBJ. 4

Gursoy Photography Company prepared the following trial balance as of July 31 of the current year:

Cash	5,935	
Accounts Receivable	9,800	
Supplies	1,450	
Prepaid Insurance	220	
Equipment	11,750	
Notes Payable		10,000
Accounts Payable		4,750
Capital Stock		11,500
Retained Earnings		890
Dividends	9,000	
Sales		86,950
Wages Expense	52,400	
Rent Expense	750	
Advertising Expense	5,250	
Gas, Electricity, and Water Expense	4,950	
	101,505	114,090

The debit and credit totals are not equal as a result of the following errors:

(a) The balance of cash was overstated by $1,000.
(b) A cash payment of $750 was posted as a credit to Cash of $570.
(c) A debit of $175 to Accounts Receivable was not posted.
(d) A return of $725 of defective supplies was erroneously posted as a $275 credit to Supplies.
(e) An insurance policy acquired at a cost of $400 was posted as a credit to Prepaid Insurance.
(f) The balance of Notes Payable was overstated by $2,500.
(g) A debit of $150 in Accounts Payable was overlooked when the balance of the account was determined.
(h) A debit of $1,500 for dividends was posted as a credit to Capital Stock.
(i) The balance of $7,500 in Rent Expense was entered as $750 in the trial balance.
(j) Miscellaneous Expense, with a balance of $840, was omitted from the trial balance.

Instructions:

Prepare a corrected trial balance as of July 31 of the current year.

MINI-CASE 2

During June through August, Ron Wood is planning to manage and operate Wood Caddy Services at the Vineyards Country Club. Ron will rent a small maintenance building from the country club for $100 per month and will offer caddy services, including cart rentals, to golfers. Ron has had no formal training in record keeping. During June, he kept notes of all receipts and expenses in a shoe box.

An examination of Ron's shoe box records for June revealed the following:

June 1. Withdrew $1,000 from personal bank account to be used to operate the caddy service.
1. Paid rent to Vineyards Country Club, $100.
1. Paid for golf supplies (practice balls, etc.), $300.
1. Paid miscellaneous expenses, $50.
1. Arranged for the rental of forty regular (pulling) golf carts and ten gasoline-driven carts for $1,000 per month. Paid $500 in advance, with the remaining $500 due June 30.
2. Purchased supplies, including gasoline, for the golf carts on account, $375. Vineyards Country Club has agreed to allow Ron to store the gasoline in one of their fuel tanks at no cost.
15. Cash receipts for June 1–15, $1,110.
15. For June 1–15, accepted IOUs from customers on account, $250.
15. Paid salary of part-time employees, $190.
17. Paid cash to creditors on account, $175.
22. Purchased supplies, including gasoline, on account, $250.
25. Received cash in payment of IOUs on account, $150.
28. Paid miscellaneous expenses, $60.
30. Cash receipts for June 16–30, $1,650.
30. For June 16–30, accepted IOUs from customers on account, $150.
30. Paid electricity (utilities) expense, $75.
30. Paid telephone (utilities) expense, $30.
30. Paid salary of part-time employees, $210.
30. Supplies on hand at the end of June, $350.
30. Paid remaining rental on golf carts, $500.

Ron has asked you several questions concerning his financial affairs to date, and he has asked you to assist him with his record keeping and reporting of financial data.

Instructions:

(1) To assist Ron with his record keeping, prepare a chart of accounts that would be appropriate for Wood Caddy Services. Note: Small business enterprises such as Wood Caddy Services are often organized as sole proprietorships. The accounting for sole proprietorships is similar to that for a corporation, except that the owner's equity accounts differ. Specifically, instead of the account Capital Stock, a capital account entitled Ron Wood, Capital is used to record investments in the business. In addition, instead of a dividends account, withdrawals from the business enterprise are debited to Ron Wood, Drawing. A sole proprietorship has no retained earnings account.

(2) Prepare an income statement for June to help Ron assess the profitability of Wood Caddy Services. For this purpose, the use of T accounts may be useful in analyzing the effects of each of the June transactions.

(3) At various times throughout June, Ron took cash from the cash receipts of the caddy service for personal use. If $750 of cash were on hand on June 30, how much did Ron withdraw from the enterprise for personal use?

ANSWERS TO SELF-EXAMINATION QUESTIONS

1. B The separate record for each financial statement item is the account (answer B), and a group of related accounts is the ledger (answer A). A listing of the accounts in a ledger is the chart of accounts (answer C).
2. A A debit may signify an increase in asset accounts (answer A) or a decrease in liability, retained earnings, and capital stock accounts. A credit may signify a decrease in asset accounts (answer B) or an increase in liability (answer C), retained earnings, and capital stock accounts (answer D).

3. C Liability, capital stock, retained earnings, and revenue (answer C) accounts have normal credit balances. Asset (answer A), dividend (answer B), and expense (answer D) accounts have normal debit balances.
4. A The receipt of cash from customers on account increases the asset Cash and decreases the asset Accounts Receivable as indicated by answer A. Answer B has the debit and credit reversed, and answers C and D involve transactions with creditors (accounts payable) and not customers (accounts receivable).
5. D The trial balance (answer D) is a listing of the balances and the titles of the accounts in the ledger on a given date, so that the equality of the debits and credits in the ledger can be verified. The income statement (answer A) is a summary of revenue and expenses for a period of time, the balance sheet (answer B) is a presentation of the assets, liabilities, and owner's equity on a given date, and the retained earnings statement (answer C) is a summary of the changes in retained earnings for a corporation over a period of time.

CHAPTER 3

CHAPTER OBJECTIVES

1 Describe and illustrate the application of the accounting period concept.

2 Discuss the matching principle as it relates to the cash basis and the accrual basis of accounting.

3 Describe the nature of the adjusting process.

4 Describe and illustrate basic procedures for adjusting the accounting records prior to the preparation of the financial statements.

5 Describe and illustrate the work sheet for summarizing the accounting data for use in preparing financial statements.

6 Describe and illustrate the preparation of financial statements.

7 Describe and illustrate journalizing and posting adjusting entries.

8 Describe and illustrate the basic procedures for preparing the accounting records for use in accumulating data for the following accounting period.

9 Describe and diagram the basic phases of the accounting cycle.

COMPLETION OF THE ACCOUNTING CYCLE

As was demonstrated in the preceding chapters, transactions are recorded during an accounting period as they occur. At the end of the period, the ledger accounts must be brought up to date (adjusted) to assure that revenues and expenses are matched properly (matching concept), so that the financial statements will fairly present the results of operations for the period and the financial condition at the end of the period.

This chapter discusses and illustrates the use of the adjusting process to achieve the proper matching of revenues and expenses in the determination of periodic net income and financial condition. The preparation of financial statements and the preparation of the accounting records for the following accounting period will also be addressed.

ACCOUNTING PERIOD

OBJECTIVE 1
Describe and illustrate the application of the accounting period concept.

Only in rare cases is a business organized with the expectation of operating for only a certain period of time. In most cases, it is not possible to determine in advance the length of life of an enterprise, and so an assumption must be made concerning the life of the business. The nature of the assumption will affect the manner of recording some of the business transactions, which in turn will affect the data reported in the financial statements.

Going Concern

It is customary to assume that a business entity has a reasonable expectation of continuing in business at a profit for an indefinite period of time. This **going concern concept** supports the treatment of prepaid expenses as assets, even though they may not be salable. To illustrate, assume that on the last day of its fiscal year, a wholesale firm receives from a printer a $20,000 order of sales catalogs. If there were no assumption that the firm is to continue in business, the catalogs would be merely scrap paper and the value reported for them on the balance sheet would be small.

Doubt as to the continued existence of a firm may be disclosed in a note to the financial statements, as indicated in the following note from the 1990 statements of Munsingwear Inc.:

> The Company's . . . financial statements have been presented on the basis that it is a going concern, which contemplates the realization of assets and the satisfaction of liabilities in the normal course of business. The Company reported net losses of $14,974,000 for the year ended January 6, 1990, and cumulative losses for the past three years of $50,790,000. As a result, a deficit [negative retained earnings] of $52,000 was reported in stockholders' equity at year end.
>
> The Company's continued existence is dependent upon its ability to achieve its 1990 operating plan . . .
>
> If management cannot achieve the 1990 operating plan because of sales shortfalls or other unfavorable events, the Company may find it necessary to dispose of . . . assets or operating entities . . .

When there is conclusive evidence that a business entity has a limited life, the accounting procedures should be appropriate to the expected terminal date of the entity. Changes in the application of normal accounting procedures may be needed for business organizations in receivership or bankruptcy, for example. In such cases, the financial statements should clearly disclose the limited life of the enterprise and should be prepared from the "quitting concern" or liquidation point of view, rather than from a "going concern" point of view.

Fiscal Year

A complete and accurate picture of an enterprise's success or failure cannot be obtained until it discontinues operations, converts its assets into cash, and pays off its debts. Then, and only then, is it possible to determine its true net income. But many decisions regarding the business must be made by management and interested outsiders during its existence. It is therefore necessary to prepare periodic reports on operations, financial position, and cash flows.

Reports may be prepared when a certain job or project is completed, but more often they are prepared at specified time intervals. For a number of reasons, including custom and various legal requirements, the maximum length of an accounting period is usually one year, which includes a complete cycle of the seasons and of business activities. Income and property taxes are also based on yearly periods and thus require that annual determinations be made.

The annual accounting period adopted by an enterprise is known as its **fiscal year.** Fiscal years ordinarily begin with the first day of the particular month selected and end on the last day of the twelfth month hence. The period most commonly adopted is the calendar year, although other periods are not unusual, particularly for incorporated businesses. For example, an enterprise may adopt a fiscal year that ends when business activities have reached the lowest point in the enterprise's annual operating cycle. Such a fiscal year is termed the **natural business year.**

The 1990 edition of *Accounting Trends & Techniques,* published by the American Institute of Certified Public Accountants, reported the following results of a survey of 600 industrial and merchandising companies concerning the month of their fiscal year end:

Percentage of companies with fiscal years ending in the month of:

Month	%	Month	%
January	4%	July	3%
February	2	August	3
March	3	September	6
April	1	October	3
May	2	November	3
June	10	December	60

The long-term financial history of a business enterprise may be shown by a succession of balance sheets, prepared every year. The history of operations for the intervening periods is presented in a series of income statements. If the life of a business enterprise is represented by a line moving from left to right, a series of balance sheets and income statements may be diagrammed as follows:

THE LIFE OF A BUSINESS

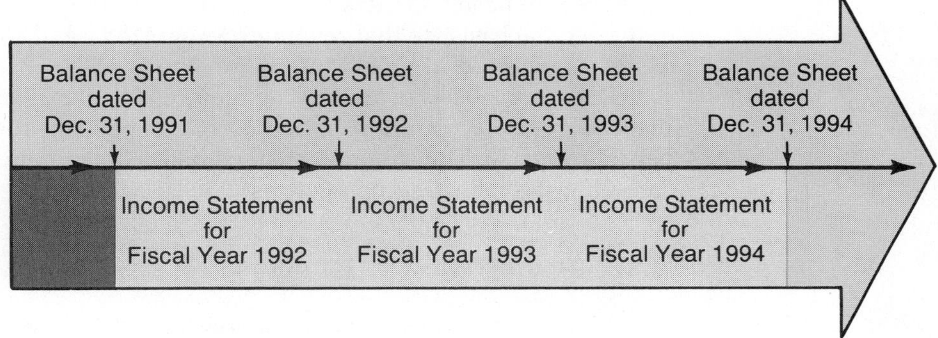

MATCHING PRINCIPLE

OBJECTIVE 2
Discuss the matching principle as it relates to the cash basis and the accrual basis of accounting.

The need for periodic financial reports creates many of the problems of accountancy. One of the major problems relates to the determination of periodic net income (or net loss). This determination relies on the **matching principle,** which requires the use of a two-step process. First, *revenues* are recognized during the period. Second the costs of assets consumed (*expenses*) in generating the revenues must be matched against those revenues in order to determine the net income (or the net loss). The periodic matching of revenues and expenses yields not only the amount of net income or net loss but also the amounts for assets, liabilities, and the owner's equity to be reported in the balance sheet as of the end of the period.

When cash is received for revenue within the same period that the revenue is earned, there is no question about the period to which the revenue relates. Similarly, when an expense is paid during the period in which the benefits from incurring the expense are received, there can be no doubt concerning the period to which the expense should be allocated. Problems occur when there are differences in the time between the earning of revenues or the incurrence of expenses and the recognition of their respective effects on assets and equities.

Revenues and expenses may be reported on the income statement by (1) the **cash basis** or (2) the **accrual basis** of accounting. When the cash basis is used, revenues are recognized in the period in which cash is received, and expenses are recognized in the period in which cash is paid. For example, fees earned would be recorded only when cash is received from customers, and salaries expense would be recorded only when cash is paid to employees. The net income (or net loss) is the difference between the cash receipts (revenues) and the cash disbursements (expenses). Small service enterprises and practicing professionals that have few receivables and payables may use the cash basis. For most businesses, however, the cash basis does not measure revenues and expenses accurately enough to be considered an acceptable method. For this reason, the cash basis will not be discussed in the remainder of the text.

Generally accepted accounting principles require the use of the accrual basis of accounting. Therefore, most enterprises use this basis, under which revenues are recognized in the period earned and expenses are recognized in the period incurred in the process of generating revenues. For example, revenue would be recognized as services are provided to customers and not when the cash is received from customers. Likewise, supplies expense would be recognized when the supplies are used and not when the cash is paid for supplies purchased. Generally accepted accounting principles require the use of the accrual basis, so that revenues recognized are matched with the related expenses incurred in producing the revenues.

The accrual basis of accounting requires the use of an adjusting process at the end of the accounting period to match revenues and expenses for the period properly. The common characteristics of the adjusting process are discussed in the following paragraphs.

NATURE OF THE ADJUSTING PROCESS

OBJECTIVE 3
Describe the nature of the adjusting process.

At the end of the accounting period, many of the amounts listed on the trial balance can be transferred, without change, to the financial statements. For example, the balance of the cash account is normally the amount of that asset owned by the enterprise on the last day of the accounting period. Similarly, the balance in Notes Payable is likely to be the total amount of that type of liability owed by the enterprise on the last day of the accounting period.

All trial balance amounts are not necessarily correct. The amounts listed for prepaid expenses are normally overstated. The reason for the overstatement is that the day-to-day consumption or expiration of these assets has not been recorded. For example, the balance in the supplies account represents the cost of the inventory of supplies at the beginning of the period plus the cost of those acquired during the period. Some of the supplies would have been used during the period; hence, the balance listed on the trial balance is overstated. In the same manner, the balance in Prepaid Insurance represents the beginning balance plus the cost of insurance policies acquired during the period, and no entries were made for the premiums as they expired. To make entries on a day-to-day basis would be costly and unnecessary. There are two effects on the ledger when the daily reduction in prepaid expenses is not recorded: (1) asset accounts are overstated and (2) expense accounts are understated.

Other data needed for the financial statements may be entirely omitted from the trial balance because revenue or expense related to the period has not been recorded. For example, salary expense incurred between the last payday and the end of the accounting period would not ordinarily be recorded in the accounts because salaries are customarily recorded only when they are paid. However, such accrued salaries are an expense of the period because the services were rendered during the period. They also represent a liability as of the last day of the period because they are owed to the employees.

The entries required at the end of an accounting period to bring the accounts up to date and to assure the proper matching of revenues and expenses are called **adjusting entries.** In a broad sense, they may be called corrections to the ledger. But bringing the ledger up to date at the end of a period is part of the accounting procedure; it is not caused by errors. The term "adjusting entries" is therefore more appropriate than the term "correcting entries."

ILLUSTRATIONS OF ADJUSTING ENTRIES

OBJECTIVE 4
Describe and illustrate basic procedures for adjusting the accounting records prior to the preparation of the financial statements.

The illustrations of adjusting entries that follow are based on the ledger of Hill Photographic Studio Inc. as reported in the March 31 trial balance presented below. T accounts are used for illustrative purposes and the adjusting entries, which are shown in the accounts, appear in color to separate them from items that were posted during the month.

Hill Photographic Studio Inc.
Trial Balance
March 31, 1992

Cash	1,631.00	
Accounts Receivable	1,775.00	
Supplies	1,850.00	
Prepaid Rent	2,400.00	
Photographic Equipment	17,500.00	
Accounts Payable		2,000.00
Capital Stock		20,650.00
Dividends	1,500.00	
Sales		5,525.00
Salary Expense	1,150.00	
Miscellaneous Expense	369.00	
	28,175.00	28,175.00

Prepaid Expenses

Prepaid expenses are the costs of goods and services that have been purchased but not used at the end of the accounting period. The portion of the asset that has been used during the period has become an expense; the remainder will not become an expense until some time in the future. Prepaid expenses include such items as prepaid insurance, prepaid rent, prepaid advertising, prepaid interest, and various kinds of supplies.

According to Hill's trial balance, the balance in the supplies account on March 31 is $1,850. Some of these supplies (film, developing agents, etc.) have been used during the past month and some are still in stock. If the amount of either is known, the other can be readily determined. It is more practical to determine the cost of the supplies on hand at the end of the month than it is to keep a record of those used from day to day. Assuming that the inventory of supplies on March 31 is determined to be $890, the amount to be moved from the asset account to the expense account is computed as follows:

Supplies available (balance of account)	$1,850
Supplies on hand (inventory)	890
Supplies used (amount of adjustment)	$ 960

Increases in expense accounts are recorded as debits and decreases in asset accounts are recorded as credits. Hence at the end of March, the supplies expense account should be debited for $960 and the supplies account should be credited for $960 to recognize the supplies used during March. The adjusting entry is illustrated in the following T accounts:

Adjustment of Prepaid Expense—Supplies

Supplies				→	Supplies Expense		
Mar. 1	1,200	Mar. 31	960	→	Mar. 31	960	
20	650						
890	*1,850*						

After the adjustment, the asset account has a debit balance of $890 and the expense account has a debit balance of $960.

The debit balance of $2,400 in the prepaid rent account represents a prepayment on March 1 of rent for three months: March, April, and May. At the end of March, the rent expense account should be increased (debited) and the prepaid rent account should be decreased (credited) by $800, the rental for one month. The adjusting entry is illustrated in the following T accounts:

Adjustment of Prepaid Expense—Rent

Prepaid Rent				→	Rent Expense		
Mar. 1	2,400	Mar. 31	800	→	Mar. 31	800	
1,600							

The prepaid rent account now has a debit balance of $1,600, which is an asset. The rent expense account has a debit balance of $800, which is an expense.

If the preceding adjustments for supplies ($960) and rent ($800) are not recorded, the financial statements prepared as of March 31 will be incorrect to the extent indicated as follows:

Income statement	
Expenses will be understated	$1,760
Net income will be overstated	1,760
Retained earnings statement	
Net income will be overstated	$1,760
Ending retained earnings will be overstated	1,760
Balance sheet	
Assets will be overstated	$1,760
Owner's equity will be overstated	1,760

The cost of supplies, prepaid rent, and other prepayments of expenses of future periods may be recorded as assets at the time of payment, as in the preceding illustration.[1] However, prepayments of expenses of one accounting period are sometimes made at the beginning of the period to which they apply. When this is the case, the expenditure is ordinarily recorded as an expense rather than as an asset. During the accounting period, the expense account debited will include an amount that represents an asset, but it will be

[1] The concepts and procedures for recording prepaid expenses initially as expenses are presented in Appendix C at the end of the text.

wholly expense at the end of the period. For example, if rent for March is paid on March 1, it is an asset at the time of payment. The asset expires gradually from day to day, and at the end of the month the entire amount has become an expense. Therefore, if the expenditure is initially recorded as a debit to Rent Expense, no additional entries are needed at the end of the period.

Plant Assets

Tangible assets that are permanent or have a relatively long life and are used in the business are called **plant assets** or **fixed assets.** For Hill Photographic Studio Inc., the plant assets consist of equipment which is used in operations much as the supplies are used. Unlike supplies, there is no visible reduction in the quantity of the equipment. As time passes, however, equipment does lose its capacity to provide useful services. This decrease in usefulness is a business expense, which is called **depreciation.** The factors involved in computing depreciation are discussed in a later chapter.

The adjusting entry to record depreciation is similar to the entry illustrated in the preceding section, in which an expense account is debited and an asset account is credited. The account debited is a depreciation expense account, which is reported on the income statement. However, because it is common practice to report on the balance sheet both the original cost of a plant asset and the amount of depreciation recorded since its acquisition, the account credited is an **accumulated depreciation** account. An accumulated depreciation account is a **contra account** because it is "offset against" another account. Accumulated depreciation accounts may be referred to as **contra asset accounts** because they are offset against asset accounts.

Typical titles for plant asset accounts and their related contra asset accounts are as follows:

Plant Asset	Contra Asset
Land	*None—land does not usually depreciate*
Buildings	Accumulated Depreciation—Buildings
Equipment	Accumulated Depreciation—Equipment

The ledger could show more detail by having a separate account for each of a number of buildings. Equipment may also be subdivided according to function, such as Delivery Equipment, Store Equipment, and Office Equipment, with a related accumulated depreciation account for each plant asset account.

The adjusting entry to record depreciation for March for Hill Photographic Studio Inc. is illustrated in the following T accounts. The estimated amount of depreciation for the month is assumed to be $175.

Adjustment for Depreciation

Photographic Equipment

Debit		Credit	
Mar. 1	15,000		
4	2,500		
	17,500		

Accumulated Depreciation

Debit		Credit	
		Mar. 31	175

Depreciation Expense

Debit		Credit	
Mar. 31	175		

The $175 increase in the accumulated depreciation account represents a subtraction from the $17,500 cost recorded in the related plant asset account.

The difference between the two balances is the unexpired or undepreciated cost and is called the **book value of the asset.** The book value may be presented on the balance sheet in the following manner:

Plant assets:		
Photographic equipment	$17,500	
Less accumulated depreciation	175	$17,325

If the previous adjustment for depreciation ($175) is not recorded, the financial statements as of March 31 will be incorrect to the extent indicated as follows:

Income statement	
Expenses will be understated	$175
Net income will be overstated	175
Retained earnings statement	
Net income will be overstated	$175
Ending retained earnings will be overstated	175
Balance Sheet	
Assets will be overstated	$175
Owner's equity will be overstated	175

Accrued Expenses (Accrued Liabilities)

It is customary to pay for some types of services, such as insurance and rent, before they are used. Other types of services are paid for after the service has been performed. Services performed by employees is an example of this type of situation. The wage or salary expense accumulates or accrues as a legal claim hour by hour and day by day, but payment is made only weekly, biweekly, or in accordance with some other period of time. The amount of such an accrued but unpaid item at the end of the accounting period is both an expense and a liability. For this reason, such accruals are called **accrued expenses** or **accrued liabilities.** In the case of the wage or salary expense, if the last day of a pay period is not the last day of the accounting period, the accrued expense and the related liability must be recorded in the accounts by an adjusting entry.

The data in the following T accounts were taken from the ledger of Hill Photographic Studio Inc. The debits of $575 on March 13 and 27 in the salary expense account were biweekly payments on alternate Fridays for the payroll periods ended on those days. The salaries earned on Monday and Tuesday, March 30 and 31, total $115. This amount is an additional expense of March and is debited to the salary expense account. It is also a liability as of March 31 and is therefore credited to Salaries Payable.

Adjustment for Accrued Expense

Salaries Payable

Debit	Credit
	Mar. 31 115

Salary Expense

Debit	Credit
Mar. 13 575	
27 575	
31 115	
1,265	

After the adjustment, the debit balance of the salary expense account is $1,265, which is the actual expense for the month. The credit balance of $115 in Salaries Payable is the amount of the liability for salaries owed as of March 31. If the previous adjustment for salaries ($115) is not recorded, the financial statements as of March 31 will be incorrect to the extent indicated as follows:

Income statement	
Expenses will be understated	$115
Net income will be overstated	115
Retained earnings statement	
Net income will be overstated	$115
Ending retained earnings will be overstated	115
Balance sheet	
Liabilities will be understated	$115
Owner's equity will be overstated	115

WORK SHEET FOR FINANCIAL STATEMENTS

OBJECTIVE 5
Describe and illustrate the work sheet for summarizing the accounting data for use in preparing financial statements.

Before journalizing and posting adjustments similar to those just described, it is necessary to determine and assemble the relevant data. For example, it is necessary to determine the cost of supplies on hand and the salaries accrued at the end of the period. Such collections of data, preliminary drafts of financial statements, and other useful analyses prepared by accountants are generally called **working papers.**

A type of working paper frequently used by accountants prior to the preparation of financial statements is called a **work sheet.** Its use reduces the possibility of overlooking the need for an adjustment, provides a convenient means of verifying arithmetical accuracy, provides for the arrangement of data in a logical form, and provides the source data for the financial statements.

The work sheet is identified by (1) the name of the enterprise, (2) the nature of the form (work sheet), and (3) the period of time involved. A form commonly used has an account title column and eight money columns arranged in four pairs of debit and credit columns. The main headings of the four sets of money columns are as follows:

1. Trial Balance
2. Adjustments
3. Income Statement
4. Balance Sheet

The preparation of work sheets is facilitated by the use of a computer software program, especially a spreadsheet program. Using computers, the procedures described and illustrated in the following paragraphs are programmed into the software, so that the completion of work sheets requires only the entry of data.

Trial Balance Columns

The trial balance data may be assembled directly on the work sheet form or they may be prepared on another sheet first and then copied onto the work sheet form. The work sheet for Hill Photographic Studio Inc., with the trial balance data recorded, is presented below and on page 109.

Adjustments Columns

Both the debit and the credit parts of an adjustment should be inserted on the appropriate lines before going on to another adjustment, as indicated on the work sheet for Hill Photographic Studio Inc. appearing on pages 110 and 111. Cross-referencing the related debit and credit of each adjustment by letters is useful to anyone who may have occasion to review the work sheet. It is also helpful later when the adjusting entries are recorded in the journal. The sequence of adjustments is not important, except that there is a time and accuracy advantage in following the order in which the adjustment data are assembled. If the titles of some of the accounts to be adjusted do not appear in the trial balance because they had no balance prior to adjustment, they should be inserted in the Account Title column, below the trial balance totals, as they are needed.

The adjusting entries for Hill Photographic Studio Inc. were explained and illustrated by T accounts earlier in the chapter. In practice, the adjustments are inserted directly on the work sheet on the basis of the data assembled by the accounting department.

Work Sheet with Trial Balance Recorded

Hill Photographic
Work
For Month Ended

	ACCOUNT TITLE	TRIAL BALANCE	
		DEBIT	CREDIT
1	Cash	1631 00	
2	Accounts Receivable	1775 00	
3	Supplies	1850 00	
4	Prepaid Rent	2400 00	
5	Photographic Equipment	17500 00	
6	Accounts Payable		2000 00
7	Capital Stock		20650 00
8	Dividends	1500 00	
9	Sales		5525 00
10	Salary Expense	1150 00	
11	Miscellaneous Expense	369 00	
12		28175 00	28175 00
13			
14			
15			
16			
17			
18			
19			
20			
21			
22			
23			

Explanatory notes for the entries in the Adjustments columns of the work sheet follow:

(a) **Supplies.** The supplies account has a debit balance of $1,850; the cost of the supplies on hand at the end of the period is $890; therefore, the supplies expense for March is the difference between the two amounts, or $960. The adjustment is entered by writing (1) *Supplies Expense* in the Account Title column, (2) *$960* in the Adjustments Debit column on the same line, and (3) *$960* in the Adjustments Credit column on the line with Supplies.

(b) **Rent.** The prepaid rent account has a debit balance of $2,400, which represents a payment for three months beginning with March; therefore, the rent expense for March is $800. The adjustment is entered by writing (1) *Rent Expense* in the Account Title column, (2) *$800* in the Adjustments Debit column on the same line, and (3) *$800* in the Adjustments Credit column on the line with Prepaid Rent.

(c) **Depreciation.** Depreciation of the photographic equipment is estimated at $175 for the month. This expired portion of the cost of the equipment is both an expense and a reduction in the asset. The adjustment is entered by writing (1) *Depreciation Expense* in the Account Title column, (2) *$175* in the Adjustments Debit column on the same line, (3) *Accumulated Depreciation*

Studio Inc.

Sheet

March 31, 1992

ADJUSTMENTS		INCOME STATEMENT		BALANCE SHEET	
DEBIT	CREDIT	DEBIT	CREDIT	DEBIT	CREDIT

in the Account Title column, and (4) *$175* in the Adjustments Credit column on the same line.

(d) **Salaries.** Salaries accrued but not paid at the end of March amount to $115. This is an increase in expense and an increase in liabilities. The adjustment is entered by writing (1) *$115* in the Adjustments Debit column on the same line with Salary Expense, (2) *Salaries Payable* in the Account Title column, and (3) *$115* in the Adjustments Credit column on the same line.

The final step in completing the Adjustments columns is to prove the equality of debits and credits by totaling and ruling the two columns.

Income Statement and Balance Sheet Columns

The data in the Trial Balance columns are combined with the adjustments data and extended to one of the remaining four columns as indicated on the work sheet for Hill Photographic Studio Inc. appearing on pages 112 and 113. The amounts of assets, liabilities, owner's equity, and dividends are extended to the Balance Sheet columns, and the revenues and expenses are extended to

Work Sheet with Trial Balance and Adjustments Recorded

Hill Photographic
Work
For Month Ended

	ACCOUNT TITLE	TRIAL BALANCE	
		DEBIT	CREDIT
1	Cash	1,631 00	
2	Accounts Receivable	1,775 00	
3	Supplies	1,850 00	
4	Prepaid Rent	2,400 00	
5	Photographic Equipment	17,500 00	
6	Accounts Payable		2,000 00
7	Capital Stock		20,650 00
8	Dividends	1,500 00	
9	Sales		5,525 00
10	Salary Expense	1,150 00	
11	Miscellaneous Expense	369 00	
12		28,175 00	28,175 00
13	Supplies Expense		
14	Rent Expense		
15	Depreciation Expense		
16	Accumulated Depreciation		
17	Salaries Payable		
18			
19			
20			
21			
22			
23			

the Income Statement columns. An advantage in time and accuracy can be achieved by beginning at the top and proceeding down the page in sequential order.

In the illustrative work sheet, the first account listed is Cash and the balance appearing in the Trial Balance Debit column is $1,631. This amount should be extended to the appropriate column since no adjustments affected the account. Cash is an asset, it is listed on the balance sheet, and it has a debit balance. Accordingly, the $1,631 amount is extended to the Debit column of the balance sheet section. The balance of Accounts Receivable is extended in similar fashion. Supplies has an initial balance of $1,850 and a credit adjustment (decrease) of $960. The amount to be extended to the Debit column of the balance sheet section is the debit balance of $890. The same procedure is continued until all account balances have been extended to the appropriate columns. The balance of the Dividends account is extended to the Balance Sheet columns, because this work sheet does not provide for separate Retained Earnings Statement columns.

After all of the balances have been extended, each of the four columns is totaled. The net income or the net loss for the period is the amount of the difference between the totals of the two Income Statement columns. If the Credit column total is greater than the Debit column total, the excess is the net

Studio Inc.

Sheet

March 31, 1992

ADJUSTMENTS		INCOME STATEMENT		BALANCE SHEET		
DEBIT	CREDIT	DEBIT	CREDIT	DEBIT	CREDIT	
						1
						2
	(a) 960 00					3
	(b) 800 00					4
						5
						6
						7
						8
						9
(d) 115 00						10
						11
						12
(a) 960 00						13
(b) 800 00						14
(c) 175 00						15
	(c) 175 00					16
	(d) 115 00					17
2050 00	2050 00					18
						19
						20
						21
						22
						23

income. For the work sheet presented below, the computation of net income is as follows:

Total of Credit column (revenue)	$5,525
Total of Debit column (expenses)	3,569
Net income (excess of revenue over expenses)	$1,956

Revenue and expense accounts, which are subdivisions of owner's equity, are temporary in nature. They are used during the accounting period to aid in the accumulation of detailed operating data. After they have served their purpose, the net balance will be transferred to the retained earnings account in the ledger. This transfer is accomplished on the work sheet by entries in the Income Statement Debit column and the Balance Sheet Credit column, with the description of the amount, "Net Income," inserted in the Account Title column, as illustrated below. If there had been a net loss instead of a net income, the amount would have been entered in the Income Statement Credit column and the Balance Sheet Debit column, and described as "Net Loss" in the Account Title column.

Work Sheet Completed For Hill Photographic Studio Inc.

Hill Photographic

Work

For Month Ended

	ACCOUNT TITLE	TRIAL BALANCE	
		DEBIT	CREDIT
1	Cash	1631 00	
2	Accounts Receivable	1775 00	
3	Supplies	1850 00	
4	Prepaid Rent	2400 00	
5	Photographic Equipment	17500 00	
6	Accounts Payable		2000 00
7	Capital Stock		20650 00
8	Dividends	1500 00	
9	Sales		5525 00
10	Salary Expense	1150 00	
11	Miscellaneous Expense	369 00	
12		28175 00	28175 00
13	Supplies Expense		
14	Rent Expense		
15	Depreciation Expense		
16	Accumulated Depreciation		
17	Salaries Payable		
18			
19	Net income		
20			
21			
22			
23			

After the final entry is made on the work sheet, each of the four statement columns is totaled to verify the arithmetic accuracy of the amount of net income or net loss transferred from the income statement to the balance sheet. The totals of the two Income Statement columns must be equal, as must the totals of the two Balance Sheet columns. The work sheet may be expanded by the addition of a pair of columns solely for the retained earnings statement data. However, because of the very few items involved, this variation is not illustrated.

FINANCIAL STATEMENTS

OBJECTIVE 6
Describe and illustrate the preparation of financial statements.

The work sheet is an aid in preparing the financial statements. The income statement, retained earnings statement, and balance sheet prepared from the work sheet of Hill Photographic Studio Inc. appear on page 114.[2] Their basic forms correspond to the statements presented in Chapter 1. Some minor variations are illustrated; others will be introduced in later chapters. The remaining portions of this section are devoted to the sources of the data and the manner in which they are reported on the statements.

[2]The basic nature of the statement of cash flows was also discussed in Chapter 1. An in-depth discussion of the preparation and use of the statement of cash flows is presented in Chapter 14 after various necessary concepts and principles have been explained and illustrated.

Studio Inc.
Sheet
March 31, 1992

ADJUSTMENTS		INCOME STATEMENT		BALANCE SHEET		
DEBIT	CREDIT	DEBIT	CREDIT	DEBIT	CREDIT	
				1631 00		1
				1775 00		2
	(a) 960 00			890 00		3
	(b) 800 00			1600 00		4
				17500 00		5
					2000 00	6
					20650 00	7
				1500 00		8
			5525 00			9
(d) 115 00		1265 00				10
		369 00				11
						12
(a) 960 00		960 00				13
(b) 800 00		800 00				14
(c) 175 00		175 00				15
	(c) 175 00				175 00	16
	(d) 115 00				115 00	17
2050 00	2050 00	3569 00	5525 00	24896 00	22940 00	18
		1956 00			1956 00	19
		5525 00	5525 00	24896 00	24896 00	20
						21
						22
						23

Income Statement

Hill Photographic Studio Inc. Income Statement For Month Ended March 31, 1992		
Sales		$ 5,525.00
Operating expenses:		
Salary expense	$ 1,265.00	
Supplies expense	960.00	
Rent expense	800.00	
Depreciation expense	175.00	
Miscellaneous expense	369.00	
Total operating expenses		3,569.00
Net income		$ 1,956.00

Retained Earnings Statement

Hill Photographic Studio Inc. Retained Earnings Statement For Month Ended March 31, 1992	
Net income for month	$ 1,956.00
Less dividends	1,500.00
Retained earnings, March 31, 1992	$ 456.00

Balance Sheet

Hill Photographic Studio Inc. Balance Sheet March 31, 1992		
Assets		
Current assets:		
Cash	$ 1,631.00	
Accounts receivable	1,775.00	
Supplies	890.00	
Prepaid rent	1,600.00	
Total current assets		$ 5,896.00
Plant assets:		
Photographic equipment	$17,500.00	
Less accumulated depreciation	175.00	17,325.00
Total assets		$23,221.00
Liabilities		
Current liabilities:		
Accounts payable	$ 2,000.00	
Salaries payable	115.00	
Total liabilities		$ 2,115.00
Stockholders' Equity		
Capital stock	$20,650.00	
Retained earnings	456.00	
Total stockholders' equity		21,106.00
Total liabilities and stockholders' equity		$23,221.00

Income Statement

The work sheet is the source of all of the data reported on the income statement. The sequence of expenses as listed on the work sheet may be changed in order to present them on the income statement in the order of size.

Retained Earnings Statement

The work sheet provides the data for the retained earnings statement for Hill Photographic Studio Inc. Since dividend payments were debited to Dividends, they appear on the work sheet. However, some accountants prefer to debit dividends directly to Retained Earnings. When this is the case, it is necessary to refer to the ledger to determine the beginning balance of Retained Earnings and the amount of the dividends debited during the period.

Balance Sheet

The work sheet is the source of all the data reported on the balance sheet, with the exception of the amount of the retained earnings, which can be obtained from the retained earnings statement. The balance sheet illustrated on page 114 was expanded by the addition of various sections which are discussed briefly in the paragraphs that follow. Additional sections are introduced in later chapters.

Assets. Any physical thing (tangible) or right (intangible) that has a monetary value is an asset. Assets are customarily divided into groups for presentation on the balance sheet. The two groups used most often are (1) current assets and (2) plant assets.

Current Assets. Cash and other assets that may reasonably be expected to be realized in cash or sold or used up usually within one year or less, through the normal operations of the business, are called **current assets.** Cash is any medium of exchange that a bank will accept at face value. It includes bank deposits, currency, checks, bank drafts, and money orders. In additon to cash, current assets include accounts receivable and notes receivable (claims against debtors, evidenced by the debtor's written promise to pay a sum of money at a definite time). Supplies and other prepaid expenses, such as insurance and property taxes, are also included in the current assets category.

Plant Assets. Plant assets include equipment, machinery, buildings, and land. With the exception of land, such assets depreciate and the cost, accumulated depreciation, and book value are listed. In the illustration on page 114, the plant assets are made up entirely of photographic equipment. When there are two or more categories of plant assets, the cost, accumulated depreciation, and book value of each category should be listed, and the total amount of plant assets should be shown. This presentation is illustrated as follows:

Plant assets:			
Equipment	$40,600		
Less accumulated depreciation	12,100	$28,500	
Automobiles	$22,500		
Less accumulated depreciation	9,600	12,900	
Total plant assets			$41,400

Liabilities. Liabilities are debts owed to outsiders (creditors) and are frequently described on the balance sheet by titles that include the word "payable." The two categories occurring most frequently are (1) current liabilities and (2) long-term liabilities.

Current Liabilities. Liabilities that will be due within a short time (usually one year or less) and that are to be paid out of current assets are called **current liabilities.** The most common liabilities in this group are **notes payable** and **accounts payable,** which are exactly like their receivable counterparts except that the debtor-creditor relationship is reversed. Other common current liabilities are Salaries Payable, Interest Payable, and Taxes Payable.

Long-Term Liabilities. Liabilities that will not be due for a comparatively long time (usually more than one year) are called **long-term liabilities** or **fixed liabilities.** As they come within the one-year range and are to be paid, such liabilities become current. If the obligation is to be renewed rather than paid at maturity, however, it would continue to be classed as long-term. When payment of a long-term debt is to be spread over a number of years, the installments due within one year from a balance sheet date are classed as a current liability. When a note is accompanied by security in the form of a mortgage, the obligation may be referred to as *mortgage note payable* or *mortgage payable.*

Stockholders' Equity. For a corporation the owner's equity is frequently called stockholders' equity, shareholders' equity, or stockholders' investment. Capital stock represents the investment of the stockholders, and retained earnings represents the net income retained in the business.

JOURNALIZING AND POSTING ADJUSTING ENTRIES

OBJECTIVE 7
Describe and illustrate journalizing and posting adjusting entries.

At the end of the accounting period, the adjusting entries appearing in the work sheet are recorded in the journal and posted to the ledger. This procedure brings the ledger into agreement with the data reported on the financial statements. The adjusting entries are dated as of the last day of the period, even though they are usually recorded at a later date. Each entry may be supported by an explanation, but a suitable caption above the first adjusting entry is sufficient.

The adjusting entries in the journal of Hill Photographic Studio Inc. are presented as follows. The accounts to which they have been posted appear in the ledger beginning on page 119.

Adjusting Entries

JOURNAL PAGE 2

	DATE		DESCRIPTION	POST. REF.	DEBIT	CREDIT	
11			Adjusting Entries				11
12	Mar.	31	Supplies Expense	51	960 00		12
13			Supplies	14		960 00	13
14							14
15		31	Rent Expense	53	800 00		15
16			Prepaid Rent	15		800 00	16
17							17
18		31	Depreciation Expense	54	175 00		18
19			Accumulated Depreciation	19		175 00	19
20							20
21		31	Salary Expense	52	115 00		21
22			Salaries Payable	22		115 00	22
23							23

NATURE OF THE CLOSING PROCESS

OBJECTIVE 8
Describe and illustrate the basic procedures for preparing the accounting records for use in accumulating data for the following accounting period.

The revenue, expense, and dividends accounts are temporary accounts used in classifying and summarizing changes in the owner's equity during the accounting period. At the end of the period, the net effect of the balances in these accounts must be recorded in the retained earnings account. The balances must also be removed from the temporary accounts, so that they will be ready for use in accumulating data for the following accounting period. Both of these goals are accomplished by a series of entries called **closing entries.**

CLOSING THE BOOKS

Habit is a wonderful saver of mental effort. But too close adherence to habit in business limits efficiency by shutting off initiative.

This is particularly true in the adherence of general business to the habit of following a fixed date for closing the so-called "fiscal" year.

The best date for closing the books and preparing financial statements for the "fiscal" year is when business is in its most liquid condition—when bank loans and other liabilities are lowest, accounts receivable reduced, and, especially, when the inventory [unsold merchandise] is at a minimum.

The most logical date for closing *your* "fiscal" year is that time when *your* business is logically over for the twelve months—when stocks are lowest—when prices are normal—when selling is not being forced—when you are not buying heavily—when profits can be most accurately determined—when your accounting department is not working nights, or your bank is not burdened with December 31st reports. In other words, close *your* books when *your* business is most naturally through with the rush of *your* year, when proper time and attention can be given, and your public accountants can serve you best.

Source: Management and Administration (May, 1924), p. 503.

Journalizing and Posting Closing Entries

An account titled **Income Summary** is used for summarizing the data in the revenue and expense accounts. It is used only at the end of the accounting period and is both opened and closed during the closing process. Other account titles used for the summarizing account are Expense and Revenue Summary, Profit and Loss Summary, and Income and Expense Summary.

Four entries are required in order to close the temporary accounts of a corporation at the end of the period. They are as follows:

1. Each revenue account is debited for the amount of its balance, and Income Summary is credited for the total revenue.
2. Each expense account is credited for the amount of its balance, and Income Summary is debited for the total expense.
3. Income Summary is debited for the amount of its balance (net income), and the retained earnings account is credited for the same amount. (Debit and credit are reversed if there is a net loss.)
4. The dividends account is credited for the amount of its balance, and the retained earnings account is debited for the same amount.

The account titles and amounts needed in journalizing the closing entries may be obtained from any one of three sources: (1) work sheet, (2) income statement and retained earnings statement, and (3) ledger. When the work sheet is used, the data for the first two entries are taken from the Income Statement columns. The amount for the third entry is the net income or net loss appearing at the bottom of the work sheet. Reference to the dividends account balance appearing in the Balance Sheet Debit column of the work sheet supplies the information for the fourth, and final, entry.

The process of closing the temporary accounts of Hill Photographic Studio Inc. is illustrated by the following flowchart:

Flowchart of Closing Process

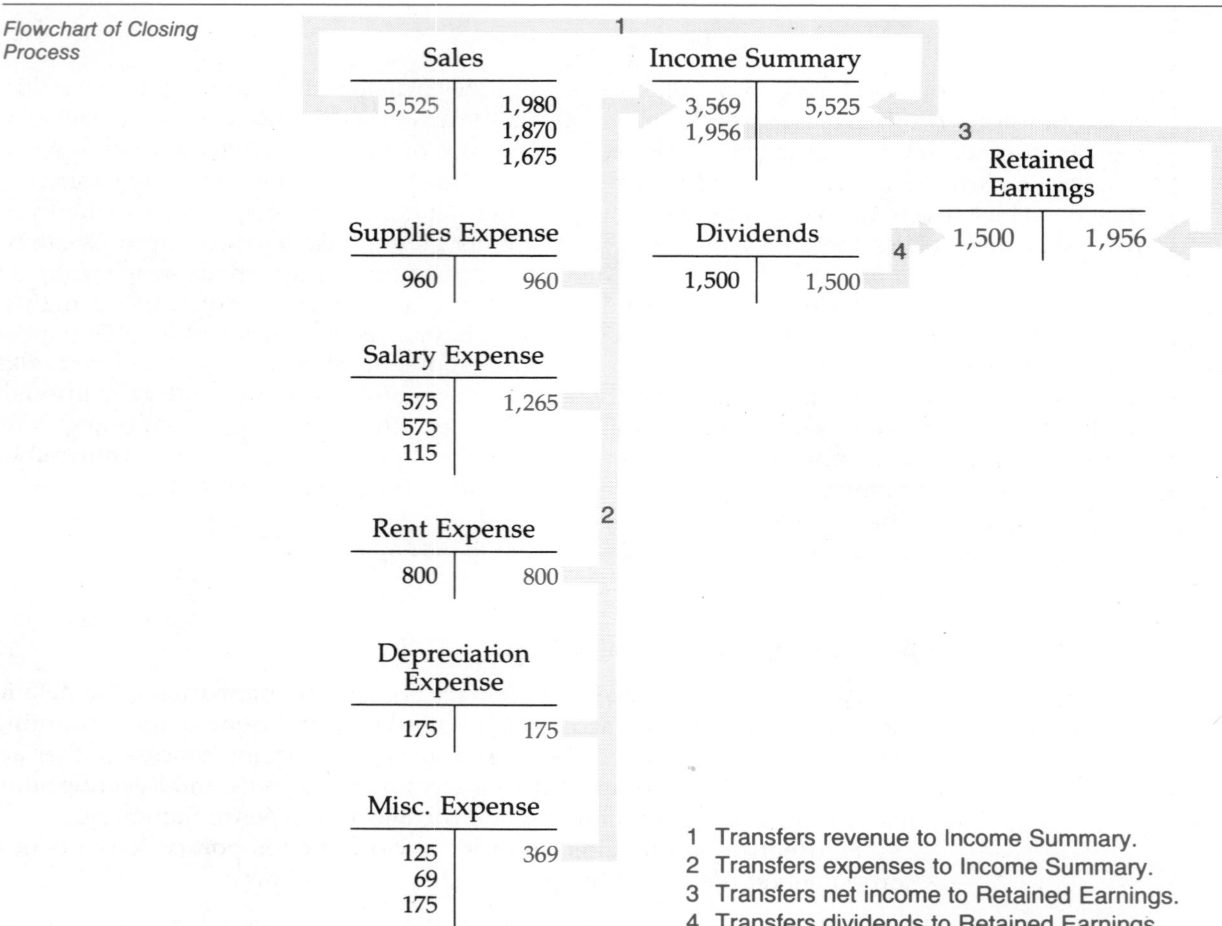

After the closing entries have been journalized, illustrated as follows, and posted to the ledger, the balance in the retained earnings account will correspond to the amounts reported on the retained earnings statement and balance sheet. In addition, the revenue, expense, and dividends accounts will have zero balances.

Closing Entries

	JOURNAL					PAGE 2	
	DATE		DESCRIPTION	POST. REF.	DEBIT	CREDIT	
24			Closing Entries				24
25	Mar.	31	Sales	41	5525 00		25
26			Income Summary	34		5525 00	26
27							27
28		31	Income Summary	34	3569 00		28
29			Salary Expense	52		1265 00	29
30			Miscellaneous Expense	59		369 00	30
31			Supplies Expense	51		960 00	31
32			Rent Expense	53		800 00	32
33			Depreciation Expense	54		175 00	33
34							34
35		31	Income Summary	34	1956 00		35
36			Retained Earnings	32		1956 00	36
37							37
38		31	Retained Earnings	32	1500 00		38
39			Dividends	33		1500 00	39
40							40
41							41

The ledger of Hill Photographic Studio Inc. after the adjusting and closing entries have been posted begins below and continues on pages 120-122. Each posting of an adjusting entry and a closing entry is identified in the item section of the account as an aid to the student. It is not necessary that this be done in actual practice.

Ledger after the Accounts Have Been Adjusted and Closed

ACCOUNT Cash — ACCOUNT NO. 11

DATE		ITEM	POST. REF.	DEBIT	CREDIT	BALANCE DEBIT	BALANCE CREDIT
1992 Mar.	1		1	3500 00		3500 00	
	1		1		2400 00	1100 00	
	5		1	850 00		1950 00	
	6		1		125 00	1825 00	
	10		1		500 00	1325 00	
	13		1		575 00	750 00	
	16		1	1980 00		2730 00	
	20		1		650 00	2080 00	
	27		1		575 00	1505 00	
	31		1		69 00	1436 00	
	31		1		175 00	1261 00	
	31		2	1870 00		3131 00	
	31		2		1500 00	1631 00	

ACCOUNT Accounts Receivable — ACCOUNT NO. 12

DATE		ITEM	POST. REF.	DEBIT	CREDIT	BALANCE DEBIT	BALANCE CREDIT
1992 Mar.	1		1	950 00		950 00	
	5		1		850 00	100 00	
	31		2	1675 00		1775 00	

Ledger after the Accounts Have Been Adjusted and Closed (Continued)

ACCOUNT Supplies — ACCOUNT NO. 14

DATE		ITEM	POST. REF.	DEBIT	CREDIT	BALANCE DEBIT	BALANCE CREDIT
1992 Mar.	1		1	1200 00		1200 00	
	20		1	650 00		1850 00	
	31	Adjusting	2		960 00	890 00	

ACCOUNT Prepaid Rent — ACCOUNT NO. 15

DATE		ITEM	POST. REF.	DEBIT	CREDIT	BALANCE DEBIT	BALANCE CREDIT
1992 Mar.	1		1	2400 00		2400 00	
	31	Adjusting	2		800 00	1600 00	

ACCOUNT Photographic Equipment — ACCOUNT NO. 18

DATE		ITEM	POST. REF.	DEBIT	CREDIT	BALANCE DEBIT	BALANCE CREDIT
1992 Mar.	1		1	15000 00		15000 00	
	4		1	2500 00		17500 00	

ACCOUNT Accumulated Depreciation — ACCOUNT NO. 19

DATE		ITEM	POST. REF.	DEBIT	CREDIT	BALANCE DEBIT	BALANCE CREDIT
1992 Mar.	31	Adjusting	2		175 00		175 00

ACCOUNT Accounts Payable — ACCOUNT NO. 21

DATE		ITEM	POST. REF.	DEBIT	CREDIT	BALANCE DEBIT	BALANCE CREDIT
1992 Mar.	4		1		2500 00		2500 00
	10		1	500 00			2000 00

ACCOUNT Salaries Payable — ACCOUNT NO. 22

DATE		ITEM	POST. REF.	DEBIT	CREDIT	BALANCE DEBIT	BALANCE CREDIT
1992 Mar.	31	Adjusting	2		115 00		115 00

ACCOUNT Capital Stock — ACCOUNT NO. 31

DATE		ITEM	POST. REF.	DEBIT	CREDIT	BALANCE DEBIT	BALANCE CREDIT
1992 Mar.	1		1		20650 00		20650 00

ACCOUNT Retained Earnings — ACCOUNT NO. 32

DATE		ITEM	POST. REF.	DEBIT	CREDIT	BALANCE DEBIT	BALANCE CREDIT
1992 Mar.	31	Closing	2		1956 00		1956 00
	31	Closing	2	1500 00			456 00

Ledger after the Accounts Have Been Adjusted and Closed (Continued)

ACCOUNT Dividends — ACCOUNT NO. 33

DATE		ITEM	POST. REF.	DEBIT	CREDIT	BALANCE DEBIT	BALANCE CREDIT
1992 Mar.	31		2	1500 00		1500 00	
	31	Closing	2		1500 00	—	—

ACCOUNT Income Summary — ACCOUNT NO. 34

DATE		ITEM	POST. REF.	DEBIT	CREDIT	BALANCE DEBIT	BALANCE CREDIT
1992 Mar.	31	Closing	2		5525 00		5525 00
	31	Closing	2	3569 00			1956 00
	31	Closing	2	1956 00		—	—

ACCOUNT Sales — ACCOUNT NO. 41

DATE		ITEM	POST. REF.	DEBIT	CREDIT	BALANCE DEBIT	BALANCE CREDIT
1992 Mar.	16		1		1980 00		1980 00
	31		2		1870 00		3850 00
	31		2		1675 00		5525 00
	31	Closing	2	5525 00		—	—

ACCOUNT Supplies Expense — ACCOUNT NO. 51

DATE		ITEM	POST. REF.	DEBIT	CREDIT	BALANCE DEBIT	BALANCE CREDIT
1992 Mar.	31	Adjusting	2	960 00		960 00	
	31	Closing	2		960 00	—	—

ACCOUNT Salary Expense — ACCOUNT NO. 52

DATE		ITEM	POST. REF.	DEBIT	CREDIT	BALANCE DEBIT	BALANCE CREDIT
1992 Mar.	13		1	575 00		575 00	
	27		1	575 00		1150 00	
	31	Adjusting	2	115 00		1265 00	
	31	Closing	2		1265 00	—	—

ACCOUNT Rent Expense — ACCOUNT NO. 53

DATE		ITEM	POST. REF.	DEBIT	CREDIT	BALANCE DEBIT	BALANCE CREDIT
1992 Mar.	31	Adjusting	2	800 00		800 00	
	31	Closing	2		800 00	—	—

ACCOUNT Depreciation Expense — ACCOUNT NO. 54

DATE		ITEM	POST. REF.	DEBIT	CREDIT	BALANCE DEBIT	BALANCE CREDIT
1992 Mar.	31	Adjusting	2	175 00		175 00	
	31	Closing	2		175 00	—	—

Ledger after the Accounts Have Been Adjusted and Closed (Concluded)

ACCOUNT Miscellaneous Expense ACCOUNT NO. 59

DATE		ITEM	POST. REF.	DEBIT	CREDIT	BALANCE DEBIT	BALANCE CREDIT
1992 Mar.	6		1	125 00		125 00	
	31		1	69 00		194 00	
	31		1	175 00		369 00	
	31	Closing	2		369 00	—	—

As the entry to close an account is posted, a line should be inserted in both Balance columns opposite the final entry, as illustrated by Dividends and the remaining temporary accounts. Transactions affecting the accounts in the following period will be posted in the spaces immediately below the closing entry.

Post-Closing Trial Balance

The last procedure of the accounting cycle is the preparation of a trial balance after all of the temporary accounts have been closed. The purpose of the **post-closing** (after closing) **trial balance,** which is illustrated as follows, is to make sure that the ledger is in balance at the beginning of the new accounting period. The accounts and amounts should agree exactly with the accounts and amounts listed on the balance sheet at the end of the period.

Post-Closing Trial Balance

Hill Photographic Studio Inc.
Post-Closing Trial Balance
March 31, 1992

Cash	1,631.00	
Accounts Receivable	1,775.00	
Supplies	890.00	
Prepaid Rent	1,600.00	
Photographic Equipment	17,500.00	
Accumulated Depreciation		175.00
Accounts Payable		2,000.00
Salaries Payable		115.00
Capital Stock		20,650.00
Retained Earnings		456.00
	23,396.00	23,396.00

Instead of preparing a formalized post-closing trial balance, it is possible to proceed directly from the ledger to a calculator to determine the equality of debit and credit balances in the ledger. A calculator providing a tape record of the amounts should be used—the tape becoming, in effect, the post-closing trial balance. Without such a tape, there are no efficient means of determining whether the cause of an inequality of trial balance totals is due to errors in manipulating the keys or to errors in the ledger.

ACCOUNTING CYCLE

OBJECTIVE 9
Describe and diagram the basic phases of the accounting cycle.

The principal accounting procedures of a fiscal period have been presented in this and the preceding chapter. The sequence of procedures is frequently called the **accounting cycle.** It begins with the analysis and the journalizing of transactions and ends with the post-closing trial balance. The most significant output of the accounting cycle is, of course, the financial statements.

An understanding of all phases of the accounting cycle is essential as a foundation for further study of accounting principles and the uses of accounting data by management. The basic phases of the cycle are shown, by number, in the flowchart below:

Accounting Cycle

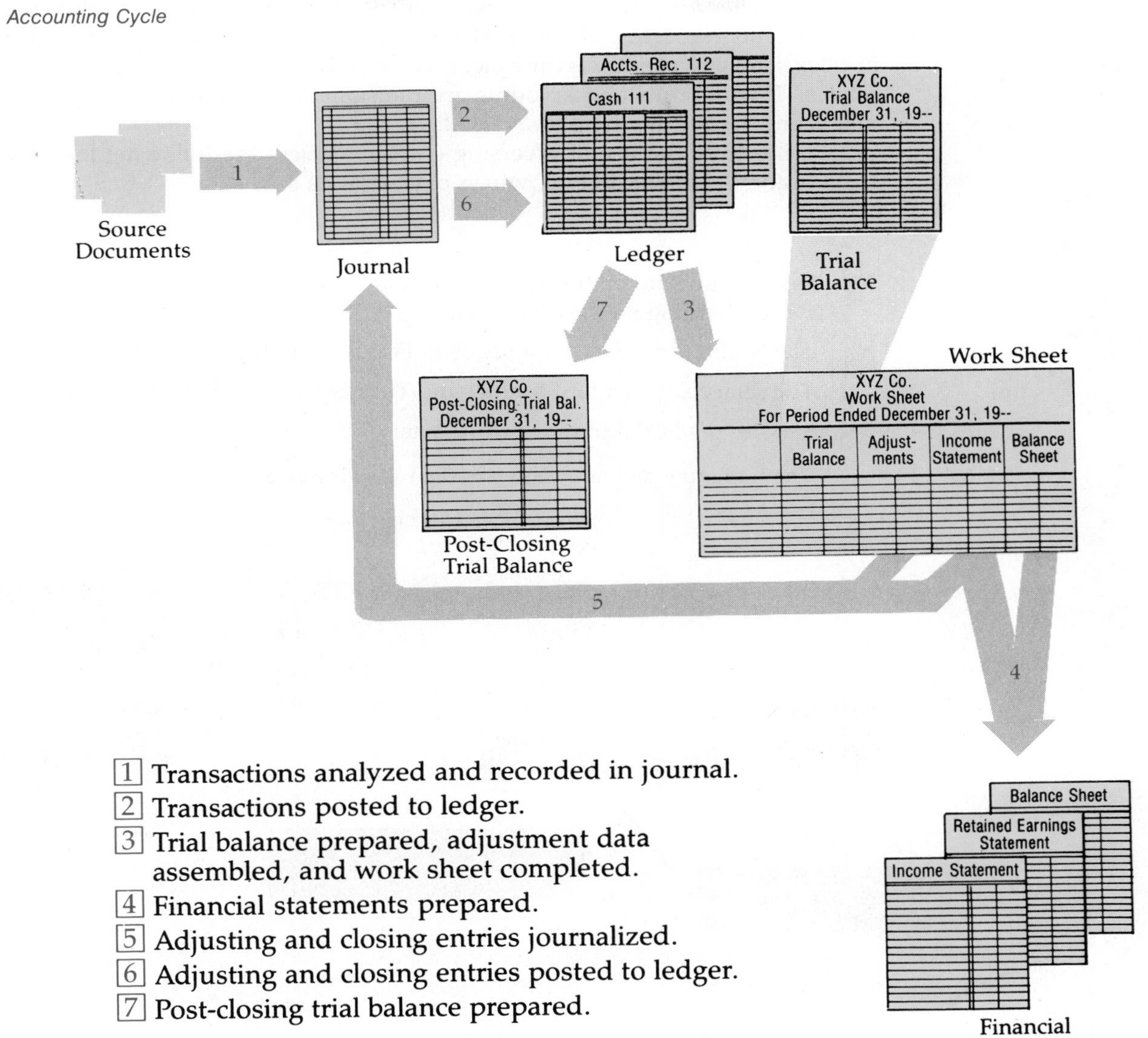

APPENDIX

REVERSING ENTRIES

Some of the adjusting entries recorded at the end of an accounting period have an important effect on otherwise routine transactions that occur in the following period. A typical example is accrued salaries owed to employees at the end of a period. If there has been an adjusting entry for accrued salaries, the first payment of salaries in the following period will include the accrual. In the absence of some special provision, Salaries Payable must be debited for the amount owed for the earlier period, and Salary Expense must be debited for the portion of the payroll that represents expense for the later period. However, an *optional* entry—the **reversing entry**—may be used to simplify the analysis and recording of this first payroll entry in a period. As the term implies, a reversing entry is the exact reverse of the adjusting entry to which it relates. The amounts and accounts are the same as the adjusting entry; the debits and credits are merely reversed.

To illustrate the use of reversing entries, assume the following facts for Hill Photographic Studio Inc., which pays salaries biweekly:

1. Salaries are paid on the second and fourth Fridays for the two-week periods ending on those Fridays.
2. The balance in Salary Expense as of Friday, March 27, is $1,150.
3. The salary accrued for Monday and Tuesday, March 30 and 31, is $115.
4. Salaries paid on Friday, April 10, total $575.

The foregoing data are shown in the following calendars:

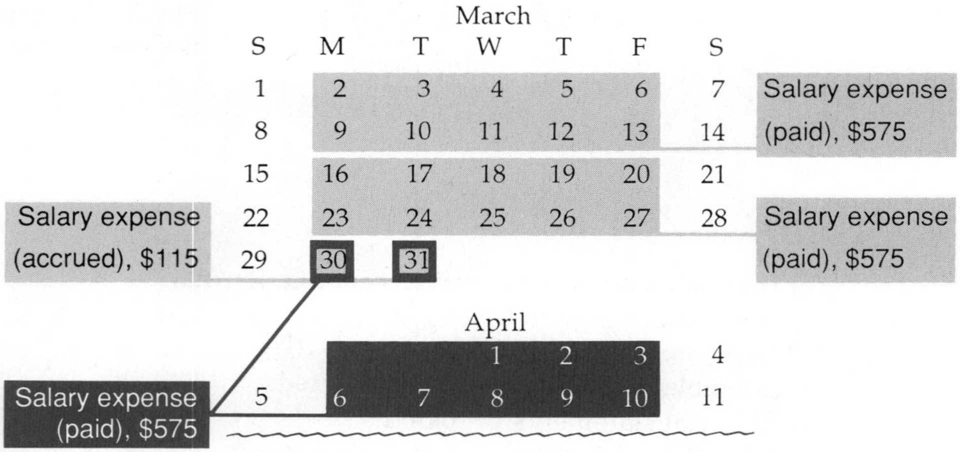

March

	S	M	T	W	T	F	S	
	1	2	3	4	5	6	7	Salary expense
	8	9	10	11	12	13	14	(paid), $575
	15	16	17	18	19	20	21	
Salary expense	22	23	24	25	26	27	28	Salary expense
(accrued), $115	29	30	31					(paid), $575

April

	S	M	T	W	T	F	S
				1	2	3	4
Salary expense (paid), $575	5	6	7	8	9	10	11

The adjusting entry to record the accrued salary expense and salaries payable for Monday and Tuesday, March 30 and 31, is as follows:

20							20
21	Mar.	31	Salary Expense	52	1 1 5 00		21
22			Salaries Payable	22		1 1 5 00	22
23							23

After the adjusting entry has been posted, Salary Expense will have a debit balance of $1,265 ($1,150 + $115) and Salaries Payable will have a credit balance of $115. After the closing process is completed, Salary Expense is in balance and ready for entries of the following year, but Salaries Payable continues to have a credit balance of $115. As matters now stand, it would be necessary to record the $575 payroll on April 10 as a debit of $115 to Salaries Payable and a debit of $460 to Salary Expense. This means that the employee who records payroll entries must not only record this particular payroll in a different manner from all other weekly payrolls for the year, but must also refer to the adjusting entries in the journal or the ledger to determine the amount of the $575 payment to be debited to each of the two accounts.

The need to refer to earlier entries and to divide the debit between two accounts can be avoided by recording a reversing entry as of the first day of the following fiscal period. Continuing with the illustration, the reversing entry for the accrued salaries is as follows:

	Date		Description	Post. Ref.	Debit	Credit	
1	Apr.	1	Salaries Payable	22	115 00		1
2			Salary Expense	52		115 00	2
3							3

The effect of the reversing entry is to transfer the $115 liability from Salaries Payable to the credit side of Salary Expense. The real nature of the $115 balance is unchanged; it remains a liability. When the payroll is paid on April 10, Salary Expense will be debited and Cash will be credited for $575, the entire amount of the weekly salaries. After the entry is posted, Salary Expense will have a debit balance of $460, which is the amount of expense incurred for April 1-10. The sequence of entries, including adjusting, closing, and reversing entries, may be traced in the following accounts:

Adjustment and Reversal for Accrued Salaries

ACCOUNT Salary Expense ACCOUNT NO. 52

Date		Item	Post. Ref.	Debit	Credit	Balance Debit	Balance Credit
1992 Mar.	13		1	575 00		575 00	
	27		1	575 00		1150 00	
	31	Adjusting	2	115 00		1265 00	
	31	Closing	2		1265 00	—	
Apr.	1	Reversing	3		115 00		115 00
	10		4	575 00		460 00	

ACCOUNT Salaries Payable ACCOUNT NO. 22

Date		Item	Post. Ref.	Debit	Credit	Balance Debit	Balance Credit
1992 Mar.	31	Adjusting	2		115 00		115 00
Apr.	1	Reversing	3	115 00		115 00	—

As discussed previously, the use of reversing entries is an optional procedure. However, with the increased computerization of accounting systems, data entry personnel may be inputting routine accounting entries. In such an environment, reversing entries may be useful, since these individuals may not recognize the impact of adjusting entries on related transactions in the following period.

CHAPTER REVIEW

KEY POINTS

OBJECTIVE 1

Accounting Period

Only in rare cases is a business organized with the expectation of operating for only a certain period of time. In most cases, it is not possible to determine in advance the length of life of an enterprise, so an assumption must be made. The going concern concept assumes that a business entity has a reasonable expectation of continuing in business at a profit for an indefinite period of time. The annual accounting period adopted by an enterprise is known as the fiscal year. The period most commonly adopted is the calendar year, although other periods corresponding to the enterprise's natural business year may be used, particularly for incorporated enterprises.

OBJECTIVE 2

Matching Principle

Revenues and expenses may be reported on the income statement by (1) the cash basis or (2) the accrual basis of accounting. When the cash basis is used, revenues are reported in the period in which cash is received, and expenses are reported in the period in which cash is paid. Most enterprises, however, use the accrual basis of accounting. Under the accrual method, revenues are reported in the period in which they are earned, and expenses are reported in the period in which they are incurred in the process of generating revenues. The accrual basis of accounting requires the use of an adjusting process at the end of the accounting period to match properly the revenues and expenses within the period.

OBJECTIVE 3, 4

Nature of the Adjusting Process

At the end of the accounting period, some of the amounts listed on the trial balance are not necessarily correct. For example, amounts listed for prepaid expenses are normally overstated because the day-to-day consumption or expiration of these assets has not been recorded. Likewise, some revenue or expense items related to the period may not be recorded, since these items are customarily recorded only when cash has been received or paid. The entries required at the end of the accounting period to bring the accounts up to date and to insure the proper matching of revenues and expenses under the accrual method are called adjusting entries. The posting of the adjusting entries will bring the ledger up to date as a planned part of the accounting cycle.

OBJECTIVE 5, 6

Work Sheet and Financial Statements

Before adjustments are journalized and posted, it is necessary to determine and assemble the relevant data. A type of working paper that is used frequently by accountants to summarize these data is called a work sheet. The work sheet is also an aid in preparing the income statement, retained earnings statement, and balance sheet.

OBJECTIVE 7

Journalizing and Posting Adjusting Entries

At the end of the accounting period, the adjusting entries are recorded in the journal and posted to the ledger. This procedure brings the ledger into agreement with the data reported on the financial statements.

OBJECTIVE 8

Nature of the Closing Process

The revenue, expense, and dividends accounts are temporary accounts used in classifying and summarizing changes in owner's equity during an accounting period. At the end of the period, the net effect of the balances in these accounts must be recorded in a retained earnings account. The balances must also be removed from the temporary accounts so that they will be ready for use to accumulate data for the following accounting period. Both of these goals are accomplished by the journalizing and posting of closing entries.

In preparing the closing entries, an account titled Income Summary is used for summarizing the data in the revenue and expense accounts. The balance of this account is then closed to the retained earnings account. Finally, the dividends account is closed to the retained earnings account. After the closing entries have been journalized and posted to the ledger, the balance in the retained earnings account will correspond to the amounts reported on the retained earnings statement and balance sheet.

The last procedure of the accounting cycle is the preparation of a trial balance after all of the temporary accounts have been closed. The purpose of the post-closing trial balance is to make sure the ledger is in balance at the beginning of the new accounting period. The accounts and amounts should agree exactly with the accounts and amounts listed on the balance sheet at the end of the period.

OBJECTIVE 9

Accounting Cycle

The sequence of accounting procedures during a fiscal period is called the accounting cycle. It begins with the analysis of transactions and ends with the post-closing trial balance. The most significant output of the accounting cycle is the financial statements.

KEY TERMS

going concern concept 99
fiscal year 100
natural business year 100
matching principle 101
cash basis 101
accrual basis 101
adjusting entries 103
prepaid expenses 103
plant assets 105
depreciation 105
accumulated depreciation 105
contra account 105
accrued expenses 106
accrued liabilities 106
work sheet 107
current assets 115
current liabilities 116
long-term liabilities 116
closing entries 117
Income Summary 117
post-closing trial balance 122
accounting cycle 122

SELF-EXAMINATION QUESTIONS

Answers at end of chapter.

1. If the supplies account, before adjustment on May 31, indicated a balance of $2,250, and an inventory of supplies on hand at May 31 totaled $950, the adjusting entry would be:
   A. debit Supplies, $950; credit Supplies Expense, $950
   B. debit Supplies, $1,300; credit Supplies Expense, $1,300
   C. debit Supplies Expense, $950; credit Supplies, $950
   D. debit Supplies Expense, $1,300; credit Supplies, $1,300

2. If the estimated amount of depreciation on equipment for a period is $2,000, the adjusting entry to record depreciation would be:
   A. debit Depreciation Expense, $2,000; credit Equipment, $2,000
   B. debit Equipment, $2,000; credit Depreciation Expense, $2,000
   C. debit Depreciation Expense, $2,000; credit Accumulated Depreciation, $2,000
   D. debit Accumulated Depreciation, $2,000; credit Depreciation Expense, $2,000

3. If the equipment account has a balance of $22,500 and its accumulated depreciation account has a balance of $14,000, the book value of the equipment is:
   A. $36,500
   B. $22,500
   C. $14,000
   D. $8,500

4. The current asset category would include:
   A. cash
   B. accounts receivable
   C. supplies on hand
   D. all of the above

5. Which of the following accounts would be closed to the income summary account at the end of a period?
   A. Sales
   B. Salary Expense
   C. Both Sales and Salary Expense
   D. Neither Sales nor Salary Expense

ILLUSTRATIVE PROBLEM

Two years ago, K.L. Waters organized Star Laundromat Company as a corporation. At March 31, 1993, the end of the current fiscal year, the trial balance of Star Laundromat Company is as follows:

Star Laundromat Company
Trial Balance
March 31, 1993

Cash	2,425.00	
Laundry Supplies	1,870.00	
Prepaid Insurance	620.00	
Laundry Equipment	37,650.00	
Accumulated Depreciation		9,700.00
Accounts Payable		925.00
Capital Stock		20,000.00
Retained Earnings		2,180.00
Dividends	10,200.00	
Laundry Revenue		39,125.00
Wages Expense	12,415.00	
Rent Expense	3,600.00	
Utilities Expense	2,715.00	
Miscellaneous Expense	435.00	
	71,930.00	71,930.00

The data needed to determine year-end adjustments are as follows:

(a) Inventory of laundry supplies at March 31, 1993	$ 480
(b) Insurance premiums expired during the year	315
(c) Depreciation on equipment during the year	1,950
(d) Wages accrued but not paid at March 31, 1993	140

Instructions:

1. Record the trial balance on a work sheet and complete the work sheet.
2. Prepare an income statement, a retained earnings statement, and a balance sheet.
3. On the basis of the adjustments data in the work sheet, journalize the adjusting entries.
4. On the basis of the data in the work sheet, journalize the closing entries.

SOLUTION

(1) See pages 130 and 131.

(2)

Star Laundromat Company
Income Statement
For Year Ended March 31, 1993

Laundry revenue		$39,125.00
Operating expenses:		
Wages expense	$12,555.00	
Rent expense	3,600.00	
Utilities expense	2,715.00	
Depreciation expense	1,950.00	
Laundry supplies expense	1,390.00	
Insurance expense	315.00	
Miscellaneous expense	435.00	
Total operating expenses		22,960.00
Net income		$16,165.00

Star Laundromat Company
Retained Earnings Statement
For Year Ended March 31, 1993

Retained earnings, April 1, 1992		$2,180.00
Net income for the year	$16,165.00	
Less dividends	10,200.00	
Increase in retained earnings		5,965.00
Retained earnings, March 31, 1993		$8,145.00

Star Laundromat Company
Balance Sheet
March 31, 1993

Assets		
Current assets:		
Cash	$ 2,425.00	
Laundry supplies	480.00	
Prepaid insurance	305.00	
Total current assets		$ 3,210.00
Plant assets:		
Laundry equipment	$37,650.00	
Less accumulated depreciation	11,650.00	26,000.00
Total assets		$29,210.00
Liabilities		
Current liabilities:		
Accounts payable	$ 925.00	
Wages payable	140.00	
Total liabilities		$ 1,065.00
Stockholders' Equity		
Capital stock	$20,000.00	
Retained earnings	8,145.00	
Total stockholders' equity		28,145.00
Total liabilities and stockholders' equity		$29,210.00

(1)

Star

Work

For Year Ended

	ACCOUNT TITLE	TRIAL BALANCE DEBIT	TRIAL BALANCE CREDIT
1	Cash	2425 00	
2	Laundry Supplies	1870 00	
3	Prepaid Insurance	620 00	
4	Laundry Equipment	37650 00	
5	Accumulated Depreciation		9700 00
6	Accounts Payable		925 00
7	Capital Stock		20000 00
8	Retained Earnings		2180 00
9	Dividends	10200 00	
10	Laundry Revenue		39125 00
11	Wages Expense	12415 00	
12	Rent Expense	3600 00	
13	Utilities Expense	2715 00	
14	Miscellaneous Expense	435 00	
15		71930 00	71930 00
16	Laundry Supplies Expense		
17	Insurance Expense		
18	Depreciation Expense		
19	Wages Payable		
20			
21	Net Income		
22			

(3)

JOURNAL PAGE

	DATE		DESCRIPTION	POST. REF.	DEBIT	CREDIT	
1			Adjusting Entries				1
2	1993 Mar.	31	Laundry Supplies Expense		1 3 9 0 00		2
3			Laundry Supplies			1 3 9 0 00	3
4							4
5		31	Insurance Expense		3 1 5 00		5
6			Prepaid Insurance			3 1 5 00	6
7							7
8		31	Depreciation Expense		1 9 5 0 00		8
9			Accumulated Depreciation			1 9 5 0 00	9
10							10
11		31	Wages Expense		1 4 0 00		11
12			Wages Payable			1 4 0 00	12

Laundromat Company
Sheet
March 31, 1993

ADJUSTMENTS DEBIT	ADJUSTMENTS CREDIT	INCOME STATEMENT DEBIT	INCOME STATEMENT CREDIT	BALANCE SHEET DEBIT	BALANCE SHEET CREDIT	
				2425 00		1
	(a) 1390 00			480 00		2
	(b) 315 00			305 00		3
				37650 00		4
	(c) 1950 00				11650 00	5
					925 00	6
					20000 00	7
					2180 00	8
				10200 00		9
			39125 00			10
(d) 140 00		12555 00				11
		3600 00				12
		2715 00				13
		435 00				14
						15
(a) 1390 00		1390 00				16
(b) 315 00		315 00				17
(c) 1950 00		1950 00				18
	(d) 140 00				140 00	19
3795 00	3795 00	22960 00	39125 00	51060 00	34895 00	20
		16165 00			16165 00	21
		39125 00	39125 00	51060 00	51060 00	22

(4)

JOURNAL PAGE

	DATE		DESCRIPTION	POST. REF.	DEBIT	CREDIT
14			Closing Entries			
15	1993 Mar.	31	Laundry Revenue		39 1 2 5 00	
16			Income Summary			39 1 2 5 00
17						
18		31	Income Summary		22 9 6 0 00	
19			Wages Expense			12 5 5 5 00
20			Rent Expense			3 6 0 0 00
21			Utilities Expense			2 7 1 5 00
22			Miscellaneous Expense			4 3 5 00
23			Laundry Supplies Expense			1 3 9 0 00
24			Insurance Expense			3 1 5 00
25			Depreciation Expense			1 9 5 0 00
26						
27		31	Income Summary		16 1 6 5 00	
28			Retained Earnings			16 1 6 5 00
29						
30		31	Retained Earnings		10 2 0 0 00	
31			Dividends			10 2 0 0 00

DISCUSSION QUESTIONS

3–1. For accounting purposes, what is the nature of the assumption as to the length of life of an enterprise?

3–2. What term is applied to the annual accounting period adopted by a business enterprise?

3–3. How are revenues and expenses reported on the income statement under (a) cash basis accounting and (b) accrual basis accounting?

3–4. Is the balance listed on the trial balance for supplies, before the accounts have been adjusted, normally the amount that should be reported on the balance sheet? Explain.

3–5. Why are adjusting entries needed at the end of an accounting period?

3–6. What is the nature of the balance in the prepaid insurance account at the end of the accounting period (a) before adjustment? (b) after adjustment?

3–7. If the effect of the credit portion of an adjusting entry is to increase the balance of a liability account, which of the following statements describes the effect of the debit portion of the entry?
(a) increases the balance of a revenue account.
(b) increases the balance of an expense account.
(c) increases the balance of an asset account.

3–8. Does every adjusting entry have an effect on the determination of the amount of net income for a period? Explain.

3–9. On July 1 of the current year, an enterprise paid the July rent on the building that it occupies. (a) Do the rights acquired at July 1 represent an asset or an expense? (b) What is the justification for debiting Rent Expense at the time of payment?

3–10. At the end of January, the first month of the fiscal year, the usual adjusting entry transferring supplies used to an expense account is inadvertently omitted. Which items will be incorrectly stated, because of the error, on (a) the income statement for January and (b) the balance sheet as of January 31? Also indicate whether the items in error will be overstated or understated.

3–11. In accounting for depreciation on equipment, what is the name of the account that would be referred to as a contra asset account?

3–12. (a) Explain the purpose of the two accounts: Depreciation Expense and Accumulated Depreciation. (b) What is the normal balance of each account? (c) Is it customary for the balances of the two accounts to be equal in amount? (d) In what financial statements, if any, will each account appear?

3–13. What term is applied to the difference between the balance in a plant asset account and its related accumulated depreciation account?

3–14. If the balance in the equipment account is $25,000 and the balance in the accumulated depreciation—equipment account is $10,000, what is the book value of the equipment?

3–15. Accrued salaries of $7,500 owed to employees for December 29, 30, and 31 are not taken into consideration in preparing the financial statements for the fiscal year ended December 31. Which items will be erroneously stated, because of the error, on (a) the income statement for the year and (b) the balance sheet as of

December 31? Also indicate whether the items in error will be overstated or understated.

3–16. Assume that the error in Question 3–15 was not corrected and that the $7,500 of accrued salaries was included in the first salary payment in January. Which items will be erroneously stated, because of failure to correct the initial error, on (a) the income statement for the month of January and (b) the balance sheet as of January 31?

3–17. Is the work sheet a substitute for the financial statements? Discuss.

3–18. In the Balance Sheet columns of the work sheet for C. D. Parker Company for the current year, the Debit column total is $29,750 greater than the Credit column total. Would the income statement report a net income or a net loss? Explain.

3–19. Describe the nature of the assets that compose the following categories: (a) current assets, (b) plant assets.

3–20. Identify each of the following as (a) a current asset or (b) a plant asset: (1) equipment, (2) cash, (3) building, (4) accounts receivable, (5) supplies, (6) land.

3–21. As of the time a balance sheet is being prepared, a business enterprise owes a mortgage note payable of $200,000, the terms of which provide for monthly payments of $5,000. How should the liability be classified on the balance sheet?

3–22. Why are closing entries required at the end of an accounting period?

3–23. What type of accounts are closed by transferring their balances to Income Summary (a) as a debit, (b) as a credit?

3–24. To what account is the income summary account closed?

3–25. To what account is the account Dividends periodically closed?

3–26. From the following list, identify the accounts that should be closed to Income Summary at the end of the fiscal year: (a) Accounts Payable, (b) Salaries Payable, (c) Capital Stock, (d) Salaries Expense, (e) Depreciation Expense—Buildings, (f) Supplies, (g) Equipment, (h) Supplies Expense, (i) Retained Earnings, (j) Sales, (k) Land, (l) Accumulated Depreciation—Buildings.

3–27. Are adjusting and closing entries in the journal dated as of the last day of the fiscal period or as of the day the entries are actually made? Explain.

3–28. Which of the following accounts will ordinarily appear in the post–closing trial balance? (a) Accounts Receivable, (b) Accumulated Depreciation, (c) Cash, (d) Supplies, (e) Depreciation Expense, (f) Wages Payable, (g) Equipment, (h) Retained Earnings, (i) Dividends, (j) Capital Stock, (k) Wages Expense, (l) Sales.

Real World Focus

3–29. The fiscal years for several well-known companies were as follows:

Company	Fiscal Year Ending
K Mart	January 30
J. C. Penney	January 26
Toys "R" Us, Inc.	February 3
Federated Department Stores	February 2
The Limited, Inc.	February 2

What general characteristic of these companies explains why they do not have fiscal years ending December 31?

Real World Focus

3–30. The balance sheet for Tandy Corporation as of June 30, 1990, includes the following accrued expenses as current liabilities:

Accrued payroll and bonuses	$59,841,000
Accrued sales and payroll taxes	20,470,000
Accrued insurance	33,032,000
Accrued interest	11,124,000

The net income for Tandy Corporation for the year ended June 30, 1990, was $290,347,000. (a) If the accrued expenses had *not* been recorded at June 30, 1990, how much would net income have been misstated for the fiscal year ended June 30, 1990? (b) What is the percentage of the misstatement in (a) to the reported net income of $290,347,000?

Real World Focus

3–31. The current asset and current liability data adapted from The Proctor & Gamble Company balance sheet as of June 30, 1990, are as follows:

Current assets (in millions):	
Cash and equivalents	$1,407
Accounts receivable	2,647
Inventories	2,865
Prepaid expenses and other current assets	725
	$7,644

Current liabilities (in millions):	
Accounts payable–trade	$2,035
Accounts payable–other	350
Accrued liabilities	1,690
Taxes payable	445
Debt due within one year	897
	$5,417

(a) Based upon the preceding data, determine (1) the difference between the total current assets and the total current liabilities as of June 30, 1990, and (2) the ratio of the total current assets to the total current liabilities as of June 30, 1990. (b) Based upon the solution in (a), is it likely that The Proctor & Gamble Company will be able to pay its current liabilities as they become due?

Ethics Discussion Case

3–32. McRee Company's fiscal year ends October 31. During the first week of November, McRee Company's accountant prepared the work sheet for the year ended October 31, 1992. After the financial statements were prepared, the accountant journalized and posted the adjusting and closing entries. The accountant dated the adjusting and closing entries October 31, 1992, even though the entries were actually prepared and entered on November 6, 1992.

Evaluate whether the accountant behaved in an ethical manner by dating the adjusting and closing entries October 31, 1992.

EXERCISES

Ex. 3–33.
Adjusting entries for prepaid insurance.
OBJ. 4

The balance in the prepaid insurance account, before adjustment at the end of the year, is $7,225. Journalize the adjusting entry required under each of the following alternative means of determining the amount of the adjustment: (a) the amount of insurance expired during the year is $4,900; (b) the amount of unexpired insurance applicable to future periods is $2,325.

Ex. 3–34.
Adjusting entries for accrued salaries.
OBJ. 4

A business enterprise pays weekly salaries of $12,000 on Friday for a five-day week ending on that day. Journalize the necessary adjusting entry at the end of the fiscal period, assuming that the fiscal period ends (a) on Monday, (b) on Wednesday.

Ex. 3–35.
Adjusting entries for prepaid and accrued taxes.
OBJ. 4

A business enterprise was organized on April 1 of the current year. On April 2, the enterprise paid $9,600 to the city for taxes (license fees) for the next 12 months, and debited the prepaid taxes account. The same enterprise is also required to pay in January an annual tax (on property) for the previous calendar year. The estimated amount of the property tax for the current year is $9,950. (a) Journalize the two adjusting entries required to bring the accounts affected by the two taxes up to date as of December 31, the end of the current year. (b) What is the amount of tax expense for the current year?

Ex. 3–36.
Adjusting entries for supplies and depreciation.
OBJ. 4

The balance in the supplies account, before adjustment at the end of the year, is $2,750. The inventory of supplies at the end of the year was determined to be $600. The estimated depreciation on equipment used during the year is $1,600. Journalize the adjusting entries required at the end of the year to recognize (a) supplies used during the year and (b) depreciation expense for the year.

Ex. 3–37.
Adjusting entries for depreciation; effect of error.
OBJ. 4

On December 31, a business enterprise estimates depreciation on equipment used during the first year of operations to be $3,200. (a) Journalize the adjusting entry required as of December 31. (b) If the adjusting entry in (a) were omitted, which items would be erroneously stated on (1) the income statement for the year and (2) the balance sheet as of December 31?

Ex. 3–38.
Balance sheet.
OBJ. 6

After all of the accounts have been closed on June 30, the end of the current fiscal year, the balances of selected accounts from the ledger of Bards Company are as follows:

Accounts Payable	$9,250
Accounts Receivable	9,920
Accumulated Depreciation—Equipment	21,100
Cash	6,150
Equipment	57,600
Prepaid Insurance	3,100
Prepaid Rent	2,400
Salaries Payable	2,750
Supplies	4,750
Capital Stock	40,000
Retained Earnings	10,820

Prepare a balance sheet in report form.

Ex. 3–39.
Retained earnings statement.
OBJ. 6
SPREADSHEET PROBLEM

Selected accounts from the ledger of Bennett-Hill Inc., for the current fiscal year ended June 30, 1993, are as follows:

Capital Stock

Debit		Credit	
		July 1	200,000

Dividends

Debit		Credit	
Aug. 1	8,000	June 30	36,000
Nov. 1	8,000		
Feb. 1	10,000		
May 1	10,000		

Retained Earnings

Debit		Credit	
June 30	36,000	July 1	94,500
		June 30	42,850

Income Summary

Debit		Credit	
June 30	808,300	June 30	851,150
30	42,850		

Prepare a retained earnings statement for the year.

Ex. 3–40.
Closing entries.
OBJ. 8

After all revenue and expense accounts have been closed at the end of the fiscal year, Income Summary has a debit of $992,150 and a credit of $980,000. As of the same date, Retained Earnings has a credit balance of $245,750, and Dividends has a balance of $25,000. (a) Journalize the entries required to complete the closing of the accounts. (b) State the amount of Retained Earnings at the end of the period.

Appendix Ex. 3–41.
Entries posted to the salary expense account; reversing entry.

Portions of the salary expense account of an enterprise are as follows:

ACCOUNT Salary Expense ACCOUNT NO. 54

Date		Item	Post. Ref.	Dr.	Cr.	Balance Dr.	Balance Cr.
19--							
Jan.	1		24		1,375		1,375
	5		24	6,500		5,125	
Dec.	27	(1)	51	7,500		245,500	
	31	(2)	51	2,500		248,000	
	31	(3)	52		248,000	—	—
19--							
Jan.	1	(4)	52		2,500		2,500
	4	(5)	53	7,500		5,000	

(a) Indicate the nature of the entry (payment, adjusting, closing, reversing) from which each numbered posting was made. (b) Present the complete journal entry from which each numbered posting was made.

Appendix Ex. 3–42.
Adjusting and reversing entries.

Sales salaries are uniformly $10,000 for a five-day workweek, ending on Friday. The last payday of the year was Friday, June 27, 1993. Journalize (a) the adjusting entries at June 30, 1993, the end of the current fiscal year, and (b) the reversing entry on July 1, 1993, the first day of the following year.

PROBLEMS

Pb. 3–43.
Work sheet and related items.
OBJ. 4, 5, 6, 7, 8

The trial balance of Westside Laundromat Inc. at July 31, 1993, the end of the current fiscal year, and the data needed to determine year-end adjustments are as follows:

Westside Laundromat Inc.
Trial Balance
July 31, 1993

Cash	7,790	
Laundry Supplies	4,750	
Prepaid Insurance	2,825	
Laundry Equipment	85,600	
Accumulated Depreciation		55,700
Accounts Payable		4,950
Capital Stock		25,000
Retained Earnings		5,900
Dividends	18,000	
Laundry Revenue		76,900
Wages Expense	24,500	
Rent Expense	15,575	
Utilities Expense	8,500	
Miscellaneous Expense	910	
	168,450	168,450

Adjustment data:

(a) Inventory of laundry supplies at July 31	$1,840
(b) Insurance premiums expired during the year	1,500
(c) Depreciation on equipment during the year	5,720
(d) Wages accrued but not paid at July 31	850

Instructions:

(1) Record the trial balance on a work sheet and complete the work sheet.
(2) Prepare an income statement, a retained earnings statement, and a balance sheet.
(3) On the basis of the adjustment data in the work sheet, journalize the adjusting entries.
(4) On the basis of the data in the work sheet, journalize the closing entries.

Pb. 3–44.
Adjusting and closing entries; retained earnings statement.
OBJ. 4, 6, 7, 8

As of December 31, the end of the current fiscal year, the accountant for Buchanan Company prepared a trial balance, journalized and posted the adjusting entries, prepared an adjusted trial balance, prepared the statements, and completed the other procedures required at the end of the accounting cycle. The two trial balances as of December 31, one before adjustments and the other after adjustments, are as follows:

Buchanan Company
Trial Balance
December 31, 19—

	Unadjusted		Adjusted	
Cash	19,750		19,750	
Supplies	9,880		3,460	
Prepaid Rent	10,400		800	
Prepaid Insurance	2,700		700	
Land	47,500		47,500	
Buildings	118,000		118,000	
Accumulated Depreciation—Buildings		79,600		84,400
Trucks	72,000		72,000	
Accumulated Depreciation—Trucks		32,800		50,900
Accounts Payable		8,920		9,520
Salaries Payable		—		1,450
Taxes Payable		—		920
Capital Stock		50,000		50,000
Retained Earnings		51,390		51,390
Dividends	24,000		24,000	
Service Fees Earned		170,680		170,680
Salary Expense	81,200		82,650	
Depreciation Expense—Trucks	—		18,100	
Rent Expense	—		9,600	
Supplies Expense	—		6,420	
Utilities Expense	6,200		6,800	
Depreciation Expense—Buildings	—		4,800	
Taxes Expense	800		1,720	
Insurance Expense	—		2,000	
Miscellaneous Expense	960		960	
	393,390	393,390	419,260	419,260

Instructions:

(1) Present the eight journal entries that were required to adjust the accounts at December 31. None of the accounts was affected by more than one adjusting entry.
(2) Present the journal entries that were required to close the accounts at December 31.
(3) Prepare a retained earnings statement for the fiscal year ended December 31.

If the working papers correlating with this textbook are not used, omit Pb. 3–45.

Pb. 3–45.
Ledger accounts, work sheet, and related items.
OBJ. 4, 5, 6, 7, 8

The ledger and trial balance of Eastland Company as of July 31, 1993, the end of the first month of its current fiscal year, are presented in the working papers.

Instructions:

(1) Complete the work sheet. Data needed to determine the necessary adjusting entries are as follows:

Inventory of supplies at July 31	$590.00
Insurance premiums expired during July	95.00
Depreciation on the building during July	125.00
Depreciation on equipment during July	140.00
Wages accrued but not paid at July 31	975.00

(2) Prepare an income statement, a retained earnings statement, and a balance sheet.
(3) Journalize and post the adjusting entries, inserting balances in the accounts affected.
(4) Journalize and post the closing entries. Indicate closed accounts by inserting a line in both Balance columns opposite the closing entry. Insert the new balance of the retained earnings account.
(5) Prepare a post-closing trial balance.

Pb. 3–46.
Ledger accounts, work sheet, and related items.
OBJ. 4, 5, 6, 7, 8

The trial balance of Lopez Company at December 31, 1993, the end of the current year, and the data needed to determine year-end adjustments are as follows:

Lopez Company
Trial Balance
December 31, 1993

Cash	7,525	
Supplies	4,870	
Prepaid Insurance	1,950	
Equipment	31,500	
Accumulated Depreciation—Equipment		9,750
Trucks	42,000	
Accumulated Depreciation—Trucks		26,400
Accounts Payable		4,015
Capital Stock		10,000
Retained Earnings		15,800
Dividends	18,000	
Service Revenue		99,950
Wages Expense	37,925	
Rent Expense	9,600	
Truck Expense	9,350	
Miscellaneous Expense	3,195	
	165,915	165,915

Adjustment data:

(a) Inventory of supplies at December 31	$ 910
(b) Insurance premiums expired during year	1,050
(c) Depreciation on equipment during year	5,380
(d) Depreciation on truck during year	6,200
(e) Wages accrued but not paid at December 31	700

Instructions:

(1) Open a ledger of standard accounts, using the following account titles and numbers: Cash, 11; Supplies, 13; Prepaid Insurance, 14; Equipment, 16; Accumulated Depreciation—Equipment, 17; Trucks, 18; Accumulated Depreciation—Trucks, 19; Accounts Payable, 21; Wages Payable, 22; Capital Stock, 31; Retained Earnings, 32; Dividends, 33; Income Summary, 34; Service Revenue, 41; Wages Expense, 51; Supplies Expense, 52; Rent Expense, 53; Depreciation Expense—Equipment, 54; Truck Expense, 55; Depreciation Expense—Trucks, 56; Insurance Expense, 57; Miscellaneous Expense, 59.
(2) For the accounts listed in the trial balance, enter the balances in the appropriate balance columns and place a check mark (✔) in the posting reference column.
(3) Record the trial balance on a work sheet and complete the work sheet.
(4) Prepare an income statement, a retained earnings statement, and a balance sheet.
(5) Journalize and post the adjusting entries, inserting balances in the accounts affected.
(6) Journalize and post the closing entries. Indicate closed accounts by inserting a line in both Balance columns opposite the closing entry. Insert the new balance of the retained earnings account.
(7) Prepare a post-closing trial balance.

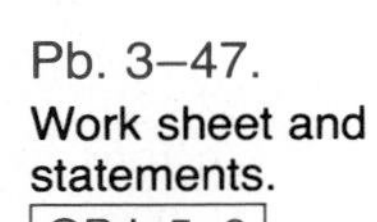

Pb. 3–47.
Work sheet and statements.
OBJ. 5, 6

Berkshire Bowl Inc. prepared the following trial balance at June 30, 1993, the end of the current fiscal year:

Berkshire Bowl Inc.
Trial Balance
June 30, 1993

Cash	13,700	
Prepaid Insurance	3,400	
Supplies	1,950	
Land	50,000	
Building	137,500	
Accumulated Depreciation—Building		51,700
Equipment	90,100	
Accumulated Depreciation—Equipment		35,300
Accounts Payable		7,500
Capital Stock		100,000
Retained Earnings		66,700
Dividends	20,000	
Bowling Revenue		198,400
Salaries and Wages Expense	80,200	
Utilities Expense	28,200	
Advertising Expense	19,000	
Repairs Expense	11,500	
Miscellaneous Expense	4,050	
	459,600	459,600

The data needed to determine year-end adjustments are as follows:

(a) Insurance expired during the year	$2,700
(b) Inventory of supplies at June 30	450
(c) Depreciation of building for the year	1,620
(d) Depreciation of equipment for the year	5,500
(e) Accrued salaries and wages at June 30	2,000

Instructions:

(1) Record the trial balance on a work sheet and complete the work sheet.
(2) Prepare an income statement for the year ended June 30.

(continued)

(3) Prepare a retained earnings statement for the year ended June 30.
(4) Prepare a balance sheet as of June 30.
(5) Compute the percent of net income to revenue for the year.
(6) Compute the percent of net income for the year ended June 30 to total stockholders' equity as of the beginning of the fiscal year. The capital stock account remained unchanged during the year.

ALTERNATE PROBLEMS

Pb. 3–43A.
Work sheet and related items.
OBJ. 4, 5, 6, 7, 8

SOLUTIONS SOFTWARE
SPREADSHEET PROBLEM

The trial balance of Parkview Laundry Company at October 31, 1993, the end of the current fiscal year, and the data needed to determine year-end adjustments are as follows:

Parkview Laundry Company
Trial Balance
October 31, 1993

Cash	9,950	
Laundry Supplies	7,200	
Prepaid Insurance	2,750	
Laundry Equipment	72,500	
Accumulated Depreciation		37,100
Accounts Payable		6,100
Capital Stock		15,000
Retained Earnings		11,500
Dividends	18,000	
Laundry Revenue		151,800
Wages Expense	50,150	
Rent Expense	36,000	
Utilities Expense	22,250	
Miscellaneous Expense	2,700	
	221,500	221,500

Adjustment data:

(a) Inventory of laundry supplies at October 31	$1,600
(b) Insurance premiums expired during the year	1,800
(c) Depreciation on equipment during the year	7,700
(d) Wages accrued but not paid at October 31	1,750

Instructions:

(1) Record the trial balance on a work sheet and complete the work sheet.
(2) Prepare an income statement, a retained earnings statement, and a balance sheet.
(3) On the basis of the adjustment data in the work sheet, journalize the adjusting entries.
(4) On the basis of the data in the work sheet, journalize the closing entries.

Pb. 3–44A.
Adjusting and closing entries; retained earnings statement.
OBJ. 4, 6, 7, 8

SPREADSHEET PROBLEM

As of June 30, the end of the current fiscal year, the accountant for Fidelity Company prepared a trial balance, journalized and posted the adjusting entries, prepared an adjusted trial balance, prepared the statements, and completed the other procedures required at the end of the accounting cycle. The two trial balances as of June 30, one before adjustments and the other after adjustments, are shown on page 141.

Fidelity Company
Trial Balance
June 30, 19—

	Unadjusted		Adjusted	
Cash	12,825		12,825	
Supplies	8,950		3,635	
Prepaid Rent	19,500		1,500	
Prepaid Insurance	3,750		1,250	
Equipment	92,150		92,150	
Accum. Depreciation—Equipment		53,480		66,270
Automobiles	56,500		56,500	
Accum. Depreciation—Automobiles		28,250		36,900
Accounts Payable		8,310		8,730
Salaries Payable		—		3,400
Taxes Payable		—		1,225
Capital Stock		25,000		25,000
Retained Earnings		16,245		16,245
Dividends	18,600		18,600	
Service Fees Earned		261,200		261,200
Salary Expense	172,300		175,700	
Rent Expense	—		18,000	
Supplies Expense	—		5,315	
Depreciation Expense—Equipment	—		12,790	
Depreciation Expense—Automobiles	—		8,650	
Utilities Expense	4,700		5,120	
Taxes Expense	1,500		2,725	
Insurance Expense	—		2,500	
Miscellaneous Expense	1,710		1,710	
	392,485	392,485	418,970	418,970

Instructions:

(1) Present the eight journal entries that were required to adjust the accounts at June 30. None of the accounts was affected by more than one adjusting entry.
(2) Present the journal entries that were required to close the accounts at June 30.
(3) Prepare a retained earnings statement for the fiscal year ended June 30.

If the working papers correlating with this textbook are not used, omit Pb. 3–45A.

Pb. 3–45A.
Ledger accounts, work sheet, and related items.
OBJ. 4, 5, 6, 7, 8

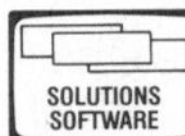

The ledger and trial balance of Eastland Company as of July 31, 1993, the end of the first month of its current fiscal year, are presented in the working papers.

Instructions:

(1) Complete the work sheet. Data needed to determine the necessary adjusting entries are as follows:

Inventory of supplies at July 31	$900.00
Insurance premiums expired during July	80.10
Depreciation on the building during July	125.00
Depreciation on equipment during July	95.00
Wages accrued but not paid at July 31	250.00

(2) Prepare an income statement, a retained earnings statement, and a balance sheet.
(3) Journalize and post the adjusting entries, inserting balances in the accounts affected.
(4) Journalize and post the closing entries. Indicate closed accounts by inserting a line in both Balance columns opposite the closing entry. Insert the new balance of the retained earnings account.
(5) Prepare a post-closing trial balance.

Pb. 3–46A.
Ledger accounts, work sheet, and related items.
OBJ. 4, 5, 6, 7, 8

The trial balance of D. D. Dyne Company at July 31, 1993, the end of the current year, and the data needed to determine year-end adjustments are as follows:

D. D. Dyne Company
Trial Balance
July 31, 1993

Cash	6,500	
Supplies	4,295	
Prepaid Insurance	1,735	
Equipment	30,650	
Accumulated Depreciation—Equipment		9,750
Trucks	23,300	
Accumulated Depreciation—Trucks		6,400
Accounts Payable		2,015
Capital Stock		20,000
Retained Earnings		10,435
Dividends	18,000	
Service Revenue		89,950
Wages Expense	33,925	
Rent Expense	9,600	
Truck Expense	8,350	
Miscellaneous Expense	2,195	
	138,550	138,550

Adjustment data:

(a) Inventory of supplies at July 31	$ 302
(b) Insurance premiums expired during year	990
(c) Depreciation on equipment during year	3,380
(d) Depreciation on truck during year	4,400
(e) Wages accrued but not paid at July 31	693

Instructions:

(1) Open a ledger of standard accounts, using the following account titles and numbers: Cash, 11; Supplies, 13; Prepaid Insurance, 14; Equipment, 16; Accumulated Depreciation—Equipment, 17; Trucks, 18; Accumulated Depreciation—Trucks, 19; Accounts Payable, 21; Wages Payable, 22; Capital Stock, 31; Retained Earnings, 32; Dividends, 33; Income Summary, 34; Service Revenue, 41; Wages Expense, 51; Supplies Expense, 52; Rent Expense, 53; Depreciation Expense—Equipment, 54; Truck Expense, 55; Depreciation Expense—Trucks, 56; Insurance Expense, 57; Miscellaneous Expense, 59.
(2) For the accounts listed in the trial balance, enter the balances in the appropriate balance columns and place a check mark (✓) in the posting reference column.
(3) Record the trial balance on a work sheet and complete the work sheet.
(4) Prepare an income statement, a retained earnings statement, and a balance sheet.
(5) Journalize and post the adjusting entries, inserting balances in the accounts affected.
(6) Journalize and post the closing entries. Indicate closed accounts by inserting a line in both Balance columns opposite the closing entry. Insert the new balance of the retained earnings account.
(7) Prepare a post-closing trial balance.

Pb. 3–47A.
Work sheet and statements.
OBJ. 5, 6

Stacey Bowl Inc. prepared the following trial balance at June 30, 1993, the end of the current fiscal year:

Stacey Bowl Inc.
Trial Balance
June 30, 1993

Cash	11,500	
Prepaid Insurance	2,400	
Supplies	1,950	
Land	40,000	
Building	122,000	
Accumulated Depreciation—Building		31,700
Equipment	72,400	
Accumulated Depreciation—Equipment		15,300
Accounts Payable		6,100
Capital Stock		100,000
Retained Earnings		60,500
Dividends	15,000	
Bowling Revenue		161,200
Salaries and Wages Expense	60,200	
Advertising Expense	19,000	
Utilities Expense	18,200	
Repairs Expense	8,100	
Miscellaneous Expense	4,050	
	374,800	374,800

The data needed to determine year-end adjustments are as follows:

(a)	Insurance expired during the year	$1,050
(b)	Inventory of supplies at June 30	450
(c)	Depreciation of building for the year	1,620
(d)	Depreciation of equipment for the year	5,160
(e)	Accrued salaries and wages at June 30	1,950

Instructions:

(1) Record the trial balance on a work sheet and complete the work sheet.
(2) Prepare an income statement for the year ended June 30.
(3) Prepare a retained earnings statement for the year ended June 30.
(4) Prepare a balance sheet as of June 30.
(5) Compute the percent of net income to revenue for the year.
(6) Compute the percent of net income for the year ended June 30 to total stockholders' equity as of the beginning of the fiscal year. The capital stock account remained unchanged during the year.

MINI-CASE 3

Assume that you recently accepted a position with the American National Bank as an assistant loan officer. As one of your first duties, you have been assigned the responsibility of evaluating a loan request for $100,000 from Antipest, a small corporation. In support of the loan application, Don Shuman, president, submitted the following "Statement of Accounts" (trial balance) for the first year of operations ended December 31, 1992:

Antipest
Statement of Accounts
December 31, 1992

Cash	5,765	
Billings Due from Others	10,835	
Supplies (chemicals, etc.)	20,930	
Trucks	45,850	
Equipment	22,610	
Amounts Owed to Others		6,580
Capital Stock Issued		50,000
Income Reinvested		16,500
Service Revenue		136,710
Wages Expense	84,140	
Utilities Expense	9,660	
Rent Expense	6,720	
Insurance Expense	1,960	
Other Expenses	1,320	
	209,790	209,790

Instructions:

(1) Explain to Don Shuman why a set of financial statements (income statement, retained earnings statement, and a balance sheet) would be useful to you in evaluating the loan request.
(2) In discussing the "Statement of Accounts" with Don Shuman, you discovered that the accounts had not been adjusted at December 31. Through analysis of the "Statement of Accounts," indicate possible adjusting entries that might be necessary before an accurate set of financial statements could be prepared.
(3) Assuming that an accurate set of financial statements will be submitted by Don Shuman in a few days, what other considerations or information would you require before making a decision on the loan request?

COMPREHENSIVE PROBLEM 1

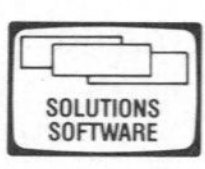

For the past several years, John Abrams has operated a television repair service in his home on a part-time basis. As of September 1, Abrams decided to move to rented quarters and to incorporate the business, which was to be known as A-1 TV Inc. A-1 TV Inc. entered into the following transactions during September:

Sept. 1. The following assets were received from John Abrams in exchange for $20,650 of capital stock: cash, $7,500; accounts receivable, $900; supplies, $1,250; and service equipment, $11,000. There were no liabilities received.
1. Paid three months' rent on a lease rental contract, $2,250.
2. Paid the premiums on property and casualty insurance policies, $1,740.
4. Purchased additional service equipment on account from Halsted Company, $2,500.
6. Received cash from customers on account, $500.
9. Paid cash for a newspaper advertisement, $110.
11. Paid Halsted Company for part of the debt incurred on September 4, $1,250.

Sept. 12. Recorded sales on account for the period September 1-12, $1,000.
13. Paid receptionist for two weeks' salary, $500.
17. Recorded cash from cash customers for service revenue earned during the first half of September, $1,100.
17. Paid cash for supplies, $950.
20. Recorded sales on account for the period September 13-20, $700.
24. Recorded cash from cash customers for service revenue earned for the period September 17-24, $1,850.
27. Received cash from customers on account, $1,200.
27. Paid receptionist for two weeks' salary, $500.
30. Paid telephone bill for September, $75.
30. Paid electricity bill for September, $140.
30. Recorded cash from cash customers for service revenue earned for the period September 25-30, $950.
30. Recorded sales on account for the remainder of September, $800.
30. Paid $1,500 in dividends.

Instructions:

(1) Open a ledger of standard accounts for A-1 TV Inc., using the following titles and account numbers: Cash, 11; Accounts Receivable, 12; Supplies, 14; Prepaid Rent, 15; Prepaid Insurance, 16; Service Equipment, 18; Accumulated Depreciation, 19; Accounts Payable, 21; Salaries Payable, 22; Capital Stock, 31; Retained Earnings, 32; Dividends, 33; Income Summary, 34; Service Revenue, 41; Salary Expense, 51; Rent Expense, 52; Supplies Expense, 53; Depreciation Expense, 54; Insurance Expense, 55; Miscellaneous Expense, 59.
(2) Record the transactions in a journal.
(3) Post the journal to the ledger, extending the month-end balances to the appropriate balance columns after all posting is completed.
(4) Prepare a trial balance as of September 30, on a work sheet, listing all the accounts in the order given in the ledger. Complete the work sheet, using the following adjustment data:

(a) Insurance expired during September	$ 145
(b) Inventory of supplies on September 30	1,520
(c) Depreciation of store equipment for September	200
(d) Accrued receptionist salary on September 30	100
(e) Rent expired during September	750

(5) Prepare an income statement, a retained earnings statement, and a balance sheet.
(6) Journalize and post the adjusting entries.
(7) Journalize and post the closing entries. Indicate closed accounts by inserting a line in both Balance columns opposite the closing entry. Insert the new balance in the retained earnings account.
(8) Prepare a post-closing trial balance.

ANSWERS TO SELF-EXAMINATION QUESTIONS

1. D The balance in the supplies account, before adjustment, represents the amount of supplies available. From this amount ($2,250) is subtracted the amount of supplies on hand ($950) to determine the supplies used ($1,300). Since increases in expense accounts are recorded by debits and decreases in asset accounts are recorded by credits, answer D is the correct entry.
2. C Since increases in expense accounts (such as depreciation expense) are recorded by debits and it is customary to record the decreases in usefulness of plant assets as credits to accumulated depreciation accounts, answer C is the correct entry.

3. D The book value of a plant asset is the difference between the balance in the asset account and the balance in the related accumulated depreciation account, or \$22,500 − \$14,000, as indicated by answer D (\$8,500).
4. D The current asset category includes cash and other assets that may reasonably be expected to be realized in cash or sold or consumed usually within a year or less, and therefore would include cash (answer A), accounts receivable (answer B), and supplies on hand (answer C).
5. C Since all revenue and expense accounts are closed at the end of the period, both Sales (revenue) and Salary Expense (expense) would be closed to Income Summary (answer C).

CHAPTER 4

CHAPTER OBJECTIVES

1 Describe and illustrate the accounting for merchandising transactions, including:
   a Purchases of merchandise
   b Sales of merchandise
   c Transportation costs

2 Describe two merchandise inventory systems.

3 Describe and illustrate the cost of merchandise sold section of an income statement.

4 Describe the year-end procedures for a merchandising enterprise.

5 Describe and illustrate alternative formats and terminology for the income statement, retained earnings statement, and balance sheet of a merchandising enterprise.

6 Describe and illustrate the preparation of adjusting and closing entries for a merchandising enterprise.

4

ACCOUNTING FOR A MERCHANDISING ENTERPRISE

Merchandising enterprises, such as grocery stores, acquire merchandise for resale to customers. The selling of merchandise, instead of a service, makes the activities of merchandising enterprises differ from the activities of service enterprises. This chapter focuses on the accounting principles and concepts that are unique to merchandising enterprises—accounting for transactions between the buyers and sellers of merchandise.[1] In addition, the necessary year-end procedures and the financial statements for a merchandising enterprise are presented.

ACCOUNTING FOR PURCHASES

OBJECTIVE 1a
Describe and illustrate the accounting for purchases of merchandise.

Purchases of merchandise are usually identified in the ledger as *Purchases*. A more exact account title, such as "Purchases of Merchandise," could be used, but the briefer title is customarily used. Thus a merchandising enterprise can accumulate in the purchases account the cost of all merchandise purchased for resale during the accounting period.

When purchases are made for cash, the transaction may be recorded in the journal as follows:

Jan. 3	Purchases	510	
	Cash		510

Most purchases of merchandise are made on account and may be recorded as follows:

Jan. 4	Purchases	925	
	Accounts Payable		925

Purchases Discounts

The arrangements agreed upon by the buyer and the seller as to when payment for merchandise is to be made are called the **credit terms**. If payment

[1] The illustrations in this chapter employ the periodic method of accounting for merchandise. The appendix at the end of the chapter uses the alternate method, called the perpetual method, in the illustration of accounting for merchandising transactions. Both methods are discussed in more depth in later chapters.

is required immediately upon delivery, the terms are said to be "cash" or "net cash." Otherwise, the buyer is allowed a certain amount of time, known as the **credit period**, in which to pay.

Usually the credit period begins with the date of the sale as shown by the date of the **invoice** or **bill**. If payment is due within a stated number of days after the date of the invoice, for example 30 days, the terms are said to be "net 30 days," which may be written as "n/30."[2] If payment is due by the end of the month in which the sale was made, it may be expressed as "n/eom."

As a means of encouraging payment before the end of the credit period, the seller may offer a discount for the early payment of cash. Thus the expression "2/10, n/30" means that, although the credit period is 30 days, the buyer may deduct 2% of the amount of the invoice if payment is made within 10 days of the invoice date. This deduction is known as a **cash discount.** The essentials of credit terms of 2/10, n/30 are summarized in the following diagram:

Credit Terms

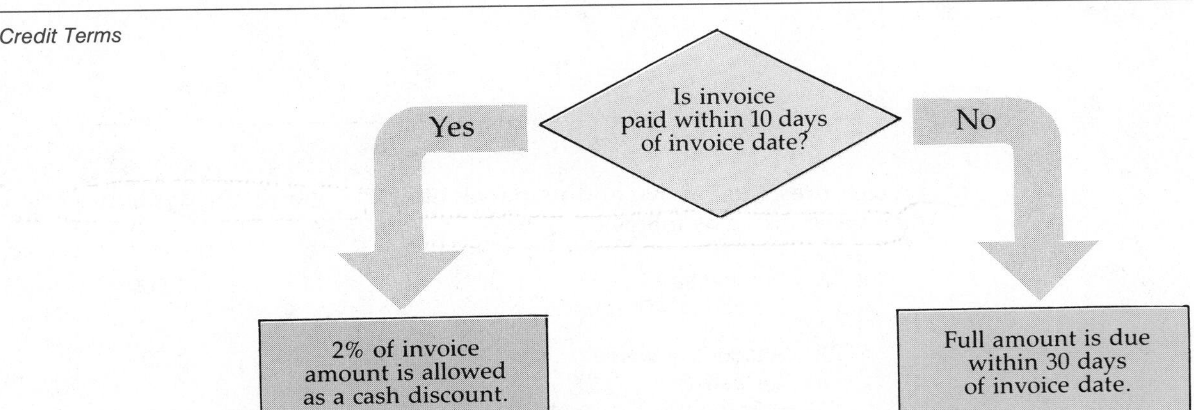

From the buyer's standpoint, it is important to take advantage of all available discounts, even though it may be necessary to borrow the money to make the payment. To illustrate, assume that the invoice for $1,500 shown at the top of page 150 is received by Valley Electric Company. The invoice, with terms of 2/10, n/30, is to be paid within the discount period with money borrowed for the remaining 20 days of the credit period. If an annual interest rate of 12% is assumed, the net savings to the buyer is $20.20, determined as follows:

Discount of 2% on $1,500	$30.00
Interest for 20 days at rate of 12% on $1,470 ($1,500 − $30)	9.80[3]
Savings effected by borrowing	$20.20

Discounts taken by the buyer for early payment of an invoice are called **purchases discounts.** They are recorded by crediting the purchases discounts account and are usually viewed as a deduction from the amount initially recorded in Purchases. In this sense, the purchases discounts account is a contra (or offsetting) account to Purchases. To illustrate, the receipt of the purchase

[2] The word "net" in this context does not have the usual meaning of a remainder after all relevant deductions have been subtracted, as in "net income," for example.

[3] Following the usual commercial practice of using 360 days as a year, the interest of $9.80 is computed as follows: $\$1,470 \times 12/100 \times 20/360 = \$9.80$

Invoice

Wallace Electronics Supply
3800 MISSION STREET
SAN FRANCISCO, CA 94110-1732

Customer's Order No. & Date: 412 Oct. 9, 1992
Refer to Invoice No.: 106-8
Invoice Date: Oct. 11, 1992
Vendor's Nos.

SOLD TO Valley Electric Company
1200 San Vicente Blvd.
Los Angeles, CA 90019-2350

Date Shipped: Oct. 11, 1992 From: San Francisco
Prepaid or Collect?: Prepaid
How Shipped and Route: Western Trucking Co.
F.O.B.: Los Angeles
Terms: 2/10, n/30
Made in U. S. A.

FOR CUSTOMER'S USE ONLY
Calculations Checked: W.M.L.
Price Approved
Material Received: 10-13 19 92 — A.S. — Rec. Cl. (Date / Signature / Title)
Audited: L.R.A.
Final Approval

QUANTITY	DESCRIPTION	UNIT PRICE	AMOUNT
20	392E Transformers	75.00	1,500.00

invoice presented above and its payment at the end of the discount period may be recorded as follows:

Oct. 11	Purchases	1,500	
	Accounts Payable		1,500
21	Accounts Payable	1,500	
	Cash		1,470
	Purchases Discounts		30

Purchases Returns and Allowances

When merchandise is returned **(purchases return)** or a price adjustment **(purchases allowance)** is requested, the buyer usually communicates with the seller in writing. The details may be stated in a letter, or the buyer (debtor) may use a **debit memorandum** form. This form, illustrated on page 151, is a convenient way to inform the seller (creditor) of the amount the buyer proposes to debit to the accounts payable account. It also states the reasons for the return or request for a price reduction.

The debtor may use a copy of the debit memorandum as the basis for an entry or may wait for confirmation from the creditor, which is usually in the form of a **credit memorandum.** In either event, Accounts Payable must be debited and Purchases Returns and Allowances must be credited.[4] The purchases returns and allowances account can be viewed as a deduction from the amount initially recorded in Purchases. In this sense, like Purchases Discounts, the purchases returns and allowances account is a contra (or offsetting) account to Purchases. To illustrate, the entry by Martin and Thomas Inc.

[4] Many businesses credit the purchases returns and allowances account for merchandise returned and allowances granted. However, some businesses prefer to credit the purchases account. If this alternative is used, the balance of the purchases account will be a net amount—the total purchases less the total returns and allowances for the period.

Debit Memorandum

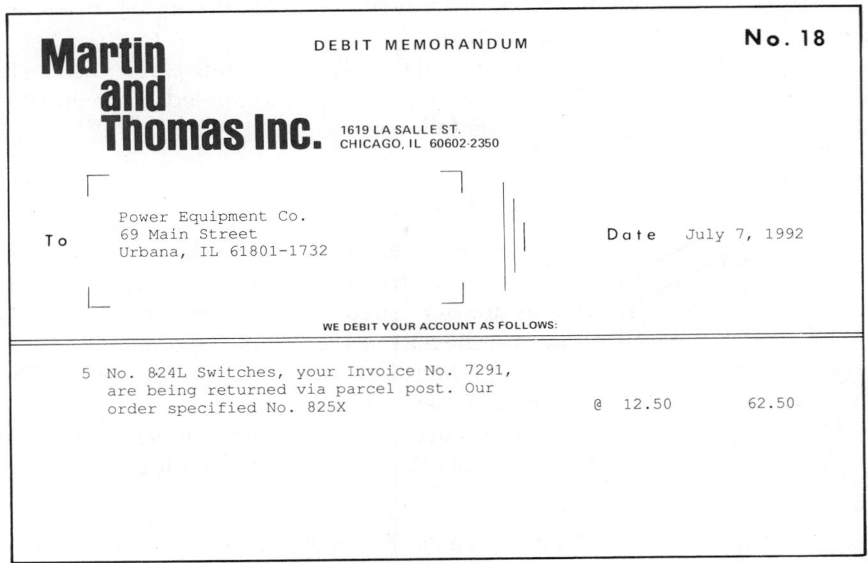

Martin and Thomas Inc. 1619 LA SALLE ST. CHICAGO, IL 60602-2350

DEBIT MEMORANDUM

No. 18

To Power Equipment Co.
69 Main Street
Urbana, IL 61801-1732

Date July 7, 1992

WE DEBIT YOUR ACCOUNT AS FOLLOWS:

5 No. 824L Switches, your Invoice No. 7291, are being returned via parcel post. Our order specified No. 825X @ 12.50 62.50

to record the return of the merchandise identified in the debit memo above would be as follows:

July 7	Accounts Payable	62.50	
	Purchases Returns and Allowances		62.50

When a buyer returns merchandise or has been granted an allowance prior to the payment of the invoice, the amount of the debit memorandum is deducted from the invoice amount before the purchases discount is computed. For example, assume that the details related to the amount payable to Power Equipment Co., for which the debit memo illustrated above was issued, are as follows:

Invoice No. 7291 dated July 1 (terms 2/10, n/30)	$2,045.00
Debit Memo No. 18 dated July 7	62.50
Balance of account	$1,982.50
Discount (2% of $1,982.50)	39.65
Cash payment, July 11	$1,942.85

The cash payment may be recorded by Martin and Thomas Inc. as follows:

July 11	Accounts Payable	1,982.50	
	Cash		1,942.85
	Purchases Discounts		39.65

ACCOUNTING FOR SALES

OBJECTIVE 1b
Describe and illustrate the accounting for sales of merchandise.

Merchandise sales usually are identified in the ledger as *Sales*, or *Sales of Merchandise*. Sales are recorded in the accounting records based upon the **realization principle.** Under this principle, sales are generally recorded when the title to the merchandise passes to the buyer in exchange for cash or claims to cash. The passing of title usually occurs when the merchandise has been delivered to the buyer or when the merchandise has been placed in the custody of a shipping agent, such as a freight company. Usually at that time, rather than when a sales order is received, the buyer incurs a specific obligation to pay for the merchandise.

A business may sell merchandise for cash. These sales are generally "rung up" on a cash register and totaled at the end of the day. Such sales may be recorded as follows:

Jan. 7	Cash	1,872.50	
	Sales		1,872.50

Sales to customers who use bank credit cards (such as MasterCard and VISA) are generally treated as cash sales. The credit card invoices representing these sales are deposited by the seller directly into the bank, along with the currency and checks received from customers. Periodically, the bank charges a service fee for handling these credit card sales. The service fee should be debited to an expense account.

A business may also sell merchandise on account. Such sales result in a debit to Accounts Receivable and a credit to Sales, as illustrated in the following entry:

Jan. 12	Accounts Receivable	510	
	Sales		510

Sales made by the use of nonbank credit cards (such as American Express) generally must be reported periodically to the card company before cash is received. Therefore, such sales create a receivable with the card company. Before the card company remits cash, it normally deducts a service fee. To illustrate, assume that nonbank credit card sales of $1,000 are made and reported to the card company on January 20. On January 27, the company deducts a service fee of $50 and remits $950. The transactions may be recorded as follows:

Jan. 20	Accounts Receivable	1,000	
	Sales		1,000
Jan. 27	Cash	950	
	Credit Card Collection Expense	50	
	Accounts Receivable		1,000

CREDIT CARDS AND CASH DISCOUNTS

The extensive use of credit cards by the American consumer has led some analysts to predict that the "cashless society" is on the horizon. In an effort to reduce operating costs, however, many businesses have encouraged consumers to use cash rather than credit cards. For example, some oil companies are now offering incentives for their customers to use cash, described as follows in an article that appeared in the *Harvard Business Review:*

... Exxon, Amoco, Sohio, and Mobil have been trying out various ways of offering discounts for cash in lieu of credit card sales. Mobil has lowered its wholesale price while adding a 3% processing fee for credit card sales to induce station managers to favor cash sales. As a result, ... Mobil stations [are] offering consumers gasoline at 4 cents a gallon less if they pay cash. ...

The idea received a boost in the summer of 1981 when Congress passed the Cash Discount Act, permitting business to give discounts exceeding 5% to consumers paying cash. Previously, a rebate of more than 5% was considered a finance charge levied against credit card users and was therefore illegal.

> *The retailer incurs two costs in each credit card transaction: the [collection] fee to convert the charge to cash and the interest expense arising from the time lag between the sale and collection of funds. If, for example, [the retailer's] cost of [funds] is 20%, if an average six days elapse between the sale and the collection of the proceeds, and if the [collector's] fee is 5%, then $10,000 in credit sales are equivalent to $9,472 in cash sales. The retailer could offer a cash discount of 5.3% and still be as well off as with a credit card sale.*
>
> *Although many retailers might like to reject credit cards altogether because of their expense, up to now they have been ill-advised to take this step unless most of their competitors followed suit. Otherwise, they could suffer a . . . disadvantage.*
>
> *Source:* Michael Levy and Charles A. Ingene, "Retailers: Head off Credit Cards with Cash Discounts?" *Harvard Business Review* (May-June, 1983), pp. 18–22.

Sales Taxes

Almost all states and many other taxing units levy a tax on retail sales of merchandise. Sales of merchandise that will be resold are normally not taxed. The liability for the sales tax is ordinarily incurred at the time the sale is made, regardless of the terms of the sale.

At the time of a cash sale, the seller collects the sales tax. When a sale is made on account, the buyer is charged for the tax. The seller credits the sales account for only the amount of the sale, and credits the tax to Sales Tax Payable. For example, a sale of $100 on account, subject to a tax of 6%, may be recorded by the following entry:

Aug. 12	Accounts Receivable	106	
	Sales		100
	Sales Tax Payable		6

Periodically, the appropriate amount of the sales tax is paid to the taxing unit, and Sales Tax Payable is debited.

Sales Discounts

The seller refers to the discounts taken by the buyer for early payment of an invoice as **sales discounts.** They are recorded by debiting the sales discounts account and are considered to be a reduction in the amount initially recorded in Sales. In this sense, the balance of the sales discounts account is viewed as a contra (or offsetting) account to Sales. To illustrate, if cash is received within the discount period from a previously recorded credit sale of $500, 2/10, n/30, the transaction may be recorded as follows:

June 10	Cash	490	
	Sales Discounts	10	
	Accounts Receivable		500

Sales Returns and Allowances

Merchandise sold may be returned by the buyer **(sales return)** or, because of defects or for other reasons, the buyer may be allowed a reduction from the original price at which the goods were sold **(sales allowance).** If the return or allowance is for a sale on account, the seller usually gives the buyer a **credit memorandum.** This memorandum shows the amount for which the buyer is to be credited and the reason therefor. A typical credit memorandum is illustrated at the top of page 154.

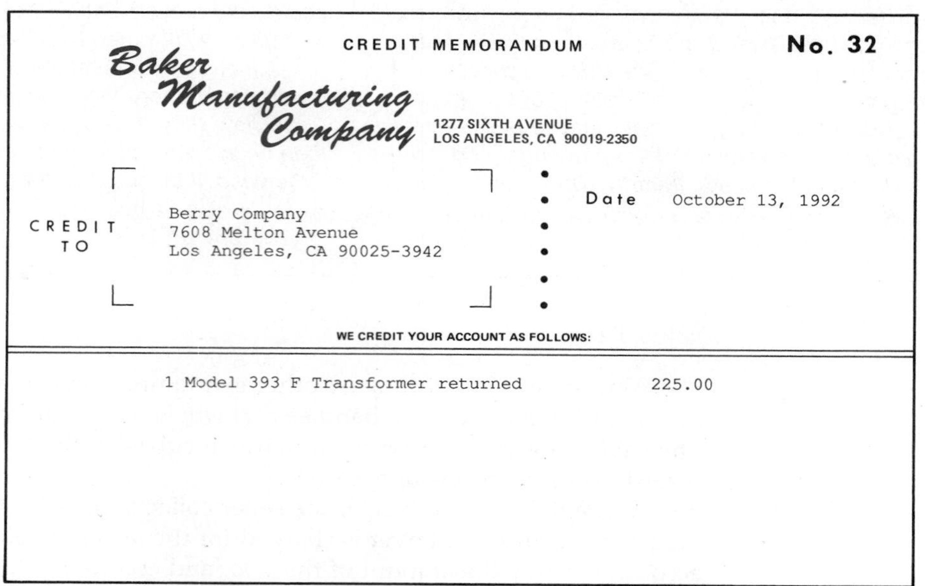
CREDIT MEMORANDUM

No. 32

Baker Manufacturing Company
1277 SIXTH AVENUE
LOS ANGELES, CA 90019-2350

CREDIT TO
Berry Company
7608 Melton Avenue
Los Angeles, CA 90025-3942

Date October 13, 1992

WE CREDIT YOUR ACCOUNT AS FOLLOWS:

1 Model 393 F Transformer returned 225.00

The effect of a sales return or allowance is a reduction in sales revenue and a reduction in cash or accounts receivable. If the sales account is debited, however, the balance of the account at the end of the period will represent net sales, and the volume of returns and allowances will not be disclosed. Because of the loss in revenue resulting from allowances, and the various expenses (transportation, unpacking, repairing, reselling, etc.) related to returns, it is advisable that management know the amount of such transactions. Such a policy will allow management to determine the causes of returns and allowances, should they become excessive, and to take corrective action. It is therefore preferable to debit an account entitled Sales Returns and Allowances. If the original sale is on account, the remainder of the transaction is recorded as a credit to Accounts Receivable. Because sales returns and allowances are viewed as reductions of the amount initially recorded in Sales, the sales returns and allowances account is a contra (or offsetting) account to Sales. To illustrate, the entry made by Baker Manufacturing Company for the credit memo presented above may be recorded as follows:

Oct. 13	Sales Returns and Allowances	225	
	Accounts Receivable		225

If a cash refund is made because of merchandise returned or for an allowance, Sales Returns and Allowances is debited and Cash is credited.

TRANSPORTATION COSTS

OBJECTIVE 1c
Describe and illustrate the accounting for transportation costs for merchandise purchases and sales.

The terms of the agreement between buyer and seller include provisions concerning (1) when the ownership (title) of the merchandise passes to the buyer and (2) which party is to bear the cost of delivering the merchandise to the buyer. If the ownership passes to the buyer when the seller delivers the merchandise to the shipper, the buyer is to absorb the transportation costs and the terms are said to be **FOB shipping point.** FOB shipping point means that the seller places the merchandise "free on board" at the shipping point and the buyer is responsible for the transportation costs beyond that point. If ownership passes to the buyer when the merchandise is received by the buyer, the seller is to assume the costs of transportation and the terms are said to be **FOB destination.** FOB destination means that the seller places the merchandise "free on board" to its destination by paying the delivery costs. The relationship of the shipping terms to the passage of ownership and who is to bear the costs of transportation is summarized in the following table:

Shipping Terms

	FOB Shipping Point	FOB Destination
Ownership (title) passes to buyer when merchandise is	delivered to shipper	delivered to buyer
Transportation costs are borne by	buyer	seller

When merchandise is purchased on terms of FOB shipping point, the transportation costs paid by the buyer should be debited to Transportation In or Freight In and credited to Cash. The balance of the transportation in or freight in account should be added to net purchases in determining the total cost of merchandise purchased.[5]

In some cases, the seller may prepay the transportation costs and add them to the invoice, as an accommodation or courtesy to the buyer, even though the agreement states that the buyer bear such costs (terms FOB shipping point). If the seller prepays the transportation charges, the buyer will debit Transportation In for the transportation costs. To illustrate, assume that on June 10, Durban Co. purchases merchandise from Bell Corp. on account, $900, terms FOB shipping point, 2/10, n/30, with prepaid transportation costs of $50 added to the invoice. The entry by Durban Co. may be recorded as follows:

June 10	Purchases	900	
	Transportation In	50	
	Accounts Payable		950

When the terms provide for a discount for early payment, the discount is based on the amount of the sale rather than on the invoice total. To illustrate, if Durban Co. pays the amount due on the purchase of June 10 within 10 days, the amount of the discount and the amount of the payment may be determined as follows:

Invoice from Bell Corp., including prepaid transportation of $50 . . .		$950
Amount subject to discount	$900	
Rate of discount	2%	
Amount of purchases discount		18
Amount of payment		$932

[5] Some businesses prefer to debit the purchases account for transportation charges paid on merchandise purchased FOB shipping point. If this alternative is used, the balance of the purchases account will include the transportation costs borne by the buyer. The total cost of merchandise purchased will be the same as when a separate transportation in or freight in account is used.

Durban Co. may record the payment as follows:

June 20	Accounts Payable	950	
	Cash		932
	Purchases Discounts		18

When the seller prepays the transportation costs and the terms are FOB shipping point, as in the illustration above, the seller adds these costs to the invoice that is sent to the buyer. Therefore, the seller records the payment of the transportation costs by debiting Accounts Receivable. In the illustration above, for example, Bell Corp. records the following entry on June 10, in addition to the entry to record the sale to Durban Co.:

June 10	Accounts Receivable	50	
	Cash		50

When the agreement states that the seller is to bear the delivery costs (FOB destination), the amounts paid by the seller for delivery are debited to Transportation Out, Delivery Expense, or a similarly titled account. The total of such costs incurred during a period is reported on the seller's income statement as an expense.

MERCHANDISE INVENTORY SYSTEMS

OBJECTIVE 2
Describe two merchandise inventory systems.

In a merchandising business, some of the merchandise purchased during the period may have been sold, and some may be unsold at the end of the period (ending inventory). This ending inventory becomes the beginning inventory for the next period and it must be accounted for properly to match revenues and expenses.

There are two main systems for accounting for merchandise: **periodic** and **perpetual.** Many merchandising enterprises use the periodic system. In this system, the revenues from sales are recorded when sales are made, but no attempt is made on the sales date to record the cost of the merchandise sold. It is only by a detailed listing of the merchandise on hand (called a **physical inventory**) at the end of the accounting period that a determination is made of (1) the cost of the merchandise sold during the period and (2) the cost of the inventory on hand at the end of the period. The periodic system is used in illustrations in this chapter.

Under the perpetual system, both the sales amount and the cost of merchandise sold amount are recorded when each item of merchandise is sold. In this manner, the accounting records continuously (perpetually) disclose the inventory on hand.[6]

COST OF MERCHANDISE SOLD

OBJECTIVE 3
Describe and illustrate the cost of merchandise sold section of an income statement.

For merchandising enterprises that use the periodic system, the cost of merchandise sold during a period is reported in a separate section in the income statement. To illustrate, assume that Cox Co. began its business operations on January 3, 1991, and purchased $340,000 of merchandise during the year. If the inventory at December 31, 1991, the end of the year, is $59,700, the cost of merchandise sold during 1991 would be reported as follows:

---

[6] The perpetual system is discussed in the appendix at the end of the chapter and in later chapters.

Cost of merchandise sold:		
Purchases	$340,000	
Less merchandise inventory, December 31, 1991	59,700	
Cost of merchandise sold		$280,300

To continue the illustration, assume that during 1992 Cox Co. purchases additional merchandise of $521,980, receives credit for purchases returns and allowances of $9,100, takes purchases discounts of $2,525, and pays transportation costs of $17,400. The purchases returns and allowances and the purchases discounts are deducted from the total purchases to yield the **net purchases**, and the transportation costs are added to the net purchases to yield the **cost of merchandise purchased**. These amounts would be reported in the cost of merchandise sold section of Cox Co.'s income statement for 1992 as follows:

Purchases		$521,980	
Less: Purchases returns and allowances	$9,100		
Purchases discounts	2,525	11,625	
Net purchases		$510,355	
Add transportation in		17,400	
Cost of merchandise purchased			$527,755

The ending inventory of Cox Co. on December 31, 1991, **$59,700**, becomes the beginning inventory for 1992. In the cost of merchandise sold section of the income statement for 1992, this beginning inventory is added to the cost of merchandise purchased to yield the **merchandise available for sale**. The ending inventory, which is assumed to be **$62,150**, is then subtracted from the merchandise available for sale to yield the **cost of merchandise sold.** The cost of merchandise sold during 1992 would be reported as follows:

Cost of Merchandise Sold for Year Ended December 31, 1992—Cox Co.

Cost of merchandise sold:				
Merchandise inventory, January 1, 1992			**$59,700**	
Purchases		$521,980		
Less: Purchases returns and allowances	$9,100			
Purchases discounts	2,525	11,625		
Net purchases		$510,355		
Add transportation in		17,400		
Cost of merchandise purchased			527,755	
Merchandise available for sale			$587,455	
Less merchandise inventory, December 31, 1992			**62,150**	
Cost of merchandise sold				$525,305

PERIODIC REPORTING FOR MERCHANDISING ENTERPRISES

OBJECTIVE 4
Describe the year-end procedures for a merchandising enterprise.

At yearly intervals throughout the life of a business enterprise, the operating data for the fiscal year must be summarized and reported for the use of managers, owners, creditors, various governmental agencies, and other interested persons. The ledger, which contains the basic data for the reports, must then be brought up to date through proper adjusting entries. Finally, the accounts must be prepared to receive entries for transactions that will occur in the following year.

Although the year-end procedures described and illustrated in this chapter are similar to those discussed in the preceding chapter, a number of differences should be noted. For the most part these differences relate to the type of business enterprise being discussed. In Chapter 3, the periodic reporting for a service enterprise was discussed. In this chapter the discussion relates to a merchandising enterprise.

Work Sheet for Merchandising Enterprises

After year-end posting of the journal is completed, a work sheet is used to assist in performing the year-end procedures, including the preparation of adjusting entries, closing entries, and financial statements.[7] In the work sheet presented on pages 160 and 161,[8] the trial balance for Cox Co. as of December 31, 1992, differs slightly from trial balances illustrated earlier. All of the accounts in the ledger are listed in sequential order, including titles of accounts that have no balances.

The data needed for adjusting the accounts of Cox Co. are summarized as follows:

(a) Office supplies as of December 31, 1992		$ 480
(b) Insurance expired during 1992		1,910
(c) Depreciation during 1992 on store equipment		3,100
(d) Depreciation during 1992 on office equipment		2,490
(e) Salaries accrued on December 31, 1992:		
Sales salaries	$780	
Office salaries	360	1,140
(f) Interest accrued on notes receivable on December 31, 1992		200
(g) Rent income earned during 1992		600

The use of adjusting entries at the end of the accounting period to match properly the revenues and expenses for the period was first discussed in Chapter 3. In that chapter, the adjusting entries for supplies, prepaid expenses (rent), depreciation, and accrued salaries were described and illustrated. The Cox Co. adjusting entries for these items, (a), (b), (c), (d), and (e) above, have been entered on the work sheet without further discussion. Two additional types of adjusting entries for Cox Co.—for accrued assets (item f) and unearned revenues (item g)—are discussed in the following paragraphs.

Adjusting Entries for Accrued Assets (Accrued Revenues). All assets belonging to the business at the end of an accounting period and all revenues earned during the period should be recorded in the ledger. But during a fiscal period it is common to record some types of revenue only as the cash is received; consequently, at the end of the period there may be items of revenue that have not been recorded. In such cases, the amount of the accrued revenue must be recorded by debiting an asset account and crediting a revenue account. Because of the dual nature of such accruals, they are called **accrued assets** or **accrued revenues.**

---

[7] As discussed in Chapter 3, computer software packages may be used to facilitate the preparation of the work sheet.

[8] The work sheet and other end-of-period procedures illustrated in this chapter employ the periodic inventory system. The end-of-period procedures under the perpetual inventory system are described and illustrated in the appendix at the end of the chapter.

To illustrate the adjusting entry for an accrued asset, assume that on December 31, 1992, the end of the fiscal year, Cox Co. has an interest-bearing note receivable. All interest income will be collected in 1993, when payment is due on the note. Assume further that the interest earned but not collected as of December 31, 1992, is $200 (item f). The entry to record this increase in the amount of interest due (receivable) on the note and the revenue earned is as follows:

Adjusting Entry

Dec. 31	Interest Receivable	200	
	Interest Income		200

After the entry has been posted, the interest receivable account will have a balance of $200, which would be reported as an asset in the balance sheet for Cox Co. The interest income would be reported on the income statement.

Adjusting Entries for Unearned Revenues. Revenue received during a particular period may be only partly earned by the end of the period. Items of revenue that are received in advance represent a liability that may be termed **unearned revenue.** The portion of the liability that is discharged during the period through delivery of goods or services has been earned; the remainder will be earned in the future. For example, magazine publishers usually receive advance payment for subscriptions covering periods ranging from a few months to a number of years. At the end of an accounting period, that portion of the receipts which is related to future periods has not been earned and should, therefore, appear in the balance sheet as a liability.

Other examples of unearned revenue are rent received in advance on property rented, premiums received in advance by an insurance company, tuition received in advance by a school, an annual retainer fee received in advance by an attorney, and amounts received in advance by an advertising firm for advertising services to be rendered in the future.

By accepting advance payment of a good or service, a business commits itself to furnish the good or the service at some future time. At the end of the accounting period, if some portion of the good or the service has been furnished, part of the revenue has been earned. The earned portion appears in the income statement. The unearned portion represents a liability of the business to furnish the good or the service in a future period and is reported in the balance sheet as a liability.

When revenue is received in advance, it may be credited to a liability account.[9] To illustrate, assume that on October 1, 1992, Cox Co. rents a portion of a building that it has been leasing for a period of one year, receiving $2,400 in payment for the entire year's rental. Assume also that the transaction was originally recorded by a debit to Cash and a credit to the liability account Unearned Rent. On December 31, 1992, the end of the fiscal year, one fourth of the amount has been earned (item g), and three fourths of the amount remains a liability. The entry to record the revenue and reduce the liability appears as follows:

Adjusting Entry

Dec. 31	Unearned Rent	600	
	Rent Income		600

---

[9] The concepts and procedures for recording unearned revenues initially as revenues are discussed in Appendix D at the end of the text.

Cox
Work
For Year Ended

	ACCOUNT TITLE	TRIAL BALANCE DEBIT	TRIAL BALANCE CREDIT	
1	Cash	62,950		1
2	Notes Receivable	40,000		2
3	Accounts Receivable	60,880		3
4	Interest Receivable			4
5	Merchandise Inventory	59,700		5
6	Office Supplies	1,090		6
7	Prepaid Insurance	4,560		7
8	Store Equipment	27,100		8
9	Accumulated Depreciation—Store Equipment		2,600	9
10	Office Equipment	15,570		10
11	Accumulated Depreciation—Office Equipment		2,230	11
12	Accounts Payable		22,420	12
13	Salaries Payable			13
14	Unearned Rent		2,400	14
15	Note Payable (final payment, 1996)		25,000	15
16	Capital Stock		100,000	16
17	Retained Earnings		53,800	17
18	Dividends	18,000		18
19	Sales		720,185	19
20	Sales Returns and Allowances	6,140		20
21	Sales Discounts	5,790		21
22	Purchases	521,980		22
23	Purchases Returns and Allowances		9,100	23
24	Purchases Discounts		2,525	24
25	Transportation In	17,400		25
26	Sales Salaries Expense	59,250		26
27	Advertising Expense	10,860		27
28	Depreciation Expense—Store Equipment			28
29	Miscellaneous Selling Expense	630		29
30	Office Salaries Expense	20,660		30
31	Rent Expense	8,100		31
32	Depreciation Expense—Office Equipment			32
33	Insurance Expense			33
34	Office Supplies Expense			34
35	Miscellaneous Administrative Expense	760		35
36	Rent Income			36
37	Interest Income		3,600	37
38	Interest Expense	2,440		38
39		943,860	943,860	39
40	Net Income			40
41				41

Co.
Sheet
December 31, 1992

	ADJUSTMENTS		INCOME STATEMENT		BALANCE SHEET		
	DEBIT	CREDIT	DEBIT	CREDIT	DEBIT	CREDIT	
1					62,950		1
2					40,000		2
3			Beginning inventory	Ending Inventory	60,880		3
4	(f) 200				200		4
5			59,700	62,150	62,150		5
6		(a) 610			480		6
7		(b) 1,910			2,650		7
8					27,100		8
9		(c) 3,100				5,700	9
10					15,570		10
11		(d) 2,490				4,720	11
12						22,420	12
13		(e) 1,140				1,140	13
14	(g) 600					1,800	14
15						25,000	15
16						100,000	16
17						53,800	17
18					18,000		18
19				720,185			19
20			6,140				20
21			5,790				21
22			521,980				22
23				9,100			23
24				2,525			24
25			17,400				25
26	(e) 780		60,030				26
27			10,860				27
28	(c) 3,100		3,100				28
29			630				29
30	(e) 360		21,020				30
31			8,100				31
32	(d) 2,490		2,490				32
33	(b) 1,910		1,910				33
34	(a) 610		610				34
35			760				35
36		(g) 600		600			36
37		(f) 200		3,800			37
38			2,440				38
39	10,050	10,050	722,960	798,360	289,980	214,580	39
40			75,400			75,400	40
41			798,360	798,360	289,980	289,980	41

(a) Office supplies used, $610 ($1,090 – $480).
(b) Insurance expired, $1,910.
(c) Depreciation of store equipment, $3,100.
(d) Depreciation of office equipment, $2,490.
(e) Salaries accrued but not paid (sales salaries, $780; office salaries, $360), $1,140.
(f) Interest earned but not received on notes receivable, $200.
(g) Rent earned from amount received in advance, $600.

After this entry has been posted, the unearned rent account will have a balance of $1,800 ($2,400 − $600), which will be reported as a liability on Cox Co.'s balance sheet. The rent income account will have a balance of $600 and that amount will be reported on the income statement.

Completing the Work Sheet

The data in the trial balance columns are combined with the adjustments data and extended to one of the remaining four columns. The amounts of assets, liabilities, and stockholders' equity (including dividends) are extended to the Balance Sheet columns. The revenues and expenses are extended to the Income Statement columns. This procedure must be applied to the balance of each account listed.

An exception to the usual practice of extending account balances is made for the merchandise inventory account. This exception is best illustrated by referring to the manner in which the beginning and ending merchandise inventory amounts are reported as part of the cost of merchandise sold section of the income statement. For Cox Co. the cost of merchandise sold section was illustrated on page 157 and is presented below.

Cost of merchandise sold:				
Merchandise inventory, January 1, 1992			$ 59,700	
Purchases		$521,980		
Less: Purchases returns and allowances	$9,100			
Purchases discounts	2,525	11,625		
Net purchases		$510,355		
Add transportation in		17,400		
Cost of merchandise purchased			527,755	
Merchandise available for sale			$587,455	
Less merchandise inventory, December 31, 1992			62,150	
Cost of merchandise sold				$525,305

The merchandise inventory amount of $59,700 on January 1, the beginning of the period, is added to the cost of merchandise purchased during the period, $527,755 to determine the merchandise available for sale, $587,455. The merchandise inventory amount of $62,150 on December 31, the end of the period, is subtracted from the merchandise available for sale to determine the cost of merchandise sold during the period, $525,305. The effect of the beginning and the ending merchandise inventories on the determination of the cost of merchandise sold influences how merchandise inventory is treated in completing the work sheet.

For Cox Co., the amount reported as merchandise inventory in the Trial Balance Debit column, $59,700, represents the unsold merchandise held for sale at the beginning of the year. Since this amount will be added to the cost of merchandise purchased in determining the cost of merchandise sold, it therefore is extended from the Trial Balance Debit column to the Income Statement Debit column. Likewise, since the merchandise on hand at the end of the year, $62,150, is subtracted in determining the cost of merchandise sold, it is entered on the work sheet as a credit in the Income Statement Credit column. Since the inventory at the end of the year also will be reported on the balance sheet as an asset, the ending merchandise inventory amount, $62,150, is also entered on the work sheet in the Balance Sheet Debit column. Note that the amount for the ending inventory is placed on the same line as that used for the beginning merchandise inventory.

After all of the items have been extended into the statement sections of the work sheet, the four columns are totaled and the net income or net loss is determined. In the illustration, the difference between the credit and the debit columns of the Income Statement section is $75,400, the amount of the net income. The difference between the debit and the credit columns of the Balance Sheet section is also $75,400, which is the increase in retained earnings as a result of the net income. Agreement between the two balancing amounts is evidence of debit-credit equality and arithmetical accuracy.

FINANCIAL STATEMENTS FOR MERCHANDISING ENTERPRISES

OBJECTIVE 5
Describe and illustrate alternative formats and terminology for the income statement, retained earnings statement, and balance sheet of a merchandising enterprise.

The basic financial statements for a merchandising enterprise, including the income statement, retained earnings statement, and balance sheet, are similar to those of a service enterprise. The basic differences between the financial statements of a merchandising enterprise and a service enterprise include the cost of merchandise sold section of the income statement, which was illustrated on page 157, and the inclusion of merchandise inventory on the balance sheet as a current asset.

The financial statements are prepared from the account titles and the data in the statement columns of the work sheet. Many variations are possible in the general format of the principal financial statements, in the terminology used, and in the extent to which details are presented. In preparing financial statements, however, the basic accounting principle of **adequate disclosure** should be followed. This principle requires that financial statements and their accompanying footnotes or other explanatory materials should contain all pertinent data believed essential to the reader's understanding of the enterprise's financial status. Criteria for standards of disclosure often must be based on value judgments rather than on objective facts.

The use of headings and subheadings and the merging of items in significant categories in the financial statements are illustrated in the following paragraphs. These illustrations are examples of adequate disclosure. Additional examples will be presented in many of the remaining chapters as more complex accounting matters are presented.[10] The work sheet of Cox Co., presented on pages 160 and 161, is used as a basis for illustration and discussion.

Income Statement

There are two widely used forms for the income statement: multiple-step and single-step. The 1990 edition of *Accounting Trends & Techniques* reported that 61% of the 600 industrial and merchandising companies surveyed use the multiple-step form, while 39% use the single-step form.

Multiple-Step Form. The **multiple-step income statement** is so called because of its many sections, subsections, and intermediate balances. In practice, there is considerable variation in the amount of detail presented in these sections. For example, instead of reporting separately the gross sales and the related returns, allowances, and discounts, the statement may begin with net

[10] Examples of alternative forms are also presented in Appendix H, Specimen Financial Statements.

sales. Similarly, the supporting data for the determination of the cost of merchandise sold may be omitted from the statement. The various sections of a multiple-step income statement for Cox Co., presented on page 165, are discussed briefly in the paragraphs that follow.

Revenue From Sales. The total of all charges to customers for merchandise sold, both for cash and on account, is reported in this section. Sales returns and allowances and sales discounts are deducted from the gross amount to yield net sales.

Cost of Merchandise Sold. The determination and reporting of the cost of merchandise sold, which is often the largest item deducted from revenues, was explained and illustrated on page 162. Other descriptive terms frequently used are **cost of goods sold** and **cost of sales.**

Gross Profit. The excess of the net revenue from sales over the cost of merchandise sold is called **gross profit, gross profit on sales**, or **gross margin**. It is called *gross* because operating expenses must be deducted from it.

Operating Expenses. The operating expenses of a business may be grouped under any desired number of headings and subheadings. In a retail business of the kind that has been used for illustrative purposes, it is usually satisfactory to subdivide operating expenses into two categories: selling and administrative.

Expenses that are incurred directly and entirely in connection with the sale of merchandise are classified as **selling expenses.** They include such expenses as salaries of the sales force, store supplies used, depreciation of store equipment, and advertising.

Expenses incurred in the administration or general operations of the business are classified as **administrative expenses** or **general expenses**. Examples of these expenses are office salaries, depreciation of office equipment, and office supplies used. Expenses that are partly connected with selling and partly connected with the administrative operations of the business may be divided between the two categories. In a small business, however, such expenses as rent, insurance, and taxes are commonly reported as administrative expenses.

Expenses of relatively small amounts that cannot be identified with the principal accounts are usually accumulated in accounts entitled Miscellaneous Selling Expense and Miscellaneous Administrative Expense.

Income from Operations. The excess of gross profit over total operating expenses is called **income from operations,** or **operating income**. The amount of the income from operations and its relationship to capital investment and to net sales are important factors in judging the efficiency of management and the degree of profitability of an enterprise. If operating expenses are greater than the gross profit, the excess is called **loss from operations**.

Other Income. Revenue from sources other than the principal activity of a business is classified as **other income,** or **nonoperating income**. In a merchandising business, this category often includes income from interest, rent, dividends, and gains resulting from the sale of plant assets.

Other Expense. Expenses that cannot be associated definitely with operations are identified as **other expense,** or **nonoperating expense.** Interest expense that results from financing activities and losses incurred in the disposal of plant assets are examples of items that are reported in this section.

The two categories of nonoperating items are offset against each other on the income statement. If the total of other income exceeds the total of other expense, the difference is added to income from operations. If the reverse is true, the difference is subtracted from income from operations.

Multiple-Step Form of Income Statement

Cox Co.
Income Statement
For Year Ended December 31, 1992

Revenue from sales:				
Sales			$720,185	
Less: Sales returns and allowances		$ 6,140		
Sales discounts		5,790	11,930	
Net sales				$708,255
Cost of merchandise sold:				
Merchandise inventory, January 1, 1992			$ 59,700	
Purchases		$521,980		
Less: Purchases returns and allowances	$9,100			
Purchases discounts	2,525	11,625		
Net purchases		$510,355		
Add transportation in		17,400		
Cost of merchandise purchased			527,755	
Merchandise available for sale			$587,455	
Less merchandise inventory, December 31, 1992			62,150	
Cost of merchandise sold				525,305
Gross profit				$182,950
Operating expenses:				
Selling expenses:				
Sales salaries expense		$ 60,030		
Advertising expense		10,860		
Depreciation expense–store equipment		3,100		
Miscellaneous selling expense		630		
Total selling expenses			$ 74,620	
Administrative expenses:				
Office salaries expense		$ 21,020		
Rent expense		8,100		
Depreciation expense–office equipment		2,490		
Insurance expense		1,910		
Office supplies expense		610		
Miscellaneous administrative expense		760		
Total administrative expenses			34,890	
Total operating expenses				109,510
Income from operations				$ 73,440
Other income:				
Interest income		$ 3,800		
Rent income		600		
Total other income			$ 4,400	
Other expense:				
Interest expense			2,440	1,960
Net income[11]				$ 75,400

[11] This amount is further reduced by corporation income tax. The discussion of income taxes levied on corporate entities is reserved for later chapters.

Net Income. The final figure on the income statement is labeled **net income** (or **net loss**). It is the net increase (or net decrease) in retained earnings as a result of profit-making activities.

Single-Step Form. The **single-step form of income statement** derives its name from the fact that the total of all expenses is deducted from the total of all revenues. Such a statement is illustrated as follows for Cox Co. The illustration has been condensed to focus attention on its principal features. Such condensation is not an essential characteristic of the single-step form.

Single-Step Form of Income Statement

Cox Co.
Income Statement
For Year Ended December 31, 1992

Revenues:		
Net sales		$708,255
Interest income		3,800
Rent income		600
Total revenues		$712,655
Expenses:		
Cost of merchandise sold	$525,305	
Selling expenses	74,620	
Administrative expenses	34,890	
Interest expense	2,440	
Total expenses		637,255
Net income		$ 75,400

The single-step form has the advantage of being simple and it emphasizes total revenues and total expenses as the factors that determine net income. An objection to the single-step form is that such relationships as gross profit to sales and income from operations to sales are not as readily determinable as they are when the multiple-step form is used.

Retained Earnings Statement

The **retained earnings statement** summarizes the changes which have occurred in the retained earnings account during the fiscal period. The retained earnings statement for Cox Co. is illustrated as follows:

Retained Earnings Statement

Cox Co.
Retained Earnings Statement
For Year Ended December 31, 1992

Retained earnings, January 1, 1992		$ 53,800
Net income for the year	$75,400	
Less dividends	18,000	
Increase in retained earnings		57,400
Retained earnings, December 31, 1992		$111,200

The analysis of retained earnings may be added at the bottom of the income statement to form a **combined income and retained earnings statement**. This combined form was used by 6% of the 600 industrial and merchandising companies surveyed in the 1990 edition of *Accounting Trends & Techniques*. The income statement portion of the combined statement may be shown either in multiple-step form or in a single-step form, as in the following illustration:

Combined Income and Retained Earnings Statement

Cox Co. Income and Retained Earnings Statement For Year Ended December 31, 1992		
Revenues:		
Net sales		$708,255
Interest income		3,800
Rent income		600
Total revenues		$712,655
Expenses:		
Cost of merchandise sold	$525,305	
Selling expenses	74,620	
Administrative expenses	34,890	
Interest expense	2,440	
Total expenses		637,255
Net income		$ 75,400
Retained earnings, January 1, 1992		53,800
		$129,200
Less dividends		18,000
Retained earnings, December 31, 1992		$111,200

The combined statement form emphasizes net income as the connecting link between the income statement and the retained earnings portion of owner's equity and thus helps the reader's understanding. A criticism of the combined statement is that the net income figure is buried in the body of the statement.

Balance Sheet

There are two widely used forms for the balance sheet: **report form** and **account form.** The 1990 edition of *Accounting Trends & Techniques* reported that 67% of the 600 industrial and merchandising companies surveyed use the report form, while 33% use the account form. The report form, with assets followed by liabilities and stockholders' equity in a downward sequence, was illustrated in earlier chapters. The account form, with assets on the left-hand side of the balance sheet and liabilities and stockholders' equity on the right-hand side, is illustrated in the balance sheet for Cox Co. on pages 168 and 169.

ADJUSTING AND CLOSING ENTRIES

OBJECTIVE 6
Describe and illustrate the preparation of adjusting and closing entries for a merchandising enterprise.

At the end of the accounting period, the adjusting entries appearing in the work sheet must be recorded in the journal and posted to the ledger. This procedure brings the ledger into agreement with the data reported on the financial statements. In addition, the ledger must be prepared to receive entries for transactions that will occur in the following period.

Adjusting Entries

The analyses required to make the adjustments were completed during the process of preparing the work sheet. It is therefore unnecessary to refer again to the basic data when recording the adjusting entries in the journal. The adjusting entries for Cox Co. are as follows:

Adjusting Entries

1992 Dec. 31	Office Supplies Expense	610.00	
	Office Supplies		610.00
31	Insurance Expense	1,910.00	
	Prepaid Insurance		1,910.00
31	Depreciation Expense—Store Equip.	3,100.00	
	Accumulated Depr.—Store Equip.		3,100.00
31	Depreciation Expense—Office Equip.	2,490.00	
	Accumulated Depr.—Office Equip.		2,490.00
31	Sales Salaries Expense	780.00	
	Office Salaries Expense	360.00	
	Salaries Payable		1,140.00
31	Interest Receivable	200.00	
	Interest Income		200.00
31	Unearned Rent	600.00	
	Rent Income		600.00

Closing Entries

The closing entries are recorded in the journal immediately following the adjusting entries. All of the temporary owner's equity accounts are cleared of their balances, reducing them to zero. In addition, the closing entries close out the beginning inventory and replace it with the ending inventory.[12] The final

[12] An alternative method of recording merchandise inventory is presented in Appendix E. This alternative method is sometimes referred to as the adjusting method. Under this method, the entries for beginning and ending merchandise inventory are classified as adjusting entries rather than closing entries.

Account Form of Balance Sheet

Cox
Balance
December

Assets			
Current assets:			
Cash		$ 62,950	
Notes receivable		40,000	
Accounts receivable		60,880	
Interest receivable		200	
Merchandise inventory		62,150	
Office supplies		480	
Prepaid insurance		2,650	
Total current assets			$229,310
Plant assets:			
Store equipment	$27,100		
Less accumulated depreciation	5,700	$ 21,400	
Office equipment	$15,570		
Less accumulated depreciation	4,720	10,850	
Total plant assets			32,250
Total assets			$261,560

effect of closing out such balances is a net increase or a net decrease in the retained earnings account. The closing entries for Cox Co. are as follows:

Closing Entries

1992				
Dec.	31	Merchandise Inventory	62,150.00	
		Sales	720,185.00	
		Purchases Returns and Allowances	9,100.00	
		Purchases Discounts	2,525.00	
		Interest Income	3,800.00	
		Rent Income	600.00	
		Income Summary		798,360.00
	31	Income Summary	722,960.00	
		Merchandise Inventory		59,700.00
		Sales Returns and Allowances		6,140.00
		Sales Discounts		5,790.00
		Purchases		521,980.00
		Transportation In		17,400.00
		Sales Salaries Expense		60,030.00
		Advertising Expense		10,860.00
		Depreciation Exp.—Store Equip.		3,100.00
		Miscellaneous Selling Expense		630.00
		Office Salaries Expense		21,020.00
		Rent Expense		8,100.00
		Depreciation Exp.—Office Equip.		2,490.00
		Insurance Expense		1,910.00
		Office Supplies Expense		610.00
		Miscellaneous Administrative Expense		760.00
		Interest Expense		2,440.00
	31	Income Summary	75,400.00	
		Retained Earnings		75,400.00
	31	Retained Earnings	18,000.00	
		Dividends		18,000.00

Co.
Sheet
31, 1992

Liabilities

Current liabilities:		
Accounts payable	$ 22,420	
Note payable (current portion)	5,000	
Salaries payable	1,140	
Unearned rent	1,800	
Total current liabilities		$ 30,360
Long-term liabilities:		
Note payable (final payment, 1996)		20,000
Total liabilities		$ 50,360

Stockholders' Equity

Capital stock	$100,000	
Retained earnings	111,200	
Total stockholders' equity		211,200
Total liabilities and stockholders' equity		$261,560

The effect of each of these four entries may be described as follows:

1. The first entry closes all accounts with balances in the Income Statement *credit* column of the work sheet by transferring the total to the *credit* side of Income Summary.
2. The second entry closes all accounts with balances in the Income Statement *debit* column of the work sheet by transferring the total to the *debit* side of Income Summary.
3. The third entry closes Income Summary by transferring its balance, the net income for the year, to Retained Earnings.
4. The fourth entry closes Dividends by transferring its balance to Retained Earnings.

The income summary account, as it will appear after the closing entries have been posted, is as follows. Each item in the account is identified as an aid to understanding. Such notations are not an essential part of the posting procedure.

Income Summary Account

ACCOUNT Income Summary ACCOUNT NO. 313

DATE		ITEM	POST. REF.	DEBIT	CREDIT	BALANCE	
						DEBIT	CREDIT
1992 Dec.	31	Revenue, etc.			798 3 6 0 00		798 3 6 0 00
	31	Expense, etc.		722 9 6 0 00			75 4 0 0 00
	31	Net Income		75 4 0 0 00			

After all temporary owner's equity accounts have been closed, the only accounts with balances are the asset, contra asset, liability, capital stock, and retained earnings accounts. It is advisable to take a post-closing trial balance to verify the debit-credit equality of the balances of these accounts, which should correspond exactly with the amounts appearing on the balance sheet on pages 168 and 169.

APPENDIX

THE PERPETUAL INVENTORY SYSTEM

In recording the merchandising transactions in this chapter, the periodic inventory system of accounting for unsold merchandise (inventory) was used.

In addition, the end-of-period procedures for a merchandising enterprise that uses the periodic inventory system were described and illustrated. This appendix describes and illustrates an alternative system, the perpetual inventory system.[13]

In a periodic inventory system, purchases of merchandise are recorded in a purchases account. On the date of the sale of the merchandise, no attempt is made to record the cost of the merchandise sold. At the end of the accounting period, a detailed listing of the merchandise on hand is prepared. The results of this physical inventory are used in determining (1) the cost of the merchandise sold during the period and (2) the cost of the inventory on hand at the end of the period.

In contrast to the periodic system, the perpetual inventory system uses accounting records that continuously disclose the amount of merchandise on hand (inventory). Purchases of merchandise are debited to a merchandise inventory account, and the cost of sales of merchandise are credited to the inventory account.

The periodic system is often used by a retailer, such as a locally owned hardware store, which sells many kinds of low-unit-cost merchandise. For such businesses, maintaining perpetual inventory records is too costly. If the accounting system is computerized, however, the retailer often uses the perpetual system in conjunction with bar codes, such as the one on the back of this textbook. A scanner reads the bar codes on the merchandise and records purchases and sales. Examples of such retailers are K Mart, Sears, and grocery store chains.

Perpetual inventory systems are also frequently used by businesses that sell a relatively small number of high-unit-cost items, such as office equipment, automobiles, or jewelry. In such cases, a manual system of maintaining perpetual inventory records can be used at a relatively low cost.

Recording Merchandise Transactions in a Perpetual Inventory System

In a perpetual inventory system, all increases and decreases related to merchandise are recorded directly in the merchandise inventory account. Thus, accounts for purchases, purchases returns and allowances, purchases discounts, and transportation in are not used in a perpetual system. To illustrate the recording of merchandise transactions in a perpetual system, the following selected transactions for Taylor Inc. are used:

June 5. Purchased $30,000 of merchandise on account from Owen Clothing, terms 2/10, n/30.

June 5	Merchandise Inventory	30,000.00	
	Accounts Payable		30,000.00

Under the perpetual system, purchases of merchandise are recorded in the merchandise inventory account.

June 8. Returned merchandise purchased on account from Owen Clothing on June 5, $500.

[13] The perpetual system is described in more detail in Chapter 7.

June 8	Accounts Payable	500.00	
	Merchandise Inventory		500.00

The merchandise inventory account must be reduced by the cost of the merchandise returned.

June 15. Paid Owen Clothing for purchase of June 5 on account, less return of $500 and discount of $590 [($30,000 − $500) × 2%].

June 15	Accounts Payable	29,500.00	
	Cash		28,910.00
	Merchandise Inventory		590.00

Under the perpetual system, purchases discounts are treated as a reduction in the cost of merchandise inventory.

June 15. Sales on account totaled $12,500 for the first half of June.[14] All sales are made with terms 1/10, n/30. The cost of the merchandise sold was $9,000.

June 15	Accounts Receivable	12,500.00	
	Sales		12,500.00
15	Cost of Merchandise Sold	9,000.00	
	Merchandise Inventory		9,000.00

The entry to record the sale of $12,500 is the same under both the perpetual and periodic systems. Under the perpetual system, however, the cost of the merchandise sold and the reduction of the inventory are also recorded at the date of the sale.

June 19. Received merchandise returned on account, $4,000. The cost of the merchandise returned was $2,800.

June 19	Sales Returns and Allowances	4,000.00	
	Accounts Receivable		4,000.00
19	Merchandise Inventory	2,800.00	
	Cost of Merchandise Sold		2,800.00

The entry to record the sales return is the same under both the perpetual and periodic systems. Since the inventory records must be kept up to date in a perpetual system, however, the cost of the merchandise returned must be added to the merchandise inventory. The cost of the merchandise must also be credited to Cost of Merchandise Sold, since this account was debited when the original sale was recorded.

June 22. Purchased merchandise from Norcross Clothiers, $15,000, terms FOB shipping point, 2/15, n/30, with prepaid transportation charges of $750 added to the invoice.

June 22	Merchandise Inventory	15,750.00	
	Accounts Payable		15,750.00

[14] To simplify the illustration, the sales transactions are recorded in summary form. Normally, under a perpetual inventory system, sales would be recorded as they occur.

This entry is similar to the June 5 entry for the purchase of merchandise. Since the transportation terms were FOB shipping point, the prepaid charges of $750 must be added to the invoice cost of $15,000, and the total cost of the purchase is $15,750.

June 30. Received $19,600 from cash sales for June. The cost of merchandise sold was $13,800.

June 30	Cash	19,600.00	
	Sales		19,600.00
30	Cost of Merchandise Sold	13,800.00	
	Merchandise Inventory		13,800.00

This entry is similar to the June 15 entry for sales made on account except that Cash is debited in place of Accounts Receivable.

End-of-Period Procedures In a Perpetual Inventory System

The end-of-period procedures are generally the same for an enterprise that uses the perpetual inventory system as for an enterprise that uses the periodic inventory system. The differences in the procedures for the two systems, which affect the work sheet, the income statement, and the closing entries, are described and illustrated in the remainder of this appendix, using the Cox Co. data presented in this chapter.

Work Sheet for Financial Statements. As discussed in this appendix, the ledger for a merchandising enterprise that uses a perpetual inventory system would not have accounts for purchases, purchases returns and allowances, purchases discounts, and transportation in. Transactions that involve these items would be recorded in the merchandise inventory account. The balance of the merchandise inventory account at the end of the period represents the cost of merchandise on hand. Thus on the partial work sheet for Cox Co. on page 174, the merchandise inventory amount shown in the trial balance, $62,150, is extended to the Balance Sheet debit column.

Under the perpetual system, the cost of merchandise sold is accumulated in a cost of merchandise sold account. At the end of a period, the balance of this account is reported on the income statement. Thus, the balance in the cost of merchandise sold account in the trial balance for Cox Co., $525,305, is extended to the Income Statement debit column.

The differences in the work sheet for an enterprise that uses the perpetual inventory system are highlighted in the partial work sheet for Cox Co. Note that the net income is the same under both the perpetual and the periodic systems. The portions of the work sheet that are not shown also would be the same under both systems.

Preparation of Financial Statements. The financial statements for Cox Co. would be essentially the same under both the perpetual and periodic inventory systems. The major difference is that the cost of merchandise sold is reported on the income statement as a single amount when the perpetual system is used.

Adjusting and Closing Entries. The adjusting entries would be the same under both the perpetual and periodic inventory systems. The closing entries would differ under the perpetual system in that the balance of the cost of

Work sheet

Cox Co.
Work Sheet
For Year Ended December 31, 1992

ACCOUNT TITLE	TRIAL BALANCE		ADJUSTMENTS		INCOME STATEMENT		BALANCE SHEET	
	DEBIT	CREDIT	DEBIT	CREDIT	DEBIT	CREDIT	DEBIT	CREDIT
Cash	62,950						62,950	
Notes Receivable	40,000						40,000	
Accounts Receivable	60,880						60,880	
Interest Receivable			(f) 200				200	
Merchandise Inventory	62,150						62,150	
Office Supplies	1,090			(b) 610			480	
Sales		720,185				720,185		
Sales Returns and Allowances	6,140				6,140			
Sales Discounts	5,790				5,790			
Cost of Merchandise Sold	525,305				525,305			
Sales Salaries Expense	59,250		(e) 780		60,030			
Advertising Expense	10,860				10,860			
Rent Income				(g) 600		600		
Interest Income		3,600		(f) 200		3,800		
Interest Expense	2,440				2,440			
	932,235	932,235	10,050	10,050	649,185	724,585	289,980	214,580
Net Income					75,400			75,400
					724,585	724,585	289,980	289,980

merchandise sold account would be closed to Income Summary. Also, the merchandise inventory account would not be updated as part of the closing process, as it is under the periodic system, since the account is continuously updated under the perpetual system. To illustrate, the closing entries for Cox Co. under the perpetual system are shown below.

Closing Entries

Date	Account	Debit	Credit
1992 Dec. 31	Sales	720,185.00	
	Interest Income	3,800.00	
	Rent Income	600.00	
	Income Summary		724,585.00
31	Income Summary	649,185.00	
	Sales Returns and Allowances		6,140.00
	Sales Discounts		5,790.00
	Cost of Merchandise Sold		525,305.00
	Sales Salaries Expense		60,030.00
	Advertising Expense		10,860.00
	Depreciation Exp.—Store Equip.		3,100.00
	Miscellaneous Selling Expense		630.00
	Office Salaries Expense		21,020.00
	Rent Expense		8,100.00
	Depreciation Exp.—Office Equip.		2,490.00
	Insurance Expense		1,910.00
	Office Supplies Expense		610.00
	Miscellaneous Administrative Exp.		760.00
	Interest Expense		2,440.00
31	Income Summary	75,400.00	
	Retained Earnings		75,400.00
31	Retained Earnings	18,000.00	
	Dividends		18,000.00

CHAPTER REVIEW

KEY POINTS

OBJECTIVE 1

Accounting for Merchandising Transactions

Merchandising enterprises acquire merchandise for resale to customers. It is the selling of merchandise, instead of a service, that makes the activities of merchandising enterprises differ from the activities of service enterprises. The accounting system for a merchandising enterprise must accommodate the recording of transactions between buyers and sellers of merchandise.

OBJECTIVE 1a

Accounting for Purchases

Purchases of merchandise, which may be made for cash or on account, are usually identified in the ledger as Purchases. For purchases of merchandise on account, the credit terms may allow cash discounts for early payment. Such discounts are recorded by the buyer as purchases discounts and are usually viewed as a deduction from the amount initially recorded in Purchases. Likewise, when merchandise is returned or a price adjustment is granted, the buyer records the adjustment as a purchases return and allowance.

OBJECTIVE 1b

Accounting for Sales

Merchandise sales, which may be for cash or on account, are usually identified in the ledger as Sales. The liability for the sales tax is ordinarily incurred at the time the sale is made and is recorded by the seller as a credit to the sales tax payable account. The offsetting debit will be to Accounts Receivable if the merchandise is purchased on account, or to Cash if the cash is collected at the time of the sale. The seller refers to the discounts taken by the buyer for early payment as sales discounts, which are viewed as a reduction in the amount initially recorded in Sales. Merchandise returned or an allowance for reduction in the original price at which the goods were sold is treated as a sales return or allowance. Like sales discounts, sales returns and allowances are treated as a reduction in the initial amount recorded in Sales.

OBJECTIVE 1c

Transportation Costs

The terms of a sale between a buyer and seller will include provisions concerning when ownership of the merchandise passes to the buyer and which party is to bear the cost of delivering merchandise to the buyer. If the ownership passes to the buyer when the seller delivers the merchandise to the shipper, the buyer is to absorb the transportation costs and the terms are said to be FOB shipping point. If the ownership passes to the buyer when the merchandise is received by the buyer, the seller is to assume the cost of transportation and the terms are said to be FOB destination.

OBJECTIVE 2, 3

Merchandise Inventory Systems and Cost of Merchandise Sold

Under the periodic system of accounting for merchandise, no attempt is made to record the cost of merchandise sold until the end of the period. It is only by a detailed listing of merchandise on hand (called a physical inventory) at the end of the accounting period that a determination is made of (1) the cost of merchandise sold during the period and (2) the cost of inventory on hand at the end of the period. Under the periodic system, the cost of merchandise sold and the beginning and ending inventories are reported in the income statement. Under the perpetual system of accounting for merchandise inventory, both the sales amount and the cost of merchandise sold amount are recorded when each item of merchandise is sold.

OBJECTIVE 4

Periodic Reporting for Merchandising Enterprises

The summarization and reporting procedures for a merchandising enterprise are similar to those of a service enterprise. In a merchandising enterprise, however, merchandise purchased during the period will be recorded in a purchases account. To properly match revenues and expenses, an accounting must be made for both the sold and the unsold merchandise.

The work sheet for a merchandising enterprise is completed in a similar fashion to that of a service enterprise. The primary difference is in the treatment of the beginning and ending merchandise inventories. The beginning inventory appears in the income statement debit column. The ending inventory appears in both the income statement credit and the balance sheet debit columns.

OBJECTIVE 5

Financial Statements for Merchandising Enterprises

The basic financial statements for a merchandising enterprise are the income statement, retained earnings statement, and balance sheet.

There are two widely used forms for the income statement: multiple-step and single-step. The multiple-step income statement is so called because of its many sections, subsections, and intermediate balances. The single-step income statement derives its name from the fact that the total of all expenses is deducted from the total of all revenues.

The retained earnings statement summarizes the changes that have occurred in the retained earnings account during a fiscal period. It is not unusual to add the analysis of retained earnings at the bottom of the income statement to form a combined income and retained earnings statement.

The balance sheet may be prepared using the account form or the report form. The account form lists assets on the left-hand side of the statement, with liabilities and stockholders' equity on the right-hand side. The report form lists assets, liabilities, and stockholders' equity in a downward sequence.

OBJECTIVE 6

Adjusting Entries and Closing Entries

The adjusting entries are prepared from the work sheet adjustments columns. After the adjusting entries have been posted, the balances of all asset, liability, revenue, and expense accounts correspond exactly to the amounts reported in the financial statements. The closing entries are recorded in the journal immediately following the adjusting entries. All the temporary owner's equity accounts are cleared of their balances, reducing them to zero. The final effect of closing out such balances is a net increase or decrease in the retained earnings account. The final closing entry reduces the dividends account to a zero balance by transferring it to retained earnings.

After the adjusting and closing entries have been recorded, it is advisable to take another trial balance to verify the debit-credit equality of the ledger as of the beginning of the following year.

KEY TERMS

invoice 149
cash discount 149
purchases discounts 149
purchases returns and allowances 150
debit memorandum 150
credit memorandum 150
realization principle 151
sales discounts 153
sales returns and allowances 153
FOB shipping point 154
FOB destination 155
periodic inventory system 156
perpetual inventory system 156
physical inventory 156
cost of merchandise sold 157
accrued assets 158
accrued revenues 158
unearned revenues 159
adequate disclosure 163
multiple-step income statement 163
gross profit 164
selling expenses 164
administrative expenses 164
income from operations 164
other income 164
other expense 164
net income 166
net loss 166
single-step income statement 166
report form of balance sheet 167
account form of balance sheet 167

SELF-EXAMINATION QUESTIONS

Answers at end of chapter.

1. If merchandise purchased on account is returned, the buyer may inform the seller of the details by issuing:
   A. a debit memorandum
   B. a credit memorandum
   C. an invoice
   D. a bill

2. If merchandise is sold on account to a customer for $1,000, terms FOB shipping point, 1/10, n/30, and the seller prepays $50 in transportation costs, the amount of the discount for early payment would be:
   A. $0
   B. $5.00
   C. $10.00
   D. $10.50

3. For an enterprise using the periodic inventory system, which of the following is added to merchandise inventory at the beginning of the period in computing the cost of merchandise sold?
   A. Purchases discounts
   B. Purchases returns and allowances
   C. Merchandise inventory at the end of the period
   D. None of the above.

4. The balance in Unearned Rent at the end of a period represents:
   A. an asset
   B. a liability
   C. a revenue
   D. an expense

5. On a multiple-step income statement, the excess of net sales over the cost of merchandise sold is called:
   A. operating income
   B. income from operations
   C. gross profit
   D. net income

ILLUSTRATIVE PROBLEM

A partially completed work sheet for Hadley Inc., including all adjustments, is presented on page 179.

Instructions:

1. Complete the work sheet for Hadley Inc. The merchandise inventory at October 31, 1992, as determined by a physical count, was $156,000.
2. Prepare a multiple-step income statement.
3. Prepare a retained earnings statement.
4. Prepare an account form of balance sheet, assuming that the current portion of the mortgage note payable is $7,500.
5. Journalize the adjusting entries.
6. Journalize the closing entries.

Hadley Inc.

Work Sheet

For Year Ended October 31, 1992

	ACCOUNT TITLE	TRIAL BALANCE		ADJUSTMENTS	
		DEBIT	CREDIT	DEBIT	CREDIT
1	Cash	26,400.00			
2	Notes Receivable	10,000.00			
3	Accounts Receivable	50,100.00			
4	Interest Receivable			(a) 300.00	
5	Merchandise Inventory	141,300.00			
6	Prepaid Insurance	6,800.00			(b) 4,300.00
7	Store Supplies	1,250.00			(c) 660.00
8	Office Supplies	800.00			(d) 480.00
9	Store Equipment	65,000.00			
10	Accumulated Depreciation—Store Equipment		20,100.00		(e) 5,850.00
11	Office Equipment	19,600.00			
12	Accumulated Depreciation—Office Equipment		8,100.00		(f) 2,160.00
13	Accounts Payable		31,000.00		
14	Salaries Payable				(g) 2,700.00
15	Unearned Rent		4,800.00	(h) 1,200.00	
16	Note Payable (final payment, 2001)		75,000.00		
17	Capital Stock		50,000.00		
18	Retained Earnings		63,420.00		
19	Dividends	8,000.00			
20	Sales		540,000.00		
21	Sales Returns and Allowances	4,300.00			
22	Sales Discounts	2,500.00			
23	Purchases	360,000.00			
24	Purchases Returns and Allowances		9,000.00		
25	Purchases Discounts		4,680.00		
26	Transportation In	1,800.00			
27	Sales Salaries Expense	43,200.00		(g) 1,800.00	
28	Advertising Expense	15,000.00			
29	Depreciation Expense—Store Equipment			(e) 5,850.00	
30	Store Supplies Expense			(c) 660.00	
31	Miscellaneous Selling Expense	970.00			
32	Office Salaries Expense	32,100.00		(g) 900.00	
33	Rent Expense	8,500.00			
34	Insurance Expense			(b) 4,300.00	
35	Depreciation Expense—Office Equipment			(f) 2,160.00	
36	Office Supplies Expense			(d) 480.00	
37	Miscellaneous Administrative Expense	830.00			
38	Rent Income				(h) 1,200.00
39	Interest Income		600.00		(a) 300.00
40	Interest Expense	8,250.00			
41		806,700.00	806,700.00	17,650.00	17,650.00
42	Net Income				
43					

SOLUTION

(1)

Hadley

Work

For Year Ended

	ACCOUNT TITLE	TRIAL BALANCE	
		DEBIT	CREDIT
1	Cash	26,400.00	
2	Notes Receivable	10,000.00	
3	Accounts Receivable	50,100.00	
4	Interest Receivable		
5	Merchandise Inventory	141,300.00	
6	Prepaid Insurance	6,800.00	
7	Store Supplies	1,250.00	
8	Office Supplies	800.00	
9	Store Equipment	65,000.00	
10	Accumulated Depreciation—Store Equipment		20,100.00
11	Office Equipment	19,600.00	
12	Accumulated Depreciation—Office Equipment		8,100.00
13	Accounts Payable		31,000.00
14	Salaries Payable		
15	Unearned Rent		4,800.00
16	Note Payable (final payment, 2001)		75,000.00
17	Capital Stock		50,000.00
18	Retained Earnings		63,420.00
19	Dividends	8,000.00	
20	Sales		540,000.00
21	Sales Returns and Allowances	4,300.00	
22	Sales Discounts	2,500.00	
23	Purchases	360,000.00	
24	Purchases Returns and Allowances		9,000.00
25	Purchases Discounts		4,680.00
26	Transportation In	1,800.00	
27	Sales Salaries Expense	43,200.00	
28	Advertising Expense	15,000.00	
29	Depreciation Expense—Store Equipment		
30	Store Supplies Expense		
31	Miscellaneous Selling Expense	970.00	
32	Office Salaries Expense	32,100.00	
33	Rent Expense	8,500.00	
34	Insurance Expense		
35	Depreciation Expense—Office Equipment		
36	Office Supplies Expense		
37	Miscellaneous Administrative Expense	830.00	
38	Rent Income		
39	Interest Income		600.00
40	Interest Expense	8,250.00	
41		806,700.00	806,700.00
42	Net Income		
43			

Inc.

Sheet

October 31, 1992

ADJUSTMENTS		INCOME STATEMENT		BALANCE SHEET		
DEBIT	CREDIT	DEBIT	CREDIT	DEBIT	CREDIT	
				26,400.00		1
				10,000.00		2
				50,100.00		3
(a) 300.00				300.00		4
		141,300.00	156,000.00	156,000.00		5
	(b) 4,300.00			2500.00		6
	(c) 660.00			590.00		7
	(d) 480.00			320.00		8
				65,000.00		9
	(e) 5,850.00				25,950.00	10
				19,600.00		11
	(f) 2,160.00				10,260.00	12
					31,000.00	13
	(g) 2,700.00				2,700.00	14
(h) 1,200.00					3,600.00	15
					75,000.00	16
					50,000.00	17
					63,420.00	18
				8,000.00		19
			540,000.00			20
		4,300.00				21
		2,500.00				22
		360,000.00				23
			9,000.00			24
			4,680.00			25
		1,800.00				26
(g) 1,800.00		45,000.00				27
		15,000.00				28
(e) 5,850.00		5,850.00				29
(c) 660.00		660.00				30
		970.00				31
(g) 900.00		33,000.00				32
		8,500.00				33
(b) 4,300.00		4,300.00				34
(f) 2,160.00		2,160.00				35
(d) 480.00		480.00				36
		830.00				37
	(h) 1,200.00		1,200.00			38
	(a) 300.00		900.00			39
		8,250.00				40
17,650.00	17,650.00	634,900.00	711,780.00	338,810.00	261,930.00	41
		76,880.00			76,880.00	42
		711,780.00	711,780.00	338,810.00	338,810.00	43

(2)

Hadley Inc.
Income Statement
For Year Ended October 31, 1992

Revenue from sales:				
Sales			$540,000	
Less: Sales returns and allowances		$ 4,300		
Sales discounts		2,500	6,800	
Net sales				$533,200
Cost of merchandise sold:				
Merchandise inventory, November 1, 1991			$141,300	
Purchases		$360,000		
Less: Purchases returns and allowances	$9,000			
Purchases discounts	4,680	13,680		
Net purchases		$346,320		
Add transportation in		1,800		
Cost of merchandise purchased			348,120	
Merchandise available for sale			$489,420	
Less merchandise inventory, October 31, 1992			156,000	
Cost of merchandise sold				333,420
Gross profit				$199,780
Operating expenses:				
Selling expenses:				
Sales salaries expense		$45,000		
Advertising expense		15,000		
Depreciation expense—store equipment		5,850		
Store supplies expense		660		
Miscellaneous selling expense		970		
Total selling expenses			$ 67,480	
Administrative expenses:				
Office salaries expense		$ 33,000		
Rent expense		8,500		
Insurance expense		4,300		
Depreciation expense—office equipment		2,160		
Office supplies expense		480		
Miscellaneous administrative expense		830		
Total administrative expenses			49,270	
Total operating expenses				116,750
Income from operations				$ 83,030
Other income:				
Rent income		$ 1,200		
Interest income		900		
Total other income			$ 2,100	
Other expense:				
Interest expense			8,250	6,150
Net income				$ 76,880

(3)

Hadley Inc.
Retained Earnings Statement
For Year Ended October 31, 1992

Retained earnings, November 1, 1991		$ 63,420
Net income for the year	$76,880	
Less dividends	8,000	
Increase in retained earnings		68,880
Retained earnings, October 31, 1992		$132,300

(4) See page 184.

(5)

Adjusting Entries

Date	Account	Debit	Credit
1992 Oct. 31	Interest Receivable	300.00	
	Interest Income		300.00
31	Insurance Expense	4,300.00	
	Prepaid Insurance		4,300.00
31	Store Supplies Expense	660.00	
	Store Supplies		660.00
31	Office Supplies Expense	480.00	
	Office Supplies		480.00
31	Depr. Expense—Store Equipment	5,850.00	
	Accumulated Depr.—Store Equip.		5,850.00
31	Depr. Expense—Office Equipment	2,160.00	
	Accumulated Depr.—Office Equip.		2,160.00
31	Sales Salaries Expense	1,800.00	
	Office Salaries Expense	900.00	
	Salaries Payable		2,700.00
31	Unearned Rent	1,200.00	
	Rent Income		1,200.00

(4)

Hadley
Balance
October 31

Assets			
Current assets:			
Cash		$ 26,400	
Notes receivable		10,000	
Accounts receivable		50,100	
Interest receivable		300	
Merchandise inventory		156,000	
Prepaid insurance		2,500	
Store supplies		590	
Office supplies		320	
Total current assets			$246,210
Plant assets:			
Store equipment	$65,000		
Less accumulated depreciation	25,950	$39,050	
Office equipment	$19,600		
Less accumulated depreciation	10,260	9,340	
Total plant assets			48,390
Total assets			$294,600

(6)

Closing Entries

Date	Account	Debit	Credit
1992 Oct. 31	Merchandise Inventory	156,000.00	
	Sales	540,000.00	
	Purchases Returns and Allowances	9,000.00	
	Purchases Discounts	4,680.00	
	Rent Income	1,200.00	
	Interest Income	900.00	
	Income Summary		711,780.00
31	Income Summary	634,900.00	
	Merchandise Inventory		141,300.00
	Sales Returns and Allowances		4,300.00
	Sales Discounts		2,500.00
	Purchases		360,000.00
	Transportation In		1,800.00
	Sales Salaries Expense		45,000.00
	Advertising Expense		15,000.00
	Depr. Expense—Store Equipment		5,850.00
	Store Supplies Expense		660.00
	Miscellaneous Selling Expense		970.00
	Office Salaries Expense		33,000.00
	Rent Expense		8,500.00
	Insurance Expense		4,300.00
	Depr. Expense—Office Equipment		2,160.00
	Office Supplies Expense		480.00
	Miscellaneous Administrative Exp.		830.00
	Interest Expense		8,250.00
31	Income Summary	76,880.00	
	Retained Earnings		76,880.00
31	Retained Earnings	8,000.00	
	Dividends		8,000.00

Inc.
Sheet
1992

Liabilities		
Current liabilities:		
Accounts payable	$ 31,000	
Note payable (current portion)	7,500	
Salaries payable	2,700	
Unearned rent	3,600	
Total current liabilities		$ 44,800
Long-term liabilities:		
Note payable (final payment, 2001)		67,500
Total liabilities		$112,300
Stockholders' Equity		
Capital stock	$ 50,000	
Retained earnings	132,300	
Total stockholders' equity		182,300
Total liabilities and stockholders' equity		$294,600

DISCUSSION QUESTIONS

4–1. What distinguishes a merchandising enterprise from a service enterprise?

4–2. What is the name of the account in which purchases of merchandise are recorded?

4–3. The credit period during which the purchaser of merchandise is allowed to pay usually begins with what date?

4–4. Pruitt Inc. ordered $5,000 of merchandise on account on May 12, terms 2/10, n/30. Although the supplier shipped the merchandise on May 13, the merchandise was not received by Pruitt Inc. until May 16. The invoice received with the merchandise by Pruitt Inc. was dated May 13. What is the last date Pruitt Inc. could pay the invoice and still receive the discount?

4–5. What is the meaning of (a) 2/10, n/60; (b) n/30; (c) n/eom?

4–6. What is the term applied to discounts for early payment by (a) the buyer; (b) the seller?

4–7. Carter Company purchased merchandise on account from a supplier for $5,000, terms 1/10, n/30. Carter Company returned $500 of the merchandise and received full credit. (a) If Carter Company pays the invoice within the discount period, what is the amount of cash required for the payment? (b) What accounts are credited by Carter Company to record the return and the cash discount?

4–8. The debits and credits from four related transactions are presented in the following T accounts. (a) Describe each transaction. (b) What is the rate of the discount and on what amount was it computed?

Cash

		(2)	175
		(4)	6,860

Accounts Payable

(3)	500	(1)	7,500
(4)	7,000		

Purchases

(1)	7,500		

Purchases Discounts

		(4)	140

Transportation In

(2)	175		

Purchases Returns and Allowances

		(3)	500

4–9. How does the accounting for sales to customers using bank credit cards, such as MasterCard and VISA, differ from accounting for sales to customers using nonbank credit cards, such as American Express?

4–10. A sale of merchandise on account for $500 is subject to a 6% sales tax. (a) Should the sales tax be recorded at the time of sale or when payment is received? (b) What is the amount of the sale? (c) What is the amount debited to Accounts Receivable? (d) What is the title of the account to which the $30 is credited?

4–11. After the amount due on a sale of $2,000, terms 2/10, n/eom, is received from a customer within the discount period, the seller consents to the return of the entire shipment. (a) What is the amount of the refund owed to the customer? (b) What accounts should be debited and credited by the seller to record the return and the refund?

4–12. Who bears the transportation costs when the terms of sale are (a) FOB shipping point, (b) FOB destination?

4–13. Merchandise is sold on account to a customer for $10,000, terms FOB shipping point, 2/10, n/30, the seller paying the transportation costs of $400. Determine the following: (a) amount of the sale, (b) amount debited to Accounts Receivable, (c) amount of the discount for early payment, (d) amount of the remittance due within the discount period.

4–14. A retailer is considering the purchase of 20 units of a specific commodity from either of two suppliers. Their offers are as follows:
A: $100 a unit, total of $2,000, 2/10, n/30, plus transportation costs of $250.
B: $110 a unit, total of $2,200, 1/10, n/30, no charge for transportation.
Which of the two offers, A or B, yields the lower price?

4–15. In which type of system for accounting for merchandise held for sale is there no attempt to record the cost of merchandise sold until the end of the period, when a physical inventory is taken?

4–16. In which type of system for accounting for merchandise held for sale do the accounting records continuously disclose the inventory on hand?

4–17. The account Merchandise Inventory is listed at $225,000 on the trial balance (before adjustments) as of July 31, the end of the first month in the fiscal year. Which one of the following phrases describes the item correctly?

(a) Inventory of merchandise at July 1, beginning of the month.
(b) Purchases of merchandise during July.
(c) Merchandise available for sale during July.
(d) Inventory of merchandise at July 31, end of the month.
(e) Cost of merchandise sold during July.

4–18. On January 2, an enterprise received $24,000 from a tenant as rent for the current calendar year and credited Unearned Rent for $24,000. The fiscal year of the enterprise is from April 1 to March 31. On March 31 of the current year, the enterprise has accrued fees income of $16,500. Prepare the adjusting entry on March 31 of the current year for (a) unearned revenues, (b) accrued assets.

4–19. What basic accounting principle requires that the financial statements and their accompanying notes contain all of the pertinent data essential to the readers' understanding of an enterprise's financial status?

4–20. The following revenues and expenses were recorded by a merchandising enterprise during the year. In which revenue or expense section of the income statement should each be reported: (a) selling, (b) administrative, or (c) other?
(1) Interest income on notes receivable.
(2) Salaries of office personnel.
(3) Insurance expense on store equipment.
(4) Advertising expense.
(5) Office supplies used.
(6) Depreciation expense on office equipment.
(7) Rent expense on office building.
(8) Salary of sales manager.

4–21. Differentiate between the multiple-step and the single-step forms of the income statement.

4–22. What major advantages and disadvantages does the single-step form of income statement have in comparison to the multiple-step statement?

4–23. (a) What two financial statements are frequently combined and presented as a single statement? (b) What is the major criticism directed at the combined statement?

4–24. Describe the four entries made from the work sheet to close the accounts of a merchandising enterprise.

Real World Focus

4–25. It is not unusual for a customer to drive into a Texaco or Mobil gasoline station and discover that the cash price per gallon is 3 or 4 cents lower than the credit price per gallon. As a result, many customers pay cash rather than use their credit cards. Why would a gasoline station owner establish such a policy?

Real World Focus

4–26. A recent trend in retailing is the establishment of warehouse clubs. These clubs offer name-brand merchandise at prices ranging from 20 to 40 percent below discount store prices to their members who pay a nominal yearly fee. The Price Club, with projected annual sales of over $1 billion, is one of the leaders in this growing area of retailing. The following graph compares the gross profit as a percent of sales of The Price Club with that of K Mart Corp.:

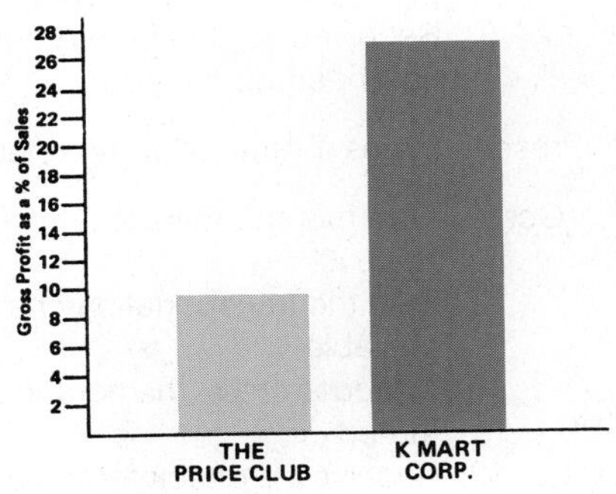

How can the Price Club remain profitable with a gross profit percentage less than one half that of K Mart Corp.?

Ethics Discussion Case

4–27. On March 1, 1992, Henning Inc. purchased $10,000 of merchandise, terms 2/10, n/30, from Dodson Company. Even though the discount period had expired on March 15, 1992, Kay Williams subtracted the discount of $200 when she processed the documents for payment by the treasurer.

Discuss whether Kay Williams behaved in an ethical manner by subtracting the discount, even though the discount period had expired.

EXERCISES

Ex. 4–28.
Purchase-related transactions.
OBJ. 1

Kramer Co. purchases $5,000 of merchandise from a supplier on account, terms FOB shipping point, 1/10, n/30. The supplier adds transportation charges of $180 to the invoice. Kramer Co. returns some of the merchandise, receiving a credit memorandum for $500, and then pays the amount due within the discount period. Present Kramer Co.'s entries to record (a) the purchase, (b) the merchandise return, and (c) the payment.

Ex. 4–29.
Determination of amounts to be paid on invoices.
OBJ. 1

Determine the amount to be paid in full settlement of each of the following invoices, assuming that credit for returns and allowances was received prior to payment and that all invoices were paid within the discount period.

	Purchase Invoice			
	Merchandise	Transportation	Terms	Returns and Allowances
(a)	$8,000	—	FOB destination, n/30	$ 500
(b)	5,000	—	FOB destination, 1/10, n/30	—
(c)	7,500	—	FOB shipping point, 2/10, n/30	1,000
(d)	4,000	$50	FOB shipping point, 1/10, n/30	100
(e)	4,750	90	FOB shipping point, 2/10, n/30	750

Ex. 4–30.
Sales-related transactions, including the use of credit cards.
OBJ. 1

Present entries for the following transactions of C.D. McDonald Inc.:

(a) Sold merchandise for cash, $7,500.
(b) Sold merchandise on account, $16,000.
(c) Sold merchandise to customers who used MasterCard and VISA, $4,250.
(d) Sold merchandise to customers who used American Express, $2,750.
(e) Paid an invoice from First National Bank for $250, representing a service fee for processing of MasterCard and VISA sales.
(f) Received $2,590 from American Express Company after a $160 collection fee had been deducted.

Ex. 4–31.
Sales-related transactions.
OBJ. 1

Present entries for the following related transactions:

Oct. 2. Sold merchandise to a customer for $10,000, terms FOB shipping point, 1/10, n/30.
2. Paid the transportation charges of $195, debiting the amount to Accounts Receivable.
6. Issued a credit memorandum for $1,000 to the customer for merchandise returned.
12. Received a check for the amount due from the sale.

Ex. 4–32.
Sales-related transactions.
OBJ. 1

Tavel Corp. sells merchandise to Graf Co. on account, $8,500, FOB shipping point, 1/10, n/30. Tavel Corp. pays the transportation charges of $250 as an accommodation and adds it to the invoice. Tavel Corp. issues a credit memorandum for $500 for merchandise returned and subsequently receives the amount due within the discount period. Present Tavel Corp.'s entries to record (a) the sale and the transportation costs, (b) the credit memorandum, and (c) the receipt of the check for the amount due.

Ex. 4–33.
Purchase-related transactions.
OBJ. 1

Based upon the data presented in Exercise 4–32, present Graf Co.'s entries to record (a) the purchase, including the transportation charges, (b) the return of the merchandise for credit, and (c) the payment of the invoice within the discount period.

Ex. 4–34.
Purchase-related transactions.
OBJ. 1

Present entries for the following related transactions of R & R Inc.:

(a) Purchased $9,000 of merchandise from Baxter Co. on account, terms 2/10, n/30.
(b) Paid the amount owed on the invoice within the discount period.
(c) Discovered that some of the merchandise was defective and returned items with an invoice price of $1,000, receiving credit.
(d) Purchased an additional $750 of merchandise from Baxter Co. on account, terms 2/10, n/30.
(e) Received a check for the balance owed from the return in (c), after deducting for the purchase in (d).

Ex. 4–35.
Sales tax-related transactions.
OBJ. 1

Present entries to record the following related transactions of Collier Electric Co.:

(a) Purchased merchandise on account, $15,000, terms 2/10, n/30.
(b) Sold $3,000 of merchandise on account, subject to a sales tax of 6%.
(c) Paid the amount owed in (a) within the discount period.
(d) Paid $1,650 to the state revenue department for sales taxes collected.

Ex. 4–36.
Cost of merchandise sold section of income statement.
OBJ. 3

On the basis of the following data, prepare the cost of merchandise sold section of the income statement for the fiscal year ended July 31, 1993, for Coldwell Inc.

Merchandise Inventory, July 31, 1993	$125,000
Merchandise Inventory, August 1, 1992	115,000
Purchases	550,000
Purchases Returns and Allowances	4,250
Purchases Discounts	3,200
Transportation In	3,950

Ex. 4–37.
Adjusting entries for unearned revenues and accrued assets.
OBJ. 4

In their first year of operations, the Buckley Gazette received $172,500 from magazine subscriptions, crediting the amount to Unearned Subscriptions. At the end of the year, $47,500 was unearned. Also at the end of the year, interest accrued on notes receivable was $320. Prepare the two adjusting entries that should be made at the end of the year.

Ex. 4–38.
Identification of items missing from income statement.
OBJ. 5

For (a) through (i), identify the items designated by "X".

(a) Sales − (X + X) = Net sales
(b) Purchases − (X + X) = Net purchases
(c) Net purchases + X = Cost of merchandise purchased
(d) Merchandise inventory (beginning) + cost of merchandise purchased = X
(e) Merchandise available for sale − X = Cost of merchandise sold
(f) Net sales − cost of merchandise sold = X
(g) X + X = Operating expenses
(h) Gross profit − operating expenses = X
(i) Income from operations + X − X = Net income

Ex. 4–39.
Determination of amounts for items omitted from income statement.
OBJ. 5

Three items are omitted in each of the following tabulations of income statement data. Determine the amounts of the missing items, identifying them by letter.

Sales	$ (a)	$575,000	$985,000	$755,000
Sales returns and allowances	12,000	17,000	(g)	28,000
Sales discounts	2,000	8,000	5,000	(j)
Net sales	110,000	(d)	965,000	(k)
Beginning inventory	(b)	125,000	215,000	(l)
Cost of merchandise purchased	70,000	(e)	600,000	580,000
Ending inventory	30,000	105,000	(h)	120,000
Cost of merchandise sold	65,000	340,000	(i)	540,000
Gross profit	(c)	(f)	390,000	180,000

Ex. 4–40.
Single-step income statement.
OBJ. 5

Summary operating data for X-L Inc. during the current year ended September 30, 1993, are as follows: cost of merchandise sold, $895,000; administrative expenses, $150,000; interest expense, $27,500; rent income, $30,000; net sales, $1,470,000; and selling expenses, $205,000. Prepare a single-step income statement.

Ex. 4–41.
Combined income and retained earnings statement.
OBJ. 5

From the data presented in Exercise 4–40 and assuming that the balance of Retained Earnings was $425,000 on October 1, 1992, and that $80,000 of dividends were paid during the year, prepare a combined income and retained earnings statement for X-L Inc. (Use the single-step form for the income statement portion.)

Ex. 4–42.
Closing entries.
OBJ. 6

After all revenue and expense accounts have been closed at the end of the fiscal year, Income Summary has a debit of $919,750 and a credit of $987,500. As of the same date, Retained Earnings has a credit balance of $310,600, and Dividends has a balance of $25,000. (a) Journalize the entries required to complete the closing of the acounts. (b) State the amount of Retained Earnings at the end of the period.

Ex. 4–43.
Multiple-step income statement and closing entries.
OBJ. 5, 6

Selected account titles and related amounts appearing in the income statement and balance sheet columns of the work sheet of Shuman Company for the year ended December 31 are listed in alphabetical order as follows:

Administrative Expenses	$ 87,200
Building	295,000
Capital Stock	300,000
Cash	60,600
Dividends	55,000
Interest Expense	2,500
Merchandise Inventory (1/1)	225,000
Merchandise Inventory (12/31)	230,000
Notes Payable	25,000
Office Supplies	8,500
Purchases	850,000
Purchases Discounts	8,000
Purchases Returns and Allowances	12,000
Retained Earnings	148,080
Salaries Payable	3,720
Sales	1,275,000
Sales Discounts	9,500
Sales Returns and Allowances	35,000
Selling Expenses	125,000
Store Supplies	7,200
Transportation In	11,300

All selling expenses have been recorded in the account entitled "Selling Expenses," and all administrative expenses have been recorded in the account entitled "Administrative Expenses."

(a) Prepare a multiple-step income statement for the year.
(b) Determine the amount of retained earnings to be reported in the balance sheet at the end of the year.
(c) Journalize the closing entries.

Appendix
Ex. 4–44.
Sales-related transactions—perpetual inventory system.

Coyles Corp. sells merchandise to Westbury Inc. on account, $6,900, 2/15, n/30. The cost of the merchandise sold was $3,900. Coyles Corp. issues a credit memorandum for $750 for merchandise returned and subsequently receives the amount due within the discount period. The cost of the merchandise returned was $450. Assuming that Coyles Corp. uses the perpetual inventory system, present Coyles Corp.'s entries to record (a) the sale, including the cost of the merchandise sold, (b) the credit memorandum, including the cost of the returned merchandise, and (c) the receipt of the check for the amount due.

Appendix
Ex. 4–45.
Purchase-related transactions—perpetual inventory system.

Based upon the data presented in Ex. 4–44, present Westbury Inc.'s entries using the perpetual inventory system to record (a) the purchase, (b) the return of the merchandise for credit, and (c) the payment of the invoice within the discount period.

Appendix
Ex. 4–46.
Single-step income statement and closing entries—perpetual inventory system.

Selected account titles and related amounts appearing in the income statement and balance sheet columns of the work sheet of Kelly Inc. for the year ended March 31 are listed in alphabetical order as follows:

Account	Amount
Administrative Expenses	$ 42,300
Building	147,500
Capital Stock	120,000
Cash	30,200
Cost of Merchandise Sold	382,500
Dividends	15,000
Interest Expense	3,600
Interest Income	5,000
Merchandise Inventory	112,000
Notes Payable	30,000
Office Supplies	6,200
Retained Earnings	80,590
Salaries Payable	2,810
Sales	637,500
Sales Discounts	11,200
Sales Returns and Allowances	21,750
Selling Expense	95,600
Store Supplies	8,050

All selling expenses have been recorded in the account entitled "Selling Expenses," and all administrative expenses have been recorded in the account entitled "Administrative Expenses." Kelly Inc. uses the perpetual inventory system.

(a) Prepare a single-step income statement for the year.
(b) Determine the amount of retained earnings to be reported in the balance sheet at the end of the year.
(c) Journalize the closing entries.

PROBLEMS

Pb. 4–47.
Purchase-related and sales-related transactions.
OBJ. 1

The following selected transactions were completed during July between Norman Company and Ruiz Inc.:

July 2. Norman Company sold merchandise on account to Ruiz Inc., $15,000, terms FOB shipping point, 1/10, n/30. Norman Company prepaid transportation costs of $500 which were added to the invoice.
8. Norman Company sold merchandise on account to Ruiz Inc., $10,000, terms FOB destination, 1/15, n/eom.
8. Norman Company paid transportation costs of $300 for delivery of merchandise sold to Ruiz Inc. on July 8.
11. Ruiz Inc. returned merchandise purchased on account on July 8 from Norman Company, $4,000.
12. Ruiz Inc. paid Norman Company for purchases of July 2, less discount.
23. Ruiz Inc. paid Norman Company for purchases of July 8, less discount and less return of July 11.
23. Norman Company sold merchandise on account to Ruiz Inc., $8,000, terms FOB shipping point, n/eom.
24. Ruiz Inc. paid transportation charges of $300 on July 23 purchase from Norman Company.
31. Ruiz Inc. paid Norman Company on account for purchases of July 23.

Instructions:

Journalize the July transactions for (1) Norman Company and (2) Ruiz Inc.

Pb. 4–48.
Purchase-related and sales-related transactions.
OBJ. 1

The following were selected from among the transactions completed by Varro Company during May of the current year:

May 1. Purchased merchandise on account from Green Inc., $5,000, terms FOB shipping point, 2/10, n/30, with prepaid transportation costs of $225 added to the invoice.
5. Purchased merchandise on account from Faulk Co., $7,500; terms FOB destination, 1/10, n/30.
6. Sold merchandise on account to R & R Inc., $4,100, terms 2/10, n/30.
8. Purchased office supplies for cash, $475.
10. Returned merchandise purchased on May 5 from Faulk Co., $1,500.
11. Paid Green Inc. on account for purchases of May 1, less discount.
14. Purchased merchandise for cash, $14,000.
15. Paid Faulk Co. on account for purchases of May 5, less return of May 10 and discount.
16. Received cash on account from sale of May 6 to R & R Inc., less discount.
21. Sold merchandise on nonbank credit cards and reported accounts to the card company, $3,750.
22. Sold merchandise on account to Comer Co., $3,480, terms 2/10, n/30.
26. Sold merchandise for cash, $6,125.
26. Received merchandise returned by Comer Co. from sale of May 22, $1,480.
30. Received cash from card company for nonbank credit card sales of May 21, less $215 service fee.

Instructions:

Journalize the transactions.

Pb. 4–49.
Purchase-related and sales-related transactions; ledger accounts.
OBJ. 1
SOLUTIONS SOFTWARE

The account balances at June 1 of the current year of Allen Company are as follows:

11	Cash	$17,990
12	Accounts Receivable	32,350
13	Merchandise Inventory	81,100
14	Prepaid Insurance	3,000
15	Store Supplies	2,200

21	Accounts Payable	$28,300
31	Capital Stock	75,000
32	Retained Earnings	33,340
33	Dividends	—
41	Sales	—
42	Sales Returns and Allowances	—
43	Sales Discounts	—
51	Purchases	—
52	Purchases Returns and Allowances	—
53	Purchases Discounts	—
54	Transportation In	—
55	Sales Salaries Expense	—
56	Advertising Expense	—
57	Store Supplies Expense	—
58	Miscellaneous Selling Expense	—
59	Office Salaries Expense	—
60	Rent Expense	—
61	Insurance Expense	—
62	Miscellaneous Administrative Expense	—

The following transactions were completed during June of the current year:

June 1. Paid rent for month, $3,000.
2. Purchased merchandise on account, $12,500.
4. Purchased merchandise on account, FOB shipping point, $20,100.
7. Sold merchandise on account, $16,000.
9. Paid transportation charges on the purchase of June 4, $525.
10. Received $12,250 cash from customers on account, after discounts of $250 were deducted.
11. Paid creditors $16,700 on account, after discounts of $280 had been deducted.
14. Sold merchandise for cash, $9,500.
15. Received merchandise returned on account, $800.
16. Paid sales salaries of $3,950 and office salaries of $1,280.
17. Paid creditors $12,750 on account, after discounts of $200 had been deducted.
18. Received $9,800 cash from customers on account, after discounts of $200 had been deducted.
21. Purchased merchandise on account, $15,200.
22. Paid advertising expense, $4,250.
23. Sold merchandise for cash, $11,600.
24. Returned merchandise purchased on account, $2,200.
25. Sold merchandise on account, $30,200.
28. Sold merchandise for cash, $8,200.
28. Refunded $350 cash on sales made for cash.
29. Paid sales salaries of $3,800 and office salaries of $1,280.
30. Paid creditors $10,900 on account, no discount.
30. Received $12,500 cash from customers on account, no discount.

Instructions:

(1) Open a ledger of standard accounts for the accounts listed. Record the balances in the appropriate balance column as of June 1, write "Balance" in the item section, and place a check mark (✔) in the posting reference column.
(2) Record the transactions for June.
(3) Post to the ledger, extending the month-end balances to the appropriate balance columns after all posting is completed.
(4) Prepare a trial balance of the ledger as of June 30.

4-194 **Pb. 4–50.**

Work sheet; cost of merchandise sold section.

OBJ. 3, 4

The accounts and their balances in the ledger of Miller Company on December 31 of the current year are as follows:

Cash	$ 38,500
Notes Receivable	5,000
Accounts Receivable	83,300
Interest Receivable	—
Merchandise Inventory	113,800
Prepaid Insurance	9,500
Store Supplies	2,300
Office Supplies	1,500
Store Equipment	86,600
Accumulated Depreciation—Store Equipment	28,000
Office Equipment	29,300
Accumulated Depreciation—Office Equipment	12,000
Accounts Payable	89,500
Salaries Payable	—
Unearned Rent	2,400
Note Payable (due 1999)	100,000
Capital Stock	50,000
Retained Earnings	29,800
Dividends	48,000
Sales	760,000
Sales Returns and Allowances	12,000
Sales Discounts	7,500
Purchases	500,000
Purchases Returns and Allowances	12,500
Purchases Discounts	6,500
Transportation In	2,400
Sales Salaries Expense	64,000
Advertising Expense	18,000
Depreciation Expense—Store Equipment	—
Store Supplies Expense	—
Miscellaneous Selling Expense	1,400
Office Salaries Expense	31,000
Rent Expense	24,000
Depreciation Expense—Office Equipment	—
Insurance Expense	—
Office Supplies Expense	—
Miscellaneous Administrative Expense	1,100
Rent Income	—
Interest Income	—
Interest Expense	11,500

The data for year-end adjustments on December 31 are as follows:

Interest accrued on notes receivable on December 31		$ 100
Insurance expired during the year		6,900
Inventory of supplies on December 31:		
Store supplies		900
Office supplies		500
Depreciation for the year:		
Store equipment		8,100
Office equipment		3,000
Salaries payable on December 31:		
Sales salaries	$2,500	
Office salaries	1,200	3,700
Rent income earned for the year		600

Instructions:

(1) Prepare a work sheet for the fiscal year ended December 31. The merchandise inventory on December 31 is $107,500.
(2) Prepare the cost of merchandise sold section of the income statement from the data presented in the income statement columns of the work sheet.

Pb. 4–51.
Preparation of multiple-step income statement and account form of balance sheet.
OBJ. 5
SOLUTIONS SOFTWARE

The following selected accounts and their normal balances appear in the income statement and balance sheet columns of the work sheet of Wilcox Inc. for the fiscal year ended December 31, 1992:

Cash	$ 87,250
Notes Receivable	50,000
Accounts Receivable	97,000
Interest Receivable	500
Merchandise Inventory, Jan. 1, 1992	75,000
Merchandise Inventory, Dec. 31, 1992	85,000
Office Supplies	2,600
Prepaid Insurance	9,800
Office Equipment	27,750
Accumulated Depreciation—Office Equipment	10,800
Store Equipment	50,000
Accumulated Depreciation—Store Equipment	18,900
Accounts Payable	34,000
Salaries Payable	2,500
Unearned Rent	1,000
Note Payable (final payment, 2002)	25,000
Capital Stock	150,000
Retained Earnings	138,210
Dividends	25,000
Sales	975,000
Sales Returns and Allowances	9,000
Sales Discounts	8,500
Purchases	775,000
Purchases Returns and Allowances	16,200
Purchases Discounts	3,800
Transportation In	10,300
Sales Salaries Expense	83,000
Advertising Expense	16,300
Depreciation Expense—Store Equipment	4,800
Miscellaneous Selling Expense	1,000
Office Salaries Expense	25,900
Rent Expense	12,150
Depreciation Expense—Office Equipment	3,500
Insurance Expense	2,750
Office Supplies Expense	900
Miscellaneous Administrative Expense	1,150
Interest Income	5,000
Rent Income	2,000
Interest Expense	3,260

Instructions:

(1) Prepare a multiple-step income statement.
(2) Prepare a retained earnings statement.
(3) Prepare an account form of balance sheet, assuming that the current portion of the note payable is $2,500.

Pb. 4–52.
Preparation of single-step income statement and combined income and retained earnings statement.
OBJ. 5

Selected accounts and related amounts for Wilcox Inc. for the fiscal year ended December 31, 1992, are presented in Pb. 4–51.

Instructions:

(1) Prepare a single-step income statement.
(2) Prepare a combined income and retained earnings statement, using the single-step form for the income statement portion.

Pb. 4–53.
Combined income and retained earnings statement; balance sheet.

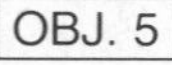

The following data for Marr Co. were selected from the ledger after adjustment at December 31, the end of the current fiscal year:

Account	Amount
Accounts payable	$ 70,900
Accounts receivable	161,100
Accumulated depreciation—office equipment	40,800
Accumulated Depreciation—store equipment	75,200
Administrative expenses	247,250
Capital stock	200,000
Cash	105,600
Cost of merchandise sold	825,500
Dividends	75,000
Dividends payable	15,000
Interest expense	18,000
Merchandise inventory	200,000
Note payable (due in 2003)	150,000
Office equipment	72,200
Prepaid insurance	10,700
Rent income	15,500
Retained earnings	156,100
Salaries payable	9,750
Sales	1,470,000
Selling expenses	283,250
Store equipment	204,650

Instructions:

(1) Prepare a combined income and retained earnings statement, using the single-step form for the income statement portion.
(2) Prepare a balance sheet in account form.

If the working papers correlating with this textbook are not used, omit Pb. 4–54.

Pb. 4–54.
Completion of work sheet and preparation of financial statements
OBJ. 4, 5

A partially completed work sheet for Magan Inc. is presented in the working papers. All adjustments have been entered on the work sheet.

Instructions:

(1) Complete the work sheet.
(2) Prepare a multiple-step income statement.
(3) Prepare a retained earnings statement.
(4) Prepare a report form of balance sheet, assuming that the current portion of the note payable is $10,000.

Pb. 4–55.
Closing entries from work sheet.
OBJ. 6

The account balances taken from the Income Statement columns of the work sheet for Wagner Corporation at the end of the current fiscal year are as follows:

	Debit	Credit
Merchandise Inventory	260,500	241,650
Sales		1,240,700
Sales Returns and Allowances	31,400	
Sales Discounts	12,900	
Purchases	770,650	
Purchases Returns and Allowances		18,050
Purchases Discounts		8,600
Transportation In	12,100	
Sales Salaries Expense	120,750	
Depreciation Expense—Store Equipment	11,800	
Supplies Expense	2,040	
Miscellaneous Selling Expense	1,600	
Office Salaries Expense	50,300	
Rent Expense	38,600	
Heating and Lighting Expense	13,420	
Insurance Expense	11,500	
Depreciation Expense—Office Equipment	5,180	
Miscellaneous Administrative Expense	1,900	
Interest Expense	21,600	
	1,361,240	1,509,000

Instructions:

Journalize the closing entries, assuming that the balance in the dividends account at the end of the current fiscal year was $60,000.

Pb. 4–56.
Preparation of work sheet, financial statements, and adjusting and closing entries.
OBJ. 4, 5, 6

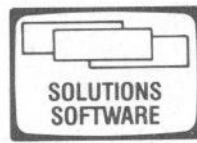

The accounts and their balances in the ledger of Gove Company on December 31 of the current year are as follows:

Cash	$ 61,075
Notes Receivable	15,000
Accounts Receivable	99,600
Interest Receivable	—
Merchandise Inventory	180,000
Prepaid Insurance	10,600
Store Supplies	3,750
Office Supplies	1,700
Store Equipment	115,000
Accumulated Depreciation—Store Equipment	40,300
Office Equipment	52,000
Accumulated Depreciation—Office Equipment	17,200
Accounts Payable	66,700
Salaries Payable	—
Unearned Rent	1,200
Note Payable (final payment, 1999)	105,000
Capital Stock	150,000
Retained Earnings	70,510
Dividends	40,000
Sales	997,500
Sales Returns and Allowances	15,000
Sales Discounts	6,500
Purchases	637,500
Purchases Returns and Allowances	9,500
Purchases Discounts	8,000
Transportation In	6,200
Sales Salaries Expense	86,400
Advertising Expense	29,450
Depreciation Expense—Store Equipment	—

Store Supplies Expense	—
Miscellaneous Selling Expense	$ 1,885
Office Salaries Expense	60,000
Rent Expense	30,000
Insurance Expense	—
Depreciation Expense—Office Equipment	—
Office Supplies Expense	—
Miscellaneous Administrative Expense	1,650
Rent Income	—
Interest Income	—
Interest Expense	12,600

The data for year-end adjustments on December 31 are as follows:

Interest accrued on notes receivable on December 31		$ 150
Insurance expired during the year		7,260
Inventory of supplies on December 31:		
Store supplies		1,700
Office supplies		400
Depreciation for the year:		
Store equipment		9,500
Office equipment		4,800
Salaries payable on December 31:		
Sales salaries	$2,750	
Office salaries	1,150	3,900
Unearned rent on December 31		400

Instructions:

(1) Prepare a work sheet for the fiscal year ended December 31, listing all accounts in the order given. The merchandise inventory on December 31 is $220,000.
(2) Prepare a multiple-step income statement.
(3) Prepare a retained earnings statement.
(4) Prepare a report form of balance sheet, assuming that the current portion of the note payable is $15,000.
(5) Journalize the adjusting entries.
(6) Journalize the closing entries.

Appendix
Pb. 4–57.
Purchase-related and sales-related transactions—perpetual inventory system.

The following were selected from among the transactions completed by Curran Corp. during May of the current year. Curran Corp. uses the perpetual inventory system.

May 4. Purchased merchandise on account from Godwin Co., $12,000, terms FOB destination, 1/10, n/30.
7. Purchased merchandise on account from Berry Inc., $5,800, terms FOB shipping point, 2/15, n/30, with prepaid transportation costs of $120 added to the invoice.
8. Sold merchandise on account to E. G. Drews Co., $3,000, terms 2/10, n/30. The cost of the merchandise sold was $1,800.
9. Purchased office supplies for cash, $380.
10. Returned merchandise purchased on May 4 from Godwin Co., $1,500.
14. Paid Godwin Co. on account for purchases of May 4, less return of May 10 and discount.
15. Purchased merchandise for cash, $6,980.
18. Received cash on account from sale of May 8 to E. G. Drews Co., less discount.
19. Sold merchandise on nonbank credit cards and reported accounts to the card company, $6,300. The cost of the merchandise sold was $3,780.
22. Paid Berry Inc. on account for purchases of May 7, less discount.
23. Sold merchandise on account to Stevens Inc., $2,750, terms 2/10, n/30. The cost of the merchandise sold was $1,650.

May 24. Sold merchandise for cash, $1,350. The cost of the merchandise sold was $800.
29. Received merchandise returned by Stevens Inc. from sale of May 23, $1,200. The cost of the returned merchandise was $720.
31. Received cash from card company for nonbank credit card sales of May 19, less $315 service fee.

Instructions:

Journalize the transactions.

Appendix
Pb. 4–58.
Work sheet using perpetual inventory system.

The accounts in the ledger of Iyer Inc., with the unadjusted balances on July 31, the end of the current fiscal year, are as follows:

Cash	$ 18,500
Notes Receivable	50,000
Accounts Receivable	53,340
Merchandise Inventory	80,000
Prepaid Insurance	4,200
Store Supplies	2,100
Store Equipment	164,200
Accumulated Depreciation—Store Equipment	84,600
Accounts Payable	32,000
Salaries Payable	—
Unearned Rent	7,600
Capital Stock	150,000
Retained Earnings	91,640
Dividends	16,000
Sales	790,500
Cost of Merchandise Sold	474,300
Sales Salaries Expense	79,800
Advertising Expense	34,850
Depreciation Expense—Store Equipment	—
Store Supplies Expense	—
Miscellaneous Selling Expense	1,600
Office Salaries Expense	83,700
Rent Expense	45,000
Heating and Lighting Expense	37,400
Taxes Expense	7,850
Insurance Expense	—
Miscellaneous Administrative Expense	3,500
Rent Income	—

The data needed for year-end adjustments on July 31 are as follows:

Insurance expired during the year		$ 1,060
Store supplies inventory on July 31		820
Depreciation for the current year		9,300
Accrued salaries on July 31:		
Sales salaries	$1,500	
Office salaries	1,200	2,700
Rent income earned during the year		3,800

Instructions:

Prepare a work sheet for the fiscal year ended July 31. List all accounts in the order given. Iyer Inc. uses the perpetual inventory system.

Appendix Pb. 4–59.

Work sheet, income statement, and closing entries—perpetual inventory system.

Sycamore Corp. uses the perpetual inventory system. A partially completed work sheet for the Sycamore Corp. for the current year ended April 30 is as follows:

Sycamore Corp.
Work Sheet
For Year Ended April 30, 19--

Account Title	Trial Balance Dr.	Trial Balance Cr.	Adjustments Dr.	Adjustments Cr.
Cash	28,500			
Accounts Receivable	88,300			
Merchandise Inventory	105,200			
Prepaid Insurance	11,500			(a) 6,900
Store Supplies	2,300			(b) 1,400
Office Supplies	1,500			(c) 900
Store Equipment	186,600			
Accum. Depr.—Store Equip.		68,000		(d) 8,100
Office Equipment	49,300			
Accum. Depr.—Office Equip.		12,000		(e) 3,000
Accounts Payable		29,500		
Salaries Payable				(f) 4,700
Unearned Rent		2,400	(g) 1,600	
Note Payable (due 1999)		100,000		
Capital Stock		100,000		
Retained Earnings		36,100		
Dividends	10,000			
Sales		760,000		
Sales Returns and Allowances	12,000			
Sales Discounts	7,500			
Cost of Merchandise Sold	456,300			
Sales Salaries Expense	64,000		(f) 3,500	
Advertising Expense	13,000			
Depr. Expense—Store Equip.			(d) 8,100	
Store Supplies Expense			(b) 1,400	
Misc. Selling Expense	4,400			
Office Salaries Expense	31,000		(f) 1,200	
Rent Expense	24,000			
Depr. Expense—Office Equip.			(e) 3,000	
Insurance Expense			(a) 6,900	
Office Supplies Expense			(c) 900	
Misc. Administrative Expense	1,100			
Rent Income				(g) 1,600
Interest Expense	11,500			
	1,108,000	1,108,000	26,600	26,600
Net Income				

Instructions:

(1) Complete the work sheet for Sycamore Corp.
(2) Prepare a single-step income statement for the year ended April 30.
(3) Prepare the closing entries for Sycamore Corp.

ALTERNATE PROBLEMS

Pb. 4–47A.
Purchase-related and sales-related transactions.
OBJ. 1

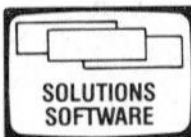

The following selected transactions were completed during February between Cary Company and Lynn Inc.:

Feb. 3. Cary Company sold merchandise on account to Lynn Inc., $15,000, terms FOB destination, 2/15, n/eom.
3. Cary Company paid transportation costs of $300 for delivery of merchandise sold to Lynn Inc. on February 3.
10. Cary Company sold merchandise on account to Lynn Inc., $10,000, terms FOB shipping point, n/eom.
12. Lynn Inc. returned merchandise purchased on account on February 10 from Cary Company, $2,000.
12. Lynn Inc. paid transportation charges of $700 on February 10 purchase from Cary Company.
18. Cary Company sold merchandise on account to Lynn Inc., $18,000, terms FOB shipping point, 2/10, n/30. Cary Company prepaid transportation costs of $1,500 which were added to the invoice.
18. Lynn Inc. paid Cary Company on account for purchases of February 3, less discount.
24. Lynn Inc. paid Cary Company on account for purchases of February 18, less discount.
28. Lynn Inc. paid Cary Company on account for purchases of February 10, less return of February 12.

Instructions:

Journalize the February transactions for (1) Cary Company and (2) Lynn Inc.

Pb. 4–48A.
Purchase-related and sales-related transactions.
OBJ. 1

The following were selected from among the transactions completed by Langerman Co. during November of the current year:

Nov. 1. Purchased office supplies for cash, $850.
2. Purchased merchandise on account from Gant Co., $10,500, terms FOB destination, 1/10, n/30.
6. Sold merchandise for cash, $4,450.
7. Purchased merchandise on account from Liebman Co., $6,900, terms FOB shipping point, 2/10, n/30, with prepaid transportation costs of $190 added to the invoice.
7. Returned merchandise purchased on November 2 from Gant Co., $500.
11. Sold merchandise on account to Bowles Co., $1,800, terms 1/10, n/30.
12. Paid Gant Co. on account for purchases of November 2, less return of November 7 and discount.
16. Sold merchandise on nonbank credit cards and reported accounts to the card company, $3,850.
17. Paid Liebman Co. on account for purchases of November 7, less discount.
19. Purchased merchandise for cash, $3,500.
21. Received cash on account from sale of November 11 to Bowles Co., less discount.
24. Sold merchandise on account to Hall Inc., $4,800, terms 1/10, n/30.
28. Received cash from card company for nonbank credit card sales of November 16, less $220 service fee.
30. Received merchandise returned by Hall Inc. from sale of November 24, $1,750.

Instructions:

Journalize the transactions.

4-202 **Pb. 4–49A.**

Purchase-related and sales-related transactions; ledger accounts.

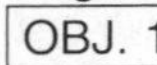

The account balances at July 1 of the current year of Haynes Company are as follows:

11	Cash	$ 20,640
12	Accounts Receivable	33,300
13	Merchandise Inventory	82,600
14	Prepaid Insurance	2,500
15	Store Supplies	1,700
21	Accounts Payable	30,800
31	Capital Stock	75,000
32	Retained Earnings	34,940
33	Dividends	—
41	Sales	—
42	Sales Returns and Allowances	—
43	Sales Discounts	—
51	Purchases	—
52	Purchases Returns and Allowances	—
53	Purchases Discounts	—
54	Transportation In	—
55	Sales Salaries Expense	—
56	Advertising Expense	—
57	Store Supplies Expense	—
58	Miscellaneous Selling Expense	—
59	Office Salaries Expense	—
60	Rent Expense	—
61	Insurance Expense	—
62	Miscellaneous Administrative Expense	—

The following transactions were completed during July of the current year:

July 1. Paid rent for month, $3,000.
3. Purchased merchandise on account, $8,000.
5. Purchased merchandise on account, FOB shipping point, $21,800.
8. Sold merchandise on account, $15,500.
9. Paid transportation charges on the purchase of July 5, $450.
10. Received $14,750 cash from customers on account, after discounts of $250 were deducted.
11. Paid creditors $16,700 on account, after discounts of $280 had been deducted.
14. Sold merchandise for cash, $7,250.
15. Received merchandise returned on account, $800.
16. Paid sales salaries of $3,400 and office salaries of $1,100.
17. Paid creditors $12,750 on account, after discounts of $200 had been deducted.
18. Received $9,500 cash from customers on account, after discounts of $120 had been deducted.
21. Purchased merchandise on account, $15,200.
22. Paid advertising expense, $2,500.
23. Sold merchandise for cash, $8,100.
24. Returned merchandise purchased on account, $6,800.
25. Sold merchandise for cash, $4,600.
28. Sold merchandise on account, $27,300.
28. Refunded $350 cash on sales made for cash.
29. Paid sales salaries of $2,800 and office salaries of $1,100.
30. Paid creditors $10,900 on account, no discount.
31. Received $12,500 cash from customers on account, no discount.

Instructions:

(1) Open a ledger of standard accounts for the accounts listed. Record the balances in the appropriate balance column as of July 1, write "Balance" in the item section, and place a check mark (✔) in the posting reference column.
(2) Record the transactions for July in a journal.
(3) Post to the ledger, extending the month-end balances to the appropriate balance columns after all posting is completed.
(4) Prepare a trial balance of the ledger as of July 31.

Pb. 4–50A.
Work sheet; cost of merchandise sold section.
OBJ. 3, 4

The accounts and their balances in the ledger of Orion Company on December 31 of the current year are as follows:

Cash	$ 34,400
Notes Receivable	10,000
Accounts Receivable	76,300
Interest Receivable	—
Merchandise Inventory	111,300
Prepaid Insurance	10,500
Store Supplies	2,800
Office Supplies	1,200
Store Equipment	79,600
Accumulated Depreciation—Store Equipment	23,000
Office Equipment	27,300
Accumulated Depreciation—Office Equipment	12,000
Accounts Payable	50,500
Salaries Payable	—
Unearned Rent	2,400
Note Payable (due 1999)	100,000
Capital Stock	50,000
Retained Earnings	39,400
Dividends	48,000
Sales	760,000
Sales Returns and Allowances	7,000
Sales Discounts	8,500
Purchases	500,000
Purchases Returns and Allowances	12,500
Purchases Discounts	6,500
Transportation In	2,400
Sales Salaries Expense	70,000
Advertising Expense	18,000
Depreciation Expense—Store Equipment	—
Store Supplies Expense	—
Miscellaneous Selling Expense	1,400
Office Salaries Expense	25,000
Rent Expense	10,000
Depreciation Expense—Office Equipment	—
Insurance Expense	—
Office Supplies Expense	—
Miscellaneous Administrative Expense	1,100
Rent Income	—
Interest Income	—
Interest Expense	11,500

The data for year-end adjustments on December 31 are as follows:

Interest accrued on notes receivable on December 31		$ 300
Insurance expired during the year		6,500
Inventory of supplies on December 31:		
Store supplies		1,600
Office supplies		450
Depreciation for the year:		
Store equipment		7,500
Office equipment		2,800
Salaries payable on December 31:		
Sales salaries	$3,200	
Office salaries	900	4,100
Rent income earned for the year		600

Instructions:

(1) Prepare a work sheet for the fiscal year ended December 31. The merchandise inventory on December 31 is $115,200.

(2) Prepare the cost of merchandise sold section of the income statement from the data presented in the income statement columns of the work sheet.

Pb. 4–51A.
Preparation of multiple-step income statement and account form of balance sheet.
OBJ. 5

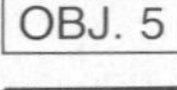

The following selected accounts and their normal balances appear in the income statement and balance sheet columns of the work sheet of Maddox Inc. for the fiscal year ended March 31, 1992:

Cash	$ 42,750
Notes Receivable	100,000
Accounts Receivable	225,000
Interest Receivable	1,000
Merchandise Inventory, April 1, 1991	125,000
Merchandise Inventory, March 31, 1992	120,000
Office Supplies	7,900
Prepaid Insurance	4,500
Office Equipment	35,000
Accumulated Depreciation—Office Equipment ...	12,800
Store Equipment	77,500
Accumulated Depreciation—Store Equipment	29,700
Accounts Payable	48,000
Salaries Payable	3,900
Unearned Rent	2,000
Note Payable (final payment, 2000)	80,000
Capital Stock	250,000
Retained Earnings	143,250
Dividends	40,000
Sales	1,450,000
Sales Returns and Allowances	12,100
Sales Discounts	11,900
Purchases	1,125,000
Purchases Returns and Allowances	24,600
Purchases Discounts	15,400
Transportation In	10,000
Sales Salaries Expense	133,200
Advertising Expense	22,800
Depreciation Expense—Store Equipment	6,400
Miscellaneous Selling Expense	1,600
Office Salaries Expense	40,150
Rent Expense	26,350

Depreciation Expense—Office Equipment	$	12,700
Insurance Expense		3,900
Office Supplies Expense		1,300
Miscellaneous Administrative Expense		1,600
Interest Income		12,000
Rent Income		4,000
Interest Expense		8,000

Instructions:

(1) Prepare a multiple-step income statement.
(2) Prepare a retained earnings statement.
(3) Prepare an account form balance sheet, assuming that the current portion of the note payable is $10,000.

Pb. 4–52A.
Preparation of single-step income statement and combined income and retained earnings statement.
OBJ. 5

Selected accounts and related amounts for Maddox Inc. for the fiscal year ended March 31, 1992, are presented in Pb. 4–51A.

Instructions:

(1) Prepare a single-step income statement.
(2) Prepare a combined income and retained earnings statement, using the single-step form for the income statement portion.

Pb. 4–53A.
Combined income and retained earnings statement; balance sheet.
OBJ. 5

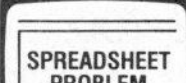

The following data for Lusk Co. were selected from the ledger after adjustment at April 30, 1992, the end of the current fiscal year:

Accounts payable	$	83,700
Accounts receivable		122,100
Accumulated depreciation—office equipment		30,750
Accumulated depreciation—store equipment		91,050
Administrative expenses		113,220
Capital stock		100,000
Cash		40,100
Cost of merchandise sold		990,890
Dividends		60,000
Dividends payable		15,000
Interest expense		18,000
Merchandise inventory		280,200
Note payable (due in 2001)		150,000
Office equipment		111,000
Prepaid insurance		5,250
Rent income		8,700
Retained earnings		281,500
Salaries payable		4,640
Sales		1,390,750
Selling expenses		175,080
Store equipment		240,250

Instructions:

(1) Prepare a combined income and retained earnings statement, using the single-step form for the income statement portion.
(2) Prepare a balance sheet in account form.

If the working papers correlating with this textbook are not used, omit Pb. 4–54A.

Pb. 4–54A.
Completion of work sheet and preparation of financial statements.
OBJ. 4, 5

A partially completed work sheet for Magan Inc. is presented in the working papers. All adjustments have been entered on the work sheet.

Instructions:

(1) Complete the work sheet.
(2) Prepare a multiple-step income statement.
(3) Prepare a retained earnings statement.
(4) Prepare a report form of balance sheet, assuming that the current portion of the note payable is $20,000.

Pb. 4–55A.
Closing entries from work sheet.
OBJ. 6

The account balances taken from the Income Statement columns of the work sheet for Woodward Corporation at the end of the current fiscal year are as follows:

	Debit	Credit
Merchandise Inventory	354,000	335,000
Sales		1,020,000
Sales Returns and Allowances	12,000	
Sales Discounts	8,500	
Purchases	617,720	
Purchases Returns and Allowances		14,650
Purchases Discounts		10,140
Transportation In	7,230	
Sales Salaries Expense	124,000	
Depreciation Expense—Store Equipment	16,460	
Supplies Expense	960	
Miscellaneous Selling Expense	3,800	
Office Salaries Expense	70,000	
Rent Expense	36,000	
Heating and Lighting Expense	21,750	
Insurance Expense	4,100	
Depreciation Expense—Office Equipment	5,180	
Miscellaneous Administrative Expense	2,900	
Interest Expense	30,000	
	1,314,600	1,379,790

Instructions:

Journalize the closing entries, assuming that the balance in the dividends account at the end of the current fiscal year was $40,000.

Pb. 4–56A.
Preparation of work sheet, financial statements, and adjusting and closing entries.
OBJ. 4, 5, 6

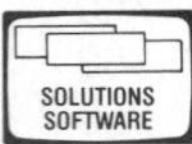

The accounts and their balances in the ledger of Bower Company on December 31 of the current year are as follows:

Cash	$ 53,160
Notes Receivable	25,000
Accounts Receivable	100,000
Interest Receivable	—
Merchandise Inventory	180,000
Prepaid Insurance	9,540
Store Supplies	2,500
Office Supplies	1,700
Store Equipment	134,000
Accumulated Depreciation—Store Equipment	40,300
Office Equipment	40,000
Accumulated Depreciation—Office Equipment	17,200
Accounts Payable	58,040
Salaries Payable	—
Unearned Rent	3,000
Note Payable (final payment, 1999)	105,000

Capital Stock	$ 150,000
Retained Earnings	70,510
Dividends	40,000
Sales	1,080,000
Sales Returns and Allowances	12,500
Sales Discounts	6,500
Purchases	720,000
Purchases Returns and Allowances	8,200
Purchases Discounts	6,800
Transportation In	5,000
Sales Salaries Expense	86,400
Advertising Expense	30,000
Depreciation Expense—Store Equipment	—
Store Supplies Expense	—
Miscellaneous Selling Expense	2,000
Office Salaries Expense	60,000
Rent Expense	18,000
Insurance Expense	—
Depreciation Expense—Office Equipment	—
Office Supplies Expense	—
Miscellaneous Administrative Expense	1,650
Interest Income	1,500
Rent Income	—
Interest Expense	12,600

The data for year-end adjustments on December 31 are as follows:

Interest accrued on notes receivable on December 31		$ 500
Insurance expired during the year		5,900
Inventory of supplies on December 31:		
Store supplies		950
Office supplies		250
Depreciation for the year:		
Store equipment		12,400
Office equipment		5,500
Salaries payable on December 31:		
Sales salaries	$2,750	
Office salaries	2,150	4,900
Unearned rent on December 31		1,500

Instructions:

(1) Prepare a work sheet for the fiscal year ended December 31, listing all accounts in the order given. The merchandise inventory on December 31 is $220,000.
(2) Prepare a multiple-step income statement.
(3) Prepare a retained earnings statement.
(4) Prepare a report form of balance sheet, assuming that the current portion of the note payable is $15,000.
(5) Journalize the adjusting entries.
(6) Journalize the closing entries.

Appendix Pb. 4–57A. **Purchase-related and sales-related transactions—perpetual inventory system.**

The following were selected from among the transactions completed by Notte Corp. during November of the current year. Notte Corp. uses the perpetual inventory system.

Nov. 2. Purchased merchandise on account from Wizner Co., $24,500, terms FOB destination, 2/10, n/30.

3. Purchased merchandise on account from Martin Inc., $16,000, terms FOB shipping point, 1/15, n/30, with prepaid transportation costs of $400 added to the invoice.

Nov. 6. Sold merchandise on account to Curtis Co., $7,800, terms 2/10, n/30. The cost of the merchandise sold was $4,700.
7. Purchased office supplies for cash, $90.
8. Returned merchandise purchased on May 2 from Wizner Co., $3,600.
12. Paid Wizner Co. on account for purchases of November 2, less return of November 8 and discount.
14. Purchased merchandise for cash, $8,350.
16. Received cash on account from sale of November 6 to Curtis Co., less discount.
17. Sold merchandise on nonbank credit cards and reported accounts to the card company, $15,200. The cost of the merchandise sold was $9,100.
18. Paid Martin Inc. on account for purchases of November 3, less discount.
23. Sold merchandise on account to Harris Inc., $11,650, terms 2/10, n/30. The cost of the merchandise sold was $7,000.
26. Sold merchandise for cash, $7,900. The cost of the merchandise sold was $4,740.
29. Received merchandise returned by Harris Inc. from sale of November 23, $2,100. The cost of the returned merchandise was $1,260.
30. Received cash from card company for nonbank credit card sales of November 17, less $430 service fee.

Instructions:

Journalize the transactions.

Appendix Pb. 4–58A.
Work sheet using perpetual inventory system.

The accounts in the ledger of Marden Inc., with the unadjusted balances on June 30 of the current fiscal year are as follows:

Cash	$ 15,100
Notes Receivable	50,000
Accounts Receivable	67,600
Merchandise Inventory	91,700
Prepaid Insurance	5,800
Store Supplies	4,950
Store Equipment	50,500
Accumulated Depreciation—Store Equipment	30,130
Accounts Payable	26,800
Salaries Payable	—
Unearned Rent	4,600
Capital Stock	100,000
Retained Earnings	69,870
Dividends	15,000
Sales	600,500
Cost of Merchandise Sold	360,300
Sales Salaries Expense	61,500
Advertising Expense	25,800
Depreciation Expense—Store Equipment	—
Store Supplies Expense	—
Miscellaneous Selling Expense	3,750
Office Salaries Expense	39,000
Rent Expense	24,000
Heating and Lighting Expense	9,660
Taxes Expense	5,100
Insurance Expense	—
Miscellaneous Administrative Expense	2,140
Rent Income	—

The data for year-end adjustments on June 30 are as follows:

Insurance expired during the year		$ 3,800
Store supplies inventory on June 30		870
Depreciation for the current year		10,500
Accrued salaries on June 30:		
Sales salaries	$2,600	
Office salaries	1,650	4,250
Rent income earned during the year		3,800

Instructions:

Prepare a work sheet for the fiscal year ended June 30, listing all accounts in the order given. Marden Inc. uses the perpetual inventory system.

Appendix Pb. 4–59A. Work sheet, income statement, and closing entries—perpetual inventory system.

MacNair Inc. uses the perpetual inventory system. A partially completed work sheet for MacNair Inc. for the current year ended October 31 is as follows:

MacNair Inc.
Work Sheet
For Year Ended October 31, 19--

Account Title	Trial Balance Dr.	Trial Balance Cr.	Adjustments Dr.	Adjustments Cr.
Cash	14,400			
Accounts Receivable	86,300			
Merchandise Inventory	108,400			
Prepaid Insurance	10,500			(a) 7,600
Store Supplies	3,800			(b) 2,200
Office Supplies	1,200			(c) 750
Store Equipment	179,600			
Accum. Depr.—Store Equip.		53,000		(d) 10,500
Office Equipment	47,300			
Accum. Depr.—Office Equip.		12,000		(e) 3,800
Accounts Payable		30,500		
Salaries Payable				(f) 4,100
Unearned Rent		2,400	(g) 1,600	
Note Payable (due 1999)		80,000		
Capital Stock		100,000		
Retained Earnings		49,200		
Dividends	9,000			
Sales		820,000		
Sales Returns and Allowances	7,000			
Sales Discounts	8,500			
Cost of Merchandise Sold	515,000			
Sales Salaries Expense	70,000		(f) 3,200	
Advertising Expense	28,000			
Depr. Expense—Store Equip.			(d) 10,500	
Store Supplies Expense			(b) 2,200	
Misc. Selling Expense	2,400			
Office Salaries Expense	35,000		(f) 900	
Rent Expense	10,000			
Depr. Expense—Office Equip.			(e) 3,800	
Insurance Expense			(a) 7,600	
Office Supplies Expense			(c) 750	
Misc. Administrative Expense	1,100			
Rent Income				(g) 1,600
Interest Expense	9,600			
	1,147,100	1,147,100	30,550	30,550
Net Income				

Instructions:

(1) Complete the work sheet for MacNair Inc.
(2) Prepare a single-step income statement for the year ended October 31.
(3) Prepare the closing entries for MacNair Inc.

MINI-CASE 4

GIANT DISCOUNT INC.

For the past twenty years, your father has managed and operated Giant Discount Inc., a regional chain of retail stores. You have recently accepted a position with Giant Discount Inc. as a special assistant to the president. As a first assignment, you are to review the purchasing and disbursing policies of the enterprise.

For your analysis, the controller has gathered the following data covering the past three years:

	19X3	19X2	19X1
Purchases	$22,500,000	$20,200,000	$17,900,000
Purchases returns and allowances	300,000	250,000	100,000
Transportation in	562,200	534,200	489,000

After reviewing these data, you ask the controller why no purchases discounts are shown for the three-year period. The controller responded as follows:

> Your father won't let us take purchases discounts. It doesn't make sense to me. The industry standard is 2/10, n/30. Your father always has believed in paying the bills on the final due date and not a day before. I've tried to convince him that we should take the discounts, but he won't budge.

The controller also indicated that the company has recently entered into a store expansion program that will likely create a cash shortage. Because of this situation, the company has negotiated a $1,250,000 line of credit with its bank at an interest rate of 12%.

Instructions:

(1) Prepare an analysis indicating the net savings that the company could have earned from taking all discounts for the past three years. Assume that discounts are available on all purchases. In addition, assume that the company had sufficient cash to pay all invoices without borrowing and that the average rates at which the excess cash could have been invested in each of the past three years were as follows:

19X3	10%
19X2	12%
19X1	13%

(Hint: You should take into consideration the interest income the company would have forgone by paying the invoices within the discount period.)

(2) Assume that you are able to convince your father to use the new line of credit to pay all invoices within the discount period during 19X4. The net purchases for 19X4 are projected to increase 10% over the net purchases for 19X3. Compute the expected net savings for 19X4 by taking all the available purchases discounts.

(3) Based upon the purchase data for 19X3, 19X2, and 19X1, what other questions might you raise concerning the company's purchasing and disbursing policies?

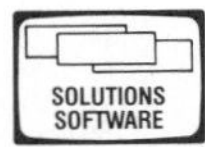

COMPREHENSIVE PROBLEM 2

The account balances for Dyson Inc. are as follows. All balances are stated as of May 1, 1992, unless otherwise indicated.

101	Cash	$ 34,160
102	Notes Receivable	—
103	Accounts Receivable	55,320
104	Interest Receivable	—
105	Merchandise Inventory, June 1, 1991	123,900
106	Prepaid Insurance	4,250
107	Store Supplies	2,550
111	Store Equipment	43,800
112	Accumulated Depreciation	12,600
201	Accounts Payable	38,000
202	Salaries Payable	—
203	Unearned Rent	500
301	Capital Stock	100,000
302	Retained Earnings, June 1, 1991	59,420
303	Dividends	6,000
305	Income Summary	—
401	Sales	792,000
402	Sales Returns and Allowances	13,600
403	Sales Discounts	5,200
501	Purchases	570,000
502	Purchases Returns and Allowances	15,600
503	Purchases Discounts	5,760
504	Transportation In	5,800
601	Sales Salaries Expense	74,400
602	Advertising Expense	18,000
603	Depreciation Expense	—
604	Store Supplies Expense	—
605	Miscellaneous Selling Expense	2,800
611	Office Salaries Expense	29,400
612	Rent Expense	33,000
613	Insurance Expense	—
614	Miscellaneous Administrative Expense	1,800
701	Interest Income	100
702	Rent Income	—

During May, the last month of Dyson Inc.'s fiscal year, the following transactions were completed:

May 1. Paid rent for May, $3,000.
1. Received a $10,000 note receivable from a customer on account.
2. Purchased merchandise on account, terms 1/10, n/30, FOB shipping point, $25,000.
3. Paid transportation charges on purchase of May 2, $710.
4. Purchased merchandise on account, terms 2/10, n/30, FOB destination, $17,500.
5. Sold merchandise on account, terms 2/10, n/30, FOB shipping point, $8,000.
8. Received $14,750 cash from customers on account, no discount.
10. Sold merchandise for cash, $19,500
11. Paid $12,800 to creditors on account, after discounts of $200 had been deducted.
12. Paid for merchandise purchased on May 2, less discount.
13. Received merchandise returned on sale of May 5, $500.
14. Paid advertising expense for last half of May, $1,500.

May 15. Received cash from sale of May 5, less return and discount.
15. Paid sales salaries of $3,500 and office salaries of $900.
18. Received $28,500 cash from customers on account, after discounts of $400 had been deducted.
19. Purchased merchandise for cash, $6,400.
19. Paid $13,150 to creditors on account, after discounts of $250 had been deducted.
20. Sold merchandise on account, terms 1/10, n/30, FOB shipping point, $16,000.
21. Purchased merchandise on account, terms 1/10, n/30, FOB destination, $15,000.
22. Paid for merchandise purchased on May 4.
24. Returned damaged merchandise purchased on May 21, receiving credit from the seller, $3,000.
25. Refunded cash on sales made for cash, $400.
29. Paid sales salaries of $3,500 and office salaries of $900.
29. Sold merchandise on account, terms 2/10, n/30, FOB shipping point, $24,700.
29. Purchased store supplies for cash, $350.
30. Received cash from sale of May 20, less discount.
31. Paid for purchase of May 21, less return and discount.
31. Sold merchandise on account, terms 2/10, n/30, FOB shipping point, $19,250.
31. Purchased merchandise on account, terms 1/10, n/30, FOB destination, $18,150.

Instructions:

(1) Record the balances of each of the accounts as of May 1 in the appropriate balance column of a four-column account. Write "Balance" in the item section, and place a check mark (✔) in the posting reference column.
(2) Record the transactions for May in a journal.
(3) Post to the ledger, extending the month-end balances to the appropriate balance columns after all posting is completed.
(4) Prepare a trial balance as of May 31 on a work sheet, listing all the accounts in the order given in the ledger. Complete the work sheet for the fiscal year ended May 31, using the following adjustment data:

(a) Interest accrued on notes receivable on May 31		$ 100
(b) Insurance expired during the year		2,750
(c) Store supplies inventory on May 31		750
(d) Depreciation for the current year		5,360
(e) Accrued salaries on May 31:		
Sales salaries	$700	
Office salaries	175	875
(f) Unearned rent on May 31		250

The physical count of merchandise on hand on May 31 totaled $134,150.
(5) Prepare a multiple-step income statement, a retained earnings statement, and an account form of balance sheet.
(6) Journalize and post the adjusting entries.
(7) Journalize and post the closing entries. Indicate closed accounts by inserting a line in both balance columns opposite the closing entry. Insert the new balance in the retained earnings account.
(8) Prepare a post-closing trial balance.

ANSWERS TO SELF-EXAMINATION QUESTIONS

1. A A debit memorandum (answer A), issued by the buyer, indicates the amount the buyer proposes to debit to the accounts payable account. A credit memorandum (answer B), issued by the seller, indicates the amount the seller proposes to credit

to the accounts receivable account. An invoice (answer C) or a bill (answer D), issued by the seller, indicates the amount and terms of the sale.

2. C The amount of discount for early payment is $10 (answer C), or 1% of $1,000. Although the $50 of transportation costs paid by the seller are debited to the customer's account, the customer is not entitled to a discount on that amount.
3. D Purchases discounts (answer A), purchases returns and allowances (answer B), and merchandise inventory at the end of the period (answer C) are all subtracted from the sum of merchandise inventory at the beginning of the period and purchases in determining the cost of merchandise sold.
4. B Unearned revenues are revenues received in advance that will be earned in the future. They represent a liability (answer B) of the business to furnish goods or services in a future period.
5. C Gross profit (answer C) is the excess of net sales over the cost of merchandise sold. Operating income (answer A) or income from operations (answer B) is the excess of gross profit over operating expenses. Net income (answer D) is the final figure on the income statement after all revenues and expenses have been reported.

PART 2

FINANCIAL ACCOUNTING SYSTEMS

CHAPTER 5

CHAPTER OBJECTIVES

1 Describe the principles of properly designed accounting systems.

2 Describe the three phases of accounting system installation and revision.

3 Describe and illustrate the principles of internal control.

4 Describe and illustrate the use of a bank account for controlling cash, including the preparation of a bank reconciliation.

5 Describe and illustrate internal controls for cash receipts, including:
Use of a cash short and over account
Use of cash change funds.

6 Describe and illustrate internal controls for cash payments, including use of a:
Voucher system
Discounts lost account
Petty cash account.

7 Describe recent trends in the use of electronic funds transfer to process cash transactions.

ACCOUNTING SYSTEMS & CASH

The way in which management is given the information for use in conducting the affairs of the business and in reporting to owners, creditors, and other interested parties is called the **accounting system.** In a general sense, an accounting system includes the entire network of communications used by a business organization to provide needed information.

In this chapter, the qualities of a properly designed accounting system and the principles of internal control for directing operations are discussed. The chapter also presents the application of these internal control principles to the design of an effective system for controlling cash and accounting for cash transactions.

PRINCIPLES OF ACCOUNTING SYSTEMS

OBJECTIVE 1
Describe the principles of properly designed accounting systems.

The entire amount of data needed by an enterprise is called its **data base.** Depending upon the enterprise, the variety and amount of data included in the data base, and the uses made of the data, various accounting systems— manual and computerized—may be used.

In preceding chapters, manual accounting systems were illustrated because they are the easiest systems to understand. If the data base is relatively small, the manual system illustrated may serve a business reasonably well. As an enterprise becomes larger and more complex, the manual system can be modified in order to make the system more efficient and to better meet the needs of the enterprise. For example, as the number of sales on account increases, including in the ledger with all of the other accounts an account for each customer may result in a ledger that is unwieldy. In such a case, the individual customers' accounts could be placed in a separate ledger called a **subsidiary ledger.** This subsidiary ledger would be represented in the principal ledger (now called the **general ledger**) by a summarizing account called a **controlling account.** The balance in the accounts receivable controlling account in the general ledger would agree with the total of the balances of all of the customers' accounts in the subsidiary ledger.[1]

The concept of the subsidary ledger can be extended to any group of individual accounts with a common characteristic, when it is desirable to reduce the number of accounts in the principal ledger. For example, a subsidiary ledger for creditors' accounts payable could be used, with Accounts Payable serving as the controlling account in the general ledger.

When the data base for an enterprise becomes too large and complex for the manual system to handle efficiently, the manual accounting system may be replaced by a computerized system. Regardless of whether the accounting system for a particular enterprise uses manual or computerized procedures to process its transactions, however, there are basic principles of accounting systems that are applicable in all cases. These principles are discussed in the following paragraphs.

Cost-Effectiveness Balance

An accounting system must be tailored to meet the specific needs of each business. Since costs must be incurred in meeting these needs, one of the major considerations in developing an accounting system is cost effectiveness. For example, although the reports produced by an accounting system are a valuable end product of the system, the value of the reports produced should be at least equal to the cost of producing them. No matter how detailed or informational a report may be, it should not be produced if it costs more than the benefits received by those who use it.

Flexibility to Meet Future Needs

A characteristic of the modern business environment is change. Each business must adapt to the constantly changing environment in which it operates. Whether the changes are the result of new government regulations, changes in accounting principles, organizational changes necessary to meet practices of competing businesses, changes in data processing technology, or other factors, the accounting system must be flexible enough to meet the changing demands made of it. For example, regulatory agencies, such as the Securities and Exchange Commission, often require a continually changing variety of reports that require changes in the accounting system.

Adequate Internal Controls

An accounting system must provide the information needed by management in reporting to owners, creditors, and other interested parties. In addition, the system should aid management in directing operations. The detailed policies and procedures used to direct operations and provide reasonable assurance that the entity's objectives are achieved are called **internal controls.** The broad principles for an internal control structure are discussed later in the chapter.

---

[1]Another means by which the manual system can be modified in order to reduce costs and more efficiently process accounting data is to use special journals, in which selected kinds of transactions are recorded. The basic features of special journals and a more detailed discussion of subsidiary ledgers are presented in Appendix F.

Effective Reporting

Users of the information provided by the accounting system rely on various reports for relevant information presented in an understandable manner. When these reports are prepared, the requirements and knowledge of the user should be recognized. For example, management may need detailed reports for controlling operations on a weekly or even daily basis, and regulatory agencies often require uniform data and establish certain deadlines for the submission of certain reports.

Adaptation to Organizational Structure

Only by effectively using and adapting to the human resources of a business can the accounting system meet information needs at the lowest cost. Since no two businesses are structured alike, the accounting system must be tailored to the organizational structure of each business. The lines of authority and responsibility will affect the information requirements of each business. In addition, an effective system needs the approval and support of all levels of management.

ACCOUNTING SYSTEM INSTALLATION AND REVISION

OBJECTIVE 2
Describe the three phases of accounting system installation and revision.

Before designing and installing an accounting system for an enterprise, the designer must have a complete knowledge of the business' operations. However, the designer should recognize that some areas of the system, such as the types and design of the forms needed and the number and titles of the accounts required, may be affected by factors that are not known when a business is first organized. As new information about a business is obtained and as a business "outgrows" its accounting system when it expands to new operational areas, the system will need to be revised.

Many large businesses continually review their accounting system and may constantly be involved in changing some part of it. The job of installing or changing an accounting system, either in its entirety or only in part, is made up of three phases: (1) analysis, (2) design, and (3) implementation.

Systems Analysis

The goal of **systems analysis** is to determine information needs, the sources of such information, and the deficiencies in procedures and data processing methods presently used. The analysis usually begins with a review of the organizational structure and the job descriptions of the personnel affected. This review is followed by a study of the forms, records, procedures, processing methods, and reports used by the enterprise. The source of such information is usually the firm's *Systems Manual*.

In addition to looking at the shortcomings of the present system, the analyst should determine management's plans for changes in operations (volume, products, territories, etc.) in the foreseeable future.

Systems Design

Accounting systems are changed as a result of the kind of analysis previously described. The design of the new system may involve only minor changes from the existing system, such as revision of a particular form and the related procedures and processing methods, or it may be a complete revision of the entire system. Systems designers must have a general knowledge of the qualities of different kinds of data processing equipment, and the ability to evaluate alternatives. Although successful systems design depends to a large extent upon the creativity, imagination, and general capabilities of the designer, observance of the broad principles previously discussed is necessary.

Systems Implementation

The final phase of the creation or revision of an accounting system is to carry out, or implement, the proposals. New or revised forms, records, procedures, and equipment must be installed, and any that are no longer useful must be withdrawn. All personnel responsible for operating the system must be carefully trained and closely supervised until satisfactory efficiency is achieved.

For a large organization, a major revision such as a change from an obsolete to a modern computer processing system is usually done gradually over an extended period rather than all at once. With such a procedure, there is less likelihood that the flow of useful data will be seriously slowed down during the critical phase of implementation. Weaknesses and conflicting or unnecessary elements in the design may also become apparent during the implementation phase. They are more easily seen and corrected when changes in a system are adopted gradually, and possible chaos is thereby avoided.

ACCOUNTING SYSTEMS, PROFIT MEASUREMENT, AND MANAGEMENT

A Greek restaurant owner in Canada had his own system of accounting. He kept his accounts payable in a cigar box on the left-hand side of his cash register, his daily cash returns in the cash register, and his receipts for paid bills in another cigar box on the right.

When his youngest son graduated as an accountant, he was appalled by his father's primitive methods. "I don't know how you can run a business that way," he said. "How do you know what your profits are?"

"Well, son," the father replied, "when I got off the boat from Greece, I had nothing but the pants I was wearing. Today, your brother is a doctor. You are an accountant. Your sister is a speech therapist. Your mother and I have a nice car, and city house, a country home. We have a good business, and everything is paid for. . ."

"So, you add all that together, subtract the pants, and there's your profit!"

Source: Anonymous.

INTERNAL CONTROL STRUCTURE

OBJECTIVE 3
Describe and illustrate the principles of internal control.

An enterprise's internal control structure consists of the policies and procedures established to provide reasonable assurance that the enterprise's goals and objectives will be achieved. This internal control structure can be divided into three elements: (1) the control environment, (2) the control procedures, and (3) the accounting system.[2] The basic principles underlying an

[2] *Statements on Auditing Standards, No. 55,* "Consideration of the Internal Control Structure in a Financial Statement Audit" (New York: American Institute of Certified Public Accountants, 1988).

effective internal control structure are briefly discussed in the following paragraphs. It should be noted that the policies and procedures of an internal control structure will vary according to the size and type of business enterprise. In a small business where it is possible for the owner-manager to supervise the employees personally and direct the affairs of the business, few control policies and procedures are necessary. As the number of employees and the complexities of an enterprise increase, it becomes more difficult for management to maintain control over all phases of operations. As a firm grows, management needs to delegate authority and to place more reliance on the control structure in order to achieve adherence to enterprise goals and objectives.

The Control Environment

The control environment of an enterprise represents an overall attitude toward and awareness of the importance of controls by both management and other employees. Factors influencing the control environment of an enterprise include management's philosophy and operating style, the organizational structure of the enterprise, and personnel policies and practices.

Management's philosophy and operating style includes management's attitude concerning controls. For example, if top management routinely violates established control policies and procedures, the control environment could be adversely affected because lower management and employees may view controls as unimportant. On the other hand, a top management that emphasizes the importance of controls in dealing with operating personnel and encourages adherence to control policies and procedures will create a favorable control environment.

The organizational structure of an enterprise establishes the framework for planning and controlling operations. For example, a merchandising enterprise might organize each of its stores as relatively separate business units, with each store manager given full authority over pricing and other operating activities. Included with this authority is the responsibility for establishing a control environment for achieving the enterprise's goals and objectives.

Personnel policies and procedures includes the hiring, training, evaluation, promotion, and compensation of employees to accomplish an enterprise's goals and objectives. Common personnel policies that impact on the control environment include the establishment of codes of ethics for employee conduct and conflict of interest policies.

The Control Procedures

Control procedures are those policies and procedures that management has established within the control environment in order to provide reasonable assurance that enterprise goals will be achieved. General control procedures which can be integrated throughout the accounting system and which apply to all enterprises are briefly discussed in the following sections.

Competent Personnel and Rotation of Duties. The successful operation of an accounting system requires procedures to ensure that people are able to perform the duties to which they are assigned. Hence, it is necessary that all accounting employees be adequately trained and supervised to perform their jobs. It is also advisable to rotate clerical personnel periodically from job to job. In addition to broadening their understanding of the system, the knowledge that others may in the future perform their jobs tends to discourage deviations from prescribed procedures. Rotation of duties is also very helpful in disclosing any irregularities that may have occurred.

Assignment of Responsibility. If employees are to work efficiently, their responsibilities must be clearly defined. Control procedures should exist to guarantee that no overlapping or undefined areas of responsibility exist. For example, if a certain cash register is to be used by two or more salesclerks, each one should be assigned a separate cash drawer and register key. Thus, a daily proof of cash can be obtained for each clerk.

Separation of Responsibility for Related Operations. To decrease the possibility of inefficiency, errors, and fraud, control procedures should exist to guarantee that responsibility for a sequence of related operations is divided among two or more persons. For example, no one individual should be authorized to order merchandise, verify the receipt of the merchandise, and pay the supplier. To do so would invite abuses such as the following:

1. Placing orders with a supplier on the basis of friendship rather than on price, quality, and other objective factors.
2. Indifferent and routine verification of the quantity and the quality of goods received.
3. Conversion of goods to the personal use of the employee.
4. Carelessness in verifying the validity and the accuracy of invoices.
5. Payment of false invoices.

When the responsibility for purchasing, receiving, and paying are divided among three persons or departments, the possibilities of such abuses are minimized.

The "checks and balances" provided by distributing responsibility among various departments requires no duplication of effort. The business documents prepared as a result of the work of each department must "fit" with those prepared by the other departments.

Separation of Operations and Accounting. Control procedures should exist to ensure that responsibility for maintaining the accounting records are separated from the responsibility for engaging in business transactions and for the custody of the firm's assets. By such separation, the accounting records serve as an independent check on the business operations. For example, the employees entrusted with handling cash receipts from credit customers should not have access to the journal or ledger. Separation of the two functions reduces the possibilities of errors and embezzlement.

Proofs and Security Measures. Proofs and security measures should be used to safeguard business assets and assure reliable accounting data. This control procedure applies to many different techniques, such as the use of a bank account and other safekeeping measures for cash and other valuable documents. Cash registers are widely used in making the initial record of cash sales. The conditioning of the public to observe the amount recorded as the sale or to accept a printed receipt from the salesclerk increases the machine's effectiveness as a part of the internal control structure.

The use of fidelity insurance is also an aid to developing an effective internal control structure. It insures against losses caused by fraud on the part of employees who are entrusted with company assets.

Independent Review. To determine whether internal control procedures are being effectively applied, the control structure should be periodically reviewed and evaluated by internal auditors. These auditors must be independent of the employees responsible for operations. An example of the use of internal auditors for review of internal control procedures is described in the annual report of Rose's Stores Inc., as follows:

> To meet its responsibilities with respect to financial information, management maintains and enforces internal accounting policies, procedures, and controls which are designed to provide reasonable assurance that assets are safeguarded and that transactions are properly recorded and executed in accordance with management's authorization. The concept of reasonable assurance is based on the recognition that the cost of controls should not exceed the expected benefits. Management maintains an internal audit function and an internal control function which are responsible for evaluating the adequacy and application of financial and operating controls and for testing compliance with Company policies and procedures.

Internal auditors should report any weaknesses and recommend changes to correct them. For example, a review of cash disbursements may disclose that invoices were not paid within the discount period, even though enough cash was available.

The Accounting System

The accounting system is an integral part of the internal control structure of an enterprise. Without the information generated by the accounting system, management would lack the ability to plan and direct operations in achieving enterprise goals. The principles of an effective accounting system were discussed earlier in this chapter.

CONTROL OVER CASH

OBJECTIVE 4
Describe and illustrate the use of a bank account for controlling cash, including the preparation of a bank reconciliation.

Because of the ease with which money can be transferred, cash is the asset most likely to be diverted and used improperly by employees. In addition, many transactions either directly or indirectly affect the receipt or payment of cash. It is therefore necessary that cash be effectively safeguarded by special controls.

The Bank Account as a Tool for Controlling Cash

One of the major devices for maintaining control over cash is the bank account. To get the most benefit from a bank account, all cash received must be deposited in the bank and all payments must be made by checks drawn on the bank or from special cash funds. When such a system is strictly followed, there is a double record of cash, one maintained by the business and the other by the bank.

In some cases, a bank may require a business to maintain in a bank account a minimum cash balance, called a **compensating balance.** This requirement is generally imposed by the bank as a part of a loan agreement or line of credit (an amount the bank is willing to lend). Compensating balance requirements should be disclosed in notes to the financial statements, as indicated in the following note taken from the financial statements for K mart Corporation:

> *... In support of lines of credit, it is expected that compensating balances will be maintained on deposit with the banks, which will average 10% of the line to the*

extent that it is not in use and an additional 10% on the portion in use, whereas other lines require fees in lieu of compensating balances....

The forms used by a business in connection with a bank account are a signature card, deposit ticket, check, and record of checks drawn. These forms are described in the following paragraphs.

Signature Card. At the time an account is opened, an identifying number is assigned to the account, and a **signature card** must be signed by each person authorized to sign checks drawn on the account. The card is used by the bank to determine the authenticity of the signature on checks presented to it for payment.

Deposit Ticket. The details of a deposit are listed by the depositor on a printed form supplied by the bank. **Deposit tickets** may be prepared in duplicate, in which case the copy is stamped or initialed by the bank's teller and given to the depositor as a receipt. The receipt of a deposit may be indicated by means other than a duplicate deposit ticket, but all methods give the depositor written proof of the date and the total amount of the deposit.

Check. A **check** is a written instrument signed by the depositor, ordering the bank to pay a certain sum of money to the order of a designated person. There are three parties to a check: the **drawer,** the one who signs the check; the **drawee,** the bank on which the check is drawn; and the **payee,** the one to whose order the check is drawn. When checks are issued to pay bills, they are recorded as credits to Cash on the day issued, even though they are not presented to the drawer's bank until some later time. When checks are received from customers, they are recorded as debits to Cash, on the assumption that the customer has enough money on deposit.

Check forms may be obtained in many styles. The name and the address of the depositor are often printed on each check, and the checks are usually numbered in sequence to facilitate the depositor's internal control. Most banks use automatic sorting and posting equipment and, therefore, provide check forms on which the bank's identification number and the depositor's account number are printed along the lower margin in machine-readable magnetic ink. When the check is presented for payment, the amount for which it is drawn is inserted next to the account number, also in magnetic ink.

Record of Checks Drawn. A memorandum record of the basic details of a check should be prepared at the time the check is written. The record may be a stub from which the check is detached or it may be a small booklet designed to be kept with the check forms. Each type of record also provides spaces for recording deposits and the current bank balance.

Business firms may prepare a copy of each check drawn and then use it as a basis for recording the transaction. Checks issued to a creditor on account are usually accompanied by a notification of the specific invoice that is being paid. The purpose of such notification, sometimes called a **remittance advice,** is to make sure that proper credit is recorded in the accounts of the creditor. Mistakes are less likely to happen and the possible need for exchange of correspondence is reduced. The invoice number or other descriptive data may be inserted in spaces provided on the face or on the back of the check or on an attachment to the check, as in the illustration on page 225.

Before depositing the check at the bank, the payee removes the part of the check containing the remittance information. The removed part may then be used by the payee as written proof of the details of the cash receipt.

Check and Remittance Advice

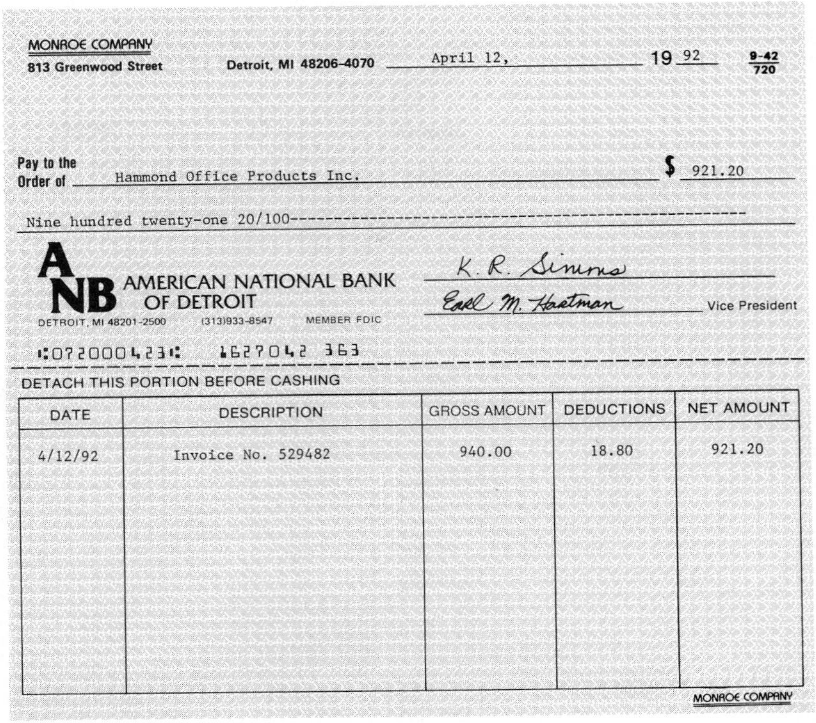

MONROE COMPANY
813 Greenwood Street Detroit, MI 48206-4070 April 12, 19 92 9-42/720

Pay to the Order of Hammond Office Products Inc. $ 921.20

Nine hundred twenty-one 20/100----------

AMERICAN NATIONAL BANK OF DETROIT
DETROIT, MI 48201-2500 (313)933-8547 MEMBER FDIC

K. R. Simms
Earl M. Hartman Vice President

⑈072000423⑆ 1627042 363

DETACH THIS PORTION BEFORE CASHING

DATE	DESCRIPTION	GROSS AMOUNT	DEDUCTIONS	NET AMOUNT
4/12/92	Invoice No. 529482	940.00	18.80	921.20

MONROE COMPANY

Bank Statement

Although there are some differences in procedure, banks usually maintain an original and a copy of all checking account transactions. When this is done, the original becomes the statement of account that is mailed to the depositor, usually once each month. Like any account with a customer or a creditor, the bank statement shows the beginning balance, checks and other debits (deductions by the bank), deposits and other credits (additions by the bank), and the balance at the end of the period. The depositor's checks received by the bank during the period may accompany the bank statement, arranged in the order of payment. The paid or canceled checks are perforated or stamped "Paid," together with the date of payment.

Debit or credit memorandums describing other entries in the depositor's account may also be enclosed with the statement. For example, the bank may have debited the depositor's account for service charges or for deposited checks returned because of insufficient funds. It may have credited the account for receipts from notes receivable left for collection, for loans to the depositor, or for interest.[3] A typical bank statement is illustrated on page 226.

Bank Reconciliation

When all cash receipts are deposited in the bank and all payments are made by check, the cash account is often called Cash in Bank. This account in the depositor's ledger is the reciprocal of the account with the depositor in

[3]Although interest-bearing checking accounts are common for individuals, Federal Reserve Regulation Q prohibits the paying of interest on corporate checking accounts.

Bank Statement

ANB
MEMBER FDIC
AMERICAN NATIONAL BANK
OF DETROIT
DETROIT, MI 48201-2500 (313)933-8547

MONROE COMPANY
813 GREENWOOD STREET
DETROIT, MI 48206-4070

PAGE 1
ACCOUNT NUMBER 1627042
FROM 6/30/92 TO 7/31/92

	BALANCE	4,218.60
22	DEPOSITS	13,749.75
52	WITHDRAWALS	15,013.57
2	OTHER DEBITS AND CREDITS	405.00CR
	NEW BALANCE	3,359.78

--CHECKS AND OTHER DEBITS---			---DEPOSITS--*	--DATE--*	--BALANCE--*
819.40	122.54		585.75	07/01	3,862.41
369.50	732.26	20.15	421.53	07/02	3,162.03
600.00	190.70	52.50	781.30	07/03	3,100.13
25.93	160.00		662.50	07/05	3,576.70
36.80	181.02		503.18	07/07	3,862.06
32.26	535.09		932.00	07/29	3,389.40
21.10	126.20		705.21	07/30	3,947.31
		SC 3.00	MS 408.00	07/30	4,352.31
26.12	1,615.13		648.72	07/31	3,359.78

EC--ERROR CORRECTION
MS--MISCELLANEOUS
NSF--NOT SUFFICIENT FUNDS

OD--OVERDRAFT
PS--PAYMENT STOPPED
SC--SERVICE CHARGE

*** *** ***

THE RECONCILEMENT OF THIS STATEMENT WITH YOUR RECORDS IS ESSENTIAL.
ANY ERROR OR EXCEPTION SHOULD BE REPORTED IMMEDIATELY.

the bank's ledger. Cash in Bank in the depositor's ledger is an asset with a debit balance, and the account with the depositor in the bank's ledger is a liability with a credit balance.

It might seem that the two balances should be equal, but they are not likely to be equal on any specific date because of either or both of the following: (1) delay by either party in recording transactions and (2) errors by either party in recording transactions. Ordinarily, there is a time lag of one day or more between the date a check is written and the date that it is presented to the bank for payment. If the depositor mails deposits to the bank or uses the night depository, a time lag between the date of the deposit and the date that it is recorded by the bank is also probable. Conversely, the bank may debit or credit the depositor's account for transactions about which the depositor will not be informed until later. Examples are service or collection fees charged by the bank and the proceeds of notes receivable sent to the bank for collection.

To determine the reasons for any difference and to correct any errors that may have been made by the bank or the depositor, the depositor's own records should be reconciled with the bank statement. The **bank reconciliation** is divided into two major sections: one section begins with the balance according to the bank statement and ends with the adjusted balance; the other section begins with the balance according to the depositor's records and also ends with the adjusted balance. The two amounts designated as the adjusted balance must be equal. The form and the content of the bank reconciliation are outlined as follows:

Format for Bank Reconciliation

Bank balance according to bank statement		$XXX
Add: Additions by depositor not on bank statement	$XX	
Bank errors	XX	XX
		$XXX
Deduct: Deductions by depositor not on bank statement	$XX	
Bank errors	XX	XX
Adjusted balance		$XXX
Bank balance according to depositor's records		$XXX
Add: Additions by bank not recorded by depositor	$XX	
Depositor errors	XX	XX
		$XXX
Deduct: Deductions by bank not recorded by depositor	$XX	
Depositor errors	XX	XX
Adjusted balance		$XXX

The following procedures are used in finding the reconciling items and determining the adjusted balance of Cash in Bank:

1. Individual deposits listed on the bank statement are compared with unrecorded deposits appearing in the preceding reconciliation and with deposit receipts or other records of deposits. Deposits not recorded by the bank are added to the balance according to the bank statement.
2. Paid checks are compared with outstanding checks appearing on the preceding reconciliation and with the record of checks written. Checks issued that have not been paid by the bank are outstanding and are deducted from the balance according to the bank statement.
3. Bank credit memorandums, representing additions made by the bank, are traced to the records of cash receipts. Credit memorandums that have not been recorded are added to the balance according to the depositor's records.
4. Bank debit memorandums, representing deductions made by the bank, are traced to the records of cash payments. Debit memorandums that have not been recorded are deducted from the balance according to the depositor's records.
5. Errors discovered during the process of making the foregoing comparisons are listed separately on the reconciliation. For example, if the amount for which a check was written had been recorded erroneously by the depositor, the amount of the error should be added to or deducted from the balance according to the depositor's records. Similarly, errors by the bank should be added to or deducted from the balance according to the bank statement.

Illustration of Bank Reconciliation. The bank statement for Monroe Company, reproduced on page 226, indicates a balance of $3,359.78 as of July 31. The balance in Cash in Bank in Monroe Company's ledger as of the same date is $2,234.99. Use of the procedures outlined above reveals the following reconciling items:

Deposit of July 31 not recorded on bank statement	$ 816.20
Checks outstanding: No. 812, $1,061.00; No. 878, $435.39; No. 883, $48.60	1,544.99

Note from Wilson Co. plus interest of $8 collected by bank (credit memorandum), not recorded by Monroe Company	$ 408.00
Bank service charges (debit memorandum) not recorded by Monroe Company	3.00
Check No. 879 for $732.26 to Taylor Co. on account, recorded by Monroe Company as $723.26	9.00

The bank reconciliation based on the bank statement and the reconciling items is as follows:

Monroe Company
Bank Reconciliation
July 31, 1992

Balance per bank statement		$3,359.78
Add deposit of July 31, not recorded by bank		816.20
		$4,175.98
Deduct outstanding checks:		
No. 812	$1,061.00	
No. 878	435.39	
No. 883	48.60	1,544.99
Adjusted balance		$2,630.99
Balance per depositor's records		$2,234.99
Add note and interest collected by bank		408.00
		$2,642.99
Deduct: Bank service charges	$ 3.00	
Error in recording Check No. 879	9.00	12.00
Adjusted balance		$2,630.99

Entries Based on Bank Reconciliation. Bank memorandums not recorded by the depositor and depositor's errors shown by the bank reconciliation require that entries be made in the accounts. The entries for Monroe Company, based on the bank reconciliation above, are as follows:

July 31	Cash in Bank	408	
	Notes Receivable		400
	Interest Income		8
	Note collected by bank.		
31	Miscellaneous Administrative Expense	3	
	Accounts Payable—Taylor Co.	9	
	Cash in Bank		12
	Bank service charges and error in recording Check No. 879.		

The data needed for these entries are provided by the section of the bank reconciliation that begins with the balance per depositor's records. No entries are necessary on the depositor's books as a result of the information included in the section that begins with the balance per bank statement.

After the foregoing entries are posted, the cash in bank account will have a debit balance of $2,630.99, which agrees with the adjusted balance shown on the bank reconciliation. This is the amount of cash available for use as of July 31 and the amount that would be reported on the balance sheet on that date.

Importance of Bank Reconciliation. The bank reconciliation is an important part of the system of internal control because it is a means of comparing recorded cash, as shown by the accounting records, with the amount of cash reported by the bank. It thus provides for finding and correcting errors and irregularities. Greater internal control is achieved when the bank reconciliation is prepared by an employee who does not take part in or record cash transactions with the bank. Without a proper separation of these duties, cash is more likely to be embezzled. For example, an employee who takes part in all of these duties could prepare an unauthorized check, omit it from the accounts, and cash it. Then to account for the canceled check when returned by the bank, the employee could understate the amount of the outstanding checks on future bank reconciliations by the amount of the embezzlement.

INTERNAL CONTROL OF CASH RECEIPTS

OBJECTIVE 5
Describe and illustrate internal controls for cash receipts.

Department stores and other retail businesses ordinarily receive cash from two main sources: (1) over the counter from cash customers and (2) by mail from charge customers making payments on account. At the end of the business day, each salesclerk counts the cash in the assigned cash drawer and records the amount on a memorandum form. An employee from the cashier's department removes the cash register tapes on which total receipts were recorded for each cash drawer, counts the cash, and compares the total with the memorandum and the tape, noting any differences. The cash is then taken to the cashier's office and the tapes and memorandum forms are forwarded to the accounting department, where they become the basis for journal entries.

The employees who open incoming mail compare the amount of cash received with the amount shown on the accompanying remittance advice to be certain that the two amounts agree. If there is no separate remittance advice, an employee prepares one on a form designed for such use. All cash received, usually in the form of checks and money orders, is sent to the cashier's department, where it is combined with the receipts from cash sales and a deposit ticket is prepared. The remittance advices are delivered to the accounting department, where they become the basis for journal entries.

The duplicate deposit tickets or other bank receipt forms obtained by the cashier are sent to the controller or other financial officer, who compares the total amount with that reported by the accounting department as the total debit to Cash in Bank for the period.

Cash Short and Over

The amount of cash actually received during a day often does not agree with the record of cash receipts. Whenever there is a difference between the record and the actual cash and no error can be found in the record, it must be assumed that the mistake occurred in making change. The cash shortage or overage is recorded in an account entitled Cash Short and Over. For example, if the actual cash received from cash sales is less than the amount indicated by the register tally, the entry would include a debit to Cash Short and Over. An example for one day's receipts follows:

Cash in Bank	4,577.60	
Cash Short and Over	3.16	
Sales		4,580.76

If there is a debit balance in the cash short and over account at the end of the fiscal period, it is an expense and may be included in "Miscellaneous administrative expense" on the income statement. If there is a credit balance, it is revenue and may be listed in the "Other income" section. If the balance becomes larger than may be accounted for by minor errors in making change, the management should take corrective measures.

Cash Change Funds

Retail stores and other businesses that receive cash directly from customers must maintain a fund of currency and coins in order to make change. The fund may be established by drawing a check for the required amount, debiting Cash on Hand and crediting Cash in Bank. No additional charges or credits to the cash on hand account are necessary unless the amount of the fund is to be increased or decreased. At the end of each business day, the total amount of cash received during the day is deposited and the original amount of the change fund is retained. The desired composition of the fund is maintained by exchanging bills or coins for those of other denominations at the bank.

INTERNAL CONTROL OF CASH PAYMENTS

OBJECTIVE 6
Describe and illustrate internal controls for cash payments.

It is common practice for business enterprises to require that every payment of cash be evidenced by a check signed by a designated official. As an additional control, some firms require two signatures on all checks or only on checks which are larger than a certain amount. It is also common to use a check protector, which produces amounts on the check that are not easily removed or changed.

When the owner of a business has personal knowledge of all goods and services purchased, the owner may sign checks, with the assurance that the creditors have followed the terms of their contracts and that the exact amount of the obligation is being paid. Disbursing officials are seldom able to have such a complete knowledge of affairs, however. In enterprises of even moderate size, the responsibility for issuing purchase orders, inspecting goods received, and verifying contractual and arithmetical details of invoices is divided among the employees of several departments. It is desirable, therefore, to coordinate these related activities and to link them with the final issuance of checks to creditors. One of the best systems used for this purpose is the voucher system.

The Voucher System

A **voucher system** is made up of records, methods, and procedures used in proving and recording liabilities and in paying and recording cash payments. A voucher system uses (1) vouchers, (2) a file for unpaid vouchers, and (3) a file for paid vouchers. As in all areas of accounting systems and internal controls, many differences in detail are possible. The discussion that follows refers to a medium-size merchandising enterprise with separate departments for purchasing, receiving, accounting, and disbursing.

Vouchers. The term **voucher** is widely used in accounting. In a general sense, it means any document that serves as proof of authority to pay cash, such as an invoice approved for payment, or as evidence that cash has been paid, such as a canceled check. The term has a narrower meaning when applied to the voucher system: a voucher is a special form on which is recorded relevant data about a liability and the details of its payment.

An important characteristic of the voucher system is the requirement that a voucher be prepared for each expenditure. In fact, a check may not be issued except in payment of a properly authorized voucher. Vouchers may be paid immediately after they are prepared or at a later date, depending upon the circumstances and the credit terms.

A voucher form is illustrated below. The face of the voucher provides space for the name and address of the creditor, the date and number of the voucher, and basic details of the invoice or other supporting document, such as the vendor's invoice number and the amount and terms of the invoice. One half of the back of the voucher is devoted to the account distribution and the other half to summaries of the voucher and the details of payment. Spaces are also provided for the signature or initials of certain employees.

Voucher

VOUCHER — JANSEN AUTO SUPPLY INC.

Date July 1, 1992 Voucher No. 451

Payee Allied Manufacturing Company
683 Fairmont Road
Chicago, IL 60630-3168

DATE	DETAILS	AMOUNT
June 28, 1992	Invoice No. 4693-C FOB Chicago, 2/10, n/30	450.00

Attach Supporting Documents

ACCOUNT DISTRIBUTION

DEBIT	AMOUNT
PURCHASES	450 00
SUPPLIES	
ADVERTISING EXPENSE	
DELIVERY EXPENSE	
MISC. SELLING EXPENSE	
MISC. GENERAL EXPENSE	
CREDIT ACCOUNTS PAYABLE	450 00

DISTRIBUTION APPROVED *L. Donnelly*

NO. 451
DATE 7/1/92 DUE 7/8/92

Allied Manufacturing Company
683 Fairmont Road
Chicago, IL 60630-3168

VOUCHER SUMMARY

AMOUNT	450 00
ADJUSTMENT	
DISCOUNT	9 00
NET	441 00

APPROVED *H. C. Leshen* CONTROLLER
RECORDED *WB*

PAYMENT SUMMARY

DATE 7/8/92
AMOUNT 441.00
CHECK NO. 863
APPROVED *A. T. Wood*
RECORDED *L. K. R.* *A. S.*

Vouchers are customarily prepared by the accounting department on the basis of an invoice or a memorandum that serves as proof of an expenditure. This is usually done only after the following comparisons and verifications have been completed and noted on the invoice:

1. Comparison of the invoice with a copy of the purchase order to verify quantities, prices, and terms.
2. Comparison of the invoice with the receiving report to verify receipt of the items billed.
3. Verification of the arithmetical accuracy of the invoice.

After all data except details of payment have been inserted, the invoice or other supporting evidence is attached to the face of the voucher, which is then folded with the account distribution and summaries on the outside. The voucher is then given to the designated official or officials for final approval.

Unpaid Voucher File. After approval by the designated official, each voucher is recorded as a credit to Accounts Payable and a debit to the appropriate account or accounts. For example, the entry to record the voucher prepared by Jansen Auto Supply Inc., illustrated above, is as follows:

Purchases	450	
Accounts Payable		450

After the voucher is recorded, it is filed in an unpaid voucher file, where it remains until it is paid. The amount due on each voucher represents the credit balance of an account payable.

All voucher systems include some way to assure payment within the discount period or on the last day of the credit period. A simple but effective method is to file each voucher in the unpaid voucher file according to the earliest date that consideration should be given to its payment. The file may be made up of a group of folders, numbered from 1 to 31, the numbers representing days of a month. Such a system brings to the attention of the disbursing official the vouchers that are to be paid on each day. It also provides management with a convenient means of forecasting the amount of cash needed to meet maturing obligations.

When a voucher is to be paid, it is removed from the unpaid voucher file and a check is issued in payment. The date, the number, and the amount of the check are listed on the back of the voucher for use in recording the payment. Paid vouchers and the supporting documents are often run through a canceling machine to prevent accidental or intentional reuse.

An exception to the general rule that vouchers be prepared for all expenditures may be made for bank charges shown by debit memorandums or notations on the bank statement. For example, such items as bank service charges, safe-deposit box rentals, and returned NSF (Not Sufficient Funds) checks from customers may be charged to the depositor's account without either a formal voucher or a check. For large expenditures, such as the repayment of a bank loan, a supporting voucher may be prepared, if desired, even though a check is not written. The paid note may then be attached to the voucher as evidence of the obligation. All bank debit memorandums are the equivalent of checks as evidence of payment.

Paid Voucher File. The payment of a voucher is recorded in the same manner as payment of an account payable. For example, the entry to record the check issued in payment of the Jansen Auto Supply Inc. voucher would be as follows:

Accounts Payable	450	
Cash in Bank		441
Purchases Discounts		9

After payment, vouchers are usually filed in numerical order in a paid voucher file. They are then readily available for examination by employees or independent auditors needing information about a certain expenditure. Eventually the paid vouchers are destroyed according to the firm's policies concerning the retention of records.

Voucher System and Management. The voucher system not only provides effective accounting controls but also aids management in discharging other responsibilities. For example, the voucher system gives greater assurance that all payments are in liquidation of valid liabilities. In addition, current information is always available for use in determining future cash requirements which in turn enables management to make the best use of cash resources. Invoices on which cash discounts are allowed can be paid within the discount period and other invoices can be paid on the final day of the credit period, thus reducing costs and maintaining a favorable credit standing. Seasonal borrowing for working capital purposes can also be planned more accurately, with a consequent saving in interest costs.

Purchases Discounts

In earlier chapters, purchases of merchandise were recorded at the invoice price, and cash discounts taken were credited to the purchases discounts account at the time of payment. There are two opposing views on how discounts taken should be reported in the income statement.

The most widely accepted view, which has been followed in this textbook, is that purchases discounts should be reported as a deduction from purchases. For example, the cost of merchandise with an invoice price of $1,000, subject to terms of 2/10, n/30, is recorded initially at $1,000. If payment is made within the discount period, the discount of $20 reduces the cost to $980. If the invoice is not paid within the discount period, the cost of the merchandise remains $1,000. This treatment of purchases discounts may be attacked on the grounds that the date of payment should not affect the cost of a commodity. The additional payment required beyond the discount period adds nothing to the value of the commodities purchased.

The second view reports discounts taken as "other income." In terms of the preceding example, the cost of the merchandise is considered to be $1,000, regardless of the time of payment. If payment is made within the discount period, revenue of $20 is considered to be realized. The objection to this procedure lies in the recognition of revenue from the act of purchasing and paying for a commodity. Theoretically, an enterprise might make no sales of merchandise during an accounting period and yet might report as revenue the amount of cash discounts taken.

A major disadvantage of recording purchases at the invoice price and recognizing purchases discounts at the time of payment is that this method does not measure the cost of failing to take discounts. Well-managed enterprises maintain enough cash to pay within the discount period all invoices subject to a discount, and view the failure to take a discount as an inefficiency. To measure the cost of this inefficiency, purchases invoices may be recorded at the net amount, assuming that all discounts will be taken. Any discounts *not* taken are then recorded in an expense account called Discounts Lost. This method measures the cost of failure to take cash discounts and gives management an opportunity to take remedial action. Again assuming the same data, the invoice for $1,000 would be recorded as a debit to Purchases of $980 and a credit to Accounts Payable for the same amount. If the invoice is not paid until after the discount period has passed, the entry would be as follows:

Accounts Payable	980	
Discounts Lost	20	
Cash in Bank		1,000

When this method is used with the voucher system, all vouchers are prepared and recorded at the net amount. Any discount lost is noted on the related voucher and recorded in the journal when the voucher is paid.

Another advantage of this treatment of purchases discounts is that all merchandise purchased is recorded initially at the net price, and hence no later adjustments to cost are necessary. An objection, however, is that the amount reported as accounts payable in the balance sheet may be less than the amount needed to discharge the liability.

Petty Cash

In most businesses there is a frequent need for the payment of relatively small amounts, such as for postage due, for transportation charges, or for the purchase of urgently needed supplies at a nearby retail store. Payment by check in such cases would result in delay, annoyance, and excessive expense of maintaining the records. Yet because these small payments may occur frequently and therefore amount to a considerable total sum, it is desirable to retain close control over such payments. This may be done by maintaining a special cash fund called **petty cash**.

In establishing a petty cash fund, the first step is to estimate the amount of cash needed for disbursements of relatively small amounts during a certain period, such as a week or a month. If the voucher system is used, a voucher is then prepared for this amount and it is recorded as a debit to Petty Cash and a credit to Accounts Payable. The check drawn to pay the voucher is recorded as a debit to Accounts Payable and a credit to Cash in Bank.

The money obtained from cashing the check is placed in the custody of a specific employee who is authorized to disburse the fund according to restrictions as to maximum amount and purpose. Each time a disbursement is made from the fund, the employee records the essential details on a receipt form, obtains the signature of the payee as proof of the payment, and initials the completed form.

When the amount of money in the petty cash fund is reduced to the predetermined minimum amount, the fund is replenished. If the voucher system is used, the accounts debited on the replenishing voucher are those indicated by a summary of expenditures. The voucher is then recorded as a debit to the various expense and asset accounts and a credit to Accounts Payable. The check in payment of the voucher is recorded in the usual manner.

To illustrate the entries that would be made in accounting for petty cash, assume that a voucher system is used and that a petty cash fund of $100 is established on August 1. At the end of August, the petty cash receipts indicate expenditures for the following items: office supplies, $28; postage (office supplies), $22; store supplies, $35; and daily newspaper (miscellaneous administrative expense), $3.70. To record the establishment and replenishment of the petty cash fund, the entries would be as follows:

Aug.	1	Petty Cash	100.00	
		Accounts Payable		100.00
	1	Accounts Payable	100.00	
		Cash in Bank		100.00
	31	Office Supplies	50.00	
		Store Supplies	35.00	
		Miscellaneous Administrative Expense	3.70	
		Accounts Payable		88.70
	31	Accounts Payable	88.70	
		Cash in Bank		88.70

Replenishing the petty cash fund restores it to its original amount. It should be noted that the only entry in the petty cash account will be the initial debit, unless at some later time the standard amount of the fund is increased or decreased.

Because disbursements are not recorded in the accounts until the fund is replenished, petty cash funds and other special funds that operate in a like manner should always be replenished at the end of an accounting period. The amount of money actually in the fund will then agree with the balance in the related fund account, and the expenses and the assets for which payment has been made will be recorded in the proper period.

Other Cash Funds

Cash funds may also be established to meet other special needs of a business. For example, money may be advanced for travel expenses as needed. Then periodically, after expense reports have been received, the expenses are recorded and the fund is replenished. A similar procedure may be used to provide a working fund for a sales office located in another city. The amount of the fund may be deposited in a local bank and the sales representative may be authorized to draw checks for payment of rent, salaries, and other operating expenses. Each month, the representative sends the invoices, bank statement, paid checks, bank reconciliation, and other business documents to the home office. The data are audited, the expenditures are recorded, and a reimbursing check is returned for deposit in the local bank.

CASH TRANSACTIONS AND ELECTRONIC FUNDS TRANSFER

OBJECTIVE 7
Describe recent trends in the use of electronic funds transfer to process cash transactions.

Currently most cash transactions are in the form of currency or check. The broad principles discussed in earlier sections provide the basis for developing an effective system to control such cash transactions. However, the development of **electronic funds transfer (EFT)** may eventually change the form in which many cash transactions are executed and could affect the processing and controlling of cash transactions.

EFT can be defined as a payment system that uses computerized electronic impulses rather than paper (money, checks, etc.) to effect a cash transaction. For example, a business may pay its employees by means of EFT. Under such a system, employees who want their payroll checks deposited directly in a checking account sign an authorization form. For each pay period, the business' computer produces a payroll file with computer-sensitive notations for relevant payroll data. The file is transmitted over telephone lines to the banks designated by the employees. The banks then credit each employee's account. Similar cash payments might be made for other preauthorized payments. The federal government currently processes several million social security checks through EFT.

EFT is also beginning to play a role in retail sales. Through a point-of-sale (POS) system, a customer pays for goods at the time of purchase by presenting a plastic card. The card is used to activate a terminal in the store and thereby effect an immediate transfer from the customer's checking account to the retailer's account at the bank.

Some companies are using EFT systems to process both cash payments and cash receipts. For example, General Electric Co. estimates that 40–50% of its payments to creditors and its collections from customers are processed by EFT systems. Studies have indicated that EFT systems may reduce the cost of processing certain cash transactions and contribute to better control over cash receipts and cash payments. Offsetting these potential advantages are problems of protecting the privacy of information stored in computers, and difficulties in documenting purchase and sale transactions. In any event, developments with EFT systems are likely to be followed very closely by most businesses over the next few years.

CONTROLLING EFT SYSTEMS

Many companies use EFT to transfer cash among various corporate bank accounts, to make investments, and to pay vendors. Control weaknesses and some relatively simple steps to safeguard electronically transferred funds were described in a *Journal of Accountancy* article, as follows:

The key element in most EFT systems is the telephone. Once a corporate cash manager has established an EFT facility with a bank, he or she usually only needs to call the bank (or make contact through a computer hookup), identify himself and specify the dollar amount to be transferred from a particular account at the disbursing bank, as well as the account and bank to which funds are to be transferred.... As a result of these calls, hundreds of billions of dollars are transferred through the banking system every business day....

...When cash disbursements are made by written check, most companies' control procedures... [provide] reasonable assurance that cash disbursements... are being made [properly. When an EFT system is used]...several relatively inexpensive and easily implemented control procedures can be added to traditional controls to reduce the risk of losing funds during electronic transfers....

- *Passwords. Companies should instruct banks not to accept transfer instructions from any caller who is unable to provide an established password....*
- *Additional authorization. The vast majority of fund transfers by most companies are routine, such as transfers between their own bank accounts and transfers to investment accounts in the company's name. These reasonably could be considered relatively low risk, since funds never leave the company's accounts. Transfers to outside accounts, on the other hand, generally are much less frequent and obviously involve much higher risk.*

  To minimize the risk of lost funds... additional authorizations [should be required] before unusual transfers are completed....
- *After the transfer. The traditional bank account reconciliation process is an effective control except for the time lag involved.... To overcome this weakness, an ongoing reconciliation system can be used with EFTs. Banks should be instructed to provide the transaction advice for each fund transfer on a timely basis....*

  Transaction advices should be sent directly to a person not involved in the EFT process. This person should be instructed to match the advices on the day they are received with the internal cash receipt or disbursement records, as well as with required internal documentation....

Source: Michael J. Fischer, "Electronic Funds Transfers: Controlling the Risk," *The Journal of Accountancy* (June 1988), pp. 130–134.

CHAPTER REVIEW

KEY POINTS

OBJECTIVE 1

Principles of Accounting Systems

Although accounting systems will vary from business to business, the following broad principles will apply to all systems: cost-effectiveness balance; flexibility to meet future needs; adequate internal controls; effective reporting; and adaptation to organizational structure.

OBJECTIVE 2

Accounting System Installation and Revision

Accounting system installation and revision involves three phases: (1) analysis of information needs, (2) design of the new system, and (3) implementation of proposals.

OBJECTIVE 3

Internal Control Structure

The internal control structure of an enterprise consists of the detailed policies and procedures which provide reasonable assurance that an entity's objectives will be achieved. The internal control structure consists of three elements: (1) the control environment, (2) the control procedures, and (3) the accounting system.

The control environment refers to the overall attitude toward and awareness of the importance of controls by both management and other employees. Control procedures are those policies and procedures that management has established within the control environment in order to provide reasonable assurance that enterprise goals will be achieved. General control procedures which can be integrated throughout the accounting system include the following: competent personnel and rotation of duties, assignment of responsibility, separation of responsibility for related operations, separation of operations and accounting, proofs and security measures, and independent review. The accounting system is an integral part of the control structure because it provides the information needed by management to plan and direct operations in achieving enterprise goals.

OBJECTIVE 4

Control Over Cash

It is necessary to safeguard cash effectively because of the ease with which it can be transferred. One of the major devices for maintaining control over cash is the bank account. To obtain the most benefit from a bank account, all cash received must be deposited in the bank and all payments must be made by checks drawn on the bank or from special cash funds.

Periodically, the bank mails to the depositor a statement of account. This statement of account should be reconciled with the depositor's records by preparing a bank reconciliation. The bank reconciliation is divided into two major sections: one section begins with the balance according to the bank statement and ends with an adjusted balance; the other section begins with the balance according to the depositor's records and also ends with an adjusted balance. After all reconciling items have been considered, the two amounts designated as the adjusted balance must be equal.

After a bank reconciliation has been prepared, the items which appear in the section of the bank reconciliation beginning with the balance according to the depositor's records must be entered into the accounting records through the use of journal entries.

OBJECTIVE 5

Internal Control of Cash Receipts

The bank reconciliation is an important part of the system of internal control over cash. Other controls of cash receipts include the separation of responsibilities for recording cash transactions from the handling of cash, the use of a cash short and over account for differences between recorded receipts and actual receipts, and the use of cash change funds.

OBJECTIVE 6

Internal Control of Cash Payments

One of the best systems for establishing control of cash payments is the use of a voucher system. A voucher system is made up of records, methods, and procedures used in proving and recording liabilities and in making and recording cash payments. A voucher system uses (1) vouchers, (2) a file for unpaid vouchers, and (3) a file for paid vouchers.

Because of the importance of taking advantage of all purchases discounts, a business may use a separate account, called Discounts Lost, to account for any discounts not taken during the discount period. When this method is used with the voucher system, all vouchers are prepared and recorded at the net amount, assuming that the discount will be taken.

A special cash fund, called petty cash, may be used by a business to make small payments that occur frequently, for which payment by check would cause delay, annoyance, or excessive expense of maintaining records. The amount of money maintained in a petty cash fund is placed in the custody of a specific employee, who authorizes disbursement of the fund according to specific restrictions as to maximum amount and purpose. When the amount of money in the petty cash fund is reduced to a predetermined minimum amount, the fund is replenished. Other cash funds may be established by businesses for purposes such as travel expenses, selling expenses, and other operating expenses.

OBJECTIVE 7 Cash Transactions and Electronic Funds Transfer

Electronic funds transfer is a payment system that uses computerized electronic impulses rather than paper (money, checks, etc.) to effect cash transactions. EFT is beginning to play an important role in retail sales and in processing cash payments and cash receipts.

KEY TERMS

accounting system 217
data base 217
subsidiary ledger 217
general ledger 217
controlling account 217
internal controls 218
bank reconciliation 226
voucher system 230
voucher 230
petty cash 234
electronic funds transfer (EFT) 235

SELF-EXAMINATION QUESTIONS

Answers at end of chapter.

1. The detailed procedures adopted by management to direct operations so that enterprise goals can be achieved are termed:
   A. internal controls
   B. systems analysis
   C. systems design
   D. system implementation

2. In preparing a bank reconciliation, the amount of checks outstanding would be:
   A. added to the bank balance according to the bank statement
   B. deducted from the bank balance according to the bank statement
   C. added to the bank balance according to the depositor's records
   D. deducted from the bank balance according to the depositor's records

3. Journal entries based on the bank reconciliation are required for:
   A. additions to the bank balance according to the depositor's records
   B. deductions from the bank balance according to the depositor's records
   C. both A and B
   D. neither A nor B

4. A voucher system is used, all vouchers for purchases are recorded at the net amount, and a purchase is made for $500 under terms 1/10, n/30.
   A. Purchases would be debited for $495 to record the purchase.
   B. Discounts Lost would be debited for $5 if the voucher is not paid within the discount period.
   C. If the voucher is not paid until after the discount period has expired, the discount lost would be reported as an expense on the income statement.
   D. All of the above

5. A petty cash fund is:
   A. used to pay relatively small amounts
   B. established by estimating the amount of cash needed for disbursements of relatively small amounts during a specified period
   C. reimbursed when the amount of money in the fund is reduced to a predetermined minimum amount
   D. all of the above

ILLUSTRATIVE PROBLEM

The bank statement for Dunlap Company for April 30 indicates a balance of $10,443.11. The Dunlap Company employs the voucher system in controlling expenditures and disbursements. All cash receipts are deposited each evening in a night depository, after banking hours. The accounting records indicate the following summary data for April:

Cash balance as of April 1	$ 5,143.50
Total cash receipts for April	28,971.60
Total amount of checks issued in April..................	26,060.85

Comparison of the bank statement and the accompanying canceled checks and memorandums with the records revealed the following reconciling items:

(a) The bank had collected for Dunlap Company $912 on a note left for collection. The face of the note was $900.
(b) A deposit of $1,852.21, representing receipts of April 30, had been made too late to appear on the bank statement.
(c) Checks outstanding totaled $3,265.27.
(d) A check drawn for $79 had been erroneously charged by the bank as $97.
(e) A check for $10 returned with the statement had been recorded in the records as $100. The check was for the payment of an obligation to Davis Equipment Company for the purchase of office supplies on account.
(f) Bank service charges for April amounted to $8.20.

Instructions:

1. Prepare a bank reconciliation for April.
2. Journalize the entries that should be made by Dunlap Company.

SOLUTION

(1)

Dunlap Company
Bank Reconciliation
April 30, 19--

Balance per bank statement		$10,443.11
Add: Deposit of April 30 not recorded by bank	$1,852.21	
Bank error in charging check for $97 instead of $79	18.00	1,870.21
		$12,313.32
Deduct: Outstanding checks		3,265.27
Adjusted balance..		$ 9,048.05
Balance per depositor's records.......................		$ 8,054.25*
Add: Proceeds of note collected by bank including $12 interest	$ 912.00	
Error in recording check........................	90.00	1,002.00
		$ 9,056.25
Deduct: Bank service charges..........................		8.20
Adjusted balance..		$ 9,048.05

*$5,143.50 + $28,971.60 − $26,060.85

(2)

Cash in Bank	1,002.00	
Notes Receivable		900.00
Interest Income		12.00
Accounts Payable		90.00
Miscellaneous Administrative Expense	8.20	
Cash in Bank		8.20

DISCUSSION QUESTIONS

5–1. Why is the accounting system of an enterprise an information system?

5–2. What are internal controls?

5–3. What is the objective of systems analysis?

5–4. What is included in an enterprise's *Systems Manual*?

5–5. Name and describe the three elements of the internal control structure.

5–6. How does a policy of rotating clerical employees from job to job aid in strengthening internal control?

5–7. Why should the responsibility for a sequence of related operations be divided among different persons?

5–8. The ticket seller at a movie theater doubles as ticket taker for a few minutes each day while the ticket taker is on a "break." Which principle of internal control is violated in this situation?

5–9. Why should the responsibility for maintaining the accounting records be separated from the responsibility for operations?

5–10. How can the use of fidelity insurance aid internal control?

5–11. How does a periodic review by internal auditors strengthen the system of internal control?

5–12. Why is cash the asset that often warrants the most attention in the design of an effective internal control system?

5–13. (a) What is meant by the term *compensating balance* as applied to the checking account of a firm? (b) How is the compensating balance reported in the financial statements?

5–14. What name is often given to the notification attached to a check that indicates the specific invoice that is being paid?

5–15. When checks are received, they are recorded as debits to Cash, the assumption being that the drawer has sufficient funds on deposit. What entry should be made if a check received from a customer and deposited is returned by the bank for lack of sufficient funds (NSF)?

5–16. Do items reported on the bank statement as debits represent (a) deductions made by the bank from the depositor's balance, or (a) additions made by the bank to the depositor's balance?

5–17. What is the purpose of preparing a bank reconciliation?

5–18. Identify each of the following reconciling items as: (a) an addition to the balance per bank statement, (b) a deduction from the balance per bank statement, (c) an addition to the balance per depositor's records, or (d) a deduction from the balance per depositor's records. (None of the transactions reported by bank debit and credit memorandums have been recorded by the depositor.)

(1) Deposit in transit, $4,725.10.
(2) Note collected by bank, $6,090.00.
(3) Outstanding checks, $8,515.50.
(4) Check for $100 charged by bank as $1,000.
(5) Check drawn by depositor for $25 but recorded as $250.
(6) Bank service charges, $30.15.
(7) Check of a customer returned by bank to depositor because of insufficient funds, $83.20.

5-19. Which of the reconciling items listed in Question 5-18 require an entry in the depositor's accounts?

5-20. The procedures employed by Martino's for over-the-counter receipts are as follows: At the close of each day's business, the salesclerks count the cash in their respective cash drawers, after which they determine the amount recorded on the cash register tapes and prepare the memorandum cash form, noting any discrepancies. An employee from the cashier's office counts the cash, compares the total with the memorandum, and takes the cash to the cashier's office. (a) Indicate the weak link in internal control. (b) How can the weakness be corrected?

5-21. The mailroom employees of Clark Company send all remittances and remittance advices to the cashier. The cashier deposits the cash in the bank and forwards the remittance advices and duplicate deposit slips to the accounting department. (a) Indicate the weak link in internal control in the handling of cash receipts. (b) How can the weakness be corrected?

5-22. The combined cash count of all cash registers at the close of business is $3.50 more than the cash sales indicated by the cash register tapes. (a) In what account is the cash overage recorded? (b) Are cash overages debited or credited to this account?

5-23. In which section of the income statement would a credit balance in Cash Short and Over be reported?

5-24. The bookkeeper pays all obligations by prenumbered checks. What are the strengths and weaknesses in the internal control over cash disbursements in this situation?

5-25. What is meant by the term *voucher* as applied to the voucher system?

5-26. Before a voucher for the purchase of merchandise is approved for payment, three documents should be compared to verify the accuracy of the liability. Name these three documents.

5-27. The controller approves all vouchers before they are submitted to the treasurer for payment. What procedure can the controller add to the system to assure that the documents accompanying the vouchers and supporting the expenditures are not "reused" to support future vouchers improperly?

5-28. In what order are vouchers ordinarily filed (a) in the unpaid voucher file, and (b) in the paid voucher file? Give reasons for the answers.

5-29. What are the two possibilities for reporting purchases discounts on the income statement?

5-30. Merchandise with an invoice price of $5,000 is purchased subject to terms of 1/10, n/30. Determine the cost of the merchandise according to each of the following systems:

(a) Discounts taken are treated as deductions from the invoice price.
   (1) The invoice is paid within the discount period.
   (2) The invoice is paid after the discount period has expired.

(b) Discounts taken are treated as other income.
   (1) The invoice is paid within the discount period.
   (2) The invoice is paid after the discount period has expired.

(c) Discounts allowable are treated as deductions from the invoice price, regardless of when payment is made.
   (1) The invoice is paid within the discount period.
   (2) The invoice is paid after the discount period has expired.

5-31. What account or accounts are debited when recording the voucher (a) establishing a petty cash fund and (b) replenishing a petty cash fund?

5-32. The petty cash account has a debit balance of $500. At the end of the accounting period, there is $42 in the petty cash fund along with petty cash receipts totaling $458. Should the fund be replenished as of the last day of the period? Discuss.

5-33. What is meant by electronic funds transfer?

Real World Focus

5-34. Between September 3 and September 22, seventeen prenumbered checks totaling $1,129,232.39 were forged and cashed on the accounts of Perini Corporation, a construction company based in the Boston suburb of Framingham. Perini Corporation kept its supply of blank prenumbered checks in an unlocked storeroom with items such as styrofoam coffee cups. Every clerk and secretary had access to this storeroom. It was later discovered that someone had apparently stolen two boxes of prenumbered checks. The numbers of the missing checks matched the numbers of the out-of-sequence checks cashed by the banks. What fundamental principle of control over cash was violated in this case?

Ethics Discussion Case

5–35. Mark Wetzstein, assistant to the controller of Hibbitt Co., has discovered during the reconciliation of Hibbitt's bank account that Jones County National Bank erroneously recorded a $1,500 check written by Hibbitt Co. as $1,000. Mark has decided not to notify the bank, but to wait to see if the bank eventually detects the error. Mark plans to record the $500 error as Other Income if the bank fails to detect the error within the next three months.

Discuss whether Mark Wetzstein is behaving in an ethical manner.

EXERCISES

Ex. 5–36.
Bank reconciliation.
OBJ. 4

The following data are accumulated for use in reconciling the bank account of Meg Nance and Company for June:

(a) Balance per bank statement at June 30, $7,929.50.
(b) Balance per depositor's records at June 30, $6,017.05.
(c) Checks outstanding, $2,510.40.
(d) A check for $230 in payment of a voucher was erroneously recorded as $320.
(e) Deposit in transit, not recorded by bank, $671.25.
(f) Bank debit memorandum for service charges, $16.70.

Prepare a bank reconciliation.

Ex. 5–37.
Entries for bank reconciliation.
OBJ. 4

Using the data presented in Ex. 5–36, prepare the entry or entries that should be made by the depositor.

Ex. 5–38.
Entries for note collected by bank.
OBJ. 4

Accompanying a bank statement for Conrad Company is a credit memorandum for $4,080, representing the principal ($4,000) and interest ($80) on a note that had been collected by the bank. The depositor had been notified by the bank at the time of the collection, but had made no entries. Present the entry that should be made by the depositor.

Ex. 5–39.
Entry for cash sales.
OBJ. 5

The actual cash received from cash sales for D. D. Clausen Company was $5,754.75, and the amount indicated by the cash register total was $5,750.25. Prepare the entry to record the cash receipts and cash sales.

Ex. 5–40.
Cash change fund entries.
OBJ. 5

Present entries to record the following transactions:

(a) Voucher No. 126 is prepared to establish a change fund of $500.
(b) Check No. 120 is issued in payment of Voucher No. 126.
(c) Cash sales for the day, according to the cash register tapes, were $4,655.30, and cash on hand is $5,153.50. A bank deposit ticket was prepared for $4,653.50.

Ex. 5–41.
Entries for vouchers and checks; purchases at gross amount.
OBJ. 6

Present entries for the following selected transactions. All invoices are recorded at invoice price.

June 1. Recorded Voucher No. 421 for $5,000, payable to Wilson Co., for merchandise purchased, terms 2/10, n/30.
7. Recorded Voucher No. 430 for $1,500, payable to J. J. Franco Co., for merchandise purchased, terms 1/10, n/30.
16. Issued Check No. 419 in payment of Voucher No. 430.
17. Recorded Voucher No. 450 for $2,500, payable to Glos Inc., for merchandise purchased, terms 2/10, n/30.
26. Issued Check No. 441 in payment of Voucher No. 450.
30. Recorded Voucher No. 459 for $221.90 to replenish the petty cash fund for the following disbursements: store supplies, $77.50; office supplies, $51.25; miscellaneous administrative expense, $46.10; miscellaneous selling expense, $47.05.
30. Issued Check No. 448 in payment of Voucher No. 459.
30. Issued Check No. 449 in payment of Voucher No. 421.

Ex. 5–42.
Entries for purchases at net amount.
OBJ. 6

Record the following related transactions, assuming that invoices for commodities purchased are recorded at their net price after deducting the allowable discount:

May 5. Voucher No. 799 is prepared for merchandise purchased from Close Co., $6,000, terms 2/10, n/30.
15. Voucher No. 811 is prepared for merchandise purchased from Bridge's Co., $2,500, terms 1/10, n/30.
25. Check No. 798 is issued in payment of Voucher No. 811.
June 3. Check No. 808 is issued in payment of Voucher No. 799.

Ex. 5–43.
Petty cash fund entries.
OBJ. 6

Prepare entries to record the following:

(a) Voucher No. 8 is prepared to establish a petty cash fund of $250.
(b) Check No. 6 is issued in payment of Voucher No. 8.
(c) The amount of cash in the petty cash fund is now $27.30. Voucher No. 62 is prepared to replenish the fund, based on the following summary of petty cash receipts: office supplies, $82.15; miscellaneous selling expense, $80.60; miscellaneous administrative expense, $58.70. (Since the amount of the check to replenish the fund plus the balance in the fund do not equal $250, record the discrepancy in the cash short and over account.)
(d) Check No. 57 is issued by the disbursing officer in payment of Voucher No. 62. The check is cashed and the money is placed in the fund.

Ex. 5–44.
Procedures for internal control of cash payments.
OBJ. 6

H. L. Stricker Corp. is a medium-size merchandising enterprise. When its current income statement was reviewed, it was noted that the amount of purchases discounts was disproportionately small in comparison with earlier periods. Further investigation revealed that in spite of a sufficient bank balance, a significant amount of available cash discounts had been lost because of failure to make timely payments. In addition, it was discovered that several purchases invoices had been paid twice.

Outline procedures for the payment of vendor's invoices so that the possibilities of losing available cash discounts and of paying an invoice a second time will be minimized.

PROBLEMS

Pb. 5–45.
Bank reconciliation and entries.
OBJ. 4

The cash in bank account for J. D. Casler Co. at May 31 of the current year indicated a balance of $13,215.80. The bank statement indicated a balance of $19,513.90 on May 31. Comparison of the bank statement and the accompanying canceled checks and memorandums with the records revealed the following reconciling items:

(a) Checks outstanding totaled $7,070.10.
(b) A deposit of $3,915.20, representing receipts of May 31, had been made too late to appear on the bank statement.
(c) The bank had collected $3,120 on an interest-bearing note left for collection. The face of the note was $3,000.
(d) A check for $69 returned with the statement had been recorded erroneously as $96. The check was for the payment of an obligation to Lee & Co. for the purchase of office supplies on account.
(e) A check drawn for $42 had been erroneously charged by the bank as $24.
(f) Bank service charges for May amounted to $21.80.

Instructions:

(1) Prepare a bank reconciliation.
(2) Record the necessary entries. The accounts have not been closed. The voucher system is used.

Pb. 5–46.
Bank reconciliation and entries.
OBJ. 4

The cash in bank account for Reese Co. at April 1 of the current year indicated a balance of $8,881.40. Cash deposited and checks written during April totaled $20,500.40 and $18,850.47, respectively. The bank statement indicated a balance of $13,408.45 on April 30. Comparison of the bank statement, the canceled checks, and the accompanying memorandums with the records revealed the following reconciling items:

(a) Checks outstanding totaled $4,180.27.
(b) A deposit of $2,481.70, representing receipts of April 30, had been made too late to appear on the bank statement.
(c) A check for $190 had been erroneously charged by the bank as $100.
(d) A check for $57.45 returned with the statement had been recorded by Reese Co. as $75.45. The check was for the payment of an obligation to Baker and Son for the purchase of office supplies on account.
(e) The bank had collected for Reese Co. $1,090 on a note left for collection. The face of the note was $1,000.
(f) Bank service charges for April amounted to $19.45.

Instructions:

(1) Prepare a bank reconcilation as of April 30.
(2) Journalize the necessary entries. The accounts have not been closed.

Pb. 5–47.
Bank reconciliation and related entries.
OBJ. 4

Pierce Company employs the voucher system in controlling expenditures and disbursements. All cash receipts are deposited each Wednesday and Friday in a night depository after banking hours. The data required to reconcile the bank statement as of July 31 have been abstracted from various documents and records and are reproduced as follows:

CASH IN BANK ACCOUNT:
Balance as of July 1 .... $10,705.50

CASH RECEIPTS FOR MONTH OF JULY .... $ 6,105.10

DUPLICATE DEPOSIT TICKETS:
Date and amount of each deposit in July:

Date	Amount	Date	Amount	Date	Amount
July 2	$725.40	July 12	$516.70	July 23	$731.45
5	634.90	16	697.60	26	601.50
9	819.24	19	701.26	30	677.05

CHECKS WRITTEN:
Number and amount of each check issued in July:

Check No.	Amount	Check No.	Amount	Check No.	Amount
614	$132.50	621	$399.50	628	$737.70
615	700.10	622	VOID	629	329.90
616	279.90	623	VOID	630	882.80
617	395.50	624	818.01	631	981.56
618	535.40	625	658.63	632	62.40
619	220.10	626	550.03	633	310.08
620	238.87	627	318.73	634	103.30

Total amount of checks issued in July $8,655.01

JULY BANK STATEMENT:

Balance as of July 1	$10,550.30
Deposits and other credits	11,308.85
Checks and other debits	(8,623.61)
Balance as of July 31	$13,235.54

Date and amount of each deposit in July:

Date	Amount	Date	Amount	Date	Amount
July 1	$780.80	July 11	$819.24	July 21	$701.26
3	725.40	13	516.70	24	731.45
6	634.90	17	697.60	28	601.50

CHECKS ACCOMPANYING JULY BANK STATEMENT:
Number and amount of each check, rearranged in numerical sequence:

Check No.	Amount	Check No.	Amount	Check No.	Amount
580	$310.10	618	$535.40	626	$550.03
612	92.50	619	220.10	627	318.73
613	137.50	620	238.87	629	339.90
614	132.50	621	399.50	630	882.80
615	700.10	624	818.01	631	981.56
616	279.90	625	658.63	632	62.40
617	395.50			633	310.08

BANK MEMORANDUMS ACCOMPANYING JULY BANK STATEMENT:

Date, description, and amount of each memorandum:

Date	Description	Amount
July 9	Bank credit memo for note collected:	
	Principal	$5,000.00
	Interest	100.00
16	Bank debit memo for check returned because of insufficient funds	240.10
31	Bank debit memo for service charges	19.40

BANK RECONCILIATION FOR PRECEDING MONTH:

Pierce Company
Bank Reconciliation
June 30, 19--

Balance per bank statement		$10,550.30
Add deposit of June 30, not recorded by bank		780.80
		$11,331.10
Deduct outstanding checks:		
No. 580	$310.10	
602	85.50	
612	92.50	
613	137.50	625.60
Adjusted balance		$10,705.50
Balance per depositor's records		$10,723.20
Deduct service charges		17.70
Adjusted balance		$10,705.50

Instructions:

(1) Prepare a bank reconciliation as of July 31. If errors in recording deposits or checks are discovered, assume that the errors were made by the company. Assume that all deposits are from cash sales. All checks are in payment of vouchers.
(2) Record the necessary entries. The accounts have not been closed.
(3) What is the amount of cash in bank that should appear on the balance sheet as of July 31?

Pb. 5–48.
Transactions for petty cash, advances to salespersons fund; cash short and over.
OBJ. 5, 6

Martin Company has just adopted the policy of depositing all cash receipts in the bank and of making all payments by check in conjunction with the voucher system. The following transactions were selected from those completed in June of the current year:

June 1. Recorded Voucher No. 1 to establish a petty cash fund of $200 and a change fund of $500.
1. Issued Check No. 725 in payment of Voucher No. 1.
3. Recorded Voucher No. 4 to establish an advances to salespersons fund of $1,000.
4. Issued Check No. 728 in payment of Voucher No. 4.
15. The cash sales for the day, according to the cash register tapes, totaled $3,097.40. The combined count of all cash on hand (including the change fund) totaled $3,600.
27. Recorded Voucher No. 40 to reimburse the petty cash fund for the following disbursements, each evidenced by a petty cash receipt:
June 4. Store supplies, $16.50.
6. Express charges on merchandise purchased, $15.50.
8. Office supplies, $14.75.
9. Office supplies, $9.20.
12. Postage stamps, $25 (Office Supplies).

June 12. Repair to adding machine, $29.50 (Miscellaneous Administrative Expense).
16. Repair to typewriter, $21.50 (Miscellaneous Administrative Expense).
18. Postage due on special delivery letter, $1.05 (Miscellaneous Administrative Expense).
20. Express charges on merchandise purchased, $19.50.
26. Telegram charges, $7.75 (Miscellaneous Selling Expense).

June 27. Issued Check No. 759 in payment of Voucher No. 40.
28. The cash sales for the day, according to the cash register tapes, totaled $2,609.50. The count of all cash on hand (including the change fund) totaled $3,105.60.
30. Recorded Voucher No. 43 to replenish the advances to salespersons fund for the following expenditures for travel: Gloria Griffin, $202.50; Nick Lane, $297.40; Teresa Palmer, $311.15.
30. Issued Check No. 765 in payment of Voucher No. 43.

Instructions:

Record the transactions.

Pb. 5–49.
Entries for voucher system.
OBJ. 6

The following selected transactions were completed by a company that uses a voucher system, with all invoices recorded at their net price.

May 1. Recorded Voucher No. 615 for $2,500, payable to Davis Supply Co., for office supplies purchased on terms n/30.
3. Recorded Voucher No. 620 for $5,000, payable to A. Adair Co., for merchandise purchased on terms 2/10, n/30.
7. Recorded Voucher No. 628 for $1,500, payable to Kennedy Inc., for merchandise purchased on terms 1/10, n/30.
17. Issued Check No. 595 in payment of Voucher No. 628.
22. Recorded Voucher No. 640 for $239.84 to replenish the petty cash fund for the following disbursements: store supplies, $92.88; office supplies, $69.95; miscellaneous administrative expense, $42.45; miscellaneous selling expense, $34.56.
23. Issued Check No. 606 in payment of Voucher No. 640.
31. Issued Check No. 621 in payment of Voucher No. 620.
31. Issued Check No. 635 in payment of Voucher No. 615.

Instructions:

Record the transactions.

ALTERNATE PROBLEMS

Pb. 5–45A.
Bank reconciliation and entries.
OBJ. 4

The cash in bank account for C. M. Ennis Co. at June 30 of the current year indicated a balance of $19,650.30. The bank statement indicated a balance of $30,606.30 on June 30. Comparison of the bank statement and the accompanying canceled checks and memorandums with the records revealed the following reconciling items:

(a) Checks outstanding totaled $14,941.50.
(b) A deposit of $6,467.75, representing receipts of June 30, had been made too late to appear on the bank statement.
(c) The bank had collected $3,090 on a note left for collection. The face of the note was $3,000.
(d) A check for $91 returned with the statement had been recorded erroneously as $19. The check was for the payment of an obligation to Allen Supply Company for the purchase of office equipment on account.
(e) A check drawn for $55 had been erroneously charged by the bank as $550.
(f) Bank service charges for June amounted to $40.75.

Instructions:

(1) Prepare a bank reconciliation.
(2) Record the necessary entries. The accounts have not been closed. The voucher system is used.

Pb. 5–46A.
Bank reconciliation and entries.
OBJ. 4

The cash in bank account for Baker Co. at July 1 of the current year indicated a balance of $13,443.90. Cash deposited and checks written during July totaled $20,650.75 and $21,770.25, respectively. The bank statement indicated a balance of $20,465.50 on July 31. Comparison of the bank statement, the canceled checks, and the accompanying memorandums with the records revealed the following reconciling items:

(a) Checks outstanding totaled $8,003.84.
(b) A deposit of $2,148.21, representing receipts of July 31, had been made too late to appear on the bank statement.
(c) The bank had collected for Baker Co. $2,650 on a note left for collection. The face of the note was $2,500.
(d) A check drawn for $470 had been erroneously charged by the bank as $740.
(e) A check for $84.20 returned with the statement had been recorded by Baker Co. as $8.42. The check was for the payment of an obligation to Bartles Company on account.
(f) Bank service charges for July amounted to $18.75.

Instructions:

(1) Prepare a bank reconciliation as of July 31.
(2) Journalize the necessary entries. The accounts have not been closed.

Pb. 5–47A.
Bank reconciliation and related entries.
OBJ. 4

Pinter Corporation employs the voucher system in controlling expenditures and disbursements. All cash receipts are deposited each Wednesday and Friday in a night depository after banking hours. The data required to reconcile the bank statement as of April 30 have been abstracted from various documents and records and are reproduced as follows.

CASH IN BANK ACCOUNT:
Balance as of April 1 .... $7,817.40

CASH RECEIPTS FOR MONTH OF APRIL $7,829.58

DUPLICATE DEPOSIT TICKETS:
Date and amount of each deposit in April:

Date	Amount	Date	Amount	Date	Amount
April 1	$848.63	April 10	$971.71	April 22	$897.34
3	914.04	15	957.85	24	942.71
8	840.50	17	946.74	29	510.06

CHECKS WRITTEN:
Number and amount of each check issued in April:

Check No.	Amount	Check No.	Amount	Check No.	Amount
740	$287.50	747	Void	754	$249.75
741	555.15	748	$490.90	755	172.75
742	501.90	749	640.13	756	113.95
743	671.30	750	376.77	757	907.95
744	506.88	751	299.37	758	359.60
745	117.25	752	537.01	759	601.50
746	298.66	753	380.95	760	486.39

Total amount of checks issued in April $8,555.66

APRIL BANK STATEMENT:

Balance as of April 1	$ 7,947.20
Deposits and other credits	10,652.77
Checks and other debits	(8,232.21)
Balance as of April 30	$10,367.76

Date and amount of each deposit in April:

Date	Amount	Date	Amount	Date	Amount
April 1	$690.25	April 9	$840.50	April 18	$946.74
2	848.63	11	971.71	23	897.34
4	914.04	16	975.85	25	942.71

CHECKS ACCOMPANYING APRIL BANK STATEMENT:
Number and amount of each check, rearranged in numerical sequence:

Check No.	Amount	Check No.	Amount	Check No.	Amount
731	$162.15	744	$506.88	751	$299.37
738	251.40	745	117.25	752	537.01
739	60.55	746	298.66	753	380.95
740	287.50	748	490.90	754	249.75
741	555.15	749	640.13	756	113.95
742	501.90	750	376.77	757	907.95
743	671.30			760	486.39

BANK MEMORANDUMS ACCOMPANYING APRIL BANK STATEMENT:
Date, description, and amount of each memorandum:

Date	Description	Amount
April 4	Bank credit memo for note collected:	
	Principal	$2,500.00
	Interest	125.00
24	Bank debit memo for check returned because of insufficient funds	311.80
30	Bank debit memo for service charges	24.50

BANK RECONCILIATION FOR PRECEDING MONTH:

Pinter Corporation
Bank Reconciliation
March 31, 19--

Balance per bank statement		$7,947.20
Add deposit for March 31, not recorded by bank		690.25
		$8,637.45
Deduct outstanding checks:		
No. 731	$162.15	
736	345.95	
738	251.40	
739	60.55	820.05
Adjusted balance		$7,817.40
Balance per depositor's records		$7,832.50
Deduct service charges		15.10
Adjusted balance		$7,817.40

Instructions:

(1) Prepare a bank reconciliation as of April 30. If errors in recording deposits or checks are discovered, assume that the errors were made by the company. Assume that all deposits are from cash sales. All checks are in payment of vouchers.

(2) Record the necessary entries. The accounts have not been closed.
(3) What is the amount of cash in bank that should appear on the balance sheet as of April 30?

Pb. 5–48A.
Transactions for petty cash, advances to salespersons fund; cash short and over.
OBJ. 5, 6

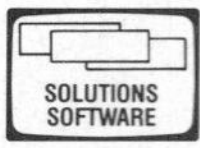

Perkins Company has just adopted the policy of depositing all cash receipts in the bank and of making all payments by check in conjunction with the voucher system. The following transactions were selected from those completed in June of the current year:

June 2. Recorded Voucher No. 1 to establish a petty cash fund of $250 and a change fund of $500.
2. Issued Check No. 350 in payment of Voucher No. 1.
7. Recorded Voucher No. 6 to establish an advances to salespersons fund of $1,000.
7. Issued Check No. 353 in payment of Voucher No. 6.
10. The cash sales for the day, according to the cash register tapes, totaled $4,707.90. The combined count of all cash on hand (including the change fund) totaled $5,210.50.
25. Recorded Voucher No. 35 to reimburse the petty cash fund for the following disbursements, each evidenced by a petty cash receipt:
    June 3. Store supplies, $19.00.
    7. Express charges on merchandise purchased, $16.00.
    8. Office supplies, $12.75.
    9. Office supplies, $9.20.
    12. Postage stamps, $45 (Office Supplies).
    15. Repair to adding machine, $37.50 (Miscellaneous Administrative Expense).
    16. Repair to typewriter, $30.50 (Miscellaneous Administrative Expense).
    18. Postage due on special delivery letter, $1.05 (Miscellaneous Administrative Expense).
    20. Express charges on merchandise purchased, $19.50.
    24. Telegram charges, $7.75 (Miscellaneous Selling Expense).
25. Issued Check No. 383 in payment of Voucher No. 35.
28. The cash sales for the day, according to the cash register tapes, totaled $4,205.50. The count of all cash on hand (including the change fund) totaled $4,701.60.
30. Recorded Voucher No. 40 to replenish the advances to salespersons fund for the following expenditures for travel: Liz Geraci, $207.50; Mark Felix, $287.40; Sara Duffin, $351.15.
30. Issued Check No. 390 in payment of Voucher No. 40.

Instructions:

Record the transactions.

Pb. 5–49A.
Entries for voucher system.
OBJ. 6

The following selected transactions were completed by a company that uses a voucher system, with all invoices recorded at their net price.

July 2. Recorded Voucher No. 240 for $750, payable to Allen Supply Co., for office supplies purchased on terms n/30.
5. Recorded Voucher No. 242 for $7,000, payable to Cox Co., for merchandise purchased on terms 1/10, n/30.
7. Recorded Voucher No. 248 for $1,400 payable to Collins Inc., for merchandise purchased on terms 2/10, n/30.
17. Issued Check No. 364 in payment of Voucher No. 248.
22. Recorded Voucher No. 260 for $225.14 to replenish the petty cash fund for the following disbursements: store supplies, $92.88; office supplies,

$84.95; miscellaneous administrative expense, $42.45; miscellaneous selling expense, $34.86.

July 23. Issued Check No. 370 in payment of Voucher No. 260.
31. Issued Check No. 377 in payment of Voucher No. 242.
31. Issued Check No. 389 in payment of Voucher No. 240.

Instructions:

Record the transactions.

MINI-CASE 5

The records of Rossiter Company indicate a May 31 cash in bank balance of $24,231.05, which includes undeposited receipts for May 30 and 31. The cash balance on the bank statement as of May 31 is $22,540. This balance includes a note of $3,000 plus $90 interest collected by the bank but not recorded in the journal. Checks outstanding on May 31 were as follows: No. 421, $843.40; No. 488, $430; No. 522, $652.40; No. 992, $955.15; No. 995, $457.70; and No. 996, $596.10.

On May 12, the cashier resigned, effective at the end of the month. Before leaving on May 31, the cashier prepared the following bank reconciliation:

Balance per books, May 31		$24,231.05
Add outstanding checks:		
992	$955.15	
995	457.70	
996	596.10	1,808.95
		$26,040.00
Less undeposited receipts		3,500.00
Balance per bank, May 31		$22,540.00
Deduct unrecorded note with interest		3,090.00
True cash, May 31		$19,450.00

Calculator Tape of Outstanding Checks

0.	*
955.15	+
457.70	+
596.10	+
1,808.95	*

Subsequently, the owner of Rossiter Company discovered that the cashier had stolen all undeposited receipts in excess of the $3,500 on hand on May 31. The owner, a close family friend, has asked your help in determining the amount that the former cashier has stolen.

Instructions:

(1) Determine the amount the cashier stole from Rossiter Company. Show your computations in good form.
(2) How did the cashier attempt to conceal the theft?
(3) (a) Identify two major weaknesses in Rossiter Company's internal controls which allowed the cashier to steal the undeposited cash receipts.
(b) Recommend improvements in Rossiter Company's internal controls, so that similar types of thefts of undeposited cash receipts could be prevented.

(AICPA adapted)

ANSWERS TO SELF-EXAMINATION QUESTIONS

1. A The policies and procedures established by an enterprise to provide reasonable assurance that the enterprise's goals will be achieved are called internal controls (answer A). The three phases of installing or changing an accounting system are (1) analysis (answer B), (2) design (answer C), and (3) implementation (answer D). Systems analysis is the determination of the informational needs, sources of such information, and deficiencies in the procedures and data processing methods presently used. Systems design refers to the design of a new system or change in the present system based on the systems analysis. The carrying out of proposals for the design of a system is referred to as systems implementation.
2. B On any specific date, the cash in bank account in a depositor's ledger may not agree with the reciprocal account in the bank's ledger because of delays and/or errors by either party in recording transactions. The purpose of a bank reconciliation, therefore, is to determine the reasons for any discrepancies between the two account balances. All errors should then be corrected by the depositor or the bank as appropriate. In arriving at the adjusted (correct) balance according to the bank statement, outstanding checks must be deducted (answer B) to adjust for checks that have been written by the depositor but that have not yet been presented to the bank for payment.
3. C All reconciling items that are added to and deducted from the "balance per depositor's records" on the bank reconciliation (answer C) require that journal entries be made by the depositor to correct errors made in recording transactions or to bring the cash account up to date for delays in recording transactions.
4. D A major advantage of recording purchases at the net amount (answer A) is that the cost of failing to take discounts is recorded in the accounts (answer B) and then reported as an expense on the income statement (answer C).
5. D To avoid the delay, annoyance, and expense that is associated with paying all obligations by check, relatively small amounts (answer A) are paid from a petty cash fund. The fund is established by estimating the amount of cash needed to pay these small amounts during a specified period (answer B) and it is then reimbursed when the amount of money in the fund is reduced to a predetermined minimum amount (answer C).

CHAPTER 6

CHAPTER OBJECTIVES

1. Describe the common classifications of receivables.
2. Describe the basic principles of internal control over receivables.
3. Describe the common characteristics of notes receivable.
4. Describe and illustrate the accounting for notes receivable, including the discounting of notes receivable and dishonored notes receivable.
5. Describe the basic concepts in accounting for uncollectible receivables.
6. Describe and illustrate the allowance method of accounting for uncollectible receivables, including the estimation of uncollectibles based on sales and an analysis of receivables.
7. Describe and illustrate the direct write-off method of accounting for uncollectible receivables.
8. Describe and illustrate the accounting for receivables from installment sales.
9. Describe and illustrate the accounting for temporary investments.
10. Describe and illustrate the presentation of temporary investments and receivables in the balance sheet.

6

RECEIVABLES & TEMPORARY INVESTMENTS

For many businesses, the revenue from sales on a credit basis is the largest factor influencing the amount of net income. As credit is granted, businesses must account for the resulting receivables, which may represent a substantial portion of the total current assets. As the receivables are collected, the cash realized is accounted for in the manner discussed in Chapter 5. If the amount of cash on hand exceeds immediate cash requirements, the excess cash might be invested in securities until needed. These securities are accounted for as temporary investments.

CLASSIFICATION OF RECEIVABLES

OBJECTIVE 1
Describe the common classifications of receivables.

The term **receivables** includes all money claims against people, organizations, or other debtors. Receivables are acquired by a business enterprise in various kinds of transactions, the most common being the sale of merchandise or services on a credit basis.

Credit may be granted on open account or on the basis of a formal instrument of credit, such as a promissory note. A **promissory note,** frequently referred to as a **note,** is a written promise to pay a sum of money on demand or at a definite time. Notes are usually used for credit periods of more than sixty days, as in sales of equipment on the installment plan, and for transactions of relatively large dollar amounts. Notes may also be used in settlement of an open account and in borrowing or lending money.

From the point of view of the creditor, a claim evidenced by a note has some advantages over a claim in the form of an account receivable. By signing a note, the debtor acknowledges the debt and agrees to pay it according to the terms given. The note is therefore a stronger legal claim if there is court action. It is also more liquid than an open account because the holder can usually transfer it more readily to a bank or other financial agency in exchange for cash.

The enterprise owning a note refers to it as a **note receivable.** If notes and accounts receivable originate from sales transactions, they are sometimes called **trade receivables.** In the absence of other descriptive words or phrases, accounts and notes receivable may be assumed to have originated from sales in the usual course of the business.

Other receivables include interest receivable, loans to officers or employees, and loans to affiliated companies. To facilitate their classification and presentation on the balance sheet, a general ledger account should be maintained for each type of receivable, with proper subsidiary ledgers.

All receivables that are expected to be realized in cash within a year are presented in the current assets section of the balance sheet. Those that are not currently collectible, such as long-term loans, should be listed under the caption "Investments" below the current assets section.

CONTROL OVER RECEIVABLES

OBJECTIVE 2
Describe the basic principles of internal control over receivables.

As is the case for all assets, the broad principles of internal control discussed in Chapter 5 can be used to establish procedures to safeguard receivables. These controls would include the separation of the business operations and the accounting for receivables, so that the accounting records can serve as an independent check on operations. Thus the employee who handles the accounting for notes and accounts receivable should not be involved with credit approvals or collections of receivables. Separation of these functions reduces the possibility of errors and embezzlement. The controls would also include the separation of responsibility for related functions, so that the work of one employee can serve as a check on the work of another employee.

For most businesses, the principal receivables are notes receivable and accounts receivable. Generally, notes receivable are recorded in a single general ledger account. If there are numerous notes, the general ledger account can be supported by a notes receivable register. The register would contain details of each note, such as the name of the maker, place of payment, amount, term, interest rate, and due date. Frequent reference to the due date section directs attention to those notes that are due for payment. In this way, the maker of the note can be notified when the note is due, and the risk that the maker will overlook the due date can be minimized.

Adequate control over accounts receivable begins with the approval of the sale by a responsible company official or the credit department, after the customer's credit rating has been reviewed. Likewise, adjustments of accounts receivable, such as for sales returns and allowances and sales discounts, should be authorized or reviewed by a responsible party. Effective collection procedures should also be established to ensure timely collection of accounts receivable and to minimize losses from uncollectible accounts.

EFFECTIVE CONTROL OF ACCOUNTS RECEIVABLE

Companies should make every effort to speed up the process of changing receivables into cash, as well as establish controls that help assure the quality of the receivables. These aspects of effective receivables control were addressed in the following paragraph from an article in *CFO:*

[A] common mistake . . . is having customers send payments to the company. "Checks sit on someone's desk for a few days, then they are sent through the mail, then they are processed at the bank, and then they sit for a while until they clear," says Andrea Bierce, manager for Peat, Marwick, Mitchell & Co.'s financial management division in

New York City. Instead, she says, have customers send payments directly to a bank lockbox. "I've seen companies free up $100,000 to $1 million this way," says Bierce. Anthony Timiraos, manager of the accounting and business advisory service department in Laventhol & Horwath's Boston office, tells clients strapped for financial manpower to split up the cash management responsibilities. "Sometimes the salespeople make a sale to someone just to make their department look good," he observes. "They don't always check with the credit manager to approve the sale." Next thing you know, says Timiraos, goods are going out to customers who can't pay their bills. Instead, he says, "Small companies need to split up cash management responbilities among different departments." Managers should work out collection goals for the sales and marketing department, for instance, to help them determine the validity of sales. . . .

Source: Leslie Schultz, "Which Ever Way the Cash Flows," *CFO* (March, 1986), p. 20.

CHARACTERISTICS OF NOTES RECEIVABLE

OBJECTIVE 3
Describe the common characteristics of notes receivable.

As indicated earlier in the chapter, a note is a written promise to pay a sum of money on demand or at a definite time. As in the case of a check, it must be payable to the order of a certain person or firm, or to bearer. It must also be signed by the person or firm that makes the promise. The one to whose order the note is payable is called the **payee**, and the one making the promise is called the **maker.** In the following illustration, Pearland Company is the payee and Selig Corporation is the maker.

Promissory Note

$ 2,500.00 Fresno, California March 16, 19 92

Ninety days AFTER DATE We PROMISE TO PAY TO

THE ORDER OF Pearland Company

Two thousand five hundred 00/100---------------------- DOLLARS

PAYABLE AT First National Bank

VALUE RECEIVED WITH INTEREST AT 10%

NO. 14 DUE June 14, 1992

SELIG CORPORATION
H. B. Lane
TREASURER

Notes have several characteristics that have accounting implications. These characteristics are described in the following paragraphs.

Due Date

The date a note is to be paid is called the due date or maturity date. The period of time between the issuance date and the due date of a short-term note may be stated in either days or months. When the term of a note is stated in days, the due date is the specified number of days after its issuance. To illustrate, the due date of the 90-day note presented above may be determined as shown on page 257.

When the term of a note is stated as a certain number of months after the issuance date, the due date is determined by counting the number of months from the issuance date. Thus, a 3-month note dated June 5 would be due on September 5. In those cases in which there is no date in the month of maturity that corresponds to the issuance date, the due date becomes the last day of the month. For example, a 2-month note dated July 31 would be due on September 30.

Determination of Due Date of Note

Term of the note		90
March (days)	31	
Date of note	16	15
Number of days remaining		75
April (days)		30
		45
May (days)		31
Due date, June		14

Interest-Bearing Notes and Non-Interest-Bearing Notes

A note that provides for the payment of interest for the period between the issuance date and the due date is called an **interest-bearing note.** If a note makes no provision for interest, it is said to be **non-interest-bearing.** The note illustrated on page 256 is an interest-bearing note.

Interest

Interest rates for interest-bearing notes are usually stated in terms of a period of one year, regardless of the actual period of time involved. Thus the interest on $2,000 for one year at 12% would be $240 (12% of $2,000); the interest on $2,000 for one fourth of one year at 12% would be $60 (¼ of $240).

Notes covering a period of time longer than one year ordinarily provide that the interest be paid semiannually, quarterly, or at some other stated interval. The time involved in commercial credit transactions is usually less than one year, and the interest provided for by a note is payable at the time the note is paid. In computing interest for a period of less than one year, agencies of the federal government use the actual number of days in the year. For example, 90 days is considered to be 90/365 of one year. The usual commercial practice is to use 360 as the denominator of the fraction; thus 90 days is considered to be 90/360 of one year.

The basic formula for computing interest is as follows:

$$\text{Principal} \times \text{Rate} \times \text{Time} = \text{Interest}$$

To illustrate the use of the formula, the $62.50 interest for the $2,500, 90-day, 10% note presented on page 256 is computed as follows:

$$\$2{,}500 \times \frac{10}{100} \times \frac{90}{360} = \$62.50 \text{ interest}$$

One of the commonly used shortcut methods of computing interest is called the 60-day, 6% method. The 6% annual rate is converted to the effective rate of 1% for a 60-day period (60/360 of 6%). Accordingly, the interest on any amount for 60 days at 6% is determined by moving the decimal point in the principal two places to the left. For example, the interest on $1,500 at 6% for 60 days is $15. The amount obtained by moving the decimal point must be adjusted (1) for interest rates greater or less than 6% and (2) for periods of time greater or less than 60 days. For example, the interest on $1,500 at 6% for 90 days is $22.50 (90/60 of $15). The interest on $1,500 at 12% for 60 days is $30 (12/6 of $15).

Comprehensive interest tables are available and are commonly used by financial institutions and other enterprises that require frequent interest calculations. Nevertheless, students of business should know the mechanics of interest computations well enough to use them with complete accuracy and to recognize major errors in interest amounts that come to their attention.

When the term of a note is stated in months instead of in days, each month may be considered as being 1/12 of a year, or, alternatively, the actual number of days in the term may be counted. For example, the interest on a 3-month note dated June 1 could be computed on the basis of 3/12 of a year or on the basis of 92/360 of a year. It is the usual commercial practice to use the first method, while banks usually charge interest for the exact number of days. For the sake of simplicity, the usual commercial practice will be assumed in all cases.

THE BOBTAILED YEAR

The practice of using the 360-day year for determining interest has a surprisingly significant effect on the economy as a whole. Both the background of the practice and its effect are described in the following excerpts from an article in *The Wall Street Journal:*

In 46 B.C., Julius Caesar proclaimed that a year would be pegged at 365 days, with an extra day added every fourth year. What was good enough for Caesar has been good enough for the rest of us ever since except for the nation's bankers.

A lot of bankers are using a 360-day year to compute the interest they charge to borrowers on commercial and corporate loans. This means, in effect, that they are collecting a smidgin more interest on these loans than their stated "annual" interest rates would indicate. . . .

Though only small amounts of money are involved in the difference between 365- and 360-day charges on any one loan, the nickels and dimes add up to an impressive pile. . . . [In fact, the overcharges that result from the use of the bobtailed year have been estimated to be at least $145 million a year.]

According to the bankers, use of the bobtailed year began before the widespread use of adding machines; clerks who had to do the computations with pencil and paper found it a lot easier to multiply and divide by 360 rather than 365 or 366. Since nobody seemed to care much, the 360-day base continued in use through the age of calculators and now is imbedded in the banks' computer programs. "Converting our computers to a 365-day year would be a massive job," says one officer of a major bank.

Source: James F. Carberry, "365 Days May Have Been Good Enough For Caesar, But Lenders Find That 360 Provide More Profit," *The Wall Street Journal*, March 30, 1973.

Maturity Value

The amount that is due at the maturity or due date is called the **maturity value.** The maturity value of a non-interest-bearing note is the face amount. The maturity value of an interest-bearing note is the sum of the face amount and the interest. In the note presented on page 256, the maturity value is $2,562.50 ($2,500 face amount plus $62.50 interest).

ACCOUNTING FOR NOTES RECEIVABLE

OBJECTIVE 4
Describe and illustrate the accounting for notes receivable, including the discounting of notes receivable and dishonored notes receivable.

FYI

The typical retail enterprise makes most of its sales for cash or on account. If the account of a customer becomes delinquent, the creditor may insist that the account be converted into a note. In this way, the debtor is given more time, and if the creditor needs more funds, the note may be endorsed and transferred to a bank or other financial agency. Notes may also be received by retail firms that sell merchandise on long-term credit. For example, a dealer in household appliances may require a down payment at the time of sale and accept a note or a series of notes for the remainder. Such arrangements usually provide for monthly payments. Wholesale firms and manufacturers are likely to receive notes more often than retailers, although here, too, much depends upon the kind of product and the length of the credit period.

When a note is received from a customer to apply on account, the facts are recorded by debiting the notes receivable account and crediting the accounts receivable controlling account and the account of the customer from whom the note is received. To illustrate, assume that the account of Glenn Enterprises, which has a balance of $9,200, is past due. A 90-day non-interest-bearing note for that amount, dated May 16, 1992, is accepted in settlement of the account. The note receivable is recorded at its face value and the entry to record the transaction is as follows:

May 16	Notes Receivable	9,200	
	Accounts Receivable—		
	Glenn Enterprises		9,200
	Received 90-day, non-interest-bearing note dated May 16, 1992.		

When the $9,200 due on the note is collected, the following entry would be recorded in the journal:

Aug. 14	Cash	9,200	
	Notes Receivable		9,200

Interest-Bearing Notes Receivable

If the note received from a customer on account is interest bearing, interest must be recorded as appropriate. To illustrate, assume that a 30-day, 12% note dated November 21, 1992, is accepted in settlement of the account of W. A. Bunn Co., which has a balance of $6,000. The entry to record the transaction is as follows:

Nov. 21	Notes Receivable	6,000	
	Accounts Receivable—W. A. Bunn Co. ...		6,000
	Received 30-day, 12% note dated November 21, 1992.		

At the time the note matures, the entry to record the receipt of $6,060 ($6,000 principal plus $60 interest) is as follows:

Dec. 21	Cash	6,060	
	Notes Receivable		6,000
	Interest Income		60

The interest income account is closed at December 31 and the amount is reported in the Other Income section of the income statement for the year ended December 31, 1992.

Discounting Notes Receivable

Although it is not a common transaction, a company in need of cash may transfer its notes receivable to a bank by endorsement. The **discount** (interest) charged by the bank is computed on the maturity value of the note for the period of time the bank must hold the note, namely the time that will pass between the date of the transfer and the due date of the note. The amount of the **proceeds** paid to the endorser is the excess of the maturity value over the discount.

To illustrate, assume that a 90-day, 12% note receivable for $1,800, dated November 8, is discounted at the payee's bank on December 3 at the rate of 14%. The data used in determining the effect of the transaction are as follows:

Face value of note dated Nov. 8		$1,800.00
Interest on note—90 days at 12%		54.00
Maturity value of note due Feb. 6		$1,854.00
Discount period—Dec. 3 to Feb. 6	65 days	
Discount on maturity value—65 days at 14%		46.87
Proceeds		$1,807.13

The same information is presented graphically in the following flow diagram. In reading the data, follow the direction of the arrows.

Diagram of Discounting a Note Receivable

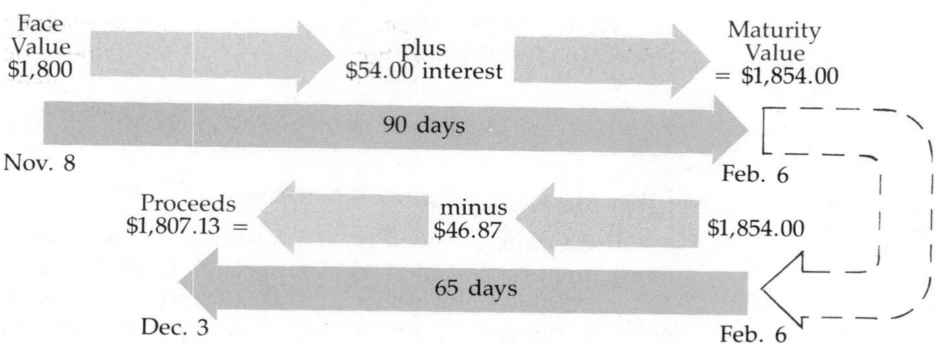

The excess of the proceeds from discounting the note, $1,807.13, over its face value, $1,800, is recorded as interest income. The entry for the transaction is as follows:

Dec. 3	Cash	1,807.13	
	Notes Receivable		1,800.00
	Interest Income		7.13

It should be observed that the proceeds from discounting a note receivable may be less than the face value. When this situation occurs, the excess of the face value over the proceeds is recorded as interest expense. The amount and direction of the difference between the interest rate and the discount rate will affect the result, as will the relationship between the full term of the note and the length of the discount period.

Without a statement limiting responsibility, the endorser of a note is committed to paying the note if the maker should default. Such potential obligations that will become actual liabilities only if certain events occur in the future are called **contingent liabilities.** Thus, the endorser of a note that has been discounted has a contingent liability that is in effect until the due date. If the maker pays the promised amount at maturity, the contingent liability is removed without any action on the part of the endorser. If, on the other hand, the maker defaults and the endorser is notified according to legal requirements, the liability becomes an actual one.

Significant contingent liabilities should be disclosed on the balance sheet or in an accompanying note. Disclosure requirements for contingent liabilities are discussed and illustrated in Chapter 9.

Dishonored Notes Receivable

If the maker of a note fails to pay the debt on the due date, the note is said to be **dishonored.** A dishonored note receivable is no longer negotiable, and for that reason the holder usually transfers the claim, including any interest due, to the accounts receivable account. For example, if the $6,000, 30-day, 12% note received and recorded on November 21 (page 260) had been dishonored at maturity, the entry to charge the note, including the interest, back to the customer's account would have been as follows:

Dec. 21	Accounts Receivable—W. A. Bunn Co.	6,060	
	Notes Receivable		6,000
	Interest Income		60
	Dishonored note and interest.		

If there had been some assurance that the maker would pay the note within a relatively short time, action would have been delayed until the matter was resolved. However, for future guidance in extending credit, it may be desirable that the customer's account disclose the dishonor of the note.

When a discounted note receivable is dishonored, the holder usually notifies the endorser of such fact and asks for payment. If the request for payment and notification of dishonor are timely, the endorser is legally obligated to pay the amount due on the note. The entire amount paid to the holder by the endorser, including the interest, should be debited to the account receivable of the maker. To illustrate, assume that the $1,800, 90-day, 12% note discounted on December 3 (page 260) is dishonored at maturity by the maker, Pryor & Co. The entry to record the payment by the endorser would be as follows:

Feb. 6	Accounts Receivable—Pryor & Co...........	1,854	
	Cash		1,854

In some cases, the holder of a dishonored note gives the endorser a notarized statement of the facts of the dishonor. The fee for this statement, known as a **protest fee,** is charged to the endorser, who in turn charges it to the maker of the note. If there had been a protest fee of $6 in connection with the dishonor and the payment previously recorded, the debit to the maker's account and the credit to Cash would have been $1,860.

UNCOLLECTIBLE RECEIVABLES

OBJECTIVE 5
Describe the basic concepts in accounting for uncollectible receivables.

When merchandise or services are sold without the immediate receipt of cash, a part of the claims against customers usually proves to be uncollectible. This situation is common, regardless of the care used in granting credit and the effectiveness of the collection procedures used. The operating expense incurred because of the failure to collect receivables is called an expense or a loss from **uncollectible accounts, doubtful accounts,** or **bad debts.**[1]

---

[1]If both notes and accounts are involved, both may be included in the title, as in "uncollectible notes and accounts expense," or the general term "uncollectible receivables expense" may be substituted. Because of its wide usage and simplicity, "uncollectible accounts expense" will be used in this text.

There is no single general rule for determining when an account or a note becomes uncollectible. The fact that a debtor fails to pay an account according to a sales contract or dishonors a note on the due date does not necessarily mean that the account will be uncollectible. Bankruptcy of the debtor is one of the most positive indications of partial or complete worthlessness of a receivable. Other evidence includes closing of the debtor's business, disappearance of the debtor, failure of repeated attempts to collect, and the barring of collection by the statute of limitations.

There are two methods of accounting for receivables that are believed to be uncollectible. The **allowance method,** which is sometimes called the **reserve method,** provides in advance for uncollectible receivables.[2] The other procedure, called the **direct write-off method** or **direct charge-off method,** recognizes the expense only when certain accounts are judged to be worthless.

ALLOWANCE METHOD OF ACCOUNTING FOR UNCOLLECTIBLES

OBJECTIVE 6
Describe and illustrate the allowance method of accounting for uncollectible receivables, including the estimation of uncollectibles based on sales and on an analysis of receivables.

Most large business enterprises provide currently for the amount of their trade receivables estimated to become uncollectible in the future. The provision for future uncollectibility is made by an adjusting entry at the end of the fiscal period. As with all periodic adjustments, the entry serves two purposes. In this instance, it provides for (1) the reduction of the value of the receivables to the amount of cash expected to be realized from them in the future, and (2) the allocation to the current period of the expected expense resulting from such reduction.

Assumed data for a new business firm, Richards Company, will be used to explain and illustrate the allowance method. The enterprise began business in August and chose to use the calendar year as its fiscal year. The accounts receivable account, illustrated below, has a balance of $105,000 at the end of the period.

ACCOUNT ACCOUNTS RECEIVABLE ACCOUNT NO. 114

Date		Post. Item	Debit	Credit	Balance	
					Debit	Credit
19--						
Aug.	31		20,000		20,000	
Sept.	30		25,000		45,000	
	30			15,000	30,000	
Oct.	31		40,000		70,000	
	31			25,000	45,000	
Nov.	30		38,000		83,000	
	30			23,000	60,000	
Dec.	31		75,000		135,000	
	31			30,000	105,000	

Among the individual customers accounts making up the $105,000 balance in Accounts Receivable are a number of balances which are a varying number of days past due. No specific accounts are believed to be wholly uncollectible at this time, but it seems likely that some will be collected only in part and that others are likely to become entirely worthless. Based on a careful study, it is estimated that a total of $3,000 will eventually prove to be un-

[2] The allowance (reserve) method is not acceptable for determining the federal income tax.

collectible. The amount expected to be realized from the accounts receivable is, therefore, $102,000 ($105,000 − $3,000), and the $3,000 reduction in value is the uncollectible accounts expense for the period.

The $3,000 reduction in accounts receivable cannot yet be identified with specific customer accounts and should therefore not be credited to the accounts receivable account. The customary practice is to use a contra asset account entitled Allowance for Doubtful Accounts. The adjusting entry to record the expense and the reduction in the asset is as follows:

Adjusting Entry

Dec. 31	Uncollectible Accounts Expense	3,000	
	Allowance for Doubtful Accounts...............		3,000

The two accounts to which the entry is posted are illustrated as follows:

ACCOUNT UNCOLLECTIBLE ACCOUNTS EXPENSE — ACCOUNT NO. 717

Date		Item	Debit	Credit	Balance Debit	Balance Credit
19-- Dec.	31	Adjusting	3,000		3,000	

ACCOUNT ALLOWANCE FOR DOUBTFUL ACCOUNTS — ACCOUNT NO. 115

Date		Item	Debit	Credit	Balance Debit	Balance Credit
19-- Dec.	31	Adjusting		3,000		3,000

The debit balance of $105,000 in Accounts Receivable is the amount of the total claims against customers on open account, and the credit balance of $3,000 in Allowance for Doubtful Accounts is the amount to be deducted from Accounts Receivable to determine the **expected realizable value.** The $3,000 reduction in the asset was transferred to Uncollectible Accounts Expense, which will in turn be closed to Income Summary.

Uncollectible accounts expense is generally reported on the income statement as an administrative expense, because the credit-granting and collection duties are the responsibilities of departments within the general administrative framework. The accounts receivable may be listed on the balance sheet at the net amount of $102,000, with a notation in parentheses showing the amount of the allowance, or the details may be presented as shown on the following partial balance sheet. When the allowance account includes provision for doubtful notes as well as accounts, it should be deducted from the total of Notes Receivable and Accounts Receivable.

Accounts Receivable on the Balance Sheet

Richards Company
Balance Sheet
December 31, 19—

Assets

Current assets:		
Cash..		$ 21,600
Accounts receivable...	$105,000	
Less allowance for doubtful accounts..................	3,000	102,000

Write-Offs to the Allowance Account

When an account is believed to be uncollectible, it is written off against the allowance account as in the following entry:

Jan. 21	Allowance for Doubtful Accounts..............	110	
	Accounts Receivable—John Parker		110
	To write off the uncollectible account.		

During the year, as more accounts or portions of accounts are determined to be uncollectible, they are written off against Allowance for Doubtful Accounts in the same manner. Instructions for write-offs should originate with the credit manager or other designated official. The authorizations, which should always be written, serve as objective evidence in support of the accounting entry.

Naturally enough, the total amount written off against the allowance account during the period will rarely be equal to the amount in the account at the beginning of the period. The allowance account will have a credit balance at the end of the period if the write-offs during the period amount to less than the beginning balance. It will have a debit balance if the write-offs exceed the beginning balance. After the year-end adjusting entry is recorded, the allowance account will have a credit balance.

An account receivable that has been written off against the allowance account may later be collected. In such cases, the account should be reinstated by an entry that is the exact reverse of the write-off entry. For example, assume that the account of $110 written off in the preceding journal entry is later collected. The entry to reinstate the account would be as follows:

June 10	Accounts Receivable—John Parker	110	
	Allowance for Doubtful Accounts...........		110
	To reinstate account written off earlier in the year.		

The cash received in payment would be recorded as a receipt on account. Although it is possible to combine the reinstatement and the receipt of cash into a single debit and credit, the entries in the customer's account, with a proper notation, provide useful credit information.

Estimating Uncollectibles

The estimate of uncollectibles at the end of the fiscal period is based on past experience and forecasts of future business activity. When the trend of general sales volume is upward and there is relatively full employment, the amount of the expense should usually be less than when the trend is in the opposite direction. The estimate is customarily based on either (1) the amount of sales for the entire fiscal period or (2) the amount and the age of the receivable accounts at the end of the fiscal period.

Estimate Based on Sales. Accounts receivable are acquired as a result of sales on account. The amount of such sales during the year may therefore be used to determine the probable amount of the accounts that will be uncollectible. The amount of this estimate is added to whatever balance exists in Allowance for Doubtful Accounts. To illustrate, assume that the allowance account has a credit balance of $700 before adjustment. If it is known from past experience that about 1% of charge sales will be uncollectible and the charge sales for a certain year amount to $300,000, the adjusting entry for uncollectible accounts at the end of the year would be as follows:

Adjusting Entry

Dec. 31	Uncollectible Accounts Expense	3,000	
	Allowance for Doubtful Accounts		3,000

After the adjusting entry is posted, the balance in the allowance account is $3,700. If there had been a debit balance of $200 in the allowance account before the year-end adjustment, the amount of the adjustment would still have been $3,000. The balance in the allowance account, after the adjusting entry is posted, would be $2,800 ($3,000 − $200).

Instead of charge sales, total sales (including those made for cash) may be used in developing the percentage. Total sales is obtainable from the ledger without the analysis that may be needed to determine charge sales. If the ratio of sales on account to cash sales does not change very much from year to year, the results obtained will be equally satisfactory. If in the above example the balance of the sales account at the end of the year is assumed to be $400,000, the application of 3/4 of 1% to that amount would also yield an estimate of $3,000.

If it becomes apparent over a period of time that the amount of write-offs is always greater or less than the amount provided by the adjusting entry, the percentage applied to sales data should be changed accordingly. A newly established business enterprise, having no record of credit experience, may obtain data on the probable amount of the expense from trade association journals and other publications containing information on credit and collections.

The estimate-based-on-sales method of determining the uncollectible accounts expense is widely used. It is simple and it provides the best basis for charging uncollectible accounts expense to the period in which the related sales were made.

Estimate Based on Analysis of Receivables. The process of analyzing the receivable accounts in terms of the length of time past due is sometimes called **aging the receivables.** The base point for determining age is the due date of the account. The number and breadth of the time intervals used will vary according to the credit terms granted to customers. A portion of a typical analysis is as follows:

Analysis of Accounts Receivable

		NOT	DAYS PAST DUE					
CUSTOMER	BALANCE	DUE	1–30	31–60	61–90	91–180	181–365	over 365
Ashby & Co.	$ 150			$ 150				
B. T. Barr	610					$ 350	$260	
Brock Co.	470	$ 470						
J. Zimmer Co. .	160							160
Total	$86,300	$75,000	$4,000	$3,100	$1,900	$1,200	$800	$300

The analysis is completed by adding the columns to determine the total amount of receivables in each age group. A sliding scale of percentages, based on experience, is next applied to obtain the estimated amount of uncollectibles in each group. The manner in which the data may be presented is illustrated as follows:

Estimate of Uncollectible Accounts

Age Interval	Balance	Estimated Uncollectible Accounts	
		Percent	*Amount*
Not due	$75,000	2%	$1,500
1–30 days past due	4,000	5	200
31–60 days past due	3,100	10	310
61–90 days past due	1,900	20	380
91–180 days past due.......	1,200	30	360
181–365 days past due.....	800	50	400
Over 365 days past due	300	80	240
Total	$86,300		$3,390

The estimate of uncollectible accounts, $3,390 in the example above, is the amount to be deducted from accounts receivable to yield their expected realizable value. It is thus the amount of the desired balance of the allowance account after adjustment. The excess of this figure over the balance of the allowance account before adjustment is the amount of the adjustment to be made for uncollectible accounts expense.

To continue the illustration, assume that the allowance account has a credit balance of $510 before adjustment. The amount to be added to this balance is therefore $2,880 ($3,390 − $510), and the adjusting entry is as follows:

Adjusting Entry

Dec. 31	Uncollectible Accounts Expense	2,880	
	Allowance for Doubtful Accounts...........		2,880

After the adjusting entry is posted, the credit balance in the allowance account will be $3,390, which is the desired amount. If there had been a debit balance of $300 in the allowance account before the year-end adjustment, the amount of the adjustment would have been $3,690 ($3,390 desired balance + $300 negative balance).

Estimations of uncollectible accounts expense based on an analysis of receivables are less common than estimations based on sales volume. Estimations based on receivables analyses are sometimes preferred because they give more accurate estimates of the current realizable values of the receivables.

THE OLDER IT GETS

A properly designed accounting system should provide for the careful screening of credit, prompt reporting of delinquent accounts, and effective collection procedures for delinquent accounts. As illustrated in the following article from a public accounting firm's newsletter, collection success depends on quick collection efforts.

There is a direct relationship between the age of outstanding receivables and the chance of successfully collecting [them]. Recently the Commercial Law League of America published the following data showing the precise correlation between the age of the receivable and the chance of collection:

Period of Delinquency	*Collection Likelihood*
1 month	*94%*
2 months	*85%*
3 months	*74%*
6 months	*48%*
9 months	*43%*
1 year	*27%*
2 years	*14%*

Source: "The Older It Gets," *The Advisor* (Spring, 1988), p. 2.

DIRECT WRITE-OFF METHOD OF ACCOUNTING FOR UNCOLLECTIBLES

OBJECTIVE 7
Describe and illustrate the direct write-off method of accounting for uncollectible receivables.

The use of the allowance method, as previously illustrated, results in the uncollectible accounts expense being reported in the period in which the sales are made. This matching of expenses with related revenue is the preferred method of accounting for uncollectible receivables. However, there are situations in which it is impossible to estimate, with reasonable accuracy, the uncollectibles at the end of the period. Also, if an enterprise sells most of its goods or services on a cash basis, the amount of its expense from uncollectible accounts is usually small in relation to its revenue. The amount of its receivables at any time is also likely to represent a relatively small part of its total current assets. In such cases, it is satisfactory to delay recognition of uncollectibility until the period in which certain amounts are believed to be worthless and are actually written off as an expense. Accordingly, an allowance account or an adjusting entry is not needed at the end of the period. The entry to write off an account when it is believed to be uncollectible is as follows:

May 10	Uncollectible Accounts Expense	42	
	Accounts Receivable — D. L. Ross..........		42
	To write off uncollectible account.		

If an account that has been written off is collected later, the account should be reinstated. If the recovery is in the same fiscal year as the write-off, the earlier entry should be reversed to reinstate the account. To illustrate, assume that the account written off in the May 10 entry is collected in November of the same fiscal year. The entry to reinstate the account would be as follows:

Nov. 21	Accounts Receivable — D. L. Ross............	42	
	Uncollectible Accounts Expense		42
	To reinstate account written off earlier in the year.		

The receipt of cash in payment of the reinstated amount would be recorded in the usual manner.

When an account that has been written off is collected in a later fiscal year, it may be reinstated by an entry like that just illustrated. An alternative is to credit some other appropriately titled account, such as Recovery of Uncollectible Accounts Written Off. The credit balance in such an account at the end of the year may then be reported on the income statement as a deduction from Uncollectible Accounts Expense, or the net expense only may be reported. Such amounts are likely to be small compared to net income.

RECEIVABLES FROM INSTALLMENT SALES

OBJECTIVE 8
Describe and illustrate the accounting for receivables from installment sales.

In some businesses, especially in the retail field, it is common to make sales on the installment plan. In the typical installment sale, the buyer makes a down payment and agrees to pay the remainder in specified amounts at stated intervals over a period of time. The seller may retain technical title to the goods or may take other means to make repossession easier in the event that the purchaser defaults on the payments. Despite such provisions, installment sales should ordinarily be treated in the same manner as any other sale on account. For such sales, revenue is usually determined by the **point of sale method** under which revenue is considered to be realized at the time title to the merchandise passes to the buyer.

In some exceptional cases, the circumstances are such that the collection of receivables is not reasonably assured. In these cases, the **installment method** of determining revenue may be used.[3] Under this method, each receipt of cash is considered to be revenue and to be composed of partial amounts of (1) the cost of merchandise sold and (2) gross profit on the sale.

As a basis for illustration, assume that in the first year of operations, a dealer in household appliances had total installment sales of $300,000, and the cost of the merchandise sold amounted to $180,000. Assume also that collections of the installment accounts receivable were spread over three years as follows: 1st year, $140,000; 2d year, $100,000; 3d year, $60,000. According to the point of sale method, all of the revenue would be recognized in the first year and the gross profit realized in that year would be determined as follows:

Point of Sale Method

Installment sales	$300,000
Cost of merchandise sold	180,000
Gross profit	$120,000

Under the installment method, gross profit is allocated according to the amount of receivables collected in each year, based on the percent of gross profit to sales. The rate of gross profit to sales is determined as follows:

$$\frac{\text{Gross Profit}}{\text{Installment Sales}} = \frac{\$120{,}000}{\$300{,}000} = 40\%$$

The amounts reported as gross profit for each of the three years based on collections of installment accounts receivable, are as follows:

Installment Method

1st year collections:	$140,000 × 40%	$ 56,000
2d year collections:	$100,000 × 40%	40,000
3d year collections:	$ 60,000 × 40%	24,000
Total	$300,000	$120,000

TEMPORARY INVESTMENTS

OBJECTIVE 9
Describe and illustrate the accounting for temporary investments.

A business may have a large amount of cash on hand that is not needed immediately, but this cash may be needed later in operating the business, possibly within the coming year. Rather than allow this excess cash to lie idle until it is actually needed, the business may put all or a part of it into income-yielding investments, such as certificates of deposit and money market funds. In many cases, the idle cash is invested in securities that can be quickly sold when cash is needed. Such securities are known as **temporary investments** or **marketable securities.** Although they may be retained as an investment for a number of years, they continue to be classified as temporary, provided that: (1) the securities are readily marketable and thus can be sold for cash at any time, and (2) management intends to sell them at such time as the enterprise needs more cash for normal operations.

[3] *Opinions of the Accounting Principles Board, No. 10,* "Omnibus Opinion—1966" (New York: American Institute of Certified Public Accountants, 1966), par. 12.

Temporary investments in securities include stocks and bonds. **Stocks** are equity securities issued by corporations, and **bonds** are debt securities issued by corporations and various government agencies. Stocks and bonds held as temporary investments are classified on the balance sheet as current assets. They may be listed after "Cash," or they may be combined with cash and described as "Cash and marketable securities."

A temporary investment in a portfolio of debt securities is usually carried at cost. However, the **carrying amount** (also called **basis**) of a temporary investment in a portfolio of equity securities is the lower of its total cost or market value, determined at the date of the balance sheet.[4] Note that in the following illustration, the carrying amount is based on the comparison between the *total* cost and the *total* market value of the portfolio, rather than the lower of cost or market price of *each item*.

Temporary Investment Portfolio	Cost	Market	Unrealized Gain (Loss)
Equity security A	$150,000	$100,000	$(50,000)
Equity security B	200,000	200,000	—
Equity security C	180,000	210,000	30,000
Equity security D	160,000	150,000	(10,000)
Total	$690,000	$660,000	$(30,000)

The marketable equity securities would be reported in the current assets section of the balance sheet at a cost of $690,000 less an allowance for decline to market value of $30,000 to yield a carrying amount of $660,000. The unrealized loss of $30,000 is included in the determination of net income and reported as a separate item on the income statement. If the market value of the portfolio later rises, the unrealized loss is reversed and included in net income, but only to the extent that it does not exceed the original cost. In such cases, the increase is reported separately in the Other Income section of the income statement, and the amount reported on the balance sheet is likewise adjusted.[5]

Some accountants believe that marketable equity securities should be valued at their current market prices, regardless of whether these prices are above or below cost. They argue for current market prices because (1) the securities are readily marketable, (2) the current market prices can be objectively and simply determined, and (3) current market prices are more useful as an indication of the amount of cash that can be made available for normal operations. Although the merits of the valuation of marketable equity securities at current market prices continues to be debated within the profession, the lower of cost or market price method is the current generally accepted method of valuation. To date, only certain industries, such as securities brokers and mutual fund dealers, are permitted to report their marketable equity securities at current market prices.

[4]*Statement of Financial Accounting Standards, No. 12*, "Accounting for Certain Marketable Securities" (Stamford: Financial Accounting Standards Board, 1975), par. 8.
[5]*Ibid.*, par. 11.

TEMPORARY INVESTMENTS AND RECEIVABLES IN THE BALANCE SHEET

OBJECTIVE 10
Describe and illustrate the presentation of temporary investments and receivables in the balance sheet.

Temporary investments and all receivables that are expected to be realized in cash within a year are presented in the current assets section of the balance sheet. It is customary to list the assets in the order of their liquidity, that is, in the order in which they can be converted to cash in normal operations. An illustration of the presentation of receivables and temporary investments is shown in the following partial balance sheet for Pilar Enterprises Inc.:

Temporary Investments and Receivables in Balance Sheet

Pilar Enterprises Inc.
Balance Sheet
December 31, 19—

Assets		
Current assets:		
Cash		$119,500
Marketable equity securities	$690,000	
Less allowance for decline to market	30,000	660,000
Notes receivable		250,000
Accounts receivable	$445,000	
Less allowance for doubtful accounts	15,000	430,000
Interest receivable		14,500

CHAPTER REVIEW

KEY POINTS

OBJECTIVE 1

Classification of Receivables

The term receivables includes all money claims against people, organizations, or other debtors. A promissory note is a written promise to pay a sum of money on demand or at a definite time. Accounts and notes receivable originating from sales transactions are called trade receivables.

OBJECTIVE 2

Control Over Receivables

The internal controls that apply to receivables include the separation of responsibility for related functions, so that the work of one employee can serve as a check on the work of another employee. For most businesses, the principal receivables are notes receivable and accounts receivable. If there are numerous notes receivable, a general ledger account for notes receivable should be supported by a notes receivable register.

OBJECTIVE 3

Characteristics of Notes Receivable

The period of time between the issuance date and the maturity date of a short-term note may be stated in either days or months. When the term of a note is stated in days, the due date is the specified number of days after its issuance. When the term of a note is stated as a number of months after the issuance date, the due date is determined by counting the number of months from the issuance date.

Interest rates for interest-bearing notes are usually stated in terms of a period of one year, regardless of the actual period of time involved. Notes covering a period of time longer than one year ordinarily provide that the interest be paid semiannually, quarterly, or at some other stated interval. The basic formula for computing interest is as follows: Principal × Rate × Time = Interest.

The amount that is due at the maturity date of a note is the maturity value. The maturity value of an interest-bearing note is the sum of the face amount and the interest.

OBJECTIVE 4

Accounting for Notes Receivable

Notes may be received by retail firms that sell merchandise on long-term credit. Such notes usually provide for monthly payments. In addition, if an account receivable becomes delinquent, the account may be converted to a note. Instead of retaining the note receivable until maturity, a note receivable may be transferred to a bank by endorsement. This transfer to a bank is called discounting the note receivable. The discount (interest) charged by the bank is computed on the maturity value of the note for the period of time the bank must hold the note until the due date. The amount of the proceeds paid to the endorser is the excess of the maturity value over the discount. Without a statement limiting responsibility, the endorser of a note is committed to paying the note if the maker should default. Such potential obligations that will become actual liabilities only if certain events occur in the future are called contingent liabilities.

If the maker of a note fails to pay the debt on the due date, the note is said to be dishonored. A dishonored note receivable is no longer negotiable, and the amount of the claim against the maker is transferred to an accounts receivable account.

OBJECTIVE 5

Uncollectible Receivables

When merchandise or services are sold on credit, a part of the claims against customers may prove to be uncollectible. The operating expense incurred because of the failure to collect receivables is called uncollectible accounts expense. There are two methods of accounting for receivables that are believed to be uncollectible: the allowance method and the direct write-off method.

OBJECTIVE 6

Allowance Method of Accounting for Uncollectibles

Most large business enterprises provide currently for the amount of their trade receivables estimated to become uncollectible. The estimate of the amount of uncollectibles may be based on either (1) the amount of sales for the entire fiscal period, or (2) the amount and the age of the receivable accounts at the end of the fiscal period. An adjusting entry made at the end of the fiscal period provides for (1) the reduction of the value of the receivables to the amount of cash expected to be realized from them in the future and (2) the allocation to the current period of the expected expense resulting from such reduction. The adjusting entry debits Uncollectible Accounts Expense and credits Allowance for Doubtful Accounts. When an account is believed to be uncollectible, it is written off against the allowance account.

The allowance account, which will normally have a credit balance after the adjusting entry has been posted, is a contra asset account. The uncollectible accounts expense is generally reported on the income statement as an administrative expense.

OBJECTIVE 7

Direct Write-Off Method of Accounting for Uncollectibles

If it is impossible to estimate uncollectibles with reasonable accuracy or if most sales are made on a cash basis, it is satisfactory to delay recognition of the uncollectibility of accounts receivable until the period in which certain accounts are believed to be worthless and are actually written off as an expense. Accordingly, under this method neither an allowance account nor an adjusting entry is needed at the end of the period. The entry in this case to write off an account debits Uncollectible Accounts Expense and credits Accounts Receivable.

OBJECTIVE 8

Receivables from Installment Sales

Revenue from sales made on the installment plan should ordinarily be accounted for by the point of sale method, under which revenue is realized at the time title passes to the buyer. When the collection of the receivables is not reasonably assured, the installment method may be used. Under this method, the gross profit from installment sales is recognized according to the amount of receivables collected in each year, based on the percent of gross profit to sales.

OBJECTIVE 9

Temporary Investments

A business may put all or part of any excess cash on hand into income-yielding investments that are readily marketable and are known as temporary investments or marketable securities. These investments may include stocks and bonds. Stocks are equity securities issued by corporations, and bonds are debt securities issued by corporations and various governmental agencies. A temporary investment of debt securities is usually carried in the records at cost. However, a temporary investment in equity securities must be carried at the lower of its total cost or market value at the balance sheet date.

OBJECTIVE 10

Temporary Investments and Receivables in the Balance Sheet

Temporary investments and all receivables that are expected to be realized in cash within a year are presented in the current assets section of the balance sheet. It is customary to list the assets in the order of their liquidity, that is, in the order in which they can be converted to cash in normal operations.

KEY TERMS

promissory (note) 254
note receivable 254
maturity value 258
discount 259
proceeds 259
contingent liabilities 260
dishonored 261
allowance method 262
direct write-off method 262
aging the receivables 265
point of sale method 268
installment method 268
temporary investments 268
marketable securities 268
carrying amount 269

SELF-EXAMINATION QUESTIONS

Answers at end of chapter.

1. What is the maturity value of a 90-day, 12% note for $10,000?
   A. $8,800
   B. $10,000
   C. $10,300
   D. $11,200

2. On June 16, an enterprise discounts a 60-day, 10% note receivable for $15,000, dated June 1, at the rate of 12%. The proceeds are:
   A. $15,000.00
   B. $15,021.25
   C. $15,250.00
   D. $15,478.75

3. At the end of the fiscal year, before the accounts are adjusted, Accounts Receivable has a balance of $200,000 and Allowance for Doubtful Accounts has a credit balance of $2,500. If the estimate of uncollectible accounts determined by aging the receivables is $8,500, the current provision to be made for uncollectible accounts expense would be:
   A. $2,500
   B. $6,000
   C. $8,500
   D. $200,000

4. At the end of the fiscal year, after the accounts are adjusted, Accounts Receivable has a balance of $100,000 and Allowance for Doubtful Accounts has a balance of $7,000. The expected realizable value of the accounts receivable is:
   A. $7,000
   B. $93,000
   C. $100,000
   D. $107,000

5. Under what caption would a temporary investment in stock be reported in the balance sheet?
   A. Current assets
   B. Plant assets
   C. Investments
   D. None of the above

ILLUSTRATIVE PROBLEM

Selected transactions completed by Rodriguez Company are as follows. Rodriguez Company uses the allowance method of accounting for uncollectible accounts receivable.

Jan. 28. Sold merchandise on account to Lakeland Inc., $10,000.
Mar. 1. Accepted a 60-day, 12% note for $10,000 from Lakeland Inc. on account.
Apr. 11. Wrote off a $4,500 account from Exdel Inc. as uncollectible.
16. Loaned $7,500 cash to Thomas Glazer, receiving a 90-day, 14% note.
30. Received the interest due from Lakeland Inc. and a new 90-day, 14% note as a renewal of the loan. (Record both the debit and credit to the notes receivable account.)
May 1. Discounted the note from Thomas Glazer at the First National Bank at 10%.
June 13. Reinstated the account of Exdel Inc., written off on April 11, and received $4,500 in full payment.
July 15. Received notice from First National Bank that Thomas Glazer dishonored his note. Paid the bank the maturity value of the note plus a $20 protest fee.
29. Received from Lakeland Inc. the amount due on its note of April 30.
Aug. 14. Received from Thomas Glazer the amount owed on the dishonored note, plus interest for 30 days at 15%, computed on the maturity value of the note and the protest fee.
Dec. 31. It is estimated that 2% of the credit sales of $958,600 for the year ended December 31 will be uncollectible.

Instructions:

Present entries to record the transactions.

SOLUTION

Date		Account	Debit	Credit
Jan.	28	Accounts Receivable—Lakeland Inc.	10,000.00	
		Sales		10,000.00
Mar.	1	Notes Receivable—Lakeland Inc.	10,000.00	
		Accounts Receivable—Lakeland Inc.		10,000.00
Apr.	11	Allowance for Doubtful Accounts	4,500.00	
		Accounts Receivable—Exdel Inc.		4,500.00
Apr.	16	Notes Receivable—Thomas Glazer	7,500.00	
		Cash		7,500.00
	30	Notes Receivable—Lakeland Inc.	10,000.00	
		Cash	200.00	
		Notes Receivable—Lakeland Inc.		10,000.00
		Interest Income		200.00

May 1	Cash	7,600.78	
	Notes Receivable—Thomas Glazer		7,500.00
	Interest Income		100.78
	Face value $7,500.00		
	Interest on note (90 days at 14%) 262.50		
	Maturity value $7,762.50		
	Discount on maturity value (75 days at 10%) 161.72		
	Proceeds $7,600.78		
June 13	Accounts Receivable—Exdel Inc.	4,500.00	
	Allowance for Doubtful Accounts		4,500.00
13	Cash	4,500.00	
	Accounts Receivable—Exdel Inc.		4,500.00
July 15	Accounts Receivable—Thomas Glazer	7,782.50	
	Cash		7,782.50
29	Cash	10,350.00	
	Notes Receivable—Lakeland Inc.		10,000.00
	Interest Income		350.00
Aug. 14	Cash	7,879.78	
	Accounts Receivable—Thomas Glazer		7,782.50
	Interest Income ($7,782.50 × 15% × 30/360)		97.28
Dec. 31	Uncollectible Accounts Expense	19,172.00	
	Allowance for Doubtful Accounts		19,172.00

DISCUSSION QUESTIONS

6–1. What are the advantages, to the creditor, of a note receivable in comparison to an account receivable?

6–2. What are trade receivables?

6–3. In what section of the balance sheet should a note receivable be listed if its term is (a) 60 days, (b) 3 years?

6–4. The accounting clerk who maintains the accounts receivable records is also responsible for handling cash receipts. Which principle of internal control is violated in this situation?

6–5. Robinson Corporation issued a promissory note to Gantt Company. (a) Who is the payee? (b) What is the title of the account employed by Gantt Company in recording the note?

6–6. If a note provides for payment of principal of $5,000 and interest at the rate of 10%, will the interest amount to $500? Explain.

6–7. The following questions refer to a 60-day, 12% note for $10,000, dated July 1: (a) What is the face value of the note? (b) What is the amount of interest payable at maturity? (c) What is the maturity value of the note? (d) What is the due date of the note?

6–8. The payee of a 90-day, 10% note for $5,000, dated April 10, endorses it to a bank on May 10. The bank discounts the note at 12%, paying the endorser

$5,022.50. Identify or determine the following as they relate to the note: (a) face value, (b) maturity value, (c) due date, (d) number of days in the discount period, (e) proceeds, (f) interest income or expense recorded by endorser, (g) amount payable to the bank if the maker should default.

6–9. During the year, notes receivable of $175,000 were discounted at a bank by an enterprise. By the end of the year, $150,000 of these notes have matured. What is the amount of the endorser's contingent liability for notes receivable discounted at the end of the year?

6–10. The maker of a $4,000, 12%, 60-day note receivable failed to pay the note on the due date. What entry should be made in the accounts of the payee to record the dishonored note receivable?

6–11. A discounted note receivable is dishonored by the maker and the endorser pays the bank the face of the note, $5,000, the interest, $300, and a protest fee of $15. What entry should be made in the accounts of the endorser to record the payment?

6–12. The series of six transactions recorded in the following T accounts were related to a sale to a customer on account and receipt of the amount owed. Briefly describe each transaction.

Cash	
(4) 9,420	(5) 9,155
(6) 9,200	

Notes Receivable	
(3) 9,500	(4) 9,500

Accounts Receivable	
(1) 10,000	(2) 500
(5) 9,155	(3) 9,500
	(6) 9,155

Sales	
(2) 500	(1) 10,000

Interest Income	
	(6) 45

Interest Expense	
(4) 80	

6–13. Which of the two methods of accounting for uncollectible accounts provides for the recognition of the expense at the earlier date?

6–14. What kind of an account (asset, liability, etc.) is Allowance for Doubtful Accounts, and is its normal balance a debit or a credit?

6–15. Give the adjusting entry to increase Allowance for Doubtful Accounts by $7,225.

6–16. After the accounts are adjusted and closed at the end of the fiscal year, Accounts Receivable has a balance of $197,500 and Allowance for Doubtful Accounts has a balance of $8,500.
(a) What is the expected realizable value of the accounts receivable?
(b) If an account receivable of $900 is written off against the allowance account, what will be the expected realizable value of the accounts receivable after the write-off, assuming that no other changes in either account have occurred in the meantime?

6–17. A firm has consistently adjusted its allowance account at the end of the fiscal year by adding a fixed percent of the period's net sales on account. After five years, the balance in Allowance for Doubtful Accounts has become disproportionately large in relationship to the balance in Accounts Receivable. Give two possible explanations.

6–18. The $400 balance of an account owed by a customer is considered to be uncollectible and is to be written off. Give the entry to record the write-off in the general ledger (a) assuming that the allowance method is used and (b) assuming that the direct write-off method is used.

6–19. Which of the two methods of estimating uncollectibles, when advance provision for uncollectible receivables is made, provides for the most accurate estimate of the current realizable value of the receivables?

6–20. Is revenue from sales of merchandise on account more commonly recognized at the time of sale or at the time of cash receipt?

6–21. During the current year, merchandise costing $225,000 was sold on the installment plan for $375,000. The down payments and the installment payments received during the current year totaled $150,000. What is the amount of gross profit considered to be realized in the current year, applying (a) the point of sale method and (b) the installment method of revenue recognition?

6–22. Under what caption should securities held as a temporary investment be reported on the balance sheet?

6–23. A corporation has two equity securities which it holds as a temporary investment. If they have a total cost of $190,000 and a fair market value of $185,000, at what amount should these securities be reported in the Current Assets section of the corporation's balance sheet?

Real World Focus

6–24. Hilton Hotels Corporation owns and operates casinos at several of its hotels, located primarily in Nevada. For the year ended December 31, 1989, the following accounts and notes receivable were reported:

(In millions)	1989	1988
Hotel accounts and notes receivable	$102.5	$88.4
Less allowance for doubtful accounts	8.3	7.9
	$ 94.2	$80.5
Casino accounts receivable	$ 43.4	$47.9
Less allowance for doubtful accounts	7.6	9.1
	$ 35.8	$38.8

(a) Compute the December 31, 1989 percentage of allowance for doubtful accounts to the gross hotel accounts and notes receivable. (b) Compute the December 31, 1989 percentage of the allowance for doubtful accounts to the gross casino accounts receivable. (c) Explain any difference in the two ratios computed in (a) and (b).

Ethics Discussion Case

6–25. Cathy Stanfield, controller of Federal Savings Bank of Bogart, has instructed the bank's computer programmer to program the bank's computers to calculate interest on depository accounts (payables) using the 365-day year and to calculate interest on loans (receivables) using the 360-day year.

Discuss whether Cathy Stanfield is behaving in an ethical manner.

EXERCISES

Ex. 6–26.
Determination of due date and interest on notes.

OBJ. 3

Determine the due date and the amount of interest due at maturity on the following notes:

Date of Note	Face Amount	Term of Note	Interest Rate
(a) April 5	$ 5,000	60 days	9%
(b) May 20	8,000	90 days	11%
(c) June 30	10,000	75 days	12%
(d) August 9	3,000	120 days	10%
(e) October 11	7,500	60 days	12%

Ex. 6–27.
Entries for notes receivable.

OBJ. 3, 4

Winger Company issued a 60-day, 12% note for $10,000, dated May 10, to Loggia Corporation on account.

(a) Determine the due date of the note.
(b) Determine the maturity value of the note.
(c) Present entries to record the following:
  (1) Receipt of the note by the payee.
  (2) Receipt by payee of payment of the note at maturity.

Ex. 6–28.
Discounting note receivable.

OBJ. 4

Bosley Co. holds a 90-day, 10% note for $20,000, dated April 20, that was received from a customer on account. On May 20, the note is discounted at the First National Bank at the rate of 12%.

(a) Determine the maturity value of the note.
(b) Determine the number of days in the discount period.
(c) Determine the amount of the discount.
(d) Determine the amount of the proceeds.
(e) Present the entry to record the discounting of the note on May 20.

Ex. 6–29.
Entries for receipt and discounting of note receivable and dishonored note.

OBJ. 4

Record the following transactions in the accounts of L. Keaton Co.

March 1. Received an $8,000, 60-day, 12% note dated March 1 from Hoskins Company on account.
21. Discounted the note at Paxton National Bank at 13%.
April 30. The note is dishonored; paid the bank the amount due on the note plus a protest fee of $15.
May 20. Received the amount due on the dishonored note plus interest for 20 days at 12% on the total amount charged to Hoskins Company on April 30.

Ex. 6–30.
Entries for receipt and dishonor of notes receivable.

OBJ. 4

Record the following transactions in the accounts of Reinhold Co.

May 1. Received a $25,000, 30-day, 12% note dated May 1 from Southwest Corp. on account.
10. Received a $12,000, 60-day, 14% note dated May 10 from Cara Young Co. on account.
31. The note dated May 1 from Southwest Corp. is dishonored and the customer's account is charged for the note, including interest.
July 9. The note dated May 10 from Cara Young Co. is dishonored and the customer's account is charged for the note, including interest.
Aug. 11. Cash is received for the amount due on the dishonored note dated May 1 plus interest for 72 days at 12% on the total amount debited to Southwest Corp. on May 31.
30. Wrote off against the allowance account the amount charged to Cara Young Co. on July 9 for the dishonored note dated May 10.

Ex. 6–31.
Provision for doubtful accounts.

OBJ. 6

At the end of the current year, the accounts receivable account has a debit balance of $112,500, and net sales for the year total $1,200,000. Determine the amount of the adjusting entry to record the provision for doubtful accounts under each of the following assumptions:

(a) The allowance account before adjustment has a credit balance of $750.
  (1) Uncollectible accounts expense is estimated at 1% of net sales.
  (2) Analysis of the accounts in the customers ledger indicates doubtful accounts of $12,450.
(b) The allowance account before adjustment has a debit balance of $500.
  (1) Uncollectible accounts expense is estimated at 3/4 of 1% of net sales.
  (2) Analysis of the accounts in the customers ledger indicates doubtful accounts of $8,850.

Ex. 6–32.
Entries for uncollectible receivables using allowance method.

OBJ. 6

Present entries to record the following transactions in the accounts of Baker Corporation, which uses the allowance method of accounting for uncollectible receivables.

Jan. 30. Sold merchandise on account to C. F. Danson, $3,300.
July 11. Received $1,980 from C. F. Danson and wrote off the remainder owed on the sale of January 30 as uncollectible.
Dec. 15. Reinstated the account of C. F. Danson that had been written off on July 11 and received $1,320 cash in full payment.

Ex. 6–33.
Entries for uncollectible accounts, using direct write-off method.

OBJ. 7

Record the following transactions in the accounts of F. L. Winston and Co., which uses the direct write-off method of accounting for uncollectible receivables.

Feb. 20. Sold merchandise on account to J. P. Sands, $2,500.
July 1. Received $1,500 from J. P. Sands and wrote off the remainder owed on the sale of February 20 as uncollectible.
Dec. 10. Reinstated the account of J. P. Sands that had been written off on July 1 and received $1,000 cash in full payment.

Ex. 6–34.
Gross profit by point of sale and installment methods.

OBJ. 8

Stratton Company makes all sales on the installment plan. Data related to merchandise sold during the current fiscal year are as follows:

Sales	$900,000
Cash received on the $900,000 of installment contracts	325,000
Merchandise inventory, beginning of year	162,500
Merchandise inventory, end of year	167,500
Purchases	635,000

Determine the amount of gross profit that would be recognized for the current fiscal year according to (a) the point of sale method and (b) the installment method.

Ex. 6–35.
Temporary equity securities in financial statements.

OBJ. 9

As of December 31 of the first year of operations, Godell Corporation has the following portfolio of temporary equity securities:

	Cost	Market
Security M	$30,500	$28,750
Security N	19,200	22,100
Security O	21,600	23,900
Security P	70,300	65,250

Describe how the portfolio of temporary equity securities would affect the year-end balance sheet and income statement of Godell Corporation.

PROBLEMS

Pb. 6–36.
Sales, notes receivable, discounting notes receivable transactions.

OBJ. 4

The following were selected from among the transactions completed by C. J. Yeager Co. during the current year:

Mar. 1. Sold merchandise on account to Kerr Co., $15,000.
30. Accepted a 60-day, 12% note for $15,000 from Kerr Co. on account.
May 29. Received from Kerr Co. the amount due on the note of March 30.
June 1. Sold merchandise on account to Robeson's for $5,000.
5. Loaned $6,000 cash to Frank Nelson, receiving a 30-day, 14% note.
11. Received from Robeson's the amount due on the invoice of June 1, less 1% discount.
July 5. Received the interest due from Frank Nelson and a new 60-day, 14% note as a renewal of the loan of June 5. (Record both the debit and the credit to the notes receivable account.)

Sept. 3. Received from Frank Nelson the amount due on his note of July 5.
16. Sold merchandise on account to Alice Rijo, $4,000.
Oct. 16. Accepted a 60-day, 12% note for $4,000 from Alice Rijo on account.
Nov. 15. Discounted the note from Alice Rijo at the Second National Bank at 10%.
Dec. 15. Received notice from Second National Bank that Alice Rijo had dishonored its note. Paid the bank the maturity value of the note.
30. Received from Alice Rijo the amount owed on the dishonored note, plus interest for 15 days at 10% computed on the maturity value of the note.

Instructions:

Present the entries to record the transactions.

Pb. 6–37.
Details of notes receivable, including discounting.

OBJ. 4

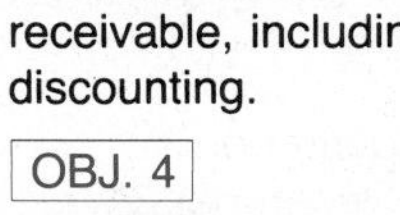

During the last six months of the current fiscal year, Mitchell Co. received the following notes. Notes (1), (2), (3), and (4) were discounted on the dates and at the rates indicated.

Date	Face Amount	Term	Interest Rate	Date Discounted	Discount Rate
(1) April 10	$15,000	60 days	12%	April 30	10%
(2) May 30	8,000	60 days	12%	June 9	15%
(3) July 1	45,000	90 days	10%	July 31	12%
(4) Sept. 1	10,800	60 days	11%	Oct. 11	12%
(5) Dec. 11	18,000	30 days	14%	—	—
(6) Dec. 21	36,000	60 days	13%	—	—

Instructions:

(1) Determine for each note (a) the due date and (b) the amount of interest due at maturity, identifying each note by number.
(2) Determine for each of the first four notes (a) the maturity value, (b) the discount period, (c) the discount, (d) the proceeds, and (e) the interest income or interest expense, identifying each note by number.
(3) Present the entries to record the discounting of notes (2) and (3) at a bank.
(4) Assuming that notes (5) and (6) are held until maturity, determine for each the amount of interest earned (a) in the current fiscal year and (b) in the following fiscal year.

Pb. 6–38.
Entries related to uncollectible accounts.

OBJ. 6

The following transactions, adjusting entries, and closing entries were completed during the current fiscal year ended December 31:

Jan. 19. Reinstated the account of Andrew Bowen, which had been written off in the preceding year as uncollectible. Recorded the receipt of $565 cash in full payment of Bowen's account.
Feb. 28. Wrote off the $4,650 balance owed by Picci Co., which is bankrupt.
May 7. Received 40% of the $5,000 balance owed by C. D. Clark Corp., a bankrupt business, and wrote off the remainder as uncollectible.
Oct. 19. Reinstated the account of Bob Johnson, which had been written off two years earlier as uncollectible. Recorded the receipt of $750 cash in full payment.
Dec. 30. Wrote off the following accounts as uncollectible (compound entry): Adams Co., $910; Dawson Co., $1,900; Keck Furniture, $2,775; Briana Parker, $620.
Dec. 31. Based on an analysis of the $212,750 of accounts receivable, it was estimated that $12,500 will be uncollectible. Recorded the adjusting entry.
31. Recorded the entry to close the appropriate account to Income Summary.

Instructions:

(1) Open the following selected accounts, recording the credit balance indicated as of January 1 of the current fiscal year:

115	Allowance for Doubtful Accounts	$12,900
313	Income Summary	—
718	Uncollectible Accounts Expense	—

(2) Record the transactions and the adjusting and closing entries described. After each entry, post to the three selected accounts affected and extend the new balances.

(3) Determine the expected realizable value of the accounts receivable as of December 31.

(4) Assuming that, instead of basing the provision for uncollectible accounts on an analysis of receivables, the adjusting entry on December 31 had been based on an estimated loss of 1/2 of 1% of the net sales of $2,500,000 for the year, determine the following:
(a) Uncollectible accounts expense for the year.
(b) Balance in the allowance account after the adjustment of December 31.
(c) Expected realizable value of the accounts receivable as of December 31.

Pb. 6–39.
Comparison of two methods of accounting for uncollectible receivables.

OBJ. 6, 7

Reissen Corporation has just completed its fourth year of operations. The direct write-off method of recording uncollectible accounts expense has been employed during the entire period. Because of substantial increases in sales volume and amount of uncollectible accounts, the firm is considering the possibility of changing to the allowance method. Information is requested as to the effect that an annual provision of 1% of sales would have had on the amount of uncollectible accounts expense reported for each of the past four years. It is also considered desirable to know what the balance of Allowance for Doubtful Accounts would have been at the end of each year. The following data have been obtained from the accounts:

			Year of Origin of Accounts Receivable Written off as Uncollectible			
Year	Sales	Uncollectible Accounts Written Off	1st	2d	3d	4th
1st	$500,000	$2,250	$2,250			
2d	750,000	3,300	1,750	$1,550		
3d	850,000	5,600	1,200	2,900	$1,500	
4th	950,000	6,550		2,800	1,950	$1,800

Instructions:

(1) Assemble the desired data, using the following columnar captions:

	Uncollectible Accounts Expense			
Year	Expense Actually Reported	Expense Based on Estimate	Increase in Amount of Expense	Balance of Allowance Account, End of Year

(2) Experience during the first four years of operation indicated that the receivables were either collected within two years or had to be written off as uncollectible. Does the estimate of 1% of sales appear to be reasonably close to the actual experience with uncollectible accounts originating during the first two years?

Pb. 6–40.
Installment sales.

OBJ. 8

Menter Co. makes all sales on the installment basis and recognizes revenue at the point of sale. Condensed income statements and the amounts collected from customers for each of the first three years of operations are as follows:

	First Year	Second Year	Third Year
Sales	$402,500	$340,000	$372,000
Cost of merchandise sold	265,650	227,800	241,800
Gross profit	$136,850	$112,200	$130,200
Operating expenses	64,000	51,500	60,700
Net income	$ 72,850	$ 60,700	$ 69,500
Collected from sales of first year	$125,000	$157,500	$120,000
Collected from sales of second year		95,000	145,000
Collected from sales of third year			110,000

Instructions:

Determine the amount of net income that would have been reported in each year if the installment method of recognizing revenue had been employed, ignoring the possible effects of uncollectible accounts on the computation. Present figures in good order.

Pb. 6–41.
Installment sale and repossession.
OBJ. 8

Cone Video employs the installment method of recognizing gross profit for sales made on the installment plan. Details of a particular installment sale, amounts collected from the buyer, and the repossession of the item sold are as follows:

First year:
Sold for $1,200 a color television set having a cost of $960; received a down payment of $200.
Second year:
Received 12 monthly payments of $40 each.
Third year:
The buyer defaulted on the monthly payments, the set was repossessed, and the remaining 13 installments were canceled. The set was estimated to be worth $450.

Instructions:

(1) Determine the gross profit to be recognized in the first year.
(2) Determine the gross profit to be recognized in the second year.
(3) Determine the gain or loss to be recognized from the repossession of the set. (*Suggestion:* First determine the amount of the unrecovered cost in the canceled installments. The gain or loss on repossession will then be the difference between this unrecovered cost and the value of the repossessed set.)

Pb. 6–42.
Financial statements for corporation.
OBJ. 10

The following data for B. N. Collins Company were selected from the ledger, after adjustment at December 31, the end of the current fiscal year:

Accounts payable	$ 24,250
Accounts receivable	48,000
Accumulated depreciation—building	162,500
Accumulated depreciation—office equipment	47,250
Administrative expenses	72,250
Allowance for decline to market of marketable securities	1,400
Allowance for doubtful accounts	2,400
Building	310,000
Capital stock	250,000
Cash	34,600
Cost of merchandise sold	514,000
Dividends	60,000
Interest and dividend income	6,100
Land	80,000
Marketable equity securities	55,000

Notes receivable	$ 40,000
Office equipment	79,750
Office supplies	5,500
Prepaid insurance	7,000
Retained earnings	203,400
Salaries payable	3,950
Sales	795,000
Sales discounts	6,500
Selling expenses	107,250
Unrealized loss from decline to market of marketable securities	1,400

Instructions:

(1) Prepare an income statement in multiple-step form. The merchandise inventory at December 31 is $75,000.
(2) Prepare a retained earnings statement.
(3) Prepare a balance sheet in report form.

ALTERNATE PROBLEMS

Pb. 6–36A.
Sales, notes receivable, discounting notes receivable transactions.

OBJ. 4

The following were selected from among the transactions completed by Drysdale Co. during the current year:

Jan. 10. Loaned $5,000 cash to Susan Butler, receiving a 90-day, 12% note.
Feb. 8. Sold merchandise on account to Warren Enterprises, $8,000.
20. Sold merchandise on account to C. D. Connors Co., $7,100.
Mar. 2. Received from C. D. Connors Co. the amount of the invoice of February 20, less 2% discount.
10. Accepted a 60-day, 15% note for $8,000 from Warren Enterprises on account.
Apr. 10. Received the interest due from Susan Butler and a new 90-day, 14% note as a renewal of the loan of January 10. (Record both the debit and the credit to the notes receivable account.)
May 9. Received from Warren Enterprises the amount due on the note of March 10.
July 2. Sold merchandise on account to Swartz and Sons, $20,000.
9. Received from Susan Butler the amount due on her note of April 10.
Aug. 1. Accepted a 60-day, 12% note for $20,000 from Swartz and Sons on account.
31. Discounted the note from Swartz and Sons at the American National Bank at 14%.
Sept. 30. Received notice from the American National Bank that Swartz and Sons had dishonored its note. Paid the bank the maturity value of the note.
Oct. 30. Received from Swartz and Sons the amount owed on the dishonored note, plus interest for 30 days at 12% computed on the maturity value of the note.

Instructions:

Present entries to record the transactions.

Pb. 6–37A.
Details of notes receivable, including discounting.

OBJ. 4

During the last three months of the current fiscal year, Donahoe Co. received the following notes. Notes (1), (2), (3), and (4) were discounted on the dates and at the rates indicated.

	Date	Face Amount	Term	Interest Rate	Date Discounted	Discount Rate
(1)	Oct. 10	$ 9,600	60 days	14%	Oct. 30	12%
(2)	Oct. 21	19,000	30 days	12%	Nov. 5	14%
(3)	Oct. 28	6,200	90 days	14%	Dec. 27	15%
(4)	Nov. 8	8,000	60 days	12%	Nov. 23	16%
(5)	Dec. 16	12,000	60 days	11%	—	—
(6)	Dec. 21	15,000	30 days	12%	—	—

Instructions:

(1) Determine for each note (a) the due date and (b) the amount of interest due at maturity, identifying each note by number.
(2) Determine for each of the first four notes (a) the maturity value, (b) the discount period, (c) the discount, (d) the proceeds, and (e) the interest income or interest expense, identifying each note by number.
(3) Present the entries to record the discounting of notes (2) and (4) at a bank.
(4) Assuming that notes (5) and (6) are held until maturity, determine for each the amount of interest earned (a) in the current fiscal year and (b) in the following fiscal year.

Pb. 6–38A.
Entries related to uncollectible accounts.

OBJ. 6

The following transactions, adjusting entries, and closing entries were completed during the current fiscal year ended December 31:

Jan. 22. Received 70% of the $5,000 balance owed by White Co., a bankrupt business, and wrote off the remainder as uncollectible.
Mar. 5. Reinstated the account of Patrick Lynskey, which had been written off in the preceding year as uncollectible. Recorded the receipt of $725 cash in full payment of Lynskey's account.
July 27. Wrote off the $8,900 balance owed by Martin Corp., which has no assets.
Sept. 7. Reinstated the account of W. W. Bacon Inc., which had been written off in the preceding year as uncollectible. Recorded the receipt of $2,950 cash in full payment of the account.
Dec. 30. Wrote off the following accounts as uncollectible (compound entry): Davis Co., $3,950; Nance Inc., $4,600; Powell Distributors, $6,500; J. J. Stevens, $4,200.
31. Based on an analysis of the $580,000 of accounts receivable, it was estimated that $31,250 will be uncollectible. Recorded the adjusting entry.
31. Recorded the entry to close the appropriate account to Income Summary.

Instructions:

(1) Open the following selected accounts, recording the credit balance indicated as of January 1 of the current fiscal year:

115	Allowance for Doubtful Accounts	$28,250
313	Income Summary	—
718	Uncollectible Accounts Expense	—

(2) Record the transactions and the adjusting and closing entries previously described. After each entry, post to the three selected accounts affected and extend the new balances.

(continued)

(3) Determine the expected realizable value of the accounts receivable as of December 31.

(4) Assuming that, instead of basing the provision for uncollectible accounts on an analysis of receivables, the adjusting entry on December 31 had been based on an estimated loss of 1/2 of 1% of the net sales of $5,500,000 for the year, determine the following:
 (a) Uncollectible accounts expense for the year.
 (b) Balance in the allowance account after the adjustment of December 31.
 (c) Expected realizable value of the accounts receivable as of December 31.

Pb. 6–39A.
Comparison of two methods of accounting for receivables.
OBJ. 6,7
SPREADSHEET PROBLEM

Lebaron Corporation has just completed its fourth year of operations. The direct write-off method of recording uncollectible accounts expense has been employed during the entire period. Because of substantial increases in sales volume and amount of uncollectible accounts, the firm is considering the possibility of changing to the allowance method. Information is requested as to the effect that an annual provision of 1% of sales would have had on the amount of uncollectible accounts expense reported for each of the past four years. It is also considered desirable to know what the balance of Allowance for Doubtful Accounts would have been at the end of each year. The following data have been obtained from the accounts:

		Uncollectible Accounts Written	Year of Origin of Accounts Receivable Written off as Uncollectible			
Year	Sales	Off	1st	2d	3d	4th
1st	$400,000	$2,000	$2,000			
2d	600,000	2,950	1,500	$1,450		
3d	850,000	4,700	700	2,400	$1,600	
4th	900,000	6,000		1,900	2,500	$1,600

Instructions:

(1) Assemble the desired data, using the following columnar captions:

	Uncollectible Accounts Expense			
Year	Expense Actually Reported	Expense Based on Estimate	Increase in Amount of Expense	Balance of Allowance Account, End of Year

(2) Experience during the first four years of operation indicated that the receivables were either collected within two years or had to be written off as uncollectible. Does the estimate of 1% of sales appear to be reasonably close to the actual experience with uncollectible accounts originating during the first two years?

Pb. 6–40A.
Installment sales.
OBJ. 8

J. A. Oquendo Inc. makes all sales on the installment basis and recognizes revenue at the point of sale. Condensed income statements and the amounts collected from customers for each of the first three years of operations are as follows:

	First Year	Second Year	Third Year
Sales	$310,000	$340,000	$400,000
Cost of merchandise sold	201,500	224,400	256,000
Gross profit	$108,500	$115,600	$144,000
Operating expenses	64,000	68,500	90,500
Net income	$ 44,500	$ 47,100	$ 53,500
Collected from sales of first year	$ 75,000	$125,000	$100,000
Collected from sales of second year		110,000	161,000
Collected from sales of third year			150,000

Instructions:

Determine the amount of net income that would have been reported in each year if the installment method of recognizing revenue had been employed, ignoring the possible effects of uncollectible accounts on the computation. Present figures in good order.

Pb. 6–41A.
Installment sale and repossession.

OBJ. 8

Martino TV Company employs the installment method of recognizing gross profit for sales made on the installment plan. Details of a particular installment sale, amounts collected from the buyer, and the repossession of the item sold are as follows.

First year:
Sold for $800 a color television set having a cost of $640; received a down payment of $150.
Second year:
Received 12 monthly payments of $25 each.
Third year:
The buyer defaulted on the monthly payments, the set was repossessed, and the remaining 14 installments were canceled. The set was estimated to be worth $250.

Instructions:

(1) Determine the gross profit to be recognized in the first year.
(2) Determine the gross profit to be recognized in the second year.
(3) Determine the gain or loss to be recognized from the repossession of the set. (*Suggestion:* First determine the amount of the unrecovered cost in the canceled installments. The gain or loss on repossession then will be the difference between this unrecovered cost and the value of the repossessed set.)

Pb. 6–42A.
Financial statements for corporation.

OBJ. 10

The following data for Chen Company were selected from the ledger, after adjustment at December 31, the end of the current fiscal year.

Accounts payable	$ 26,100
Accounts receivable	57,500
Accumulated depreciation—building	175,000
Accumulated depreciation—office equipment	49,750
Administrative expenses	73,500
Allowance for decline to market of marketable securities	1,100
Allowance for doubtful accounts	1,500
Building	335,000
Capital stock	300,000
Cash	29,500
Cost of merchandise sold	520,000
Dividends	60,000
Interest and dividend income	6,100
Land	65,000
Marketable equity securities	60,000
Notes receivable	40,000
Office equipment	79,750
Office supplies	5,600
Prepaid insurance	5,200
Retained earnings	155,900
Salaries payable	2,900
Sales	805,000
Sales discounts	6,500
Selling expenses	110,500
Unrealized loss from decline to market of marketable securities	1,100

Instructions:

(1) Prepare an income statement in multiple-step form. The merchandise inventory at December 31 is $74,200.

(2) Prepare a retained earnings statement.
(3) Prepare a balance sheet in report form.

MINI-CASE 6

For several years, Myers' sales have been on a "cash only" basis. On January 1, 1988, however, Myers began offering credit on terms of n/30. The amount of the adjusting entry to record the estimated uncollectible receivables at the end of each year has been 1/2 of 1% of credit sales, which is the rate reported as the average for the industry. Credit sales and the year-end credit balances in Allowance for Doubtful Accounts for the past four years are as follows:

Year	Credit Sales	Allowance for Doubtful Accounts
1988	$5,000,000	$ 7,500
1989	4,700,000	10,000
1990	5,200,000	14,500
1991	4,500,000	18,000

Ethyl Myers, president of Myers, is concerned that the method used to account for and write off uncollectible receivables is unsatisfactory. She has asked for your advice in the analysis of past operations in this area and for recommendations for change.

Instructions:

(1) Determine the amount of (a) the addition to Allowance for Doubtful Accounts and (b) the accounts written off for each of the four years.
(2) Advise Ethyl Myers as to whether the estimate of 1/2 of 1% of credit sales appears reasonable.
(3) Assume that after discussing item (2) with Ethyl Myers, she asked you what action might be taken to determine what the balance of Allowance for Doubtful Accounts should be at December 31, 1991, and possible changes, if any, you might recommend in accounting for uncollectible receivables. How would you respond?

ANSWERS TO SELF-EXAMINATION QUESTIONS

1. C Maturity value is the amount that is due at the maturity or due date. The maturity value of $10,300 (answer C) is determined as follows:

Face amount of note	$10,000
Plus interest ($10,000 × 12/100 × 90/360)	300
Maturity value of note	$10,300

2. B The proceeds of $15,021.25 (answer B) are determined as follows:

Face value of note dated June 1	$15,000.00
Interest on note (60 days at 10%)	250.00
Maturity value of note due July 31	$15,250.00
Discount on maturity value (45 days, from June 16 to July 31 at 12%)	228.75
Proceeds	$15,021.25

3. B The estimate of uncollectible accounts, $8,500 (answer C), is the amount of the desired balance of Allowance for Doubtful Accounts *after adjustment*. The amount of the current provision to be made for uncollectible accounts expense is thus $6,000 (answer B), which is the amount that must be added to the Allowance for Doubtful Accounts credit balance of $2,500 (answer A), so that the account will have the desired balance of $8,500.
4. B The amount expected to be realized from accounts receivable is the balance of Accounts Receivable, $100,000, less the balance of Allowance for Doubtful Accounts, $7,000, or $93,000 (answer B).
5. A Securities held as temporary investments are classified on the balance sheet as current assets (answer A).

CHAPTER 7

CHAPTER OBJECTIVES

1 Describe and illustrate the effect of inventory on the financial statements of the current period and the following period.

2 Identify and describe the two principal inventory systems.

3 Identify and illustrate the procedures for determining the actual quantities in inventory.

4 Describe and illustrate the determination of the cost of inventory.

5 Describe and illustrate the most common inventory costing methods under a periodic system, including the comparison of the effect of the methods on operating results.

6 Describe and illustrate the accounting for inventory under the perpetual system.

7 Describe and illustrate the valuation of inventory at other than cost, including valuation at the lower of cost or market.

8 Identify and illustrate the proper presentation of inventory in the financial statements.

9 Describe and illustrate methods of estimating the cost of inventory.

10 Describe and illustrate inventories of manufacturing enterprises.

11 Describe and illustrate accounting for long-term construction contracts.

INVENTORIES

The term **inventories** is used to designate (1) merchandise held for sale in the normal course of business, and (2) materials in the process of production or held for such use. This chapter discusses the determination of the inventory of merchandise purchased for resale, commonly called **merchandise inventory.** Inventories of raw materials and partially processed materials of a manufacturing enterprise are also discussed.

IMPORTANCE OF INVENTORIES

OBJECTIVE 1
Describe and illustrate the effect of inventory on the financial statements of the current period and the following period.

Merchandise, being continually purchased and sold, is one of the most active elements in the operation of wholesale and retail businesses. The sale of merchandise provides the principal source of revenue for such enterprises. When the net income is determined, the cost of merchandise sold is normally the largest deduction from sales. In fact, it is usually larger than all other deductions combined. In addition, a substantial part of a merchandising firm's resources is invested in inventory. It is frequently the largest of the current assets of such a firm.

The Effect of Inventory on the Current Period's Statements

Inventory determination plays an important role in matching expired costs with revenues of the period. As was explained and illustrated in Chapter 4, the total cost of merchandise available for sale during a period of time must be divided into two parts at the end of the period. The cost of the merchandise determined to be in the inventory will appear on the balance sheet as a current asset. The other element, which is the cost of the merchandise sold, will be reported on the income statement as a deduction from net sales to yield gross profit. An error in the determination of the inventory amount at the end of the period will cause an equal misstatement of gross profit and net income, and the amount reported for both assets and owner's equity in the balance sheet will be incorrect by the same amount. The effects of understatements and overstatements of merchandise inventory at the end of the period are demonstrated in the following three sets of condensed income statements and balance sheets. The first set of statements is based on a correct ending inventory of $20,000; the second set, on an *incorrect ending inventory of $12,000;* and the third set, on an *incorrect ending inventory of $27,000.* In all three cases, net sales are $200,000, merchandise available for sale is $140,000, and expenses are $55,000.

Income Statement for the Year		Balance Sheet at End of Year	
1. Inventory at end of period correctly stated at $20,000.			
Net sales	$200,000	Merchandise inventory	$ 20,000
Cost of merchandise sold	120,000	Other assets	80,000
Gross profit	$ 80,000	Total	$100,000
Expenses	55,000		
Net income	$ 25,000	Liabilities	$ 30,000
		Owner's equity	70,000
		Total	$100,000
2. Inventory at end of period incorrectly stated at $12,000; (understated by $8,000).			
Net sales	$200,000	Merchandise inventory	$ 12,000
Cost of merchandise sold	128,000	Other assets	80,000
Gross profit	$ 72,000	Total	$ 92,000
Expenses	55,000		
Net income	$ 17,000	Liabilities	$ 30,000
		Owner's equity	62,000
		Total	$ 92,000
3. Inventory at end of period incorrectly stated at $27,000; (overstated by $7,000).			
Net sales	$200,000	Merchandise inventory	$ 27,000
Cost of merchandise sold	113,000	Other assets	80,000
Gross profit	$ 87,000	Total	$107,000
Expenses	55,000		
Net income	$ 32,000	Liabilities	$ 30,000
		Owner's equity	77,000
		Total	$107,000

Note that in the illustration the total cost of merchandise available for sale was constant at $140,000. It was the way in which the cost was allocated that varied. The variations in allocating the $140,000 of merchandise cost are summarized as follows:

	Merchandise Available		
	Total	*Inventory*	*Sold*
1. Inventory correctly stated	$140,000	$20,000	$120,000
2. Inventory understated by $8,000	140,000	12,000	128,000
3. Inventory overstated by $7,000	140,000	27,000	113,000

The effect of the errors on net income, assets, and owner's equity may also be summarized. Comparison of the financial statements in *2* and *3* with the financial statements in *1* yields the following:

	Net Income	Assets	Owner's Equity
2. Ending inventory understated $8,000	Understated $8,000	Understated $8,000	Understated $8,000
3. Ending inventory overstated $7,000	Overstated $7,000	Overstated $7,000	Overstated $7,000

The Effect of Inventory on the Following Period's Statements

The inventory at the end of one period becomes the inventory for the beginning of the following period. Thus, if the inventory is incorrectly stated at the end of the period, the net income of that period will be misstated and so will the net income for the following period. The amount of the two misstatements will be equal and in opposite directions. Therefore, the effect on net income of an incorrectly stated inventory, if not corrected, is limited to the period of the error and the following period. At the end of this following period, assuming no additional errors, both assets and owner's equity will be correctly stated. To illustrate, assume that the ending inventory for period *1* was understated by $10,000, and no other errors are made. The gross profit (and net income) would be understated for period *1* and overstated for period *2* by $10,000, indicated as follows:

	Period 1				Period 2			
	No Error		*Error*		*Error*		*No Error*	
Net sales		$90,000		$90,000		$85,000		$85,000
Cost of merchandise sold:								
Beginning inventory	$25,000		$25,000		$20,000		$30,000	
Purchases	70,000		70,000		65,000		65,000	
Merchandise available for sale	$95,000		$95,000		$85,000		$95,000	
Less ending inventory	30,000		20,000		28,000		28,000	
Cost of merchandise sold		65,000		75,000		57,000		67,000
Gross profit		$25,000		$15,000		$28,000		$18,000
				Understated $10,000		Overstated $10,000		

In the illustration, the $10,000 understatement of inventory at the end of period *1* resulted in an overstatement of the cost of merchandise sold and thus an understatement of gross profit by $10,000. On the balance sheet, merchandise inventory and owner's equity would both be understated by $10,000. Because the ending inventory of period *1* becomes the beginning inventory for period *2*, the cost of merchandise sold was understated and gross profit was overstated by $10,000 for period *2*. Both merchandise inventory and owner's equity will be correct at the end of period *2*.

FALSIFIED INVENTORY AND INCOME INFLATE COMPANY'S VALUE

The importance of inventory to financial statements is recognized even by those who attempt to manipulate a company's statements in a fraudulent manner. One example of such inventory fraud is described in the following excerpt from an article in *The Wall Street Journal:*

Until last year, Crazy Eddie Inc. steadily recorded superb gains in sales and earnings, apparently because of rapid expansion of its electronics stores, adept sales-floor techniques and catchy commercials.

But the now-troubled company's latest court and regulatory filings suggest another element: a possible scheme by founder Eddie Antar and others to falsify inventory and profit reports. . . .

. . . Crazy Eddie says its former management—led by Mr. Antar—created "phantom" inventory and profits, then destroyed records in a cover-up. The purpose, the company says . . . was to "artificially inflate the net worth of the company"

and the value of stock owned by Mr. Antar and others.

For instance, Crazy Eddie says the former management inflated the March 1987 inventory count at one warehouse by $10 million, by drafting phony count sheets and, among other things, improperly including $4 million in merchandise that was [recorded as] being returned to suppliers. Stores were also packed with unrecorded [purchases] prior to physical [inventory] counts. . . .

Source: Jeffrey A. Tannenbaum, "Filings by Crazy Eddie Suggest Founder Led Scheme to Inflate Company's Value," *The Wall Street Journal* (May 31, 1988), p. 28.

INVENTORY SYSTEMS

OBJECTIVE 2
Identify and describe the two principal inventory systems.

As discussed in Chapter 4, there are two principal systems of inventory accounting— periodic and perpetual. When the **periodic inventory system** is used, only the revenue from sales is recorded each time a sale is made. No entry is made at the time of the sale to record the cost of the merchandise that has been sold. Consequently, a **physical inventory** must be taken in order to determine the cost of the inventory at the end of an accounting period. Ordinarily, it is practical to take a complete physical inventory only at the end of the fiscal year. In the earlier chapters dealing with purchases and sales of merchandise, the use of the periodic system was assumed.

In contrast to the periodic system, the **perpetual inventory system** uses accounting records that continuously disclose the amount of the inventory. A separate account for each type of merchandise is maintained in a subsidiary ledger. Increases in inventory items are recorded as debits to the proper accounts, and decreases are recorded as credits. The balances of the accounts are called the **book inventories** of the items on hand. Regardless of the care with which the perpetual inventory records are maintained, their accuracy must be tested by taking a physical inventory of each type of commodity at least once a year. The records are then compared with the actual quantities on hand and any differences are corrected.

The periodic inventory system is often used by retail enterprises that sell many kinds of low unit cost merchandise, such as groceries, hardware, and drugs. The expense of maintaining perpetual inventory records may be prohibitive in such cases. In recent years, however, the use of computerized systems in such businesses has reduced this expense considerably. Firms selling a relatively small number of high unit cost items, such as office equipment, automobiles, or fur garments, are more likely to use the perpetual system.

Although much of the discussion that follows applies to both systems, the use of the periodic inventory system will be assumed. Later in the chapter, principles and procedures related only to the perpetual inventory system will be presented.

DETERMINING ACTUAL QUANTITIES IN THE INVENTORY

OBJECTIVE 3
Identify and illustrate the procedures for determining the actual quantities in inventory.

The first stage in the process of "taking" an inventory is to determine the quantity of each kind of merchandise owned by the enterprise. When the periodic system is used, the counting, weighing, and measuring should be done at the end of the accounting period. To accomplish this, the inventory crew may work during the night, or business operations may be stopped until the count is finished.

The details of the specific procedures for determining quantities and assembling the data differ among companies. A common practice is to use teams made up of two persons. One person counts, weighs, or otherwise determines quantity, and the other lists the description and the quantity on inventory sheets. The quantity indicated for high-cost items is verified by a third person at some time during the inventory-taking period. It is also advisable for the third person to verify other items selected at random from the inventory sheets.

All of the merchandise owned by the business on the inventory date, and only such merchandise, should be included in the inventory. It may be necessary to examine purchase and sales invoices of the last few days of the accounting period and the first few days of the following period to determine who has legal title to merchandise in transit on the inventory date. When goods are purchased or sold **FOB shipping point,** title usually passes to the buyer when the goods are shipped. When the terms are **FOB destination,** title usually does not pass to the buyer until the goods are delivered. To illustrate, assume that merchandise purchased FOB shipping point is shipped by the seller on the last day of the buyer's fiscal period. The merchandise does not arrive until the following period and hence is not available for "counting" by the inventory crew. However, such merchandise should be included in the buyer's inventory because title has passed. It is also evident that a debit to Purchases and a credit to Accounts Payable should be recorded by the buyer as of the end of the current period, rather than recording it as a transaction of the following period.

Another example, although less common, will further show the importance of closely examining transactions involving shipments of merchandise. Manufacturers sometimes ship merchandise on a consignment basis to retailers who act as the manufacturer's agent when selling the merchandise. The manufacturer retains title until the goods are sold. Obviously, such unsold merchandise is a part of the manufacturer's (consignor's) inventory, even though the manufacturer does not have physical possession. It is just as obvious that the consigned merchandise should not be included in the retailer's (consignee's) inventory.

DETERMINING THE COST OF INVENTORY

OBJECTIVE 4
Describe and illustrate the determination of the cost of inventory.

The cost of merchandise inventory is made up of the purchase price and all expenditures incurred in acquiring such merchandise, including transportation, customs duties, and insurance against losses in transit. The purchase price can be readily determined, as may some of the other costs. Those that are difficult to associate with specific inventory items may be prorated on some equitable basis. Minor costs that are difficult to allocate may be left out entirely from inventory cost and treated as operating expenses of the period.

If purchases discounts are treated as a deduction from purchases on the income statement, they should also be deducted from the purchase price of items in the inventory. If it is not possible to determine the exact amount of discount applicable to each inventory item, a pro rata amount of the total discount for the period may be deducted instead. For example, if net purchases and purchases discounts for the period amount to $200,000 and $3,000, respectively, the discounts represent 1½% of net purchases. If the inventory cost, before considering the cash discounts is $30,000, the amount may be reduced by 1½%, or $450, to yield an inventory cost of $29,550.

INVENTORY COSTING METHODS UNDER A PERIODIC SYSTEM

OBJECTIVE 5
Describe and illustrate the most common inventory costing methods under a periodic system, including the comparison of the effect of the methods on operating results.

One of the most significant problems in determining inventory cost comes about when identical units of a certain commodity have been acquired at different unit cost prices during the period. In such cases, it is necessary to determine the unit prices of the items still on hand. To illustrate this problem and its relationship to the determination of net income and inventory cost, assume that three identical units of Commodity X were available for sale to customers during the fiscal year. One of these units was in the inventory at the beginning of the year, and the other two were purchased on March 4 and May 9 respectively. The costs per unit are as follows:

Commodity X	Units	Cost
Jan. 1 Inventory	1	$ 9
Mar. 4 Purchase	1	13
May 9 Purchase	1	14
Total	3	$36
Average cost per unit		$12

During the year, two units of Commodity X were sold, leaving one unit in the inventory at the end of the year. In the illustration, the units are easily identified with specific expenditures because both the variety of merchandise carried in stock and the volume of sales are relatively small. Since these conditions do not usually exist in actual practice, businesses are not likely to use **specific identification** procedures except with the aid of computerized accounting systems and equipment that can read inventory labels (bar codes). When specific identification procedures are too costly to justify their use, it is customary to use an arbitrary assumption as to the *flow of costs* of merchandise through the enterprise. The three most common assumptions of determining the cost of the merchandise sold are as follows:

1. Cost flow is in the order in which the expenditures were made—first-in, first-out.
2. Cost flow is in the reverse order in which the expenditures were made—last-in, first-out.
3. Cost flow is an average of the expenditures.

Details of the cost of the two units of Commodity X assumed to be sold and the cost of the one unit remaining, determined in accordance with each of these assumptions, are as follows:

	Commodity X Costs				
	Units Available		*Units Sold*		*Unit Remaining*
1. In order of expenditures (first-in, first-out)	$36	–	($ 9 + $13)	=	$14
2. In reverse order of expenditures (last-in, first-out).	36	–	(14 + 13)	=	9
3. In accordance with average expenditures	36	–	(12 + 12)	=	12

The three most widely used inventory costing methods (which correspond to the three assumptions of cost flows illustrated) are:

1. **First-in, first-out (fifo)**
2. **Last-in, first-out (lifo)**
3. **Average**

The extent of the use of these three methods is indicated by the chart below.

Inventory Costing Methods

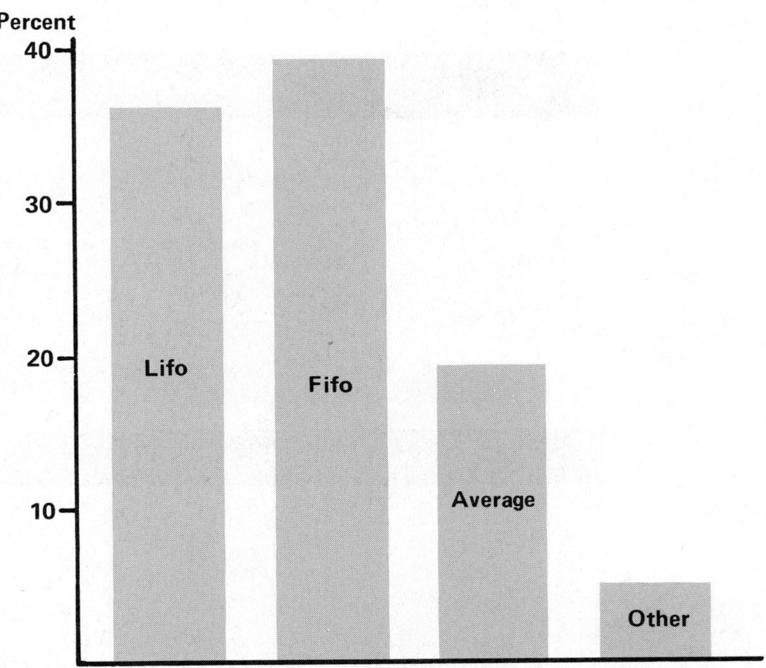

Source: Accounting Trends & Techniques, 44th ed. (New York: American Institute of Certified Public Accountants, 1990).

First-In, First-Out Method

The **first-in, first-out (fifo) method** of costing inventory is based on the assumption that costs should be charged against revenue in the order in which they were incurred. Hence the inventory remaining is assumed to be made up of the most recent costs. The illustration of the application of this method is based on the following data for a particular commodity:

Jan. 1	Inventory	200 units at $ 9	$ 1,800
Mar. 10	Purchase	300 units at 10	3,000
Sept. 21	Purchase	400 units at 11	4,400
Nov. 18	Purchase	100 units at 12	1,200
	Available for sale during year	1,000	$10,400

The physical count on December 31 shows that 300 units of the particular commodity are on hand. In accordance with the assumption that the inventory is composed of the most recent costs, the cost of the 300 units is determined as follows:

Most recent costs, Nov. 18	100 units at $12	$1,200
Next most recent costs, Sept. 21	200 units at 11	2,200
Inventory, Dec. 31	300	$3,400

Deduction of the inventory of $3,400 from the $10,400 of merchandise available for sale yields $7,000 as the cost of merchandise sold, which represents the earliest costs incurred for this commodity. The relationship of the inventory at December 31 and the cost of merchandise sold during the year is illustrated in the following diagram:

In most businesses, there is a tendency to dispose of goods in the order of their acquisition. This would be particularly true of perishable merchandise and goods in which style or model changes are frequent. Thus, the fifo method is generally in harmony with the physical movement of merchandise in an enterprise. To the extent that this is the case, the fifo method approximates the results that would be obtained by the specific identification of costs.

Last-In, First-Out Method

The **last-in, first-out (lifo) method** is based on the assumption that the most recent costs incurred should be charged against revenue. Hence the inventory remaining is assumed to be composed of the earliest costs. Based on the illustrative data presented in the preceding section, the cost of the 300 units of inventory is determined in the following manner:

Earliest costs, Jan. 1	200 units at $ 9	$1,800
Next earliest costs, Mar. 10	100 units at 10	1,000
Inventory, Dec. 31	300	$2,800

Deduction of the inventory of $2,800 from the $10,400 of merchandise available for sale yields $7,600 as the cost of merchandise sold, which represents the most recent costs incurred for this particular commodity. The relationship of the inventory at December 31 and the cost of merchandise sold during the year is illustrated in the following diagram:

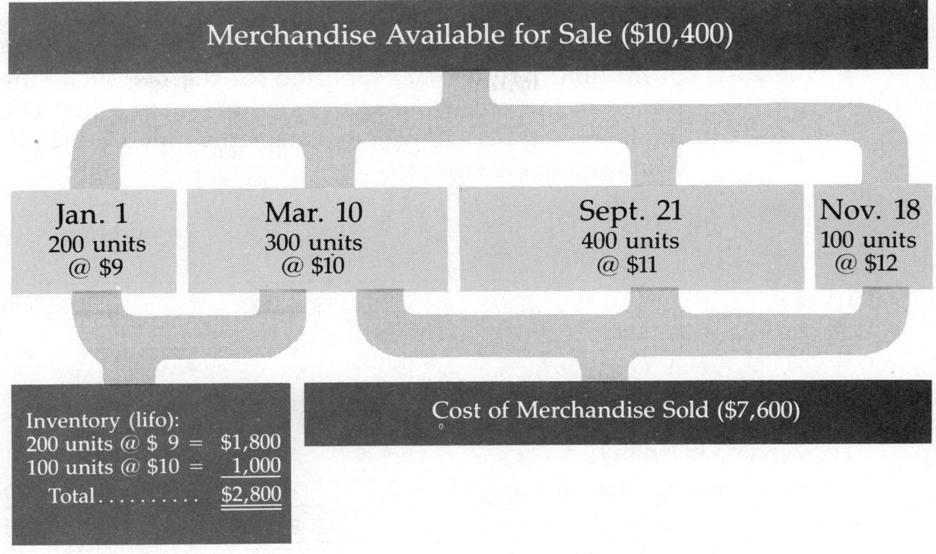

The use of the lifo method was originally confined to the relatively rare situations in which the units sold were taken from the most recently acquired stock. Because of tax considerations, its use has greatly increased during the past few decades, and it is now often used even when it does not represent the physical flow of goods.

Average Cost Method

The **average cost method,** sometimes called the **weighted average method,** is based on the assumption that costs should be charged against revenue according to the weighted average unit costs of the goods sold. The same weighted average unit costs are used in determining the cost of the merchandise remaining in the inventory. The weighted average unit cost is determined by dividing the total cost of the identical units of each commodity available for sale during the period by the related number of units of that commodity. Assuming the same cost data as in the preceding illustrations, the average cost of the 1,000 units and the cost of the 300 units in inventory are determined as follows:

Average unit cost.............	$10,400 ÷ 1,000 = $10.40	
Inventory, Dec. 31............	300 units at $10.40........................	$3,120

Deduction of the inventory of $3,120 from the $10,400 of merchandise available for sale yields $7,280 as the cost of merchandise sold, which represents the average of the costs incurred for this commodity.

For businesses in which various purchases of identical units of a commodity are mingled, the average method has some relationship to the physical flow of goods.

Comparison of Inventory Costing Methods

Each of the three alternative methods of costing inventories under the periodic system is based on a different assumption as to the flow of costs. If the cost of units and prices at which they were sold had remained stable, all three methods would have yielded the same results. Prices do change, however, and as a consequence the three methods will usually yield different amounts for (1) the inventory reported on the balance sheet at the end of the period, (2) the cost of the merchandise sold for the period, and (3) the gross profit (and net income) reported for the period. Using the examples presented in the preceding sections and assuming that net sales were $15,000, the following partial income statements indicate the effects of each method when prices are rising:

	First-In, First-Out		Average Cost		Last-In, First-Out	
Net sales		$15,000		$15,000		$15,000
Cost of merchandise sold:						
Beginning inventory	$ 1,800		$ 1,800		$ 1,800	
Purchases	8,600		8,600		8,600	
Merchandise available for sale	$10,400		$10,400		$10,400	
Less ending inventory	**3,400**		**3,120**		**2,800**	
Cost of merchandise sold		**7,000**		**7,280**		**7,600**
Gross profit		**$ 8,000**		**$ 7,720**		**$ 7,400**

As shown in the income statements, the fifo method yielded the lowest amount for the cost of merchandise sold and the highest amount for gross profit (and net income). It also yielded the highest amount for the ending inventory. On the other hand, the lifo method yielded the highest amount for the cost of merchandise sold, the lowest amount for gross profit (and net income), and the lowest amount for ending inventory. The average cost method yielded results that were between those of fifo and lifo.

Use of the First-In, First-Out Method. During a period of inflation or rising prices, the use of the fifo method will result in the effects shown in the illustration because the costs of the units sold are assumed to be in the order in which they were incurred, and the earlier unit costs were lower than the more recent unit costs. Much of the benefit of the larger amount of gross profit is lost, however, as the inventory is continually replenished at ever higher prices. During the 1970s, when the rate of inflation increased to double-digit percentages, the larger gross profits that resulted were frequently referred to as *inventory profits* or *illusory profits.*

In a period of deflation or declining prices, the effect described above is reversed, and the fifo method yields the lowest amount of gross profit. The major criticism of the fifo method is this tendency to maximize the effect of inflationary and deflationary trends on amounts reported as gross profit. However, the dollar amount reported as merchandise inventory on the balance sheet will usually be about the same as its current replacement cost.

Use of the Last-In, First-Out Method. During a period of rising prices, the use of the last-in, first-out method will result in a lower amount of inventory at the end of the period, a higher amount of cost of merchandise sold, and a lower amount of gross profit than the other two methods. The reason for these effects is that the cost of the most recently acquired units most nearly approximates the cost of their replacement, and the more recent unit costs were higher than the earlier unit costs. Thus, it can be argued that the use of the lifo method more nearly matches current costs with current revenues. This latter point was one reason that Chrysler Corporation changed from the fifo method to the lifo method in 1984, as stated in the following footnote that accompanied Chrysler's financial statements for 1984:

> Effective January 1, 1984, Chrysler changed its method of accounting from first-in, first-out (fifo) to last-in, first-out (lifo) for substantially all of its domestic productive inventories. The change to lifo was made to more accurately match current costs with current revenues. Had the inventory, at December 31, 1984, been valued on the fifo basis, it would have been $29.7 million higher than reported.

During periods of rising prices, the use of lifo offers a savings in income taxes. The income tax savings results because lifo reports the lowest amount of net income of the three methods. During the accelerated inflationary trend of the 1970s, many business enterprises changed from fifo to lifo to take advantage of this tax savings.

In a period of deflation or falling price levels, the effect described above is reversed and the lifo method yields the highest amount of gross profit. The major justification for lifo is this tendency to minimize the effect of price trends on reported gross profit and, therefore, to exert a stabilizing influence on the economy. A criticism of the use of lifo is that the dollar amount reported for merchandise inventory on the balance sheet may be quite far removed from the current replacement cost. In such situations, however, it is customary to indicate in a note accompanying the published financial statements the approximate difference between the lifo inventory amount and the inventory amount if fifo had been used. The following note accompanying the 1990 statements of The Walgreen Co. is illustrative:

> Inventories are valued on a last-in, first out (LIFO) cost basis. At August 31, 1990 and 1989, inventories would have been greater by $285,143,000 and $246,362,000 respectively, if they had been valued on a lower of first-in, first-out (FIFO) cost or market basis.

INFLATION AND ADOPTION OF LIFO

The effects of using lifo and some of the reasons that the method is adopted (or not adopted) by businesses were discussed in an article in *Management Accounting*. Some excerpts from that article follow.

. . . The primary advantage of lifo is that in today's inflationary environment lifo defers (not avoids) income taxes by reducing income. The improved cash flow, then, can be profitably invested or used to reduce borrowings. . . .

In addition to deferring income taxes, though, lifo has a great deal of theoretical justification. By matching current costs against current sales, lifo produces a truer picture of income; that is, the quality of income produced by the use of lifo is higher because it more nearly approximates disposable income. . . .

Even though the primary advantage of lifo— reduced tax payments— is a function of lower income, the negative earnings impact ironically continues to cloud corporate managers' decisions about the adoption of lifo. Managers fear that lower reported earnings will [have unfavorable effects on the stock price, executive compensation contracts, and credit ratings. However,] there is little evidence to suggest that stock price is adversely affected by lifo adoption. Furthermore, [lifo should have no effect on executive compensation contracts or credit ratings.]

The Internal Revenue Code . . . and Treasury Regulations . . . [mandate] that taxpayers who avail themselves of the federal income tax benefits of the lifo method also must use lifo ". . . for credit purposes or for purposes of reports to shareholders, partners, or other proprietors, or to beneficia-

ries. . . ." Thus, the lifo conformity requirement is the culprit behind the negative earnings impact issue. However, regulations adopted in January, 1981, although not going to the extent of allowing the use of lifo in tax returns and a non-lifo method elsewhere, did relax the conformity requirement significantly, such that it is now possible to present non-lifo information very favorably in lifo-based reports. . . .

. . . [The] non-lifo data may be presented in the notes to the financial statements as in the . . . Merck & Co. Inc. Annual Report: ". . . Lifo had the effect of reducing . . . net income by $21,108,000 ($.28 per share) . . . with a positive increase to cash flow of $19,500,000 . . . as a result of decreased U.S. taxes."

. . . Another concern about lifo commonly expressed by corporate managers is misstatement of the inventories on the lifo balance sheet. Particularly over a period of rapidly rising inventory quantities and prices, the use of lifo can lead to a valuation of inventories that is significantly less than current replacement cost. However, this misstatement can be mitigated by presenting inventories valued on a non-lifo basis and deducting the lifo valuation [allowance to reduce the balance sheet inventory to the lifo amount, as follows:]

Inventory	XXX
Less reduction to lifo cost	XXX
Total	XXX

Source: Clayton T. Rumble, "So You Still Have Not Adopted Lifo," *Management Accounting* (October, 1983), pp. 59–67.

Use of the Average Cost Method. The average cost method of inventory costing is, in a sense, a compromise between fifo and lifo. The effect of price trends is averaged, both in the determination of gross profit and in the determination of inventory cost. For any given series of acquisitions, the average cost will be the same, regardless of the direction of price trends. For example, a complete reversal of the sequence of unit costs presented in the illustration on page 294 would not affect the reported gross profit or the inventory cost. The time required to assemble the data is likely to be greater for the average cost method than for the other two methods. The additional expense incurred could be large if there are many purchases of a wide variety of merchandise items.

Selection of an Inventory Costing Method. The foregoing comparisons show the importance attached to the selection of the inventory costing method. It is not unusual for manufacturing enterprises to apply one method to a particular class of inventory, such as merchandise ready for sale, and a different method to another class, such as raw materials purchased. The method(s) used may be changed for a valid reason. The effect of any change in method and the reason for the change should be fully disclosed in the financial statements for the fiscal period in which the change occurred.

ACCOUNTING FOR AND REPORTING INVENTORY UNDER A PERPETUAL SYSTEM

OBJECTIVE 6
Describe and illustrate the accounting for inventory under the perpetual system.

Under the periodic inventory system, as described in earlier chapters, the merchandise inventory account at the beginning of an accounting period reflects the merchandise on hand on that date. Purchases of merchandise are recorded in the purchases account, and sales of merchandise are recorded in the sales account. The cost of the merchandise sold is not determined for each sale. Instead, at the end of an accounting period, when a physical inventory is taken, the beginning inventory is removed from the merchandise inventory account and is replaced by the ending inventory. This ending balance of merchandise inventory is reported on the balance sheet. The cost of merchandise sold is then determined, and this amount is reported on the income statement.

Under the perpetual inventory system, all merchandise increases and decreases are recorded in a manner somewhat similar to the recording of increases and decreases in cash. The merchandise inventory account at the beginning of an accounting period reflects the merchandise on hand on that date. Sales are recorded in the sales account and, on the date of each sale, the cost of the merchandise sold is recorded by debiting Cost of Merchandise Sold and crediting Merchandise Inventory. Thus, in the perpetual system, the merchandise inventory account continuously (perpetually) discloses the balance of merchandise on hand. At the end of the period, the balance in the merchandise inventory account is reported on the balance sheet, and the balance in the cost of merchandise sold account is reported on the income statement.

The accounting for and reporting of merchandise inventory transactions under the periodic and perpetual systems are compared and illustrated as follows:

Comparison of Periodic and Perpetual Systems

Inventory, Purchases, and Sales Data

January 1	Merchandise inventory (beginning)	$52,500
1–31	Purchases (on account)	26,200
1–31	Sales (on account)—selling price	49,750
	Sales—cost price	28,000
31	Merchandise inventory (ending)	50,700

Periodic			Perpetual		
January 1 Merchandise Inventory					
Merchandise inventory account reflects inventory on hand, $52,500.			Merchandise inventory account reflects inventory on hand, $52,500.		
Entries to Record Purchases, January 1–31					
Purchases	26,200		Merchandise Inventory	26,200	
Accounts Payable		26,200	Accounts Payable		26,200
Entries to Record Sales, January 1–31					
Accounts Receivable	49,750		Accounts Receivable	49,750	
Sales		49,750	Sales		49,750
			Cost of Merchandise Sold	28,000	
			Merchandise Inventory		28,000
January 31 Merchandise Inventory					
Merchandise inventory account will reflect the inventory on hand at January 31, $50,700, after the accounts are closed.			Merchandise inventory account perpetually discloses the inventory on hand, which at January 31 is $50,700.		

Periodic			Perpetual	
Reporting Cost of Merchandise Sold in January on Income Statement				
Cost of merchandise sold:			Cost of merchandise sold...........	$28,000
Jan. 1 inventory........	$52,500			
January purchases....	26,200			
Merchandise available for sale................	$78,700			
Less Jan. 31 inventory	50,700			
Cost of merchandise sold		$28,000		
Reporting Merchandise Inventory, January 31, on Balance Sheet				
Merchandise inventory		$50,700	Merchandise inventory................	$50,700

Inventory Costing Methods Under a Perpetual System

Unlike cash, merchandise is a mixed mass of goods. Details of the cost of each type of merchandise purchased and sold, together with such related transactions as returns and allowances, must be maintained in a subsidiary **inventory ledger,** with a separate account for each type. Whether this ledger is computerized or maintained manually, it is customary to use one of the three costing methods—first-in, first-out; last-in, first-out; or average.

In the following paragraphs, the fifo and lifo methods in a perpetual system are discussed and illustrated. The average cost method is briefly discussed also, but an illustration is reserved for advanced texts.

The basis for the fifo and lifo illustrations is the following data for merchandise identified as Commodity 127B:

			Units	Cost
Jan.	1	Inventory	10	$20
	4	Sale..	7	
	10	Purchase	8	21
	22	Sale..	4	
	28	Sale..	2	
	30	Purchase	10	22

First-In, First-Out Method. To illustrate the first-in, first-out method of cost flow in a perpetual inventory system, the inventory ledger account for Commodity 127B is shown at the top of page 303. The number of units on hand after each transaction, together with total costs and unit costs, appears in the inventory section of the account.

Note that after the 7 units of the commodity were sold on January 4, there was a remaining inventory of 3 units at $20 each. The 8 units purchased on January 10 were acquired at a unit cost of $21, instead of $20, and hence could not be combined with the 3 units. The inventory after the January 10 purchase is therefore reported on two lines, 3 units at $20 each and 8 units at $21 each. Next, it should be noted that the $81 cost of the 4 units sold on January 22 is composed of the remaining 3 units at $20 each and 1 unit at $21. At this point, 7 units remain in inventory at a cost of $21 per unit. The remainder of the illustration is explained in a similar manner.

Perpetual Inventory Account (FIFO)

Commodity 127B

Date	Purchases			Cost of Merchandise Sold			Inventory		
	Quantity	Unit Cost	Total Cost	Quantity	Unit Cost	Total Cost	Quantity	Unit Cost	Total Cost
Jan. 1							10	20	200
4				7	20	140	3	20	60
10	8	21	168				3 8	20 21	60 168
22				3 1	20 21	60 21	7	21	147
28				2	21	42	5	21	105
30	10	22	220				5 10	21 22	105 220

Last-In, First-Out Method. When the last-in, first-out method is used in a perpetual inventory system, the cost of the units sold is the cost of the most recent purchases. To illustrate, the ledger account for Commodity 127B, prepared on a lifo basis, is as follows:

Perpetual Inventory Account (LIFO)

Commodity 127B

Date	Purchases			Cost of Merchandise Sold			Inventory		
	Quantity	Unit Cost	Total Cost	Quantity	Unit Cost	Total Cost	Quantity	Unit Cost	Total Cost
Jan. 1							10	20	200
4				7	20	140	3	20	60
10	8	21	168				3 8	20 21	60 168
22				4	21	84	3 4	20 21	60 84
28				2	21	42	3 2	20 21	60 42
30	10	22	220				3 2 10	20 21 22	60 42 220

A comparison of the ledger accounts for the fifo perpetual system and the lifo perpetual system indicates that the accounts are the same through the January 10 purchase. Using the lifo perpetual system, however, the cost of the 4 units sold on January 22 is the cost of the units from the January 10 purchase ($21 per unit). The cost of the 7 units in inventory after the sale on January 22 is the cost of the 3 units remaining from the beginning inventory and the cost of the 4 units remaining from the January 10 purchase. The remainder of the lifo illustration is explained in a similar manner.

Average Cost Method. When the average cost method is used in a perpetual inventory system, an average unit cost for each type of commodity is computed each time a purchase is made, rather than at the end of the period. This unit cost is then used to determine the cost of each sale, until another purchase is made and a new average is computed. This averaging technique is called a **moving average.**

Internal Control and Perpetual Inventory Systems

The use of a perpetual inventory system for merchandise provides the most effective means of control over this important asset. Although it is possible to maintain a perpetual inventory in memorandum records only or to limit the data to quantities, a complete set of records integrated with the general ledger is preferable. With the widespread use of computers, integrated perpetual inventory systems are being used by more and more companies.

The control feature is the most important advantage of the perpetual system. The inventory of each type of merchandise is always readily available in the subsidiary ledger. A physical count of any type of merchandise can be made at any time and compared with the balance of the subsidiary account to determine the existence and seriousness of any shortages. When a shortage is discovered, an entry is made debiting Inventory Shortages and crediting Merchandise Inventory for the cost. If the balance of the inventory shortages account at the end of a fiscal period is relatively small, it may be included in miscellaneous administrative expense on the income statement. Otherwise it may be separately reported in the administrative expense section.

In addition to the usefulness of the perpetual inventory system in the preparation of interim statements, the subsidiary ledger can be an aid in maintaining inventory quantities at an optimum level. Frequent comparisons of balances with predetermined maximum and minimum levels facilitate the timely reordering of merchandise to avoid loss of sales and the avoidance of excess inventory.

Automated Perpetual Inventory Records

A perpetual inventory system may be maintained using manually kept records. However, such a system is often too costly and too time consuming for enterprises with a large number of inventory items and/or with many purchase and sales transactions. In such cases, because of the mass of data to be processed, the frequently recurring and routine nature of the processing, and the importance of speed and accuracy, the record keeping is often computerized. A computerized inventory system operates with little human intervention.

One use of computers in maintaining perpetual inventory records for retail stores is described in the following outline:

1. The quantity of inventory for each commodity, along with its color, unit size or other descriptive data, and any other information desired, is stored in the computer.

2. Each time a commodity is purchased or returned by a customer, the data are recorded and processed by the computer, so that the inventory records are updated.
3. Each time a commodity is sold, a salesclerk passes an electronic wand over the price tag attached to the merchandise. The electronic wand "reads" the magnetic code on the price tag. The information provided in the magnetic code is used by the computer to update the inventory records.
4. Data from a physical inventory count are periodically entered into the computer. These data are compared with the current balances and a listing of the overages and shortages is printed. The appropriate commodity balances are adjusted to the quantities determined by the physical count.

By entering additional data, the system described above can be extended to aid in maintaining inventory quantities at optimum levels. For example, data on the most economical quantity to be purchased in a single order and the minimum quantity to be maintained for each commodity can be entered into the computer. The equipment is then programmed to compare these data with data on actual inventory and to start the purchasing activity by preparing purchase orders.

The system can also be extended to aid in processing the related accounting transactions. For example, as cash sales are entered on an electronic cash register, the sales data can be accumulated and used for the appropriate accounting entries. These entries would include a debit to Cash and a credit to Sales as well as a debit to Cost of Merchandise Sold and a credit to Merchandise Inventory.

VALUATION OF INVENTORY AT OTHER THAN COST

OBJECTIVE 7
Describe and illustrate the valuation of inventory at other than cost, including valuation at the lower of cost or market.

As discussed in the preceding sections, cost is the primary basis for the valuation of inventories. Under certain circumstances, however, inventory is valued at other than cost. Two such circumstances arise when (1) the cost of replacing items in inventory is below recorded cost, and (2) the inventory is not salable at normal sales prices because of imperfections, shop wear, style changes, or other causes.

Valuation at Lower of Cost or Market

If the market price of an item in inventory is lower than its cost, the **lower of cost or market** method is used to value inventory. It should be noted that regardless of the method used (cost, or lower of cost or market), it is first necessary to determine the cost of the inventory. "Market," as used in the phrase *lower of cost or market,* is interpreted to mean the cost to replace the merchandise on the inventory date, based on quantities typically purchased from the usual source of supply. In the discussion that follows, the salability of the merchandise at normal sales prices will be assumed. Articles that have to be sold at a price below their cost would be valued at their net realizable value, as described on page 307.

If the replacement price of an item in the inventory is lower than its cost, the use of the lower of cost or market method provides two advantages: (1) the gross profit (and net income) are reduced for the period in which the decline occurred and (2) an approximately normal gross profit is realized during the period in which the item is sold. To illustrate, assume that merchandise with a unit cost of $70 has sold at $100 during the period, yielding a gross profit of $30 a unit, or 30% of sales. Assume also that at the end of the year, there is a single unit of the commodity in the inventory and that its replacement price has declined to $63. Under such circumstances it would be reasonable to expect that the selling price would also decline, if indeed it had not already done so. Assuming a reduction in selling price to $90, the gross profit based on replacement cost of $63 would be $27, which is also 30% of the selling price. Accordingly, valuation of the unit in the inventory at $63 reduces gross profit of the past period by $7 and permits a normal gross profit of $27 to be realized on its sale in the following period. If the unit had been valued at its original cost of $70, the gross profit determined for the past year would have been $7 greater, and the gross profit attributable to the sale of the item in the following period would have been $7 less.

It would be possible to apply the lower of cost or market basis (1) to each item in the inventory, (2) to major classes or categories, or (3) to the inventory as a whole. The first procedure is the one usually followed in practice. To illustrate the application of the lower of cost or market to individual items, assume that there are 400 identical units of Commodity A in the inventory, each acquired at a unit cost of $10.25. If at the inventory date the commodity would cost $10.50 to replace, the cost price of $10.25 would be multiplied by 400 to determine the inventory value. On the other hand, if the commodity could be replaced at $9.50 a unit, the replacement price of $9.50 would be used for valuation purposes. The following tabulation illustrates one of the forms that may be followed in assembling inventory data:

Determination of Inventory at Lower of Cost or Market

Description	Quantity	Unit Cost Price	Unit Market Price	Total	
				Cost	*Lower of C or M*
Commodity A	400	$10.25	$ 9.50	$ 4,100	$ 3,800
Commodity B	120	22.50	24.10	2,700	2,700
Commodity C	600	8.00	7.75	4,800	4,650
Commodity D	280	14.00	14.00	3,920	3,920
Total				$15,520	$15,070

Although it is not essential to accumulate the data for total cost, as in the illustration, it permits the measurement of the reduction in inventory value as a result of a decline in market prices. When the amount of the market decline is known ($15,520 − $15,070, or $450), it may be reported as a separate item on the income statement. Otherwise, the market decline will be included in the amount reported as the cost of merchandise sold and will reduce gross profit by a corresponding amount. In any event, the amount reported as net income will not be affected. It will be the same, regardless of whether the amount of the market decline is determined and separately stated.

As with the method elected for the determination of inventory cost (first-in, first-out; last-in, first out; or average cost), the method elected for inventory valuation (cost, or lower of cost or market) should be followed consistently from year to year.

Valuation at Net Realizable Value

Obsolete, spoiled, or damaged merchandise and other merchandise that can be sold only at prices below cost should be valued at **net realizable value.** For this purpose, net realizable value is the estimated selling price less any direct cost of disposition, such as sales commissions. To illustrate, assume that damaged merchandise that had a cost of $1,000 can be sold for only $800, and direct selling expenses are estimated at $150. This inventory would be valued at $650 ($800 − $150), which is its net realizable value.

PRESENTATION OF MERCHANDISE INVENTORY ON THE BALANCE SHEET

OBJECTIVE 8
Identify and illustrate the proper presentation of inventory in the financial statements.

Merchandise inventory is usually presented on the balance sheet immediately following receivables. Both the method of determining the cost of the inventory (fifo, lifo, or average) and the method of valuing the inventory (cost, or lower of cost or market) should be shown. Both are important to the reader. The details may be disclosed by a parenthetical notation or a footnote. The use of a parenthetical notation is illustrated by the following partial balance sheet:

Merchandise Inventory on Balance Sheet

Afro-Arts Company
Balance Sheet
December 31, 1992

Assets		
Current assets:		
Cash		$ 19,400
Accounts receivable	$80,000	
Less allowance for doubtful accounts	3,000	77,000
Merchandise inventory—at lower of cost (first-in, first-out method) or market		216,300

It is not unusual for large enterprises with diversified activities to use different costing methods for different segments of their inventories. The following note taken from the financial statements of Chrysler Corp. is illustrative:

> Automotive inventories are valued at the lower of cost or market. The cost of substantially all domestic automotive inventories is recorded on a Last-In, First-Out (LIFO) basis.
>
> Aerospace inventories are stated at the lower of cost or market, with cost recognized on a First-In, First-Out (FIFO) basis. In accordance with aerospace industry practice, inventoried costs relating to aircraft programs are stated at actual . . . costs, . . .

ESTIMATING INVENTORY COST

OBJECTIVE 9
Describe and illustrate methods of estimating the cost of inventory.

In practice, an inventory amount may be needed in order to prepare an income statement when it is impractical or impossible to take a physical inventory or to maintain perpetual inventory records. For example, taking a physical inventory each month may be too costly, even though monthly income statements are desired. Taking a physical inventory may be impossible when a catastrophe, such as a fire, has destroyed the inventory. In such cases, the inventory cost might be estimated for use in preparing the income statement. Two commonly used methods of estimating inventory cost are (1) the retail method and (2) the gross profit method.

Retail Method of Inventory Costing

The **retail inventory method** of inventory costing is widely used by retail businesses, particularly department stores. It is based on the relationship of the cost of merchandise available for sale to the retail price of the same merchandise. The retail prices of all merchandise acquired are accumulated in supplementary records, and the inventory at retail is determined by deducting sales for the period from the retail price of the goods that were available for sale during the period. The inventory at retail is then converted to cost on the basis of the ratio of cost to selling (retail) price for the merchandise available for sale. Determination of inventory by the retail method is illustrated as follows:

Determination of Inventory by Retail Method

	Cost	Retail
Merchandise inventory, January 1	$19,400	$ 36,000
Purchases in January (net)	42,600	64,000
Merchandise available for sale..................................	$62,000	$100,000
Ratio of cost to retail price: $\frac{\$62,000}{\$100,000} = 62\%$		
Sales for January (net)..		70,000
Merchandise inventory, January 31, at retail................		$ 30,000
Merchandise inventory, January 31, at estimated cost ($30,000 × 62%)		$ 18,600

There is an inherent assumption in the retail method of inventory costing that the composition or "mix" of the commodities in the ending inventory, in terms of percent of cost to selling price, is comparable to the entire stock of merchandise available for sale. In the illustration, for example, it is unlikely that the retail price of every item was composed of exactly 62% cost and 38% gross profit. It is assumed, however, that the weighted average of the cost percentages of the merchandise in the inventory ($30,000) is the same as in the merchandise available for sale ($100,000). When the inventory is made up of different classes of merchandise with very different gross profit rates, the cost percentages and the inventory should be developed separately for each class.

One of the major advantages of the retail method is that it provides inventory figures for use in preparing interim statements. Department stores and similar merchandisers usually determine gross profit and operating income each month but take a physical inventory only once a year. In addition to facilitating frequent income determinations, a comparison of the computed ending inventory with the physical ending inventory, both at retail prices, will help identify inventory shortages resulting from shoplifting and other causes. The appropriate corrective measures then can be taken.

The retail method also can be used in conjunction with the periodic system when a physical inventory is taken at the end of the year. In such a case, the items counted are recorded on the inventory sheets at their selling prices instead of their cost prices. The physical inventory at selling price is then converted to cost by applying the ratio of cost to selling (retail) price for the merchandise available for sale. To illustrate, assume that the data presented in the example above are for an entire fiscal year rather than for the first month of the year only. If the physical inventory taken on December 31 totaled $29,000, priced at retail, it would be this amount rather than the $30,000 that would be converted to cost. Accordingly, the inventory at cost would be $17,980 ($29,000 × 62%) instead of $18,600 ($30,000 × 62%). The $17,980 is generally accepted for use on the year-end financial statements and for income tax purposes.

Gross Profit Method of Estimating Inventories

The **gross profit method** uses an estimate of the gross profit realized during the period to estimate the inventory at the end of the period. By using the rate of gross profit, the dollar amount of sales for a period can be divided into its two components: (1) gross profit and (2) cost of merchandise sold. The latter may then be deducted from the cost of merchandise available for sale to yield the estimated inventory of merchandise on hand.

To illustrate this method, assume that the inventory on January 1 is $57,000, that net purchases during the month are $180,000, that net sales during the month are $250,000, and finally that gross profit is *estimated* to be 30% of net sales. The inventory on January 31 may be estimated as follows:

Estimate of Inventory by Gross Profit Method

Merchandise inventory, January 1		$ 57,000
Purchases in January (net)		180,000
Merchandise available for sale		$237,000
Sales in January (net)	$250,000	
Less estimated gross profit ($250,000 × 30%)	75,000	
Estimated cost of merchandise sold		175,000
Estimated merchandise inventory, January 31		$ 62,000

The estimate of the rate of gross profit is ordinarily based on the actual rate for the preceding year, adjusted for any changes made in the cost and prices during the current period. Inventories estimated in this manner are useful in preparing interim statements. The method also may be used in establishing an estimate of the cost of merchandise destroyed by fire or other disaster.

INVENTORIES OF MANUFACTURING ENTERPRISES

OBJECTIVE 10
Describe and illustrate inventories of manufacturing enterprises.

In the preceding discussion, the principles and procedures for inventory were presented in the context of a merchandising enterprise. These same principles and procedures, with some modification, also apply to inventories of a manufacturing enterprise. Although attention is directed to these basic principles and procedures in the following paragraphs, it should be noted that they are discussed in more detail in later chapters.

Manufacturing businesses maintain three inventory accounts instead of a single merchandise inventory account. Separate accounts are maintained for (1) goods in the state in which they are to be sold, (2) goods in the process of manufacture, and (3) goods in the state in which they were acquired.

These inventories are called respectively **finished goods, work in process,** and **materials.** The balances in the inventory accounts may be presented in the balance sheet in the following manner:

Inventories:		
Finished goods	$300,000	
Work in process	55,000	
Materials	123,000	$478,000

The finished goods inventory and work in process inventory are composed of three separate categories of manufacturing costs: direct materials, direct labor, and factory overhead. **Direct materials** represent the delivered cost of the materials that enter directly into the finished product. **Direct labor** represents the wages of the factory workers who change the materials into a finished product. **Factory overhead** includes all of the remaining costs of operating the factory, such as wages for factory supervision, supplies used in the factory but not entering directly into the finished product, and taxes, insurance, depreciation, and maintenance related to factory plant and equipment.

LONG-TERM CONSTRUCTION CONTRACTS

OBJECTIVE 11
Describe and illustrate accounting for long-term construction contracts.

Enterprises engaged in large construction projects may devote several years to the completion of a particular contract or project. In such cases, the costs incurred in construction may be accumulated in a work in process account, called Construction in Progress, until the project is completed. After the project is completed and accepted by the customer, the full revenue and the related net income are recognized. This **completed-contract method** of determining revenue recognizes the entire net income at the point of sale or, in this case, when the project is completed. To illustrate, assume that a contractor engages in a project that will require three years to complete, for a contract price of $50,000,000. If the total costs accumulated during construction total $44,000,000, the revenue of $50,000,000 and the net income of $6,000,000 would be reported in the third year.

Whenever the total cost of a long-term contract and the extent of the project's progress can be reasonably estimated, it is preferable to consider the revenue as being realized over the entire life of the contract.[1] The amount of revenue to be recognized in any particular period is then determined on the basis of the estimated percentage of the contract that has been completed during the period. The estimated percentage of completion can be developed by comparing the incurred costs with the most recent estimates of total costs or by estimates by engineers, architects, or other qualified personnel of the progress of the work performed. To continue with the illustration, assume that by the end of the first fiscal year the contract is estimated to be one-fourth completed and the costs incurred during the year were $11,200,000. According to the **percentage-of-completion method,** the revenue to be recognized and the income for the year would be determined as follows:

[1]*Accounting Research and Terminology Bulletins—Final Edition,* "No. 45, Long-term Construction-type Contracts" (New York: American Institute of Certified Public Accountants, 1961), par. 15.

Revenue ($50,000,000 × 25%)	$12,500,000
Costs incurred	11,200,000
Income (Year 1)	$ 1,300,000

The cost actually incurred during the year (rather than one fourth of the original cost estimate of $44,000,000, or $11,000,000) are deducted from the revenue recognized.

The 1990 edition of *Accounting Trends & Techniques* indicated that 69% of the surveyed companies with long-term contracts used the percentage-of-completion method. Although the use of this method involves some subjectivity, and hence possible error, in the determination of the amount of reported revenue, the financial statements may be more informative and more useful than they would be if none of the revenue was recognized until completion of the contract.

The method used to recognize revenue on a long-term contract should be noted in the financial statements, as indicated in the following excerpt taken from a note to the financial statements of Martin Marietta Corporation:

> Revenue Recognition. Sales under long-term contracts generally are recognized under the percentage-of-completion method, and include a proportion of the earnings expected to be realized on the contract. . . . Other sales are recorded upon shipment of products or performance of services.

CHAPTER REVIEW

KEY POINTS

OBJECTIVE 1

Importance of Inventories

Inventory determination plays an important role in matching expired costs with revenues of the period. An error in the determination of the inventory amount at the end of the period will cause an equal misstatement of gross profit and net income. The amount reported for both assets and owner's equity in the balance sheet will also be incorrect by the same amount. In addition, because the inventory at the end of one period becomes the inventory for the beginning of the following period, an error in inventory at the end of the period will cause the net income of the following period to be misstated. The effect of the two misstatements in income will be equal and in opposite directions. Therefore, the effect on net income of an incorrectly stated inventory is limited to the period of the error and the following period. At the end of this following period, assuming no additional errors, both assets and owner's equity will be correctly stated.

OBJECTIVE 2

Inventory Systems

There are two principal systems of inventory accounting — periodic and perpetual. In the periodic system, only the revenue from sales is recorded at the time a sale is made. No entry is made until the end of the period to record the cost of merchandise sold. In the perpetual inventory system, sales and cost of merchandise sold are recorded at the time each sale is made. In this way, the accounting records continuously disclose the amount of inventory on hand. In a perpetual inventory system, a subsidiary ledger is maintained with a separate account for each type of merchandise.

OBJECTIVE 3

Determining Actual Quantities in the Inventory

All the merchandise owned by a business on the inventory date, and only such merchandise, should be included in the inventory. The first step in "taking" an inventory is to count the merchandise on hand. To this count is added merchandise in transit that is owned. Therefore, it is normally necessary to examine purchases and sales invoices of the last few days of the accounting period and the first few days of the following period to determine who has legal title to merchandise in transit on the inventory date.

OBJECTIVE 4

Determining the Cost of Inventory

The cost of merchandise inventory is made up of the purchase price and all expenditures incurred in acquiring such merchandise, including transportation, customs duties, and insurance against losses in transit.

OBJECTIVE 5

Inventory Costing Methods Under a Periodic System

In determining the cost of merchandise sold and the inventory cost at the end of the period, it is customary to use an assumption as to the flow of costs of merchandise through an enterprise. The three most common assumptions of determining the cost of merchandise sold are as follows: first-in, first-out (fifo), last-in, first-out (lifo), and average cost. The fifo method of costing inventory is based on the assumption that costs should be charged against revenue in the order in which they were incurred. The lifo method is based on the assumption that the most recent costs incurred should be charged against revenues. The average cost method, sometimes called the weighted average method, is based on the assumption that costs should be charged against revenue according to the weighted average unit costs of the goods sold.

If the cost of units and the prices at which they are sold remain stable, all three inventory costing methods will yield the same results. However, during a period of rising prices, the use of the fifo method will result in a higher amount of gross profit than the other two methods. In a period of declining prices, the use of the lifo method will result in a higher amount of gross profit than the other two methods. The average cost method of inventory costing is often viewed as a compromise between the fifo and lifo methods.

OBJECTIVE 6

Accounting for Inventory Under a Perpetual System

Under a perpetual inventory system, sales are recorded in the sales account. On the date of each sale, the cost of the merchandise sold is also recorded by debiting Cost of Merchandise Sold and crediting Merchandise Inventory.

In a perpetual system, the details of merchandise increases and decreases are maintained in a subsidiary ledger, called an inventory ledger, with a separate account for each type of merchandise. As in a periodic system, it is customary to use one of the three costing methods — fifo, lifo, or average.

The use of a perpetual inventory system for merchandise provides the most effective means of control over this important asset. In a perpetual system, the existence of shortages can be determined by taking a physical count of the merchandise and comparing the count with the balance of the subsidiary ledger. The timely reordering of merchandise to avoid excess inventory and loss of sales can be accomplished by comparing the balance of the subsidiary ledger with predetermined maximum and minimum levels of inventory.

The basic inventory records in a perpetual inventory system may be maintained by using a computer. The system can be extended to aid in maintaining inventory quantities at optimum levels and in processing the inventory-related accounting transactions.

OBJECTIVE 7

Valuation of Inventory at Other than Cost

If the market price of an item in inventory is lower than its cost, the lower of cost or market method is used to value inventory. Market, as used in the phrase *lower of cost or market,* is interpreted to mean the cost to replace the merchandise on the inventory date. It is possible to apply the lower of cost or market basis to each item in the inventory, to major classes or categories, or to the inventory as a whole.

Merchandise that can be sold only at prices below cost should be valued at net realizable value, which is the estimated selling price less any direct cost of disposition.

OBJECTIVE 8

Presentation of Merchandise Inventory on the Balance Sheet

Merchandise inventory is usually presented in the current assets section of the balance sheet immediately following receivables. Both the method of determining the cost of the inventory (lifo, fifo, or average) and the method of valuing the inventory (cost, or lower of cost or market) should be shown.

OBJECTIVE 9

Estimating Inventory Cost

When it is impractical or impossible to take a physical inventory or to maintain perpetual inventory records, two commonly used methods of estimating inventory may be used: (1) the retail method and (2) the gross profit method. The retail method of inventory estimation is based on the relationship of the cost of merchandise available for sale to the retail price of the same merchandise. The inventory at retail is determined by deducting sales for the period from the retail price of the goods that were available for sale during the period. The inventory at retail is then converted to cost on the basis of the ratio of cost to selling (retail) price for the merchandise available for sale.

The gross profit method of estimating inventory is based upon the historical relationship of the gross profit to the dollar amount of sales. The rate of gross profit is multiplied by the current period sales in order to estimate the gross profit for the period. To determine the estimate of the cost of merchandise sold, the estimated gross profit is then subtracted from the sales of the period. The estimated cost of merchandise sold can then be subtracted from the merchandise available for sale for the period to determine an estimate of the ending inventory.

OBJECTIVE 10

Inventories of Manufacturing Enterprises

Manufacturing enterprises maintain three separate inventory accounts for (1) goods in the state in which they are to be sold (finished goods), (2) goods in the process of manufacture (work in process), and (3) goods in the state in which they were acquired (materials). The finished goods inventory and work in process inventory are composed of three separate manufacturing costs: direct mateirals, direct labor, and factory overhead.

OBJECTIVE 11 Long-Term Construction Contracts

Enterprises engaged in large, long-term construction projects may determine revenue and income by the percentage-of-completion method. Under this method, the revenue to be recognized each year of the life of the contract is based on the estimated percentage of the contract that has been completed during each year.

KEY TERMS

merchandise inventory 289
periodic inventory system 292
physical inventory 292
perpetual inventory system 292
first-in, first-out (fifo) method 295
last-in, first-out (lifo) method 296
average cost method 297
lower of cost or market 305
net realizable value 307
retail inventory method 308
gross profit method 309
finished goods 310
work in process 310
materials 310
direct materials 310
direct labor 310
factory overhead 310
completed-contract method 310
percentage-of-completion method 310

SELF-EXAMINATION QUESTIONS

Answers at end of chapter.

1. If the merchandise inventory at the end of the year is overstated by $7,500, the error will cause an:
   A. overstatement of cost of merchandise sold for the year by $7,500
   B. understatement of gross profit for the year by $7,500
   C. overstatement of net income for the year by $7,500
   D. understatement of net income for the year by $7,500

2. The inventory system employing accounting records that continuously disclose the amount of inventory is called:
   A. periodic
   B. perpetual
   C. physical
   D. retail

3. The inventory costing method that is based on the assumption that costs should be charged against revenue in the order in which they were incurred is:
   A. fifo
   B. lifo
   C. average cost
   D. perpetual inventory

4. The following units of a particular commodity were available for sale during the period:

Beginning inventory	40 units at $20
First purchase	50 units at $21
Second purchase	50 units at $22
Third purchase	50 units at $23

   What is the unit cost of the 35 units on hand at the end of the period as determined under the periodic system by the fifo costing method?
   A. $20
   B. $21
   C. $22
   D. $23

5. If merchandise inventory is being valued at cost and the price level is steadily rising, the method of costing that will yield the highest net income is:
   A. lifo
   B. fifo
   C. average
   D. periodic

ILLUSTRATIVE PROBLEM

Stewart Inc.'s beginning inventory and purchases during the fiscal year ended March 31, 1993, were as follows:

		Units	Unit Cost	Total Cost
April 1, 1992	Inventory	1,000	$50.00	$ 50,000
April 10, 1992	Purchase	1,200	52.50	63,000
May 30, 1992	Purchase	800	55.00	44,000
August 26, 1992	Purchase	2,000	56.00	112,000
October 15, 1992	Purchase	1,500	57.00	85,500
December 31, 1992	Purchase	700	58.00	40,600
January 18, 1993	Purchase	1,350	60.00	81,000
March 21, 1993	Purchase	450	62.00	27,900
Total		9,000		$504,000

Stewart Inc. uses the periodic inventory system, and there are 3,200 units of inventory on hand on March 31, 1993.

Instructions:

1. Determine the cost of inventory on March 31, 1993, under each of the following inventory costing methods:
   a. First-in, first-out
   b. Last-in, first-out
   c. Average cost
2. Assume that during the fiscal year ended March 31, 1993, sales of $536,000 were made at an estimated gross profit rate of 40%. Estimate the ending inventory at March 31, 1993, using the gross profit method.

SOLUTION

(1)

(a) First-in, first-out method:

450 units @ $62	$ 27,900
1,350 units @ $60	81,000
700 units @ $58	40,600
700 units @ $57	39,900
3,200 units	$189,400

(b) Last-in, first-out method:

1,000 units @ $50.00	$ 50,000
1,200 units @ $52.50	63,000
800 units @ $55.00	44,000
200 units @ $56.00	11,200
3,200 units	$168,200

(c) Average cost method:

Average cost per unit . $504,000 ÷ 9,000 units = $56

Inventory, March 31, 1993 . . 3,200 units at $56 .... $179,200

(2)		
Merchandise inventory, April 1, 1992		$ 50,000
Purchases (net), April 1, 1992–March 31, 1993		454,000
Merchandise available for sale		$504,000
Sales (net), April 1, 1992–March 31, 1993	$536,000	
Less estimated gross profit ($536,000 × 40%)	214,400	
Estimated cost of merchandise sold		321,600
Estimated merchandise inventory, March 31, 1993		$182,400

DISCUSSION QUESTIONS

7–1. The merchandise inventory at the end of the year was inadvertently understated by $10,000. (a) Did the error cause an overstatement or an understatement of the gross profit for the year? (b) Which items on the balance sheet at the end of the year were overstated or understated as a result of the error?

7–2. The $10,000 inventory error in Question 7–1 was not discovered, and the inventory at the end of the following year was correctly stated. (a) Will the earlier error cause an overstatement or an understatement of the gross profit for the following year? (b) Which items on the balance sheet at the end of the following year will be overstated or understated as a result of the error in the earlier year?

7–3. Under which inventory accounting system—periodic or perpetual—must a physical inventory be taken to determine the cost of inventory at the end of an accounting period?

7–4. (a) Differentiate between the periodic system and the perpetual system of inventory determination. (b) Which system is more costly to maintain?

7–5. If the perpetual inventory system is used, is it desirable to take a physical inventory? Discuss.

7–6. What is the meaning of each of the following terms: (a) physical inventory; (b) book inventory?

7–7. In which of the following types of businesses would a perpetual inventory system ordinarily be used: (a) retail hardware store, (b) retail yacht dealer, (c) retail sports car dealer, (d) retail drugstore?

7–8. When does title to merchandise pass from the seller to the buyer if the terms of shipment are (a) FOB shipping point; (b) FOB destination?

7–9. A manufacturer ships merchandise to a retailer on a consignment basis. If the merchandise is unsold at the end of the period, in whose inventory should the merchandise be included?

7–10. Which of the three methods of inventory costing—fifo, lifo, or average cost—is based on the assumption that costs should be charged against revenue in the reverse order in which they were incurred?

7–11. Do the terms *fifo* and *lifo* refer to techniques employed in determining quantities of the various classes of merchandise on hand? Explain.

7–12. Does the term *last-in* in the lifo method mean that the items in the inventory are assumed to be the most recent (last) acquisitions? Explain.

7–13. Under which method of cost flow are (a) the earliest costs assigned to inventory; (b) the most recent costs assigned to inventory; (c) average costs assigned to inventory?

7–14. The following units of a particular commodity were available for sale during the year:

Beginning inventory................................	6 units at $111
First purchase.......................................	10 units at $117
Second purchase...................................	5 units at $120

The firm uses the periodic system, and there are 4 units of the commodity on hand at the end of the year. What is their unit cost according to (a) fifo, (b) lifo, (c) average cost?

7–15. If merchandise inventory is being valued at cost and the price level is steadily rising, which of the three methods of costing—fifo, lifo, or average cost—will yield (a) the highest inventory cost, (b) the lowest inventory cost, (c) the highest gross profit, (d) the lowest gross profit?

7–16. Which of the three methods of inventory costing—fifo, lifo, or average cost—will in general yield an inventory cost most nearly approximating current replacement cost?

7–17. An enterprise using a perpetual inventory system sells merchandise to a customer on account for $360; the cost of the merchandise was $270.
(a) What entries would be made in the accounts as a result of the transaction?
(b) What is the amount and direction of the net change in the amount of assets and owner's equity resulting from the transaction?

7–18. What are the three most important advantages of the perpetual inventory system over the periodic system?

7–19. In the phrase *lower of cost or market,* what is meant by "market"?

7–20. The cost of a particular inventory item is $275, the current replacement cost is $260, and the selling price is $350. At what amount should the item be included in the inventory according to the lower of cost or market basis?

7–21. Because of imperfections, an item of merchandise cannot be sold at its normal selling price. How should this item be valued for financial statement purposes?

7–22. An enterprise using the retail method of inventory costing determines that merchandise inventory at retail is $300,000. If the ratio of cost to retail price is 65%, what is the amount of inventory to be reported on the financial statements?

7–23. What uses can be made of the estimate of the cost of inventory determined by the gross profit method?

7–24. Name the three inventory accounts for a manufacturing business and describe what each balance represents at the end of an accounting period.

7–25. Name and describe the three categories of manufacturing costs included in the cost of finished goods and the cost of work in process.

7–26. What are the advantages and disadvantages of using the percentage-of-completion method for reporting income on long-term construction projects?

Real World Focus

7–27. The following footnote was taken from the 1990 financial statements of The Walgreen Co.:

> Inventories are valued on a last-in, first-out (LIFO) cost basis. At August 31, 1990 and 1989, inventories would have been greater by $285,143,000 and $246,362,000 respectively, if they had been valued on a lower of first-in, first-out (FIFO) cost or market basis.

Additional data are as follows:

Earnings before income taxes, 1990	$280,923,000
Total lifo inventories, August 31, 1990......	827,997,000

Based on the preceding data, determine (a) what the total inventories at August 31, 1990, would have been, using the fifo method, and (b) what the earnings before income taxes for the year ended August 31, 1990 would have been if fifo had been used instead of lifo.

Ethics Discussion Case

7–28. Webb Inc. is experiencing a decrease in sales and operating income for the fiscal year ending December 31, 1992. Shirley Gilreath, controller of Webb Inc., has suggested that all orders received before the end of the fiscal year be shipped by midnight, December 31, 1992, even if the shipping department must work overtime. Since Webb Inc. ships all merchandise FOB shipping point, Webb Inc. would record all such shipments as sales for the year ending December 31, 1992, thereby offsetting some of the decreases in sales and operating income.

Discuss whether Shirley Gilreath is behaving in an ethical manner.

EXERCISES

Ex. 7–29.
Periodic inventory by three methods.
OBJ. 5

The beginning inventory and the purchases of an item during the year were as follows:

Jan. 1.	Inventory...	20 units at $78
Mar 15.	Purchase...	15 units at $80
June 1.	Purchase...	20 units at $84
Sept. 30.	Purchase...	15 units at $82

There are 25 units of the commodity in the physical inventory at December 31. The periodic system is used. Determine the inventory cost and the cost of merchandise sold by three methods, presenting your answers in the following form:

	Cost	
Inventory Method	Merchandise Inventory	Merchandise Sold
(1) First-in, first-out	$	$
(2) Last-in, first-out		
(3) Average cost		

Ex. 7–30.
Perpetual inventory using fifo.
OBJ. 6

Beginning inventory, purchases, and sales data for Commodity D45 are as follows:

Jan. 1.	Inventory	15 units at $40
5.	Sold..	5 units
10.	Purchased	10 units at $41
17.	Sold..	12 units
22.	Sold..	3 units
30.	Purchased	10 units at $42

The enterprise maintains a perpetual inventory system, costing by the first-in, first-out method. Determine the cost of the merchandise sold in each sale and the inventory balance after each sale, presenting the data in the form illustrated on page 303.

Ex. 7–31.
Perpetual inventory using lifo.
OBJ. 6

Beginning inventory, purchases, and sales data for Commodity R71 for July are as follows:

Inventory:	
July 1	25 units at $50
Sales:	
July 7	15 units
18	10 units
27	12 units
Purchases:	
July 3	20 units at $51
20	15 units at $52

Assuming that the perpetual inventory system is used, costing by the lifo method, determine the cost of the inventory balance at July 31, presenting data in the form illustrated on page 303.

Ex. 7–32.
Perpetual inventory entries.
OBJ. 6

The perpetual inventory system is used, and the merchandise inventory account (controlling) had a balance of $175,500 on January 1, the beginning of the current year. The account was debited for $659,500 for purchases made during the year.

(a) Journalize the entries required to record sales for the year (all sales are made on account): sales price, $995,000; cost, $676,600.
(b) If a physical count of inventory on December 31 revealed a cost of $157,150, prepare the entry to record the inventory shortage.

Ex. 7–33.
Lower of cost or market inventory.
OBJ. 7

On the basis of the following data, determine the value of the inventory at the lower of cost or market. Assemble the data in the form illustrated on page 306.

Commodity	Inventory Quantity	Unit Cost	Unit Market Price
27C	12	$ 90	$ 92
42H	6	550	525
91K	25	110	115
11S	35	70	65
50V	20	250	260

Ex. 7–34.
Retail inventory method.
OBJ. 9

On the basis of the following data, estimate the cost of the merchandise inventory at July 31 by the retail method:

		Cost	Retail
July 1	Merchandise inventory	$283,970	$417,500
July 1–31	Purchases (net)	215,150	316,500
July 1–31	Sales (net)		330,000

Ex. 7–35.
Gross profit inventory method.
OBJ. 9

The merchandise inventory of Armstead Company was destroyed by fire on April 29. The following data were obtained from the accounting records:

Jan. 1	Merchandise inventory	$110,650
Jan. 1–April 29	Purchases (net)	175,150
	Sales (net)	300,000
	Estimated gross profit rate	35%

Estimate the cost of the merchandise destroyed.

Ex. 7–36.
Percentage-of-completion method
OBJ. 11

During the current year, Chandler Construction Company obtained a contract to build an apartment building. The total contract price was $8,000,000, and the estimated construction costs were $6,550,000. During the current year, the project was estimated to be 40% completed, and the costs incurred totaled $2,990,000. Under the percentage-of-completion method of revenue recognition, what amount of (a) revenue, (b) cost, and (c) income should be recognized from the contract for the current year?

PROBLEMS

Pb. 7–37.
Corrections to inventory; revised income statement.
OBJ. 1, 3

The following preliminary income statement of Saxton Company was prepared before the accounts were adjusted or closed at the end of the fiscal year. The company uses the periodic inventory system.

Saxton Company
Income Statement
For Year Ended December 31, 19--

Sales (net)		$917,500
Cost of merchandise sold:		
Merchandise inventory, January 1, 19--	$195,000	
Purchases (net)	625,000	
Merchandise available for sale	$820,000	
Less merchandise inventory, December 31, 19--	187,500	
Cost of merchandise sold		632,500
Gross profit		$285,000
Operating expenses		202,500
Net income		$ 82,500

The following errors in the ledger and on the inventory sheets were discovered by the independent CPA retained to conduct the annual audit:

(a) A number of errors were discovered in pricing inventory items, in extending amounts, and in footing inventory sheets. The net effect of the errors, exclusive of those described below, was to understate by $7,500 the amount of ending inventory on the income statement.

(b) A purchases invoice for merchandise of $2,000, dated December 30, was not received until January 3 and had not been recorded by December 31. However, the merchandise, to which title had passed, had arrived and had been included in the December 31 inventory.

(c) A purchases invoice for merchandise of $2,500, dated December 31, had been received and correctly recorded, but the merchandise was not received until January 4 and had not been included in the December 31 inventory. Title had passed to Saxton Company on December 31.

(d) A sales invoice for $1,750, dated December 30, had not been recorded. The merchandise was shipped on December 30, FOB shipping point, and its cost, $1,150, was excluded from the December 31 inventory.

(e) A sales order for $7,500, dated December 31, had been recorded as a sale on that date, but title did not pass to the buyer until shipment was made on January 3. The merchandise, which had cost $5,000, was excluded from the December 31 inventory.

(f) An item of office equipment, received on December 27, was erroneously included in the December 31 merchandise inventory at its cost of $4,750. The invoice had been recorded correctly.

Instructions:

(1) Determine the correct inventory for December 31, beginning your analysis with the $187,500 inventory shown on the preliminary income statement. Assemble the corrections in two groupings, "Additions" and "Deductions," allowing six lines for each group. Identify each correction by the appropriate letter.

(2) Prepare a revised income statement.

Pb. 7–38.
Periodic inventory by three methods.
OBJ. 5

Allen Stereo employs the periodic inventory system. Details regarding the inventory of television sets at January 1, purchases invoices during the year, and the inventory count at December 31 are summarized as follows:

Model	Inventory, January 1	Purchases Invoices 1st	2d	3d	Inventory Count, December 31
A24	6 at $240	6 at $241	8 at $245	7 at $245	5
C11	3 at 305	3 at 310	5 at 317	4 at 320	3
F35	2 at 520	2 at 530	2 at 530	2 at 536	3
H51	6 at 520	8 at 531	4 at 549	6 at 542	9
L60	9 at 213	7 at 215	6 at 222	6 at 225	8
R71	6 at 305	3 at 310	3 at 316	4 at 321	5
V82	—	4 at 570	4 at 600	—	2

Instructions:

(1) Determine the cost of the inventory on December 31 by the first-in, first-out method. Present data in columnar form, using the following headings:

Model	Quantity	Unit Cost	Total Cost

If the inventory of a particular model is composed of an entire lot plus a portion of another lot acquired at a different unit cost, use a separate line for each lot.

(2) Determine the cost of the inventory on December 31 by the last-in, first-out method, following the procedures indicated in (1).

(3) Determine the cost of the inventory on December 31 by the average cost method, using the columnar headings indicated in (1).

Pb. 7–39.
Fifo and lifo perpetual inventory.
OBJ. 6

The beginning inventory of Commodity CB9 and data on purchases and sales for a three-month period are as follows:

Date		Transaction	Number of Units	Per Unit	Total
April	1.	Inventory	12	$220	$2,640
	8.	Purchase	20	225	4,500
	12.	Sale	15	340	5,100•
	22.	Sale	5	340	1,700•
May	4.	Purchase	10	230	2,300
	11.	Sale	5	350	1,750
	21.	Sale	4	350	1,400
	28.	Purchase	15	235	3,525
June	5.	Sale	7	355	2,485
	13.	Sale	10	355	3,550
	19.	Purchase	10	240	2,400
	26.	Sale	8	360	2,880

Instructions:

(1) Record the inventory, purchases, and cost of merchandise sold data in a perpetual inventory record similar to the one illustrated on page 303, using the first-in, first-out method.

(2) Determine the total sales and the total cost of Commodity CB9 sold for the period and indicate their effect on the general ledger by two journal entries. Assume that all sales were on account.

(3) Determine the gross profit from sales of Commodity CB9 for the period.

(4) Record the inventory, purchases, and cost of merchandise sold data in a perpetual inventory record similar to the one illustrated on page 303, using the last-in, first-out method.

If the working papers correlating with the textbook are not used, omit Pb. 7–40.

Pb. 7–40.
Lower of cost or market inventory.
OBJ. 7

Data on the physical inventory of E. W. Mahan Co. as of December 31, the end of the current fiscal year, are presented in the working papers. The quantity of each commodity on hand has been determined and recorded on the inventory sheet. Unit market prices have also been determined as of December 31 and recorded on the sheet. The inventory is to be determined at cost and also at the lower of cost or market, using the first-in, first-out method. Quantity and cost data from the last purchases invoice of the year and the next-to-the-last purchases invoice are summarized below.

	Last Purchases Invoice		Next-to-the-Last Purchases Invoice	
Description	Quantity Purchased	Unit Cost	Quantity Purchased	Unit Cost
A96	10	$ 40	15	$ 39
C11	15	290	15	290
E37	15	145	15	142
F52	100	30	75	31
H90	6	550	15	540
J19	150	12	100	13
K41	8	800	5	790
P21	500	7	500	8
P72	70	17	50	16
T15	5	250	4	260
V55	1,000	5	500	5
BC4	80	45	100	46
DD7	5	410	5	400
EA4	100	20	100	19
FB3	50	15	40	16
HH2	40	29	50	28
JB9	25	30	25	29
MN5	6	690	5	700

Instructions:

Record the appropriate unit costs on the inventory sheet and complete the pricing of the inventory. When there are two different unit costs applicable to a commodity, proceed as follows:

(1) Draw a line through the quantity and insert the quantity and unit cost of the last purchase.
(2) On the following line, insert the quantity and unit cost of the next-to-the-last purchase. The first item on the inventory sheet has been completed as an example.

Pb. 7–41.
Retail method; gross profit method.
OBJ. 9

Selected data on merchandise inventory, purchases, and sales for Morheim Co. and Queens Supply Co. are as follows:

Morheim Co.

	Cost	Retail
Merchandise inventory, January 1	$292,520	$456,000
Transactions during January:		
Purchases	177,250	274,500
Purchases discounts	2,250	
Sales		267,500
Sales returns and allowances		5,000

Queens Supply Co.

Merchandise inventory, July 1	$425,200
Transactions during July and August:	
Purchases	310,500
Purchases discounts	5,500
Sales	476,900
Sales returns and allowances	3,900
Estimated gross profit rate	35%

Instructions:

(1) Determine the estimated cost of the merchandise inventory of Morheim Co. on January 31 by the retail method, presenting details of the computations.
(2) Estimate the cost of the merchandise inventory of Queens Supply Co. on August 31 by the gross profit method, presenting details of the computations.

Pb. 7–42.
Percentage-of-completion method.
OBJ. 11

SPREADSHEET PROBLEM

Sweeney Company began construction on three contracts during 1991. The contract prices and construction activities for 1991, 1992, and 1993 were as follows:

		1991		1992		1993	
Contract	Contract Price	Costs Incurred	Percent Completed	Costs Incurred	Percent Completed	Costs Incurred	Percent Completed
1	$15,000,000	$5,575,000	40%	$4,900,000	35%	$3,400,000	25%
2	10,000,000	2,550,000	30	2,625,000	30	2,695,000	30
3	8,000,000	3,710,000	50	3,815,000	50	—	—

Instructions:

Determine the amount of revenue and the income to be recognized for each of the years, 1991, 1992, and 1993. Revenue is to be recognized by the percentage-of-completion method. Present computations in good order.

ALTERNATE PROBLEMS

Pb. 7–37A.
Corrections to inventory; revised income statement.
OBJ. 1, 3

The following preliminary income statement of Poole Enterprises Inc. was prepared after the accounts were adjusted and closed at the end of the fiscal year. The company uses the periodic inventory system.

Poole Enterprises Inc.
Income Statement
For Year Ended December 31, 19--

Sales (net)		$996,750
Cost of merchandise sold:		
Merchandise inventory, January 1, 19--	$190,000	
Purchases (net)	695,000	
Merchandise available for sale	$885,000	
Less merchandise inventory, December 31, 19--	205,000	
Cost of merchandise sold		680,000
Gross profit		$316,750
Operating expenses		202,250
Net income		$114,500

The following errors in the ledger and on the inventory sheets for the physical inventory on December 31 were discovered by the independent CPA retained to conduct the annual audit:

(a) A number of errors were discovered in pricing inventory items, in extending amounts, and in footing inventory sheets. The net effect of the errors, exclusive of those described below, was to overstate by $3,500 the amount of ending inventory on the income statement.
(b) A purchases invoice for merchandise of $1,500, dated December 30, had been received and correctly recorded, but the merchandise was not received until January 3 and had not been included in the December 31 inventory. Title had passed to Poole Enterprises Inc. on December 30.
(c) A purchases invoice for merchandise of $4,250, dated December 31, was not received until January 4 and had not been recorded by December 31. However, the merchandise, to which title had passed, had arrived and had been included in the December 31 inventory.
(d) A sales order for $9,500, dated December 31, had been recorded as a sale on that date, but title did not pass to the buyer until shipment was made on January 3. The merchandise, which had cost $6,500, was excluded from the December 31 inventory.
(e) A sales invoice for $1,250, dated December 30, had not been recorded. The merchandise was shipped on December 30, FOB shipping point, and its cost, $775, was excluded from the December 31 inventory.
(f) An item of office equipment, received on December 27, was erroneously included in the December 31 merchandise inventory at its cost of $8,500. The invoice had been recorded correctly.

Instructions:

(1) Determine the correct inventory for December 31, beginning your analysis with the $205,000 inventory shown on the preliminary income statement. Assemble the corrections in two groupings, "Additions" and "Deductions," allowing six lines for each group. Identify each correction by the appropriate letter.
(2) Prepare a revised income statement.

Pb. 7–38A.
Periodic inventory by three methods.
OBJ. 5

A-1 Television employs the periodic inventory system. Details regarding the inventory of television sets at July 1, 1991, purchases invoices during the year, and the inventory count at June 30, 1992, are summarized as follows:

Model	Inventory, July 1	Purchases Invoices 1st	2d	3d	Inventory Count, June 30
B44	2 at $253	4 at $255	4 at $260	4 at $265	5
E17	8 at 80	10 at 84	8 at 90	8 at 99	10
G32	2 at 510	2 at 521	3 at 526	3 at 530	3
J60	8 at 120	4 at 105	3 at 105	6 at 99	8
M91	2 at 250	2 at 260	4 at 271	4 at 275	4
R55	5 at 160	4 at 170	4 at 175	7 at 180	8
T20	—	4 at 320	4 at 330	2 at 340	3

Instructions:

(1) Determine the cost of the inventory on June 30, 1992, by the first-in, first-out method. Present data in columnar form, using the following headings:

Model	Quantity	Unit Cost	Total Cost

If the inventory of a particular model is composed of an entire lot plus a portion of another lot acquired at a different unit cost, use a separate line for each lot.
(2) Determine the cost of the inventory on June 30, 1992, by the last-in, first-out method, following the procedures indicated in (1).
(3) Determine the cost of the inventory on June 30, 1992, by the average cost method, using the columnar headings indicated in (1).

Pb. 7–39A.
Fifo and lifo perpetual inventory.
OBJ. 6

The beginning inventory of soybeans at the Savoy Co-Op and data on purchases and sales for a three-month period are as follows:

Date		Transaction	Number of Bushels	Per Unit	Total
July	1.	Inventory	35,000	$7.50	$262,500
	6.	Purchase	70,000	7.55	528,500
	16.	Sale	40,000	8.50	340,000
	25.	Sale	30,000	8.50	255,000
Aug.	8.	Sale	10,000	8.60	86,000
	12.	Purchase	50,000	7.60	380,000
	20.	Sale	35,000	8.70	304,500
	28.	Sale	25,000	8.65	216,250
Sept.	5.	Purchase	60,000	7.55	453,000
	11.	Sale	40,000	8.50	340,000
	20.	Purchase	30,000	7.40	222,000
	30.	Sale	45,000	8.50	382,500

Instructions:

(1) Record the inventory, purchases, and cost of merchandise sold data in a perpetual inventory record similar to the one illustrated on page 303, using the first-in, first-out method.
(2) Determine the total sales and the total cost of soybeans sold for the period and indicate their effect on the general ledger by preparing two journal entries. Assume that all sales were on account.
(3) Determine the gross profit from sales of soybeans for the period.
(4) Record the inventory, purchases, and cost of merchandise sold data in a perpetual inventory record similar to the one illustrated on page 303, using the last-in, first-out method.

If the working papers correlating with the textbook are not used, omit Pb. 7–40A.

Pb. 7–40A.
Lower of cost or market inventory.
OBJ. 7

Data on the physical inventory of Dent Corporation as of December 31, the end of the current fiscal year, are presented in the working papers. The quantity of each commodity on hand has been determined and recorded on the inventory sheet. Unit market prices have also been determined as of December 31 and recorded on the sheet. The inventory is to be determined at cost and also at the lower of cost or market, using the first-in, first-out method. Quantity and cost data from the last purchases invoice of the year and the next-to-the-last purchases invoice are summarized as follows:

	Last Purchases Invoice		Next-to-the-Last Purchases Invoice	
Description	Quantity Purchased	Unit Cost	Quantity Purchased	Unit Cost
A96	10	$ 40	15	$ 39
C11	5	315	5	325
E37	10	145	10	142
F52	100	30	100	29
H90	10	560	10	570
J19	150	15	100	13
K41	5	800	5	785
P21	500	6	500	6
R72	80	17	50	18
T15	5	250	4	260
V55	1,000	6	500	6
BC4	75	45	75	46
DD7	5	420	5	425

Description	Last Purchases Invoice: Quantity Purchased	Last Purchases Invoice: Unit Cost	Next-to-the-Last Purchases Invoice: Quantity Purchased	Next-to-the-Last Purchases Invoice: Unit Cost
EA4	100	$ 20	75	$ 19
FB3	60	16	40	17
HH2	50	29	25	28
JB9	50	26	50	25
MN5	5	710	5	715

Instructions:

Record the appropriate unit costs on the inventory sheet and complete the pricing of the inventory. When there are two different unit costs applicable to a commodity, proceed as follows:

(1) Draw a line through the quantity and insert the quantity and unit cost of the last purchase.

(2) On the following line, insert the quantity and unit cost of the next-to-the-last purchase. The first item on the inventory sheet has been completed as an example.

Pb. 7–41A.
Retail method; gross profit method.
OBJ. 9
SPREADSHEET PROBLEM

Selected data on merchandise inventory, purchases, and sales for Alton Co. and Zimmer Co. are as follows:

Alton Co.

	Cost	Retail
Merchandise inventory, July 1	$214,000	$307,500
Transactions during July:		
Purchases	175,500	242,500
Purchases discounts	4,500	
Sales		250,000
Sales returns and allowances		5,000

Zimmer Co.

Merchandise inventory, April 1	$602,500
Transactions during April and May:	
Purchases	399,750
Purchases discounts	2,750
Sales	625,000
Sales returns and allowances	5,000
Estimated gross profit rate	40%

Instructions:

(1) Determine the estimated cost of the merchandise inventory of Alton Co. on July 31 by the retail method, presenting details of the computations.

(2) Estimate the cost of the merchandise inventory of Zimmer Co. on May 31 by the gross profit method, presenting details of the computations.

Pb. 7–42A.
Percentage-of-completion method.
OBJ. 11
SPREADSHEET PROBLEM

McCarver Company began construction on three contracts during 1991. The contract prices and construction activities for each of the years 1991, 1992, and 1993 were as follows:

Contract	Contract Price	1991 Costs Incurred	1991 Percent Completed	1992 Costs Incurred	1992 Percent Completed	1993 Costs Incurred	1993 Percent Completed
1	$6,000,000	$2,175,000	40%	$3,250,000	60%	—	—
2	8,000,000	1,200,000	20	2,750,000	40	$3,000,000	40%
3	3,500,000	455,000	15	985,000	30	1,575,000	50

Instructions:

Determine the amount of revenue and income to be recognized from the contracts for each of the years 1991, 1992, and 1993. Revenue is to be recognized by the percentage-of-completion method. Present computations in good order.

MINI-CASE 7

Drew Company began operations in 1991 by selling a single product. Data on purchases and sales for the year were as follows:

Purchases

Date	Units Purchased	Unit Cost	Total Cost
April 12	2,500	$26.40	$ 66,000
May 17	3,000	27.25	81,750
June 8	2,000	29.00	58,000
July 18	2,000	30.00	60,000
August 20	2,000	31.00	62,000
October 25	1,000	31.00	31,000
November 20	500	31.50	15,750
December 15	500	34.00	17,000
	13,500		$391,500

Sales

April	1,000 units	September	1,475 units
May	1,000	October	1,400
June	1,750	November	1,125
July	2,000	December	500
August	1,750		
Total sales	$501,000		

On January 2, 1992, the president of the company, Becky Drew, asked for your advice on costing the 1,500-unit physical inventory that was taken on December 31, 1991. Also, since the firm plans to expand its product line, she asked for your advice on the use of a perpetual inventory system in the future.

Instructions:

(1) Determine the cost of the December 31, 1991 inventory under the periodic system, using the (a) first-in, first-out method, (b) last-in, first-out method, and (c) average cost method.
(2) Determine the gross profit for the year under each of the three methods in (1).
(3) (a) In your opinion, which of the three inventory costing methods best reflects the results of operations for 1991? Why?
(b) In your opinion, which of the three inventory costing methods best reflects the replacement cost of the inventory on the balance sheet as of December 31, 1991? Why?
(c) Which inventory costing method would you choose to use for income tax purposes? Why?
(4) Discuss the advantages and disadvantages of using a perpetual inventory system. From the data presented in this case, is there any indication of the adequacy of inventory levels during the year?

ANSWERS TO SELF-EXAMINATION QUESTIONS

1. C The overstatement of inventory by $7,500 at the end of a period will cause the cost of merchandise sold for the period to be understated by $7,500, the gross profit for the period to be overstated by $7,500, and the net income for the period to be overstated by $7,500 (answer C).
2. B The perpetual system (answer B) continuously discloses the amount of inventory. The periodic inventory system (answer A) relies upon a detailed listing of the merchandise on hand, called a physical inventory (answer C), to determine the cost of inventory at the end of a period. The retail inventory method (answer D) is employed in connection with the periodic system and is based on the relationship of the cost of merchandise available for sale to the retail price of the same merchandise.
3. A The fifo method (answer A) is based on the assumption that costs are charged against revenue in the order in which they were incurred. The lifo method (answer B) charges the most recent costs incurred against revenue, and the average cost method (answer C) charges a weighted average of unit costs of commodities sold against revenue. The perpetual inventory system (answer D) is a system that continuously discloses the amount of inventory.
4. D The fifo method of costing is based on the assumption that costs should be charged against revenue in the order in which they were incurred (first-in, first-out). Thus the most recent costs are assigned to inventory. The 35 units would be assigned a unit cost of $23 (answer D).
5. B When the price level is steadily rising, the earlier unit costs are lower than recent unit costs. Under the fifo method (answer B), these earlier costs are matched against revenue to yield the highest possible net income. The periodic inventory system (answer D) is a system and not a method of costing.

CHAPTER 8

CHAPTER OBJECTIVES

1 Describe and illustrate the accounting for the acquisition of plant assets.

2 Describe the nature of depreciation.

3 Describe and illustrate the accounting for depreciation.

4 Describe and illustrate the composite-rate depreciation method.

5 Describe and illustrate the accounting for capital and revenue expenditures.

6 Describe and illustrate the accounting for plant asset disposals.

7 Describe and illustrate the accounting for the leasing of plant assets.

8 Describe and illustrate the accounting for depletion.

9 Describe and illustrate the accounting for intangible assets.

10 Describe and illustrate the reporting of depreciation expense, plant assets, and intangible assets in the financial statements.

11 Describe and illustrate the use of replacement cost of plant assets.

8

PLANT ASSETS & INTANGIBLE ASSETS

Long-lived is a general term that may be applied to assets of a permanent or relatively fixed nature owned by a business enterprise. As discussed in previous chapters, long-lived tangible assets that are of a permanent nature, used in the operations of the business, and not held for sale in the ordinary course of the business are classified on the balance sheet as **plant assets** or **fixed assets.** Other descriptive titles frequently used are **property, plant, and equipment,** used either alone or in various combinations. The properties most frequently included in plant assets may be described in more specific terms as equipment, furniture, tools, machinery, buildings, and land. Long-lived assets that are without physical characteristics, are not held for sale, but are useful in the operations of an enterprise are classified as **intangible assets.** Intangible assets often include patents, copyrights, and goodwill. This chapter focuses on the accounting principles and concepts for both tangible (plant) assets and intangible assets.

Although there is no standard criterion as to the minimum length of life necessary for classification as plant assets or intangible assets, such assets must be capable of repeated use or benefit and are ordinarily expected to last more than a year. However, the asset need not actually be used continuously or used often. For example, items of standby equipment held for use in the event of a breakdown of regular equipment or for use only during peak periods of activity are included in plant assets.

Assets acquired for resale in the normal course of business cannot be characterized as plant assets, regardless of their durability or the length of time they are held. For example, undeveloped land or other real estate acquired as a speculation should be listed on the balance sheet in the asset section entitled "Investments."

ACQUISITION OF PLANT ASSETS

OBJECTIVE 1
Describe and illustrate the accounting for the acquisition of plant assets.

The cost of acquiring a plant asset includes all expenditures *necessary* to get it in place and ready for use. Sales tax, transportation charges, insurance on the asset while in transit, special foundations, and installation costs should be added to the purchase price of the related plant asset. Similarly, when a secondhand asset is purchased, the initial costs of getting it ready for use, such as expenditures for new parts, repairs, and painting, are debited to the asset account. On the other hand, costs associated with the acquisition of a plant asset should be excluded from the asset account if they are not necessary for getting the asset ready for use and therefore do not increase the asset's usefulness. Expenditures resulting from carelessness or errors in installing the asset, from vandalism, or from other unusual occurrences do not increase the usefulness of the asset and should be treated as an expense.

The cost of constructing a building includes the fees paid to architects and engineers for plans and supervision, insurance incurred during construction, and all other needed expenditures related to the project. Generally, interest incurred during the construction period on money borrowed to finance construction should also be treated as part of the cost of the building.[1]

The cost of land includes not only the negotiated price but also broker's commissions, title fees, surveying fees, and other expenditures connected with securing title. If delinquent real estate taxes are assumed by the buyer, they also are chargeable to the land account. If unwanted buildings are located on land acquired for a plant site, the cost of their razing or removal, less any salvage recovered, is properly chargeable to the land account. The cost of leveling or otherwise permanently changing the contour is also an additional cost of the land.

Other expenditures related to the land may be charged to Land, Buildings, or Land Improvements, depending upon the circumstances. If the property owner bears the initial cost of paving the public street bordering the land, either by direct payment or by special tax assessment, the paving may be considered to be as permanent as the land. On the other hand, the cost of constructing walkways to and around the building may be added to the building account if the walkways are expected to last as long as the building. Expenditures for improvements that are neither as permanent as the land nor directly associated with the building may be set apart in a land improvements account and depreciated according to their different life spans. Some of the more usual items of this nature are trees and shrubs, fences, outdoor lighting systems, and paved parking areas.

NATURE OF DEPRECIATION

OBJECTIVE 2
Describe the nature of depreciation.

As time passes, all plant assets with the exception of land lose their capacity to yield services.[2] Accordingly, the cost of such assets should be transferred to the related expense accounts in an orderly manner during their expected useful life. This periodic cost expiration is called **depreciation.**

Factors contributing to a decline in usefulness may be divided into two categories: *physical* depreciation, which includes wear from use and deterioration from the action of the elements, and *functional* depreciation, which includes inadequacy and obsolescence. A plant asset becomes inadequate if its capacity is not sufficient to meet the demands of increased production. A plant asset is obsolete if the commodity that it produces is no longer in demand or if a newer machine can produce a commodity of better quality or at a great reduction in cost. The continued growth of technological progress

[1] *Statement of Financial Accounting Standards, No. 34,* "Capitalization of Interest Cost" (Stamford: Financial Accounting Standards Board, 1979), par. 6.

[2] Land is here assumed to be used only as a site. Consideration will be given later in the chapter to land acquired for its mineral deposits or other natural resources.

during this century has made obsolescence an increasingly important part of depreciation. Although the several factors comprising depreciation can be defined, it is not feasible to identify them when recording depreciation expense.

The meaning of the term "depreciation" as used in accounting is often misunderstood because the same term is also commonly used in business to mean a decline in the market value of an asset. The amount of unexpired cost of plant assets reported in the balance sheet is not likely to agree with the amount that could be realized from their sale. Plant assets are held for use in the enterprise rather than for sale. It is assumed that the enterprise will continue forever as a **going concern**. Consequently, the decision to dispose of a plant asset is based mainly on its usefulness to the enterprise and not on its market value.

Another common misunderstanding is that depreciation accounting automatically provides the cash needed to replace plant assets as they wear out. The cash account is neither increased nor decreased by the periodic entries that transfer the cost of plant assets to depreciation expense accounts. The misconception probably occurs because depreciation expense, unlike most expenses, does not require an equivalent outlay of cash in the period in which the expense is recorded.

ACCOUNTING FOR DEPRECIATION

OBJECTIVE 3
Describe and illustrate the accounting for depreciation.

If a plant asset is expected to have no value at the time that it is retired from service, its entire initial cost should be spread over the expected useful life of the asset as depreciation expense. Also, if a plant asset's value at the time of retirement is expected to be very small in comparison with the cost of the asset, this value may be ignored and the entire cost spread over the asset's expected useful life. If a plant asset is expected to have a significant value at the time that it is retired from service, the difference between its initial cost and this value is the cost (depreciable cost) that should be spread over the useful life of the asset as depreciation expense. The plant asset's estimated value at the time that it is to be retired from service is called its **residual value, scrap value, salvage value,** or **trade-in value.**

In determining the amount of depreciable cost that is to be recognized as periodic depreciation expense, three factors need to be considered: the plant asset's (a) initial cost, (b) residual value, and (c) useful life. The relationship between these three factors and the periodic depreciation expense is presented in the following diagram:

Factors that Determine Depreciation Expense

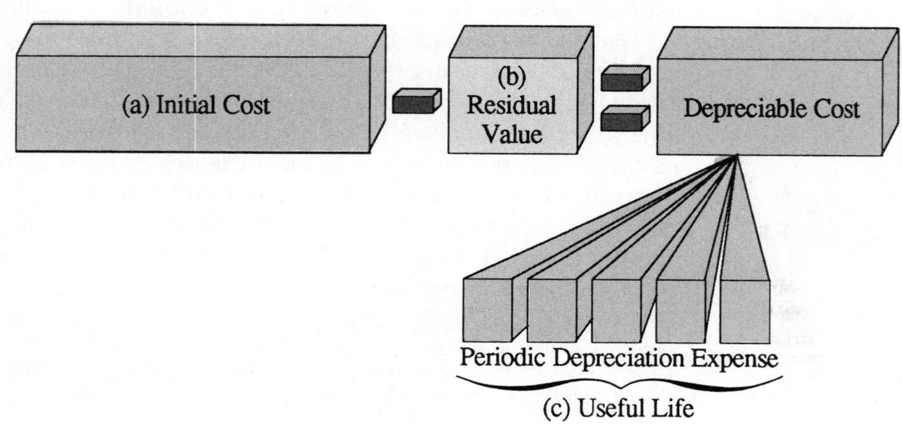

Neither the period of usefulness of a plant asset nor its residual value at the end of that period can be accurately determined until the asset is retired. However, in determining the amount of the periodic depreciation, these two related factors must be estimated at the time the asset is placed in service.

There are no hard-and-fast rules for estimating either factor, and both factors may be greatly affected by management policies. For example, the estimates of a company that provides its sales representatives with a new automobile every year will differ from those of a firm that keeps its cars for three years. Such variables as climate, frequency of use, maintenance, and minimum standards of efficiency will also affect the estimates.

Life estimates for depreciable assets are available in various trade association and other publications. For federal income tax purposes, the Internal Revenue Service also has established guidelines for life estimates. These guidelines may be useful in determining depreciation for financial reporting purposes.

In addition to the many factors that may influence the life estimate of an asset, there is a wide range in the degree of exactness used in the computation. A calendar month is ordinarily the smallest unit of time used. When this period of time is used, all assets placed in service or retired from service during the first half of a month are treated as if the event had occurred on the first day of that month. Similarly, all plant asset additions and reductions during the second half of a month are considered to have occurred on the first day of the next month. In the absence of any statement to the contrary, this practice will be assumed throughout this chapter.

It is not necessary that an enterprise use a single method of computing depreciation for all classes of its depreciable assets. The methods used in the accounts and financial statements also may differ from the methods used in determining income taxes and property taxes. The four methods used most often are straight-line, units-of-production, declining-balance, and sum-of-the-years-digits. The extent of the use of these methods in financial statements is presented in the following chart:

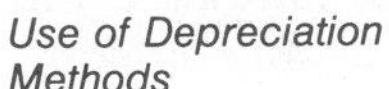

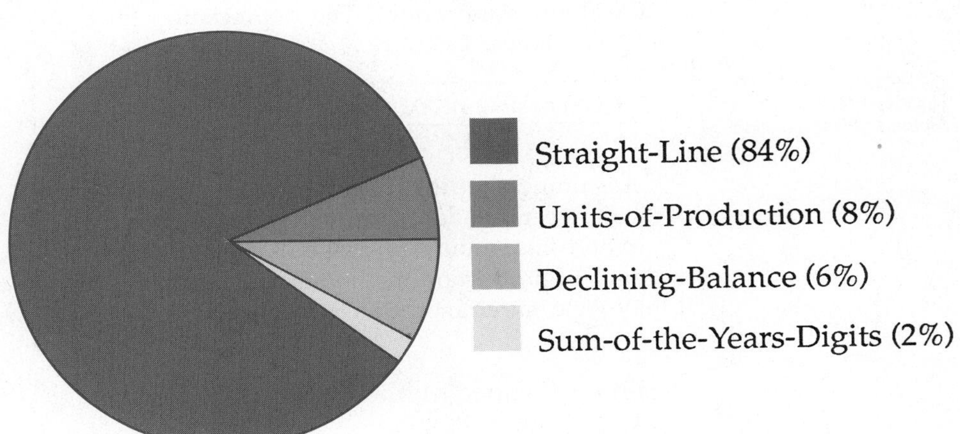

Straight-Line Method

The **straight-line method** of determining depreciation provides for equal periodic charges to expense over the estimated life of the asset. To illustrate this method, assume that the cost of a depreciable asset is $16,000, its estimated residual value is $1,000, and its estimated life is 5 years. The annual depreciation is computed as follows:

Straight-Line Method of Depreciation

$$\frac{\$16{,}000 \text{ cost} - \$1{,}000 \text{ estimated residual value}}{5 \text{ years estimated life}} = \$3{,}000 \text{ annual depreciation}$$

The annual depreciation of $3,000 would be prorated for the first and the last partial years of use. Assuming a fiscal year ending on December 31 and first use of the asset on October 15, the depreciation for that fiscal year would be $750 (3 months). If usage had begun on October 16, the depreciation for the year would be $500 (2 months).

The annual straight-line depreciation may be converted to a percentage rate, determined on the basis of cost and the estimated life of the asset without regard to residual value. The conversion to an annual percentage rate is accomplished by dividing 100 by the number of years of life. Thus a life of 50 years is equivalent to a 2% depreciation rate, 20 years is equivalent to a 5% rate, 8 years is equivalent to a 12½% rate, and so on.

The straight-line method is widely used because of its simplicity. In addition, it provides a reasonable allocation of costs to periodic revenue when usage is relatively the same from period to period.

Units-of-Production Method

The **units-of-production method** yields a depreciation charge that varies with the amount of asset usage. To apply this method, the length of life of the asset is expressed in terms of productive capacity, such as hours, miles, or number of units. Depreciation is first computed for the appropriate unit of production, and the depreciation for each accounting period is then determined by multiplying the unit depreciation by the number of units used during the period. To illustrate, assume that a machine with a cost of $16,000 and estimated residual value of $1,000 is expected to have an estimated life of 10,000 operating hours. The depreciation for a unit of one hour is computed as follows:

Units-of-Production Method of Depreciation

$$\frac{\$16{,}000 \text{ cost} - \$1{,}000 \text{ estimated residual value}}{10{,}000 \text{ estimated hours}} = \$1.50 \text{ hourly depreciation}$$

Assuming that the machine was in operation for 2,200 hours during a particular year, the depreciation for that year would be $3,300 ($1.50 × 2,200).

When the amount of usage of a plant asset changes from year to year, the units-of-production method is more logical than the straight-line method. It may yield fairer allocations of cost against periodic revenue.

Declining-Balance Method

The **declining-balance method** yields a declining periodic depreciation charge over the estimated life of the asset. The most common technique is to double the straight-line depreciation rate, computed as explained previously, and apply the resulting rate to the cost of the asset less its accumulated depreciation. For example, the declining-balance rate for an asset with an estimated life of five years would be double the straight-line rate of 20%, or 40%. This rate is then applied to the cost of the asset for the first year of its use and thereafter to the declining book value (cost minus accumulated depreciation). The method is illustrated in the following table:

Declining-Balance Method of Depreciation

Year	Cost	Accumulated Depreciation at Beginning of Year	Book Value at Beginning of Year	Rate	Depreciation for Year	Book Value at End of Year
1	$16,000	—	$16,000.00	40%	$6,400.00	$9,600.00
2	16,000	$ 6,400.00	9,600.00	40%	3,840.00	5,760.00
3	16,000	10,240.00	5,760.00	40%	2,304.00	3,456.00
4	16,000	12,544.00	3,456.00	40%	1,382.40	2,073.60
5	16,000	13,926.40	2,073.60	40%	829.44	1,244.16

Note that estimated residual value is not considered in determining the depreciation rate. It is also ignored in computing periodic depreciation, except that the asset should not be depreciated below the estimated residual value. In the above example, it was assumed that the estimated residual value at the end of the fifth year approximates the book value of $1,244.16. If the residual value had been estimated at $1,500, the depreciation for the fifth year would have been $573.60 ($2,073.60 – $1,500) instead of $829.44.

There was an implicit assumption in the above illustration that the first use of the asset coincided with the beginning of the fiscal year. This would usually not occur in actual practice, however, and would require a slight change in the computation for the first partial year of use. If the asset in the example had been placed in service at the end of the third month of the fiscal year, only the pro rata portion of the first full year's depreciation, $4,800 (9/12 × 40% × $16,000), would be allocated to the first fiscal year. The method of computing the depreciation for the following years would not be affected. Thus, the depreciation for the second fiscal year would be $4,480 [40% × ($16,000 – $4,800)].

Sum-of-the-Years-Digits Method

The **sum-of-the-years-digits method** yields results like those obtained by use of the declining-balance method. The periodic charge for depreciation declines steadily over the estimated life of the asset because a successively smaller fraction is applied each year to the original cost of the asset less the estimated residual value. The denominator of the fraction, which remains the same, is the sum of the digits representing the years of life. The numerator of the fraction, which changes each year, is the number of years of life remaining at the beginning of the year for which depreciation is being computed. For an asset with an estimated life of 5 years, the denominator is 5 + 4 + 3 + 2 + 1, or 15.[3] For the first year, the numerator is 5, for the second year 4, and so on. The method is illustrated by the following deprecia-

[3]The denominator can also be determined from the following formula, where S = sum of the digits and N = number of years of estimated life: $S = N[(N + 1) \div 2]$.

tion schedule for an asset with an assumed cost of $16,000, residual value of $1,000, and life of 5 years:

Sum-of-the-Years-Digits Method of Depreciation

Year	Cost Less Residual Value	Rate	Depreciation for Year	Accumulated Depreciation at End of Year	Book Value at End of Year
1	$15,000	5/15	$5,000	$ 5,000	$11,000
2	15,000	4/15	4,000	9,000	7,000
3	15,000	3/15	3,000	12,000	4,000
4	15,000	2/15	2,000	14,000	2,000
5	15,000	1/15	1,000	15,000	1,000

When the first use of the asset does not coincide with the beginning of a fiscal year, it is necessary to allocate each full year's depreciation between the two fiscal years benefited. Assuming that the asset in the example was placed in service after three months of the fiscal year had elapsed, the depreciation for that fiscal year would be $3,750 (9/12 × 5/15 × $15,000). The depreciation for the second year would be $4,250, computed as follows:

3/12 × 5/15 × $15,000	$1,250
9/12 × 4/15 × $15,000	3,000
Total, second fiscal year	$4,250

Comparison of Depreciation Methods

The straight-line method provides for uniform periodic charges to depreciation expense over the life of the asset. The units-of-production method provides for periodic charges to depreciation expense that may vary considerably, depending upon the amount of usage of the asset.

Both the declining-balance and the sum-of-the-years-digits methods provide for a higher depreciation charge in the first year of use of the asset and a gradually declining periodic charge thereafter. For this reason they are frequently referred to as **accelerated depreciation methods.** These methods are most appropriate for situations in which the decline in productivity or earning power of the asset is proportionately greater in the early years of its use than in later years. Further justification for their use is based on the tendency of repairs to increase with the age of an asset. The reduced amounts of depreciation in later years are therefore offset to some extent by increased maintenance expenses.

The periodic depreciation charges for the straight-line method and the accelerated methods are compared in the chart on page 337. This chart is based on an asset cost of $16,000, an estimated life of 5 years, and an estimated residual value of $1,000.

Depreciation for Federal Income Tax

Each of the four depreciation methods described in the preceding paragraphs can be used to determine the amount of depreciation for federal income tax purposes for plant assets acquired prior to 1981. The accelerated depreciation methods are widely used. Acceleration of the "write-off" of the asset reduces the income tax liability in the earlier years and thus increases the amount of cash available in those years to pay for the asset or for other purposes.

Comparison of Depreciation Methods

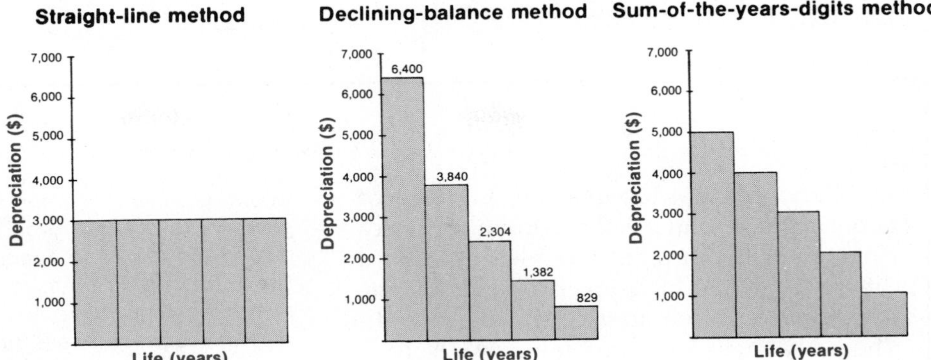

For plant assets acquired after 1980 and before 1987, either the straight-line method or the Accelerated Cost Recovery System (ACRS) could be used for federal income tax purposes. ACRS provided for depreciation deductions that approximated the depreciation calculated by the 150-percent declining-balance method. For most business property, ACRS also provided for three classes of useful life. Each class of useful life was often much shorter than the actual useful life of the asset in that class.

Under the Tax Reform Act of 1986, Modified ACRS (MACRS) provides for eight classes of useful life for plant assets acquired after 1986. The two most common classes, other than real estate, are the 5-year class and the 7-year class.[4] The 5-year class includes automobiles and light-duty trucks, and the 7-year class includes most machinery and equipment. The depreciation deduction for these two classes approximates the use of the 200-percent declining-balance method.

The Internal Revenue Service has prescribed methods that result in annual percentages to be used in determining depreciation for each class. In using these rates, salvage value is ignored, and all plant assets are assumed to be placed in service in the middle of the year and taken out of service in the middle of the year. Thus, for the 5-year-class assets, for example, depreciation is spread over six years, as shown in the following schedule of MACRS depreciation rates:

MACRS Depreciation Rate Schedule

Year	5-Year-Class Depreciation Rates
1	20.0%
2	32.0
3	19.2
4	11.5
5	11.5
6	5.8
	100.0%

The use of ACRS and MACRS may not be acceptable for computing depreciation under generally accepted accounting principles. The accounting

[4]Real estate is classified into 27 1/2-year and 31 1/2-year classes and is depreciated by the straight-line method.

issues raised because of different depreciation amounts being used for federal income tax purposes and financial reporting purposes are discussed in Chapter 11.

TWO (LEGAL) SETS OF BOOKS

Many companies use one method of depreciation for financial reporting purposes (frequently the straight-line method) and a different method of depreciation for income tax purposes (often an accelerated method). The advantages of maintaining two sets of accounts is addressed in the following excerpts from an article in *The Wall Street Journal:*

. . . When you're dealing with the tax folks, quick depreciation . . . of equipment outlays makes a lot of sense. It cuts . . . profits and [therefore cuts] taxes. . . . [Such a policy also] leaves more cash for other uses. But good tax strategy can be bad business strategy.

David A. Tonneson, a Wakefield, Mass., accountant who specializes in advising small businesses, says the biggest mistake his clients make is to immediately deduct too much from profits [for depreciation on] equipment and installation costs. This results in undervalued [bases for] assets and makes borrowing more funds or selling the company more difficult. Small start-up companies would be wiser to [spread depreciation over future years more evenly]. Though this boosts reported income [in the early years], it boosts their asset base, permitting them to borrow more and sell their concern for more.

Mr. Tonneson says one of his clients lost a chance for a $1 million contract because it had used accelerated depreciation for its equipment. Using straight-line depreciation, the equipment would have been valued on the books at $525,000, or enough to collateralize a $420,000 loan from a bank. But after accelerated depreciation, the books only showed the equipment at $300,000, so the bank would supply only a $240,000 loan. The company needed $400,000 to gear up for the new order. It lost the sale.

Many new small-business owners aren't aware that they can use accelerated depreciation [MACRS] to report income to the tax authorities but can keep their asset [book] values up by using straight-line depreciation to report to shareholders. . . . While this does entail keeping two sets of books, "it's well worth it."

Source: Lee Berton, "Dos and Don'ts," *The Wall Street Journal* (June 10, 1988), p. 34R.

Revision of Periodic Depreciation

Earlier in this chapter, it was noted that two of the factors that must be considered in computing the periodic depreciation of a plant asset — its residual value at the time it is retired from service and its useful life — must be estimated at the time the asset is placed in service. Minor errors resulting from the use of these estimates are normal and tend to be recurring.[5] When such errors occur, the revised estimates are used to determine the amount of the remaining undepreciated asset cost to be charged as an expense in future periods.

To illustrate, assume that a plant asset purchased for $130,000 and originally estimated to have a useful life of 30 years and a residual value of $10,000 has been depreciated for 10 years by the straight-line method. At the end of ten years, its book value (undepreciated cost) would be $90,000, determined as follows:

[5]The correction of material or large errors made in computing depreciation is discussed in Chapter 11.

Asset cost	$130,000
Less accumulated depreciation ($4,000 per year × 10 years)	40,000
Book value (undepreciated cost), end of tenth year	$ 90,000

If during the eleventh year it is estimated that the remaining useful life is 25 years (instead of 20) and that the residual value is $5,000 (instead of $10,000), the depreciation expense for each of the remaining 25 years would be $3,400, determined as follows:

Book value (undepreciated cost), end of tenth year	$90,000
Less revised estimated residual value	5,000
Revised remaining depreciation	$85,000
Revised annual depreciation expense ($85,000 ÷ 25)	$ 3,400

Note that the correction of minor errors in the estimates used in the determination of depreciation does not affect the amounts of depreciation expense recorded in earlier years. The use of estimates, and the resulting likelihood of minor errors in such estimates, is inherent in the accounting process. Therefore when such errors do occur, the amounts recorded for depreciation expense in the past are not corrected; only future depreciation expense amounts are affected.

Recording Depreciation

Depreciation may be recorded by an entry at the end of each month, or the adjustment may be delayed until the end of the year. As illustrated on page 105, the part of the entry that records the decrease in the plant asset is credited to a contra asset account entitled Accumulated Depreciation or Allowance for Depreciation. The use of a contra asset account permits the original cost to remain unchanged in the plant asset account. This facilitates the computation of periodic depreciation, the listing of both cost and accumulated depreciation on the balance sheet, and the reporting required for property tax and income tax purposes.

An exception to the general procedure of recording depreciation monthly or annually is often made when a plant asset is sold, traded in, or scrapped. As discussed and illustrated later in the chapter, the disposal is recorded by removing from the accounts both the cost of the asset and its related accumulated depreciation as of the date of the disposal. Hence, it is advisable to record the additional depreciation on the item for the current period before recording the transaction disposing of the asset. A further advantage of recording the depreciation at the time of the disposal of the asset is that no additional attention need be given the transaction when the amount of the periodic depreciation adjustment for the other plant assets is later determined.

Subsidiary Ledgers for Plant Assets

When depreciation is to be computed individually on a large number of assets making up a functional group, it is advisable to maintain a subsidiary ledger. To illustrate, assume that an enterprise owns about 200 items of office equipment with a total cost of about $100,000. Unless the business is newly organized, the equipment would have been acquired over a number of years. The individual cost, estimated residual value, and estimated useful life would be different in each case, and the makeup of the group will continually change because of acquisitions and disposals.

There are many variations in the form of subsidiary records for depreciable assets. Multicolumn analysis sheets may be used, or a separate ledger account may be maintained for each asset. The form should be designed to provide spaces for recording the acquisition and the disposal of the asset, the depreciation charged each period, the accumulated depreciation to date, and any other pertinent data desired. An example of a subsidiary ledger account for a plant asset is shown below.

An Account in the Office Equipment Ledger

Plant Asset Record

Account No.: 123-215 General Ledger Account: Office Equipment
Item: SF 490 COPIER
Serial No.: AT 47-3926
From Whom Purchased: Hamilton Office Machines Co. Inc.
Estimated Useful Life: 10 Years Estimated Residual Value: $500 Depreciation per Year: $240

	Asset			Accumulated Depreciation			Book
Date	Debit	Credit	Balance	Debit	Credit	Balance	Value
04/08/92	2,900		2,900				2,900
12/31/92					180	180	2,720
12/31/93					240	420	2,480

The number assigned to the account illustrated is made up of the number of the office equipment account in the general ledger (123) followed by the number assigned to the specific item of office equipment purchased (215). An identification tag or plaque with the corresponding account number is attached to the asset. Depreciation for the year in which the asset was acquired, computed for nine months on a straight-line basis, is $180; for the following year it is $240. These amounts, together with the corresponding amounts from all other accounts in the subsidiary ledger, provide the figures for the respective year-end adjusting entries debiting the depreciation expense account and crediting the accumulated depreciation account.

The sum of the asset balances and the sum of the accumulated depreciation balances in all of the accounts should be compared periodically with the balances of their respective controlling accounts in the general ledger. When a certain asset is disposed of, the asset section of the subsidiary account is credited and the accumulated depreciation section is debited. This reduces the balances of both sections to zero. The account is then removed from the ledger and filed for possible future reference.

Subsidiary ledgers for plant assets are useful to the accounting department in (1) determining the periodic depreciation expense, (2) recording the disposal of individual items, (3) preparing tax returns, and (4) preparing insurance claims in the event of insured losses. The forms may also be expanded to provide spaces for accumulating data on the operating efficiency of the asset. Such information as number of breakdowns, length of time out of service, and cost of repairs is useful in comparing similar equipment produced by different manufacturers. When new equipment is to be purchased, the data are useful to management in deciding upon size, model, and other specifications and the best source of supply.

Regardless of whether subsidiary equipment ledgers are maintained, plant assets should be inspected periodically in order to determine their state of repair and whether or not they are still in use.

Depreciation of Plant Assets of Low Unit Cost

Subsidiary ledgers are not usually maintained for classes of plant assets that are made up of individual items of low unit cost, such as hand tools and portable equipment. Because of hard usage, breakage, and pilferage, such assets may be relatively short-lived and may require constant replacement. In such cases, the usual depreciation methods are not practical. One common method of determining cost expiration is to take a periodic inventory of the items on hand, estimate their fair value based on original cost, and transfer the remaining amount from the asset account to an appropriately titled account, such as Tools Expense. Other categories to which the same method is often applied are dies, molds, patterns, and spare parts.

COMPOSITE-RATE DEPRECIATION METHOD

OBJECTIVE 4
Describe and illustrate the composite-rate depreciation method.

In the preceding illustrations, depreciation has been computed on each individual plant asset and, unless otherwise stated, this procedure will be assumed in the problem materials at the end of the chapter. Another procedure, called the **composite-rate depreciation method,** is to determine depreciation for entire groups of assets by use of a single rate. The basis for grouping may be similarity in life estimates or other common traits, or it may be broadened to include all assets within a functional class, such as office equipment or factory equipment.

When depreciation is computed on the basis of a composite group of assets of differing life spans, a rate based on averages must be developed. This may be done by (1) computing the annual depreciation for each asset, (2) determining the total annual depreciation, and (3) dividing the sum thus determined by the total cost of the assets. The procedure is illustrated as follows:

Composite-Rate Method of Depreciation

Asset No.	Cost	Estimated Residual Value	Estimated Life	Annual Depreciation
101	$ 20,000	$4,000	10 years	$ 1,600
102	15,600	1,500	15 years	940
~~	~~~	~~~	~~~	~~~
147	41,000	1,000	8 years	5,000
Total	$473,400			$49,707

$$\frac{\$49{,}707 \text{ annual depreciation}}{\$473{,}400 \text{ cost}} = 10.5\% \text{ composite rate}$$

Although new assets of differing life spans and residual values will be added to the group and old assets will be retired, the "mix" is assumed to remain relatively unchanged. Accordingly, a depreciation rate based on averages (10.5% in the illustration) also remains unchanged for an indefinite time in the future.

When a composite rate is used, it may be applied against total asset cost on a monthly basis, or some reasonable assumption may be made regarding the timing of increases and decreases in the group. A common practice is to assume that all additions and retirements have occurred uniformly throughout the year. The composite rate is then applied to the average of the beginning and the ending balances of the account. Another acceptable averaging technique is to assume that all additions and retirements during the first half of the year occurred as of the first day of the year, and that all additions and retirements during the second half of the year occurred on the first day of the following year.

When assets within the composite group are retired, no gain or loss should be recognized. Instead, the asset account is credited for the cost of the asset and the accumulated depreciation account is debited for the excess of cost over the amount realized from the disposal. Any deficiency in the amount of depreciation recorded on the shorter-lived assets is presumed to be balanced by excessive depreciation on the longer-lived assets.

Regardless of whether depreciation is computed for each individual unit or for composite groups, the periodic depreciation charge is based on estimates. The effect of obsolescence and inadequacy on the life of plant assets is particularly difficult to forecast. Any system that provides for the allocation of depreciation in a systematic and rational manner fulfills the requirements of good accounting.

CAPITAL AND REVENUE EXPENDITURES

OBJECTIVE 5
Describe and illustrate the accounting for capital and revenue expenditures.

Expenditures for acquiring plant assets or for additions to plant assets and expenditures that add to the utility of plant assets for more than one accounting period are called **capital expenditures**. Such expenditures are debited to the asset account or to a related accumulated depreciation account. Expenditures that benefit only the current period and that are made in order to maintain normal operating efficiency are called **revenue expenditures.** Such expenditures are debited to expense accounts. Although it may be difficult to distinguish between capital and revenue expenditures, care should be exercised so that revenues and expenses will be matched properly. Capital expenditures will affect the depreciation expense of more than one period, while revenue expenditures will affect the expenses of only the current period.

Capital Expenditures

The accounting for the initial costs of acquiring plant assets was discussed earlier in the chapter. The accounting for other common capital expenditures related to plant assets — (a) additions, (b) betterments, and (c) extraordinary repairs — are discussed in the following paragraphs.

Additions to Plant Assets. Expenditures for additions to existing plant assets would be debited to the plant asset accounts as discussed earlier in the chapter for the initial costs of acquiring plant assets. The costs of additions would be depreciated over the estimated useful life of the additions. For example, the costs of adding an air conditioning system to a building or of adding a wing to a building would be treated as capital expenditures.

Betterments. Expenditures that increase operating efficiency or capacity for the remaining useful life of a plant asset are called **betterments.** Such expenditures would be added to the plant asset account. For example, if the power unit attached to a machine is replaced by one of greater capacity, the cost would be debited to the plant asset account. Also, the cost and the accumulated depreciation related to the old power unit would be removed from the accounts. The cost of the new power unit would be depreciated over its estimated useful life.

Extraordinary Repairs. Expenditures that increase the useful life of an asset beyond the original estimate are called **extraordinary repairs**. They should be debited to the appropriate accumulated depreciation account, however, rather than to the asset account. In such circumstances, the extraordinary repairs may be said to restore or "make good" a portion of the depreciation accumulated in prior years. In addition, the periodic depreciation for future periods would be redetermined on the basis of the revised book value of the asset and the revised estimate of the remaining useful life.

To illustrate, assume that a machine costing $50,000, with no residual value and a useful life of 10 years, has been depreciated for 6 years by the straight-line method ($5,000 annual depreciation). If at the beginning of the seventh year, an $11,500 extraordinary repair increases the remaining useful life of the machine to 7 years (instead of 4), the $11,500 would be debited to accumulated depreciation. The annual depreciation for the remaining 7 years of use would be $4,500, determined as follows:

Cost of machine		$50,000
Less accumulated depreciation balance:		
Depreciation for first 6 years ($5,000 × 6)	$30,000	
Deduct debit for extraordinary repairs	11,500	
Balance of accumulated depreciation		18,500
Revised book value of machine after extraordinary repair		$31,500
Annual depreciation ($31,500 ÷ 7 years remaining useful life)		$ 4,500

Revenue Expenditures

Expenditures for ordinary maintenance and repairs of a recurring nature should be classified as revenue expenditures and debited to expense accounts. For example, the cost of replacing spark plugs in an automobile or the cost of repainting a building should be debited to proper expense accounts.

Small expenditures are usually treated as repair expense, even though they may have the characteristics of capital expenditures. The saving in time and clerical expenses justifies the sacrifice of the small degree of accuracy. Some businesses establish a minimum amount required to classify an item as a capital expenditure.

Summary of Capital and Revenue Expenditures

The initial cost of acquiring a plant asset is debited to a plant asset account. Subsequent to the initial expenditures, the accounting for expenditures related to the plant asset is summarized in the diagram on page 344.

DISPOSAL OF PLANT ASSETS

OBJECTIVE 6
Describe and illustrate the accounting for plant asset disposals.

Plant assets that are no longer useful may be discarded, sold, or applied toward the purchase of other plant assets. The details of the entry to record a disposal will vary, but in all cases it is necessary to remove the book value of the asset from the accounts. This is done by debiting the proper accumu-

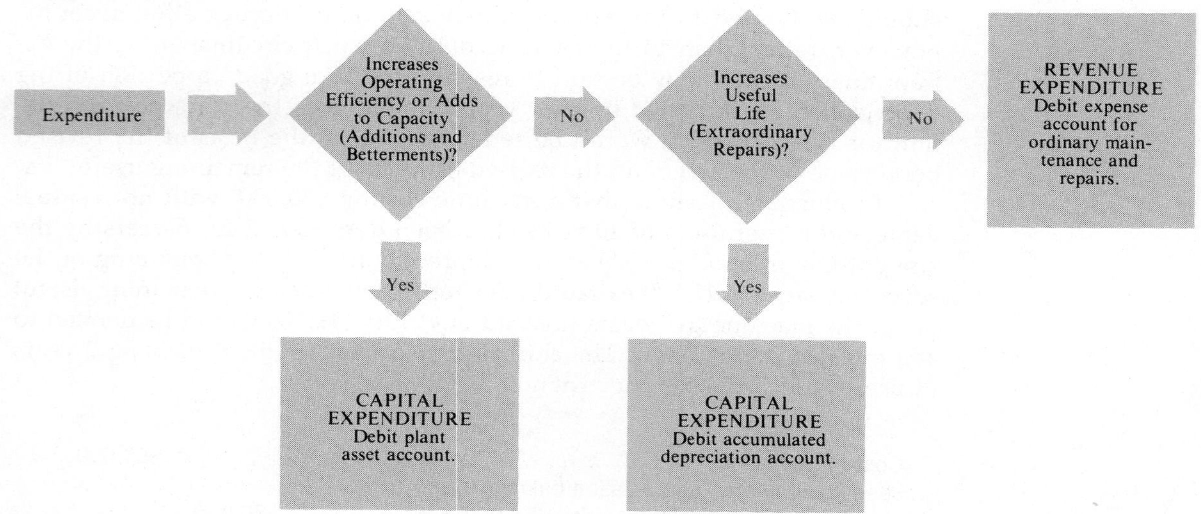

lated depreciation account for the total depreciation to the date of disposal and crediting the asset account for the cost of the asset.

A plant asset should not be removed from the accounts only because it has been depreciated for the full period of its estimated life. If the asset is still useful to the enterprise, the cost and accumulated depreciation should remain in the ledger. Otherwise the accounts would contain no evidence of the continued existence of such plant assets and the control function of the ledger would be impaired. In addition, the cost and the accumulated depreciation data on such assets are often needed in reporting for property tax and income tax purposes.

Discarding Plant Assets

When plant assets are no longer useful to the business and have no market value, they are discarded. If the asset has been fully depreciated, no loss is realized. To illustrate, assume that an item of equipment acquired at a cost of $6,000 became fully depreciated at December 31, the end of the preceding fiscal year, and is now to be discarded as worthless. The entry to record the disposal is as follows:

Mar. 24	Accumulated Depreciation—Equipment.....	6,000	
	Equipment..		6,000
	To write off equipment discarded.		

If the accumulated depreciation applicable to the $6,000 of discarded equipment had been less than $6,000, there would have been a loss on its disposal. Furthermore, it would have been necessary to record depreciation for the three months of use in the current period before recording the disposal. To illustrate these differences, assume that annual depreciation on the equipment is computed at 10% of cost and that the accumulated depreciation balance is $4,750 after the annual adjusting entry at the end of the preceding year. The entry to record depreciation of $150 for the three months of the current period is as follows:

Mar. 24	Depreciation Expense—Equipment..........	150	
	Accumulated Depreciation—Equipment..		150
	To record current depreciation on equipment discarded.		

The equipment is then removed from the accounts and the loss is recorded by the following entry:

Mar. 24	Accumulated Depreciation—Equipment.....	4,900	
	Loss on Disposal of Plant Assets..............	1,100	
	Equipment.......................................		6,000
	To write off equipment discarded.		

Ordinary losses and gains on the disposal of plant assets are nonoperating items and may be reported in the Other Expense and Other Income sections, respectively, of the income statement.

Sale of Plant Assets

The entry to record the sale of a plant asset is like the entries illustrated in the preceding section, except that the cash or other asset received must also be recorded. If the selling price is more than the book value of the asset, the transaction results in a gain; if the selling price is less than the book value, there is a loss. To illustrate some possibilities, assume that equipment acquired at a cost of $10,000 and depreciated at the annual rate of 10% of cost is sold for cash on October 12 of the eighth year of its use. The accumulated depreciation in the account as of the preceding December 31 is $7,000. The entry to record the depreciation for the nine months of the current year is as follows:

Oct. 12	Depreciation Expense—Equipment..............	750	
	Accumulated Depreciation—Equipment......		750
	To record current depreciation on equipment sold.		

After the current depreciation is recorded, the book value of the asset is $2,250. The entries to record the sale under three different assumptions as to selling price are as follows:

Sold at book value, for $2,250. No gain or loss.

Oct. 12	Cash..	2,250	
	Accumulated Depreciation—Equipment.........	7,750	
	Equipment..		10,000

Sold below book value, for $1,000. Loss of $1,250.

Oct. 12	Cash..	1,000	
	Accumulated Depreciation—Equipment.........	7,750	
	Loss on Disposal of Plant Assets..................	1,250	
	Equipment..		10,000

Sold above book value, for $3,000. Gain of $750.

Oct. 12	Cash	3,000	
	Accumulated Depreciation—Equipment	7,750	
	Equipment		10,000
	Gain on Disposal of Plant Assets		750

Exchange of Plant Assets

Old equipment is often traded in for new equipment having a similar use. The trade-in allowance is deducted from the price of the new equipment, and the balance owed **(boot)** is paid according to the credit terms. The trade-in allowance given by the seller is often greater or less than the book value of the old equipment traded in. In the past, it was acceptable for financial reporting purposes to recognize the difference between the trade-in allowance and the book value as a gain or a loss. For example, a trade-in allowance of $1,500 on equipment with a book value of $1,000 would have yielded a recognized gain of $500. Such treatment is no longer acceptable for financial reporting purposes on the theory that revenue occurs from the production and sale of items produced by plant assets and not from the exchange of similar plant assets. However, if the trade-in allowance is less than the book value of the old equipment, the loss is recognized immediately.

Nonrecognition of Gain. The acceptable method of accounting for an exchange in which the trade-in allowance exceeds the book value of the old plant asset requires that the cost of the new asset be determined by adding the amount of boot given to the book value of the old asset. To illustrate, assume an exchange based on the following data:

Equipment traded in (old):	
Cost of old equipment	$4,000
Accumulated depreciation at date of exchange	3,200
Book value at June 19, date of exchange	$ 800

Similar equipment acquired (new):	
Price of new equipment	$5,000
Trade-in allowance on old equipment	1,100
Boot given (cash)	$3,900

The cost basis of the new equipment is **$4,700**, which is determined by adding the boot given **($3,900)** to the book value of the old equipment **($800)**. The compound entry to record the exchange and the payment of cash is as follows:

June 19	Accumulated Depreciation—Equipment	3,200	
	Equipment	4,700	
	Equipment		4,000
	Cash		3,900

It should be noted that the nonrecognition of the $300 gain ($1,100 trade-in allowance minus $800 book value) at the time of the exchange is really a postponement. The periodic depreciation expense is based on a cost of $4,700 rather than on the quoted price of $5,000. The unrecognized gain of $300 at the time of the exchange will be matched by a reduction of $300 in the total amount of depreciation taken during the life of the equipment.

Recognition of Loss. To illustrate the accounting for a loss on the exchange of one plant asset for another which is similar in use, assume an exchange based on the following data:

Equipment traded in (old):	
Cost of old equipment	$ 7,000
Accumulated depreciation at date of exchange	4,600
Book value at September 7, date of exchange	$ 2,400

Similar equipment acquired (new):	
Price of new equipment	$10,000
Trade-in allowance on old equipment	2,000
Boot given (cash)	$ 8,000

The amount of the loss to be recognized on the exchange is the excess of the book value of the equipment traded in **($2,400)** over the trade-in allowance **($2,000)**, or **$400.** The entry to record the exchange is as follows:

Sept. 7	Accumulated Depreciation—Equipment	4,600	
	Equipment	10,000	
	Loss on Disposal of Plant Assets	400	
	Equipment		7,000
	Cash		8,000

Federal Income Tax Requirements. The Internal Revenue Code (IRC) requires that neither gains nor losses be recognized for income tax purposes if (1) the asset acquired by the taxpayer is similar in use to the asset given in exchange and (2) any boot involved is given (rather than received) by the taxpayer. Thus, the treatment of a nonrecognized gain corresponds to the acceptable method prescribed for financial reporting purposes, the boot given being added to the book value of the old equipment. In the first illustration, the cost basis for federal income tax purposes corresponds to the amount recorded as the cost of the new equipment, namely $4,700.

The cost basis of the new equipment in the second illustration, for federal income tax purposes, is determined in a like manner. The boot given ($8,000) is added to the book value of the old equipment ($2,400), yielding a cost basis of $10,400. The unrecognized loss of $400 at the time of the exchange will be matched by an increase of $400 in the total amount of depreciation allowed for income tax purposes during the life of the asset.

ACQUISITION OF PLANT ASSETS THROUGH LEASING

OBJECTIVE 7
Describe and illustrate the accounting for the leasing of plant assets.

Instead of owning a plant asset, a business may acquire the use of a plant asset through a lease. A **lease** is a contractual agreement that conveys the right to use an asset for a stated period of time. The two parties to a lease contract are the **lessor** and the **lessee.** The lessor is the party who legally owns the asset and who conveys the rights to use the asset to the lessee. Typical lease transactions include the leasing of automobiles, computers, airplanes, and communication satellites.

In agreeing to a lease, the lessee incurs an obligation to make periodic rent payments for the lease term. In accounting for lease obligations, all leases are classified by the lessee as either capital leases or operating leases. **Capital leases** are defined as leases which include one or more of the following provisions: (1) the lease transfers ownership of the leased asset to the lessee at the end of the lease term; (2) the lease contains an option for a bargain purchase of the leased asset by the lessee; (3) the lease term extends over most of the economic life of the leased asset; and/or (4) the lease requires rental payments which approximate the fair market value of the leased asset.[6] Leases which do not meet the preceding criteria for a capital lease are classified as **operating leases.**

A capital lease is accounted for as if the lessee has, in fact, purchased the asset. Accordingly, when a lease is executed, the lessee would debit an asset account for the fair market value of the leased asset and would credit a long-term lease liability account. The complex accounting procedures applicable to capital leases are discussed in detail in more advanced accounting texts.

In accounting for operating leases, rent expense is recognized as the leased asset is used. Neither future lease obligations nor the future rights to use the leased asset are recognized in the accounts. However, the lessee must disclose future lease commitments in footnotes to the financial statements.[7] An example of the disclosure of future lease commitments taken from the 1990 annual report of Walgreens is as follows:

Minimum rental commitments at August 31, 1990, under all leases having an initial or remaining non-cancelable term of more than one year are shown below *(in thousands):*

Year	
1991	$ 144,105
1992	149,597
1993	145,417
1994	140,625
1995	134,128
After 1995	1,219,593
Total minimum lease payments	$1,933,465

DEPLETION

OBJECTIVE 8
Describe and illustrate the accounting for depletion.

The periodic allocation of the cost of metal ores and other minerals removed from the earth is called **depletion.** The amount of the periodic cost allocation is based on the relationship of the cost to the estimated size of the mineral deposit and on the quantity extracted during the particular period. To illustrate, assume that the cost of certain mineral rights is $400,000 and that the deposit is estimated at 1,000,000 tons of ore of uniform grade. The depletion rate would be $400,000 ÷ 1,000,000, or $.40 a ton. If 90,000 tons are mined during the year, the depletion, amounting to $36,000, would be recorded by the following entry:

Adjusting Entry

Dec. 31	Depletion Expense	36,000	
	Accumulated Depletion		36,000

[6]*Statement of Financial Accounting Standards, No. 13,* "Accounting for Leases" (Stamford: Financial Accounting Standards Board, 1976), par. 7.
[7]*Ibid.,* par. 16.

The accumulated depletion account is a contra asset account and is presented in the balance sheet as a deduction from the cost of the mineral deposit.

In determining income subject to the federal income tax, the IRC permits, with certain limitations, a depletion deduction equal to a specified percent of gross income from the extractive operations. Thus, for income tax purposes, it is possible for total depletion deductions to be more than the cost of the property. A detailed examination of the tax law and regulations regarding "percentage depletion" is beyond the scope of this discussion, however.

INTANGIBLE ASSETS

OBJECTIVE 9
Describe and illustrate the accounting for intangible assets.

The basic principles of accounting for intangible assets are like those described earlier for plant assets. The major concerns are the determination of the acquisition costs and the recognition of periodic cost expiration, called **amortization,** due to the passage of time or a decline in usefulness. These concerns as they affect patents, copyrights, and goodwill are discussed in the following paragraphs.

Patents

Manufacturers may acquire exclusive rights to produce and sell goods with one or more unique features. Such rights are evidenced by **patents,** which are issued to inventors by the federal government. They continue in effect for 17 years. An enterprise may purchase patent rights from others or it may obtain patents on new products developed in its own research laboratories.

The initial cost of a purchased patent should be debited to an asset account and then written off, or amortized, over the years of its expected usefulness. This period of time may be less than the remaining legal life of the patent, and the expectations are also subject to change in the future. The straight-line method of amortization should be used unless it can be shown that another method is more appropriate.[8]

A separate contra asset account is normally not credited for the write-off or amortization of patents. In most situations, the credit is recorded directly in the patents account. This practice is common for all intangible assets. To illustrate, assume that at the beginning of its fiscal year an enterprise acquires for $100,000 a patent granted six years earlier. Although the patent will not expire for another eleven years, it is expected to be of value for only five years. The entry to amortize the patent at the end of the fiscal year is as follows:

Adjusting Entry

Dec. 31	Amortization Expense — Patents................	20,000	
	Patents...		20,000

Continuing the illustration, assume that after two years of use it appears that the patent will have no value at the end of an additional two

---

[8]*Opinions of the Accounting Principles Board, No. 17,* "Intangible Assets" (New York: American Institute of Certified Public Accountants, 1970), par. 30.

years. The cost to be amortized in the third year would be the balance of the asset account, $60,000, divided by the remaining two years, or $30,000.

An enterprise that develops patentable products in its own research laboratories often incurs substantial costs for the experimental work involved. In theory, some accountants believe that such costs, normally referred to as **research and development costs,** should be treated as an asset in the same manner as patent rights purchased from others. However, business enterprises are generally required to treat expenditures for research and development as current operating expenses.[9] The reason for this requirement is that there is a high degree of uncertainty about their future benefits, and therefore expensing these costs as incurred seems most appropriate. In addition, from a practical standpoint, a reasonably fair cost figure for each patent is difficult to establish because a number of research projects may be in process at the same time or work on some projects may extend over a number of years. As a result, a specific relationship between research and development costs and future revenue seldom can be established.

Whether patent rights are purchased from others or result from the effort of its own research laboratories, an enterprise often incurs substantial legal fees related to the patents. For example, legal fees may be incurred in establishing the legal validity of the patents. Such fees should be debited to an asset account and then amortized over the years of the usefulness of the patents.

Copyrights

The exclusive right to publish and sell a literary, artistic, or musical composition is obtained by a **copyright.** Copyrights are issued by the federal government and extend for 50 years beyond the author's death. The costs assigned to a copyright include all costs of creating the work plus the cost of obtaining the copyright. A copyright that is purchased from another should be recorded at the price paid for it. Because of the uncertainty regarding the useful life of a copyright, it is usually amortized over a relatively short period of time.

Goodwill

In the sense that it is used in business, **goodwill** is an intangible asset that attaches to a business as a result of such favorable factors as location, product superiority, reputation, and managerial skill. Its existence is evidenced by the ability of the business to earn a rate of return on the investment that is in excess of the normal rate for other firms in the same line of business.

Accountants are in general agreement that goodwill should be recognized in the accounts only if it can be objectively determined by an event or transaction, such as the purchase or sale of a business. Accountants also agree that the value of goodwill eventually disappears and that the recorded costs should be amortized over the years during which the goodwill is expected to be of value. This period, however, should not exceed 40 years.[10]

---

[9] *Statement of Financial Accounting Standards, No. 2,* "Accounting for Research and Development Costs" (Stamford: Financial Accounting Standards Board, 1974), par. 12.

[10] *Opinions of the Accounting Principles Board, No. 17,* "Intangible Assets," *op. cit.,* par. 29.

REPORTING DEPRECIATION EXPENSE, PLANT ASSETS, AND INTANGIBLE ASSETS IN THE FINANCIAL STATEMENTS

OBJECTIVE 10
Describe and illustrate the reporting of depreciation expense, plant assets, and intangible assets in the financial statements.

The amount of depreciation expense of a period should be set forth separately in the income statement or disclosed in some other manner. A general description of the method or methods used in computing depreciation should also accompany the financial statements.[11]

The balance of each major class of depreciable assets should be disclosed in the balance sheet or in notes thereto, together with the related accumulated depreciation, either by major class or in total.[12] When there are too many classes of plant assets to permit such a detailed listing in the balance sheet, a single figure may be presented, supported by a separate schedule.

Intangible assets are usually presented in the balance sheet in a separate section immediately following plant assets. The balance of each major class of intangible assets should be disclosed at an amount net of amortization taken to date.

An illustration of the presentation of plant assets and intangible assets is shown in the following partial balance sheet:

Plant Assets and Intangible Assets in the Balance Sheet

Clinton Door Inc.
Balance Sheet
December 31, 19--

Assets

	Cost	Accumulated Depreciation	Book Value	
Total current assets...				$462,500
Plant assets:				
Land..........................	$ 30,000	—	$ 30,000	
Buildings	110,000	$ 26,000	84,000	
Factory equipment........	650,000	192,000	458,000	
Office equipment..........	120,000	13,000	107,000	
Total plant assets......	$910,000	$231,000		679,000
Intangible assets:				
Patents			$ 75,000	
Goodwill			50,000	
Total intangible assets.				125,000

REPLACEMENT COST OF PLANT ASSETS

OBJECTIVE 11
Describe and illustrate the use of replacement cost of plant assets.

In preceding illustrations, plant assets were recorded at the cost actually incurred in acquiring them (historical cost), and depreciation was based on this cost. This principle is generally accepted for financial reporting purposes. The basic financial statements, therefore, do not indicate the effect of changes in price levels on plant assets and depreciation. In periods of inflation, which have been common in the past, many accountants have ques-

[11] *Opinions of the Accounting Principles Board, No. 22*, "Disclosure of Accounting Policies" (New York: American Institute of Certified Public Accountants, 1972), par. 13.

[12] *Opinions of the Accounting Principles Board, No. 12*, "Omnibus Opinion—1967" (New York: American Institute of Certified Public Accountants, 1967), par. 5.

tioned the usefulness of financial statements that ignore the effects of inflation on operations.

To indicate the nature of the problem, assume that plant assets acquired by an enterprise ten years ago for $1,000,000 are now to be replaced with similar assets which, at present price levels, will cost $2,000,000. Assume further that during the ten-year period the plant assets had been fully depreciated and that the net income of the enterprise had amounted to $5,000,000. Although the initial outlay of $1,000,000 for the plant assets was recovered through depreciation charges, the amount represents only one half of the cost of replacing the assets. Instead of considering the current value of the new assets to have doubled compared to a decade earlier, the dollars recovered can be said to have declined to one half of their earlier value. From either point of view, the firm has suffered a loss in purchasing power, which is the same as a loss of capital. In addition, $1,000,000 of the net income reported during the period might be said to be illusory, since it must be used to replace the assets.

The use of historical cost in accounting for plant assets insures objectivity. Therefore, in spite of inflationary trends, historical-cost financial statements are considered to be better than statements based on movements in the price level. Many accountants, however, recommend that businesses provide supplemental information that indicates the replacement cost, or current cost, of plant assets and the depreciation based on such cost. This supplemental information would match current costs for depreciation against current revenues and would therefore give a net income figure that would be useful in evaluating operating results. For example, a net income figure that has been determined after considering plant asset depreciation based on replacement cost would be especially useful in evaluating the amount of net income that should be made available for dividends.

There are many obstacles to the use of replacement costs for accounting for plant assets. For many businesses, such as a steel company with its many buildings and special machinery and equipment, it would be difficult to determine replacement costs with reasonable accuracy. In addition, if replacement costs were used, the process of estimating costs would have to be repeated each year, which would further increase the subjectivity of the accounting method. For reasons such as these, the use of replacement costs in accounting for plant assets has been generally restricted to experimental situations involving supplementary data.

REPLACEMENT COSTS FOR ASSETS

Over the years, there has been much discussion and controversy over the relevance of using original cost for reporting plant assets on the balance sheet and for determining depreciation expense for the income statement. The Securities and Exchange Commission views on this topic are addressed in the following excerpts from an article in *The Wall Street Journal:*

Under federal law, the SEC has the mandate to determine accounting principles for publicly traded companies. But it has generally ceded that authority to private-sector accounting bodies such as the Financial Accounting Standards Board. However, the SEC may now be shaking up the world of accounting. . . .

Although no one is suggesting that the SEC will revamp financial statements altogether, it wants to force companies to go a long way toward putting up-to-date values on assets currently on their books at historical cost—the original purchase price. It has launched an aggressive campaign in Congress and with the accounting profession to get fast action. . . .

At the root of SEC's new zeal are lessons drawn from the thrift [savings and loan] crisis. [SEC Chairman Richard C.] Breeden cites 1978 numbers that show the thrift industry with a positive net worth. But a harder look—using current instead of historical accounting—shows that the industry was already ailing, with a negative net worth of as much as $118 billion. . . .

A major advantage of historical-cost accounting, . . . argues [John Robbins, a managing partner at the accounting firm of Kenneth Leventhal & Co.], is that value is determined by competing interests—a buyer and a seller agreeing on a price. Relying on a company's current valuation requires appraisals. "There's only one danger with doing an appraisal: Believing it," he says. The wild real-estate appraisals emerging from the devastated thrift industry have increased that anxiety.

But that hasn't stopped some companies from relying more heavily on internal systems of current accounting. "We may not be accurate in our current cost estimates," says David G. Harmer, FMC Corp.'s comptroller, "but we're a hell of a lot closer than erroneous historical-cost basis. We know [those] are understated." . . .

Mr. Harmer cites a metal-fabrication press, which bends and shapes metal. To determine the replacement cost of a press bought in 1982 for $522,000, the company would add 19%—the change in the wholesale price index over the seven years—to arrive at a replacement cost of $621,000.

Since the company assumes that the press has a 12-year life, it then would deduct depreciation from both numbers, putting the replacement value at $257,000. That's still 19% higher than what accounting rules force the company to show on its books. . . .

. . . FMC's numbers . . . also show why many companies oppose the plan: FMC estimates that 1989 operating profit (before interest expense and taxes), reported at $347 million, would have been 10% to 15% lower using current-cost accounting. . . .

. . . SEC [Commissioner Philip] Lochner sees [some other] stumbling block[s]. "What is the current value of Coca-Cola's trademarks? Your guess is as good as theirs," he says. "But we all know it's worth more than the $1 or so it's carried for on Coke's books." (Actually, it's on the books at zero.) . . .

Source: Kevin G. Salwen and Robin Goldwyn Blumenthal, "What's It Worth? Tackling Accounting, SEC Pushes Changes with Broad Impact," *The Wall Street Journal* (September 27, 1990), p. 1.

CHAPTER REVIEW

KEY POINTS

OBJECTIVE 1

Acquisition of Plant Assets

Long-lived assets that are tangible in nature, used in the operations of the business, and not held for sale in the ordinary course of the business are called plant assets or fixed assets. The initial cost of a plant asset includes all expenditures necessary to get it in place and ready for use. Such expenditures include sales taxes, transportation charges, insurance on the asset while in transit, special foundations, installation costs, broker's commissions, and title fees.

OBJECTIVE 2

Nature of Depreciation

As time passes, all plant assets with the exception of land lose their capacity to yield services. This expiration of the cost of plant assets is called depreciation.

OBJECTIVE 3

Accounting for Depreciation

In determining the amount of depreciation, three factors need to be considered: (1) the plant asset's initial cost, (2) the residual value of the asset, and (3) the useful life of the asset. The difference between a plant asset's initial cost and its residual value is the cost that is to be spread over the useful life of the asset.

The four methods of depreciation used most often are summarized as follows:

Straight-line	Provides for equal periodic charges to expense over the estimated useful life of the asset.
Units-of-production............	Yields a depreciation charge that varies with the amount of asset usage. Length of useful life of asset expressed in terms of productive capacity.
Declining-balance	Yields a declining periodic depreciation charge over the estimated useful life of the asset. Rate of depreciation usually twice the straight-line rate computed without regard to residual value. Resulting rate applied to cost of asset less accumulated depreciation.
Sum-of-the-years-digits........	Yields a steadily declining periodic depreciation charge over the estimated useful life of the asset. Successively smaller fraction applied each year to the original cost of the asset less the estimated residual value.

All four depreciation methods will yield the same total depreciation over the life of the asset. However, each method will yield periodic charges which may vary significantly. Because the declining-balance and the sum-of-the-years-digits methods provide a higher depreciation charge in the early years of the life of the asset and a gradually declining charge thereafter, they are referred to as accelerated depreciation methods.

Each of the four depreciation methods can be used to determine the amount of depreciation for federal income tax purposes for plant assets acquired prior to 1981. For plant assets acquired after 1980 and before 1987, either the straight-line method or the Accelerated Cost Recovery System (ACRS) may be used. Under the Tax Reform Act of 1986, modified ACRS (MACRS) must be used for plant assets acquired after 1986.

Minor errors resulting from incorrect estimates of a plant asset's useful life and residual value are corrected by revising estimates used to determine the amount of remaining undepreciated asset cost to be charged to expense in future periods.

When depreciation is to be computed individually on a large number of assets making up a functional group, it is advisable to maintain a subsidiary ledger. Subsidiary ledgers for plant assets are useful in determining the periodic depreciation expense, recording the disposal of individual items, preparing tax returns, and preparing insurance claims in the event of insured losses.

Subsidiary ledgers are not usually maintained for classes of plant assets that are made up of individual items of low unit cost. For such items, depreciation is often determined by periodically taking an inventory of items on hand, estimating their fair value based on original cost, and transferring the remaining amount from the asset account to an expense account.

OBJECTIVE 4

Composite-Rate Depreciation Method

Depreciation determined for an entire group of assets by use of a single rate is referred to as composite-rate depreciation. When this method is used to compute depreciation on a group of assets of differing life spans, a rate based on averages must be developed.

OBJECTIVE 5

Capital and Revenue Expenditures

In addition to the initial cost of acquiring a plant asset, costs for additions made to the asset and other costs related to its efficiency or capacity are called capital expenditures. Costs for additions are debited to an asset account. Costs that add to the utility of the asset for more than one period (called betterments) are also debited to an asset account. Expenditures that increase the useful life of an asset beyond the original estimate are called extraordinary repairs and are debited to the appropriate accumulated depreciation account. Expenditures that benefit only the current period and that maintain normal operating efficiency are chargeable to expense accounts and are called revenue expenditures.

OBJECTIVE 6

Disposal of Plant Assets

Plant assets that are no longer useful may be discarded, sold, or traded in on other plant assets. When disposal of a plant asset occurs, the cost of the plant asset and the accumulated depreciation must be removed from the accounts and any related gain or loss recognized.

OBJECTIVE 7

Acquisition of Plant Assets Through Leasing

Instead of owning a plant asset, a business may acquire the use of a plant asset through a lease. A lease agreement conveys the right to use an asset for a stated period of time. A capital lease is accounted for as if the lessee has, in fact, purchased the asset. An operating lease recognizes lease payments as rent expense for the lessee and as rent income for the lessor.

OBJECTIVE 8

Depletion

The periodic allocation of the cost of metal ores and other minerals removed from the earth is called depletion. The amount of the periodic cost allocation is based on the relationship of the cost to the estimated size of the mineral deposit, and on the quantity extracted during the particular period. An accumulated depletion account is maintained as a contra account to the original cost of the mineral deposit.

OBJECTIVE 9

Intangible Assets

Long-lived assets that are useful in the operations of an enterprise, not held for sale, and without physical qualities usually are classified as intangible assets. The initial cost of an intangible asset normally is amortized over its useful life. Intangible assets include patents, copyrights, and goodwill.

OBJECTIVE 10

Reporting Depreciation Expense, Plant Assets, and Intangible Assets in the Financial Statements

The amount of depreciation expense and the method or methods used in computing depreciation should be disclosed in the financial statements. In addition, each major class of depreciable assets should be disclosed, along with the related accumulated depreciation. Intangible assets are usually presented in the balance sheet in a separate section immediately following plant assets. Each major class of intangible assets should be disclosed at an amount net of amortization taken to date.

OBJECTIVE 11

Replacement Cost of Plant Assets

Plant assets are recorded at cost, and depreciation is based on this cost for financial reporting purposes. However, many accountants recommend that businesses provide supplemental information that indicates the replacement cost, or current cost, of plant assets and the depreciation based on such costs. Such supplemental information would be especially useful in evaluating operating results in periods of inflation.

KEY TERMS

plant assets 330
intangible assets 330
depreciation 331
residual value 332
straight-line method 334
units-of-production method 334
declining-balance method 334
sum-of-the-years-digits method 335
accelerated depreciation methods 336
composite-rate depreciation method 341
capital expenditures 342
revenue expenditures 342
betterments 342
extraordinary repairs 343
boot 346
capital leases 347
operating leases 348
depletion 348
amortization 349
goodwill 350

SELF-EXAMINATION QUESTIONS

Answers at end of chapter.

1. Which of the following expenditures incurred in connection with the acquisition of machinery is a proper charge to the asset account?
   A. Transportation charges
   B. Installation costs
   C. Both A and B
   D. Neither A nor B

2. What is the amount of depreciation, using the sum-of-the-years-digits method, for the first year of use for equipment costing $9,500, with an estimated residual value of $500 and an estimated life of 3 years?
   A. $4,500.00
   B. $3,166.67
   C. $3,000.00
   D. None of the above

3. An example of an accelerated depreciation method is:
   A. straight-line
   B. sum-of-the-years-digits
   C. units-of-production
   D. none of the above

4. A plant asset priced at $100,000 is acquired by trading in a similar asset that has a book value of $25,000. Assuming that the trade-in allowance is $30,000 and that $70,000 cash is paid for the new asset, what is the cost basis for the new asset for financial reporting purposes?
   A. $100,000
   B. $70,000
   C. $30,000
   D. None of the above

5. Which of the following is an example of an intangible asset?
   A. Patents
   B. Goodwill
   C. Copyrights
   D. All of the above

ILLUSTRATIVE PROBLEM

Florence Company acquired new equipment at a cost of $75,000 at the beginning of the fiscal year. The equipment has an estimated life of five years and an estimated residual value of $6,000. The president, John C. Florence, has requested information regarding the alternative depreciation methods.

Instructions:

1. Determine the annual depreciation for each of the five years of estimated useful life of the equipment, the accumulated depreciation at the end of each year, and the book value of the equipment at the end of each year by (a) the straight-line method, (b) the declining-balance method (at twice the straight-line rate), and (c) the sum-of-the-years-digits method.

2. Assume that the equipment was depreciated under the declining-balance method. In the first week of the fifth year, the equipment was traded in for similar equipment priced at $90,000. The trade-in allowance on the old equipment was $8,000, and cash was paid for the balance.
   a. Prepare the journal entry to record the exchange.
   b. What is the cost basis of the new equipment for computing the amount of depreciation allowable for income tax purposes?

SOLUTION

(1)

	Year	Depreciation Expense	Accumulated Depreciation, End of Year	Book Value, End of Year
(a)	1	$13,800	$13,800	$61,200
	2	13,800	27,600	47,400
	3	13,800	41,400	33,600
	4	13,800	55,200	19,800
	5	13,800	69,000	6,000
(b)	1	$30,000	$30,000	$45,000
	2	18,000	48,000	27,000
	3	10,800	58,800	16,200
	4	6,480	65,280	9,720
	5	3,720*	69,000	6,000
(c)	1	$23,000	$23,000	$52,000
	2	18,400	41,400	33,600
	3	13,800	55,200	19,800
	4	9,200	64,400	10,600
	5	4,600	69,000	6,000

*The asset is not depreciated below the estimated residual value of $6,000.

(2)(a)		
Accumulated Depreciation—Equipment	65,280	
Equipment..........	90,000	
Loss on Disposal of Plant Assets..........	1,720	
Equipment..........		75,000
Cash..........		82,000

(b)	
Book value of old equipment..........	$ 9,720
Boot given (cash)..........	82,000
Cost basis of new equipment for income tax purposes.....	$91,720

or

Price of new equipment..........	$90,000
Plus unrecognized loss on old equipment..........	1,720
Cost basis of new equipment for income tax purposes	$91,720

DISCUSSION QUESTIONS

8–1. Which of the following qualities are characteristic of plant assets? (a) intangible, (b) tangible, (c) capable of repeated use in the operations of the business, (d) held for sale in the normal course of business, (e) used continuously in the operations of the business, (f) long-lived.

8–2. Walton Office Equipment Co. has a fleet of automobiles and trucks for use by salespersons and for delivery of office supplies and equipment. Sullivan Auto Sales Inc. has automobiles and trucks for sale. Under what caption would the automobiles and trucks be reported on the balance sheet of (a) Walton Office Equipment Co., (b) Sullivan Auto Sales Inc.?

8–3. Tomlin Company acquired an adjacent vacant lot as a speculation. The lot will hopefully be sold in the future at a gain. Where should such real estate be listed in the balance sheet?

8–4. Which of the following expenditures incurred in connection with the acquisition of a lathe should be charged to the asset account? (a) sales tax on purchase price, (b) freight charges, (c) cost of special foundation, (d) new parts to replace those damaged in unloading, (e) fee paid to factory representative for installation, (f) insurance while in transit.

8–5. Which of the following expenditures incurred in connection with the purchase of a secondhand printing press should be debited to the asset account? (a) freight charges, (b) repair of vandalism damages that occurred during installation, (c) replacement of worn-out parts, (d) installation costs.

8–6. To increase its parking area, Westex Shopping Center acquired adjoining land for $70,000 and a building located on the land for $35,000. The net cost of razing the building and leveling the land was $8,000, after amounts received from the sale of salvaged building materials were deducted. What accounts should be debited for (a) the cost of the land ($70,000), (b) the cost of the building ($35,000), (c) the net cost of preparing the land ($8,000)?

8–7. Are the amounts at which plant assets are reported in the balance sheet their approximate market values as of the balance sheet date? Discuss.

8–8. (a) Does the recognition of depreciation in the accounts provide a special cash fund for the replacement of plant assets? Explain. (b) Describe the nature of depreciation as the term is used in accounting.

8–9. Name the three factors that need to be considered in determining the amount of periodic depreciation.

8–10. Is it necessary for an enterprise to use the same method of computing depreciation (a) for all classes of its depreciable assets, (b) in the financial statements and in the determination of income taxes?

8–11. Of the four common depreciation methods, which is most widely used?

8–12. Convert each of the following estimates of useful life to a straight-line depreciation rate, stated as a percent, assuming that the residual value of the plant asset is to be ignored: (a) 4 years, (b) 5 years, (c) 10 years, (d) 20 years, (e) 25 years, (f) 40 years, (g) 50 years.

8–13. A plant asset with a cost of $95,000 has an estimated residual value of $5,000 and an estimated useful life of 6 years. What is the amount of the annual depreciation, computed by the straight-line method?

8–14. A plant asset with a cost of $65,000 has an estimated residual value of $5,000 and an estimated productive capacity of 600,000 units. What is the amount of annual depreciation, computed by the units-of-production method, for a year in which production is (a) 60,000 units, (b) 90,000 units?

8–15. The declining-balance method, at double the straight-line rate, is to be used for an asset with a cost of $100,000, estimated residual value of $10,000, and estimated useful life of 5 years. What is the depreciation for the first fiscal year, assuming that the asset was placed in service at the beginning of the year?

8–16. An asset with a cost of $22,000, an estimated residual value of $1,000, and an estimated useful life of 6 years is to be depreciated by the sum-of-the-years-digits method. (a) What is the denominator of the depreciation fraction? (b) What is the amount of depreciation for the first full year of use? (c) What is the amount of depreciation for the second full year of use?

8–17. (a) Name the two accelerated depreciation methods described in this chapter. (b) Why are the accelerated depreciation methods used frequently for income tax purposes? (c) What is the Modified Accelerated Cost Recovery System (MACRS), and under what conditions is it used?

8–18. A plant asset with a cost of $245,000 has an estimated residual value of $5,000, an estimated useful life of 40 years, and is depreciated by the straight-line method. (a) What is the amount of the annual depreciation? (b) What is the book value at the end of the twentieth year of use? (c) If at the start of the twenty-first year it is estimated that the remaining life is 25 years and that the residual value is $5,000, what is the depreciation expense for each of the remaining 25 years?

8–19. The cost of a composite group of equipment is $600,000 and the annual depreciation, computed on the individual items, totals $60,000. (a) What is the composite straight-line depreciation rate? (b) What would the rate be if the total depreciation amounted to $66,000 instead of $60,000?

8–20. (a) Differentiate between capital expenditures and revenue expenditures. (b) Why are some items that have the characteristics of capital expenditures treated as revenue expenditures?

8–21. Immediately after a used truck is acquired, a new motor is installed and the tires are replaced at a total cost of $4,150. Is this a capital expenditure or a revenue expenditure?

8–22. For a number of plant asset ledger accounts of an enterprise, the balance in accumulated depreciation is exactly equal to the cost of the asset. (a) Is it permissible to record additional depreciation on the assets if they are still useful to the enterprise? Explain. (b) When should an entry be made to remove the cost and accumulated depreciation from the accounts?

8–23. In what sections of the income statement are gains and losses from the disposal of plant assets presented?

8–24. A plant asset priced at $100,000 is acquired by trading in a similar asset and paying cash for the remainder. (a) Assuming that the trade-in allowance is $20,000, what is the amount of boot given? (b) Assuming that the book value of the asset traded in is $30,000, what is the cost basis of the new asset for financial reporting purposes? (c) What is the cost basis of the new asset for the computation of depreciation for federal income tax purposes?

8–25. Assume the same facts as in Question 8–24, except that the book value of the asset traded in is $10,000. (a) What is the cost basis of the new asset for financial reporting purposes? (b) What is the cost basis of the new asset for the computation of depreciation for federal income tax purposes?

8–26. Differentiate between a capital lease and an operating lease.

8–27. What is the term applied to the periodic charge for (a) ore removed from a mine, (b) the write-off of the cost of an intangible asset?

8–28. (a) Over what period of time should the cost of a patent acquired by purchase be amortized? (b) In general, what is the required treatment for research and development costs?

Real World Focus

8–29. Is the use of replacement cost generally accepted for accounting for plant assets and depreciation?

8–30. A corporation purchased land and the building on the land with the intent of razing the building. Would the costs of demolition be reflected as part of the cost of the land? (Adapted from "Technical Issues Feature," *Journal of Accountancy* (December, 1987), p. 80.)

Real World Focus

8–31. A company has developed a tract of land into a ski resort. The company has cut the trees, cleared and graded the land and hills, and constructed ski lifts. (a) Should the tree cutting, land clearing, and grading costs of constructing the ski slopes be debited to the land account? (b) If such costs are debited to Land, should they be depreciated? (Adapted from "Technical Issues Feature," *Journal of Accountancy* (December, 1987), p. 82.)

Real World Focus

8–32. The financial statements of La-Z-Boy Chair Company contain the following footnote:

> The Company has several long-term leases covering manufacturing facilities. The lease agreements require the Company to insure and maintain the facilities and provide for annual payments, which include interest. These leases give the Company the option to purchase the facilities for nominal amounts, or in some instances to renew the leases for extended periods at nominal annual rentals.

Would these leases be classified as operating or capital leases? Discuss.

Ethics Discussion Case

8–33. Ken Cantrell, CPA, is an assistant to the controller of Sinclair Inc. In his spare time, Ken also prepares tax returns and performs general accounting services for clients. Frequently, Ken performs these services after his normal working hours, using Sinclair Inc.'s microcomputers and laser printers. Occasionally, Ken's clients will call him at the office during regular working hours.

Discuss whether Ken Cantrell is performing in an ethical manner.

EXERCISES

Ex. 8–34. Depreciation by three methods. OBJ. 3

A plant asset acquired on January 2 at a cost of $275,000 has an estimated useful life of 10 years. Assuming that it will have no residual value, determine the depreciation for each of the first two years (a) by the straight-line method, (b) by the declining-balance method, using twice the straight-line rate, and (c) by the sum-of-the-years-digits method.

Ex. 8–35. Depreciation by units-of-production method. OBJ. 3

A diesel-powered generator with a cost of $170,000 and estimated salvage value of $10,000 is expected to have a useful operating life of 40,000 hours. During May, the generator was operated 320 hours. Determine the depreciation for the month.

Ex. 8–36. Depreciation by units-of-production method. OBJ. 3

Balances in Trucks and in Accumulated Depreciation—Trucks at the end of the year, prior to adjustment, are $159,500 and $49,600, respectively. Details of the subsidiary ledger are as follows:

Truck No.	Cost	Estimated Residual Value	Estimated Useful Life in Miles	Accumulated Depreciation at Beginning of Year	Miles Operated During Year
1	$67,500	$7,500	200,000	$18,600	30,000
2	45,000	5,000	200,000	7,700	20,000
3	28,000	4,000	150,000	23,300	4,500
4	19,000	1,000	150,000	—	17,500

(a) Determine the depreciation rates per mile and the amount to be credited to the accumulated depreciation section of each of the subsidiary accounts for the current year. (b) Present the journal entry to record depreciation for the year.

Ex. 8–37.
Depreciation by three methods.
OBJ. 3

An item of equipment acquired at the beginning of the fiscal year at a cost of $52,400 has an estimated residual value of $2,000 and an estimated useful life of 8 years. Determine the following: (a) the amount of annual depreciation by the straight-line method, (b) the amount of depreciation for the second year computed by the declining-balance method (at twice the straight-line rate), (c) the amount of depreciation for the second year computed by the sum-of-the-years-digits method.

Ex. 8–38.
Depreciation by accelerated depreciation methods.
OBJ. 3

A piece of machinery acquired at a cost of $40,000 has an estimated residual value of $4,000 and an estimated useful life of 5 years. It was placed in service on April 1 of the current fiscal year, which ends on December 31. Determine the depreciation for the current fiscal year and for the following fiscal year by (a) the declining-balance method, at twice the straight-line rate, and (b) the sum-of-the-years-digits method.

Ex. 8–39.
Revision of depreciation.
OBJ. 3

An item of equipment acquired on January 4, 1988, at a cost of $35,000 has an estimated residual value of $5,000 and an estimated useful life of 10 years. Depreciation has been recorded for the first four years ended December 31, 1991, by the straight-line method. Determine the amount of depreciation for the current year ended December 31, 1992, if the revised estimated residual value is $3,800 and the revised estimated remaining useful life (including the current year) is 8 years.

Ex. 8–40.
Composite depreciation rate.
OBJ. 4

A composite depreciation rate of 15% is applied annually to a plant asset account. Details of the account for the fiscal year ended December 31 are as follows:

Delivery Equipment

Jan. 1	Balance	297,750	Feb. 27	16,500
Feb. 19		19,650	Aug. 15	10,700
May 3		21,600	Dec. 20	16,550
July 30		17,000		
Dec. 1		21,000		

Determine the depreciation for the year according to each of the following assumptions: (a) that all additions and retirements have occurred uniformly throughout the year, (b) that additions and retirements during the first half of the year occurred on the first day of that year and those during the second half occurred on the first day of the succeeding year.

Ex. 8–41.
Major repair to plant asset.
OBJ. 5

A number of major structural repairs completed at the beginning of the current fiscal year at a cost of $130,000 are expected to extend the life of a building 10 years beyond the original estimate. The original cost of the building was $1,000,000, and it has been depreciated by the straight-line method for 25 years. Residual value is expected to be negligible and has been ignored. The balance of the related accumulated depreciation account after the depreciation adjustment at the end of the preceding year is $500,000. (a) What has the amount of annual depreciation been in past years? (b) To what account should the cost of repairs ($130,000) be debited? (c) What is the book value of the building after the repairs have been recorded? (d) What is the amount of depreciation for the current year, using the straight-line method (assume that the repairs were completed at the very beginning of the year)?

Ex. 8–42.
Entries for sale of plant asset.
OBJ. 6

A piece of equipment acquired on January 2, 1989, at a cost of $55,000 has an estimated useful life of 5 years, an estimated residual value of $5,000, and is depreciated by the straight-line method. (a) What was the book value of the equipment at December 31, 1992, the end of the fiscal year? (b) Assuming that the equipment was sold on July 1, 1993, for $7,500, prepare journal entries to record (1) depreciation for the six months of the current year ending December 31, 1993, and (2) the sale of the equipment.

Ex. 8–43.
Disposal of plant asset.
OBJ. 6

A piece of equipment acquired on January 3, 1989, at a cost of $22,500 has an estimated useful life of 4 years and an estimated residual value of $2,500. (a) What was the annual amount of depreciation for the years 1989, 1990, and 1991, assuming the use of the straight-line method of depreciation? (b) What was the book value of the equipment on January 1, 1992? (c) Assuming that the equipment was sold on January 2, 1992, for $6,000, prepare the journal entry to record the sale. (d) Assuming that the equipment had been sold for $9,000 on January 2, 1992, instead of $6,000, prepare the journal entry to record the sale.

Ex. 8–44.
Entries for loss on trade of plant asset.
OBJ. 6

On July 1, Farrell Co. acquired a new computer with a list price of $75,000. Farrell received a trade-in allowance of $15,000 on an old computer of a similar type, paid cash of $10,000, and gave a series of five notes payable for the remainder. The following information about the old computer is obtained from the account in the office equipment ledger: cost, $53,750; accumulated depreciation on December 31, the end of the preceding fiscal year, $32,500; annual depreciation, $10,000. Present entries to record: (a) the current depreciation on the old computer to the date of trade-in, (b) the transaction on July 1 for financial reporting purposes.

Ex. 8–45.
Entries for gain on trade of plant asset.
OBJ. 6

On July 1, Ross Co. acquired a new computer with a list price of $125,000. Ross received a trade-in allowance of $15,000 on an old computer of a similar type, paid cash of $30,000, and gave a series of five notes payable for the remainder. The following information about the old computer is obtained from the account in the office equipment ledger: cost, $82,500; accumulated depreciation on December 31, the end of the preceding fiscal year, $62,500; annual depreciation, $15,000. Present entries to record: (a) the current depreciation on the old computer to the date of trade-in, (b) the transaction on July 1 for financial reporting purposes.

Ex. 8–46.
Depreciation on asset acquired by exchange.
OBJ. 6

On the first day of the fiscal year, a delivery truck with a list price of $32,000 was acquired in an exchange for an old delivery truck and $27,500 cash. The old truck has a book value of $3,000 at the date of the exchange. The new truck is to be depreciated over 5 years by the straight-line method. The estimated residual value is $2,000. Determine the following: (a) annual depreciation for financial reporting purposes, (b) annual depreciation for income tax purposes, (c) annual depreciation for financial reporting purposes, assuming that the book value of the old delivery truck was $5,500, (d) annual depreciation for income tax purposes, assuming the same book value as indicated in (c).

Ex. 8–47.
Amortization and depletion entries.
OBJ. 8, 9

On July 1 of the current fiscal year ended December 31, Stone Co. acquired a patent for $75,000 and mineral rights for $250,000. The patent, which expires in 7 years, is expected to have value for 5 years. The mineral deposit is estimated at 500,000 tons of ore of uniform grade. Present entries to record the following for the current year: (a) amortization of the patent, (b) depletion, assuming that 75,000 tons were mined during the year.

Ex. 8–48.
Amortization and depletion entries.
OBJ. 8, 9

For each of the following unrelated transactions, (a) determine the amount of the amortization or depletion expense for the current year, and (b) present the adjusting entries required to record each expense.

(1) Timber rights on a tract of land were purchased for $90,000. The stand of timber is estimated at 300,000 board feet. During the current year, 50,000 board feet of timber were cut.

(2) Governmental and legal costs of $34,100 were incurred at midyear in obtaining a patent with an estimated economic life of 11 years. Amortization is to be for one-half year.

(3) Goodwill in the amount of $120,000 was purchased on January 5, the first month of the fiscal year. It is decided to amortize over the maximum period allowable.

PROBLEMS

Pb. 8–49.
Allocation of expenditures and receipts to plant asset accounts.
OBJ. 1

The following expenditures and receipts are related to land, land improvements, and buildings acquired for use in a business enterprise. The receipts are identified by an asterisk.

(a)	Cost of real estate acquired as a plant site: Land	$ 210,000
	Building	60,000
(b)	Finder's fee paid to real estate agency	18,900
(c)	Fee paid to attorney for title search	$ 1,500
(d)	Delinquent real estate taxes on property, assumed by purchaser	11,250
(e)	Cost of razing and removing the building	8,500
(f)	Proceeds from sale of salvage materials from old building	1,500*
(g)	Cost of land fill and grading	13,500
(h)	Architect's and engineer's fees for plans and supervision	95,000
(i)	Premium on 1-year insurance policy during construction	9,000
(j)	Cost of paving parking lot to be used by customers	17,500
(k)	Cost of trees and shrubbery planted	15,000
(l)	Special assessment paid to city for extension of water main to the property	7,500
(m)	Cost of repairing windstorm damage during construction	2,250
(n)	Cost of repairing vandalism damage during construction	500
(o)	Proceeds from insurance company for windstorm and vandalism damage	2,200*
(p)	Interest incurred on building loan during construction	85,000
(q)	Money borrowed to pay building contractor	1,000,000*
(r)	Paid to building contractor for new building	1,250,000
(s)	Refund of premium on insurance policy (i) canceled after 11 months	750*

Instructions:

Assign each expenditure and receipt (indicate receipts by an asterisk) to Land (permanently capitalized), Land Improvements (limited life), Building, or Other Accounts. Identify each item by letter and list the amounts in columnar form, as follows:

Item	Land	Land Improvements	Building	Other Accounts
	$	$	$	$

Pb. 8–50.
Depreciation by four methods.
OBJ. 3

Jacobsen Company purchased equipment on July 1, 1991, for $90,000. The equipment was expected to have a useful life of 3 years, or 7,000 operating hours, and a residual value of $6,000. The equipment was used for 700 hours during 1991 and for 2,800, 2,400 and 1,100 hours for 1992, 1993, and 1994, respectively.

Instructions:

Determine the amount of depreciation expense for the years ended December 31, 1991, 1992, 1993, and 1994 by (a) the straight-line method, (b) the declining-balance method, using twice the straight-line rate, (c) the sum-of-the-years-digits method, and (d) the units-of-production method.

Pb. 8–51.
Determination of depreciation by three methods; trade of plant asset.
OBJ. 3, 6

An item of new equipment, acquired at a cost of $160,000 at the beginning of a fiscal year, has an estimated useful life of 4 years and an estimated residual value of $10,000. The manager requested information regarding the effect of alternative methods on the amount of depreciation expense each year. Upon the basis of the data presented to the manager, the declining-balance method was selected.

In the first week of the fourth year, the equipment was traded in for similar equipment priced at $225,000. The trade-in allowance on the old equipment was $25,000, cash of $50,000 was paid, and a note payable was issued for the balance.

Instructions:

(1) Determine the annual depreciation expense for each of the estimated 4 years of use, the accumulated depreciation at the end of each year, and the book value of the equipment at the end of each year by (a) the straight-line method, (b) the declining-balance method (at twice the straight-line rate), and (c) the sum-of-the-years-digits method. The following columnar headings are suggested for each schedule:

Year	Depreciation Expense	Accumulated Depreciation, End of Year	Book Value, End of Year

(2) For financial reporting purposes, determine the cost basis of the new equipment acquired in the exchange.
(3) Present the entry to record the exchange.
(4) What is the cost basis of the new equipment for purposes of computing the amount of depreciation allowable for income tax purposes?
(5) Present the entry to record the exchange, assuming that the trade-in allowance was $15,000 instead of $25,000.
(6) What is the cost basis of the new equipment for purposes of computing the amount of depreciation allowable for income tax purposes, assuming the data presented in Instruction (5)?

Pb. 8–52.
Correcting entries.
OBJ. 1, 5, 6

The following recording errors occurred and were discovered during the current year:

(a) The $1,100 cost of repairing factory equipment damaged in the process of installation was charged to Factory Equipment.
(b) Office equipment with a book value of $6,700 was traded in for similar equipment with a list price of $50,000. The trade-in allowance on the old equipment was $10,500, and a note payable was given for the balance. A gain on disposal of plant assets of $3,800 was recorded.
(c) Property taxes of $5,000 were paid on real estate acquired during the year and were debited to Property Tax Expense. Of this amount, $2,000 was for taxes that were delinquent at the time the property was acquired.
(d) The sale of a computer for $875 was recorded by an $875 credit to Office Equipment. The original cost of the computer was $3,900, and the related balance in Accumulated Depreciation at the beginning of the current year was $3,000. Depreciation of $400 accrued during the current year, prior to the sale, had not been recorded.
(e) The $1,900 cost of a major motor overhaul expected to prolong the life of a truck two years beyond the original estimate was debited to Delivery Expense. The truck was acquired new four years earlier.
(f) The $11,100 cost of repainting several interior rooms of a building was debited to Building. The building had been owned and occupied for 20 years.
(g) The cost of a razed building, $25,000, was debited to Loss on Disposal of Plant Assets and credited to Building. The building and the land on which it was located had been acquired at a total cost of $100,000 ($75,000 debited to Land, $25,000 debited to Building) as a parking area for the adjacent plant.
(h) The fee of $7,500 paid to the wrecking contractor to raze the building in (g) was debited to Miscellaneous Expense.
(i) A $350 charge for incoming transportation on an item of factory equipment was debited to Transportation In.

Instructions:

Journalize the entries to correct the errors during the current year. Identify each entry by letter.

Pb. 8–53. **Transactions for plant assets, including trade.** OBJ. 1, 5, 6

The following transactions, adjusting entries, and closing entries were completed by Rhodes Furniture Co. during 3 fiscal years ending on June 30. All are related to the use of delivery equipment. The declining-balance method (twice the straight-line rate) of depreciation is used:

1991–1992 Fiscal Year

July 1. Purchased a used delivery truck for $18,500, paying cash.
3. Paid $1,500 to replace the automatic transmission and install new brakes on the truck. (Debit Delivery Equipment.)
Dec. 20. Paid garage $220 for changing the oil, replacing the oil filter, and tuning the engine on the delivery truck.
June 30. Recorded depreciation on the truck for the fiscal year. The estimated useful life of the truck is 8 years, with a residual value of $3,000.
30. Closed the appropriate accounts to the income summary account.

1992–1993 Fiscal Year

Sept. 2. Paid garage $235 to tune the engine and make other minor repairs on the truck.
Oct. 31. Traded in the used truck for a new truck priced at $30,250, receiving a trade-in allowance of $14,000 and paying the balance in cash. (Record depreciation to date in 1992.)
June 30. Recorded depreciation on the truck. It has an estimated trade-in value of $2,750 and an estimated life of 10 years.
30. Closed the appropriate accounts to the income summary account.

1993–1994 Fiscal Year

Apr. 1. Purchased a new truck for $36,000, paying cash.
2. Sold the truck purchased October 31, 1992, for $22,500. (Record depreciation for the year.)
June 30. Recorded depreciation on the remaining truck. It has an estimated residual value of $4,500 and an estimated useful life of 8 years.
30. Closed the appropriate accounts to the income summary account.

Instructions:

(1) Open the following accounts in the ledger:
122 Delivery Equipment
123 Accumulated Depreciation—Delivery Equipment
616 Depreciation Expense—Delivery Equipment
617 Truck Repair Expense
812 Gain on Disposal of Plant Assets
(2) Record the transactions and the adjusting and closing entries. Post to the accounts and extend the balances after each posting.

If the working papers correlating with the textbook are not used, omit Pb. 8–54.

Pb. 8–54. **Plant asset transactions and subsidiary plant ledger.** OBJ. 3, 6

Lasorta Press Co. maintains a subsidiary equipment ledger for the printing equipment and accumulated depreciation accounts in the general ledger. A small portion of the subsidiary ledger, the two controlling accounts, and a journal are presented in the working papers. The company computes depreciation on each individual item of equipment. Transactions and adjusting entries affecting the printing equipment are described as follows:

1991
July 2. Purchased a binder (Model G, Serial No. 19752) from Maas Manufacturing Co. on account for $102,000. The estimated useful life of the asset is 12 years, it is expected to have no residual value, and the straight-line method of depreciation is to be used. (This is the only transaction of the year that directly affected the printing equipment account.)

Dec. 31. Recorded depreciation for the year in subsidiary accounts 120-22 to 120-24, and inserted the new balances. (An assistant recorded the depreciation and the new balances in accounts 120-1 to 120-21.)

31. Journalized and posted the annual adjusting entry for depreciation on printing equipment. The depreciation for the year, recorded in subsidiary accounts 120-1 to 120-21, totaled $51,500 to which was added the depreciation entered in accounts 120-22 to 120-24.

1992

Sept. 30. Purchased a Model P rotary press from Birk Press Inc., priced at $60,000, giving the Model 11 Linotype (Account No. 120-23) in exchange, plus $15,000 cash and a series of ten $3,000 notes payable, maturing at 6-month intervals. The estimated useful life of the new press is 10 years, and it is expected to have a residual value of $6,250. (Recorded depreciation to date in 1992 on item traded in.)

Instructions:

(1) Journalize the transaction of July 2. Post to Printing Equipment in the general ledger and to Account No. 120-24 in the subsidiary ledger.
(2) Journalize the adjusting entry on December 31 and post to Accumulated Depreciation — Printing Equipment in the general ledger.
(3) Journalize the entries required by the purchase of printing equipment on September 30. Post to Printing Equipment and to Accumulated Depreciation — Printing Equipment in the general ledger and to Account Nos. 120-23 and 120-25 in the subsidiary ledger.
(4) If the rotary press purchased on September 30 had been depreciated by the declining-balance method at twice the straight-line rate, determine the depreciation on this press for the fiscal years ending (a) December 31, 1992, and (b) December 31, 1993.

Pb. 8–55. Income statement and balance sheet for corporation.

OBJ. 4, 9, 10

The trial balance of Staub Corporation at the end of the current calendar year, before adjustments, is as follows:

Cash	27,700	
Accounts Receivable	62,600	
Allowance for Doubtful Accounts		500
Merchandise Inventory	179,200	
Prepaid Expense	10,750	
Land	50,000	
Buildings	225,000	
Accumulated Depreciation — Buildings		90,000
Office Equipment	41,100	
Accumulated Depreciation — Office Equipment		17,600
Store Equipment	52,200	
Accumulated Depreciation — Store Equipment		22,100
Delivery Equipment	57,850	
Accumulated Depreciation — Delivery Equipment		21,750
Patents	18,000	
Accounts Payable		40,200
Notes Payable (short-term)		25,000
Capital Stock		250,000
Retained Earnings		180,250
Dividends	70,000	
Sales (net)		999,750
Purchases (net)	706,550	
Operating Expenses (controlling account)	144,600	
Interest Expense	1,600	
	1,647,150	1,647,150

Data needed for year-end adjustments:

(a) Estimated uncollectible accounts at December 31, $7,200.
(b) Insurance and other prepaid operating expenses expired during the year, $6,750.
(c) Depreciation is computed at composite rates on the average of the beginning and the ending balances of the plant asset accounts. The beginning balances and rates are as follows:

Office Equipment, $37,900; 10% — Delivery Equipment, $57,150; 20%
Store Equipment, $49,200; 8% — Buildings, $225,000; 2%

(d) Amortization of patents computed for the year, $3,000.
(e) Accrued liabilities at the end of the year, $2,000, of which $250 is for interest on the notes and $1,750 is for wages and other operating expenses.

Instructions:

(1) Prepare a multiple-step income statement for the current year. The merchandise inventory at December 31 is $171,000.
(2) Prepare a balance sheet in report form, presenting the plant assets in the manner illustrated in this chapter.

ALTERNATE PROBLEMS

Pb. 8–49A.
Allocation of expenditures and receipts to plant asset accounts.
OBJ. 1
SPREADSHEET PROBLEM

The following expenditures and receipts are related to land, land improvements, and buildings acquired for use in a business enterprise. The receipts are identified by an asterisk.

(a)	Cost of real estate acquired as a plant site: Land	$140,000
	Building	65,000
(b)	Delinquent real estate taxes on property assumed by purchaser	11,250
(c)	Cost of razing and removing the building	6,400
(d)	Fee paid to attorney for title search	2,750
(e)	Cost of land fill and grading	14,500
(f)	Architect's and engineer's fees for plans and supervision	54,000
(g)	Premium on 1-year insurance policy during construction	4,200
(h)	Paid to building contractor for new building	600,000
(i)	Cost of repairing windstorm damage during construction	1,250
(j)	Cost of paving parking lot to be used by customers	20,000
(k)	Cost of trees and shrubbery planted	32,500
(l)	Special assessment paid to city for extension of water main to the property	7,500
(m)	Cost of repairing vandalism damage during construction	500
(n)	Interest incurred on building loan during construction	40,000
(o)	Cost of floodlights installed on parking lot	13,500
(p)	Proceeds from sale of salvage materials from old building	1,100*
(q)	Money borrowed to pay building contractor	500,000*
(r)	Proceeds from insurance company for windstorm damage	1,000*
(s)	Refund of premium on insurance policy (g) canceled after 11 months	350*

Instructions:

Assign each expenditure and receipt (indicate receipts by an asterisk) to Land (permanently capitalized), Land Improvements (limited life), Building, or Other Accounts. Identify each item by letter and list the amount in columnar form, as follows:

Item	Land	Land Improvements	Building	Other Accounts
	$	$	$	$

Pb. 8–50A.
Depreciation by four methods.
OBJ. 3

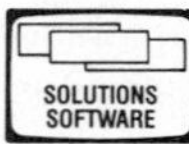

Thompson Company purchased equipment on January 2, 1992, for $80,000. The equipment was expected to have a useful life of 4 years, or 14,800 operating hours, and a residual value of $6,000. The equipment was used for 3,200 hours during 1992 and for 4,000, 3,800, and 3,800 hours for 1993, 1994, and 1995, respectively.

Instructions:

Determine the amount of depreciation expense for the years ending December 31, 1992, 1993, 1994, and 1995 by (a) the straight-line method, (b) the declining-balance method, using twice the straight-line rate, (c) the sum-of-the-years-digits method, and (d) the units-of-production method.

Pb. 8–51A.
Depreciation by three methods; trade of plant asset.
OBJ. 3, 6

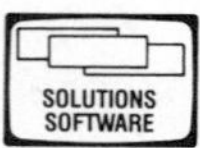

An item of new equipment, acquired at a cost of $150,000 at the beginning of a fiscal year, has an estimated useful life of 5 years and an estimated residual value of $15,000. The manager requested information regarding the effect of alternative methods on the amount of depreciation expense each year. Upon the basis of the data presented to the manager, the declining-balance method was selected.

In the first week of the fifth year, the equipment was traded in for similar equipment priced at $170,000. The trade-in allowance on the old equipment was $20,000, cash of $25,000 was paid, and a note payable was issued for the balance.

Instructions:

(1) Determine the annual depreciation expense for each of the estimated 5 years of use, the accumulated depreciation at the end of each year, and the book value of the equipment at the end of each year by (a) the straight-line method, (b) the sum-of-the-years-digits method, and (c) the declining-balance method (at twice the straight-line rate). The following columnar headings are suggested for each schedule:

Year	Depreciation Expense	Accumulated Depreciation, End of Year	Book Value, End of Year

(2) For financial reporting purposes, determine the cost basis of the new equipment acquired in the exchange.
(3) Present the entry to record the exchange.
(4) What is the cost basis of the new equipment for purposes of computing the amount of depreciation allowable for income tax purposes?
(5) Present the entry to record the exchange, assuming that the trade-in allowance was $10,000 instead of $20,000.
(6) What is the cost basis of the new equipment for purposes of computing the amount of depreciation allowable for income tax purposes, assuming the data presented in Instruction (5)?

Pb. 8–52A.
Correcting entries.
OBJ. 1, 5, 6

The following recording errors occurred and were discovered during the current year:

(a) The $1,100 cost of repairing computer equipment damaged in the process of installation was charged to Office Equipment.
(b) The sale of an electronic typewriter for $475 was recorded by a $475 credit to Office Equipment. The original cost of the machine was $1,300, and the related balance in Accumulated Depreciation at the beginning of the current year was $775. Depreciation of $100 accrued during the current year, prior to the sale, had not been recorded.
(c) Property taxes of $5,000 were paid on real estate acquired during the year and were debited to Property Tax Expense. Of this amount, $3,500 was for taxes that were delinquent at the time the property was acquired.
(d) Office equipment with a book value of $10,000 was traded in for similar equipment with a list price of $62,500. The trade-in allowance on the old equipment was $15,000, and a note payable was given for the balance. A gain on disposal of plant assets of $5,000 was recorded.

(e) The $1,450 cost of a major motor overhaul expected to prolong the life of a truck two years beyond the original estimate was debited to Delivery Expense. The truck was acquired new four years earlier.
(f) A $450 charge for incoming transportation on the purchase of merchandise was debited to Factory Equipment.
(g) The cost of a razed building, $45,000 was debited to Loss on Disposal of Plant Assets and credited to Building. The building and the land on which it was located had been acquired at a total cost of $110,000 ($65,000 debited to Land, $45,000 debited to Building) as a parking area for the adjacent plant.
(h) The fee of $7,500 paid to the wrecking contractor to raze the building in (g) was debited to Miscellaneous Expense.
(i) The $9,000 cost of repainting several interior rooms of a building was debited to Building. The building had been owned and occupied for 20 years.

Instructions:

Journalize the entries to correct the errors during the curent year. Identify each entry by letter.

Pb. 8–53A.
Transactions for plant assets, including trade.
OBJ. 1, 5, 6

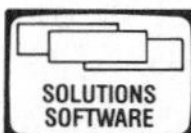

The following transactions, adjusting entries, and closing entries were completed by Robb Furniture Co. during a 3-year period. All are related to the use of delivery equipment. The declining-balance method (twice the straight-line rate) of depreciation is used.

1991
Jan. 4. Purchased a used delivery truck for $12,800, paying cash.
7. Paid $1,600 for major repairs to the truck.
Aug. 11. Paid garage $195 for miscellaneous repairs to the truck.
Dec. 31. Recorded depreciation on the truck for the fiscal year. The estimated useful life of the truck is 4 years, with a residual value of $2,000.
31. Closed the appropriate accounts to the income summary account.

1992
June 30. Traded in the used truck for a new truck priced at $26,000, receiving a trade-in allowance of $6,000 and paying the balance in cash. (Record depreciation to date in 1992.)
Nov. 4. Paid garage $195 for miscellaneous repairs to the truck.
Dec. 31. Recorded depreciation on the truck. It has an estimated residual value of $5,250 and an estimated useful life of 5 years.
31. Closed the appropriate accounts to the income summary account.

1993
Oct. 1. Purchased a new truck for $24,400, paying cash.
2. Sold the truck purchased in 1992 for $16,000. (Record depreciation to date in 1992.)
Dec. 31. Recorded depreciation on the remaining truck. It has an estimated residual value of $1,500 and an estimated useful life of 8 years.
31. Closed the appropriate accounts to the income summary account.

Instructions:

(1) Open the following accounts in the ledger:

122 Delivery Equipment
123 Accumulated Depreciation—Delivery Equipment
616 Depreciation Expense—Delivery Equipment
617 Truck Repair Expense
812 Gain on Disposal of Plant Assets

(2) Record the transactions and the adjusting and closing entries. Post to the accounts and extend the balances after each posting.

If the working papers correlating with the textbook are not used, omit Pb. 8–54A.

Pb. 8–54A.
Plant asset transactions and subsidiary plant asset ledger.
OBJ. 3, 6

Cosby Press Inc. maintains a subsidiary equipment ledger for the printing equipment and accumulated depreciation accounts in the general ledger. A small portion of the subsidiary ledger, the two controlling accounts, and a journal are presented in the working papers. The company computes depreciation on each individual item of equipment. Transactions and adjusting entries affecting the printing equipment are described as follows:

1991
Sept. 1. Purchased a binder (Model C6, Serial No. 2795) from Weiss Manufacturing Co. on account for $90,000. The estimated useful life of the asset is 10 years, it is expected to have no residual value, and the straight-line method of depreciation is to be used. (This is the only transaction of the year that directly affected the printing equipment account.)
Dec. 31. Recorded depreciation for the year in subsidiary accounts 120-22 to 120-24, and inserted the balances. (An assistant recorded the depreciation and the new balances in accounts 120-1 to 120-21.)
31. Journalized and posted the annual adjusting entry for depreciation on printing equipment. The depreciation for the year, recorded in subsidiary accounts 120-1 to 120-21, totaled $56,200, to which was added the depreciation entered in accounts 120-22 to 120-24.

1992
Mar. 31. Purchased a Model 17 rotary press from Clark Press Inc., priced at $50,000, giving the Model 11 Linotype (Account No. 120-23) in exchange plus $7,500 cash and a series of four $5,000 notes payable, maturing at 6-month intervals. The estimated useful life of the new press is 10 years, and it is expected to have a residual value of $1,750. (Recorded depreciation to date in 1992 on item traded in.)

Instructions:

(1) Journalize the transaction of September 1. Post to Printing Equipment in the general ledger and to Account No. 120-24 in the subsidiary ledger.
(2) Journalize the adjusting entry required on December 31 and post to Accumulated Depreciation—Printing Equipment in the general ledger.
(3) Journalize the entries required by the purchase of printing equipment on March 31. Post to Printing Equipment and to Accumulated Depreciation—Printing Equipment in the general ledger and to Account Nos. 120-23 and 120-25 in the subsidiary ledger.
(4) If the rotary press purchased on March 31 had been depreciated by the declining-balance method at twice the straight-line rate, determine the depreciation on this press for the fiscal years ending (a) December 31, 1992, and (b) December 31, 1993.

Pb. 8–55A.
Income statement and balance sheet.
OBJ. 4, 9, 10

The trial balance of Rollins Corporation at the end of the fiscal year, before adjustments, is shown on page 371. The data needed for year-end adjustments are as follows:

(a) Estimated uncollectible accounts at December 31, $6,100.
(b) Insurance and other prepaid operating expenses expired during the year, $7,250.
(c) Depreciation is computed at composite rates on the average of the beginning and the ending balances of the plant asset accounts. The beginning balances and rates are as follows:

Office Equipment, $27,900; 10%	Delivery Equipment, $57,150; 20%
Store Equipment, $48,500; 8%	Buildings, $230,000; 2%

(d) Amortization of patents computed for the year, $3,000.
(e) Accrued liabilities at the end of the year, $3,000, of which $350 is for interest on the notes and $2,650 is for wages and other operating expenses.

Cash	30,400	
Accounts Receivable	59,900	
Allowance for Doubtful Accounts		500
Merchandise Inventory	178,700	
Prepaid Expense	11,250	
Land	45,000	
Buildings	230,000	
Accumulated Depreciation — Buildings		86,000
Office Equipment	31,100	
Accumulated Depreciation — Office Equipment		11,600
Store Equipment	51,500	
Accumulated Depreciation — Store Equipment		21,400
Delivery Equipment	57,850	
Accumulated Depreciation — Delivery Equipment		21,750
Patents	18,000	
Accounts Payable		35,200
Notes Payable (short-term)		25,000
Capital Stock		250,000
Retained Earnings		179,750
Dividends	70,000	
Sales (net)		986,750
Purchases (net)	692,150	
Operating Expenses (controlling account)	140,500	
Interest Expense	1,600	
	1,617,950	1,617,950

Instructions:

(1) Prepare a multiple-step income statement for the current year. The merchandise inventory at December 31 is $171,000.

(2) Prepare a balance sheet in report form, presenting the plant assets in the manner illustrated in this chapter.

MINI-CASE 8

Frank Cramer, president of Frank Cramer and Company, is considering the purchase of twelve light-duty trucks on July 1, 1992, for $120,000. The trucks have a useful life of 5 years and no residual value. In the past, all plant assets have been leased. For tax purposes, Cramer was considering depreciating the trucks by the straight-line method. He discussed the matter with his CPA and learned that, although the straight-line method could be elected, it was to his advantage to use the modified accelerated cost recovery system (MACRS) for tax purposes. He has asked for your advice as to which method to use for tax purposes.

Instructions:

(1) Compute depreciation for each of the years (1992, 1993, 1994, 1995, 1996, and 1997) of useful life by (a) the straight-line method and (b) MACRS. In using the straight-line method, one-half year's depreciation should be computed for 1992 and 1997. The rates to be used for MACRS are presented on page 337.
(2) Assuming that income before depreciation and income tax is estimated to be $100,000 uniformly per year, and that the income tax rate is 30%, compute the net income for each of the years 1992, 1993, 1994, 1995, 1996, and 1997 if (a) the straight-line method is used and (b) MACRS is used.
(3) What factors would you present for Cramer's consideration in the selection of a depreciation method?

ANSWERS TO SELF-EXAMINATION QUESTIONS

1. C All expenditures necessary to get a plant asset (such as machinery) in place and ready for use are proper charges to the asset account. In the case of machinery acquired, the transportation costs (answer A) and the installation costs (answer B) are both (answer C) proper charges to the machinery accounts.
2. A The periodic charge for depreciation under the sum-of-the-years-digits method is determined by multiplying a fraction by the original cost of the asset after the estimated residual value has been subtracted. The denominator of the fraction, which remains constant, is the sum of the digits representing the years of life, or 6(3 + 2 + 1), in the question. The numerator of the fraction, which changes each year, is the number of years of life remaining at the beginning of the year for which depreciation is being computed, or 3 for the first year, 2 for the second year, and 1 for the third year in the question. The $4,500 (answer A) of depreciation for the first year is determined as follows:

$$\frac{\text{Years of Life Remaining at Beginning of Year}}{\text{Sum of Digits for Years of Life}} \times \left[\text{Cost} - \begin{matrix}\text{Estimated}\\ \text{Residual Value}\end{matrix}\right]$$

$$\frac{3}{3 + 2 + 1} \times (\$9{,}500 - \$500)$$

$$= \frac{1}{2} \times \$9{,}000 = \$4{,}500$$

3. B Depreciation methods that provide for a higher depreciation charge in the first year of the use of an asset and a gradually declining periodic charge thereafter are referred to as accelerated depreciation methods. Examples of such methods are the sum-of-the-years-digits (answer B) and the declining-balance methods.
4. D The acceptable method of accounting for an exchange of similar assets in which the trade-in allowance ($30,000) exceeds the book value of the old asset ($25,000) requires that the cost of the new asset be determined by adding the amount of boot given ($70,000) to the book value of the old asset ($25,000), which totals $95,000.
5. D Long-lived assets that are useful in operations, not held for sale, and without physical qualities are referred to as intangible assets. Patents, goodwill, and copyrights are examples of intangible assets (answer D).

CHAPTER 9

CHAPTER OBJECTIVES

1. Describe and illustrate the determination of payrolls, including liabilities arising from employee earnings and deductions from earnings.
2. Describe and illustrate accounting systems for payroll and payroll taxes.
3. Describe and illustrate accounting for employee fringe benefits, including vacation pay, pensions, and stock options.
4. Describe and illustrate accounting for short-term notes payable.
5. Describe and illustrate accounting for product warranties.
6. Describe and illustrate accounting for contingent liabilities.

9

PAYROLL, NOTES PAYABLE, & OTHER CURRENT LIABILITIES

Payables are the opposite of receivables. They are debts owed by an enterprise to its creditors. Money claims against a firm may originate in many ways, such as purchases of merchandise or services on account, loans from banks, and purchases of equipment and marketable securities on a credit basis. At any particular moment, a business may also owe its employees for wages or salaries accrued, banks or other creditors for interest accrued on notes, and governmental agencies for taxes.

In addition to known liabilities of a definite or reasonably approximate amount, there may be potential obligations that will materialize only if certain events take place in the future. Such uncertain liabilities are termed **contingent liabilities.**

Some types of current liabilities, such as accounts payable, have been discussed in earlier chapters. Additional types of current liabilities, including liabilities arising from payrolls, pensions, and notes payable, are discussed in this chapter. Contingent liabilities are also discussed. Long-term liabilities are presented in Chapter 12.

PAYROLL AND PAYROLL TAXES

OBJECTIVE 1
Describe and illustrate the determination of payrolls, including liabilities arising from employee earnings and deductions from earnings.

The term **payroll** is often used to refer to the total amount paid to employees for a certain period. Payroll expenditures are usually significant for several reasons. First, employees are sensitive to payroll errors or irregularities, and maintaining good employee morale requires that the payroll be paid on a timely, accurate basis. Second, payroll expenditures are subject to various federal and state regulations. Finally, the amount of these payroll expenditures and related payroll taxes has a significant effect on the net income of most business enterprises. Although the degree of importance of such expenses varies widely, it is not unusual for a business to expend nearly a third of its sales revenue for payroll and payroll-related expenses. These expenses and their related liabilities are discussed in the following sections.

Liability for Employee Earnings

The term **salary** is usually applied to payment for managerial, administrative, or similar services. The rate of salary is ordinarily expressed in terms of a month or a year. Remuneration for manual labor, both skilled and unskilled, is commonly called **wages** and is stated on an hourly, weekly, or piecework basis. In practice, the terms salary and wages are often used interchangeably.

The basic salary or wage of an employee may be supplemented by commissions, bonuses, profit sharing, or cost-of-living adjustments. The form in which remuneration is paid generally has no effect on the manner in which it is treated by either the employer or the employee. Although payment is usually in terms of cash, it may take such forms as securities, notes, lodging, or other property or services.

Salary and wage rates are determined, in general, by agreement between the employer and the employees. Enterprises engaged in interstate commerce must also follow the requirements of the Fair Labor Standards Act. Employers covered by this legislation, which is commonly called the Federal Wage and Hour Law, are required to pay a minimum rate of 1½ times the regular rate for all hours worked in excess of 40 hours per week. Exemptions from the requirements are provided for executive, administrative, and certain supervisory positions. Premium rates for overtime or for working at night or other less desirable times are fairly common, even when not required by law, and the premium rates may be as much as twice the base rate.

Determination of Employee Earnings. To illustrate the computation of the earnings of an employee, it is assumed that John T. McGrath is employed at the rate of $20 per hour for the first 40 hours in the weekly pay period and at $30 ($20 + $10) per hour for any additional hours. His time card shows that he worked 46 hours during the week ended December 27. His earnings for that week are computed as follows:

Earnings at base rate (40 × $20)	$800.00
Earnings at overtime rate (6 × $30)	180.00
Total earnings	$980.00

In general, when the hours worked and the hourly rate is known for each employee, the earnings of each employee can be determined accurately and speedily at the end of a payroll period. The use of computers makes it possible to process a payroll routinely, regardless of its size.

Determination of Profit-Sharing Bonuses. Many enterprises pay their employees an annual bonus in addition to their regular salary or wage. The amount of the bonus is often based on the productivity of the employees, as measured by the net income of the enterprise. Such profit-sharing bonuses are treated in the same manner as wages and salaries.

The method used in determining the amount of a profit-sharing bonus is usually stated in the agreement between the employer and the employees. When the amount of the bonus is measured by a certain percentage of income, there are four basic formulas for the computation. The percentage may be applied (1) to income before deducting the bonus and income taxes, (2) to income after deducting the bonus but before deducting income taxes, (3) to income before deducting the bonus but after deducting income taxes, or (4) to net income after deducting both the bonus and income taxes.

Determination of a 10% bonus according to each of the four methods is illustrated as follows, based on the assumption that the employer's income before deducting the bonus and income taxes amounts to $150,000, and that income taxes are levied at the rate of 40% of income. Bonus and income taxes are abbreviated as B and T respectively.

(1) Bonus based on income before deducting bonus and taxes.

B =	.10 ($150,000)
Bonus =	$15,000

(2) Bonus based on income after deducting bonus but before deducting taxes.

	B =	.10 ($150,000 − B)
Simplifying:	B =	$15,000 − .10B
Transposing:	1.10B =	$15,000
	Bonus =	$13,636.36

(3) Bonus based on income before deducting bonus but after deducting taxes.

B equation:	B =	.10 ($150,000 − T)
T equation:	T =	.40 ($150,000 − B)

Substituting for T in the B equation and solving for B:

	B =	.10 [$150,000 − .40 ($150,000 − B)]
Simplifying:	B =	.10 ($150,000 − $60,000 + .40B)
Simplifying:	B =	$15,000 − $6,000 + .04B
Transposing:	.96B =	$9,000
	Bonus =	$9,375

(4) Bonus based on net income after deducting bonus and taxes.

B equation:	B =	.10 ($150,000 − B − T)
T equation:	T =	.40 ($150,000 − B)

Substituting for T in the B equation and solving for B:

	B =	.10 [$150,000 − B − .40 ($150,000 − B)]
Simplifying:	B =	.10 ($150,000 − B − $60,000 + .40B)
Simplifying:	B =	$15,000 − .10B − $6,000 + .04B
Transposing:	1.06B =	$9,000
	Bonus =	$8,490.57

With the amount of the bonus possibilities ranging from the high of $15,000 to the low of $8,490.57, the importance of strictly following the bonus agreement is evident. If the bonus is to be shared by all of the employees, the agreement must also provide for the manner by which the bonus is divided among them. A common method is to express the bonus as a percentage of total earnings for the year. For example, if the bonus were computed to be $15,000 and employee earnings before the bonus had been $100,000, the bonus for each of the employees could be stated as 15% of their earnings.

MANAGERS' REWARDS FOR CORPORATE PERFORMANCE

The role of bonuses in compensation plans is becoming increasingly important in many companies. Examples of how and why companies are using bonuses, particularly for their executives, were given in articles in *The Wall Street Journal*, excerpts from which are as follows:

David Margolis works for a [very] generous company... [In 1985,] Mr. Margolis, the president, chairman and chief executive officer of Colt Industries Inc., received a bonus of $555,000, more than double the average bonus for chief executives of similar-sized companies. And that bonus was $115,680 more than his base salary. Total compensation: close to $1 million.

...On top of his regular salary of $363,931, [Paul Fireman, Chairman of Reebok International Ltd.] received a bonus of $12.7 million... [for 1986.]

That sum reflects an agreement under which Mr. Fireman is entitled to an annual bonus equal to 5% of the amount by which the company's annual pre-tax earnings exceeds $20 million. Pre-tax earnings for the maker of athletic shoes soared to $261.2 million in 1986 from $78.1 million in 1985...

...After years of regularly receiving hefty increases in salary and bonus—regardless of their company's success or failure—more top executives are now finding their compensation linked directly to corporate performance...

"There's been so much scrutiny that boards have been taking a closer look" at compensation, says Pete Smith, national director of Wyatt Co.'s compensation consulting business. As a result, companies are relying less on salary and more on bonuses and other performance-linked compensation to reward executives. They are also tightening the criteria for earning those rewards.... [For example,] more compensation is being pegged to three-year or five-year gains in... performance....

Some companies also want to extend bonuses, which are usually limited to senior executives, to lower-level managers. Specialists believe that bonuses work successfully as incentives only if they amount to 15% or more of total compensation. But most lower-level managers are unwilling to risk that large a portion of their income....

The solution—adding bonuses to existing salaries—means a big increase in costs. But some executives say those costs are worth it to retain first-class management. Says David Jones, chairman and chief executive of Humana Corp.: "You don't pay executives with cornflakes. There's always costs of employing executives. If the costs are reasonable, you pay them. You have to pay what the marketplace demands."

Source: Amanda Bennet, "More Managers Find Salary, Bonus Are Tied Directly to Performance," *The Wall Street Journal,* February 28, 1986 and Christopher J. Chipello, "Reebok's Chairman Got Bonuses Totaling $12.7 Million in '86," *The Wall Street Journal,* April 14, 1987.

Deductions from Employee Earnings

The total earnings of an employee for a payroll period, including bonuses and overtime pay, are often called the **gross pay.** From this amount is subtracted one or more **deductions** to arrive at the **net pay,** which is the amount the employer must pay the employee. The deductions for federal taxes are of the widest applicability and usually the largest in amount. Deductions may also be needed for state or local income taxes and for contributions to state unemployment compensation programs. Other deductions may be made for contributions to pension plans and for items authorized by individual employees.

FICA Tax. Most employers are required by the Federal Insurance Contributions Act (FICA) to withhold a portion of the earnings of each of their employees. The amount of **FICA tax** withheld is the employees' contribution to the combined federal programs for old-age and disability benefits, insurance benefits to survivors, and health insurance for the aged (medicare). With very few exceptions, employers are required to withhold from each employee a tax at a specified rate on earnings up to a specified amount paid in the calendar year. Although both the schedule of future tax rates and the maximum amount subject to tax are revised often by Congress, such changes have no effect on the basic outline of the payroll system.[1] In the text, a rate of 7.5% on the first $55,000 of annual earnings and a rate of 1.5% on annual earnings from $55,000 to $125,000 will be used. To illustrate, assume that an employee's annual earnings prior to the current payroll period total

[1] Current tax rates and the amount of earnings subject to tax may be located in Internal Revenue Service publications and in standard tax reporting services. As of January 1, 1991, the FICA tax rate was 7.65% on the first $53,400 of annual earnings and 1.45% on earnings from $53,400 to $125,000.

$54,100 and the current period's earnings are $1,200. The FICA tax of $72 is determined as follows:

Earnings subject to 7.5% FICA tax ($55,000 − $54,100)	$900	
FICA tax rate	7.5%	
FICA tax		$67.50
Earnings subject to 1.5% FICA tax ($54,100 + $1,200 − $55,000)	$300	
FICA tax rate	1.5%	
FICA tax		4.50
Total FICA tax		$72.00

Federal Income Tax. Except for certain types of employment, all employers must withhold a portion of the earnings of their employees for payment of the employees' liability for federal income tax. The amount that must be withheld from each employee differs according to the amount of gross pay, marital status, and the estimated deductions and exemptions claimed when filing the annual income tax return.

Other Deductions. Deductions from gross earnings for payment of taxes are compulsory. Neither the employer nor the employee has any choice in the matter. In addition, however, there may be other deductions authorized by individual employees or by the union representing them. For example, an employee may authorize deductions for the purchase of United States savings bonds, for contributions to a United Fund or other charitable organization, for payment of premiums on various types of employee insurance, or for the purchase of a retirement annuity. The union contract may also require the deduction of union dues or other deductions for group benefits.

Computation of Employee Net Pay

Gross earnings for a payroll period less the payroll deductions yields the amount to be paid to the employee, which is often called the **net pay** or **take-home pay.** The net pay of employee John T. McGrath for the week ended December 27 is $694.80, based on the following summary:

Gross earnings for the week		$980.00
Deductions:		
FICA tax	$ 73.50	
Federal income tax	186.70	
U.S. savings bonds	20.00	
United Fund	5.00	
Total deductions		285.20
Net pay		$694.80

Reference to McGrath's earnings record shows cumulative earnings of $49,500 prior to the current week's earnings of $980. The entire amount of the current week's earnings is therefore subject to FICA tax of 7.5% and the FICA tax to be withheld is $73.50 (7.5% of $980.).

The amount of federal income tax withheld would be determined by reference to official withholding tax tables issued by the Internal Revenue Service. For purposes of this illustration, the amount of federal income tax withheld was assumed to be $186.70. The deductions for the purchase of bonds and for the charitable contribution were in accordance with McGrath's authorizations.

As in the determination of gross earnings when overtime rates are a factor, the computations for deductions can be generalized and programmed into a computer. In this way, the processing of payroll can be performed accurately and quickly at the end of each pay period.

Liability for Employer's Payroll Taxes

Thus far the discussion of taxes has been limited to those levied against employees and withheld by employers. Most employers are subject to federal and state taxes based on the amount of remuneration earned by their employees. Such taxes are an operating expense of the business and may amount to a relatively large sum.

FICA Tax. Employers are required to contribute to the Federal Insurance Contributions Act program for each employee. The tax rates are the same as those applicable to employees. For purposes of illustration, these rates are assumed to be 7.5% on the first $55,000 of annual earnings and 1.5% on annual earnings from $55,000 to $125,000.

YOUR SOCIAL SECURITY TAXES

In its 1936 publication, *Security in Your Old Age,* the Social Security Board set forth the following explanation of how the social security tax would affect a worker's paycheck:

The taxes called for in this law will be paid both by your employer and by you. For the next 3 years you will pay maybe 15 cents a week, maybe 25 cents a week, maybe 30 cents or more, according to what you earn. That is to say, during the next 3 years, beginning January 1, 1937, you will pay 1 cent for every dollar you earn, and at the same time your employer will pay 1 cent for every dollar you earn, up to $3,000 a year. Twenty-six million other workers and their employers will be paying at the same time.

After the first 3 years—that is to say, beginning in 1940—you will pay, and your employer will pay, 1½ cents for each dollar you earn, up to $3,000 a year. This will be the tax for 3 years, and then beginning in 1943, you will pay 2 cents, and so will your employer, for every dollar you earn for the next three years. After that, you and your employer will each pay half a cent more for 3 years, and finally, beginning in 1949, twelve years from now, you and your employer will each pay 3 cents on each dollar you earn, up to $3,000 a year. That is the most you will ever pay.

The rate on January 1, 1991, is 7.65 cents for each dollar of the first $53,400 earned and 1.45 cents for each dollar earned from $53,400 to $125,000.

Source: Adapted from Arthur Lodge, "That Is the Most You Will Ever Pay," *Journal of Accountancy* (October, 1985), p. 44.

Federal Unemployment Compensation Tax. Unemployment insurance provides temporary relief to those who become unemployed as a result of economic forces beyond their control. Types of employment subject to the unemployment insurance program are similar to those covered by the FICA tax. The tax of .8% is levied on employers only, rather than on both employers and employees.[2] It is applicable only to the first $7,000 of the remuneration of each covered employee during a calendar year. As with the FICA tax, the rate and the maximum amount subject to federal unemployment com-

[2]The rate on January 1, 1991 was 6.2%, which may be reduced to .8% for credits for state unemployment compensation tax.

pensation tax are revised often by Congress. The funds collected by the federal government are not paid out as benefits to the unemployed, but are allocated among the states for use in administering state programs.

State Unemployment Compensation Tax. The amounts paid as benefits to unemployed persons are obtained, for the most part, by taxes levied upon employers only. A very few states also require employee contributions. The rates of tax and the tax base vary, and in most states, employers who provide steady employment for their employees are awarded reduced rates. The employment experience and the status of each employer's tax account are reviewed annually, and the merit ratings and tax rates are revised accordingly.[3]

ACCOUNTING SYSTEMS FOR PAYROLL AND PAYROLL TAXES

OBJECTIVE 2
Describe and illustrate accounting systems for payroll and payroll taxes.

Accounting systems for payroll and payroll taxes are concerned with the records and reports associated with the employer-employee relationship. It is important that the accounting system provide safeguards to insure that payments are in accord with management's general plans and its specific authorizations.

All employees of a firm expect and are entitled to receive their remuneration at regular intervals following the close of each payroll period. Regardless of the number of employees and the difficulties in computing the amounts to be paid, the payroll system must be designed to process the necessary data quickly and assure payment of the correct amount to each employee. The system must also provide adequate safeguards against payments to fictitious persons and other misappropriations of funds.

Various federal, state, and local laws require that employers accumulate certain specified data in their payroll records, not only for each payroll period but also for each employee. Periodic reports of such data must be submitted to the appropriate governmental agencies and remittances made for amounts withheld from employees and for taxes levied on the employer. The records must be retained for specified periods of time and be available for inspection by those responsible for enforcement of the laws. In addition, payroll data may be useful in negotiations with labor unions, in settling employee grievances, and in determining rights to vacations, sick leaves, and retirement pensions.

Although complex organizational structures may necessitate the use of detailed subsystems, the major parts common to most payroll systems are the payroll register, employee's earnings record, and payroll checks. Each of these major payroll components is described briefly in the following sections.

Payroll Register

A form frequently used in assembling and summarizing the data needed at the end of each payroll period is the **payroll register.** Its design varies according to the number and classes of employees and the extent to which computers are used. The payroll register normally is prepared at the end of each pay period and includes for each employee the following data:

1. The total hours worked during the period.
2. The gross earnings for the employee including any overtime to be paid for the period.

---

[3]As of January 1, 1991, the maximum state rate recognized by the federal unemployment system was 5.4% of the first $7,000 of each employee's earnings during a calendar year.

3. Itemized deductions for each employee including such items as FICA tax, federal and state income tax withholdings, health insurance premiums, union dues, and charitable contributions.
4. The net amount to be paid to each employee.
5. The distribution of the employee's gross pay to the accounts to be debited, or "charged," for the expense of the employee's pay. Two accounts frequently debited for payroll for a merchandising enterprise are Sales Salaries Expense and Office Salaries Expense.

Although the preceding data commonly are included in a payroll register for most business enterprises, modifications may be made in actual practice depending upon the needs of the business enterprise.[4]

Recording Employees' Earnings. The payroll register may be used as a supporting record for a journal entry that records the employees' earnings for a pay period. Such an entry is illustrated as follows:

Dec. 27	Sales Salaries Expense	11,122.16	
	Office Salaries Expense	2,780.54	
	FICA Tax Payable		851.60
	Employees Federal Income Tax Payable		3,332.18
	Bond Deductions Payable		680.00
	United Fund Deductions Payable		520.00
	Salaries Payable		8,518.92

The total expense incurred for the services of employees is recorded by the debits to the salary expense accounts. The credits in the entry represent increases in specific liability accounts.

Recording and Paying Payroll Taxes. Each time a payroll is prepared, the amounts of employer payroll taxes must be determined and the related expense and liabilities recorded. The employer payroll taxes are computed by multiplying each employee's earnings subject to the tax by the applicable tax rate.

Computations of employer payroll taxes for FICA and federal and state unemployment compensation for a payroll period are illustrated as follows:

	Taxable Earnings	Tax Rate	Payroll Tax
FICA	$11,354.70	7.5%	$ 851.60
State unemployment compensation tax	2,710.00	5.4	146.34
Federal unemployment compensation tax	2,710.00	.8	21.68
Total payroll taxes			$1,019.62

The journal entry to record the payroll tax expense and the liability for the taxes accrued is as follows:

Dec. 27	Payroll Taxes Expense	1,019.62	
	FICA Tax Payable		851.60
	State Unemployment Tax Payable		146.34
	Federal Unemployment Tax Payable		21.68

Payment of the liability for each of the taxes is recorded in the same manner as the payment of other liabilities. Employers are required to com-

[4]The payroll register is further described and illustrated in the appendix at the end of this chapter.

pute and report all payroll taxes on the calendar-year basis, regardless of the fiscal year they may use for financial reporting and income tax purposes. Details of the federal income tax and FICA tax withheld from employees are combined with the employer's FICA tax on a single return accompanied by the amount of tax due. Payments are required on a weekly, semimonthly, monthly, or quarterly basis, depending on the amount of the combined taxes. Unemployment compensation tax returns and payments are required by the federal government on an annual basis. Earlier payments are required when the tax exceeds a certain minimum. Unemployment compensation tax returns and payments are required by most states on a basis similar to that required by the federal government.

All payroll taxes levied against employers become liabilities at the time the related remuneration is *paid* to employees, rather than at the time the liability to the employees is incurred. Observance of this requirement may cause a problem of expense allocation between fiscal periods. To illustrate, assume that an enterprise using the calendar year as its fiscal year pays its employees on Friday for a weekly payroll period ending the preceding Wednesday, the two-day lag between Wednesday and Friday being needed to process the payroll. Regardless of the day of the week on which the year ends, there will be some accrued wages. If it ends on a Thursday, the accrual will cover a full week plus an extra day. Logically, the unpaid wages and the related payroll taxes should both be charged to the period that benefited from the services performed by the employees. On the other hand, there is legally no liability for the payroll taxes until the wages are paid in January, when a new cycle of earnings subject to tax is begun. The distortion of net income that would result from failure to accrue the payroll taxes might well be insignificant. The practice adopted should be followed consistently.

Employee's Earnings Record

The necessity of having the cumulative amount of each employee's earnings readily available at the end of each payroll period was discussed earlier. Without such information there would be no means of determining the appropriate amount of FICA tax to withhold from current earnings. It is essential, therefore, that detailed records be maintained for each employee. An **employee's earnings record** normally is used for this purpose.

An employee's earnings record usually includes for each pay period during the year the hours worked, the gross earnings, the deductions, and the net pay. Subtotals throughout the year and yearly totals may be shown for use in preparing various reports for tax, insurance, and other purposes. One such annual report, known as Form W-2 Wage and Tax Statement, must be given to each employee as well as to the Social Security Administration.[5]

Payroll Checks

One of the principal outputs of most payroll systems is a series of **payroll checks** at the end of each pay period. The data needed for this purpose

---

[5]An employee's earnings record and related Form W-2 Wage and Tax Statement are described further and illustrated in the appendix at the end of this chapter.

normally are provided by the payroll register. The customary practice is to provide each employee with a statement of the details of the payroll computation. The statement may be entirely separate from the check or it may be in the form of a detachable stub attached to the check.

When employees are paid by checks drawn on the regular bank account and the voucher system is used, it is necessary to prepare a voucher for the net amount to be paid the employees. The voucher is then recorded as a debit to Salaries Payable and a credit to Accounts Payable, and the payment is recorded in the usual manner. If the voucher system is not used, the payment would be recorded by a debit to Salaries Payable and a credit to Cash. It should be noted that the recording of these entries would be preceded by the recording of the journal entry for payroll expense, such as the entry illustrated on page 381.

Most employers with a large number of employees use a special bank account and payroll checks designed specifically for the purpose. After the data for the payroll period have been recorded and summarized, a single check for the total amount to be paid is drawn on the firm's regular bank account and deposited in a special account. The individual payroll checks are then drawn against the special payroll account.

The use of special payroll checks relieves the treasurer or other executives of the task of signing a large number of regular checks each payday. The responsibility for signing payroll checks may be given to the paymaster, or mechanical means of signing the checks may be used. Another advantage of this system is that reconciling the regular bank statement is simplified. The paid payroll checks are returned by the bank separately from regular checks and are accompanied by a statement of the special bank account. Any balance shown on the bank's statement will correspond to the sum of the payroll checks outstanding because the amount of each deposit is exactly the same as the total amount of checks drawn. The recording procedures are the same as when checks on the regular bank account are used.

Currency is sometimes used as the medium of payment when the payroll is paid each week or when the business location or the time of payment is such that banking or check-cashing facilities are not readily available to employees. In such cases, a single check, payable to Payroll, is drawn for the entire amount to be paid. The check is then cashed at the bank and the money is inserted in individual pay envelopes. Each employee should be required to sign a receipt which serves as evidence of payment. The procedures for recording the payment correspond to those outlined for payroll checks.

Payroll System Diagram

The flow of data within segments of an accounting system may be shown by diagrams such as the one illustrated on page 384. It depicts the interrelationships of the principal parts of the payroll system described in this chapter. The requirement of constant updating of the employee's earnings record is indicated by the dotted line.

Attention thus far has been directed to the end product or *output* of a payroll system, including the payroll register, the checks payable to individual employees, the earnings records for each employee, and reports for tax and other purposes. The basic data entering the payroll systems are sometimes called the *input* of the system. Input data that remain relatively unchanged and do not need to be reintroduced into the system for each payroll

Flow Diagram of a Payroll System

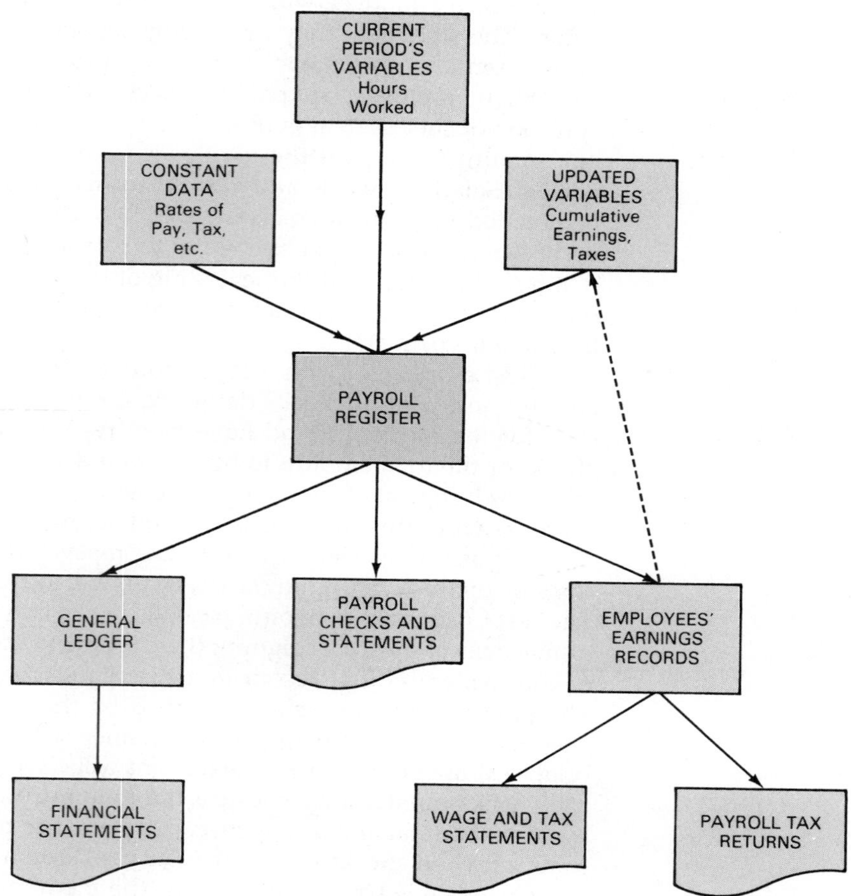

period are characterized as *constants*. Those data that differ from period to period are termed *variables*.

Constants include such data for each employee as name and social security number, marital status, number of income tax withholding allowances claimed, rate of pay, function category (office, sales, etc.), and department where employed. The FICA tax rates and various tax tables are also constants which apply to all employees. The variable data for each employee include the number of hours or days worked during each payroll period, days of sick leave with pay, vacation credits, and cumulative amounts of earnings and taxes withheld. If salespersons are employed on a commission basis, the amount of their sales would also vary from period to period. The forms used in initially recording both the constant and the variable data vary widely according to the complexities of the payroll system and the processing methods used.

Internal Controls for Payroll Systems

The large amount of data and the computations necessary to process the payroll are evident. As the number of employees and the mass of data increase, the number of individuals needed to manage and process payroll data likewise increases. Such characteristics, together with the relative magnitude of labor costs, indicate the need for controls that will assure the reliability of the data and minimize the opportunity for misuse of funds.

The cash disbursement controls discussed in Chapter 5 are applicable to payrolls. Thus, the use of the voucher system and the requirement that all payments be supported by vouchers are desirable. The addition or deletion of names on the payroll should be supported by written authorizations from the personnel department. It is also essential that employees' attendance records be controlled in such a manner as to prevent errors and abuses. Perhaps the most basic and widely used records are "In and Out" cards, whereby employees indicate, often by "punching" a time clock, their time of arrival and departure. Employee identification cards or badges may also be used in this connection to assure that all salaries and wages are paid to the proper individuals.

LIABILITY FOR EMPLOYEES' FRINGE BENEFITS

OBJECTIVE 3
Describe and illustrate accounting for employee fringe benefits, including vacation pay, pensions, and stock options.

Many companies provide a variety of benefits to their employees in addition to salary and wages earned. These benefits, often referred to as **fringe benefits,** may take many forms, such as vacations, employee pension plans, and health, life, and disability insurance. If the employer pays part or all of the cost of the fringe benefits and revenues and expenses are to be matched properly, the estimated cost of these benefits must be recognized as an expense of the period during which the employee earns the benefit. The application of accounting principles to fringe benefits is described in the following paragraphs, using vacation pay, pensions, and stock options as examples.

Liability for Vacation Pay

Most employees are granted some vacation privileges. To match revenue and expense properly, the employer should accrue the vacation pay liability as the vacation privilege is earned, if the payment is probable and can be reasonably estimated.[6] To illustrate the accounting for vacation absences, frequently referred to as compensated absences, assume that all employees earn two weeks of vacation for each 50 weeks worked during the year, and the total vacation pay expense for the year is $100,000. Since this expense is actually incurred during the 50 weeks the employees work during the year, the expense and the liability could be recorded by an adjusting entry at the end of the accounting period, or recorded each pay period, illustrated as follows:

May 5	Vacation Pay Expense	2,000	
	Vacation Pay Payable		2,000
	Vacation pay for week ended May 5 (1/50 of annual vacation pay of $100,000).		

Depending upon when it is to be paid, the vacation liability will be classified in the balance sheet as either a current liability or a long-term liability. When the payroll in which the employees are paid for their vacations is prepared, Vacation Pay Payable would be debited, and Salaries Payable and the appropriate accounts for recording taxes and withholdings would be credited.

---

[6] *Statement of Financial Accounting Standards, No. 43,* "Accounting for Compensated Absences" (Stamford: Financial Accounting Standards Board, 1980), par. 6.

Liability for Pensions

In recent years, retirement pension plans have increased rapidly in number, variety, and complexity. Although the details of the plans vary from employer to employer, pension benefits are usually based on factors such as employee age, years of service, and salary level. In 1974, Congress enacted the Employee Retirement Income Security Act (ERISA), which established guidelines for safeguarding employee benefits.

Pension plans may be classified as contributory or noncontributory, funded or unfunded, and qualified or unqualified. A **contributory plan** requires the employer to withhold a portion of each employee's earnings as a contribution to the plan. The employer then makes a contribution according to the provisions of the plan. A **noncontributory plan** requires the employer to bear the entire cost. A **funded plan** requires the employer to set aside funds to meet future pension benefits by making payments to an independent funding agency. The funding agency is responsible for managing the assets of the pension fund and for disbursing the pension benefits to employees. For many pension plans, insurance companies serve as the funding agency. An **unfunded plan** is managed entirely by the employer instead of by an independent agency. A **qualified plan** is designed to comply with federal income tax requirements which allow the employer to deduct pension contributions for tax purposes and which exempt pension fund income from tax. Most pension plans are qualified.

The accounting for pension plans can be complex due to the uncertainties of projecting future pension obligations. Future pension obligations depend upon such factors as employee life expectancies, expected employee compensation levels, and investment income on pension contributions. Pension funding requirements are estimated by individuals known as actuaries, who use sophisticated mathematical and statistical models.

The employer's cost of an employee's pension plan in a given year, referred to as the **net periodic pension cost**, is debited to an operating expense account, Pension Expense.[7] The credit is to Cash if the pension cost is fully funded. If the pension cost is partially funded, any unfunded amount is credited to Unfunded Accrued Pension Cost. To illustrate, assume that the pension plan of Flossmoor Industries requires an annual pension cost of $25,000, and Flossmoor Industries pays $15,000 to the fund trustee, Equity Insurance Company. The entry to record the transaction is as follows:

Pension Expense	25,000	
Cash		15,000
Unfunded Accrued Pension Cost		10,000

Depending upon when the pension liability (unfunded accrued pension cost) is to be paid, the $10,000 will be classified on the balance sheet as either a long-term or a current liability.

An entity's financial statements should fully disclose the nature of its pension plans and pension obligations. The financial statement disclosures should include the net periodic pension cost for the year and a description of the pension plan, including such items as the employee groups covered,

[7] *Statement of Financial Accounting Standards, No. 87,* "Employers' Accounting for Pensions" (Stamford: Financial Accounting Standards Board, 1985), par. 6.

the entity's accounting and funding policies, and any pension changes affecting comparability among years.

When an employer first adopts or changes a pension plan, the employer must consider whether to grant employees credit for prior years service. If a company does grant credit to employees for prior service, a prior service cost obligation must be recognized. The funding of prior service cost is normally provided for over a number of years, thus creating a long-term prior service pension cost liability. The complex nature of accounting for prior service costs is left for more advanced accounting study.

Employee Stock Options

Stock options are rights given by a corporation to its employees to purchase shares of the corporation's stock at a stated price. Employee stock options generally involve an element of salary expense when the employees have the right to purchase the corporation's stock at a price below market value. In such a case, the expense is the difference between the market price of the stock and the amount the employees are required to pay for it. The amount of the expense is debited to an appropriate expense account and credited to an owner's equity account. The details of accounting for employee stock options are discussed in more advanced accounting texts.

SHORT-TERM NOTES PAYABLE

OBJECTIVE 4
Describe and illustrate accounting for short-term notes payable.

Notes may be issued to creditors in temporary satisfaction of an account payable created earlier, or they may be issued at the time merchandise or other assets are purchased. To illustrate the former, assume that an enterprise issues to Gilmer Co. a 90-day, 12% note for $1,000, dated August 1, 1992, in settlement of a $1,000 overdue account. The entry to record the transaction is as follows:

Aug. 1	Accounts Payable—Gilmer Co.	1,000	
	Notes Payable		1,000
	Issued a 90-day, 12% note on account.		

At the time the note matures, the entry to record the payment of $1,030 ($1,000 principal plus $30 interest) is as follows:

Oct. 30	Notes Payable	1,000	
	Interest Expense	30	
	Cash		1,030

The interest expense account is closed at December 31, and the amount is reported in the Other Expense section of the income statement for the year ended December 31, 1992.

Notes may also be issued when money is borrowed from banks. Although there are many variations in interest and repayment terms, the most direct procedure is for the borrower to issue an interest-bearing note for the amount of the loan. For example, assume that on September 19 a firm borrows $4,000 from the City National Bank, with the loan evidenced by the firm's 90-day, 15% note. The effect of this transaction is as follows:

Sept. 19	Cash	4,000	
	Notes Payable		4,000

On the due date of the note, ninety days later, the borrower owes $4,000, the face amount of the note, and interest of $150. The accounts are affected by the payment as follows:

Dec. 18	Notes Payable	4,000	
	Interest Expense	150	
	Cash		4,150

A variant of the bank loan transaction just illustrated is to issue a non-interest-bearing note for the amount that is to be paid at maturity. Although the note issued is non-interest-bearing, interest is deducted from the maturity value of the note and the borrower receives the remainder. The deduction of interest from a future value is termed **discounting.** The rate used in computing the interest may be termed the **discount rate**, the deduction may be called the **discount**, and the net amount available to the borrower is called the **proceeds.**

To illustrate the discounting of a note payable, assume that on August 10 an enterprise issued to a bank a $4,000, 90-day, non-interest-bearing note and that the bank discount rate is 15%. The amount of the discount is $150, and the proceeds are $3,850. The entry to record the transaction is as follows:

Aug. 10	Cash	3,850	
	Interest Expense	150	
	Notes Payable		4,000

The note payable is recorded at its face value, which is also its maturity value, and the interest expense is recorded at the time the note is issued. When the note is paid, the following entry is recorded:

Nov. 8	Notes Payable	4,000	
	Cash		4,000

PRODUCT WARRANTY LIABILITY

OBJECTIVE 5
Describe and illustrate accounting for product warranties.

At the time of sale, a company may grant a warranty on a product. If revenues and expenses are to be matched properly, a liability to cover the warranty must be recorded in the period of the sale.[8] Later, when the product is repaired or replaced, the liability will be reduced. To illustrate, assume that during June a company sells $60,000 of a product, on which there is a 36-month warranty for repairing defects in the product. If past experience indicates that the average cost to repair defects is 5% of the sales price, the entry to record the product warranty liability would be as follows:

June 30	Product Warranty Expense	3,000	
	Product Warranty Payable		3,000
	Product warranty for June, 5% × $60,000.		

When the defective product is repaired, the repair costs would be recorded by debiting Product Warranty Payable and crediting Cash, Supplies, or other appropriate account.

[8]*Statement of Financial Accounting Standards, No. 5,* "Accounting for Contingencies" (Stamford: Financial Accounting Standards Board, 1975), pars. 8, 24.

CONTINGENT LIABILITIES

OBJECTIVE 6
Describe and illustrate accounting for contingent liabilities.

As discussed in Chapter 6, contingent liabilities are potential obligations that will materialize only if certain events occur in the future. If the liability is *probable* and the amount of the liability can be *estimated reasonably*, it should be recorded in the accounts. Such liabilities discussed in preceding paragraphs include vacation pay payable and product warranty payable. Although the vacation pay liability is dependent on employees taking vacations, the liability is probable and is estimated reasonably. Likewise, although the product warranty liability is dependent upon customers presenting products for repair, the product warranty liability is probable and is estimated reasonably.

If the amount of the potential obligation cannot be estimated reasonably, the details of the contingency should be disclosed.[9] The most common contingent liabilities disclosed in notes to the financial statements—from litigation, guarantees, and discounting receivables—are discussed in the following paragraphs. The 1990 edition of *Accounting Trends & Techniques* indicated that 63% of the surveyed companies disclosed contingencies for litigations, 29% for guarantees, and 11% for discounting receivables.

Litigation

Lawsuits are being filed against companies with increasing frequency. In many cases, litigation takes many months or years to complete. Although it is often difficult to estimate the amount of the liability, the details should be disclosed. Following is an example of a note in the 1990 financial statements of Tandy Corporation, disclosing a contingent liability arising from litigation:

Note 19—Litigation

There are various claims, lawsuits, disputes with third parties, investigations and pending actions involving allegations of negligence, product defects, discrimination, patent infringement, tax deficiencies and breach of contract against the Company and its subsidiaries incident to the operation of its business. The liability, if any, associated with these matters was not determinable at June 30, 1990. While certain of these matters involve substantial amounts, it is the opinion of management that their ultimate resolution will not have a materially adverse effect on Tandy's financial position or results of operations.

In June, 1990, the Superior Court for the City and County of San Francisco, California, entered summary adjudications against the Company in a class action filed in 1988 by Karl and Cathleen Czechowski vs. Tandy Corporation seeking payment of unused vacation pay to all California employees terminated since October, 1983, penalties under California law and punitive damages. Several issues, including damages, members of the class and notice to the class, remain unresolved. A trial is currently set for April, 1991. Tandy is vigorously defending this action and intends to appeal the court's action. The Company's liability, if any, associated with this dispute is not determinable at this time. The Company believes that any award of damages in the action would not have a materially adverse effect on the financial condition of the Company or its results of operations.

---

[9]*Ibid.*, pars. 8, 10, 12.

Guarantees

Companies sometimes guarantee a loan for another company, often a supplier or favored customer. In such cases, the company is obligated to pay the loan if the borrower fails to make payment. Such a contingency can be disclosed as illustrated in the following note from the financial statements of Briggs & Stratton Corporation:

(7) Guarantees and Commitments:

The Company is a 50% guarantor on bank loans of an unconsolidated Japanese joint venture for the manufacture of engines which has not yet begun operations. These bank loans totaled approximately $15,400,000 at June 30, 1988.

Discounted Receivables

In Chapter 6, the contingent liability arising from discounting a note receivable was discussed. A similar potential obligation may also arise from the sale of receivables. The contingent liability that exists until the due date for discounted receivables can be disclosed as illustrated by the following note from the financial statements of John Deere & Company:

Commitments and Contingent Liabilities

On October 31, 1989, the company was contingently liable for recourse of approximately $36 million on credit receivables sold to financial institutions.

APPENDIX

PAYROLL REGISTER AND EMPLOYEE'S EARNINGS RECORD

This chapter described and discussed the major elements common to most payroll systems, including the payroll register and the employee's earnings record. This appendix further describes and illustrates the payroll register and the employee's earnings record.

PAYROLL REGISTER

Although the form of the payroll register will differ among businesses, a form suitable for a small number of employees is illustrated on page 391. The nature of most of the data appearing in this payroll register is evident from the columnar headings. The number of hours worked and the earnings and deduction data are inserted in the appropriate columns. The sum of the deductions applicable to an employee is then deducted from the total earnings to yield the amount to be paid. Recording the check numbers in the payroll register as the checks are written eliminates the need to maintain other detailed records of the payments. The last two columns of the payroll register are used to accumulate the total wages or salaries to be

PAYROLL FOR WEEK ENDING DECEMBER 27, 19—

		EARNINGS			DEDUCTIONS					PAID		ACCOUNTS DEBITED	
NAME	TOTAL HOURS	REGULAR	OVER-TIME	TOTAL	FICA TAX	FEDERAL INCOME TAX	U.S SAVINGS BOND	MISCEL-LANEOUS	TOTAL	NET AMOUNT	CHECK NO.	SALES SALARIES EXPENSE	OFFICE SALARIES EXPENSE
ABRAMS, JULIE S.	40	500.00		500.00	37.50	74.10	20.00	UF 10.00	141.60	358.40	6857	500.00	
ELROD, FRED G.	44	392.00	58.80	450.80	33.81	62.60		UF 50.00	146.41	304.39	6858		450.80
GOMEZ, JOSE C.		840.00		840.00	12.60	173.70	25.00	UF 10.00	221.30	618.70	6859	840.00	
McGRATH, JOHN T.	46	800.00	180.00	980.00	73.50	186.70	20.00	UF 5.00	285.20	694.80	6860	980.00	
WILKES, GLENN K.	40	480.00		480.00	36.00	69.20	10.00		115.20	364.80	6880	480.00	
ZUMPANO, MICHAEL W.		600.00		600.00	45.00	71.36	5.00	UF 2.00	123.36	476.64	6881		600.00
TOTAL		13,328.70	574.00	13,902.70	851.60	3,332.18	680.00	UF 520.00	5,383.78	8,518.92		11,122.16	2,780.54

MISCELLANEOUS DEDUCTIONS: UF—UNITED FUND

charged to the expense accounts. This process is usually termed **payroll distribution.**

The format of the illustrative payroll register aids the determination of arithmetic accuracy before checks are issued to employees and before the summary amounts are formally recorded. Specifically, all columnar totals should be cross-verified. The following tabulation illustrates the method of cross-verification:

Earnings:		
Regular	$13,328.70	
Overtime	574.00	
Total		$13,902.70
Deductions:		
FICA tax	$ 851.60	
Federal income tax	3,332.18	
U.S. savings bonds	680.00	
United Fund	520.00	
Total		5,383.78
Paid—net amount		$ 8,518.92
Accounts debited:		
Sales Salaries Expense		$11,122.16
Office Salaries Expense		2,780.54
Total (as above)		$13,902.70

The entry to record the total expense incurred for the services of employees, the amounts withheld from employees' earnings, and the net pay, based on the payroll register, is as follows:

Dec. 27	Sales Salaries Expense	11,122.16	
	Office Salaries Expense	2,780.54	
	FICA Tax Payable		851.60
	Employees Federal Income Tax Payable		3,332.18
	Bond Deductions Payable		680.00
	United Fund Deductions Payable		520.00
	Salaries Payable		8,518.92

Employee's Earnings Record

An employee's earnings record suitable for most businesses is illustrated below and on page 393. The relationship between this record and the payroll register can be seen by tracing the amounts entered on McGrath's earnings record for December 27 back to its source, which is the fourth line of the payroll register illustrated on page 391.

As described within the chapter, the employee's earnings record is the source for the preparation of various reports for tax, insurance, and other purposes. The illustrated employee's earnings record for McGrath was the source of the amounts inserted in the W-2 Wage and Tax Statement on page 393. A similar Form W-2 must be submitted annually to each employee.

Employee's Earnings Record

JOHN T. MCGRATH
1830 FOURTH ST. PHONE: 555-1679
CLINTON, IA 52732-6142

MARRIED | NUMBER OF WITHHOLDING ALLOWANCES: 4 | PAY RATE: $800.00 PER WEEK

OCCUPATION: SALESPERSON | EQUIVALENT HOURLY RATE: $20

			EARNINGS			
LINE NO.	PERIOD ENDED	TOTAL HOURS	REGULAR EARNINGS	OVERTIME	TOTAL EARNINGS	CUMULATIVE TOTAL
39	SEPT. 27	51	800.00	330.00	1,130.00	38,250.00
THIRD QUARTER			10,400.00	1,770.00	12,170.00	
40	OCT. 4	40	800.00		800.00	39,050.00
46	NOV. 15	41	800.00	30.00	830.00	45,020.00
47	NOV. 22	40	800.00		800.00	45,820.00
48	NOV. 29	42	800.00	60.00	860.00	46,680.00
49	DEC. 6	50	800.00	300.00	1,100.00	47,780.00
50	DEC. 13	40	800.00		800.00	48,580.00
51	DEC. 20	44	800.00	120.00	920.00	49,500.00
52	DEC. 27	46	800.00	180.00	980.00	50,480.00
FOURTH QUARTER			10,400.00	1,830.00	12,230.00	
YEARLY TOTAL			41,600.00	8,880.00	50,480.00	

Wage and Tax Statement

1 Control number		OMB No. 1545-0008	
2 Employer's name, address, and ZIP code McDermott Supply Co. 415 Fifth Avenue So. Dubuque, IA 52736-0142		6 Statutory employee ☐ Deceased ☐ Pension plan ☐ Legal rep. ☐ 942 emp. ☐ Subtotal ☐ Deferred compensation ☐ Void ☐	
		7 Allocated tips	8 Advance EIC payment
		9 Federal income tax withheld $8,942.06	10 Wages, tips, other compensation $50,480.00
3 Employer's identification number 61-843652	4 Employer's state I.D. number	11 Social security tax withheld $3,786.00	12 Social security wages $50,480.00
5 Employee's social security number 381-48-9120		13 Social security tips	14 Medicare wages and tips
19 Employee's name, address, and ZIP code John T. McGrath 1830 Fourth Street Clinton, IA 52732-6142		15 Medicare tax withheld	16 Nonqualified plans
		17 See Instrs. for Box 17	18 Other
20	21	22 Dependent care benefits	23 Benefits included in Box 10

24 State income tax	25 State wages, tips, etc.	26 Name of state	27 Local income tax	28 Local wages, tips, etc.	29 Name of locality

Copy B To Be Filed With Employee's FEDERAL Tax Return Department of the Treasury—Internal Revenue Service

Form **W-2 Wage and Tax Statement 19--**

This information is being furnished to the Internal Revenue Service.

SOC. SEC. NO.: 381-48-9120 EMPLOYEE NO.: 814

DATE EMPLOYED: FEBRUARY 15, 1974

DATE OF BIRTH: OCTOBER 4, 1952

DATE EMPLOYMENT TERMINATED:

DEDUCTIONS					PAID		
FICA TAX	FEDERAL INCOME TAX	U.S. BONDS	OTHER	TOTAL	NET AMOUNT	CHECK NO.	LINE NO.
84.75	213.60	20.00		318.35	811.65	6175	39
912.75	2,238.30	260.00	UF 40.00	3,451.05	8,718.95		
60.00	150.82	20.00	UF 5.00	235.82	564.18	6225	40
62.25	156.11	20.00		238.36	591.64	6530	46
60.00	150.82	20.00		230.82	569.18	6582	47
64.50	162.41	20.00		246.91	613.09	6640	48
82.50	210.00	20.00	UF 5.00	317.50	782.50	6688	49
60.00	150.82	20.00		230.82	569.18	6743	50
69.00	174.99	20.00		263.99	656.01	6801	51
73.50	186.70	20.00	UF 5.00	285.20	694.80	6860	52
917.25	2,244.60	260.00	UF 15.00	3,436.85	8,793.15		
3,786.00	8,942.06	1,040.00	UF100.00	13,868.06	36,611.94		

CHAPTER REVIEW

KEY POINTS

OBJECTIVE 1

Payroll and Payroll Taxes

The term payroll is used to refer to the total amount paid to employees for a certain period. Payroll includes amounts paid for salaries to managerial or administrative employees as well as wages paid for manual labor.

Many enterprises pay their employees an annual bonus in addition to their regular salary or wage. The amount of the bonus may be measured by a certain percentage of income, which may be computed in a variety of ways.

The total earnings of an employee for a payroll period, including bonuses and overtime pay, are often called the gross pay. From this amount is subtracted one or more deductions to arrive at the net pay. Deductions normally include FICA tax, federal income tax, and state and local income taxes, and may include union dues, charitable contributions, or employee insurance.

Most employers are subject to federal and state taxes based on the amount of remuneration earned by their employees. Such taxes include FICA tax, federal unemployment compensation tax, and state unemployment compensation tax.

OBJECTIVE 2

Accounting Systems for Payroll and Payroll Taxes

Although payroll systems will vary, the major parts common to most payroll systems include the payroll register, payroll checks, and employee's earnings record. Based upon the data in the payroll register, a compound journal entry is usually prepared to record the payroll for a period. At this time, the employer's payroll taxes are also recorded. The payment of the payroll liabilities is recorded in the usual manner. The payment of the payroll is usually accomplished through the use of payroll checks.

The employee's earnings record is updated after each payroll period and is used for preparing reports for tax, insurance, and other purposes.

Cash disbursement controls are applicable to payrolls. Thus, the use of the voucher system and the requirement that all payments be supported by vouchers is desirable. Additional controls, such as the maintenance of employees' attendance records, are also desirable.

OBJECTIVE 3

Liability for Employees' Fringe Benefits

Most companies provide a variety of benefits to their employees in addition to salary and wages earned. These benefits are referred to as fringe benefits and may take the form of vacations, employee pension plans, stock options, health insurance, etc. The estimated cost of these benefits should be recognized as an expense of the period during which the employee earns the benefit.

OBJECTIVE 4

Short-Term Notes Payable

Notes may be issued to creditors in temporary satisfaction of an account payable created earlier, or they may be issued at the time merchandise or other assets are purchased. Notes may also be issued to borrow money from banks. The notes may be interest-bearing or non-interest-bearing. In the case of non-interest-bearing notes, the interest (discount) is deducted from the face of the note and the borrower receives the balance (proceeds).

OBJECTIVE 5

Product Warranty Liability

At the time of sale, a company may grant a warranty on a product. A liability to cover the warranty should be recorded during the period of the sale.

OBJECTIVE 6 Contingent Liabilities

Contingent liabilities are potential obligations that will materialize only if certain events occur in the future. If the liability is probable and the amount of the liability can be reasonably estimated, it should be recorded in the accounts. If the amount cannot be reasonably estimated, the details of the contingency should be disclosed in the financial statements.

KEY TERMS

contingent liabilities 374
payroll 374
gross pay 377
net pay 377
FICA tax 377
payroll register 380
employee's earnings record 382
stock options 387
discount rate 388
discount 388
proceeds 388

SELF-EXAMINATION QUESTIONS

Answers at end of chapter.

1. An employee's rate of pay is $20 per hour, with time and a half for all hours worked in excess of 40 during a week. The following data are available:

Hours worked during current week	44
Year's cumulative earnings prior to current week	$49,400
FICA rate on first $55,000 of annual earnings	7.5%
Federal income tax withheld	$ 212

Based on these data, the amount of the employee's net pay for the current week is:
A. $639
B. $708
C. $800
D. $920

2. Which of the following taxes are employers usually required to withhold from employees?
A. Federal income tax
B. Federal unemployment compensation tax
C. State unemployment compensation tax
D. All of the above

3. With limitations on the maximum earnings subject to the tax, employers incur operating costs for which of the following payroll taxes?
A. FICA tax
B. Federal unemployment compensation tax
C. State unemployment compensation tax
D. All of the above

4. An enterprise issued a $5,000, 60-day, 12% note to the bank. The amount due at maturity is:
A. $4,900
B. $5,000
C. $5,100
D. $5,600

5. An enterprise issued a $5,000, 60-day, non-interest-bearing note to the bank, and the bank discounts the note at 12%. The proceeds are:
A. $4,400
B. $4,900
C. $5,000
D. $5,100

ILLUSTRATIVE PROBLEM

Selected transactions of Grainger Company, completed during the fiscal year ended December 31, are as follows:

Mar. 1. Purchased merchandise on account from Perry Inc., $15,000.
Apr. 10. Issued a 60-day, 12% note for $15,000 to Perry Inc., on account.
June 9. Paid Perry Inc. the amount owed on the note of April 10.
Aug. 1. Issued a 90-day, non-interest-bearing note for $30,000 to Atlantic Coast National Bank. The bank discounted the note at 15%.
Oct. 30. Paid Atlantic Coast National Bank the amount due on the note of August 1.
Dec. 27. Prepared the entry to record the biweekly payroll. A summary of the payroll record follows:

Deductions:	
FICA tax	$ 4,820
Federal income tax withheld	13,280
State income tax withheld	3,840
Savings bond deductions	630
Medical insurance deductions	960
Salary distribution:	
Sales	$50,800
Officers	25,800
Office	6,400
Net amount	$59,470

30. Issued a check in payment of employees' federal income tax of $13,280 and FICA tax of $9,640 due.
31. Issued a check for $8,600 to the pension fund trustee to fully fund the pension cost for December.
31. Prepared the entry to record the employees' accrued vacation pay, $32,200.
31. Prepared the entry to record the estimated accrued product warranty liability, $41,360.

Instructions:

Record the preceding transactions.

SOLUTION

Date	Account	Debit	Credit
Mar. 1	Purchases	15,000	
	Accounts Payable—Perry Inc.		15,000
Apr. 10	Accounts Payable—Perry Inc.	15,000	
	Notes Payable		15,000
June 9	Notes Payable	15,000	
	Interest Expense	300	
	Cash		15,300
Aug. 1	Cash	28,875	
	Interest Expense	1,125	
	Notes Payable		30,000
Oct. 30	Notes Payable	30,000	
	Cash		30,000

		Debit	Credit
Dec. 27	Sales Salaries Expense	50,800	
	Officers Salaries Expense	25,800	
	Office Salaries Expense	6,400	
	FICA Tax Payable		4,820
	Employees Federal Income Tax Payable		13,280
	Employees State Income Tax Payable		3,840
	Bond Deductions Payable		630
	Medical Insurance Payable		960
	Salaries Payable		59,470
30	Employees Federal Income Tax Payable	13,280	
	FICA Tax Payable	9,640	
	Cash		22,920
31	Pension Expense	8,600	
	Cash		8,600
31	Vacation Pay Expense	32,200	
	Vacation Pay Payable		32,200
31	Product Warranty Expense	41,360	
	Product Warranty Payable		41,360

DISCUSSION QUESTIONS

9–1. What term is frequently used to refer to the total amount paid to employees for a certain period?

9–2. If an employee is granted a profit-sharing bonus, is the amount of the bonus (a) part of the employee's earnings and (b) deductible as an expense of the enterprise in determining the federal income tax?

9–3. The general manager of a business enterprise is entitled to an annual profit-sharing bonus of 8%. For the current year, income before bonus and income taxes is $200,000, and income taxes are estimated at 35% of income before income taxes. Determine the amount of the bonus, assuming that the bonus is based on net income after deducting both bonus and income taxes.

9–4. What is (a) gross pay? (b) net or take-home pay?

9–5. (a) Identify the federal taxes that most employers are required to withhold from employees. (b) Give the titles of the accounts to which the amounts withheld are credited.

9–6. For each of the following payroll-related taxes, indicate whether there is a ceiling on the annual earnings subject to the tax: (a) FICA tax, (b) federal income tax, (c) federal unemployment compensation tax.

9–7. An employee earns $20 per hour with 1½ times the regular rate for all hours in excess of 40 per week. If the employee worked 50 hours during the current week, what was the gross pay for the week?

9–8. Based on the data presented in Question 9–7, determine the net pay for the current week, assuming that gross pay prior to the current week totaled $49,760, the FICA tax rate was 7.5% (with earnings up to $55,000 subject to the 7.5% rate) and federal income tax to be withheld was $215.

9–9. Identify the payroll taxes levied against employers.

9–10. Do payroll taxes levied against employers become liabilities at the time the liabilities for wages are incurred or at the time the wages are paid?

9–11. For each of the following payroll-related taxes, indicate whether they generally apply to (a) employees only, (b) employers only, (c) both employees and employers: (1) FICA tax, (2) federal income tax, (3) federal unemployment compensation tax, (4) state unemployment compensation tax.

9–12. Indicate the principal functions served by the employee's earnings record.

9–13. An employer pays the employees in currency and the pay envelopes are prepared by an employee rather than by the bank. (a) Why would it be advisable to obtain from the bank the exact amount of money needed for a payroll? (b) How could the exact number of each bill and coin denomination needed be determined efficiently in advance?

9–14. A company uses a weekly payroll period and a special bank account for payroll. (a) When should deposits be made in the account? (b) How is the amount of the deposit determined? (c) Is it necessary to have in the general ledger an account entitled "Cash—Special Payroll Account"? Explain. (d) The bank statement for the payroll bank account for the month ended July 31 indicates a bank balance of $9,972.50. Assuming that the bank has made no errors, what does this amount represent?

9–15. In a payroll system diagram, what type of input data are referred to as (a) constants, (b) variables?

9–16. To strengthen internal controls, what department should provide written authorizations for the addition of names to the payroll?

9–17. Explain how a payroll system that is properly designed and operated tends to give assurance (a) that wages paid are based upon hours actually worked, and (b) that payroll checks are not issued to fictitious employees.

9–18. To match revenues and expenses properly, should the expense for employee vacation pay be recorded in the period during which the vacation privilege is earned or during the period in which the vacation is taken? Discuss.

9–19. Differentiate between a contributory and a noncontributory pension plan.

9–20. Identify several factors which influence the future pension obligation of an enterprise.

9–21. How does prior service cost arise in a new or revised pension plan?

9–22. Where should the unfunded accrued pension cost be reported on the balance sheet?

9–23. What are employee stock options?

9–24. A business enterprise issued a 60-day, 12% note for $15,000 to a creditor on account. Give the entries to record (a) the issuance of the note and (b) the payment of the note at maturity, including interest of $300.

9–25. In borrowing money from a bank, an enterprise issued a $75,000, 90-day, non-interest-bearing note, which the bank discounted at 13%. Are the proceeds $75,000? Explain.

9–26. When should the liability associated with a product warranty be recorded? Discuss.

9–27. A business firm is contesting a suit for damages of a substantial amount, brought by a customer for an alleged faulty product. Is this a contingent liability for the defendant? If so, should it be disclosed in financial statements issued during the period of litigation? Discuss.

Real World Focus

9–28. The 1990 annual report for Zenith Electronics Corporation reported in the liability section of the December 31, 1989 balance sheet the following data with respect to product warranties:

Current Liabilities:
Product warranty 24,700,000

(a) What entry would have been made to record the accrued product warranty costs at December 31, 1989, assuming that no entry had been made in prior years? (b) How would costs of repairing a defective product be recorded?

Real World Focus

9–29. The "Questions and Answers Technical Hotline" in the June, 1988 *Journal of Accountancy* included the following question:

Several years ago, Company B instituted legal action against Company A. Under a memorandum of settlement and agreement, Company A agreed to pay Company B a total of $17,500 in three installments—$5,000 on March 1, $7,500 on July 1 and the remaining $5,000 on December 31. Company A paid the first two installments during its fiscal year ended September 30. Should the unpaid amount of $5,000 be presented as a current liability at September 30?

Ethics Discussion Case

9–30. How would you answer this question?

Ed Kirkland, a CPA and staff assistant for a local CPA firm, noticed on his payroll stub covering the two-week period of March 2–March 16 that his overtime pay had been computed on the basis of 2 times his regular pay rate, rather than 1 1/2 times his regular rate. Ed has decided to cash the payroll check. If his employer later catches the error, Ed plans to deny having originally noticed the mistake.
Discuss whether Ed Kirkland is behaving in an ethical manner.

EXERCISES

Ex. 9–31.
Profit-sharing bonus.
OBJ. 1

The general manager of a business enterprise is entitled to an annual profit-sharing bonus of 6%. For the current year, income before bonus and income taxes is $500,000, and income taxes are estimated at 35% of income before income taxes. Determine the amount of the bonus, assuming that (a) the bonus is based on income before deductions for bonus and income taxes and (b) the bonus is based on income after deduction for both bonus and income taxes.

Ex. 9–32.
Summary payroll data.
OBJ. 1, 2

In the following summary of data for a payroll period, some amounts have been intentionally omitted:

Earnings:		Deductions:	
(1) At regular rate......	?	(4) FICA tax..............	$ 4,962.25
(2) At overtime rate....	$ 4,760.00	(5) Income tax withheld.	10,673.15
(3) Total earnings	?	(6) Medical insurance..	816.50
		(7) Union dues...........	?
		(8) Total deductions....	18,130.90
		(9) Net amount paid....	67,948.50

Accounts debited:	
(10) Factory Wages ...	$62,080.50
(11) Sales Salaries.....	?
(12) Office Salaries....	5,600.00

(a) Determine the amounts omitted in lines (1), (3), (7), and (11). (b) Present the journal entry to record the payroll. (c) Present the entry to record the voucher for the payroll. (d) Present the entry to record the payment of the voucher. (e) From the data given in this exercise and your answer to (a), would you conclude that this payroll was paid sometime during the first few weeks of the calendar year? Explain.

Ex. 9–33.
Payroll tax entries.
OBJ. 2

According to a summary of the payroll of McFarlane Publishing Co., the amount of earnings for the four weekly payrolls paid in November of the current year was $540,000. Of this amount, $510,000 was subject to the 7.5% FICA tax rate and $30,000 was subject to the 1.5% FICA tax rate. Also $15,000 was subject to state and federal unemployment taxes. (a) Determine the employer's payroll taxes expense for the month, using the following rates: state unemployment, 4.8%; federal unemployment, 8%. (b) Present the entry to record the accrual of payroll taxes for the month of November.

Ex. 9–34.
Accrued vacation pay and product warranty.
OBJ. 3, 5

A business enterprise provides its employees with varying amounts of vacation per year, depending on the length of employment. It also warrants its products for one year. The estimated total amount of the current year's vacation pay is $216,000, and the estimated product warranty is 2% of sales. If sales were $950,000 for January, prepare the adjusting entries required at January 31, the end of the first month of the current year, to record (a) the accrued vacation pay and (b) the accrued product warranty.

Ex. 9–35.
Pension plan entries.
OBJ. 3

Bair Corporation maintains a funded pension plan for its employees. The plan requires quarterly installments to be paid to the funding agent, Powers Insurance Company, by the fifteenth of the month following the end of each quarter. If the pension cost is $60,000 for the quarter ended December 31, prepare entries to record (a) the accrued pension liability on December 31 and (b) the payment to the funding agent on January 15.

Ex. 9–36.
Entries for discounting notes.
OBJ. 4

Gerhardt Co. issues a 90-day, non-interest-bearing note for $100,000 to Tyson Bank and Trust Co., and the bank discounts the note at 14%. (a) Present the maker's entries to record (1) the issuance of the note and (2) the payment of the note at maturity. (b) Present the payee's entries to record (1) the receipt of the note and (2) the receipt of payment of the note at maturity.

Ex. 9–37.
Determination of interest on notes issued.
OBJ. 4

In negotiating a 90-day loan, an enterprise has the option of either (1) issuing a $250,000, non-interest-bearing note that will be discounted at the rate of 12%, or (2) issuing a $250,000 note that bears interest at the rate of 12% and that will be accepted at face value.

(a) Determine the amount of the interest expense for each option.
(b) Determine the amount of the proceeds for each option.
(c) Indicate the option that is more favorable to the borrower.

Ex. 9–38.
Plant asset purchases with note.
OBJ. 4

On June 30, Jenkins Company purchased land for $120,000 and a building for $480,000, paying $150,000 cash and issuing a 12% note for the balance, secured by a mortgage on the property. The terms of the note provide for 18 semiannual payments of $25,000 on the principal plus the interest accrued from the date of the preceding payment. Present the entry to record (a) the transaction on June 30, (b) the payment of the first installment on December 31, and (c) the payment of the second installment the following June 30.

PROBLEMS

Pb. 9–39.
Profit-sharing bonuses.
OBJ. 1

The Chief Operating Officer (COO) of Shulman Company is entitled to an annual profit-sharing bonus of 4%. For the current year, income before bonus and income taxes is $750,000, and income taxes are estimated at 35% of income before income taxes.

Instructions:

(1) Determine the amount of the bonus, assuming that:
- (a) The bonus is based on income before deductions for bonus and income taxes.
- (b) The bonus is based on income after deduction for bonus but before deduction for income taxes.
- (c) The bonus is based on income after deduction for income taxes but before deduction for bonus.
- (d) The bonus is based on income after deduction for both bonus and income taxes.

(2) (a) Which bonus plan would the COO prefer? (b) Would this plan always be the COO's choice, regardless of Shulman Company's income level?

Pb. 9–40.
Entries for payroll and payroll taxes.
OBJ. 1, 2

The following information relative to the payroll for the week ended October 1 was obtained from the records of Griffin Enterprises Inc.:

Salaries:		Deductions:	
Sales salaries	$150,250	Income tax withheld	$34,200
Warehouse salaries	22,500	FICA tax withheld	14,100
Office salaries	15,250	U.S. savings bonds	4,500
	$188,000	Group insurance	3,300

Tax rates assumed:
State unemployment (employer only), 3.8%
Federal unemployment, .8%

Instructions:

(1) Present the entry to record the payroll.
(2) Present the entry to record the employer's payroll taxes. Of the total payroll, $15,000 is subject to unemployment compensation taxes.

9-402

Pb. 9–41.
Payroll entries.
OBJ. 1, 2

The following accounts, with the balances indicated, appear in the ledger of Zeigler Company on December 1 of the current year:

212	Salaries Payable	—
213	FICA Tax Payable	$ 7,100
214	Employees Federal Income Tax Payable	8,520
215	Employees State Income Tax Payable	14,586
216	State Unemployment Tax Payable	1,881
217	Federal Unemployment Tax Payable	396
218	Bond Deductions Payable	750
219	Medical Insurance Payable	4,265
611	Sales Salaries Expense	694,430
711	Officers Salaries Expense	342,980
712	Office Salaries Expense	94,050
719	Payroll Taxes Expense	101,673

The following transactions relating to payroll, payroll deductions, and payroll taxes occurred during December:

Dec. 2. Prepared Voucher No. 749 for $750, payable to Monroe National Bank, to purchase United States savings bonds for employees.

2. Issued Check No. 732 in payment of Voucher No. 749.

3. Prepared Voucher No. 750 for $15,620, payable to Monroe National Bank for $8,520 of employees' federal income tax and $7,100 of FICA tax due.

3. Issued Check No. 733 in payment of Voucher No. 750.

14. Prepared a journal entry to record the biweekly payroll. A summary of the payroll record follows:

Deductions:	
FICA tax	$ 3,575
Federal income tax withheld	8,569
State income tax withheld	2,112
Savings bond deductions	375
Medical insurance deductions	528
Salary distributions:	
Sales	$33,660
Officers	16,720
Office	4,180
Net amount	$39,401

14. Prepared Voucher No. 757, payable to Payroll Bank Account, for the net amount of the biweekly payroll.

14. Issued Check No. 738 in payment of Voucher No. 757.

14. Prepared a journal entry to record employer's payroll taxes on earnings of December 14: FICA, $3,575; state unemployment tax, $162; federal unemployment tax, $35.

17. Prepared Voucher No. 758 for $15,719, payable to Monroe National Bank for $8,569 of employees' federal income tax and $7,150 of FICA tax due.

17. Issued Check No. 744 in payment of Voucher No. 758.

18. Prepared Voucher No. 760 for $4,265, payable to Wilson Insurance Company, for the semiannual premium on the group medical insurance policy.

Dec. 19. Issued Check No. 750 in payment of Voucher No. 760.

28. Prepared a journal entry to record the biweekly payroll. A summary of the payroll record follows:

Deductions:	
FICA tax	$ 3,311
Federal income tax withheld	8,322
State income tax withheld	2,029
Savings bond deductions	375
Salary distribution:	
Sales	$31,350
Officers	16,720
Office	4,180
Net amount	$38,213

28. Prepared Voucher No. 795, payable to Payroll Bank Account, for the net amount of the biweekly payroll.
28. Issued check No. 782 in payment of Voucher No. 795.
28. Prepared a journal entry to record the employer's payroll taxes on earnings of December 28: FICA, $3,311; state unemployment tax, $161; federal unemployment tax, $33.
30. Prepared Voucher No. 801 for $750, payable to Monroe National Bank, to purchase United States savings bonds for employees.
30. Issued Check No. 791 in payment of Voucher No. 801.
30. Prepared Voucher No. 802 for $14,586, payable to Monroe National Bank, for employees' state income tax due on December 31.
30. Issued Check No. 792 in payment of Voucher No. 802.

Instructions:

(1) Record the transactions in a journal.
(2) Journalize the adjusting entry on December 31 to record salaries for the incomplete payroll period. Salaries accrued are as follows: sales salaries, $3,245; officers salaries, $1,800; office salaries, $450. The payroll taxes are immaterial and are not accrued.

Pb. 9–42.
Wage and Tax Statement data and employer FICA tax.
OBJ. 1, 2

SPREADSHEET PROBLEM

Dilla Company began business on January 2 of last year. Salaries were paid to employees on the last day of each month, and both FICA tax and federal income tax were withheld in the required amounts. An employee who is hired in the middle of the month receives half the monthly salary for that month. All required payroll tax reports were filed and the correct amount of payroll taxes was remitted by the company for the calendar year. Before the Wage and Tax Statements (Form W-2) could be prepared for distributing to employees and filing with the Social Security Administration, the employees' earnings records were inadvertently destroyed.

None of the employees resigned or were discharged during the year, and there were no changes in salary rates. The FICA tax was withheld at the rate of 7.5% on the first $55,000 of salary and at the rate of 1.5% on salary from $55,000 to $125,000. Data on dates of employment, salary rates, and employees' income taxes withheld, which are summarized as follows, were obtained from personnel records and payroll records.

Employee	Date First Employed	Monthly Salary	Monthly Income Tax Withheld
Brown	Jan. 2	$4,200	$ 854.50
Davis	June 2	2,500	417.50
Jung	Apr. 15	2,800	461.10
O'Leary	Jan. 2	4,000	810.10
Silhan	Dec. 1	3,600	652.30
Reese	Mar. 1	3,800	748.15
Silvas	Feb. 1	5,200	1,261.40

Instructions:

(1) Determine the following amounts which would be reported on each employee's Wage and Tax Statement (Form W-2) for the year, arranging the data in the following form:

Employee	Gross Earnings	Federal Income Tax Withheld	FICA Tax Withheld

(2) Determine the following employer payroll taxes for the year: (a) FICA; (b) state unemployment compensation at 3.8% on the first $7,000 of each employee's earnings; (c) federal unemployment compensation at .8% of the first $7,000 of each employee's earnings; (d) total.

Pb.9–43.
Notes payable, vacation pay, product warranty, and pension transactions.
OBJ. 3, 4, 5

The following items were selected from among the transactions completed by Brokow Co. during the current year:

Feb. 6. Purchased merchandise on account from Matlock Company, $7,500.
Mar. 18. Issued a 60-day, 12% note for $7,500 to Matlock Company, on account.
May 10. Issued a 120-day, non-interest-bearing note for $45,000 to Garden City Bank. The bank discounted the note at the rate of 14%.
17. Paid Matlock Company the amount owed on the note of March 18.
Aug. 5. Borrowed $15,000 from First Federal Savings, issuing a 60-day, 14% note for that amount.
Sept. 7. Paid Garden City Bank the amount due on the note of May 10.
Oct. 4. Paid First Federal Savings the interest due on the note of August 5 and renewed the loan by issuing a new 30-day, 16% note for $15,000. (Record both the debit and the credit to the notes payable account.)
Nov. 3. Paid First Federal Savings the amount due on the note of October 4.
15. Purchased store equipment from Ames Equipment Co. for $50,000, paying $15,000 and issuing a series of seven 12% notes for $5,000 each, coming due at 30-day intervals.
Dec. 15. Paid the amount due Ames Equipment Co. on the first note in the series issued on November 15.
31. Paid $27,500 of the annual pension cost of $40,000. (Record both the payment and the unfunded pension cost.)

Instructions:

(1) Record the transactions.
(2) Record the adjusting journal entries for each of the following accrued expenses for the current year:
(a) Vacation pay $15,000
(b) Product warranty cost 12,750

(3) Record the adjusting journal entry for the accrued interest at December 31 on the six notes owed to Ames Equipment Co.
(4) Assume that a single note for $35,000 had been issued on November 15 instead of the series of seven notes, and that its terms required principal payments of $5,000 each 30 days, with interest at 12% on the principal balance before applying the $5,000 payment. Determine the amount that would have been due and payable on December 15.

If the working papers correlating with the textbook are not used, omit Appendix Pb. 9–44.

Appendix Pb. 9–44.
Payroll register.

The payroll register for Ayres Company for the week ended December 21 of the current fiscal year is presented in the working papers.

Instructions:

(1) Journalize the entry to record the payroll for the week.
(2) Assuming the use of a voucher system and payment by regular check, present the entries to record the payroll voucher and the issuance of the checks to employees.
(3) Journalize the entry to record the employer's payroll taxes for the week. Assume the following tax rates: state unemployment, 3.8%; federal unemployment, .8%. Of the earnings, $1,020 is subject to unemployment taxes.
(4) Present the entries to record the following selected transactions:

Dec. 15. Prepared a voucher, payable to Arnaz National Bank, for employees income taxes, $1,275.40, and FICA taxes, $816.50.
15. Issued a check to Arnaz National Bank in payment of the voucher.

ALTERNATE PROBLEMS

Pb. 9–39A.
Profit-sharing bonuses.
OBJ. 1

The president of Beaver Products is entitled to an annual profit-sharing bonus of 5%. For the current year, income before bonus and income taxes is $500,000, and income taxes are estimated at 35% of income before income taxes.

Instructions:

(1) Determine the amount of the bonus, assuming that:
(a) The bonus is based on income before deductions for bonus and income taxes.
(b) The bonus is based on income after deduction for bonus but before deduction for income taxes.
(c) The bonus is based on income after deduction for income taxes but before deduction for bonus.
(d) The bonus is based on income after deduction for both bonus and income taxes.
(2) (a) Which bonus would the president prefer? (b) Would this plan always be the president's choice, regardless of Beaver Product's income level?

Pb. 9–40A.
Entries for payroll and payroll taxes.
OBJ. 1, 2

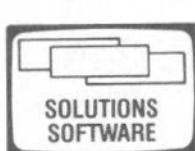

The following information relative to the payroll for the week ended September 30 was obtained from the records of T.T. Grasso Co.:

Salaries:		Deductions:	
Sales salaries	$ 90,000	Income tax withheld	$19,250
Warehouse salaries	18,980	FICA tax withheld	9,000
Office salaries	11,020	Group insurance	1,500
	$120,000	U.S. savings bonds	1,200

Tax rates assumed:
State unemployment (employer only), 4.2%
Federal unemployment, .8%

Instructions:

(1) Present the entry to record the payroll.
(2) Present the entry to record the employer's payroll taxes. Of the total payroll, $9,000 is subject to unemployment compensation taxes.

Pb. 9–41A.
Payroll entries.
OBJ. 1, 2

The following accounts, with the balances indicated, appear in the ledger of King Company on December 1 of the current year:

212	Salaries Payable	—
213	FICA Tax Payable	$ 7,455
214	Employees Federal Income Tax Payable	22,400
215	Employees State Income Tax Payable	13,260
216	State Unemployment Tax Payable	1,710
217	Federal Unemployment Tax Payable	360
218	Bond Deductions Payable	715
219	Medical Insurance Payable	3,875
611	Sales Salaries Expense	631,300
711	Officers Salaries Expense	311,800
712	Office Salaries Expense	85,500
719	Payroll Taxes Expense	92,430

The following transactions relating to payroll, payroll deductions, and payroll taxes occurred during December:

Dec. 2. Prepared Voucher No. 638 for $715, payable to Southeast National Bank, to purchase United States savings bonds for employees.
2. Issued Check No. 621 in payment of Voucher No. 638.
3. Prepared Voucher No. 639 for $29,855, payable to Southeast National Bank for $22,400 of employees' federal income tax and $7,455 of FICA tax due.
3. Issued Check No. 622 in payment of Voucher No. 639.
14. Prepared a journal entry to record the biweekly payroll. A summary of the payroll record follows:

Deductions:	
FICA tax	$ 3,250
Federal income tax withheld	7,790
State income tax withheld	1,920
Savings bond deductions	315
Medical insurance deductions	480
Salary distributions:	
Sales	$30,600
Officers	15,200
Office	3,800
Net amount	$35,845

Dec. 14. Prepared Voucher No. 646, payable to Payroll Bank Account, for the net amount of the biweekly payroll.

Dec. 14. Issued Check No. 627 in payment of Voucher No. 646.

14. Prepared a journal entry to record employer's payroll taxes on earnings of December 14: FICA, $3,250; state unemployment tax, $81; federal unemployment tax, $18.

17. Prepared Voucher No. 647 for $14,290, payable to Southeast National Bank for $7,790 of employees' federal income tax and $6,500 of FICA tax due.

17. Issued Check No. 628 in payment of Voucher No. 647.

18. Prepared Voucher No. 650 for $3,875, payable to Wilson Insurance Company, for the semiannual premium on the group medical insurance policy.

19. Issued Check No. 639 in payment of Voucher No. 650.

28. Prepared a journal entry to record the biweekly payroll. A summary of the payroll record follows:

Deductions:	
FICA tax	$ 3,010
Federal income tax withheld	7,565
State income tax withheld	1,845
Savings bond deductions	315
Salary distribution:	
Sales	$28,500
Officers	15,200
Office	3,800
Net amount	$34,765

28. Prepared Voucher No. 684, payable to Payroll Bank Account, for the net amount of the biweekly payroll.

28. Issued Check No. 671 in payment of Voucher No. 684.

28. Prepared a journal entry to record the employer's payroll taxes on earnings of December 28: FICA, $3,010; state unemployment tax, $80; federal unemployment tax, $17.

30. Prepared Voucher No. 690 for $630, payable to Southeast National Bank, to purchase United States savings bonds for employees.

30. Issued Check No. 680 in payment of Voucher No. 690.

30. Prepared Voucher No. 691 for $13,260, payable to Southeast National Bank, for employees' state income tax due on December 31.

30. Issued Check No. 681 in payment of Voucher No. 691.

Instructions:

(1) Record the transactions in a journal.

(2) Journalize the adjusting entry on December 31 to record salaries for the incomplete payroll period. Salaries accrued are as follows: sales salaries, $2,950; officers salaries, $1,640; office salaries, $410. The payroll taxes are immaterial and are not accrued.

Pb. 9–42A.
Wage and Tax Statement data and employer FICA tax.
OBJ. 1, 2

Stoner Company began business on January 2 of last year. Salaries were paid to employees on the last day of each month, and both FICA tax and federal income tax were withheld in the required amounts. An employee who is hired in the middle of the month receives half the monthly salary for that month. All required payroll tax reports were filed and the correct amount of payroll taxes was remitted by the company for the calendar year. Before the Wage and Tax Statements (Form W-2) could be prepared for distributing to employees and filing with the Social Security Administration, the employees' earnings records were inadvertently destroyed.

None of the employees resigned or were discharged during the year, and there were no changes in salary rates. The FICA tax was withheld at the rate of 7.5% on the first $55,000 of salary and at the rate of 1.5% on salary from $55,000 to $125,000. Data on dates of employment, salary rates, and employees' income taxes withheld, which are summarized as follows, were obtained from personnel records and payroll records.

Employee	Date First Employed	Monthly Salary	Monthly Income Tax Withheld
Allan	Mar. 1	$3,220	$ 541.88
Bork	Jan. 2	4,200	895.60
Faulk	Nov. 1	2,500	394.25
Helms	Aug. 1	3,740	700.15
Omar	Jan. 2	5,400	1,374.10
Ruiz	May 1	3,600	652.30
Yeager	Feb. 16	4,000	864.10

Instructions:

(1) Determine the following amounts which would be reported on each employee's Wage and Tax Statement (Form W-2) for the year, arranging the data in the following form:

Employee	Gross Earnings	Federal Income Tax Withheld	FICA Tax Withheld

(2) Determine the following employer payroll taxes for the year: (a) FICA; (b) state unemployment compensation at 4.2% on the first $7,000 of each employee's earnings; (c) federal unemployment compensation at .8% of the first $7,000 of each employee's earnings; (d) total.

Pb. 9–43A.
Notes payable, vacation pay, product warranty, and pension transactions.
OBJ. 3, 4, 5

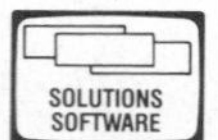

The following items were selected from among the transactions completed by Douglas Co. during the current year:

Jan. 15. Purchased merchandise on account from Davis Co., $7,800.
Feb. 28. Issued a 60-day, 12% note for $7,800 to Davis Co., on account.
Apr. 29. Paid Davis Co. the amount owed on the note of February 28.
July 15. Borrowed $8,000 from Keyes National Bank, issuing a 90-day, 13% note for that amount.
25. Issued a 120-day, non-interest-bearing note for $40,000 to Mid-State Bank. The bank discounted the note at the rate of 15%.
Oct. 13. Paid Keyes National Bank the interest due on the note of July 15 and renewed the loan by issuing a new 30-day, 15% note for $8,000. (Record both the debit and credit to the notes payable account.)
Nov. 12. Paid Keyes State Bank the amount due on the note of October 13.
22. Paid Mid-State Bank the amount due on the note of July 25.
Dec. 1. Purchased office equipment from Bunn Equipment Co. for $60,000, paying $10,000 and issuing a series of ten 12% notes for $5,000 each, coming due at 30-day intervals.
31. Paid the amount due Bunn Equipment Co. on the first note in the series issued on December 1.
31. Paid $32,400 of the year's pension cost of $45,000. (Record both the payment and the unfunded pension cost.)

Instructions:

(1) Record the transactions.
(2) Record the adjusting journal entries for each of the following accrued expenses for the current year:
(a) Vacation pay $17,900
(b) Product warranty cost 15,000

(3) Record the adjusting entry for the accrued interest at December 31 on the nine notes owed to Bunn Equipment Co.

(4) Assume that a single note for $50,000 had been issued on December 1 instead of the series of ten notes, and that its terms required principal payments of $5,000 each 30 days, with interest at 12% on the principal balance before applying the $5,000 payment. Determine the amount that would have been due and payable on December 31.

If the working papers correlating with the textbook are not used, omit Appendix Pb. 9–44A.

Appendix Pb. 9–44A.
Payroll register.

The payroll register for Amy Garrow Co. for the week ending December 21 of the current fiscal year is presented in the working papers.

Instructions:

(1) Journalize the entry to record the payroll for the week.
(2) Assuming the use of a voucher system and payment by regular check, present the entries to record the payroll voucher and the issuance of the checks to employees.
(3) Journalize the entry to record the employer's payroll taxes for the week. Assume the following tax rates: state unemployment, 3.1%; federal unemployment, .8%. Of the earnings, $500 is subject to unemployment taxes.
(4) Present the entries to record the following selected transactions:

Dec. 16. Prepared a voucher, payable to Weiss National Bank, for employees income taxes, $1,217.50, and FICA taxes, $401.50.
16. Issued a check to Weiss National Bank in payment of the above voucher.

MINI-CASE 9

In 1991, your father retired as president of the family-owned business, MG Inc., and a new president was recruited by an executive search firm. The new president's contract called for an annual base salary of $60,000 plus a bonus of 12% of income after deducting the bonus but before deducting income taxes.

In 1992, the first full year under the new president, MG Inc. reported income of $966,000 before deducting the bonus and income taxes. After being fired on January 2, 1993, the new president demanded immediate payment of a $115,920 bonus for 1992.

Your father was concerned about the accounting practices used during 1992, and he has asked you to help him in reviewing the accounting records before the bonus is paid. Upon investigation, you have discovered the following facts:

(a) The payroll for December 28–31, 1992, was not accrued at the end of the year. The salaries for the four-day period and the applicable payroll taxes are as follows:

Sales salaries	$7,000
Office salaries	3,000
FICA tax	750
State unemployment tax (employer only)	320
Federal unemployment tax	80

The payroll was paid on January 4, 1993, for the period December 28, 1992, through January 3, 1993.

(b) The semiannual pension cost of $25,000 was not accrued for the last half of 1992. The pension cost was paid to Equity Insurance Company on January 15, 1993, and was recorded by a debit to Pension Expense and a credit to Cash for $25,000.
(c) The estimated product warranty liability of $12,500 for products sold during the year ended December 31, 1992, was not recorded.
(d) On April 1, 1992, MG Inc. purchased a one-year insurance policy for $9,640, debiting the cost to Prepaid Insurance. No adjusting entry was made for insurance expired at December 31, 1992.
(e) The vacation pay liability of $10,120 for the year ended December, 1992, was not recorded.

Instructions:

(1) Based on reported 1992 income of $966,000 before deducting the bonus and income taxes, was the president's calculation of the $115,920 bonus correct? Explain.
(2) What accounting errors were made in 1992 which would affect the amount of the president's bonus?
(3) Based on the employment contract and your answer to (2), what is the correct amount of the president's bonus for 1992?
(4) How much did the president's demand for a $115,920 bonus exceed the correct amount of the bonus under the employment contract?
(5) Describe the major advantage and disadvantage of using profit-sharing bonuses in employment contracts.

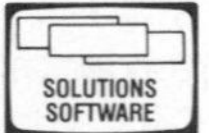

COMPREHENSIVE PROBLEM 3

Selected transactions completed by Hogan Company during its first fiscal year ending December 31 were as follows:

(a) Prepared a voucher to establish a petty cash fund of $250 and issued a check in payment of the voucher. (Prepare two journal entries.)
(b) Prepared a voucher to replenish the petty cash fund, based on the following summary of petty cash receipts: office supplies, $55; miscellaneous selling expense, $97; miscellaneous administrative expense, $80.
(c) Prepared a voucher to record the purchase of $10,000 of merchandise, 2/10, n/30. Purchase invoices are recorded at the net amount.
(d) Paid the invoice in (c) after the discount period had passed.
(e) Received cash from daily cash sales for $8,750. The amount indicated by the cash register tally was $8,755.
(f) Received a 60-day, 10% note for $30,000 on account.
(g) Discounted note received in (f) at bank, 30 days prior to maturity, at 12%.

(h) Received notice from bank that note discounted in (g) had been dishonored. Paid the bank the maturity value of the note.
(i) Received amount owed on dishonored note in (h) plus interest for 36 days at 10% computed on the maturity value of the note.
(j) Received $1,200 on account and wrote off the remainder owed on a $2,000 accounts receivable balance. (The allowance method is used in accounting for uncollectible receivables.)
(k) Reinstated the account written off in (j) and received $800 cash in full payment.
(l) Traded office equipment on July 1 for new equipment with a list price of $125,000. A trade-in allowance of $80,000 was received on the old equipment that had cost $90,000 and had accumulated depreciation of $15,000 as of July 1. A voucher was prepared for the amount owed of $45,000.
(m) Recorded the monthly payroll for November, based on the following data:

Salaries:		Deductions:	
Sales salaries	$ 9,500	Income tax withheld	$2,950
Office salaries	4,500	FICA tax withheld	900
	$14,000		

Tax rates assumed:
State unemployment, 3.8%
Federal unemployment, .8%
Amount subject to unemployment taxes:

State unemployment	$2,000
Federal unemployment	2,000

(n) Recorded the employer's payroll taxes on the payroll in (m).
(o) Issued a 90-day, non-interest-bearing note for $50,000 to the bank, which discounted it at 12%.
(p) Recorded voucher for payment of the note in (o) at maturity.
(q) The pension cost for the year was $12,000 and a voucher was prepared for $10,000, payable to the trustee for the funded portion.

Instructions:

(1) Prepare entries to record the selected transactions.
(2) Based on the following data, prepare a bank reconciliation for November of the current year:
   (a) Balance per bank statement at November 30, $90,530.
   (b) Balance per ledger at November 30, $58,340.
   (c) Checks outstanding at November 30, $60,500.
   (d) Deposit in transit, not recorded by bank, $28,200.
   (e) Bank debit memorandum for service charges, $20.
   (f) A check for $100 in payment of a voucher was erroneously recorded in the accounts as $10.
(3) Based on the bank reconciliation prepared in (2), prepare the entry or entries to be made by Hogan Company.
(4) Based on the following selected data, prepare the adjusting entries as of December 31 of the current year:
   (a) Estimated uncollectible accounts at December 31, $6,100. The balance of Allowance for Doubtful Accounts at December 31 was $1,500 (debit).
   (b) Prepaid insurance expired during the year, $17,250.
   (c) Office supplies used during the year, $4,500.

(d) Depreciation is computed as follows:

Asset	Cost	Residual Value	Acquisition Date	Useful Life in Years	Depreciation Method Used
Buildings	$225,000	0	January 2	50	Straight-line
Office Equipment	120,000	$12,000	July 1	5	Sum-of-the-years-digits
Store Equipment	60,000	10,000	January 3	8	Declining-balance (at twice the straight-line rate)

(e) A patent costing $18,000 when acquired on January 2 has a remaining legal life of 9 years, and was expected to have value for 6 years.

(f) The cost of mineral rights was $50,000. Of the estimated deposit of 25,000 tons of ore, 6,000 tons were mined during the year.

(g) Total vacation pay expense for the year, $7,000.

(h) A product warranty was granted beginning December 1 and covering a one-year period. The estimated cost is 3% of sales, which totaled $150,000 in December.

(5) Based on the following post-closing trial balance and other data, prepare a balance sheet in report form at December 31 of the current year:

Hogan Company
Post-Closing Trial Balance
December 31, 19--

Petty Cash	250	
Cash	60,500	
Marketable Equity Securities	40,000	
Allowance for Decline to Market		4,360
Notes Receivable	50,000	
Accounts Receivable	151,100	
Allowance for Doubtful Accounts		6,100
Merchandise Inventory	220,250	
Prepaid Insurance	13,750	
Office Supplies	1,500	
Land	50,000	
Buildings	225,000	
Accumulated Depreciation—Buildings		4,500
Office Equipment	120,000	
Accumulated Depreciation—Office Equipment		18,000
Store Equipment	60,000	
Accumulated Depreciation—Store Equipment		15,000
Mineral Rights	50,000	
Accumulated Depletion		12,000
Patents	15,000	
FICA Tax Payable		1,800
Employees Federal Income Tax Payable		2,950
State Unemployment Tax Payable		1,520
Federal Unemployment Tax Payable		320
Salaries Payable		14,000
Accounts Payable		88,300
Product Warranty Payable		4,500
Vacation Pay Payable		7,000
Unfunded Accrued Pension Cost		2,000
Notes Payable		450,000
Capital Stock		320,000
Retained Earnings		105,000
	1,057,350	1,057,350

The following information relating to the balance sheet accounts at December 31 is obtained from supplementary records:

Notes receivable, current asset	
Merchandise inventory, at cost by lifo method	
Product warranty payable, current liability	
Vacation pay payable:	
Current liability	$ 5,000
Long-term liability	2,000
Unfunded accrued pension cost, long-term liability	
Notes payable:	
Current liability	50,000
Long-term liability	400,000

(6) Assuming that the general manager had been granted a 5% profit-sharing bonus (based on income after deduction for the bonus) and income before the bonus was $105,000, what would have been the amount of the bonus?

(7) On February 15 of the following year, the merchandise inventory was destroyed by fire. Based on the following data obtained from the accounting records, estimate the cost of the merchandise destroyed:

Jan. 1	Merchandise inventory	$220,250
Jan. 1–Feb. 15	Purchases (net)	192,250
	Sales (net)	380,000
	Estimated gross profit rate	40%

ANSWERS TO SELF-EXAMINATION QUESTIONS

1. A The amount of net pay of $639 (answer A) is determined as follows:

Gross pay:		
40 hours at $20	$800	
4 hours at $30	120	$920
Deductions:		
Federal income tax withheld	$212	
FICA ($920 × .075)	69	281
Net pay		$639

2. A Employers are usually required to withhold a portion of the earnings of their employees for payment of federal income taxes (answer A). Generally, federal (answer B) and state (answer C) unemployment compensation taxes are levied against the employer only and thus are not deducted from employee earnings.

3. D The employer incurs operating costs for FICA tax (answer A), federal unemployment compensation tax (answer B), and state unemployment compensation tax (answer C). These costs add significantly to the total labor costs for most businesses.

4. C The maturity value is $5,100, determined as follows:

Face amount of note	$5,000
Plus interest ($5,000 × 12/100 × 60/360)	100
Maturity value	$5,100

5. B The net amount available to a borrower from discounting a note payable is termed the proceeds. The proceeds of $4,900 (answer B) is determined as follows:

Face amount of note	$5,000
Less discount ($5,000 × 12/100 × 60/360)	100
Proceeds	$4,900

PART

3

ACCOUNTING FOR EQUITY RIGHTS

CHAPTER 10

CHAPTER OBJECTIVES

1 Identify basic sole proprietorship characteristics which have accounting implications.

2 Describe and illustrate the accounting for sole proprietorships.

3 Identify basic partnership characteristics which have accounting implications.

4 Describe and illustrate the accounting for partnerships.

5 Identify basic corporation characteristics which have accounting implications.

6 Describe and illustrate the accounting for corporations.

7 Describe and illustrate the computation of equity per share of stock.

8 Describe and illustrate the accounting for organization costs.

FORMS OF BUSINESS ORGANIZATION

In preceding chapters, the corporate enterprise was used in illustrations. The transactions affecting the stockholders' equity of these enterprises focused on basic accounting concepts and principles. In this chapter, consideration will be given to the two other types of business organizations — sole proprietorships and partnerships. In addition, the accounting for more complex corporation transactions affecting stockholders' equity will be discussed.

CHARACTERISTICS OF SOLE PROPRIETORSHIPS

OBJECTIVE 1
Identify basic sole proprietorship characteristics which have accounting implications.

A sole proprietorship is a business enterprise owned by one individual. Approximately 74% of all business enterprises in the United States are sole proprietorships. However, sole proprietorships account for only 7% of all business revenues. These statistics indicate that sole proprietorships, although numerous, consist mostly of small enterprises.

A business may be started and operated relatively easily as a sole proprietorship. There are few legal restrictions to establishing a sole proprietorship, and the individual owner can usually make all business decisions without being accountable to others. This ability to be one's own boss is a major reason why many individuals organize their business enterprises as sole proprietorships.

A sole proprietorship is a separate entity for accounting purposes, and when the owner dies or retires, the sole proprietorship ceases to exist. For federal income tax purposes, however, the sole proprietorship is not treated as a separate taxable entity. The income (or loss) is allocated to the owner and is included on the owner's personal tax return.

A primary disadvantage of a sole proprietorship may be the difficulty in raising funds. Investment in the business is limited to the amounts that the owner can provide from personal resources, plus any additional amounts that can be raised through borrowing. The owner is also personally liable for any debts of the business. Thus, if the business becomes insolvent, creditors have rights to the personal assets of the owner, regardless of the amount of the owner's investment in the enterprise.

ACCOUNTING FOR SOLE PROPRIETORSHIPS

OBJECTIVE 2
Describe and illustrate the accounting for sole proprietorships.

Since the sole proprietorship is a separate business entity for accounting purposes, the transactions of the sole proprietorship must be kept separate from the personal financial affairs of the owner. Only in this way can the financial condition and the results of operations of the sole proprietorship be accurately measured and reported.

The day-to-day accounting entries for a sole proprietorship are much the same as for a corporation. The primary differences in accounting for a sole proprietorship include the use of an owner's **capital account,** rather than a capital stock account, to record investments in the enterprise. In addition, this capital account, rather than a retained earnings account, is used to record changes in owner's equity from net income or net loss. Finally, instead of a dividends account, distributions to the owner are recorded in the owner's **drawing account.** At the end of the period, the drawing account is closed to the owner's capital account, and a statement of owner's equity is prepared. The **statement of owner's equity** thus summarizes changes in owner's equity that have occurred during a specific period of time.

CHARACTERISTICS OF PARTNERSHIPS

OBJECTIVE 3
Identify basic partnership characteristics which have accounting implications.

The Uniform Partnership Act, which has been adopted by more than ninety percent of the states, defines a partnership as "an association of two or more persons to carry on as co-owners a business for profit." The partnership form of business organization is widely used for comparatively small businesses that wish to take advantage of the combined capital, managerial talent, and experience of two or more persons. In many cases, the alternative to securing the amount of investment needed or the various skills needed to operate a business is to adopt the corporate form of organization. The typical corporate form of organization is sometimes not permitted, however, because of restrictions in state laws. In addition, a group of physicians, attorneys, or certified public accountants who wish to band together to practice a profession often organize as a partnership. Medical and legal partnerships made up of 20 or more partners are not unusual, and the number of partners in some CPA firms exceeds 1,000.

Partnerships have several characteristics that have accounting implications. These characteristics are described in the following paragraphs.

A partnership has a **limited life.** Dissolution of a partnership occurs whenever a partner ceases to be a member of the firm for any reason, including withdrawal, bankruptcy, incapacity, or death. Similarly, admission of a new partner dissolves the old partnership. In case of dissolution, a new partnership must be formed if the operations of the business are to be continued without interruption. This situation frequently occurs with professional partnerships. Their composition may change often as new partners are admitted and others are retired.

Most partnerships are *general partnerships,* in which the partners have **unlimited liability.** Each partner is individually liable to creditors for debts incurred by the partnership. Thus, if a partnership becomes insolvent, the partners must contribute sufficient personal assets to settle the debts of the partnership. In some states, a *limited partnership* may be formed, in which the liability of some partners may be limited to the amount of their capital investment. However, a limited partnership must have at least one general partner who has unlimited liability. In this chapter, the discussion is focused on the general partnership.

Partners have **co-ownership of partnership property.** The property invested in a partnership by a partner becomes the joint property of all the partners. Upon dissolution of the partnership and distribution of its assets, the partners' claims against the assets are measured by the amount of the balances in their capital accounts.

Another characteristic of a partnership is **mutual agency.** This feature means that each partner is an agent of the partnership, with the authority to enter into contracts for the partnership. Thus, the acts of each partner bind the partnership and become the responsibility of all partners.

A significant right of partners is **participation in income** of the partnership. Net income and net loss are distributed among the partners according to their agreement. In the absence of any agreement, all partners share equally. If the agreement specifies profit distribution but is silent as to losses, the losses are shared in the same manner as profits.

A partnership, like a sole proprietorship, is a **nontaxable entity** and is therefore not required to pay federal income taxes. However, revenue and expense and other financial details of partnership operations must be reported annually on official Internal Revenue Service forms known as *information returns*. The individual partners must report their distributive share of partnership income on their personal tax returns.

A partnership is created by a voluntary contract containing all the elements essential to any other enforceable contract. It is not necessary that this contract be in writing, nor even that its terms be specifically expressed. However, good business practice dictates that the contract should be in writing and should clearly express the intentions of the partners. The contract, known as the **articles of partnership** or **partnership agreement,** should contain provisions regarding such matters as the amount of investment to be made, limitations on withdrawals of funds, the manner in which net income and net loss are to be divided, and the admission and withdrawal of partners.

PARTNERS' LIABILITY—A REALITY

Many CPAs practice as partners in a partnership. Laventhol & Horwath was the nation's seventh largest public accounting firm, with 350 partners in more than fifty offices, when it filed for bankruptcy in November, 1990. Since each partner is individually liable to creditors for debts incurred by the partnership, the bankruptcy will not relieve the partners of their liability to creditors. This harsh reality is discussed in the following excerpts from an article in *The Wall Street Journal*.

Partners of Laventhol & Horwath, which said it would file for bankruptcy court protection this week, face a long and complicated process that could lead to personal bankruptcy for some of them . . .

When a [corporation] files for bankruptcy court protection, its creditors are permitted only to make claims against the corporation, rather than against its shareholders. But when partnerships such as Laventhol file, creditors can sue individual partners in an effort to recover their money.

. . . Laventhol's creditors, which include banks, landlords, suppliers and plaintiffs in litigation, are expected to try to recover money from partners . . . if Laventhol is unable to satisfy their claims with its remaining assets.

If a partner was at Laventhol "when a potential liability arose, he's on the hook," said Leslie Corwin, a partner at the New York law firm of Morrison Cohen Singer & Weinstein. . . .

If a Laventhol partner joins another accounting firm, the partner remains personally liable for his share of any Laventhol debt. . . .

It is likely to take Laventhol a particularly long time to achieve a plan for paying off debts, largely because the firm doesn't know the extent of its liabilities. Laventhol still faces a number of lawsuits brought by former clients claiming faulty accounting practices; in one, the PTL, the religious organization of imprisoned evangelist Jim Bakker, is seeking $184 million in damages from Laventhol and other defendants.

Until such claims are settled, say bankruptcy lawyers, Laventhol won't be able to escape from bankruptcy proceedings. . . .

Source: Laurie P. Cohen, "Laventhol Partners Face Long Process That Could End in Personal Bankruptcy," *The Wall Street Journal*, November 20, 1990.

ACCOUNTING FOR PARTNERSHIPS

OBJECTIVE 4
Describe and illustrate the accounting for partnerships.

Most of the day-to-day accounting for a partnership is the same as the accounting for a corporation. The primary differences in accounting for a partnership include the recording of investments in the enterprise in owner's equity accounts, one for each partner, rather than in a capital stock account. In addition, changes in the owner's equity from net income or net loss are recorded in the capital accounts of each individual partner. As mentioned previously, the partnership agreement normally provides the manner in which net income and net loss are to be divided among the partners. In the absence of such an agreement, net income and net losses are divided equally among the partners.

Distributions of assets to owners are recorded in each partner's drawing account, which is similar to the dividends account for a corporation. At the end of the period, each partner's drawing account is closed to the partner's capital account and a statement of owner's equity is prepared. The statement of owner's equity, sometimes referred to as the statement of partners' equity, summarizes changes in the partners' capital accounts during a specific period of time.[1]

CHARACTERISTICS OF A CORPORATION

OBJECTIVE 5
Identify basic corporation characteristics which have accounting implications.

In the Dartmouth College case in 1819, Chief Justice Marshall stated: "A corporation is an artificial being, invisible, intangible, and existing only in contemplation of the law." The concept underlying this definition has become the foundation for the prevailing legal doctrine that a corporation is an artificial person, created by law and having a distinct existence separate and apart from the natural persons who are responsible for its creation and operation. Almost all large business enterprises in the United States are organized as corporations.

Corporations may be classified as **not-for-profit** or **profit**. Not-for-profit corporations include those organized for recreational, educational, charitable, or other philanthropic purposes. For their continuation, they depend upon dues from their members or upon gifts and grants from the public at large. Other not-for-profit corporations include those which render services to the public for a fee, such as cooperative-owned utility companies, but

[1]The accounting for partnership formation, income distribution, dissolution, and liquidation are described and illustrated in the appendix at the end of this chapter.

whose objective is rendering services to the public on a cost basis rather than earning a profit.

Profit corporations are engaged in business activities. They depend upon profitable operations for their continued existence. Large profit corporations whose shares of stock are widely distributed and traded in a public market are often called **public corporations**. Corporations whose shares are owned by a small group are often called **nonpublic corporations**. Regardless of their nature or purpose, profit corporations are created according to state or federal statutes and are separate legal entities.

As a legal entity, the corporation has certain characteristics that make it different from other types of business organizations. The most important characteristics with accounting implications are described briefly in the following paragraphs.

A corporation has a **separate legal existence.** It may acquire, own, and dispose of property in its corporate name. It may also incur liabilities and enter into other types of contracts according to the provisions of its **charter** (also called **articles of incorporation**).

The ownership of a corporation, of which there may be several categories or classes, is divided into **transferable units** known as **shares of stock.** Each share of stock of a certain class has the same rights and privileges as every other share of the same class. The owners of the corporation, or **stockholders** (also called **shareholders**), may buy and sell shares without interfering with the activities of the corporation. The millions of transactions that occur daily on stock exchanges are independent transactions between buyers and sellers. Thus, in contrast to the partnership, the existence of the corporation is not affected by changes in ownership.

The stockholders of a corporation have **limited liability.** A corporation is responsible for its own acts and obligations, and therefore its creditors usually may not look beyond the assets of the corporation for satisfaction of their claims. Thus, the financial loss that a stockholder may suffer is limited to the amount invested. The phenomenal growth of the corporate form of business would not have been possible without this limited liability feature.

The stockholders, who are, in fact, the owners of the corporation, exercise control over the management of corporate affairs indirectly by electing a **board of directors.** It is the responsibility of the board of directors to meet from time to time to determine the corporate policies and to select the officers who manage the corporation. The following chart shows the **organizational structure** of a corporation:

Organizational Structure of a Corporate Enterprise

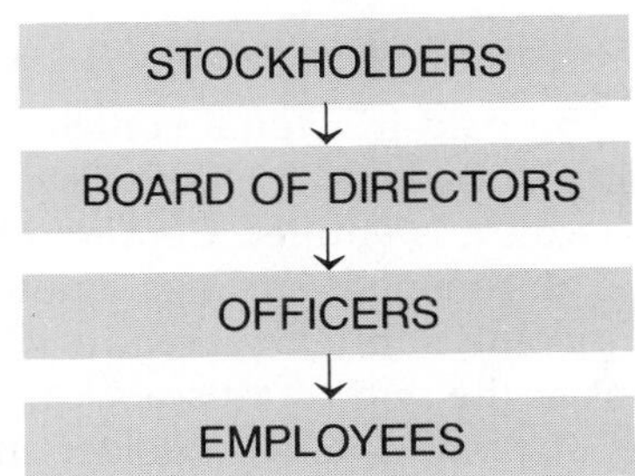

As a separate entity, a corporation is subject to **additional taxes.** It must pay a charter fee to the state at the time of its organization and annual taxes thereafter. If the corporation does business in states other than the one in which it is incorporated, it may also be required to pay annual taxes to such states. The earnings of a corporation may also be subject to a state income tax.

The earnings of a corporation are subject to the federal income tax. When the remaining earnings are distributed to stockholders as dividends, they are again taxed as income to the individuals receiving them. Under certain conditions specified in the Internal Revenue Code, a corporation with a few stockholders may elect to be treated in a manner similar to a partnership for income tax purposes. A corporation electing this optional treatment does not pay federal income taxes. Instead, its stockholders include their distributive shares of corporate income in their own taxable income, regardless of whether the income is distributed to them.

Being a creature of the state and being owned by stockholders who have limited liability, a corporation has less freedom of action than a sole proprietorship and a partnership. There may be **government regulations** in such matters as ownership of real estate, retention of earnings, and purchase of its own stock.

ACCOUNTING FOR CORPORATIONS

OBJECTIVE 6
Describe and illustrate the accounting for corporations.

Corporations may have more complex capital structures than those used in the illustrations in previous chapters. The following paragraphs include discussion and illustrations that focus on some of the features that complicate corporate structures, including preferred stock, special rights granted to preferred stockholders, issuing stock at a price other than par value, and treasury stock.

Stockholders' Equity

The owners' equity in a corporation is commonly called **stockholders' equity, shareholders' equity, shareholders' investment,** or **capital.** The two main sources of stockholders' equity are (1) investments contributed by the stockholders, called **paid-in capital** or **contributed capital,** and (2) net income retained in the business, called **retained earnings.** As shown in the following illustration, the stockholders' equity section of corporation balance sheets is divided into subsections based on these two sources.

Stockholders' Equity		
Paid-in capital:		
Common stock	$330,000	
Retained earnings	80,000	
Total stockholders' equity		$410,000

The paid-in capital contributed by the stockholders is recorded in accounts maintained for each class of stock. If there is only one class of stock, the account is entitled Common Stock or Capital Stock.

The retained earnings amount results from transferring the balance in the income summary account (the net income) to a retained earnings account at the end of a fiscal year. The dividends account, to which distributions of earnings to stockholders have been debited, is also closed to Retained Earnings. If the occurrence of net losses results in a debit balance in Retained Earnings, it is termed a **deficit.** In the stockholders' equity section of the balance sheet, a deficit is deducted from paid-in capital to determine total stockholders' equity.

There are a number of acceptable variants of the term "retained earnings," among which are *earnings retained for use in the business, earnings reinvested in the business, earnings employed in the business,* and *accumulated earnings.* For many years, the term applied to retained earnings was *earned surplus.* However, the use of this term in published financial statements has generally been discontinued. Because of its connotation as an excess, or something left over, "surplus" was sometimes erroneously interpreted by readers of financial statements to mean "cash available for dividends."

Characteristics of Capital Stock

The general term applied to the shares of ownership of a corporation is **capital stock.** The number of shares that a corporation is *authorized* to issue is set forth in its charter. The term *issued* is applied to the shares issued to the stockholders. A corporation may, under circumstances discussed later in the chapter, reacquire some of the stock that it has issued. The stock remaining in the hands of the stockholders is then referred to as the **stock outstanding.**

The shares of capital stock are often assigned an arbitrary monetary figure, known as **par.** The par amount is printed on the **stock certificate,** which is the evidence of ownership issued to the stockholder. Stock may also be issued without par, in which case it is called **no-par** stock. Many states provide that the board of directors must assign a **stated value** to no-par stock, which makes it similar to par stock.

Because of the limited liability feature, the creditors of a corporation have no claim against the personal assets of stockholders. However, the law requires that some specific minimum contribution by the stockholders be retained by the corporation for the protection of its creditors. This amount, called **legal capital,** varies among the states but usually includes the par or stated value of the shares of capital stock issued.

Classes of Stock. The major basic rights that accompany ownership of a share of stock are (1) the right to vote in matters concerning the corporation, (2) the right to share in distributions of earnings, (3) the **preemptive right,** which is the right to maintain the same fractional interest in the corporation by purchasing a proportionate number of shares of any additional issuances of stock,[2] and (4) the right to share in assets upon liquidation.

If a corporation issues only **common stock,** each share generally has equal rights. In order to appeal to a broader investment market, a corporation may provide for one or more classes of stock with various preferential rights. The preference usually relates to the right to share in distributions of earnings. Such stock is generally called **preferred stock.**

The board of directors has the sole authority to distribute earnings to the stockholders. When such action is taken, the directors are said to *declare a dividend.* A corporation cannot guarantee that its operations will be profitable and hence it cannot guarantee dividends to its stockholders. Furthermore, the directors have wide discretionary powers in determining the extent to which earnings should be retained by the corporation to provide for expansion, to offset possible future losses, or to provide for other contingencies.

---

[2]In recent years the stockholders of a significant number of corporations have, by formal action, given up their preemptive rights.

A corporation with both preferred stock and common stock may declare dividends on the common only after it meets the requirements of the stated dividend on the preferred (which may be stated in monetary terms or as a percent of par). To illustrate, assume that a corporation has 1,000 shares of $10 preferred stock (that is, the preferred has a prior claim to an annual $10 per share dividend) and 4,000 shares of common stock outstanding. Assume also that in the first three years of operations, net income was $30,000, $55,000, and $100,000, respectively. The directors authorize the retention of a portion of each year's earnings and the distribution of the remainder. Details of the dividend distribution are presented in the following tabulation:

	First Year	Second Year	Third Year
Net income	$30,000	$55,000	$100,000
Amount retained	10,000	20,000	40,000
Amount distributed	$20,000	$35,000	$ 60,000
Preferred dividend (1,000 shares)	10,000	10,000	10,000
Common dividend (4,000 shares)	$10,000	$25,000	$ 50,000
Dividends per share:			
Preferred	$10.00	$10.00	$10.00
Common	$ 2.50	$ 6.25	$12.50

Participating and Nonparticipating Preferred Stock. In the foregoing illustration, the holders of preferred stock received an annual dividend of $10 per share, in contrast to the common stockholders, whose annual per share dividends were $2.50, $6.25, and $12.50, respectively. It is apparent from the example that holders of preferred stock have relatively greater assurance than common stockholders of receiving dividends regularly. On the other hand, holders of common stock have the possibility of receiving larger dividends than preferred stockholders. The preferred stockholders' preferential right to dividends is usually limited to a certain amount, which was assumed to be the case in the preceding example. Such stock is said to be **nonparticipating.**

Preferred stock which provides for the possibility of dividends in excess of a certain amount is said to be **participating.** Preferred shares may participate with common shares to varying degrees, and the agreement with the shareholders must be examined to determine the extent of this participation. To illustrate, assume that the contract covering the preferred stock of the corporation in the preceding illustration provides that if the total dividends to be distributed exceed the regular preferred dividend and a comparable dividend on common, the preferred shall share in the excess ratably on a share-for-share basis with the common. According to such terms, the $60,000 dividend distribution in the third year would be allocated as follows:

	Preferred Dividend	Common Dividend	Total Dividends
Regular dividend to preferred (1,000 × $10)	$10,000	—	$10,000
Comparable dividend to common (4,000 × $10)	—	$40,000	40,000
Remainder to 5,000 shares ratably ($2 per share)	2,000	8,000	10,000
Total	$12,000	$48,000	$60,000
Dividends per share	$12	$12	

Cumulative and Noncumulative Preferred Stock. As was indicated in the preceding section, most preferred stock is nonparticipating. Provision is usually made, however, to assure the continuation of the preferential dividend right if at any time the directors *pass* (do not declare) the usual dividend. The preferential dividend right is assured by providing that dividends may not be paid on the common stock if any preferred dividends have been passed (are in *arrears*). Such preferred stock is said to be **cumulative.** To illustrate, assume that a corporation has outstanding 5,000 shares of cumulative preferred 9% stock of $100 par (that is, the preferred stockholders have a prior claim to an annual 9% dividend, or $9 per share). In addition, assume that dividends have been passed for the preceding two years. In the current year, no dividend may be declared on the common stock unless the directors first declare preferred dividends of $90,000 for the past two years and $45,000 for the current year. Preferred stock not having this cumulative right is called **noncumulative.**

Other Preferential Rights. Thus far the discussion of preferential rights of preferred stock has related to dividend distributions. Preferred stock may also be given a preference in its claim to assets upon liquidation of the corporation. If the assets remaining after payment of creditors are not sufficient to return the capital contributions of both classes of stock, payment would first be made to the preferred stockholders and any balance remaining would go to the common stockholders. Another difference between preferred and common stock is that the former may have no voting rights. A corporation may also have more than one class of preferred stock, with differences as to the amount of dividends, priority of claims upon liquidation,

PREFERRED STOCK—RISKS VS. REWARDS

Preferred stocks shield shareholders somewhat from the lows of corporate fortunes. If dividend payments must be reduced, preferred stockholders receive dividends before common shareholders. However, preferred stockholders often miss out on the highs of corporate fortunes. If dividend payments are large, because most preferred stock is nonparticipating, preferred shareholders receive a fixed dividend and the bulk of the large dividends go to common shareholders. These "safe-but-stodgy" equities can offer dramatic profits, however, as described in the following excerpt from an article in *Business Week:*

> *...In times of grave financial trouble, dividends on preferreds are often suspended and placed in arrears.... If and when the company reinstates dividends, current shareholders are entitled to all the back payments, whether or not they owned stock during the arrearage period—if the preferred is cumulative....*
>
> *The gains [from purchasing preferred stock with dividends in arrears] can be impressive. Bethlehem Steel announced in April that it would pay $22.5 million in arrears and resume the regular quarterly dividend on its two classes of preferred stock. Because Bethlehem had missed four payments, investors receive an extra year's worth of dividends: One class that usually pays $1.25 quarterly will return $6.25—not bad on a stock that traded in the low 30s just a few months ago.*
>
> *Playing preferreds in arrears requires patience. Long Island Lighting, for instance, recently announced that it would try to resume paying dividends next year after a four-year hiatus. But the larger concern lies in the fact that you're betting on a turnaround. And all bets are off if the company goes bankrupt: You not only lose arrearages but you're also sure to see the share price plummet. On the repayment totem pole, preferreds occupy the second-lowest notch—before the common shareholders but after the creditors and bondholders....*

Source: Troy Segal, "Preferred Stock: The Risky Hunt for Hidden Rewards," *Business Week* (June 13, 1988), p. 114

and voting rights. In any particular case, the rights of a class of stock may be determined by reference to the charter, the stock certificate, or some other abstract of the agreement.

Issuing Capital Stock

The entries to record investments of stockholders in a corporation are like those for investments by owners of other types of business organizations, in that cash and other assets received are debited and any liabilities assumed are credited. The credit to stockholders' equity differs, however, in that there are accounts for each class of stock. To illustrate, assume that a corporation, with an authorization of 10,000 shares of preferred stock of $100 par and 100,000 shares of common stock of $20 par, issues one half of each authorization at par for cash. The entry to record the stockholders' investment and the receipt of the cash is as follows:

Cash	1,500,000	
Preferred Stock		500,000
Common Stock		1,000,000

The capital stock accounts (Preferred Stock, Common Stock) are controlling accounts. It is necessary to maintain records of each stockholder's name, address, and number of shares held in order to issue dividend checks, proxy forms, and financial reports. Individual stockholders accounts are kept in a subsidiary ledger known as the **stockholders ledger.**

Par stock is often issued by a corporation at a price other than par. When it is issued for more than par, the excess of the contract price over par is termed a **premium** on stock. When it is issued at a price that is below par, the difference is called a **discount** on stock. Thus, if stock with a par of $50 is issued at $60, the amount of the premium is $10. If the same stock is issued at $45, the amount of the discount is $5.

Theoretically, there is no reason for a newly organized corporation to issue stock at a price other than par. The par designation is merely a part of the plan of dividing owners' equity into a number of units of ownership. Hence, a group of persons investing their funds in a new corporation might all be expected to pay par for the shares. The fortunes of an enterprise do not remain the same, however, even when it is still in the process of organizing. The changing prospects for its future success may affect the price per share at which the incorporators can secure other investors.

A need for additional paid-in capital may arise long after a corporation has become established. Losses during prior fiscal periods may have depleted operating funds or the operations may have been successful enough to warrant a substantial expansion of plant and equipment. If the funds are to be obtained by the issuance of additional stock, it is apparent that the current price at which the original stock is selling in the market will affect the price that can be obtained for the new shares.

Generally speaking, the price at which stock can be sold by a corporation is influenced by (1) the financial condition, the earnings record, and the dividend record of the corporation, (2) its potential earning power, (3) the availability of money for investment purposes, and (4) general business and economic conditions and prospects.

Premium and Discount on Stock. When capital stock is issued at a premium, cash or other assets are debited for the amount received. The stock account is then credited for the par amount, and an account generally called Paid-In Capital in Excess of Par is credited for the amount of the premium.[3] For example, if Caldwell Company issues 2,000 shares of $50 par preferred stock for cash at $55, the entry to record the transaction would be as follows:

Cash	110,000	
Preferred Stock		100,000
Paid-In Capital in Excess of Par—Preferred Stock		10,000

The premium of $10,000 is a part of the investment of the stockholders and is therefore a part of paid-in capital. It is distinguished from the capital stock account because usually it is not a part of legal capital and in many states may be used as a basis for dividends to stockholders. However, if the premium is returned to stockholders as a dividend at a later date, it should be emphasized that the dividend is a return of paid-in capital rather than a distribution of earnings.

Most states do not permit the issuance of stock at a discount. In others, it may be done only under certain conditions. When stock is issued at less than its par, it is considered to be fully paid as between the corporation and the stockholder. In some states, however, the stockholders are contingently liable to creditors for the amount of the discount. If the corporation is liquidated and there are not enough assets to pay creditors in full, the stockholders may be assessed for an additional contribution up to the amount of the discount on their stock.

When capital stock is issued at a discount, cash or other assets are debited for the amount received, and a discount account is debited for the amount of the discount. The discount on capital stock is deducted from the par amount of capital stock in the paid-in capital subsection of stockholders' equity. Since capital stock is not often issued at a discount, transactions involving discounts are not illustrated.

Premium on Capital Stock on the Balance Sheet. The manner in which premiums on capital stock may be presented in the stockholders' equity section of the balance sheet is illustrated as follows:

Stockholders' Equity			
Paid-in capital:			
Preferred 10% stock, cumulative, $50 par (2,000 shares authorized and issued)	$100,000		
Excess of issue price over par	10,000	$110,000	
Common stock, $25 par (50,000 shares authorized, 20,000 shares issued)	$500,000		
Excess of issue price over par	40,000	540,000	
Total paid-in capital		$650,000	
Retained earnings		175,000	
Total stockholders' equity			$825,000

[3]Although the formal name of the account is Paid-In Capital in Excess of Par, the shorter term "premium" will often be used in the discussion.

The following stockholders' equity section illustrates the reporting of a deficit and some differences in terminology from that in the foregoing example:

Shareholders' Equity

Paid-in capital:			
Preferred $3 stock, cumulative, $25 par (10,000 shares authorized and issued)	$ 250,000		
Premium on preferred stock	20,000	$ 270,000	
Common stock, $10 par (200,000 shares authorized, 100,000 shares issued)	$1,000,000		
Premium on common stock	100,000	1,100,000	
Total paid in by stockholders		$1,370,000	
Less deficit		75,000	
Total shareholders' equity			$1,295,000

Issuing Stock for Assets Other than Cash. When capital stock is issued in exchange for assets other than cash, such as land, buildings, and equipment, the assets acquired should be recorded at their fair market price or at the fair market price of the stock issued, whichever is more objectively determinable. The determination of the values to be assigned to the assets is the responsibility of the board of directors.

As a basis for illustration, assume that a corporation acquired land for which the fair market price is not determinable. In exchange, the corporation issued 10,000 shares of its $10 par common stock with a current market price of $12 per share. The transaction could be recorded as follows:

Dec. 5	Land	120,000	
	Common Stock		100,000
	Paid-In Capital in Excess of Par—Common Stock		20,000

No-Par Stock. In the early days of rapid industrial expansion and increasing use of the corporate form of business organization, it was customary to assign a par of $100 to shares of stock. It is not surprising that unsophisticated investors, mistakenly considering "par value" to be the equivalent of "value," were often induced to invest in mining and other highly speculative enterprises by the simple means of being offered $100 par stock at "bargain" prices. Another misleading practice was the use of par in assigning highly inflated values to assets acquired in exchange for stock. For example, stock with a total par of $1,000,000 might be issued in exchange for patents, mineral rights, or other properties with a conservatively estimated value of $50,000. The assets would be recorded at the full par of $1,000,000, whereas in reality the stock had been issued at a discount of $950,000. Balance sheets that were "window-dressed" in this manner were obviously deceptive.

To combat such abuses and also to eliminate the troublesome discount liability of stockholders, stock without par was conceived. The issuance of stock without par was first permitted by New York in 1912. Its use is now authorized in nearly all of the states.

Over the years, questionable practices in the issuance of securities have been virtually eliminated. Today federal and state laws and rules imposed by organized stock exchanges and governmental agencies such as the Securities and Exchange Commission combine to protect the investor from misrepresentations that were common in earlier days.

In most states, both preferred and common stock may be issued without a par designation. However, preferred stock is usually assigned a par. When no-par stock is issued, the entire proceeds may be credited to the capital stock account, even though the issuance price varies from time to time. For example, if at the time of organization a corporation issues 10,000 shares of no-par common stock at $40 a share and at a later date issues 1,000 additional shares at $36, the entries would be as follows:

Original issuance of 10,000 shares of no-par common at $40.	Cash	400,000	
	Common Stock		400,000
Subsequent issuance of 1,000 shares of no-par common at $36.	Cash	36,000	
	Common Stock		36,000

The laws of some states require that the entire proceeds from the issuance of no-par stock be regarded as legal capital. The preceding entries conform to this principle, which also conforms to the original concept of no-par stock. In other states, no-par stock may be assigned a stated value per share, and the excess of the proceeds over the stated value may be credited to Paid-In Capital in Excess of Stated Value. Assuming that in the previous example the stated value is $25 and the board of directors wishes to credit the common stock for stated value, the transactions would be recorded as follows. From these entries it is readily apparent that the accounting for no-par stock with a stated value may follow the same pattern as the accounting for par stock.

Original issuance of 10,000 shares of no-par common, stated value $25, at $40.	Cash	400,000	
	Common Stock		250,000
	Paid-In Capital in Excess of Stated Value		150,000
Subsequent issuance of 1,000 shares of no-par common, stated value $25, at $36.	Cash	36,000	
	Common Stock		25,000
	Paid-In Capital in Excess of Stated Value		11,000

Treasury Stock

Although there are some legal restrictions on the practice, a corporation may purchase shares of its own outstanding stock from stockholders. It may also accept shares of its own stock in payment of a debt owed by a stockholder, which in essence is much the same as acquisition by purchase. A corporation may buy its own stock in order to provide shares for resale to employees, to provide shares for reissuance to employees as a bonus, or to support the market price of the stock. In March, 1986, for example, General Motors announced that it would buy back as much as $1.95 billion of its common stock. General Motors officials stated that two primary uses of the treasury stock would be for incentive compensation plans and employee savings plans.

The term **treasury stock** may be applied only to the issuing corporation's stock that (1) has been issued as fully paid, (2) has later been reacquired by the corporation, and (3) has not been canceled or reissued. In the past, corporations would occasionally list treasury stock on the balance sheet as an asset. The justification for such treatment was that the stock could be reissued and was thus like an investment in the stock of another corporation. The same argument, though indefensible, might well be extended to authorized but unissued stock.

Today, it is agreed among most accountants that treasury stock should not be reported as an asset. A corporation cannot own a part of itself. Treasury stock has no voting rights, it does not have the preemptive right to participate in additional issuances of stock, nor does it generally participate in cash dividends. When a corporation purchases its own stock, it is returning capital to the stockholders from whom the purchase was made.

There are several methods of accounting for the purchase and the resale of treasury stock. A commonly used method is the **cost basis.** When the stock is purchased by the corporation, the account Treasury Stock is debited for the price paid for it. The par and the price at which the stock was originally issued are ignored. When the stock is resold, Treasury Stock is credited at the price paid for it, and the difference between the price paid and the selling price is debited or credited to an account entitled Paid-In Capital from Sale of Treasury Stock.

As a basis for illustrating the cost method, assume that the paid-in capital of a corporation is composed of common stock issued at a premium, detailed as follows:

Common stock, $25 par (20,000 shares authorized and issued)	$500,000
Excess of issue price over par	150,000

The assumed transactions involving treasury stock and the required entries are as follows:

		Debit	Credit
Purchased 1,000 shares of treasury stock at $45.	Treasury Stock	45,000	
	Cash		45,000
Sold 200 shares of treasury stock at $60.	Cash	12,000	
	Treasury Stock		9,000
	Paid-In Capital from Sale of Treasury Stock		3,000
Sold 200 shares of treasury stock at $40.	Cash	8,000	
	Paid-In Capital from Sale of Treasury Stock	1,000	
	Treasury Stock		9,000

Paid-In Capital from Sale of Treasury Stock is reported in the paid-in capital section of the balance sheet. Treasury Stock is deducted from the total of the paid-in capital and retained earnings. After the foregoing transactions are completed, the stockholders' equity section of the balance sheet would appear as follows:

Stockholders' Equity

Paid-in capital:			
Common stock, $25 par			
(20,000 shares authorized and issued) ...	$500,000		
Excess of issue price over par — common stock	150,000	$650,000	
From sale of treasury stock		2,000	
Total paid-in capital		$652,000	
Retained earnings		130,000	
Total		$782,000	
Deduct treasury stock (600 shares at cost)...		27,000	
Total stockholders' equity			$755,000

The stockholders' equity section of the balance sheet indicates that 20,000 shares of stock were issued, of which 600 are held as treasury stock. The number of shares outstanding is therefore 19,400. If cash dividends are declared at this time, the declaration would apply to only 19,400 shares of stock. Similarly, 19,400 shares could be voted at a stockholders' meeting.

If sales of treasury stock result in a net decrease in paid-in capital, the decrease would be debited to the retained earnings account.

EQUITY PER SHARE

OBJECTIVE 7
Describe and illustrate the computation of equity per share of stock

The amount appearing on the balance sheet as total stockholders' equity can be stated in terms of the **equity per share.** Another term sometimes used in referring to the equity allocable to a single share of stock is **book value per share.** The latter term is not only less accurate but its use of "value" may also be interpreted by nonaccountants to mean "market value" or "actual worth."

When there is only one class of stock, the equity per share is determined by dividing total stockholders' equity by the number of shares outstanding. For a corporation with both preferred and common stock, it is necessary first to allocate the total equity between the two classes. In making the allocation, consideration must be given to the liquidation rights of the preferred stock, including any participating and cumulative dividend features. After the total is allocated to the two classes, the equity per share of each class may then be determined by dividing the respective amounts by the related number of shares outstanding.

To illustrate, assume that as of the end of the current fiscal year, a corporation has both preferred and common shares outstanding, that there are no preferred dividends in arrears, and that the preferred stock is entitled to receive $105 per share upon liquidation. The amounts of the stockholders' equity accounts of the corporation and the computation of the equity per share are as follows:

Stockholders' Equity

Preferred $9 stock, cumulative, $100 par	
(1,000 shares outstanding)	$100,000
Excess of issue price over par—preferred stock	2,000
Common stock, $10 par (50,000 shares outstanding)	500,000
Excess of issue price over par—common stock	50,000
Retained earnings	253,000
Total equity	$905,000

Allocation of Total Equity to Preferred and Common Stock

Total equity	$905,000
Allocated to preferred stock:	
Liquidation price	105,000
Allocated to common stock	$800,000

Equity Per Share

Preferred stock: $105,000 ÷ 1,000 shares = $105 per share
Common stock: $800,000 ÷ 50,000 shares = $ 16 per share

If it is assumed that the preferred stock is entitled to dividends in arrears in the event of liquidation, and that there is an arrearage of two years, the computations for the foregoing illustration would be as follows:

Allocation of Total Equity to Preferred and Common Stock

Total equity		$905,000
Allocated to preferred stock:		
Liquidation price	$105,000	
Dividends in arrears	18,000	123,000
Allocated to common stock		$782,000

Equity Per Share

Preferred stock: $123,000 ÷ 1,000 shares = $123.00 per share
Common stock: $782,000 ÷ 50,000 shares = $ 15.64 per share

Equity per share, particularly of common stock, is often stated in corporation reports to stockholders and quoted in the financial press. It is one of the many factors affecting the **market price,** that is, the price at which a share is bought and sold at a particular moment. However, it should be noted that earning capacity, dividend rates, and prospects for the future usually affect the market price of listed stocks to a much greater extent than does equity per share. So-called "glamour" stocks may at times sell at more than ten times the amount of the equity per share. On the other hand, stock in corporations that have suffered severe declines in earnings or whose future prospects appear to be unfavorable may sell at prices which are much less than the equity per share.

ORGANIZATION COSTS

OBJECTIVE 8
Describe and illustrate the accounting for organization costs.

Expenditures incurred in organizing a corporation, such as legal fees, taxes and fees paid to the state, and promotional costs, are charged to an intangible asset account entitled Organization Costs. Although such costs have no realizable value upon liquidation, they are as essential as plant and equipment, for without the expenditures the corporation could not have been created. If the life of a corporation is limited to a definite period of time, the organization costs should be amortized over the period by annual charges to an expense account. However, at the time of incorporation the length of life of most corporations is indeterminate.

There are two possible extreme viewpoints on the proper accounting for organization costs and other intangibles of indeterminate life. One extreme would consider the cost of intangibles as a permanent asset until there was convincing evidence of loss in value. The other extreme would consider the cost of intangibles as an expense in the period in which the cost is incurred. The practical solution to the problem is expressed in the following quotation:

> *. . . . Allocating the cost of goodwill or other intangible assets with an indeterminate life over time is necessary because the value almost inevitably becomes zero at some future date. Since the date at which the value becomes zero is indeterminate, the end of the useful life must necessarily be set arbitrarily at some point or within some range of time for accounting purposes.*[4]

[4]*Opinions of the Accounting Principles Board, No. 17,* "Intangible Assets" (New York: American Institute of Certified Public Accountants, 1970), par. 23.

The Internal Revenue Code permits the amortization of organization costs equally over a period of not less than sixty months beginning with the month the corporation commences business. Since the amount of such costs is generally small in relation to total assets and the effect on net income is ordinarily not significant, amortization of organization costs over sixty months is generally accepted in accounting practice.

APPENDIX

PARTNERSHIP ACCOUNTING

As discussed in this chapter, most of the day-to-day accounting for a partnership is the same as the accounting for a corporation. It is in the areas of the formation, income distribution, dissolution, and liquidation that transactions peculiar to partnerships arise. The accounting concepts for each of these areas are described and illustrated in this appendix.

PARTNERSHIP FORMATION

A separate entry is made for the investment of each partner in a partnership. The various assets contributed by a partner are debited to the proper asset accounts. If liabilities are assumed by the partnership, the appropriate liability accounts are credited. The partner's capital account is credited for the net amount.

To illustrate the entry to record an initial investment, assume that Joseph A. Stevens and Earl S. Foster, who are sole owners of competing hardware stores, agree to combine their businesses in a partnership. Each is to contribute certain amounts of cash and other business assets. It is also agreed that the partnership is to assume the liabilities of the separate businesses. The entry to record the assets contributed and the liabilities transferred by Joseph A. Stevens is as follows:

Apr. 1	Cash	7,200	
	Accounts Receivable	16,300	
	Merchandise Inventory	28,700	
	Store Equipment	5,400	
	Office Equipment	1,500	
	Allowance for Doubtful Accounts		1,500
	Accounts Payable		2,600
	Joseph A. Stevens, Capital		55,000

The monetary amounts at which the noncash assets are stated are those agreed upon by the partners. In arriving at an appropriate amount for such assets, consideration should be given to their market values at the time the partnership is formed. The values agreed upon represent the acquisition cost to the accounting entity created by the formation of the partnership. These amounts may differ from the balances appearing in the accounts of the separate businesses before the partnership was organized.

DIVISION OF NET INCOME OR NET LOSS

The net income of a partnership may be said to include a return for the services of the owners, for the capital invested, and for economic or pure profit. Partners are not legally employees of the partnership, nor are their capital contributions a loan. If each of two partners is to contribute equal services and amounts of capital, an equal sharing in partnership net income would be equitable. But if one partner is to contribute a larger portion of capital than the other, provision for unequal capital contributions should be given recognition in the agreement for dividing net income. Or, if the services of one partner are much more valuable to the partnership than those of the other, provision for unequal service contributions should be given recognition in their agreement.

To illustrate the division of net income and the accounting for this division, assume that Stone and Mills (1) are allowed monthly salaries of $2,500 and $2,000, respectively; (2) are allowed interest at 12% on capital balances at January 1 of the current fiscal year, which amounted to $80,000 and $60,000, respectively; and (3) divide the remainder of net income equally. A report of the division of net income may be presented as a separate statement accompanying the balance sheet and the income statement, or it may be added at the bottom of the income statement. If the latter procedure is adopted, the lower part of the income statement would appear as follows:

Net income			$75,000
	J. L. Stone	C. R. Mills	Total
Division of net income:			
Salary allowance	$30,000	$24,000	$54,000
Interest allowance	9,600	7,200	16,800
Remaining income	2,100	2,100	4,200
Net income	$41,700	$33,300	$75,000

The division of net income is recorded as a closing entry, regardless of whether the partners actually withdraw any amounts from the partnership. The entry for the division of net income is as follows:

Dec. 31	Income Summary	75,000	
	Jennifer L. Stone, Capital		41,700
	Crystal R. Mills, Capital		33,300

If Stone and Mills had withdrawn any amounts, the withdrawals would have accumulated as debits in the drawing accounts during the year. At the end of the year, the debit balances in their drawing accounts would be transferred to their respective capital accounts.

In the above illustration, the net income exceeded the sum of the allowances for salary and interest. If the net income is less than the total of the special allowances, the "remaining balance" will be a negative figure that must be divided among the partners as though it were a net loss. The effect of this situation may be illustrated by assuming the same salary and interest allowances as in the preceding illustration, but changing the amount of net income to $50,000. The salary and interest allowances to Stone total $39,600 and the comparable figure for Mills is $31,200. The sum of these amounts, $70,800, exceeds the net income of $50,000 by $20,800. It is therefore necessary to deduct $10,400 (½ of $20,800) from each partner's share to arrive at the net income, as follows:

	J. L. Stone	C. R. Mills	Total
Net income			$50,000
Division of net income:			
Salary allowance	$30,000	$24,000	$54,000
Interest allowance	9,600	7,200	16,800
Total	$39,600	$31,200	$70,800
Excess of allowances over income	10,400	10,400	20,800
Net income	$29,200	$20,800	$50,000

In closing Income Summary at the end of the year, $29,200 would be credited to Jennifer L. Stone, Capital, and $20,800 would be credited to Crystal R. Mills, Capital.

PARTNERSHIP DISSOLUTION

One of the basic characteristics of the partnership form of organization is its limited life. Any change in the personnel of the ownership results in the dissolution of the partnership. Thus, admission of a new partner dissolves the old firm. Similarly, death, bankruptcy, or withdrawal of a partner causes dissolution.

Dissolution of the partnership is not necessarily followed by the winding up of the affairs of the business. For example, a partnership composed of two partners may admit an additional partner. Or if one of three partners in a business withdraws, the remaining two partners may continue to operate the business.

Admission of a Partner

An additional person may be admitted to a partnership enterprise only with the consent of all the current partners. It does not follow, however, that a partner's interest, or part of that interest, cannot be disposed of without the consent of the remaining partners. Under common law, if a partner's interest was assigned to an outside party, the partnership was automatically dissolved. Under the Uniform Partnership Act, a partner's interest can be disposed of without the consent of the remaining partners. The person who buys the interest acquires the selling partner's rights to share in net income and in assets upon liquidation. The buyer does not automatically become a partner, however, and has no voice in partnership affairs unless admitted to the firm.

An additional person may be admitted to a partnership through either of two procedures:

1. Purchase of an interest from one or more of the current partners.
2. Contribution of assets to the partnership.

When the first procedure is followed, the capital interest of the incoming partner is obtained from current partners, and *neither the total assets nor the total owner's equity of the business is affected.* When the second procedure is followed, *both the total assets and the total owner's equity of the business are increased.*

Admission by Purchase of an Interest. When an additional person is admitted to a firm by purchasing an interest from one or more of the partners, the purchase price is paid directly to the selling partners. Payment is for partnership equity owned by the partners as individuals, and hence the cash or other consideration paid is not recorded in the accounts of the partnership. The only entry needed is the transfer of the proper amounts of owner's equity from the capital accounts of the selling partners to the capital account established for the incoming partner.

As an example, assume that partners Tom Andrews and Nathan Bell have capital balances of $50,000 each. On June 1, each sells one fifth of his respective equity to Joe Canter for $10,000 in cash. The exchange of cash is not a partnership transaction and thus is not recorded by the partnership. The only entry required in the partnership accounts is as follows:

June 1	Tom Andrews, Capital	10,000	
	Nathan Bell, Capital	10,000	
	Joe Canter, Capital		20,000

The effect of the transaction on the partnership accounts is presented in the following diagram:

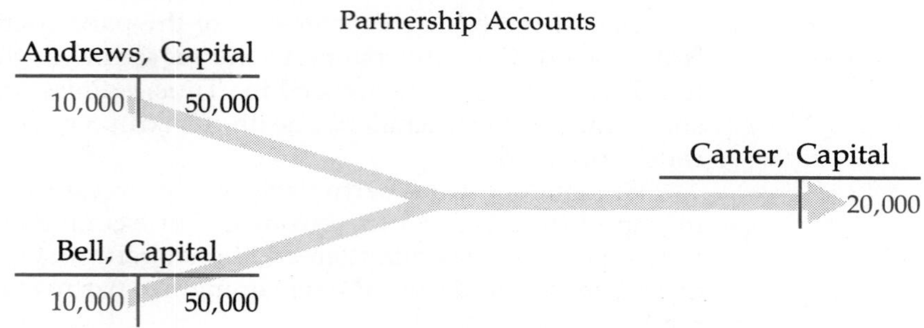

The foregoing entry is not affected by the amount paid by Canter for the one-fifth interest. If the firm had been earning a high rate of return on the investment and Canter had been very eager to obtain the one-fifth interest, he might have paid considerably more than $20,000. Had other circumstances prevailed, he might have acquired the one-fifth interest for considerably less than $20,000. In either event, the entry to transfer the capital interests would be as illustrated.

After the admission of Canter, the total owner's equity of the firm is $100,000, of which Canter has a one-fifth interest, or $20,000. It does not necessarily follow that he will be entitled to a similar share of the partnership net income. Division of net income or net loss will be in accordance with the new partnership agreement.

Admission by Contribution of Assets. Instead of buying an interest from the current partners, the incoming partner may contribute assets to the partnership. In this case, both the assets and the owner's equity of the firm are increased. To illustrate, assume that Donald Lewis and Gerald Morton are partners with capital accounts of $35,000 and $25,000, respectively. On June 1, Sharon Nelson invests $20,000 cash in the business, for which she is to receive an ownership equity of $20,000. The entry to record this transaction is as follows:

June 1	Cash	20,000	
	Sharon Nelson, Capital		20,000

The major difference between the circumstances of the admission of Nelson and the admission of Canter in the preceding example may be observed by comparing the following diagram with the one on page 436.

Partnership Accounts

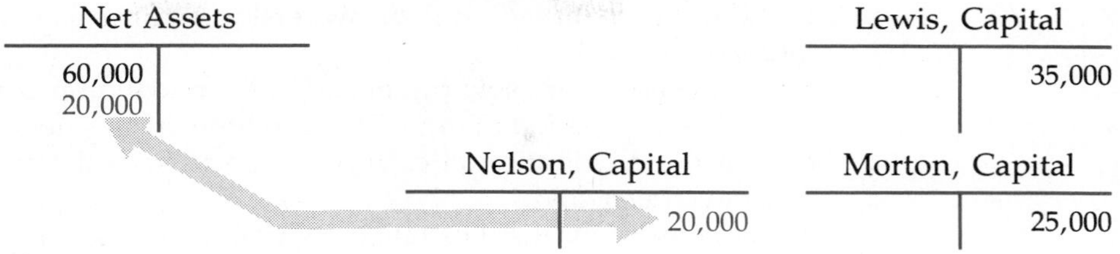

Net Assets	
60,000	
20,000	

Lewis, Capital	
	35,000

Nelson, Capital	
	20,000

Morton, Capital	
	25,000

With the admission of Nelson, the total owners' equity of the new partnership becomes $80,000, of which Nelson has a one-fourth interest, or $20,000. The extent of her participation in partnership net income will be governed by the articles of partnership.

Withdrawal of a Partner

When a partner retires or for some other reason wishes to withdraw from the firm, one or more of the remaining partners may purchase the withdrawing partner's interest and the business may be continued without apparent interruption. In such cases, settlement for the purchase and sale is made between the partners as individuals, in a manner similar to the admission of a new partner by purchase of an interest, and thus is not recorded by the partnership. The only entry required by the partnership is a debit to the capital account of the partner withdrawing and a credit to the capital account of the partner or partners acquiring the interest.

If the settlement with the withdrawing partner is made by the partnership, the effect is to reduce the assets and the owner's equity of the firm. To determine the ownership equity of the withdrawing partner, the asset accounts should be adjusted to current market prices. The net amount of the adjustments should be divided among the capital accounts of the partners according to the income-sharing ratio. In the event that the cash or the other available assets are insufficient to make complete payment at the time of withdrawal, a liability account should be credited for the balance owed to the withdrawing partner.

Death of a Partner

The death of a partner dissolves the partnership. In the absence of any contrary agreement, the accounts should be closed as of the date of death, and the net income for the fractional part of the year should be transferred to the capital accounts. It is not unusual, however, for the partnership agreement to stipulate that the accounts remain open to the end of the fiscal year or until the affairs are wound up, if that should occur earlier. The net income of the entire period is then divided, as provided by the agreement, between the respective periods occurring before and after dissolution.

The balance in the capital account of the deceased partner is then transferred to a liability account with the deceased's estate. The surviving partner or partners may continue the business or the affairs may be wound up. If the former course is followed, the procedures for settling with the estate will conform to those outlined earlier for the withdrawal of a partner from the business.

PARTNERSHIP LIQUIDATION

When a partnership goes out of business, it usually sells most of the assets. As cash is realized, it is applied first to the payment of the claims of creditors. After all liabilities have been paid, the remaining cash is distributed to the partners, based on their ownership equities as indicated by their capital accounts.

If the assets are sold piecemeal, the liquidation process may extend over a considerable period of time. This situation creates no special problem, however, if the distribution of cash to the partners is delayed until all of the assets have been sold.

As a basis for the illustration, assume that Farley, Greene, and Hill decide to liquidate their partnership. Their income-sharing ratio is 5:3:2 (5/10, 3/10, 2/10). On April 9, after discontinuing the ordinary business operations and closing the accounts, the following summary of the general ledger is prepared:

Cash	$11,000	
Noncash Assets	64,000	
Liabilities		$ 9,000
Jane Farley, Capital		22,000
Brad Greene, Capital		22,000
Alice Hill, Capital		22,000
Total	$75,000	$75,000

For the sake of brevity, it will be assumed that all noncash assets are disposed of in a single transaction and that all liabilities are paid at one time. In addition, Noncash Assets and Liabilities will be used as account titles in place of the various asset, contra asset, and liability accounts that in actual practice would be affected by the transactions.

Between April 10 and April 30 of the current year, Farley, Greene, and Hill sell all noncash assets for $72,000, realizing a gain of $8,000 ($72,000 − $64,000). The gain is divided among the capital accounts in the income-sharing ratio of 5:3:2. The liabilities are paid, and *the remaining cash is distributed to the partners according to the balances in their capital accounts.* A statement of partnership liquidation, which summarizes the liquidation process, follows:

Farley, Greene, and Hill
Statement of Partnership Liquidation
For Period April 10–30, 19--

	Cash	+	Noncash Assets	=	Liabilities	+	Capital Farley (50%)	+	Capital Greene (30%)	+	Capital Hill (20%)
Balances before realization	$11,000		$64,000		$9,000		$22,000		$22,000		$22,000
Sale of noncash assets and division of gain	+72,000		−64,000		—		+ 4,000		+ 2,400		+ 1,600
Balances after realization	$83,000		0		$9,000		$26,000		$24,400		$23,600
Payment of liabilities	− 9,000		—		−9,000		—		—		—
Balances after payment of liabilities	$74,000		0		0		$26,000		$24,400		$23,600
Distribution of cash to partners	−74,000		—		—		−26,000		−24,400		−23,600
Final balances	0		0		0		0		0		0

As shown in the foregoing illustration, the distribution of the cash among the partners is determined by reference to the balances of their respective capital accounts after the gain on realization has been allocated. Under no circumstances should the income-sharing ratio be used as a basis for distributing the cash.

If the sale of assets were to result in a loss, the loss would be divided among the partners' capital accounts in the income-sharing ratio. The cash would then be applied first to the payment of the claims of creditors and the remainder would be distributed to the partners according to the balances in their respective capital accounts.

CHAPTER REVIEW

KEY POINTS

OBJECTIVE 1

Characteristics of Sole Proprietorships

A sole proprietorship, which is a business owned by one individual, is a separate entity for accounting purposes. There are few legal restrictions to establishing a sole proprietorship, and the individual owner can usually make all business decisions without being accountable to others. A primary disadvantage of a sole proprietorship may be the difficulty in raising funds.

OBJECTIVE 2

Accounting for Sole Proprietorships

The primary differences in accounting for a sole proprietorship as compared with a corporation include the use of an owner's capital account (rather than a capital stock account) to record investments in the enterprise. This capital account is also used to record changes in owner's equity from net income or net loss. Instead of a dividends account, distributions to the owner are recorded in the owner's drawing account.

OBJECTIVE 3

Characteristics of Partnerships

Partnership characteristics that have accounting implications are: limited life, unlimited liability, co-ownership of property, mutual agency, and participation in income. In addition, a partnership is a nontaxable entity and is therefore not required to pay federal income taxes. Individual partners must report their distributive share of partnership income on their personal returns.

OBJECTIVE 4

Accounting for Partnerships

Most of the day-to-day accounting for a partnership is the same as the accounting for a corporation. The primary differences in accounting for a partnership include the recording of investments in the enterprise in owner's equity accounts, one for each partner, rather than in a capital stock account. In addition, changes in the owner's equity from net income or net loss are recorded in the capital accounts of each individual partner. Distributions of assets to owners are recorded in each partner's drawing account, which is similar to the dividends account for a corporation.

OBJECTIVE 5

Characteristics of a Corporation

The most important corporation characteristics with accounting implications are the following: separate legal existence, transferable units of stock, limited liability, and organizational structure. In addition, a corporation as a separate entity is subject to federal income taxes.

OBJECTIVE 6

Accounting for Corporations

The stockholders' equity section of a corporation balance sheet is divided into two subsections: paid-in capital and retained earnings.

The stock of a corporation may be classified according to its par, right to vote, preference as to dividends, and preference as to liquidation rights. Various types of stock include par common stock, no-par common stock, participating preferred stock, nonparticipating preferred stock, cumulative preferred stock, and noncumulative preferred stock.

When a corporation issues stock at par, each class of stock is credited for its par amount. When a corporation issues stock at more than par, the premium is recorded by crediting Paid-In Capital in Excess of Par. Balances in the premium accounts appear with their related class of stock in the stockholders' equity section of the balance sheet.

When capital stock is issued and exchanged for assets other than cash, the assets acquired should be recorded at their fair market price or at the fair market price of the stock issued, whichever is more objectively determinable.

When no-par stock is issued, the entire proceeds may be credited to the capital stock account, even though the issue price varies from time to time. In some cases, no-par stock may be assigned a stated value per share, and the excess of the proceeds over the stated value may be credited to a separate paid-in capital account.

A corporation may purchase shares of its own outstanding stock from stockholders. Any treasury stock held at the end of an accounting period is deducted from the total of the paid-in capital and retained earnings of the corporation. Any difference between the price paid for and the selling price of the treasury stock is usually recorded in a paid-in capital account for treasury stock transactions.

OBJECTIVE 7

Equity per Share

The amount appearing on the balance sheet as total stockholders' equity can be stated in terms of the equity per share. For a corporation with both preferred and common stock outstanding, it is necessary to allocate the total equity between the two classes of stock. The equity allocated to each class is divided by the number of shares outstanding of the respective class to determine the equity per share.

OBJECTIVE 8

Organization Costs

Expenditures incurred in organizing a corporation are charged to an intangible asset account entitled Organization Costs. The generally accepted accounting practice is to amortize organization costs over a period of sixty months, which conforms with federal income tax regulations.

KEY TERMS

articles of partnership 419
stockholders 421
stockholers' equity 422
paid-in capital 422
retained earnings 422
deficit 422
capital stock 423
stock outstanding 423
par 423
stated value 423
preemptive right 423
common stock 423
preferred stock 423
participating preferred stock 424
cumulative preferred stock 425
premium on stock 426
discount on stock 426
treasury stock 429
equity per share 431

SELF-EXAMINATION QUESTIONS

Answers at end of chapter.

1. The owners' equity in a corporation is commonly called:
   A. stockholders' equity
   B. shareholders' investment
   C. capital
   D. all of the above

2. If a corporation has outstanding 1,000 shares of $9 cumulative preferred stock of $100 par and dividends have been passed for the preceding three years, what is the amount of preferred dividends that must be declared in the current year before a dividend can be declared on common stock?
   A. $9,000
   B. $27,000
   C. $36,000
   D. None of the above

3. The stockholders' equity section of the balance sheet may include:
   A. Common Stock
   B. Paid-In Capital in Excess of Par
   C. Preferred Stock
   D. all of the above

4. If a corporation reacquires its own stock, the stock is listed on the balance sheet in the:
   A. current assets section
   B. long-term liabilities section
   C. stockholders' equity section
   D. none of the above

5. A corporation's balance sheet includes 10,000 outstanding shares of $8 cumulative preferred stock of $100 par; 100,000 outstanding shares of $20 par common stock; paid-in capital in excess of par—common stock of $100,000; and retained earnings of $540,000. If preferred dividends are three years in arrears and the preferred stock is entitled to dividends in arrears plus $110 per share in the event of liquidation, what is the equity per common share?
   A. $20.00
   B. $23.00
   C. $25.40
   D. None of the above

ILLUSTRATIVE PROBLEM

The stockholders' equity and related accounts of Rockton Manufacturing Corporation as of November 1, 1992, the beginning of the fiscal year, are as follows:

Preferred 8% Stock, $50 par (100,000 shares authorized, 23,000 shares issued)	$1,150,000
Paid-In Capital in Excess of Par—Preferred Stock	80,000
Common Stock, $25 par (500,000 shares authorized, 100,000 shares issued)	2,500,000
Paid-In Capital in Excess of Par—Common Stock	600,000
Retained Earnings	3,150,000

During the fiscal year ended October 31, 1993, Rockton Manufacturing Corporation completed the following transactions affecting stockholders' equity:

(a) Purchased 5,000 shares of treasury common for $130,000 ($26 per share).
(b) Sold 3,000 shares of treasury common for $81,000 ($27 per share).
(c) Issued 40,000 shares of common stock at $27, receiving cash.
(d) Sold 1,000 shares of treasury common for $24,000 ($24 per share).

Instructions:

1. Prepare the journal entries to record the transactions listed, identifying each transaction by the appropriate letter.
2. Prepare the stockholders' equity section for the October 31, 1993 balance sheet. The beginning retained earnings balance must be increased by the net income for the year, $710,000, and reduced by the dividends declared and paid, $280,000.

SOLUTION

(1)

	Debit	Credit
(a) Treasury Stock	130,000	
Cash		130,000
(b) Cash	81,000	
Treasury Stock		78,000
Paid-In Capital from Sale of Treasury Stock		3,000
(c) Cash	1,080,000	
Common Stock		1,000,000
Paid-In Capital in Excess of Par—Common Stock		80,000
(d) Cash	24,000	
Paid-In Capital from Sale of Treasury Stock	2,000	
Treasury Stock		26,000

(2)

Stockholders' Equity

Paid-in capital:			
Preferred 8% stock, $50 par (100,000 shares authorized, 23,000 shares issued)	$1,150,000		
Excess of issue price over par—preferred stock	80,000	$1,230,000	
Common stock, $25 par (500,000 shares authorized, 140,000 shares issued)	$3,500,000		
Excess of issue price over par—common stock	680,000	4,180,000	
From sale of treasury stock		1,000	
Total paid-in capital		$5,411,000	
Retained earnings		3,580,000	
Total		$8,991,000	
Deduct treasury common stock (1,000 shares at cost)		26,000	
Total stockholders' equity			$8,965,000

DISCUSSION QUESTIONS

10–1. What form of business organization is used most frequently in the United States?

10–2. What is the primary disadvantage of organizing a business enterprise as a sole proprietorship?

10–3. What are the primary differences in accounting for a sole proprietorship and accounting for a corporation?

10–4. At the end of the accounting period for a sole proprietorship, the owner's drawing account is closed to what account?

10–5. Ceal Burk and Frank Edwards joined together to form a partnership. Is it possible for them to lose a greater amount than the amount of their investment in the partnership enterprise? Explain.

10–6. Must a partnership (a) file a federal income tax return or (b) pay federal income taxes? Explain.

10–7. The partnership agreement between Barr and Chou provides for the sharing of partnership net income in the ratio of 2:1. Since the agreement is silent concerning the sharing of net losses, in what ratio will they be shared?

10–8. In the absence of an agreement, how will the net income be distributed between Jose Mandosa and Vincent Shore, partners in the firm of Mandosa and Shore Consultants?

10–9. Steven Kent, Eric Brooks, and Kurt Ross are contemplating the formation of a partnership. According to the partnership agreement, Kent is to invest $75,000 and devote one-half time, Brooks is to invest $50,000 and devote three-fourths time, and Ross is to make no investment and devote full time. Would Ross be correct in assuming that, since he is not contributing any assets to the firm, he is risking nothing? Explain.

10–10. What are the disadvantages of the partnership over the corporation as a form of organization for a profit-making business enterprise?

10–11. Contrast the owners' liability to creditors of (a) a partnership (partners) and (b) a corporation (stockholders).

10–12. Why is it said that the earnings of a corporation are subject to "double taxation"? Discuss.

10–13. Why are most large business enterprises organized as corporations?

10–14. What are the two principal sources of stockholders' equity?

10–15. The retained earnings account of a corporation at the beginning of the year had a credit balance of $90,000. The only other entry in the account during the year was a debit of $105,000 transferred from the income summary account at the end of the year. (a) What is the term applied to the $105,000 debit? (b) What is the balance in Retained Earnings at the end of the year? (c) What is the term applied to the balance determined in (b)?

10–16. The charter of a corporation provides for the issuance of a maximum of 100,000 shares of common stock. The corporation issued 80,000 shares of common stock, and two years later it reacquired 5,000 shares. After the reacquisition, what is the number of shares of stock (a) authorized, (b) issued, and (c) outstanding?

10–17. Of two corporations organized at approximately the same time and engaged in competing businesses, one issued $20 par common stock and the other issued $10 par common stock. Do the par designations provide any indication as to which stock is preferable as an investment? Explain.

10–18. What are the four basic rights that accompany ownership of a share of common stock?

10–19. (a) Differentiate between common stock and preferred stock. (b) Describe briefly (1) participating preferred stock and (2) cumulative preferred stock.

10–20. Assume that a corporation has had outstanding 100,000 shares of $2 cumulative preferred stock of $25 par and dividends were passed for the preceding three years. What amount of total dividends must be paid to the preferred stockholders before the common stockholders are entitled to any dividends in the current year?

10–21. If common stock of $25 par is sold for $30, what is the $5 difference between the issue price and par called?

10–22. What are some of the factors that influence the market price of a corporation's stock?

10–23. When a corporation issues stock at a premium, does the premium constitute income? Explain.

10–24. In which section of the corporation balance sheet would Paid-In Capital in Excess of Par—Preferred Stock appear?

10–25. The stockholders' equity section of a corporation balance sheet is composed of the following items:

Preferred $10 stock, $100 par	$500,000			
Excess of issue price over par—preferred stock .	40,000	$540,000		
Common stock, $20 par	$800,000			
Excess of issue price over par—common stock ..	70,000	870,000	$1,410,000	
Retained earnings.......			330,000	$1,740,000

What is the amount of each of the following: (a) paid-in capital attributable to preferred stock, (b) paid-in capital attributable to common stock, (c) earnings retained for use in the business, and (d) total stockholders' equity?

10–26. Land is acquired by a corporation for 10,000 shares of its $10 par common stock, which is currently selling for $35 per share on a national stock exchange. (a) At what value should the land be recorded? (b) What accounts and amounts should be credited to record the transaction?

10–27. (a) In what respect does treasury stock differ from unissued stock? (b) For what reasons might a company purchase treasury stock? (c) How should treasury stock be presented on the balance sheet?

10–28. A corporation reacquires 1,000 shares of its own $50 par common stock for $75,000, recording it at cost. (a) What effect does this transaction have on revenue or expense of the period? (b) What effect does it have on stockholders' equity?

10–29. The treasury stock in Question 10–28 is resold for $90,000. (a) What is the effect on the corporation's revenue of the period? (b) What is the effect on stockholders' equity?

10–30. A corporation that had issued 50,000 shares of $10 par common stock subsequently reacquired 5,000 shares, which it now holds as treasury stock. If the board of directors declares a cash dividend of $1 per share, what will be the total amount of the dividend?

10–31. At the end of the current period, a corporation has 5,000 shares of preferred stock and 50,000 shares of common stock outstanding. Assuming that there are no preferred dividends in arrears, that the preferred stock is entitled to receive $110 per share upon liquidation, and that total stockholders' equity is $2,750,000, determine the following amounts: (a) equity per share of preferred stock and (b) equity per share of common stock.

10–32. Common stock has a par of $20 per share, the current equity per share is $32.50, and the market price per share is $55. Suggest reasons for the comparatively high market price in relation to par and to equity per share.

10–33. (a) What type of expenditure is charged to the organization costs account? (b) Give examples of such expenditures. (c) In what section of the balance sheet is the balance of Organization Costs listed?

10–34. Identify each of the following accounts as asset, liability, stockholders' equity, revenue, or expense, and indicate the normal balance of each:
(1) Preferred Stock
(2) Paid-In Capital from Sale of Treasury Stock
(3) Treasury Stock
(4) Organization Costs
(5) Paid-In Capital in Excess of Par—Common Stock
(6) Common Stock
(7) Paid-In Capital in Excess of Par—Preferred Stock
(8) Retained Earnings

Real World Focus

10–35. In November, 1990, the CPA firm of Laventhol & Horwath filed for bankruptcy. At the time of filing for bankruptcy, the firm had at least 100 lawsuits pending against it for claims totaling perhaps as much as $2 billion. If Laventhol & Horwath should have to pay all these damages and if the firm itself had no assets after paying existing liabilities, approximately how much would each of the 350 partners have to pay out of their personal assets?

Ethics Discussion Case

10–36. Miguel Gallardo and Joseph Keker are organizing Mines Unlimited Inc. to undertake a high-risk gold mining venture in Mexico. Gallardo and Keker tentatively plan to request authorization for 100,000,000 shares of common stock to be sold to the general public. Gallardo and Keker have decided to establish a par value of $.10 per share in order to appeal to a wide variety of potential investors. Gallardo and Keker felt that investors would be more willing to invest in the company if they received a large quantity of shares for what might appear to be a "bargain" price.

Discuss whether Gallardo and Keker are behaving in an ethical manner.

EXERCISES

Ex. 10–37.
Dividends per share.
OBJ. 6

H. L. Baxter Company has stock outstanding as follows: 20,000 shares of $4 cumulative, nonparticipating preferred stock of $50 par, and 100,000 shares of $20 par common. During its first five years of operations, the following amounts were distributed as dividends: first year, none; second year, $100,000; third year, $150,000; fourth year, $200,000; fifth year, $250,000. Determine the dividends per share on each class of stock for each of the five years.

Ex. 10–38.
Dividends per share.
OBJ. 6

C. C. Werner Inc. has outstanding stock composed of 1,000 shares of $9 participating preferred stock of $100 par and 10,000 shares of no-par common stock. The preferred stock is entitled to participate equally with the common, on a share-for-share basis, in any dividend distributions which exceed the regular preferred dividend and a $2 per share common dividend. The directors declare dividends of $40,000 for the current year. Determine the amount of the dividend per share on (a) the preferred stock and (b) the common stock.

Ex. 10–39.
Entries for stock issuance.
OBJ. 6

On March 10, Abrams Company issued for cash 5,000 shares of no-par common stock (with a stated value of $10) at $14, and on August 7 it issued for cash 1,000 shares of $50 par preferred stock at $54. (a) Give the entries for March 10 and August 7, assuming that the common stock is to be credited with the stated value. (b) What is the total amount invested by all stockholders as of August 7?

Ex. 10–40.
Treasury stock transactions.
OBJ. 6

On January 11 of the current year, Slezak Company reacquired 1,000 shares of its common stock at $30 per share. On July 2, 500 of the reacquired shares were sold at $28 per share. The remaining 500 shares were sold at $35 per share on December 19. (a) Record the transactions of January 11, July 2, and December 19. (b) What is the balance in Paid-In Capital from Sale of Treasury Stock on December 31 of the current year? (c) Where will the balance in Paid-In Capital from Sale of Treasury Stock be reported on the balance sheet?

Ex. 10–41.
Equity per share.
OBJ. 7

The stockholders' equity accounts of De Vito Company at the end of the current fiscal year are as follows: Preferred $10 Stock, $100 par, $1,000,000; Common Stock, $10 par, $5,000,000; Paid-In Capital in Excess of Par—Common Stock, $200,000; Paid-In Capital in Excess of Par—Preferred Stock, $40,000; Retained Earnings, $935,000. (a) Determine the equity per share of each class of stock, assuming that the preferred stock is entitled to receive $120 upon liquidation. (b) Determine the equity per share of each class of stock, assuming that the preferred stock is to receive $120 per share plus the dividends in arrears in the event of liquidation, and that only the dividends for the current year are in arrears.

Ex. 10–42.
Treasury stock and equity per share.
OBJ. 6, 7

The following items were listed in the stockholders' equity section of the balance sheet of June 30: Common stock, $25 par (20,000 shares outstanding), $500,000; Paid-in capital in excess of par—common stock, $120,000; Retained earnings, $180,000. On July 1, the corporation purchased 1,000 shares of its stock for $35,250. (a) Determine the equity per share of stock on June 30. (b) Present the entry to record the purchase of the stock on July 1. (c) Determine the equity per share on July 1.

Ex. 10–43.
Equity per share; liquidation amounts.
OBJ. 7

The following items were listed in the stockholders' equity section of the balance sheet on July 31: Preferred stock, $100 par, $500,000; Common stock, $20 par, $2,000,000; Paid-in capital in excess of par—common stock, $150,000; Deficit, $250,000. On August 1, the board of directors voted to dissolve the corporation immediately. A short time later, after all noncash assets were sold and liabilities were paid, cash of $1,550,000 remained for distribution to stockholders. (a) Assuming that preferred stock is entitled to preference in liquidation of $110 per share, determine the equity per share on July 31 of (1) preferred stock and (2) common stock. (b) Determine the amount of the $1,550,000 that will be distributed for each share of (1) preferred stock and (2) common stock. (c) Explain the reason for the difference between the common stock equity per share on July 31 and the amount of the cash distribution per common share.

Ex. 10–44.
Corporate organization; stockholders' equity section.
OBJ. 6, 8

Pryor Products Inc. was organized on February 17 of the current year, with an authorization of 10,000 shares of $11 noncumulative preferred stock, $100 par, and 100,000 shares of $10 par common stock.

The following selected transactions were completed during the first year of operations:

Feb. 17. Issued 25,000 shares of common stock at par for cash.
17. Issued 750 shares of common stock to an attorney in payment of legal fees for organizing the corporation.
Mar. 4. Issued 30,000 shares of common stock in exchange for land, buildings, and equipment with fair market prices of $75,000, $205,000, and $30,000, respectively.
Aug. 15. Issued 2,000 shares of preferred stock at $106 for cash.

(a) Record the transactions. (b) Prepare the stockholders' equity section of the balance sheet as of December 31, the end of the current year. The net income for the year amounted to $64,000.

Appendix Ex. 10–45.
Division of partnership income.

Charles Berger and Mary Curren formed a partnership, investing $50,000 and $100,000, respectively. Determine their participation in the year's net income of $60,000 under each of the following assumptions: (a) no agreement concerning division of net income; (b) divided in the ratio of original capital investment; (c) interest at the rate of 12% allowed on original investments and the remainder divided in the ratio of 2:3;

(d) salary allowances of $15,000 and $30,000, respectively, and the balance divided equally; (e) allowance of interest at the rate of 12% on original investments, salary allowances of $15,000 and $30,000, respectively, and the remainder divided equally.

Appendix Ex. 10–46.
Division of partnership income.

Determine the participation of Berger and Curren in the year's net income of $90,000, according to each of the five assumptions as to income division listed in Appendix Ex. 10–45.

Appendix Ex. 10–47.
Admission of new partners.

The capital accounts of Mike Cash and Ed Doerr have balances of $56,000 and $100,000, respectively. Paula Goles and Julie Howell are to be admitted to the partnership. Goles purchases one fourth of Cash's interest for $22,500 and one fifth of Doerr's interest for $30,000. Howell contributes $60,000 cash to the partnership, for which she is to receive an ownership equity of $60,000. (a) Present the entries to record the admission of (1) Goles and (2) Howell. (b) What are the capital balances of each partner after the admission of the new partners?

Appendix Ex. 10–48.
Distribution of cash on liquidation.

Jim Omer and Gil Arthur, with capital balances of $49,500 and $37,500, respectively, decided to liquidate their partnership. After selling the noncash assets and paying the liabilities, there is $55,000 of cash remaining. If the partners share income and losses equally, how should the cash be distributed?

PROBLEMS

Pb. 10–49.
Dividends on preferred and common stock.
OBJ. 6
SPREADSHEET PROBLEM

The annual dividends declared by C. L. Adler Company during a six-year period are presented in the following table:

		Preferred Dividends		Common Dividends	
Year	Total Dividends	Total	Per Share	Total	Per Share
1989	$ 3,000				
1990	11,000				
1991	28,000				
1992	77,000				
1993	83,000				
1994	8,000				

During the entire period, the outstanding stock of the company was composed of 1,000 shares of cumulative, participating, $9 preferred stock, $100 par, and 10,000 shares of common stock, $50 par. The preferred stock contract provides that the preferred stock shall participate in distributions of additional dividends after allowance of a $5 dividend per share on the common stock, the additional dividends to be prorated among common and preferred shares on the basis of the total par of the stock outstanding.

Instructions:

(1) Determine the total dividends and the per share dividends declared on each class of stock for each of the six years, using the headings presented above. There were no dividends in arrears on January 1, 1989.
(2) Determine the average annual dividend per share for each class of stock for the six-year period.
(3) Assuming that the preferred stock was sold at par and common stock was sold at $62.50 at the beginning of the six-year period, determine the percentage return on initial shareholders' investment, based on the average annual dividend per share (a) for preferred stock and (b) for common stock.

Pb. 10–50.
Corporate expansion; stockholders' equity section.
OBJ. 6

The following accounts and their balances appear in the ledger of A and G Inc. on June 30 of the current year:

Preferred $8 Stock, $100 par (10,000 shares authorized, 7,000 shares issued)	$ 700,000
Paid-In Capital in Excess of Par—Preferred Stock	30,000
Common Stock, $20 par (100,000 shares authorized, 75,000 shares issued)	1,500,000
Paid-In Capital in Excess of Par—Common Stock	250,000
Retained Earnings	375,000

At the annual stockholders' meeting on July 2, the board of directors presented a plan for modernizing and expanding plant operations at a cost of approximately $700,000. The plan provided (a) that the corporation borrow $250,000, (b) that 2,000 shares of the unissued preferred stock be issued through an underwriter, and (c) that a building, valued at $190,000, and the land on which it is located, valued at $50,000, be acquired in accordance with preliminary negotiations by the issuance of 10,000 shares of common stock. The plan was approved by the stockholders and accomplished by the following transactions:

July 24. Issued 10,000 shares of common stock in exchange for land and building in accordance with the plan.
30. Issued 2,000 shares of preferred stock, receiving $105 per share in cash from the underwriter.
31. Borrowed $250,000 from First National Bank, giving a 13% mortgage note.

Instructions:

Assuming for the purpose of the problem that no other transactions occurred during July:

(1) Prepare the entries to record the foregoing transactions.
(2) Prepare the stockholders' equity section of the balance sheet as of July 31.

Pb. 10–51.
Stock transactions; stockholders' equity section.
OBJ. 6

The following selected accounts appear in the ledger of Lowry Corporation on July 1, the beginning of the current fiscal year:

Preferred 10% Stock, $50 par (10,000 shares authorized, 9,000 shares issued)	$450,000
Paid-In Capital in Excess of Par—Preferred Stock	35,000
Common Stock, $20 par (50,000 shares authorized, 25,000 shares issued)	500,000
Paid-In Capital in Excess of Par—Common Stock	90,000
Retained Earnings	337,000

During the year, the corporation completed a number of transactions affecting the stockholders' equity. They are summarized as follows:

(a) Purchased 1,000 shares of treasury common for $30,000.
(b) Sold 500 shares of treasury common for $16,250.
(c) Issued 2,500 shares of common stock at $35, receiving cash.
(d) Sold 250 shares of treasury common for $7,125.

Instructions:

(1) Prepare entries to record the transactions. Identify each entry by letter. (The use of T accounts for stockholders' equity accounts will facilitate the determination of the amounts needed in recording some of the transactions and in completing Instruction (2).)
(2) Prepare the stockholders' equity section of the balance sheet as of June 30, the end of the current fiscal year. The net income for the year was $210,000, and cash dividends declared and paid during the year were $130,000.

Pb. 10–52.
Corporation organization; stockholders' equity section.
OBJ. 6, 8

Vineyards Corp. was organized by Ferber, Garr, and Hopper. The charter authorized 100,000 shares of common stock with a par of $10. The following transactions affecting stockholders' equity were completed during the first year of operations:

(a) Issued 10,000 shares of stock at par to Ferber for cash.
(b) Issued 500 shares of stock at par to Garr for promotional services rendered in connection with the organization of the corporation, and issued 7,500 shares of stock at par to Garr for cash.
(c) Purchased land and a building from Hopper. The building is encumbered by a 12%, 15-year mortgage of $100,000, and there is accrued interest of $4,000 on the mortgage note at the time of the purchase. It is agreed that the land is to be priced at $50,000 and the building at $125,000, and that Hopper's equity will be exchanged for stock at par. The corporation agreed to assume responsibility for paying the mortgage note and the accrued interest.
(d) Issued 10,000 shares of stock at $12 to various investors for cash.
(e) Purchased equipment for $75,000. The seller accepted a 6-month, 13% note for $25,000 and 5,000 shares of stock in exchange for the equipment.

Instructions:

(1) Prepare entries to record the transactions.
(2) Prepare the stockholders' equity section of the balance sheet as of the end of the first year of operations. The retained earnings balance is the net income for the year, $90,000, less dividends declared and paid during the year, $1 per share on each share of stock issued.

Pb. 10–53.
Stock transactions and corrections; balance sheet.
OBJ. 6, 7, 8

Schultz Company was organized on April 15 of the current year and prepared its first financial statement, a balance sheet, the following December 31, the date that had been adopted as the end of the fiscal year. The balance sheet that was prepared by the accounting clerk is as follows:

Schultz Company
Balance Sheet
April 15 to December 31, 19--

Assets		Liabilities	
Cash	$ 70,100	Accounts payable	$ 93,000
Accounts receivable	190,500	Preferred stock	200,000
Merchandise inventory	122,500	Common stock	300,000
Prepaid insurance	9,100	Paid-in capital in excess	
Treasury common stock	20,000	of par—common stock	30,000
Equipment	130,000		
Retained earnings (deficit)	80,800		
Total assets	$623,000	Total liabilities	$623,000

You are retained by the board of directors to audit the accounts and to prepare a revised balance sheet. The relevant facts developed during the course of your engagement are:

(a) Stock authorized: 10,000 shares of $50 par, $5 preferred, and 50,000 shares of $20 par common.
(b) Stock issued: 4,000 shares of fully paid preferred at $51.25 and 15,000 shares of common at $22. The premium on preferred stock was credited to Retained Earnings.
(c) The company reacquired 1,000 shares of the issued common stock at $25. The difference between par and the price paid was debited to Retained Earnings. (It is decided that the treasury stock is to be recorded at cost.)
(d) Included in merchandise inventory is $3,000 of office supplies.
(e) Land to be used as a future building site cost $30,000 and was debited to Equipment.

(f) No depreciation has been recognized. The equipment is to be depreciated for 9 months by the straight-line method, using an estimated life of 10 years, and assuming no residual value.
(g) Organization costs of $6,000 were debited to Advertising Expense. (The organization costs are to be amortized over 60 months beginning with May 1 of the current year.)
(h) No dividends have been declared or paid.

Instructions:

(1) Prepare journal entries where necessary to record the corrections. Corrections of net income should be recorded as adjustments to retained earnings.
(2) Prepare a six-column work sheet, with columns for (a) balances per balance sheet, (b) corrections, and (c) corrected balances. In listing the accounts, leave an extra line blank following the retained earnings account. Complete the work sheet.
(3) Prepare a corrected balance sheet in report form as of the end of the fiscal year.

Pb. 10–54.
Equity per share.
OBJ. 7

Selected data from the balance sheets of six corporations, identified by letter, are as follows:

A. Common stock, $10 par .... $ 250,000
Paid-in capital in excess of par—common stock 50,000
Deficit 25,000

B. Preferred $5 stock, $50 par $1,000,000
Common stock, $20 par 3,000,000
Paid-in capital in excess of par—common stock 260,000
Retained earnings 415,000
Preferred stock has prior claim to assets on liquidation to the extent of par.

C. Preferred $9 stock, $100 par $1,000,000
Paid-in capital in excess of par—preferred stock 100,000
Common stock, no par, 25,000 shares outstanding 1,250,000
Deficit 350,000
Preferred stock has prior claim to assets on liquidation to the extent of par.

D. Preferred 11% stock, $50 par $1,000,000
Paid-in capital in excess of par—preferred stock 275,000
Common stock, $25 par 3,000,000
Retained earnings 425,000
Preferred stock has prior claim to assets on liquidation to the extent of 110% of par.

E. Preferred 9% stock, $100 par $1,200,000
Common stock, $50 par 4,000,000
Paid-in capital in excess of par—common stock 340,000
Retained earnings 108,000
Dividends on preferred stock are in arrears for 2 years, including the dividend passed during the current year. Preferred stock is entitled to par plus unpaid cumulative dividends upon liquidation to the extent of retained earnings.

F. Preferred $2 stock, $25 par .... $ 500,000
Common stock, $10 par 2,000,000
Deficit 130,000
Dividends on preferred stock are in arrears for 3 years, including the dividend passed during the current year. Preferred stock is entitled to par plus unpaid cumulative dividends upon liquidation, regardless of the availability of retained earnings.

Instructions:

Determine for each corporation the equity per share of each class of stock, presenting the total shareholders' equity allocated to each class and the number of shares outstanding.

Appendix Pb. 10–55. **Division of partnership income.**

Chin and Dyke have decided to form a partnership. They have agreed that Chin is to invest $60,000 and that Dyke is to invest $30,000. Chin is to devote one-half time to the business and Dyke is to devote full time. The following plans for the division of income are being considered:

(a) Equal division.
(b) In the ratio of original investments.
(c) In the ratio of time devoted to the business.
(d) Interest of 12% on original investments and the remainder equally.
(e) Interest of 12% on original investments, salaries of $20,000 to Chin and $30,000 to Dyke, and the remainder equally.
(f) Plan (e), except that Dyke is also to be allowed a bonus equal to 25% of the amount by which net income exceeds the salary allowances.

Instructions:

For each plan, determine the division of the net income under each of the following assumptions: (1) net income of $42,000 and (2) net income of $120,000. Present the data in tabular form, using the following columnar headings:

	$42,000		$120,000	
Plan	Chin	Dyke	Chin	Dyke

Appendix Pb. 10–56. **Statement of partnership liquidation.**

After closing the accounts on June 1, prior to liquidating the partnership, the capital account balances of Gertz, Hart, and Imes are $13,000, $26,000, and $31,000, respectively. Cash, noncash assets, and liabilities total $17,000, $83,000, and $30,000, respectively. Between June 1 and June 30, the noncash assets are sold for $41,000, the liabilities are paid, and the remaining cash is distributed to the partners. The partners share net income and loss in the ratio of 1:2:3.

Instructions:

Prepare a statement of partnership liquidation for the period June 1–30.

ALTERNATE PROBLEMS

Pb. 10–49A. **Dividends on preferred and common stock.** OBJ. 6

The annual dividends declared by Merlin Company during a six-year period are presented in the following table:

		Preferred Dividends		Common Dividends	
Year	Total Dividends	Total	Per Share	Total	Per Share
1989	$ 72,000				
1990	138,000				
1991	12,000				
1992	5,000				
1993	6,000				
1994	43,000				

During the entire period, the outstanding stock of the company was composed of 1,000 shares of cumulative, participating, $10 preferred stock, $100 par, and 10,000 shares of common stock, $20 par. The preferred stock contract provides that the preferred stock shall participate in distributions of additional dividends after allowance of a $5 dividend per share on the common stock, the additional dividends to be prorated among common and preferred shares on the basis of the total par of the stock outstanding.

Instructions:

(1) Determine the total dividends and the per share dividends declared on each class of stock for each of the six years, using the headings presented above. There were no dividends in arrears on January 1, 1989.

(2) Determine the average annual dividend per share for each class of stock for the six-year period.
(3) Assuming that the preferred stock was sold at par and common stock was sold at $31 at the beginning of the six-year period, determine the percentage return on initial shareholders' investment, based on the average annual dividend per share (a) for preferred stock and (b) for common stock.

Pb. 10–50A.
Corporate expansion; stockholders' equity section.
OBJ. 6

The following accounts and their balances appear in the ledger of Janet Combs and Co. on March 31 of the current year:

Preferred $9 Stock, $100 par (10,000 shares authorized, 5,000 shares issued)	$ 500,000
Paid-in Capital in Excess of Par—Preferred Stock	20,000
Common Stock, $20 par (100,000 shares authorized, 75,000 shares issued)	1,500,000
Paid-in Capital in Excess of Par—Common Stock	225,000
Retained Earnings	305,000

At the annual stockholders' meeting on April 11, the board of directors presented a plan for modernizing and expanding plant operations at a cost of approximately $500,000. The plan provided (a) that the corporation borrow $175,000, (b) that 1,000 shares of the unissued preferred stock be issued through an underwriter, and (c) that a building, valued at $180,000, and the land on which it is located, valued at $40,000, be acquired in accordance with preliminary negotiations by the issuance of 10,000 shares of common stock. The plan was approved by the stockholders and accomplished by the following transactions:

May 7. Issued 10,000 shares of common stock in exchange for land and building in accordance with the plan.
20. Issued 1,000 shares of preferred stock, receiving $105 per share in cash from the underwriter.
31. Borrowed $175,000 from Highland National Bank, giving a 12% mortgage note.

Instructions:

Assuming for the purpose of the problem that no other transactions occurred during May:

(1) Prepare the entries to record the foregoing transactions.
(2) Prepare the stockholders' equity section of the balance sheet as of May 31.

Pb. 10–51A.
Stock transactions; stockholders' equity section.
OBJ. 6

The following selected accounts appear in the ledger of Wayne Corporation on July 1, the beginning of the current fiscal year:

Preferred $9 Stock, $100 par (20,000 shares authorized, 12,500 shares issued)	1,250,000
Paid-In Capital in Excess of Par—Preferred Stock	55,000
Common Stock, $10 par (500,000 shares authorized, 300,000 shares issued)	3,000,000
Paid-In Capital in Excess of Par—Common Stock	600,000
Retained Earnings	975,000

During the year, the corporation completed a number of transactions affecting the stockholders' equity. They are summarized as follows:

(a) Purchased 7,500 shares of treasury common for $90,000.
(b) Sold 1,500 shares of treasury common for $22,500.
(c) Issued 50,000 shares of common stock at $15, receiving cash.
(d) Sold 1,000 shares of treasury common for $11,000.

Instructions:

(1) Prepare entries to record the transactions. Identify each entry by letter. (The use of T accounts for the stockholders' equity accounts will facilitate the determination

of the amounts needed in recording some of the transactions and in completing Instruction (2).)

(2) Prepare the stockholders' equity section of the balance sheet as of June 30, the end of the current fiscal year. The net income for the year was $600,000, and cash dividends declared and paid during the year were $462,500.

Pb. 10–52A.
Corporation organization; stockholders' equity section.
OBJ. 6, 8

Payne Company was organized by Bows, Howe, and Radner. The charter authorized 10,000 shares of common stock with a par of $50. The following transactions affecting stockholders' equity were completed during the first year of operations:

(a) Issued 1,000 shares of stock at par to Bows for cash.
(b) Issued 100 shares of stock at par to Howe for promotional services rendered in connection with the organization of the corporation, and issued 900 shares of stock at par to Howe for cash.
(c) Purchased land and a building from Radner. The building is encumbered by a 12%, 22-year mortgage of $125,000, and there is accrued interest of $4,000 on the mortgage note at the time of the purchase. It is agreed that the land is to be priced at $49,000 and the building at $130,000, and that Radner's equity will be exchanged for stock at par. The corporation agreed to assume responsibility for paying the mortgage note and the accrued interest.
(d) Issued 2,000 shares of stock at $60 to various investors for cash.
(e) Purchased equipment for $75,000. The seller accepted a 6-month, 11% note for $25,000 and 1,000 shares of stock in exchange for the equipment.

Instructions:

(1) Prepare entries to record the transactions.
(2) Prepare the stockholders' equity section of the balance sheet as of the end of the first year of operations. The retained earnings balance is the net income for the year, $67,200, less dividends declared and paid during the year, $5 per share.

Pb. 10–53A.
Stock transactions and corrections; balance sheet.
OBJ. 6, 7, 8

Grady Company was organized on March 1 of the current year and prepared its first financial statement, a balance sheet, the following December 31, the date that had been adopted as the end of the fiscal year. The balance sheet that was prepared by the accounting clerk is as follows:

Grady Company
Balance Sheet
March 1 to December 31, 19--

Assets		Liabilities	
Cash	$ 51,700	Accounts payable	$ 93,000
Accounts receivable	208,900	Preferred stock	200,000
Merchandise inventory	122,500	Common stock	300,000
Prepaid insurance	9,100	Paid-in capital in excess of par—common stock	30,000
Treasury common stock	20,000		
Equipment	130,000		
Retained earnings (deficit)	80,800		
Total assets	$623,000	Total liabilities	$623,000

You are retained by the board of directors to audit the accounts and to prepare a revised balance sheet. The relevant facts developed during the course of your engagement are:

(a) Stock authorized: 5,000 shares of $100 par, $8 preferred, and 50,000 shares of $20 par common.
(b) Stock issued: 2,000 shares of fully paid preferred at $102.50 and 15,000 shares of common at $22. The premium on preferred stock was credited to Retained Earnings.
(c) The company reacquired 1,000 shares of the issued common stock at $25. The difference between par and the price paid was debited to Retained Earnings. (It is decided that the treasury stock is to be recorded at cost.)

(d) Included in merchandise inventory is $4,000 of office supplies.
(e) Land to be used as a future building site cost $30,000 and was debited to Equipment.
(f) No depreciation has been recognized. The equipment is to be depreciated for 9 months by the straight-line method, using an estimated life of 10 years and assuming no residual value.
(g) Organization costs of $12,000 were debited to Advertising Expense. (The organization costs are to be amortized over 60 months beginning with March 1 of the current year.)
(h) No dividends have been declared or paid.

Instructions:

(1) Prepare journal entries where necessary to record the corrections. Corrections of net income should be recorded as adjustments to retained earnings.
(2) Prepare a six-column work sheet, with columns for (a) balances per balance sheet, (b) corrections, and (c) corrected balances. In listing the accounts, leave an extra line blank following the retained earnings account. Complete the work sheet.
(3) Prepare a corrected balance sheet in report form as of the end of the fiscal year.

Pb. 10–54A.
Equity per share.
OBJ. 7

Selected data from the balance sheets of six corporations, identified by letter, are as follows:

A. Common stock, no par, 100,000 shares outstanding .... $ 900,000
Deficit 70,000

B. Preferred $2 stock, $25 par .... $ 500,000
Common stock, $10 par 2,000,000
Paid-in capital in excess of par—common stock 75,000
Retained earnings 525,000
Preferred stock has prior claim to assets on liquidation to the extent of par.

C. Preferred $12 stock, $100 par .... $ 750,000
Paid-in capital in excess of par—preferred stock 40,000
Common stock, $5 par 1,000,000
Paid-in capital in excess of par—common stock 55,000
Deficit 95,000
Preferred stock has prior claim to assets on liquidation to the extent of par.

D. Preferred 10% stock, $100 par .... $ 750,000
Paid-in capital in excess of par—preferred stock 100,000
Common stock, $20 par 2,500,000
Deficit 75,000
Preferred stock has prior claim to assets on liquidation to the extent of 110% of par.

E. Preferred 11% stock, $100 par .... $ 800,000
Common stock, $5 par 2,000,000
Paid-in capital in excess of par—common stock 240,000
Retained earnings 104,000
Dividends on preferred stock are in arrears for 2 years, including the dividend passed during the current year. Preferred stock is entitled to par plus unpaid cumulative dividends upon liquidation to the extent of retained earnings.

F. Preferred $2 stock, $25 par .... $ 500,000
Paid-in capital in excess of par—preferred stock 15,000
Common stock, $10 par 1,500,000
Deficit 75,000
Dividends on preferred stock are in arrears for 3 years, including the dividend passed during the current year. Preferred stock is entitled to par plus

unpaid cumulative dividends upon liquidation, regardless of the availability of retained earnings.

Instructions:

Determine for each corporation the equity per share of each class of stock, presenting the total stockholders' equity allocated to each class and the number of shares outstanding.

Appendix Pb. 10–55A. Division of partnership income.

Gwen Cole and Carol Brown have decided to form a partnership. They have agreed that Cole is to invest $40,000 and that Brown is to invest $60,000. Cole is to devote full time to the business and Brown is to devote one-half time. The following plans for the division of income are being considered:

(a) Equal division.
(b) In the ratio of original investments.
(c) In the ratio of time devoted to the business.
(d) Interest of 10% on original investments and the remainder in the ratio of 3:2.
(e) Interest of 10% on original investments, salary allowances of $40,000 to Cole and $20,000 to Brown, and the remainder equally.
(f) Plan (e), except that Cole is also to be allowed a bonus equal to 20% of the amount by which net income exceeds the salary allowances.

Instructions:

For each plan, determine the division of the net income under each of the following assumptions: (1) net income of $90,000 and (2) net income of $45,000. Present the data in tabular form, using the following columnar headings:

	$90,000		$45,000	
Plan	Cole	Brown	Cole	Brown

Appendix Pb. 10–56A. Statement of partnership liquidation.

After closing the accounts on April 1, prior to liquidating the partnership, the capital account balances of Bowen, Carr, and Davis are $21,000, $26,000, and $13,000, respectively. Cash, noncash assets, and liabilities total $23,000, $79,000, and $42,000, respectively. Between April 1 and April 30, the noncash assets are sold for $55,000, the liabilities are paid, and the remaining cash is distributed to the partners. The partners share net income and loss in the ratio of 3:2:1.

Instructions:

Prepare a statement of partnership liquidation for the period April 1–30.

MINI-CASE 10

Miami Valley Cooperative Electric Corporation needs $5,000,000 to finance a major plant expansion. To raise the $5,000,000, the chairman of the board of directors suggested that the cooperative first offer common stock for sale at a price equal to the January 1, 1992 equity per share of common stock. The chairman indicated that by setting the price in this way, the value of the current common stockholders' interest in the cooperative would be preserved. Any additional funds that might be needed after this offer expired could be obtained from the issuance of preferred stock.

Since no preferred stock is authorized, the board is considering characteristics of the stock, such as the dividend rate and the cumulative and participating features. So as not to jeopardize common stockholder dividends, the board of directors tentatively approved a dividend rate of 4% for the preferred stock. The board agreed to delay any final action on other aspects of the financing plan until the legal counsel can be contacted to determine the procedures necessary to seek authorization of the preferred stock.

As of January 1, 1992, the stockholders' equity is as follows:

Paid-in capital:		
Common stock, $20 par (500,000 shares authorized, 300,000 shares issued)	$6,000,000	
Excess of issue price over par	450,000	
Total paid-in capital		$6,450,000
Retained earnings		1,650,000
Total stockholders' equity		$8,100,000

Instructions:

(1) Determine the equity per share of common stock on January 1, 1992.

(2) During the board meeting, the chairman asked for your opinion of the suggestion for determining the selling price of the common stock. How would you respond?

(3) What characteristics might you suggest the board consider in designing the preferred stock? Comment on the low preferred stock dividend rate tentatively approved by the board.

ANSWERS TO SELF-EXAMINATION QUESTIONS

1. D The owners' equity in a corporation is commonly called stockholders' equity (answer A), shareholders' investment (answer B), capital (answer C), or shareholders' equity.
2. C If a corporation has cumulative preferred stock outstanding, dividends that have been passed for prior years plus the dividend for the current year must be paid before dividends may be declared on common stock. In this case, dividends of $27,000 ($9,000 × 3) have been passed for the preceding three years and the current year's dividends are $9,000, making a total of $36,000 (answer C) that must be paid to preferred stockholders before dividends can be declared on common stock.
3. D The stockholders' equity section of corporate balance sheets is divided into two principal subsections: (1) investments contributed by the stockholders and (2) net income retained in the business. Included as part of the investments by stockholders is the par of common stock (answer A); paid-in capital in excess of par (answer B); and the par of preferred stock (answer C).
4. C Reacquired stock, known as treasury stock, should be listed in the stockholders' equity section (answer C) of the balance sheet. The price paid for the treasury stock is deducted from the total of all of the stockholders' equity accounts.
5. B The total stockholders' equity is determined as follows:

Preferred stock	$1,000,000
Common stock	2,000,000
Excess of issue price over par—common stock	100,000
Retained earnings	540,000
Total equity	$3,640,000

The amount allocated to common stock is determined as follows:

Total equity		$3,640,000
Allocated to preferred stock:		
Liquidation price	$1,100,000	
Dividends in arrears	240,000	1,340,000
Allocated to common stock		$2,300,000

The equity per common share is determined as follows:

$2,300,000 ÷ 100,000 shares = $23 per share

CHAPTER 11

CHAPTER OBJECTIVES

1 Identify and illustrate alternative terminology used in the paid-in capital section of the balance sheet.

2 Describe and illustrate the accounting for corporate earnings and income taxes.

3 Describe and illustrate the allocation of income tax between periods.

4 Describe and illustrate the accounting for unusual items in the financial statements.

5 Describe and illustrate the computation of earnings per share.

6 Describe and illustrate the accounting for appropriations of retained earnings and the preparation of a retained earnings statement.

7 Describe and illustrate the accounting for dividends, including cash dividends, stock dividends, and liquidating dividends.

8 Describe and illustrate the accounting for stock splits.

9 Describe the accounting for dividends and stock splits for treasury stock.

STOCKHOLDERS' EQUITY, EARNINGS, & DIVIDENDS

As has been indicated, the stockholders' equity section of the balance sheet is divided into two major subdivisions, *paid-in capital* (or contributed capital) and *retained earnings*. Although in practice there is wide variation in the amount of detail presented and the descriptive captions used, sources of significant amounts of stockholders' equity should be disclosed properly.

The emphasis on disclosure and clarity of expression by the accounting profession has been relatively recent. In earlier days, it was not unusual to present for stockholders' equity only the amount of the par of the preferred and common stock outstanding and a balancing amount described simply as "Surplus." Readers of the balance sheet could only assume that par represented the amount paid in by stockholders and that surplus represented retained earnings. Although it was possible for a "surplus" of $1,000,000, for example, to be composed solely of retained earnings, it could represent paid-in capital from premiums on stock issued or even an excess of $1,200,000 of such premiums over an accumulated deficit of $200,000 of retained earnings.

PAID-IN CAPITAL

OBJECTIVE 1
Identify and illustrate alternative terminology used in the paid-in capital section of the balance sheet.

As illustrated in Chapter 10, the main credits to paid-in capital accounts result from the issuance of stock. If par stock is issued at a price above or below par, the difference is recorded in a separate paid-in capital account. It is also common to use two accounts in recording the issuance of no-par stock, one for the stated value and the other for the excess over stated value. Another account for paid-in capital discussed in the preceding chapter was Paid-In Capital from Sale of Treasury Stock.

Paid-in capital may also originate from donated real estate and redemptions of a corporation's own stock. Civic organizations sometimes give land or land and buildings to a corporate enterprise as an inducement to locate in the community. In such cases, the assets are recorded in the corporate accounts at fair market value, with a credit to Donated Capital. Preferred stock contracts may give to the issuing corporation the right to redeem the stock at varying redemption prices at varying future dates. If the redemption price paid to the stockholder is greater than the original issuance price, the excess is considered to be a distribution of retained earnings. On the other hand, if the amount paid is less than the amount originally received by the corporation, the difference is a retention of capital and should be credited to Paid-In Capital from Preferred Stock Redemption or a similarly titled account.

As with other sections of the balance sheet, there are many variations in terminology and arrangement of the paid-in capital section. Some of these variations are illustrated by the following three examples. The details of each class of stock, including related stock premium or discount, are commonly listed first, followed by the other paid-in capital accounts. Instead of describing the source of each amount in excess of par or stated value, a common practice is to combine all such accounts into a single amount. It is then listed below the capital stock accounts and described as "Additional paid-in capital," "Capital in excess of par (or stated value) of shares," or by a similarly descriptive phrase.

Stockholders' Equity

Paid-in capital:			
Common stock, $20 par (50,000 shares authorized, 45,000 shares issued)	$900,000		
Excess of issue price over par	132,000	$1,032,000	
From stock redemption		60,000	
From sale of treasury stock		25,000	
Total paid-in capital			$1,117,000

Shareholders' Equity

Paid-in capital:			
Common stock, $20 par (50,000 shares authorized, 45,000 shares issued)		$ 900,000	
Premium on common stock	$132,000		
From redemption of common stock	60,000		
From transactions in own stock	25,000	217,000	
Total paid-in capital			$1,117,000

Shareholders' Investment

Contributed capital:		
Common stock, $20 par (50,000 shares authorized, 45,000 shares issued)	$ 900,000	
Additional paid-in capital	217,000	
Total contributed capital		$1,117,000

Significant changes in paid-in capital during the period should also be disclosed. The details of these changes may be presented either in a separate paid-in capital statement or in notes to other financial statements.

CORPORATE EARNINGS AND INCOME TAXES

OBJECTIVE 2
Describe and illustrate the accounting for corporate earnings and income taxes.

The determination of the net income or net loss of a corporation is comparable, in most respects, to that of other forms of business organization. Unlike sole proprietorships and partnerships, however, corporations are distinct legal entities. In general, they are subject to the federal income tax and, in many cases, to income taxes levied by states or other political subdivisions. Although the discussion that follows is limited to the income tax levied by the federal government, the basic concepts apply also to state and local income taxes.

For several years, most corporations have been required to estimate the amount of their federal income tax expense for the year and to make advance payments, usually in four installments. To illustrate, assume that a calendar-year corporation estimates its income tax expense for the year to be $84,000. The required entry for each of the four payments of $21,000 (1/4 of $84,000) would be as follows:

Income Tax	21,000	
Cash		21,000

At year end, the actual taxable income and the actual tax are determined. If an additional amount is owed, this liability must be recorded. Continuing with the illustration, assume that the corporation's actual tax, based on actual taxable income, is $86,000 instead of $84,000. The following entry would be required in order to include the income tax expense in the fiscal year in which the related income was earned:

Dec. 31	Income Tax	2,000	
	Income Tax Payable		2,000

If the amount of the advance payments exceeds the tax liability based on actual income, the amount of the overpayment would be debited to a receivable account and credited to Income Tax.

Income tax returns and related records and documents are subject to review by the taxing authority, usually for a period of three years after the return is filed. Consequently, the determination made by the taxpayer is provisional rather than final. In recognition of the possibility of an assessment for a tax deficiency, the liability for income taxes is sometimes described in the current liability section of the balance sheet as "Estimated income tax payable."

Because of its substantial size in relationship to net income, income tax is often reported on the income statement as a special deduction, as follows:

Palmer Corporation
Income Statement
For Year Ended December 31, 19--

Sales	$980,000
...	
Income before income tax	$200,000
Income tax	82,500
Net income	$117,500

ALLOCATION OF INCOME TAX BETWEEN PERIODS

OBJECTIVE 3
Describe and illustrate the allocation of income tax between periods.

The **taxable income** of a corporation, determined according to the tax laws, is often different from the amount of income (before income tax) reported in the income statement. As a result, the amount of income tax payable based upon a corporation's income tax return may differ from the amount of income tax reported in the income statement. This difference may need to be allocated between periods, depending upon the nature of the items causing the differences.

Some items create differences between income before income tax and taxable income because the items are recognized in one period for income statement purposes and in another period for tax purposes. Such differences, called **temporary differences,** reverse or turn around in later years. Some examples of items which create temporary differences are described as follows:[1]

1. Revenues or gains that are taxable after they are reported in the income statement. Example: The point of sale method is used for reporting purposes and the installment method of determining revenue is used in determining taxable income.
2. Expenses or losses that are deducted in determining taxable income after they are reported in the income statement. Example: Product warranty expense estimated and reported in the year of the sale for reporting purposes, but is only deductible for tax purposes when paid.
3. Revenues or gains that are taxable before they are reported in the income statement. Example: Cash received in advance for magazine subscriptions is included in taxable income of the current period when received, but included in the income statement of a future period when earned.
4. Expenses or losses that are deducted in determining taxable income before they are reported in the income statement. Example: An accelerated depreciation method is used for tax purposes, and the straight-line method is used for financial reporting purposes.

Temporary differences require that the amount of the tax liability be computed at the end of each year and that the proper amount of current and postponed (deferred) liability be recognized. To illustrate the effect of temporary differences and their related effect on the amount of income tax reported in corporate financial statements, assume that a corporation that sells its product on the installment basis recognizes the revenue at the time of sale and maintains its accounts accordingly. At the end of the first year of operations, the income before income tax according to the ledger is $300,000. Realizing the advantage of reducing current income tax, the corporation elects the installment method of determining revenue and cost of merchandise sold, which yields taxable income of only $100,000. Assuming an income tax rate of 40%, the income tax on $300,000 of income would amount to $120,000.[2] The income tax actually due for the year would only be $40,000 (40% of $100,000). The $80,000 difference between the two amounts is due to the timing difference in recognizing revenue. It represents a deferment of $80,000 of income tax to future years. As the installment accounts receivable are collected in later years, the additional $200,000 of income will be included in the taxable income, and the $80,000 deferment (40% of $200,000)

---

[1]*Statement of Financial Accounting Standards No. 96,* "Accounting for Income Taxes" (Stamford: Financial Accounting Standards Board, 1987), par. 10.

[2]For purposes of illustration, the 40% tax rate is assumed to include all federal, state, and local income taxes.

will become a tax liability of those years.[3] The situation may be summarized as follows:

Income deferred to future years	$200,000
Income tax deferred to future years (40% × $200,000)	$ 80,000

In this example, the proof of the $80,000 deferred tax credit is shown in the following computation:

Income tax based on $300,000 reported income at 40%	$120,000
Income tax based on $100,000 taxable income at 40%	40,000
Income tax deferred to future years	$ 80,000

The income tax to be reported on the income statement should be the total tax ($120,000 in the illustration) expected to result from the net income of the year. In this manner, the revenue reported on the income statement will be matched with the expenses (including income tax) related to that revenue, regardless of when the tax will become an actual liability to be paid. Applying the concept of the allocation of income tax between periods to the illustrative data yields the following results, stated in terms of a journal entry:

Income Tax	120,000	
Income Tax Payable		40,000
Deferred Income Tax Payable		80,000

Continuing with the illustration, the $80,000 in Deferred Income Tax Payable will be transferred to Income Tax Payable as the remaining $200,000 of income becomes taxable in later years. If, for example, $120,000 of untaxed income of the first year of the corporation's operations becomes taxable in the second year, the effect would be as follows, stated as a journal entry:

Deferred Income Tax Payable	48,000	
Income Tax Payable		48,000

In the illustration, the amount in Deferred Income Tax Payable at the end of a year will be reported as a liability. The amount due within one year will be classified as a current liability, and the remainder will be classified as a long-term liability or reported in a Deferred Credits section following the Long-Term Liabilities section.[4]

During periods of growth, the amount of deferred income taxes for an enterprise may increase rapidly and can become a significant amount. The

[3]If the tax rates change, companies are required to recompute their tax liabilities and to recognize the effect of the change in net income. This topic is discussed in more detail in advanced texts.

[4]In some cases, a deferred tax asset may arise for tax benefits to be received in the future. Such deferred tax assets would be reported as either a current or long-term asset, depending upon when the expected benefits are expected to be realized.

amounts of deferred income taxes listed as long-term liabilities on the 1990 annual reports of nine major companies were as follows:

Walgreen Co.	$ 156,364,000
Alcoa	763,500,000
Circus Circus Enterprises, Inc.	42,586,000
Tandy Corporation	68,971,000
The Quaker Oats Company	327,700,000
PepsiCo	942,800,000
Whirlpool Corp.	167,000,000
Boeing Company	161,000,000
IBM	3,861,000,000

Differences between taxable income and income (before tax) reported on the income statement may also arise because certain revenues are exempt from tax and certain expenses are not deductible in determining taxable income.[5] For example, interest income on municipal bonds may be exempt from taxation. Such differences create no special financial reporting problems, since the amount of income tax determined in accordance with the tax laws is the amount reported on the income statement.

ARE DEFERRED TAXES REALLY A LIABILITY?

For those companies that show a significant amount of deferred taxes on their balance sheets, the question that may arise is whether such amounts are really liabilities. For example, the reporting of a liability for "deferred income taxes, $267.7 million," on an Anheuser-Busch balance sheet was discussed in *Forbes*. In this article, excerpts from which follow, it was noted that Anheuser-Busch's deferred tax liability was equal to 19% of the total liabilities and 26% of the stockholders' equity.

. . . Says Harvey D. Moskowitz, national director of accounting and auditing for Seidman & Seidman, "The deferred taxes on the balance sheet bear no relationship to what is actually going to be owed. So the current method of income tax accounting makes it impossible for the investor to evaluate a company's liquidity, solvency or cash flow."

Here's the explanation for this curious state of affairs: Anheuser-Busch had pretax income of $271.5 million, so, using standard corporate tax rates (less credits), it owed $99.7 million to Uncle Sam. That's what it set aside as "provision for income taxes" on its income statement. But it's not what the company actually paid. Like most businesses Anheuser keeps two sets of books, one for tax purposes, one for stock owners. It uses accelerated depreciation for taxes but straight line for reporting to investors. . . . So, out-of-pocket, it really had to pay only $31.9 million in taxes . . . the line marked "current" on the income statement. The other $67.8 million, called "deferred," represents cash that's squirreled away in liabilities on the balance sheet, under the assumption that the company will pay those taxes eventually—when accelerated depreciation runs out, for example.

That assumption is probably wrong, though. As long as the company keeps growing—in real terms or because of inflation—it will keep adding new assets and new interest costs to replace the ones that are running out. That means those deferred taxes, instead of getting paid, will simply roll over. And over and over and over. It could almost make you dizzy.

Source: Jane Carmichael, "Rollover," *Forbes* (January 18, 1982), pp. 75, 78.

[5]Such differences, which will not reverse with the passage of time, are sometimes referred to as permanent differences.

OBJECTIVE 4
Describe and illustrate the accounting for unusual items in the financial statements.

Professional accounting organizations have devoted much time to the development of guidelines for reporting unusual items in the financial statements. Generally, unusual items affect the determination of either current or prior year's net income. Accordingly, these items may be described as (1) items that affect the current year's net income and are therefore reported on the current year's income statement and (2) items that affect a prior year's net income and are therefore reported on the current year's retained earnings statement. Each of these types of unusual items are described and illustrated in the following paragraphs.

Unusual Items that Affect the Income Statement

In preparing the income statement, a company's records may show three well-defined categories of unusual items which should be presented separately from other items. These categories, which are briefly described and illustrated in the following paragraphs, are as follows:

1. The results of discontinued operations.
2. Extraordinary items of gain or loss.
3. A change from one generally accepted accounting principle to another.

Discontinued Operations. A gain or loss resulting from the disposal of a segment of a business should be identified on the income statement as a gain or loss from **discontinued operations**. The term *discontinued* refers to "the operations of a segment of a business . . . that has been sold, abandoned, spun off, or otherwise disposed of or . . . is the subject of a formal plan for disposal."[6] The term "segment of a business" refers to a part of an enterprise whose activities represent a major line of business, such as a division or department or a certain class of customer.[7] For example, if an enterprise owning newspapers, television stations, and radio stations were to sell its radio stations, the results of the sale would be reported as a gain or loss on discontinued operations.

When an enterprise discontinues a segment of its operations and identifies the gain or loss therefrom, the results of "continuing operations" should also be identified in the income statement. The net income or loss from continuing operations is presented first, beginning with sales and followed by the enterprise's customary analysis of its costs and expenses. In addition to the data on discontinued operations presented in the body of the statement, such details as the identity of the segment disposed of, the disposal date, a description of the assets and liabilities involved, and the manner of disposal should be disclosed in a note to the financial statements.[8]

Extraordinary Items. Extraordinary gains and losses result from "events and transactions that are distinguished by their unusual nature *and* by the infrequency of their occurrence."[9] Such gains and losses, other than those from the disposal of a segment of a business, should be identified in the in-

---

[6] *Opinions of the Accounting Principles Board, No. 30,* "Reporting the Results of Operations" (New York: American Institute of Certified Public Accountants, 1973), par. 8.

[7] *Ibid.*, par. 13.

[8] *Ibid.*, par. 18.

[9] *Ibid.*, par. 20.

come statement as **extraordinary items**. To be so classified, an event or transaction must meet both of the following criteria:

1. Unusual nature—*the underlying event or transaction should possess a high degree of abnormality and be of a type clearly unrelated to, or only incidentally related to, the ordinary and typical activities of the entity, taking into account the environment in which the entity operates.*
2. Infrequency of occurrence—*the underlying event or transaction should be of a type that would not reasonably be expected to recur in the foreseeable future, taking into account the environment in which the entity operates.*[10]

Transactions that meet both of the criteria are uncommon. For example, the 1990 edition of *Accounting Trends & Techniques* indicated that only 49 of the 600 industrial and merchandising companies surveyed reported extraordinary items on their income statements. Usually, extraordinary items result from major casualties, such as floods, earthquakes, and other rare catastrophes not expected to recur. In addition, gains or losses that result when land or buildings are condemned for public use are considered extraordinary.

Occasionally, extraordinary events create unusual reporting in the financial statements. For example, in its 1989 income statement, Delta Air Lines reported an extraordinary gain of over $5.5 million as the result of the crash of a 727 earlier in the fiscal year. The plane that crashed was insured for $6.5 million, but its book value in Delta's accounting records was $962,000.

Gains and losses on the disposal of plant assets do not qualify as extraordinary items because (1) they are not unusual and (2) they recur from time to time in the ordinary course of business activities. Similarly, gains and losses incurred on the sale of investments are usual and recurring for most enterprises. However, if a company had owned only one investment during its entire existence, a gain or loss on its sale might qualify as an extraordinary item, provided there was no intention of acquiring other investments in the foreseeable future.

Changes in Accounting Principles. A number of accepted alternative principles affecting the determination of income statement and balance sheet amounts were presented in preceding chapters. Recognizing that different methods may be used under varying circumstances, some guide or standard is needed to assure that the periodic financial statements of an enterprise can be compared. It is common practice to compare an enterprise's current income statement and balance sheet with the statements of the preceding year. Therefore, interested persons should be able to assume that successive financial statements of an enterprise are based consistently on the same generally accepted accounting principles. If the principles are not applied consistently, the trends indicated could be the result of changes in the principles used rather than the result of changes in business conditions or managerial effectiveness.

The concept of **consistency** does not completely prohibit changes in the accounting principles used. Changes are permissible when it is believed that the use of a different principle will state net income and financial position more fairly. In such cases, the nature of the change, the justification for the change, and its effect on income should be disclosed in the financial statements of the period in which the change in principle is made.

The generally accepted procedures for disclosing the effect on net income of a change in principle are as follows: (1) report the cumulative effect

---

[10]*Ibid.*

of the change on net income of prior periods as a special item on the income statement and (2) report the effect of the change on net income of the current period. If the financial statements for prior periods are presented in conjunction with the current statements, the effect of the change in accounting principle should also be applied retroactively to the published statements of the prior periods and reported either on their face or in accompanying notes.

The amount of the cumulative effect on net income of prior periods should be reported in a special section of the income statement located immediately prior to the net income. If an extraordinary item or items are reported on the statement, the amount related to the change in principle should follow the extraordinary items.

The procedures should be modified for a change from the last-in, first-out assumption for inventory costing to another method or for a change in the method of accounting for long-term construction contracts. For these changes in principle, the cumulative effect on prior years' income is not reported as a special item on the income statement. Instead, the newly adopted principle should be applied retroactively to the income statements of the prior periods and the effect on income disclosed, either on the face of the statements or in accompanying notes. Financial statements of subsequent periods need not repeat the disclosures.[11]

Allocation of Income Tax to Unusual Items. The amount reported as a gain or loss from a discontinued operation, an extraordinary item, or the cumulative effect of a change in accounting principle should be net of the related income tax. The amount of income tax allocable to each of these items may be disclosed on the face of the appropriate financial statement or by an accompanying note.

Presentation of Unusual Items in the Income Statement. The manner in which gains or losses from discontinued operations, extraordinary items, and the cumulative effect of a change in accounting principle may be presented in the income statement is illustrated for Jones Corporation on page 468. Many variations in terminology and format are possible.

Unusual Items that Affect the Retained Earnings Statement

Most accountants agree that it is preferable to report all revenue and expense items occurring in the current period in the current year's income statement. Unusual or nonrecurring items, such as those described in the preceding paragraphs, are also identified and disclosed in the income statement. If nonrecurring items were "buried" in the retained earnings statement, they would likely be overlooked by financial statement readers. In addition, if they were included in the retained earnings statement, the total amount of the periodic net income reported over the entire life of an enterprise could not be determined from its income statements. An exception, however, is made for errors discovered in the determination of a prior period's net income.

Material errors may result from mathematical mistakes and from mistakes in the application of accounting principles or oversight or misuse of facts that existed at the time transactions were recorded. The effect of material errors that are not discovered within the same fiscal period in which they occurred should not be included in the determination of net income for the current period. Corrections of this type of error, usually called **prior**

---

[11] *Ibid.*, pars. 27 and 28.

Jones Corporation
Income Statement
For the Year Ended August 31, 19--

Net sales	$9,600,950
~~	
Income from continuing operations before income tax	$1,310,000
Income tax	620,000
Income from continuing operations	$ 690,000
Loss on discontinued operations (Note A)	100,000
Income before extraordinary item and cumulative effect of a change in accounting principle	$ 590,000
Extraordinary item:	
Gain on condemnation of land, net of applicable income tax of $65,000	150,000
Cumulative effect on prior years of changing to a different depreciation method (Note B)	92,000
Net income	$ 832,000

Note A. On July 1 of the current year, the entire electrical products division of the corporation was sold at a loss of $100,000, net of applicable income tax of $50,000. The net sales of the division for the current year were $2,900,000. The assets sold were composed of inventories, equipment, and plant totaling $2,100,000, and the liabilities assumed by the purchaser amounted to $600,000.

Note B. Depreciation of property, plant, and equipment has been computed by the straight-line method at all manufacturing facilities in 19--. Prior to 19--, depreciation of equipment for one of the divisions had been computed on the double-declining balance method. In 19--, the straight-line method was adopted for this division in order to achieve uniformity and to more appropriately match the remaining depreciation charges with the estimated economic utility of such assets. Pursuant to APB Opinion 20, this change in depreciation has been applied retroactively to prior years. The effect of the change was to increase income before extraordinary items for 19-- by approximately $30,000. The adjustment of $92,000 (after reduction for income tax of $88,000) to apply retroactively the new method is also included in income for 19--.

period adjustments, should be reported as an adjustment of the retained earnings balance at the beginning of the period in which the correction is made.[12] Prior period adjustments would include, for example, the correction of a material error in computing depreciation expense for a prior period. In addition, a change from an unacceptable accounting principle to an acceptable accounting principle is considered to be a correction of a material error and should be treated as a prior period adjustment. An example of such a situation would be the correction resulting from changing from the cash basis to the accrual basis of accounting for a business enterprise that buys and sells merchandise.

Prior period adjustments should be distinguished from differences arising from the use of estimates. The use of estimates is inherent in the ac-

[12] *Statement of Financial Accounting Standards, No. 16,* "Prior Period Adjustments" (Stamford: Financial Accounting Standards Board, 1977), par. 11.

counting process. For example, income taxes and uncollectible accounts receivable must be estimated for the timely preparation of financial statements. As a consequence, differences between the estimated and actual amounts may arise. These differences are normally minor in amount. They are not considered errors or prior period adjustments, but are included in the determination of the current period's net income.

The manner in which a prior period adjustment is presented in the retained earnings statement is illustrated as follows:

Casper Company Retained Earnings Statement For Year Ended December 31, 1992		
Retained earnings, January 1, 1992		$310,500
Less prior period adjustment:		
Correction of error in depreciation expense in 1991, net of applicable income tax of $13,000		29,200
Corrected retained earnings, January 1, 1992		$281,300
Net income for year	$77,350	
Less dividends	40,000	
Increase in retained earnings		37,350
Retained earnings, December 31, 1992		$318,650

Note that the amount reported as a prior period adjustment is reported net of the related income tax. In addition, if financial statements are presented only for the current period, the effect of the adjustment on the net income of the preceding period should also be disclosed. If financial statements for prior periods are presented, as is preferable, the statements should be adjusted and the amount of each adjustment should be disclosed.

Adjustments applicable to prior periods that meet the criteria for a prior period adjustment are rare in modern financial accounting. Annual audits by independent public accountants, combined with the internal control features of accounting systems, lessen the chances of errors justifying such treatment.

EARNINGS PER COMMON SHARE

OBJECTIVE 5
Describe and illustrate the computation of earnings per share.

The absolute amounts of net income are often useful in evaluating a company's profitability. However, these absolute amounts are difficult to use in comparing companies of different sizes. For example, a net income of $750,000 may be satisfactory for a small computer manufacturer, but it may be unsatisfactory for a very large computer manufacturer. Likewise, the absolute amount of net income is difficult to use in evaluating a company's profitability when the amount of stockholders' equity changes significantly. In such cases, the profitability of a company expressed as earnings per share may be more useful. The term **earnings per share** refers to the net income per share of common stock outstanding during a given period. For public corporations, data on earnings per share of common stock must be reported on the income statement.[13] Earnings per share is often the item of greatest

[13]Nonpublic corporations are exempt from this requirement, according to *Statement of Financial Accounting Standards, No. 21*, "Suspension of the Reporting of Earnings per Share and Segment Information by Nonpublic Enterprises" (Stamford: Financial Accounting Standards Board, 1978).

interest contained in corporate financial statements. These data are also often reported by the financial press and by various statistical services.

If a company has only common stock outstanding, the earnings per share of common stock is determined by dividing net income by the number of common shares outstanding. If preferred stock is outstanding, the net income must be reduced by the amount of any preferred dividend requirements before dividing by the number of common shares outstanding.

The effect of nonrecurring additions to or deductions from income of a period should be considered in computing earnings per share. Otherwise, a single per share amount based on net income would be misleading. To illustrate this point, assume that Jones Corporation, whose partial income statement for the current year was presented on page 468, reported net income of $700,000 for the preceding year, with no extraordinary or other special items. Assume also that the corporation's capital stock was composed of 200,000 common shares outstanding during the entire two-year period. If the earnings per share of $3.50 ($700,000 ÷ 200,000) for the preceding year were compared with the earnings per share of $4.16 ($832,000 ÷ 200,000) for the current year, it would appear that operations had improved greatly. However, the current year's per share amount that is comparable to $3.50 is in reality $3.45 ($690,000 ÷ 200,000), which indicates a slight downward trend in normal operations.

Data on earnings per share should be presented in conjunction with the income statement. If there are nonrecurring items on the statement, the per share amounts should be presented for (1) income from continuing operations, (2) income before extraordinary items and the cumulative effect of a change in accounting principle, (3) the cumulative effect of a change in accounting principle, and (4) net income.[14] Presentation of per share amounts is optional for the gain or loss on discontinued operations and for extraordinary items. The per share data may be shown in parentheses or added at the bottom of the statement, as in the following illustration for Jones Corporation:

Jones Corporation
Income Statement
For the Year Ended August 31, 19--

Income from continuing operations	$690,000
Net income	$832,000
Earnings per common share:	
Income from continuing operations	$3.45
Loss on discontinued operations	.50
Income before extraordinary item and cumulative effect of a change in accounting principle	$2.95
Extraordinary item	.75
Cumulative effect on prior years of changing to a different depreciation method	.46
Net income	$4.16

[14] *Opinions of the Accounting Principles Board, No. 15,* "Earnings per Share" (New York: American Institute of Certified Public Accountants, 1969) as amended by *Opinions of the Accounting Principles Board, No. 20,* and *Opinions of the Accounting Principles Board, No. 30.*

In computing the earnings per share of common stock, all factors that affect the number of common shares outstanding must be considered. If there is an issue of preferred stock or bonds (debt) with the privilege of converting to common stock, two different amounts of per share earnings should ordinarily be reported. One amount is computed without regard to the conversion privilege and is referred to as "Earnings per common share—assuming no dilution" or "Primary earnings per share." The other computation is based on the assumption that the convertible preferred stock or bonds are converted to common stock, and the amount is referred to as "Earnings per common share—assuming full dilution" or "Fully diluted earnings per share."[15]

The details of the computation of earnings per share should be disclosed in notes to the financial statements, as indicated by the following note adapted from the annual report of The Pillsbury Company:

> *Net earnings per share are computed using the weighted average number of common shares, including common share equivalents of stock options, outstanding during each year. Net earnings per share assuming full dilution would be substantially the same.*

The complexities of the computation of earnings per share and other complexities of capital structure are discussed in more advanced accounting texts.

APPROPRIATION OF RETAINED EARNINGS

OBJECTIVE 6
Describe and illustrate the accounting for appropriations of retained earnings and the preparation of a retained earnings statement.

The amount of a corporation's retained earnings available for distribution to its shareholders may be limited by action of the board of directors. The amount restricted, which is called an **appropriation** or a **reserve**, remains a part of retained earnings and should be so classified in the financial statements. An appropriation can be effected by transferring the desired amount from Retained Earnings to a special account designating its purpose, such as Appropriation for Plant Expansion.

Appropriations may be initiated by the directors, or they may be required by law or contract. Some states require that a corporation retain earnings equal to the amount paid for treasury stock. For example, if a corporation with accumulated earnings of $200,000 purchases shares of its own issued stock for $50,000, the corporation would not be permitted to pay more than $150,000 in dividends. The restriction is equal to the $50,000 paid for the treasury stock and assures that legal capital will not be impaired by a declaration of dividends. The entry to record the appropriation would be:

Apr. 24	Retained Earnings	50,000	
	Appropriation for Treasury Stock		50,000

When a part or all of an appropriation is no longer needed, the amount should be transferred back to the retained earnings account. Thus, if the corporation in the above illustration sells the treasury stock, the appropriation would be eliminated by the following entry:

Nov. 10	Appropriation for Treasury Stock	50,000	
	Retained Earnings		50,000

---

[15] *Opinions of the Accounting Principles Board, No. 15,* "Earnings per Share" (New York: American Institute of Certified Public Accountants, 1969) par. 16.

When a corporation borrows a large amount through the issuance of bonds (debt), the agreement may provide for restrictions on dividends until the debt is paid. The contract may stipulate that retained earnings equal to the amount borrowed be restricted during the entire period of the loan, or it may require that the restriction be built up by annual appropriations. For example, assume that a corporation borrows $700,000 on ten-year bonds. If equal annual appropriations were to be made over the life of the bonds, there would be a series of ten entries, each in the amount of $70,000, debiting Retained Earnings and crediting an appropriation account entitled Appropriation for Bonded Indebtedness. Even if the bond agreement did not require the restriction on retained earnings, the directors might decide to establish the appropriation. In that case, it would be a *discretionary* rather than a *contractual* appropriation. The entries would be the same in either case.

It must be clearly understood that the appropriation account is not directly related to any certain group of asset accounts. Its existence does not imply that there is an equivalent amount of cash or other assets set aside in a special fund. The appropriation serves the purpose of restricting dividends, but it does not assure that the cash that might otherwise be distributed as dividends will not be invested in additional inventories or other assets, or used to reduce liabilities.

Appropriations of retained earnings may be accompanied by a segregation of cash or marketable securities, in which case the appropriation is said to be **funded.** Accumulation of such funds is discussed in Chapter 12.

There are other purposes for which the directors may consider appropriations desirable. A company may earmark earnings for specific contingencies, such as inventory price declines or an adverse decision on a pending lawsuit. Some companies with properties in many locations may assume their own risk of losses from fire, windstorm, and other casualties rather than obtain protection from insurance companies. In such cases, the appropriation account would be entitled Appropriation for Self-Insurance. Such an appropriation is likely to be permanent, although its amount may vary as the total value of properties and the extent of casualty protection change. If a loss occurs, it should be debited to a special loss account rather than to the appropriation account. It is definitely a loss of the particular period and should be reported in the income statement.

The details of retained earnings may be presented in the balance sheet in the following manner. The item designated "Unappropriated" is the balance of the retained earnings account.

Retained earnings:		
Appropriated:		
For plant expansion	$ 250,000	
Unappropriated	1,800,000	
Total retained earnings		$2,050,000

Restrictions on retained earnings do not need to be formalized in the ledger. However, following legal requirements and contractual restrictions is necessary, and the nature and the amount of all restrictions should always be disclosed in the balance sheet. For example, the appropriations data appearing in the foregoing illustration could be presented in a note accompanying the balance sheet. Such an alternative might also be used as a means of simplifying or condensing the balance sheet, even though appropriation accounts are maintained in the ledger. The alternative balance sheet presentation, including the note, might appear as follows:

Retained earnings (see note)	$2,050,000

Note: Retained earnings in the amount of $250,000 are appropriated for expansion of plant facilities; the remaining $1,800,000 is unrestricted.

When there are accounts for appropriations, it is customary to divide the retained earnings statement into two major sections: (1) appropriated and (2) unappropriated. The first section is composed of an analysis of all appropriation accounts, beginning with the opening balance, followed by the additions or the deductions during the period, and ending with the closing balance. The second section is composed of an analysis of the retained earnings account, beginning with the opening balance, followed by the period's net income, dividends, and transfers to and from the appropriation accounts, and ending with the closing balance. The final figure on the statement is the total retained earnings as of the last day of the period. This form of the statement is illustrated for Lester Corporation as follows:

Retained Earnings Statement

Lester Corporation
Retained Earnings Statement
For Year Ended December 31, 19--

Appropriated:			
Appropriation for plant expansion, January 1, 19--.....		$ 180,000	
Additional appropriation (see below)		100,000	
Retained earnings appropriated, December 31, 19-- ..			$ 280,000
Unappropriated:			
Balance, January 1, 19--....................................	$1,414,500		
Net income for the year....................................	580,000	$1,994,500	
Cash dividends declared	$ 125,000		
Transfer to appropriation for plant expansion (see above)...	100,000	225,000	
Retained earnings unappropriated, December 31, 19--			1,769,500
Total retained earnings, December 31, 19--................			$2,049,500

There are many possible variations in the form of the retained earnings statement. It may also be added to the income statement to form a combined statement of income and retained earnings, as illustrated in Chapter 4.

NATURE OF DIVIDENDS

OBJECTIVE 7
Describe and illustrate the accounting for dividends, including cash dividends, stock dividends, and liquidating dividends.

A **dividend** is a distribution by a corporation to its shareholders. On common shares, the dividend is usually stated in terms of dollars and cents rather than as a percentage of par. On preferred shares, the dividend may be stated either in monetary terms or as a percentage of par. For example, the annual dividend rate on a particular $100 par preferred stock may be stated as either $10 or 10%.

A dividend usually represents a distribution from retained earnings, and may be paid in cash, in stock of the company, or in other property. A dividend may also represent a distribution from paid-in capital. The types of dividends are discussed in the following paragraphs.

Cash Dividends

A cash distribution of earnings by a corporation to its shareholders is called a **cash dividend.** Cash dividends are the most common form of dividend. Usually there are three prerequisites to paying a cash dividend:

1. Sufficient unappropriated retained earnings,
2. Sufficient cash, and
3. Formal action by the board of directors.

A large amount of accumulated earnings does not always mean that a corporation is able to pay dividends. There must also be enough cash in excess of routine requirements. The amount of retained earnings, which represents net income retained in the business, is not directly related to cash. The cash provided by the net income may have been used to purchase assets, to reduce liabilities, or for other purposes. The directors are not required by law to declare dividends, even when both retained earnings and cash appear to be sufficient. When a dividend has been declared, however, it becomes a liability of the corporation.

Corporations with a wide distribution of stock usually try to maintain a stable dividend record. They may retain a large part of earnings in good years in order to be able to continue dividend payments in lean years. Dividends may be paid once a year or on a semiannual or quarterly basis. The tendency is to pay quarterly dividends on both common and preferred stock. In particularly good years, the directors may declare an "extra" dividend on common stock. It may be paid at one of the usual dividend dates or at some other date. The designation "extra" indicates that the board of directors does not anticipate an increase in the amount of the "regular" dividend.

Notice of a dividend declaration is usually reported in financial publications and newspapers. The notice identifies three different dates related to a declaration:

1. The date of declaration,
2. The date of record, and
3. The date of payment.

The first is the date the directors take formal action declaring the dividend, the second is the date as of which ownership of shares is to be determined, and the third is the date payment is to be made. For example, a notice read: "On June 26, the board of directors of Campbell Soup Co. declared a quarterly cash dividend of $.33 per common share to stockholders of record as of the close of business on July 8, payable on July 31."

The liability for a dividend is recorded on the declaration date, when the formal action is taken by the directors. No entry is required on the date of record, which merely fixes the date for determining the identity of the stockholders entitled to receive the dividend. The period of time between the record date and the payment date is provided to permit completion of postings to the stockholders ledger and preparation of the dividend checks. The liability of the corporation is paid by the mailing of the checks.

To illustrate the entries required in the declaration and the payment of cash dividends, assume that on December 1 the board of directors of Hiber Corporation declares the regular quarterly dividend of $2.50 on the 5,000 shares of $100 par, 10% preferred stock outstanding (total dividend of $12,500), and a quarterly dividend of 30¢ on the 100,000 shares of $10 par common stock outstanding (total dividend of $30,000). Both dividends are to stockholders of record on December 10, and checks are to be issued to stockholders on January 2. The entry to record the declaration of the dividends is as follows:

Dec. 1	Cash Dividends....................................	42,500	
	Cash Dividends Payable......................		42,500

The balance in Cash Dividends would be transferred to Retained Earnings as a part of the closing process and Cash Dividends Payable would be listed on the balance sheet as a current liability. Payment of the liability on January 2 would be recorded in the usual manner as a debit to Cash Dividends Payable and a credit to Cash for $42,500.

Dividends on cumulative preferred stock do not become a liability of the corporation until formal action is taken by the board of directors. However, dividends in arrears at a balance sheet date should be disclosed by a footnote, a parenthetical notation, or a segregation of retained earnings similar to the following:

Retained earnings:		
Required to meet dividends in arrears on preferred stock	$ 50,000	
Remainder, unrestricted	116,000	
Total retained earnings....................................		$166,000

Stock Dividends

A pro rata distribution of shares of stock of a company to the stockholders, accompanied by a transfer of retained earnings to paid-in capital accounts, is called a **stock dividend.** Such distributions are usually in common stock and are issued to holders of common stock. It is possible to issue common stock to preferred stockholders or vice versa, but such stock dividends are too unusual to warrant their consideration here.

Stock dividends are quite unlike cash dividends, in that there is no distribution of cash or other corporate assets to the stockholders. They are ordinarily issued by corporations that "plow back" (retain) earnings for use in acquiring new facilities or for expanding their operations.

The effect of a stock dividend on the capital structure of the issuing corporation is to transfer accumulated earnings to paid-in capital. The statutes of most states require that an amount equivalent to the par or stated value of a stock dividend be transferred from the retained earnings account to the common stock account. Compliance with this minimum requirement is considered by accountants to be satisfactory for a nonpublic corporation, whose stockholders are presumed to have enough knowledge of the corporation's affairs to recognize the true import of the dividend. However, many investors in the stock of public corporations are often less knowledgeable. An analysis of this latter situation, and the widely accepted viewpoint of professional accountants, has been expressed as follows:

> *...many recipients of stock dividends look upon them as distributions of corporate earnings and usually in an amount equivalent to the fair value of the additional shares received. Furthermore, it is to be presumed that such views of recipients are materially strengthened in those instances, which are by far the most numerous, where the issuances are so small in comparison with the shares previously outstanding that they do not have any apparent effect upon the share market price and, consequently, the market value of the shares previously held remains substantially unchanged. The committee therefore believes that where*

these circumstances exist the corporation should in the public interest account for the transaction by transferring from [retained earnings] to the category of permanent capitalization... an amount equal to the fair value of the additional shares issued. Unless this is done, the amount of earnings which the shareholder may believe to have been distributed to him will be left, except to the extent otherwise dictated by legal requirements, in [retained earnings] subject to possible further similar stock issuances or cash distributions. [16]

To illustrate the issuance of a stock dividend according to the procedure recommended above, assume the following balances in the stockholders' equity accounts of Hendrix Corporation as of December 15:

Common Stock, $20 par (2,000,000 shares issued)	$40,000,000
Premium on Common Stock	9,000,000
Retained Earnings	26,600,000

On December 15, the board of directors declares a 5% stock dividend (100,000 shares, $20 par), to be issued on January 10. Assuming that the average of the high and low market prices on the declaration date is $31 a share, the entry to record the declaration would be as follows:

Dec. 15	Stock Dividends	3,100,000	
	Stock Dividends Distributable		2,000,000
	Paid-In Capital in Excess of Par—Common Stock		1,100,000

The $3,100,000 debit to Stock Dividends would be transferred to Retained Earnings as a part of the closing process. The issuance of the stock certificates would be recorded on January 10 as follows:

Jan. 10	Stock Dividends Distributable	2,000,000	
	Common Stock		2,000,000

The effect of the stock dividend is to transfer $3,100,000 from the retained earnings account to paid-in capital accounts and to increase by 100,000 the number of shares outstanding. There is no change in the assets, liabilities, or total stockholders' equity of the corporation. If financial statements are prepared between the date of declaration and the date of issuance, the stock dividends distributable account should be listed in the paid-in capital section of the balance sheet.

The issuance of the additional shares does not affect the total amount of a stockholder's equity and proportionate interest in the corporation. The effect of the stock dividend on the accounts of a corporation and on the equity of a stockholder owning 1,000 shares is demonstrated by the following tabulation:

The Corporation	Before Stock Dividend	After Stock Dividend
Common stock	$40,000,000	$42,000,000
Excess of issue price over par	9,000,000	10,100,000
Retained earnings	26,600,000	23,500,000
Total stockholders' equity	$75,600,000	$75,600,000
Number of shares outstanding	2,000,000	2,100,000
Equity per share	$37.80	$36.00

[16] *Accounting Research and Terminology Bulletins—Final Edition,* "No. 43, Restatement and Revision of Accounting Research Bulletins" (New York: American Institute of Certified Public Accountants, 1961), Ch. 7, Sec. B, par. 10.

A Stockholder	Before Stock Dividend	After Stock Dividend
Number of shares owned	1,000	1,050
Total equity	$37,800	$37,800
Portion of corporation owned	.05%	.05%

Liquidating Dividends

The term **liquidating dividend** is applied to a distribution to stockholders from paid-in capital. Such dividends are unusual, but in many states they may be declared from the excess of paid-in capital over par or stated value. Liquidating dividends are usually paid when a corporation permanently reduces its operations or winds up its affairs completely. Since dividends are normally paid from retained earnings, dividends that reduce paid-in capital should be identified as liquidating dividends when paid.

STOCK SPLITS

OBJECTIVE 8
Describe and illustrate the accounting for stock splits.

Corporations sometimes reduce the par or stated value of their common stock and issue a proportionate number of additional shares. Such a procedure is called a **stock split** or **stock split-up.** The primary purpose of a stock split is to bring about a reduction in the market price per share and thus to encourage more investors to enter the market for the company's shares.

To illustrate a stock split, assume that the board of directors of Rojek Corporation, which has 10,000 shares of $100 par stock outstanding, reduces the par to $20 and increases the number of shares to 50,000. The amount of stock outstanding is $1,000,000 both before and after the stock split. Only the number of shares and the par per share are changed. Since there are no changes in the balances of any of the corporation's accounts, no entry to record the stock split is required.

Each shareholder in a corporation whose stock is split owns the same total par amount of stock before and after the stock split. For example, a Rojek Corporation stockholder who owned 100 shares of $100 par stock before the split (total par of $10,000) would own 500 shares of $20 par stock after the split (total par of $10,000).

2 FOR 1 STOCK SPLIT

Some extra mail sacks will leave the Harris Trust and Savings Bank in Chicago, Ill., on Nov. 7 and, as they go, the number of General Mills common shares outstanding will double. Acting as General Mills' stock transfer agent, the bank is responsible for effecting the company's recently declared 2-for-1 stock split. . . .

General Mills shareholders of record on Oct. 10 will receive one additional share for every share they owned on that date. . . . [This] does not result in any gain or loss to shareholders for federal income tax purposes.

. . . At the company's annual meeting of shareholders, Chairman Bruce Atwater said this action recognized "the company's strong equity market performance, our promising outlook, and our strong commitment to maintaining a market price for our shares in a range attractive to individual investors."

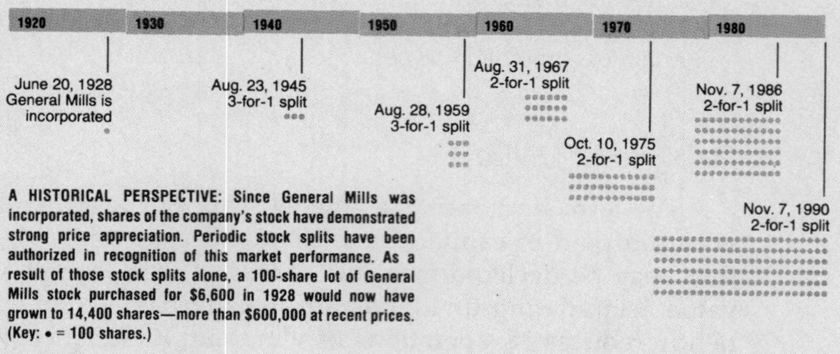

A HISTORICAL PERSPECTIVE: Since General Mills was incorporated, shares of the company's stock have demonstrated strong price appreciation. Periodic stock splits have been authorized in recognition of this market performance. As a result of those stock splits alone, a 100-share lot of General Mills stock purchased for $6,600 in 1928 would now have grown to 14,400 shares—more than $600,000 at recent prices. (Key: • = 100 shares.)

Source: General Mills Review, first quarter 1991, page 9.

DIVIDENDS AND STOCK SPLITS FOR TREASURY STOCK

OBJECTIVE 9
Describe the accounting for dividends and stock splits for treasury stock.

Cash or property dividends are not paid on treasury stock. To do so would place the corporation in the position of earning income through dealing with itself. Accordingly, the total amount of a cash (or property) dividend should be based on the number of shares outstanding at the record date.

When a corporation holding treasury stock declares a stock dividend, the number of shares to be issued may be based on either (1) the number of shares outstanding or (2) the number of shares issued. In practice, the number of shares held as treasury stock represents a small percent of the number of shares issued. Also, the rate of dividend is usually small, so that the difference between the end results of both methods is usually not significant.

There is no legal, theoretical, or practical reason for excluding treasury stock when computing the number of shares to be issued in a stock split. The reduction in par or stated value would apply to all shares of the class, including the unissued, issued, and treasury shares.

CHAPTER REVIEW

KEY POINTS

OBJECTIVE 1

Paid-In Capital

Although paid-in capital usually results from the issuance of stock, it may also originate from donated assets and redemptions of a corporation's own stock. Many variations in terminology and arrangement of the paid-in capital section of the balance sheet exist. Significant changes in paid-in capital during a period should be disclosed.

OBJECTIVE 2

Corporate Earnings and Income Taxes

Unlike sole proprietorships and partnerships, corporations are subject to federal income tax and, in many cases, to income taxes levied by states or other political subdivisions. Most corporations are required to estimate the amount of their federal income tax expense for the year and make advance payment, usually in four installments. At the end of the year, the actual taxable income and the actual tax are determined. If an additional amount is owed, a liability is recorded. If an overpayment occurs, the amount would be debited to a receivable account and credited to Income Tax.

OBJECTIVE 3

Allocation of Income Tax Between Periods

The taxable income of a corporation, determined according to the tax laws, is often different from the amount of income (before income tax) reported in the income statement. This difference may need to be allocated between periods, depending upon the nature of the items causing the difference.

Some items create differences between income before income tax and taxable income because the items are recognized in one period for income statement purposes and in another period for tax purposes. These temporary differences turn around in later years. They require special treatment in the accounts. The income tax to be reported on the income statement should be the total tax expected to result from the net income reported for that period. The amount of the income tax postponed (deferred) is accounted for in a deferred tax liability account. The deferred income tax liability is reported on the balance sheet as a current liability or a long-term liability, depending on when the items to which it relates will reverse their effects on taxable income.

OBJECTIVE 4

Reporting Unusual Items in the Financial Statements

General guidelines have been developed for reporting unusual items in the financial statements. These items may be described as (1) items that affect the current year's net income and are therefore reported on the current year's income statement and (2) items that affect a prior year's net income and are therefore reported on the current year's retained earnings statement.

A gain or loss resulting from the disposal of a segment of a business should be identified on the income statement as a gain or loss from discontinued operations. In addition, the results of continuing operations should be identified in the income statement. Details of the discontinued operations should also be disclosed in a note to the financial statements.

Extraordinary gains and losses result from events and transactions that are distinguished by their unusual nature and the infrequency of their occurrence. Such gains and losses, other than those from the disposal of a segment of a business, should be identified in the income statement as extraordinary items.

A number of acceptable alternative principles affecting the determination of income statement and balance sheet amounts exist. The concept of consistency implies that the financial statements should be prepared by applying the same principles year after year. If a change in principle occurs, the effect of the change on net income in the current period, as well as the cumulative effect on income of prior periods, should be disclosed. Details describing the change in accounting principle are also normally disclosed in an accompanying note to the financial statements.

The amount reported as a gain or loss from discontinued operations, an extraordinary item, the cumulative effect of a change in accounting principle, or a prior period adjustment should be net of the related income tax. The amount of income tax allocable to each of these items should be disclosed on the face of the appropriate financial statement or by an accompanying note.

Material errors related to a prior period are termed prior period adjustments and are reported as an adjustment on the retained earnings balance at the beginning of the period in which the correction is made. Any financial statements presented for the prior period should be restated, and the current period financial statements should clearly set forth the adjustment necessary to the retained earnings account.

OBJECTIVE 5

Earnings per Common Share

Data on earnings per share of common stock are reported on the income statements of public corporations. If preferred stock is outstanding, the net income must be reduced by the amount of any preferred dividend requirements before dividing by the number of common shares outstanding. If there are nonrecurring items on the income statement, the per share amount should be presented for (1) income from continuing operations, (2) income before extraordinary items and the cumulative effect of a change in accounting principle, (3) the cumulative effect of a change in accounting principle, and (4) net income. Presentation of per share amounts is optional for a gain or loss on discontinued operations and for extraordinary items.

OBJECTIVE 6

Appropriation of Retained Earnings

The amount of a corporation's retained earnings available for distribution to its shareholders may be limited by action of the board of directors or by law or contract. The amount restricted, called an appropriation or a reserve, remains a part of retained earnings. An appropriation of retained earnings is not directly related to any certain group of assets, and its existence does not imply that there is an equivalent amount of cash or other assets set aside in a special fund. However, appropriations may be accompanied by a segregation of cash or marketable securities, in which case the appropriation is said to be funded. Appropriations of retained earnings should be clearly set forth in the retained earnings statement and should be properly identified on the face of the balance sheet or in an accompanying note.

It is customary to divide the retained earnings statement into two major sections: (1) appropriated and (2) unappropriated. Each of these sections should identify the beginning balance and any additions or deductions during the period.

OBJECTIVE 7

Nature of Dividends

A dividend is a distribution by a corporation to its shareholders. Dividends may be paid in cash, in stock of the company, or in other property. Three dates are important in the distribution of dividends. (1) The date of declaration is the date on which the directors take formal action to declare the dividend and on which the dividend is recorded in the accounting records. (2) The date of record is the date on which ownership of shares is to be determined for purposes of distribution of the dividend. (3) The date of payment is the date on which the dividend is to be distributed or paid.

Dividends on cumulative preferred stock do not become a liability of the corporation until formal action is taken by the board of directors. However, dividends in arrears at a balance sheet date should be disclosed by a footnote, a parenthetical notation, or a segregation of retained earnings.

A stock dividend is a pro rata distribution of shares of stock to stockholders. The effect of a stock dividend on the capital structure of the issuing corporation is to transfer accumulated earnings to paid-in capital. There is no change in the assets, liabilities, or total stockholders' equity of the corporation.

A dividend distribution to stockholders from paid-in capital is known as a liquidating dividend. Such dividends are usually paid when a corporation permanently reduces its operations or winds up its affairs completely. Because of the unusual nature of liquidating dividends, they should be clearly identified in the financial statements.

OBJECTIVE 8

Stock Splits

When a corporation reduces the par or stated value of its common stock and issues a proportionate number of additional shares, a stock split or stock split-up has occurred. Because only the number of shares and the par amount per share of stock is changed during a stock split, there are no changes in the balances of any corporation accounts, and no entry is required. Each shareholder owns the same total par amount of stock before and after a stock split. The primary purpose of a stock split is to reduce the market price per share and encourage more investors to enter the market for the company's shares.

OBJECTIVE 9 Dividends and Stock Splits for Treasury Stock

Cash or property dividends are not paid on treasury stock. To do so would place the corporation in a position of earning income through dealing with itself. However, when a stock dividend or a stock split occurs, treasury shares may or may not participate, depending upon action of the board of directors.

KEY TERMS

taxable income 461
temporary differences 462
discontinued operations 465
extraordinary items 466
consistency concept 466
prior period adjustments 468
earnings per share 469
appropriation of retained earnings 471
funded 472
dividend 473
cash dividend 474
stock dividend 475
liquidating dividend 477
stock split 477

SELF-EXAMINATION QUESTIONS

Answers at end of chapter.

1. Paid-in capital for a corporation may originate from which of the following sources?
   A. Real estate donated to the corporation
   B. Redemption of the corporation's own stock
   C. Sale of the corporation's treasury stock
   D. All of the above

2. During its first year of operations, a corporation elected to use the straight-line method of depreciation for financial reporting purposes and the sum-of-the-years-digits method in determining taxable income. If the income tax is 40% and the amount of depreciation expense is $60,000 under the straight-line method and $100,000 under the sum-of-the-years-digits method, what is the amount of income tax deferred to future years?
   A. $16,000
   B. $24,000
   C. $40,000
   D. None of the above

3. A material gain resulting from the condemnation of land for public use would be reported on the income statement as:
   A. an extraordinary item
   B. an other income item
   C. an item of revenue from sales
   D. none of the above

4. An item treated as a prior period adjustment should be reported in the financial statements as:
   A. an extraordinary item
   B. an other expense item
   C. an adjustment of the beginning balance of retained earnings
   D. none of the above

5. An appropriation for plant expansion would be reported on the balance sheet in:
   A. the plant assets section
   B. the long-term liabilities section
   C. the stockholders' equity section
   D. none of the above

ILLUSTRATIVE PROBLEM

During its current fiscal year ended December 31, Block Inc. completed the following selected transactions:

Jan. 9. Purchased 1,500 shares of own common stock at $16, recording the stock at cost. (Prior to the purchase there were 70,000 shares of $10 par common stock outstanding.)

Mar. 16. Discovered that a receipt of $500 cash on account from I. Jonson had been posted in error to the account of I. Johnson. The transaction was recorded correctly in the journal.

May 18. Declared a semiannual dividend of $1 on the 10,000 shares of preferred stock and a 20¢ dividend on the common stock to stockholders of record on May 28, payable on June 10.

June 10. Paid the cash dividends.

Aug. 23. Sold 1,000 shares of treasury stock at $18, receiving cash.

Nov. 12. Declared semiannual dividends of $1 on the preferred stock and 20¢ on the common stock. In addition, a 5% common stock dividend was declared on the common stock outstanding, to be capitalized at the fair market value of the common stock, which is estimated at $16.

Dec. 4. Paid the cash dividends and issued the certificates for the common stock dividend.

31. Recorded $75,000 additional federal income tax allocable to net income for the year. Of this amount, $65,600 is a current liability and $9,400 is deferred.

31. The board of directors authorized the appropriation necessitated by the holding of treasury stock.

Instructions:

Prepare the journal entries to record the transactions for Block Inc.

SOLUTION

Date	Account	Debit	Credit
Jan. 9	Treasury Stock	24,000	
	Cash		24,000
Mar. 16	No entry. Error can be corrected by revising the postings in the subsidiary accounts receivable ledger.		
May 18	Cash Dividends	23,700	
	Cash Dividends Payable		23,700
June 10	Cash Dividends Payable	23,700	
	Cash		23,700
Aug. 23	Cash	18,000	
	Treasury Stock		16,000
	Paid-In Capital from Sale of Treasury Stock		2,000
Nov. 12	Cash Dividends	23,900	
	Stock Dividends	55,600	
	Cash Dividends Payable		23,900
	Stock Dividends Distributable		34,750
	Premium on Common Stock		20,850
Dec. 4	Cash Dividends Payable	23,900	
	Stock Dividends Distributable	34,750	
	Cash		23,900
	Common Stock		34,750

Dec. 31	Income Tax	75,000	
	Income Tax Payable		65,600
	Deferred Income Tax Payable		9,400
31	Retained Earnings	8,000	
	Appropriation for Treasury Stock		8,000

DISCUSSION QUESTIONS

11–1. What are the titles of the two principal subdivisions of the stockholders' equity section of a corporate balance sheet?

11–2. If a corporation is given land as an inducement to locate in a particular community, (a) how should the amount of the debit to the land account be determined, and (b) what is the title of the account that should be credited for the same amount?

11–3. A corporation has paid $200,000 of federal income tax during the year on the basis of its estimated income. What entry should be recorded as of the end of the year if it determines that (a) it owes an additional $30,000; (b) it overpaid its tax by $10,000?

11–4. The income before income tax reported on the income statement for the year is $750,000. Because of temporary differences between accounting and tax methods, the taxable income for the same year is $620,000. Assuming an income tax rate of 40%, determine (a) the amount of income tax to be deducted from the $750,000 on the income statement, (b) the amount of the actual income tax that should be paid for the year, and (c) the amount of the deferred income tax liability.

11–5. How would the amount of deferred income tax payable be reported in the balance sheet if (a) it is payable within one year, and (b) if it is payable beyond one year?

11–6. Indicate where the following should be reported in the financial statements, assuming that financial statements are presented only for the current year:
(a) Loss on disposal of equipment considered to be obsolete.
(b) Uninsured loss on building due to hurricane damage. The firm was organized in 1915, and had not previously incurred hurricane damage.

11–7. Classify each of the following revenue and expense items as either (a) normally recurring or (b) extraordinary. Assume that the amount of each item is material.
(1) Interest income on notes receivable.
(2) Loss on sale of plant assets.
(3) Salaries of corporate officers.
(4) Uninsured flood loss. (Flood insurance is unavailable because of periodic flooding in the area.)
(5) Uncollectible accounts expense.
(6) Gain on sale of land condemned for public use.

11–8. During the current year, twenty acres of land which cost $180,000 were condemned for construction of an interstate highway. Assuming that an award of $200,000 in cash was received and that the applicable income tax on this transaction is 25%, how would this information be presented in the income statement?

11–9. If significant changes are made in the accounting principles applied from one period to the next, why should the effect of these changes be disclosed in the financial statements?

11–10. Indicate how prior period adjustments would be reported on the financial statements presented only for the current period.

11–11. A corporation reports earnings per share of $12.10 for the most recent year and $9.60 for the preceding year. The $12.10 includes $3.00 per share gain from a sale of the only investment owned since the business was organized in 1946. (a) Should the composition of the $12.10 be disclosed in the financial reports? (b) What is the earnings per share amount for the most recent year that is comparable to the $9.60 earnings per share of the preceding year? (c) On the basis of the limited information presented, would you conclude that operations had improved or declined?

11–12. Appropriations of retained earnings may be (a) required by law, (b) required by contract, or (c) made at the discretion of the board of directors. Give an illustration of each type of appropriation.

11–13. A credit balance in Retained Earnings does not represent cash. Explain.

11–14. The board of directors votes to appropriate $500,000 of retained earnings for bonded indebtedness. What is the effect of this action on (a) cash, (b) total retained earnings, and (c) retained earnings available for dividends?

11–15. What are the three prerequisites of the declaration and the payment of a cash dividend?

11–16. The dates in connection with the declaration of a cash dividend are September 1, October 15, and October 30. Identify each date.

11–17. A corporation with both cumulative preferred stock and common stock outstanding has a substantial credit balance in its retained earnings account at the beginning of the current fiscal year. Although net income for the current year is sufficient to pay the preferred dividend of $100,000 each quarter and a common dividend of $400,000 each quarter, the board of directors declares dividends only on the preferred stock. Suggest possible reasons for passing the dividends on the common stock.

11–18. State the effect of the following actions on a corporation's total assets, liabilities, and stockholders' equity: (a) declaration of a cash dividend; (b) payment of the cash dividend declared in (a); (c) declaration of a stock dividend; (d) issuance of stock certificates for the stock dividend declared in (c); (e) authorization and issuance of stock certificates in a stock split.

11–19. An owner of 500 shares of Randall Company common stock receives a stock dividend of 20 shares. (a) What is the effect of the stock dividend on the equity per share of the stock? (b) How does the total equity of 520 shares compare with the total equity of 500 shares before the stock dividend?

11–20. What term is used to identify a distribution to stockholders from paid-in capital?

11–21. A corporation with 10,000 shares of no-par common stock issued, of which 3,000 shares are held as treasury stock, declares a cash dividend of $2 a share. What is the total amount of the dividend?

11–22. If a corporation with 5,000 shares of common stock outstanding has a 6-for-1 stock split (5 additional shares of each share issued), what will be the number of shares outstanding after the split?

11–23. If the common stock in Question 11-22 had a market price of $150 per share before the stock split, what would be an approximate market price per share after the split?

Real World Focus

11–24. The annual report of Entertainment, Marketing, Incorporated disclosed the discontinuance of the company's televised home shopping operation. The estimated loss on disposal of this segment of the company is $2,567,597, net of an estimated income tax benefit of $1,641,578. Indicate how the loss from discontinued operations should be reported by Entertainment, Marketing, Incorporated on its income statement.

Real World Focus

11–25. Corporation A received an insurance refund of $45,000 in December 1991. After a limited investigation into why the money was received, Corporation A concluded the refund was an adjustment of premiums previously paid. The $45,000 was reflected in the income statement for the year ended December 31, 1991, as a reduction of insurance expense.

Subsequently in 1992, Corporation A was notified that the amount had been refunded in error and paid the insurance company $45,000. How should it be reported in the financial statements for the year ended December 31, 1992? Adapted from "Technical Hotline," *Journal of Accountancy* (June, 1989), p. 31.

Real World Focus

11–26. Corporation X realized a material gain when its facilities at a designated floodway were acquired by the urban renewal agency. How should the gain be reported in the income statement? Adapted from "Technical Hotline," *Journal of Accountancy* (June, 1989), p. 32.

Ethics Discussion Case

11–27. Sikes Inc. discontinued its cellular telephone operations on July 1, 1992. In preparing the income statement for the year ended December 31, 1992, Thomas Reeves, the controller, omitted the earnings per share amount for the discontinued operations. The per share loss on the discontinued operations was $1.05, while the net income per share was $4.20.

Discuss whether Thomas Reeves is behaving in an ethical manner.

EXERCISES

Ex. 11–28.
Income tax entries.
OBJ. 2, 3

Present entries to record the following selected transactions of Ayres Inc.:

Apr. 15. Paid the first installment of the estimated income tax for the current fiscal year ending December 31, $200,000. No entry had been made to record the liability.

June 15. Paid the second installment of $200,000.

Dec. 31. Recorded the additional income tax liability for the year just ended and the deferred income tax liability, based on the two transactions above and the following data:

Income tax rate	40%
Income before income tax	$2,100,000
Taxable income according to tax return	2,010,000
Third installment paid on September 15	200,000
Fourth installment paid on December 15	200,000

Ex. 11–29.
Retained earnings statement with prior period adjustment.
OBJ. 4

Leslie Heart and Company reported the following results of transactions affecting retained earnings for the current year ended March 31, 1992:

Net income	$136,500
Dividends	30,000
Prior period adjustment for understatement of merchandise inventory on March 31, 1991, net of applicable income tax of $8,000	12,000

Assuming that the retained earnings balance reported on the retained earnings statement as of March 31, 1991, was $300,000, prepare a retained earnings statement for the year ended March 31, 1992.

Ex. 11–30.
Income statement.
OBJ. 4, 5

On the basis of the following data for the current fiscal year ended April 30, prepare an income statement for Bryant Company, including an analysis of earnings per share in the form illustrated in this chapter. There were 100,000 shares of $20 par common stock outstanding throughout the year.

Administrative expenses	$ 55,300
Cost of merchandise sold	730,000
Cumulative effect on prior years of changing to a different depreciation method	80,600
Gain on condemnation of land (extraordinary item)	70,100
Income tax applicable to change in depreciation method	24,600
Income tax applicable to gain on condemnation of land	20,100
Income tax reduction applicable to loss from discontinued operations	27,000
Income tax applicable to ordinary income	110,000
Loss on discontinued operations	89,000
Sales	1,180,000
Selling expenses	89,700

Ex. 11–31.
Entries for treasury stock.
OBJ. 6

A corporation purchased for cash 3,000 shares of its own $5 par common stock at $7 a share. In the following year, it sold 1,000 of the treasury shares at $10 a share for cash. (a) Present the entries (1) to record the purchase (treasury stock is recorded at cost) and (2) to provide for the appropriation of retained earnings. (b) Present the entries (1) to record the sale of the stock and (2) to reduce the appropriation.

Ex. 11–32.
Retained earnings statement.
OBJ. 6

Farmer Corporation reports the following results of transactions affecting net income and retained earnings for its first fiscal year of operations ended on December 31:

Appropriation for plant expansion	$ 40,000
Cash dividends declared	15,000
Income before income tax	240,000
Income tax	95,500

Prepare a retained earnings statement for the fiscal year ended December 31.

Ex. 11–33.
Entries for cash dividends.
OBJ. 7

The dates in connection with a cash dividend of $18,000 on a corporation's common stock are January 12, February 2, and February 20. Present the entries required on each date.

Ex. 11–34.
Stock dividends; equity per share.
OBJ. 7

The following account balances appear on the balance sheet of Kennedy Company: Common stock (10,000 shares authorized), $100 par, $500,000; Paid-in capital in excess of par—common stock, $8,000; and Retained earnings, $51,000. The board of directors declared a 4% stock dividend when the market price of the stock was $120 a share. (a) Present entries to record (1) the declaration of the dividend, capitalizing an amount equal to market value, and (2) the issuance of the stock certificates. (b) Determine the equity per share (1) before the stock dividend and (2) after the stock dividend. (c) Nancy Long owned 250 shares of the common stock before the stock dividend was declared. Determine the total equity of her holdings (1) before the stock dividend and (2) after the stock dividend.

Ex. 11–35.
Stock split.
OBJ. 8

The board of directors of Pike Corporation authorized the reduction of par of its common shares from $50 to $10, increasing the number of outstanding shares to 500,000. The market price of the stock immediately before the stock split was $175 a share. (a) Determine the number of outstanding shares prior to the stock split. (b) Present the entry to record the stock split. (c) At approximately what price would a share of stock be expected to sell immediately after the stock split?

PROBLEMS

Pb. 11–36.
Income tax allocation.
OBJ. 3

Differences between the accounting methods applied to accounts and financial reports and those used in determining taxable income yielded the following amounts for the first four years of a corporation's operations:

	First Year	Second Year	Third Year	Fourth Year
Income before income tax......	$380,000	$480,000	$600,000	$570,000
Taxable income	310,000	440,000	620,000	615,500

The income tax rate for each of the four years was 40% of taxable income, and each year's taxes were promptly paid.

Instructions:

(1) Determine for each year the amounts described in the following columnar captions, presenting the information in the form indicated:

			Deferred Income Tax Payable	
Year	Income Tax Deducted on Income Statement	Income Tax Payments for the Year	Year's Addition (Deduction)	Year-End Balance

(2) Total the first three amount columns.

Pb. 11–37.
Income statement.
OBJ. 4, 5

The following data were selected from the records of Leiter Inc. for the current fiscal year ended August 31, 1992:

Advertising expense	$ 30,000
Delivery expense	11,800
Depreciation expense—office equipment	5,100
Depreciation expense—store equipment	13,200
Gain on condemnation of land	60,000
Income tax:	
Applicable to continuing operations	68,800
Applicable to loss from disposal of a segment of a business (reduction)	6,000
Applicable to gain on condemnation of land	17,000
Insurance expense	11,000
Interest income	16,500
Loss from disposal of a segment of the business	30,000
Merchandise inventory (September 1, 1991)	118,300
Merchandise inventory (August 31, 1992)	126,000
Miscellaneous administrative expense	3,500
Miscellaneous selling expense	4,200
Office salaries expense	55,200
Office supplies expense	2,100
Purchases	722,700
Rent expense	36,000
Sales	1,185,000
Sales commissions expense	54,800
Sales salaries expense	67,600
Store supplies expense	3,200

Instructions:

Prepare a multiple-step income statement, concluding with a section for earnings per share in the form illustrated in this chapter. There were 100,000 shares of common stock (no preferred) outstanding throughout the year. Assume that the condemnation of land is an extraordinary item.

Pb. 11–38.
Retained earnings statement.
OBJ. 6, 7

The retained earnings accounts of Palm Bay Corporation for the current fiscal year ended December 31 are as follows:

ACCOUNT APPROPRIATION FOR PLANT EXPANSION — ACCOUNT NO. 3201

Date		Item	Debit	Credit	Balance Debit	Balance Credit
19--						
Jan.	1	Balance				300,000
Dec.	31	Retained earnings		65,000		365,000

ACCOUNT APPROPRIATION FOR TREASURY STOCK — ACCOUNT NO. 3202

Date		Item	Debit	Credit	Balance Debit	Balance Credit
19--						
Jan.	1	Balance				500,000
Dec.	31	Retained earnings	50,000			450,000

ACCOUNT RETAINED EARNINGS — ACCOUNT NO. 3301

Date		Item	Debit	Credit	Balance Debit	Balance Credit
19--						
Jan.	1	Balance				875,000
Dec.	31	Income summary		315,000		1,190,000
	31	Appropriation for plant expansion	65,000			1,125,000
	31	Appropriation for treasury stock		50,000		1,175,000
	31	Cash dividends	100,000			1,075,000
	31	Stock dividends	250,000			825,000

ACCOUNT CASH DIVIDENDS — ACCOUNT NO. 3302

Date		Item	Debit	Credit	Balance Debit	Balance Credit
19--						
Apr.	12		50,000		50,000	
Oct.	17		50,000		100,000	
Dec.	31	Retained earnings		100,000	—	—

ACCOUNT STOCK DIVIDENDS — ACCOUNT NO. 3303

Date		Item	Debit	Credit	Balance Debit	Balance Credit
19--						
Sept.	17		250,000		250,000	
Dec.	31	Retained earnings		250,000	—	—

Instructions:

Prepare a retained earnings statement for the fiscal year ended December 31.

Pb. 11–39.
Entries for selected corporate transactions.
OBJ. 6, 7

The stockholders' equity accounts of O'Tell Enterprises Inc., with balances on January 1 of the current fiscal year, are as follows:

Common Stock, stated value $20 (100,000 shares authorized, 45,000 shares issued)	$900,000
Paid-In Capital in Excess of Stated Value	60,000
Appropriation for Plant Expansion	200,000

Appropriation for Treasury Stock	$ 12,500
Retained Earnings	735,000
Treasury Stock (500 shares, at cost)	12,500

The following selected transactions occurred during the year:

Jan. 8. Paid cash dividends of $1 per share on the common stock. The dividend had been properly recorded when declared on December 10 of the preceding fiscal year.
Feb. 18. Sold all of the treasury stock for $14,000.
Apr. 25. Issued 5,000 shares of common stock for $150,000 cash.
May 11. Received land with an estimated fair market value of $40,000 from the Columbia City Council as a donation.
June 30. Declared a 4% stock dividend on common stock, to be capitalized at the market price of the stock, which is $30 a share.
July 31. Issued the certificates for the dividend declared on June 30.
Nov. 10. Purchased 1,000 shares of treasury stock for $32,000.
Dec. 15. Declared a $1 per share dividend on common stock.
15. The board of directors authorized the increase of the appropriation for plant expansion by $50,000.
20. Increased the appropriation for treasury stock to $32,000.
31. Closed the credit balance of the income summary account, $186,000.
31. Closed the two dividends accounts to Retained Earnings.

Instructions:

(1) Open T accounts for the stockholders' equity accounts listed and enter the balances as of January 1. Also open T accounts for the following: Paid-In Capital from Sale of Treasury Stock; Donated Capital; Stock Dividends Distributable; Stock Dividends; Cash Dividends.
(2) Prepare entries to record the transactions and post to the eleven selected accounts.
(3) Prepare the stockholders' equity section of the balance sheet as of December 31 of the current fiscal year.

Pb. 11–40.
Stockholders' equity transactions and statements.
OBJ. 6, 7

The stockholders' equity section of the balance sheet of Dixon Industries as of January 1 is as follows:

Stockholders' Equity

Paid-in capital:			
Common stock, $10 par (100,000 shares authorized, 60,000 shares issued)	$600,000		
Excess of issue price over par	120,000		
Total paid-in capital		$ 720,000	
Retained earnings:			
Appropriated for bonded indebtedness	$400,000		
Unappropriated	880,000		
Total retained earnings		1,280,000	
Total		$2,000,000	
Deduct treasury stock (5,000 shares at cost)		220,000	
Total stockholders' equity			$1,780,000

The following selected transactions occurred during the fiscal year:

Mar. 15. Sold all of the treasury stock for $250,000.
Apr. 5. Issued 20,000 shares of stock in exchange for land and buildings with an estimated fair market value of $100,000 and $220,000 respectively. The property was encumbered by a mortgage of $80,000, and the company agreed to assume the responsibility for paying the mortgage note.
June 10. Declared a cash dividend of $1 per share to stockholders of record on July 10, payable on July 31.

July 31. Paid the cash dividend declared on June 10.
Sept. 12. Received additional land valued at $70,000. The land was donated for a plant site by the Fort Aikens Industrial Development Council.
Dec. 4. Issued 1,000 shares of stock to officers as a salary bonus. Market price of the stock is $13 a share. (Debit Officers Salaries Expense.)
13. Declared a 2% stock dividend on the stock outstanding to stockholders of record on December 28 to be issued on January 28. The market price of the stock is $13 a share.
31. Increased the appropriation for bonded indebtedness by $50,000.
31. Closed the income summary account. After closing all revenue and expense accounts, Income Summary has a credit balance of $315,000.
31. Closed the two dividends accounts to Retained Earnings.

Instructions:

(1) Open T accounts for the accounts appearing in the stockholders' equity section of the balance sheet and enter the balances as of January 1. Also open T accounts for the following: Paid-In Capital from Sale of Treasury Stock; Donated Capital; Cash Dividends; Stock Dividends; Stock Dividends Distributable.
(2) Prepare entries to record the transactions and post to the ten selected accounts.
(3) Prepare the stockholders' equity section of the balance sheet as of December 31, the end of the fiscal year.
(4) Prepare a retained earnings statement for the fiscal year ended December 31.

Pb. 11–41.
Correcting entries and financial statements.
OBJ. 2, 4, 5, 6, 7

Oberkfell Company is in need of additional cash to expand operations. To raise the needed funds, the company is applying to Hill County Bank for a loan. For this purpose, the bank requests that the financial statements be audited. To assist the auditor, Oberkfell Company's accountant prepared a work sheet that was used to prepare the following financial statements related to the current year:

Oberkfell Company
Balance Sheet
December 31, 19--

Current assets:		
Cash	$ 67,500	
Accounts receivable	77,400	
Merchandise inventory	102,900	
Supplies	8,700	$ 256,500
Plant assets:		
Land	$148,000	
Buildings	390,000	
Equipment	159,000	
Patents	54,000	751,000
Total assets		$1,007,500
Current liabilities:		
Accounts payable	$ 55,800	
Salaries payable	4,200	$ 60,000
Deferred charges:		
Accumulated depreciation—buildings	$ 87,000	
Accumulated depreciation—equipment	42,500	
Allowance for doubtful accounts	4,500	134,000
Stockholders' equity:		
Common stock (50,000 shares authorized, $20 par)	$460,000	
Excess of issue price over par	54,000	
Retained earnings	198,000	
Net income	101,500	813,500
Total liabilities and stockholders' equity		$1,007,500

Oberkfell Company
Income Statement
For Year Ended December 31, 19--

Revenues:		
Net sales	$867,000	
Gain on expropriation of land	50,400	
Total revenues		$917,400
Expenses:		
Cost of merchandise sold	$528,600	
Salary expense	72,300	
Depreciation expense—buildings	44,300	
Loss on discontinued operations	42,600	
Utilities expense	24,900	
Insurance expense	12,500	
Depreciation expense—equipment	10,200	
Amortization expense—patents	6,000	
Uncollectible accounts expense	4,500	
Miscellaneous administrative expense	4,000	
Income tax	36,000	
Dividends expense	30,000	
Total expenses		815,900
Net income		$101,500

In the course of the audit, the auditor examined the common stock and retained earnings accounts, which appeared as follows:

ACCOUNT COMMON STOCK ($20 Par) ACCOUNT NO. 3200

Date		Item	Debit	Credit	Balance Debit	Balance Credit
19--						
Jan.	1	Balance—20,000 shares				400,000
	3	Issued 1,000 shares for patents		60,000		460,000

ACCOUNT RETAINED EARNINGS ACCOUNT NO. 3300

Date		Item	Debit	Credit	Balance Debit	Balance Credit
19--						
Jan.	1	Balance				117,000
Mar.	1	Donation of land		60,000		177,000
	20	Error correction	9,000			168,000
Dec.	30	Appropriation for land acquisition		30,000		198,000

A closer examination of the transactions in these and other accounts revealed the following details:

(a) The patent acquired on January 3 by an issuance of 1,000 shares of common stock had a fair market value of $60,000 and an estimated useful life of 10 years.

(b) On March 1, the company received a donation of land. The land account was debited for $60,000, the fair market value of the land at that date.

(c) A computational error was made in the calculation of a prior year's dividend. The corrected amount of the dividend was paid on March 20 and debited to the retained earnings account.

(d) In anticipation of further land acquisition, the board of directors on December 30 authorized a $30,000 appropriation of retained earnings that resulted in a debit to Land and a credit to Retained Earnings.

(e) After three years of using the straight-line method of depreciation for the buildings, the company changed to the sum-of-the-years-digits method. The following entry recorded this change:

Depreciation Expense — Buildings....................	32,300	
Accumulated Depreciation — Buildings...........		32,300

(f) A $1 cash dividend declared on December 30 and payable on January 31 of the next fiscal year, was not recorded. The $30,000 of dividends expense represents the mid-year cash dividend paid on July 31 of the current year.

(g) The income tax of $36,000 is the estimated tax paid during the year. The tax based on the corrected net income was determined to be $37,300, allocated as follows:

(1) Income from continuing operations..............................	$53,400
(2) Loss from discontinued operations	17,400
(3) Gain on expropriation of land	14,700
(4) Cumulative effect of change in depreciation method.......	13,400

The tax owed of $1,300 at December 31 had not been recorded.

Instructions:

(1) Prepare the necessary correcting entries for the items discovered by the independent auditor. Assume that the accounts have not been closed for the current fiscal year.
(2) Prepare a multiple-step income statement for the current fiscal year, including the appropriate earnings per share disclosure. Operating expenses need not be divided into selling and administrative expense categories.
(3) Prepare the retained earnings statement for the current fiscal year.
(4) Prepare a balance sheet as of the end of the current fiscal year.

Pb. 11–42.
Entries for selected corporate transactions.
OBJ. 3, 6, 7, 8, 9

Selected transactions completed by Power Corporation during the current fiscal year are as follows:

Jan. 8. Split the common stock 4 for 1 and reduced the par from $100 to $25 per share. After the split, there were 200,000 common shares outstanding.

Feb. 1. Declared semiannual dividends of $2 on 50,000 shares of preferred stock and $1 on the 200,000 shares of $25 par common stock to stockholders of record on February 20, payable on February 27.

27. Paid the cash dividends.

Mar. 12. Purchased 25,000 shares of the corporation's own common stock at $30, recording the stock at cost.

Apr. 9. Discovered that a receipt of $4,500 cash on account from L. T. Fulton Co. had been posted in error to the account of T. Fuller Inc. The transaction was recorded correctly in the journal.

June 10. Sold 5,000 shares of treasury stock at $34, receiving cash.

July 18. Declared semiannual dividends of $2 on the preferred stock and $1 on the common stock. In addition, a 5% common stock dividend was declared on the common stock outstanding. The fair market value of the common stock, is estimated at $36.

Aug. 28. Paid the cash dividends and issued the certificates for the common stock dividend.

Oct. 15. Discovered that an invoice of $3,250 for utilities expense for the month of September was debited to Office Supplies.

Dec. 31. Recorded $168,000 additional federal income tax allocable to net income for the year. Of this amount, $92,500 is a current liability and $75,500 is deferred.

31. The board of directors authorized the appropriation necessitated by the holding of treasury stock.

Instructions:

Record the transactions.

ALTERNATE PROBLEMS

Pb. 11–36A.
Income tax allocation.
OBJ. 3

Differences between the accounting methods applied to accounts and financial reports and those used in determining taxable income yielded the following amounts for the first four years of a corporation's operations:

	First Year	Second Year	Third Year	Fourth Year
Income before income tax	$168,500	$240,000	$360,000	$390,500
Taxable income	120,000	200,000	320,500	425,500

The income tax rate for each of the four years was 40% of taxable income, and each year's taxes were promptly paid.

Instructions:

(1) Determine for each year the amounts described in the following columnar captions, presenting the information in the form indicated:

			Deferred Income Tax Payable	
Year	Income Tax Deducted on Income Statement	Income Tax Payments for the Year	Year's Addition (Deduction)	Year-End Balance

(2) Total the first three amount columns.

Pb. 11–37A.
Income statement.
OBJ. 4, 5

The following data were selected from the records of Birkbeck Co. for the current fiscal year ended March 31, 1992:

Advertising expense	$ 40,800
Delivery expense	30,600
Depreciation expense — office equipment	7,800
Depreciation expense — store equipment	13,500
Gain on condemnation of land	30,000
Income tax:	
Applicable to continuing operations	70,400
Applicable to loss from disposal of a segment of a business (reduction)	12,300
Applicable to gain on condemnation of land	6,000
Insurance expense	13,400
Interest expense	35,000
Loss from disposal of a segment of the business	60,300
Merchandise inventory (April 1, 1991)	195,000
Merchandise inventory (March 31, 1992)	203,200
Miscellaneous administrative expense	6,800
Miscellaneous selling expense	12,900
Office salaries expense	64,100
Office supplies expense	2,500
Purchases	908,400
Rent expense	30,000

Sales	$1,500,000
Sales commissions expense	80,200
Sales salaries expense	63,700
Store supplies expense	11,100

Instructions:

Prepare a multiple-step income statement, concluding with a section for earnings per share in the form illustrated in this chapter. There were 50.000 shares of common stock (no preferred) outstanding throughout the year. Assume that the gain or condemnation of land is an extraordinary item.

Pb. 11–38A.
Retained earnings statement.
OBJ. 6, 7

The retained earnings accounts of Bedrosian Corporation for the current fiscal year ended December 31 are as follows:

ACCOUNT APPROPRIATION FOR PLANT EXPANSION — ACCOUNT NO. 3201

Date		Item	Debit	Credit	Balance Debit	Balance Credit
19--						
Jan.	1	Balance				100,000
Dec.	31	Retained earnings		75,000		175,000

ACCOUNT APPROPRIATION FOR TREASURY STOCK — ACCOUNT NO. 3202

Date		Item	Debit	Credit	Balance Debit	Balance Credit
19--						
Jan.	1	Balance				350,000
Dec.	31	Retained earnings	80,000			270,000

ACCOUNT RETAINED EARNINGS — ACCOUNT NO. 3301

Date		Item	Debit	Credit	Balance Debit	Balance Credit
19--						
Jan.	1	Balance				815,000
Dec.	31	Income summary		163,500		978,500
	31	Appropriation for plant expansion	75,000			903,500
	31	Appropriation for treasury stock		80,000		983,500
	31	Cash dividends	50,000			933,500
	31	Stock dividends	40,000			893,500

ACCOUNT CASH DIVIDENDS — ACCOUNT NO. 3302

Date		Item	Debit	Credit	Balance Debit	Balance Credit
19--						
Nov.	22		50,000		50,000	
Dec.	31	Retained earnings		50,000	—	—

ACCOUNT STOCK DIVIDENDS ACCOUNT NO. 3303

Date		Item	Debit	Credit	Balance	
					Debit	Credit
19--						
Nov.	22		40,000		40,000	
Dec.	31	Retained earnings		40,000	—	—

Instructions:

Prepare a retained earnings statement for the fiscal year ended December 31.

Pb. 11–39A.
Entries for selected corporate transactions.
OBJ. 6, 7

The stockholders' equity accounts of Thurman Enterprises Inc., with balances on January 1 of the current fiscal year, are as follows:

Common Stock, stated value $100 (10,000 shares authorized, 4,000 shares issued)	$400,000
Paid-In Capital in Excess of Stated Value	150,000
Appropriation for Plant Expansion	50,000
Appropriation for Treasury Stock	25,000
Retained Earnings	372,000
Treasury Stock (200 shares, at cost)	25,000

The following selected transactions occurred during the year:

Jan. 20. Received land with an estimated fair market value of $20,000 from the city as a donation.
Feb. 1. Paid cash dividends of $5 per share on the common stock. The dividend had been properly recorded when declared on December 30 of the preceding fiscal year for $19,000.
Mar. 7. Sold all of the treasury stock for $28,000.
May 12. Issued 1,000 shares of common stock for $145,000.
Apr. 3. Sold all of the treasury stock for $150,000.
July 1. Declared a cash dividend of $1 per share to stockholders of record on July 15, payable on July 30.
July 30. Paid the cash dividend declared on July 1.
Sept. 2. Received additional land valued at $50,000. The land was donated for a plant site by the Sabal Bay Development Council.
July 10. Declared a 2% stock dividend on common stock, which has a market price of $150 a share.
Aug. 11. Issued the certificates for the dividend declared on July 10.
Oct. 30. Purchased 500 shares of treasury stock for $75,000.
Dec. 19. The board of directors authorized an increase of the appropriation for plant expansion by $40,000.
19. Declared a $4 per share dividend on common stock.
19. Increased the appropriation for treasury stock to $75,000.
31. Closed the credit balance of the income summary account, $108,500.
31. Closed the two dividends accounts to Retained Earnings.

Instructions:

(1) Open T accounts for the stockholders' equity accounts listed and enter the balances as of January 1. Also open T accounts for the following: Paid-in Capital from Sale of Treasury Stock; Donated Capital; Stock Dividends Distributable; Stock Dividends; Cash Dividends.
(2) Prepare entries to record the transactions and post to the eleven selected accounts.
(3) Prepare the stockholders' equity section of the balance sheet as of December 31 of the current fiscal year.

Pb. 11–40A.
Stockholders' equity transactions and statements.
OBJ. 6, 7

The stockholders' equity section of the balance sheet of Ames Corporation as of January 1 is as follows:

Stockholders' Equity

Paid-in capital:			
Common stock, $10 par (200,000 shares authorized, 80,000 shares issued) ...	$800,000		
Excess of issue price over par	75,000		
Total paid-in capital......................		$ 875,000	
Retained earnings:			
Appropriated for bonded indebtedness .	$275,000		
Unappropriated	425,000		
Total retained earnings		700,000	
Total		$1,575,000	
Deduct treasury stock (10,000 shares at cost).		125,000	
Total stockholders' equity			$1,450,000

The following selected transactions occured during the fiscal year:

Jan. 21. Issued 20,000 shares of stock in exchange for land and buildings with an estimated fair market value of $100,000 and $275,000, respectively. The property was encumbered by a mortgage of $125,000, and the company agreed to assume the responsibility for paying the mortgage note.

Dec. 1. Issued 2,000 shares of stock to officers as a salary bonus. Market price of the stock is $15 a share. (Debit Officers Salaries Expense.)

5. Declared a 4% stock dividend on the stock outstanding to stockholders of record on December 20 to be issued on January 20. The stock dividend is to be capitalized at the market price of $15 a share.

31. Increased the appropriation for bonded indebtedness by $25,000.

31. Closed the income summary account. After closing all revenue and expense accounts, Income Summary has a credit balance of $195,000.

31. Closed the two dividends accounts to Retained Earnings.

Instructions:

(1) Open T accounts for the accounts appearing in the stockholders' equity section of the balance sheet and enter the balances as of January 1. Also open T accounts for the following: Paid-In Capital from Sale of Treasury Stock; Donated Capital; Cash Dividends; Stock Dividends; Stock Dividends Distributable.
(2) Prepare entries to record the transactions and post to the ten selected accounts.
(3) Prepare the stockholders' equity section of the balance sheet as of December 31, the end of the fiscal year.
(4) Prepare a retained earnings statement for the fiscal year ended December 31.

Pb. 11–41A.
Correcting entries and financial statements.
OBJ. 2, 4, 5, 6, 7

B. G. Cox Company is in need of additional cash to expand operations. To raise the needed funds, the company is applying to the Barnett County Bank for a loan. For this purpose, the bank requests that the financial statements be audited. To assist the auditor, B. G. Cox Company's accountant prepared a work sheet that was used to prepare the following financial statements related to the current year:

B. G. Cox Company
Balance Sheet
December 31, 19--

Current assets:		
Cash	$ 55,650	
Accounts receivable	65,900	
Merchandise inventory	86,250	
Supplies	6,750	$214,550
Plant assets:		
Land	$100,000	
Buildings	315,000	
Equipment	132,500	
Patents	45,000	592,500
Total assets		$807,050
Current liabilities:		
Accounts payable	$ 46,400	
Salaries payable	3,600	$ 50,000
Deferred charges:		
Accumulated depreciation — buildings	$ 72,500	
Accumulated depreciation — equipment	37,500	
Allowance for doubtful accounts	4,500	114,500
Stockholders' equity:		
Common stock (100,000 shares authorized, $20 par)	$350,000	
Excess of issue price over par	45,000	
Retained earnings	165,000	
Net income	82,550	642,550
Total liabilities and stockholders' equity		$807,050

B. G. Cox Company
Income Statement
For Year Ended December 31, 19--

Revenues:		
Net sales	$802,500	
Gain on expropriation of land	42,000	
Total revenues		$844,500
Expenses:		
Cost of merchandise sold	$500,500	
Salary expense	72,000	
Depreciation expense — buildings	36,900	
Loss on discontinued operations	35,550	
Utilities expense	19,000	
Insurance expense	15,400	
Depreciation expense — equipment	8,500	
Amortization expense — patents	5,000	
Uncollectible accounts expense	3,750	
Miscellaneous administrative expense	8,350	
Income tax	32,000	
Dividends expense	25,000	
Total expenses		761,950
Net income		$ 82,550

In the course of the audit, the auditor examined the common stock and retained earnings accounts, which appeared as follows:

ACCOUNT COMMON STOCK ($20 Par) ACCOUNT NO. 3200

Date		Item	Debit	Credit	Balance Debit	Balance Credit
19--						
Jan.	1	Balance — 15,000 shares				300,000
July	2	Issued 1,500 shares for patents		50,000		350,000

ACCOUNT RETAINED EARNINGS ACCOUNT NO. 3300

Date		Item	Debit	Credit	Balance Debit	Balance Credit
19--						
Jan.	1	Balance				97,500
Feb.	1	Donation of land		50,000		147,500
	10	Error correction	7,500			140,000
Dec.	28	Appropriation for land acquisition		25,000		165,000

A closer examination of the transactions in these and other accounts revealed the following details:

(a) A computational error was made in the calculation of a prior year's dividend. The corrected amount of the dividend was paid on February 10 and debited to the retained earnings account.
(b) On February 1, the company received a donation of land. The land account was debited for $50,000, the fair market value of the land at that date.
(c) The patent acquired on July 2 by an issuance of 1,500 shares of common stock had a fair market value of $50,000 and an estimated useful life of 5 years.
(d) A $2 cash dividend declared on December 10 and payable on January 20 the next fiscal year was not recorded. The $25,000 of dividends expense represents the mid-year cash dividend paid on July 30 of the current year.
(e) After three years of using the straight-line method of depreciation for the buildings, the company changed to the sum-of-the-years-digits method. The following entry recorded this change:

Depreciation Expense — Buildings	26,900	
Accumulated Depreciation — Buildings		26,900

(f) In anticipation of further land acquisition, the board of directors on December 28 authorized a $25,000 appropriation of retained earnings that resulted in a debit to Land and a credit to Retained Earnings.
(g) The income tax of $32,000 is the estimated tax paid during the year. The tax based on the corrected net income was determined to be $33,950, allocated as follows:

(1) Income from continuing operations	$44,500
(2) Loss from discontinued operations	14,100
(3) Gain on expropriation of land	12,300
(4) Cumulative effect of change in depreciation method	8,750

The tax owed of $1,950 at December 31 had not been recorded.

Instructions:

(1) Prepare the necessary correcting entries for the items discovered by the independent auditor. Assume that the accounts have not been closed for the current fiscal year.

(2) Prepare a multiple-step income statement for the current fiscal year, including the appropriate earnings per share disclosure. Operating expenses need not be divided into selling and administrative expense categories.
(3) Prepare the retained earnings statement for the current fiscal year.
(4) Prepare a balance sheet as of the end of the current fiscal year.

Pb. 11–42A.
Entries for selected corporate transactions.
OBJ. 3, 6, 7, 8, 9

SOLUTIONS SOFTWARE

Selected transactions completed by Stewart Company during the current fiscal year are as follows:

Jan. 12. Split the common stock 2 for 1 and reduced the par from $100 to $50 per share. After the split, there were 60,000 common shares outstanding.
Feb. 13. Purchased 4,000 shares of the corporation's own common stock at $55, recording the stock at cost.
Mar. 20. Discovered that a receipt of $1,500 cash on account from C. Spencer had been posted in error to the account of C. Spense. The transaction was recorded correctly in the journal.
May 9. Declared semiannual dividends of $1 on 10,000 shares of preferred stock and $2 on the common stock to stockholders of record on May 30, payable on June 22.
June 22. Paid the cash dividends.
Aug. 18. Sold 1,500 shares of treasury stock at $60, receiving cash.
Nov. 10. Declared semiannual dividends of $1 on the preferred stock and $2.20 on the common stock. In addition, a 2% common stock dividend was declared on the common stock outstanding, which had a fair market value of $62.
Dec. 30. Paid the cash dividends and issued the certificates for the common stock dividend.
30. Recorded $92,600 additional federal income tax allocable to net income for the year. Of this amount, $61,400 is a current liability and $31,200 is deferred.
30. The board of directors authorized the appropriation necessitated by the holding of treasury stock.

Instructions:

Record the transactions.

MINI-CASE 11

Kahn Co. has paid quarterly cash dividends since 1985. These dividends have steadily increased from $.10 per share to the latest dividend declaration of $1.25 per share. The board of directors would like to continue this trend and are hesitant to suspend or decrease the amount of quarterly dividends. Unfortunately, sales of Kahn Co. dropped sharply in the fourth quarter of 1992 due to worsening economic conditions and increased competition. As a result, the board is uncertain as to whether it should declare a dividend for the last quarter of 1992.

On October 1, 1992, Kahn Co. borrowed $1,000,000 from Frye National Bank to use in modernizing its retail stores and to expand its product line in reaction to its competition. The terms of the 10-year, 12% loan require Kahn Co. to

(a) Pay monthly the total interest due,
(b) Pay $100,000 of the principal each October 1, beginning in 1993,
(c) Maintain a current ratio (current assets ÷ current liabilities) of 2:1,

(d) Appropriate $1,000,000 of retained earnings until the loan is fully paid, and

(e) Maintain a minimum balance of $20,000 (called a compensating balance) in its Frye National Bank account.

On December 31, 1992, 30% of the $1,000,000 loan had been disbursed in modernization of the retail stores and in expansion of the product line, and the remainder is temporarily invested in U.S. Treasury notes. Kahn Co.'s balance sheet as of December 31, 1992, is as follows:

Kahn Co.
Balance Sheet
December 31, 1992

Assets			
Current assets:			
Cash		$ 50,000	
Marketable securities, at cost (market price, $706,500)		700,000	
Accounts receivable	$ 163,000		
Less allowance for doubtful accounts	13,000	150,000	
Merchandise inventory		291,000	
Prepaid expenses		9,000	
Total current assets			$1,200,000
Plant assets:			
Land		$ 350,000	
Buildings	$1,900,000		
Less accumulated depreciation	430,000	1,470,000	
Equipment	$ 920,000		
Less accumulated depreciation	220,000	700,000	
Total plant assets			2,520,000
Total assets			$3,720,000
Liabilities			
Current liabilities:			
Accounts payable	$ 143,600		
Notes payable (Frye National Bank)	100,000		
Salaries payable	6,400		
Total current liabilities		$ 250,000	
Long-term liabilities:			
Notes payable (Frye National Bank)		900,000	
Total liabilities			$1,150,000
Stockholders' Equity			
Paid-in capital:			
Common stock, $50 par (50,000 shares authorized, 20,000 shares issued)	$1,000,000		
Excess of issue price over par	80,000		
Total paid-in capital		$1,080,000	
Retained earnings:			
Appropriated for provision of Frye National Bank loan	$1,000,000		
Unappropriated	490,000		
Total retained earnings		1,490,000	
Total stockholders' equity			2,570,000
Total liabilities and stockholders' equity			$3,720,000

The board of directors is scheduled to meet January 8, 1993, to discuss the results of operations for 1992 and to consider the declaration of dividends for the fourth quarter of 1992. The chairman of the board has asked for your advice on the declaration of dividends.

Instructions:

(1) What factors should the board consider in deciding whether to declare a cash dividend?
(2) The board is considering the declaration of a stock dividend instead of a cash dividend. Discuss the issuance of a stock dividend from the point of view of (a) a stockholder and (b) the board of directors.

ANSWERS TO SELF-EXAMINATION QUESTIONS

1. D Paid-in capital is one of the two major subdivisions of the stockholders' equity of a corporation. It may result from many sources, including the receipt of donated real estate (answer A), the redemption of a corporation's own stock (answer B), and the sale of a corporation's treasury stock (answer C).
2. A The amount of income tax deferred to future years is $16,000 (answer A), determined as follows:

Depreciation expense, sum-of-the-years-digits method	$100,000
Depreciation expense, straight-line method	60,000
Excess expense in determination of taxable income	$ 40,000
Income tax rate	× 40%
Income tax deferred to future years	$ 16,000

3. A Events and transactions that are distinguished by their unusual nature and by the infrequency of their occurrence, such as a gain on condemnation of land for public use, are reported in the income statement as extraordinary items (answer A).
4. C The correction of a material error related to a prior period should be excluded from the determination of net income of the current period and reported as an adjustment of the balance of retained earnings at the beginning of the current period (answer C).
5. C An appropriation for plant expansion is a portion of total retained earnings and would be reported in the stockholder's equity section of the balance sheet (answer C).

CHAPTER 12

CHAPTER OBJECTIVES

1. Describe and illustrate the impact of borrowing on a long-term basis as a means of financing corporations.
2. Describe the characteristics of bonds.
3. Describe the present value concept.
4. Describe and illustrate the present value concept for bonds payable.
5. Describe and illustrate the accounting for bonds payable.
6. Describe and illustrate the use of and accounting for bond sinking funds.
7. Describe and illustrate the accounting for an appropriation for bonded indebtedness.
8. Describe and illustrate the accounting for bond redemption.
9. Describe the balance sheet presentation of bonds payable.
10. Describe and illustrate the accounting for investments in bonds.

LONG-TERM LIABILITIES & INVESTMENTS IN BONDS

The acquisition of cash and other assets by a corporation through the issuance of its stock has been discussed in earlier chapters. Expansion of corporate enterprises through the retention of earnings, in some instances accompanied by the issuance of stock dividends, has also been explored. In addition to these two methods of obtaining relatively permanent funds, corporations may also borrow money on a long-term basis by issuing notes or **bonds**, which are a form of interest-bearing note. Long-term notes may be issued to relatively few lending agencies or to a single investor such as an insurance company. Bonds are usually sold to underwriters (dealers and brokers in securities), who in turn sell them to investors. Although the discussion that follows will be limited to bonds, the accounting principles involved apply equally to long-term notes.

When funds are borrowed through the issuance of bonds, there is a definite commitment to pay interest and to repay the principal at a stated future date. Bondholders are creditors of the issuing corporation and their claims for interest and for repayment of principal rank ahead of the claims of stockholders.

FINANCING CORPORATIONS

OBJECTIVE 1
Describe and illustrate the impact of borrowing on a long-term basis as a means of financing corporations.

Many factors influence the incorporators or the board of directors in deciding upon the best means of obtaining funds. The subject will be limited here to a brief illustration of the effect of different financing methods on the income of a corporation and the common stockholders. To illustrate, assume that three different plans for financing a $4,000,000 corporation are under consideration by its organizers, and that in each case the securities will be issued at their par or face amount. The incorporators estimate that the enterprise will earn $800,000 annually, before deducting interest on the bonds and income tax estimated at 40% of income. The following tabulation indi-

12-504 cates the amount of earnings that would be available to common stockholders under each of the three plans:

	Plan 1	Plan 2	Plan 3
12% bonds	—	—	$2,000,000
Preferred 9% stock, $50 par	—	$2,000,000	1,000,000
Common stock, $10 par	$4,000,000	2,000,000	1,000,000
Total	$4,000,000	$4,000,000	$4,000,000
Earnings before interest and income tax	$ 800,000	$ 800,000	$ 800,000
Deduct interest on bonds	—	—	240,000
Income before income tax	$ 800,000	$ 800,000	$ 560,000
Deduct income tax	320,000	320,000	224,000
Net income	$ 480,000	$ 480,000	$ 336,000
Dividends on preferred stock	—	180,000	90,000
Available for dividends on common stock	$ 480,000	$ 300,000	$ 246,000
Shares of common stock outstanding	400,000	200,000	100,000
Earnings per share on common stock	$1.20	$1.50	$2.46

If Plan 1 is adopted and the entire financing is from the issuance of common stock, the earnings per share on the common stock would be $1.20 per share. Under Plan 2, the effect of using 9% preferred stock for half of the capitalization would result in $1.50 earnings per common share. The issuance of 12% bonds in Plan 3, with the remaining capitalization split between preferred and common stock, would yield a return of $2.46 per share on common stock.

Under the assumed conditions, Plan 3 would obviously be the most attractive for common stockholders. If the anticipated earnings should increase beyond $800,000, the spread between the earnings per share to common stockholders under Plan 1 and Plan 3 would become even greater. But if successively smaller amounts of earnings are assumed, the attractiveness of Plan 2 and Plan 3 decreases. The effect of lower earnings is illustrated by the following tabulation, in which earnings, before interest and income tax are deducted, are assumed to be $440,000 instead of $800,000.

	Plan 1	Plan 2	Plan 3
12% bonds	—	—	$2,000,000
Preferred 9% stock, $50 par	—	$2,000,000	1,000,000
Common stock, $10 par	$4,000,000	2,000,000	1,000,000
Total	$4,000,000	$4,000,000	$4,000,000
Earnings before interest and income tax	$ 440,000	$ 440,000	$ 440,000
Deduct interest on bonds	—	—	240,000
Income before income tax	$ 440,000	$ 440,000	$ 200,000
Deduct income tax	176,000	176,000	80,000
Net income	$ 264,000	$ 264,000	$ 120,000
Dividends on preferred stock	—	180,000	90,000
Available for dividends on common stock	$ 264,000	$ 84,000	$ 30,000
Shares of common stock outstanding	400,000	200,000	100,000
Earnings per share on common stock	$.66	$.42	$.30

The preceding analysis focused attention on the effect of the different plans on earnings per share of common stock. There are other factors that must be considered when different methods of financing are evaluated. The issuance of bonds represents a fixed annual interest charge that, in contrast to dividends, is not subject to corporate control. Provision must also be made for the eventual repayment of the principal amount of the bonds, in contrast to the absence of any such obligation to stockholders. On the other hand, a decision to finance entirely by an issuance of common stock would require substantial investment by a single stockholder or small group of stockholders who desire to control the corporation.

HOW REFINANCING WORKS

Some of the same factors that influence a corporation's decision on financing will also be considered when a company refinances, or changes the structure of its debt and stockholders' equity. In refinancing, however, both management and the stockholders are concerned about the effect of *changes* in the debt and equity relationship. These concerns are described in the following excerpt from an article in *USA TODAY:*

When a major company like Allegis Corp. announces that it is "recapitalizing" [refinancing], many shareholders may be baffled.... Recapitalization plans aren't as complicated as they seem, however. Here are some basic questions and answers:

What is capital?

Simply put, it's a company's money. It can come from two sources: stockholders and lenders.

The stockholders' share is called equity. It represents cash the company has raised by selling stock, and profits the company has built up.

The other part of capital is money borrowed from banks or raised by selling bonds.

How companies balance equity and debt is up to them. At IBM Corp., only 11% of total capital is debt. Sears, Roebuck and Co. has 46% debt. The level of debt a company keeps depends on the risk its managers are willing to assume.

What does risk have to do with it?

It's no different for a company than for an individual. The more debt you have, the greater the risk. Reason: Any profit you earn first must go to meet interest payments. If earnings aren't sufficient to cover the interest owed, you'll have to deplete your savings—or sell something—to raise the needed cash.

What happens in a recapitalization?

A company decides to borrow heavily to raise cash for a large, one-time cash... payment to shareholders.... [In addition,]... shareholders also receive new shares to replace their old shares in the company.... [In] the process, the company generally [reduces its equity]. It's replaced with debt.

How can the company afford the debt load?

The company is forced to operate more efficiently than ever. It will have to slash expenses to keep earnings up in the face of higher interest expenses. Owens-Corning Fiberglas Corp., for example, pared its research costs significantly after its recapitalization last year....

Is there any advantage in being so heavily in debt?

Debt does have a good side. By borrowing, you gain "leverage"—the ability to control more assets by using someone else's money. That can magnify the return to shareholders, if business is good and the firm operates efficiently....

Source: Neil Budde, "How Company Recapitalization Plans Work," *USA TODAY,* (June 8, 1987).

CHARACTERISTICS OF BONDS

OBJECTIVE 2
Describe the characteristics of bonds.

When a corporation issues bonds, it executes a contract with the bondholders known as a **bond indenture** or **trust indenture.** The entire issue is divided into a number of individual bonds, which may be of varying denominations. Usually the principal of each bond, also called the **face value,** is $1,000 or a multiple thereof. The interest on bonds may be payable at annual, semiannual, or quarterly intervals. Most bonds provide for payment on a semiannual basis.

Registered bonds may be transferred from one owner to another only by endorsement on the bond certificate, and the issuing corporation must maintain a record of the name and the address of each bondholder. Interest payments are made by check to the owner of record. Title to **bearer bonds,** which are also called **coupon bonds,** is transferred merely by delivery, and the issuing corporation does not know the identity of the bondholders. Interest coupons for the entire term, in the form of checks or drafts payable to bearer, are attached to the bond certificate. At each interest date, the holder detaches the appropriate coupon and presents it to a bank for payment. Although bearer bonds once were issued frequently, they rarely are issued today.

When all bonds of an issue mature at the same time, they are called **term bonds.** If the maturities are spread over several dates, they are called **serial bonds.** For example, one tenth of an issue of $1,000,000, or $100,000, may mature eleven years from the issuance date, another $100,000 may mature twelve years from the issuance date, and so on until the final $100,000 matures at the end of the twentieth year.

Bonds that may be exchanged for other securities under certain conditions are called **convertible bonds.** Bonds issued by a corporation that reserves the right to redeem them before maturity are referred to as **callable bonds.**

A **secured bond** is one that gives the bondholder a claim on specific assets in case the issuing corporation fails to meet its obligations on the bonds. The properties mortgaged or pledged may be specific buildings and equipment, the entire plant, or stocks and bonds of other companies owned by the debtor corporation. Unsecured bonds issued on the basis of the general credit of the corporation are called **debenture bonds.**

PRESENT VALUE CONCEPTS

OBJECTIVE 3
Describe the present value concept.

The concept of present value plays an important role in many accounting analyses and business decisions. For example, accounting analyses based on the present value concept are useful for evaluating proposals for long-term investments in plant and equipment. Such analyses are discussed in managerial accounting textbooks. In this chapter, the concept of present value will be discussed in the context of the role that it plays in determining the selling price of bonds.

The concept of **present value** is that an amount of cash to be received at some date in the future is not the equivalent of the same amount of cash held at an earlier date. In other words, a sum of cash to be received in the future is not as valuable as the same sum on hand today, because cash on hand today can be invested to earn income. For example, $100 on hand today would be more valuable than $100 to be received a year from today. In this case, if the $100 cash on hand today can be invested to earn 10% per year, the $100 will accumulate to $110 ($100 plus $10 earnings) by one year from today. The $100 on hand today can be referred to as the present value amount that is equivalent to $110 to be received a year from today.

PRESENT VALUE CONCEPTS FOR BONDS PAYABLE

OBJECTIVE 4
Describe and illustrate the present value concept for bonds payable.

When a corporation issues bonds, it usually incurs two distinct obligations: (1) to pay the face amount of the bonds at a specified maturity date, and (2) to pay periodic interest at a specified percentage of the face amount. The price that a buyer is willing to pay for these future benefits is the sum of

(1) the *present value* of the face amount of the bonds at the maturity date and (2) the *present value* of the periodic interest payments.

Present Value of $1

The present value of the face amount of bonds at the maturity date is the value today of the promise to pay the face amount at some future date. To illustrate, assume that $1,000 is to be paid in one year and that the rate of earnings is 12%. The present value amount is $892.86 ($1,000 ÷ 1.12). If the $1,000 is to be paid one year later (two years in all), with the earnings compounded at the end of the first year, the present value amount would be $797.20 ($892.86 ÷ 1.12).

Instead of determining the present value of a future cash sum by a series of divisions in the manner just illustrated, it is customary to use a table of present values to find the present value of $1 for the appropriate number of periods, and to multiply that present value factor by the amount of the future cash sum. A partial table of the present value of $1 appears as follows:[1]

Present Value of $1 at Compound Interest

Periods	5%	5½%	6%	6½%	7%	10%	11%	12%	13%	14%
1	0.9524	0.9479	0.9434	0.9390	0.9346	0.9091	0.9009	0.8929	0.8850	0.8772
2	0.9070	0.8985	0.8900	0.8817	0.8734	0.8264	0.8116	0.7972	0.7831	0.7695
3	0.8638	0.8516	0.8396	0.8278	0.8163	0.7513	0.7312	0.7118	0.6931	0.6750
4	0.8227	0.8072	0.7921	0.7773	0.7629	0.6830	0.6587	0.6355	0.6133	0.5921
5	0.7835	0.7651	0.7473	0.7299	0.7130	0.6209	0.5935	0.5674	0.5428	0.5194
6	0.7462	0.7252	0.7050	0.6853	0.6663	0.5645	0.5346	0.5066	0.4803	0.4556
7	0.7107	0.6874	0.6651	0.6435	0.6228	0.5132	0.4817	0.4523	0.4251	0.3996
8	0.6768	0.6516	0.6274	0.6042	0.5820	0.4665	0.4339	0.4039	0.3762	0.3506
9	0.6446	0.6176	0.5919	0.5674	0.5439	0.4241	0.3909	0.3606	0.3329	0.3075
10	0.6139	0.5854	0.5584	0.5327	0.5083	0.3855	0.3522	0.3220	0.2946	0.2697
11	0.5847	0.5549	0.5268	0.5002	0.4751	0.3505	0.3173	0.2875	0.2607	0.2366
12	0.5568	0.5260	0.4970	0.4697	0.4440	0.3186	0.2858	0.2567	0.2307	0.2076
13	0.5303	0.4986	0.4688	0.4410	0.4150	0.2897	0.2575	0.2292	0.2042	0.1821
14	0.5051	0.4726	0.4423	0.4141	0.3878	0.2633	0.2320	0.2046	0.1807	0.1597
15	0.4810	0.4479	0.4173	0.3888	0.3624	0.2394	0.2090	0.1827	0.1599	0.1401
16	0.4581	0.4246	0.3936	0.3651	0.3387	0.2176	0.1883	0.1631	0.1415	0.1229
17	0.4363	0.4024	0.3714	0.3428	0.3166	0.1978	0.1696	0.1456	0.1252	0.1078
18	0.4155	0.3815	0.3503	0.3219	0.2959	0.1799	0.1528	0.1300	0.1108	0.0946
19	0.3957	0.3616	0.3305	0.3022	0.2765	0.1635	0.1377	0.1161	0.0981	0.0829
20	0.3769	0.3427	0.3118	0.2838	0.2584	0.1486	0.1240	0.1037	0.0868	0.0728

For the previous example, the table indicates that the present value of $1 to be received two years hence, with earnings at the rate of 12% a year, is .7972. Multiplying $1,000 by .7972 yields $797.20, which is the same amount that was determined previously by two successive divisions. In using the table, it should be noted that the "periods" column represents the number of compounding periods, while the "percentage" columns represent the compound interest rate per period. For example, 12% for two years compounded annually, as in the preceding illustration, is 12% for two periods; 12% for two years compounded semiannually would be 6% (12% per year ÷ 2 semiannual

[1]The tables illustrated are limited to 20 periods for a small number of interest rates, and the amounts are carried to only four decimal places. Books of tables are available with as many as 360 periods, 45 interest rates (including many fractional rates), and amounts carried to eight decimal places. More complete interest tables are provided in Appendix A.

periods) for four periods (2 years × 2 semiannual periods); and 12% for three years compounded semiannually would be 6% (12% ÷ 2) for six periods (3 years × 2 semiannual periods).

Present Value of Annuity of $1

The present value of the periodic interest payments on bonds is the value today of the promise to pay a fixed amount of interest at the end of each of a number of periods. Such a series of fixed payments at fixed intervals is called an **annuity**.

The following partial table of the present value of an annuity of $1 at compound interest indicates the value now (present value) of $1 to be received at the end of *each* period at various compound rates of interest. For example, the present value of $1,000 to be received at the end of each of the next 5 periods at 10% compound interest per period is $3,790.80 (3.7908 × $1,000).

Present Value of Annuity of $1 at Compound Interest

Periods	5%	5½%	6%	6½%	7%	10%	11%	12%	13%	14%
1	0.9524	0.9479	0.9434	0.9390	0.9346	0.9091	0.9009	0.8929	0.8850	0.8772
2	1.8594	1.8463	1.8334	1.8206	1.8080	1.7355	1.7125	1.6901	1.6681	1.6467
3	2.7232	2.6979	2.6730	2.6485	2.6243	2.4869	2.4437	2.4018	2.3612	2.3216
4	3.5460	3.5052	3.4651	3.4258	3.3872	3.1699	3.1024	3.0373	2.9745	2.9137
5	4.3295	4.2703	4.2124	4.1557	4.1002	3.7908	3.6959	3.6048	3.5172	3.4331
6	5.0757	4.9955	4.9173	4.8410	4.7665	4.3553	4.2305	4.1114	3.9976	3.8887
7	5.7864	5.6830	5.5824	5.4845	5.3893	4.8684	4.7122	4.5638	4.4226	4.2883
8	6.4632	6.3346	6.2098	6.0888	5.9713	5.3349	5.1461	4.9676	4.7988	4.6389
9	7.1078	6.9522	6.8017	6.6561	6.5152	5.7590	5.5370	5.3283	5.1317	4.9464
10	7.7217	7.5376	7.3601	7.1888	7.0236	6.1446	5.8892	5.6502	5.4262	5.2161
11	8.3064	8.0925	7.8869	7.6890	7.4987	6.4951	6.2065	5.9377	5.6869	5.4527
12	8.8633	8.6185	8.3838	8.1587	7.9427	6.8137	6.4924	6.1944	5.9176	5.6603
13	9.3936	9.1171	8.8527	8.5997	8.3577	7.1034	6.7499	6.4235	6.1218	5.8424
14	9.8986	9.5896	9.2950	9.0138	8.7455	7.3667	6.9819	6.6282	6.3025	6.0021
15	10.3797	10.0376	9.7123	9.4027	9.1079	7.6061	7.1909	6.8109	6.4624	6.1422
16	10.8378	10.4622	10.1059	9.7678	9.4467	7.8237	7.3792	6.9740	6.6039	6.2651
17	11.2741	10.8646	10.4773	10.1106	9.7632	8.0216	7.5488	7.1196	6.7291	6.3729
18	11.6896	11.2461	10.8276	10.4325	10.0591	8.2014	7.7016	7.2497	6.8399	6.4674
19	12.0853	11.6077	11.1581	10.7347	10.3356	8.3649	7.8393	7.3658	6.9380	6.5504
20	12.4622	11.9504	11.4699	11.0185	10.5940	8.5136	7.9633	7.4694	7.0248	6.6231

ACCOUNTING FOR BONDS PAYABLE

OBJECTIVE 5
Describe and illustrate the accounting for bonds payable.

The interest rate specified in the bond indenture is called the **contract** or **coupon rate,** which may differ from the rate prevailing in the market at the time the bonds are issued. If the **market** or **effective rate** is higher than the contract rate, the bonds will sell at a **discount,** or less than their face amount. This discount results because buyers are unwilling to pay the face amount for bonds whose contract rate is lower than the prevailing market rate. The discount, therefore, represents the amount necessary to make up for the difference in the market and the contract interest rates. Conversely, if the market rate is lower than the contract rate, the bonds will sell at a **premium,** or more than their face amount. In this case, buyers are willing to pay more than the face amount for bonds whose contract rate is higher than the market rate.

Bonds Issued at Face Amount

To illustrate an issuance of bonds, assume that on January 1 a corporation issues for cash $100,000 of 12%, five-year bonds, with interest of $6,000 payable semiannually. The market rate of interest at the time the bonds are issued is 12%. Since the contract rate and the market rate of interest are the same, the bonds will sell at their face amount. This amount, calculated as follows, is the sum of (1) the present value of the face amount of $100,000 to be repaid in 5 years and (2) the present value of 10 semiannual interest payments of $6,000 each.[2]

Present value of face amount of $100,000 due in 5 years, at 12% compounded semiannually: $100,000 × .5584 (present value of $1 for 10 periods at 6%)	$ 55,840
Present value of 10 semiannual interest payments of $6,000, at 12% compounded semiannually: $6,000 × 7.3601 (present value of annuity of $1 for 10 periods at 6%)	44,160
Total present value of bonds	$100,000

The basic data for computing the two present values totaling $100,000 were obtained from the two present value tables presented on pages 507 and 508. The first of the two amounts, **$55,840**, is the present value of the $100,000 that is to be repaid in 5 years. The $55,840 is determined by locating the present value of $1 for 10 periods (5 years of semiannual payments) at 6% semiannually (12% annual rate) in the present value of $1 table and multiplying by $100,000. If the bond indenture provided that no interest would be paid during the entire 5-year period, the bonds would be worth only $55,840 at the time of their issuance. To express the concept of present value from a different viewpoint, if $55,840 were invested today, with interest at 12% compounded semiannually, the sum accumulated at the end of 10 semiannual periods would be $100,000.

The second of the two amounts, **$44,160**, is the present value of the series of ten $6,000 payments. The $44,160 is determined by locating the present value of an annuity of $1 for 10 periods (5 years of semiannual payments) at 6% semiannually (12% annual rate) in the present value of an annuity of $1 table and multiplying by $6,000. The present value of $44,160 can also be viewed as the amount of a current deposit earning 12% that would yield ten semiannual withdrawals of $6,000, with the original deposit being reduced to zero by the tenth withdrawal.

The entry to record the issuance of the $100,000 bonds at their face amount is as follows:

Jan. 1	Cash	100,000	
	Bonds Payable		100,000

At six-month intervals following the issuance of the 12% bonds, the interest payment of $6,000 is recorded in the usual manner by a debit to Interest Expense and a credit to Cash. At the maturity date, the payment of the principal sum of $100,000 would be recorded by a debit to Bonds Payable and a credit to Cash.

[2]Because the present value tables are rounded to four decimal places, minor rounding errors may appear in the illustrations.

Bonds Issued at a Discount

If the market rate of interest is 13% and the contract rate is 12%, the bonds will sell at a discount. The present value of the five-year, $100,000 bonds with a market rate of 13% may be calculated as follows:

Present value of $100,000 due in 5 years, at 13% compounded semiannually: $100,000 × .5327 (present value of $1 for 10 periods at 6 1/2%)	$53,270
Present value of 10 semiannual interest payments of $6,000 at 13% compounded semiannually: $6,000 × 7.1888 (present value of an annuity of $1 for 10 periods at 6 1/2%)	43,133
Total present value of bonds	$96,403

The two present values that make up the total are both somewhat less than the comparable amounts in the first illustration, where the contract rate and the market rate were exactly the same. The reason for the lesser present value is that the value now of a future amount becomes less and less as the interest rate rises. In other words, the sum that would have to be invested today to equal a fixed future amount becomes less and less as the interest rate earned on the investment rises.

In the following entry to record the issuance of the 12% bonds, the bond liability is recorded at the face amount, and the discount is recorded in a separate contra account:

Jan. 1	Cash	96,403	
	Discount on Bonds Payable	3,597	
	Bonds Payable		100,000

The $3,597 discount may be viewed as the amount that is needed to compensate the investor for accepting a contract rate of interest that is below the prevailing market rate. From another view, the $3,597 represents the additional amount that must be returned by the issuer at maturity; that is, the issuer received $96,403 at the sale date but must return $100,000 at the maturity date. The $3,597 discount must therefore be amortized as additional interest expense over the five-year life of the bonds. There are two widely used methods of allocating bond discount to the various periods: (1) **straight-line** and (2) **interest.** Although the interest method is the recommended method, the straight-line method is acceptable if the results obtained by its use do not materially differ from the results that would be obtained by the use of the interest method.[3]

Amortization of Discount by the Straight-Line Method. The straight-line method is the simpler of the two methods and provides for amortization in equal periodic amounts. Application of this method to the illustration would yield amortization of 1/10 of $3,597, or $359.70, each half year. The amount of the interest expense on the bonds would remain constant for each half year at $6,000 plus $359.70, or $6,359.70. The entry to record the first interest payment and the amortization of the related amount of discount is as follows:

June 30	Interest Expense	6,359.70	
	Discount on Bonds Payable		359.70
	Cash		6,000.00

[3]*Opinions of the Accounting Principles Board, No. 21,* "Interest on Receivables and Payables" (New York: American Institute of Certified Public Accountants, 1971), par. 14.

As an alternative to recording the amortization each time the interest is paid, it may be recorded only at the end of the year. When this procedure is used, each interest payment is recorded as a debit to Interest Expense and a credit to Cash. In terms of the illustration, the entry to amortize the discount at the end of the first year would be as follows:

Dec. 31	Interest Expense	719.40	
	Discount on Bonds Payable		719.40

The amount of the discount amortized, $719.40, is made up of the two semiannual amortization amounts of $359.70.

Amortization of Discount by the Interest Method. In contrast to the straight-line method, which provides for a constant *amount* of interest expense, the interest method provides for a constant *rate* of interest on the **carrying amount** (also called **book value**) of the bonds at the beginning of each period. The interest rate used in the computation is the market rate as of the date the bonds were issued, and the carrying amount of the bonds is their face amount minus the unamortized discount. The difference between the interest expense computed in this manner and the amount of the periodic interest payment is the amount of discount to be amortized for the period. Application of this method to the illustration yields the following data:

Amortization of Discount on Bonds Payable

Interest Payment	A Interest Paid (6% of Face Amount)	B Interest Expense (6½% of Bond Carrying Amount)	C Discount Amortization (B–A)	D Unamortized Discount (D–C)	E Bond Carrying Amount ($100,000–D)
				$3,597	$ 96,403
1	$6,000	$6,266(6½% of $96,403)	$266	3,331	96,669
2	6,000	6,284(6½% of $96,669)	284	3,047	96,953
3	6,000	6,302(6½% of $96,953)	302	2,745	97,255
4	6,000	6,322(6½% of $97,255)	322	2,423	97,577
5	6,000	6,343(6½% of $97,577)	343	2,080	97,920
6	6,000	6,365(6½% of $97,920)	365	1,715	98,285
7	6,000	6,389(6½% of $98,285)	389	1,326	98,674
8	6,000	6,415(6½% of $98,674)	415	911	99,089
9	6,000	6,441(6½% of $99,089)	441	470	99,530
10	6,000	6,470(6½% of $99,530)	470	—	100,000

The following important details should be observed:

1. The interest paid (column A) remains constant at 6% of $100,000, the face amount of the bonds.
2. The interest expense (column B) is computed at 6 1/2% of the bond carrying amount at the beginning of each period, yielding a gradually increasing amount.
3. The excess of the interest expense over the interest payment of $6,000 is the amount of discount to be amortized (column C).
4. The unamortized discount (column D) decreases from the initial balance, $3,597, to a zero balance at the maturity date of the bonds.
5. The carrying amount (column E) increases from $96,403, the amount received for the bonds, to $100,000 at maturity.

The entry to record the first interest payment and the amortization of the related amount of discount is as follows:

June 30	Interest Expense	6,266	
	Discount on Bonds Payable		266
	Cash		6,000

If the amortization is recorded only at the end of the year, the amount of the discount amortized on December 31 would be $550, which is the sum of the first two semiannual amortization amounts ($266 and $284) from the preceding table.

Bonds Issued at a Premium

If the market rate of interest is 11% and the contract rate is 12%, the bonds will sell at a premium. The present value of the five-year, $100,000 bonds, with a market rate of 11%, may be calculated as follows:

Present value of $100,000 due in 5 years, at 11% compounded semiannually: $100,000 × .5854 (present value of $1 for 10 periods at 5 1/2%)	$ 58,540
Present value of 10 semiannual interest payments of $6,000, at 11% compounded semiannually: $6,000 × 7.5376 (present value of an annuity of $1 for 10 periods at 5 1/2%)	45,226
Total present value of bonds	$103,766

The entry to record the issuance of the bonds is as follows:

Jan. 1	Cash	103,766	
	Bonds Payable		100,000
	Premium on Bonds Payable		3,766

Procedures for amortization of the premium and determination of the periodic interest expense are basically the same as those used for bonds issued at a discount.

Amortization of Premium by the Straight-Line Method. Application of the straight-line method to the illustration would yield amortization of 1/10 of $3,766, or $376.60, each half year. Just as bond discount can be viewed as additional interest expense, bond premium can be viewed as a reduction in the amount of interest expense. The entry to record the first interest payment and the amortization of the related amount of premium is as follows:

June 30	Interest Expense	5,623.40	
	Premium on Bonds Payable	376.60	
	Cash		6,000.00

If the amortization of the premium is recorded only at the end of the year, each interest payment would be recorded by debiting Interest Expense and crediting Cash. The amortization of the premium at the end of the year, in the illustration, would then be recorded as follows:

Dec. 31	Premium on Bonds Payable	753.20	
	Interest Expense		753.20

The amount of the premium amortized, $753.20, is the sum of the two semiannual amounts of $376.60.

Amortization of Premium by the Interest Method. Application of the interest method of amortization yields the following data:

Amortization of Premium on Bonds Payable

Interest Payment	A Interest Paid (6% of Face Amount)	B Interest Expense (5½% of Bond Carrying Amount)	C Premium Amortization (A–B)	D Unamortized Premium (D–C)	E Bond Carrying Amount ($100,000 + D)
				$3,766	$103,766
1	$6,000	$5,707(5½% of $103,766)	$293	3,473	103,473
2	6,000	$5,691(5½% of $103,473)	309	3,164	103,164
3	6,000	$5,674(5½% of $103,164)	326	2,838	102,838
4	6,000	$5,657(5½% of $102,838)	343	2,495	102,495
5	6,000	$5,638(5½% of $102,495)	362	2,133	102,133
6	6,000	$5,618(5½% of $102,133)	382	1,751	101,751
7	6,000	$5,597(5½% of $101,751)	403	1,348	101,348
8	6,000	$5,575(5½% of $101,348)	425	923	100,923
9	6,000	$5,551(5½% of $100,923)	449	474	100,474
10	6,000	$5,526(5½% of $100,474)	474	—	100,000

The following important details should be observed:

1. The interest paid (column A) remains constant at 6% of $100,000, the face amount of the bonds.
2. The interest expense (column B) is computed at 5 1/2% of the bond carrying amount at the beginning of each period, yielding a gradually decreasing amount.
3. The excess of the periodic interest payment of $6,000 over the interest expense is the amount of premium to be amortized (column C).
4. The unamortized premium (column D) decreases from the initial balance, $3,766, to a zero balance at the maturity date of the bonds.
5. The carrying amount (column E) decreases from $103,766, the amount received for the bonds, to $100,000 at maturity.

The entry to record the first payment and the amortization of the related amount of premium is as follows:

June 30	Interest Expense	5,707	
	Premium on Bonds Payable	293	
	Cash		6,000

If the amortization is recorded only at the end of the year, the amount of the premium amortized on December 31 would be $602, which is the sum of the first two semiannual amounts ($293 and $309) from the preceding table.

Zero-Coupon Bonds

During the 1980s, some enterprises issued bonds that did not provide for periodic interest payments. In its 1987 financial statements, for example, PepsiCo Inc. reported such bonds, called **zero-coupon bonds,** with a face value of $1.1 billion and due between 1989 and 2012.

Zero-coupon bonds provide for only the payment of the face amount of the bonds at the maturity date. Because the bonds do not provide for periodic interest payments, they sell at a large discount. To illustrate, if the market rate of interest for five-year bonds which pay interest semiannually is 13%, the present value of $100,000 zero-coupon, five-year bonds may be calculated as follows:

Present value of $100,000 due in 5 years, at 13% compounded semiannually:	
$100,000 × .5327 (present value of $1 for 10 periods at 6 1/2%)	$53,270

The accounting for zero-coupon bonds is similar to that for interest-bearing bonds that have been sold at a discount. The entry to record the issuance of the bonds is as follows:

Cash..	53,270	
Discount on Bonds Payable...................................	46,730	
Bonds Payable..		100,000

The discount of $46,730 is amortized as interest expense over the life of the bonds, using either the straight-line method or the interest method, as illustrated on pages 510-512.

BOND SINKING FUND

OBJECTIVE 6
Describe and illustrate the use of and accounting for bond sinking funds.

The bond indenture may provide that funds for the payment of bonds at maturity be accumulated over the life of the issue. The amounts set aside are kept separate from other assets in a special fund called a **sinking fund.** Cash deposited in the fund is usually invested in income-producing securities. The periodic deposits plus the earnings on the investments should approximately equal the face amount of the bonds at maturity. In determining the amount of these periodic deposits, the concept of future value can be used.

Future Value Concepts

Future value is the amount that will accumulate at some future date as a result of an investment or a series of investments. For example, if $1,000 is invested to earn 10% per year, the future value at the end of a year will be $1,100 ($1,000 plus $100 earnings). If the $1,100 is left to accumulate additional compounded earnings for three years, the future value at the end of the second year will be $1,210 ($1,100 plus $110 earnings), and at the end of the third year, $1,331 ($1,210 plus $121 earnings).

The future value of an investment can also be determined by using a table of future values to find the future value of $1 for the appropriate number of periods, and then multiplying the amount of the investment by this future value factor. A partial table of the future value of $1 appears as follows:

Future Value of $1 at Compound Interest

Periods	5%	5½%	6%	6½%	7%	10%	11%	12%	13%	14%
1	1.0500	1.0550	1.0600	1.0650	1.0700	1.1000	1.1100	1.1200	1.1300	1.1400
2	1.1025	1.1130	1.1236	1.1342	1.1449	1.2100	1.2321	1.2544	1.2769	1.2996
3	1.1576	1.1742	1.1910	1.2080	1.2250	1.3310	1.3676	1.4049	1.4429	1.4815
4	1.2155	1.2388	1.2625	1.2865	1.3108	1.4641	1.5181	1.5735	1.6305	1.6890
5	1.2763	1.3070	1.3382	1.3701	1.4026	1.6105	1.6851	1.7623	1.8424	1.9254
6	1.3401	1.3788	1.4185	1.4591	1.5007	1.7716	1.8704	1.9738	2.0820	2.1950
7	1.4071	1.4547	1.5036	1.5540	1.6058	1.9487	2.0762	2.2107	2.3526	2.5023
8	1.4775	1.5347	1.5939	1.6550	1.7182	2.1436	2.3045	2.4760	2.6584	2.8526
9	1.5513	1.6191	1.6895	1.7626	1.8385	2.3580	2.5580	2.7731	3.0040	3.2520
10	1.6289	1.7081	1.7909	1.8771	1.9672	2.5937	2.8394	3.1059	3.3946	3.7072
11	1.7103	1.8021	1.8983	1.9992	2.1049	2.8531	3.1518	3.4786	3.8359	4.2262
12	1.7959	1.9012	2.0122	2.1291	2.2522	3.1384	3.4985	3.8960	4.3345	4.8179
13	1.8857	2.0058	2.1329	2.2675	2.4099	3.4523	3.8833	4.3635	4.8980	5.4924
14	1.9799	2.1161	2.2609	2.4149	2.5785	3.7975	4.3104	4.8871	5.5348	6.2614
15	2.0789	2.2325	2.3966	2.5718	2.7590	4.1773	4.7846	5.4736	6.2543	7.1379
16	2.1829	2.3553	2.5404	2.7390	2.9522	4.5950	5.3109	6.1304	7.0673	8.1373
17	2.2920	2.4848	2.6928	2.9171	3.1588	5.0545	5.8951	6.8660	7.9861	9.2765
18	2.4066	2.6215	2.8543	3.1067	3.3799	5.5599	6.5436	7.6900	9.0243	10.5752
19	2.5270	2.7657	3.0256	3.3086	3.6165	6.1159	7.2633	8.6128	10.1974	12.0557
20	2.6533	2.9178	3.2071	3.5237	3.8697	6.7275	8.0623	9.6463	11.5231	13.7435

For the previous example, the table indicates that the future value of $1 three years (periods) hence, with earnings at the rate of 10% a year, is 1.331. Multiplying $1,000 by 1.331 yields $1,331, which is the same amount as determined previously.

Future value may also arise from a series of equal investments made at fixed intervals (an annuity).[4] For example, if $1,000 is invested at the end of each year to earn 10% per year compounded annually, the future value of the annuity at the end of the third year would be $3,310, determined as follows:

Year	Beginning Balance	Earnings During Year (10% × Beginning Balance)	Annual Deposit (End of Year)	Accumulation at End of Year
1	—	—	$1,000	$1,000
2	$1,000	$100	1,000	2,100
3	2,100	210	1,000	3,310

The future value of a series of investments can also be determined by using a table of future values to find the future value of an annuity of $1 for the appropriate number of periods, and then multiplying the amount of the

[4]As discussed in a preceding section, a series of fixed payments or investments at fixed intervals is called an annuity.

investment by the future value factor. A partial table of the future value of an annuity of $1 appears as follows:

Future Value of Annuity of $1 at Compound Interest (Investments at End of Period)

Periods	5%	5½%	6%	6½%	7%	10%	11%	12%	13%	14%
1	1.0000	1.0000	1.0000	1.0000	1.0000	1.0000	1.0000	1.0000	1.0000	1.0000
2	2.0500	2.0550	2.0600	2.0650	2.0700	2.1000	2.1100	2.1200	2.1300	2.1400
3	3.1525	3.1680	3.1836	3.1992	3.2149	3.3100	3.3421	3.3744	3.4069	3.4396
4	4.3101	4.3423	4.3746	4.4072	4.4399	4.6410	4.7097	4.7793	4.8498	4.9211
5	5.5256	5.5811	5.6371	5.6936	5.7507	6.1051	6.2278	6.3529	6.4803	6.6101
6	6.8019	6.8881	6.9753	7.0637	7.1533	7.7156	7.9129	8.1152	8.3227	8.5355
7	8.1420	8.2669	8.3938	8.5229	8.6540	9.4872	9.7833	10.0890	10.4047	10.7305
8	9.5491	9.7216	9.8975	10.0769	10.2598	11.4359	11.8594	12.2997	12.7573	13.2328
9	11.0266	11.2563	11.4913	11.7319	11.9780	13.5795	14.1640	14.7757	15.4157	16.0854
10	12.5779	12.8754	13.1808	13.4944	13.8165	15.9374	16.7220	17.5487	18.4198	19.3373
11	14.2068	14.5835	14.9716	15.3716	15.7836	18.5312	19.5614	20.6546	21.8143	23.0445
12	15.9171	16.3856	16.8699	17.3707	17.8885	21.3843	22.7132	24.1331	25.6502	27.2708
13	17.7130	18.2868	18.8821	19.4998	20.1406	24.5227	26.2116	28.0291	29.9847	32.0887
14	19.5986	20.2926	21.0151	21.7673	22.5505	27.9750	30.0949	32.3926	34.8827	37.5811
15	21.5786	22.4087	23.2760	24.1822	25.1290	31.7725	34.4054	37.2797	40.4175	43.8424
16	23.6575	24.6411	25.6725	26.7540	27.8881	35.9497	39.1900	42.7533	46.6717	50.9804
17	25.8404	26.9964	28.2129	29.4930	30.8402	40.5447	44.5008	48.8837	53.7391	59.1176
18	28.1324	29.4812	30.9057	32.4104	33.9990	45.5992	50.3959	55.7497	61.7251	68.3941
19	30.5390	32.1027	33.7600	35.5167	37.3790	51.1591	56.9395	63.4397	70.7494	78.9692
20	33.0660	34.8683	36.7856	38.8253	40.9955	57.2750	64.2028	72.0524	80.9468	91.0249

For the previous example, the table indicates that the future value of an annuity of $1 three years (periods) hence, with earnings at the rate of 10% a year, is 3.310. Multiplying $1,000 by 3.310 yields $3,310, which is the same amount as determined previously.

To illustrate the concept of the future value of an annuity for the periodic deposits in a bond sinking fund, assume that a corporation issues $100,000 of 10-year bonds, dated January 1. A bond sinking fund for the payment of the bonds at maturity is established, with deposits to be made at the end of each year. If the deposits are expected to earn 14% per year, the annual deposit would be $5,171, determined as follows:

$$\text{Annual Deposit} = \frac{\text{Maturity Value of Bonds}}{\text{Future Value of Annuity of \$1 for 10 Periods at 14\%}}$$

$$\text{Annual Deposit} = \frac{\$100{,}000}{19.3373}$$

$$\text{Annual Deposit} = \$5{,}171 \text{ (rounded)}$$

Accounting for Bond Sinking Fund

When cash is transferred to the sinking fund, an account called Sinking Fund Cash is debited and Cash is credited. The purchase of investments is recorded by a debit to Sinking Fund Investments and a credit to Sinking Fund Cash. As income (interest or dividends) is received, the cash is debited to Sinking Fund Cash and Sinking Fund Income is credited.

The accounting for a bond sinking fund is illustrated by using the preceding example, in which a corporation issues $100,000 of 10-year bonds dated January 1. As indicated in the preceding section, annual deposits of $5,171, invested in securities that will yield approximately 14% per year, are sufficient to provide a fund of approximately $100,000 at the end of 10 years.

A few of the typical transactions and the related entries affecting the sinking fund during the 10-year period are illustrated as follows:

Deposit of cash in the fund

Sinking Fund Cash	5,171	
Cash		5,171

The first deposit in the sinking fund is recorded. A similar entry would be recorded as deposits are made at the end of each of the 9 remaining years.

Purchase of investments

Sinking Fund Investments	5,000	
Sinking Fund Cash		5,000

The purchases of securities after the first deposit was made are recorded in a summary entry. The time of purchase and the amount invested at any one time vary, depending upon market conditions and the unit price of securities purchased.

Receipt of income from investments

Sinking Fund Cash	700	
Sinking Fund Income		700

The receipt of income for the year on the securities purchased is recorded in a summary entry. Interest and dividends are received at different times during the year, and the amount earned per year normally increases as the fund increases.

Sale of investments

Sinking Fund Cash	85,100	
Sinking Fund Investments		82,480
Gain on Sale of Investments		2,620

The sale of all securities at the end of the tenth year is recorded. Investments may be sold from time to time and the proceeds reinvested. Prior to maturity, all investments are converted into cash.

Payment of bonds

Bonds Payable	100,000	
Cash	1,791	
Sinking Fund Cash		101,791

The payment of the bonds and the transfer of the remaining sinking fund cash to the cash account is recorded. The cash available in the fund at the end of the tenth year is assumed to be composed of the following:

Proceeds from sale of investments	$ 85,100
Income earned during tenth year	11,520
Last annual deposit	5,171
Total	$101,791

In the illustration, the amount of the fund exceeded the amount of the liability by $1,791. This excess was transferred to the regular cash account. If the fund had been less than the amount of the liability, $99,500 for example, the regular cash account would have been drawn upon for the $500 deficiency.

Sinking fund income represents earnings of the corporation and is reported in the income statement as "Other income." The cash and the securities making up the sinking fund are classified in the balance sheet as "Investments," which usually appears immediately below the current assets section.

APPROPRIATION FOR BONDED INDEBTEDNESS

OBJECTIVE 7
Describe and illustrate the accounting for an appropriation for bond indebtedness.

The restriction of dividends during the life of a bond issue is another means of increasing the assurance that the obligation will be paid at maturity. Assuming that the corporation in the preceding example is required by the bond indenture to appropriate $10,000 of retained earnings each year for the 10-year life of the bonds, the following entry would be made annually:

Dec. 31	Retained Earnings	10,000	
	Appropriation for Bonded Indebtedness ..		10,000

As was indicated in Chapter 11, an appropriation has no direct relationship to a sinking fund. Each is independent of the other. When there is both a fund and an appropriation for the same purpose, the appropriation may be said to be **funded.**

BOND REDEMPTION

OBJECTIVE 8
Describe and illustrate the accounting for bond redemption.

Callable bonds are redeemable by the issuing corporation within the period of time and at the price stated in the bond indenture. Usually the call price is above the face value. If the market rate of interest declines after the issuance of the bonds, the corporation may sell new bonds at a lower interest rate and use the funds to redeem the original issue. The reduction of future interest expense is always an incentive for bond redemption. A corporation may also redeem all or a portion of its bonds before maturity by purchasing them on the open market.

When a corporation redeems bonds at a price below their carrying amount, the corporation realizes a gain. If the price is in excess of the carrying amount, a loss is incurred.[5] To illustrate redemption, assume that on June 30 a corporation has a bond issue of $100,000 outstanding, on which there is an unamortized premium of $4,000. The corporation has the option of calling the bonds for $105,000, which it exercises on this date. The entry to record the redemption is:

June 30	Bonds Payable......................................	100,000	
	Premium on Bonds Payable	4,000	
	Loss on Redemption of Bonds.................	1,000	
	Cash		105,000

If the bonds were not callable, the corporation might purchase a portion on the open market. Assuming that the corporation purchases one fourth ($25,000) of the bonds for $24,000 on June 30, the entry to record the redemption would be as follows:

June 30	Bonds Payable......................................	25,000	
	Premium on Bonds Payable	1,000	
	Cash		24,000
	Gain on Redemption of Bonds..............		2,000

Note that only the portion of the premium relating to the bonds redeemed is written off. The excess of the carrying amount of the bonds purchased, $26,000, over the cash paid, $24,000, is recognized as a gain.

[5]Gains and losses on the redemption of bonds are reported in the income statement as extraordinary items. See *Statement of Financial Accounting Standards, No. 4,* "Reporting Gains and Losses from Extinguishment of Debt" (Stamford: Financial Accounting Standards Board, 1975), par. 8.

BALANCE SHEET PRESENTATION OF BONDS PAYABLE

OBJECTIVE 9
Describe the balance sheet presentation of bonds payable.

Bonds payable are usually reported on the balance sheet as long-term liabilities. If there are two or more bond issues, separate accounts should be maintained and the details of each should be reported on the balance sheet or in a supporting schedule or note. When the balance sheet date is within one year of the bond maturity date, the bonds should be transferred to the current liability classification if they are to be paid out of current assets. If they are to be paid with funds that have been set aside or if they are to be replaced with another bond issue, they should remain in the noncurrent category and their anticipated liquidation disclosed in an explanatory note.

The balance in a discount account should be reported in the balance sheet as a deduction from the related bonds payable. Conversely, the balance in a premium account should be reported as an addition to the related bonds payable. Either in the financial statements or in accompanying notes, the description of the bonds (terms, security, due date, etc.) should also include the effective interest rate and the maturities and sinking fund requirements for each of the next five years.[6]

INVESTMENTS IN BONDS

OBJECTIVE 10
Describe and illustrate the accounting for investments in bonds.

The issuance of bonds and related transactions were discussed in the preceding paragraphs from the standpoint of the issuing corporation. Whenever a corporation records a transaction between itself and the owners of its bonds, there is a reciprocal entry in the accounts of the investor.

In the following discussion, attention will be given to the principles underlying the accounting for investments in **debt securities** (bonds and notes) that are identified as long-term investments. **Long-term investments** are investments that are not intended as a ready source of cash in the normal operations of the business. These long-term investments are listed in the balance sheet under the caption "Investments," which usually follows the current assets. By contrast, temporary investments or marketable securities, which were discussed in Chapter 6, are available to meet the needs for additional cash for normal operations and are classified as current assets.

A business may make long-term investments simply because it has cash that is not needed in its normal operations. As discussed previously, cash and securities in bond sinking funds are considered long-term investments, since they are accumulated for the purpose of paying the bond liability. A corporation may also purchase bonds as a means of establishing or maintaining business relations with the issuing company.

Investments in corporate bonds may be purchased directly from the issuing corporation or from other investors. The services of a broker are usually employed in buying and selling bonds listed on the organized exchanges. The record of transactions on bond exchanges is reported daily in the financial pages of newspapers. This record usually includes data on the bond interest rate, maturity date, volume of sales, and the closing price for each corporation's bonds traded during the day. Prices for bonds are quoted as a percentage of the face amount. Thus, the price of a $1,000 bond quoted at 104 1/2 would be $1,045.

---

[6] *Statement of Financial Accounting Standards, No. 47,* "Disclosure of Long-Term Obligations" (Stamford: Financial Accounting Standards Board, 1981), par. 10.

Accounting for Bond Investments — Purchase, Interest, and Amortization

A long-term investment in debt securities is customarily carried at cost. The cost of bonds purchased includes the amount paid to the seller plus other costs related to the purchase, such as the broker's commission. When bonds are purchased between interest dates, the buyer pays the seller the interest accrued from the last interest payment date to the date of purchase. The amount of the interest paid should be debited to Interest Income, since it is an offsetting amount against the amount that will be received at the next interest date. To illustrate, assume that a $1,000 bond is purchased at 102 plus a brokerage fee of $5.30 and accrued interest of $10.20. The transaction is recorded by the following entry. Note that the cost of the bond is recorded in a single account, i.e., the face amount of the bond and the premium paid are not recorded in separate accounts.

Apr. 2	Investment in Lewis Co. Bonds	1,025.30	
	Interest Income	10.20	
	Cash		1,035.50

As discussed previously, the price investors pay for bonds may be much greater or less than the face amount or the original issuance price. When bonds held as long-term investments are purchased at a price other than the face amount, the discount or premium should be amortized over the remaining life of the bonds. The amortization of discount increases the amount of the investment account and interest income. The amortization of premium decreases the amount of the investment account and interest income. The procedures for determining the amount of amortization each period correspond to those described and illustrated on pages 510 to 513.

Interest received on bond investments is recorded by a debit to Cash and a credit to Interest Income. At the end of a fiscal year, the interest accrued should be recorded by a debit to Interest Receivable and a credit to Interest Income.

As a basis for illustrating the transactions associated with long-term investments in bonds, assume that $50,000 of 8% bonds of Nowell Corporation, due in 8 3/4 years, are purchased on July 1 to yield approximately 11%. The purchase price is $41,706 plus interest of $1,000 accrued from April 1, the date of the last semiannual interest payment. Entries in the accounts of the purchaser at the time of purchase and for the remainder of the fiscal year, ending December 31, are as follows:

July 1
Payment for investment in bonds and accrued interest

Investment in Nowell Corp. Bonds	41,706	
Interest Income	1,000	
Cash		42,706

Cost of $50,000 of Nowell Corp. bonds	$41,706
Interest accrued on $50,000 at 8%, April 1–July 1 (3 months)	1,000
Total	$42,706

October 1
Receipt of semiannual interest

Cash	2,000	
Interest Income		2,000

Interest on $50,000 at 8%, April 1–October 1 (6 months), $2,000.

December 31
Adjusting entries

Interest Receivable	1,000	
Interest Income		1,000

Interest accrued on $50,000 at 8%, October 1–December 31 (3 months), $1,000.

Investment in Nowell Corp. Bonds	294	
Interest Income		294

Discount to be amortized by interest method, July 1–December 31 (6 months):

Interest income (5 1/2% of bond carrying amount of $41,706)	$2,294
Less interest received (4% of face amount of $50,000)	2,000
Amount to be amortized	$ 294

The entries in the interest income account in the above illustration may be summarized as follows:

July 1	Paid accrued interest—3 months	$(1,000)
Oct. 1	Received interest payment—6 months	2,000
Dec. 31	Recorded accrued interest—3 months	1,000
31	Recorded amortization of discount—6 months	294
	Interest earned—6 months	$ 2,294

Accounting for Bond Investments—Sale

When bonds held as long-term investments are sold, the seller will receive the sales price (less commissions and other selling costs) plus the interest accrued since the last payment date. Before recording the proceeds, the seller should record the appropriate amount of the amortization of discount or premium for the current period, up to the date of sale. Then, in recording the proceeds, any gain or loss incurred on the sale can be recognized. To illustrate the recording of a sale of bonds held as a long-term investment, assume that the Nowell Corporation bonds of the preceding example are sold for $47,350 plus accrued interest on June 30, seven years after their purchase. The carrying amount of the bonds (cost plus amortized discount) as of January 1 of the year of sale is $47,080. The entries to record the amortization of discount for the current year and the sale of the bonds are as follows:

June 30
Amortization of discount for current year

Investment in Nowell Corp. Bonds	589	
Interest Income		589

Discount to be amortized by the interest method, January 1–June 30, $589.

June 30
Receipt of interest and sale of bonds

Cash	48,350	
Loss on Sale of Investments	319	
Interest Income		1,000
Investment in Nowell Corp. Bonds		47,669

Interest accrued on $50,000 at 8%, April 1–June 30 (3 months), $1,000

Carrying amount of bonds on January 1 of current year	$47,080
Discount amortized in current year	589
Carrying amount of bonds on June 30	$47,669
Proceeds of sale	47,350
Loss on sale	$ 319

CHAPTER REVIEW

KEY POINTS

OBJECTIVE 1

Financing Corporations

Business enterprises may raise funds for long-term financing in various ways. They may sell capital stock or issue notes or bonds, which are a form of interest-bearing note. When funds are borrowed through the issuance of bonds, there is a definite commitment to pay periodic interest and to repay the principal at a stated future date. There are many factors that must be considered when different methods of financing are evaluated. One such factor is the impact on the corporation's earnings per share of common stock.

OBJECTIVE 2

Characteristics of Bonds

When a corporation issues bonds, it executes a contract, known as a bond indenture or trust indenture, with bondholders. The principal amount of each bond is called its face value and is usually a multiple of $1,000. Different types of bonds that may be issued by a corporation include registered bonds, bearer bonds, coupon bonds, term bonds, serial bonds, convertible bonds, callable bonds, secured bonds, and debenture bonds.

OBJECTIVE 3

Present Value Concepts

The concept of present value plays an important role in many accounting analyses and business decisions. The concept of present value is that an amount of cash to be received at some date in the future is not the equivalent of the same amount of cash held at an earlier date. In other words, a sum of cash to be received in the future is not as valuable as the same sum on hand today, because cash on hand today can be invested to earn income.

OBJECTIVE 4

Present Value Concepts for Bonds Payable

When a corporation issues bonds, it incurs two distinct obligations: (1) to pay the face amount of the bonds at a specified maturity date, and (2) to pay periodic interest at a specified percentage of the face amount. A price that a buyer is willing to pay for these future benefits is the sum of (1) the present value of the face amount of the bonds at the maturity date and (2) the present value of the periodic interest payments. The present value of $1 table is used to compute the present value of the face amount of the bonds at the maturity date. The present value of an annuity of $1 table is used to compute the present value of the periodic interest payments on the bonds.

OBJECTIVE 5

Accounting for Bonds Payable

The interest rate specified in the bond indenture is called the contract or coupon rate, which may differ from the rate prevailing in the market at the time the bonds are issued. If the market or effective rate is higher than the contract rate, the bonds will sell at a discount, or less than their face amount. The discount results because buyers are unwilling to pay the face amount for bonds whose contract rate is lower than the prevailing market rate. If the market rate is lower than the contract rate, the bonds will sell at a premium, or more than their face amount. In this case, buyers are willing to pay more than the face amount for bonds whose contract rate is higher than the market rate.

When bonds are issued at a discount, Discount on Bonds Payable is debited for the amount of the discount. When bonds are issued at a premium, Premium on Bonds Payable is credited for the amount of the premium. The amount of the discount or premium must be allocated to interest expense over the life of the bonds by using either the straight-line method or the interest method. The straight-line method provides for a constant amount of interest expense. The interest method provides for a constant rate of interest. A discount is amortized by crediting Discount on Bonds Payable. A premium is amortized by debiting Premium on Bonds Payable. The amortization of a discount increases interest expense, and the amortization of a premium decreases interest expense. The amortization entry may be recorded at either the date of periodic interest payments or the end of the accounting period.

OBJECTIVE 6

Bond Sinking Fund

The bond indenture may provide that funds for the payment of bonds at maturity be accumulated over the life of the issue. The amounts set aside are accounted for separately from other assets in a special fund called a sinking fund. Cash deposited in this fund is usually invested in income-producing securities. The periodic deposits plus the earnings on the investments should approximately equal the face amount of the bonds at maturity. The concept of future value may be used to determine the amount of the periodic deposits.

OBJECTIVE 7

Appropriation for Bonded Indebtedness

The bond indenture may require a board of directors to restrict dividends during the life of a bond issue through the use of an appropriation of retained earnings. This action may also be taken voluntarily. When there is both a bond sinking fund and an appropriation of retained earnings for the purpose of redeeming bonds at maturity, the appropriation is said to be funded.

OBJECTIVE 8

Bond Redemption

Callable bonds are redeemable by the issuing corporation at the price stated in the bond indenture. If the bonds are not callable, they may be purchased on the open market. When a corporation redeems bonds, any gain or loss on the redemption is recognized in the accounts.

OBJECTIVE 9

Balance Sheet Presentation of Bonds Payable

Bonds payable are usually reported on the balance sheet as long-term liabilities. When the balance sheet date is within one year of the bond maturity date, the bonds should be transferred to the current liability classification if they are to be paid out of current assets. If they are to be paid with funds that have been set aside or if they are to be replaced with another bond issue, they should remain in the noncurrent category and their anticipated liquidation disclosed in an explanatory note. The balance in a discount account should be reported in the balance sheet as a deduction from the related bonds payable, and the balance in a premium account should be reported as an addition to the related bonds payable.

OBJECTIVE 10

Investments in Bonds

A corporation may purchase bonds of another corporation as a long-term investment that is not intended as a ready source of cash in the normal operations of the business. These long-term investments are listed in the balance sheet under the caption "Investments," following the Current Assets section.

A long-term investment in debt securities is customarily carried at cost. The cost of the bonds purchased includes the amount paid to the seller plus other costs related to the purchase, such as the broker's commission. When bonds are purchased between interest dates, the buyer pays the seller the interest accrued from the last interest payment date to the date of the purchase. The amount of the interest paid should be debited to Interest Income, since it is an offset against the amount that will be received at the next interest date. When bonds held as long-term investments are purchased at a price other than the face amount, the discount or premium should be amortized over the remaining life of the bonds. The procedures for determining the amount of amortization are similar to those for bonds payable. The amortization of a discount increases the amount of the investment account and interest income. The amortization of a premium decreases the amount of the investment account and interest income.

When bonds held as long-term investments are sold, the seller will receive the sales price (less commissions and other selling costs) plus the interest accrued since the last payment date. Before recording the proceeds, the seller should record the appropriate amount of the amortization of discount or premium for the current period, up to the date of sale. Then, in recording the proceeds, any gain or loss incurred on the sale can be recognized.

KEY TERMS

bonds 503
bond indenture 505
present value 506
annuity 508
contract rate of interest 508
effective rate of interest 508
bond discount 508
bond premium 508
carrying amount 511
sinking fund 514
future value 514
debt securities 519
long-term investments 519

SELF-EXAMINATION QUESTIONS

Answers at end of chapter.

1. If a corporation plans to issue $1,000,000 of 12% bonds at a time when the market rate for similar bonds is 10%, the bonds can be expected to sell:
   A. at their face amount
   B. at a premium
   C. at a discount
   D. at a price below their face amount

2. If the bonds payable account has a balance of $500,000 and the discount on bonds payable account has a balance of $40,000, what is the carrying amount of the bonds?
   A. $460,000
   B. $500,000
   C. $540,000
   D. None of the above

3. The cash and the securities comprising the sinking fund established for the payment of bonds at maturity are classified on the balance sheet as:
   A. current assets
   B. investments
   C. long-term liabilities
   D. none of the above

4. If a firm purchases $100,000 of bonds of X Company at 101 plus accrued interest of $2,000 and pays broker's commissions of $50, the amount debited to Investment in X Company Bonds would be:
   A. $100,000
   B. $101,050
   C. $103,000
   D. none of the above

5. The balance in the discount on bonds payable account would usually be reported in the balance sheet in the:
   A. current assets section
   B. current liabilities section
   C. long-term liabilities section
   D. none of the above

ILLUSTRATIVE PROBLEM

Dent Inc.'s fiscal year ends December 31. Selected transactions for the period 1992 through 1999 involving bonds payable issued by Dent Inc. are as follows:

1992
June 30. Issued $4,000,000 of 25-year, 9% callable bonds dated June 30, 1992, for cash of $3,840,000. Interest is payable semiannually on December 31 and June 30.

Dec. 31. Paid the semiannual interest on the bonds.
31. Recorded amortization of $3,200 discount on the bonds.
31. Closed the interest expense account.

1993

June 30. Paid the semiannual interest on the bonds.

Dec. 31. Paid the semiannual interest on the bonds.
31. Recorded amortization of $6,400 discount on the bonds.
31. Closed the interest expense account.

1999

June 30. Recorded the redemption of the bonds, which were called at 102. The balance in the bond discount account is $115,200 after the payment of interest and amortization of discount have been recorded. (Record the redemption only.)

Instructions:

1. Prepare journal entries to record the preceding transactions.
2. Determine the amount of interest expense for 1992.
3. Estimate the effective annual interest rate by dividing the interest expense for 1992 by the bond carrying amount at the time of issuance and multiplying by 2.
4. Determine the carrying amount of the bonds as of December 31, 1993.

SOLUTION

(1)

Date	Account	Debit	Credit
1992			
June 30	Cash	3,840,000	
	Discount on Bonds Payable	160,000	
	Bonds Payable		4,000,000
Dec. 31	Interest Expense	180,000	
	Cash		180,000
31	Interest Expense	3,200	
	Discount on Bonds Payable		3,200
31	Income Summary	183,200	
	Interest Expense		183,200
1993			
June 30	Interest Expense	180,000	
	Cash		180,000
Dec. 31	Interest Expense	180,000	
	Cash		180,000
31	Interest Expense	6,400	
	Discount on Bonds Payable		6,400
31	Income Summary	366,400	
	Interest Expense		366,400
1999			
June 30	Bonds Payable	4,000,000	
	Loss on Redemption of Bonds Payable	195,200	
	Discount on Bonds Payable		115,200
	Cash		4,080,000

(2) $183,200

(3) $183,200 ÷ $3,840,000 = 4.8% rate for six months of a year
4.8% × 2 = 9.6% annual rate

(4) Initial carrying amount of bonds	$3,840,000
Discount amortized on December 31, 1992	3,200
Discount amortized on December 31, 1993	6,400
Carrying amount of bonds, December 31, 1993	$3,849,600

DISCUSSION QUESTIONS

12–1. When underwriters are used by the corporation issuing bonds, what function do the underwriters perform?

12–2. How are interest payments made to holders of (a) bearer or coupon bonds and (b) registered bonds?

12–3. Explain the meaning of each of the following terms as they relate to a bond issue: (a) secured, (b) convertible, (c) callable, and (d) debenture.

12–4. Describe the two distinct obligations incurred by a corporation when issuing bonds.

12–5. A corporation issues $10,000,000 of 11% coupon bonds to yield interest at the rate of 10%. (a) Was the amount of cash received from the sale of the bonds greater or less than $10,000,000? (b) Identify the following terms related to the bond issue: (1) face amount, (2) market or effective rate of interest, (3) contract or coupon rate of interest, and (4) maturity amount.

12–6. If bonds issued by a corporation are sold at a discount, is the market rate of interest greater or less that the coupon rate?

12–7. What is the present value of $1,000 due in 3 years, if the market rate of interest is 12%?

12–8. What is the present value of $1,000 to be received in each of the next 3 years, if the market rate of interest is 12%?

12–9. If the bonds payable account has a balance of $500,000 and the discount on bonds payable account has a balance of $24,500, what is the carrying amount of the bonds?

12–10. The following data are related to a $1,000,000, 14% bond issue for a selected semiannual interest period:

Bond carrying amount at beginning of period	$1,120,000
Interest paid at end of period	70,000
Interest expense allocable to the period	64,000

(a) Were the bonds issued at a discount or at a premium? (b) What is the balance of the discount or premium account at the beginning of the period? (c) How much amortization of discount or premium is allocable to the period?

12–11. A corporation issues 12%, 10-year debenture bonds, with a face amount of $2,000,000, for 101 1/2 at the beginning of the current year. Assuming that the premium is to be amortized on a straight-line basis, what is the total amount of interest expense for the current year?

12–12. Indicate the title of (a) the account to be debited and (b) the account to be credited in the entry made at year end for amortization of (1) discount on bonds payable and (2) premium on bonds payable.

12–13. When the premium on bonds payable is amortized by the interest method, does the interest expense increase or decrease over the amortization period?

12–14. What is the purpose of a bond sinking fund?

12–15. What would be the value at the end of the second year for a $1,000 investment if the earnings rate is 12% compounded annually?

12–16. What would be the value at the end of the sixth year for a $5,000 investment if the earnings rate is 10% compounded annually? Use the table of the future value of $1 presented in this chapter to determine the value.

12–17. What would be the value at the end of the second year from a series of investments of $10,000 each to be made at the end of each of the first two years, with earnings of 12% compounded annually?

12–18. If Cowan Company invests $10,000 at the end of each of the next 5 years in a sinking fund, what is the value of the fund at the end of 5 years if the fund investments yield 12% per year, compounded annually? Use the table of the future value of an annuity of $1 presented in this chapter to determine the value.

12–19. What amount must be invested at the end of each of the next 5 years, in a sinking fund that earns 12% compounded annually, to accumulate to $10,000 at the end of the fifth year? Use the table of the future value of an annuity of $1 presented in this chapter to determine the amount.

12–20. If the amount accumulated in a sinking fund account exceeds the amount of liability at the redemption date, to what account is the excess transferred?

12–21. How are cash and securities comprising a sinking fund classified on the balance sheet?

12–22. Bonds Payable has a balance of $400,000 and Discount on Bonds Payable has a balance of $8,500. If the issuing corporation redeems the bonds at 98, what is the amount of gain or loss on redemption?

12–23. Indicate how the following accounts should be reported in the balance sheet: (a) Premium on Bonds Payable and (b) Discount on Bonds Payable.

12–24. Under what caption are "Long-term investments in bonds" listed on the balance sheet?

12–25. The quoted price of Prater Corp. bonds on June 1 is 104. On the same day the interest accrued is 5% of the face amount. (a) Does the quoted price include accrued interest? (b) If $10,000 face amount of Prater Corp. bonds is purchased on June 1 at the quoted price, what is the cost of the bonds, exclusive of commission?

12–26. An investor sells $50,000 of bonds of Frasier Corp. carried at $51,000 for $52,100 plus accrued interest of $500. The broker remits the balance due after deducting a commission of $250. Present the entry to record this transaction.

Real World Focus

12–27. Xerox Corporation 8 5/8% sinking fund debenture bonds due in 1999 were reported in *The Wall Street Journal* as selling for 93 1/2 on May 3, 1990. (a) Were the bonds selling at a premium or at a discount on May 3, 1990? (b) Was the market rate of interest for similar quality bonds higher or lower than 8 5/8% on May 3, 1990?

Real World Focus

12–28. A company purchased a $1,000, 20-year zero-coupon bond for $189 to yield 8.5% to maturity. How is the interest income computed? Adapted from "Technical Hotline," *Journal of Accountancy* (January 1989), p. 100.

Ethics Discussion Case

12–29. Fleming Inc. has outstanding a $25,000,000, 25-year, 12% debenture bond issue dated July 1, 1977. The bond issue is due June 30, 2000. The bond indenture requires a sinking fund which, as of February 1, 1992, has a balance of $8,000,000. Fleming Inc. is currently experiencing a shortage of funds due to a recent plant expansion. Kim Arnold, treasurer of Fleming, has suggested using the sinking fund cash to temporarily alleviate the shortage of funds. Arnold's brother-in-law, who is trustee of the sinking fund, would be willing to loan Fleming Inc. the necessary funds from the sinking fund.

Discuss whether Kim Arnold is behaving in an ethical manner.

EXERCISES

Ex. 12–30.
Effect of financing on earnings per share.
OBJ. 1

Two companies are financed as follows:

	Jeter Inc.	Vessels Co.
Bonds payable, 10% (issued at face value)	$1,000,000	$ 500,000
Preferred 6% stock (nonparticipating)	1,000,000	500,000
Common stock, $10 par	1,000,000	2,000,000

Income tax is estimated at 40% of income. Determine for each company the earnings per share of common stock, assuming that the income before bond interest and income tax for each company is (a) $200,000, (b) $500,000, and (c) $1,000,000.

Ex. 12–31.
Entries for bond issuance; amortization of discount by straight-line method.
OBJ. 5

On the first day of its fiscal year, Swindel Inc. issued $5,000,000 of 10-year, 8% bonds, interest payable semiannually, at an effective interest rate of 10%, receiving cash of $4,376,940.

(a) Present the journal entries to record the following:
  (1) Sale of the bonds.
  (2) First semiannual interest payment. (Amortization of discount is to be recorded annually.)
  (3) Second semiannual interest payment.
  (4) Amortization of discount at the end of the first year, using the straight-line method.
(b) Determine the amount of the bond interest expense for the first year.

Ex. 12–32.
Amortization of discount by interest method.
OBJ. 5

Using the data presented in Ex. 12–31, compute the following:

(a) Amortization of discount at the end of the first year, using the interest method. (Round to the nearest dollar.)
(b) The amount of the bond interest expense for the first year.

Ex. 12–33.
Computation of bond proceeds, entries for bond issuance, and amortization of premium by straight-line method.
OBJ. 5

On May 1, 1992, Pugh Corporation issued $1,000,000 of 10-year, 14% bonds at an effective interest rate of 13%. Interest is payable semiannually on May 1 and November 1. Present the journal entries to record the following:

(a) Sale of bonds on May 1, 1992. (Use the tables of present values appearing in the chapter to determine the bond proceeds.)
(b) First interest payment on November 1, 1992, including amortization of bond premium for 6 months, using the straight-line method. (Round to the nearest dollar.)

Ex. 12–34.
Computation of bond proceeds, amortization of premium by interest method, and interest expense.
OBJ. 5

On the first day of its fiscal year, Primm Co. issued $4,000,000 of 10-year, 13% bonds at an effective interest rate of 12%, with interest payable semiannually. Compute the following, presenting figures used in your computations and rounding to the nearest dollar:

(a) The amount of cash proceeds from the sale of the bonds. (Use the tables of present values appearing in the chapter.)
(b) The amount of premium to be amortized for the first semiannual interest payment period, using the interest method.

(c) The amount of premium to be amortized for the second semiannual interest payment period, using the interest method.
(d) The amount of the bond interest expense for the first year.

Ex. 12–35.
Computation of amortization of bond discount by both straight-line and interest methods.
OBJ. 5

On July 1 of the current fiscal year, Diaz Company purchased $750,000 of 10-year, 8% bonds as a long-term investment directly from the issuing company for $656,541. The effective rate of interest is 10%, and the interest is payable semiannually. Compute the amount of discount to be amortized for the first semiannual interest payment period using (a) the straight-line method and (b) the interest method.

Ex. 12–36.
Determination of sinking fund deposit and entry.
OBJ. 6

C. C. Cutler Co. issued $10,000,000 of 20-year bonds on January 1 of the current year. The bond indenture requires that equal deposits be made in a bond sinking fund at the end of each of the 20 years. The fund is expected to be invested in securities that will yield 12% per year compounded annually.

(a) Determine the amount of each of the 20 deposits to be made in the bond sinking fund.
(b) Prepare the entry to record the first deposit made in the sinking fund.

Ex. 12–37.
Entries for bond sinking fund and appropriation of retained earnings.
OBJ. 6, 7

Mixon Corporation issued $10,000,000 of 10-year bonds on the first day of the fiscal year. The bond indenture provides that a sinking fund be accumulated, assuming 10% interest, by 10 annual deposits of $627,455, beginning at the end of the first year.

Present the journal entries to record the following selected transactions related to the bond issue:

(a) The required amount is deposited in the sinking fund.
(b) Investments in securities from the first sinking fund deposit total $600,000.
(c) Appropriated $1,000,000 of retained earnings for bonded indebtedness.
(d) The sinking fund earned $61,500 during the year following the first deposit (summarizing entry).
(e) The bonds are paid at maturity, and excess cash of $43,800 in the fund is transferred to the cash account.
(f) Transferred the appropriation for bonded indebtedness balance of $10,000,000 back to retained earnings.

Ex. 12–38.
Entries for issuance and calling of bonds.
OBJ. 5, 8

T. R. Bethel Inc. issued $10,000,000 of 20-year, 11% callable bonds on April 1, 1992, with interest payable on April 1 and October 1. The fiscal year of the company is the calendar year. Present the journal entries to record the following selected transactions:

1992
Apr. 1. Issued the bonds for cash at their face amount.
Oct. 1. Paid the interest on the bonds.

1997
Oct. 1. Called the bond issue at 101 1/2, the rate provided in the bond indenture. (Omit entry for payment of interest.)

Ex. 12–39.
Entries for purchase and sale of investment in bonds.
OBJ. 10

Present journal entries to record the following selected transactions of Lauren Corporation:

(a) Purchased for cash $500,000 of Varon Co. 12% bonds at 103 plus accrued interest of $10,000.
(b) Received first semiannual interest.
(c) Amortized $750 on the bond investment at the end of the first year.
(d) Sold the bonds at 101 plus accrued interest of $5,000. The bonds were carried at $511,250 at the time of the sale.

PROBLEMS

Pb. 12–40.
Effect of financing on earnings per share.
OBJ. 1

Three different plans for financing a $10,000,000 corporation are under consideration by its organizers. Under each of the following plans, the securities will be issued at their par or face amount and the income tax rate is estimated at 40% of income:

	Plan 1	Plan 2	Plan 3
14% bonds			$ 5,000,000
Preferred 8% stock, $100 par		$ 5,000,000	2,500,000
Common stock, $25 par	$10,000,000	5,000,000	2,500,000
Total	$10,000,000	$10,000,000	$10,000,000

Instructions:

(1) Determine for each plan the earnings per share of common stock, assuming that the income before bond interest and income tax is $1,500,000.
(2) Determine for each plan the earnings per share of common stock, assuming that the income before bond interest and income tax is $1,100,000.
(3) What are the advantages and disadvantages of each plan?

Pb. 12–41.
Entries for bonds payable transactions.
OBJ. 5

On July 1, 1992, Jones Corporation issued $10,000,000 of 10-year, 11% bonds at an effective interest rate of 10%. Interest on the bonds is payable semiannually on December 31 and June 30. The fiscal year of the company is the calendar year.

Instructions:

(1) Present the journal entry to record the amount of the cash proceeds from the sale of the bonds. Use the tables of present values appearing in this chapter to compute the cash proceeds, rounding to the nearest dollar.
(2) Present the journal entries to record the following:
   (a) The first semiannual interest payment on December 31, 1992, including the amortization of the bond premium, using the interest method.
   (b) The interest payment on June 30, 1993, including the amortization of the bond premium, using the interest method.
(3) Present the entries for Instruction (2), using the straight-line method of amortization.
(4) Determine the total interest expense for 1992 under (a) the interest method of premium amortization and (b) the straight-line method of premium amortization. (c) Will the annual interest expense using the interest method of premium amortization always be greater than the annual interest expense using the straight-line method of premium amortization?

Pb. 12–42.
Entries for bond and sinking fund transactions.
OBJ. 5, 6

The following transactions relate to the issuance of $6,000,000 of 10-year, 9% bonds dated January 1, 1982, and the accumulations in a sinking fund to redeem the bonds at maturity. Interest on the bonds is payable on June 30 and December 31.

1982
Jan. 2. Sold the bond issue at 100.
June 30. Paid semiannual interest on bonds.
Dec. 31. Paid semiannual interest on bonds and deposited $435,000 in a bond sinking fund.

1983
Jan. 7. Purchased $367,500 of investments with bond sinking fund cash.
June 30. Paid semiannual interest on bonds.
Nov. 30. Received $38,725 income on investments.
Dec. 31. Paid semiannual interest on bonds.

(Assume that all intervening transactions have been properly recorded.)

1992
Jan. 2. Sold all investments in the bond sinking fund for $5,957,400. The sinking fund investments had a carrying value of $5,999,800.

Jan. 11. Paid the bonds at maturity from the sinking fund cash and the regular cash account. The cash available in the sinking fund at this date was $5,960,000.

Instructions:

Prepare journal entries to record the foregoing transactions.

Pb. 12–43.
Entries for bond and sinking fund transactions, including appropriation of retained earnings.
OBJ. 5, 6, 7

During 1992 and 1993, Jordan Company completed the following transactions relating to its $30,000,000 issue of 20-year, 14% bonds dated May 1, 1992. Interest is payable on May 1 and November 1. The corporation's fiscal year is the calendar year.

1992
May 1. Sold the bond issue for $31,200,000 cash.
Nov. 1. Paid the semiannual interest on the bonds.
Dec. 31. Recorded the adjusting entry for interest payable.
31. Recorded bond premium amortization of $40,000, which was determined by using the straight-line method.
31. Deposited $350,000 cash in a bond sinking fund.
31. Appropriated $1,000,000 of retained earnings for bonded indebtedness.
31. Closed the interest expense account.

1993
Jan. 15. Purchased various securities with sinking fund cash, cost $330,000.
May 1. Paid the semiannual interest on the bonds.
Nov. 1. Paid the semiannual interest on the bonds.
Dec. 18. Recorded the receipt of $22,300 of income on sinking fund securities, depositing the cash in the sinking fund.
31. Recorded the adjusting entry for interest payable.
31. Recorded bond premium amortization of $60,000, which was determined by using the straight-line method.
31. Deposited $525,000 cash in the sinking fund.
31. Appropriated $1,500,000 of retained earnings for bonded indebtedness.
31. Closed the interest expense account.

Instructions:

(1) Prepare journal entries to record the foregoing transactions.
(2) Prepare a columnar table, using the following headings, and list the information for each of the two years.

		Account Balances at End of Year					
					Sinking Fund		
Year	Bond Interest Expense for Year	Sinking Fund Income for Year	Bonds Payable	Premium on Bonds	Cash	Investments	Appropriation for Bonded Indebtedness

Pb. 12–44.
Entries for bonds payable transactions.
OBJ. 5, 8

The following transactions were completed by Weis Industries Inc., whose fiscal year is the calendar year:

1992
July 1. Issued $5,000,000 of 10-year, 8% callable bonds dated July 1, 1992, at an effective rate of 10%, receiving cash of $4,376,940. Interest is payable semiannually on December 31 and June 30.

Dec. 31. Paid the semiannual interest on the bonds.
31. Recorded bond discount amortization of $18,847, which was determined by using the interest method.
31. Closed the interest expense account.

1993
June 30. Paid the semiannual interest on the bonds.
Dec. 31. Paid the semiannual interest on the bonds.
31. Recorded bond discount amortization of $40,568, which was determined by using the interest method.
31. Closed the interest expense account.

2000
June 30. Recorded the redemption of the bonds, which were called at 101. The balance in the bond discount account is $177,184 after the payment of interest and amortization of discount have been recorded. (Record the redemption only.)

Instructions:

(1) Prepare journal entries to record the foregoing transactions.
(2) Indicate the amount of the interest expense in (a) 1992 and (b) 1993.
(3) Determine the effective interest rate by dividing the interest expense for 1992 by the bond carrying amount at the time of issuance and converting the result to an annual rate.
(4) Determine the carrying amount of the bonds as of December 31, 1993.

Pb. 12–45.
Entries for bond investments.
OBJ. 10

The following selected transactions relate to certain securities acquired as a long-term investment by Gresham Company, whose fiscal year ends on December 31:

1992
Sep. 1. Purchased $300,000 of Clarke Company 10-year, 14% bonds dated July 1, 1992, directly from the issuing company for $305,900 plus accrued interest of $7,000.
Dec. 31. Received the semiannual interest on the Clarke Company bonds.
31. Recorded bond premium amortization of $200 on the Clarke Company bonds. The amortization amount was determined by using the straight-line method.

(Assume that all intervening transactions and adjustments have been recorded properly, and that the number of bonds owned has not changed from December 31, 1992, to December 31, 1997.)

1998
June 30. Received the semiannual interest on the Clarke Company bonds.
July 31. Sold one half of the Clarke Company bonds at 102 plus accrued interest. The broker deducted $700 for commission, etc., remitting the balance. Before the sale was recorded, $175 of premium on one half of the bonds was amortized, reducing the carrying amount of those bonds to $151,175.
Dec. 31. Received the semiannual interest on the Clarke Company bonds.
31. Recorded bond premium amortization of $300 on the Clarke Company bonds.

Instructions:

Prepare journal entries to record the foregoing transactions.

ALTERNATE PROBLEMS

Pb. 12–40A.
Effect of financing on earnings per share.
OBJ. 1

Three different plans for financing a $10,000,000 corporation are under consideration by its organizers. Under each of the following plans, the securities will be issued at their par or face amount and the income tax rate is estimated at 40% of income:

	Plan 1	Plan 2	Plan 3
12% bonds			$ 5,000,000
Preferred 8% stock, $100 par......		$ 5,000,000	2,500,000
Common stock, $20 par............	$10,000,000	5,000,000	2,500,000
Total	$10,000,000	$10,000,000	$10,000,000

Instructions:

(1) Determine for each plan the earnings per share of common stock, assuming that the income before bond interest and income tax is $1,500,000.
(2) Determine for each plan the earnings per share of common stock, assuming that the income before bond interest and income tax is $1,100,000.
(3) What are the advantages and disadvantages of each plan?

Pb. 12–41A.
Entries for bonds payable transactions.
OBJ. 5

On July 1, 1992, Raven Corporation issued $15,000,000 of 10-year, 10% bonds at an effective interest rate of 12%. Interest on the bonds is payable semiannually on December 31 and June 30. The fiscal year of the company is the calendar year.

Instructions:

(1) Present the journal entry to record the amount of the cash proceeds from the sale of the bonds. Use the tables of present values appearing in this chapter to compute the cash proceeds, rounding to the nearest dollar.
(2) Present the journal entries to record the following selected transactions for 1992 and 1993:
   (a) The entry for the payment of interest and the amortization of the bond discount on December 31, 1992, using the interest method.
   (b) The semiannual interest payment on June 30, 1993, including the amortization of the bond discount, using the interest method.
(3) Present the entries for Instruction (2), using the straight-line method of discount amortization.
(4) What is the total interest expense for 1992 for (a) the interest method of discount amortization and (b) the straight-line method of discount amortization? (c) Will the annual interest expense using the interest method of discount amortization always be less than the annual interest expense using the straight-line method of discount amortization?

Pb. 12–42A.
Entries for bond and sinking fund transactions.
OBJ. 5, 6

The following transactions relate to the issuance of $1,000,000 of 10-year, 10% bonds dated January 1, 1983, and the accumulations in a sinking fund to redeem the bonds at maturity. Interest on the bonds is payable on June 30 and December 31.

1983
Jan. 2. Sold the bond issue at 100.
June 30. Paid semiannual interest on bonds.
Dec. 31. Paid semiannual interest on bonds and deposited $58,000 in a bond sinking fund.

1984
Jan. 13. Purchased $56,100 of investments with bond sinking fund cash.
June 30. Paid semiannual interest on bonds.
Oct. 22. Received $4,125 income on investments.
Dec. 31. Paid semiannual interest on bonds.

(Assume that all intervening transactions have been recorded properly.)

1993
Jan. 2. Sold all investments in the bond sinking fund for $980,500. The sinking fund investments had a book carrying value of $999,200.
4. Paid the bonds at maturity from the sinking fund cash and the regular cash account. The cash available in the sinking fund at this date was $991,900.

Instructions:

Prepare entries to record the foregoing transactions.

Pb. 12–43A.
Entries for bond and sinking fund transactions, including appropriation of retained earnings.
OBJ. 5, 6, 7

During 1992 and 1993, Bridges Company completed the following transactions relating to its $12,000,000 issue of 25-year, 10% bonds dated September 1, 1992. Interest is payable on September 1 and March 1. The corporation's fiscal year is the calendar year.

1992
Sept. 1. Sold the bond issue for $11,760,000.
Dec. 31. Recorded the adjusting entry for interest payable.
31. Recorded bond discount amortization of $3,200, which was determined by using the straight-line method.
31. Deposited $41,700 cash in a bond sinking fund.
31. Appropriated $160,000 of retained earnings for bonded indebtedness.
31. Closed the interest expense account.

1993
Jan. 15. Purchased various securities with sinking fund cash, cost $40,000.
Mar. 1. Paid the semiannual interest on the bonds.
Sept. 1. Paid the semiannual interest on the bonds.
Dec. 15. Recorded the receipt of $3,120 of income on sinking fund securities, depositing the cash in the sinking fund.
31. Recorded the adjusting entry for interest payable.
31. Recorded bond discount amortization of $9,600, which was determined by using the straight-line method.
31. Deposited $125,000 cash in the sinking fund.
31. Appropriated $480,000 of retained earnings for bonded indebtedness.
31. Closed the interest expense account.

Instructions:

(1) Prepare journal entries to record the foregoing transactions.
(2) Prepare a columnar table, using the following headings, and list the information for each of the two years.

			Account Balances at End of Year				
					Sinking Fund		
Year	Bond Interest Expense for Year	Sinking Fund Income for Year	Bonds Payable	Discount on Bonds	Cash	Investments	Appropriation for Bonded Indebtedness

Pb. 12–44A.
Entries for bonds payable transactions.
OBJ. 5, 8

The following transactions were completed by Skeean Co., whose fiscal year is the calendar year:

1992
July 1. Issued $20,000,000 of 10-year, 14% callable bonds dated July 1, 1992, at an effective rate of 12%, receiving cash of $22,293,860. Interest is payable semiannually on December 31 and June 30.

Dec. 31. Paid the semiannual interest on the bonds.
31. Recorded bond premium amortization of $62,368, which was determined using the interest method.
31. Closed the interest expense account.

1993
June 30. Paid the semiannual interest on the bonds.
Dec. 31. Paid the semiannual interest on the bonds.
31. Recorded bond premium amortization of $136,187, which was determined by using the interest method.
31. Closed the interest expense account.

1998
July. 1. Recorded the redemption of the bonds, which were called at 106. The balance in the bond premium account is $1,360,103 after the payment of interest and amortization of premium have been recorded. (Record the redemption only.)

Instructions:

(1) Prepare journal entries to record the foregoing transactions.
(2) Indicate the amount of the interest expense in (a) 1992 and (b) 1993.
(3) Determine the effective interest rate by dividing the interest expense for 1992 by the bond carrying amount at the time of issuance and converting the result to an annual rate.
(4) Determine the carrying amount of the bonds as of December 31, 1993.

Pb. 12–45A.
Entries for bond investments.
OBJ. 10

The following selected transactions relate to certain securities acquired by Armour Company, whose fiscal year ends on December 31:

1992
Sep. 1. Purchased $500,000 of Sewell Company 20-year, 9% bonds dated July 1, 1992, directly from the issuing company for $476,200 plus $7,500 accrued interest.
Dec. 31. Received the semiannual interest on the Sewell Company bonds.
31. Recorded bond discount amortization of $400 on the Sewell Company bonds. The amortization amount was determined by using the straight-line method.

(Assume that all intervening transactions and adjustments have been recorded properly, and that the number of bonds owned has not changed from December 31, 1992, to December 31, 1996.)

1997
June 30. Received the semiannual interest on the Sewell Company bonds.
July 31. Sold one half of the Sewell Company bonds at 95 plus accrued interest. The broker deducted $750 for commission, etc., remitting the balance. Before the sale was recorded, $350 of discount on one half of the bonds was amortized, increasing the carrying amount of those bonds to $241,050.
Dec. 31. Received the semiannual interest on the Sewell Company bonds.
31. Recorded bond discount amortization of $600 on the Sewell Company bonds.

Instructions:

Prepare journal entries to record the foregoing transactions.

MINI-CASE 12

You hold a 20% common stock interest in the family-owned business, a soft drink bottling distributorship. Your father, who is the manager, has proposed an expansion of plant facilities at an expected cost of $2,000,000. Two alternative plans have been suggested as methods of financing the expansion. Each plan is briefly described as follows:

Plan 1. Issue an additional 25,000 shares of $25 par common stock at $40 per share, and $1,000,000 of 20-year, 13% bonds at face amount.

Plan 2. Issue $2,000,000 of 20-year, 13% bonds at face amount.

The balance sheet as of the end of the previous fiscal year is as follows:

CU Bottling Co.
Balance Sheet
December 31, 19--

Assets	
Current assets	$ 1,800,000
Plant assets	8,700,000
Total assets	$10,500,000
Liabilities and Stockholders' Equity	
Current liabilities	$ 2,700,000
Common stock, $25	1,875,000
Excess of issue price over par	225,000
Retained earnings	5,700,000
Total liabilities and stockholders' equity	$10,500,000

Net income has remained relatively constant over the past several years. The expansion program is expected to increase yearly income before bond interest and income tax from $800,000 to $1,200,000.

Your father has asked you, as the company treasurer, to prepare an analysis of each financing plan.

Instructions:

(1) Prepare a tabulation indicating the expected earnings per share on the common stock under each plan. Assume an income tax rate of 40%.
(2) List factors other than earnings per share that should be considered in evaluating the two plans.
(3) Which plan offers the greater benefit to the present stockholders? Give reasons for your opinion.

COMPREHENSIVE PROBLEM 4

Selected transactions completed by Sharp Inc. during the fiscal year ending March 31, 1992, were as follows:

(a) Issued 10,000 shares of $25 par common stock at $45, receiving cash.
(b) Issued 5,000 shares of $100 par preferred 8% stock at $120, receiving cash.

(c) Recorded $58,900 additional federal income tax allocable to net income for the fiscal year ending March 31, 1992. Of this amount, $55,900 is a current liability and $3,000 is deferred.
(d) Declared a dividend of $.25 per share on common stock and $2 per share on preferred stock. On the date of record, 100,000 shares of common stock were outstanding, no treasury shares were held, and 15,000 shares of preferred stock were outstanding.
(e) Paid the cash dividends.
(f) Redeemed $500,000 of 8-year, 16% bonds at 97 1/2. The balance in the bond discount account is $6,400 after the payment of interest and amortization of discount have been recorded. (Record only the redemption of the bonds payable.)
(g) Transferred $500,000 of the appropriation for bonded indebtedness back to retained earnings for the bonds redeemed in (f).
(h) Purchased 2,000 shares of treasury common stock at $40 per share.
(i) Issued $1,000,000 of 10-year, 12% bonds at an effective interest rate of 10%, with interest payable semiannually.
(j) Declared 5% stock dividend on common stock and a $2 cash dividend per share on preferred stock. On the date of declaration, the market value of the common stock was $41 per share. On the date of record, 100,000 shares of common stock were outstanding, 2,000 shares of treasury common stock were held, and 15,000 shares of preferred stock were outstanding.
(k) Issued the stock certificates for the stock dividends declared in (j) and paid the cash dividends to the preferred stockholders.
(l) Sold, at $42 per share, 1,000 shares of treasury common stock purchased in (h).
(m) Purchased $50,000 of Wilson Inc. 10-year, 15% bonds directly from the issuing company for $48,500 plus accrued interest of $1,875.
(n) Recorded the payment of semiannual interest on the bonds issued in (i) and the amortization of the premium for six months. The amortization was determined using the interest method. (Round the amortization to the nearest dollar.)
(o) Deposited $15,000 in a bond sinking fund.
(p) Appropriated $1,000,000 of retained earnings for bonded indebtedness.
(q) Accrued interest for four months on the Wilson Inc. bonds purchased in (m). Also recorded amortization of $50.

Instructions:

(1) Record the selected transactions.
(2) After all of the transactions for the year ended March 31, 1992 had been posted (including the transactions recorded in (1) and all adjusting entries), the following data were selected from the records of Sharp Inc.:

Income statement data:

Advertising expense	$ 90,000
Delivery expense	12,000
Depreciation expense—office equipment	12,600
Depreciation expense—store equipment	45,000
Gain on redemption of bonds	6,100
Income tax:	
Applicable to continuing operations	308,975
Applicable to loss from disposal of a segment of the business	21,100
Applicable to gain from redemption of bonds	1,150
Interest expense	68,500
Interest income	675
Loss from disposal of a segment of the business	80,500
Merchandise inventory (April 1, 1991)	380,000

Merchandise inventory (March 31, 1992)	$ 430,000
Miscellaneous administrative expenses	1,600
Miscellaneous selling expenses	6,300
Office rent expense	25,000
Office salaries expense	85,000
Office supplies expense	5,800
Purchases	4,050,000
Sales	5,400,000
Sales commissions	125,000
Sales salaries expense	150,000
Store supplies expense	9,500

Retained earnings and balance sheet data:

Accounts payable	$ 151,000
Accounts receivable	280,500
Accumulated depreciation — office equipment	835,250
Accumulated depreciation — store equipment	2,214,750
Allowance for doubtful accounts	11,500
Bond sinking fund cash	15,000
Bonds payable, 12%, due 2001	1,000,000
Cash	120,000
Common stock, $25 par (400,000 shares authorized; 105,000 shares issued)	2,625,000
Deferred income tax payable (current portion, $3,200)	22,600
Dividends:	
Cash dividends for common stock	75,000
Cash dividends for preferred stock	100,000
Stock dividends for common stock	200,900
Dividends payable	25,000
Income tax payable	55,900
Interest receivable	2,500
Investment in Wilson Inc. bonds (long-term)	48,550
Marketable securities at cost, held as a short-term investment (market value, $88,300)	75,000
Merchandise inventory (March 31, 1992), at lower of cost (fifo) or market	430,000
Office equipment	2,410,100
Organization costs	60,000
Paid-in capital from sale of treasury stock	2,000
Paid-in capital in excess of par—common stock	450,000
Paid-in capital in excess of par—preferred stock	240,000
Preferred 8% stock, $100 par (30,000 shares authorized; 15,000 shares issued)	1,500,000
Premium on bonds payable	120,000
Prepaid expenses	15,900
Retained earnings:	
Appropriated for bonded indebtedness (April 1, 1991)	500,000
Appropriated for bonded indebtedness (March 31, 1992)	1,000,000
Appropriated for treasury stock (April 1, 1991)	—
Appropriated for treasury stock (March 31, 1992)	40,000
Unappropriated, April 1, 1991	2,448,450
Store equipment	8,603,950
Treasury stock (1,000 shares of common stock at cost of $40 per share)	40,000

(a) Prepare a multiple-step income statement for the year ended March 31, 1992, concluding with earnings per share. In computing earnings per share, assume that the average number of common shares outstanding was 100,000 and preferred dividends were $100,000.

(b) Prepare a retained earnings statement for the year ended March 31, 1992.

(c) Prepare a balance sheet in report form as of March 31, 1992.

ANSWERS TO SELF-EXAMINATION QUESTIONS

1. B Since the contract rate on the bonds is higher than the prevailing market rate, a rational investor would be willing to pay more than the face amount, or a premium (answer B), for the bonds. If the contract rate and the market rate were equal, the bonds could be expected to sell at their face amount (answer A). Likewise, if the market rate is higher than the contract rate, the bonds would sell at a price below their face amount (answer D) or at a discount (answer C).
2. A The bond carrying amount, sometimes called the book value, is the face amount plus unamortized premium or less unamortized discount. For this question, the carrying amount is $500,000 less $40,000, or $460,000 (answer A).
3. B Although the sinking fund may consist of cash as well as securities, the fund is listed on the balance sheet as an investment (answer B) because it is to be used to pay the long-term liability at maturity.
4. B The amount debited to the investment account is the cost of the bonds, which includes the amount paid to the seller for the bonds (101% × $100,000) plus broker's commissions ($50), or $101,050 (answer B). The $2,000 of accrued interest that is paid to the seller should be debited to Interest Income, since it is an offset against the amount that will be received as interest at the next interest date.
5. C The balance of Discount on Bonds Payable is usually reported as a deduction from Bonds Payable in the Long-Term Liabilities section (answer C) of the balance sheet. Likewise, a balance in a premium on bonds payable account would usually be reported as an addition to Bonds Payable in the Long-Term Liabilities section of the balance sheet.

CHAPTER 13

CHAPTER OBJECTIVES

1 Describe investments in stocks.

2 Describe and illustrate the accounting for long-term investments.

3 Describe alternative methods of combining businesses.

4 Describe the accounting for parent-subsidiary affiliations.

5 Describe and illustrate the basic principles of consolidation of financial statements.

6 Illustrate a statement of stockholders' equity and a consolidated balance sheet.

7 Describe and illustrate the accounting for international operations.

INVESTMENTS IN STOCKS; CONSOLIDATIONS; INTERNATIONAL OPERATIONS

In the preceding chapter, the principles of accounting for long-term investments in bonds were discussed. In this chapter, the principles of accounting for long-term investments in stocks will be presented. Accounting for the combining of operations of two corporations and the expansion of operations into international markets will also be discussed.

INVESTMENTS IN STOCKS

OBJECTIVE 1
Describe investments in stocks.

A business may make long-term investments in **equity securities** (preferred and common shares), simply because it has cash that it does not need for normal operations. A corporation may also purchase stocks as a means of establishing or maintaining business relations with the issuing company. In some cases, a corporation may acquire all or a large part of the voting stock of another corporation in order to control its activities. Similarly, a corporation may organize a new corporation for the purpose of marketing a new product or for some other business reason, receiving stock in exchange for the assets transferred to the new corporation.

Investments in stocks may be purchased directly from the issuing corporation or from other investors. Both preferred and common stocks may be *listed* on an organized stock exchange, or they may be *unlisted*, in which case they are said to be bought or sold *over the counter.* The services of a broker are usually used in buying and selling both listed and unlisted securities.

The record of transactions on the stock exchanges is reported daily by the financial press. For each stock traded, this record usually includes the high and low price for the past year, the current annual dividend, the volume of sales for the day, and the high, low, and closing price for the day. Prices for stocks are quoted in terms of fractional dollars, with 1/8 of a dollar being the usual minimum fraction, although some low-priced stocks are sold in lower fractions of a dollar, such as 1/16 or 1/32. Thus, a price of 40 3/8 per share means $40.375; a price of 40 1/2 means $40.50.

In the following discussion, attention will be given to the principles underlying the accounting for investments in stocks that are not intended as a ready source of cash in the normal operations of the business. Such investments are identified as long-term investments and are reported in the balance sheet under the caption "Investments." The principles underlying the accounting for investments in stocks that are classified as temporary investments or marketable securities were discussed in Chapter 6.

MORE AMERICANS THAN EVER BEFORE OWN STOCK

About 47 million Americans own stock, more than ever before, but many are participants through stock mutual funds, according to a New York Stock Exchange survey.

The survey said the 47 million investors tallied as of mid-1985 were an 11 percent increase over the 42 million found in the exchange's last survey in mid-1983.

That means that one in five Americans is now a stock investor, as opposed to one of every six two years ago.

Women account for 57 percent of the new investors, the survey said; typically, she is married, employed in a technical or professional job, has an annual household income of $35,000 and a portfolio of $2,200.

Source: "More Americans Than Ever Before Own Stock," *Champaign-Urbana News Gazette,* December 5, 1985. © Associated Press.

ACCOUNTING FOR LONG-TERM INVESTMENTS IN STOCK

OBJECTIVE 2
Describe and illustrate the accounting for long-term investments.

There are two methods of accounting for long-term investments in stock: (1) the **cost method** and (2) the **equity method.** The method used depends upon whether the investor owns enough of the voting stock of the investee (company whose stock is owned by the investor) to have a significant influence over its operating and financing policies. If the investor does not have a significant influence, the cost method (with the lower of cost or market rule) must be used. If the investor can exercise a significant influence in a long-term investment situation, the equity method must be used. Evidence of such influence includes, but is not limited to, representation on the board of directors, material intercompany transactions, and interchange of managerial personnel. Guidelines to be applied in making the election are as follows:

> *In order to achieve a reasonable degree of uniformity in application, the Board concludes that an investment (direct or indirect) of 20% or more of the voting stock of an investee should lead to a presumption that in the absence of evidence to the contrary an investor has the ability to exercise significant influence over an investee. Conversely, an investment of less than 20% of the voting stock of an investee should lead to a presumption that an investor does not have the ability to exercise significant influence unless such ability can be demonstrated.*[1]

Cost Method

The cost of stocks purchased includes not only the amount paid to the seller but also other costs related to the purchase, such as the broker's commission and postage charges for delivery. When stocks are purchased between dividend dates, there is no separate charge for the pro rata amount of the dividend. Dividends do not accrue from day to day, since they become an obligation of the issuing corporation only when they are declared by the

[1]*Opinions of the Accounting Principles Board, No. 18,* "The Equity Method of Accounting for Investments in Common Stock" (New York: American Institute of Certified Public Accountants, 1971), par. 17.

board of directors. The prices of stocks may be affected by the anticipated dividend as the usual declaration date approaches, but this anticipated dividend is only one of many factors that influence stock prices.

The total cost of stocks purchased should be debited to an investment account. When the cost method is used, cash dividends on capital stock held as an investment may be recorded as an increase in the appropriate income and asset accounts. To illustrate, assume that Makowski Corporation purchases 100 shares of Compton Corporation common stock at 55 plus a brokerage fee of $42. At the end of the year, Compton Corporation declares a $2 per share cash dividend. Entries in the accounts of Makowski Corporation, the investor, are as follows:

		Debit	Credit
Record purchase of Compton Corp. common stock	Investment in Compton Corp. Stock	5,542	
	Cash		5,542
Record share of cash dividends paid by Compton Corp.	Cash	200	
	Dividend Income		200

In the illustration, the dividend was recorded when the cash was received. An alternative would be to record the cash dividend when it is declared by the investee corporation. If this alternative had been used, Makowski Corporation would have debited Dividends Receivable and credited Dividend Income when the dividend was declared. When the dividend was paid, Makowski Corporation would have debited Cash and credited the receivable.

A dividend in the form of additional shares of stock is usually not income, and therefore no entry is needed beyond a notation as to the additional number of shares acquired. The receipt of a stock dividend does, however, affect the carrying amount of each share of stock. Thus, if a 5-share common stock dividend is received on 100 shares of common stock with a current carrying amount of $4,200 ($42 per share), the unit carrying amount of the 105 shares becomes $40 per share ($4,200 ÷ 105).

Long-term investments in stocks of a company over which the investor does not exercise significant influence are subject to the lower of cost or market rule. In applying the rule, the carrying amount of a long-term investment in a portfolio of equity securities is the lower of the *total* cost or *total* market price of the portfolio at the date of the balance sheet. Any market value changes that are recognized are not included in net income, but are reported as a separate item in the stockholders' equity section of the balance sheet.[2] If the decline in market value below cost of an individual security as of the balance sheet date is other than temporary, the cost basis of the individual security is written down and the amount of the write-down is accounted for as a realized loss. After the write-down, the carrying amount of the individual security cannot be changed for subsequent recoveries in market value.[3]

Equity Method

When the equity method of accounting is used, a stock purchase is recorded at cost as under the cost method. The features that distinguish the

---

[2]*Statement of Financial Accounting Standards, No. 12,* "Accounting for Certain Marketable Securities" (Stamford: Financial Accounting Standards Board, 1975), par. 11.

[3]*Ibid.*, par. 21.

equity method from the cost method relate to the net income and cash dividends of the investee and are summarized as follows:

1. The investor records its share of the periodic net income of the investee as an increase in the investment account and as revenue of the period. Conversely, the investor's share of the investee's periodic loss is recorded as a decrease in the investment and a loss of the period.
2. The investor records its share of cash or property dividends on the stock as a decrease in the investment account and an increase in the appropriate asset accounts.

To illustrate the foregoing, assume that as of the beginning of the fiscal years of Hally Corporation and Brock Corporation, Hally acquires 40% of the common (voting) stock of Brock for $350,000 in cash, that Brock reports net income of $105,000 for the year, and that Brock declared and paid $45,000 in cash dividends during the year. Entries in the accounts of the investor to record these transactions are as follows:

		Debit	Credit
Record purchase of 40% of Brock Corp. common stock	Investment in Brock Corp. Stock	350,000	
	Cash		350,000
Record 40% of Brock Corp. net income of $105,000	Investment in Brock Corp. Stock	42,000	
	Income of Brock Corp.		42,000
Record 40% of cash dividends of $45,000 paid by Brock Corp.	Cash	18,000	
	Investment in Brock Corp. Stock		18,000

The combined effect of recording 40% of Brock Corporation's income and the dividends received was to increase Cash by $18,000, Investment in Brock Corp. Stock by $24,000, and Income of Brock Corp. by $42,000.

Sale of Long-Term Investments in Stocks

When shares of stock held as a long-term investment are sold, the investment account is credited for the carrying amount of the shares sold and the cash or appropriate receivable account is debited for the proceeds (sales price less commission and other selling costs). Any difference between the proceeds and the carrying amount is recorded as a gain or loss on the sale. To illustrate, assume that an investment in Drey Corporation stock has a carrying amount of $15,700. If the proceeds from the sale of the stock are $17,500, the entry to record the transaction is as follows:

	Debit	Credit
Cash	17,500	
Investment in Drey Corp. Stock		15,700
Gain on Sale of Investments		1,800

BUSINESS COMBINATIONS

OBJECTIVE 3
Describe alternative methods of combining businesses.

The history of business organization in the United States has been characterized by continuous growth in the size of business entities and the combining of separate enterprises to form even larger operating units. Over the past several years, the combining of businesses has increased dramatically both in numbers and dollars. In 1987, for example, more than 3,500 combinations took place, involving the exchange of cash, debt obligations, or capital stock of approximately $170 billion.[4] These combinations were influenced by such objectives as efficiencies of large-scale production, broadening of markets and sales volume, reduction of competition, diversification of product lines, and savings in income taxes.

The combining of businesses that are engaged either in similar types of activity or in totally different kinds of pursuits may be effected (1) through a joining of two or more corporations to form a single unit by merger or by consolidation or (2) through common control of two or more corporations by means of stock ownership that results in a parent-subsidiary affiliation. These methods of combining separate corporations into larger operating units are complex. Therefore, the discussion that follows is intended to be introductory, with major emphasis on the financial statements of business combinations.

Mergers and Consolidations

When one corporation acquires the properties of another corporation and the latter then dissolves, the joining of the two enterprises is called a **merger.** Usually, all of the assets of the acquired company, as well as its liabilities, are taken over by the acquiring company, which continues its operations as a single unit. Payment may be in the form of cash, obligations, or capital stock of the acquiring corporation, or there may be a combination of several kinds of consideration. In any event, the consideration received by the dissolving corporation is distributed to its stockholders in final liquidation.

When two or more corporations transfer their assets and liabilities to a corporation which has been created for purposes of the takeover, the combination is called a **consolidation.** The new corporation usually issues its own securities in exchange for the properties acquired, and the original corporations are dissolved.

There are many legal, financial, managerial, and accounting problems associated with mergers and consolidations. Perhaps the most important matter is the determination of the class and amount of securities to be issued to the owners of the dissolving corporations. In resolving this problem, several factors are considered, including the relative value of the net assets contributed, the relative earning capacities, and the market price of the securities of the respective companies. Bargaining between the parties to the combination may also affect the final outcome.

Parent and Subsidiary Corporations

A common means of achieving a business combination is by one corporation owning a controlling share of the outstanding voting stock of one or more other corporations. When this method is used, none of the participants dissolves. All continue as separate legal entities. The corporation owning all or a majority of the voting stock of another corporation is known as the **parent company.** The corporation that is controlled is known as the **subsidiary company.** Two or more corporations closely related through stock ownership are sometimes called **affiliated** or **associated** companies.

The relationship of a parent and a subsidiary may be established by "purchase" or by a "pooling of interests." When a corporation acquires a controlling share of the voting common stock of another corporation in exchange

---

[4]"Takeovers + Divestitures: Full Speed Ahead," Edward T. O'Toole, *Barron's*, May 23, 1988.

for cash, other assets, issuance of notes or other debt obligations, or by a combination of these items, the transaction is treated as a purchase. It is accounted for by the **purchase method.** When this method of effecting a parent-subsidiary affiliation is used, the stockholders of the acquired company transfer their stock to the parent corporation.

Alternatively, when two corporations become affiliated by means of an exchange of voting common stock of one corporation (the parent) for substantially all (at least 90%) of the voting common stock of the other corporation (the subsidiary), the transaction is termed a pooling of interests. It is accounted for by the **pooling of interests method.** When this method of effecting a parent-subsidiary affiliation is used, the former stockholders of the subsidiary become stockholders of the parent company.

The accounting implications of the two affiliation methods are very different. The method first described is a "sale-purchase" transaction in contrast to the second method, in which there is a "joining of ownership interests" in the two companies.

The Accounting Principles Board established very strict criteria that must be met before the pooling of interests method can be used.[5] As a result, most business combinations are accounted for as a purchase. The 1990 edition of *Accounting Trends & Techniques* reported that of the applicable companies surveyed, 92% of the business combinatins were accounted for by the purchase method and 8% wre accounted for by the pooling of interests method.

ACCOUNTING FOR PARENT-SUBSIDIARY AFFILIATIONS

OBJECTIVE 4
Describe the accounting for parent-subsidiary affiliations.

Although the corporations that make up a parent-subsidiary affiliation may operate as a single economic unit, they continue to maintain separate accounting records and prepare their own periodic financial statements. The parent corporation uses the equity method of accounting for its investment in the stock of a subsidiary.

After the parent-subsidiary relationship has been established, the investment account of the parent is periodically increased by its share of the subsidiary's net income and decreased by its share of dividends received from the subsidiary. At the end of each fiscal year, the parent reports the investment account balance on its own balance sheet as a long-term investment, and its current share of the subsidiary's net income on its own income statement as a separate item.

In addition to the interrelationship through stock ownership, there are usually other intercorporate transactions which have an effect on the financial statements of both the parent and the subsidiary. For example, either may own bonds or other evidences of indebtedness issued by the other and either may purchase or sell goods or services to the other.

Because of the central managerial control factor and the intertwining of relationships, the results of operations and the financial position of a parent company and its subsidiaries usually should be presented as if the group were a single company with one or more branches or divisions. Such statements are likely to be more meaningful to stockholders of the parent company than separate statements for each corporation.

---

[5] *Opinions of the Accounting Principles Board, No. 16,* "Business Combinations" (New York: American Institute of Certified Public Accountants, 1970).

The financial statements resulting from the combining of parent and subsidiary statements are generally called **consolidated statements.** Specifically, such statements may be identified by the addition of "and subsidiary(ies)" to the name of the parent corporation or by modification of the title of the respective statement, as in *consolidated balance sheet* or *consolidated income statement.*[6]

BASIC PRINCIPLES OF CONSOLIDATION OF FINANCIAL STATEMENTS

OBJECTIVE 5
Describe and illustrate the basic principles of consolidation of financial statements.

When the data on the financial statements of the parent corporation and its subsidiaries are combined to form the consolidated statements, special attention should be given to the ties of relationship between the separate corporations. These ties are represented by the intercompany items appearing in their respective ledgers and statements. Examples of such intercompany items include notes receivable and notes payable, accounts receivable and accounts payable, interest receivable and interest payable, sales and purchases (or cost of merchandise sold), and interest expense and interest income. The intercompany items, which are called **reciprocals,** must be eliminated from the statements that are to be consolidated. For example, a note representing a loan by a parent corporation to its subsidiary would appear as a note receivable in the parent's balance sheet and a note payable in the subsidiary's balance sheet. When the two balance sheets are combined, the note receivable and the note payable would be eliminated because the consolidated balance sheet is prepared as if the parent and subsidiary were one operating unit. After the proper eliminations are made, the remaining items on the financial statements of the subsidiary are combined with the like items on the financial statements of the parent.

The intercompany accounts of a parent and its subsidiaries may not be entirely reciprocal in amount. Differences may be caused by the manner in which the parent-subsidiary relationship was created, by the extent of the parent's ownership of the subsidiary, or by the nature of their subsequent intercompany transactions. Such factors must be considered when the financial statements of affiliated corporations are consolidated.

To direct attention to the basic concepts of consolidation, most of the data appearing in financial statements will be omitted from many of the illustrations in the following paragraphs. The term "net assets" will be used as a substitute for the specific assets and liabilities that appear in the balance sheet. Explanations will also be simplified by using the term "book equity" in referring to the monetary amount of the stockholders' equity of the subsidiary acquired by the parent. The illustrative companies will be identified as Parent and Subsidiary.

Purchase Method

When a parent-subsidiary affiliation is effected as a purchase, the parent corporation is deemed to have purchased all or a major part of the subsidiary corporation's net assets. Accordingly, the principles of accounting for a sale-purchase transaction are applied to the consolidation of the parent and the subsidiary.

---

[6] Examples of consolidated statements are presented in Appendix H.

Consolidated Balance Sheet at Date of Acquisition. At the date of acquisition, the assets of the subsidiary should be reported on the consolidated balance sheet at their cost to the parent, as measured by the amount of the consideration given in acquiring the stock. In the subsidiary's ledger, the reciprocal of the investment account at the date of acquisition is the composite of all of the subsidiary's stockholders' equity accounts. Any difference between the cost to the parent and the amounts reported on the subsidiary's balance sheet must be given recognition on the consolidated balance sheet.

Income from an investment in assets does not accrue to an investor until after the assets have been purchased. Therefore, subsidiary company earnings accumulated prior to the date of the parent-subsidiary purchase affiliation must be excluded from the consolidated balance sheet and the income statement. Only those earnings of the subsidiary realized subsequent to the affiliation are includable in the consolidated statements.

Wholly Owned Subsidiary Acquired at a Cost Equal to Book Equity. Assume that Parent creates Subsidiary, transferring to it $120,000 of assets and $20,000 of liabilities, and taking in exchange 10,000 shares of $10 par common stock of Subsidiary. The effect of the transaction on Parent's ledger is to replace the various assets and liabilities (net assets of $100,000) with a single account: Investment in Subsidiary, $100,000. The effect on the balance sheet of Parent, together with the balance sheet of Subsidiary prepared immediately after the transaction, is as follows:

	Assets	Stockholders' Equity
Parent:		
Investment in Subsidiary, 10,000 shares..........	$100,000	
Subsidiary:		
Net assets	$100,000	
Common stock, 10,000 shares, $10 par		$100,000

When the balance sheets of the two corporations are consolidated, the reciprocal accounts Investment in Subsidiary and Common Stock are offset against each other, or *eliminated.* The individual assets (Cash, Equipment, etc.) and the individual liabilities (Accounts Payable, etc.) making up the $100,000 of net assets on the balance sheet of Subsidiary are then added to the corresponding items on the balance sheet of Parent. The consolidated balance sheet is completed by listing Parent's paid-in capital accounts and retained earnings.

Wholly Owned Subsidiary Acquired at a Cost Above Book Equity. Instead of creating a new subsidiary, a corporation may acquire an already established corporation by purchasing its stock. In such cases, the subsidiary stock's total cost to the parent usually differs from the book equity of such stock. To illustrate, assume that Parent acquires for $180,000 all of the outstanding stock of Subsidiary, a going concern, from Subsidiary's stockholders. Assume further that the stockholders' equity of Subsidiary is made up of common stock of $100,000 (10,000 shares, $10 par) and $50,000 of retained earnings. Parent records the investment at its cost of $180,000, regardless of the amount of the book equity of Subsidiary. It should also be noted that the $180,000 paid to Subsidiary's stockholders has no effect on the assets, liabilities, or stockholders' equity of Subsidiary. The situation immediately after the transaction may be presented as follows:

	Assets	Stockholders' Equity
Parent:		
Investment in Subsidiary, 10,000 shares..........	$180,000	
Subsidiary:		
Net assets	$150,000	
Common stock, 10,000 shares, $10 par		$100,000
Retained earnings		50,000

GOODWILL AND THE BALANCE SHEET

Goodwill is usually listed as an intangible asset on the balance sheet. For many companies, as described in the following article from *Business Week,* goodwill is a significant percentage of their net worth. When the goodwill is written off in future years, it can also have a major effect on reported earnings.

When Philip Morris Cos. gobbled up Kraft Inc. for $12.9 billion . . . it acquired a passel of prizes that are household names to nearly every shopper in America: Velveeta cheese and Chiffon margarine, to mention just a few. Wall Street has applauded vigorously, sending Philip Morris stock up more than 50%. But according to accountants, Philip Morris was taken to the cleaners. The fair value of the Kraft assets, say the bean counters, was only $1.3 billion. The difference, a staggering $11.6 billion, or 90% of the purchase price, is a wispy, intangible asset known as goodwill.

. . . Because of the Kraft deal, Philip Morris' goodwill climbed to $15 billion from $4 billion. That's nearly triple its net worth . . . [The table shows that,] for many . . . companies, especially those in consumer products and media, goodwill is becoming an ever larger piece of the balance sheet.

Company	Intangible assets	
	Millions of dollars	Percentage of net worth
VIACOM	$2,468	721%
FRUIT OF THE LOOM	908	352
TELE-COMMUNICATIONS	3,143	261
PHILIP MORRIS	15,071	196
COCA-COLA ENTERPRISES	2,935	188
BAXTER INTERNATIONAL	2,705	87
GANNETT	1,526	85
DOW JONES	964	83
PEPSICO	2,582	82
SHEARSON LEHMAN HUTTON	1,758	76
CAPITAL CITIES/ABC	2,217	73
EASTMAN KODAK	4,610	68
McGRAW-HILL	507	55
GENERAL ELECTRIC	8,552	46
WASTE MANAGEMENT	838	38
CHRYSLER	2,688	35
AMERICAN HOME PRODUCTS	643	22
XEROX	1,089	20
GENERAL MOTORS	5,392	15
IBM	717	2

DATA STANDARD & POOR'S COMPUSTAT SERVICES INC.

. . . All that goodwill is bad news for reported earnings. U.S. corporations must "amortize" or write it off—without the benefit of a tax deduction.

No one's advocating doing away with goodwill entirely . . . Kraft spent decades building up its food products, and consumer loyalty to the Kraft label is a valuable asset.

But will the value of the Kraft name decline to zero in 40 years? That's how Philip Morris has to treat it, deducting $290 million a year from earnings—about $1.25 a share. While assets such as machines deteriorate visibly, it's not so easy to pinpoint when an intangible is losing value.

The goodwill rules also have a vastly different impact on different industries. In capital-intensive businesses, the bulk of the purchase price can be attributed to physical assets. Goodwill is not a major factor and the write-off does not chew up earnings.

But in consumer products and media, the bulk of the purchase price is goodwill . . .

Source: Jeffrey M. Laderman, Leah J. Nathans, Mark Maremont, and Ted Holden, "Goodwill is Making A Lot of People Angry," *Business Week* (July 31, 1989), pp. 73–74.

It is readily apparent that the reciprocal items on the separate balance sheets differ by $30,000. If the reciprocals were eliminated, as in the preceding illustration, and were replaced solely by Subsidiary's net assets of $150,000, the consolidated balance sheet would be out of balance.

The treatment of the $30,000 difference depends upon the reason that Parent paid more than book equity for Subsidiary's stock. When the amount paid above book equity is due to an excess of fair market value over book value of Subsidiary's assets, the values of the appropriate assets should be revised upward by $30,000. For example, if land that Subsidiary had acquired several years previously at a cost of $50,000 (book value) has a current fair market value of $80,000, the book amount should be increased from $50,000 to $80,000 when the asset is reported on the consolidated balance sheet. When Parent has paid more for Subsidiary's stock because Subsidiary has prospects for high future earnings, the $30,000 should be reported on the consolidated balance sheet under a description such as "Goodwill" or "Excess of fair cost of business acquired over related net assets."

When the amount paid above book equity is due to both an excess of fair market value over book value of assets and high future earnings prospects, the excess of cost over book equity should be allocated accordingly.[7] To illustrate, assume that the $30,000 difference in the illustration is due to a $20,000 excess of fair market value over book value of Subsidiary's land and Subsidiary prospects for high future earnings. The book amount of the land, which had cost $50,000, would be increased to $70,000, and goodwill of $10,000 would be reported on the consolidated balance sheet.

Wholly Owned Subsidiary Acquired at a Cost Below Book Equity. All of the stock of a corporation may be acquired from its stockholders at a cost that is less than book equity. To illustrate, assume that the stock in Subsidiary is acquired for $130,000 and that the composition of the stockholders' equity of Subsidiary is the same as in the preceding illustration. Parent records the investment at its cost of $130,000. The situation immediately after the transaction is as follows:

	Assets	Stockholders' Equity
Parent:		
Investment in Subsidiary, 10,000 shares	$130,000	
Subsidiary:		
Net assets	$150,000	
Common stock, 10,000 shares, $10 par..........		$100,000
Retained earnings		50,000

Elimination of the reciprocal accounts and reporting the $150,000 of net assets of Subsidiary on the consolidated balance sheet creates an imbalance of $20,000. The possible reasons for the apparent "bargain" purchase and the treatment of the imbalance are generally the reverse of those given in explaining acquisition at a price higher than book equity. The complexities that might arise in some instances are discussed in advanced texts.

Partially Owned Subsidiary Acquired at a Cost Above or Below Book Equity. When one corporation seeks to gain control over another by purchase of its stock, it is not necessary and often not possible to acquire all of

[7] *Opinions of the Accounting Principles Board, No. 16, op. cit.*, par. 87.

the stock. To illustrate this situation, assume that Parent acquires, at a total cost of $190,000, 80% of the stock of Subsidiary, whose book equity is composed of common stock of $100,000 (10,000 shares, $10 par) and $80,000 of retained earnings. The relevant data immediately after the acquisition of the stock are as follows:

	Assets	Stockholders' Equity
Parent:		
Investment in Subsidiary, 8,000 shares	$190,000	
Subsidiary:		
Net assets	$180,000	
Common stock, 10,000 shares, $10 par..........		$100,000
Retained earnings..........		80,000

The explanation of the $10,000 imbalance in the reciprocal items in this illustration is more complex than in the preceding illustrations. Two factors are involved: (1) the amount paid for the stock is greater than 80% of Subsidiary's book equity and (2) only 80% of Subsidiary's stock was purchased. Since Parent acquired 8,000 shares or 80% of the outstanding shares of Subsidiary, only 80% of the stockholders' equity accounts of Subsidiary can be eliminated. The remaining 20% of the stock is owned by outsiders, who are called collectively the **minority interest.** The eliminations from the partially reciprocal accounts and the amounts to be reported on the consolidated balance sheet, including the minority interest, are determined as follows:

Parent:		
Investment in Subsidiary..........		$190,000
Eliminate 80% of Subsidiary stock..........	$ 80,000	
Eliminate 80% of Subsidiary retained earnings	64,000	144,000
Excess of cost over book equity of Subsidiary interest..........		$ 46,000
Subsidiary:		
Common stock	$100,000	
Eliminate 80% of Subsidiary stock..........	80,000	
Remainder..........		$ 20,000
Retained earnings..........	$ 80,000	
Eliminate 80% of Subsidiary retained earnings	64,000	
Remainder..........		16,000
Minority interest		$ 36,000

The excess cost of $46,000 is reported on the consolidated balance sheet as goodwill or the valuation placed on other assets is increased by $46,000, according to the principles explained earlier. The minority interest of $36,000, which is the amount of Subsidiary's book equity allocable to outsiders, is reported on the consolidated balance sheet, usually preceding the stockholders' equity accounts of Parent. The 1989 edition of *Accounting Trends & Techniques* indicates that minority interest normally is reported in the long-term liabilities section.

Consolidated Balance Sheet Subsequent to Acquisition. Subsequent to acquisition of a subsidiary, the parent company uses the equity method to account for its investment in the subsidiary. Thus, the parent company's investment account is increased periodically for its share of the subsidiary's earnings and decreased for the related dividends received. Correspondingly, the retained earnings account of the subsidiary will be increased periodically by the amount of its net income and reduced by dividend distributions. Because of these periodic changes in the balances of the reciprocal accounts, the eliminations required in preparing a consolidated balance sheet will change each year.

To illustrate consolidation of balance sheets subsequent to acquisition, assume that Subsidiary in the preceding illustration earned net income of $50,000 and paid dividends of $20,000 during the year subsequent to Parent's acquisition of 80% of its stock. The net effect of the year's transactions on Subsidiary were as follows:

	Net Assets	Common Stock	Retained Earnings
Subsidiary:			
Date of acquisition	$180,000	$100,000	$ 80,000
Add net income	50,000		50,000
Deduct dividends	(20,000)		(20,000)
Date subsequent to acquisition	$210,000	$100,000	$110,000

Parent's entries to record its 80% share of subsidiary's net income and dividends are as follows:

Parent entries

	Debit	Credit
Investment in Subsidiary	40,000	
Income of Subsidiary		40,000
Cash	16,000	
Investment in Subsidiary		16,000

The net effect of the foregoing entries on Parent's investment account is to increase the balance by $24,000, as follows:

Parent:		
Investment in subsidiary, 8,000 shares:		
Date of acquisition		$190,000
Add 80% of Subsidiary's net income	$40,000	
Deduct 80% of Subsidiary's dividends	(16,000)	24,000
One year subsequent to acquisition		$214,000

Continuing the illustration, the eliminations from the partially reciprocal accounts and the amounts to be reported on the consolidated balance sheet are determined as follows:

Parent:		
Investment in Subsidiary		$214,000
Eliminate 80% of Subsidiary stock	$ 80,000	
Eliminate 80% of Subsidiary retained earnings	88,000	168,000
Excess of cost over book equity of Subsidiary interest		$ 46,000
Subsidiary:		
Common stock	$100,000	
Eliminate 80% of Subsidiary stock	80,000	
Remainder		$ 20,000
Retained earnings	$110,000	
Eliminate 80% of Subsidiary retained earnings	88,000	
Remainder		22,000
Minority interest		$ 42,000

A comparison of the data with the analysis as of the date of acquisition shows the following:

1. Minority interest increased $6,000 (from $36,000 to $42,000), which is equivalent to 20% of the $30,000 net increase ($50,000 of net income less $20,000 of dividends) in Subsidiary's retained earnings.
2. Excess of cost over book equity of the subsidiary interest remained unchanged at $46,000.

To avoid additional complexities, it was assumed that the $46,000 excess at the date of acquisition was not due to goodwill or to assets subject to depreciation or amortization.[8]

Work Sheet for Consolidated Balance Sheet. The preceding discussion focused on the basic concepts associated with the process of preparing consolidated balance sheets. If the consolidation process becomes quite complex or if the amount of data to be processed is substantial, all of the relevant data for the consolidated statements may be assembled on work sheets. Although a work sheet is not essential, it is used in the following illustration to show an alternate method of accumulating all relevant data for the consolidated balance sheet. Whether or not a work sheet is used, the basic concepts and the consolidated balance sheet would not be affected.

To illustrate the use of the work sheet, assume that (as was the case in the illustration in the preceding section) Parent had purchased 80% of Subsidiary stock for $190,000. Any excess of the cost of the investment over book equity is due to the excess of fair market value over book value of Subsidiary's land. For the year since the acquisition, Parent had debited the investment account for its share of Subsidiary earnings and had credited the investment account for its share of dividends declared by Subsidiary. Balance sheet data for Parent and Subsidiary as of December 31 of the year subsequent to acquisition appear as follows. Although these data include amounts for land, other assets, and liabilities, the net assets and stockholders' equity for Subsidiary are the same as in the preceding illustration.

	Parent	Subsidiary
Investment in Subsidiary	$214,000	
Land	100,000	$ 60,000
Other assets	400,000	200,000
	$714,000	$260,000
Liabilities	$164,000	$ 50,000
Common stock:		
Parent	300,000	
Subsidiary		100,000
Retained earnings:		
Parent	250,000	
Subsidiary		110,000
	$714,000	$260,000

[8]Any portion of the excess of cost over book equity assigned to goodwill must be amortized according to *Opinions of the Accounting Principles Board, No. 17,* "Intangible Assets." Similarly, any excess of cost over book equity assigned to plant assets of limited life must be gradually reduced by depreciation. The application of such amortization and depreciation techniques to consolidated statements goes beyond the scope of the discussion here.

The account balances at December 31 and the eliminations from the reciprocal accounts would be entered on the work sheet and the appropriate amounts extended to the Consolidated Balance Sheet column as follows:

Parent and Subsidiary
Work Sheet for Consolidated Balance Sheet
December 31, 19--

	Parent	Subsidiary	Eliminations		Consolidated Balance Sheet	
			Debit	Credit		
Investment in Subsidiary...	214,000			(a) 168,000 (b) 46,000		
Land............................	100,000	60,000	(b) 46,000		206,000	
Other Assets..................	400,000	200,000			600,000	
	714,000	260,000			806,000	
Liabilities.......................	164,000	50,000			214,000	
Common Stock:						
Parent.........................	300,000				300,000	
Subsidiary...................		100,000	(a) 80,000		20,000	minority interest
Retained Earnings:						
Parent.........................	250,000				250,000	
Subsidiary...................		110,000	(a) 88,000		22,000	minority interest
	714,000	260,000	214,000	214,000	806,000	

Explanations for the entries in the Eliminations columns of the work sheet are as follows:

(a) This entry eliminates from the investment in subsidiary account Parent's share of Subsidiary's common stock and retained earnings. As discussed in the preceding paragraphs, Parent's share of Subsidiary's common stock is $80,000, and Parent's share of the retained earnings is $88,000. After these two amounts are eliminated on the work sheet, the remaining balances in Subsidiary's common stock and retained earnings accounts represent minority interest. The minority interests of $20,000 and $22,000 are identified in the Consolidated Balance Sheet column of the work sheet as an aid in the preparation of the consolidated balance sheet.

(b) This entry eliminates the remainder of the investment in subsidiary account and allocates the excess of cost over book equity according to the principles explained earlier. In this illustration, since the $46,000 excess of cost over book equity is due to an excess of fair market value over book value of Subsidiary's land, the land account is debited for $46,000.

In the following consolidated balance sheet, the amount reported for land is $206,000 and the amount reported for minority interest is $42,000. Both of these amounts were identified on the work sheet.

It should be noted that the work sheet is only an aid for accumulating the data for the consolidated balance sheet. It is not the consolidated balance sheet. Also, if there are other intercompany items that must be eliminated from the statements that are to be consolidated, those eliminations would be entered in the Eliminations columns of the work sheet. For example, a loan by a parent to its subsidiary on a note would require an elimination of the amount of the note from both notes receivable and notes payable in the work sheet.

Parent and Subsidiary
Consolidated Balance Sheet
December 31, 19--

Assets	
Land	$206,000
Other assets	600,000
Total assets	$806,000
Liabilities and Stockholders' Equity	
Liabilities	$214,000
Minority interest in subsidiary	42,000
Common stock	300,000
Retained earnings	250,000
Total liabilities and stockholders' equity	$806,000

Pooling of Interests Method

When a parent-subsidiary affiliation is effected as a pooling of interests, the ownership of the two companies is joined together in the parent corporation. The parent deems its investment in the subsidiary to be equal to the carrying amount of the subsidiary's net assets. Any difference that may exist between such carrying amount and the fair market value of the subsidiary's assets does not affect the amount recorded by the parent as the investment.

Consolidated Balance Sheet at Date of Affiliation. Since the parent's investment in the subsidiary is equal to the carrying amount of the subsidiary's net assets, no change is needed in the amounts at which the subsidiary's assets should be included in the consolidated balance sheet prepared at the date of affiliation. The subsidiary's assets are reported as they appear in the subsidiary's separate balance sheet.

The credit to the parent company's stockholders' equity accounts for the stock issued in exchange for the subsidiary company's stock corresponds to the amount debited to the investment account. In addition to the common stock account, the paid-in capital accounts may be affected, as well as the retained earnings account. According to the concept of continuity of ownership interests, subsidiary earnings accumulated prior to the affiliation should be combined with those of the parent on the consolidated balance sheet. It is as though there had been a single economic unit from the time the enterprises had begun.

To illustrate the procedure for consolidating the balance sheets of two corporations by the pooling of interests method, their respective financial positions immediately prior to the exchange of stock are assumed to be as follows:

	Assets	Stockholders' Equity
Parent:		
Net assets	$230,000	
Common stock, 4,000 shares, $25 par		$100,000
Retained earnings		130,000
Subsidiary:		
Net assets	$150,000	
Common stock, 10,000 shares, $10 par		$100,000
Retained earnings		50,000

Since poolings must involve substantially all (90% or more) of the stock of the subsidiary, the illustration will assume an exchange of 100% of the stock. It is also assumed that the fair market value of the net assets of both companies is greater than the amounts reported above and that there appears to be an element of goodwill in both cases. Based on recent price quotations, it is agreed that for the purpose of the exchange, Parent's common stock is to be valued at $45 a share and Subsidiary's at $18 a share.[9] According to the agreement, the exchange of stock is brought about as follows:

Parent issues 4,000 shares valued at $45 per share	$180,000
in exchange for	
Subsidiary's 10,000 shares valued at $18 per share	$180,000

The excess of the $180,000 value of Parent's stock issued over the $150,000 of net assets of Subsidiary may be ignored and the investment recorded as follows:

Parent entry

Investment in Subsidiary	150,000	
Common Stock		100,000
Retained Earnings		50,000

After the foregoing entry has been recorded, the basic balance sheet data of the two companies are as follows:

	Assets	Stockholders' Equity
Parent:		
Investment in Subsidiary, 10,000 shares	$150,000	
Other net assets	230,000	
Common stock, 8,000 shares, $25 par		$200,000
Retained earnings		180,000
Subsidiary:		
Net assets	$150,000	
Common stock, 10,000 shares, $10 par		$100,000
Retained earnings		50,000

To consolidate the balance sheets of the two companies, Parent's investment account and Subsidiary's common stock and retained earnings ac-

[9] In practice, it may be necessary to pay cash for fractional shares or for subsidiary shares held by dissenting stockholders.

counts are eliminated. The net assets of the two companies, $230,000 and $150,000, are combined without any changes in valuation, making a total of $380,000. The consolidated stockholders' equity is composed of common stock of $200,000 and retained earnings of $180,000, for a total of $380,000.

Consolidated Balance Sheet Subsequent to Affiliation. The equity method is used by the parent corporation in recording changes in its investment account subsequent to acquisition. Thus, the account is increased by the parent's share of the subsidiary's earnings and decreased by its share of dividends. Continuing the illustration of the preceding section, assume that Subsidiary's net income and dividends paid during the year subsequent to affiliation with Parent are $20,000 and $5,000 respectively. After Parent has recorded Subsidiary's net income and dividends, the Parent's investment in Subsidiary increases by $15,000, and the Subsidiary's net assets and retained earnings increase by $15,000, yielding the following account balances:

	Assets	Stockholders' Equity
Parent:		
Investment in Subsidiary, 10,000 shares..........	$165,000	
Subsidiary:		
Net assets	$165,000	
Common stock, 10,000 shares, $10 par..........		$100,000
Retained earnings		65,000

When the balance sheets of the affiliated corporations are consolidated, the reciprocal accounts are eliminated and the $165,000 of net assets of Subsidiary are combined with those of Parent.

Work Sheet for Consolidated Balance Sheet. To illustrate the use of the work sheet to assemble the relevant data for the consolidated balance sheet for an affiliation effected as a pooling of interests, assume that (as was the case in the illustration in the preceding section) Parent had exchanged 4,000 shares of its common stock for all of the 10,000 shares of Subsidiary common stock. For the year since the acquisition, Parent had debited the investment account for its share (100%) of Subsidiary earnings and had credited the investment account for its share (100%) of dividends declared by Subsidiary. Balance sheet data for Parent and Subsidiary as of December 31 of the year subsequent to acquisition appear as follows. As in the purchase illustration, amounts for land, other assets, and liabilities have been added, but the amounts for net assets and stockholders' equity for Subsidiary are the same as in the preceding illustration.

	Parent	Subsidiary
Investment in Subsidiary..........	$165,000	
Land..........	80,000	$ 40,000
Other assets	325,000	175,000
	$570,000	$215,000
Liabilities	$140,000	$ 50,000
Common stock:		
Parent..........	200,000	
Subsidiary..........		100,000
Retained earnings:		
Parent..........	230,000	
Subsidiary..........		65,000
	$570,000	$215,000

The account balances at December 31 and the eliminations from the reciprocal accounts would be entered on the work sheet and the amounts determined for the consolidated balance sheet items as follows:

Parent and Subsidiary
Work Sheet for Consolidated Balance Sheet
December 31, 19--

	Parent	Subsidiary	Eliminations Debit	Eliminations Credit	Consolidated Balance Sheet
Investment in Subsidiary......	165,000			165,000	
Land..............................	80,000	40,000			120,000
Other Assets......................	325,000	175,000			500,000
	570,000	215,000			620,000
Liabilities..........................	140,000	50,000			190,000
Common Stock:					
Parent..............................	200,000				200,000
Subsidiary.........................		100,000	100,000		
Retained Earnings:					
Parent..............................	230,000				230,000
Subsidiary.........................		65,000	65,000		
	570,000	215,000	165,000	165,000	620,000

After 100% of Subsidiary common stock and Subsidiary retained earnings is eliminated against Investment in Subsidiary, as indicated in the eliminations columns of the work sheet, the amounts for the two companies are combined, without any changes in valuation, and are then reported on the consolidated balance sheet.

As previously discussed, the work sheet is only an aid for accumulating the data for the consolidated balance sheet. These data are the basis for the consolidated balance sheet, which is prepared in the normal manner.

Consolidated Income Statement and Other Statements

Consolidation of income statements and other statements of affiliated companies usually presents fewer difficulties than those encountered in balance sheet consolidations. The difference is largely because of the inherent nature of the statements. The balance sheet reports cumulative effects of all transactions from the very beginning of an enterprise to a current date, whereas the income statement, the retained earnings statement, and the statement of cash flows report selected transactions only and are for a limited period of time, usually one year.

The principles used in the consolidation of the income statements of a parent and its subsidiaries are the same, regardless of whether the affiliation is deemed to be a purchase or a pooling of interests. When the income statements are consolidated, all amounts resulting from intercompany transactions, such as management fees or interest on loans charged by one affiliate to another, must be eliminated. Any intercompany profit included in inventories must also be eliminated. The remaining amounts of sales, cost of merchandise sold, operating expenses, and other revenues and expenses reported on the income statements of the affiliated corporations are then combined.

The eliminations required in consolidating the retained earnings statement and other statements are based largely on data assembled in consolidating the balance sheet and income statement.

CORPORATION FINANCIAL STATEMENTS

OBJECTIVE 6
Illustrate a statement of stockholders' equity and a consolidated balance sheet.

The financial statements for corporate enterprises were described and illustrated in preceding chapters. For example, sections of the income statement affected by the corporate form of organization, the combined income and retained earnings statement, and the balance sheet were illustrated. In addition to the basic financial statements, significant changes in stockholders' equity other than retained earnings should be reported for the period in which they occur. These changes may be reported in a **statement of stockholders' equity,** such as the following statement from the annual report of Colgate-Palmolive Company:

	Common Stock		Additional Paid-In	Treasury Stock	
Dollars In Millions	Shares	Amount	Capital	Shares	Amount
Balance, January 1, 1988	68,600,329	$83.7	$126.4	15,090,324	$477.2
Shares issued for stock options	411,071	.4	13.5	—	—
Treasury stock acquired	(57,391)	—	—	57,391	2.6
Other	114,993	—	—	(114,993)	(4.5)
Balance, December 21, 1988	69,069,002	84.1	139.9	15,032,722	475.3
Shares issued for stock options	827,555	.8	37.8	—	—
Treasury stock acquired	(3,913,466)	—	—	3,913,466	229.8
Other	110,077	—	—	(107,734)	(6.4)
Balance, December 31, 1989	66,093,168	84.9	177.7	18,838,454	698.7
Shares issued for stock options	642,107	.7	31.4	—	—
Treasury stock acquired	(236,434)	—	—	236,434	13.8
Other	104,767	—	—	(104,767)	(6.0)
Balance, December 31, 1990	66,603,608	$85.6	$209.1	18,970,121	$706.5

The consolidated balance sheet on pages 560-561 illustrates for a corporation the balance sheet presentation of many of the items discussed in this and preceding chapters. These items include bond sinking funds, investments in bonds, goodwill, deferred income taxes, bonds payable and unamortized discount, minority interesst in subsidiaries, and appropriation of retained earnings.

ACCOUNTING FOR INTERNATIONAL OPERATIONS

OBJECTIVE 7
Describe and illustrate the accounting for international operations.

In an effort to expand operations, many U.S. companies conduct business in foreign countries. If the operations of these multinational companies involve currencies other than the dollar, special accounting problems may arise (1) in accounting for transactions with the foreign companies and (2) in the preparation of consolidated statements for domestic and foreign companies that are affiliated. The basic principles used in such situations are presented in the following paragraphs. Details and complexities are reserved for advanced texts.

Accounting for Transactions with Foreign Companies

If transactions with foreign companies are executed in dollars, no special accounting problems arise. Such transactions would be recorded as illustrated

Balance Sheet of a Corporation

Escoe Corporation
Consolidated
December

Assets				
Current assets:				
Cash			$ 255,000	
Marketable securities, at cost (market price, $160,000)			152,500	
Accounts and notes receivable		$ 722,000		
Less allowance for doubtful receivables		37,000	685,000	
Inventories, at lower of cost (first-in, first-out) or market			917,500	
Prepaid expenses			70,000	
Total current assets				$2,080,000
Investments:				
Bond sinking fund			$ 422,500	
Investment in bonds of Dalton Company			240,000	
Total investments				662,500

	Cost	Accumulated Depreciation	Book Value	
Plant assets (depreciated by the straight-line method):				
Land	$ 250,000	—	$ 250,000	
Buildings	920,000	$ 379,955	540,045	
Machinery and equipment	2,764,400	766,200	1,998,200	
Total plant assets	$3,934,400	$1,146,155		2,788,245
Intangible assets:				
Goodwill			$ 300,000	
Organization costs			50,000	
Total intangible assets				350,000
Total assets				$5,880,745

in the text. For example, the sale of merchandise to a Japanese company that is billed in and paid in dollars would be recorded by the U.S. company in the normal manner, using dollar amounts. However, if transactions involve receivables or payables that are to be received or paid in a foreign currency, the U.S. company may incur an exchange gain or loss.

Realized Currency Exchange Gains and Losses. When a U.S. company executes a transaction with a company in a foreign country using a currency other than the dollar, one currency needs to be converted into another to settle the transaction. For example, a U.S. company purchasing merchandise from a British company that requires payment in British pounds must exchange dollars ($) for pounds (£) to settle the transaction. This exchange of one currency into another involves the use of an exchange rate. The **exchange rate**

and Subsidiaries
Balance Sheet
31, 19--

Liabilities				
Current liabilities:				
Accounts payable			$ 508,810	
Income tax payable			120,500	
Dividends payable			94,000	
Accrued liabilities			81,400	
Deferred income tax payable			10,000	
Total current liabilities				$ 814,710
Long-term liabilities:				
Debenture 8% bonds payable, due December 31, 19--		$1,000,000		
Less unamortized discount		60,000	$ 940,000	
Minority interest in subsidiaries			115,000	
Total long-term liabilities				1,055,000
Deferred credits:				
Deferred income tax payable				85,500
Total liabilities				$1,955,210
Stockholders' Equity				
Paid-in capital:				
Common stock, $20 par (250,000 shares authorized, 100,000 shares issued)		$2,000,000		
Excess of issue price over par—common stock		320,000		
Total paid-in capital			$2,320,000	
Retained earnings:				
Appropriated:				
For bonded indebtedness	$250,000			
For plant expansion	750,000	$1,000,000		
Unappropriated		605,535		
Total retained earnings			1,605,535	
Total stockholders' equity				3,925,535
Total liabilities and stockholders' equity				$5,880,745

is the rate at which one unit of currency (the dollar, for example) can be converted into another currency (the British pound, for example). To continue with the illustration, if the U.S. company had purchased merchandise for £1,000 from a British company on June 1, when the exchange rate was $1.40 per British pound, $1,400 would need to be exchanged for £1,000 to make the purchase.[10] Since the U.S. company maintains its accounts in dollars, the transaction would be recorded as follows:

[10]Foreign exchange rates are quoted in major financial reporting services. Because the exchange rates are quite volatile, those used in this chapter are assumed rates which do not necessarily reflect current rates.

June 1	Purchases	1,400	
	Cash		1,400
	Payment of Invoice No. 1725 from W. A. Sterling Co., £1,000; exchange rate, $1.40 per British pound.		

Special accounting problems arise when the exchange rate fluctuates between the date of the original transaction (such as a purchase on account) and the settlement of that transaction in cash in the foreign currency (such as the payment of an account payable). In practice, such fluctuations are frequent. To illustrate, assume that on July 10, when the exchange rate was $.004 per yen (Y), a purchase for Y100,000 was made from a Japanese company. Since the U.S. company maintains its accounts in dollars, the entry would be recorded at $400 (Y100,000 × $.004), as follows:

July 10	Purchases	400	
	Accounts Payable—M. Suzuki and Son		400
	Invoice No. 818, Y100,000, exchange rate, $.004 per yen.		

If on the date of payment, August 9, the exchange rate had increased to $.005 per yen, the Y100,000 account payable must be settled by exchanging $500 (Y100,000 × $.005) for Y100,000. In such a case, the U.S. company incurs an exchange loss of $100, because $500 was needed to settle a $400 debt (account payable). The cash payment would be recorded as follows:

Aug. 9	Accounts Payable—M. Suzuki and Son	400	
	Exchange Loss	100	
	Cash		500
	Cash paid on Invoice No. 818, for Y100,000, or $400, when exchange rate was $.005 per yen.		

All transactions with foreign companies can be analyzed in the manner described above. For example, assume that on May 1, when the exchange rate was $.25 per Swiss franc (F), a sale on account for $1,000 to a Swiss company was billed in Swiss francs. The transaction would be recorded as follows:

May 1	Accounts Receivable—D. W. Robinson Co.	1,000	
	Sales		1,000
	Invoice No. 9772, F4,000; exchange rate, $.25 per Swiss franc.		

If the exchange rate had increased to $.30 per Swiss franc on May 31, the date of receipt of cash, the U.S. company would realize an exchange gain of $200. The gain was realized because the F4,000, which had a value of $1,000 on the date of sale, had increased in value to $1,200 (F4,000 × $.30) on May 31 when payment was received. The receipt of the cash would be recorded as follows:

May 31	Cash	1,200	
	Accounts Receivable—D. W. Robinson Co.		1,000
	Exchange Gain		200
	Cash received on Invoice No. 9772, for F4,000, or $1,000, when exchange rate was $.30 per Swiss franc.		

Unrealized Currency Exchange Gains and Losses. In the previous illustrations, the transactions were completed by either the receipt or the payment of cash. Therefore, any exchange gain or loss was realized and, in an accounting sense, was "recognized" at the date of the cash receipt or cash payment. However, if financial statements are prepared between the date of the original transaction (sale or purchase on account, for example) and the date of the cash receipt or cash payment, and the exchange rate has changed since the original transaction, an unrealized gain or loss must be recognized in the statements. To illustrate, assume that a sale on account for $1,000 had been made to a German company on December 20, when the exchange rate was $.50 per deutsche mark (DM), and that the transaction had been recorded as follows:

Dec. 20	Accounts Receivable—T. A. Mueller Inc.	1,000	
	Sales		1,000
	Invoice No. 1793, DM2,000; exchange rate, $.50 per deutsche mark.		

If the exchange rate had decreased to $.45 per deutsche mark on December 31, the date of the balance sheet, the $1,000 account receivable would have a value of only $900 (DM2,000 × $.45). This "unrealized" loss would be recorded as follows:

Dec. 31	Exchange Loss	100	
	Accounts Receivable—T. A. Mueller Inc. .		100
	Invoice No. 1793, DM2,000 × $.05 decrease in exchange rate.		

Assuming that DM2,000 are received on January 19 in the following year, when the exchange rate is $.42, the additional decline in the exchange rate from $.45 to $.42 per deutsche mark must be recognized. The cash receipt would be recorded as follows:

Jan. 19	Cash	840	
	Exchange Loss ($.03 × DM2,000)............	60	
	Accounts Receivable—T. A. Mueller Inc. .		900
	Cash received on Invoice No. 1793, for DM2,000, or $900, when exchange rate was $.42 per deutsche mark.		

If the exchange rate had increased between December 31 and January 19, an exchange gain would be recorded on January 19. For example, if the exchange rate had increased from $.45 to $.47 per deutsche mark during this period, Exchange Gain would be credited for $40 ($.02 × DM2,000).

A balance in the exchange loss account at the end of the fiscal period should be reported in the Other Expense section of the income statement. A balance in the exchange gain account should be reported in the Other Income section.

Consolidated Financial Statements with Foreign Subsidiaries

Before the financial statements of domestic and foreign companies are consolidated, the amounts shown on the statements for the foreign companies must be converted to U.S. dollars. Asset and liability amounts are normally converted to U.S. dollars by using the exchange rates as of the balance sheet date. Revenues and expenses are normally converted by using the exchange rates that were in effect when those transactions were executed. (For practical purposes, a weighted average rate for the period generally is used.) The adjustments (gains or losses) resulting from the conversion are reported as a separate item in the stockholders' equity section of the balance sheets of the foreign companies.[11]

After the foreign company statements have been converted to U.S. dollars, the financial statements of U.S. and foreign subsidiaries are consolidated in the normal manner as described previously in this chapter.

CHAPTER REVIEW

KEY POINTS

OBJECTIVE 1

Investments in Stocks

A business may make long-term investments in equity securities (preferred and common shares) with cash that it does not need for normal operations. A corporation may also purchase stocks as a means of establishing or maintaining business relations with the issuing company. In other cases, a corporation may acquire all or a large part of the voting stock of another corporation in order to control its activities.

OBJECTIVE 2

Accounting for Long-Term Investments in Stock

There are two methods of accounting for long-term investments in stock: (1) the cost method and (2) the equity method. The method used depends upon whether the investor owns enough of the voting stock of the investee (company whose stock is owned by the investor) to have a significant influence over its operating and financing policies. If the investor does not have a significant influence, the cost method (with the lower of cost or market rule) must be used. If the investor can exercise significant influence in a long-term investment situation, the equity method must be used.

The cost of stocks purchased includes not only the amount paid to the seller but also other costs related to the purchase, such as the broker's commission and postage charges for delivery. When the cost method is used, cash dividends on capital stock held as an investment may be recorded as an increase in the appropriate income and asset accounts. Under the cost method, the lower of cost or market rule must be applied to the total cost or total market price of the stock as of the date of the balance sheet. Any market value changes that are recognized are not included in net income, but are reported as a separate item in the stockholders' equity section of the balance sheet. If the decline in market value below cost for an individual security as of the balance sheet date is other than temporary, the cost basis of the individual security is written down and the amount of the write-down is accounted for as a realized loss. After the write-down, the carrying amount of the individual security cannot be changed for subsequent recoveries in market value.

When the equity method of accounting is used, a stock purchase is recorded at cost. The investor records its share of periodic net income of the investee as an increase in the investment account and as revenue of the period. Conversely, the investor's share of the investee's periodic loss is recorded as a decrease in the investment and a loss of the period. In addition, the investor records its share of cash or

---

[11]*Statement of Financial Accounting Standards, No. 52*, "Foreign Currency Translation" (Stamford: Financial Accounting Standards Board, 1981).

property dividends on the stock as a decrease in the investment account and as an increase in the appropriate asset accounts.

When shares of stock held as a long-term investment are sold, the investment account is credited for the carrying amount of the shares sold and the cash or appropriate receivable account is debited for the proceeds (sales price less commission and other selling costs). Any difference between the proceeds and the carrying amount is recorded as a gain or loss on the sale.

OBJECTIVE 3

Business Combinations

Combinations of businesses may be effected (1) through a joining of two or more corporations to form a single unit by either merger or consolidation or (2) through common control of two or more corporations by means of stock ownership that results in a parent-subsidiary affiliation. When a corporation acquires the properties of another corporation and the latter then dissolves, the joining of the two enterprises is called a merger. When two or more corporations transfer their assets and liabilities to a corporation which has been created for purposes of the takeover, the combination is called a consolidation. When a business combination is effected by one corporation acquiring a controlling share of the outstanding voting stock of one or more other corporations, the corporation owning the majority of the voting stock is known as the parent company. The corporation that is controlled is known as the subsidiary company. When a corporation acquires a controlling share of the voting stock of another corporation in exchange for cash, other assets, issuance of notes or other debt obligations, or by a combination of these items, the transaction is accounted for by the purchase method. When two corporations are combined by exchanging the voting common stock of one corporation (the parent) for substantially all (at least 90%) of the voting common stock of the other corporation (the subsidiary), the transaction is accounted for by the pooling of interests method.

OBJECTIVE 4

Accounting for Parent-Subsidiary Affiliations

Although the corporations that make up a parent-subsidiary affiliation may operate as a single economic unit, they usually continue to maintain separate accounting records and prepare their own periodic financial statements. The parent corporation uses the equity method of accounting for its investment in the stock of the subsidiary. The financial statements resulting from combining the parent and subsidiary statements generally are called consolidated statements.

OBJECTIVE 5

Basic Principles of Consolidation of Financial Statements

When the data on the financial statements of the parent corporation and its subsidiaries are combined to form the consolidated statements, special attention should be given to the intercompany items appearing on the separate corporation financial statements. These intercompany items must be eliminated in preparing financial statements for the consolidated entity.

When a parent-subsidiary affiliation is effected as a purchase, the parent corporation is deemed to have purchased all or a major part of the subsidiary corporation's net assets. Accordingly, the assets of the subsidiary should be reported on the consolidated balance sheet at their cost to the parent. In the subsidiary's ledger, the reciprocal of the investment account at the date of acquisition is the composite of all the subsidiary's stockholders' equity accounts. In some cases, a parent corporation may pay an amount above the book equity of a subsidiary because the subsidiary has prospects for high future earnings. The amount of this excess should be identified on the consolidated balance sheet as goodwill. When a parent corporation purchases less than 100% of the subsidiary's stock, the remaining stockholders' equity is identified as minority interest. The minority interest is reported on the consolidated balance sheet, usually preceding the stockholders' equity accounts of the parent.

When a parent-subsidiary affiliation is effected as a pooling of interests, the ownership of the two companies is joined together in the parent corporation. The parent deems its investment in the subsidiary to be equal to the carrying amount of the subsidiary's net assets. Any difference that may exist between such carrying amount and the fair market value of the subsidiary's assets does not affect the amount recorded by the parent as the investment. Consequently, no change is needed in the amounts at which the subsidiary's assets should be included in the consolidated balance sheet.

The principles used in the consolidation of income statements of a parent and its subsidiary are the same, regardless of whether the affiliation is deemed to be a purchase or a pooling of interests. When the income statements are consolidated, all amounts resulting from intercompany transactions, such as management fees or interest on loans charged by one affiliate to another, must be eliminated. Any intercompany profit included in inventories must also be eliminated.

OBJECTIVE 6

Corporation Financial Statements

Significant changes in stockholders' equity other than retained earnings may be reported in a statement of stockholders' equity. A consolidated balance sheet of a corporation, containing many of the items discussed in this and preceding chapters, is presented on pages 560-561.

OBJECTIVE 7

Accounting for International Operations

When U.S. companies conduct business in foreign countries, special accounting problems may arise (1) in accounting for transactions with foreign companies and (2) in the preparation of consolidated statements for domestic and foreign companies that are affiliated. When a U.S. company executes a transaction with a company in a foreign country using a currency other than the dollar, an exchange rate should be used to convert one currency into another to settle the transaction. Because of this conversion process, gains and losses on foreign transactions may arise. If a foreign transaction has not been completed by the end of the year, an unrealized currency exchange gain or loss may need to be recognized, depending upon fluctuations in the exchange rates.

Before the financial statements of domestic and foreign countries are consolidated, the statements of the foreign companies must be converted to U.S. dollars. Asset and liability amounts are normally converted to U.S. dollars by using the exchange rates as of the balance sheet date. Revenues and expenses are normally converted by using the exchange rates that were in effect when those transactions were executed.

KEY TERMS

equity securities 541
cost method 542
equity method 542
merger 545
consolidation 545
parent company 545
subsidiary company 545
purchase method 546
pooling of interests method 546
consolidated statements 547
minority interest 551
exchange rate 560

SELF-EXAMINATION QUESTIONS

Answers at end of chapter.

1. Which of the following are characteristic of a parent-subsidiary relationship known as a pooling of interests?
   A. Parent acquires substantially all of the voting stock of subsidiary in exchange for cash
   B. Parent acquires substantially all of the voting stock of subsidiary in exchange for its bonds payable

C. Parent acquires substantially all of the voting stock of subsidiary in exchange for its voting common stock
D. All of the above

2. P Co. purchased the entire outstanding stock of S Co. for $1,000,000 in cash. If at the date of acquisition S Co.'s stockholders' equity consisted of $750,000 of common stock and $150,000 of retained earnings, what is the amount of the difference between cost and book equity of the subsidiary interest?
   A. Excess of cost over book equity of subsidiary interest, $250,000
   B. Excess of cost over book equity of subsidiary interest, $100,000
   C. Excess of book equity over cost of subsidiary interest, $250,000
   D. None of the above

3. If in Question 2, P Co. had purchased 90% of the outstanding stock of S Co. for $1,000,000, what is the amount of the difference between cost and book equity of subsidiary interest?
   A. Excess of cost over book equity of subsidiary interest, $100,000
   B. Excess of cost over book equity of subsidiary interest, $190,000
   C. Excess of cost over book equity of subsidiary interest, $250,000
   D. None of the above

4. Based on the data in Question 3, what is the amount of the minority interest at the date of acquisition?
   A. $15,000
   B. $75,000
   C. $100,000
   D. None of the above

5. On July 9, 1992, a sale on account for $10,000 to a Mexican company was billed for 25,000,000 pesos. The exchange rate was $.0004 per peso on July 9 and $.0005 per peso on August 8, 1992, when the cash was received on account. Which of the following statements identifies the exchange gain or loss for the fiscal year ended December 31, 1992?
   A. Realized exchange loss, $2,500
   B. Realized exchange gain, $2,500
   C. Unrealized exchange loss, $2,500
   D. Unrealized exchange gain, $2,500

ILLUSTRATIVE PROBLEM

All of Stereophonic Inc.'s outstanding shares of stock were acquired on October 1, 1992, by Piedmont Inc. After lengthy negotiations with Stereophonic Inc.'s major shareholder, it was agreed that (1) the current management of Stereophonic Inc. would be retained for a minimum of five years, (2) Stereophonic Inc. would be operated as an independent subsidiary, and (3) Piedmont Inc. would issue 1,200 of its own $100 par common stock in exchange for all of Stereophonic Inc.'s stock.

The balance sheets of the two corporations on September 30, 1992, were as follows:

	Piedmont Inc.	Stereophonic Inc.
Assets		
Cash	$ 124,200	$ 18,120
Accounts receivable	238,150	36,810
Inventory	405,750	61,300
Land	120,000	50,000
Plant and equipment (net)	612,300	120,450
	$1,500,400	$286,680
Liabilities and Stockholders' Equity		
Accounts payable	$ 136,400	$ 41,500
Common stock	900,000	120,000
Retained earnings	464,000	125,180
	$1,500,400	$286,680

Instructions:

1. Prepare the entry that should be made by Piedmont Inc. to record the combination as a pooling of interests.
2. Assuming the business combination is to be recorded as a pooling of interests, prepare a consolidated balance sheet for Piedmont Inc. and Stereophonic Inc. as of October 1, 1992.
3. Assume that Piedmont Inc. paid $106,000 in cash and issued 1,500 shares of Piedmont Inc. common stock with a market value of $212,000 for all the common stock of Stereophonic Inc. Prepare the journal entry for Piedmont Inc. to record the combination as a purchase.
4. Assuming that the business combination is to be recorded as a purchase and that the book values of the net assets of Stereophonic Inc. are approximately equal to their market values, prepare a consolidated balance sheet for Piedmont Inc. and Stereophonic Inc. as of October 1, 1992.

SOLUTION

(1)

Investment in Stereophonic Inc.	245,180	
Common Stock		120,000
Retained Earnings		125,180

(2)

Piedmont Inc. and Subsidiary Stereophonic Inc.
Consolidated Balance Sheet
October 1, 1992

Assets		
Current assets:		
Cash	$ 142,320	
Accounts receivable	274,960	
Inventory	467,050	
Total current assets		$ 884,330
Plant assets:		
Land	$ 170,000	
Plant and equipment (net)	732,750	
Total plant assets		902,750
Total assets		$1,787,080
Liabilities		
Accounts payable		$ 177,900
Stockholders' Equity		
Common stock	$1,020,000	
Retained earnings	589,180	
Total stockholders' equity		1,609,180
Total liabilities and stockholders' equity		$1,787,080

(3)

Investment in Stereophonic Inc.	318,000	
Cash		106,000
Common Stock		150,000
Paid-In Capital in Excess of Par—Common Stock		62,000

(4)

Piedmont Inc. and Subsidiary Stereophonic Inc.
Consolidated Balance Sheet
October 1, 1992

Assets		
Current assets:		
Cash ($124,200 + $18,120 − $106,000)	$ 36,320	
Accounts receivable	274,960	
Inventory	467,050	
Total current assets		$ 778,330
Plant assets:		
Land	$ 170,000	
Plant and equipment (net)	732,750	
Total plant assets		902,750
Intangible assets:		
Goodwill ($318,000 − $245,180)		72,820
Total assets		$1,753,900
Liabilities		
Accounts payable		$ 177,900
Stockholders' Equity		
Common stock	$1,050,000	
Premium on common stock	62,000	
Retained earnings	464,000	
Total stockholders' equity		1,576,000
Total liabilities and stockholders' equity		$1,753,900

DISCUSSION QUESTIONS

13–1. (a) What are two methods of accounting for long-term investments in stock? (b) Under what caption are long-term investments in stock reported on the balance sheet?

13–2. When stocks are purchased between dividend dates, does the purchaser pay the seller the dividend accrued since the last dividend payment date? Explain.

13–3. A stockholder owning 400 shares of Haines Co. common stock, acquired at a total cost of $11,550, receives a common stock dividend of 20 shares. What is the carrying amount per share after the stock dividend?

13–4. What terms are applied to the following: (a) a corporation that is controlled by another corporation through ownership of a controlling interest in its stock; (b) a corporation that owns a controlling interest in the voting stock of another corporation; (c) a group of corporations related through stock ownership?

13–5. What are the two methods by which the relationship of parent-subsidiary may be established?

13–6. P Company purchases for $12,000,000 the entire common stock of S Corporation. What type of accounts on S's balance sheet are reciprocal to the investment account on P's balance sheet?

13–7. Are the eliminations of the reciprocal accounts in consolidating the balance sheets of P and S in Question 13–6 recorded in the respective ledgers of the two companies? Explain.

13–8. Parks Company purchased from stockholders the entire outstanding stock of Sapp Inc. for a total of $5,150,000 in cash. At the date of acquisition, Sapp Inc. had $3,600,000 of liabilities and total stockholders' equity of $5,000,000. (a) As of the acquisition date, what was the total amount of the assets of Sapp Inc.? (b) As of the acquisition date, what was the amount of the net assets of Sapp Inc.? (c) What is the amount of difference between the investment account and the book equity of the subsidiary interest acquired by Parks Company?

13–9. What is the possible explanation of the difference determined in Question 13–8(c) and how will it affect the reporting of the difference on the consolidated balance sheet?

13–10. If, in Question 13–8, Parks Company had paid only $4,880,000 for the stock of Sapp Inc., what would the solution to part (c) have been?

13–11. Parent Corporation owns 85% of the outstanding common stock of Subsidiary Corporation, which has no preferred stock. (a) What is the term applied to the remaining 15% interest? (b) If the total stockholders' equity of Subsidiary Corporation is $878,000, what is the amount of Subsidiary's book equity allocable to outsiders? (c) Where is the amount determined in part (b) reported on the consolidated balance sheet?

13–12. P Corporation owns 90% of the outstanding common stock of S Co., which has no preferred stock. Net income of S Co. was $500,000 for the year, and cash dividends declared and paid during the year amounted to $100,000. What entries should be made by P Corporation to record its share of S Co.'s (a) net income and (b) dividends? (c) What is the amount of the net increase in the equity of the minority interest?

13–13. (a) What purpose is served by the work sheet for a consolidated balance sheet? (b) Is the work sheet a substitute for the consolidated balance sheet?

13–14. At the end of the fiscal year, the amount of notes receivable and notes payable reported on the respective balance sheets of a parent and its wholly owned subsidiary are as follows:

	Parent	Subsidiary
Notes Receivable..........	$550,000	$100,000
Notes Payable..............	200,000	120,000

If $75,000 of Subsidiary's notes receivable are owed by Parent, determine the amount of notes receivable and notes payable to be reported on the consolidated balance sheet.

13–15. Sales and purchases of merchandise by a parent corporation and its wholly owned subsidiary during the year were as follows:

	Parent	Subsidiary
Sales	$8,250,000	$1,200,000
Purchases	4,950,000	720,000

If $110,000 of the sales of Parent were made to Subsidiary, determine the amount of sales and purchases to be reported on the consolidated income statement.

13–16. The relationships of parent and subsidiary were established by the following transactions. Identify each affiliation as a "purchase" or a "pooling of interests."

(a) Company P receives 75% of the voting common stock of Company S in exchange for voting common stock of Company P.
(b) Company P receives 90% of the voting common stock of Company S in exchange for cash.
(c) Company P receives 100% of the voting common stock of Company S in exchange for cash and long-term bonds payable.
(d) Company P receives 95% of the voting common stock of Company S in exchange for voting common stock of Company P.

13–17. Which of the following procedures for consolidating the balance sheet of a parent and wholly owned subsidiary are characteristic of acquisition of control by purchase and which are characteristic of a pooling of interests? (a) Retained earnings of subsidiary at date of acquisition are eliminated. (b) Retained earnings of subsidiary at date of acquisition are combined with retained earnings of parent. (c) Assets are not revalued. (d) Goodwill may not be recognized.

13–18. On March 31, Parrott Corp. issued 8,000 shares of its $100 par common stock, with a total market value of $1,000,000 to the stockholders of Shutt Inc. in exchange for all of Shutt's common stock. Parrott Corp. records its investment at $900,000. The net assets and stockholders' equities of the two companies just prior to the affiliation are summarized as follows:

	Parrott Corp.	Shutt Inc.
Net assets	$3,200,000	$900,000
Common stock	$2,000,000	$350,000
Retained earnings	1,200,000	550,000
	$3,200,000	$900,000

(a) At what amounts would the following be reported on the consolidated balance sheet as of March 31, applying the pooling of interests method: (1) Net assets, (2) Retained earnings?
(b) Assume that, instead of issuing shares of stock, Parrott Corp. had given $1,000,000 in cash and long-term notes. At what amounts would the following be reported on the consolidated balance sheet as of March 31: (1) Net assets, (2) Retained earnings?

13–19. Can a U.S. company incur an exchange gain or loss because of fluctuations in the exchange rate if its transactions with foreign countries, involving receivables or payables, are executed in (a) dollars, (b) the foreign currency?

13–20. A U.S. company purchased merchandise for 90,000 francs on account from a French company. If the exchange rate was $.18 per franc on the date of purchase and $.16 per franc on the date of payment of the account, what was the amount of exchange gain or loss realized by the U.S. company?

13–21. What two conditions give rise to unrealized currency exchange gains and losses from sales and purchases on account that are to be settled in the foreign currency?

Real World Focus

13–22. The following data were taken from the footnotes of Triton Energy Corporation's 1989 annual report:

"... At May 31, 1989 ... the Company owned approximately 49 1/2% of Crusader, an Australian public company engaged in oil and gas exploration and production, coal mining and gas processing. The Company's investment in Crusader's common stock, which is accounted for using the equity method, was $27,810,000 ... at May 31, 1989. ... the Company's equity in Crusader's earnings ... was $4,266,000 in 1989 ... the Company's share of dividends declared by Crusader was $947,000 in 1989 ..."

(a) Prepare the journal entry that Triton Energy Corporation would have made to record its interest in the 1989 earnings of Crusader. (b) Prepare the journal entry that Triton Energy Corporation would have made to record its share of the dividends of Crusader that were paid in cash during 1989.

Ethics Discussion Case

13–23. Marchant Company has recently begun selling merchandise to foreign customers. Roberta Douglas, the controller, has implemented a policy that requires all foreign transactions to be executed in United States dollars. In this way, Douglas transfers to the customers all risks of foreign exchange fluctuations on sales to foreign markets.

Discuss whether Roberta Douglas's policy is ethical.

EXERCISES

Ex. 13–24.
Entries for investment in stock, receipt of dividends, and sale of shares.
OBJ. 2

On May 3, Niemyer Corporation acquired 1,000 shares of the 100,000 outstanding shares of Grace Co. common stock at 74 1/2 plus commission and postage charges of $380. On August 31, a cash dividend of $1.75 per share and a 4% stock dividend were received. On December 15, 400 shares were sold at 76 1/4 less commission and postage charges of $180. Present entries to record (a) the purchase of the stock, (b) the receipt of the dividends, and (c) the sale of the 400 shares.

Ex. 13–25.
Entries using equity method for stock investment.
OBJ. 2

At a total cost of $1,760,000, Conn Corporation acquired 80,000 shares of Maxi-Systems Co. common stock as a long-term investment. Conn Corporation uses the equity method of accounting for this investment. Maxi-Systems Co. has 320,000 shares of common stock outstanding, including the shares acquired by Conn Corporation. Present the entries by Conn Corporation to record the following information:

(a) Maxi-Systems Co. reports net income of $500,000 for the current period.
(b) A cash dividend of $.40 per common share is paid by Maxi-Systems Co. during the current period.

Ex. 13–26.
Determination and reporting of items related to consolidated statements.
OBJ. 5

On the last day of the fiscal year, Powell Inc. purchased 90% of the common stock of Singer Company for $575,000, at which time Singer Company reported the following on its balance sheet: assets, $1,000,000; liabilities, $400,000; common stock, $100 par, $100,000; retained earnings, $500,000. In negotiating the stock sale, it was determined that the book carrying amounts of Singer's recorded assets and equities approximated their current market values.

(a) Indicate for each of the following the section, the title of the item, and the amount to be reported on the consolidated balance sheet as of the date of acquisition:
(1) Difference between cost and book equity of subsidiary interest.
(2) Minority interest.
(b) During the following year, Powell Inc. realized net income of $1,250,000, exclusive of the income of the subsidiary, and Singer Company realized

net income of $380,000. In preparing a consolidated income statement, indicate in what amounts the following would be reported:
(1) Minority interest's share of net income.
(2) Consolidated net income.

Ex. 13–27.
Consolidated balance sheet from affiliation effected as a purchase.
OBJ. 5

On December 31 of the current year, P Corporation purchased 85% of the stock of S Company. The data reported on their separate balance sheets immediately after the acquisition are as follows:

	P Corporation	S Company
Assets		
Cash	$ 48,300	$ 32,100
Accounts receivable (net)	76,200	52,500
Inventories	211,500	93,600
Investment in S Company	555,000	—
Equipment (net)	600,000	437,300
	$1,491,000	$615,500
Liabilities and Stockholders' Equity		
Accounts payable	$ 148,500	$ 75,500
Common stock, $100 par	1,125,000	375,000
Retained earnings	217,500	165,000
	$1,491,000	$615,500

The fair market value of S Company's assets corresponds to their book carrying amounts, except for equipment, which is valued at $480,000 for consolidation purposes. Prepare a consolidated balance sheet as of December 31, in report form, omitting captions for current assets, plant assets, etc. (A work sheet need not be used.)

Ex. 13–28.
Consolidated balance sheet from affiliation effected as a pooling.
OBJ. 5

As of October 31 of the current year, Pittman Corporation exchanged 2,500 shares of its $30 par common stock for the 15,000 shares of Sisk Company $5 par common stock held by Sisk stockholders. The separate balance sheets of the two enterprises, immediately after the exchange of shares, are as follows:

	Pittman Corporation	Sisk Company
Assets		
Cash	$ 31,500	$ 21,700
Accounts receivable (net)	38,150	28,000
Inventories	106,050	45,850
Investment in Sisk Company	122,500	—
Equipment (net)	460,600	61,950
	$758,800	$157,500
Liabilities and Stockholders' Equity		
Accounts payable	$107,800	$ 35,000
Common stock	400,000	75,000
Retained earnings	251,000	47,500
	$758,800	$157,500

Prepare a consolidated balance sheet as of October 31, in report form, omitting captions for current assets, plant assets, etc. (A work sheet need not be used.)

Ex. 13–29.
Consolidated income statement.
OBJ. 5

For the current year ended April 30, the results of operations of Palay Corporation and its wholly owned subsidiary, Sigler Enterprises, are as follows:

	Palay Corporation		Sigler Enterprises	
Sales		$1,200,000		$500,000
Cost of merchandise sold	$790,000		$300,000	
Selling expenses	180,000		72,000	
Administrative expenses	100,000		48,000	
Interest expense (income)	(15,000)	1,055,000	15,000	435,000
Net income		$ 145,000		$ 65,000

During the year, Palay sold merchandise to Sigler for $90,000. The merchandise was sold by Sigler to nonaffiliated companies for $120,000. Palay's interest income was realized from a long-term loan to Sigler.

(a) Prepare a consolidated income statement for the current year for Palay and its subsidiary. Use the single-step form and disregard income taxes. (A work sheet need not be used.)

(b) Assuming that none of the merchandise sold by Palay to Sigler had been sold during the year to nonaffiliated companies, and that Palay's cost of the merchandise had been $54,000, determine the amounts that would have been reported for the following items on the consolidated income statement: (1) sales, (2) cost of merchandise sold, (3) net income.

Ex. 13–30.
Determination of consolidated balance sheet amounts for affiliation effected as a pooling and as a purchase.
OBJ. 5

Summarized data from the balance sheets of Peach Company and Stover Inc., as of June 30 of the current year, are as follows:

	Peach Company	Stover Inc.
Net assets	$5,000,000	$400,000
Common stock:		
25,000 shares, $50 par	1,250,000	
5,000 shares, $30 par		150,000
Retained earnings	3,750,000	250,000

(a) On July 1 of the current year, the two companies combine. Peach Company issues 3,000 shares of its $50 par common stock, valued at $450,000, to Stover's stockholders in exchange for the 5,000 shares of Stover's $30 par common stock, also valued at $450,000. Assuming that the affiliation is effected as a pooling of interests, what are the amounts that would be reported for net assets, common stock, and retained earnings as of July 1 of the current year?

(b) Assume that Peach Company had paid cash of $450,000 for all of Stover Inc.'s common stock on July 1 of the current year and that the book value of the net assets of Stover Inc. is deemed to reflect fair market value. (1) What are the amounts that would be reported for net assets, common stock, and retained earnings as of July 1 of the current year, using the purchase method? (2) How much goodwill will be reported on the combined balance sheet?

Ex. 13–31.
Entries for sales made in foreign currency.
OBJ. 7

Jarvis Company makes sales on account to several Israeli companies which it bills in shekels. Record the journal entries for the following selected transactions completed during the current year:

Mar. 3. Sold merchandise on account, 40,000 shekels; exchange rate, $.63 per shekel.
Apr. 8. Received cash from sale of March 3, 40,000 shekels; exchange rate, $.64 per shekel.
June 20. Sold merchandise on account, 70,000 shekels; exchange rate, $.64 per shekel.
July 31. Received cash from sale of June 20, 70,000 shekels; exchange rate, $.62 per shekel.

Ex. 13–32.
Entries for purchases made in foreign currency.
OBJ. 7

Gunter Company purchases merchandise from a German company that requires payment in deutsche marks. Record the journal entries for the following selected transactions completed during the current year:

Aug. 15. Purchased merchandise on account, net 30, 10,000 deutsche marks; exchange rate, $.58 per deutsche mark.
Sept. 14. Paid invoice of August 15; exchange rate, $.59 per deutsche mark.
Nov. 13. Purchased merchandise on account, net 30, 80,000 deutsche marks; exchange rate, $.59 per deutsche mark.
Dec. 13. Paid invoice of November 13; exchange rate, $.55 per deutsche mark.

PROBLEMS

Pb. 13–33.
Entries for investments in stock.
OBJ. 2

The following transactions relate to certain securities acquired by Norton Company, whose fiscal year ends on December 31:

1992
Jan. 7. Purchased 500 shares of the 20,000 outstanding common shares of McGinnis Corporation at 20 3/4 plus commission and other costs of $335.
Apr. 29. Received the regular cash dividend of 90¢ a share on McGinnis Corporation stock.
Oct. 30. Received the regular cash dividend of 90¢ a share plus an extra dividend of 5¢ a share on McGinnis Corporation stock.

(Assume that all intervening transactions have been recorded properly, and that the number of shares of stock owned have not changed from December 31, 1992, to December 31, 1996.)

1997
Apr. 30. Received the regular cash dividend of 90¢ a share and a 2% stock dividend on the McGinnis Corporation stock.
Aug. 10. Sold 250 shares of McGinnis Corporation stock at 31 1/2. The broker deducted commission and other costs of $75, remitting the balance.
Oct. 31. Received a cash dividend at the new rate of 95¢ a share on the McGinnis Corporation stock.

Instructions:

Record the journal entries for the foregoing transactions.

Pb. 13–34.
Work sheet and consolidated balance sheet from affiliation effected as a purchase.
OBJ. 5

On May 31 of the current year, Petty Company purchased 95% of the stock of Sawyer Company. On the same date, Petty Company loaned Sawyer Company $100,000 on a 90-day note. The data reported on their separate balance sheets immediately after the acquisition and loan are as follows:

	Petty Company	Sawyer Company
Assets		
Cash	$ 90,400	$ 88,000
Accounts receivable (net)	122,400	112,000
Notes receivable	120,000	—
Inventories	286,800	156,800
Investment in Sawyer Company	862,000	—
Equipment (net)	680,000	688,000
	$2,161,600	$1,044,800
Liabilities and Stockholders' Equity		
Accounts payable	$ 336,000	$ 92,800
Notes payable	—	100,000
Common stock, $40 par	1,280,000	—
Common stock, $10 par	—	600,000
Retained earnings	545,600	252,000
	$2,161,600	$1,044,800

The fair market value of Sawyer Company's assets corresponds to the book carrying amounts, except for equipment, which is valued at $700,000 for consolidation purposes.

Instructions:

(1) Prepare a work sheet for a consolidated balance sheet as of May 31 of the current year.
(2) Prepare in report form a consolidated balance sheet as of May 31, omitting captions for current assets, plant assets, etc.

Pb. 13–35.
Consolidated balance sheet from both pooling and purchase methods.
OBJ. 5

On July 1 of the current year, after several months of negotiations, Pear Company issued 20,000 shares of its own $10 par common stock for all of Schwab Inc.'s outstanding shares of stock. The fair market value of the Pear Company shares issued is $18.75 per share, or a total of $375,000. Schwab Inc. is to be operated as a separate subsidiary. The balance sheets of the two firms on June 30 of the current year are as follows:

	Pear Company	Schwab Inc.
Assets		
Cash	$ 243,000	$ 28,200
Accounts receivable (net)	294,000	50,300
Inventory	513,900	71,800
Land	144,000	55,000
Plant and equipment (net)	605,100	204,700
	$1,800,000	$410,000
Liabilities and Stockholders' Equity		
Accounts payable	$ 174,000	$ 60,000
Common stock ($10 par)	1,000,000	200,000
Retained earnings	626,000	150,000
	$1,800,000	$410,000

Instructions:

(1) (a) What entry would be made by Pear Company to record the combination as a pooling of interests? (b) Prepare a consolidated balance sheet for Pear Com-

pany and Schwab Inc. as of July 1 of the current year, assuming that the business combination has been recorded as a pooling of interests. (A work sheet is not required.)

(2) (a) Assume that Pear Company paid $75,000 in cash and issued 16,000 shares of Pear common stock with a fair market value of $300,000 for all the common stock of Schwab Inc. What entry would Pear Company make to record the combination as a purchase? (b) Prepare a consolidated balance sheet as of July 1 of the current year, assuming that the business combination has been recorded as a purchase, and that the book values of the net assets of Schwab Inc. are deemed to represent fair market value. (A work sheet is not required.)

(3) Assume the same situation as in (2), except that the fair market value of the land of Schwab Inc. was $70,000 for consolidation purposes. Prepare a consolidated balance sheet as of July 1 of the current year. (A work sheet is not required.)

Pb. 13–36.
Eliminations for and preparation of consolidated balance sheet and income statement.
OBJ. 5

On January 2 of the current year, Purdy Corporation exchanged 32,000 shares of its $12.50 par common stock for 8,000 shares (the entire issue) of Salters Company's $50 par common stock. Salters purchased from Purdy Corporation $100,000 of its $300,000 issue of bonds payable, at face amount. All of the items for "interest" appearing on the balance sheets and income statements of both corporations are related to the bonds.

During the year, Purdy Corporation sold merchandise with a cost of $240,000 to Salters Company for $320,000, all of which was sold by Salters Company before the end of the year.

Purdy Corporation has correctly recorded the income and dividends reported for the year by Salters Company. Data for the income statements for both companies for the current year are as follows:

	Purdy Corporation	Salters Company
Revenues:		
Sales	$1,920,000	$600,000
Income of subsidiary	126,000	—
Interest income	—	12,000
	$2,046,000	$612,000
Expenses:		
Cost of merchandise sold	$1,140,000	$336,000
Selling expenses	199,200	62,400
Administrative expenses	150,000	44,400
Interest expense	36,000	—
Income tax	84,000	43,200
	$1,609,200	$486,000
Net Income	$ 436,800	$126,000

Data for the balance sheets of both companies as of the end of the current year are as follows:

	Purdy Corporation	Salters Company
Assets		
Cash	$ 75,000	$ 31,000
Accounts receivable (net)	200,000	62,200
Dividends receivable	60,000	—
Interest receivable	—	3,000
Inventories	330,000	151,600
Investment in Salters Co. (8,000 shares)	800,000	—
Investment in Purdy Corp. bonds (at face amount)	—	100,000
Plant and equipment	1,380,000	682,400
Accumulated depreciation	(780,000)	(130,200)
	$2,065,000	$900,000

Liabilities and Stockholders' Equity	Purdy Corporation	Salters Company
Accounts payable	$ 80,300	$ 33,200
Income tax payable	34,600	6,800
Dividends payable	36,000	60,000
Interest payable	9,000	—
Bonds payable, 12% (due in 2010)	300,000	—
Common stock, $12.50 par	1,200,000	—
Common stock, $50 par	—	400,000
Excess of issue price over par—common stock	120,000	40,000
Retained earnings	285,100	360,000
	$2,065,000	$900,000

Instructions:

(1) Determine the amounts to be eliminated from the following items in preparing the consolidated balance sheet as of December 31 of the current year: (a) dividends receivable and dividends payable; (b) interest receivable and interest payable; (c) investment in Salters Co. and stockholders' equity; (d) investment in Purdy Corp. bonds and bonds payable.

(2) Prepare a detailed consolidated balance sheet as of December 31 in report form.

(3) Determine the amounts to be eliminated from the following items in preparing the consolidated income statement for the current year ended December 31: (a) sales and cost of merchandise sold; (b) interest income and interest expense; (c) income of subsidiary and net income.

(4) Prepare a single-step consolidated income statement, inserting the earnings per share in parentheses on the same line with net income.

(5) Determine the amount of the reduction in consolidated inventories, net income, and retained earnings if Salters Company's inventory had included $80,000 of the merchandise purchased from Purdy Corporation.

Pb. 13–37.
Work sheet and consolidated balance sheet; year-end minority interest; increase in investment account during year.
OBJ. 5, 6

On October 31, Pruitt Company purchased 90% of the outstanding stock of Sorells Company for $975,000. Balance sheet data for the two corporations immediately after the transaction are as follows:

	Pruitt Company	Sorells Company
Assets		
Cash and marketable securities	$ 385,300	$ 53,500
Accounts receivable	554,700	138,900
Allowance for doubtful accounts	(45,200)	(18,600)
Inventories	893,600	274,700
Investment in Sorells Company	975,000	—
Land	315,000	168,750
Building and equipment	1,641,400	1,112,850
Accumulated depreciation	(522,800)	(590,100)
	$4,197,000	$1,140,000
Liabilities and Stockholders' Equity		
Accounts payable	$ 347,500	$ 126,400
Income tax payable	94,500	13,600
Bonds payable (due in 2010)	900,000	—
Common stock, $100 par	1,600,000	—
Common stock, $5 par	—	700,000
Retained earnings	1,255,000	300,000
	$4,197,000	$1,140,000

Instructions:

(1) Prepare a work sheet for a consolidated balance sheet as of the date of acquisition. The fair market value of Sorells Company's assets are deemed to correspond to the book carrying amounts, except for land, which is to be increased by $31,250.

(2) Prepare in report form a detailed consolidated balance sheet as of the date of acquisition.
(3) Assuming that Sorells Company earns net income of $180,500 and pays cash dividends of $42,000 during the following fiscal year and that Pruitt Company records its share of the earnings and dividends, determine the following as of the end of the year:
   (a) The net amount added to Pruitt Company's investment account as a result of Sorells Company's earnings and dividends.
   (b) The amount of the minority interest.

Pb. 13–38. Consolidated balance sheet from affiliation effected as a purchase.
OBJ. 5, 6

Several years ago, Pirkle Corporation purchased 19,000 shares of the 20,000 outstanding shares of stock of Shell Company. Since the date of acquisition, Pirkle Corporation has debited the investment account for its share of the subsidiary's earnings and has credited the account for its share of dividends declared. Balance sheet data for the two corporations as of December 31 of the current year are as follows:

	Pirkle Corp.	Shell Co.
Assets		
Cash	$ 69,300	$ 25,300
Notes receivable	45,000	18,000
Accounts receivable (net)	170,900	59,600
Interest receivable	3,600	800
Dividends receivable	5,700	—
Inventories	240,400	82,800
Prepaid expenses	6,200	2,000
Investment in Shell Co.	225,000	—
Land	90,000	54,000
Buildings and equipment	492,900	288,000
Accumulated depreciation	(240,000)	(115,500)
	$1,109,000	$415,000
Liabilities and Stockholders' Equity		
Notes payable	$ 54,000	$ 60,000
Accounts payable	119,400	78,600
Income tax payable	42,000	15,600
Dividends payable	18,000	6,000
Interest payable	3,100	4,800
Common stock, $50 par	720,000	—
Common stock, $10 par	—	120,000
Excess of issue price over par—common stock	—	30,000
Retained earnings	152,500	100,000
	$1,109,000	$415,000

Pirkle Corporation holds $45,000 of short-term notes of Shell Company, on which there is accrued interest of $3,600. Shell Company owes Pirkle Corporation $30,000 for a management advisory fee for the year. It has been recorded by both corporations in their respective accounts payable and accounts receivable accounts.

Instructions:

Prepare in report form a detailed consolidated balance sheet as of December 31 of the current year. (A work sheet is not required.) The excess of book equity in Shell Company over the balance of the Pirkle Corporation's investment account is attributable to overvaluation of Shell Company's land.

Pb. 13–39.
Consolidated balance sheet.
OBJ. 6

The following data were extracted from the records of Marin Inc. after adjustment at January 31, 1992, the end of the current fiscal year:

Accounts and notes receivable	$ 360,000
Accounts payable	250,000
Accrued liabilities	40,750
Accumulated depreciation — buildings	190,600
Accumulated depreciation — machinery and equipment	583,100
Allowance for doubtful receivables	18,500
Appropriation for bonded indebtedness	500,000
Appropriation for plant expansion	250,000
Bonds payable, 10% debenture bonds due January 31, 1998	500,000
Bond sinking fund	210,500
Buildings	500,000
Cash	127,500
Common stock, $10 par, 500,000 shares authorized, 100,000 shares issued	1,000,000
Deferred income tax payable ($5,000 due within one year)	45,000
Discount on bonds payable	15,000
Dividends payable	12,500
Goodwill	400,000
Income tax payable	60,250
Inventories (lower of cost, first-in, first-out, or market)	460,750
Investment in bonds of Span Company	100,000
Land	150,000
Machinery and equipment	1,382,200
Marketable securities (at lower of cost or market; original cost, $80,000)	76,250
Minority interest in subsidiaries	57,500
Organization costs	100,000
Paid-in capital in excess of par — common stock	160,000
Prepaid expenses	20,000
Retained earnings (unappropriated)	234,000

Instructions:

Prepare a report form consolidated balance sheet for Marin Inc.

Pb. 13–40.
Foreign currency transactions.
OBJ. 7

Nealy Company sells merchandise to and purchases merchandise from various Canadian and French companies. These transactions are settled in the foreign currency. The following selected transactions were completed during the current fiscal year:

Feb. 14. Sold merchandise on account to Korn Company, net 30, 400,000 francs; exchange rate, $.17 per French franc.
Mar. 16. Received cash from Korn Company; exchange rate, $.16 per French franc.
May 1. Purchased merchandise on account from Hunt Company, net 30, $12,000 Canadian; exchange rate, $.83 per Canadian dollar.
June 1. Issued check for amount owed to Hunt Company; exchange rate, $.82 per Canadian dollar.
July 31. Sold merchandise on account to Pierre Company, net 30, 150,000 francs; exchange rate, $.15 per French franc.
Aug. 30. Received cash from Pierre Company; exchange rate, $.18 per French franc.
Sept. 8. Purchased merchandise on account from Dryson Company, net 30, $30,000 Canadian; exchange rate, $.84 per Canadian dollar.
Oct. 8. Issued check for amount owed to Dryson Company; exchange rate, $.85 per Canadian dollar.
Dec. 12. Sold merchandise on account to Kammer Company, net 45, $75,000 Canadian; exchange rate, $.85 per Canadian dollar.
24. Purchased merchandise on account from Toulouise Company, net 30, 120,000 francs; exchange rate, $.18 per French franc.

Dec. 31. Recorded unrealized currency exchange gain and/or loss on transactions of December 12 and 24. Exchange rates on December 31: $.87 per Canadian dollar; $.19 per French franc.

Instructions:

(1) Present entries to record the transactions and adjusting entries for the year.
(2) Present entries to record the payment of the December 24 purchase, on January 23, when the exchange rate was $.17 per French franc, and the receipt of cash from the December 12 sale, on January 26, when the exchange rate was $.88 per Canadian dollar.

ALTERNATE PROBLEMS

Pb. 13–33A.
Entries for investments in stock.
OBJ. 2

The following transactions relate to certain securities acquired by Hidy Company, whose fiscal year ends on December 31:

1992
Feb. 11. Purchased 1,000 shares of the 25,000 outstanding common shares of Huston Corporation at 35 plus commission and other costs of $175.
June 5. Received the regular cash dividend of $1 a share on Huston Corporation stock.
Dec. 5. Received the regular cash dividend of $1 a share plus an extra dividend of 25¢ a share on Huston Corporation stock.

(Assume that all intervening transactions have been recorded properly, and that the number of shares of stock owned has not changed from December 31, 1992, to December 31, 1996.)

1997
June 7. Received the regular cash dividend of $1 a share and a 5% stock dividend on the Huston Corporation stock.
July 20. Sold 500 shares of Huston Corporation stock at 40. The broker deducted commission and other costs of $125, remitting the balance.
Dec. 9. Received a cash dividend at the new rate of $1.10 a share on the Huston Corporation stock.

Instructions:

Record the entries for the foregoing transactions.

Pb. 13–34A.
Work sheet and consolidated balance sheet from affiliation effected as a purchase.
OBJ. 5

On February 1 of the current year, Parson Company purchased 85% of the stock of Stern Company. On the same date, Parson Company loaned Stern Company $80,000 on a 120-day note. The data reported on their separate balance sheets immediately after the acquisition and loan are as follows:

	Parson Company	Stern Company
Assets		
Cash	$ 81,200	$ 41,200
Accounts receivable (net)	77,600	51,200
Notes receivable	80,000	—
Inventories	263,600	83,600
Investment in Stern Company	400,000	—
Equipment (net)	608,000	344,000
	$1,510,400	$520,000

	Parson Company	Stern Company
Liabilities and Stockholders' Equity		
Accounts payable	$ 280,000	$ 40,000
Notes payable	—	80,000
Common stock, $50 par	800,000	—
Common stock, $10 par	—	320,000
Retained earnings	430,400	80,000
	$1,510,400	$520,000

The fair value of Stern Company's assets corresponds to the book carrying amounts, except for equipment, which is valued at $360,000 for consolidation purposes.

Instructions:

(1) Prepare a work sheet for a consolidated balance sheet as of February 1 of the current year.
(2) Prepare in report form a consolidated balance sheet as of February 1, omitting captions for current assets, plant assets, etc.

Pb. 13–35A. **Consolidated balance sheet from both pooling and purchase methods.** OBJ. 5

On April 30 of the current year, after several months of negotiations, Power Company issued 7,500 shares of its own $20 par common stock for all of Sabo Inc.'s outstanding shares of stock. The fair market value of the Power Company shares issued is $45 per share, or a total of $337,500. Sabo Inc. is to be operated as a separate subsidiary. The balance sheets of the two firms on April 30 of the current year are as follows:

	Power Company	Sabo Inc.
Assets		
Cash	$ 192,500	$ 19,500
Accounts receivable (net)	255,000	45,900
Inventory	428,250	61,450
Land	120,000	50,000
Plant and equipment (net)	504,250	123,150
	$1,500,000	$300,000
Liabilities and Stockholders' Equity		
Accounts payable	$ 145,000	$ 52,500
Common stock ($20 par)	1,000,000	150,000
Retained earnings	355,000	97,500
	$1,500,000	$300,000

Instructions:

(1) (a) What entry would be made by Power Company to record the combination as a pooling of interests? (b) Prepare a consolidated balance sheet for Power Company and Sabo Inc. as of April 30 of the current year, assuming that the business combination has been recorded as a pooling of interests. (A work sheet is not required.)
(2) (a) Assume that Power Company paid $150,000 in cash and issued 6,250 shares of Power common stock with a market value of $187,500 for all the common stock of Sabo Inc. What entry would Power Company make to record the combination as a purchase? (b) Prepare a consolidated balance sheet as of April 30 of the current year, assuming that the business combination has been recorded as a purchase, and that the book values of the net assets of Sabo Inc. are deemed to represent fair market value. (A work sheet is not required.)
(3) Assume the same situation as in (2), except that the fair market value of the land of Sabo Inc. was $60,000. Prepare a consolidated balance sheet as of April 30 of the current year. (A work sheet is not required.)

Pb. 13–36A.

Eliminations for and preparation of consolidated balance sheet and income statement.

OBJ. 5

On January 1 of the current year, Pulp Corporation exchanged 30,000 shares of its $10 par common stock for 15,000 shares (the entire issue) of Sego Company's $20 par common stock. Later in the year, Sego Company purchased from Pulp Corporation $50,000 of its $400,000 issue of bonds payable, at face amount. All of the items for "interest" appearing on the balance sheets and income statements of both corporations are related to the bonds.

During the year, Pulp Corporation sold merchandise with a cost of $108,000 to Sego Company for $180,000, all of which was sold by Sego Company before the end of the year.

Pulp Corporation has correctly recorded the income and dividends reported for the year by Sego Company. Data for the income statements for both companies for the current year are as follows:

	Pulp Corporation	Sego Company
Revenues:		
Sales	$1,520,000	$500,000
Income of subsidiary	111,500	—
Interest income	—	4,500
	$1,631,500	$504,500
Expenses:		
Cost of merchandise sold	$ 975,400	$252,600
Selling expenses	148,000	49,800
Administrative expenses	110,000	29,600
Interest expense	36,000	—
Income tax	104,100	61,000
	$1,373,500	$393,000
Net income	$ 258,000	$111,500

Data for the balance sheets of both companies as of the end of the current year are as follows:

	Pulp Corporation	Sego Company
Assets		
Cash	$ 70,100	$ 29,700
Accounts receivable (net)	212,400	50,100
Dividends receivable	10,000	—
Interest receivable	—	750
Inventories	405,300	159,200
Investment in Sego Co. (15,000 shares)	480,100	—
Investment in Pulp Corp. bonds (at face amount)	—	50,000
Plant and equipment	970,300	357,600
Accumulated depreciation	(184,700)	(131,850)
	$1,963,500	$515,500
Liabilities and Stockholders' Equity		
Accounts payable	$ 123,500	$ 20,900
Income tax payable	26,000	4,500
Dividends payable	18,000	10,000
Interest payable	6,000	—
Bonds payable, 9% (due in 2014)	400,000	—
Common stock, $10 par	1,000,000	—
Common stock, $20 par	—	300,000
Excess of issue price over par—common stock	120,000	40,000
Retained earnings	270,000	140,100
	$1,963,500	$515,500

Instructions:

(1) Determine the amounts to be eliminated from the following items in preparing the consolidated balance sheet as of December 31 of the current year: (a) dividends receivable and dividends payable; (b) interest receivable and interest payable; (c) investment in Sego Co. and stockholders' equity; (d) investment in Pulp Corp. bonds and bonds payable.
(2) Prepare a detailed consolidated balance sheet as of December 31 in report form.
(3) Determine the amounts to be eliminated from the following items in preparing the consolidated income statement for the current year ended December 31: (a) sales and cost of merchandise sold; (b) interest income and interest expense; (c) income of subsidiary and net income.
(4) Prepare a single-step consolidated income statement, inserting the earnings per share in parentheses on the same line with net income.
(5) Determine the amount of the reduction in consolidated inventories, net income, and retained earnings if Sego Company's inventory had included $40,000 of the merchandise purchased from Pulp Corporation.

Pb. 13–37A.
Work sheet and consolidated balance sheet; year-end minority interest; increase in investment account during year.
OBJ. 5, 6

On April 30, Price Company purchased 85% of the outstanding stock of Sales Company for $650,000. Balance sheet data for the two corporations immediately after the transaction are as follows:

	Price Company	Sales Company
Assets		
Cash and marketable securities	$ 173,400	$ 65,100
Accounts receivable	240,100	118,300
Allowance for doubtful accounts	(19,000)	(6,400)
Inventories	950,000	230,800
Investment in Sales Company	650,000	—
Land	860,000	45,000
Building and equipment	2,381,000	600,000
Accumulated depreciation	(1,451,500)	(232,800)
	$3,784,000	$820,000
Liabilities and Stockholders' Equity		
Accounts payable	$ 310,000	$108,800
Income tax payable	83,500	11,200
Bonds payable (due in 2015)	640,000	—
Common stock, $200 par	1,000,000	—
Common stock, $10 par	—	200,000
Retained earnings	1,750,500	500,000
	$3,784,000	$820,000

Instructions:

(1) Prepare a work sheet for a consolidated balance sheet as of the date of acquisition. The fair value of Sales Company's assets is deemed to correspond to the book carrying amounts, except for land, which is to be increased by $5,000 for consolidation purposes.
(2) Prepare in report form a detailed consolidated balance sheet as of the date of acquisition.
(3) Assuming that Sales Company earns net income of $75,000 and pays cash dividends of $10,000 during the fiscal year and that Price Company records its share of the earnings and dividends, determine the following as of the end of the year:
    (a) The net amount added to Price Company's investment account as a result of Sales Company's earnings and dividends.
    (b) The amount of the minority interest.

Pb. 13–38A.
Consolidated balance sheet from affiliation effected as a purchase.
OBJ. 5, 6

Several years ago, Pond Corporation purchased 18,000 shares of the 20,000 outstanding shares of stock of Sax Company. Since the date of acquisition, Pond Corporation has debited the investment account for its share of the subsidiary's earnings and has credited the account for its share of dividends declared. Balance sheet data for the two corporations as of December 31 of the current year are as follows:

	Pond Corp.	Sax Co.
Assets		
Cash	$ 62,750	$ 16,050
Notes receivable	35,000	15,000
Accounts receivable (net)	140,750	49,650
Interest receivable	3,000	600
Dividends receivable	4,500	—
Inventories	199,500	70,000
Prepaid expenses	5,100	1,700
Investment in Sax Co.	180,180	—
Land	75,000	45,000
Buildings and equipment	411,000	240,000
Accumulated depreciation	(200,000)	(95,400)
	$916,780	$342,600
Liabilities and Stockholders' Equity		
Notes payable	$ 45,000	$ 35,000
Accounts payable	99,500	80,500
Income tax payable	35,000	13,900
Dividends payable	15,000	5,000
Interest payable	2,450	3,000
Common stock, $20 par	600,000	—
Common stock, $5 par	—	100,000
Paid-in Capital in excess of par—common stock	—	25,000
Retained earnings	119,830	80,200
	$916,780	$342,600

Pond Corporation holds $35,000 of short-term notes of Sax Company, on which there is accrued interest of $3,000. Sax Company owes Pond Corporation $15,000 for a management advisory fee for the year. It has been recorded by both corporations in their respective accounts payable and accounts receivable accounts.

Instructions:

Prepare in report form a detailed consolidated balance sheet as of December 31 of the current year. (A work sheet is not required.) The excess of book equity in Sax Company over the balance of the Pond Corporation's investment account is attributable to overvaluation of Sax Company's land.

Pb. 13–39A.
Consolidated balance sheet.
OBJ. 6

The following data were extracted from the records of Furstner Inc. after adjustment at December 31, 1992, the end of the current fiscal year:

Accounts and notes receivable	$ 400,000
Accounts payable	290,000
Accrued liabilities	40,750
Accumulated depreciation — buildings	240,600
Accumulated depreciation — machinery and equipment	583,100
Allowance for doubtful receivables	18,500
Appropriation for bonded indebtedness	300,000
Appropriation for plant expansion	250,000
Bonds payable, 12% debenture bonds due March 1, 2000	500,000
Bond sinking fund	260,500

Buildings	$ 550,000
Cash	132,500
Common stock, $10 par, 500,000 shares authorized, 125,000 shares issued	1,250,000
Deferred income tax payable ($10,000 due within one year)	50,000
Discount on bonds payable	15,000
Dividends payable	12,500
Goodwill	400,000
Income tax payable	60,250
Inventories (lower of cost, first-in, first-out, or market)	460,750
Investment in bonds of Maxwell Company	100,000
Land	150,000
Machinery and equipment	1,382,200
Marketable securities (at lower of cost or market; original cost, $80,000)	76,250
Minority interest in subsidiaries	57,500
Organization costs	100,000
Paid-in capital in excess of par—common stock	160,000
Prepaid expenses	20,000
Retained earnings (unappropriated)	234,000

Instructions:

Prepare a report form consolidated balance sheet for Furstner Inc.

Pb. 13–40A.
Foreign currency transactions.
OBJ. 7

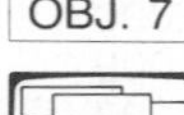

Mills Company sells merchandise to and purchases merchandise from various Canadian and Japanese companies. These transactions are settled in the foreign currency. The following selected transactions were completed during the current fiscal year:

Jan. 8. Purchased merchandise on account from Pierce Company, net 30, $40,000 Canadian; exchange rate, $.84 per Canadian dollar.
Feb. 17. Issued check for amount owed to Pierce Company; exchange rate, $.86 per Canadian dollar.
Mar. 27. Sold merchandise on account to Nakato Company, net 30, 600,000 yen; exchange rate, $.008 per Japanese yen.
Apr. 26. Received cash from Nakato Company; exchange rate, $.009 per Japanese yen.
May 7. Purchased merchandise on account from Rutland Company, net 30, $31,000 Canadian; exchange rate, $.87 per Canadian dollar.
June 6. Issued check for amount owed to Rutland Company; exchange rate, $.86 per Canadian dollar.
Oct. 3. Sold merchandise on account to Oh Company, net 30, 1,000,000 yen; exchange rate, $.0085 per Japanese yen.
Nov. 3. Received cash from Oh Company; exchange rate, $.007 per Japanese yen.
Dec. 16. Sold merchandise on account to Claude Company, net 45, $8,000 Canadian; exchange rate, $.85 per Canadian dollar.
20. Purchased merchandise on account from Toko Company, net 30, 3,000,000 yen; exchange rate, $.006 per Japanese yen.
31. Recorded unrealized currency exchange gain and/or loss on transactions of December 16 and 20. Exchange rates on December 31: $.83 per Canadian dollar; $.005 per Japanese yen.

Instructions:

(1) Present the journal entries to record the transactions and adjustments for the year.
(2) Present the journal entries to record the payment of the December 20th purchase on January 19, when the exchange rate was $.0055 per Japanese yen, and the receipt of cash from the December 16th sale, on January 20, when the exchange rate was $.82 per Canadian dollar.

MINI-CASE 13

Maxine McNeal

Your grandmother recently retired, sold her home in Hartford, and moved to a retirement community in Scottsdale. With some of the proceeds from the sale of her home, she is considering investing $300,000 in the stock market.

In the process of selecting among alternative stock investments, your grandmother collected annual reports from twenty different companies. In reviewing these reports, however, she has become confused and has questions concerning several items which appear in the financial reports. She has asked for your help and has written down the following questions for you to answer:

(a) "In reviewing the annual reports, I noticed many references to 'consolidated financial statements.' What are consolidated financial statements?"

(b) "'Excess of cost of business acquired over related net assets' appears on the consolidated balance sheets in several annual reports. What does this mean? Is it an asset (it appears with other assets)?"

(c) "What is minority interest?"

(d) "A footnote to one of the consolidated statements indicated interest and the amount of a loan from one company to another had been eliminated. Is this good accounting? A loan is a loan. How can a company just eliminate a loan that hasn't been paid off?"

(e) "How can financial statements for an American company (in dollars) be combined with a British subsidiary (in pounds)?"

Instructions:

(1) Briefly respond to each of your grandmother's questions.
(2) While discussing the items in (1) with your grandmother, she asked for your advice on whether she should limit her investment to one stock. What would you advise?

ANSWERS TO SELF-EXAMINATION QUESTIONS

1. C When parent acquires substantially all of the voting stock of subsidiary in exchange for its voting common stock (answer C), the affiliation is termed a "pooling of interests." When parent acquires substantially all of the voting stock of subsidiary in exchange for cash (answer A), other assets, issuances of debt obligations (answer B), or a combination of the foregoing, it is termed a "purchase."
2. B The excess of cost over book equity of interest in S Co. is $100,000 (answer B), determined as follows:

Investment in S Co. (cost)	$1,000,000
Eliminate 100% of S Co. stock	(750,000)
Eliminate 100% of S Co. retained earnings	(150,000)
Excess of cost over book equity of subsidiary interest	$ 100,000

3. B The excess of cost over book equity of interest in S Co. is $190,000 (answer B), determined as follows:

Investment in S Co. (cost)	$1,000,000
Eliminate 90% of S Co. stock	(675,000)
Eliminate 90% of S Co. retained earnings	(135,000)
Excess of cost over book equity of subsidiary interest	$ 190,000

4. D The 10% of the stock owned by outsiders is referred to as the minority interest. It amounts to $90,000, determined as follows:

10% of common stock	$75,000
10% of retained earnings	15,000
Total minority interest	$90,000

5. B The 25,000,000 pesos ($10,000 ÷ $.0004) representing the billed price, which had a value of $10,000 on July 9, 1990, had increased in value to $12,500 (25,000,000 pesos × $.0005) on August 8, 1990, when payment was received. The gain, which was realized because the transaction was completed by the receipt of cash, was $2,500 (answer B).

PART 4

REPORTING CHANGES IN CASH FLOWS

CHAPTER 14

CHAPTER OBJECTIVES

1 Describe the nature of the statement of cash flows.

2 Describe and illustrate the reporting of cash flows, including:
  - Cash flows from operating activities
  - Cash flows from investing activities
  - Cash flows from financing activities

3 Describe and illustrate the preparation of the statement of cash flows.

STATEMENT OF CASH FLOWS

The four basic financial statements are the balance sheet, the income statement, the retained earnings statement (statement of owner's equity), and the statement of cash flows. The preparation and use of the first three statements were thoroughly discussed in preceding chapters. In Chapter 1, the statement of cash flows was briefly described and illustrated for a small service enterprise. In this chapter, the nature, purpose, and preparation of the statement of cash flows are further discussed and illustrated.

NATURE OF THE STATEMENT OF CASH FLOWS

OBJECTIVE 1
Describe the nature of the statement of cash flows.

In 1987, the Financial Accounting Standards Board (FASB) issued Statement of Financial Accounting Standards No. 95, which requires the inclusion of a statement of cash flows as part of the basic set of financial statements. Such a statement is useful to managers in evaluating past and planning future investing and financing activities. It is also useful to creditors and investors in their analysis of a firm's financial condition and profitability.

The statement of cash flows replaces the statement of changes in financial position (frequently called the funds statement). The statement of changes in financial position reported a firm's significant investing and financing activities for a period. These activities were generally described in terms of the inflow or outflow of "funds," with funds defined either as "cash" or "working capital" (current assets — current liabilities). After considerable research and experimentation, the FASB decided that a statement of cash flows would better meet the objectives of financial reporting, expressed as follows:

> *Financial reporting should provide information to help present and potential investors and creditors and other users in assessing the amounts, timing, and uncertainty of prospective cash receipts from dividends or interest and the proceeds from the sale, redemption, or maturity of securities or loans. The prospects for those cash receipts are affected by an enterprise's ability to gen-*

erate enough cash to meet its obligations when due and its other cash operating needs, to reinvest in operations, and to pay cash dividends....[1]

The **statement of cash flows** reports a firm's major sources of cash receipts and major uses of cash payments for a period.[2] Such a statement provides useful information about a firm's activities in generating cash from operations, maintaining and expanding operating capacity, meeting its financial obligations, and paying dividends. Such information, when used in conjunction with the other financial statements, assists investors, creditors, and others in assessing the entity's profitability and solvency (the ability to meet currently maturing debt). For example, the receipt of cash from issuing bonds indicates that the firm is not only committed to the payment of periodic interest expense (which affects profitability and solvency), but also to the redemption of the bonds at maturity (which affects solvency). Thus, the statement of cash flows is useful in analyzing both past and future profitability and solvency of the firm.

FOCUS ON CASH FLOW

In the past, investors have relied almost exclusively on a company's earnings information in judging the company's performance. But this information may be misleading. Therefore, as described in the following excerpt from an article in *The Wall Street Journal*, more and more investors are focusing on cash flows.

Follow the money.

That's a guiding principle for the increasing number of stock analysts and investors who study corporate cash flows. While none of them advocates using cash-flow analysis by itself, they say it can be an important tool in piercing the camouflage that sometimes makes reported earnings misleading.

As the term suggests, cash flow is basically a measure of the money flowing into—or out of—a business. If large companies were run, like lemonade stands, on a cash basis, earnings and cash flow would be identical.

Every major corporation, however, keeps its books on an accrual basis. When it builds a new plant or receives a large multiyear contract, it generally staggers the expense or income over a period of years. That can give a truer picture of corporate profitability, but sometimes it obscures important developments.

Take a company that spent $140 million on new machinery last year. If it depreciates the equipment over a seven-year period, it will be subtracting $20 million from reported profits each year.

But if the machines will stay up-to-date and useful for 25 years, the company's reported earnings may understate its true strength....

...Sometimes the reverse is true. If a company has been neglecting capital spending, its earnings may look good. But on a cash-flow basis, it will look no better, perhaps worse, than its competitors.

Thus, focusing on cash flow makes the investor confront an important question: whether... assets being depreciated really do wear out as rapidly as they are being depreciated....

...Joseph Battipaglia, an analyst with Gruntal & Co. in New York, says that cash-flow trends gave alert investors an early warning of the auto industry's problems in the 1970's. By the end of the decade, he notes, poor earnings made those problems apparent to everyone. But by then, he says, "everyone was going through the same door at the same time."

Source: John R. Dorfman, "Stock Analysts Increase Focus on Cash Flow," *The Wall Street Journal* (February 17, 1987), Section 2, page 1.

---

[1]*Statement of Financial Accounting Concepts, No. 1,* "Objectives of Financial Reporting by Business Enterprises" (Stamford: Financial Accounting Standards Board, 1978), par. 37.

[2]Cash is the most useful concept for the statement of cash flows. However, cash in excess of immediate needs may be invested in income-producing, short-term, highly liquid investments, called cash equivalents, such as Treasury bills and money market funds. In such cases, the statement of cash flows may report changes during the period in cash and cash equivalents.

REPORTING CASH FLOWS

OBJECTIVE 2
Describe and illustrate the reporting of cash flows, including:
Cash flows from operating activities
Cash flows from investing activities
Cash flows from financing activities

The statement of cash flows classifies cash receipts and cash payments by three types of activities:

1. **Cash flows from operating activities,** which include cash transactions that enter into the determination of net income.
2. **Cash flows from investing activities,** which include receipts from the sale of investments and plant assets and other noncurrent assets; and payments for the acquisition of investments and plant assets and other noncurrent assets.
3. **Cash flows from financing activities,** which include receipts from the issuance of equity and debt securities; and payments for dividends, repurchase of equity securities, and redemption of debt securities.

By grouping cash flows by operating, investing, and financing activities, significant relationships within and among the activities can be evaluated. For example, cash receipts from borrowings can easily be related to repayments of borrowings when both are reported as financing activities. Also, the impact of each of the three activities (operating, investing, and financing) on cash flows can be evaluated. Such relationships assist investors and creditors in evaluating the effects of cash flows on profitability and solvency.

The common transactions giving rise to cash flows that would be reported in one of the three sections of the statement of cash flows are presented in the diagram below and are discussed in the following paragraphs. The focus in this chapter is on presenting the basic concept of cash flows and on providing an understanding of the preparation, interpretation, and use of the statement of cash flows.

Cash Flows

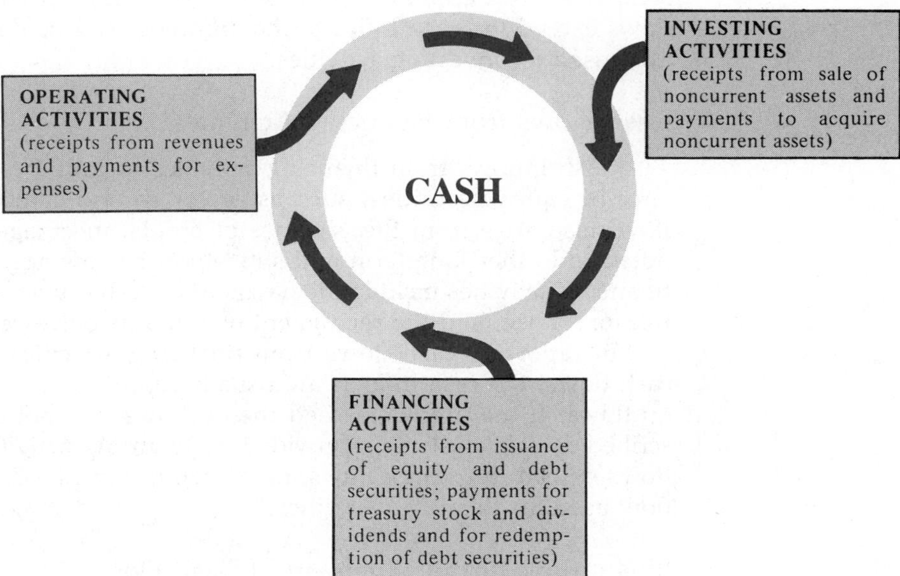

Cash Flows from Operating Activities

The most frequent and often the most important cash flows relate to the operating activities entered into for the purpose of earning net income. There are two alternatives to reporting cash flows from such operating activities in the statement of cash flows: (1) the direct method and (2) the indirect method. The **direct method** reports the major classes of operating cash receipts (cash collected from customers and cash received from interest and dividends, for example) and of operating cash payments (cash paid to suppliers for merchandise and services, to employees for wages, and to creditors for interest, for example). The difference between these operating cash receipts and cash payments would be reported as the net cash flow from operating activities. The principal advantage of the direct method is that it presents the major categories of cash receipts and cash payments. Its principal disadvantage is that the necessary data are often costly to accumulate.

When the **indirect method** is used, the effects of all deferrals of past cash receipts and payments and all accruals of expected future cash receipts and payments are removed from the net income reported on the income statement. This removal is accomplished by adjusting the amount reported as net income upward or downward to determine the net amount of cash flows from operating activities. One of the major advantages of the indirect method is that it focuses on the differences between net income and cash flows from operating activities. In addition, the data needed for the indirect method are generally more readily available and less costly to obtain than the data needed for the direct method.

Cash Flows from Investing Activities

Cash inflows from investing activities generally arise from the sale of investments, plant assets, and intangible assets. Cash outflows generally include payments to acquire investments, plant assets, and intangible assets.

In reporting cash flows from investing activities on the statement of cash flows, the cash inflows are usually reported first, followed by the cash outflows. If the inflows exceed the outflows, the net cash flow can be described as "Net cash flow provided by investing activities." If the cash outflows exceed the cash inflows, the difference can be described as "Net cash flow used for investing activities."

Cash Flows from Financing Activities

Cash inflows from financing activities include proceeds from the issuance of equity securities, such as preferred and common stocks. Cash inflows also arise from the issuance of bonds, mortgage notes payable, and notes and other long-term and short-term borrowings. Cash outflows from financing activities include the payment of cash dividends, the acquisition of treasury stock, and the repayment of amounts borrowed.

In reporting cash flows from financing activities on the statement of cash flows, the cash inflows are usually reported first, followed by the cash outflows. If the inflows exceed the outflows, the net cash flow can be described as "Net cash flow provided by financing activities." If the cash outflows exceed the cash inflows, the difference can be described as "Net cash flow used for financing activities."

Illustrations of the Statement of Cash Flows

As described in the preceding paragraphs, the statement of cash flows is divided into three sections—cash flows from operating activities, cash flows from investing activities, and cash flows from financing activities. Although different formats are possible, the cash flows from operating activities is generally presented first, followed by the cash flows from investing activities and the cash flows from financing activities. The total of the net cash flow from these activities is the net increase or decrease in cash for the period. The cash balance at the beginning of the period is added to the net increase or decrease in cash for the period to arrive at the cash balance at the end of the period.

Two illustrations of the statement of cash flows are presented below. The first illustration is the Gramm Corporation statement that was presented in Chapter 1 and that reports cash flows from operating activities by the direct method. The second illustration is also the Gramm Corporation statment, but with cash flows from operating activities reported by the indirect method. Note that regardless of which method is used, the same amount of net cash flow from operating activities is reported in the statement of cash flows.

Statement of Cash Flows—Direct Method

Gramm Corporation
Statement of Cash Flows
For Month Ended January 31, 1992

Cash flows from operating activities:		
Cash received from customers	$62,000	
Deduct cash payments for expenses and payments to creditors................................	51,500	
Net cash flow from operating activities		$10,500
Cash flows from investing activities:		
Cash payments for acquisition of land..............		(40,000)
Cash flows from financing activities:		
Cash received from sale of capital stock...........		$60,000
Net cash flows and January 31, 1992 cash balance .		$30,500

Statement of Cash Flows—Indirect Method

Gramm Corporation
Statement of Cash Flows
For Month Ended January 31, 1992

Cash flows from operating activities:		
Net income, per income statement	$11,000	
Add increase in accounts payable	4,000	
	$15,000	
Deduct increase in supplies	4,500	
Net cash flow from operating activities		$10,500
Cash flows from investing activities:		
Cash payments for acquisition of land..............		(40,000)
Cash flows from financing activities:		
Cash received from sale of capital stock...........		$60,000
Net cash flows and January 31, 1992 cash balance		$30,500

For small enterprises with few transactions, such as Gramm Corporation, the direct method of reporting cash flows from operating activities can be easily used in preparing the statement of cash flows. For large enterprises with numerous transactions, the direct method is not widely used. Therefore, the indirect method will be used in the remainder of this chapter.[3]

Noncash Investing and Financing Activities

In addition to the investing and financing activities described in the preceding sections, investing and financing may be affected by transactions that do not involve cash. If such transactions have occurred during the period, their effect, if significant, should be reported in a separate schedule to accompany the statement of cash flows. This broadened concept recognizes that some investing and financing transactions do not involve cash receipts and payments, but have a significant effect on future cash flows. For example, the issuance of common stock to retire long-term debt has no effect on cash. However, the transaction will eliminate the future cash payments to retire the bonds and future cash payments for interest. Therefore, it should be reported.

A complete discussion of the kinds of noncash transactions that usually have a significant effect on investing and financing activities is beyond the scope of discussion here. Two examples of the many possibilities are the acquisition of plant assets by the issuance of bonds or capital stock and the issuance of common stock in exchange for convertible preferred stock.

Cash Flow per Share

The term "cash flow per share" is sometimes encountered in the financial press. In many cases, the reference is to cash flows from operations per share. Such reporting of cash flow per share might mislead readers into thinking that cash flow is equivalent to or perhaps superior to earnings per share in appraising the relative success of operations. For example, users might interpret the cash flow from operations per share as being the amount available for dividends, when most of the cash generated by operations may be required for repaying loans or for reinvesting in the business. Therefore, the financial statements, including the statement of cash flows, should not report a cash flow per share amount.

ASSEMBLING DATA AND PREPARING THE STATEMENT OF CASH FLOWS

OBJECTIVE 3
Describe and illustrate the preparation of the statement of cash flows.

To collect the data for the statement of cash flows, all the cash receipts and disbursements for a period could be analyzed and then reported by activity (operating, investing, or financing) on the statement. However, this direct method of analyzing and reporting cash flows is expensive and time consuming. An indirect method is generally the more efficient procedure of examining the noncash balance sheet accounts and determining the type of cash flow activity that leads to changes in these accounts during the period. In performing this analysis, supplementary explanatory data can be obtained from the income statement and other records as needed. Such a procedure is

[3]An appendix that further discusses and illustrates the direct method of reporting cash flows from operating activities is presented at the end of this chapter.

not only efficient but logical, because all transactions eventually affect balance sheet accounts. For example, although revenues and expenses are not shown directly on the balance sheet, the retained earnings account on the balance sheet is affected as revenues and expenses are closed at the end of a period.

Although there is no order in which the noncash balance sheet accounts must be analyzed, one can save time and achieve greater accuracy by selecting the accounts in the reverse order in which they appear on the balance sheet. Therefore, the retained earnings account provides the starting point for determining the cash flows from operating activities that normally appear first on the statement of cash flows.

To illustrate this approach to assembling the data for the statement of cash flows, the comparative balance sheet presented below for Message Corporation for the year ended December 31, 1992, will be used. Selected ledger

Comparative Balance Sheet

Message Corporation
Comparative Balance Sheet
December 31, 1992 and 1991

	1992	1991	Increase Decrease*
Assets			
Cash	$ 49,000	$ 26,000	$ 23,000
Trade receivables (net)	74,000	65,000	9,000
Inventories	172,000	180,000	8,000*
Prepaid expenses	4,000	3,000	1,000
Investments (long-term)	—	45,000	45,000*
Land	90,000	40,000	50,000
Building	200,000	200,000	—
Accumulated depreciation—building	(36,000)	(30,000)	(6,000)
Equipment	290,000	142,000	148,000
Accumulated depreciation—equipment	(43,000)	(40,000)	(3,000)
Total assets	$800,000	$631,000	$169,000
Liabilities			
Accounts payable (merchandise creditors)	$ 50,000	$ 32,000	$ 18,000
Income tax payable	2,500	4,000	1,500*
Dividends payable	15,000	8,000	7,000
Bonds payable	120,000	245,000	125,000*
Total liabilities	$187,500	$289,000	$101,500*
Stockholders' Equity			
Preferred stock	$150,000	—	$150,000
Excess of issue price over par—preferred stock	10,000	—	10,000
Common stock	280,000	$230,000	50,000
Retained earnings	172,500	112,000	60,500
Total stockholders' equity	$612,500	$342,000	$270,500
Total liabilities and stockholders' equity	$800,000	$631,000	$169,000

accounts will be presented as needed, along with supplementary data taken from the income statement.[4]

Retained Earnings

According to the comparative balance sheet for Message Corporation there was an increase of $60,500 in retained earnings during the year. The retained earnings account, as shown below, indicates the nature of the entries made during the year that resulted in this increase.

ACCOUNT RETAINED EARNINGS ACCOUNT NO.

Date		Item	Debit	Credit	Balance	
					Debit	Credit
1992						
Jan.	1	Balance				112,000
Dec.	31	Net income		90,500		
	31	Cash dividends	30,000			172,500

The retained earnings account indicates net income of $90,500 and cash dividends declared of $30,000. The determination of the amount of cash flows from operating activities and the cash flows for the payment of dividends is discussed in the following paragraphs. Note that there may be entries in the retained earnings account that do not affect cash, such as a transfer of retained earnings to paid-in capital accounts for the issuance of a stock dividend. Similarly, transfers between the retained earnings account and appropriations accounts have no effect on cash. Such transactions would not be reported on the statement of cash flows.

Cash Flows from Operating Activities. The amount of net income, $90,500, which is reported on the income statement, was determined by the accrual method of accounting. Therefore it is necessary to recognize the relationship of the accrual method to the movement of cash. Usually, a part of some of the costs and expenses reported on the income statement, as well as a part of the revenue earned, is not accompanied by cash outflow or inflow.

There is often a period of time between the accrual of a revenue and the receipt of the related cash. Perhaps the most common example is the sale of merchandise or a service on account, for which payment is received at a later point in time. Hence, the amount reported on the income statement as revenue from sales is not likely to correspond with the amount of the related cash inflow for the same period.

Timing differences between the incurrence of an expense and the related cash outflow must also be considered in determining the amount of cash flows from operating activities. For example, the amount reported on the income statement as insurance expense is the amount of insurance premiums expired rather than the amount of premiums paid during the period.

---

[4]When the volume of data is substantial, experienced accountants may first assemble all relevant facts in working papers designed for the purpose. Specialized working papers are not essential, however. Because of their complexity, they may obscure the basic concepts of cash flow analysis for anyone who is not already familiar with the subject. For this reason, special working papers will not be used in the following discussion. Instead, the emphasis will be on the basic analyses. An appendix that discusses the use of a work sheet as an aid in assembling data for the statement of cash flows is presented at the end of this chapter.

Similarly, supplies paid for in one year may be used and thus converted to an expense in a later year. Conversely, a portion of some of the expenses incurred near the end of one period, such as wages and taxes, may not require a cash outlay until the following period.

Some revenues and expenses related to noncurrent accounts do not provide or use cash. For example, depreciation expense is a proper expense for the purpose of determining net income, but it does not require an outlay of cash.

To determine the amount of cash flows from operating activities, the accrual basis net income, as reported on the income statement, must be converted to the cash basis. For purposes of illustration, the types of accounts that must be analyzed to convert net income from the accrual basis to the cash basis can be placed in two categories, described as follows:

1. Expenses affecting noncurrent accounts but not cash. For example, depreciation of plant assets and amortization of intangible assets are deducted from revenue but have no effect on cash. Similarly, the amortization of premium on bonds payable, which decreases interest expense and therefore increases operating income, does not affect cash.
2. Revenues and expenses affecting current asset and current liability accounts in amounts that differ from cash flows. For example, a sale of $10,000 on account, on which $8,000 has subsequently been collected, increases revenue by $10,000 but increases cash by only $8,000. In this case, to convert the revenue reported on the income statement ($10,000) to the cash basis, the increase in accounts receivable of $2,000 ($10,000 sale less $8,000 collection) can be deducted from the $10,000 of revenue to yield a cash flow of $8,000.

Generally accepted accounting principles require that cash flows be classified according to the nature of the underlying transaction.[5] This requirement means that cash flows from operating activities should not include transactions which are investing activities or financing activities. For example, the gain or loss from the sale of noncurrent assets would be reported as part of the total cash flows from investing activities arising from the sale of noncurrent assets. To illustrate, assume that land costing $50,000 was sold for $90,000 (a gain of $40,000). The sale should be reported in the investing activities section as "Cash receipts from the sale of land, $90,000." Since the $40,000 gain on the sale of the land is reported in the income statement, the $40,000 must be deducted from net income in converting the reported net income to cash flows from operations. Otherwise, the $40,000 gain would be reported twice on the statement of cash flows. Similarly, losses resulting from such transactions would be added to net income in determining the net cash flow from operating activities. Also, gains or losses arising from the retirement of debt would need to be deducted from or added to net income as reported on the income statement to determine the net cash flow from operating activities.

---

[5] *Statement of Financial Accounting Standards, No. 95,* "Statement of Cash Flows" (Stamford: Financial Accounting Standards Board, 1987).

The conversion of the net income reported on the income statement to cash flows from operating activities can be summarized as follows:

Net income, per income statement		$XX
Add: Depreciation of plant assets	$XX	
Amortization of bond payable discount and intangible assets	XX	
Decreases in current assets (receivables, inventories, prepaid expenses)	XX	
Increases in current liabilities (accounts and notes payable, accrued liabilities)	XX	
Losses on disposal of assets and retirement of debt	XX	XX
Deduct: Amortization of bond payable premium	$XX	
Increases in current assets (receivables, inventories, prepaid expenses)	XX	
Decreases in current liabilities (accounts and notes payable, accrued liabilities)	XX	
Gains on disposal of assets and retirement of debt	XX	XX
Net cash flow from operating activities		$XX

Note that two current accounts—cash and dividends payable—are not included in this conversion schedule. Cash is omitted because it is the focus of the analysis. Dividends payable is omitted because dividends are a distribution of earnings and do not affect net income. The treatment of dividends as they affect the statement of cash flows will be discussed later in the chapter. In the following paragraphs, the manner in which the net income reported by Message Corporation is converted to "Cash flows from operating activities" is discussed.

Depreciation. The comparative balance sheet for Message Corporation indicates that Accumulated Depreciation—Equipment increased by $3,000, and Accumulated Depreciation—Building increased by $6,000. Reference to these two accounts, shown as follows, indicates that depreciation for the year was $12,000 for the equipment and $6,000 for the building, or a total of $18,000.

ACCOUNT ACCUMULATED DEPRECIATION—EQUIPMENT ACCOUNT NO.

Date		Item	Debit	Credit	Balance Debit	Balance Credit
1992						
Jan.	1	Balance				40,000
May	9	Discarded, no salvage	9,000			
Dec.	31	Depreciation for year		12,000		43,000

ACCOUNT ACCUMULATED DEPRECIATION—BUILDING ACCOUNT NO.

Date		Item	Debit	Credit	Balance Debit	Balance Credit
1992						
Jan.	1	Balance				30,000
Dec.	31	Depreciation for year		6,000		36,000

Since the $18,000 of depreciation expense reduces net income but did not require an outlay of cash, $18,000 is added to net income in the process of determining the cash flows from operating activities, as follows:

Cash flows from operating activities:		
Net income	$90,500	
Add: Depreciation	18,000	$108,500

Current Assets and Current Liabilities. In the process of determining cash flows from operating activities, decreases in the noncash current assets and increases in the current liabilities must be added to the amount reported as net income. Conversely, increases in the noncash current assets and decreases in the current liabilities must be deducted from the amount reported as net income. The relevant current asset and current liability accounts of Message Corporation are as follows:

Accounts	December 31 1992	December 31 1991	Increase Decrease*
Trade receivables (net)	$ 74,000	$ 65,000	$ 9,000
Inventories	172,000	180,000	8,000*
Prepaid expenses	4,000	3,000	1,000
Accounts payable (merchandise creditors)	50,000	32,000	18,000
Income tax payable	2,500	4,000	1,500*

The additions to **trade receivables** for sales on account during the year were $9,000 more than the deductions for amounts collected from customers on account. The amount reported on the income statement as sales therefore included $9,000 that did not yield cash inflow during the year. Accordingly, $9,000 must be deducted from net income.

The $8,000 decrease in **inventories** indicates that the merchandise sold exceeded the cost of the merchandise purchased by $8,000. The amount reported on the income statement as a deduction from the revenue therefore included $8,000 that did not require cash outflow during the year. Accordingly, $8,000 must be added to net income.

The outlay of cash for **prepaid expenses** exceeded by $1,000 the amount deducted as an expense during the year. Hence, $1,000 must be deducted from net income.

The effect of the increase in **accounts payable**, which is the amount owed creditors for goods and services, was to include in expired costs and expenses the sum of $18,000 for which there had been no cash outlay during the year. Income was thereby reduced by $18,000, though there was no cash outlay. Hence, $18,000 must be added to net income.

The outlay of cash for **income taxes** exceeded by $1,500 the amount of income tax deducted as an expense during the period. Accordingly, $1,500 must be deducted from net income.

The foregoing adjustments to income, including the adjustment for depreciation, may be summarized as follows:

Cash flows from operating activities:			
Net income		$ 90,500	
Add: Depreciation	$18,000		
Decrease in inventories	8,000		
Increase in accounts payable	18,000	44,000	
		$134,500	
Deduct: Increase in trade receivables	$ 9,000		
Increase in prepaid expenses	1,000		
Decrease in income tax payable	1,500	11,500	$123,000

Gain on Sale of Investments. Reference to the ledger or income statement would indicate that the sale of investments resulted in a gain of $30,000. As discussed in preceding paragraphs, to avoid the double reporting of this

$30,000 in the statement of cash flows, it must be deducted from the net income reported on the income statement as follows:[6]

Cash flows from operating activities:		
Net income	$90,500	
Deduct: Gain on sale of investments..........	30,000	$60,500

Reporting Cash Flows from Operating Activities. All the adjustments that are necessary to convert the net income to cash flows from operating activities for Message Corporation are presented in a format suitable for the statement of cash flows, as follows:

Cash flows from operating activities:			
Net income, per income statement		$ 90,500	
Add: Depreciation..........	$18,000		
Decrease in inventories..........	8,000		
Increase in accounts payable..........	18,000	44,000	
		$134,500	
Deduct: Increase in trade receivables	$ 9,000		
Increase in prepaid expenses..........	1,000		
Decrease in income tax payable..........	1,500		
Gain on sale of investments..........	30,000	41,500	
Net cash flow from operating activities			$93,000

Cash Flows for Payment of Dividends. According to the retained earnings account of Message Corporation (page 597), cash dividends of $30,000 were declared during the year. However, according to the dividends payable account, shown as follows, dividend payments during the year totaled $23,000, revealing a timing difference between the declaration and the payment.

ACCOUNT DIVIDENDS PAYABLE ACCOUNT NO.

Date		Item	Debit	Credit	Balance Debit	Balance Credit
1992						
Jan.	1	Balance				8,000
	10	Cash paid	8,000		—	—
June	20	Dividend declared		15,000		15,000
July	10	Cash paid	15,000		—	—
Dec.	20	Dividend declared		15,000		15,000

The $23,000 of cash dividend payments would be reported in the financing activities section and may be noted on the statement of cash flows as follows:

Cash flows from financing activities:	
Cash paid for dividends..........	$23,000

Common Stock

The increase of $50,000 in the common stock account, shown as follows, is the result of stock being issued in exchange for land valued at $50,000.

[6]The reporting of the cash flows from the sale of investments, which is an investing activity, is discussed in a later paragraph.

ACCOUNT COMMON STOCK ACCOUNT NO.

Date		Item	Debit	Credit	Balance Debit	Balance Credit
1992						
Jan.	1	Balance				230,000
Dec.	28	Issued at par in exchange for land		50,000		280,000

Although cash was not involved, the transaction represents a significant investing and financing transaction that should be reported in a separate schedule to the statement of cash flows, as discussed previously. In this schedule, the transaction may be noted as follows:

Noncash investing and financing activities:
Acquisition of land by issuance of common stock $50,000

Preferred Stock

The increase of $150,000 in the preferred stock account and the increase of $10,000 in the premium on preferred stock account, shown as follows, is the result of an issuance of preferred stock for $160,000.

ACCOUNT PREFERRED STOCK, $50 PAR ACCOUNT NO.

Date		Item	Debit	Credit	Balance Debit	Balance Credit
1992						
Nov.	1	3,000 shares issued for cash		150,000		150,000

ACCOUNT PAID-IN CAPITAL IN EXCESS OF PAR—PREFERRED STOCK ACCOUNT NO.

Date		Item	Debit	Credit	Balance Debit	Balance Credit
1992						
Nov.	1	3,000 shares issued for cash		10,000		10,000

This cash flow would be reported in the financing activities section and may be noted on the statement of cash flows as follows:

Cash flows from financing activities:
Cash received from sale of preferred stock $160,000

Bonds Payable

The next item listed on the balance sheet, bonds payable, decreased $125,000 during the year. Examination of the bonds payable account, which appears as follows, indicates that $125,000 of the bonds payable were retired by a cash payment for the face amount.

ACCOUNT BONDS PAYABLE ACCOUNT NO.

Date		Item	Debit	Credit	Balance Debit	Balance Credit
1992						
Jan.	1	Balance				245,000
June	30	Retired by payment of cash at face amount	125,000			120,000

This cash flow would be reported in the financing activities section and may be noted as follows:

Cash flows from financing activities:
Cash paid to retire bonds payable $125,000

Equipment

The comparative balance sheet indicates that the cost of equipment increased $148,000. The following equipment account and the accumulated depreciation account reveal that the net change of $148,000 was the result of two separate transactions — the discarding of equipment that had cost $9,000 and the purchase of equipment for $157,000. The equipment discarded had been fully depreciated, as indicated by the debit of $9,000 in the accumulated depreciation account, and no salvage was realized from its disposal. Hence, the transaction had no effect on cash and is not reported on the statement of cash flows.

ACCOUNT EQUIPMENT ACCOUNT NO.

Date		Item	Debit	Credit	Balance	
					Debit	Credit
1992						
Jan.	1	Balance			142,000	
May	9	Discarded, no salvage		9,000		
Dec.	7	Purchased for cash	157,000		290,000	

ACCOUNT ACCUMULATED DEPRECIATION—EQUIPMENT ACCOUNT NO.

Date		Item	Debit	Credit	Balance	
					Debit	Credit
1992						
Jan.	1	Balance				40,000
May	9	Discarded, no salvage	9,000			
Dec.	31	Depreciation for year		12,000		43,000

The effect on cash flows from the purchase of equipment for $157,000 would be reported in the investing activities section and may be noted as follows:

Cash flows from investing activities:
Cash paid for purchase of equipment $157,000

The credit in the accumulated depreciation account had the effect of reducing the book value of equipment by $12,000 but caused no change in cash. The depreciation was treated previously as an addition to net income in determining cash flows from operating activities.

Building

According to the comparative balance sheet, there was no change in the $200,000 balance in the building account between the beginning and end of the year. Reference to the ledger confirms the absence of entries in the building account during the year, and hence the account is not shown here. The credit in the related accumulated depreciation account reduced the book value of the building, but, as indicated previously, cash was not affected. The depreciation was treated previously as an addition to net income in determining cash flows from operating activities.

Land

The comparative balance sheet indicates that land increased by $50,000. The notation in the land account, which follows, indicates that the land was acquired by issuance of common stock at par.

ACCOUNT LAND — ACCOUNT NO.

Date		Item	Debit	Credit	Balance Debit	Balance Credit
1992						
Jan.	1	Balance			40,000	
Dec.	28	Acquired by issuance of common stock at par	50,000		90,000	

Although cash was not involved in this transaction, as indicated previously, the acquisition represents a significant investing and financing activity. Therefore, the transaction would be reported in a separate schedule as follows:

Noncash investing and financing activities:
Acquisition of land by issuance of common stock $50,000

Investments

The comparative balance sheet indicates that investments decreased by $45,000. The notation in the following investments account indicates that the investments were sold for $75,000 in cash.

ACCOUNT INVESTMENTS — ACCOUNT NO.

Date		Item	Debit	Credit	Balance Debit	Balance Credit
1992						
Jan.	1	Balance			45,000	
June	8	Sold for $75,000 cash		45,000	—	—

The $75,000 received from the sale of the investments must be reported as a cash flow from investing activities. Accordingly, the notation in the statement of cash flows is as follows:

Cash flows from investing activities:
Cash received from sale of investments (includes $30,000 gain reported in net income) $75,000

Note that the $30,000 gain on the sale is included in the net income reported on the income statement. As indicated previously, this gain was deducted from the net income in determining the cash flows from operating activities.

Preparing the Statement of Cash Flows

The statement of cash flows for Message Corporation can be prepared from the data assembled and analyzed in the preceding paragraphs. Using the indirect method of reporting cash flows from operating activities, the statement of cash flows for Message Corporation is shown below. An analysis of the statement indicates that the cash position increased by $23,000 during the year. The most significant increase in net cash flows, $93,000, was from operating activities, while the most significant use of cash, $82,000, was for investing activities.

Statement of Cash Flows

Message Corporation
Statement of Cash Flows
For Year Ended December 31, 1992

Cash flows from operating activities:			
Net income, per income statement		$ 90,500	
Add: Depreciation	$ 18,000		
Decrease in inventories	8,000		
Increase in accounts payable	18,000	44,000	
		$134,500	
Deduct: Increase in trade receivables	$ 9,000		
Increase in prepaid expenses	1,000		
Decrease in income tax payable	1,500		
Gain on sale of investments	30,000	41,500	
Net cash flow from operating activities			$93,000
Cash flows from investing activities:			
Cash received from sale of investments		$ 75,000	
Less: Cash paid for purchase of equipment		157,000	
Net cash flow used for investing activities			(82,000)
Cash flows from financing activities:			
Cash received from sale of preferred stock		$160,000	
Less: Cash paid for dividends	$ 23,000		
Cash paid to retire bonds payable	125,000	148,000	
Net cash flow provided by financing activities			12,000
Increase in cash			$23,000
Cash at the beginning of the year			26,000
Cash at the end of the year			$49,000

Schedule of Noncash Investing and Financing Activities

Acquisition of land by issuance of common stock	$50,000

APPENDIX

THE DIRECT METHOD OF REPORTING CASH FLOWS FROM OPERATING ACTIVITIES

There are two alternative formats for reporting cash flows from operating activities on the statement of cash flows: (1) the indirect method and (2) the direct method. The amount reported as the net cash flow from operating activities will not be affected by the format used. The indirect method is more widely used in practice and was discussed and illustrated in this chapter. The basic concepts of reporting cash flows from operating activities by the direct method are briefly discussed in this appendix.

In reporting cash flows from operating activities by the direct method, the major classes of operating cash receipts (cash received from customers, for example) and operating cash payments (cash payments to suppliers for merchandise, for example) are presented on the statement of cash flows. The difference between the total cash receipts by major classes and the total cash payments by major classes is the net cash flow from operating activities.[7]

ASSEMBLING DATA FOR CASH FLOWS FROM OPERATING ACTIVITIES

To collect data for reporting cash flows from operating activities by the direct method, all of the operating cash receipts and operating cash payments for a period could be analyzed and classified for reporting on the statement of cash flows. However, this procedure would be expensive and time-consuming. A more efficient procedure is to examine the revenues and expenses reported on the income statement and to determine the cash flows related to these revenues and expenses. In performing this analysis, supplementary data can be obtained from other records as needed. To illustrate, the following data for Johnson Company, showing the change in relevant account balances from the beginning to the end of 1992, and the income statement for the year ended December 31, 1992, will be used.

Accounts	December 31 1992	December 31 1991	Increase Decrease*
Trade receivables	$ 72,500	$ 65,000	$ 7,500
Inventories	155,000	165,000	10,000*
Prepaid expenses	6,500	5,000	1,500
Accounts payable (merchandise creditors)	60,000	46,000	14,000
Accrued operating expenses	13,000	8,500	4,500
Income tax payable	5,500	7,500	2,000*

[7] A reconciliation of net income and net cash flow from operating activities, as illustrated on page 601, should be included as a supplement to the cash flow statement when the direct method of reporting cash flows from operating activities is used.

Johnson Company Income Statement For Year Ended December 31, 1992		
Sales		$990,000
Cost of merchandise sold		580,000
Gross profit		$410,000
Operating expenses:		
Depreciation expense	$ 38,000	
Other operating expenses	256,500	
Total operating expenses		294,500
Income before income tax		$115,500
Income tax		27,500
Net income		$ 88,000

The determination of the cash receipts and cash payments by major classes are discussed and illustrated in the following paragraphs.

Cash Received from Customers

The $990,000 of sales reported on the income statement for Johnson Company is determined by the accrual method. To determine the cash received from sales made to customers, the $990,000 must be converted to the cash basis. The procedure to convert the sales reported on the income statement to the cash received from customers can be summarized as follows:

Sales (reported on the income statement)	....	+ decrease in trade receivables or − increase in trade receivables	=	Cash Received from Customers

For Johnson Company, the cash received from customers is $982,500, determined as follows:

Sales	$990,000
Less increase in trade receivables	7,500
Cash received from customers	$982,500

The additions to **trade receivables** for sales on account during the year were $7,500 more than the deductions for amounts collected from customers on account. The amount reported on the income statement as sales therefore included $7,500 that did not yield cash inflow during the year. In other words, the increase in trade receivables of $7,500 during 1992 indicates that sales exceeded cash received from customers by $7,500. Accordingly, $7,500 must be deducted from sales to determine the cash received from customers.

The $982,500 of cash received from customers would be reported in the cash flows from operating activities section of the cash flow statement. For Johnson Company, this section is presented on page 610.

Cash Payments for Merchandise

The $580,000 of cost of merchandise sold reported on the income statement for Johnson Company is determined by the accrual method. The conversion of the cost of merchandise sold to the cash payments made during 1992 for merchandise can be summarized as follows:

	+ increase in inventories		
	or		
Cost of Merchandise Sold (reported on the income statement)	− decrease in inventories	=	Cash Payments for Merchandise
	AND		
	+ decrease in accounts payable		
	or		
	− increase in accounts payable		

In the illustration for Johnson Company, the cash payments for merchandise is $556,000, determined as follows:

Cost of merchandise sold		$580,000
Deduct: Decrease in inventories	$10,000	
Increase in accounts payable	14,000	24,000
Cash payments for merchandise		$556,000

The $10,000 decrease in **inventories** indicates that the merchandise sold exceeded the cost of the merchandise purchased by $10,000. The amount reported on the income statement as a deduction from sales revenue therefore included $10,000 that did not require cash outflow during the year. Accordingly, $10,000 must be deducted from cost of merchandise sold in determining the cash payments for merchandise.

The effect of the increase in **accounts payable**, which is the amount owed creditors for merchandise, was to include in merchandise purchases the sum of $14,000 for which there had been no cash outlay during the year. In other words, the increase in accounts payable indicates that cash payments for merchandise were $14,000 less than purchases made during 1992. Hence, $14,000 must be deducted from the cost of merchandise sold in determining the cash payments for merchandise.

Cash Payments for Operating Expenses

Since the $38,000 of depreciation expense reported on the income statement did not require an outlay of cash, it is not reported on the statement of cash flows. The conversion of the $256,500 reported for the other operating expenses to cash payments for operating expenses can be summarized as follows:

	+ increase in prepaid expenses		
	or		
Operating Expenses other than Depreciation (reported on the income statement)	− decrease in prepaid expenses	=	Cash Payments for Operating Expenses
	AND		
	+ decrease in accrued expenses		
	or		
	− increase in accrued expenses		

For Johnson Company, the cash payments for operating expenses is $253,500, determined as follows:

Operating expenses other than depreciation	$256,500
Add increase in prepaid expenses	1,500
	$258,000
Deduct increase in accrued operating expenses	4,500
Cash payments for operating expenses	$253,500

The outlay of cash for **prepaid expenses** exceeded by $1,500 the amount deducted as an expense during the year. Hence, $1,500 must be added to the amount of operating expenses (other than depreciation) reported on the income statement in determining the cash payments for operating expenses.

The increase in **accrued operating expenses** indicates that the amount reported as an expense during the year exceeded the cash payments by $4,500. Hence, $4,500 must be deducted from the amount of operating expenses on the income statement in determining the cash payments for operating expenses.

Cash Payments for Income Taxes

The procedure to convert the amount of income tax reported on the income statement to the cash basis can be summarized as follows:

Income Tax (reported on income statement)	......	+ decrease in income tax payable or − increase in income tax payable	=	Cash Payments for Income Tax

For Johnson Company, the cash payments for income tax is $29,500, determined as follows:

Income tax	$27,500
Add decrease in income tax payable	2,000
Cash payments for income tax	$29,500

The outlay of cash for **income taxes** exceeded by $2,000 the amount of income tax deducted as an expense during the period. Accordingly, $2,000 must be added to the amount of income tax reported on the income statement to determine the cash payments for income tax.

REPORTING CASH FLOWS FROM OPERATING ACTIVITIES

The main classes of operating cash receipts and operating cash payments for Johnson Company, as determined in the preceding paragraphs, may be reported in the statement of cash flows as follows:

Cash flows from operating activities:			
Cash received from customers		$982,500	
Deduct: Cash payments for merchandise	$556,000		
Cash payments for operating expenses	253,500		
Cash payments for income tax	29,500	839,000	
Net cash flow from operating activities			$143,500

Regardless of whether the direct method or the indirect method is used, the same amount of net cash flow from operating activities will be reported in the statement of cash flows. When the direct method is used, a reconciliation of net income and net cash flow from operating activities should be reported in a separate schedule to accompany the statement of cash flows.[8] This schedule is similar to the cash flows from operating activities section of the statement of cash flows that would be presented when the indirect method is used. For Johnson Company, such a schedule would appear as follows:

Net income, per income statement		$ 88,000	
Add: Depreciation	$38,000		
Decrease in inventories	10,000		
Increase in accounts payable	14,000		
Increase in accrued operating expenses	4,500	66,500	
		$154,500	
Deduct: Increase in trade receivables	$ 7,500		
Increase in prepaid expenses	1,500		
Decrease in income tax payable	2,000	11,000	
Net cash flow from operating activities			$143,500

APPENDIX

WORK SHEET FOR STATEMENT OF CASH FLOWS

Some accountants prefer to use a work sheet to assist them in assembling data for the statement of cash flows. Although a work sheet is not essential, it is especially useful when a large number of transactions must be analyzed. The concept of cash flows and the statement of cash flows are not affected regardless of whether or not a work sheet is used.

The following sections describe and illustrate the use of the work sheet in preparing the statement of cash flows for Message Corporation, based on the data in this chapter.

WORK SHEET PROCEDURES FOR STATEMENT OF CASH FLOWS

The comparative balance sheet and additional data obtained from the accounts of Message Corporation are presented on page 612. The work sheet prepared from these data is presented on page 613. The procedures to prepare the work sheet for the statement of cash flows are outlined as follows:

1. List the titles of each balance sheet account in the Accounts column. For each account, enter the balance as of December 31, 1991, in the first column, and the balance as of December 31, 1992, in the last column. Distinguish the debit balances from the credit balances by placing the credit balances in parentheses.
2. Total the balances for both the first and last columns. The total of the debit balances should equal the total of the credit balances; thus, the totals of the first and last columns should equal zero.
3. Provide space in the bottom portion of the work sheet for later use in identifying the various cash flows from (1) operating activities, (2) investing

[8]*Statement of Financial Accounting Standards, No. 95,* "Statement of Cash Flows" (Stamford: Financial Accounting Standards Board, 1987), par. 30.

activities, and (3) financing activities. Also, provide space at the end of the work sheet for later use in identifying items for the schedule of noncash investing and financing activities.

4. Analyze the change during the year in each account to determine the net increase (decrease) in cash and cash flows by type of activity. Record these activities in the bottom portion of the work sheet by means of entries in the work sheet Transactions columns.
5. Complete the work sheet.

The procedures for using the work sheet are explained in detail in the following paragraphs.

Message Corporation
Comparative Balance Sheet
December 31, 1992 and 1991

	1992	1991
Assets		
Cash	$ 49,000	$ 26,000
Trade receivables (net)	74,000	65,000
Inventories	172,000	180,000
Prepaid expenses	4,000	3,000
Investments (long-term)	—	45,000
Land	90,000	40,000
Building	200,000	200,000
Accumulated depreciation—building	(36,000)	(30,000)
Equipment	290,000	142,000
Accumulated depreciation—equipment	(43,000)	(40,000)
Total assets	$800,000	$631,000
Liabilities		
Accounts payable (merchandise creditors)	$ 50,000	$ 32,000
Income tax payable	2,500	4,000
Dividends payable	15,000	8,000
Bonds payable	120,000	245,000
Total liabilities	$187,500	$289,000
Stockholders' Equity		
Preferred stock	$150,000	—
Excess of issue price over par—preferred stock	10,000	—
Common stock	280,000	$230,000
Retained earnings	172,500	112,000
Total stockholders' equity	$612,500	$342,000
Total liabilities and stockholders' equity	$800,000	$631,000

Additional data:

(1) Net income, $90,500.
(2) Cash dividends declared, $30,000.
(3) Common stock issued at par for land, $50,000.
(4) Preferred stock issued for cash, $160,000.
(5) Bonds payable retired for cash, $125,000.
(6) Depreciation for year: equipment, $12,000; building, $6,000.
(7) Fully depreciated equipment discarded, $9,000.
(8) Equipment purchased for cash, $157,000.
(9) Book value of investments sold for $75,000 cash, $45,000.

Account Balances

Since cash flows can be determined by analyses of transactions affecting balance sheet accounts, the balance sheet account balances as of December 31, 1991 and 1992 are entered in the first and last columns of the work sheet. To

Work Sheet for Statement of Cash Flows

Message Corporation
Work Sheet for Statement of Cash Flows
For Year Ended December 31, 1992

Accounts	Balance, Dec. 31, 1991	Transactions Debit	Transactions Credit	Balance, Dec. 31, 1992
Cash	26,000	(r) 23,000		49,000
Trade Receivables	65,000	(q) 9,000		74,000
Inventories	180,000		(p) 8,000	172,000
Prepaid Expenses	3,000	(o) 1,000		4,000
Investments	45,000		(n) 45,000	—
Land	40,000	(m) 50,000		90,000
Building	200,000			200,000
Accumulated Depreciation—Building	(30,000)		(l) 6,000	(36,000)
Equipment	142,000	(k) 157,000	(j) 9,000	290,000
Accumulated Depreciation—Equipment	(40,000)	(j) 9,000	(i) 12,000	(43,000)
Accounts Payable	(32,000)		(h) 18,000	(50,000)
Income Tax Payable	(4,000)	(g) 1,500		(2,500)
Dividends Payable	(8,000)		(f) 7,000	(15,000)
Bonds Payable	(245,000)	(e) 125,000		(120,000)
Preferred Stock	—		(d) 150,000	(150,000)
Paid-In Capital in Excess of Par—Preferred Stock	—		(d) 10,000	(10,000)
Common Stock	(230,000)		(c) 50,000	(280,000)
Retained Earnings	(112,000)	(b) 30,000	(a) 90,500	(172,500)
Totals	0	405,500	405,500	0
Operating activities:				
Net Income		(a) 90,500		
Decrease in income tax payable			(g) 1,500	
Increase in accounts payable		(h) 18,000		
Depreciation of equipment		(i) 12,000		
Depreciation of building		(l) 6,000		
Gain on sale of investments			(n) 30,000	
Increase in prepaid expenses			(o) 1,000	
Decrease in inventories		(p) 8,000		
Increase in trade receivables			(q) 9,000	
Investing activities:				
Purchase of equipment			(k) 157,000	
Sale of investments		(n) 75,000		
Financing activities:				
Declaration of cash dividends			(b) 30,000	
Issuance of preferred stock		(d) 160,000		
Retirement of bonds payable			(e) 125,000	
Increase in dividends payable		(f) 7,000		
Schedule of noncash investing and financing activities:				
Acquisition of land by issuance of common stock		(c) 50,000	(m) 50,000	
Net increase in cash			(r) 23,000	
Totals		426,500	426,500	

reduce the size of the work sheet, both debit and credit balances are entered in the same column. Credit balances are identified with parentheses. The totals for both columns should equal zero, since the total of the debits in a column should equal the total of the credits in a column.

Cash Flow Activities

After the Balance columns are totaled and ruled, "Operating activities," "Investing activities," and "Financing activities" are written in the bottom portion of the work sheet. Several lines should be skipped between each category so that at a later time the various cash flows can be entered by type of activity. In addition, "Schedule of noncash investing and financing activities" is written near the bottom of the work sheet so that noncash transactions that have a significant effect on investing and financing activities can also be identified separately on the work sheet. When the work sheet is completed, the bottom portion of the work sheet will contain the data necessary to prepare the statement of cash flows.

Analysis of Accounts

As was discussed in this chapter, an efficient method of determining cash flows is to determine the type of cash flow activity that led to changes in balance sheet accounts during the period. As each noncash account is analyzed to make this determination, entries that relate specific types of cash flow activity to the noncash accounts are made in the work sheet. After all the noncash accounts have been analyzed, an entry is made to recognize the increase (decrease) in cash for the period. It should be noted that the work sheet entries are not entered into the accounts. They are, as is the entire work sheet, strictly an aid in assembling the data for later use in preparing the statement.

The sequence in which the accounts are analyzed is unimportant. However, because it is more convenient and efficient and the chance for errors is reduced, the analysis illustrated will begin with the retained earnings account and proceed upward in the listing in sequential order.

Retained Earnings. The work sheet indicates a balance of $112,000 at December 31, 1991, and $172,500 at December 31, 1992, for an increase of $60,500 in retained earnings for the year. The additional data, taken from an examination of the account, indicate that the increase was the result of two factors: (1) net income of $90,500 and (2) declaration of cash dividends of $30,000. To identify the cash flows by activity, two entries are made on the work sheet. These entries also serve to account for, or explain in terms of cash flows, the increase of $60,500.

Net Income. In closing the accounts at the end of the year, the retained earnings account was credited for $90,500, representing the net income. The $90,500 is also reported on the statement of cash flows as "cash flows from operating activities." An entry in the Transactions columns on the work sheet to debit "Operating activities—net income" and to credit retained earnings accomplishes the following: (1) the credit portion of the closing entry (to retained earnings) is accounted for and (2) the cash flow is identified in the bottom portion of the work sheet. The entry on the work sheet is as follows:

(a) Operating Activities—Net Income	90,500	
Retained Earnings...		90,500

Dividends. In closing the accounts at the end of the year, the retained earnings account was debited for $30,000, representing the cash dividends declared. The $30,000 is also reported on the statement as a financing activity. An entry on the work sheet to debit retained earnings and credit "Financing activities—declaration of cash dividends" accomplishes the following: (1) the debit portion of the closing entry (to retained earnings) is accounted for and (2) the cash flow is identified in the bottom portion of the work sheet. The entry on the work sheet is as follows:

		Debit	Credit
(b)	Retained Earnings..	30,000	
	Financing Activities—Declaration of Cash Dividends....		30,000

The cash used for the payment of dividends is also affected by a difference between the time a dividend is declared and the time it is paid. This effect is discussed later in this appendix.

Common Stock. The next item on the work sheet, common stock, increased from $230,000 to $280,000 or by $50,000 during the year. The additional data, taken from an examination of the account, indicate that the stock was exchanged for land. Although this is a noncash transaction, it should be reported in a separate schedule on the statement of cash flows. To account fully for the change of $50,000 in the common stock account and to provide the data for the separate schedule, the following entry is made on the work sheet:

		Debit	Credit
(c)	Schedule of Noncash Investing and Financing Activities:		
	Acquisition of Land by Issuance of Common Stock	50,000	
	Common Stock...		50,000

It should be noted that the effect of the exchange will also be analyzed when the land account is examined.

Preferred Stock. The work sheet indicates that the preferred stock account increased by $150,000 and the paid-in capital in excess of par—preferred stock account increased by $10,000. The additional data indicate that these increases resulted from the sale of preferred stock for $160,000. The work sheet entry to account for these increases and to identify the cash flow is as follows:

		Debit	Credit
(d)	Financing Activities—Issuance of Preferred Stock.....	160,000	
	Preferred Stock		150,000
	Paid-In Capital in Excess of Par—Preferred Stock ..		10,000

Bonds Payable. The decrease from $245,000 to $120,000 or $125,000 in the bonds payable account resulted from the retirement of the bonds for cash. The work sheet entry to record the effect of this transaction on cash is as follows:

		Debit	Credit
(e)	Bonds Payable..	125,000	
	Financing Activities—Retirement of Bonds Payable...		125,000

Dividends Payable. The increase in the dividends payable account from $8,000 to $15,000 during the year reveals a timing difference between the declaration and the payment of dividends. The additional data indicate that $30,000 of dividends had been declared, which was identified as a financing activity in entry (b). However, the increase in the dividends payable account of $7,000 indicates that only $23,000 ($30,000 − $7,000) of dividends were paid. The work sheet entry to adjust the dividends declared of $30,000 to reflect the dividends paid of $23,000 is as follows:

(f) Financing Activities—Declaration of Cash Dividends:		
Increase in Dividends Payable	7,000	
Dividends Payable		7,000

When the $7,000, which represents the increase in dividends payable, is deducted from the $30,000 of "Financing activities—declaration of cash dividends," $23,000 is subsequently reported on the statement as a cash flow from financing activity.

Income Tax Payable. The decrease from $4,000 to $2,500 in the income tax payable account indicates that the outlay of cash for income taxes exceeded by $1,500 the amount of income tax deducted as an expense during the period. Accordingly, $1,500 must be deducted from income to determine the amount of cash flows from operating activities. This procedure is indicated on the work sheet by the following entry:

(g) Income Tax Payable	1,500	
Operating Activities—Net Income:		
Decrease in Income Tax Payable		1,500

Accounts Payable. The accounts payable account increased by $18,000, from $32,000 to $50,000, during the year. The effect of the increase in the amount owed creditors for goods and services was to include in expired costs and expenses the sum of $18,000. Income was thereby reduced by $18,000 for which there had been no cash outlay during the year. Hence, $18,000 must be added to income to determine the amount of cash flows from operating activities. The work sheet entry is as follows:

(h) Operating Activities—Net Income:		
Increase in Accounts Payable	18,000	
Accounts Payable		18,000

Accumulated Depreciation—Equipment. The work sheet indicates that the accumulated depreciation—equipment account increased from $40,000 to $43,000 during the year. The additional data indicate that the increase resulted from (1) depreciation expense of $12,000 (credit) for the year and (2) discarding $9,000 (debit) of fully depreciated equipment. Since depreciation expense does not affect cash but does decrease the amount of net income, it should be added to net income to determine the amount of cash flows from operating activities. This effect is indicated on the work sheet by the following entry:

(i) Operating Activities—Net Income:		
Depreciation of Equipment	12,000	
Accumulated Depreciation—Equipment		12,000

Since the discarding of the fully depreciated equipment did not affect cash, the following entry is made on the work sheet in order to fully account for the change of $3,000 in the accumulated depreciation—equipment account:

(j) Accumulated Depreciation—Equipment	9,000	
Equipment		9,000

It should be noted that this entry, like the transaction that was recorded in the accounts, does not affect cash. It serves only to complete the accounting for all transactions that resulted in the change in the account during the year and thus helps assure that no transactions affecting cash are overlooked in the analysis.

Equipment. The work sheet indicates that the equipment account increased from $142,000 to $290,000 or by $148,000 during the year. The additional data, determined from an examination of the ledger account, indicates that the increase resulted from (1) discarding $9,000 of fully depreciated equipment and (2) purchasing $157,000 of equipment. The discarding of the equipment was included in, or accounted for, in (j) and needs no additional attention. The use of cash to purchase equipment is recognized by the following entry on the work sheet:

(k)	Equipment	157,000	
	Investing Activities—Purchase of Equipment		157,000

Accumulated Depreciation—Building. The work sheet indicates that the accumulated depreciation—building account increased from $30,000 to $36,000 during the year. This $6,000 increase in the accumulated depreciation—building account during the year resulted from the entry to record depreciation expense. Since depreciation expense does not affect cash but does decrease the amount of net income, it should be added to net income to determine the amount of cash flows from operating activities. This effect is accomplished by the following entry on the work sheet:

(l)	Operating Activities—Net Income:		
	Depreciation of Building	6,000	
	Accumulated Depreciation—Building		6,000

Building. There was no change in the balance of the building account during the year, and reference to the account confirms that no entries were made in it during the year. Hence, no entry is necessary on the work sheet.

As indicated in the analysis of the common stock account, the $50,000 increase in land resulted from an acquisition by issuance of common stock. To account fully for the change of $50,000 in the land account and to provide the data for the separate schedule reporting this noncash transaction, the following entry is made on the work sheet:

(m)	Land	50,000	
	Schedule of Noncash Investing and Financing Activities: Acquisition of Land by Issuance of Common Stock		50,000

Investments. The work sheet indicates that investments decreased from a balance of $45,000 to zero during the year. The examination of the ledger account indicates that investments were sold for $75,000. As was explained on page 605, the $30,000 gain on the sale is included in net income and must be deducted from the net income in the operating activities section. The $75,000 of cash flows from investments sold would be reported as an investing activity. To indicate this cash flow on the work sheet, the following entry is made:

(n)	Investing Activities—Sale of Investments	75,000	
	Operating Activities—Net Income:		
	Gain on Sale of Investments		30,000
	Investments		45,000

Prepaid Expenses. The work sheet indicates that the prepaid expenses account increased from a balance of $3,000 to $4,000 during the year. Thus, the outlay of cash for prepaid expenses exceeded by $1,000 the amount deducted as an expense during the year. Hence $1,000 must be deducted from income to determine the amount of cash flows from operating activities. The work sheet entry is as follows:

(o) Prepaid Expenses	1,000	
Operating Activities—Net Income:		
Increase in Prepaid Expenses		1,000

Inventories. The work sheet indicates that the inventories account decreased from $180,000 to $172,000 during the year. This $8,000 decrease indicates that the merchandise sold exceeded the cost of the merchandise purchased by $8,000. The amount reported on the income statement as a deduction from the revenue therefore included $8,000 that did not require cash outflow during the year. Accordingly, $8,000 must be added to income to determine the amount of cash flows from operations. The work sheet entry is as follows:

(p) Operating Activities—Net Income:		
Decrease in Inventories..	8,000	
Inventories..		8,000

Trade Receivables (Net). The work sheet indicates that the trade receivables account increased from $65,000 to $74,000 during the year. This $9,000 increase indicates that the additions to trade receivables for sales on account during the year exceeded by $9,000 the deductions for amounts collected from customers on account. The amount reported on the income statement as sales therefore included $9,000 that did not yield cash inflow during the year. Accordingly, $9,000 must be deducted from income to determine the amount of cash flows from operating activities. The work sheet entry is as follows:

(q) Trade Receivables	9,000	
Operating Activities—Net Income:		
Increase in Trade Receivables..		9,000

Cash. The work sheet indicates that the cash account increased from $26,000 to $49,000 during the year. This $23,000 increase in cash is identified in the work sheet by the following entry:

(r) Cash	23,000	
Net Increase in Cash..		23,000

The credit portion of the entry is entered at the bottom of the work sheet. In preparing the statement of cash flows, the cash balance at the beginning of the year is added to this amount to determine the cash balance at the end of the year.

Completing the Work Sheet

After all the balance sheet accounts have been analyzed, all the operating, investing, and financing activities are identified in the bottom portion of the work sheet. To assure the accuracy of the work sheet entries, the debit and credit Transaction columns are totaled and compared for equality.

The statment of cash flows prepared from the work sheet is identical to the statement illustrated on page 606. The data for the three sections of the statement are obtained from the bottom portion of the work sheet. Some modifications are made to the work sheet data for presentation on the statement. For example, in presenting the cash flows from operating activities, the total depreciation expense ($18,000) is reported instead of the two separate amounts ($12,000 and $6,000). In preparing the cash flows for operating activities section, the effect of depreciation is normally presented first, followed by the effects of increases and decreases in current assets and current liabilities. The effects of any gains and losses on operating activities is normally presented last. The cash paid for dividends is reported as $23,000 instead of the amount of dividends declared ($30,000) less the increase in dividends payable ($7,000). The issuance of the common stock for land ($50,000) is reported in a separate schedule.

CHAPTER REVIEW

KEY POINTS

OBJECTIVE 1

Nature of the Statement of Cash Flows

The statement of cash flows reports a firm's major sources of cash receipts and major uses of cash payments for a period. The statement of cash flows provides useful information about a firm's activities in generating cash from operations, meeting its financial obligations, paying dividends, and maintaining and expanding operating capacity. When used in conjunction with the other financial statements, the statement of cash flows is useful in analyzing both past and future profits of a firm and the ability of a firm to pay its liabilities as they become due.

OBJECTIVE 2

Types of Cash Flow Activities

The statement of cash flows classifies cash receipts and cash payments by three types of activities: cash flows from operating activities, cash flows from investing activities, and cash flows from financing activities.

Cash flows from operating activities relate to cash transactions that enter into the determination of net income. There are two alternatives to reporting cash flows from such operating activities in the statement of cash flows: (1) the direct method and (2) the indirect method. Because of its more frequent usage, the indirect method was used in this chapter. Regardless of which method is used, the same amount of net cash flows from operating activities will be reported.

Cash inflows from investing activities generally arise from the sale of investments, plant assets, and intangible assets. Cash outflows generally include payments to acquire investments, plant assets, and intangible assets. In reporting cash flows from investing activities on the statement of cash flows, the cash inflows are usually reported first, followed by the cash outflows.

Cash inflows from financing activities include proceeds from the issuance of equity securities, such as preferred and common stock. Cash inflows also arise from the issuance of bonds, mortgage notes payable, and other long-term and short-term borrowings. Cash outflows from financing activities include the payment of cash dividends, the acquisition of treasury stock, and the repayment of amounts borrowed. In reporting cash flows from financing activities on the statement of cash flows, the cash inflows are usually reported first, followed by the cash outflows.

Investing and financing for an enterprise may be affected by transactions that do not involve cash. If such transactions have occurred during the period, their effect, if significant, should be reported in a separate schedule to accompany the statement of cash flows. This broadened concept recognizes that some investing and financing transactions do not involve cash receipts and payments, but have a significant effect on future cash flows. For example, the issuance of common stock to retire long-term debt has no effect on cash. However, the transaction will eliminate the future cash payments to retire the bonds and future cash payments for interest. Therefore, it should be reported.

OBJECTIVE 3

Assembling Data for and Preparing the Statement of Cash Flows

The common and most efficient procedure for determining the data for the statement of cash flows is to examine the noncash balance sheet accounts and determine the type of cash flow activity related to changes in these accounts.

The statement of cash flows is divided into three sections, with the cash flows from operating activities generally placed first, followed by the cash flows from investing activities and the cash flows from financing activities. A separate schedule is used to report noncash investing and financing activities.

KEY TERMS

statement of cash flows 592
cash flows from operating activities 593
cash flows from investing activities 593
cash flows from financing activities 593
direct method 594
indirect method 594

SELF-EXAMINATION QUESTIONS

Answers at end of chapter.

1. A full set of financial statements for a corporation would include:
   A. a balance sheet
   B. an income statement
   C. a statement of cash flows
   D. all of the above

2. An example of a cash flow from an operating activity is:
   A. receipt of cash from the sale of capital stock
   B. receipt of cash from the sale of bonds
   C. payment of cash for dividends
   D. none of the above

3. An example of a cash flow from an investing activity is:
   A. receipt of cash from the sale of equipment
   B. receipt of cash from the sale of capital stock
   C. payment of cash for dividends
   D. payment of cash to repurchase equity securities

4. An example of a cash flow from a financing activity is:
   A. receipt of cash from the sale of capital stock
   B. receipt of cash from the sale of bonds
   C. payment of cash for dividends
   D. all of the above

5. The net income reported on the income statement for the year was $55,000 and depreciation on plant assets for the year was $22,000. The balances of the current

asset and current liability accounts at the beginning and end of the year are as follows:

	End	Beginning
Cash	$ 65,000	$ 70,000
Trade receivables	100,000	90,000
Inventories	145,000	150,000
Prepaid expenses	7,500	8,000
Accounts payable (merchandise creditors)	51,000	58,000

The total amount reported for cash flows from operating activities in the statement of cash flows would be:

A. $33,000
B. $55,000
C. $77,000
D. none of the above

ILLUSTRATIVE PROBLEM

The comparative balance sheet of Jones Inc. for December 31, 1992 and 1991, is as follows:

Assets	1992	1991
Cash	$ 65,100	$ 42,500
Trade receivables (net)	91,350	61,150
Inventories	104,500	109,500
Prepaid expenses	3,600	2,700
Land	30,000	50,000
Buildings	345,000	245,000
Accumulated depreciation—buildings	(120,600)	(110,400)
Machinery and equipment	255,000	255,000
Accumulated depreciation—machinery and equipment	(92,000)	(65,000)
Patents	35,000	40,000
	$716,950	$630,450

Liabilities and Stockholders' Equity		
Accounts payable (merchandise creditors)	$ 61,150	$ 75,000
Dividends payable	15,000	10,000
Salaries payable	6,650	7,550
Mortgage note payable, due 1997	60,000	—
Bonds payable	—	75,000
Common stock, $20 par	300,000	250,000
Excess of issue price over par—common stock	100,000	75,000
Retained earnings	174,150	137,900
	$716,950	$630,450

An examination of the income statement and the accounting records revealed the following additional information applicable to 1992:

(a) Net income, $96,250.
(b) Depreciation expense reported on the income statement: buildings, $10,200; machinery and equipment, $27,000.
(c) Land costing $20,000 was sold for $20,000.
(d) Patent amortization reported on the income statement, $5,000.
(e) A mortgage note was issued for $60,000.
(f) A building costing $100,000 was constructed.

(g) 2,500 shares of common stock were issued at 30 in exchange for the bonds payable.
(h) Cash dividends declared, $60,000.

Instructions:

Prepare a statement of cash flows.

SOLUTION

Jones Inc.
Statement of Cash Flows
For Year Ended December 31, 1992

Cash flows from operating activities:			
Net income, per income statement		$ 96,250	
Add: Depreciation.............................	$ 37,200		
Amortization of patents	5,000		
Decrease in inventories..............	5,000	47,200	
		$143,450	
Deduct: Increase in trade receivables (net).................................	$ 30,200		
Increase in prepaid expenses ...	900		
Decrease in accounts payable...	13,850		
Decrease in salaries payable.....	900	45,850	
Net cash flow from operating activities ...			$97,600
Cash flows from investing activities:			
Cash received from sale of land		$ 20,000	
Less: Cash paid for construction of building..............................		100,000	
Net cash flow used for investing activities..			(80,000)
Cash flows from financing activities:			
Cash received from issuance of mortgage note payable		$ 60,000	
Less: Cash paid for dividends.............		55,000	
Net cash flow provided by financing activities..			5,000
Increase in cash....................................			$22,600
Cash at the beginning of the year.............			42,500
Cash at the end of the year			$65,100

Schedule of Noncash Investing and Financing Activities

Issuance of common stock to retire bonds payable................	$75,000

DISCUSSION QUESTIONS

14–1. Which financial statement is most useful in evaluating past and planning future investing and financing activities?

14–2. What financial statement was replaced by the statement of cash flows?

14–3. For the statement of changes in financial position, the working capital basis was often employed. What is working capital?

14–4. What are the three types of activities reported on the statement of cash flows?

14–5. State the effect of each of the following transactions, considered individually, on cash flows (cash receipt or payment, and amount):
(a) Sold a new issue of $300,000 of bonds at 98.
(b) Sold equipment with a book value of $67,500 for $80,000.
(c) Sold 1,000 shares of $100 par common stock at $120 per share.
(d) Retired $100,000 of bonds on which there was $6,000 of unamortized bond discount for $102,000.

14–6. Identify each of the following as to type of cash flow activity (operating, investing, or financing):
(a) Sale of investments
(b) Issuance of common stock
(c) Purchase of buildings
(d) Net income
(e) Issuance of bonds
(f) Payment of cash dividends
(g) Purchase of treasury stock
(h) Redemption of bonds
(i) Sale of equipment
(j) Issuance of preferred stock
(k) Purchase of patents

14–7. Name the two alternatives to reporting cash flows from operating activities in the statement of cash flows.

14–8. What is the principal disadvantage of the direct method of reporting cash flows from operating activities?

14–9. What are the major advantages of the indirect method of reporting cash flows from operating activities?

14–10. On the statement of cash flows, if the cash inflows from investing activities exceed the cash outflows, how is the difference described?

14–11. On the statement of cash flows, if the cash outflows from investing activities exceed the cash inflows, how is the difference described?

14–12. On the statement of cash flows, if the cash inflows from financing activities exceed the cash outflows, how is the difference described?

14–13. On the statement of cash flows, if the cash outflows from financing activities exceed the cash inflows, how is the difference described?

14–14. A corporation issued $500,000 of common stock in exchange for $500,000 of plant assets. Where would this transaction be reported on the statement of cash flows?

14–15. A corporation acquired as a long-term investment all of the capital stock of Jackson Inc., valued at $10,000,000, by issuance of $10,000,000 of its own common stock. Where should the transaction be reported on the statement of cash flows?

14–16. (a) What is the effect on cash flows of the declaration and issuance of a stock dividend?
(b) Is the stock dividend reported on the statement of cash flows?

14–17. On its income statement for the current year, a company reported a net loss of $30,000 from operations. On its statement of cash flows, it reported $15,000 of cash flows from operating activities. Explain the seeming contradiction between the loss and the cash flows.

14–18. What is the effect on cash flows of an appropriation of retained earnings for bonded indebtedness?

14–19. Indicate whether each of the following would be added to or deducted from net income in determining net cash flow from operating activities:
(a) Depreciation of plant assets
(b) Decrease in accounts payable
(c) Gain on retirement of long-term debt
(d) Increase in notes payable due in 120 days
(e) Increase in notes receivable due in 90 days
(f) Amortization of discount on bonds payable
(g) Increase in merchandise inventory
(h) Decrease in accounts receivable
(i) Loss on disposal of plant assets
(j) Decrease in accrued salaries payable
(k) Amortization of bonds premium
(l) Amortization of patents
(m) Decrease in prepaid expenses

14–20. A retail enterprise, employing the accrual method of accounting, owed merchandise creditors (accounts payable) $175,000 at the beginning of the year and $192,000 at the end of the year. What adjustment for the $17,000 increase must be made to net income in determining the amount of cash flows from operating activities? Explain.

14–21. If revenue from sales amounted to $680,000 for the year and trade receivables totaled $55,000 and $75,000 at the beginning and end of the year, respectively, what was the amount of cash received from customers during the year?

14–22. If salaries payable was $15,000 and $22,000 at the beginning and end of the year, respectively, should $7,000 be added to or deducted from income to determine the amount of cash flows from operating activities? Explain.

14–23. The board of directors declared cash dividends totaling $90,000 during the current year. The comparative balance sheet indicates dividends payable of $20,000 at the beginning of the year and $22,500 at the end of the year. What was the amount of cash payments to stockholders during the year?

14–24. A long-term investment in bonds with a cost of $115,000 was sold for $127,500 cash. (a) What was the gain or loss on the sale? (b) What was the effect of the transaction on cash flows? (c) How should the transaction be reported in the statement of cash flows?

14–25. A corporation issued $1,000,000 of 20-year bonds for cash at 95. How would the transaction be reported on the statement of cash flows?

14–26. Fully depreciated equipment costing $150,000 was discarded. What was the effect of the transaction on cash flows if (a) $6,000 cash is received, (b) there is no salvage value?

Real World Focus

14–27. In its 1989 financial statements, Apple Computer Inc. reported the issuance of 33,812 shares of common stock having a value of $1,631,429 in conjunction with acquisitions. How would this transaction be reported on the statement of cash flows?

Ethics Discussion Case

14–28. Lee Curtis, controller of Tish Inc., has decided to add "cash flow per share" to the financial statements. He feels that such reporting, although different from past reporting, would be useful to the readers. The "cash flow per share" would be reported on the statement of cash flows. On a comparative basis with the preceding year, the "cash flow per share" figure for the current year increased by 35% (as contrasted with a slight decline in net income and earnings per share).

Discuss whether Lee Curtis is behaving in an ethical manner.

EXERCISES

Ex 14–29.
Cash flows from operating activities section.
OBJ. 2, 3

The net income reported on the income statement for the current year was $110,000. Depreciation recorded on equipment and a building amounted to $21,300 for the year. Balances of the current asset and current liability accounts at the beginning and end of the year are as follows:

	End of Year	Beginning of Year
Cash	$ 73,350	$ 70,500
Trade receivables (net)	105,000	96,000
Inventories	132,000	114,000
Prepaid expenses	8,300	9,200
Accounts payable (merchandise creditors)	93,000	87,300
Salaries payable	4,500	7,500

Prepare the cash flows from operating activities section of the statement of cash flows.

Ex. 14–30.
Cash flows from operating activities section.
OBJ. 2, 3

The net income reported on an income statement for the current year was $73,700. Depreciation recorded on store equipment for the year amounted to $23,800. Balances of the current asset and current liability accounts at the beginning and end of the year are as follows:

	End of Year	Beginning of Year
Cash	$55,800	$50,000
Trade receivable (net)	64,400	68,000
Merchandise inventory	88,000	77,600
Prepaid expenses	6,300	6,000
Accounts payable (merchandise creditors)	55,800	58,200
Wages payable	6,000	5,000

Prepare the cash flows from operating activities section of a statement of cash flows.

Ex. 14–31.
Reporting changes in equipment on statement of cash flows.
OBJ. 2, 3

An analysis of the general ledger accounts indicated that office equipment, which had cost $120,000 and on which accumulated depreciation totaled $105,000 on the date of sale, was sold for $14,000 during the year. Using this information, indicate the items to be reported on the statement of cash flows.

Ex. 14–32.
Reporting changes in equipment on statement of cash flows.
OBJ. 2, 3

An analysis of the general ledger accounts indicated that delivery equipment, which had cost $56,000 and on which accumulated depreciation totaled $47,600 on the date of sale, was sold for $11,200 during the year. Using this information, indicate the items to be reported on the statement of cash flows.

Ex. 14–33.
Reporting land transactions on statement of cash flows.
OBJ. 2, 3

On the basis of the details of the following plant asset account, indicate the items to be reported on the statement of cash flows.

ACCOUNT LAND ACCOUNT NO.

Date		Item	Debit	Credit	Balance Debit	Balance Credit
19--						
Jan.	1	Balance			800,000	
Aug.	29	Purchased for cash	250,000			
Nov.	20	Sold for $80,000		50,000	1,000,000	

Ex. 14–34.
Reporting stockholders' equity items on statement of cash flows.
OBJ. 2, 3

On the basis of the following stockholders' equity accounts, indicate the items, exclusive of net income, to be reported on the statement of cash flows. There were no unpaid dividends at either the beginning or end of the year.

ACCOUNT COMMON STOCK, $10 PAR ACCOUNT NO.

Date		Item	Debit	Credit	Balance Debit	Balance Credit
19--						
Jan.	1	Balance, 65,000 shares				650,000
	20	10,000 shares issued for cash		100,000		
June	25	3,750-share stock dividend		37,500		787,500

ACCOUNT PAID-IN CAPITAL IN EXCESS OF PAR—COMMON STOCK ACCOUNT NO.

Date		Item	Debit	Credit	Balance Debit	Balance Credit
19--						
Jan.	1	Balance				75,000
	20	10,000 shares issued for cash		20,000		
June	25	Stock dividend		7,500		102,500

ACCOUNT RETAINED EARNINGS ACCOUNT NO.

Date		Item	Debit	Credit	Balance Debit	Balance Credit
19--						
Jan.	1	Balance				300,000
June	25	Stock dividend	45,000			
Dec.	15	Cash dividend	75,000			
	31	Net income		158,500		338,500

Ex. 14–35.
Reporting land acquisition for cash and mortgage note on statement of cash flows.
OBJ. 2, 3

On the basis of the details of the following asset account, indicate the items to be reported on the statement of cash flows.

ACCOUNT LAND ACCOUNT NO.

Date		Item	Debit	Credit	Balance Debit	Balance Credit
19--						
Jan.	1	Balance			400,000	
Mar.	2	Purchased for cash	40,000			
Oct.	29	Purchased with long-term mortgage note	60,000		500,000	

Ex. 14–36. **Determination of net income from net cash flow from operating activities.** OBJ. 2, 3

Brown Inc. reported a net cash flow from operating activities of $46,500 on its statement of cash flows for the year ended December 31, 1992. The following information was reported in the cash flows from operating activities section of the statement of cash flows:

Decrease in income tax payable	$ 500
Decrease in inventories	4,000
Depreciation	9,400
Gain on sale of investments	15,000
Increase in accounts payable	8,800
Increase in prepaid expenses	700
Increase in accounts receivable	4,500

Determine the net income reported by Brown Inc. for the year ended December 31, 1992.

Ex. 14–37. **Real world focus.** OBJ. 2,3

The current asset and current liability sections of the January 28, 1990 and January 29, 1989 balance sheets of Toys "R" Us, Inc. are as follows (dollars in thousands):

	1990	1989
Current assets:		
Cash and short-term investments	40,895	122,912
Accounts and other receivables	53,098	68,030
Merchandise inventories	1,230,394	931,120
Prepaid expenses	13,965	10,822
Other assets	33,362	25,114
Current liabilities:		
Short-term notes payable to banks	205,513	76,133
Accounts payable	517,903	505,370
Accrued expenses, taxes and other liabilities	280,517	240,928
Income taxes payable	96,033	55,839

Selected data from Toys "R" Us, Inc.'s 1990 income statement (dollars in thousands) were as follows:

Net income	$321,080
Depreciation and amortization	65,839
Deferred income taxes (expense)	17,572

Instructions:

Prepare the cash flows from operating activities section of the statement of cash flows for Toys "R" Us, Inc. for the year ended January 28, 1990.

Appendix Ex. 14–38. **Cash flows from operating activities section.**

The income statement of Hackett Company for the current year ended June 30 is as follows:

Sales		$1,030,000
Cost of merchandise sold		620,000
Gross profit		$ 410,000
Operating expenses:		
Depreciation expense	$ 31,500	
Other operating expenses	248,500	
Total operating expenses		280,000
Income before income tax		$ 130,000
Income tax		40,000
Net income		$ 90,000

Changes in the balance of selected accounts from the beginning to the end of the current year are as follows:

	Increase (Decrease)
Trade receivables (net)	$(21,000)
Inventories	11,200
Prepaid expenses	(1,050)
Accounts payable (merchandise creditors)	(17,500)
Accrued operating expenses	7,000
Income tax payable	(2,100)

Prepare the cash flows from operating activities section of the statement of cash flows, using the direct method of presentation.

Appendix Ex. 14–39.
Cash flows from operating activities section.

The income statement for Morrow Co. for the current year ended August 31 and the balances of selected accounts at the end and beginning of the year are as follows:

Sales		$200,000
Cost of merchandise sold		125,000
Gross profit		$ 75,000
Operating expenses:		
Depreciation expense	$12,500	
Other operating expenses	43,000	
Total operating expenses		55,500
Income before income tax		$ 19,500
Income tax		2,600
Net income		$ 16,900

	End of Year	Beginning of Year
Trade receivables	$19,600	$17,800
Inventories	21,100	23,000
Prepaid expenses	900	600
Accounts payable (merchandise creditors)	13,500	15,000
Accrued operating expenses	1,800	1,200
Income tax payable	600	400

Prepare the cash flows from operating activities section of the statement of cash flows, using the direct method of presentation.

Appendix Ex. 14–40.
Cash flows from operating activities section.

The income statement for the current year and balances of selected accounts at the beginning and end of the current year are as follows:

Sales		$650,200
Cost of merchandise sold		382,500
Gross profit		$267,700
Operating expenses:		
Depreciation expense	$ 24,200	
Other operating expenses	160,300	
Total operating expenses		184,500
Income before income tax		$ 83,200
Income tax		17,800
Net income		$ 65,400

	End of Year	Beginning of Year
Trade receivables (net)	$65,600	$60,000
Inventories	82,500	71,500
Prepaid expenses	5,180	5,740
Accounts payable (merchandise creditors)	57,900	54,500
Accrued operating expenses	2,810	4,690
Income tax payable	800	800

Prepare the cash flows from operating activities section of the statement of cash flows, using the direct method of presentation.

Appendix Ex. 14–41.
Cash flows from operating activities section.

The income statement for the current year and the balances of selected accounts at the beginning and end of the current year are as follows:

Sales		$1,170,000
Cost of merchandise sold		684,000
Gross profit		$ 486,000
Operating expenses:		
Depreciation expense	$ 39,150	
Other operating expenses	331,100	
Total operating expenses		370,250
Operating income		$ 115,750
Other expense:		
Interest expense		8,100
Income before income tax		$ 107,650
Income tax		27,100
Net income		$ 80,550

	End of Year	Beginning of Year
Accounts receivables (trade)	$ 72,500	$76,500
Inventories	100,000	87,300
Prepaid expenses	7,110	6,700
Accounts payable (merchandise creditors)	62,730	65,430
Accrued operating expenses	6,750	5,650
Interest payable	1,400	1,400
Income tax payable	2,250	3,600

Prepare the cash flows from operating activities section of the statement of cash flows, using the direct method of presentation.

PROBLEMS

Pb.14–42.
Statement of cash flows.
OBJ. 3

The comparative balance sheet of C. W. Dodson Inc. for December 31, 1992 and 1991, is as follows:

Assets	Dec. 31, 1992	Dec. 31, 1991
Cash	$ 100,800	$ 70,700
Trade receivables (net)	123,200	112,000
Inventories	150,300	128,100
Investments	—	80,000
Land	70,000	—
Equipment	854,300	704,200
Accumulated depreciation	(208,600)	(159,600)
	$1,090,000	$935,400

Liabilities and Stockholders' Equity	Dec. 31, 1992	Dec. 31, 1991
Accounts payable (merchandise creditors)	$ 74,400	$ 70,000
Accrued operating expenses	5,400	7,000
Dividends payable	21,000	14,000
Common stock, $40 par	450,000	350,000
Excess of issue price over par—common stock	23,800	16,800
Retained earnings	515,400	477,600
	$1,090,000	$935,400

The following additional information was taken from Dodson's records:

(a) The investments were sold for $85,000 cash.
(b) Equipment and land were acquired for cash.
(c) There were no disposals of equipment during the year.
(d) The common stock was issued for cash.
(e) There was a $90,300 credit to Retained Earnings for net income.
(f) There was a $52,500 debit to Retained Earnings for cash dividends declared.

Instructions:

Prepare a statement of cash flows.

Pb. 14–43.
Statement of cash flows.
OBJ. 3

The comparative balance sheet of Wong Corporation at December 31, 1992 and 1991, is as follows:

Assets	Dec. 31, 1992	Dec. 31, 1991
Cash	$ 78,900	$ 64,600
Trade receivables (net)	70,300	73,700
Merchandise inventory	122,900	97,400
Prepaid expenses	6,660	5,860
Plant assets	472,440	425,240
Accumulated depreciation—plant assets	(138,500)	(157,500)
	$612,700	$509,300

Liabilities and Stockholders' Equity		
Accounts payable (merchandise creditors)	$ 70,100	$ 53,500
Mortgage note payable	—	60,000
Common stock, $50 par	300,000	250,000
Excess of issue price over par—common stock	34,500	31,500
Retained earnings	208,100	114,300
	$612,700	$509,300

Additional data obtained from the income statement and from an examination of the accounts in the ledger are as follows:

(a) Net income, $108,800.
(b) Depreciation reported on the income statement, $34,600.
(c) An addition to the building was constructed at a cost of $100,800, and fully depreciated equipment costing $53,600 was discarded, with no salvage realized.
(d) The mortgage note payable was not due until 1999, but the terms permitted earlier payment without penalty.
(e) 1,000 shares of common stock were issued at 53 for cash.
(f) Cash dividends declared and paid, $15,000.

Instructions:

Prepare a statement of cash flows.

Pb. 14–44.
Statement of cash flows.
OBJ. 3

SPREADSHEET PROBLEM

The comparative balance sheet of Monique Corporation at December 31, 1992 and 1991, is as follows:

Assets	Dec. 31, 1992	Dec. 31, 1991
Cash	$ 58,900	$ 50,800
Trade receivables (net)	90,300	74,200
Inventories	121,600	131,700
Prepaid expenses	4,400	3,100
Land	65,000	65,000
Buildings	381,500	291,500
Accumulated depreciation—buildings	(154,600)	(143,400)
Machinery and equipment	302,500	302,500
Accumulated depreciation—machinery and equipment	(101,200)	(71,500)
Patents	30,800	38,500
	$799,200	$742,400
Liabilities and Stockholders' Equity		
Accounts payable (merchandise creditors)	$ 58,000	$ 88,000
Dividends payable	9,400	8,250
Salaries payable	5,000	5,450
Mortgage note payable, due 1999	55,000	—
Bonds payable	—	110,000
Common stock, $20 par	450,000	350,000
Excess of issue price over par—common stock	80,000	70,000
Retained earnings	141,800	110,700
	$799,200	$742,400

An examination of the income statement and the accounting records revealed the following additional information applicable to 1992:

(a) Net income, $56,100.
(b) Depreciation expense reported on the income statement: buildings, $11,200; machinery and equipment, $29,700.
(c) A building was constructed for $90,000 cash.
(d) Patent amortization reported on the income statement, $7,700.
(e) A mortgage note for $55,000 was issued for cash.
(f) 5,000 shares of common stock were issued at 22 in exchange for the bonds payable.
(g) Cash dividends declared, $25,000.

Instructions:

Prepare a statement of cash flows.

Pb. 14–45.
Statement of cash flows.
OBJ. 3

The comparative balance sheet of Pauley Inc. at December 31, 1992 and 1991, is as follows:

Assets	Dec. 31, 1992	Dec. 31, 1991
Cash	$ 33,700	$ 36,300
Trade receivables (net)	66,300	59,600
Inventories	131,250	115,500
Prepaid expenses	3,850	4,100
Investments	—	45,000
Land	28,500	28,500
Buildings	190,000	126,000
Accumulated depreciation—buildings	(46,200)	(41,400)
Equipment	284,000	237,300
Accumulated depreciation—equipment	(86,100)	(77,400)
	$605,300	$533,500

Liabilities and Stockholders' Equity		
Accounts payable (merchandise creditors)	$ 38,700	$ 48,300
Income tax payable	3,600	2,800
Bonds payable	50,000	—
Discount on bonds payable	(2,900)	—
Common stock, $20 par	315,000	300,000
Excess of issue price over par — common stock	40,200	33,000
Appropriation for plant expansion	50,000	30,000
Retained earnings	110,700	119,400
	$605,300	$533,500

The noncurrent asset, the noncurrent liability, and the stockholders' equity accounts for 1992 are as follows:

ACCOUNT INVESTMENTS — ACCOUNT NO.

Date		Item	Debit	Credit	Balance Debit	Balance Credit
1992						
Jan.	1	Balance			45,000	
July	23	Realized $40,500 cash from sale		45,000	—	—

ACCOUNT LAND — ACCOUNT NO.

Date		Item	Debit	Credit	Balance Debit	Balance Credit
1992						
Jan.	1	Balance			28,500	

ACCOUNT BUILDINGS — ACCOUNT NO.

Date		Item	Debit	Credit	Balance Debit	Balance Credit
1992						
Jan.	1	Balance			126,000	
July	1	Acquired for cash	64,000		190,000	

ACCOUNT ACCUMULATED DEPRECIATION — BUILDINGS — ACCOUNT NO.

Date		Item	Debit	Credit	Balance Debit	Balance Credit
1992						
Jan.	1	Balance				41,400
Dec.	31	Depreciation for year		4,800		46,200

ACCOUNT EQUIPMENT — ACCOUNT NO.

Date		Item	Debit	Credit	Balance Debit	Balance Credit
1992						
Jan.	1	Balance			237,300	
Apr.	3	Discarded, no salvage		21,000		
Oct.	10	Purchased for cash	40,000			
Dec.	1	Purchased for cash	27,700		284,000	

ACCOUNT ACCUMULATED DEPRECIATION—EQUIPMENT ACCOUNT NO.

Date		Item	Debit	Credit	Balance	
					Debit	Credit
1992						
Jan.	1	Balance				77,400
Apr.	3	Equipment discarded	21,000			
Dec.	31	Depreciation for year		29,700		86,100

ACCOUNT BONDS PAYABLE ACCOUNT NO.

Date		Item	Debit	Credit	Balance	
					Debit	Credit
1992						
May	1	Issued 20-year bonds		50,000		50,000

ACCOUNT DISCOUNT ON BONDS PAYABLE ACCOUNT NO.

Date		Item	Debit	Credit	Balance	
					Debit	Credit
1992						
May	1	Bonds issued	3,000		3,000	
Dec.	31	Amortization		100	2,900	

ACCOUNT COMMON STOCK, $20 PAR ACCOUNT NO.

Date		Item	Debit	Credit	Balance	
					Debit	Credit
1992						
Jan.	1	Balance				300,000
Aug.	4	Stock dividend		15,000		315,000

ACCOUNT PAID-IN CAPITAL IN EXCESS OF PAR—COMMON STOCK ACCOUNT NO.

Date		Item	Debit	Credit	Balance	
					Debit	Credit
1992						
Jan.	1	Balance				33,000
Aug.	4	Stock dividend		7,200		40,200

ACCOUNT APPROPRIATION FOR PLANT EXPANSION ACCOUNT NO.

Date		Item	Debit	Credit	Balance	
					Debit	Credit
1992						
Jan.	1	Balance				30,000
Dec.	31	Appropriation		20,000		50,000

ACCOUNT RETAINED EARNINGS | ACCOUNT NO.

Date		Item	Debit	Credit	Balance Debit	Balance Credit
1992						
Jan.	1	Balance				119,400
Aug.	4	Stock dividend	22,200			
Dec.	31	Net income		52,400		
	31	Cash dividends	18,900			
	31	Appropriated	20,000			110,700

Instructions:

Prepare a statement of cash flows.

Pb. 14–46.
Statement of cash flows.
OBJ. 3

An income statement and a comparative balance sheet for Rogers Company are as follows:

Rogers Company
Income Statement
For Current Year Ended December 31, 1992

Sales		$1,203,100
Cost of merchandise sold		772,800
Gross profit		$ 430,300
Operating expenses (including depreciation of $39,990)		275,750
Income from operations		$ 154,550
Other income:		
Gain on sale of land	$18,750	
Gain on sale of investments	9,350	
Interest income	2,000	30,100
		$ 184,650
Interest expense		30,000
Income before income tax		$ 154,650
Income tax		43,250
Net income		$ 111,400

Rogers Company
Comparative Balance Sheet
December 31, 1992 and 1991

Assets	1992	1991
Cash	$ 49,870	$ 58,200
Trade receivables (net)	137,180	117,800
Inventories	211,500	190,150
Prepaid expenses	5,160	6,120
Investments	34,250	93,500
Land	87,500	75,000
Buildings	412,500	225,000
Accumulated depreciation—buildings	(91,260)	(81,220)
Equipment	493,700	437,500
Accumulated depreciation—equipment	(179,700)	(149,750)
Total assets	$1,160,700	$972,300

Liabilities and Stockholders' Equity		
Accounts payable (merchandise creditors)	$ 70,340	$ 63,000
Income tax payable	6,250	9,750
Dividends payable	15,660	12,500
Mortgage note payable	175,000	—
Bonds payable	100,000	250,000
Common stock, $50 par	450,000	375,000
Excess of issue price over par—common stock	47,250	41,250
Retained earnings	296,200	220,800
Total liabilities and stockholders' equity	$1,160,700	$972,300

The following additional information on cash flows during the year was obtained from an examination of the ledger:

(a) Investments (long-term) were purchased for $34,500.
(b) Investments (long-term) were sold for $103,100.
(c) Equipment was purchased for $56,200. There were no disposals.
(d) A building valued at $187,500 and land valued at $62,500 were acquired by a cash payment of $250,000.
(e) Land which cost $50,000 was sold for $68,750 cash.
(f) A mortgage note payable for $175,000 was issued for cash.
(g) Bonds payable of $150,000 were retired by the payment of their face amount.
(h) 1,500 shares of common stock were issued for cash at 54.
(i) Cash dividends of $36,000 were declared.

Instructions:

Prepare a statement of cash flows.

Appendix Problem 14–47.
Statement of cash flows, applying the direct method to Pb. 14–42.

The comparative balance sheet of C. W. Dodson Inc. for December 31, 1992 and 1991, is as follows:

Assets	Dec. 31, 1992	Dec. 31, 1991
Cash	$ 100,800	$ 70,700
Trade receivables (net)	123,200	112,000
Inventories	150,300	128,100
Investments	—	80,000
Land	70,000	—
Equipment	854,300	704,200
Accumulated depreciation	(208,600)	(159,600)
	$1,090,000	$935,400

Liabilities and Stockholders' Equity		
Accounts payable (merchandise creditors)	$ 74,400	$ 70,000
Accrued operating expenses	5,400	7,000
Dividends payable	21,000	14,000
Common stock, $40 par	450,000	350,000
Excess of issue price over par—common stock	23,800	16,800
Retained earnings	515,400	477,600
	$1,090,000	$935,400

The income statement for the year ended December 31, 1992, is as follows:

Sales		$1,287,300
Cost of merchandise sold		770,000
Gross profit		$ 517,300
Operating expenses:		
Depreciation expense	$ 49,000	
Other operating expenses	364,000	
Total operating expenses		413,000
Operating income		$ 104,300
Other income:		
Gain on sale of investments		5,000
Income before income tax		$ 109,300
Income tax		19,000
Net income		$ 90,300

The following additional information was taken from C. W. Dodson's records:

(a) The investments were sold for $85,000 cash at the beginning of the year.
(b) Equipment and land were acquired for cash.
(c) There were no disposals of equipment during the year.
(d) The common stock was issued for cash.
(e) There was a $52,500 debit to Retained Earnings for cash dividends declared.

Instructions:

Prepare a statement of cash flows, using the direct method of presenting cash flows from operating activities.

ALTERNATE PROBLEMS

Pb. 14–42A.
Statement of cash flows.
OBJ. 3

The comparative balance sheet of T. E. Harber Inc. for June 30, 1992 and 1991, is as follows:

Assets	June 30, 1992	June 30, 1991
Cash	$ 77,000	$ 59,800
Trade receivables (net)	109,800	96,000
Inventories	127,100	108,600
Investments	—	90,000
Land	102,000	—
Equipment	426,000	330,000
Accumulated depreciation	(178,800)	(142,800)
	$663,100	$541,600
Liabilities and Stockholders' Equity		
Accounts payable (merchandise creditors)	$ 68,900	$ 61,000
Accrued operating expenses	6,100	5,000
Dividends payable	14,400	12,000
Common stock, $20 par	360,000	300,000
Excess of issue price over par — common stock	26,400	14,400
Retained earnings	187,300	149,200
	$663,100	$541,600

The following additional information was taken from the records of T. E. Harber, Inc.:

(a) Equipment and land were acquired for cash.
(b) There were no disposals of equipment during the year.

(c) The investments were sold for $98,000 cash.
(d) The common stock was issued for cash.
(e) There was a $92,100 credit to Retained Earnings for net income.
(f) There was a $54,000 debit to Retained Earnings for cash dividends declared.

Instructions:

Prepare a statement of cash flows.

Pb. 14–43A.
Statement of cash flows.
OBJ. 3

The comparative balance sheet of Lee Inc. at June 30, 1992 and 1991, is as follows:

Assets	June 30, 1992	June 30, 1991
Cash	$ 55,100	$ 74,600
Trade receivables (net)	115,300	128,300
Merchandise inventory	344,700	336,400
Prepaid expenses	5,200	3,600
Plant assets	434,000	390,800
Accumulated depreciation—plant assets	(232,300)	(266,600)
	$722,000	$667,100

Liabilities and Stockholders' Equity	June 30, 1992	June 30, 1991
Accounts payable (merchandise creditors)	$ 72,300	$ 66,400
Mortgage note payable	—	101,300
Common stock, $30 par	300,000	270,000
Excess of issue price over par—common stock	38,800	33,800
Retained earnings	310,900	195,600
	$722,000	$667,100

Additional data obtained from the income statement and from an examination of the accounts in the ledger are as follows:

(a) Net income, $133,800.
(b) Depreciation reported on the income statement, $38,600.
(c) An addition to the building was constructed at a cost of $116,100, and fully depreciated equipment costing $72,900 was discarded, with no salvage realized.
(d) The mortgage note payable was not due until 1998, but the terms permitted earlier payment without penalty.
(e) 1,000 shares of common stock were issued at 35 for cash.
(f) Cash dividends declared and paid, $18,500.

Instructions:

Prepare a statement of cash flows.

Pb. 14–44A.
Statement of cash flows.
OBJ. 3
SPREADSHEET PROBLEM

The comparative balance sheet of M. S. Terrell Corporation at December 31, 1992 and 1991, is as follows:

Assets	Dec. 31, 1992	Dec. 31, 1991
Cash	$ 67,400	$ 61,800
Trade receivables (net)	87,900	100,500
Inventories	195,100	178,600
Prepaid expenses	3,400	2,900
Land	75,000	75,000
Buildings	480,600	316,800
Accumulated depreciation — buildings	(157,500)	(144,000)
Machinery and equipment	206,300	206,300
Accumulated depreciation — machinery and equipment	(98,000)	(81,300)
Patents	35,000	37,500
	$895,200	$754,100
Liabilities and Stockholders' Equity		
Accounts payable (merchandise creditors)	$ 27,200	$ 38,900
Dividends payable	18,800	15,000
Salaries payable	7,900	14,600
Mortgage note payable, due 1997	120,000	—
Bonds payable	—	70,000
Common stock, $15 par	412,500	360,000
Excess of issue price over par — common stock	57,500	40,000
Retained earnings	251,300	215,600
	$895,200	$754,100

An examination of the income statement and the accounting records revealed the following additional information applicable to 1992:

(a) Net income, $63,200.
(b) Depreciation expense reported on the income statement: buildings, $13,500; machinery and equipment, $16,700.
(c) Patent amortization reported on the income statement, $2,500.
(d) A building was constructed for $163,800.
(e) A mortgage note for $120,000 was issued for cash.
(f) 3,500 shares of common stock were issued at 20 in exchange for the bonds payable.
(g) Cash dividends declared, $27,500.

Instructions:

Prepare a statement of cash flows.

Pb. 14–45A.
Statement of cash flows.
OBJ. 3

The comparative balance sheet of M. T. Wade Inc. at December 31, 1992 and 1991, is as follows:

Assets	Dec. 31, 1992	Dec. 31, 1991
Cash	$ 117,100	$ 101,400
Trade receivables (net)	168,600	150,300
Income tax refund receivable	9,000	—
Inventories	257,000	270,800
Prepaid expenses	9,300	11,100
Investments	90,000	250,000
Land	130,000	180,000
Buildings	780,000	450,000
Accumulated depreciation — buildings	(207,700)	(193,800)
Equipment	608,400	470,400
Accumulated depreciation — equipment	(218,000)	(205,700)
	$1,743,700	$1,484,500

Liabilities and Stockholders' Equity		
Accounts payable (merchandise creditors)	$ 96,000	$ 108,720
Income tax payable	—	10,880
Bonds payable	350,000	—
Discount on bonds payable	(29,000)	—
Common stock, $5 par	630,000	600,000
Excess of issue price over par—common stock	81,000	72,000
Appropriation for plant expansion	250,000	200,000
Retained earnings	365,700	492,900
	$1,743,700	$1,484,500

The noncurrent asset, the noncurrent liability, and the stockholders' equity accounts for 1992 are as follows:

ACCOUNT INVESTMENTS ACCOUNT NO.

Date		Item	Debit	Credit	Balance Debit	Balance Credit
1992						
Jan.	1	Balance			250,000	
Apr.	10	Realized $180,000 cash from sale		160,000	90,000	—

ACCOUNT LAND ACCOUNT NO.

Date		Item	Debit	Credit	Balance Debit	Balance Credit
1992						
Jan.	1	Balance			180,000	
July	8	Realized $62,500 cash from sale		50,000	130,000	

ACCOUNT BUILDINGS ACCOUNT NO.

Date		Item	Debit	Credit	Balance Debit	Balance Credit
1992						
Jan.	1	Balance			450,000	
June	30	Acquired for cash	330,000		780,000	

ACCOUNT ACCUMULATED DEPRECIATION—BUILDINGS ACCOUNT NO.

Date		Item	Debit	Credit	Balance Debit	Balance Credit
1992						
Jan.	1	Balance				193,800
Dec.	31	Depreciation for year		13,900		207,700

ACCOUNT EQUIPMENT ACCOUNT NO.

Date		Item	Debit	Credit	Balance Debit	Balance Credit
1992						
Jan.	1	Balance			470,400	
Feb.	5	Discarded, no salvage		48,000		
Aug.	8	Purchased for cash	96,000			
Sept.	30	Purchased for cash	90,000		608,400	

ACCOUNT ACCUMULATED DEPRECIATION—EQUIPMENT ACCOUNT NO.

Date		Item	Debit	Credit	Balance Debit	Balance Credit
1992						
Jan.	1	Balance				205,700
Feb.	5	Equipment discarded	48,000			
Dec.	31	Depreciation for year		60,300		218,000

ACCOUNT BONDS PAYABLE ACCOUNT NO.

Date		Item	Debit	Credit	Balance Debit	Balance Credit
1992						
May	1	Issued 20-year bonds		350,000		350,000

ACCOUNT DISCOUNT ON BONDS PAYABLE ACCOUNT NO.

Date		Item	Debit	Credit	Balance Debit	Balance Credit
1992						
May	1	Bonds issued	30,000		30,000	
Dec.	31	Amortization		1,000	29,000	

ACCOUNT COMMON STOCK, $5 PAR ACCOUNT NO.

Date		Item	Debit	Credit	Balance Debit	Balance Credit
1992						
Jan.	1	Balance				600,000
Nov.	1	Stock dividend		30,000		630,000

ACCOUNT PAID-IN CAPITAL IN EXCESS OF PAR—COMMON STOCK ACCOUNT NO.

Date		Item	Debit	Credit	Balance Debit	Balance Credit
1992						
Jan.	1	Balance				72,000
Nov.	1	Stock dividend		9,000		81,000

ACCOUNT APPROPRIATION FOR PLANT EXPANSION ACCOUNT NO.

Date		Item	Debit	Credit	Balance Debit	Balance Credit
1992						
Jan.	1	Balance				200,000
Dec.	31	Appropriation		50,000		250,000

ACCOUNT RETAINED EARNINGS ACCOUNT NO.

Date		Item	Debit	Credit	Balance Debit	Balance Credit
1992						
Jan.	1	Balance				492,900
Nov.	1	Stock dividend	39,000			
Dec.	31	Net loss	8,200			
	31	Cash dividends	30,000			
	31	Appropriated	50,000			365,700

Instructions:

Prepare a statement of cash flows.

Pb. 14–46A.
Statement of cash flows.
OBJ. 3

An income statement and a comparative balance sheet for DABCO Company are as follows:

DABCO Company
Income Statement
For Current Year Ended December 31, 1992

Sales		$1,520,700
Cost of merchandise sold		1,110,200
Gross profit		$ 410,500
Operating expenses (including depreciation of $39,990)		267,100
Income from operations		$ 143,400
Other income:		
Gain on sale of land	$20,500	
Gain on sale of investments	7,600	
Interest income	3,400	31,500
		$ 174,900
Interest expense		25,000
Income before income tax		$ 149,900
Income tax		38,500
Net income		$ 111,400

DABCO Company
Comparative Balance Sheet
December 31, 1992 and 1991

Assets	1992	1991
Cash	$ 57,870	$ 66,200
Trade receivables (net)	137,180	117,800
Inventories	211,500	190,150
Prepaid expenses	5,160	6,120
Investments	44,500	93,500
Land	77,250	75,000
Buildings	412,500	225,000
Accumulated depreciation—buildings	(91,260)	(81,220)
Equipment	493,700	437,500
Accumulated depreciation—equipment	(179,700)	(149,750)
Total assets	$1,168,700	$980,300
Liabilities and Stockholders' Equity		
Accounts payable (merchandise creditors)	$ 71,590	$ 64,250
Income tax payable	5,000	8,500
Dividends payable	15,660	12,500
Mortgage note payable	175,000	—
Bonds payable	100,000	250,000
Common stock, $25 par	450,000	375,000
Excess of issue price over par—common stock	47,250	41,250
Retained earnings	304,200	228,800
Total liabilities and stockholders' equity	$1,168,700	$980,300

The following additional information on cash flows during the year was obtained from an examination of the ledger:

(a) Investments (long-term) were purchased for $40,500.
(b) Investments (long-term) were sold for $97,100.
(c) Equipment was purchased for $56,200. There were no disposals.

(d) A building valued at $187,500 and land valued at $62,500 were acquired by a cash payment of $250,000.
(e) Land which cost $60,250 was sold for $80,750 cash.
(f) A mortgage note payable for $175,000 was issued for cash.
(g) Bonds payable of $150,000 were retired by the payment of their face amount.
(h) 3,000 shares of common stock were issued for cash at 27.
(i) Cash dividends of $36,000 were declared.

Instructions:

Prepare a statement of cash flows.

Appendix
Pb. 14–47A.
Statement of cash flows, applying the direct method to Pb. 14–42A.

The comparative balance sheet of T. E. Harber Inc. for June 30, 1992 and 1991, is as follows:

Assets	June 30, 1992	June 30, 1991
Cash	$ 77,000	$ 59,800
Trade receivables (net)	109,800	96,000
Inventories	127,100	108,600
Investments	—	90,000
Land	102,000	—
Equipment	426,000	330,000
Accumulated depreciation	(178,800)	(142,800)
	$663,100	$541,600
Liabilities and Stockholders' Equity		
Accounts payable (merchandise creditors)	$ 68,900	$ 61,000
Accrued operating expenses	6,100	5,000
Dividends payable	14,400	12,000
Common stock, $20 par	360,000	300,000
Excess of issue price over par—common stock	26,400	14,400
Retained earnings	187,300	149,200
	$663,100	$541,600

The income statement for the year ended June 30, 1992, is as follows:

Sales		$1,194,000
Cost of merchandise sold		708,900
Gross profit		$ 485,100
Operating expenses:		
Depreciation expense	$ 36,000	
Other operating expenses	336,000	
Total operating expenses		372,000
Operating income		$ 113,100
Other income:		
Gain on sale of investments		8,000
Income before income tax		$ 121,100
Income tax		29,000
Net income		$ 92,100

The following additional information was taken from the records of T. E. Harber Inc.:

(a) Equipment and land were acquired for cash.
(b) There were no disposals of equipment during the year.
(c) The investments were sold for $98,000.
(d) The common stock was issued for cash.
(e) There was a $54,000 debit to Retained Earnings for cash dividends declared.

Instructions:

Prepare a statement of cash flows, using the direct method of presenting cash flows from operating activities.

MINI-CASE 14

a.j.jenkinsinc.

Ann Jenkins is the president and majority shareholder of A. J. Jenkins Inc., a small retail store chain. Recently, Jenkins submitted a loan application for A. J. Jenkins Inc. to Broad State Bank. It called for a $200,000, 12%, 10-year loan to help finance the construction of a building and the purchase of store equipment costing a total of $250,000 to enable A. J. Jenkins Inc. to open a store in Cedartown. Land for this purpose was acquired last year. The bank's loan officer requested a statement of cash flows in addition to the most recent income statement, balance sheet, and retained earnings statement that Jenkins had submitted with the loan application.

As a close family friend, Jenkins asked you to prepare a statement of cash flows. From the records provided, you prepared the following statement:

A. J. Jenkins Inc.
Statement of Cash Flows
For Year Ended December 31, 19--

Cash flows from operating activities:			
Net income, per income statement		$ 45,000	
Add: Depreciation	$28,600		
Decrease in trade receivables	10,800	39,400	
		$ 84,400	
Deduct: Increase in inventory	$ 9,000		
Increase in prepaid expenses	600		
Decrease in accounts payable	2,400		
Gain on sale of investments	6,000	18,000	
Net cash flow from operating activities			$66,400
Cash flows from investing activities:			
Cash received from investments sold		$ 42,000	
Less: Cash paid for purchase of store equipment		35,000	
Net cash flow from investing activities			7,000
Cash flows from financing activities:			
Cash paid for dividends		$(20,000)	
Net cash flow used for financing activities			(20,000)
Increase in cash			$ 53,400
Cash at the beginning of the year			19,500
Cash at the end of the year			$ 72,900

Schedule of Noncash Investing and Financing Activities

Issuance of common stock at par for land	$50,000

After reviewing the statement, Jenkins telephoned you and commented, "Are you sure this statement is right?" Jenkins then raised the following questions:

(a) "How can depreciation be a cash flow?"
(b) "The issuance of common stock for the land is listed in a separate schedule. This transaction has nothing to do with cash! Shouldn't this transaction be eliminated from the statement?"
(c) "How can the gain on sale of investments be a deduction from net income in determining the cash flow from operating activities?"
(d) "Why does the bank need this statement anyway? They can compute the increase in cash from the balance sheets for the last two years."

After jotting down Jenkins' questions, you assured her that this statement was "right". However, to alleviate Jenkins' concern, you arranged a meeting for the following day.

Instructions:

(1) How would you respond to each of Jenkins' questions?
(2) Do you think that the statement of cash flows enhances the chances of A. J. Jenkins Inc. receiving the loan? Discuss.

ANSWERS TO SELF-EXAMINATION QUESTIONS

1. D A full set of financial statements for a corporation includes a balance sheet (answer A), an income statement (answer B), a statement of cash flows (answer C), and a statement of retained earnings.
2. D Cash flows from operating activities relate to transactions that enter into the determination of net income (answer D). Receipts of cash from the sale of capital stock (answer A) and the sale of bonds (answer B) and payments of cash for dividends (answer C) are cash flows from financing activities.
3. A Cash flows from investing activities include receipts from the sale of noncurrent assets, such as equipment (answer A) and payments for the acquisition of noncurrent assets. Receipts of cash from the sale of capital stock (answer B) and payments of cash for dividends (answer C) and for the repurchase of equity securities (answer D) are cash flows from financing activities.
4. D Cash flows from financing activities include receipts from the issuance of equity (answer A) and debt (answer B) securities and payments for dividends (answer C), repurchase of equity securities, and redemption of debt securities.
5. D The cash flows from operating activities section of the statement of cash flows would report net cash flow from operating activities of $65,500, determined as follows:

Net income		$55,000	
Add:			
Depreciation	$22,000		
Decrease in inventories	5,000		
Decrease in prepaid expenses	500	27,500	
		$82,500	
Deduct:			
Increase in trade receivables	$10,000		
Decrease in accounts payable	7,000	17,000	
Net cash flow from operating activities			$65,500

PART 5

MANAGERIAL ACCOUNTING CONCEPTS & SYSTEMS

CHAPTER 15

CHAPTER OBJECTIVES

1 Describe the basic functions of the management process.

2 Describe the role of managerial accounting in the management process.

3 Describe the characteristics of managerial accounting reports.

4 Describe and illustrate the basic cost concepts and terminology useful in managerial accounting:

- Direct and indirect costs
- Differential costs
- Sunk costs
- Controllable and noncontrollable costs
- Discretionary costs
- Variable and fixed costs
- Opportunity costs

5 Describe manufacturing operations, including manufacturing cost concepts and terminology.

6 Describe the major current trends in manufacturing and service enterprises.

NATURE OF MANAGERIAL ACCOUNTING; COST CONCEPTS & TERMINOLOGY

The **management** of an organization consists of those individuals charged with the responsibility for directing an enterprise toward achieving its goals. The primary goal of most enterprises is to earn a profit by rendering services or selling products. The primary goal of not-for-profit organizations, such as governmental units, churches, and the Red Cross, is to provide goods or services that fulfill a social need at the lowest possible cost. Regardless of the goals or type of organization, managers rely heavily on accounting information in attempting to achieve their goals.

The previous chapters of this text emphasized **financial accounting,** which is concerned with the recording and reporting of business transactions. Financial accounting information is provided primarily to owners, creditors, and the general public, who are not involved in the operations of the business. The remaining chapters emphasize **managerial accounting,** which is the field of accounting that specializes in providing accounting information, including financial accounting information, to managers for their use in making decisions that affect the operations of the business.

This chapter begins with a description of the nature of the management process and the key role that managerial accounting plays in this process. The chapter also describes and illustrates various accounting concepts and terms which are frequently used in reporting relevant information to management for its use in decision making. Manufacturing operations, including manufacturing cost concepts and terminology are described and illustrated. The chapter concludes with a discussion of the major current trends in manufacturing and service enterprises.

THE MANAGEMENT PROCESS

OBJECTIVE 1
Describe the basic functions of the management process.

The **management process** involves the four basic functions of (1) planning, (2) organizing and directing, (3) controlling, and (4) decision making. Although decision making has the central role in the management process, all four functions interact. As shown in the following diagram, these functions are the driving force for an enterprise's operations.

Diagram of Management Process

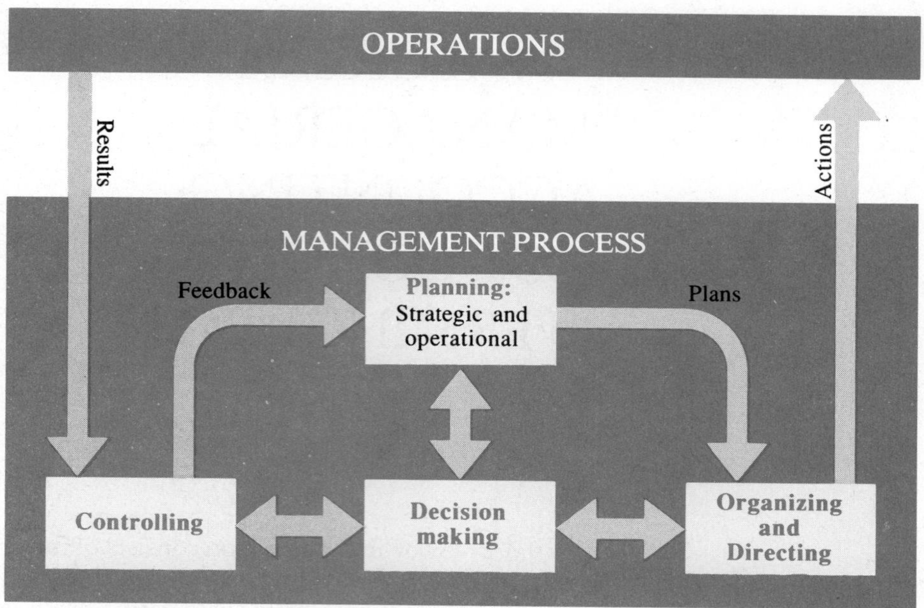

Planning

Planning is the process by which management develops a course of action to attain enterprise goals. Planning involves such activities as setting selling prices, arranging for the financing of a plant expansion, and the development of new products. Planning can be categorized as either strategic planning or operational planning.

Strategic planning is the development of a long-range course of action to achieve goals. A strategic plan often encompasses periods ranging from five to ten years. Such a plan establishes enterprise policy and priorities for such activities as research and development, marketing, financing, and plant expansion. A strategic plan serves as the basis for the commitment of enterprise resources.

A strategic plan, which is normally approved by the highest levels of management, should integrate all aspects of the enterprise operations necessary for the achievement of long-range goals. Because the strategic plan is influenced by the changing environment within which the enterprise operates, the strategic plan should be periodically reviewed and revised. For example, rising interest rates might postpone a proposed plant expansion, or rising oil prices might accelerate an enterprise's plan to expand operations into energy-saving products.

Operational planning, sometimes referred to as **tactical planning,** is the development of short-term plans to achieve goals identified in the strategic plan. Thus, operational plans complement the strategic plan and are typically established for time periods ranging from a week or a month to several years. Examples of operational planning are the setting of the current month's production levels by a manufacturer and determining the hiring needs for part-time employees during a holiday shopping period by a merchandising enterprise.

Effective communication between all levels of management within an enterprise is essential, so that operations can be coordinated to meet the operational and strategic plans. An important part of this communication is the various accounting reports that management uses in planning operations.

STRATEGIC PLANNING

Based on a survey of 180 executives selected from manufacturing corporations listed in Standard & Poor's *Register of Corporations, Directors and Executives,* the following environmental factors were considered important to include in the development of strategic plans:

Environmental Factors
To Include In Strategic Plans

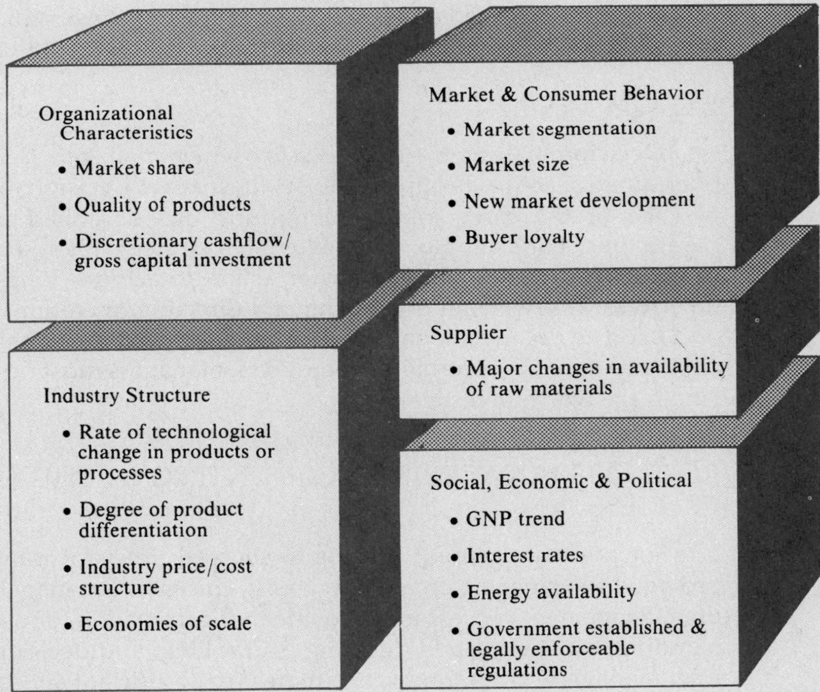

Source: James F. Brown, Jr., "How U.S. Firms Conduct Strategic Planning," *Management Accounting* (February, 1986), pp. 38–44, 55.

Organizing and Directing

Organizing is the process by which management assigns responsibility to individuals for achieving enterprise goals. Each enterprise has its own unique organizational structure that management has established to implement strategic and operational plans. Some managers favor a highly centralized and autocratic organizational structure, while other managers favor decentralized structures with significant lower-management autonomy. No one organizational structure has proven best in all situations.

Directing is the process by which managers, given their assigned level of responsibilities, run day-to-day operations. Examples of directing include a production supervisor's efforts at keeping the production line moving smoothly throughout a work shift and the credit manager's efforts at assessing the credit standing of potential customers.

Controlling

Controlling is the process by which managers attempt to achieve the goals identified in the strategic and operational plans. This process normally involves monitoring the operating results of implemented plans and comparing the expected results with the actual results. This **feedback** allows management to isolate significant variations for further investigation and possible remedial action. It may also lead to a revision of future plans. This philosophy of controlling is sometimes referred to as **management by exception.** For example, if actual materials costs incurred in manufacturing a product significantly exceed expected costs, an investigation may be conducted to determine the cause of the difference so that corrective action may be taken.

Decision Making

Decision making is the process by which managers determine to follow one course of action as opposed to an alternative. Decision making is inherent in each of the three management functions described in the preceding paragraphs. For example, in developing a strategic plan, managers must decide between competing courses of action to achieve long-range goals and objectives. Likewise, in organizing and directing operations, managers must decide on an organizational structure and on specific actions to take in day-to-day operations. In controlling operations, managers must decide whether variances are worth investigating.

ROLE OF MANAGERIAL ACCOUNTING IN THE MANAGEMENT PROCESS

OBJECTIVE 2
Describe the role of managerial accounting in the management process.

For the management process to succeed, relevant information must be provided to managers on a timely basis. The role of managerial accounting in the management process is to provide this information for use by managers in planning, organizing and directing, controlling, and decision making. In this role, managerial accounting contributes to the efficient allocation of resources within society.

Managerial accounting aids managers in **planning** by providing reports which estimate the effects of alternative actions on an enterprise's ability to achieve desired goals. For example, an enterprise might establish a 25% market share as a long-term strategic goal. To achieve this goal, the enterprise might consider increasing its advertising expenditures and/or decreasing its unit selling prices. Managerial accounting could report the estimated effects of the increased advertising, based on past experience, industry advertising statistics, market surveys, and other data, as well as the estimated effects of the decreased selling prices.

Managerial accounting aids managers in **organizing and directing** by providing reports which allow them to adjust operations for changing conditions.

For example, managerial accounting reports organized by product line may provide management with useful information on combining or eliminating product lines. Likewise, daily or weekly sales reports may be used by a retail store manager in deciding which items should be reordered and which items should not be reordered.

Managerial accounting aids managers in **controlling** operations by providing performance reports of variances between expected and actual operating results. Such reports serve as a basis for taking necessary corrective action to control operations. For example, a production supervisor might receive weekly or daily performance reports comparing actual materials cost with estimated costs. Significant variances could be isolated and corrective action could be taken. An excess of actual materials costs over estimated costs might be caused by high levels of scrap that was generated by the use of poor quality materials. To correct this problem, a change in suppliers might be warranted. Another example would be a partner in a law firm receiving weekly progress reports on the amount of staff time spent on each case. An excessive amount of staff time spent on any particular case would warrant an investigation and an explanation from the staff.

Managerial accounting aids managers in **decision making** by providing the basic information which the manager uses in selecting among alternative courses of action. For example, an accounting report indicating the contribution of the automotive service department to total store profits would aid the store manager in deciding whether to discontinue that department. Likewise, a similar accounting report would aid an ophthalmologist in deciding whether to sell eyeglass frames as a service to patients.

Managerial accounting thus provides information to management to carry out all the basic functions of the management process. Without this information, it would be difficult for managers to manage effectively. To illustrate the types of decisions made on the basis of information provided by managerial accounting, the following excerpt is taken from the article "Huge GM Write-Off Positions Auto Maker to Show New Growth," which appeared in the December 1, 1990 *Wall Street Journal:*

> *"[Write-offs to cover plant closings are], a major element in GM's long-term strategic plan to improve the competitiveness and profitability of its North American operations," said Chairman Robert C. Stempel. "That means GM intends to run fewer factories faster and make more money . . . ."*
>
> *". . . [GM intends to close] at least 7 of its 38 assembly plants in the U.S. and Canada and . . . related parts factories as well, affecting more than 20,000 workers. . . . By the time the shutdowns end, GM estimates, it will have cut roughly $1 billion from its yearly operating costs."*

Organization of the Managerial Accounting Function

In most large business enterprises, departments or similar units are assigned responsibilities for specific functions or activities. This operating structure of an enterprise can be diagrammed in an **organization chart.** An organization chart for Baker Inc., a small manufacturing enterprise, is as shown on page 652.

The individual reporting units in an enterprise can be viewed as having either (1) line responsibilities or (2) staff responsibilities. A **line** department or unit is one directly involved in the basic objectives of the organization. For Baker Inc., the vice-president of production and the managers of the Conyers

Organization Chart For Baker Inc.

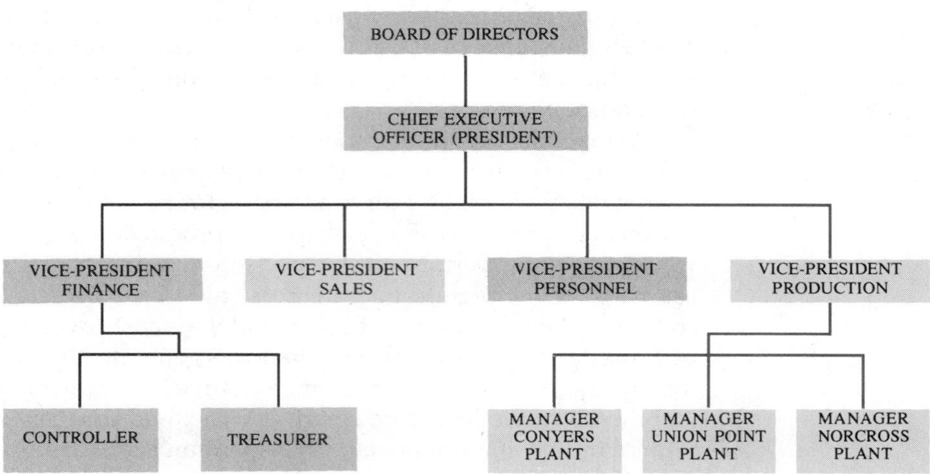

Plant, the Union Point Plant, and the Norcross Plant occupy line positions because they are responsible for the manufacture of Baker's product. Likewise, the vice-president of sales occupies a line position because the vice-president of sales is directly responsible for the generation of revenues.

A **staff** department or unit is one that provides services, assistance, and advice to the departments with line or other staff responsibilities. A staff department has no direct authority over a line department. The organization

THE MAGIC OF 3M

3M was listed along with 61 other corporate high achievers in the best seller, *In Search of Excellence,* by Thomas J. Peters and Robert H. Waterman, Jr. In *A Passion for Excellence,* by Peters and Nancy Austin, 3M was again listed as a model for product innovation and entrepreneurship.

Some of the reasons for 3M's success, based on interviews with 3M executives, are as follows:

"Financial [accounting] expertise, long recognized as one of 3M's greatest assets, is a major contributor to the corporation's success. 3M uses its [accounting] system to encourage . . . creativity . . ."

". . . we (controllers) get intimately involved with day-to-day activities . . . with forecasting and planning activities of business units. . . . Our controller's view their roles as not to always challenge management, but as being a cooperative effort to develop a better business."

"3M's (division) controllers have been able to support 3M's strategic objectives while keeping management focused on operational objectives . . . we do a fair, if not a good, job of balancing strategic and operational considerations."

"Our organization is not a negatively focused accounting organization. . . . We are supportive and positive in dealing with line management. We have tried to understand the business while doing our jobs."

"I (division controller) view the controller's function as [a] consultant . . . the person who brings to a division the financial information."

"I (vice president of finance) tell our people, 'Your job is to help the operating people achieve what they're trying to achieve. . . . The first principle is working with the operating people."

Source: Kathy Williams, "The Magic of 3M: Management Accounting Excellence," *Management Accounting* (February, 1986), pp 20–27.

chart for Baker Inc. indicates that two staff vice-president positions report to the chief executive officer. The vice-president of personnel occupies a staff position because the personnel department assists line managers and others in staffing their departments. Likewise, the vice-president of finance occupies a staff position, to which two other staff positions—the controller and the treasurer—report. In large organizations staff positions may also exist for such functions as engineering, research and development, and marketing.

In most business organizations, the chief accountant is called the **controller.** The controller has a staff relationship with others in the organization, providing advice and assistance to management but assuming no direct responsibility for the operations of the business. However, in providing information for management's use, the controller must be thoroughly familiar with the operations of the business. Because of this critical role, the controller is considered a member of top management.

The controller's staff often consists of several accountants. Each accountant is responsible for a specialized accounting function, such as systems and procedures, general accounting, budgets and budget analyses, special reports and analyses, taxes, and cost accounting. The following organization chart is typical for an accounting department that reports to the controller:

Organization Chart—Controller's Department

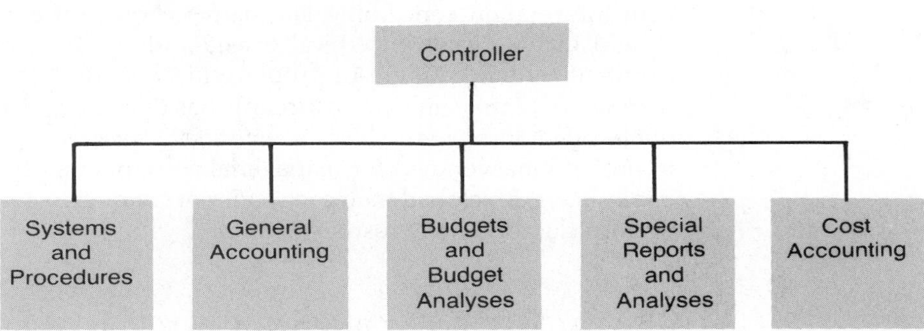

Managerial Accounting as a Profession

As described in preceding paragraphs, managerial accounting plays a major role in contributing to the effective management of business enterprises. Thus, because of its importance to the economy and to society as a whole, managerial accounting is gaining recognition as a profession. Two important characteristics of this profession—certification and ethics—have received increased emphasis and discussion in recent years. These two characteristics are briefly discussed in the following paragraphs.

Certification. To provide more recognition of managerial accounting as a profession, the Institute of Certified Management Accountants offers the **Certificate in Management Accounting (CMA)** program. The primary purpose of the CMA program is to provide evidence of competence in managerial accounting through the awarding of the CMA certificate.

The requirements for the CMA designation include education, experience, and the passing of a 2-day examination. The examination consists of the following four parts, which reflect the interdisciplinary nature of managerial accounting:

1. Economics, finance and management.
2. Financial accounting and reporting.

3. Management reporting, analysis and behavioral issues.
4. Decision analysis and information systems.

Individual holders of the CMA designation are also required to participate in a program of continuing professional education and to adhere to a professional code of ethics.

Ethics. **Ethics** are moral principles that guide the conduct of individuals, when they are acting alone, as members of a profession, or as employees of an organization. Although reasonable people may differ on what is "right" or "wrong" in a given situation, proper ethical conduct implies a responsibility beyond that required by law to act in the best interests of society. The essence of ethical conduct is, therefore, the sacrifice of one's own well-being for the benefit of society. Although it may seem contradictory, the sacrificing of one's well-being for the benefit of others not only promotes high self worth, but also is often good business. For example, a business which ignores the public welfare and intentionally pollutes the environment may find itself the focus of lawsuits and customer boycotts. Likewise, an automobile manufacturer, which fails to correct a safety defect in order to reduce costs and earn additional profits, may later suffer lost sales from the loss of consumer confidence.

Managerial accountants, as members of the management team, are in a unique position to influence management decision making by providing relevant information concerning alternative choices of action. This information should include relevant ethical considerations. In addition, managerial accountants should adhere to proper ethical conduct in their own work. The Institute of Management Accountants has developed standards of ethical conduct, called *Standards of Ethical Conduct for Management Accountants,* as a guide to professional conduct for managerial accountants.[1] In addition, many companies have developed their own codes of conduct to guide their employees in performing their daily responsibilities.[2]

CHARACTERISTICS OF MANAGERIAL ACCOUNTING REPORTS

OBJECTIVE 3
Describe the characteristics of managerial accounting reports.

As indicated, accounting reports provide much of the information useful for management in planning, organizing and directing, controlling, and decision making. The principle of "usefulness to management" is the primary criterion for the preparation of managerial accounting reports. To be useful, these reports should possess the characteristics of (1) relevance, (2) timeliness, (3) accuracy, (4) clarity, and (5) conciseness. Each of these characteristics is described in the following paragraphs.

Relevance

Relevance means that the economic information reported must be pertinent to the specific action being considered by management. In applying this concept, the accountant must be familiar with the operations of the firm and the needs of management in order to select what is important from the masses of data that are available. Especially in this modern age of the information

---

[1] These standards of ethical conduct appear in Appendix B at the end of this text.

[2] An ethics discussion case has been provided at the end of each chapter to focus attention on meaningful ethical situations which accountants often encounter in practice.

explosion, this selection process can be difficult. To accomplish this task, the accountant must determine the needs of management for the decision at hand, examine the available data, and select only the relevant data for reporting to management. To illustrate, assume that management is considering the replacement of fully depreciated equipment, which cost $100,000, with new equipment costing $150,000. It is the $150,000 that is relevant for an analysis of financing the replacement. The original cost, $100,000, is irrelevant.

In applying the concept of relevance, it is important to recognize that some accounting information may have little or no relevance for one use but may have a high degree of relevance for another use. For example, in the previous illustration, the $100,000 was irrelevant for purposes of evaluating the financing of the replacement equipment. For tax purposes, however, the $100,000 (and its accumulated depreciation) would be relevant for determining the amount of the depreciation on the new equipment.

Timeliness

Timeliness refers to the need for accounting reports to contain the most up-to-date information. In many cases, outdated data can lead to unwise decisions. For example, if prior years' costs are relied upon in setting the selling price of a product, the resulting selling price may not be sufficient to cover the current year's costs and to provide a satisfactory profit.

In some cases, the timeliness concept may require the accountants to prepare reports on a prearranged schedule, such as daily, weekly, or monthly. For example, daily reports of cash receipts and disbursements assist management in effectively managing the use of cash on a day-to-day basis. On the other hand, weekly departmental expense reports may be satisfactory to assist management in the control of expenses. In other cases, reports are prepared on an irregular basis or only when needed. For example, if management is evaluating a proposed advertising promotion for the month of May, a report of current costs and other current relevant data for this specific proposal would be needed in sufficient time for management to make and implement the decision.

Accuracy

Accuracy refers to the need for the report to be correct within the constraints of the use of the report and the inherent inaccuracies in the measurement process. If the report is not accurate, management's decision may not be prudent. For example, if an inaccurate report on a customer's past payment practices is presented to management, an unwise decision in granting credit may be made.

The concept of accuracy must be applied within the constraint of the use to be made of the report. In other words, there are occasions when accuracy should be sacrificed for less precise data that are more useful to management. For example, in planning production, estimates (forecasts) of future sales may be more useful than more accurate data from past sales. In addition, it should be noted that there are inherent inaccuracies in accounting data that are based on estimates and approximations. For example, in determining the unit cost of a product manufactured, an estimate of depreciation expense on factory equipment used in the manufacturing process must be made. Without this estimate, the cost of the product would be of limited usefulness in establishing the product selling price.

Clarity

Clarity refers to the need for reports to be clear and understandable in both format and content. Reports that are clear and understandable will enable management to focus on significant factors in planning and controlling operations. For example, for management's use in controlling the costs of manufacturing a product, a report that compares actual costs with expected costs and clearly indicates the differences enables management to give its attention to significant differences and to take any necessary corrective action.

Conciseness

Conciseness refers to the requirement that the report should be brief and to the point. Although the report must be complete and include all relevant information, the inclusion of unnecessary information wastes management's time and makes it more difficult for management to focus on the significant factors related to a decision. For example, reports prepared for the top level of management should usually be broad in scope and present summaries of data rather than small details.

Costs vs. Benefits of Managerial Accounting Reports

The characteristics of managerial accounting reports provide general guidelines for the preparation of reports to meet the various needs of management. In applying these guidelines, consideration must be given to the specific needs of each manager, and the reports should be tailored to meet these needs. In preparing reports, costs are incurred, and a primary consideration is that the value of the management reports should be greater than the cost of producing them. The relationship between the general guidelines and the cost-benefit consideration is illustrated on page 657.

Costs and benefits must be considered, no matter how much information a report may contain. A report should not be prepared if its expected cost exceeds its expected benefits.

COST CONCEPTS AND TERMINOLOGY

OBJECTIVE 4
Describe and illustrate the basic cost concepts and terminology useful in managerial accounting.

The economic information reported to management for use in decision making is very often related to the costs associated with operations. A **cost** is a disbursement of cash or its equivalent or the commitment to pay cash in the future for the purpose of generating revenues. For example, the amount of cash (or credit) used to purchase equipment is the cost of the equipment. Likewise, if equipment is purchased through the exchange of assets other than cash, the current market value of the other assets is the cost of the equipment purchased. The following paragraphs describe and illustrate common cost concepts and terminology used in managerial accounting. An understanding of these concepts and terms will provide the foundation for later discussions and illustrations of more complex, real-world decision-making situations.

Direct and Indirect Costs

For management's use in making decisions, costs are often classified in terms of how they relate to some object or segment of operations, often referred to as a **cost object**. The cost object may be a product, a sales territory, a department, or some activity such as research and development. Costs that can be traced directly to the cost object are referred to as **direct costs.** Costs that cannot be traced easily and accurately to a particular cost object are **indirect costs** with respect to that cost object.

Management determines cost objects depending upon its decision-making needs. The classification of a cost as a direct or indirect cost first requires the identification of the cost object by management. Next, a determination must be made as to whether the cost can be traced directly to the cost object. For example, if the management of Midway Taxi is evaluating the cost effectiveness of its various taxis, the cost object would be a taxi. In this case, the cost of gasoline consumed and repair parts used in operating the taxis are direct costs. On the other hand, the salary of the maintenance shop supervisor whose department repairs and services company taxis is an indirect cost of the taxi, since it cannot be traced easily to individual taxis. If the cost object was the maintenance shop, however, the salary of the maintenance shop supervisor would be a direct cost. Hence, a cost can be either direct or indirect, depending upon the cost object under consideration by management.

Differential Costs

Differential cost, sometimes referred to as **incremental cost**, is the increase or decrease in cost that is expected from a particular course of action as compared with an alternate course of action. For example, the management of a microcomputer manufacturer must decide on whether to purchase carrying cases for the computers from an outside supplier or to produce the carrying cases. If the cost of purchasing the carrying cases is $20 per case and the cost of producing the carrying case is $18 per case, the cost difference betwen the two alternatives ($2) is referred to as the differential cost. As another example, if an increase in advertising expenditures from $100,000 to $150,000 is being considered, the differential cost of the proposal would be $50,000.

Sunk Costs

Sunk costs are costs which have been incurred and cannot be reversed by subsequent decisions. Sunk costs are irrelevant for future decision making and are therefore often excluded from managerial accounting reports prepared to assist management in making such decisions. To illustrate, assume that a major airline is currently operating a fleet of Boeing 727 passenger jets, which originally cost $300 million and on which depreciation of $250 million has been taken. In considering whether to spend $500 million to upgrade its fleet of aircraft to newer, more fuel-efficient and technologically advanced 767 passenger jets, the original $300 million cost is irrelevant. The $300 million has been spent, and regardless of whether the original decision was wise or unwise, the $300 million expenditure cannot be reversed. For this reason, the $300 million original cost of the 727 jets is referred to as a sunk cost. Likewise, the $50 million book value (the original cost of $300 million less accumulated depreciation of $250 million) and the $250 million accumulated depreciation are irrelevant. The cost savings resulting from the use of the more fuel-efficient 767, when compared to the proposed expenditure of $500 million, are the relevant costs that would be considered by management in making the decision.

Controllable and Noncontrollable Costs

All costs are controllable by someone within a business enterprise, but not all costs are controllable at the same level of management. For example, plant supervisors, as members of operating management, are responsible for the use of direct materials in their departments. Since the plant supervisors have significant influence or control over direct material costs, those costs are **controllable costs** to the plant supervisors. On the other hand, the insurance premium costs related to the building housing their departments are **noncontrollable costs** to the plant supervisors because they have no significant influence or control over those costs. However, the premium costs would be controllable costs to the company treasurer. The distinction between controllable and noncontrollable costs, as applied to specific managers, is useful in fixing the responsibility for the incurrence of costs and then for reporting the cost data to those responsible for cost control.

In some cases, there is a time dimension to the classification of costs as controllable or noncontrollable. Some costs cannot be controlled in the short run but can be controlled in the long run. For example, a plant manager cannot, in the short run, control the wages of factory employees who have union contracts that cover wages and layoffs. In the long run, however, the wages and layoffs become controllable because the contracts expire and are subject to renegotiation.

Discretionary Costs

A **discretionary cost** is a cost that is not essential to short-term operations and can therefore be avoided in the short run. For example, costs incurred in continuing education courses for management are classified as discretionary. Other examples of discretionary costs include advertising expenses, management consulting fees, sponsorship of employee social events (such as a company picnic), sponsorship of local athletic teams (such as a Little League team), charitable contributions to community activities, and a subsidized employee cafeteria.

Management reviews discretionary costs periodically, usually yearly, to determine whether the costs should continue to be incurred. Discretionary costs are usually the first to be reduced or eliminated during periods of worsening economic conditions, since their discontinuance will result in an immediate increase in profit. Although discretionary costs do not have a significant effect on short-term operations, their discontinuance can have a long-term impact on the enterprise. For example, research and development costs are often viewed as discretionary, but their discontinuance could be disastrous in the long run, especially in high-tech industries such as the computer industry. Likewise, the discontinuance of management continuing education could jeopardize the quality of managerial decision making in the long run.

Variable Costs and Fixed Costs

For management's use, costs are often classified by cost behavior; that is, costs are classified as to how they respond to changes in the volume of business activity. As the volume of business activity rises or falls, some costs tend to change proportionally to the rise or fall, while other costs do not change significantly as the volume of business activity changes. For directing current operations and planning future operations, a knowledge of the response pattern of costs to changing or anticipated changes in activity levels is useful.

Variable Costs. A **variable cost** varies in total dollar amount as the level of activity changes. The level of activity is normally expressed in terms of an activity base. Materials cost is a variable cost for the number of units produced because the total materials cost varies proportionately with the number of units produced (the activity base). For example, assume that Micro-Systems Inc. produces a standard microcomputer containing a 256K memory board. If each memory board costs $50, the total materials cost of the memory boards for the production of 1,000 computers is $50,000 ($50 × 1,000); for 2,000 computers, the total cost is $100,000. Hence, materials cost is a variable cost for the number of units produced (computers).

Fixed Costs. A **fixed cost** remains constant in total dollar amount as the level of activity changes. As with variable costs, the level of activity is normally expressed in terms of an activity base. Straight-line depreciation on manufacturing equipment is a fixed cost for the number of units produced because the total annual depreciation does not vary with the number of units produced (the activity base). For example, straight-line depreciation of $15,000 per year on Micro-Systems Inc.'s assembly and testing equipment would not vary with the number of computers produced. The total straight-line depreciation would be $15,000 regardless of whether 1,000, 2,000, or 6,000 microcomputers are produced.

Mixed Costs. Some costs have both variable and fixed characteristics. These costs are often called **mixed costs** or **semivariable** or **semifixed** costs. These mixed costs can often be separated into their variable and fixed components. For example, the rental charge for a copier might be $100 per month plus $.01 per copy. The $100 per month portion of the rental charge is a fixed cost, and the $.01 per copy portion is a variable cost for the activity base of number of copies.

Opportunity Costs

An opportunity cost is unlike the cost concepts discussed in the preceding paragraphs in that a cash disbursement or equivalent has not occurred. Instead, an **opportunity cost** is the amount of income that is forgone by selecting one alternative over another. To illustrate, assume that the treasurer of Faulkner Inc. invested $100,000 in a money market account yielding 5% interest. If United States Treasury bills are currently yielding 6%, the opportunity cost of not investing in the Treasury bills is $6,000 ($100,000 × 6%) per year. Hence, the treasurer might consider switching investments to maximize the return to Faulkner Inc.

Although opportunity cost differs fundamentally from the other classifications of costs that have been discussed, opportunity costs should be considered in all decisions that management makes involving the commitment of resources. For example, in deciding whether to acquire an international subsidiary in order to expand into Eastern European markets, management should consider the opportunity costs of forgoing competing investments such as the expansion into other product lines.

Classification of Costs

Many of the costs described in the preceding paragraphs can be classified in more than one way, depending upon the decision-making needs of management. For example, in determining the cost of products manufactured, materials costs would be classified as a variable cost related to the activity base of units produced. In determining responsibility for cost control, the cost of materials used would also be classified as a controllable cost of the production supervisor. This concept is often expressed as "different costs for different purposes."

MANUFACTURING OPERATIONS: COSTS AND TERMINOLOGY

OBJECTIVE 5
Describe manufacturing operations, including manufacturing cost concepts and terminology.

The operations of all business enterprises can be classified as either service, merchandising, or manufacturing. A service enterprise renders services to its customers. A merchandising enterprise purchases goods in a form ready for sale and then retails the merchandise to consumers. A manufacturing enterprise converts raw materials into a finished product through the use of machinery and labor.

The cost concepts described and illustrated in the preceding paragraphs are used in managerial accounting for all three types of business enterprises. In addition, most of the managerial accounting concepts described in the remaining chapters of this text also are applicable to all three business types. In the following paragraphs, however, cost concepts and terms that are unique to manufacturing enterprises are described and illustrated.

Manufacturing Costs

The cost of manufacturing a product includes not only the cost of tangible materials entering into the manufacturing process, but also the costs incurred in changing the materials into a finished product ready for sale. The cost of a manufactured product normally consists of direct materials cost, direct labor cost, and factory overhead cost.

Direct materials cost. The cost of materials that are an integral part of the manufactured end product is classified as **direct materials cost**, sometimes referred to as **raw materials cost**. For example, the direct materials for Seawind Company, a manufacturer of fishing boats, would include fiberglass and paint. The cost object, in this case, is the product (a fishing boat).

As a practical matter, in order for a cost to be classified as a direct materials cost, the cost must not only be an integral part of the end product, but it must be a significant dollar portion of the total cost of the product. For Seawind Company, the costs of fiberglass and paint are a significant portion of the total cost of each boat.

Other examples of direct materials costs would normally include the cost of paper and ink for a printer, lumber for a furniture manufacturer, silicon wafers for a producer of microcomputer chips, and steel for an automobile manufacturer.

Direct labor cost. The cost of wages of employees who are directly involved in converting raw materials into the manufactured end product is classified as **direct labor cost**. As with direct materials, the cost object for direct labor cost is the product. For example, the direct labor cost of Seawind Company includes the wages of the employees who paint the boat hulls in the manufacturing process. Other examples of direct labor costs would normally include the wages of carpenters for a construction contractor, mechanics' wages in an automotive repair shop, machine operators' wages in a tool manufacturing plant, and assemblers' wages in a microcomputer manufacturing plant.

As a practical matter, for the cost of employee wages to be classified as direct labor cost, the employee must not only be directly involved in the creation of the finished product, but the wages must be a significant portion of the total product cost. For Seawind Company, the painters' wages are a significant portion of the total cost of each boat.

Factory overhead cost. Costs other than direct materials cost and direct labor cost incurred in the manufacturing process are classified as **factory overhead cost**, sometimes referred to as **manufacturing overhead** or **factory burden**. For example, factory overhead cost includes the cost of heating and lighting the factory, repair and maintenance of factory equipment, and property taxes, insurance, and depreciation on factory plant and equipment. Factory overhead cost also includes materials and labor costs which do not enter directly into the finished product. For example, the cost of oil used to lubricate machinery is a materials cost which does not enter directly into finished products. Other examples of such costs include the wages of janitorial, supervisory, and quality control personnel.

As a practical matter, if the costs of direct materials or direct labor are not a significant portion of the total product cost, these costs may be classified as factory overhead. In Seawind Company, for example, glue enters directly into the finished product (boats), but its cost is insignificant and it is therefore classified as factory overhead. For many industries, the increased use of automated machinery and robotics has decreased labor costs to a level where they are a small portion of total product costs. In this situation, direct labor costs of manufactured products are often included as part of factory overhead cost.

Prime costs and conversion costs. As previously discussed, the total cost of a manufactured product normally consists of three elements: direct materials, direct labor, and factory overhead costs. These costs are often grouped in various classifications for analysis and reporting purposes. As will be illustrated in later chapters, two common classifications of manufacturing costs often reported to management for planning and decision making purposes are prime costs and conversion costs.

Prime costs are normally the combination of direct materials and direct labor costs. **Conversion costs** are the combination of direct labor and factory overhead costs. Conversion costs are the costs of converting the materials into a finished, manufactured product.

The diagram below summarizes the classification of manufacturing costs into prime costs and conversion costs.

Prime Costs and Conversion Costs

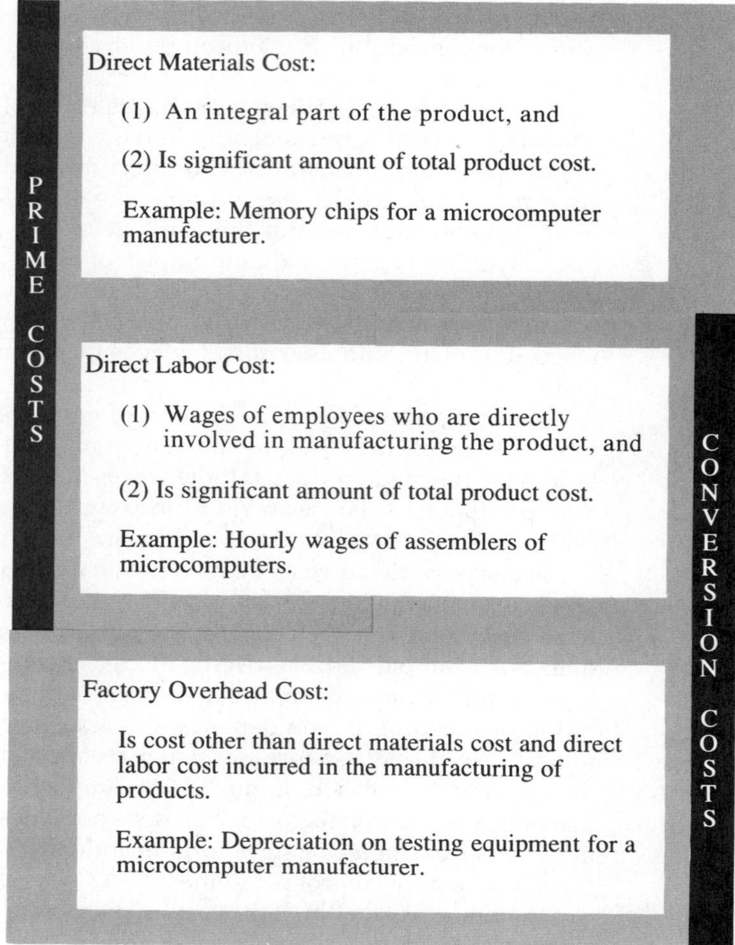

Product Costs and Period Costs

For financial reporting purposes, costs are often classified as either product costs or period costs. **Product costs** are composed of the three elements of manufacturing cost: direct materials, direct labor, and factory overhead. These costs are treated as assets until the product is sold. In other words, during the period beginning when product costs are initially incurred until the products are sold, product costs are accounted for as assets and are reported as a part of inventory on the balance sheet. In this sense, product costs are sometimes referred to as **inventoriable costs**. Thus, direct materials, direct labor, and factory overhead costs incurred in one period will not appear on the income statement as expenses until the products with which they are associated are sold.[3]

Period costs are those costs that are recognized as expenses in the period in which they arise. Period costs are generally classified into two categories: selling and administrative. **Selling costs** are costs that are incurred in marketing the product and delivering the sold product to customers. Examples of selling costs include salaries of marketing personnel, advertising expenditures, sales commissions, salespersons' salaries, and depreciation on store equipment. **Administrative costs** are costs that are incurred in the administration of the business and that are not related to the manufacturing or selling functions. Examples of administrative costs include office salaries, office supplies, and depreciation on office buildings and equipment.

The distinction between product costs and period costs is summarized in the following diagram:

Period Costs and Product Costs Distinguished

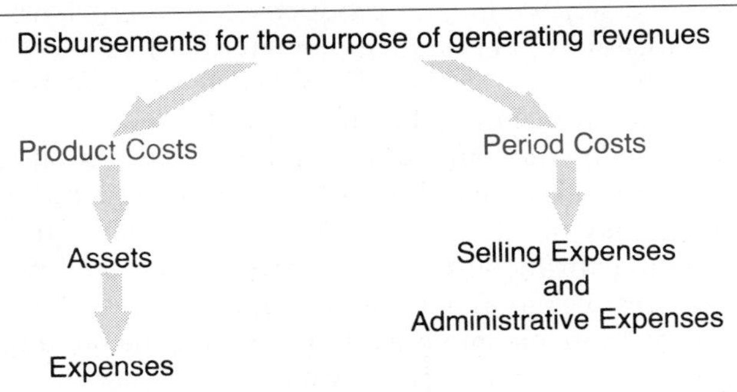

Disbursements for the purpose of generating revenues

Product Costs → Assets → Expenses

Period Costs → Selling Expenses and Administrative Expenses

By classifying period costs into selling and administrative, the managerial accountant enables management to establish accountability and control over the cost of two major functional activities: selling activities and administrative activities. Different levels of accountability for these activities may be shown in managerial reports. For example, selling costs may be reported by product, salespersons, departments, divisions, or geographic territories. Likewise, administrative costs may be reported by functional area, such as personnel, computer services, accounting, finance, or office support. The concepts and

[3] Financial statements for manufacturing enterprises are described and illustrated in the appendix at the end of this chapter.

principles discussed throughout this text for planning and controlling manufacturing costs are also applicable to selling and administrative costs.

TRENDS IN MANUFACTURING AND SERVICE ENTERPRISES

OBJECTIVE 6
Describe the major current trends in manufacturing and service enterprises.

Managerial accounting has evolved and continues to evolve in response to changes in the business environment and management philosophies. The evolution has been particularly rapid for manufacturing enterprises. Competitive world-wide pressures have forced many manufacturers to rethink their techniques and philosophies and to adopt innovative approaches to managing and manufacturing. In addition, the United States economy has increasingly become more service-oriented. This service orientation, combined with the deregulation of many service industries, has resulted in a renewed emphasis for service enterprises to apply managerial accounting concepts and techniques in order to compete more effectively in the marketplace.

The following paragraphs provide an overview of the major trends and innovations occurring in the manufacturing and service industries. The impact of each of these trends on managerial accounting is also briefly described. Additional discussions and illustrations of these trends are presented in later chapters.

Just-in-Time Manufacturing

To achieve greater productivity and efficiency, many manufacturing enterprises have begun to implement **just-in-time (JIT) manufacturing systems**, sometimes referred to as **flexible flow manufacturing systems**. These systems emphasize the manufacture of products or product components only as they are needed (demanded) by the next stage of production or by the marketplace. Because the demand launches the manufacturing process, just-in-time systems may be called "demand-pull" systems. In contrast, in more traditional manufacturing systems, materials tend to be "pushed" through the production process to avoid idle time for employees. The emphasis on keeping the production line moving often results in the buildup of manufacturing inventories to protect against unexpected bottlenecks caused by such factors as machine breakdowns or materials shortages.

Because just-in-time systems produce only what is needed by the next stage of production, inventories are often reduced to low or insignificant levels. Suppliers are required to deliver raw materials just in time to enter the production process. Materials in the process of manufacture may be reduced to a low enough level that they are insignificant and are not accounted for as a separate inventory. This low inventory allows the managerial accountant to concentrate less on inventory accounting for financial statement preparation and more on supplying information for the decision-making needs of management.

Just-in-time manufacturing places a greater focus on manufacturing quality control, since a defective part will have the effect of stopping the production line until the part can be reworked or a new part manufactured. Since one of a manufacturer's goals is to respond quickly to customer orders, just-in-time systems also focus on reducing the time required to manufacture a product from start to finish, sometimes referred to as **cycle time** or **throughput time**. As mentioned in the preceding paragraph, just-in-time systems require the timely delivery of raw materials, which requires a greater emphasis on purchasing high quality raw materials from reliable vendors who can meet strict production deadlines. Hence, in just-in-time systems, managerial accountants devote time and effort to measuring the costs and benefits of quality control systems, measuring cycle time, and assessing the reliability and performance of suppliers.

Total Quality Control

During the 1950s and 1960s, price was a primary vehicle for competition among manufacturers. During that period, for example, Japanese products were primarily known for their low prices. During the last decade, however, foreign competitiors, such as Japan, have implemented new manufacturing techniques and stringent quality control standards and have often supplied world markets with higher quality products at lower prices than those of U.S. manufacturers. As a result, many manufacturers have realized that they cannot compete in the world markets on lower prices alone, but that superior product quality must be a major manufacturing goal.

Although quality control programs are an integral part of just-in-time manufacturing systems, other manufacturers have also implemented such programs in order to improve product quality. **Total quality control (TQC)** programs begin with product design and continue through production, and they involve an ongoing commitment to improving product quality. Managerial accountants play a vital role in total quality control programs by providing information on the costs of poor quality, including the costs of reworks, scrap, defect prevention, customer dissatisfaction, and warranty obligations.

Computer-Integrated Manufacturing

Often used with a just-in-time manufacturing system, **computer-integrated manufacturing (CIM)** involves the use of automated equipment to perform routine, repetitive tasks with a minimum of human involvement. The automated equipment may be either in the form of computer-aided machinery or robots. Since some automated machines perform a variety of repetitive tasks, computer-integrated manufacturing adds flexibility to the manufacturing process and allows manufacturers to respond quickly to changing market conditions.

The use of automated equipment increases factory overhead costs through increases in depreciation, maintenance, repairs, and insurance, for example. At the same time, automation significantly reduces the amount of direct labor used in the manufacturing process. In some cases, direct labor is reduced to such a low level that it is treated as factory overhead. As a result, increased emphasis has been placed on controlling and properly accounting for overhead, which has lead to more refined attempts to trace overhead to specific activities that cause it. This latter emphasis is a critical part of "activity-based" cost accounting, which is described and illustrated in Chapter 18. In addition, increased emphasis has been placed on eliminating or significantly reducing manufacturing activities that are not critical to the manufacture of a product or that do not directly add value to the product. Such activities, re-

FACTORY AUTOMATION

In the mid-1980s, several U.S. companies were competing with Japanese companies for what was expected to be a $2 billion business in the manufacture of factory automated equipment. By 1990, most of the U.S. companies had "quit the business, whipped by the Japanese . . . " and " . . . robots installed in the U.S. . . had an estimated value of just $437 million."

"Saddled with high labor costs, the auto industry, particularly, saw robotics as a way to match Japan's lower car production costs. . . ." To meet this demand for factory automated equipment, U.S. companies focused on the development of hydraulic robots, while the Japanese companies stressed electric robots. The electric robot won out, partly because hydraulics "cost $48,000 on average, while electric robots sold for more than $70,000 . . . however, . . . it cost $12,000 a year to run a hydraulic robot, but only $6,000 for electric." Also important factors were that electric robots have 30% fewer parts and a higher reliability rate than hydraulic robots.

Source: "How U.S. Robots Lost the Market to Japan in Factory Automation," *The Wall Street Journal*, November 6, 1990.

ferred to as non-value-adding activities, include machine setups, moving materials between work stations, and machine downtime. The managerial accountant can assist managers in identifying and controlling these non-value-adding activities.

Service Industry Awareness

Primarily as a result of deregulation, the increased competition within the service sector of the economy, in such industries as trucking, airlines, and health care, has many service enterprises struggling for survival. As a result, service enterprises are increasingly looking to managerial accountants for analyses and information that will enable them to compete more effectively. Many of the managerial accounting techniques and concepts discussed in the remainder of this text are applicable to service enterprises. For example, hospital managers need accurate cost information in order to properly bill patients for such health-care services as X-rays, nursing care, and laboratory tests.

APPENDIX

FINANCIAL STATEMENTS FOR MANUFACTURING ENTERPRISES

The financial statements for manufacturing enterprises are more complex than those for service and merchandising enterprises. Since a manufacturing enterprise manufactures the products that it sells, the manufacturing costs described in this chapter must be properly accounted for and reported in the financial statements. These manufacturing costs primarily affect the preparation of the balance sheet and income statement, which are described in the following paragraphs. The retained earnings and cash flow statements for merchandising and manufacturing enterprises are similar and therefore are not discussed.

BALANCE SHEET FOR A MANUFACTURING ENTERPRISE

A manufacturing enterprise reports three types of inventory on its balance sheet: direct materials inventory, work in process inventory, and finished goods inventory. The **direct materials inventory** for a manufacturing enterprise consists of the cost of the direct materials which have not yet entered into the manufacturing process.[4] The **work in process inventory** for a manufacturing enterprise consists of the direct materials costs, the direct labor costs, and the factory overhead costs which have entered into the manufacturing process, but are associated with products that have not been finished. The **finished goods inventory** of a manufacturing enterprise consists of the finished products on hand that have not been sold.

The flow of manufacturing costs into the manufacturing process and the flow of costs to inventories of a manufacturing enterprise are illustrated in the following diagram:

Flow of Manufacturing Costs to Balance Sheet

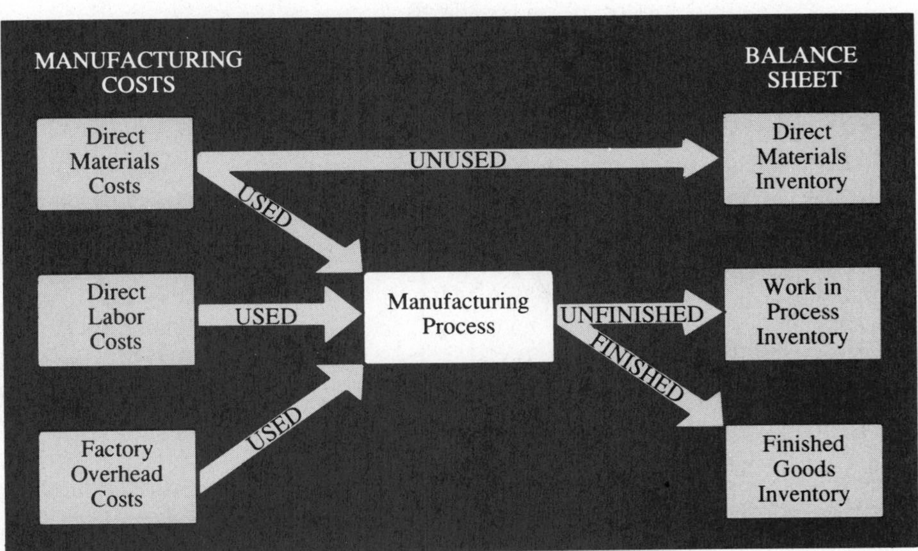

[4]Direct materials inventory, sometimes simply called materials inventory, includes only direct materials to be used in the manufacturing process. Indirect materials are classified as factory supplies.

INCOME STATEMENT FOR A MANUFACTURING ENTERPRISE

The major difference in the income statements for merchandising and manufacturing enterprises is in the reporting of cost of merchandise sold for a merchandising enterprise and cost of goods sold for a manufacturing enterprise. For a merchandising enterprise, merchandise is purchased in a finished state for resale to customers. The merchandise that is sold is called the **cost of merchandise sold**.

For a manufacturing enterprise, the product to be sold is manufactured by processing direct materials, using direct labor and factory overhead. The cost of the product sold is called the **cost of goods sold**. The costs of manufacturing the product, which are comparable to the purchases reported by a merchandising enterprise, can be reported in a **statement of cost of goods manufactured**. To illustrate the difference between the income statements for a merchandising enterprise and a manufacturing enterprise, the income statements for Loose Inc., a merchandiser, and Burleson Manufacturing Company are shown below and on the following page. The Burleson Manufacturing Company income statement is supported by a statement of cost of goods manufactured.

Merchandising Enterprise—Income Statement

Loose Inc.
Income Statement
For The Year Ended December 31, 1992

Sales		$1,100,000
Cost of merchandise sold:		
Merchandise inventory, Jan. 1, 1992	$ 90,000	
Purchases	900,000	
Merchandise available for sale	$990,000	
Less merchandise inventory, Dec. 31, 1992	120,000	
Cost of merchandise sold		870,000
Gross profit		$ 230,000
Operating expenses:		
Selling expenses	$ 85,000	
Administrative expenses	75,000	
Total operating expenses		160,000
Net income		$ 70,000

In Burleson's statement of cost of goods manufactured, the amount listed for the work in process inventory at the beginning of the period is composed of the estimated cost of the direct materials, the direct labor, and the factory overhead applicable to the inventory of partially processed products at the end of the preceding period. The cost of the direct materials placed in production is determined by adding the beginning inventory of direct materials and the net cost of the direct materials purchased and deducting the ending inventory. The amount of direct labor is then listed. The factory overhead costs are listed individually in the statement or in a separate schedule. The sum of the costs of direct materials placed in production, the direct labor, and the factory overhead represents the total manufacturing costs incurred during the period. Addition of this amount to the beginning inventory of work in process yields the total cost of the work that has been in process during the period. The estimated cost of the ending inventory of work in process is then deducted to yield the cost of goods manufactured during the period.

Manufacturing Enterprise—Income Statement

Burleson Manufacturing Company
Income Statement
For The Year Ended December 31, 1992

Sales		$915,800
Cost of goods sold:		
Finished goods inventory, January 1, 1992	$ 78,500	
Cost of goods manufactured	550,875	
Cost of finished goods available for sale	$629,375	
Less finished goods inventory, December 31, 1992	91,000	
Cost of goods sold		538,375
Gross profit		$377,425
Operating expenses:		
Selling expenses	$165,000	
Administrative expenses	84,425	
Total operating expenses		249,425
Net income		$128,000

Statement of Cost of Goods Manufactured

Burleson Manufacturing Company
Statement of Cost of Goods Manufactured
For The Year Ended December 31, 1992

Work in process inventory, January 1, 1992			$ 55,000
Direct materials:			
Inventory, January 1, 1992	$ 62,000		
Purchases	220,800		
Cost of materials available for use	$282,800		
Less inventory, December 31, 1992	58,725		
Cost of materials placed in production		$224,075	
Direct labor		218,750	
Factory overhead:			
Indirect labor	$ 49,300		
Depreciation of factory equipment	22,300		
Heat, light, and power	21,800		
Property taxes	9,750		
Depreciation of buildings	6,000		
Insurance expense	4,750		
Factory supplies expense	2,900		
Miscellaneous factory costs	2,050		
Total factory overhead		118,850	
Total manufacturing costs			561,675
Total work in process during period			$616,675
Less work in process inventory, December 31, 1992			65,800
Cost of goods manufactured			$550,875

CHAPTER REVIEW

KEY POINTS

OBJECTIVE 1

The Management Process

The management of an organization consists of those individuals charged with the responsibility of directing the enterprise toward achieving its goals. The management process involves the four basic functions of (1) planning, (2) organizing and directing, (3) controlling, and (4) decision making.

Planning is the process by which management develops a course of action to attain enterprise goals. Long-range goals involve strategic planning, while short-term goals involve operational planning. Organizing is the process by which management assigns responsibility to individuals for achieving enterprise goals, while directing is the process by which managers run day-to-day operations. Controlling is the process by which managers attempt to achieve the goals identified in the strategic and operational plans. Decision making, which involves choosing among alternative courses of action, has a central role in planning, organizing and directing, and controlling operations.

OBJECTIVE 2

Role of Managerial Accounting

The field of accounting that specializes in providing accounting information for use by managers is managerial accounting. Managerial accounting aids managers in planning (by providing reports which estimate the effects of alternative actions on an enterprise's ability to achieve desired goals), in organizing and directing (by providing information which is used to adjust operations for changing conditions), in controlling operations (by providing performance reports of variances between expected and actual operating results), and in decision making (by providing the basic information which the manager uses in selecting among alternative courses of action). Without accounting information, it would be difficult for management to manage effectively.

Departments or similar units are assigned responsibilities for specific functions or activities. This operating structure of an enterprise can be diagrammed in an organization chart. Individual units in an enterprise can be viewed as having either (1) line responsibilities or (2) staff responsibilities. A line department or unit is one directly involved in the basic objectives of the organization. A staff department or unit is one that provides services, assistance, and advice to the line departments or other staff departments.

The chief accountant in a corporation is called the controller. The controller has a staff relationship with others in the organization, providing advice and assistance to management but assuming no direct responsibility for the operations of the business. The functions most commonly provided by the controller's staff include systems and procedures, general accounting, budgets and budget analyses, special reports and analyses, taxes, and cost accounting.

Managerial accounting plays a major role in contributing to the effective management of business enterprises. Two important characteristics of the profession of managerial accounting are the Certificate in Management Accounting (CMA) program and ethics.

OBJECTIVE 3

Characteristics of Managerial Accounting Reports

The principle of usefulness to management is the primary criterion for the preparation of managerial accounting reports. In preparing useful managerial accounting reports, five characteristics should be considered. Relevance means that the economic information reported must be pertinent to the specific action being considered by management. Timeliness refers to the need for accounting reports to contain the most up-to-date information. Accuracy refers to the need for the report to be correct within the constraints of the use of the report and the inherent inaccuracies in the measurement process. Clarity refers to the need for the report to be clear and understandable in both format and content. Conciseness refers to the requirement that the report should be brief and to the point. A report should not be prepared if the cost of preparing it exceeds the benefits derived by management from its use.

OBJECTIVE 4

Cost Concepts and Terminology

A cost is a disbursement of cash or its equivalent or the commitment to pay cash in the future for the purpose of generating revenues.

For use by management, costs are often classified in terms of how they relate to some object or segment of operations, referred to as a cost object. Costs that can be traced directly to the cost object are direct costs. Costs that cannot be traced easily and accurately to a cost object are indirect costs for that cost object.

A differential cost, sometimes referred to as an incremental cost, is the difference in cost from one course of action compared to alternative courses of action. Differential costs are an important consideration for managers in deciding among alternative courses of action.

Sunk costs are costs which have been incurred and cannot be reversed by a subsequent decision. Sunk costs are irrelevant for future decision making and are therefore excluded from managerial accounting reports.

A controllable cost is one over which management has significant influence or control. Over time, all costs are controllable at some level of management. Therefore, when classifying costs as controllable or noncontrollable, the time period and level of management are critical reference points.

A discretionary cost is a cost that is not essential to short-term operations and can therefore be avoided in the short run. Management reviews discretionary costs periodically, usually yearly, to determine whether the costs should continue to be incurred. Although discretionary costs do not have a significant effect on short-term operations, their discontinuance can have a long-term impact on the enterprise.

A variable cost varies in total dollar amount as the level of activity changes. The level of activity is expressed in terms of an activity base. When the number of units produced is the activity base, materials cost is an example of a variable cost.

A fixed cost remains constant in total dollar amount as the level of activity changes. An example of a fixed cost when the activity base is the number of units produced is straight-line depreciation on manufacturing equipment. Costs that have both variable and fixed characteristics are called mixed costs or semivariable or semifixed costs.

An opportunity cost is the amount of income that is forgone by selecting one alternative over another. Opportunity cost differs fundamentally from the other classifications of costs that have been discussed because a cash disbursement or equivalent has not occurred. Opportunity costs should be considered in all decisions that management makes involving the commitment of resources.

Many of the costs described in this chapter can be classified in more than one way, depending upon the decision-making needs of management. Each specific decision-making situation must be analyzed carefully by the managerial accountant in order to classify and report costs properly for managerial use.

OBJECTIVE 5

Manufacturing Cost Concepts and Terminology

The cost of a manufactured product consists of direct materials cost, direct labor cost, and factory overhead cost. The cost of materials that are an integral part of the manufactured end product is classified as direct materials cost. For a cost to be classified as a direct materials cost, the cost must not only be an integral part of the end product, but it must also be a significant dollar amount of the total cost of the product.

The cost of wages paid to employees directly involved in converting raw materials into the manufactured end product is classified as direct labor cost. For the cost of employee wages to be classified as direct labor cost, the employee must not only be directly involved in the creation of the product, but the wages must be a significant portion of the total product cost.

Costs other than direct materials cost and direct labor cost incurred in the manufacturing process are classified as factory overhead cost. If the costs of direct materials or direct labor are not a significant portion of the total product cost, these costs may be classified as factory overhead.

Two common classifications of manufacturing costs are prime costs and conversion costs. Prime costs are the combination of direct materials cost and direct labor cost. Conversion costs are the combination of direct labor cost and factory overhead cost.

For financial reporting purposes, costs are often classified as either product costs or period costs. Product costs are composed of the three elements of manufacturing costs: direct materials, direct labor, and factory overhead. These costs are treated as assets until the product with which they are associated is sold. Product costs are sometimes referred to as inventoriable costs. Period costs are those costs that are used up in generating revenue during the current period. These costs are recognized as selling expenses or administrative expenses on the current period's income statement. Many period costs are time-oriented, in the sense that the costs are incurred or used as time passes.

OBJECTIVE 6

Trends in Manufacturing and Service Enterprises

Managerial accounting has evolved over the years as the business environment and management philosophies have changed. To achieve greater productivity and efficiency, many manufacturing enterprises have begun to implement just-in-time manufacturing systems, sometimes referred to as flexible flow manufacturing systems. The development and use of robotics, computer-aided manufacturing design, and flexible manufacturing systems have had a dramatic impact on manufacturing processes. Often used with a just-in-time system, computer-integrated manufacturing allows manufacturers to quickly respond to changing market conditions.

To improve product quality, many manufacturers have implemented total quality control programs. These programs are aimed at not only superior quality, but a continued commitment to improving product quality.

Because of increased competition within the service sector, managers of many service enterprises are looking to managerial accountants for analyses and information.

KEY TERMS

management 647
financial accounting 647
managerial accounting 647
management process 647
planning 648
strategic planning 648
operational planning 648
organizing 649
directing 650
controlling 650
management by exception 650
decision making 650
controller 653
ethics 654
cost 656
cost object 657
direct costs 657
indirect costs 657
differential cost 658
sunk costs 658
controllable cost 658
noncontrollable cost 658
discretionary cost 659
variable cost 659
fixed cost 659
mixed (semivariable or semifixed) cost 660
opportunity cost 660
direct materials cost 661
direct labor cost 661
factory overhead cost 661
prime cost 662
conversion cost 662
product costs 663
period costs 663
just-in-time manufacturing systems (JIT) 664
cycle (throughput) time 665
total quality control (TQC) 665

SELF-EXAMINATION QUESTIONS

Answers at end of chapter.

1. Which of the following is *not* one of the four basic functions of the management process?
   A. Planning
   B. Controlling
   C. Decision making
   D. Operations

2. Which of the following designations serves as evidence of professional competence in managerial accounting?
   A. Certified Public Accountant
   B. Certified Management Accountant
   C. Certified Internal Auditor
   D. Certified Financial Planner

3. Which of the following is *not* a characteristic of managerial accounting reports?
   A. Timeliness
   B. Relevance
   C. Conciseness
   D. Cost-benefit balance

4. Which of the following costs would be included as part of the factory overhead costs of a microcomputer manufacturer?
   A. The cost of memory chips
   B. Depreciation on testing equipment
   C. Wages of computer assemblers
   D. The cost of disk drives

5. When the activity base is the number of units produced, which of the following costs would normally be considered a variable cost?
   A. Direct materials cost
   B. Direct labor cost
   C. Electricity to operate factory equipment
   D. All of the above

ILLUSTRATIVE PROBLEM

The following is a list of costs that were incurred in producing this textbook:

(a) Insurance on the factory building and equipment
(b) Salary of the vice-president of finance
(c) Hourly wages of printing press operators during production
(d) Straight-line depreciation on the printing presses used to manufacture the text
(e) Electricity used to run the presses during the printing of the text
(f) Sales commissions paid to textbook representatives for each text sold
(g) Paper on which the text is printed
(h) Ink used to print the text
(i) Royalty paid to the authors for each text sold
(j) Salary of staff used to develop artwork for the text

Instructions:

With respect to the manufacture and sale of this text, classify each cost as either a product cost or a period cost. Indicate whether each product cost is a direct materials cost, a direct labor cost, or a factory overhead cost. Indicate whether each period cost is a selling expense or an administrative expense. Use the following tabular headings for your answer, placing an "X" in the appropriate column.

	Product Cost			Period Cost	
Cost	Direct Materials Cost	Direct Labor Cost	Factory Overhead Cost	Selling Expense	Administrative Expense

SOLUTION

	Product Cost			Period Cost	
Cost	Direct Materials Cost	Direct Labor Cost	Factory Overhead Cost	Selling Expense	Administrative Expense
(a)			X		
(b)					X
(c)		X			
(d)			X		
(e)			X		
(f)				X	
(g)	X				
(h)	X				
(i)				X	
(j)			X		

DISCUSSION QUESTIONS

15–1. What term refers to the individuals who are responsible for directing an enterprise?

15–2. Describe the field of managerial accounting.

15–3. What are the four basic functions of the management process?

15–4. What is the term for a plan that encompasses a period ranging from five to ten years and that serves as a basis for commitment of enterprise resources?

15–5. What is the process by which management assigns responsibility to individuals for achieving enterprise goals?

15–6. Describe what is meant by "management by exception."

15–7. (a) Differentiate between a department with line responsibility and a department with staff responsibility. (b) In an organization that has a sales department and a personnel department, among others, which of the two departments has (1) line responsibility and (2) staff responsibility?

15–8. (a) What is the role of the controller in a business organization? (b) Does the controller have a line or a staff responsibility?

15–9. (a) What do the initials CMA signify? (b) Briefly describe the requirements for the CMA designation.

15–10. Describe what proper ethical conduct implies.

15–11. What is the dominant principle that guides the managerial accountant in preparing management reports?

15–12. Chandler Inc. is contemplating the expansion of its operations through the purchase of the assets of Quality Tile Inc. Included among the assets of Quality Tile Inc. is inventory purchased for $75,000 and having a current replacement cost of $120,000. Which cost, $75,000 or $120,000, is relevant for the decision to be made by Chandler Inc.? Briefly explain the reason for your answer.

15–13. A bank loan officer is evaluating a request for a loan that is to be secured by a mortgage on the borrower's property. The property cost $100,000 thirty years ago and has a current market value of $900,000. Which amount, $100,000 or $900,000, is relevant for the loan officer's use in evaluating the request for the loan? Discuss.

15–14. What is meant by cost-benefit balance as it relates to the preparation of management reports?

15–15. What term describes a disbursement in cash (or its equivalent or the commitment to pay cash in the future) for the purpose of generating revenues?

15–16. For a company that produces microcomputers, would memory chips be considered a direct or an indirect cost of each microcomputer produced?

15–17. In deciding between the purchase of truck E or truck F, what would be the differential cost?

15–18. (a) What is meant by *sunk costs*? (b) A company is contemplating replacing an old piece of machinery which cost $620,000 and has $585,000 accumulated depreciation to date. A new machine costs $1,200,000. What are the sunk costs in this situation?

15–19. In considering the purchase of a new automobile, would the book value (the original cost less accumulated depreciation) of the automobile traded in be considered a sunk cost?

15–20. For a production line supervisor, would depreciation on the factory plant be considered a controllable or a noncontrollable cost?

15–21. How might the discontinuance or reduction of discretionary costs affect long-term operations? Use research and development costs as the basis for an example.

15–22. A variable cost remains constant in total dollar amount as the level of activity changes. Do you agree? Explain.

15–23. If the activity base is the number of units produced, classify each of the following costs as either (a) variable cost or (b) fixed cost:
(1) direct labor cost
(2) straight-line depreciation on factory equipment
(3) $3,000 per month rent on factory building used for warehouse
(4) property taxes on factory plant and equipment
(5) property insurance on factory building
(6) direct materials cost
(7) electricity (power) usage by robotic machinery
(8) monthly salary of factory supervisor

15–24. (a) What is meant by opportunity cost? (b) Crow Company is currently earning 9% on $100,000 invested in marketable securities. It proposes to use the $100,000 to acquire plant facilities to manufacture a new product line that is expected to add $8,000 annually to net income. What is the opportunity cost involved in the decision to manufacture the new product?

15–25. What three costs make up the cost of manufacturing a product?

15–26. What manufacturing cost term is used to describe the cost of materials that are an integral part of the manufactured end product?

15–27. If the cost of wages paid to employees who are directly involved in converting raw materials into a manufactured end product is not a significant portion of the total product cost, how would the wages cost be classified as to type of manufacturing cost?

15–28. Indicate whether each of the following costs of an airplane manufacturer would be classified as (a) direct materials cost, (b) direct labor cost, or (c) factory overhead cost:

(1) steel used in landing gear
(2) controls for flight deck
(3) welding machinery lubricants
(4) salary of test pilot
(5) wages of assembly-line worker
(6) tires
(7) aircraft engines
(8) depreciation on welding equipment

15–29. Distinguish between prime costs and conversion costs.

15–30. What is the difference between a product cost and a period cost?

15–31. What term is sometimes used to refer to just-in-time manufacturing systems?

15–32. Why are just-in-time manufacturing systems said to be "demand-pull" systems?

15–33. Does the amount of inventory normally increase or decrease with the implementation of a just-in-time manufacturing system?

15–34. Why does the implementation of a just-in-time manufacturing system increase the emphasis placed on quality control?

15–35. What are some of the implications of just-in-time manufacturing systems for management accounting?

15–36. What is meant by a total quality control system?

15–37. (a) Why does the increased use of automated manufacturing equipment increase factory overhead costs? (b) What is the implication of increased factory overhead costs for managerial accountants?

15–38. Why are managers of service enterprises increasingly looking to managerial accountants for analyses and information that will enable them to compete more effectively?

Real World Focus

15–39. The management of Trico Products Inc., a manufacturer of windshield wipers in Buffalo, New York, was faced with a decision on whether to locate several new plants in New York or on the Mexican border. The management decided to locate the plants on the Mexican border. Why would the employee hourly wage rate be a major differential operating cost of the two locations for purposes of this decision?

Ethics Discussion Case

15–40. Lyn Taos, assistant controller for Shepard Inc., is preparing a report for a proposed expansion of plant facilities at one of two possible locations—Morgan City and Pottersville. In preparing the report, Taos intentionally omitted the fact that Pottersville's property tax rates are significantly higher than Morgan City's. Taos has several relatives who own property in Pottersville. If the plant is built in Pottersville, property values should significantly increase. Discuss whether Lyn Taos is behaving in an ethical manner.

EXERCISES

Ex. 15–41.
Managerial accounting terminology.
OBJ. 1,2,3

From the choices presented in parentheses, choose the appropriate term for completing each of the following sentences:

(a) Long-range plans of action to achieve goals are referred to as (strategic, operational) plans.

(b) The function of the management process that involves the development of a course of action to attain enterprise goals is referred to as (planning, controlling).
(c) The function of the management process that involves the assignment of responsibility to individuals for achieving enterprise goals is (directing, organizing).
(d) The vice-president of production would occupy a (line, staff) position within a manufacturing company.
(e) (Accuracy, Conciseness) refers to the need for a managerial accounting report to be correct within the constraints of the use of the report.
(f) (Clarity, Relevance) refers to the need for a managerial accounting report to be clear and understandable in both format and content.
(g) The primary criterion for the preparation of managerial accounting reports is the principle of (timeliness, usefulness).

Ex. 15–42.
Analysis of differential costs.
OBJ. 4

Wilbanks Inc. has been manufacturing carrying cases for its laptop computers at a price of $8 per case. If Wilbanks Inc. purchases the carrying cases, the cases are expected to cost $10 per case. (a) What is the differential cost of purchasing the carrying cases, compared to the alternative of manufacturing the cases? (b) Should Wilbanks Inc. purchase or manufacture the cases? Explain.

Ex. 15–43.
Classification of costs.
OBJ. 4

The following is a list of costs that were incurred in producing this textbook. With respect to the manufacture and sale of this text, classify each cost as either variable or fixed, and as either indirect or direct. For purposes of classifying each cost as variable or fixed, use the number of books produced and sold as the activity base. For purposes of classifying each cost as direct or indirect, use the textbook as the cost object.

(a) Insurance on the factory building and equipment
(b) Wages of the vice-president of finance
(c) Hourly wages of printing press operators during production
(d) Straight-line depreciation on the printing presses used to manufacture the text
(e) Electricity used to run the presses during the printing of the text
(f) Sales commissions paid to textbook representatives for each text sold
(g) Paper on which the text is printed
(h) Ink used to print the text
(i) Royalty paid to the authors for each text sold
(j) Salary of staff used to develop artwork for the text

Ex. 15–44.
Classification as product cost or period cost.
OBJ. 5

For a manufacturing enterprise, classify each of the following costs as either a product (inventoriable) cost or a period cost:

(a) Depreciation on factory equipment
(b) Factory janitorial supplies
(c) Direct materials used during production
(d) Sales commissions
(e) Depreciation on office equipment
(f) Property taxes on factory building and equipment
(g) Advertising expenses
(h) Factory supervisors' salaries
(i) Repairs and maintenance costs for factory equipment
(j) Salary of production quality control supervisor
(k) Oil used to lubricate factory equipment
(l) Travel costs of salespersons
(m) Utility costs for office building
(n) Controller's salary
(o) Wages of assembly workers

Ex. 15–45.
Cost concepts and terminology.
OBJ. 4,5,6

From the choices presented in parenthesis, choose the appropriate term for completing each of the following sentences:

(a) Disbursements of cash or its equivalent or the commitment to pay cash in the future for the purpose of generating revenues are (costs, expenses).
(b) A product, sales territory, department, or activity to which costs are traced is referred to as a (cost driver, cost object).
(c) The increase or decrease in cost that is expected from a particular course of action as compared with an alternative is referred to as a (differential cost, sunk cost).
(d) Insurance premiums on factory equipment would be a (controllable, noncontrollable) cost for an assembly-line supervisor.
(e) Research and development costs are usually viewed as (discretionary, opportunity) costs.
(f) Factory overhead costs combined with direct labor costs are called (prime, conversion) costs.
(g) The implementation of automated, robotic factory equipment normally (increases, decreases) the direct labor component of product costs.

Ex. 15–46.
Cost concepts and terminology.
OBJ. 4,5,6

From the choices presented in parentheses, choose the appropriate term for completing each of the following sentences:

(a) A cost that has been incurred and cannot be reversed by subsequent decisions is an example of a (fixed, sunk) cost.
(b) Since the amount of overtime worked by assembly workers can be determined by the production supervisor through proper scheduling, overtime pay is considered a (controllable, noncontrollable) cost for the production supervisor.
(c) If the activity base is the number of units produced, the wages of assembly workers are considered a (fixed, variable) cost.
(d) The (opportunity, prime) cost of not investing in U.S. Treasury securities that are yielding 10% is the interest forgone on the possible investment.
(e) Direct materials costs combined with direct labor costs are called (prime, conversion) costs.
(f) The wages of an assembly worker are normally considered an inventoriable or (period, product) cost.
(g) The time required to manufacture a product from start to finish is referred to as (process time, cycle time).

Appendix Ex. 15–47.
Statement of cost of goods manufactured.

The following accounts were selected from the pre-closing trial balance of Stuart Co. at August 31, 1992, the end of the current fiscal year:

Administrative Expense	$ 65,700
Direct Labor	230,400
Direct Materials Inventory	62,000
Direct Materials Purchases	275,200
Factory Overhead	92,000
Finished Goods Inventory	91,800
Interest Expense	10,200
Sales	860,000
Selling Expense	95,000
Work in Process Inventory	67,000

Inventories at August 31 were as follows:

Finished Goods	$ 97,200
Work in Process	71,500
Direct Materials	64,800

Prepare a statement of cost of goods manufactured.

Appendix Ex. 15–48.
Cost of goods sold.

On the basis of the data presented in Ex. 15–47, prepare the cost of goods sold section of the income statement.

PROBLEMS

Pb. 15–49.
Managerial accounting terminology.
OBJ. 1,2,3,4,5,6

The following statements define, describe, or apply terms used in this chapter:

(a) The field of accounting that specializes in providing accounting information for use by managers in making decisions is (financial accounting, managerial accounting).
(b) Moral principles that guide the conduct of individuals are referred to as (ethics, laws).
(c) The development of short-term plans is referred to as (operational, strategic) planning.
(d) The function of the management process that involves the attempt to achieve the goals identified in the strategic and operational plans is referred to as (controlling, directing).
(e) The function of the management process that involves selecting one course of action from alternatives is referred to as (directing, decision making).
(f) In a merchandising enterprise, the vice-president of sales occupies a (line, staff) position within the organization.
(g) In most business organizations, the chief accountant is called the (controller, treasurer).
(h) The characteristic of managerial accounting reports that refers to the economic information reported being pertinent to the specific action being considered by management is (relevance, timeliness).
(i) The principle of (relevance, usefulness) is the primary criterion for the preparation of managerial accounting reports.
(j) Costs that cannot be traced to a specific cost object are said to be (direct, indirect) costs with respect to that cost object.
(k) Costs that are irrelevant for future decision making because they have already been incurred and cannot be reversed are called (indirect, sunk) costs.
(l) The cost of management consulting is normally considered an example of a (discretionary, sunk) cost.
(m) If the activity base is the number of units produced, the salary of a quality control inspector is normally considered a (variable, fixed) cost.
(n) The charge of $30 per day plus $.30 per mile for a rental car is an example of a (discretionary, mixed) cost.
(o) Straight-line depreciation on factory equipment is considered a (fixed, variable) cost for the activity base, number of units produced.
(p) The (opportunity, prime) cost of not investing in U.S. Treasury securities that are yielding 10% is the interest forgone on the possible investment.
(q) The cost of materials that are an integral part of the manufactured end product is classified as part of the (direct materials, factory overhead) cost.
(r) The cost of wages of employees who are directly involved in converting raw materials into the manufactured end product is classified as (direct labor, factory overhead) cost.
(s) Costs such as property taxes and insurance on factory buildings are normally classified as a (direct materials, factory overhead) cost.
(t) Prime costs include direct materials cost and (direct labor, factory overhead) cost.
(u) Product costs would normally not include (depreciation on factory equipment, salary of the controller).
(v) In a just-in-time manufacturing system, inventories usually (increase, decrease) in amount.
(w) In just-in-time manufacturing systems, managerial accountants devote considerable time in measuring (cycle time, inventory values).
(x) An example of a non-value-added manufacturing activity is (movement of materials, assembly workers' wages).

Instructions:

From the choices presented in parentheses, choose the appropriate term for completing each of the above sentences.

Pb. 15–50.
Classification of costs.
OBJ. 4

Case One: The Quality Control Department of a manufacturing enterprise is a cost object. Each of the following costs is either a direct cost or an indirect cost:

(a) Salary of the Quality Control Department supervisor
(b) Executive bonuses paid to the president and all vice-presidents of the company
(c) Depreciation of office equipment used in the Quality Control Department
(d) Payroll taxes paid on the wages of Quality Control Department employees
(e) Costs of maintaining the factory cafeteria used by all factory employees, including quality control employees

Case Two: Management is considering replacing a 1985 Ford pickup used for deliveries to customers with a 1992 Chrysler mini-van. Each of the following costs is either a differential cost or a sunk cost:

(a) Remaining book value of the 1985 truck
(b) $25 fee for transfer of the mini-van's title to the company
(c) Sales taxes on the purchase of the mini-van
(d) Cost of painting the truck last year
(e) Increase in insurance premiums on purchase of the mini-van

Case Three: For an emergency room supervisor at a local hospital, each of the following costs is either a controllable cost or a noncontrollable cost on a day-to-day basis:

(a) Salaries of emergency room doctors negotiated on a yearly basis by hospital administrators
(b) Cost of medical supplies used in treating patients
(c) Straight-line depreciation on X-ray equipment
(d) Cost of office supplies used in processing patients
(e) Health insurance premiums on emergency room staff

Case Four: Each of the following costs would normally be classified as a discretionary cost or a nondiscretionary cost for most business enterprises:

(a) Advertising costs
(b) Direct materials costs
(c) Research and development costs
(d) Depreciation on factory equipment
(e) Charitable contributions to the local United Fund

Case Five: With respect to the activity base, number of employees, each of the following costs is either a variable cost or a fixed cost:

(a) Wages of assembly workers
(b) $5,000 paid to an outside consulting firm to provide employees safety training
(c) Salary of vice-president of human resources
(d) Health insurance premiums paid on behalf of each employee
(e) Salary of production supervisors

Instructions:

For each of the preceding cases, properly classify the costs as indicated.

Pb. 15–51.
Cost identification and classification.
OBJ. 4

The management of Wadley Inc., a motorcycle retailer and distributor, is considering expanding operations by adding a Repair and Maintenance Department. Wadley Inc. constructed its building to accommodate future expansion. For the past several years, it has rented a 1,500-square-foot section of the building to Jim's Video-for-View for $750 per month. At the end of Jim's lease, this section of the building will be converted for use by the Repair and Maintenance Department.

Repair and maintenance equipment costing $6,000 will be purchased. It will be depreciated using the straight-line method. Existing store fixtures used by Jim's Video-for-View have a book value of $800 and will be converted for use by the Repair and Maintenance Department. An experienced mechanic will be hired for $1,350 per month, and an assistant mechanic will be hired for $5 per hour. A $7,500 inventory of spare parts will be ordered. Wadley Inc.'s insurance premiums are expected to increase by $100 per month, once the Repair and Maintenance Department opens for business.

To obtain as much visibility as possible, a one-time special advertising promotion is planned at a cost of $400.

Instructions:

(1) Classify the costs of the proposed Repair and Maintenance Department into the following categories:
   Variable costs when the activity base is the number of repair and maintenance orders
   Fixed costs when the activity base is the number of repair and maintenance orders
   Differential costs of expansion
   Sunk costs of expansion
(2) What is the opportunity cost of expanding operations for Wadley Inc.?

Pb. 15–52.
Classification of costs.
OBJ. 4

The following is a list of costs that were incurred in the production and sale of lawn mowers.

(a) Property taxes on the factory building and equipment
(b) Wages of vice-president of marketing
(c) Hourly wages of operators of robotic machinery used in production
(d) Factory cafeteria cashier's wages
(e) Electricity used to run the robotic machinery
(f) Commissions paid to sales representatives, based upon the number of lawn mowers sold
(g) Steel used in producing the lawn mowers
(h) Paint used to paint the lawn mowers
(i) Telephone charges for controller's office
(j) License fees for use of patent for lawn mower blade, based upon the number of lawn mowers produced
(k) Straight-line depreciation on the robotic machinery used to manufacture the lawn mowers
(l) Maintenance costs for new robotic factory equipment, based upon hours of usage
(m) Attorney fees for drafting a new lease for headquarters offices
(n) Engine oil used in mower engines prior to shipment
(o) Cost paid to outside firm for janitorial services for factory
(p) Rivets, bolts, and other fasteners used in lawn mowers
(q) Salary of quality control supervisor who inspects each lawn mower before it is shipped
(r) Plastic for outside housing of lawn mowers
(s) Cost of advertising in a national magazine
(t) Tires for lawn mowers
(u) Salary of factory supervisor
(v) Gasoline engines used for lawn mowers
(w) Premiums on insurance policy for factory buildings
(x) Cost of boxes used in storing and shipping lawn mowers
(y) Filter for spray gun used to paint the lawn mowers
(z) Payroll taxes on hourly assembly line employees

Instructions:

Classify each cost as either variable or fixed, and as either indirect or direct. For purposes of classifying each cost as variable or fixed, use the number of lawn mowers produced and sold as the activity base. For purposes of classifying each cost as direct or indirect, use the lawn mower as the cost object.

Pb. 15–53.
Classification of costs.
OBJ. 5

A list of costs incurred in the production and sale of lawn mowers is presented in Pb. 15–52.

Instructions:

Classify each cost as either a product cost or a period cost. Indicate whether each product cost is a direct materials cost, a direct labor cost, or a factory overhead cost. Indicate whether each period cost is a selling expense or an administrative expense. Use the following tabular headings for your answer, placing an "X" in the appropriate column.

	Product Cost			Period Cost	
Cost	Direct Materials Cost	Direct Labor Cost	Factory Overhead Cost	Selling Expense	Administrative Expense

Pb. 15–54.
Classification as product costs and period costs.
OBJ. 5

The following is a list of costs incurred by several business enterprises:

(a) Tires for an automobile manufacturer
(b) Shipping supplies for products sold
(c) Costs for television advertisement
(d) Disk drives for a microcomputer manufacturer
(e) Seed for grain farmer
(f) Executive bonus for vice-president of marketing
(g) Wages of a machine operator on the production line
(h) Hourly wages of controller's secretary
(i) Factory operating supplies
(j) First aid supplies for factory workers
(k) Sum-of-the-years digits depreciation on factory equipment
(l) Salary of quality control supervisor
(m) Maintenance and repair costs for factory equipment
(n) Sales commissions
(o) Cost of hogs for meat processor
(p) Health insurance premiums paid for factory workers
(q) Lumber used by furniture manufacturer
(r) Ink used by commercial printer
(s) Paper used by computer department in processing various managerial reports
(t) Hourly wages of warehouse laborers
(u) Costs of operating a research laboratory
(v) Entertainment expenses for sales representatives
(w) Protective glasses for factory machine operators
(x) Cost of telephone operators for a toll-free hotline to help customers operate products

Instructions:

Classify each of the preceding costs as product costs or period costs. Indicate whether each product cost is a direct materials cost, a direct labor cost, or a factory overhead cost. Indicate whether each period cost is a selling expense or an administrative expense. Use the following tabular headings for preparing your answer. Place an X in the appropriate column.

	Product Cost			Period Cost	
Cost	Direct Materials Cost	Direct Labor Cost	Factory Overhead Cost	Selling Expense	Administrative Expense

Appendix Pb. 15–55. **Statement of cost of goods manufactured; cost of goods sold.**

The following accounts related to manufacturing operations of Wofford Inc. were selected from the pre-closing trial balance at October 31, 1992, the end of the current fiscal year:

Depreciation of Factory Buildings	$ 60,000
Depreciation of Factory Equipment	75,200
Direct Labor	590,000
Direct Materials Inventory	155,000
Direct Materials Purchases	800,000
Factory Supplies Expense	17,200
Finished Goods Inventory	245,000
Heat, Light, and Power	80,500
Indirect Labor	132,000
Insurance Expense	25,400
Miscellaneous Factory Costs	13,500
Property Taxes	35,000
Work in Process Inventory	150,000

Inventories at October 31 were as follows:

Finished Goods	$260,000
Work in Process	175,000
Direct Materials	190,000

Instructions:

(1) Prepare a statement of cost of goods manufactured.
(2) Prepare the cost of goods sold section of the income statement.

Appendix Pb. 15–56. **Financial statements for a manufacturing enterprise.**

The following pre-closing trial balance of Howe Inc. was prepared as of July 31, 1992, the end of the current fiscal year:

Cash	35,000	
Accounts Receivable	120,000	
Allowance for Doubtful Accounts		12,000
Finished Goods Inventory	160,000	
Work in Process Inventory	55,000	
Direct Materials Inventory	42,000	
Prepaid Insurance	12,000	
Factory Supplies	7,000	
Land	100,000	
Factory Buildings	350,000	
Accumulated Depreciation—Factory Buildings		220,000
Factory Equipment	175,000	
Accumulated Depreciation—Factory Equipment		75,000
Accounts Payable		45,000
Wages Payable		18,000
Income Tax Payable		10,000
Common Stock		200,000
Retained Earnings		445,000
Dividends	30,000	
Sales		1,250,000
Direct Materials Purchases	520,000	
Direct Labor	250,000	
Indirect Factory Labor	110,000	
Factory Heat, Light, and Power	28,000	
Depreciation—Factory Equipment	20,000	
Factory Property Taxes	15,000	
Depreciation—Factory Buildings	14,000	

Insurance Expense—Factory	9,000	
Factory Supplies Expense	8,000	
Miscellaneous Factory Costs	5,000	
Selling Expenses	120,000	
Administrative Expenses	60,000	
Income Tax	30,000	
	2,275,000	2,275,000

Inventories at July 31, 1992, were as follows:

Finished Goods	$140,000
Work in Process	50,000
Direct Materials	48,000

Instructions:

(1) Prepare a statement of cost of goods manufactured.
(2) Prepare an income statement.
(3) Prepare a retained earnings statement.
(4) Prepare a balance sheet in report form.

ALTERNATE PROBLEMS

Pb. 15–49A. Managerial accounting terminology.

OBJ. 1,2,3,4,5,6

The following statements define, describe, or apply terms used in this chapter:

(a) The management process involves (three, four) basic functions.
(b) The function of the management process by which managers with assigned responsibilities run day-to-day operations is referred to as (directing, organizing).
(c) The comparisons of actual results with expected results is referred to as (controlling, feedback).
(d) Long-range plans of action to achieve goals are referred to as (strategic, operational) plans.
(e) The operating structure of an enterprise can be diagrammed in (organization, pert) charts.
(f) The controller occupies a (line, staff) position within an organization.
(g) To provide more recognition of managerial accounting as a profession, the Institute of Certified Management Accountants grants the (Certificate in Management Accounting (CMA), Certificate in Public Accounting (CPA)).
(h) The characteristic of managerial accounting reports that refers to the need for the report to be correct within the constraints of the use of the report is (accuracy, clarity).
(i) Disbursements of cash for the purpose of generating revenues are called (costs, expenses).
(j) Increases in costs that are expected from a particular course of action as compared to an alternative course of action are referred to as (differential, opportunity) costs.
(k) Costs over which a manager has no significant influence are referred to as (controllable, noncontrollable) costs for that manager.
(l) If the activity base is the number of units produced, the hourly wages of assembly workers are normally considered a (variable, fixed) cost.
(m) If the activity base is the number of patients, the yearly premium for malpractice insurance for a doctor is normally considered a (variable, fixed) cost.
(n) The amount of income forgone by selecting one alternative over another is referred to as an (indirect, opportunity) cost.
(o) Costs that can be traced to a cost object are (direct, indirect) costs with respect to that cost object.
(p) For a television manufacturer, the cost of picture tubes is a (direct materials, factory overhead) cost.

(q) An assembly line worker's hourly wages for an automobile manufacturer is an example of (direct labor, factory overhead) costs.
(r) The cost that is common to both prime costs and conversion costs is (direct materials, direct labor) cost.
(s) Conversion costs include direct labor costs and (direct materials, factory overhead) costs.
(t) Period costs would normally include (advertising costs, power costs used by factory equipment).
(u) Just-in-time manufacturing systems are often referred to as (demand-pull, demand-push) systems.
(v) The implementation of automated equipment normally (increases, decreases) factory overhead costs.
(w) Recent trends in the service sector of the economy have (increased, decreased) the demand for managerial accounting analyses and reports.
(x) Manufacturing systems that emphasize the manufacture of products only as they are needed by the next stage of production or by the market place are referred to as (job order cost, just-in-time) systems.

Instructions:

From the choices presented in parentheses, choose the appropriate term for completing each of the above sentences.

Pb. 15–50A.
Classification of costs.
OBJ.4

Case One: The hamburger at a fast food restaurant is a cost object. Each of the following costs is either a direct cost or an indirect cost:

(a) Salary of restaurant manager
(b) Hamburger patty
(c) Pickles put on each hamburger
(d) Hourly wages of cook
(e) Hamburger bun

Case Two: Management is considering whether to continue to lease office space in a downtown location or move to a suburban location. Each of the following costs is either a differential cost or a sunk cost:

(a) Cost of attorney's fees for negotiating the new lease
(b) Initial deposit of $4,000 for prepayment of one month's rent at the new suburban location
(c) Book value of lease improvements already made at the current location
(d) Costs to move to new location
(e) Nonrefundable deposit of $3,000 made under the original downtown lease agreement

Case Three: For the general manager of a professional baseball team, each of the following costs is either a controllable cost or a noncontrollable cost on a day-to-day basis:

(a) Salaries of the managers and players
(b) Annual stadium rental fee
(c) Hotel, meals, and transportation costs for away games
(d) Field maintenance and facility repair costs
(e) Executive entertainment expenses

Case Four: Each of the following costs would normally be classified as a discretionary cost or a nondiscretionary cost for most business enterprises:

(a) Sales salaries
(b) Salary of media consultant
(c) Executive bonuses
(d) Attorney fees for regulatory filings with the state
(e) Costs of sponsoring local golf tournament to benefit a community center for troubled children

Case Five: Each of the following costs would be classified as an opportunity cost or as some other type of cost:

(a) President's salary
(b) Interest that could be earned on investing in 8%, 10-year bonds instead of acquiring equipment with a 10-year life
(c) Revenues that could have been earned from renting a building rather than selling it
(d) Cost of insurance on sales representatives' automobiles
(e) Income a student could earn from working a full-time job rather than attending college

Instructions:

For each of the preceding cases, properly classify the costs as indicated.

Pb. 15–51A.
Cost identification and classification.
OBJ. 4

The management of Owens Grocery Inc., a local grocer, is considering expanding operations by adding a small Pharmacy Department. The space for the pharmacy is currently being rented by a flower shop for $5,000 per month.

New store fixtures costing $200,000 will be purchased. The new store fixtures will be depreciated using straight-line depreciation. Existing store fixtures having a book value of $350,000 will be used in the pharmacy.

An experienced pharmacist will be hired for $2,500 per month and an assistant will be hired. The assistant will be paid a sales commission of 5%. An inventory of $18,000 of medicines and drugs will be ordered. Owens Grocery Inc.'s insurance premiums are expected to increase by $200 per month, once the Pharmacy Department opens for business.

To obtain as much visibility as possible for the new pharmacy, a one-time special advertising promotion is planned at a cost of $1,000.

Instructions:

(1) Classify the costs of the proposed Pharmacy Department into the following categories:
    Direct costs
    Fixed costs when the activity base is sales dollars
    Variable costs when the activity base is sales dollars
    Differential costs
    Sunk costs
(2) What is the opportunity cost of operating a Pharmacy Department for Owens Grocery Inc.?

Pb. 15–52A.
Classification of costs.
OBJ. 4

The following is a list of costs that were incurred in the production and sale of boats:

(a) Legal department costs for the year
(b) Fiberglass for producing the boat hull
(c) Salary of president of company
(d) Paint for boats
(e) Annual fee to pro-fisherman Jim Bo Wilks to promote the boats
(f) Decals for boat hull
(g) Salary of shop supervisor
(h) Executive end-of-the-year bonuses
(i) Glue for boats
(j) Oil to lubricate factory equipment
(k) Yearly cost of maintenance contract for robotic equipment
(l) Power used by sanding equipment
(m) Masks for use by sanders in smoothing boat hulls
(n) Special advertising campaign in *BassWorld*
(o) Steering wheels
(p) Wood paneling for use in interior boat trim

(q) Straight-line depreciation on factory equipment
(r) Premiums on business interruption insurance in case of a natural disaster
(s) Hourly wages of assembly-line workers
(t) Cost of paving the employee parking lot
(u) Cost of metal hardware for boats, such as ornaments and tie-down grasps
(v) Cost of normal scrap from defective hulls
(w) Cost of electrical wiring for boats
(x) Memberships for key executives in the BassWorld Association
(y) Cost of boat for "grand prize" promotion in local bass tournament
(z) Commissions to sales representatives, based upon the number of boats sold

Instructions:

Classify each cost as either variable or fixed, and as either indirect or direct. For purposes of classifying each cost as variable or fixed, use the number of boats produced and sold as the activity base. For purposes of classifying each cost as direct or indirect, use the boat as the cost object.

Pb. 15–53A.
Classification of Costs.
OBJ. 5

A list of costs incurred in the production and sale of boats is presented in Pb. 15–52A.

Instructions:

Classify each cost as either a product cost or a period cost. Indicate whether each product cost is a direct materials cost, a direct labor cost, or a factory overhead cost. Indicate whether each period cost is a selling expense or an administrative expense. Use the following tabular headings for your answer, placing an "X" in the appropriate column.

	Product Cost			Period Cost	
Cost	Direct Materials Cost	Direct Labor Cost	Factory Overhead Cost	Selling Expense	Administrative Expense

Pb. 15–54A.
Classification as product costs and period costs.
OBJ. 5

The following is a list of costs incurred by several business enterprises:

(a) Cost of dyes used by a clothing manufacturer
(b) Salary of the vice-president of manufacturing logistics
(c) Wages of a machine operator on the production line
(d) Travel costs of marketing executives to annual sales meeting
(e) Cost of sewing machine needles used by a shirt manufacturer
(f) Depreciation on microcomputers used in the factory to coordinate and monitor the production schedules
(g) Pens, paper, and other supplies used by Accounting Department in preparing various managerial reports
(h) Electricity used to operate factory machinery
(i) Factory janitorial supplies
(j) Fees paid lawn service for office grounds
(k) Wages of computer programmer for producer and distributor of microcomputer software
(l) Depreciation on copying machines used by the Marketing Department
(m) Telephone charges by president's office
(n) Cost of plastic for a telephone manufacturer
(o) Oil lubricants for factory plant and equipment
(p) Cost of a 30-second television commercial
(q) Depreciation on robot used to assemble a product
(r) Wages of production quality control personnel
(s) Maintenance and repair costs for factory equipment
(t) Depreciation on tools used in production
(u) Rent for a warehouse used to store finished products

(v) Maintenance costs for factory equipment
(w) Fees charged by collection agency on past due customer accounts
(x) Charitable contribution to United Fund

Instructions:

Classify each of the preceding costs as product costs or period costs. Indicate whether each product cost is a direct materials cost, a direct labor cost, or a factory overhead cost. Indicate whether each period cost is a selling expense or an administrative expense. Use the following tabular headings for preparing your answer. Place an X in the appropriate column.

	Product Cost			Period Cost	
Cost	Direct Materials Cost	Direct Labor Cost	Factory Overhead Cost	Selling Expense	Administrative Expense

Appendix Pb. 15–55A. **Statement of cost of goods manufactured; cost of goods sold.**

The following accounts related to manufacturing operations of Searcy Inc. were selected from the pre-closing trial balance at November 30, 1992, the end of the current fiscal year:

Depreciation of Factory Buildings	$ 12,000
Depreciation of Factory Equipment	14,500
Direct Labor	120,000
Direct Materials Inventory	30,000
Direct Materials Purchases	150,600
Factory Supplies Expense	3,200
Finished Goods Inventory	55,000
Heat, Light, and Power	14,300
Indirect Labor	24,500
Insurance Expense	5,000
Miscellaneous Factory Costs	2,400
Property Taxes	6,100
Work in Process Inventory	38,400

Inventories at November 30 were as follows:

Finished Goods	$ 60,000
Work in Process	43,200
Direct Materials	32,500

Instructions:

(1) Prepare a statement of cost of goods manufactured.
(2) Prepare the cost of goods sold section of the income statement.

Appendix Pb. 15–56A. **Financial statements for a manufacturing enterprise.**

The following pre-closing trial balance of Hirch Inc. was prepared as of January 31, 1992, the end of the current fiscal year:

Cash	25,000	
Accounts Receivable	80,000	
Allowance for Doubtful Accounts		4,000
Finished Goods Inventory	80,000	
Work in Process Inventory	65,000	
Direct Materials Inventory	50,000	
Prepaid Insurance	9,000	
Factory Supplies	8,000	
Land	75,000	
Factory Buildings	370,000	
Accumulated Depreciation—Factory Buildings		180,000
Factory Equipment	420,000	

Account	Debit	Credit
Accumulated Depreciation—Factory Equipment		200,000
Accounts Payable		60,000
Wages Payable		8,000
Income Tax Payable		5,000
Common Stock		100,000
Retained Earnings		543,000
Dividends	20,000	
Sales		900,000
Direct Materials Purchases	250,000	
Direct Labor	175,000	
Indirect Labor	45,000	
Depreciation—Factory Equipment	32,000	
Factory Heat, Light, and Power	22,000	
Factory Property Taxes	15,000	
Depreciation—Factory Buildings	20,000	
Insurance Expense—Factory	6,000	
Factory Supplies Expense	5,000	
Miscellaneous Factory Costs	3,000	
Selling Expenses	90,000	
Administrative Expenses	75,000	
Income Tax	60,000	
	2,000,000	2,000,000

Inventories at January 31, 1992 were as follows:

Finished Goods	$85,000
Work in Process	70,000
Direct Materials	55,000

Instructions:

(1) Prepare a statement of cost of goods manufactured.
(2) Prepare an income statement.
(3) Prepare a retained earnings statement.
(4) Prepare a balance sheet in report form.

MINI-CASE 15

Prescott Computers Inc. began operations on September 5, 1992, in the garage of Scott Pressley. During the weekends, Scott assembled microcomputers from commercially available parts and components. The microcomputers were assembled according to customer needs and specifications. Because of customer demand, Scott is considering moving to a vacant office building and devoting full time to the business. Scott is currently employed as the assistant manager of Boland Food Stores, where he makes $18,000 a year.

Scott has estimated the following costs of opening the new business:

Purchase of new testing equipment	$ 6,000
Purchase of used delivery van	12,000
Purchase of tables and other furnishings	8,000
Monthly rent	1,500
Wages of assistant	8 per hour
Insurance	120 per month
Local advertising	125 per month
Business licenses	500 per year

Scott plans to move the existing equipment from his garage to the new business. The existing equipment has an original cost of $9,000 and accumulated depreciation of $5,000. Straight-line depreciation is used to depreciate all assets.

Instructions:

(1) Classify each of the preceding costs of opening the new business, using the following categories:
   Variable costs when the activity base is the number of orders
   Fixed costs when the activity base is the number of orders
   Differential costs
   Discretionary costs
   Opportunity costs
   Sunk costs
   Note: Some costs may be classified into more than one category.
(2) Assuming that Scott opens the new business, list (a) costs which are controllable on a day-to-day basis, and (b) costs which are noncontrollable on a day-to-day basis.
(3) List direct costs and indirect costs of assembling microcomputers.

ANSWERS TO SELF-EXAMINATION QUESTIONS

1. D The four basic functions of the management process are planning (answer A), organizing and directing, controlling (answer B), and decision making (answer C). Operations (answer D) is not one of the four basic functions, but is the activity which managers attempt to manage.
2. B The Certified Management Accountant designation (answer B) serves as evidence of professional competence in managerial accounting. A Certified Public Accountant (answer A) has professional competence in financial accounting and auditing. A Certified Internal Auditor (answer C) has professional competence in internal auditing. A Certified Financial Planner (answer D) has professional competence in financial planning.
3. D Cost-benefit balance (answer D) is not a characteristic of managerial accounting reports, but is a general guideline for the preparation of managerial accounting reports. Timeliness (answer A), relevance (answer B), and conciseness (answer C) are all characteristics of useful managerial accounting reports.
4. B Depreciation on testing equipment (answer B) is included as part of the factory overhead costs of the microcomputer manufacturer. The cost of memory chips (answer A) and the cost of disk drives (answer D) are both considered a part of direct materials cost. The wages of microcomputer assemblers (answer C) are part of direct labor cost.
5. D Direct materials cost (answer A), direct labor cost (answer B), and electricity to operate factory equipment (answer C) all vary with changes in the activity base, number of units produced, and are therefore variable costs.

CHAPTER 16

CHAPTER OBJECTIVES

1 Describe the usefulness of product costs.

2 Describe accounting systems used by manufacturing enterprises, including:
   General accounting systems
   Cost accounting systems

3 Describe a job order cost accounting system for a manufacturing enterprise.

4 Illustrate a job order cost accounting system for a manufacturing enterprise.

5 Describe a job order cost accounting system for a service enterprise.

16

JOB ORDER COST SYSTEMS

A variety of cost concepts and classifications were described and illustrated in Chapter 15. For manufacturing enterprises, the importance of distinguishing between period costs and product costs was emphasized. Period costs are used up in generating revenues of the current period. Product costs are composed of the three elements of manufacturing costs: direct materials, direct labor, and factory overhead. To account for product costs properly, a manufacturing enterprise must use an accounting system that will accumulate and allocate product costs to the related units of production.

This chapter briefly describes the basic types of accounting systems used by manufacturing enterprises. The chapter then focuses on a discussion and illustration of one of these systems, the job order cost system, and traditional methods of allocating factory overhead costs to products.[1] The chapter concludes with a brief description of how a job order cost accounting system can be adapted for use by service enterprises.

USEFULNESS OF PRODUCT COSTS

OBJECTIVE 1
Describe the usefulness of product costs.

In studying product costs, it is important to keep in mind that the primary function of the managerial accountant is to provide useful information to managers for planning and controlling operations. Much of this information is developed in the process of accounting for product costs.

Product costs are needed by management for a wide variety of purposes. For example, the per unit cost of finished goods inventory is useful information for the setting of long-term product prices. Product cost information is also necessary in deciding whether to continue making a product internally for use in further processing or to purchase the product from an outside supplier. A variety of other managerial decisions which require the use of product cost information will be illustrated throughout the remainder of this text. Without accurate product cost information, managers could not effectively or efficiently manage operations.

[1] Another approach to allocating costs to products—activity-based costing—as well as an in-depth discussion of traditional methods, is presented in Chapter 18.

Product costs are also used by managers in the preparation of the financial statements of the enterprise. To present materials, work in process, and finished goods inventories properly on the balance sheet and cost of goods sold on the income statement, product costs must be accounted for and allocated to the individual units in inventory.

TYPES OF ACCOUNTING SYSTEMS

OBJECTIVE 2
Describe accounting systems used by manufacturing enterprises, including:
General accounting systems.
Cost accounting systems.

Two basic accounting systems are commonly used by manufacturers: general accounting systems and cost accounting systems. A **general accounting system** is essentially an extension to manufacturing operations of the system for merchandising enterprises which use periodic inventory procedures. A **cost accounting system** uses perpetual inventory procedures and provides more detailed information concerning costs of production.

Although accounting for manufacturing operations is usually more complex than for merchandising operations, a general accounting system may be used if a single product or several similar products are manufactured. A general accounting system is essentially an extension of the periodic system of inventory accounting used in merchandising enterprises to the three manufacturing inventories: direct materials, work in process, and finished goods. Because such simple manufacturing situations are rare, the basic principles of a general accounting system for manufacturing operations are not discussed further in this chapter.

Through the use of perpetual inventory systems, a cost accounting system achieves greater accuracy in the determination of product costs than is possible with a general accounting system that uses periodic inventory procedures. Cost accounting procedures also permit far more effective control by supplying data on the costs incurred by each manufacturing department or process and the unit cost of manufacturing each type of product. Such procedures provide not only data useful to management in minimizing costs, but also other valuable information about production methods to use and quantities to produce.

Types of Cost Accounting Systems

There are two main types of cost accounting systems for manufacturing operations—job order cost and process cost. Each of the two systems is widely used, and a manufacturer may use a job order cost system for some of its products and a process cost system for others.

A **job order cost system** provides for a seperate record of the cost of each particular quantity of product that passes through the factory. It is best suited to industries that manufacture goods to fill special orders from customers and to industries that produce different lines of products for stock. It is also appropriate when standard products are manufactured in batches rather than on a continuous basis. In a job order cost system, a summary such as the following would show the cost incurred in completing a job:

Job 565
1,000 Units of Product X200

Direct materials used	$2,380
Direct labor used	4,400
Factory overhead applied	3,080
Total cost	$9,860
Unit cost ($9,860 ÷ 1,000)	$ 9.86

Under a **process cost system,** the costs are accumulated for each of the departments or processes within the factory. A process system is best used by manufacturers of like units of product that are not distinguishable from each other during a continuous production process.

Perpetual Inventory Procedures

In a cost accounting system, perpetual inventory controlling accounts and subsidiary ledgers are maintained for materials, work in process, and finished goods.[2] Each of these accounts is debited for all additions and is credited for all deductions. The balance of each account thus represents the inventory on hand.

All expenditures incidental to manufacturing move through the work in process account, the finished goods account, and eventually into the cost of goods sold account. The flow of costs through the perpetual inventory accounts and into the cost of goods sold account is illustrated as follows:

Flow of Costs Through Perpetual Inventory Accounts

Materials		Work in Process		Finished Goods	
Purchased	Dir. used a Indir. used b	a c e	Finished f	f	Sold g

Wages Payable		Factory Overhead		Costs of Goods Sold	
Paid	Dir. used c Indir. used d	b d Other costs	Applied e	g	

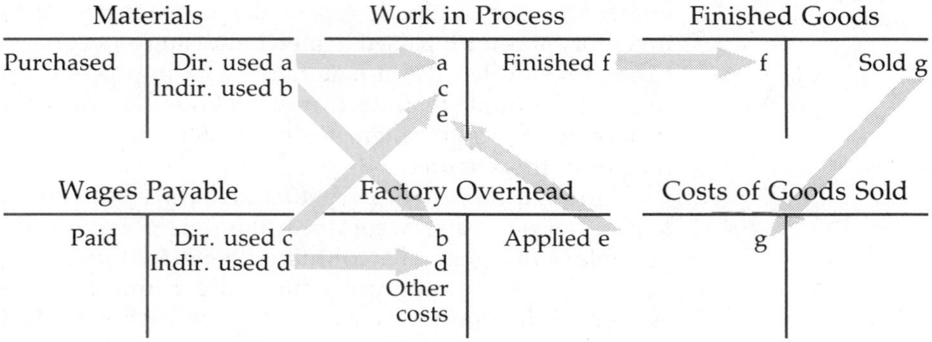

Materials and labor used in production are classified as direct and indirect. The materials and the labor that can be traced to units of product are classified as direct and are debited to Work in Process (a and c in the diagram). The materials and the labor that do not enter directly into the finished product are debited to Factory Overhead (b and d in the diagram). Examples of indirect materials are oils and greases, abrasives and polishes, cleaning supplies, gloves, and brushes. Examples of indirect labor are salaries of supervisors, inspectors, material handlers, security guards, and janitors.

Factory overhead cost is allocated (applied) to the product manufactured by using a predetermined factory overhead rate, as explained later in this chapter. The applied factory overhead cost is debited to Work in Process (e in the diagram). The costs of the goods finished are transferred from Work in Process to Finished Goods (f in the diagram). When the goods are sold, their costs are transferred from Finished Goods to Cost of Goods Sold (g in the diagram).

The number of accounts presented in the flow chart was limited in order to simplify the illustration. In practice, manufacturing operations may require many processing departments, each requiring separate work in process and factory overhead accounts.

---

[2] In this chapter and in subsequent chapters, the titles of the three manufacturing inventories will be shortened to "Materials," "Work in Process," and "Finished Goods."

OBJECTIVE 3
Describe a job order cost accounting system for a manufacturing enterprise.

The basic concepts of job order cost systems are illustrated in this chapter, while process cost systems are discussed in Chapter 17. In the following paragraphs, the discussion focuses attention on the source documents that serve as the basis for the entries in the job order cost system and on the managerial uses of cost accounting in planning and controlling operations.

Materials

Procedures used in the procurement and issuance of materials differ considerably among manufacturers and even among departments of a particular manufacturer. The discussion that follows is confined to the basic principles, however, and will disregard relatively minor variations and details.

Some time in advance of the date that production of a certain commodity is to begin, the department responsible for scheduling informs the purchasing department, by means of **purchase requisitions,** of the materials that will be needed. The purchasing department then issues the necessary **purchase orders** to suppliers. After the goods have been received and inspected, the receiving department personnel prepare a **receiving report,** showing the quantity received and its condition. Quantities, unit costs, and total costs of the goods billed, as reported on the supplier's invoice are then compared with the purchase order and the receiving report to make sure that the amounts billed agree with the materials ordered and received. After such verifications, the invoice is recorded as a debit to Materials and a credit to Accounts Payable.

The account Materials in the general ledger is a controlling account. A separate account for each type of material is maintained in a subsidiary ledger called the **materials ledger.** Details as to quantity and cost of materials received are recorded in the materials ledger on the basis of the purchase invoices, or receiving reports. A typical form of materials ledger account is illustrated as follows:

Materials Ledger Account

MATERIAL NO. 23								ORDER POINT 1,000	
RECEIVED			ISSUED				BALANCE		
REC. REPORT NO.	QUANTITY	AMOUNT	MAT. REQ. NO.	QUANTITY	AMOUNT	DATE	QUANTITY	AMOUNT	UNIT PRICE
						JAN. 1	1,200	600.00	.50
			672	500	250.00	4	700	350.00	.50
196	3,000	1,620.00				8	700	350.00	.50
							3,000	1,620.00	.54
			704	800	404.00	18	2,900	1,566.00	.54

The accounts in the materials ledger may also be used as an aid in maintaining proper inventory quantities of stock items. Frequent comparisons of quantity balances with predetermined order points enable management to avoid costly idle time caused by lack of materials. The subsidiary ledger may also include columns for recording quantities ordered and dates of the purchase orders.

Materials are transferred from the storeroom to the factory in response to **materials requisitions,** which may be issued by the manufacturing department concerned or by a central scheduling department. Storeroom personnel record the issuances on the materials requisition by inserting the physical quantity data. Transfer of responsibility for the materials is evidenced by the signature or initials of the storeroom and factory personnel concerned. The requisition is then routed to the materials ledger clerk, who inserts unit prices and amounts. A typical materials requisition is illustrated as follows:

Materials Requisition

MATERIALS REQUISITION				
Job No. 62		Requisition No. 704		
Authorized by R. A. Sanders		Date January 18, 19--		
Description	Quantity Authorized	Quantity Issued	Unit Price	Amount
Material No. 23	800	700 100	$.50 .54	$350 54
Total issued				$404
Issued by M. K.		Received by J. B.		

The completed requisition serves as the basis for posting quantities and dollar data to the materials ledger accounts. In the illustration, the first-in, first-out costing method was used. A summary of the materials requisitions completed during the month serves as the basis for transferring the cost of the materials from the controlling account in the general ledger to the controlling accounts for work in process and factory overhead. The flow of materials into production is illustrated by the following entry:

Work in Process	13,000	
Factory Overhead	840	
Materials		13,840

The perpetual inventory system for materials has three important advantages: (1) it provides for prompt and accurate charging of materials to jobs and factory overhead, (2) it permits the work of inventory-taking to be spread out rather than concentrated at the end of a fiscal period, and (3) it aids in the disclosure of inventory shortages or other irregularities. As physical quantities of the various materials are determined, the actual inventories are compared with the balances of the respective subsidiary ledger accounts. The causes of significant differences between the two should be determined and the responsibility for the differences assigned to specific individuals. Remedial action can then be taken.

Factory Labor

Unlike materials, factory labor is not tangible, nor is it acquired and stored in advance of its use. Hence, there is no perpetual inventory account for labor. The two main objectives in accounting for labor are (1) determination of the correct amount to be paid each employee for each payroll period and (2) appropriate allocation of labor costs to factory overhead and individual job orders.

The amount of time spent by an employee in the factory is usually recorded on **clock cards**, which are also called **in-and-out-cards**. The amount of time spent by each employee and labor cost incurred for each individual job, or for factory overhead, are recorded on **time tickets.** A typical time ticket form is illustrated as follows:

Time Ticket

Time Ticket

Employee Name Gail Berry — No. 4521

Employee No. 240 — Date January 18, 19--

Description of work Finishing — Job No. 62

Time Started	Time Stopped	Hours Worked	Hourly Rate	Cost
10:00	12:00	2	$6.50	$13.00
1:00	2:00	1	6.50	6.50
Total cost				$19.50

Approved by T. D.

The times reported on an employee's time tickets are compared with the related clock cards as an internal check on the accuracy of payroll disbursements. A summary of the time tickets at the end of each month serves as the basis for recording the direct and indirect labor costs incurred. The flow of labor costs into production is illustrated by the following entry:

Work in Process	10,000	
Factory Overhead	2,200	
Wages Payable		12,200

Factory Overhead

Factory overhead includes all manufacturing costs except direct materials and direct labor. Examples of factory overhead costs, in addition to indirect materials and indirect labor, are depreciation, electricity, fuel, insurance, and property taxes. It is customary to have a factory overhead controlling account in the general ledger. Details of the various types of cost are accumulated in a subsidiary ledger.

Debits to Factory Overhead come from various sources. For example, the cost of indirect materials is obtained from the summary of the materials requisitions, the cost of indirect labor is obtained from the summary of the time tickets, cost of electricity and water are obtained from invoices, and the cost of depreciation and expired insurance may be recorded as adjustments at the end of the accounting period.

Although factory overhead cannot be specifically identified with particular jobs, it is as much a part of manufacturing costs as direct materials and direct labor. As the use of machines and automation has increased, factory overhead has represented an ever larger part of total costs. Many items of factory overhead cost are incurred for the entire factory and cannot be directly related to the finished product. The problem is further complicated because some items of factory overhead cost are relatively fixed in amount while others tend to vary according to changes in productivity.

To wait until the end of an accounting period to allocate factory overhead to the various jobs would be quite acceptable from the standpoint of accuracy but highly unsatisfactory in terms of timeliness. If the cost system is to be of maximum usefulness, it is imperative that cost data be available as each job is completed, even though there is a sacrifice in accuracy. It is only through timely reporting that management can make whatever adjustments seem necessary in pricing and manufacturing methods to achieve the best possible combination of revenue and cost on future jobs. Therefore, in order that job costs may be available currently, factory overhead may be allocated or applied to production by using a **predetermined factory overhead rate.**

Predetermined Factory Overhead Rate. The factory overhead rate is determined by relating the estimated amount of factory overhead for the forthcoming year to an activity base, such as machine hours, direct labor costs, or direct labor hours. The activity base selected should represent the activity that is a significant *cause* of the factory overhead cost. The term frequently used to describe such a causal factor is **cost driver.** For example, if a machine is used in processing various jobs, machine hours would likely be a significant factor in "driving" or causing the factory overhead costs incurred in operating the machine. Once this cost driver has been identified and the factory overhead cost has been estimated, the factory overhead rate can be determined.

To illustrate the use of a predetermined overhead rate, assume that machine hours, estimated to be 20,000, is the cost driver, and the total factory overhead cost for the year is estimated to be $100,000. The predetermined factory overhead rate is $5 per machine hour, as shown in the following computation:

$$\text{Predetermined Factory Overhead Rate} = \frac{\text{Estimated Total Factory Overhead Costs}}{\text{Activity Base}}$$

$$\text{Predetermined Factory Overhead Rate} = \frac{\$100{,}000}{20{,}000 \text{ machine hours}} = \$5 \text{ per machine hour}$$

As factory overhead costs are incurred, they are debited to the factory overhead account. The factory overhead costs applied to production are periodically credited to the factory overhead account and debited to the work in process account. To illustrate the entry to record the application of factory overhead costs to production at the rate of $5 per machine hour, assume that 1,600 machine hours were used during a period, according to the machine usage reports. The entry to apply the $8,000 ($5 × 1,600 machine hours) of factory overhead is as follows:

Work in Process	8,000	
Factory Overhead		8,000

Inevitably, factory overhead costs applied and actual factory overhead costs incurred during a particular period will differ. If the amount applied exceeds the actual costs, the factory overhead account will have a credit balance and the overhead is said to be **overapplied** or **overabsorbed**. If the amount applied is less than the actual costs, the account will have a debit balance and the overhead is said to be **underapplied** or **underabsorbed**. Both cases are illustrated in the following account:

ACCOUNT FACTORY OVERHEAD ACCOUNT NO.

Date		Item	Debit	Credit	Balance	
					Debit	Credit
May	1	Balance				200
	31	Costs incurred	8,320			
	31	Cost applied		8,000	120	

Underapplied Balance

Overapplied Balance

Disposition of Factory Overhead Balance. The balance in the factory overhead account is carried forward from month to month until the end of the year. The amount of the balance is reported on interim balance sheets as a deferred item.

The nature of the balance in the factory overhead account (underapplied or overapplied), as well as the amount, may change during the year. If there is a decided trend in either direction and the amount is substantial, the reason should be determined. If the variation is caused by changes in manufacturing methods or in production goals, it may be advisable to revise the factory overhead rate. A large underapplied balance is more serious than a trend in the opposite direction and may indicate inefficiencies in production methods, excessive expenditures, or a combination of factors.

Despite any corrective actions that may be taken to avoid an underapplication or overapplication of factory overhead, the account will usually have a balance at the end of the fiscal year. Since the balance represents the underapplied or overapplied factory overhead applicable to the operations of the year just ended, it is not proper to report it in the year-end balance sheet as a deferred item.

There are two main alternatives for disposing of the balance of factory overhead at the end of the year: (1) by allocation of the balance among work in process, finished goods, and cost of goods sold accounts on the basis of the total amounts of applied factory overhead included in those accounts at the end of the year, or (2) by transfer of the balance to the cost of goods sold account. Theoretically, only the first alternative is sound because it represents a correction of the estimated overhead rate and brings the accounts into agreement with the costs actually incurred. On the other hand, much time and expense may be required to make the allocation and to revise the unit costs of the work in process and finished goods inventories. Furthermore, in most manufacturing enterprises, a very large part of the total manufacturing costs for the year passes through the work in process and the finished goods accounts into the cost of goods sold account before the end of the year. Therefore, unless the total amount of the underapplied or overapplied balance is great, it is satisfactory to transfer it to Cost of Goods Sold.

THE IMPLICATIONS OF AUTOMATION FOR ALLOCATING FACTORY OVERHEAD—A CASE STUDY

For some departments at Amerock Corporation, the allocation of overhead on the basis of direct labor became less accurate and less useful as manufacturing processes became more automated. The solution was to change from direct labor hours to machine hours for these departments.

Amerock Corporation, a manufacturer of cabinet and decorative hardware, found that the only disadvantages to using machine hours as a basis for allocating factory overhead were the time it would take to develop the system and the need for additional reporting by the machine operators. The potential benefits clearly outweighed any disadvantages. In the accounting area, a major advantage would be the ability to allocate overhead when one worker tended several machines. Better cost estimating would also be possible because overhead allocation would be more accurate. Forecasting and the calculation of actual costs would be easier. In the manufacturing area, machine utilization information would be more useful in understanding and controlling production and reporting.

Amerock Corporation's change in its overhead allocation basis has made it possible for accounting to capture cost accurately and for manufacturing to measure performance efficiently. The results have been so successful that Amerock plans to convert most of its departments to a machine hour basis as more of its plants become automated.

Source: Gregory Hakala, "Measuring Costs with Machine Hours," *Management Accounting* (October, 1985), pp. 57–61.

Work in Process

Costs incurred for the various jobs are debited to Work in Process. The job costs described in the preceding sections may be summarized as follows:

Direct materials, $13,000—Work in Process debited and Materials credited; data obtained from summary of materials requisitions.

Direct labor, $10,000—Work in Process debited and Wages Payable credited; data obtained from summary of time tickets.

Factory overhead, $8,000—Work in Process debited and Factory Overhead credited; data obtained from summary of machine usage reports.

The work in process account to which these costs were charged is illustrated as follows:

ACCOUNT WORK IN PROCESS ACCOUNT NO.

Date		Item	Debit	Credit	Balance	
					Debit	Credit
May	1	Balance			3,000	
	31	Direct materials	13,000		16,000	
	31	Direct labor	10,000		26,000	
	31	Factory overhead	8,000		34,000	
	31	Jobs completed		31,920	2,080	

The work in process account is a controlling account that contains summary information only. The details concerning the costs incurred on each job order are accumulated in a subsidiary ledger known as the **cost ledger**. Each cost ledger account, called a **job cost sheet,** has spaces for recording all direct materials and direct labor chargeable to the job and for factory overhead applied at the predetermined rate. Postings to the job cost sheets are made from materials requisitions, time tickets, and machine usage reports, or from summaries of these documents.

The four cost sheets in the subsidiary ledger for the work in process account illustrated are summarized as follows:

COST LEDGER

Job 71 (Summary)	
Balance	3,000
Direct materials	2,000
Direct labor	2,400
Factory overhead	1,920
	9,320

Job 73 (Summary)	
Direct materials	6,000
Direct labor	4,000
Factory overhead	3,200
	13,200

Job 72 (Summary)	
Direct materials	4,000
Direct labor	3,000
Factory overhead	2,400
	9,400

Job 74 (Summary)	
Direct materials	1,000
Direct labor	600
Factory overhead	480
	2,080

The relationship between the work in process controlling account on page 700 and the subsidiary cost ledger may be observed in the following tabulation:

Work in Process (Controlling)			Cost Ledger (Subsidiary)	
Beginning balance	$3,000	⟷	Beginning Balance	
			Job 71	$ 3,000
			Direct materials	
			Job 71	$ 2,000
			Job 72	4,000
Direct materials	$13,000	⟷	Job 73	6,000
			Job 74	1,000
				$13,000
			Direct labor	
			Job 71	$ 2,400
			Job 72	3,000
Direct labor	$10,000	⟷	Job 73	4,000
			Job 74	600
				$10,000

Factory overhead	$8,000	⟷	Factory overhead	
			Job 71	$ 1,920
			Job 72	2,400
			Job 73	3,200
			Job 74	480
				$ 8,000
Jobs completed	$31,920	⟷	Jobs completed	
			Job 71	$ 9,320
			Job 72	9,400
			Job 73	13,200
				$31,920
Ending balance	$2,080	⟷	Ending balance	
			Job 74	$ 2,080

The data in the cost ledger were presented in summary form for illustrative purposes. A job cost sheet for Job 72, providing for the current accumulation of cost elements entering into the job order and for a summary when the job is completed, is as follows:

Job Cost Sheet

Job No. 72 | Date May 7, 19--
Item 5,000 Type C Containers | Date wanted May 23, 19--
For Stock | Date completed May 21, 19--

DIRECT MATERIALS		DIRECT LABOR		FACTORY OVERHEAD		SUMMARY	
Mat. Req. No.	Amount	Time Summary No.	Amount	Machine Usages Summary No.	Amount	Item	Amount
834	800.00	2202	383.60	248	750.00	Direct materials	4,000.00
838	1,000.00	2204	208.40	250	1,100.00	Direct labor	3,000.00
841	1,400.00	2205	667.00	253	550.00	Factory overhead	2,400.00
864	800.00	2210	529.00		2,400.00	Total cost	9,400.00
	4,000.00	2211	798.30				
		2213	107.20				
		2216	306.50			No. of units finished	5,000
			3,000.00			Cost per unit	1.88

When Job 72 was completed, the direct materials costs, the direct labor costs, and the factory overhead costs were totaled and entered in the Summary column and the total cost of the job was determined. The total cost of the job, $9,400, divided by the number of units produced, 5,000, yielded a unit cost of $1.88 for the Type C Containers produced.

Upon the completion of Job 72, the job cost sheet was removed from the cost ledger and filed for future reference. At the end of the accounting period, the sum of the total costs on all cost sheets completed during the period is determined and the following entry is made:

Finished Goods	31,920	
Work in Process		31,920

The remaining balance in the work in process account represents the total cost charged to the uncompleted job cost sheets.

Finished Goods and Cost of Goods Sold

The finished goods account is a controlling account. The related subsidiary ledger, which has an account for each kind of commodity produced, is called the **finished goods ledger** or **stock ledger**. Each account in the subsidiary finished goods ledger provides columns for recording the quantity and the cost of goods manufactured, the quantity and the cost of goods shipped, and the quantity, the total cost, and the unit cost of goods on hand. An account in the finished goods ledger is illustrated as follows:

Finished Goods Ledger Account

ITEM: TYPE C CONTAINER

MANUFACTURED			SHIPPED			BALANCE				
JOB ORDER NO.	QUANTITY	AMOUNT	SHIP ORDER NO.	QUANTITY	AMOUNT	DATE		QUANTITY	AMOUNT	UNIT COST
						May	1	2,000	3,920.00	1.96
			643	2,000	3,920.00		8	—	—	—
72	5,000	9,400.00					21	5,000	9,400.00	1.88
			646	2,000	3,760.00		23	3,000	5,640.00	1.88

Just as there are various methods of costing materials entering into production, there are various methods of determining the cost of the finished goods sold. In the illustration, the first-in, first-out method is used. The quantities shipped are posted to the finished goods ledger from a copy of the shipping order or other memorandum. The finished goods ledger clerk then records on the copy of the shipping order the unit cost and the total amount of the commodity sold. A summary of the cost data on these shipping orders becomes the basis for the following entry:

Cost of Goods Sold	30,168	
Finished Goods		30,168

If goods are returned by a buyer and are put back in stock, it is necessary to debit Finished Goods and credit Cost of Goods Sold for the cost.

Sales

For each sale of finished goods, it is necessary to maintain a record of both the cost price and the selling price of the goods sold. As previously stated, the cost data may be recorded on the shipping orders. As each sale occurs, the cost of the goods billed is recorded by debiting Cost of Goods Sold and crediting

Finished Goods. The selling price of the goods sold is recorded by debiting Accounts Receivable (or Cash) and crediting Sales.

ILLUSTRATION OF JOB ORDER COST ACCOUNTING

OBJECTIVE 4
Illustrate a job order cost accounting system for a manufacturing enterprise.

To illustrate further a job order cost accounting system, assume that Amelia Co. has the following general ledger trial balance on January 1, the first day of the fiscal year.

Amelia Co. Trial Balance January 1, 19--		
Cash	85,000	
Accounts Receivable	73,000	
Finished Goods	40,000	
Work in Process	20,000	
Materials	30,000	
Prepaid Expenses	2,000	
Plant Assets	850,000	
Accumulated Depreciation—Plant Assets		473,000
Accounts Payable		70,000
Wages Payable		15,000
Common Stock		500,000
Retained Earnings		42,000
	1,100,000	1,100,000

Although in practice the transactions for Amelia Co. would be recorded daily, the January transactions and adjustments are summarized as follows, along with the related journal entries:

(a) Materials purchased and prepaid expenses incurred

Materials	66,000	
Prepaid Expenses	1,000	
Accounts Payable		67,000

Summary of invoices and receiving reports:

Material A	$29,000
Material B	17,000
Material C	16,000
Material D	4,000
Total	$66,000

(b) Materials requisitioned for use

Work in Process	60,000	
Factory Overhead	3,000	
Materials		63,000

Summary of requisitions:

By Use		
Job 1001	$12,000	
Job 1002	26,000	
Job 1003	22,000	$60,000
Factory Overhead		3,000
Total		$63,000

By Types

Material A	$27,000
Material B	18,000
Material C	15,000
Material D	3,000
Total	$63,000

(c) Factory labor used	Work in Process	100,000	
	Factory Overhead	20,000	
	Wages Payable		120,000

Summary of time tickets:

Job 1001	$60,000	
Job 1002	30,000	
Job 1003	10,000	$100,000
Factory Overhead		20,000
Total		$120,000

(d) Other costs incurred	Factory Overhead	56,000	
	Selling Expenses	25,000	
	Administrative Expenses	10,000	
	Accounts Payable		91,000
(e) Expiration of prepaid expenses	Factory Overhead	1,000	
	Selling Expenses	100	
	Administrative Expenses	100	
	Prepaid Expenses		1,200
(f) Depreciation	Factory Overhead	7,000	
	Selling Expenses	200	
	Administrative Expenses	100	
	Accumulated Depreciation—Plant Assets		7,300
(g) Application of factory overhead costs to jobs	Work in Process	90,000	
	Factory Overhead		90,000

The predetermined rate was $2 per machine hour. Summary of factory overhead applied:

Job 1001 ($2 × 27,000 machine hours)	$54,000
Job 1002 ($2 × 13,500 machine hours)	27,000
Job 1003 ($2 × 4,500 machine hours)	9,000
Total	$90,000

(h) Jobs completed	Finished Goods	229,000	
	Work in Process		229,000

Summary of completed job cost sheets:

Job 1001	$146,000
Job 1002	83,000
Total	$229,000

(i) Sales and cost of goods sold

Accounts Receivable	290,000	
Sales		290,000
Cost of Goods Sold	220,000	
Finished Goods		220,000

Summary of sales invoices and shipping orders:

	Sales Price	Cost Price
Product X	$ 19,600	$ 15,000
Product Y	165,100	125,000
Product Z	105,300	80,000
Total	$290,000	$220,000

(j) Cash received

Cash	300,000	
Accounts Receivable		300,000

(k) Cash disbursed

Accounts Payable	190,000	
Wages Payable	125,000	
Cash		315,000

The flow of costs through the manufacturing accounts, together with summary details of the subsidiary ledgers, is illustrated as follows. Entries in the accounts are identified by letters to facilitate comparisons with the foregoing summary journal entries.

Flow of Costs Through Job Order Cost Accounts

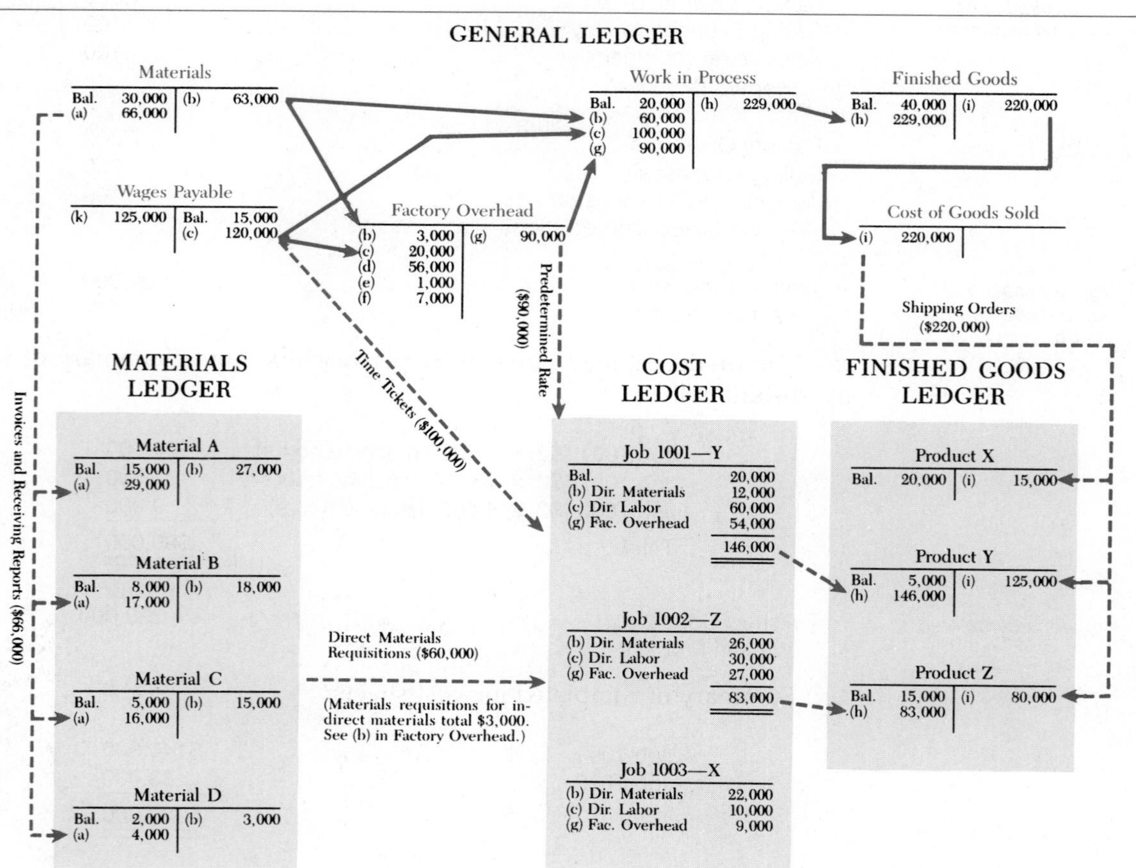

The trial balance taken from the general ledger of Amelia Co. on January 31 is as follows:

Amelia Co. Trial Balance January 31, 19--		
Cash	70,000	
Accounts Receivable	63,000	
Finished Goods	49,000	
Work in Process	41,000	
Materials	33,000	
Prepaid Expenses	1,800	
Plant Assets	850,000	
Accumulated Depreciation—Plant Assets		480,300
Accounts Payable		38,000
Wages Payable		10,000
Common Stock		500,000
Retained Earnings		42,000
Sales		290,000
Cost of Goods Sold	220,000	
Factory Overhead		3,000
Selling Expenses	25,300	
Administrative Expenses	10,200	
	1,363,300	1,363,300

The balances of the three inventory accounts—Finished Goods, Work in Process, and Materials—represent the respective ending inventories on January 31. The balances of the general ledger controlling accounts are compared with their respective subsidiary ledgers as follows:

Controlling and Subsidiary Accounts Compared

Controlling Accounts			Subsidiary Ledgers		
Account	Balance		Account		Balance
Finished Goods	$49,000	⟷	Product X	$ 5,000	
			Product Y	26,000	
			Product Z	18,000	$49,000
Work in Process	$41,000	⟷	Job 1003		$41,000
Materials	$33,000	⟷	Material A	$17,000	
			Material B	7,000	
			Material C	6,000	
			Material D	3,000	$33,000

To simplify the Amelia Co. illustration, only one work in process account and one factory overhead account were used. Usually, a manufacturing business has several processing departments, each requiring separate work in process and factory overhead accounts. In the illustration, one predetermined rate was used in applying the factory overhead to jobs. In a factory with several processing departments, a single factory overhead rate may not provide accurate product cost and effective cost control. A single rate for the entire factory cannot take into consideration such factors as differences among departments in the nature of their operations and in amounts of factory overhead incurred. In such cases, each factory department should have a separate factory overhead rate. For example, in a factory with twenty distinct operating departments, one department might have an overhead rate of $3.50 per machine hour, another a rate of 110% of direct labor cost, and another a rate of $4 per direct labor hour.

The financial statements on the next page are based on the data for Amelia Co. It should be noted that the overapplied factory overhead on January 31 is reported on the balance sheet as a deferred item.

JOB ORDER COST SYSTEMS FOR SERVICE ENTERPRISES

OBJECTIVE 5
Describe a job order cost accounting system for a service enterprise.

A job order cost accounting system may be useful to the management of a service enterprise, such as an advertising agency, in planning and controlling operations. Since the "product" of such an enterprise is service, management's focus is on direct labor and overhead costs. The cost of any materials or supplies used in rendering services for a client is usually small in amount and is normally included as part of the overhead.

The direct labor and overhead costs of rendering services to clients are accumulated in a work in process account, which is supported by a cost ledger. A job cost sheet is used to accumulate the costs for each client's job. When a job is completed and the client is billed, the costs are transferred to a cost of services account. This account is similar to the cost of merchandise sold account for a merchandising enterprise or the cost of goods sold account for a manufacturing enterprise. A finished goods account is not necessary, since the revenues associated with the services are recorded after the services have been rendered. The flow of costs through a service enterprise using a job order cost accounting system is as follows:

Flow of Costs Through a Service Enterprise

Wages Payable

Paid XXX	Direct labor XXX
	Indirect labor XXX

Work in Process

XXX	Completed jobs XXX
XXX	

Cost of Services

XXX	

Supplies

Purchased XXX	Used XXX

Overhead

XXX	Applied XXX
XXX	
Other costs XXX	

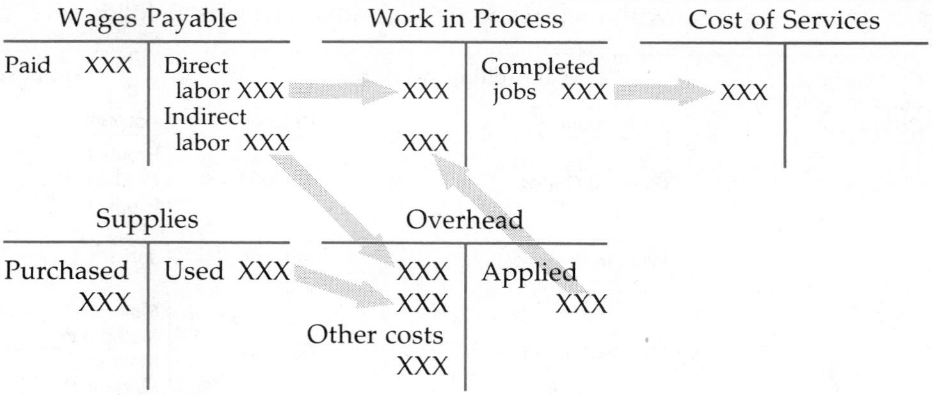

In practice, additional accounting considerations unique to service enterprises may need to be considered. For example, a service enterprise may bill clients on a weekly or monthly basis rather than waiting until a job is completed. In these situations, a portion of the costs related to each billing should be transferred from the work in process account to the cost of services account. This treatment is similar to the percentage-of-completion method used by construction contractors. A service enterprise may also have advance billings which would be accounted for as deferred revenue until the services have been completed.

Amelia Co.
Income Statement
For Month Ended January 31, 19--

Sales		$290,000
Cost of goods sold		220,000
Gross profit		$ 70,000
Operating expenses:		
Selling expenses	$25,300	
Administrative expenses	10,200	
Total operating expenses		35,500
Income from operations		$ 34,500

Amelia Co.
Retained Earnings Statement
For Month Ended January 31, 19--

Retained earnings, January 1, 19--	$42,000
Income for the month	34,500
Retained earnings, January 31, 19--	$76,500

Amelia Co.
Balance Sheet
January 31, 19--

Assets			
Current assets:			
Cash		$ 70,000	
Accounts receivable		63,000	
Inventories:			
Finished goods	$49,000		
Work in process	41,000		
Materials	33,000	123,000	
Prepaid expenses		1,800	
Total current assets			$257,800
Plant assets		$850,000	
Less accumulated depreciation		480,300	369,700
Total assets			$627,500
Liabilities			
Current liabilities:			
Accounts payable	$38,000		
Wages payable	10,000		
Total current liabilities		$ 48,000	
Deferred credits:			
Factory overhead		3,000	
Total liabilities			$ 51,000
Stockholders' Equity			
Common stock		$500,000	
Retained earnings		76,500	
Total stockholders' equity			576,500
Total liabilities and stockholders' equity			$627,500

CHAPTER REVIEW

KEY POINTS

OBJECTIVE 1

Usefulness of Product Costs

Product costs are useful to managers for the preparation of financial statements. Product costs are also needed by management for a wide variety of decisions, such as setting long-term product prices. Without accurate product cost information, managers could not effectively or efficiently manage operations.

OBJECTIVE 2

Types of Accounting Systems

Two basic accounting systems are commonly used by manufacturers: general accounting systems and cost accounting systems. A general accounting system uses periodic inventory procedures for materials, work in process, and finished goods inventories. For more complex manufacturing operations, a cost accounting system using perpetual inventory procedures is usually employed. A cost accounting system also uses controlling accounts and subsidiary ledgers for materials, work in process, and finished goods. The two main cost accounting systems are the job order cost and process cost systems.

OBJECTIVE 3, 4

Job Order Cost Systems for Manufacturing Enterprises

A job order cost system provides for a separate record of the cost of each particular quantity of product that passes through the factory. The details concerning the costs incurred on each job order are accumulated in a subsidiary ledger known as the cost ledger. Each cost ledger account, called a job cost sheet, has spaces for recording all direct materials and direct labor chargeable to the job and for the factory overhead applied at the predetermined rate. Work in Process is the controlling account for the cost ledger. As a job is finished, it is transferred to the finished goods ledger, for which Finished Goods is the controlling account.

OBJECTIVE 5

Job Order Cost Systems for Service Enterprises

A cost accounting system may be useful to management in planning and controlling the operations of a service enterprise. The cost of any materials or supplies used in rendering services for a client is usually small in amount and is normally included as part of the overhead. The direct labor and overhead costs of rendering services are accumulated in a work in process account. When a job is completed and the client is billed, the costs are transferred to a cost of services account.

KEY TERMS

general accounting system 693
cost accounting system 693
job order cost system 693
process cost system 694
purchase requisitions 695
purchase orders 695
receiving report 695
materials ledger 695
materials requisitions 696
time tickets 697
predetermined factory overhead rate 698
cost driver 698
overapplied overhead 699
underapplied overhead 699
cost ledger 701
job cost sheet 701
finished goods ledger 703

SELF-EXAMINATION QUESTIONS

Answers at end of chapter.

1. The account maintained by a manufacturing business for inventory of goods in the process of manufacture is:
   A. Finished Goods
   B. Materials
   C. Work in Process
   D. none of the above

2. For a manufacturing business, finished goods inventory includes:
   A. direct materials costs
   B. direct labor costs
   C. factory overhead costs
   D. all of the above

3. An example of a factory overhead cost is:
   A. wages of factory assembly-line workers
   B. salaries for factory plant supervisors
   C. bearings for electric motors being manufactured
   D. all of the above

4. For which of the following would the job order cost system be appropriate?
   A. Antique furniture repair shop
   B. Rubber manufacturer
   C. Coal manufacturer
   D. All of the above

5. If the factory overhead account has a credit balance, factory overhead is said to be:
   A. underapplied
   B. overapplied
   C. underabsorbed
   D. none of the above

ILLUSTRATIVE PROBLEM

Shelton Signs Inc. specializes in the production of neon signs and uses a job order cost system. The following data summarize the operations related to production for November, the first month of operations:

(a) Materials purchased on account, $21,750.
(b) Materials requisitioned and factory labor used:

	Materials	Factory Labor
Job No. 1	$2,750	$1,700
Job No. 2	3,800	2,000
Job No. 3	2,990	1,450
Job No. 4	5,950	3,800
Job No. 5	3,250	1,900
Job No. 6	900	600
For general factory use	595	500

(c) Factory overhead costs incurred on account, $4,300.
(d) Depreciation of machinery, $1,450.
(e) The factory overhead rate is 60% of direct labor cost.
(f) Jobs completed: Nos. 1, 2, 4, and 5.
(g) Jobs 1, 2, and 4 were shipped and customers were billed for $7,900, $10,500, and $18,100, respectively.

Instructions:

1. Prepare entries to record the foregoing summarized operations.
2. Determine the account balances for Work in Process and Finished Goods.
3. Prepare a schedule of unfinished jobs to support the balance in the work in process account.
4. Prepare a schedule of completed jobs on hand to support the balance in the finished goods account.

SOLUTION

		Dr.	Cr.
(1) (a)	Materials	21,750	
	Accounts Payable		21,750
(b)	Work in Process	31,090	
	Factory Overhead	1,095	
	Materials		20,235
	Wages Payable		11,950
(c)	Factory Overhead	4,300	
	Accounts Payable		4,300
(d)	Factory Overhead	1,450	
	Accumulated Depreciation—Machinery		1,450
(e)	Work in Process	6,870	
	Factory Overhead (60% of $11,450)		6,870
(f)	Finished Goods	30,790	
	Work in Process		30,790

Computation of the cost of jobs finished:

Job	Direct Materials	Direct Labor	Factory Overhead	Total
Job No. 1	$2,750	$1,700	$1,020	$ 5,470
Job No. 2	3,800	2,000	1,200	7,000
Job No. 4	5,950	3,800	2,280	12,030
Job No. 5	3,250	1,900	1,140	6,290
				$30,790

		Dr.	Cr.
(g)	Accounts Receivable	36,500	
	Sales		36,500
	Cost of Goods Sold	24,500	
	Finished Goods		24,500

Computation of the cost of jobs sold:

Job No. 1	$ 5,470
Job No. 2	7,000
Job No. 4	12,030
	$24,500

(2) Work in Process: $7,170 ($31,090 + $6,870 − $30,790)
Finished Goods: $6,290 ($30,790 − $24,500)

(3) Schedule of Unfinished Jobs

	Direct Materials	Direct Labor	Factory Overhead	Total
Job No. 3	$2,990	$1,450	$870	$5,310
Job No. 6	900	600	360	1,860
Balance of Work in Process, November 30				$7,170

(4) Schedule of Completed Jobs

Job No. 5:	Direct materials	$3,250
	Direct labor	1,900
	Factory overhead	1,140
Balance of Finished Goods, November 30		$6,290

DISCUSSION QUESTIONS

16–1. What are two important uses of product cost information by managers?

16–2. What are the two basic accounting systems commonly used by manufacturers?

16–3. (a) Name the two principal types of cost accounting systems. (b) Which system provides for a separate record of each particular quantity of product that passes through the factory? (c) Which system accumulates the costs for each department or process within the factory?

16–4. Distinguish between the purchase requisition and the purchase order used in the procurement of materials.

16–5. Briefly discuss how the purchase order, purchase invoice, and receiving report can be used to assist in controlling cash disbursements for materials acquired.

16–6. What document is the source for (a) debiting the accounts in the materials ledger and (b) crediting the accounts in the materials ledger?

16–7. Briefly discuss how the accounts in the materials ledger can be used as an aid in maintaining appropriate inventory quantities of stock items.

16–8. How does use of the materials requisition help control the issuance of materials from the storeroom?

16–9. Discuss the major advantage of a perpetual inventory system over a periodic system for materials.

16–10. (a) Differentiate between the clock card and the time ticket. (b) Why should the total time reported on an employee's time tickets for a payroll period be compared with the time reported on the employee's clock cards for the same period?

16–11. Which of the following items are properly classified as part of factory overhead?
(a) Amortization of factory patents
(b) Interest expense
(c) Factory supplies used
(d) Direct materials
(e) Sales commissions
(f) Property taxes on factory buildings

16–12. Discuss how the predetermined factory overhead rate can be used in job order cost accounting to assist management in pricing jobs.

16–13. (a) How is a predetermined factory overhead rate calculated? (b) Name three common bases used in calculating the rate.

16–14. (a) What is (1) overapplied factory overhead and (2) underapplied factory overhead? (b) If the factory overhead account has a debit balance, was factory overhead underapplied or overapplied? (c) If the factory overhead account has a credit balance at the end of the first month of the fiscal year, where will the amount of this balance be reported on the interim balance sheet?

16–15. At the end of the fiscal year, there was a relatively minor balance in the factory overhead account. What is the simplest satisfactory procedure for the disposition of the balance in the account?

16–16. What name is given to the individual accounts in the cost ledger?

16–17. What document serves as the basis for posting to (a) the direct materials section of the job cost sheet, and (b) the direct labor section of the job cost sheet?

16–18. Describe the source of the data for debiting Work in Process for (a) direct materials, (b) direct labor, and (c) factory overhead.

16–19. What account is the controlling account for (a) the materials ledger, (b) the cost ledger, and (c) the finished goods ledger or stock ledger?

16–20. In a cost accounting system for a service enterprise, the cost of any materials or supplies used in rendering services for a client is normally debited to what account?

16–21. When a job is completed and the client is billed, the costs are transferred to what account in a cost accounting system for a service enterprise?

Real World Focus

16–22. Hewlett-Packard Company manufactures printed circuit boards in which a high volume of standardized units are fabricated, machined, assembled, and tested. Is the job order cost system appropriate in this situation?

Ethics Discussion Case

16–23. Hillyard Manufacturing Enterprises allows employees to purchase, at cost, manufacturing materials, such as metal and lumber, for personal use. To purchase materials for personal use, an employee must complete a materials requisition form, which must then be approved by the employee's immediate supervisor. Jared Stepp, an assistant cost accountant, charges the employee an amount based upon Hillyard's net purchase cost.

Jared Stepp is in the process of replacing a deck on his home and has requisitioned lumber for personal use, which has been approved in accordance with company policy. In computing the cost of the lumber, Jared reviewed all the purchase invoices for the past year. He then used the lowest price to compute the amount due the company for the lumber.

Discuss whether Jared Stepp behaved in an ethical manner.

EXERCISES

Ex. 16–24.
Cost of materials issuances by fifo and lifo methods.
OBJ. 2,3

The balance of Material F on May 1 and the receipts and issuances during May are as follows:

Balance:	May 1	120 units at $12.00
Received:	May 3	300 units at $12.50
	12	240 units at $13.00
	29	180 units at $13.80
Issued:	May 5	180 units for Job 512
	19	150 units for Job 528
	30	200 units for Job 545

Determine the cost of each of the three issuances under a perpetual system, using (a) the first-in, first-out method and (b) the last-in, first-out method.

Ex. 16–25.
Entry for issuance of materials.
OBJ. 3,4

The issuances of materials for the current month are as follows:

Requisition No.	Material	Job No.	Amount
711	A-06	9001	$10,280
712	I-70	9010	3,380
713	B-11	9015	7,720
714	F-12	General factory use	1,500
715	W-29	9040	8,900

Present the journal entry to record the issuances of materials.

Ex. 16–26.
Entry for factory labor costs
OBJ. 3,4

A summary of the time tickets for the current month follows:

Job No.	Amount	Job No.	Amount
14012	$ 3,750	14016	$ 2,400
14013	24,300	Indirect labor	3,540
14014	8,010	14017	18,750
14015	13,500	14018	10,600

Present the journal entry to record the factory labor costs.

Ex. 16–27.
Factory overhead rates, entries, and account balance.
OBJ. 3,4

Milford Company, which maintains departmental accounts for work in process and factory overhead, applies factory overhead to jobs on the basis of machine hours in Department 10 and on the basis of direct labor costs in Department 20. Estimated factory overhead costs, direct labor costs, and machine hours for April are as follows:

	Department 10	Department 20
Estimated factory overhead cost for year	$200,000	$720,000
Estimated direct labor costs for year		$600,000
Estimated machine hours for year	40,000	
Actual factory overhead costs for April	$ 37,150	$ 87,680
Actual direct labor costs for April		$ 78,500
Actual machine hours for April	7,200	

(a) Determine the factory overhead rate for Department 10. (b) Determine the factory overhead rate for Department 20. (c) Prepare the journal entries to apply factory overhead to production for April. (d) Determine the balances of the departmental factory accounts as of April 30 and indicate whether the amounts represent overapplied or underapplied factory overhead.

Ex. 16–28.
Entry for jobs completed; cost of unfinished jobs.
OBJ. 3,4

The following account appears in the ledger after only part of the postings have been completed for October:

Work in Process

Balance, October 1	51,450	
Direct Materials	129,300	
Direct Labor	202,500	
Factory Overhead	111,000	

Jobs finished during October are summarized as follows:

Job 1903	$ 76,200	Job 1930	$122,400
Job 1908	136,800	Job 1941	78,300

(a) Prepare the journal entry to record the jobs completed and (b) determine the cost of the unfinished jobs at October 31.

Ex. 16–29.
Entries for factory costs and jobs completed.
OBJ. 3,4

Park Enterprises Inc. began manufacturing operations on March 1. Jobs 301 and 302 were completed during the month, and all costs applicable to them were recorded on the related cost sheets. Jobs 303 and 304 are still in process at the end of the month, and all applicable costs except factory overhead have been recorded on the related cost sheets. In addition to the materials and labor charged directly to the jobs, $21,000 of indirect materials and $50,400 of indirect labor were used during the month. The cost sheets for the four jobs entering production during the month are as follows, in summary form:

Job 301		Job 302	
Direct materials	31,500	Direct materials	56,400
Direct labor	25,200	Direct labor	40,320
Factory overhead	12,600	Factory overhead	20,160
Total	69,300	Total	116,880

Job 303	
Direct materials	42,800
Direct labor	35,280
Factory overhead	

Job 304	
Direct materials	11,000
Direct labor	15,600
Factory overhead	

Prepare an entry to record each of the following operations for the month (one entry for each operation):

(a) Direct and indirect materials used.
(b) Direct and indirect labor used.
(c) Factory overhead applied (a single overhead rate is used, based on direct labor cost).
(d) Completion of Jobs 301 and 302.

Ex. 16–30.
Job order cost accounting entries for service enterprise.
OBJ. 5

(a) Prepare journal entries to record the following selected transactions for September for Bateman and Sparkman, CPAs and (b) prepare a summary of jobs in work in process as of September 30.

(1) Labor incurred as reported by time reports for September:

Direct labor:	
Abel Inc. (Job 1)	$ 4,000
Nobel Co. (Job 2)	2,800
Anderson Co. (Job 3)	3,500
Nash Inc. (Job 4)	12,250
Thomas Inc. (Job 5)	1,250
	$23,800
Indirect labor	6,200
Total	$30,000

(2) The following other costs were incurred on account: overhead cost, $15,000; advertising expense, $3,000; rent expense, $5,000; and office supplies expense, $1,800

(3) Overhead is applied to individual jobs at a rate of $5 per computer hour. Computer hours used, as reported by usage summaries for September:

Job 1	480
Job 2	336
Job 3	420
Job 4	1,470
Job 5	150
Total	2,856

(4) Jobs completed and billed to clients:

Client	Amount Billed
Abel Inc. (Job 1)	$ 7,000
Nobel Co. (Job 2)	5,500
Anderson Co. (Job 3)	6,000
Total billings	$18,500

PROBLEMS

Pb. 16–31.
Entries and schedules for unfinished and completed jobs.
OBJ. 3,4

Keeling Printing Company uses a job order cost system. The following data summarize the operations related to production for April, the first month of operations:

(a) Materials purchased on account, $86,130.
(b) Materials requisitioned and factory labor used:

	Materials	Factory Labor
Job 401	$17,400	$13,725
Job 402	5,100	2,940
Job 403	12,780	7,035
Job 404	6,420	2,850
Job 405	10,245	4,200
Job 406	9,270	6,915
For general factory use	1,965	4,500

(c) Factory overhead costs incurred on account, $16,950.
(d) Depreciation of machinery and equipment, $8,100.
(e) The factory overhead rate is $1 per machine hour. Machine hours used:

Job 401	10,980
Job 402	2,352
Job 403	5,628
Job 404	2,280
Job 405	3,360
Job 406	5,532
Total	30,132

(f) Jobs completed: 401, 402, 403, and 405.
(g) Jobs 401, 402, and 403 were shipped and customers were billed for $70,175, $17,320, and $42,405 respectively.

Instructions:

(1) Prepare entries to record the foregoing summarized operations.
(2) Open T accounts for Work in Process and Finished Goods and post the appropriate entries, using the identifying letters as dates. Insert memorandum account balances as of the end of the month.
(3) Prepare a schedule of unfinished jobs to support the balance in the work in process account.
(4) Prepare a schedule of completed jobs on hand to support the balance in the finished goods account.

If the working papers correlating with the textbook are not used, omit Problem 16–32.

Pb. 16–32.
Job order cost sheet.
OBJ. 3,4

Douglas Furniture Company repairs, refinishes, and reupholsters furniture. A job order cost system was installed recently to facilitate (1) the determination of price quotations to prospective customers, (2) the determination of actual costs incurred on each job, and (3) cost reductions.

In response to a prospective customer's request for a price quotation on a job, the estimated cost data are inserted on an unnumbered job cost sheet. If the offer is accepted, a number is assigned to the job and the costs incurred are recorded in the usual manner on the job cost sheet. After the job is completed, reasons for the variances between the estimated and actual costs are noted on the sheet. The data are then available to management in evaluating the efficiency of operations and in preparing quotations on future jobs.

16-
718

On October 7, an estimate of $342 for reupholstering a chair and couch was given to Daryl Towns. The estimate was based on the following data:

Estimated direct materials:	
9 meters at $14 per meter	$126
Estimated direct labor:	
6 hours at $10 per hour	60
Estimated factory overhead (70% of direct labor cost)	42
Total estimated costs	$228
Markup (50% of production costs)	114
Total estimate	$342

On October 12, the chair and couch were picked up from the residence of Daryl Towns, 1340 Bald Eagle Drive, Tucson, with a commitment to return it on October 26. The job was completed on October 20.

The related materials requisitions and time tickets are summarized as follows:

Materials Requisition No.	Description	Amount
C817	9 meters at $14	$126
C819	2 meters at $14	28

Time Ticket No.	Description	Amount
7193	5 hours at $10	$ 50
7198	2 hours at $10	20

Instructions:

(1) Complete that portion of the job order cost sheet that would be prepared when the estimate is given to the customer.

(2) Assign number 90-10-17 to the job, record the costs incurred, and complete the job order cost sheet. In commenting upon the variances between actual costs and estimated costs, assume that 2 meters of materials were spoiled, the factory overhead rate has been proved to be satisfactory, and an inexperienced employee performed the work.

Pb. 16–33.
Preparation of financial statements.
OBJ. 3,4

The trial balance of Alpine Inc. at the beginning of the current fiscal year is as follows:

Alpine Inc.
Trial Balance
February 1, 19--

Cash	69,520	
Accounts Receivable	105,390	
Finished Goods	99,750	
Work in Process	36,540	
Materials	48,300	
Prepaid Expenses	12,900	
Plant Assets	873,600	
Accumulated Depreciation—Plant Assets		495,780
Accounts Payable		35,550
Wages Payable		—
Common Stock		150,000
Retained Earnings		564,670
Sales		—
Cost of Goods Sold	—	
Factory Overhead	—	
Selling Expenses	—	
Administrative Expenses	—	
	1,246,000	1,246,000

Transactions completed during February and adjustments required on February 28 are summarized as follows:

(a) Materials purchased on account		$ 41,220
(b) Materials requisitioned for factory use:		
Direct	$38,700	
Indirect	480	39,180
(c) Factory labor costs incurred:		
Direct	$19,440	
Indirect	2,760	22,200
(d) Other costs and expenses incurred on account:		
Factory overhead	$10,125	
Selling expenses	9,855	
Administrative expenses	7,200	27,180
(e) Cash disbursed:		
Accounts payable	$73,800	
Wages payable	19,950	93,750
(f) Depreciation charged:		
Factory equipment	$ 6,480	
Office equipment	540	7,020
(g) Prepaid expenses expired:		
Chargeable to factory	$ 960	
Chargeable to selling expenses	225	
Chargeable to administrative expenses	210	1,395
(h) Applied factory overhead at a predetermined rate based on machine hours		22,356
(i) Total cost of jobs completed		77,400
(j) Sales, all on account:		
Selling price		100,800
Cost		65,400
(k) Cash received on account		102,600

Instructions:

(1) Open T accounts and record the initial balances indicated in the February 1 trial balance, identifying each as "Bal."
(2) Record the transactions directly in the accounts, using the identifying letters in place of dates.
(3) Prepare an income statement for the month ended February 28, 19--.
(4) Prepare a retained earnings statement for the month ended February 28, 19--.
(5) Prepare a balance sheet as of February 28, 19--.

Pb. 16–34.
Entries, trial balance, and financial statements.
OBJ. 3,4

The trial balance of the general ledger of Mott Corporation as of March 31, the end of the first month of the current fiscal year, is shown as follows:

16-720

Mott Corporation
Trial Balance
March 31, 19--

Cash	82,300	
Accounts Receivable	166,700	
Finished Goods	160,200	
Work in Process	55,260	
Materials	66,510	
Plant Assets	711,900	
Accumulated Depreciation—Plant Assets		317,600
Accounts Payable		119,700
Wages Payable		13,500
Capital Stock		300,000
Retained Earnings		467,470
Sales		241,500
Cost of Goods Sold	180,000	
Factory Overhead	1,800	
Selling and Administrative Expenses	35,100	
	1,459,770	1,459,770

As of the same date, balances in the accounts of selected subsidiary ledgers are as follows:

Finished goods ledger:
Commodity A, 3,500 units, $63,000; Commodity B, 2,700 units, $40,500; Commodity C, 2,100 units, $56,700.

Cost ledger:
Job 318, $55,260.

Materials ledger:
Material X, $26,550; Material Y, $33,210; Material Z, $6,750.

The transactions completed during April are summarized as follows:

(a) Materials were purchased on account as follows:

Material X	$49,500
Material Y	34,650
Material Z	1,350

(b) Materials were requisitioned from stores as follows:

Job 318, Material X, $24,300; Material Y, $21,267	$45,567
Job 319, Material X, $12,420; Material Y, $4,986	17,406
Job 320, Material X, $19,080; Material Y, $15,177	34,257
For general factory use, Material Z	1,440

(c) Time tickets for the month were chargeable as follows:

Job 318	$17,640	Job 320	$14,760
Job 319	15,120	Indirect labor	5,400

(d) Factory payroll checks for $57,960 were issued.
(e) Various factory overhead charges of $20,150 were incurred on account.
(f) Depreciation of $8,100 on factory plant and equipment was recorded.
(g) Factory overhead was applied to jobs at 70% of direct labor cost.
(h) Jobs completed during the month were as follows: Job 318 produced 8,550 units of Commodity B; Job 320 produced 2,190 units of Commodity C.
(i) Selling and administrative expenses of $34,380 were incurred on account.
(j) Payments on account were $128,700.

(k) Total sales on account were $251,700. The goods sold were as follows (use first-in, first-out method): 1,500 units of Commodity A; 4,800 units of Commodity B; 2,400 units of Commodity C.

(l) Cash of $225,900 was received on accounts receivable.

Instructions:

(1) Open T accounts for the general ledger, the finished goods ledger, the cost ledger, and the materials ledger. Record directly in these accounts the balances as of March 31, identifying them as "Bal." Record the quantities as well as the dollar amounts in the finished goods ledger.

(2) Prepare entries to record the April transactions. After recording each transaction, post to the T accounts, using the identifying letters as dates. When posting to the finished goods ledger, record quantities as well as dollar amounts.

(3) Prepare a trial balance.

(4) Prepare schedules of the account balances in the finished goods ledger, the cost ledger, and the materials ledger.

(5) Prepare an income statement for the two months ended April 30.

Pb. 16–35.
Determination of amounts missing from selected accounts in job cost system.
OBJ. 3,4

Following are selected accounts for Bulla Products. For the purposes of this problem, some of the debits and credits have been omitted.

Accounts Receivable

Jan.	1 Balance	130,500	Jan. 31	Collections	192,800
	31 Sales	(A)			

Materials

Jan.	1 Balance	33,600	Jan. 31	Requisitions	(B)
	31 Purchases	66,400			

Work in Process

Jan.	1 Balance	38,400	Jan. 31	Goods finished	(E)
	31 Direct materials	(C)			
	31 Direct labor	77,600			
	31 Factory overhead	(D)			

Finished Goods

Jan.	1 Balance	20,700	Jan. 31	Cost of goods sold	(G)
	31 Goods finished	(F)			

Factory Overhead

Jan.	1 Balance	400	Jan. 31	Applied	58,200
	1–31 Costs incurred	57,900			

Cost of Goods Sold

Jan. 31		(H)			

Sales

			Jan.	31	(I)

Selected balances at January 31:

Accounts receivable	$125,000
Finished goods	35,200
Work in process	43,500
Materials	24,000

Materials requisitions for January included $2,000 of materials issued for general factory use. All sales are made on account, terms n/30.

Instructions:

(1) Determine the amounts represented by the letters (A) through (I), presenting your computations.
(2) Determine the amount of factory overhead overapplied or underapplied as of January 31.

ALTERNATE PROBLEMS

Pb. 16–31A. Entries and schedules for unfinished and completed jobs. OBJ. 3,4

Clardy Printing Company uses a job order cost system. The following data summarize the operations related to production for July, the first month of operations:

(a) Materials purchases on account, $275,400.
(b) Materials requisitioned and factory labor used:

	Materials	Factory Labor
Job 701	$39,600	$23,750
Job 702	25,950	17,600
Job 703	34,750	12,750
Job 704	52,375	33,450
Job 705	28,600	16,700
Job 706	17,750	7,250
For general factory use	5,750	4,400

(c) Factory overhead costs incurred on account, $49,000.
(d) Depreciation of machinery and equipment, $19,400.
(e) The factory overhead rate is $2.50 per machine hour. Machine hours used:

Job 701	6,650
Job 702	4,928
Job 703	3,570
Job 704	9,366
Job 705	4,676
Job 706	2,030
Total	31,220

(f) Jobs completed: 701, 702, 703, and 704.
(g) Jobs 701, 702, and 704 were shipped and customers were billed for $134,200, $94,100, and $182,100 respectively.

Instructions:

(1) Prepare entries to record the foregoing summarized operations.
(2) Open T accounts for Work in Process and Finished Goods and post the appropriate entries, using the identifying letters as dates. Insert memorandum account balances as of the end of the month.
(3) Prepare a schedule of unfinished jobs to support the balance in the work in process account.

(4) Prepare a schedule of completed jobs on hand to support the balance in the finished goods account.

If the working papers correlating with the textbook are not used, omit Problem 16–32A.

Pb. 16–32A.
Job order cost sheet.
OBJ. 3,4

Meeks Furniture Company repairs, refinishes, and reupholsters furniture. A job order cost system was installed to facilitate (1) the determination of price quotations to prospective customers, (2) the determination of actual costs incurred on each job, and (3) cost reductions.

In response to a prospective customer's request for a price quotation on a job, the estimated cost data are inserted on an unnumbered job cost sheet. If the offer is accepted, a number is assigned to the job and the costs incurred are recorded in the usual manner on the job cost sheet. After the job is completed, reasons for the variances between the estimated and actual costs are noted on the sheet. The data are then available to management in evaluating the efficiency of operations and in preparing quotations on future jobs.

On August 15, an estimate of $243 for reupholstering a couch was given to Joan Holiday. The estimate was based on the following data:

Estimated direct materials:	
5 meters at $20 per meter	$100
Estimated direct labor:	
4 hours at $16 per hour	64
Estimated factory overhead (25% of direct labor cost)	16
Total estimated costs	$180
Markup (35% of production costs)	63
Total estimate	$243

On August 16, the couch was picked up from the residence of Joan Holiday, 315 Reading Lane, Elberton, with a commitment to return it on August 30.

The job was completed on August 28. The related materials requisitions and time tickets are summarized as follows:

Materials Requisition No.	Description	Amount
2718	5 meters at $20	$100
2723	3 meters at $20	60

Time Ticket No.	Description	Amount
U8815	4 hours at $16	$ 64
U8817	2 hours at $16	32

Instructions:

(1) Complete that portion of the job order cost sheet that would be prepared when the estimate is given to the customer.
(2) Assign number U8-13 to the job, record the costs incurred, and complete the job order cost sheet. In commenting upon the variances between actual costs and estimated costs, assume that 3 meters of materials were spoiled, the factory overhead rate has been proved to be satisfactory, and an inexperienced employee performed the work.

Pb. 16–33A.
Preparation of financial statements.
OBJ. 3,4

The trial balance of Bluebill Inc. at the beginning of the current fiscal year is as follows:

16-724

Bluebill Inc.
Trial Balance
July 1, 19--

Cash	30,020	
Accounts Receivable	164,890	
Finished Goods	104,750	
Work in Process	41,540	
Materials	50,300	
Prepaid Expenses	15,400	
Plant Assets	879,100	
Accumulated Depreciation—Plant Assets		501,280
Accounts Payable		51,050
Wages Payable		—
Common Stock		300,000
Retained Earnings		433,670
Sales		—
Cost of Goods Sold	—	
Factory Overhead	—	
Selling Expenses	—	
Administrative Expenses	—	
	1,286,000	1,286,000

Transactions completed during July and adjustments required on July 31 are summarized as follows:

(a) Materials purchased on account		$ 39,200
(b) Materials requisitioned for factory use:		
Direct	$40,350	
Indirect	480	40,830
(c) Factory labor costs incurred.		
Direct	$20,200	
Indirect	2,690	22,890
(d) Other costs and expenses incurred on account:		
Factory overhead	$10,125	
Selling expenses	9,855	
Administrative expenses	7,200	27,180
(e) Cash disbursed:		
Accounts payable	$65,700	
Wages payable	18,400	84,100
(f) Prepaid expenses expired:		
Chargeable to factory	$ 960	
Chargeable to selling expenses	225	
Chargeable to administrative expenses	430	1,615
(g) Depreciation charged:		
Factory equipment	$ 6,480	
Office equipment	540	7,020
(h) Applied factory overhead at a predetermined rate based on machine hours		22,220
(i) Total cost of jobs completed		80,250

(j) Sales, all on account:

Selling price	120,900
Cost	78,800

(k) Cash received on account . . . 140,600

Instructions:

(1) Open T accounts and record the initial balances indicated in the July 1 trial balance, identifying each as "Bal."
(2) Record the transactions directly in the accounts, using the identifying letters in place of dates.
(3) Prepare an income statement for the month ended July 31, 19--.
(4) Prepare a retained earnings statement for the month ended July 31, 19--
(5) Prepare a balance sheet as of July 31, 19--.

Pb. 16–34A.
Entries, trial balance, and financial statements.
OBJ. 3,4

The trial balance of the general ledger of T. Pickett Co. as of July 31, the end of the first month of the current fiscal year, is as follows:

T. Pickett
Trial Balance
July 31, 19--

Cash	73,600	
Accounts Receivable	148,200	
Finished Goods	150,080	
Work in Process	49,600	
Materials	58,320	
Plant Assets	650,000	
Accumulated Depreciation—Plant Assets		290,000
Accounts Payable		100,000
Wages Payable		12,000
Capital Stock		100,000
Retained Earnings		556,000
Sales		250,000
Cost of Goods Sold	145,500	
Factory Overhead	700	
Selling and Administrative Expenses	32,000	
	1,308,000	1,308,000

As of the same date, balances in the accounts of selected subsidiary ledgers are as follows:

Finished goods ledger:
Commodity Q, 1,600 units, $32,000; Commodity R, 4,800 units, $72,000; Commodity S, 2,560 units, $46,080.
Cost ledger:
Job 900, $49,600.
Materials ledger:
Materials G, $30,880; Material H, $25,280; Material I, $2,160.

The transactions completed during August are summarized as follows:

(a) Materials were purchased on account as follows:

Material G	$44,000
Material H	30,800
Material I	1,200

(b) Materials were requisitioned from stores as follows:

Job 900, Material G, $16,832; Material H, $13,440	$30,272
Job 901, Material G, $21,600; Material H, $18,496	40,096
Job 902, Material G, $11,040; Material H, $4,904	15,944
For general factory use, Material I	1,280

(c) Time tickets for the month were chargeable as follows:

Job 900	$15,680	Job 902	$13,120
Job 901	13,440	Indirect labor	4,000

(d) Factory payroll checks for $47,500 were issued.
(e) Various factory overhead charges of $9,000 were incurred on account.
(f) Selling and administrative expenses of $30,600 were incurred on account.
(g) Payments on account were $120,000.
(h) Depreciation of $8,200 on factory plant and equipment was recorded.
(i) Factory overhead was applied to jobs at 60% of direct labor cost.
(j) Jobs completed during the month were as follows: Job 900 produced 5,120 units of Commodity Q; Job 901 produced 4,000 units of Commodity R.
(k) Total sales on account were $325,000. The goods sold were as follows (use first-in, first-out method): 3,680 units of Commodity Q; 6,000 units of Commodity R; 1,600 units of Commodity S.
(l) Cash of $200,000 was received on accounts receivable.

Instructions:

(1) Open T accounts for the general ledger, the finished goods ledger, the cost ledger, and the materials ledger. Record directly in these accounts the balances as of July 31, identifying them as "Bal." Record the quantities as well as the dollar amounts in the finished goods ledger.
(2) Prepare entries to record the August transactions. After recording each transaction, post to the T accounts, using the identifying letters as dates. When posting to the finished goods ledger, record quantities as well as dollar amounts.
(3) Prepare a trial balance.
(4) Prepare schedules of the account balances in the finished goods ledger, the cost ledger, and the materials ledger.
(5) Prepare an income statement for the two months ended August 31.

Pb. 16–35A.
Determination of amounts missing from selected accounts in job cost system.
OBJ. 3,4

Following are selected accounts for Watson Products. For the purposes of this problem, some of the debits and credits have been omitted.

Accounts Receivable

Nov.	1 Balance	142,800	Nov. 30	Collections	310,000
	30 Sales	(A)			

Materials

Nov.	1 Balance	34,500	Nov. 30	Requisitions	(B)
	30 Purchases	50,700			

Work in Process

Nov.	1 Balance	63,000	Nov. 30	Goods finished	(E)
	30 Direct materials	(C)			
	30 Direct labor	67,000			
	30 Factory overhead	(D)			

Finished Goods

Nov.	1 Balance	116,700	Nov. 30	Cost of goods sold	(G)
	30 Goods finished	(F)			

Factory Overhead

Nov.	1 Balance	360	Nov. 30	Applied	26,800
	1–30 Costs incurred	25,600			

Cost of Goods Sold

Nov.	30	(H)			

Sales

			Nov. 30		(I)

Selected balances at November 30:

Accounts receivable	$155,000
Finished goods	72,000
Work in process	53,400
Materials	28,500

Materials requisitions for November included $1,200 of materials issued for general factory use. All sales are made on account, terms n/30.

Instructions:

(1) Determine the amounts represented by the letters (A) through (I), presenting your computations.
(2) Determine the amount of factory overhead overapplied or underapplied as of November 30.

MINI-CASE 16

As an assistant cost accountant for Atkinson Industries, you have been assigned to review the activity base for the predetermined factory overhead rate. The president, J.C. Atkinson, has expressed concern that the over- or underapplied overhead has fluctuated excessively over the years.

An analysis of the company's operations and use of the current overhead base (direct materials usage) has narrowed the possible alternative overhead bases to direct labor cost and machine hours. For the past five years, the following data have been gathered:

	1993	1992	1991	1990	1989
Actual overhead	$ 672,000	$ 656,000	$ 720,000	$ 588,000	$ 564,000
Applied overhead	649,600	678,000	736,800	600,000	524,800
(Over) underapplied overhead	$ 22,400	$ (22,000)	$ (16,800)	$ (12,000)	$ 39,200
Direct labor cost	$2,680,000	$2,640,000	$2,900,000	$2,340,000	$2,240,000
Machine hours	530,400	516,000	580,800	477,600	455,200

Instructions:

(1) Calculate a predetermined factory overhead rate for each alternative base, assuming that the rates would have been determined by relating the amount of factory overhead for the past five years to the base.
(2) For each of the past five years, determine the over- or underapplied overhead, based on the two predetermined overhead rates developed in (1).
(3) Which predetermined overhead rate would you recommend? Discuss the basis for your recommendation.

ANSWERS TO SELF-EXAMINATION QUESTIONS

1. C Inventory accounts are maintained by manufacturing businesses for (1) goods in the process of manufacture (Work in Process—answer C), (2) goods in the state in which they are to be sold (Finished Goods—answer A), and (3) goods in the state in which they were acquired (Materials—answer B).
2. D The finished goods inventory is composed of three categories of manufacturing costs: direct materials (answer A), direct labor (answer B), and factory overhead (answer C).
3. B Factory overhead includes all manufacturing costs, except direct materials and direct labor. Salaries of plant supervisors (answer B) is an example of a factory overhead item. Wages of factory assembly-line workers (answer A) is a direct labor item, and bearings for electric motors (answer C) are direct materials.
4. A Job order cost systems are best suited to businesses manufacturing for special orders from customers, such as would be the case for a repair shop for antique furniture (answer A). A process cost system is best suited for manufacturers of homogeneous units of product, such as rubber (answer B) and coal (answer C).
5. B If the amount of factory overhead applied during a particular period exceeds the actual overhead costs, the factory overhead account will have a credit balance and is said to be overapplied (answer B) or overabsorbed. If the amount applied is less than the actual costs, the account will have a debit balance and is said to be underapplied (answer A) or underabsorbed (answer C).

CHAPTER 17

CHAPTER OBJECTIVES

1 Describe the differences between job order costing and process costing systems.

2 Describe and illustrate the flow of costs in a process cost accounting system.

3 Describe and illustrate the accounting for inventories of partially processed units.

4 Describe and illustrate the preparation and use of a cost of production report.

5 Describe and illustrate the accounting for service department costs.

6 Describe and illustrate the accounting for joint products and by-products.

7 Illustrate the accounting for product costs in a process cost accounting system.

8 Describe and illustrate the use of the average cost method of inventory costing for process cost accounting systems.

9 Describe hybrid cost accounting systems.

17

PROCESS COST SYSTEMS

There are two principal types of cost accounting systems—job order cost and process cost. The basic concepts of allocating costs to products, using the job order cost system, were described and illustrated in Chapter 16. In this chapter, these concepts are refined and modified to fit the process cost system.[1] The chapter concludes with a brief discussion of hybrid cost systems, which are a blend of job order and process costing. One of these hybrids, called operation costing, is described.

JOB ORDER COSTING AND PROCESS COSTING COMPARED

OBJECTIVE 1
Describe the differences between job order costing and process costing systems.

As discussed in the preceding chapter, the job order cost system is best suited to industries that fill special orders from customers or manufacture standard products in batches. Industries that may use job order cost systems include special-order printing, custom-made tailoring, furniture manufacturing, shipbuilding, aircraft building, and construction. The process cost system is best suited for industries that mass-produce identical units of a product which often have passed through a sequence of processes on a continuous basis. Industries that may use process cost systems include chemicals, oil, cement, meat packing, and assembly-type industries such as automobile manufacturers.

In many ways the process cost and job order cost systems are similar. Both systems provide for the accumulation of product costs—direct materials, direct labor, and factory overhead—and the allocation of these costs to the units of production. For example, perpetual inventory accounts with subsidiary ledgers for materials, work in process, and finished goods are used by both systems in accounting for product costs. Both systems also supply essential cost data to management for planning, organizing and directing, controlling, and decision making. The main difference between the two systems is the format in which the product costs are accumulated and reported.

[1] Another approach to allocating costs to products is activity-based costing, which is discussed in Chapter 18.

In a job order cost system, product costs are accumulated by individual jobs and are summarized on job order cost sheets. The job order cost sheets provide unit cost information and can be used by management for such purposes as product pricing and cost control. In the process cost system there is no need to accumulate costs by job orders, since the units of product that pass through several stages of production are identical. Therefore, in the process cost system, costs are accumulated by department or process and are summarized in a cost of production report. This cost of production report provides unit cost information and can be used by management for such purposes as cost control.

FLOW OF COSTS IN A PROCESS COST SYSTEM

OBJECTIVE 2
Describe and illustrate the flow of costs in a process cost accounting system.

In process cost accounting, costs are accumulated by department in factory overhead and work in process accounts. If there is only one processing department in a factory, the cost accounting procedures are simple. The manufacturing cost elements are charged to the single work in process account, and the unit cost of the finished product is determined by dividing the total cost by the number of units produced.

When the manufacturing procedure requires a sequence of different processes, the output of Process 1 becomes the direct materials of Process 2, the output of Process 2 becomes the direct materials of Process 3, and so on until the finished product emerges. The accumulated costs transferred from preceding departments and the costs of direct materials and direct labor incurred in each processing department are debited to the related work in process account. Each work in process account is also debited for the factory overhead applied. The costs incurred are summarized periodically, usually at the end of the month. The costs related to the output of each department during the month are then transferred to the next processing department or to Finished Goods, as the case may be. This flow of costs through a work in process account for McDermott Manufacturing Company is illustrated as follows:

Work in Process—Sanding Department

10,000 units at $9.60 from Assembly Dept.		96,000	To Polishing Dept., 10,000 units	160,000
Direct labor	36,800		Cost per unit:	
Factory overhead	27,200	64,000	$160,000 ÷ 10,000 = $16	
		160,000		160,000

The three debits in the preceding account are normally grouped into two separate categories: (1) direct materials or partially processed materials received from another department, which in this case is composed of 10,000 units received from the Assembly Department, with a total cost of $96,000, and (2) direct labor and factory overhead applied in the Sanding Department, which in this case totaled $64,000. This second group of costs, as described in Chapter 15, is called the **conversion cost** or **processing cost.**

Again referring to the illustration, all of the 10,000 units were completely processed in the Sanding Department and were passed on to the Polishing Department. The $16 unit cost of the product transferred to the Polishing Department is made up of Assembly Department cost of $9.60 ($96,000 ÷ 10,000 units) and conversion cost of $6.40 ($64,000 ÷ 10,000 units) incurred in the Sanding Department.

A NEW WAY TO BUILD CARS

One of the major industries that uses process cost accounting is the automobile manufacturing industry. Typically, cars are built as they move along an assembly line that provides little flexibility for the installation of the many options common to today's vehicles. Therefore, automakers are turning to modern technology in modifying the traditional assembly line. For example, in two assembly plants, hundreds of motorized, unmanned carriers move cars through the assembly process. The effect of using these carriers, called automated guided vehicles, in the production of cars is described in the following excerpts from an article in the *New York Times:*

When Henry Ford perfected the assembly line, he was making only one type of car, the Model T, which came in just one color, black. Since then, options have proliferated and today there can be as much as a 30 percent difference in the content of a stripped-down model and one fully loaded.

Because current lines move at a constant speed, regardless of the model mix, plant managers have had to hire enough workers to build the most complex car in the assigned amount of time. This means that some people are idle when base models come down the line. And because stopping the line to fix something would idle thousands, most workers only tag an incorrectly fitting part and hope it will be repaired at the end of the line.

With the carriers, the notion of a "line" begins to fade, although the vehicles generally follow a prescribed path, receiving their instructions from wires buried in the plant floor. If a particular car has a heavy load of options, though, the vehicle may be directed to move out of the main [path] to have those parts installed, while less heavily equipped models continue along the route. G.M. engineers call this "decoupling the line." With this flexibility, plant managers will be able to balance the work force more closely with the workload. . . .

The carriers also fit into the modular assembly concept that G.M. officials have called one of the keys to cutting manufacturing costs in its Saturn program. Instead of installing thousands of parts, one by one, on a car, a whole module, such as an instrument panel, will be built off the line, tested and only installed if it passes the tests. Since a carrier can be programmed to stop and go as needed, it could roll to the completed instrument panels and then stop to ease the installation. . . . .

"We couldn't have done this a few years ago," said . . . the director of operations for G.M.'s Chevrolet-Pontiac-Canada group. "We need computers that can keep track of hundreds of carriers and decide on a minute-by-minute basis what station to assign them to, based on variations in the model mix."

Source: John Holusha, "A New Way to Build Cars," *The New York Times,* March 13, 1986.

INVENTORIES OF PARTIALLY PROCESSED UNITS

OBJECTIVE 3
Describe and illustrate the accounting for inventories of partially processed units.

In the preceding illustration, all materials entering a process were completely processed at the end of the accounting period. In such a case, the determination of unit costs is quite simple. The total of the costs transferred from other departments, the direct materials, the direct labor, and the factory overhead charged to a department is divided by the number of units completed and passed on to the next department or to finished goods. Often, however, some partially processed materials remain in various stages of production in a department at the end of a period. In this case, the costs in work in process must be allocated between the units that have been completed and transferred to the next process or to finished goods and those that are only partially completed and remain within the department.

Flow of Materials

To allocate direct materials and transferred costs between the output completed and transferred to the next process and inventory of goods within the department, it is necessary to determine the manner in which materials are placed in production and flow through the production processes. For some products, materials may be added to production in about the same proportion as conversion costs are incurred. In still other situations, materials may enter the process at relatively few points, which may or may not be evenly spaced throughout the process. For most manufacturing processes, however, the materials are on hand when production begins, and they move through the production processes in a first-in, first-out flow; that is, the first units entering the production process are the first to be completed. Therefore, the following discussion and illustrations will assume a normal production process, whereby all materials are placed into the process in a fifo (first-in, first-out) order. The manufacturing costs associated with such a process will also be allocated by the fifo cost method. Later in the chapter, an alternate method—the average cost method—will be discussed.

Equivalent Units of Production

To allocate processing costs between the output completed and transferred to the next process and the inventory of goods within the process, it is necessary to determine the number of *equivalent units* of production during the period. The **equivalent units of production** are the number of units that could have been manufactured from start to finish during the period. To illustrate, assume that there is no inventory of goods in process in a certain processing department at the beginning of the period, that 1,000 units of materials enter the process during the period, and that at the end of the period all of the units are 75% completed. The equivalent production in the processing department for the period would be 750 units (75% of 1,000).

Usually there is an inventory of partially processed units in the department at the beginning of a period. These units are normally completed during the period and transferred to the next department along with units started and completed in the current period. Other units started in the period are only partially processed and thus make up the ending inventory. To illustrate the computation of equivalent units under such circumstances, the following data are assumed for the Polishing Department of McDermott Manufacturing Company:

Inventory within Polishing Department of March 1	600 units; 1/3 completed
Completed in Polishing Department and transferred to finished goods during March	9,800 units, completed
Inventory within Polishing Department on March 31	800 units, 2/5 completed

The equivalent units of production are determined as follows:

Determination of Equivalent Units of Production

To process units in inventory of March 1 (600 units × 2/3)	400
To process units started and completed in March (9,800 units completed − 600 units in March 1 inventory)	9,200
To process units in inventory on March 31 (800 units × 2/5)	320
Equivalent units of production in March....................................	9,920

The equivalent units of production necessary to complete the March 1 inventory is determined by multiplying the number of units, 600, by the portion that needed to be completed during March. In this example, since the 600 units were 1/3 complete on March 1, the equivalent portion that was necessary to complete production during March is 2/3. Hence, the equivalent units related to the March 1 inventory is 400 (600 units × 2/3). The units started and completed during March, 9,200, is computed by subtracting the 600 units in the March 1 inventory from the total number of units completed, 9,800. The equivalent units for the March 31 inventory is determined by multiplying the number of units, 800, by the portion that was completed during March, 2/5. The 9,920 total equivalent units of production in March represents the number of units that would have been produced if there had been no inventories within the process either at the beginning or at the end of the period.

Continuing with the illustration, the next step is to allocate the cost incurred in the Polishing Department between the units completed during March and those remaining in process at the end of the month. If all materials were introduced at the beginning of the process, the full materials cost per unit must be assigned to the uncompleted units. The conversion costs would then be allocated to the finished and the uncompleted units on the basis of equivalent units of production, as shown in the following account:

ACCOUNT WORK IN PROCESS—POLISHING DEPARTMENT ACCOUNT NO.

Date		Item	Debit	Credit	Balance Debit	Balance Credit
Mar.	1	Bal., 600 units, ⅓ completed			10,200	
	31	Sanding Dept. 10,000 units at $16	160,000		170,200	
	31	Direct labor	26,640		196,840	
	31	Factory overhead	18,000		214,840	
	31	Goods finished, 9,800 units		200,600		
	31	Bal., 800 units, ⅖ completed			14,240	

The conversion costs incurred in the Polishing Department during March total $44,640 ($26,640 + $18,000). The equivalent units of production for March, determined above, is 9,920. The conversion cost per equivalent unit is therefore $4.50 ($44,640 ÷ 9,920). Of the $214,840 debited to the Polishing Department, $200,600 was transferred to Finished Goods and $14,240 remained in the account as work in process inventory. The computation of the allocations to the finished goods and to inventory is as follows:

Allocation of Departmental Charges to Finished Goods and Inventory

Goods Finished During March

600 units:	Inventory on March 1, 1/3 completed	$10,200	
	Conversion cost in March:		
	600 × 2/3, or 400 units at $4.50	1,800	
	Total		$ 12,000
	(Unit cost: $12,000 ÷ 600 = $20)		
9,200 units:	Materials cost in March, at $16 per unit	$147,200	
	Conversion cost in March:		
	9,200 at $4.50 per unit	41,400	
	Total		188,600
	(Unit cost: $188,600 ÷ 9,200 = $20.50)		
9,800 units:	Goods finished during March		$200,600

Polishing Department Inventory on March 31

800 units:	Materials cost in March, at $16 per unit	$12,800	
	Conversion cost in March:		
	800 × 2/5, or 320 at $4.50	1,440	
800 units:	Polishing Department inventory on March 31		$ 14,240

COST OF PRODUCTION REPORT

OBJECTIVE 4
Describe and illustrate the preparation and use of a cost of production report.

A report prepared periodically for each processing department summarizes (1) the units for which the department is accountable and the disposition of these units, and (2) the costs charged to the department and the allocation of these costs. This report, termed the **cost of production report,** may be used as the source of the computation of unit production costs and the allocation of the processing costs in the general ledger to the finished and the uncompleted units. More importantly, the report is used to control costs. Each department head is held responsible for the units entering production and the costs incurred in the department. Any differences in unit product costs from one month to another are studied carefully and the causes of significant differences are determined.

The cost of production report based on the data presented in the preceding section for the Polishing Department of McDermott Manufacturing Company is shown below:

Cost of Production Report

McDermott Manufacturing Company
Cost of Production Report—Polishing Department
For the Month Ended March 31, 19--

Quantities:		
Charged to production:		
In process, March 1		600
Received from Sanding Department		10,000
Total units to be accounted for		10,600
Units accounted for:		
Transferred to finished goods		9,800
In process, March 31		800
Total units accounted for		10,600
Costs:		
Charged to production:		
In process, March 1		$ 10,200
March costs:		
Direct materials from Sanding Department ($16 per unit)		160,000
Conversion costs:		
Direct labor	$ 26,640	
Factory overhead	18,000	
Total conversion costs ($4.50 per unit)		44,640
Total costs to be accounted for		$214,840

Costs allocated as follows:		
Transferred to finished goods:		
600 units at $20	$ 12,000	
9,200 units at $20.50	188,600	
Total cost of finished goods		$200,600
In process, March 31:		
Direct materials (800 units at $16)	$ 12,800	
Conversion costs (800 units × 2/5 × $4.50)	1,440	
Total cost of inventory in process, March 31		14,240
Total costs accounted for		$214,840
Computations:		
Equivalent units of production:		
To process units in inventory on March 1:		
600 units × 2/3		400
To process units started and completed in March:		
9,800 units − 600 units		9,200
To process units in inventory on March 31:		
800 units × 2/5		320
Equivalent units of production		9,920
Unit conversion cost:		
$44,640 ÷ 9,920		$ 4.50

SERVICE DEPARTMENTS AND PROCESS COSTS

OBJECTIVE 5
Describe and illustrate the accounting for service department costs.

In a factory with several processes, there may be one or more **service departments** that do not process the materials directly. Examples of service departments are the factory office, the power plant, and the maintenance and repair shop. These departments perform services for the benefit of other production departments. The costs that they incur, therefore, are part of the total manufacturing costs and must be allocated or assigned to the processing departments. This allocation is performed periodically in order to charge the factory overhead accounts of the processing departments with their share of the costs incurred by the service departments. The period usually chosen is a month, although a different period of time may be used.

To illustrate the allocation of service department costs, assume that the Power Department of McDermott Manufacturing Company produced 600 000 kilowatt-hours (kwh) during the month at a total cost of $30,000, or 5¢ per kilowatt-hour ($30,000 ÷ 600 000). The factory overhead accounts for the departments that used the power are accordingly charged for power at the 5¢ rate. Assuming that during the month the Assembly Department used 100 000 kwh, the Sanding Department used 300 000 kwh, and the Polishing Department used 200 000 kwh, the accounts affected by the allocation of cost would appear as shown on the following page.

In the illustration, there was only one service department. In some manufacturing businesses, there may be several service departments. In addition, some service departments may render services to other service departments. For example, the power department may supply electric current to light the

Service Department Costs Charged to Processing Departments

Power Department

Fuel	12,000	To Factory Overhead—Assembly Dept.	5,000
Wages	8,500	To Factory Overhead—Sanding Dept.	15,000
Depreciation	3,000	To Factory Overhead—Polishing Dept.	10,000
Maintenance	2,500		
Insurance	2,000		
Taxes	1,500		
Miscellaneous	500		
	30,000		30,000

Factory Overhead—Assembly Dept.

Power	5,000	

Factory Overhead—Sanding Dept.

Power	15,000	

Factory Overhead—Polishing Dept.

Power	10,000	

factory office and to operate data processing equipment. At the same time, the factory office provides general supervision for the power department, maintains its payroll records, buys its fuel, and so on. The allocation of service department costs in such cases is discussed in Chapter 18.

JOINT PRODUCTS AND BY-PRODUCTS

OBJECTIVE 6
Describe and illustrate the accounting for joint products and by-products.

In some manufacturing processes, more than one product is produced. In processing cattle, for example, the meat packer produces dressed beef, hides, and other products. In processing logs, the lumber mill produces several grades of lumber in addition to scraps and sawdust. When the output of a manufacturing process consists of two or more different products, the products may be joint products, or one or more of the products may be a by-product.

When two or more goods of significant value are produced from a single principal direct material, the products are termed **joint products.** Similarly, the costs incurred in the manufacture of joint products are called **joint costs.** Common examples of joint products are gasoline, naphtha, kerosene, paraffin, benzine, and other related goods, all of which come from the processing of crude oil.

If one of the products resulting from a process has little value in relation to the main product or joint products, it is known as a **by-product.** The emergence of a by-product is only incidental to the manufacture of the main product or joint products. By-products may be leftover materials, such as sawdust and scraps of wood in a lumber mill, or they may be separated from the material at the beginning of production, as in the case of cotton-seed from raw cotton.

Accounting for Joint Products

In management decisions concerning the production and sale of joint products, only the relationship of the total revenue to be derived from the entire group to their total production cost is relevant. Nothing is to be gained from an allocation of joint costs to each product because one product cannot be produced without the others. A decision to produce a single joint product is in effect a decision to produce all of the joint products.

Since joint products come from the processing of a common parent material, the assignment of cost to each separate product cannot be based on actual expenditures. It is impossible to determine the amount of cost incurred in the manufacture of each separate product. However, for purposes of inventory valuation, it is necessary to allocate joint costs among the joint products.

One method of allocation commonly used is the **market (sales) value method.** Its main feature is the assignment of costs to the different products according to their relative sales values. To illustrate, assume that 10,000 units of Product X and 50,000 units of Product Y were produced at a total cost of $63,000. The sales values of the two products and the allocation of the joint costs are as follows:

Allocation of Joint Costs

Joint Costs	*Joint Product*	*Units Produced*	*Sales Value per Unit*	*Total Sales Value*
$63,000	X	10,000	$3.00	$30,000
	Y	50,000	1.20	60,000
Total sales value				$90,000

Allocation of joint costs:

X: $\frac{\$30,000}{\$90,000} \times \$63,000$ $21,000

Y: $\frac{\$60,000}{\$90,000} \times \$63,000$ 42,000

Unit cost:

X: $21,000 ÷ 10,000 units $2.10

Y: $42,000 ÷ 50,000 units .... .84

Accounting for By-Products

The amount of manufacturing cost usually assigned to a by-product is the sales value of the by-product reduced by any additional costs necessary to complete and sell it. The amount of cost thus determined is removed from the proper work in process account and transferred to a finished goods inventory account. To illustrate, assume that for a certain period the costs accumulated in Department 4 total $24,400, and during the same period of time, 1,000 units of by-product B emerge from the processing in Department 4. If the estimated value of the by-product is $200, after estimated completion and selling costs have been deducted, Finished Goods—Product B would be debited for $200 and Work in Process—Department 4 would be credited for the same amount, as illustrated in the following accounts:

Work in Process—Department 4		Finished Goods—Product B	
	200	200	

ILLUSTRATION OF PROCESS COST ACCOUNTING

OBJECTIVE 7
Illustrate the accounting for product costs in a process cost accounting system.

To illustrate further the basic procedures of the process costing system, assume that Dunbar Company manufactures Product A. The manufacturing activity begins in Department 1, where all materials enter production. The materials remain in Department 1 for a relatively short time, and there is usually no inventory of work in process in that department at the end of the accounting period. From Department 1, the materials are transferred to Department 2. In Department 2, there are usually inventories at the end of the accounting period. Separate factory overhead accounts are maintained for Departments 1 and 2. Factory overhead is applied at the rates of $.80 and $.50 per machine hour for Departments 1 and 2 respectively. There is one service department, Power. All inventories are costed by the first-in, first-out method.

The trial balance of the general ledger on January 1, the first day of the fiscal year, is as follows:

Dunbar Company
Trial Balance
January 1, 19--

Cash	39,400	
Accounts Receivable	45,000	
Finished Goods—Product A (1,000 units at $36.50)	36,500	
Work in Process—Department 2 (800 units, 1/2 completed)	24,600	
Materials	32,000	
Prepaid Expenses	6,150	
Plant Assets	510,000	
Accumulated Depreciation—Plant Assets		295,000
Accounts Payable		51,180
Wages Payable		3,400
Common Stock		250,000
Retained Earnings		94,070
	693,650	693,650

To reduce the illustrative entries to a manageable number and to avoid repetition, the transactions and the adjustments for January are stated as summaries. In practice, the transactions would be recorded from day to day. The descriptions of the transactions, followed in each case by the entry, are as follows:

(a) Materials purchased and prepaid expenses incurred	Materials	80,500	
	Prepaid Expenses	3,300	
	Accounts Payable		83,800
(b) Materials requisitioned for use	Power Department	6,300	
	Factory Overhead—Department 1	6,420	
	Factory Overhead—Department 2	5,700	
	Work in Process—Department 1	58,500	
	Materials		76,920
(c) Factory labor used	Power Department	4,500	
	Factory Overhead—Department 1	2,850	
	Factory Overhead—Department 2	2,100	
	Work in Process—Department 1	24,900	
	Work in Process—Department 2	37,800	
	Wages Payable		72,150

(d) Other costs incurred	Power Department	900	
	Factory Overhead—Department 1	1,800	
	Factory Overhead—Department 2	1,200	
	Selling Expenses	15,000	
	Administrative Expenses	13,500	
	Accounts Payable		32,400
(e) Expiration of prepaid expenses	Power Department	750	
	Factory Overhead—Department 1	1,350	
	Factory Overhead—Department 2	1,050	
	Selling Expenses	900	
	Administrative Expenses	600	
	Prepaid Expenses		4,650
(f) Depreciation	Power Department	1,050	
	Factory Overhead—Department 1	1,800	
	Factory Overhead—Department 2	2,700	
	Selling Expenses	600	
	Administrative Expenses	300	
	Accumulated Depreciation—Plant Assets		6,450
(g) Distribution of Power Department costs	Factory Overhead—Department 1	5,400	
	Factory Overhead—Department 2	8,100	
	Power Department		13,500

Power was provided at 5¢ per kwh for 108 000 and 162 000 kwh for Departments 1 and 2, respectively.

(h) Application of factory overhead costs to work in process	Work in Process—Department 1	19,920	
	Work in Process—Department 2	18,900	
	Factory Overhead—Department 1		19,920
	Factory Overhead—Department 2		18,900

The predetermined rates were $.80 and $.50 per machine hour for Departments 1 and 2 respectively. Machine hours totaled 24,900 and 37,800 for Departments 1 and 2 respectively.

(i) Transfer of production costs from Department 1 to Department 2	Work in Process—Department 2	103,320	
	Work in Process—Department 1		103,320

4,100 units were fully processed, and there is no work in process in Department 1 at the beginning or at the end of the month.

Total costs charged to Department 1:	
Direct materials	$ 58,500
Direct labor	24,900
Factory overhead	19,920
Total costs	$103,320

Unit cost of product transferred to Department 2:	
$103,320 ÷ 4,100	$ 25.20

(j) Transfer of production costs from Department 2 to Finished Goods	Finished Goods—Product A	153,840	
	Work in Process—Department 2		153,840

4,000 units were completed, and the remaining 900 units were 2/3 completed at the end of the month.

Equivalent units of production:		
To process units in inventory on January 1:		
800 × 1/2		400
To process units started and completed in January:		
4,000 − 800		3,200
To process units in inventory on January 31:		
900 × 2/3		600
Equivalent units of production in January		4,200

Conversion costs:		
Direct labor [transaction (c)]		$ 37,800
Factory overhead [transaction (h)]		18,900
Total conversion costs		$ 56,700
Unit conversion cost:		
$56,700 ÷ 4,200		$ 13.50

Allocation of costs of Department 2:		
Units started in December, completed in January:		
Inventory on January 1, 800 units, 1/2 completed	$24,600	
Conversion costs in January, 400 at $13.50	5,400	
Total ($30,000 ÷ 800 = $37.50 unit cost)		$30,000
Units started and completed in January:		
From Department 1, 3,200 units at $25.20	$80,640	
Conversion costs, 3,200 at $13.50	43,200	
Total ($123,840 ÷ 3,200 = $38.70 unit cost)		123,840
Total transferred to Product A		$153,840
Units started in January, 2/3 completed:		
From Department 1, 900 units at $25.20	$22,680	
Conversion costs, 600 at $13.50	8,100	
Total work in process—Department 2		30,780
Total costs charged to Department 2		$184,620

(k) Cost of goods sold	Cost of Goods Sold	143,900	
	Finished Goods—Product A		143,900

Product A, 3,800 units:	
1,000 units at $36.50	$ 36,500
800 units at $37.50	30,000
2,000 units at $38.70	77,400
Total cost of goods sold	$143,900

(l) Sales	Accounts Receivable	210,500	
	Sales		210,500
(m) Cash received	Cash	200,000	
	Accounts Receivable		200,000
(n) Cash disbursed	Accounts Payable	120,000	
	Wages Payable	72,500	
	Cash		192,500

A chart of the flow of costs from the service and processing department accounts into the finished goods account and then to the cost of goods sold account is as follows. Entries in the accounts are identified by letters to aid the comparison with the summary journal entries.

Flow of Costs Through Process Cost Accounts

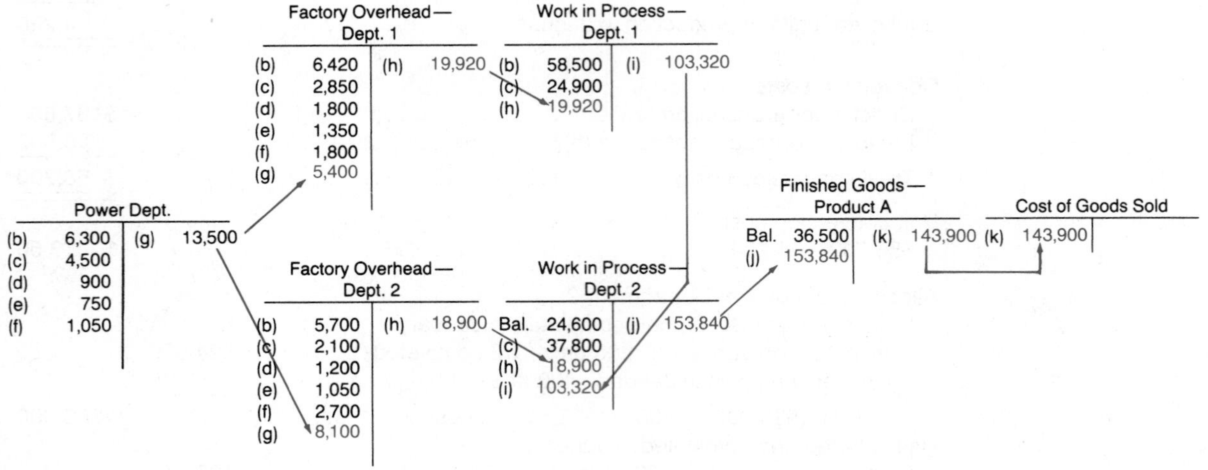

Cost of Production Reports

The cost of production reports for Departments 1 and 2 are as follows:

Dunbar Company
Cost of Production Report—Department 1
For the Month Ended January 31, 19--

Quantities:	
Units charged to production and to be accounted for	4,100
Units accounted for and transferred to Department 2	4,100
Costs:	
Costs charged to production in January:	
Direct materials	$ 58,500
Direct labor	24,900
Factory overhead	19,920
Total costs to be accounted for	$103,320
Total costs accounted for and transferred to Department 2 (4,100 units × $25.20)	$103,320

Dunbar Company
Cost of Production Report—Department 2
For the Month Ended January 31, 19--

Quantities:	
Charged to production:	
In process, January 1	800
Received from Department 1	4,100
Total units to be accounted for	4,900

Units accounted for:		
Transferred to finished goods		4,000
To process, January 31		900
Total units accounted for		4,900
Costs:		
Charged to production:		
In process, January 1		$ 24,600
January costs:		
Direct materials from Department 1 ($25.20 per unit)		103,320
Conversion costs:		
Direct labor	$ 37,800	
Factory overhead	18,900	
Total conversion costs ($13.50 per unit)		56,700
Total costs to be accounted for		$184,620
Costs allocated as follows:		
Transferred to finished goods:		
800 units at $37.50	$ 30,000	
3,200 units at $38.70	123,840	
Total cost of finished goods		$153,840
In process, January 31:		
Direct materials (900 units at $25.20)	$ 22,680	
Conversion costs (900 units × 2/3 × $13.50)	8,100	
Total cost of inventory in process, January 31		30,780
Total costs accounted for		$184,620
Computations:		
Equivalent units of production:		
To process units in inventory on January 1: 800 units × 1/2		400
To process units started and completed in January: 4,000 units − 800 units		3,200
To process units in inventory on January 31: 900 units × 2/3		600
Equivalent units of production		4,200
Unit conversion cost: $56,700 ÷ 4,200		$ 13.50

Financial Statements

The financial statements for process cost systems are similar to those for job order cost systems. To illustrate, the trial balance and the condensed financial statements for Dunbar Company are presented as follows. Note that the net underapplied factory overhead of $1,650 ($1,950 − $300) on January 31 is reported on the balance sheet as a deferred item.

Dunbar Company
Trial Balance
January 31, 19--

Cash	46,900	
Accounts Receivable	55,500	
Finished Goods—Product A (1,200 units at $38.70)	46,440	
Work in Process—Department 2 (900 units, 2/3 completed)	30,780	
Materials	35,580	
Prepaid Expenses	4,800	
Plant Assets	510,000	
Accumulated Depreciation—Plant Assets		301,450
Accounts Payable		47,380
Wages Payable		3,050
Common Stock		250,000
Retained Earnings		94,070
Sales		210,500
Cost of Goods Sold	143,900	
Factory Overhead—Department 1		300
Factory Overhead—Department 2	1,950	
Selling Expenses	16,500	
Administrative Expenses	14,400	
	906,750	906,750

Dunbar Company
Income Statement
For Month Ended January 31, 19--

Sales		$210,500
Cost of goods sold		143,900
Gross profit		$ 66,600
Operating expenses:		
Selling expenses	$16,500	
Administrative expenses	14,400	
Total operating expenses		30,900
Income from operations		$ 35,700

Dunbar Company
Retained Earnings Statement
For Month Ended January 31, 19--

Retained earnings, January 1, 19--	$ 94,070
Income for the month	35,700
Retained earnings, January 31, 19--	$129,770

Dunbar Company Balance Sheet January 31, 19--			
Assets			
Current assets:			
Cash		$ 46,900	
Accounts receivable		55,500	
Inventories:			
Finished goods	$46,440		
Work in process	30,780		
Materials	35,580	112,800	
Prepaid expenses		4,800	
Total current assets			$220,000
Plant assets		$510,000	
Less accumulated depreciation		301,450	208,550
Deferred debits:			
Factory overhead underapplied			1,650
Total assets			$430,200
Liabilities			
Current liabilities:			
Accounts payable		$ 47,380	
Wages payable		3,050	
Total liabilities			$50,430
Stockholders' Equity			
Common stock		$250,000	
Retained earnings		129,770	
Total stockholders' equity			379,770
Total liabilities and stockholders' equity			$430,200

INVENTORY COSTING METHODS

OBJECTIVE 8
Describe and illustrate the use of the average cost method of inventory costing for process cost accounting systems

In the preceding discussion and illustrations, the **first-in, first-out (fifo) cost method** was used to determine unit product costs. Another method, known as the average cost method, is sometimes used in practice. Under the **average cost method,** all costs incurred in manufacturing the goods completed during a period are averaged. This average is then used in determining the unit product cost of the goods completed during the period and the work in process at the end of the period. Although the average cost method is not as accurate and not as useful to management in controlling costs as the fifo method, it is simpler to use and is therefore encountered in practice.

First-In, First-Out (Fifo) Cost Method

In a manufacturing process, especially one that is automated, the products may flow through the process in a first-in, first-out manner; that is, the first units entering the process are the first completed. In such processes, the work in process at the beginning of the period is completed before work is completed on additional materials entered into the process. The fifo cost method is consistent with the flow of products in such manufacturing processes and is widely used.

When the fifo cost method is used, the beginning work in process inventory costs are kept separate from the costs incurred during the current period. As a result, the fifo cost method generally provides two unit cost figures for products completed during a period: (1) units completed from the beginning work in process and (2) units started and completed during the current period. These two unit cost figures are useful to management in controlling manufacturing costs because current costs are used to determine the cost of products started and completed during the current period. Management can therefore focus on these current costs in evaluating and controlling current operations.

Although using two separate costs assists in the control of costs, it adds some complexity to the calculation of unit costs. It also complicates the determination of product costs when the products completed by one process are used in subsequent processes. Primarily for these reasons, some enterprises prefer to use the average cost method.

Average Cost Method

The average cost method is *based on the assumption that the work in process at the beginning of the current period was started and completed during the current period.* Using this method, one unit cost figure for all products completed during the current period is determined. Although not as accurate as the fifo cost method, the average cost method avoids the problem of have two unit cost figures for products completed during a period. When the average cost method is used, it is more difficult for management to evaluate and control current operations, since past costs and current costs are averaged.

To illustrate the use of the average cost method, assume the following data for the Cutting Department of Perrin Company for July of the current year. In addition, assume that all materials used in the Cutting Department are added at the beginning of the process.

Inventory in process, July 1, 500 units:	
Materials cost, 500 units	$24,550
Conversion costs, 500 units, 70% completed	3,600
Materials cost for July, 1,000 units	50,000
Conversion costs for July, 1000 units	9,660
Goods finished in July (includes units in process on July 1), 1,100 units	—
Inventory in process, July 31, 400 units, 50% completed	—

To apply the average cost method in the determination of the unit cost for the 1,100 units finished in July and the 400 units that are 50% completed on July 31, the average materials cost and the average conversion cost are determined as follows:

Materials cost for 500 units in process at July 1	$24,550
Materials cost for 1,000 units for July	50,000
Total materials cost (1,500 units)	$74,550
Average materials cost per unit ($74,550 ÷ 1,500)	$ 49.70
Conversion costs for units in process at July 1	$ 3,600
Conversion costs for July	9,660
Total conversion costs	$13,260

Equivalent units of production:	
To process units in inventory on July 1	500
To process units started and completed in July (1,100 units − 500 units)	600
To process units in inventory on July 31 (400 units × 50%)	200
Equivalent units of production in July	1,300
Average conversion cost per unit ($13,260 ÷ 1,300)	$ 10.20

It should be noted that in determining the average unit materials cost, the cost of materials in work in process on July 1 (the beginning inventory) is added to the materials cost for July before dividing by the total units of materials in the cutting process during July. A similar procedure is followed for computing the average unit conversion cost. The conversion costs in work in process on July 1 (the beginning inventory) are added to the conversion costs for July before dividing by the equivalent units of production for July. As mentioned earlier, in computing these equivalent units, the units in the beginning inventory are treated as if they were all started and completed during the current period. In other words, the beginning inventory of 500 units is treated as 500 units fully completed during the current period, not 500 units 30% completed (150 units) during the current period. Alternatively, the total equivalent units, 1,300, is the total of the units completed, 1,100, and the equivalent units in the ending inventory, 200.

The average unit costs for Perrin Company are used to determine the cost of goods finished during July and the cost of the work in process on July 31 (the ending inventory) as follows:

Goods finished during July:		
1,100 units:	1,100 units at $49.70 for materials costs	$54,670
	1,100 units at $10.20 for conversion costs	11,220
	Total (1,100 units at $59.90)	$65,890

Work in process, July 31:		
400 units:	400 units at $49.70 for materials costs	$19,880
	400 units × 50% × $10.20 for conversion costs	2,040
	Total	$21,920

In many manufacturing processes, there is no significant difference between the unit cost figures determined under the average cost and the fifo cost methods. This similarity in unit costs is especially true where the beginning and ending work in process inventories are uniform and materials costs do not fluctuate widely from period to period. Therefore, the simplification of the calculations by using the average cost method and the lack of significant variation in unit costs under the two methods have been the principal reasons for the use of the average cost method. Computers, however, have removed much of the complexity from the calculations of unit product costs.

Inventory Costing Methods and Just-In-Time Manufacturing

In recent years, more and more manufacturers are using the just-in-time (JIT) manufacturing concept. In JIT manufacturing, materials are received just in time to enter production and the product is finished just in time to meet the demands of the next process or to meet customer orders. In a pure JIT system, all costs of production for a period are traced to completed products, and are not accounted for as work in process. Production costs are added to the products and transferred to the finished goods account after the manufacturing process is completed. This transfer of costs is sometimes referred to as **backflush costing**, since production costs are said to be "flushed" out of the accounting system when products are completed. The concept of JIT manufacturing is discussed in more depth in Chapters 18 and 24.

HYBRID COST ACCOUNTING SYSTEMS

OBJECTIVE 9
Describe hybrid cost accounting systems.

The two most commonly used cost systems—job order and process cost—have been described and illustrated in this and the preceding chapter. Some companies manufacture products that have production characteristics common to both job order and process systems. For example, a manufacturer of men's sport shirts may mass-produce the shirts through continuous-flow manufacturing processes (cutting materials, sewing, etc.) that are common to process systems. The shirts may then be customized by adding a customer's logo to specific batches of shirts. When continuous-flow processing is blended with custom-order processing, management is best served by a costing system that is tailored to the production system. This hybrid costing system would include characteristics of both process and job order costing.

One hybrid system, called **operation costing,** is used in practice. Under operation costing, products are typically handled in batches, with various batches having both individual characteristics and common characteristics. For example, a shoe manufacturer may make shoes in batches. Some batches may be made using leather and others may be made using vinyl. In such cases the costs of the specific materials used in production would be changed for each batch, as in job order costing. All batches may be cut and sewed using the same basic processing procedures. The conversion costs—direct labor and factory overhead—would be charged to the product, as in process costing. Thus, operation costing is well-suited to manufacturers whose products are typically produced in batches that can vary from model to model or from style to style.

CHAPTER REVIEW

KEY POINTS

OBJECTIVE 1

Job Order and Process Costing Compared

The process cost system is best suited for industries that mass-produce identical units of a product which often have passed through a sequence of processes on a continuous basis. In process cost accounting, costs are charged to processing departments, and the cost of the finished unit is determined by dividing the total cost incurred in each process among the number of units produced.

OBJECTIVE 2

Flow of Costs in a Process Cost System

The accumulated costs transferred from preceding departments and the costs of direct materials and direct labor incurred in each processing department are debited to the related work in process account in a process cost system. Each work in process account is also debited for the factory overhead applied. The direct labor and the factory overhead applied are referred to as the conversion costs.

OBJECTIVE 3

Inventories of Partially Processed Materials

Frequently, partially processed materials remain in various stages of production in a department at the end of a period. In this case, the manufacturing costs must be allocated between the units that have been completed and those that are only partially completed and remain within the department. In allocating costs between completed products and work remaining in process, either the first-in, first-out method or the average cost method may be used. To allocate processing costs between the output completed and the inventory of goods within the department, it is necessary to determine the number of equivalent units of production during the period. The equivalent units of production are the number of units that could have been manufactured from start to finish during the period.

OBJECTIVE 4

Cost of Production Report

A report prepared periodically for each processing department summarizes (1) the units for which the department is accountable and the disposition of these units and (2) the costs charged to the department and the allocation of these costs. This report, termed the cost of production report, may be used as the source of the computation of unit production costs and the allocation of the processing costs to the finished and the uncompleted units. More importantly, the report is used to control costs.

OBJECTIVE 5

Service Departments and Process Costs

In a factory with several processes, there may be one or more service departments that do not process the materials directly. Examples include the factory office, the power plant, and the maintenance and repair shop. Periodically, the costs incurred by service departments are allocated to the factory overhead accounts of the processing departments.

OBJECTIVE 6

Joint Products and By-Products

In some manufacturing processes, more than one product is produced. When the output of a manufacturing process consists of two or more different products, the products are either joint products or by-products. When two or more goods of significant value are produced from a single principal direct material, the products are termed joint products. Similarly, the costs incurred in the manufacture of joint products are called joint costs. If one of the products resulting from a process has little value in relation to the main product or joint products, it is known as a by-product.

Since joint products come from the processing of a common parent material, the allocation of cost to each separate product cannot be based on actual expenditures. The allocation of joint costs among the joint products is usually performed using the market (sales) value method. The amount of manufacturing cost usually assigned to a by-product is the sales value of the by-product reduced by any additional costs necessary to complete and sell it.

OBJECTIVE 7

Illustration of Process Cost Accounting

In a process cost accounting system, transactions are recorded throughout the period, using perpetual inventory procedures. A cost of production report is prepared at the end of the period as support for the allocation of processing costs to work in process and finished goods.

OBJECTIVE 8 Inventory Costing Methods

The first-in, first-out (fifo) cost method of accounting for manufacturing costs is consistent with the flow of product costs through most manufacturing processes. The average cost method, although not as useful for cost control as the fifo method, is also used in practice. The simplification of the computations of unit product costs under the average cost method is the major reason for use of the method. Under the average cost method, one unit cost figure (rather than two, as under the fifo method) is computed for all products completed during a period.

OBJECTIVE 9 Hybrid Cost Accounting Systems

Some production methods have characteristics common to both job order and process cost systems. Operation costing is an example of one type of hybrid system that is tailored to the production system.

KEY TERMS

conversion cost 731
equivalent units of production 733
cost of production report 735
service departments 736
joint products 737
joint costs 737
by-product 737
market (sales) value method 738
first-in, first-out (fifo) cost method 745
average cost method 745
operation costing 748

SELF-EXAMINATION QUESTIONS

Answers at end of chapter.

1. For which of the following businesses would the process cost system be most appropriate?
   A. Custom furniture manufacturer
   B. Commercial building contractor
   C. Crude oil refinery
   D. None of the above

2. The group of manufacturing costs referred to as *conversion costs* includes:
   A. direct materials and direct labor
   B. direct materials and factory overhead
   C. direct labor and factory overhead
   D. none of the above

3. Information relating to production in Department A for May is as follows:

May 1	Balance, 1,000 units, 3/4 completed	$22,150
31	Direct materials, 5,000 units	75,000
31	Direct labor	32,500
31	Factory overhead	16,250

   If 500 units were 1/4 completed at May 31, 5,500 units were completed during May, and inventories are costed by the first-in, first-out method, what was the number of equivalent units of production for May?
   A. 4,500
   B. 4,875
   C. 5,500
   D. None of the above

4. Based on the data presented in Question 3, what is the unit conversion cost?
   A. $10
   B. $15
   C. $25
   D. None of the above

5. Which of the following departments is an example of a service department?
   A. Factory office
   B. Power plant
   C. Maintenance
   D. All of the above

ILLUSTRATIVE PROBLEM

Tate Company manufactures Product A by a series of four processes, all materials being introduced in Department 1. From Department 1 the materials pass through Departments 2, 3, and 4, emerging as finished Product A. All inventories are costed by the first-in, first-out method.

The balances in the accounts Work in Process—Department 4 and Finished Goods were as follows on May 1:

Work in Process—Department 4 (1,000 units, 1/4 completed)	$17,800
Finished Goods (1,800 units at $23.50 a unit)	42,300

The following costs were charged to Work in Process—Department 4 during May:

Direct materials transferred from Department 3: 4,700 units at $16 a unit	$75,200
Direct labor	25,500
Factory overhead	15,300

During May, 5,000 units of A were completed and 4,800 units were sold. Inventories on May 31 were as follows:

Work in Process—Department 4: 700 units, 1/2 completed
Finished Goods: 2,000 units

Instructions:

Determine the following, presenting the computations in good order:

(a) Equivalent units of production for Department 4 during May.
(b) Unit conversion cost for Department 4 for May.
(c) Total and unit cost of Product A started in a prior period and finished in May.
(d) Total and unit cost of Product A started and finished in May.
(e) Total cost of goods transferred to finished goods.
(f) Work in process inventory for Department 4, May 31.
(g) Cost of goods sold (indicate number of units and unit costs).
(h) Finished goods inventory, May 31.

SOLUTION

(a) Equivalent units of production:

To process units in inventory on May 1: 1,000 units × 3/4	750
To process units started and completed in May: 5,000 units − 1,000 units	4,000
To process units in inventory on May 31: 700 units × 1/2	350
Equivalent units of production in May	5,100

(b) Unit conversion cost: $\frac{\$25,500 + \$15,300}{5,100} = \$8$

(c) Cost of Product A started in a prior period and finished in May:

1,000 units:	Inventory on May 1, 1/4 completed	$ 17,800
	Conversion cost in May, 750 × $8	6,000
	Total	$ 23,800

Unit cost: $23,800 ÷ 1,000 = $23.80

(d) Cost of Product A started and finished in May:

4,000 units: Materials from Department 3, 4,000 × $16	$ 64,000
Conversion cost in May, 4,000 × $8	32,000
Total	$ 96,000

Unit cost: $96,000 ÷ 4,000 = $24

(e) Total cost of goods transferred to finished goods:

Cost of Product A started in a prior period and finished in May (1,000 units at $23.80)	$ 23,800
Cost of Product A started and finished in May (4,000 units at $24)	96,000
Total	$119,800

(f) Work in process inventory, May 31:

700 units: Materials cost, 700 × $16	$ 11,200
Conversion costs in May, 350 × $8	2,800
Work in process inventory, May 31	$ 14,000

(g) Cost of goods sold:

1,800 units at $23.50	$ 42,300
1,000 units at $23.80	23,800
2,000 units at $24.00	48,000
4,800 units	$114,100

(h) Finished goods inventory, May 31:

2,000 units at $24	$ 48,000

DISCUSSION QUESTIONS

17–1. Which type of cost system, process or job order, would be best suited for each of the following: (a) paper manufacturer, (b) oil refinery, (c) automobile repair shop, (d) building contractor, (e) lumber mill? Give reasons for your answers.

17–2. Are perpetual inventory accounts for materials, work in process, and finished goods generally used for (a) job order cost systems and (b) process cost systems?

17–3. In job order cost accounting, the three elements of manufacturing cost are charged directly to job orders. Why is it not necessary to charge manufacturing costs in process cost accounting to job orders?

17–4. What two groups of manufacturing costs are referred to as conversion costs?

17–5. In the manufacture of 5,000 units of a product, direct materials cost incurred was $56,000, direct labor incurred was $32,000, and factory overhead applied was $11,500. (a) What is the total conversion cost? (b) What is the conversion cost per unit? (c) What is the total manufacturing cost? (d) What is the manufacturing cost per unit?

17–6. What is meant by the term "equivalent units"?

17–7. If Department F had no work in process at the beginning of the period, 16,000 units were completed during the period, and 3,000 units were 20% completed at the end of the period, what was the number of equivalent units of production for the period?

17–8. The following information concerns production in the Painting Department for March. All direct materials are placed in process at the beginning of production. Determine the number of units in work in process inventory at the end of the month.

WORK IN PROCESS—PAINTING DEPARTMENT

Date		Item	Debit	Credit	Balance	
					Debit	Credit
Mar.	1	Bal., 10,500 units ⅓ completed			17,500	
	31	Direct materials, 20,500 units	28,700			
	31	Direct labor	36,100			
	31	Factory overhead	9,300			
	31	Goods finished, 21,600 units		81,000		
	31	Bal., ____ units, ¼ completed			10,600	

17–9. For Question No. 17-8, determine the equivalent units of production for March, assuming that the first-in, first-out method is used to cost inventories.

17–10. What data are summarized in the two principal sections of the cost of production report?

17–11. What is the most important purpose of the cost of production report?

17–12. (a) How does a service department differ from a processing department? (b) Give two examples of a service department.

17–13. Jones Company maintains a cafeteria for its employees at a cost of $3,750 per month. On what basis would the company most likely allocate the cost of the cafeteria among the production departments?

17–14. Muster Company has two processing departments: A and B. The power plant provides 100 000 kilowatt-hours of its total output of 300 000 kilowatt-hours to Department A. How much of the $45,000 of total power plant costs should be allocated to Department A?

17–15. Distinguish between a joint product and a by-product.

17–16. The Cutting Department produces two products. How should the cost be allocated (a) if the products are joint products and (b) if one of the products is a by-product?

17–17. Where is net underapplied factory overhead reported on the interim balance sheet?

17–18. What are the principal advantages of using the first-in, first-out method for costing inventories for process cost systems?

17–19. What is the principal advantage of using the average method for costing inventories for process cost systems?

17–20. What is operation costing?

Real World Focus

17–21. As production processes become more and more automated in what many see as the "age of robotics," materials may enter into and leave a production process without human intervention. For example, in the manufacture of automobiles, General Motors uses state-of-the-art paint systems, which are operated from an automated video control room. The control room supervisor monitors the preparation of the bare metal body of the automobile as it is submerged in a primer. Next, the body passes through nine pairs of robot painters teamed with other robot devices that open and close doors and paint inside surfaces. (a) In this type of production environment, would direct labor hours be an appropriate base for allocation of predetermined factory overhead? (b) Can you suggest other possible factory overhead bases?

Ethics Discussion Case

17–22. Kathy Burchett, a cost accountant for Thacker Industries, has the responsibility of allocating service department costs. She allocates Power Department costs on a monthly basis to each of the producing departments, based on actual kilowatt usage. John Mercer, supervisor of the Assembly Department, recently complained to the vice-president of production that the allocations of Power Department costs were wrong and that they should be divided equally between all departments. He charges that because of the method of allocation used, his department receives a larger share and the Finishing Department receives a smaller share than is warranted. He also charges that the only reason for using the current method is that her husband is the supervisor of the Finishing Department. Discuss the ethical issues of this case.

EXERCISES

Ex. 17–23.
Flowchart of accounts related to service and processing departments.
OBJ. 2

Grey Co. manufactures two products. The entire output of Department A is transferred to Department B. Part of the fully processed goods from Department B are sold as Product X and the remainder of the goods are transferred to Department C for further processing into Product Y. The service department, Factory Office, provides services for each of the processing departments.

Prepare a chart of the flow of costs from the service and processing department accounts into the finished goods account and then into the cost of goods sold account. The relevant accounts are as follows.

Cost of Goods Sold	Finished Goods—Product X
Factory Office	Finished Goods—Product Y
Factory Overhead—Department A	Work in Process—Department A
Factory Overhead—Department B	Work in Process—Department B
Factory Overhead—Department C	Work in Process—Department C

Ex. 17–24.
Entries for flow of factory costs for process cost system.
OBJ. 2

Raser Company manufactures a single product by a continuous process, involving three production departments. The records indicate that direct materials, direct labor, and applied factory overhead were $78,000, $108,000, and $32,400, respectively. Also, work in process in the department at the beginning of the period totaled $45,000, and work in process at the end of the period totaled $42,000.

Prepare entries to record (a) the flow of costs into Department 1 during the period for (1) direct materials, (2) direct labor, and (3) factory overhead; (b) the transfer of production costs to Department 2.

Ex. 17–25.
Factory overhead rate, entry for application of factory overhead, and factory overhead account balance.
OBJ. 2

The chief cost accountant for G.C. Love Co. estimates total factory overhead cost for the Blending Department for the year at $18,000 and total direct labor costs at $48,000. During November, the actual direct labor cost totaled $4,000, and factory overhead cost incurred totaled $1,125. (a) What is the predetermined factory overhead rate based on direct labor cost? (b) Prepare the entry to apply factory overhead to production for November. (c) What is the November 30 balance of the account Factory Overhead—Blending Department? (d) Does the balance in (c) represent overapplied or underapplied factory overhead?

Ex. 17–26.
Equivalent units of production and related costs.
OBJ. 3
SPREADSHEET PROBLEM

The charges to Work in Process—Finishing Department for a period, together with information concerning production, are as follows. All direct materials are placed in process at the beginning of production, and the first-in, first-out method is used to cost inventories.

Work in Process—Finishing Department

2,500 units, 60% completed	94,000	To Dept. 2, 5,600 units	237,350
Direct materials, 3,100 at $26	80,600		
Direct labor	77,500		
Factory overhead	10,650		

Determine the following, presenting your computations: (a) equivalent units of production, (b) conversion cost per equivalent unit of production, (c) total and unit cost of product started in prior period and completed in the current period, and (d) total and unit cost of product started and completed in the current period.

Ex. 17–27.
Unit costs of product.
OBJ. 3

The debits to Work in Process—Melting Department for a period, together with information concerning production, are as follows:

Work in process, beginning of period, 4,500 units, 60% completed ...	$272,260
Materials added during period, 18,200 units	382,200
Conversion costs during period	574,000
Work in process, end of period, 4,000 units, 10% completed	—
Goods finished during period, 18,700 units	—

All direct materials are placed in process at the beginning of the process and the first-in, first-out method is used to cost inventories. Determine the following, presenting your computations: (a) equivalent units of production for the period, (b) conversion cost per equivalent unit for the period, (c) cost of goods finished during the period, and (d) cost of work in process at the end of the period.

Ex. 17–28.
Cost of production report.
OBJ. 4
SPREADSHEET PROBLEM

Prepare a cost of production report for the Assembly Department of Royal Company for June of the current fiscal year, using the following data and assuming that the first-in, first-out method is used to cost inventories:

Inventory, June 1, 8,000 units, 70% completed	$65,600
Materials from the Sanding Department, 20,800 units	87,360
Direct labor for June	78,200
Factory overhead for June	52,000
Goods finished during June (includes units in process, June 1) 21,300 units	—
Inventory (June 30, 7,500 units, 80% completed)	—

Ex. 17–29.
Entry for allocation of service department costs.
OBJ. 5

The Maintenance and Repair Department provides services to processing departments H, I, and J. During September of the current year, the total cost incurred by the Maintenance and Repair Department was $120,000. During September, it was estimated that 55% of the services were provided to Department H, 20% to Department I, and 25% to Department J.

Prepare an entry to record the allocation of the Maintenance and Repair Department cost for September to the processing departments.

Ex. 17–30.
Allocation of costs for by-product and joint products.
OBJ. 6

The charges to Work in Process—Department 3, together with units of product completed during the period, are indicated in the following account:

Work in Process—Department 3

From Department 2	326,800	By-product E, 6,000 units
Direct labor	112,300	Joint product M, 12,000 units
Factory overhead	51,400	Joint product N, 20,000 units

There is no inventory of goods in process at either the beginning or the end of the period. The value of E is $1.75 a unit; M sells at $30 a unit, and N sells at $22 a unit.

Allocate the costs to the three products and determine the unit cost of each, presenting your computations.

Ex. 17–31.
Unit costs of product by average cost method.
OBJ. 8

The debits to Work in Process—Melting Department for a period, together with information concerning production, are as follows:

Work in process, beginning of period:	
Materials costs, 4,500 units	$127,100
Conversion costs, 4,500 units, 60% completed	145,160
Materials added during period, 18,200 units	381,380
Conversion costs during period	580,640
Work in process, end of period, 4,000 units, 10% completed	—
Goods finished during period, 18,700 units	—

All direct materials are placed in process at the beginning of the process, and the average cost method is used to cost inventories. Determine the following, presenting your computations: (a) average materials cost per unit for period, (b) equivalent units of production for period, (c) average conversion cost per unit for period, (d) cost of goods finished during the period, and (e) cost of work in process at end of period.

PROBLEMS

Pb. 17–32.
Work in process account data for two months and determination of difference in unit product cost between months.
OBJ. 2,3

A process cost system is used to record the costs of manufacturing Product G, which requires a series of four processes. The inventory of Work in Process—Department 4 on April 1 and debits to the account during April were as follows:

Balance, 2,000 units, 3/4 completed	$18,025
From Department 3, 14,300 units	35,750
Direct labor	94,500
Factory overhead	10,500

During April, 2,000 units in process on April 1 were completed, and of the 14,300 units entering the department, all were completed except 3,500 units which were 1/5 completed.

Charges to Work in Process—Department 4 for May were as follows:

From Department 3, 10,500 units	$27,300
Direct labor	95,220
Factory overhead	10,580

During May, the units in process at the beginning of the month were completed, and of the 10,500 units entering the department, all were completed except 2,700 units, which were 1/3 completed. All inventories are costed by the first-in, first-out method.

Instructions:

(1) Set up an account for Work in Process—Department 4. Enter the balance as of April 1 and record the debits and the credits in the account for April. Present computations for the determination of (a) equivalent units of production, (b) unit conversion cost, (c) cost of goods finished, differentiating between units started in the prior period and units started and finished in April, and (d) work in process inventory.

(2) Record the transactions for May in the account. Present the computations listed in (1).

(3) Determine the difference in unit cost between the product started and completed in April and the product started and completed in May. Determine also the amount of the difference attributable collectively to operations in Departments 1 through 3 and the amount attributable to operations in Department 4.

Pb. 17–33.
Equivalent units and related costs; cost of production report.
OBJ. 3,4

Yeary Company manufactures Product P by a series of three processes, all materials being introduced in Department 1. From Department 1, the materials pass through Departments 2 and 3, emerging as finished Product P. All inventories are costed by the first-in, first-out method.

The balances in the accounts Work in Process—Department 3 and Finished Goods were as follows on October 1:

Work in Process—Department 3 (9,000 units, 1/2 completed)	$177,300
Finished Goods (11,000 units at $25.75 a unit)	283,250

The following costs were charged to Work in Process—Department 3 during October:

Direct materials transferred from Department 2: 33,500 units at $13.80 a unit	$462,300
Direct labor	286,130
Factory overhead	154,070

During October, 32,500 units of P were completed and 32,900 units were sold. Inventories on October 31 were as follows:

Work in Process—Department 3: 10,000 units, 3/4 completed
Finished Goods: 10,600 units

Instructions:

(1) Determine the following, presenting computations in good order:
 (a) Equivalent units of production for Department 3 during October.
 (b) Unit conversion cost for Department 3 for October.
 (c) Total and unit cost of Product P started in a prior period and finished in October.
 (d) Total and unit cost of Product P started and finished in October.
 (e) Total cost of goods transferred to finished goods.
 (f) Work in process inventory for Department 3, October 31.
 (g) Cost of goods sold (indicate number of units and unit costs).
 (h) Finished goods inventory, October 31.
(2) Prepare a cost of production report for Department 3 for October.

Pb. 17–34.
Entries for process cost system.
OBJ. 2, 3, 5, 7

Lester Company manufactures Product H. Material X is placed in process in Department 1, where it is ground and partially refined. The output of Department 1 is transferred to Department 2, where Material Y is added at the beginning of the process and the refining is completed. On April 1, Lester Company had the following inventories:

Finished Goods (6,500 units)	$136,500
Work in process—Department 1	—
Work in process—Department 2 (8,000 units, 3/4 completed)	152,400
Materials	43,700

Departmental accounts are maintained for factory overhead, and there is one service department, Factory Office. The first-in, first-out method is used to cost inventories. Manufacturing operations for April are summarized as follows:

(a) Materials purchased on account	$89,100
(b) Materials requisitioned for use:	
Material X	$67,250
Material Y	24,000
Indirect materials—Department 1	4,280
Indirect materials—Department 2	1,080
(c) Labor used:	
Direct labor—Department 1	$85,000
Direct labor—Department 2	46,500

Indirect labor—Department 1	8,400
Indirect labor—Department 2	3,800
Factory Office	2,900
(d) Depreciation charged on plant assets:	
Department 1	$37,850
Department 2	15,100
Factory Office	1,800
(e) Miscellaneous costs incurred on account:	
Department 1	$ 7,100
Department 2	2,920
Factory Office	1,200
(f) Expiration of prepaid expenses:	
Department 1	$ 2,400
Department 2	600
Factory Office	350
(g) Distribution of Factory Office costs:	
Department 1	40% of total Factory Office costs
Department 2	60% of total Factory Office costs
(h) Application of factory overhead costs based on machine hours:	
Department 1	$63,750
Department 2	27,900

(i) Production costs transferred from Department 1 to Department 2:
16,000 units were fully processed, and there was no inventory of work in process in Department 1 at April 30.

(j) Production costs transferred from Department 2 to finished goods:
15,000 units, including the inventory at April 1, were fully processed. There were 9,000 units 1/3 completed at April 30.

(k) Cost of goods sold duing April:
17,900 units (Use the first-in, first-out method in crediting the finished goods account.)

Instructions:

(1) Prepare entries to record the foregoing operations. Identify each entry by letter.
(2) Compute the April 30 work in process inventory for Department 2.

Pb. 17–35.
Cost of production report.
OBJ. 4, 7
SPREADSHEET PROBLEM

The data related to production during April of the current year for Department 2 of Lester Company are presented in Problem 17–34.

Instructions:

Prepare a cost of production report for Department 2 for April.

Pb. 17–36.
Entries for process cost system.
OBJ. 7

A.C. Joyner Products manufactures Product E. Materials are placed in production in Department 1, and after processing, are transferred to Department 2 where more materials are added. The finished product emerges from Department 2. There is one service department, Maintenance and Repair.

There were no inventories of work in process at the beginning or at the end of March. Finished goods inventory at March 1 was 10,000 units of Product E at a total cost of $180,000.

Transactions related to manufacturing operations for March are summarized as follows:

(a) Materials purchased on account, $256,900.
(b) Materials requisitioned for use: Department 1, $100,540 ($92,140 entered directly into the product); Department 2, $65,210 ($56,500 entered directly into the product); Maintenance and Repair, $3,680.
(c) Labor costs incurred: Department 1, $97,180 ($88,200 entered directly into the product); Department 2, $103,560 ($94,000 entered directly into the product); Maintenance and Repair, $6,910.

(d) Miscellaneous costs and expenses incurred on account: Department 1, $25,150; Department 2, $23,140; and Maintenance and Repair, $4,060.
(e) Depreciation charged on plant assets: Department 1, $15,320; Department 2, $14,000; and Maintenance and Repair, $2,760.
(f) Expiration of various prepaid expenses: Department 1, $1,260; Department 2, $920; and Maintenance and Repair, $340.
(g) Maintenance and repair costs allocated on the basis of services rendered: Department 1, 70%; Department 2, 30%.
(h) Factory overhead applied to production, based on machine hours: $70,560 and $61,100 for Departments 1 and 2 respectively.
(i) Output of Department 1: 25,000 units.
(j) Output of Department 2: 25,000 units of Product E.
(k) Sales on account: 26,500 units of Product E at $30. Credits to the finished goods account are to be made according to the first-in, first-out method.

Instructions:

Present entries to record the transactions, identifying each by letter. Include as an explanation for entry (k) the number of units and the unit costs for the product sold.

Pb. 17–37.
Financial statements for process cost system.
OBJ. 7

The trial balance of Raymond Inc. at March 31, the end of the first month of the current fiscal year, is as follows:

Raymond Inc.
Trial Balance
March 31, 19--

Cash	36,300	
Marketable Securities	30,000	
Accounts Receivable	122,500	
Allowance for Doubtful Accounts		5,000
Finished Goods—Product M	45,800	
Finished Goods—Product N	77,500	
Work in Process—Department 1	9,850	
Work in Process—Department 2	16,750	
Work in Process—Department 3	14,700	
Materials	30,250	
Prepaid Insurance	7,400	
Office Supplies	3,570	
Land	52,500	
Buildings	350,000	
Accumulated Depreciation—Buildings		159,600
Machinery and Equipment	171,000	
Accumulated Depreciation—Machinery and Equipment		108,300
Office Equipment	30,700	
Accumulated Depreciation—Office Equipment		12,780
Patents	33,000	
Accounts Payable		61,020
Wages Payable		9,800
Income Tax Payable		3,250
Mortgage Note Payable (due 1999)		60,000
Common Stock ($50 par)		300,000
Retained Earnings		279,910
Sales		380,000
Cost of Goods Sold	251,100	
Factory Overhead—Department 1	200	
Factory Overhead—Department 2	180	
Factory Overhead—Department 3		140
Selling Expenses	50,800	

Administrative Expenses	34,400	
Interest Expense	6,500	
Interest Income		200
Income Tax	5,000	
	1,380,000	1,380,000

Instructions:

(1) Prepare an income statement.
(2) Prepare a retained earnings statement.
(3) Prepare a balance sheet

Pb. 17–38.
Unit cost of finished product by average cost method; cost of production report
OBJ. 8

Rivero Company manufactures Product J by a series of four processes, all materials being introduced in Department 1. From Department 1, the materials pass through Departments 2, 3, and 4, emerging as finished Product J. All inventories are costed by the average cost method.

The balance in the account Work in Process—Department 4 was as follows on July 1:

Materials cost (2,000 units)	$12,390
Conversion costs (2,000 units, 1/4 completed)	6,400

The following costs were charged to Work in Process—Department 4 during July:

Direct materials transferred from Department 3: 17,500 units at $6 per unit	$105,000
Direct labor	172,800
Factory overhead	44,800

During July, 16,500 units of Product J were completed and the work in process inventory on July 31 was 3,000 units, 1/3 completed.

Instructions:

(1) Determine the following for Department 4, presenting compulations in good order:
  (a) Average materials cost per unit.
  (b) Equivalent units of production in July.
  (c) Average conversion cost per unit for July.
  (d) Cost of goods finished during July.
  (e) Cost of work in process at July 31.

(2) Prepare a cost of production report for Department 4 for July.

ALTERNATE PROBLEMS

Pb. 17–32A.
Work in process account data for two months and determination of difference in unit product cost between months.
OBJ. 2,3

A process cost system is used to record the costs of manufacturing Product Q, which requires a series of three processes. The inventory of Work in Process—Department 3 on September 1 and debits to the account during September were as follows:

Balance, 4,800 units, 1/4 completed	$ 21,840
From Department 2, 27,000 units	86,400
Direct labor	133,280
Factory overhead	23,520

During September, 4,800 units in process on September 1 were completed, and of the 27,000 units entering the department, all were completed except 5,200 units which were 1/2 completed.

Charges to Work in Process—Department 3 for October were as follows:

From Department 2, 30,800 units	$ 97,020
Direct labor	132,000
Factory overhead	33,000

During October, the units in process at the beginning of the month were completed, and of the 30,800 units entering the department, all were completed except 5,100 units, which were 1/3 completed. All inventories are costed by the first-in, first-out method.

Instructions:

(1) Set up an account for Work in Process—Department 3. Enter the balance as of September 1 and record the debits and the credits in the account for September. Present computations for the determination of (a) equivalent units of production, (b) unit conversion cost, (c) cost of goods finished, differentiating between units started in the prior period and units started and finished in September, and (d) work in process inventory.
(2) Record the transactions for October in the account. Present the computations listed in (1).
(3) Determine the difference in unit cost between the product started and completed in September and the product started and completed in October. Determine also the amount of the difference atrributable collectively to operations in Departments 1 and 2 and the amount attributable to operations in Department 3.

Pb. 17–33A.
Equivalent units and related costs; cost of production report.
OBJ. 3,4

Scotch Company manufactures Product F by a series of four processes, all materials being introduced in Department 1. From Department 1, the materials pass through Departments 2, 3, and 4, emerging as finished Product F. All inventories are costed by the first-in, first-out method.

The balances in the accounts Work in Process—Department 4 and Finished Goods were as follows on May 1:

Work in Process—Department 4 (4,500 units, 2/3 completed)	$34,200
Finished Goods (6,200 units at $9.80 a unit)	60,760

The following costs were charged to Work in Process—Department 4 during May:

Direct materials transferred from Department 3: 14,000 units at $2.50 a unit	$35,000
Direct labor	78,000
Factory overhead	19,500

During May, 14,500 units of F were completed and 15,600 units were sold. Inventories on May 31 were as follows:

Work in Process—Department 4: 4,000 units, 1/4 completed
Finished Goods: 5,100 units

Instructions:

(1) Determine the following, presenting computations in good order:
(a) Equivalent units of production for Department 4 during May.
(b) Unit conversion cost for Department 4 for May.
(c) Total and unit cost of Product F started in a prior period and finished in May.
(d) Total and unit cost of Product F started and finished in May.
(e) Total cost of goods transferred to finished goods.
(f) Work in process inventory for Department 4, May 31.
(g) Cost of goods sold (indicate number of units and unit costs).
(h) Finished goods inventory, May 31.
(2) Prepare a cost of production report for Department 4 for May.

17-762 **Pb. 17–34A.**

Entries for process cost system.

OBJ. 2,3,5,7

Holman Company manufactures Product T. Material A is placed in process in Department 1, where it is ground and partially refined. The output of Department 1 is transferred to Department 2, where Material B is added at the beginning of the process and the refining is completed. On November 1, Holman Company had the following inventories:

Finished Goods (8,000 units)	$72,000
Work in process—Department 1	—
Work in process—Department 2 (12,000 units, 1/3 completed)	90,400
Materials	26,400

Departmental accounts are maintained for factory overhead, and there is one service department, Factory Office. All inventories are costed by the first-in, first-out method. Manufacturing operations for November are summarized as follows:

(a) Materials purchased on account	$48,100
(b) Materials requisitioned for use:	
Material A	$26,080
Material B	21,600
Indirect materials—Department 1	1,700
Indirect materials—Department 2	1,240
(c) Labor used:	
Direct labor—Department 1	$53,900
Direct labor—Department 2	38,500
Indirect labor—Department 1	4,030
Indirect labor—Department 2	1,920
Factory Office	1,830
(d) Miscellaneous costs incurred on account:	
Department 1	$ 7,000
Department 2	4,100
Factory Office	2,100
(e) Expiration of prepaid expenses:	
Department 1	$ 1,050
Department 2	700
Factory Office	300
(f) Depreciation charged on plant assets:	
Department 1	$14,350
Department 2	12,250
Factory Office	900
(g) Distribution of Factory Office costs:	
Department 1	80% of total Factory Office costs
Department 2	20% of total Factory Office costs
(h) Application of factory overhead costs based on machine hours:	
Department 1	$32,340
Department 2	21,175

(i) Production costs transferred from Department 1 to Department 2:
21,600 units were fully processed, and there was no inventory of work in process in Department 1 at November 30.

(j) Production costs transferred from Department 2 to finished goods:
22,140 units, including the inventory at November 1, were fully processed. 11,460 units were 1/2 completed at November 30.

(k) Cost of goods sold during November:
25,200 units (Use the first-in, first-out method in crediting the finished goods account.)

Instructions:

(1) Prepare entries to record the foregoing operations. Identify each entry by letter.
(2) Compute the November 30 work in process inventory for Department 2.

Pb. 17–35A.
Cost of production report.
OBJ. 4,7

The data related to production during November of the current year for Department 2 of Holman Company are presented in Problem 17–34A.

Instructions:

Prepare a cost of production report for Department 2 for November.

Pb. 17–36A.
Entries for process cost system.
OBJ. 7

Irvin Manufacturing Inc. manufactures Product C. Materials are placed in production in Department 1, and after processing are transferred to Department 2 where more materials are added. The finished product emerges from Department 2. There is one service department: Maintenance and Repair.

There were no inventories of work in process at the beginning or at the end of July. Finished goods inventory at July 1 was 15,000 units of Product C at a total cost of $183,750.

Transactions related to manufacturing operations for July are summarized as follows:

(a) Materials purchased on account, $119,750.
(b) Materials requisitioned for use: Department 1, $76,100 ($67,700 entered directly into the product); Department 2, $36,700 ($28,400 entered directly into the product); Maintenance and Repair, $680.
(c) Labor costs incurred: Department 1, $95,180 ($88,200 entered directly into the product); Department 2, $103,560 ($94,000 entered directly into the product); Maintenance and Repair, $3,960.
(d) Miscellaneous costs and expenses incurred on account: Department 1, $14,150; Department 2, $12,340; and Maintenance and Repair, $2,060.
(e) Expiration of various prepaid expenses: Department 1, $1,260; Department 2, $920; and Maintenance and Repair, $340.
(f) Depreciation charged on plant assets: Department 1, $5,320; Department 2, $4,000; and Maintenance and Repair, $1,760.
(g) Maintenance and repair costs allocated on the basis of services rendered: Department 1, 60%; Department 2, 40%.
(h) Factory overhead applied to production based on machine hours: $44,100 and $37,600 for Departments 1 and 2 respectively.
(i) Output of Department 1: 30,000 units.
(j) Output of Department 2: 30,000 units of product C.
(k) Sales on account: 29,000 units of product C at $20. Credits to the finished goods account are to be made according to the first-in, first-out method.

Instructions:

Present entries to record the transactions, identifying each by letter. Include as an explanation for entry (k) the number of units and the unit costs for the product sold.

Pb. 17–37A.
Financial statements for process cost system.
OBJ. 7

The trial balance of Trier Products Inc. at July 31, the end of the first month of the current fiscal year, is as follows:

Trier Products Inc.
Trial Balance
July 31, 19--

Cash	47,900	
Marketable Securities	30,000	
Accounts Receivable	322,500	
Allowance for Doubtful Accounts		25,000
Finished Goods—Product A	62,500	
Finished Goods—Product B	60,800	
Work in Process—Department 1	19,850	
Work in Process—Department 2	8,750	
Work in Process—Department 3	12,700	
Materials	30,250	
Prepaid Insurance	7,400	
Office Supplies	3,570	
Land	52,500	
Buildings	525,000	
Accumulated Depreciation—Buildings		344,500
Machinery and Equipment	391,000	
Accumulated Depreciation—Machinery and Equipment		280,600
Office Equipment	30,700	
Accumulated Depreciation—Office Equipment		12,780
Patents	40,000	
Accounts Payable		97,750
Wages Payable		12,100
Income Tax Payable		1,200
Mortgage Note Payable (due 2001)		75,000
Common Stock ($50 par)		500,000
Retained Earnings		276,190
Sales		415,000
Cost of Goods Sold	287,500	
Factory Overhead—Department 1	250	
Factory Overhead—Department 2		310
Factory Overhead—Department 3	160	
Selling Expenses	60,250	
Administrative Expenses	39,400	
Interest Expense	750	
Interest Income		200
Income Tax	6,900	
	2,040,630	2,040,630

Instructions:

(1) Prepare an income statement.
(2) Prepare a retained earnings statement.
(3) Prepare a balance sheet.

Pb. 17–38A.
Unit cost of finished product by average cost method; cost of production report.
OBJ. 8

Waller Company manufactures Product Q by a series of four processes, all materials being introduced in Department 1. From Department 1, the materials pass through Departments 2, 3, 4, emerging as finished Product Q. All inventories are costed by the average cost method.

The balance in the account Work in Process—Department 4 was as follows on May 1:

Materials cost (3,000 units)	$18,600
Conversion costs (3,000 units, 1/4 completed)	9,600

The following costs were charged to Work in Process—Department 4 during May:

Direct materials transferred from Department 3:	
27,000 units at $6 per unit	$162,000
Direct labor	210,000
Factory overhead	163,900

During May, 28,000 units of Product Q were completed and the work in process inventory on May 31 was 2,000 units, 3/4 completed.

Instructions:

(1) Determine the following for Department 4, presenting computations in good order:
  (a) Average materials cost per unit.
  (b) Equivalent units of production in May.
  (c) Average conversion cost per unit for May.
  (d) Cost of goods finished during May.
  (e) Cost of work in process at May 31.
(2) Prepare a cost of production report for Department 4 for May.

MINI-CASE 17

H and S Inc. manufactures Product T by a series of four processes. All materials are placed in production in the Die Casting Department and, after processing, are transferred to the Tooling, Assembly, and Polishing Departments, emerging as finished Product T.

On January 1, the balance in the account Work in Process—Polishing was $213,000, determined as follows:

Direct materials: 15,000 units	$121,200
Direct labor: 15,000 units, 2/5 completed	73,440
Factory overhead: 15,000 units, 2/5 completed	18,360
Total	$213,000

The following costs were charged to Work in Process—Polishing during January:

Direct materials transferred from Assembly Dept.,	
145,000 units	$1,189,000
Direct labor	1,870,850
Factory overhead	330,150

During January, 144,000 units of T were completed and transferred to Finished Goods. On January 31, the inventory in the Polishing Department consisted of 16,000 units, one-fourth completed. All inventories are costed by the first-in, first-out method.

As a new cost accountant for H and S Inc., you have just received a phone call from Jill Stallings, the superintendent of the Polishing Department. She was extremely upset with the cost of production report, which she says does not balance. In addition, she commented:

"I give up! There reports are a waste of time. My department has always been the best department in the plant, so why should I bother with these reports? Just what purpose do they serve?"

The report to which Stallings referred is as follows:

H and S Inc.
Cost of Production Report—Polishing Department
For Month Ended January 31, 19--

Quantities:		
Charged to production:		
In process, January 1		6,000
Received from Assembly Department		145,000
Total units to be accounted for		151,000
Units accounted for:		
Transferred to finished goods		144,000
In process, January 31		4,000
Total units accounted for		148,000
Costs:		
Charged to production:		
In process, January 1		$213,000
January costs:		
Direct materials from Assembly Department ($8.20 per unit)		1,189,000
Conversion costs:		
Direct labor	$1,870,850	
Factory overhead	330,150	
Total conversion costs (14.20 per unit)		2,201,000
Total costs to be accounted for		$3,603,000
Costs allocated as follows:		
Transferred to finished goods:		
144,000 units at $22.40 ($8.20 + $14.20)		$3,225,600
In process, January 31:		
Materials (4,000 units × $8.20)	$ 32,800	
Conversion costs (4,000 units × $14.20)	56,800	
Total cost of inventory in process		89,600
Total costs accounted for		$3,315,200
Computations:		
Equivalent units of production:		
To process units in inventory in January 1: 15,000 units × 2/5		6,000
To process units started and completed in January		145,000
To process units in inventory on January 31 16,000 units × 1/4		4,000
Equivalent units of production		155,000
Unit conversion cost:		
$2,201,000 ÷ 155,000		$14.20

Instructions:

(1) Based upon the data for January, prepare a revised cost of production report for the Polishing Department.

(2) Assuming that all costs reported in the work in process account on January 1 were incurred in the preceding month, determine the unit direct materials cost and the unit conversion cost for December.

(3) Based on (2), determine the change in the unit direct materials cost and unit conversion cost for January as compared to December.
(4) Based on (3), what are some possible explanations for the changing unit costs?
(5) Describe how you would explain to Stallings that cost of production reports are useful.

ANSWERS TO SELF-EXAMINATION QUESTIONS

1. C The process cost system is most appropriate for a business where manufacturing is conducted by continuous operations and involves a series of uniform production processes, such as the processing of crude oil (answer C). The job order cost system is most appropriate for a business where the product is made to customer's specifications, such as custom furniture manufacturing (answer A) and commerical building construction (answer B).
2. C The manufacturing costs that are necessary to convert direct materials into finished products are referred to as conversion costs. The conversion costs include direct labor and factory overhead (answer C).
3. B The number of units that could have been produced from start to finish during a period is termed equivalent units. The 4,875 equivalent units (answer B) is determined as follows:

To process units in inventory on May 1: 1,000 × 1/4	250
To process units started and completed in May: 5,500 units − 1,000 units	4,500
To process units in inventory on May 31: 500 units × 1/4	125
Equivalent units of production in May	4,875

4. A The conversion costs (direct labor and factory overhead) totaling $48,750 are divided by the number of equivalent units (4,875) to determine the unit conversion cost of $10 (answer A).
5. D Service departments, such as factory office (answer A), Power plant (answer B), and Maintenance (answer C), perform services for the processing departments.

CHAPTER 18

CHAPTER OBJECTIVES

1 Describe the managerial accounting objectives of cost allocation.

2 Describe the basic principles of cost allocation.

3 Describe and illustrate service department cost allocation using the direct method and the step method.

4 Describe and illustrate the use of predetermined factory overhead rates and the potential for distorting product costs.

5 Describe and illustrate activity-based costing.

6 Describe cost allocation in just-in-time manufacturing systems.

COST ALLOCATION & ACTIVITY-BASED COSTING

Cost allocation is the assignment of costs to a cost object. A **cost object** is an activity, such as a product, service, department, or job, to which costs are allocated. Cost objects are determined by management, depending upon its decision-making needs. For example, in allocating costs for decisions involving product prices, the cost object would be a product.

Chapters 16 and 17 described and illustrated traditional cost allocations used in job order and process cost accounting systems. These chapters discussed the allocation of manufacturing (factory) overhead costs using predetermined rates, the allocation of service department costs, and the allocation of production costs to joint products and by-products. This chapter continues this discussion by focusing more specifically on cost allocation objectives and principles, and how improper cost allocations can distort product costs. Such distortions of costs can lead to disastrous results if such costs are relied upon by management for decision-making purposes. For example, if management sets product prices based upon distorted cost estimates, products may be significantly underpriced or overpriced. As a result, an enterprise's management might make incorrect decisions regarding which products to retain and which to discontinue.

This chapter also describes and illustrates the activity-based costing approach that many companies have used to achieve accurate cost allocations. The chapter concludes with a discussion of cost allocation in a just-in-time manufacturing system.

OBJECTIVES OF COST ALLOCATION

OBJECTIVE 1
Describe the managerial accounting objectives of cost allocation.

The allocation of costs may have one or more of the following objectives:

1. Evaluating manufacturing processes
2. Costing products
3. Motivating managers
4. Valuing inventories

From a managerial accounting perspective, the first three objectives are most important for planning and control. The fourth objective of valuing inventories is primarily a financial accounting objective that is necessary for the preparation of financial statements.[1]

Evaluating Manufacturing Processes

Management's evaluation of the manufacturing processes may depend upon first-hand observations as well as reports that summarize and describe the manufacturing operations. One summary report that is often used in evaluating manufacturing processes compares actual costs with budgeted (estimated) costs. These reports, which may include allocated costs, highlight unexpected cost differences for investigation. Such differences are often caused by inefficiencies within the manufacturing process. When the investigation indicates that the underlying causes are controllable, management may take appropriate action.

For cost reports to be useful in evaluating manufacturing processes, the cost object of each report must be clearly defined by management. The cost object could be a process, an operation, a product, a department, or a machine. Only those costs that are allocated to the cost object should be included within the report. The costs allocated are costs that are traceable to the cost object or are directly influenced by the cost object. For example, if the cost object is a robot, power costs could be properly allocated using metered kilowatt-hours of usage. In contrast, office salaries should not be allocated to the equipment, because they normally cannot be directly traced to individual pieces of equipment.

For reports to be useful for evaluating manufacturing processes, they must also be timely. The timeliness of a report depends upon the cost object and management's decision-making needs. For example, reports for a robot could be generated hourly, and management could make immediate changes in the manufacturing processes. In contrast, a report for a research and development department might be generated quarterly or annually, and changes in that department would most likely be long-range in nature.

Costing Products

Costs are allocated to products for the decision-making needs of management. For example, management uses product costs to determine sales prices, to determine the product mix, in deciding whether to introduce or discontinue products, and in deciding whether to accept special orders.

The manner in which costs are allocated for product costing purposes depends upon the decisions that must be made. For example, when management is deciding upon a normal sales price, all manufacturing costs would be allocated to the product, since all costs plus a reasonable profit must be covered by the sales price. If management is considering a one-time sale at a special price to a foreign distributor, only variable manufacturing costs and other costs directly traceable to the order would be allocated. In this situation, selling the product at a price that exceeds these costs would add to profits.

---

[1] For additional discussion of cost allocation objectives, see *Relevance Lost*, by H. Thomas Johnson and Robert S. Kaplan (Boston: Harvard Business School Press, 1987), and *Statements on Management Accounting (Statement 4B)*, "Allocation of Service and Administrative Costs" (Montvale, New Jersey: National Association of Accountants, 1985).

Motivating Managers

Cost allocations can also motivate managers to act in the company's best interests. For example, service department costs can be allocated to producing departments, as described and illustrated later in this chapter. The allocation of service department costs to producing departments reminds production managers of their responsibility to use the service departments wisely. Without any allocation of service department costs, the production manager's cost for using the service activities would be zero. Therefore, production managers might tend to overconsume services provided by service departments.

To illustrate, assume that a production department uses electricity provided by the Power Department. If the production department is not allocated a share of the Power Department's costs of generating electricity, the production managers would not be motivated to efficiently use electricity.

Service department cost allocations also might motivate production managers to more closely monitor the quality of service department activities, especially if the production managers have the authority to acquire the services from outside sources. In turn, service department managers might be motivated to be more sensitive and more responsive to the needs of the production departments.

Valuing Inventories

In valuing inventories for financial statements, costs are allocated according to generally accepted accounting principles. The illustrations of job order and process costing in Chapters 16 and 17 were consistent with this objective. However, cost allocation for valuing inventories may not be appropriate for the other cost allocation objectives. Therefore, managerial accountants must be careful when using inventory valuation allocations for purposes of evaluating manufacturing processes, costing products, or motivating managers. The remainder of this chapter focuses on cost allocations for these latter three objectives.

PRINCIPLES OF COST ALLOCATION

OBJECTIVE 2
Describe the basic principles of cost allocation.

Consistent with the cost allocation objectives discussed above, three basic principles of cost allocation are as follows:

1. To the extent possible, the activity that causes the cost to be incurred should be used as a basis for allocation.
2. Budgeted (planned) costs rather than actual costs should normally be allocated.
3. Fixed costs and variable costs should be allocated separately.

Cost Drivers

Using the activity that causes a cost as the basis for allocation achieves the most accurate allocation of costs. Such an activity base is referred to as a **cost driver.** For example, kilowatt-hours used by production departments might be an appropriate activity base (cost driver) for allocating the costs of a power department. Other examples of costs and possible cost drivers are as follows:

Cost	Cost Driver
Materials handling costs	Amount of material moved
Cost of reworking	Number of units reworked
Machine maintenance costs	Number of machine hours
Energy costs	Number of kilowatt-hours
Quality control costs	Number of inspections
Product design and engineering costs	Number of component parts
Purchasing costs	Number of transactions
Cafeteria services costs	Number of employees
Supervisory costs	Direct labor hours

The preceding examples are illustrative only and other cost drivers could be appropriate for the preceding costs. For example, if each movement of material involved moving approximately the same amount of material the same distance, the number of material moves might also be an appropriate cost driver for materials handling costs.

Budgeted Costs and Actual Costs

Budgeted costs are carefully estimated costs which management plans to incur. Normally, budgeted or planned costs, rather than actual costs, should be allocated for purposes of evaluating manufacturing processes, costing products, and motivating managers. The allocation of actual costs would pass operating inefficiencies or efficiencies on to the cost object receiving the allocation. As a result, a fundamental principle of performance evaluation would be violated. This principle requires that managers be held responsible only for costs they can control in their department, and not for costs resulting from the operating effectiveness or ineffectiveness of other departments.

Fixed Costs and Variable Costs

Fixed costs are different from variable costs. Specifically, fixed costs remain constant in total dollar amount as the level of activity changes, and variable costs vary in total dollar amount as the level of activity changes. Thus, since their cost drivers are often different, fixed and variable costs should be allocated separately.

The identification of an appropriate cost driver for a variable cost is usually easier than for a fixed cost, because it is easier to observe the change in a variable cost as the activity changes. For example, when coal is used in generating power, the total cost of coal increases as the number of kilowatt-hours produced increase. Thus, kilowatt-hours used would be an appropriate cost driver for allocating the cost of coal.

Appropriate cost drivers for fixed costs often relate to the long-term needs of the business. For example the initial size of a power plant is normally determined by estimating the long-term power capacity demands (needs) of the various service and producing departments. In such a case, it would be reasonable to base the allocation of the fixed costs associated with the power plant on the *original* capacity estimates for each department. Thus, kilowatt-hours of capacity would be an appropriate cost driver for allocating the power plant's fixed costs.

To illustrate the allocation of fixed and variable costs, assume that a power department provides power to two producing departments, P1 and P2. The total budgeted fixed cost for the power plant is $100,000 and variable costs are budgeted at $.05 per kilowatt-hour (kwh). Also assume the following capacity and actual power usage for Departments P1 and P2:

	Dept. P1	Dept. P2
Capacity	2 500 000 kwh	1 500 000 kwh
Actual usage..........	1 500 000 kwh	1 500 000 kwh

Using actual kilowatt-hour usage for the variable costs and capacity for the fixed costs, the power plant cost allocations are as follows:

	Dept. P1	Dept. P2
Variable costs ($.05 per kwh):		
1 500 000 kwh used × $.05................	$ 75,000	
1 500 000 kwh used × $.05................		$ 75,000
Fixed costs ($100,000):		
5/8* × $100,000.........................	62,500	
3/8* × $100,000.........................		37,500
Total allocation	$137,500	$112,500

*Allocation ratios:
Total capacity = 2 500 000 kwh + 1 500 000 kwh = 4 000 000 kwh
Dept. P1 allocation ratio: 2 500 000 kwh ÷ 4 000 000 kwh = 5/8
Dept. P2 allocation ratio: 1 500 000 kwh ÷ 4 000 000 kwh = 3/8

If both the variable and fixed power plant costs had been allocated on the basis of actual kilowatt-hour usage, each department would have been allocated the same amounts of cost ($125,000), determined as follows:

	Dept. P1	Dept. P2
Variable costs ($.05 per kwh):		
1 500 000 kwh used × $.05................	$ 75,000	
1 500 000 kwh used × $.05................		$ 75,000
Fixed costs ($100,000):		
1/2* × $100,000.........................	50,000	
1/2* × $100,000.........................		50,000
Total allocation	$125,000	$125,000

*Allocation ratios:
Actual total usage = 1 500 000 kwh + 1 500 000 kwh = 3 000 000 kwh
Dept. P1 allocation ratio: 1 500 000 kwh ÷ 3 000 000 kwh = 1/2
Dept. P2 allocation ratio: 1 500 000 kwh ÷ 3 000 000 kwh = 1/2

When the variable and fixed costs are not allocated separately, Department P2 is allocated $12,500 more power costs ($125,000 − $112,500), even though P2 operated at its original estimate of capacity. Additional costs are allocated to P2 solely because P1 failed to operate at its original estimate of capacity.

SERVICE DEPARTMENT COST ALLOCATION

OBJECTIVE 3
Describe and illustrate service department cost allocation, using the direct method and the step method.

The allocation of service department costs was briefly discussed in Chapter 17. In that discussion, only one service department was illustrated, and its costs were allocated directly to three production departments. The following paragraphs extend the discussion of Chapter 17 by describing two methods of allocating service department costs when more than one service department exists and the service departments render services to one another (interservice activities). These methods, which are widely used in practice, are the direct method and the step method. They differ in how they handle interservice activities. If there are no interservice activities, both methods yield the same cost allocations.

Direct Method

The **direct method** of service department cost allocation does not recognize any interservice activities in the allocation process. Thus, no service department costs are allocated to other service departments. Service department costs are only allocated to production departments.

To illustrate, assume that Quill Inc. has two production departments, Assembly and Finishing, and two service departments, Power and Maintenance. Budgeted cost data and the relevant cost drivers for allocating Power and Maintenance costs to the Assembly and Finishing Departments are as follows:

Departmental costs:	
Assembly Department	$300,000
Finishing Department	850,000
Power Department	400,000
Maintenance Department	150,000
Cost drivers:	
Power Department (kilowatt-hours):	
Assembly Department	6 080 kwh
Finishing Department	9 120
Maintenance Department	800
Total	16 000 kwh
Maintenance Department (machine hours):	
Assembly Department	1,050 hrs.
Finishing Department	2,450
Power Department	1,500
Total	5,000 hrs.

Using the direct method, the Power Department and Maintenance Department costs are allocated directly to the Assembly and Finishing departments. The cost allocated to each production department is computed using the percentage of the cost driver used by the department. Since interservice activities are ignored by the direct method, the allocation percentages are computed as follows, without regard for the amounts of the cost drivers used by other service departments:

Cost Driver Allocation Percentages—Direct Method

	Kilowatt-Hours	Percent Used
Power Department:		
Assembly Department	6 080	40%
Finishing Department	9 120	60
Total	15 200	100%

	Machine Hours	Percent Used
Maintenance Department:		
Assembly Department	1,050	30%
Finishing Department	2,450	70
Total	3,500	100%

The cost allocations using the direct method are as follows:

Direct Method of Allocation

	Power Dept.	Maintenance Dept.	Assembly Dept.	Finishing Dept.
Departmental costs	$400,000	$150,000	$300,000	$ 850,000
Allocated costs:				
Power Dept.	(400,000)		160,000*	240,000*
Maintenance Dept.		(150,000)	45,000**	105,000**
Total costs	$ 0	$ 0	$505,000	$1,195,000

*Power Dept. allocations:
Assembly Dept.: $400,000 × 40% = $160,000
Finishing Dept.: $400,000 × 60% = $240,000
**Maintenance Dept. allocations:
Assembly Dept.: $150,000 × 30% = $45,000
Finishing Dept.: $150,000 × 70% = $105,000

Step Method

The **step method**, sometimes referred to as the **sequential method**, recognizes some interservice activities. As the name implies, the step method allocates service department costs in a step-wise fashion. First, the costs of the service department rendering the largest amount of service to other departments are allocated to other service departments as well as to production departments. As a practical matter, the service department rendering the largest amount of service to other departments is assumed to be that department with the largest amount of costs to be allocated.

The next step is to allocate the costs of the service department rendering the second largest amount of service. This process continues until all the service department costs have been allocated. No service department costs are allocated to a service department whose costs have already been allocated.

To illustrate, assume the same data for Quill Inc. that was used for the direct method, where $400,000 of Power Department costs and $150,000 of Maintenance Department costs are to be allocated. Since the Power Department has the larger amount of costs, its costs are allocated first, followed by the allocation of Maintenance Department costs. The allocation percentages are computed as follows, using the appropriate cost drivers:

Cost Driver Allocation Percentages—Step Method

	Kilowatt-Hours	Percent Used
Power Department:		
Assembly Department	6 080	38%
Finishing Department	9 120	57
Maintenance Department	800	5
Total	16 000	100%

	Machine Hours	Percent Used
Maintenance Department:		
Assembly Department	1,050	30%
Finishing Department	2,450	70
Total	3,500	100%

The cost allocations using the step method are as follows:

Step Method of Allocation

	Power Dept.	Maintenance Dept.	Assembly Dept.	Finishing Dept.
Departmental costs	$400,000	$150,000	$300,000	$ 850,000
Allocated costs:				
Power Dept.	(400,000)	20,000*	152,000*	228,000*
Maintenance Dept.		(170,000)	51,000**	119,000**
Total costs	$ 0	$ 0	$503,000	$1,197,000

*Power Dept. allocations:
Maintenance Dept.: $400,000 × 5% = $20,000
Assembly Dept.: $400,000 × 38% = $152,000
Finishing Dept.: $400,000 × 57% = $228,000
** Maintenance Dept. allocations:
Assembly Dept.: $170,000 × 30% = $51,000
Finishing Dept.: $170,000 × 70% = $119,000

In the preceding illustration, the Maintenance Department is allocated $20,000 of the Power Department's costs. This allocation reflects the Maintenance Department's use of 5% of the kilowatt-hours provided by the Power Department. The cost allocated from the Maintenance Department is then $170,000, which is the total of its own costs of $150,000 and the $20,000 cost allocated from the Power Department. Because the step method recognizes some of the interservice activities, it is considered more accurate than the direct method. However, when the difference in the two allocations is relatively minor, the simpler direct method is often used for practical purposes.[2]

[2] A third method of service department cost allocation, the reciprocal method, is illustrated in the appendix at the end of this chapter.

OBJECTIVE 4
Describe and illustrate the use of predetermined factory overhead rates and the potential for distorting product costs.

As discussed in preceding chapters, manufacturing (factory) overhead costs may be allocated by the use of predetermined rates. Such rates are often determined and the manufacturing overhead applied on either a plant-wide or a departmental basis. In introducing manufacturing operations in the context of job order cost systems in Chapter 16, predetermined plant-wide overhead rates were used. In Chapter 17, departmental overhead rates were used in illustrating process cost systems.

The following paragraphs further discuss manufacturing overhead and illustrate its allocation among several products by the use of plant-wide and departmental rates. The appropriate uses of these rates and the product cost distortion that may result when the rates are improperly used are also discussed.

Manufacturing Overhead in Product Costing

As discussed previously, companies may use predetermined overhead rates to assign or allocate manufacturing overhead costs to products. When only one product is produced, this allocation is relatively easy. Because all the overhead costs are caused by the single product, all the budgeted overhead costs must be allocated to that product. Thus, the predetermined overhead rate is computed by dividing the total budgeted overhead costs by the number of units to be produced.

When several products are produced, each product must be allocated the manufacturing overhead costs caused by its manufacture. Improper allocations will distort product costs, which can lead to incorrect management decisions in such matters as the best mix of products to sell or whether to discontinue a product line.

Plant-Wide Overhead Rate

When a plant-wide rate is used, the total manufacturing overhead is applied to all products by that single rate. This rate is usually determined by using a volume-related activity base (cost driver), such as units produced, machine hours, direct labor hours, or direct labor dollars. To illustrate, assume that Howard Inc. manufactures two products, L and M, using two production departments, Assembly and Finishing, and two service departments, Power and Quality Control. The following overhead costs are budgeted for the production departments. The power and quality control costs are allocated costs from the service departments. The "other" costs are manufacturing overhead other than power and quality control costs, such as insurance and property taxes on machinery, indirect materials, and indirect labor.

	Assembly Dept.	Finishing Dept.	Total
Overhead costs:			
Power	$42,000	$168,000	$210,000
Quality control	30,000	30,000	60,000
Other	24,000	24,000	48,000
Total	$96,000	$222,000	$318,000

The production of each product requires 15 machine hours per unit. Thus, 60,000 machine hours were used to produce 4,000 units of Product L, and 240,000 machine hours were used to produce 16,000 units of Product M. If Howard Inc. uses machine hours as the activity base (cost driver) for a plant-wide overhead rate, the rate is computed by dividing the total budgeted manufacturing overhead ($318,000) by the total machine hours (300,000), as follows:

Plant-wide overhead rate = $318,000 ÷ 300,000 machine hours
Plant-wide overhead rate = $1.06 per machine hour

Using the plant-wide rate of $1.06 per machine hour, the manufacturing overhead cost per unit for each product is determined as follows:

	Product L	Product M
Allocated overhead costs:		
60,000 machine hrs. × $1.06	$63,600	
240,000 machine hrs. × $1.06		$254,400
Total units produced	4,000	16,000
Overhead cost per unit	$15.90	$15.90

In the illustration, the same number of machine hours per unit (15) are required for each product. Therefore, when machine hours are used as the allocation base, the overhead cost per unit for both Product L and Product M is the same, $15.90.

The use of a plant-wide overhead rate such as the one illustrated above assumes that the activities causing overhead costs are the same across all departments and products. In the illustration, if machine hours do not cause the incurrence of overhead costs in both the Assembly Department and the Finishing Department, overhead costs could be misallocated and product costs could be distorted. For example, if one of the departments was labor-intensive while the other department was capital-intensive, the activities causing overhead costs would likely be different between the two departments. The capital-intensive department would likely have high machine-related overhead costs, such as repairs and maintenance costs. The labor-intensive department would have more labor-related overhead costs, such as supervisory costs.

Departmental Overhead Rates

When production departments differ significantly in their manufacturing processes, overhead costs are likely to be incurred differently in each department. In such cases, overhead costs may be more accurately allocated by the use of departmental overhead rates than by a plant-wide rate. Management must determine whether this increased accuracy justifies the additional expense of using departmental rates.

To illustrate the use of departmental overhead rates, assume that the Assembly Department for Howard Inc. in the preceding illustration relies heavily upon direct labor, while the Finishing Department is primarily automated. In this situation, direct labor hours would be an appropriate activity base (cost driver) for the Assembly Department, and machine hours would be an appropriate activity base (cost driver) for the Finishing Department. The following direct labor hours and machine hours are budgeted for each production department:

	Direct Labor Hours	Machine Hours
Assembly Department:		
Product L	1,200	20,000
Product M	6,800	80,000
	8,000	100,000
Finishing Department:		
Product L	800	40,000
Product M	1,200	160,000
	2,000	200,000
Total	10,000	300,000

The Assembly Department utilizes 80% (8,000 ÷ 10,000) of the total direct labor hours. In contrast, the Finishing Department utilizes two-thirds (200,000 ÷ 300,000) of the total machine hours.

The Assembly Department's overhead rate is computed by dividing its total budgeted overhead costs ($96,000) by its total budgeted direct labor hours (8,000), as follows:

Assembly Department overhead rate = $96,000 ÷ 8,000 direct labor hours
Assembly Department overhead rate = $12 per direct labor hour

The Finishing Department's overhead rate is computed by dividing its total budgeted overhead costs ($222,000) by its total budgeted machine hours (200,000), as follows:

Finishing Department overhead rate = $222,000 ÷ 200,000 machine hours
Finishing Department overhead rate = $1.11 per machine hour

Using the departmental overhead rates, the manufacturing overhead cost per unit for each product is determined as follows:

	Product L	Product M
Allocated overhead costs:		
Assembly Department:		
1,200 hrs. × $12	$14,400	
6,800 hrs. × $12		$81,600
Finishing Department:		
40,000 hrs. × $1.11	44,400	
160,000 hrs. × $1.11		177,600
Total allocated overhead	$58,800	$259,200
Total units produced	4,000	16,000
Overhead cost per unit	$14.70	$16.20

The overhead costs per unit differ by $1.50 ($16.20 − $14.70). This difference is caused by using different activity bases for allocating the overhead costs of the Assembly Department (direct labor hours) and the Finishing Department (machine hours). Note also that the overhead costs per unit of Product L and Product M, determined using departmental rates, differ from the per unit amount ($15.90) determined using a plant-wide rate. This difference was also caused by using different activity bases for the plant-wide and departmental rates.

Distortions of Product Costs

If the bases used to allocate manufacturing overhead costs do not reflect the underlying causes of the overhead, misallocations may occur and product costs may be distorted. For example, Rockwell International conducted a special study after one of its best-selling axles had begun losing market share. The study found that incorrect factory overhead cost allocations had "overcosted" its highest-volume axle by roughly 20%, while underestimating the cost of other axles by as much as 40%. Since pricing was based on these estimated costs, Rockwell had underpriced its low-volume axles and overpriced its high-volume axle. As a result, competitors had begun to lure customers away from Rockwell's best-selling, high-volume axles.[3]

Manufacturing overhead may be a major portion of the total manufacturing costs for some companies, such as those that use automated, flexible manufacturing systems to produce a variety of products. In this environment, the use of plant-wide and department overhead rates may not be appropriate.

The use of a plant-wide rate assumes that all overhead is directly related to or caused by one activity representing the entire plant. In many manufacturing systems, this assumption is not realistic. Likewise, the use of departmental overhead rates assumes that all departmental overhead is directly related to or caused by one cost driver for each department. In more sophisticated and complex manufacturing systems, departmental overhead costs are usually caused by a variety of cost drivers. Thus, in today's manufacturing environment, the use of one allocation base in a plant or a department may cause product costs to be distorted.

To illustrate such distortions, the following overhead cost data from the preceding illustrations for Howard Inc. are used:

	Assembly Dept.	Finishing Dept.	Total
Overhead costs:			
Power	$42,000	$168,000	$210,000
Quality control	30,000	30,000	60,000
Other	24,000	24,000	48,000
Total	$96,000	$222,000	$318,000

The proper allocation of the power, quality control, and other overhead costs to each product requires the identification of the activities (cost drivers) which are directly related to or cause the overhead to be incurred. For example, it is likely that the power costs are directly related to the number of kilowatt-hours of power generated, and the quality control costs are directly related to the number of inspections made. Therefore, kilowatt-hours is used

[3] "Accounting Bores You? Wake Up," Ford S. Worthy, *Fortune*, October 12, 1987.

as the cost driver for power costs, and the number of inspections is used as the cost driver for quality control costs. Finally, the cost driver for the other overhead is assumed to be the number of units produced in each department. The relevant data for these cost drivers for each product are follows:

	Kilowatt-Hours Used	Number of Inspections
Product L (4,000 units):		
Assembly Department	56 000	300
Finishing Department	28 000	300
	84 000	600
Product M (16,000 units):		
Assembly Department	224 000	450
Finishing Department	112 000	450
	336 000	900
Total (20,000 units)	420 000	1,500

Based upon the cost drivers that were identified, the overhead rates for the power, quality control, and other overhead costs are as follows. Each overhead rate is determined by dividing the overhead cost by the amount of the cost driver.

Power overhead rate = $210,000 ÷ 420 000 kilowatt-hours
Power overhead rate = $ .50 per kilowatt-hour

Quality control overhead rate = $60,000 ÷ 1,500 inspections
Quality control overhead rate = $40 per inspection

Other overhead rate = $48,000 ÷ 20,000 units
Other overhead rate = $2.40 per unit

Using the above overhead rates, the overhead cost per unit for each product is determined as follows:

	Product L	Product M
Allocated overhead costs:		
Power Department overhead:		
84 000 kwh × $ .50	$42,000	
336 000 kwh × $ .50		$168,000
Quality Control Department overhead:		
600 inspections × $40	24,000	
900 inspections × $40		36,000
Other overhead:		
4,000 units × $2.40	9,600	
16,000 units × $2.40		38,400
Total allocated overhead	$75,600	$242,400
Total units produced	4,000	16,000
Overhead cost per unit	$18.90	$15.15

The overhead costs per unit, based upon the plant-wide rate, the departmental rates, and the proper cost drivers for Howard Inc., are summarized as follows:

	Product L	Product M
Overhead costs per unit:		
Plant-wide rate	$15.90	$15.90
Departmental rates	14.70	16.20
Proper rates	18.90	15.15

In the illustration, the use of the plant-wide and departmental overhead rates distorted the cost of each product. These distortions were caused by using inappropriate cost drivers. For example, the plant-wide rate allocated 20% of the overhead to Product L, which used 20% of the machine hours (60,000 hours ÷ 300,000 hours), and 80% to Product M, which used 80% of the machine hours (240,000 hours ÷ 300,000 hours). However, as measured by the number of inspections, Product L incurred 40% (600 inspections ÷ 1,500 inspections) of the quality control costs. Thus, the use of the plant-wide rate underallocated the quality control costs to Product L and overallocated the quality control costs to Product M. The use of the departmental rates caused a similar distortion.

When plant-wide and departmental overhead rates are used, the cost drivers are normally volume-based. However, some overhead costs are not directly related to volume-based cost drivers, such as units produced, machine hours, or direct labor hours. Thus, the use of plant-wide or departmental overhead rates has the potential to distort product costs significantly. Such distortions tend to allocate more overhead to the high-volume products and less overhead to the low-volume products, as in the Rockwell International example described on page 780.

ACTIVITY-BASED COSTING

OBJECTIVE 5
Describe and illustrate activity-based costing.

When the use of plant-wide or departmental overhead rates significantly distorts product costs, as discussed in the preceding paragraphs, companies may use activity-based costing. **Activity-based costing (ABC)** is a cost allocation method that initially traces or allocates costs to activities. In this first stage of product costing, manufacturing overhead costs are allocated to cost pools that represent activities, such as machine usage, inspections, and production setups. In contrast, in the first stage of product costing using traditional methods, manufacturing overhead costs are allocated to cost pools that represent individual departments or operations. For example, in the process cost illustration in Chapter 17, the manufacturing costs were initially recorded by the service and production departments. These departments were the cost objects, to which responsibility for the costs was allocated.

In the second stage of product costing, costs are traced or allocated to the finished products. In activity-based costing, the overhead cost pools are allocated to products on the basis of the number of the activities, such as number of production setups, involved in each product's manufacture. The traditional methods allocate overhead from the departmental cost pools to the products, using various predetermined rates. Although both activity-based costing and the traditional methods allocate costs to products in this second stage, activity-based costing uses many cost drivers rather than the typical one or two used by the traditional methods.

To illustrate the application of activity-based costing, assume that Weiss Inc. manufactures two products, X and Y. The production of these products requires four overhead activities—power, maintenance, quality control, and setup. The following budgeted costs for these activities are to be allocated to Products X and Y:

	Overhead Costs
Power	$360,000
Maintenance	105,000
Quality control	51,000
Setup	84,000
Total	$600,000

In applying activity-based costing, the overhead activities must be analyzed to determine how the costs for these activities are incurred. That is, the cost drivers for each activity must be identified. For Weiss Inc., the appropriate cost drivers are as follows:

	Cost Driver
Power	Kilowatt-hours
Maintenance	Machine hours
Quality control	Number of inspections
Setup	Number of setups

The amounts of the cost drivers for each product are as follows:

	Kilowatt-Hours	Machine Hours	Number of Inspections	Number of Production Setups
Product X	800 000	10,000	400	48
Product Y	3 200 000	40,000	600	72
Total	4 000 000	50,000	1,000	120

Based upon the preceding data, the overhead rates for each overhead activity are determined by dividing each overhead cost by its cost driver as indicated below.

Power overhead rate = $360,000 ÷ 4 000 000 kilowatt-hours
Power overhead rate = $.09 per kilowatt-hour

Maintenance overhead rate = $105,000 ÷ 50,000 machine hours
Maintenance overhead rate = $2.10 per machine hour

Quality control overhead rate = $51,000 ÷ 1,000 inspections
Quality control overhead rate = $51 per inspection

Setup overhead rate = $84,000 ÷ 120 setups
Setup overhead rate = $700 per setup

Using the above overhead rates, the overhead costs would be allocated to Products X and Y as shown below:

	Product X	Product Y
Overhead costs:		
Power:		
800,000 hrs. × $ .09	$ 72,000	
3,200,000 hrs. × $ .09		$288,000
Maintenance:		
10,000 hrs. × $2.10	21,000	
40,000 hrs. × $2.10		84,000
Quality control:		
400 insp. × $51	20,400	
600 insp. × $51		30,600
Setup:		
48 setups × $700	33,600	
72 setups × $700		50,400
Total	$147,000	$453,000

For Weiss Inc. a different cost driver was used for each overhead activity. In practice, many companies could identify a large number of overhead activities and it could become very costly to allocate each activity separately. For example, the preceding illustration assumed that kilowatt-hours could be traced directly to individual products. In practice, it would be very costly, if not impossible, to do so. In such cases, overhead activities may be grouped together in cost pools, and each cost pool would be allocated using a primary cost driver related to the costs within that pool. This reduces the cost of measuring a large number of cost drivers and simplifies the allocation process.

To illustrate, the percentage of each cost driver used by Product X and Product Y for Weiss Inc. is as follows:

	Kilowatt-Hours	Machine Hours	Number of Inspections	Number of Production Setups
Product X	20%*	20%**	40%***	40%****
Product Y	80 *	80 **	60 ***	60 ****
Total	100%	100%	100%	100%

*800 000 ÷ 4 000 000 (Product X) and 3 200 000 ÷ 4 000 000 (Product Y)
**10,000 ÷ 50,000 (Product X) and 40,000 ÷ 50,000 (Product Y)
***400 ÷ 1,000 (Product X) and 600 ÷ 1,000 (Product Y)
****48 ÷ 120 (Product X) and 72 ÷ 120 (Product Y)

Although each overhead cost could be allocated separately on the basis of the cost drivers identified, as illustrated previously, the expense of the allocation would be reduced by grouping activities into appropriate cost pools. These cost pools are identified in such a way that the costs within the pool are related to one primary cost driver. As shown in the above table, Product X consumes or uses 20% of the power activity measure of kilowatt-hours and 20% of the maintenance activity measure of machine hours. Similarly, Product X uses 40% of the quality control and setups activity measures. Since power and maintenance have common kilowatt-hours and machine hours usage rates of 20% for Product X and 80% for Product Y, they can be pooled and applied to the two products, using either one of the activity measures. Similarly, the quality control and setup activities may be pooled and allocated, using either the number of inspections or the number of production setups. The activity measure selected should be the one that is the least costly to identify, since the primary purpose of using cost pools is to reduce the expense of allocating overhead.

To continue the illustration, assume that Weiss Inc. uses machine hours to allocate the power and maintenance cost pool, and production setups to allocate the quality control and setup cost pool. The overhead rates for each of these cost pools would be as follows:

Power and Maintenance cost pool:		
Overhead costs:		
Power	$360,000	
Maintenance	105,000	
Total	$465,000	
Total machine hours	50,000	hours
Overhead rate	$9.30	per machine hour
Quality Control and Setup cost pool:		
Overhead costs:		
Quality control	$ 51,000	
Setup	84,000	
Total	$135,000	
Total number of production setups	120	setups
Overhead rate	$1,125	per setup

Using these rates, the overhead costs are allocated as follows. Note that the total overhead allocated to each product is the same amount that was allocated when four separate cost drivers were used, as illustrated on page 784.

	Product X	Product Y
Power and maintenance:		
10,000 hrs. × $9.30	$ 93,000	
40,000 hrs. × $9.30		$372,000
Quality control and setup:		
48 setups × $1,125	54,000	
72 setups × $1,125		81,000
Total	$147,000	$453,000

Activity-based costing may be more expensive to implement than plant-wide or departmental overhead rates because of the need to measure and accumulate more cost pools and cost drivers. However, activity-based costing usually costs products more accurately. This increased accuracy allows management to make better decisions in such matters as product pricing. In an environment where many companies manufacture a variety of diverse products, accurate product costs are essential to long-term profitability.

An additional benefit of activity-based costing is that it requires managers to focus their attention on activities that create overhead. As a result, management may often be able to identify activities that add value to the product, such as power supplied to automated equipment, as well as those activities that do not add value to the product. Managers can then focus their efforts on reducing or eliminating the non-value-adding activities. For example, the movement of materials among work stations is considered a non-value-adding activity. To reduce this movement of materials, a company could redesign its plant layout or reorganize the work stations.

COST ALLOCATION IN JUST-IN-TIME MANUFACTURING SYSTEMS

OBJECTIVE 6
Describe cost allocation in just-in-time manufacturing systems.

Many manufacturers have installed just-in-time manufacturing systems. These systems, which were mentioned briefly in Chapters 15 and 17, have important implications for cost allocation.

Product costing in a just-in-time manufacturing system is simpler and more accurate than for other manufacturing systems. Many of the traditional service department functions are performed in work centers, which are organized by combining processing functions. This arrangement generally simplifies the tracing of costs to products. Other overhead costs such as materials storage may be reduced or eliminated entirely. For example, most just-in-time systems provide for materials to be delivered directly from outside vendors to the work center. Hence, the need for a central storage function is decreased. When a work center processes only one product, all the costs traceable to that work center, such as depreciation on the work center equipment, become costs of that product. When combined with an activity-based cost system, just-in-time manufacturing systems can provide more accurate product costs.

Inventories are reduced to minimal levels in just-in-time manufacturing systems. Thus, the inventory valuation objective of cost allocation is typically not important in such systems. For example, work in process equivalent units under a process cost system would not be computed, since little, if any, work in process would exist. A cost of production report would simply list inputs and finished products.

Finally, with the emphasis on flexibility and fast response to customer orders, many just-in-time manufacturing systems are highly automated. In many cases, this increased automation reduces direct labor to such a small percentage of total product cost that all labor is treated as overhead cost.

SYMPTOMS OF A SICK COST ACCOUNTING SYSTEM

Management must continuously evaluate the effectiveness of its cost accounting system, especially in an environment that is characterized by rapid change. Some of the symptoms of a potentially sick or inadequate cost accounting system are described in the following excerpt from an article in the *Journal of Cost Management*:

Products that are very difficult to produce are reported to be very profitable even though they are not premium priced. *Not all products are easy to manufacture: some are just inherently difficult to make. . . . If the system is capturing the additional manufacturing costs, these difficult-to-manufacture products should either be selling at a premium or have low [profit] margins.*

Profit margins cannot be easily explained. *Management should usually be able to identify why some products are more profitable than others. . . . If the cost system is accurately reporting product costs, management should be able to explain the overall patterns of product profitability. If management cannot explain the pattern, yet believes it understands the market, the cost accounting system is probably to blame.*

Some products that are not sold by competitors have high reported [profit] margins. *If there is no simple explanation for this situation, the cost system may be at fault. It may be reporting phantom profits; the competitors' systems did not. . . .*

The competition's high-volume products are priced at apparently unrealistically low levels. *When smaller competitors with no apparent economic advantage are pricing high-production-volume products at very low levels and are simultaneously making good returns, the cost system is the prime suspect. . . . High-volume products are inherently less expensive to produce than low-volume products, and [the traditional] cost system may fail to accurately account for this difference. . . .*

Vendor bids for parts are considerably lower than expected. *Parts are often put out to bid because they appear to be too expensive to manufacture in-house. If vendors' bids on these parts are much lower than expected given the estimated production economies involved, the cost system may be at fault.*

Customers ignore price increases, even when there is no corresponding increase in cost. *When prices increase, customers usually react negatively. If there is little or no reaction, the cost system may be underestimating product costs. . . . If customers don't complain, they were probably paying less for the product than its perceived value. . . .*

Source: Robin Cooper, "Does Your Company Need a New Cost System?" *Journal of Cost Management*, reproduced in *Emerging Practices in Cost Management*, edited by Barry J. Brinker (Warren, Gorham & Lamont: Boston/New York, 1990).

APPENDIX

THE RECIPROCAL METHOD OF ALLOCATING SERVICE DEPARTMENT COSTS

The direct method and the step method of allocating service department costs were described and illustrated in this chapter. This appendix describes and illustrates a third method, the **reciprocal method**. Many accountants prefer the reciprocal method for service department cost allocation because it recognizes all interservice activities. Although it may be theoretically the best method, it is more difficult to apply than the direct method and the step method. Also, because the results of using these latter two methods do not, in many cases, materially differ from the results using the reciprocal method, the reciprocal method may not be used in practice.

The reciprocal method is applied in two steps. First, the total costs for each service department are determined, giving effect to all interservice activities. Second, the total costs for each service department determined in the first step are then allocated to both the other service departments and the production departments in accordance with the cost drivers.

The total costs for each service department in the first step are determined using simultaneous equations. To illustrate, the data that were used to illustrate the direct method and the step method for Quill Inc. on pages 774-776 are reproduced below:

Departmental costs:

Assembly Department	$300,000
Finishing Department	850,000
Power Department	400,000
Maintenance Department	150,000

Cost drivers:

Power Department (kilowatt-hours):

	Amount	Percent
Assembly Department	6 080 kwh	38%
Finishing Department	9 120	57
Maintenance Department	800	5
Total	16 000 kwh	100%

Maintenance Department (machine hours):

	Amount	Percent
Assembly Department	1,050 hrs.	21%
Finishing Department	2,450	49
Power Department	1,500	30
Total	5,000 hrs.	100%

The following equation represents the Power Department total cost, where P represents Power Department cost and M represents Maintenance Department cost:

$$P = \$400,000 + .30M$$

The equation indicates that the Power Department total cost is the $400,000 cost incurred in the Power Department plus 30% (1,500 hours ÷ 5,000 hours) of the Maintenance Department's total cost. Likewise, the equation representing the Maintenance Department's total cost is:

$$M = \$150,000 + .05P$$

This equation indicates that the Maintenance Department total cost is the $150,000 cost incurred in the Maintenance Department plus 5% (800 kwh ÷ 16 000 kwh) of the Power Department's total cost. By solving the two simultaneous equations, each department's total cost is determined as follows:

$$P = \$400,000 + .30M$$
$$M = \$150,000 + .05P$$

Substituting for M in the first equation and solving for P:

$$P = \$400,000 + .30\ (\$150,000 + .05P)$$

Simplifying: $$P = \$400,000 + \$45,000 + .015P$$

Transposing: $$.985\ P = \$445,000$$

$$P = \$451,777$$

Substituting for P in the second equation and solving for M:

	M = \$150,000 + .05P
Substituting:	M = \$150,000 + .05 (\$451,777)
Simplifying:	M = \$150,000 + \$22,589
	M = \$ 172,589

Once the total service department costs are determined, these costs are allocated to the service and production departments using the percentages determined by the cost drivers, as follows:

Reciprocal Method of Allocation

	Power Dept.	Maintenance Dept.	Assembly Dept.	Finishing Dept.
Costs	\$ 400,000	\$150,000	\$300,000	\$ 850,000
Allocated costs:				
Power Dept.	(451,777)	22,589*	171,675*	257,513*
Maint. Dept.	51,777**	(172,589)	36,244**	84,568**
Total costs	\$ 0	\$ 0	\$507,919	\$1,192,081

*Power Dept. allocations:
Maintenance Dept.: \$451,777 × 5% = \$22,589
Assembly Dept.: \$451,777 × 38% = \$171,675
Finishing Dept.: \$451,777 × 57% = \$257,513
**Maintenance Dept. allocations:
Power Dept.: \$172,589 × 30% = \$51,777
Assembly Dept.: \$172,589 × 21% = \$36,244
Finishing Dept.: \$172,589 × 49% = \$84,568 (rounded)

The costs allocated to each production department differs under each of the three methods of allocating service department costs. Depending upon the total direct service department costs and the amount of interservice activities, the additional accuracy of using the reciprocal method rather than the direct method or the step method may not be warranted.

CHAPTER REVIEW

KEY POINTS

OBJECTIVE 1

Objectives of Cost Allocation

Cost allocation is the assignment of costs to a cost object. Cost objects are determined by management, depending upon its decision-making needs. The allocation of costs may have one or more of the following objectives (1) evaluating manufacturing processes, (2) costing products, (3) motivating managers, and (4) valuing inventories. From a managerial accounting perspective, the first three objectives are most important for planning and control. The fourth objective of valuing inventories is primarily a financial accounting objective that is necessary for the preparation of financial statements.

OBJECTIVE 2

Principles of Cost Allocation

The three basic principles of cost allocation are as follows:

(1) To the extent possible, the activity that causes the cost to be incurred should be used as a basis for allocation.
(2) Budgeted (planned) costs rather than actual costs should normally be allocated.
(3) Fixed costs and variable costs should be allocated separately.

Using the activity that causes a cost as the basis for allocation achieves the most accurate allocation of costs. Such an activity base is referred to as a cost driver.

OBJECTIVE 3

Service Department Cost Allocation

Two methods of allocating service department costs are the direct method and the step method. These methods differ in how they handle interservice departmental activities. The direct method recognizes no interservice activities and allocates no service department costs to other service departments. The step method recognizes some interservice activities and allocates some service department costs to other service departments. If there are no interservice activities, both methods yield the same cost allocations.

The step method, sometimes referred to as the sequential method allocates service department costs in a step-wise fashion. The costs of the service department rendering the largest amount of service to other departments are allocated first, the costs of the service department rendering the second largest amount of service are allocated next, and so on. As a practical matter, the service department rendering the largest amount of service to other departments is assumed to be that department with the largest amount of costs to be allocated. No service department costs are allocated to a service department whose costs have already been allocated.

OBJECTIVE 4

Predetermined Overhead Rates and Product Costing

Manufacturing (factory) overhead costs may be allocated by the use of predetermined rates. Such rates are often determined and the manufacturing overhead applied on either a plant-wide or a departmental basis. When plant-wide and departmental overhead rates are used, the cost drivers are normally volume-based. Since some overhead costs are not directly related to volume-based cost drivers, the use of plant-wide or departmental overhead rates has the potential to distort product costs significantly.

OBJECTIVE 5

Activity-Based Costing

Activity-based costing (ABC) is a cost allocation method that initially traces or allocates costs to activities and then to the product. In this first stage of product costing, manufacturing overhead costs are allocated to cost pools that represent activities, such as hours of machine usage. In the second stage of product costing, costs are traced or allocated to the finished products.

Although each overhead cost could be allocated separately on the basis of the cost drivers identified, the expense of the allocation would be reduced by grouping activities into appropriate cost pools. These cost pools are identified in such a way that the costs within the pool can be related to one primary cost driver.

Activity-based costing usually costs products more accurately than traditional product costing methods. This increased accuracy allows management to make better decisions in such matters as product pricing. An additional benefit of activity-based costing is that it requires managers to focus their attention on activities that create overhead.

OBJECTIVE 6

Cost Allocation in Just-in-Time Manufacturing Systems

Many manufacturers have installed just-in-time manufacturing systems. Product costing in a just-in-time manufacturing system is simpler and more accurate than for other manufacturing systems. Many of the traditional service department functions are performed in work centers. This arrangement simplifies the tracing of costs to products. Because inventories are minimized, the cost allocation objective of inventory valuation is typically not important in just-in-time manufacturing systems.

KEY TERMS

cost allocation 769
cost object 769
cost driver 771
budgeted costs 772
direct method 774
step method 775
activity-based costing (ABC) 782

SELF-EXAMINATION QUESTIONS

Answers at end of chapter.

1. The assignment of costs to a cost object is referred to as:
   A. valuing inventories
   B. costing products
   C. cost allocation
   D. evaluating manufacturing processes

2. Which of the following is not one of the basic principles of cost allocation?
   A. Budgeted costs rather than actual costs should be allocated.
   B. The costs of the service department rendering the largest amount of service to other service departments should be allocated first.
   C. The activity that causes the cost to be incurred should be used as a basis for allocation.
   D. Fixed costs and variable costs should be allocated separately.

3. Which of the following is not a method of allocating service department costs?
   A. Activity-based costing
   B. Direct method
   C. Step method
   D. Sequential method

4. March Inc. uses the step method of allocating service department costs. The four service departments and their costs are as follows:

Engineering Department	$1,200
Maintenance and Repair Department	2,080
Power Department	1,950
Quality Control Department	1,700

   Which of the four service department costs would be allocated third?
   A. Engineering Department
   B. Maintenance and Repair Department
   C. Power Department
   D. Quality Control Department

5. Broun Inc. has the following budgeted overhead costs for two production departments, P1 and P2. Determine the plant-wide overhead rate based upon 150,000

budgeted machine hours (100,000 machine hours for P1 and 50,000 machine hours for P2).

	P1	P2	Total
Overhead costs:			
Power	$42,000	$190,000	$232,000
Quality control	22,000	18,000	40,000
Other	14,000	14,000	28,000
Total	$78,000	$222,000	$300,000

A. $ .52
B. $1.48
C. $2.00
D. $2.22

ILLUSTRATIVE PROBLEM

Wilks Inc. has two production departments, P1 and P2, and two service departments, Maintenance and Factory Office. Budgeted cost data and the relevant cost drivers are as follows:

Departmental costs:	
Dept. P1	$300,000
Dept. P2	850,000
Factory Office Dept.	150,000
Maintenance Dept.	120,000
Cost drivers:	
Factory Office Dept. (number of employees):	
Dept. P1	540 employees
Dept. P2	135
Maintenance Department	75
Total	750 employees
Maintenance Dept. (number of work orders):	
Dept. P1	285 orders
Dept. P2	95
Factory Office Dept.	20
Total	400 orders

Instructions:

(1) Compute the cost driver allocation percentages and then use these percentages to allocate the service department costs, using the direct method.
(2) Compute the cost driver allocation percentages and then use these percentages to allocate the service department costs, using the step method.

SOLUTION

(1) Cost driver allocation percentages:

	Number of Employees	Percent Used
Factory Office Dept.:		
Dept. P1	540	80%
Dept. P2	135	20
Total	675	100%

	Work Orders	Percent Used
Maintenance Dept.:		
Dept. P1	285	75%
Dept. P2	95	25
Total	380	100%

Service department allocations:

	Factory Office Dept.	Maintenance Dept.	Dept. P1	Dept. P2
Departmental costs	$150,000	$120,000	$300,000	$850,000
Allocated costs:				
Factory Office Dept.	(150,000)		120,000*	30,000*
Maintenance Dept.		(120,000)	90,000**	30,000**
Total costs	$ 0	$ 0	$510,000	$910,000

*Factory Office Dept. allocations:
Dept. P1: $150,000 × 80% = $120,000
Dept. P2: $150,000 × 20% = $30,000

**Maintenance Dept. allocations:
Dept. P1: $120,000 × 75% = $90,000
Dept. P2: $120,000 × 25% = $30,000

(2) Cost driver allocation percentages:

	Number of Employees	Percent Used
Factory Office Dept.:		
Dept. P1	540	72%
Dept. P2	135	18
Maintenance Dept.	75	10
Total	750	100%

	Work Orders	Percent Used
Maintenance Dept.:		
Dept. P1	285	75%
Dept. P2	95	25
Total	380	100%

Service department allocations:

	Factory Office Dept.	Maintenance Dept.	Dept. P1	Dept. P2
Departmental costs	$150,000	$120,000	$300,000	$850,000
Allocated costs:				
Factory Office Dept.	(150,000)	15,000*	108,000*	27,000*
Maintenance Dept.		(135,000)	101,250**	33,750**
Total costs	$ 0	$ 0	$509,250	$910,750

*Factory Office Dept. allocations:
Maintenance Dept.: $150,000 × 10% = $15,000
Dept. P1: $150,000 × 72% = $108,000
Dept. P2: $150,000 × 18% = $27,000

**Maintenance Dept. allocations:
Dept. P1: $135,000 × 75% = $101,250
Dept. P2: $135,000 × 25% = $33,750

DISCUSSION QUESTIONS

18–1. What is meant by the term cost allocation?

18–2. For purposes of product pricing, what is the final cost object?

18–3. Name the four cost allocation objectives.

18–4. Which of the four cost allocation objectives is primarily related to the preparation of financial statements for external reporting purposes?

18–5. What are the three basic principles of cost allocation?

18–6. Tatum Inc. allocates Personnel Department costs of $350,000 equally to its production departments. Budgeted costs for the Personnel Department were $320,000 for the year and all of the costs except for $60,000 are considered fixed costs when the activity base is the number of units produced. Which of the three principles of cost allocation, if any, has Tatum Inc. violated?

18–7. What term is used to describe an activity base that causes a cost and is used as a basis for cost allocation?

18–8. For the purpose of allocating Purchasing Department, Engineering Department, and Quality Control Department costs, which of the following cost drivers would be most appropriate for each department?
(1) number of material moves
(2) number of employees
(3) number of inspections
(4) direct labor hours
(5) number of transactions
(6) number of components

18–9. Why is it better to allocate fixed Power Department costs on the basis of capacity estimates rather than actual usage?

18–10. What two methods of service department cost allocation are frequently used in practice?

18–11. Under the direct method of service department cost allocation, which service department's costs are allocated first, second, and so on?

18–12. Under the step method of service department cost allocation, which service department's costs are allocated first, second, and so on?

18–13. Why is the allocation of manufacturing overhead cost relatively easy when only one product is produced?

18–14. What is assumed about the activities that cause overhead costs when a plant-wide overhead rate is used?

18–15. When might departmental overhead rates be more accurate than a plant-wide rate?

18–16. (a) What are some examples of volume-based cost drivers that might be used with plant-wide and departmental overhead rates? (b) When plant-wide or departmental overhead rates are used, what is the possible effect on the cost of high-volume products?

18–17. Describe activity-based costing.

18–18. Describe the two stages of product costing using traditional methods.

18–19. Contrast activity-based costing with traditional methods of product costing.

18–20. Why are cost pools normally used in activity-based costing?

18–21. Why is the tracing of costs to products often simplified in a just-in-time manufacturing system?

18–22. Is the cost allocation objective of valuing inventories more important in a traditional manufacturing system or in a just-in-time (JIT) manufacturing system?

Real World Focus

18–23. After a $100-million-a-year plumbing manufacturer began losing money on its operations, it hired a consulting firm to study its manufacturing processes. Almost 60% of the company's cost of goods sold related to manufacturing overhead. Upon further investigation, the consultant discovered that tooling costs were allocated to manufacturing departments based upon annual depreciation dollars. The Screw Machine Department was allocated the largest proportion of tooling overhead because it had the largest equipment depreciation, but screw machines required almost no Tooling Department support. The Punch Press Department, on the other hand, consumed 40% of the Tooling Department's resources and was allocated just over 9% of the Tooling Department costs. (a) How could the misallocation of manufacturing overhead affect the profitability of the company? (b) What might be a better activity base for allocating Tooling Department costs to the manufacturing departments?

Source: Michael O'Guin, "Focus the Factory With Activity-Based Costing," *Management Accounting,* February, 1990.

Ethics Discussion Case

18–24. James Nesbitt, controller for Syntel Inc., is considering whether to use number of units reworked or number of inspections for purposes of allocating Quality Control Department costs. The number of inspections is not currently recorded and would require additional recordkeeping. Based upon this cost consideration, James Nesbitt decided to allocate the Quality Control Department costs using the number of items reworked. Discuss whether it is ethical for James Nesbitt to base his allocation decision on the expense of accumulating the necessary data for the two cost drivers.

EXERCISES

Ex. 18-25.
Identification of cost drivers.
OBJ. 2

Sorel Inc. manufactures and sells corrugated boxes of various shapes and sizes. For each of the following costs, identify the most appropriate cost allocation base (cost driver). Some cost drivers may be used more than once and some may not be used.

Costs:	Possible allocation bases (cost drivers):
Food services costs	Number of employees
Repair costs	Number of equipment repair orders
Purchasing costs	Value of equipment
Shipping costs	Number of materials moves
Property taxes on equipment	Number of inspections
Personnel services	Number of transactions
Materials handling costs	Space occupied (in square feet)
Quality control costs	Number of machine hours
Production setup costs	Number of packing orders
Machinery depreciation	Number of production runs
Factory supervisory costs	Number of direct labor hours
Heating costs	Number of units produced
	Kilowatt-hours used

Ex. 18-26.
Allocation of fixed and variable costs.
OBJ. 2

The Power Department of Untz Inc. supplies power to two producing departments P1 and P2. The budgeted fixed costs of the Power Department total $500,000, and the variable costs are budgeted at $ .04 per kilowatt-hour. The capacity and actual power usage for P1 and P2 are as follows:

	Dept. P1	Dept. P2
Actual usage	1 200 000 kwh	400 000 kwh
Capacity usage	1 200 000 kwh	800 000 kwh

(a) Allocate total Power Department costs, using actual kilowatt-hours for allocating the fixed costs.
(b) Allocate total Power Department costs, using capacity kilowatt-hours for allocating the fixed costs.
(c) Which of the two allocations is best? Explain.

Ex. 18-27.
Direct method of service department cost allocation.
OBJ. 3

Chien Inc. has two service departments, Maintenance and Grounds, and two production departments, Fabrication and Finishing. Budgeted cost data and the relevant cost drivers for allocating the service department costs are as follows:

Departmental costs:	
Maintenance Department	$120,000
Grounds Department	80,000
Fabrication Department	600,000
Finishing Department	250,000
Cost drivers:	
Maintenance Department (number of work orders)	
Fabrication Department	138 orders
Finishing Department	46
Grounds Department	16
Total	200 orders
Grounds Department (square feet):	
Fabrication Department	10,260 sq. ft.
Finishing Department	6,840
Maintenance Department	900
Total	18,000 sq. ft.

Chien Inc. uses the direct method of service department cost allocation.

Instructions:

(a) Compute the cost driver allocation percentages for each service department.
(b) Allocate the Maintenance Department and Grounds Department costs to the

Fabrication Department and Finishing Department by completing the following table:

	Maintenance Dept.	Grounds Dept.	Fabrication Dept.	Finishing Dept.
Departmental costs				
Allocated costs:				
Maintenance Dept.				
Grounds Dept.				
Total costs				

Ex. 18-28.
Step method of service department cost allocation.
OBJ. 3

Chien Inc. in Ex. 18-27 uses the step method of service department cost allocation.

Instructions:

(a) Compute the cost driver allocation percentages for each service department.
(b) Allocate the Maintenance Department and Grounds Department costs to the Fabrication Department and Finishing Department by completing the following table:

	Maintenance Dept.	Grounds Dept.	Fabrication Dept.	Finishing Dept.
Departmental costs				
Allocated costs:				
Maintenance Dept.				
Grounds Dept.				
Total costs				

Ex. 18-29.
Plant-wide overhead rate.
OBJ. 4

Ng Inc. manufactures two products, X and Y, using two production departments, Foundry and Plating, and two service departments, Engineering and Factory Supervision. The following manufacturing overhead costs have been budgeted for the production departments:

	Foundry Dept.	Plating Dept.	Total
Overhead costs:			
Engineering	$34,000	$ 76,000	$110,000
Factory supervision	25,000	50,000	75,000
Other	14,500	25,500	40,000
Total	$73,500	$151,500	$225,000

The following direct labor hours and machine hours have been budgeted for each production department:

	Direct Labor Hours	Machine Hours
Foundry Department:		
Product X	1,500	1,200
Product Y	5,500	3,600
	7,000	4,800
Plating Department:		
Product X	1,200	13,000
Product Y	800	7,200
	2,000	20,200
Total	9,000	25,000

Determine a plant-wide overhead rate based upon (a) direct labor hours and (b) machine hours.

Ex. 18-30.
Departmental overhead rates.
OBJ. 4

Using the data for Ng Inc. in Ex. 18-29, determine departmental overhead rates for the Foundry and Plating Departments. Assume that the Foundry Department is labor-intensive, while the Plating Department is capital-intensive. Thus, use direct labor hours as the cost driver for the Foundry Department and machine hours as the cost driver for the Plating Department.

Ex. 18-31.
Activity-based costing.
OBJ. 5

Pita Inc. manufactures two products, R and S, which involves four overhead activities—factory supervision, maintenance, product engineering, and quality control. The budgeted costs for these activities are as follows:

Overhead costs:	
Factory supervision	$150,000
Maintenance	200,000
Product engineering	120,000
Quality control	80,000
Total	$550,000

The appropriate cost drivers and the amounts of the cost drivers for each product are as follows:

Overhead Cost	Cost Driver
Factory supervision	Number of employees
Maintenance	Machine hours
Product engineering	Number of components
Quality control	Number of inspections

	Number of Employees	Machine Hours	Number of Components	Number of Inspections
Product R	45	12,000	36	180
Product S	30	8,000	44	220
Total	75	20,000	80	400

Instructions:

(a) Develop an overhead rate for each overhead activity.
(b) Allocate the overhead costs to each product, using the overhead rates from (a).

Ex. 18-32.
Activity-based costing.
OBJ. 5

Using the data from Ex. 18-31, (a) determine the percentage of each cost driver used by each product, (b) identify appropriate cost pools and determine an overhead rate for each pool (use machine hours and the number of inspections as the cost drivers), and (c) allocate the overhead costs to products R and S, using the overhead rates identified in (b).

Appendix
Ex. 18-33.
Reciprocal method of service department cost allocation.

Chien Inc. has two service departments, Maintenance and Grounds, and two production departments, Fabrication and Finishing. Budgeted cost data and the relevant cost drivers for allocating the service department costs are as follows:

Departmental costs:	
Maintenance Department	$120,000
Grounds Department	80,000
Fabrication Department	600,000
Finishing Department	250,000

Cost drivers:

Maintenance Department (number of work orders)

Fabrication Department	138 orders
Finishing Department	46
Grounds Department	16
Total	200 orders

Grounds Department (square feet):

Fabrication Department	10,260 sq. ft.
Finishing Department	6,840
Maintenance Department	900
Total	18,000 sq. ft.

Chien Inc. uses the reciprocal method of service department cost allocation.

Instructions:

(a) Compute the cost driver allocation percentage for each service department.

(b) Allocate the Maintenance Department and Grounds Department costs to the Fabrication Department and Finishing Department by completing the following table:

	Maintenance Dept.	Grounds Dept.	Fabrication Dept.	Finishing Dept.
Departmental costs				
Allocated costs:				
Maintenance Dept.				
Grounds Dept.				
Total costs				

PROBLEMS

Pb. 18-34.
Service department cost allocation—direct method.
OBJ. 3

Sejdi Inc. has two service departments, Power and Maintenance, and two production departments, Cutting and Polishing. Budgeted cost data and the relevant cost drivers for allocating the service department costs are as follows:

Departmental costs:

Power Department	$ 860,000
Maintenance Department	140,000
Cutting Department	1,200,000
Polishing Department	750,000

Cost drivers:

Power Department (kilowatt-hours):

Cutting Department	29 700 kwh
Polishing Department	9 900
Maintenance Department	5 400
Total	45 000 kwh

Maintenance Department (machine hours):

Cutting Department	18,240 hours
Polishing Department	12,160
Power Department	1,600
Total	32,000 hours

Instructions:

(1) Assuming that Sejdi Inc. uses the direct method of service department cost allocation, compute the cost driver allocation percentages for each service department.
(2) Allocate the Power Department and Maintenance Department costs to the Cutting Department and Polishing Department, using the percentages computed in (1) and completing the following table:

	Power Dept.	Maintenance Dept.	Cutting Dept.	Polishing Dept.
Departmental costs				
Allocated costs:				
Power Dept.				
Maintenance Dept.				
Total costs				

(3) What are the advantages of using the direct method of service department cost allocation?

Pb. 18-35.
Service department cost allocation—step method.
OBJ. 3

Sejdi Inc. in Pb. 18-34 decides to use the step method of service department cost allocation.

Instructions:

(1) Compute the cost driver allocation percentages for each service department.
(2) Allocate the Power Department and Maintenance Department costs to the Cutting Department and Polishing Department, using the percentages computed in (1) and completing the following table:

	Power Dept.	Maintenance Dept.	Cutting Dept.	Polishing Dept.
Departmental costs				
Allocated costs:				
Power Dept.				
Maintenance Dept.				
Total costs				

(3) When would it be appropriate to use the step method of service department cost allocation?

Pb. 18-36.
Plant-wide and departmental overhead rates; product cost distortions.
OBJ. 4

Golin Inc. manufactures two products, S and T, using two production departments, Bindery and Stripping, and two service departments, Factory Supervision and Quality Control. The following overhead costs have been budgeted for the production departments:

	Bindery Dept.	Stripping Dept.	Total
Overhead costs:			
Factory supervision	$30,000	$20,000	$ 50,000
Quality control	18,000	22,000	40,000
Other	15,000	15,000	30,000
Total	$63,000	$57,000	$120,000

The following direct labor hours and machine hours have been budgeted for each production department:

18-801

	Direct Labor Hours	Machine Hours
Bindery Department:		
Product S	1,000	3,000
Product T	800	1,500
	1,800	4,500
Stripping Department:		
Product S	200	4,500
Product T	400	3,000
	600	7,500
Total	2,400	12,000

Assume that 1,000 units of Product S and 1,500 units of Product T are scheduled for production.

Instructions:

(1) Determine a plant-wide overhead rate based upon (a) direct labor hours and (b) machine hours.

(2) Allocate the manufacturing overhead costs to each product, based upon (a) the direct labor hour rate and (b) the machine hour rate.

(3) Determine departmental overhead rates for the Bindery and Stripping Departments. Assume that the Bindery Department is labor-intensive while the Stripping Department is capital-intensive. Thus, use direct labor hours as the cost driver for the Bindery Department and machine hours as the cost driver for the Stripping Department.

(4) Allocate the manufacturing overhead costs to each product, based upon the departmental overhead rates determined in (3).

(5) Determine the overhead rates for (a) factory supervision, based upon number of employees, (b) quality control, based upon number of inspections, and (c) other overhead, based upon number of units. The following relevant cost drivers have been identified:

	Number of Employees	Number of Inspections
Product S:		
Bindery Department	30	35
Stripping Department	10	15
	40	50
Product T:		
Bindery Department	40	50
Stripping Department	20	25
	60	75
Total	100	125

(6) Using the overhead rates in (5), allocate the manufacturing overhead costs to each product.

(7) (a) Using the following table, prepare a summary of the allocated total and per unit manufacturing overhead costs for the plant-wide overhead rates in (2), the departmental overhead rates in (4), and the cost-driver-based rates in (6):

	Product S (1,000 Units)		Product T (1,500 Units)	
	Total Allocated Cost	Per Unit Cost	Total Allocated Cost	Per Unit Cost
Plant-wide rate:				
Direct labor hours				
Machine hours				
Departmental rates				
Cost driver rates				

(b) What do the differences in the allocated costs represent?

Pb. 18-37.
Activity-based costing.
OBJ. 5

Tosha Inc. manufactures two products, A and B, which involves four overhead activities—equipment maintenance and repairs, grounds, heating and lighting, and product engineering. The budgeted costs for these activities are as follows:

Overhead costs:	
Equipment maintenance & repairs	$250,000
Grounds	80,000
Heating and lighting	320,000
Product engineering	150,000
Total	$800,000

The appropriate cost drivers and the amounts of the cost drivers for each product are as follows:

Overhead Cost	Cost Driver
Equipment maintenance & repairs	machine hours
Grounds	square feet
Heating and lighting	kilowatt-hours
Product engineering	number of components

	Machine Hours	Square Feet	Kilowatt-Hours	Number of Components
Product A	6,000	20,000	10 000	36
Product B	2,000	30,000	15 000	12
Total	8,000	50,000	25 000	48

Instructions:

(1) Determine an overhead rate for each overhead activity.
(2) Allocate the overhead costs to each product, using the overhead rates from part (1).
(3) Determine the percentage of each cost driver used by each product.
(4) Using the percentages computed in (3), (a) identify appropriate cost pools and determine an overhead rate for each pool (use machine hours and the number of square feet as the cost drivers). (b) Allocate the overhead costs to products A and B, using the overhead rates identified in (a).

Pb. 18-38.
Plant-wide overhead rates and activity-based costing.
OBJ. 4, 5

Faris Inc. manufactures two products, E and F, which involves four overhead activities—maintenance, power, production setup, and quality control. Faris Inc. uses a plant-wide overhead rate, based upon units produced, to allocate overhead costs to Products E and F. The procedure for allocating overhead was initially established when only Product E was being produced.

Although management is pleased that sales of Product F are increasing, it is concerned because sales of the previously best selling Product E are decreasing. Several former customers have indicated that Faris Inc.'s price for Product E is too high and that they can buy a competitor's product at significant savings. The president is concerned because the manufacture of Product E is costing too much, and perhaps the company should discontinue its production.

Faris Inc. has gathered the following data for use in analyzing the costs of manufacturing Products E and F:

Budgeted direct manufacturing costs (per unit):

	Product E	Product F
Direct materials	$12.00	$43.00
Direct labor	8.00	17.00
Expected production volume:	10,000 units	5,000 units

Overhead activities and costs:

Maintenance	$ 60,000
Power	40,000
Production setup	75,000
Quality control	65,000
Total	$240,000

Overhead cost drivers:

Maintenance	machine hours
Power	kilowatt-hours
Production setup	number of setups
Quality control	number of inspections

	Machine Hours	Kilowatt-Hours	Number of Setups	Number of Inspections
Product E	144,000	576 000	16	8
Product F	56,000	224 000	24	12
Total	200,000	800 000	40	20

Instructions:

(1) Determine the plant-wide overhead rate for Faris Inc., using expected production volume as the activity base.

(2) (a) Using the plant-wide overhead rate determined in (1), allocate overhead to Products E and F. (b) Determine the per unit manufacturing cost for each product, based upon the budgeted direct materials and direct labor costs and the allocated overhead.

(3) Determine the expected selling price of each product, based upon the per unit manufacturing cost determined in (2). Faris Inc. normally sets its prices at 20% above the manufacturing cost per unit.

(4) (a) Using activity-based costing, determine the percentage of each cost driver used by each product. (b) Based upon your answer to (a), identify appropriate cost pools and determine an overhead rate for each cost pool (use machine hours and the number of setups as cost drivers). (c) Allocate the overhead costs to Products E and F, using the overhead rates determined in (b). (d) Determine the manufacturing overhead cost per unit for Products E and F. (e) Determine the per unit manufacturing costs for each product, based upon the budgeted direct materials and direct labor costs and the allocated overhead.

(5) Determine the expected selling price of each product, based upon the per unit manufacturing cost determined in (4). Faris Inc. normally sets its prices at 20% above the manufacturing cost per unit.

(6) Based upon the preceding analysis, comment on possible reasons for the decreased sales of Product E and the increased sales of Product F.

Appendix Pb. 18-39. Service department cost allocation—reciprocal method.

Sejdi Inc. has two service departments, Power and Maintenance, and two production departments, Cutting and Polishing. Budgeted cost data and the relevant cost drivers for allocating the service department costs are as follows:

Departmental costs:	
Power Department	$ 860,000
Maintenance Department	140,000
Cutting Department	1,200,000
Polishing Department	750,000
Cost drivers:	
Power Department (kilowatt-hours):	
Cutting Department	29 700 kwh
Polishing Department	9 900
Maintenance Department	5 400
Total	45 000 kwh
Maintenance Department (machine hours):	
Cutting Department	18,240 hours
Polishing Department	12,160
Power Department	1,600
Total	32,000 hours

Instructions:

(1) Assuming that Sejdi Inc. uses the reciprocal method of service department cost allocation, compute the cost driver allocation percentages for each service department.

(2) Allocate the Power Department and Maintenance Department costs to the Cutting Department and the Polishing Department, using the percentages computed in (1) and completing the following table:

	Power Dept.	Maintenance Dept.	Cutting Dept.	Polishing Dept.
Departmental costs				
Allocated costs:				
Power Dept.				
Maintenance Dept.				
Total costs				

ALTERNATE PROBLEMS

Pb. 18-34A. Service department cost allocation—direct method. OBJ. 3

Yoo Sun Inc. has two service departments, Grounds and Engineering, and two production departments, Cutting and Trimming. Budgeted cost data and the relevant cost drivers for allocating the service department costs are as follows:

Departmental costs:	
Grounds Department	$ 90,000
Engineering Department	60,000
Cutting Department	800,000
Trimming Department	550,000
Cost drivers:	
Grounds Department (square feet):	
Cutting Department	41,040 sq. ft.
Trimming Department	10,260
Engineering Department	2,700
Total	54,000 sq. ft.

Engineering Department (number of work orders):	
Cutting Department	108 orders
Trimming Department	36
Grounds Department	6
Total	150 orders

Instructions:

(1) Assuming that Yoo Sun Inc. uses the direct method of service department cost allocation, compute the cost driver allocation percentages for each service department.

(2) Allocate the Grounds Department and Engineering Department costs to the Cutting Department and Trimming Department, using the percentages computed in (1) and completing the following table:

	Grounds Dept.	Engineering Dept.	Cutting Dept.	Trimming Dept.
Departmental costs				
Allocated costs:				
Grounds Dept.				
Engineering Dept.				
Total costs				

(3) What are the advantages of using the direct method of service department cost allocation?

Pb. 18-35A. **Service department cost allocation—step method.** OBJ. 3

Yoo Sun Inc. in Pb. 18-34A decides to use the step method of service department cost allocation.

Instructions:

(1) Compute the cost driver allocation percentages for each service department.

(2) Allocate the Grounds Department and Engineering Department costs to the Cutting Department and Trimming Department, using the percentages computed in (1) and completing the following table:

	Grounds Dept.	Engineering Dept.	Cutting Dept.	Trimming Dept.
Departmental costs				
Allocated costs:				
Grounds Dept.				
Engineering Dept.				
Total costs				

(3) When would it be appropriate to use the step method of service department cost allocation?

Pb. 18-36A. **Plant-wide and departmental overhead rates; product cost distortions.** OBJ. 4

Liu Inc. manufactures two products, Q and R, using two production departments, Framing and Painting, and two service departments, Maintenance and Power. The following overhead costs have been budgeted for the production departments:

	Framing Dept.	Painting Dept.	Total
Overhead costs:			
Maintenance	$ 50,000	$30,000	$ 80,000
Power	38,000	22,000	60,000
Other	20,000	20,000	40,000
Total	$108,000	$72,000	$180,000

The following direct labor hours and machine hours have been budgeted for each production department:

	Direct Labor Hours	Machine Hours
Framing Department:		
Product Q	1,200	2,600
Product R	300	1,400
	1,500	4,000
Painting Department:		
Product Q	250	5,500
Product R	250	2,500
	500	8,000
Total	2,000	12,000

Assume that 2,500 units of Product Q and 10,000 units of Product R are scheduled for production.

Instructions:

(1) Determine a plant-wide overhead rate, based upon (a) direct labor hours and (b) machine hours.
(2) Allocate the manufacturing overhead costs to each product, based upon (a) the direct labor hour rate and (b) the machine hour rate.
(3) Determine departmental overhead rates for the Framing and Painting Departments. Assume that the Framing Department is labor-intensive, while the Painting Department is capital-intensive. Thus, use direct labor hours as the cost driver for the Framing Department and machine hours as the cost driver for the Painting Department.
(4) Allocate the manufacturing overhead costs to each product, based upon the departmental overhead rates determined in (3).
(5) Determine the overhead rates for (a) maintenance, based upon number of work orders, (b) power, based upon kilowatt-hours, and (c) other overhead, based upon number of units. The following relevant cost drivers have been identified:

	Number of Work Orders	Kilowatt-Hours
Product Q:		
Framing Department	30	120 000
Painting Department	45	400 000
	75	520 000
Product R:		
Framing Department	15	50 000
Painting Department	35	230 000
	50	280 000
Total	125	800 000

(6) Using the overhead rates in (5), allocate the manufacturing overhead costs to each product.
(7) (a) Using the following table, prepare a summary of the allocated total and per unit manufacturing overhead costs for the plant-wide overhead rates in (2), the departmental overhead rates in (4), and the cost-driver-based rates in (6):

	Product Q (2,500 Units)		Product R (10,000 Units)	
	Total Allocated Cost	Per Unit Cost	Total Allocated Cost	Per Unit Cost
Plant-wide rate:				
Direct labor hours				
Machine hours				
Departmental rates				
Cost driver rates				

(b) What do the differences in the allocated costs represent?

Pb. 18-37A. **Activity-based costing.** OBJ. 5

Straub Inc. manufactures two products, W and X, which involves four overhead activities—equipment maintenance and repairs, power, production setup, and quality control. The budgeted costs for these activities are as follows:

Overhead costs:	
Equipment maintenance & repairs	$30,000
Power	24,000
Production setup	90,000
Quality control	70,000
Total	$214,000

The appropriate cost drivers and the amount of the cost drivers for each product are as follows:

Overhead Cost	Cost Driver
Equipment Maintenance & repairs	machine hours
Power	kilowatt-hours
Production setup	number of setups
Quality control	number of inspections

	Machine Hours	Kilowatt-Hours	Number of Setups	Number of Inspections
Product W	11,000	330 000	5	8
Product X	9,000	270 000	20	32
Total	20,000	600 000	25	40

Instructions:

(1) Determine an overhead rate for each overhead activity.
(2) Allocate the overhead costs to each product, using the overhead rates from part (1).
(3) Determine the percentage of each cost driver used by each product.
(4) Using the percentages computed in (3), (a) identify appropriate cost pools and determine an overhead rate for each pool (use machine hours and the number of setups as the cost drivers). (b) Allocate the overhead costs to products W and X, using the overhead rates identified in (a).

Pb. 18-38A. **Plant-wide overhead rates and activity-based costing.** OBJ. 4,5

Kirchoff Inc. manufactures two products, H and I, which involves four overhead activities—maintenance, power, production setup, and quality control. Kirchoff Inc. uses a plant-wide overhead rate, based upon units produced, to allocate overhead costs to Products H and I. The procedure for allocating overhead was initially established when only Product H was being produced.

Although management is pleased that sales of Product I are increasing, it is concerned because sales of the previously best selling Product H are decreasing. Several former customers have indicated that Kirchoff Inc.'s price for Product H is too high and that they can buy a competitor's product at significant savings. The president is concerned because it is costing too much to manufacture Product H, and perhaps the company should discontinue its production.

Kirchoff Inc. has gathered the following data for use in analyzing the cósts of manufacturing Products H and I:

Budgeted direct manufacturing costs (per unit):

	Product H	Product I
Direct materials	$15.00	$36.00
Direct labor	7.00	14.00
Expected production volume:	50,000 units	2,000 units

Overhead activities and costs:

Maintenance	$ 85,000
Power	65,000
Production setup	45,000
Quality control	65,000
Total	$260,000

Overhead cost drivers:

Maintenance	machine hours
Power	kilowatt-hours
Production setup	number of setups
Quality control	number of inspections

	Machine Hours	Kilowatt-Hours	Number of Setups	Number of Inspections
Product H	192,000	480 000	32	12
Product I	108,000	270 000	48	18
Total	300,000	750 000	80	30

Instructions:

(1) Determine the plant-wide overhead rate for Kirchoff Inc., using expected production volume as the activity base.

(2) (a) Using the plant-wide overhead rate determined in (1), allocate overhead to Products H and I. (b) Determine the per unit manufacturing cost for each product, based upon the budgeted direct materials and direct labor costs and the allocated overhead.

(3) Determine the expected selling price of each product, based upon the manufacturing cost per unit determined in (2). Kirchoff Inc. normally sets its prices at 25% above the manufacturing cost per unit.

(4) (a) Using activity-based costing, determine the percentage of each cost driver used by each product. (b) Based upon your answer to (a), identify appropriate cost pools and determine an overhead rate for each cost pool (use machine hours and the number of setups as cost drivers). (c) Allocate the overhead costs to Products H and I, using the overhead rates determined in (b). (d) Determine the manufacturing overhead cost per unit for Products H and I. (e) Determine the per unit manufacturing cost for each product, based upon the budgeted direct materials and direct labor costs and the allocated overhead.

(5) Determine the expected selling price of each product, based upon the manufacturing cost per unit determined in (4). Kirchoff Inc. normally sets its prices at 25% above the manufacturing cost per unit.

(6) Based upon the preceding analysis, comment on possible reasons for the decreased sales of Product H and the increased sales of Product I.

Appendix Pb. 18-39A.
Service department cost allocation—reciprocal method.

Yoo Sun Inc. has two service departments, Grounds and Engineering, and two production departments, Cutting and Trimming. Budgeted cost data and the relevant cost drivers for allocating the service department costs are as follows:

Departmental costs:	
Grounds Department	$ 90,000
Engineering Department	60,000
Cutting Department	800,000
Trimming Department	550,000

Cost drivers:	
Grounds Department (square feet):	
Cutting Department	41,040 sq. ft.
Trimming Department	10,260
Engineering Department	2,700
Total	54,000 sq. ft.
Engineering Department (number of work orders):	
Cutting Department	108 orders
Trimming Department	36
Grounds Department	6
Total	150 orders

Instructions:

(1) Assuming that Yoo Sun Inc. uses the reciprocal method of service department cost allocation, compute the cost driver allocation percentages for each service department.

(2) Allocate the Grounds Department and Engineering Department costs to the Cutting Department and Trimming Department, using the percentages computed in (1) and completing the following table:

	Grounds Dept.	Engineering Dept.	Cutting Dept.	Trimming Dept.
Departmental costs				
Allocated costs:				
Grounds Dept.				
Engineering Dept.				
Total costs				

MINI-CASE 18

Gateway Inc.

Andre Geer, the production engineer for Gateway, Inc., recently returned from a tour of three manufacturing plants that had recently implemented just-in-time manufacturing systems and activity-based costing. The three manufacturing plants were located in Houston, San Jose, and Seattle. Gateway Inc. is headquartered in Denver, Colorado.

Gateway Inc.'s travel policy allows for the full reimbursement of business-related travel costs. Airfare is reimbursed for only the amount for a coach fare. Andre combined the visits to the three plants with a side trip to visit his ailing mother in San Diego. Andre is uncertain as to the amount of airfare to submit for reimbursement. He has asked you to assist him in allocating a reasonable amount of the airfare costs to business travel and to personal travel. The actual amount paid for Andre's plane ticket is $1,495, broken down between destinations as follows:

Denver to Houston	$ 220
Houston to San Diego	380
San Diego to San Jose	170
San Jose to Seattle	250
Seattle to Denver	475*
Total	$1,495

*Includes $45 for first class upgrade from the basic coach fare.

The air miles among the cities are as follows:

Denver to Houston	1,000 miles
Houston to San Diego	1,500 miles
San Diego to San Jose	400 miles
San Jose to Seattle	800 miles
Seattle to Denver	1,300 miles

The air miles from Houston to San Jose, assuming that Andre had not traveled to San Diego, is 1,800 miles. The normal coach air fare from Houston to San Jose is $460.

Discuss the alternative air fare reimbursements (cost allocations) for Andre. What would you suggest as the proper air fare reimbursement?

ANSWERS TO SELF-EXAMINATION QUESTIONS

1. C The assignment of costs to a cost object is referred to as cost allocation. Valuing inventories (answer A), costing products (answer B), and evaluating manufacturing processes (answer D) are objectives of cost allocation.
2. B The costs of the service department rendering the largest amount of service to other service departments should be allocated first (answer B) is not a basic principle of cost allocation, but rather a procedure used in applying the step method of service department cost allocations. Budgeted costs rather than actual costs should be allocated (answer A), the activity that causes the cost to be incurred should be used as a basis for allocation (answer C), and fixed costs and variable costs should be allocated separately (answer D) are all basic principles of cost allocation.
3. A Activity-based costing (answer A) is a method of allocating manufacturing overhead and is not a method of allocating service department costs. The direct method (answer B) and the step method (answer C), sometimes referred to as the sequential method (answer D), are all methods of allocating service department costs.
4. D Under the step method, the costs of the service department rendering the largest amount of service to other service departments should be allocated first, followed by the department rendering the second largest amount of service, and so on. The service department rendering the largest amount of service is assumed to be the department with the largest amount of costs to be allocated. Therefore, the Maintenance and Repair Department (answer B) costs would be allocated first, the Power Department (answer C) would be allocated second, the Quality Control Department (answer D) would be allocated third, and the Engineering Department (answer A) costs would be allocated fourth.
5. C The plant-wide overhead rate is determined by dividing the total budgeted overhead costs of $300,000 by the 150,000 budgeted machine hours, as follows:

$$\text{Plant-wide overhead rate} = \frac{\$300{,}000}{150{,}000 \text{ machine hours}}$$

$$\text{Plant-wide overhead rate} = \$2.00$$

PART 6

ANALYSES FOR MANAGERIAL DECISION MAKING

CHAPTER 19

CHAPTER OBJECTIVES

1 Describe and illustrate the common classifications of costs by behavior, including:
Variable costs
Fixed costs
Mixed costs

2 Describe and illustrate the common methods for estimating costs, including:
High-low method
Scattergraph method
Least squares method

3 Describe the judgmental and engineering methods of cost estimation.

COST BEHAVIOR & COST ESTIMATION

A variety of managerial cost terms, classifications, systems, and concepts were described and illustrated in Chapters 15-18. This chapter continues this discussion by focusing on cost behavior and cost estimation and the use of these concepts in planning and controlling the operations of an enterprise. **Cost behavior** refers to the manner in which a cost changes in relation to its activity base. For example, direct materials costs vary proportionately with changes in the activity base number of units produced. If the total units produced doubles, direct materials costs will also double. **Cost estimation** refers to the methods used to estimate costs for use in managerial decision making. For example, the managerial accountant must develop reliable product cost estimates for use by managers in setting selling prices.

A thorough understanding of cost behavior and cost estimation methods is essential for planning and controlling operations. For example, classifying costs by their behavior as production varies allows management to establish standards for evaluating (controlling) the efficiency of current operations and for predicting (planning) the costs of future levels of operations. Cost estimation methods may be used to analyze past cost behavior so that future production costs can be estimated.

COST BEHAVIOR

OBJECTIVE 1
Describe and illustrate the common classifications of costs by behavior including:
Variable costs
Fixed costs
Mixed costs.

The behavior of costs can be classified in a variety of ways. The three most common cost classifications are variable costs, fixed costs, and mixed costs. Each of these classifications was briefly described in Chapter 15. This chapter expands upon this discussion to include additional issues which must be considered if the managerial accountant is to properly classify cost behavior.

Variable Costs

Variable costs are costs that vary in total in direct proportion to changes in an activity base. As mentioned in Chapter 15, direct materials and direct labor costs are generally treated as variable costs because, as production volume changes, the totals of these costs change proportionately. To illustrate, assume that Wilson Inc. produces stereophonic sound systems under the brand name of JimBo. The parts for the stereo systems are purchased from outside supplies for $10 per unit and are assembled in Wilson's Augusta plant. The direct materials costs for Model JW-12 for differing levels of production are summarized in the following table:

Number of Units of Model JW-12 Produced	Direct Materials Cost per Unit	Total Direct Materials Cost
5,000 units	$10	$ 50,000
10,000 units	10	100,000
15,000 units	10	150,000
20,000 units	10	200,000
25,000 units	10	250,000
30,000 units	10	300,000

As the table illustrates, the total direct materials cost varies in direct proportion to the number of units of Model JW-12 produced. The direct materials cost for 25,000 units ($250,000) is 5 times the direct materials cost for 5,000 units ($50,000). However, the unit direct materials cost of $10 remains constant over all levels of production. A constant per unit cost is a characteristic of variable costs.

The following graphs illustrate how the variable costs for direct materials for Model JW-12 behave in total and on a per unit basis as production changes:

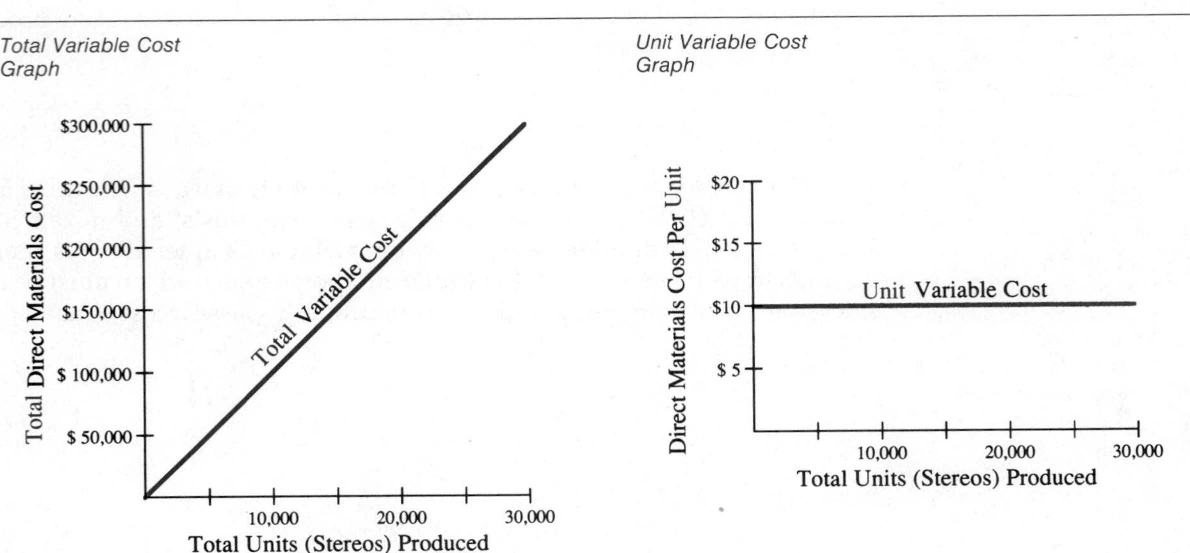

Activity Base for Variable Costs. The preceding illustration of a variable cost used units produced as the activity base. The relevant activity base for a cost depends upon which base causes or is most closely associated with the cost and the decision-making needs of management in using the cost in planning and controlling operations. To illustrate, food costs for a hospital are closely associated with the number of patients in the hospital. Thus, the number of patients would be the most appropriate activity base for making decisions related to food costs. On the other hand, because patients' diagnoses differ, the number of x-rays taken rather than the number of patients is a better activity base for decisions related to the cost of X-ray film.

To provide relevant information to management for decision making, managerial accountants must be thoroughly familiar with the operations of the entity, so that the most appropriate activity bases for various cost classifications are selected. Units sold and units produced are commonly used activity bases, but they may not always be the most appropriate. For example, miles driven rather than the number of orders delivered would be the most appropriate activity base for gasoline costs of a moving company.

Step-Wise Variable Costs. True variable costs remain constant on a per unit basis and change in total on a proportionate basis with changes in an activity base. For example, in the previous illustration of Wilson Inc., each additional Model JW-12 unit produced required $10 of direct materials. The materials cost per unit remained constant at $10, and the total materials cost increased by $10 with each additional unit produced. Hence, as the number of units of Model JW-12 produced doubled from 5,000 units to 10,000 units, the total direct materials cost doubled from $50,000 to $100,000. Likewise, as the number of units of Model JW-12 tripled, the total direct materials cost tripled.

Step-wise variable costs may not change in exact proportion to changes in the activity base, even though they may be classified as variable costs. For example, direct labor costs are generally treated as a variable cost. However, direct labor may be acquired in units that increase or decrease with a batch of products produced. In such cases, the direct labor cost is a step-wise variable cost. To illustrate, assume that Horn Inc. manufactures machine tools using semi-automated lathes. During an 8-hour work shift, a machine operator normally produces 50 tools. For each increase in production of 50 tools, an additional machine operator is required. If scheduled production for a machine operator is less than 50 tools, the operator is still paid for an 8-hour shift. Assuming that machine operators earn $12.50 per hour, the direct labor costs for increasing levels of production are summarized in the following table and the graph at the top of page 816.

Number of Units Produced	Total Direct Labor Cost
0— 50	$100
51—100	200
101—150	300
151—200	400
201—250	500
251—300	600

Total Step-Wise Variable Cost

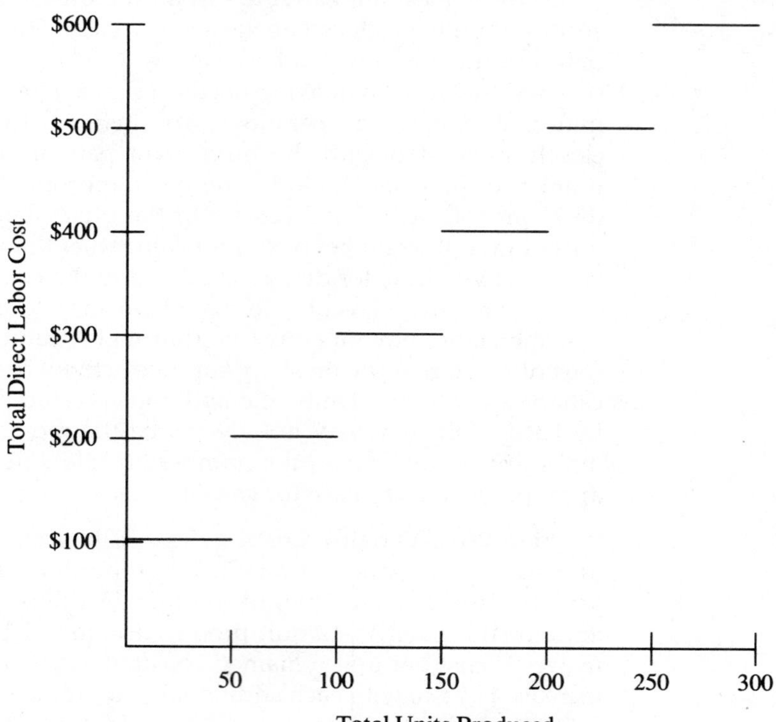

Step-wise variable costs derive their name for their step-wise nature, as indicated in the preceding graph. In practice, when the length of the steps is relatively small, step-wise variable costs are often treated as simple variable costs. For example, in the preceding illustration, the direct labor cost could be treated as a variable cost with a constant per unit cost of $2, as illustrated in the following table:

Number of Units Produced	Total Direct Labor Cost	Direct Labor Cost per Unit
50	$100	$2
100	200	2
150	300	2
200	400	2
250	500	2
300	600	2

These direct labor costs are shown in the graph at the top of page 817, where the step-wise variable cost data are indicated by dotted lines and the estimated variable cost data are indicated by a solid line.

Relevant Range for Variable Costs. Because variable costs are assumed to change in a constant proportion with changes in the activity base, the graph of a variable cost when plotted against the activity base appears as a straight line, as illustrated on page 814. In this sense, variable costs are said to be **linear** in nature.

Over a wide range of production, costs may vary in differing proportions to changes in an activity base, rather than in a constant proportion. This phe-

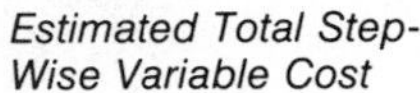

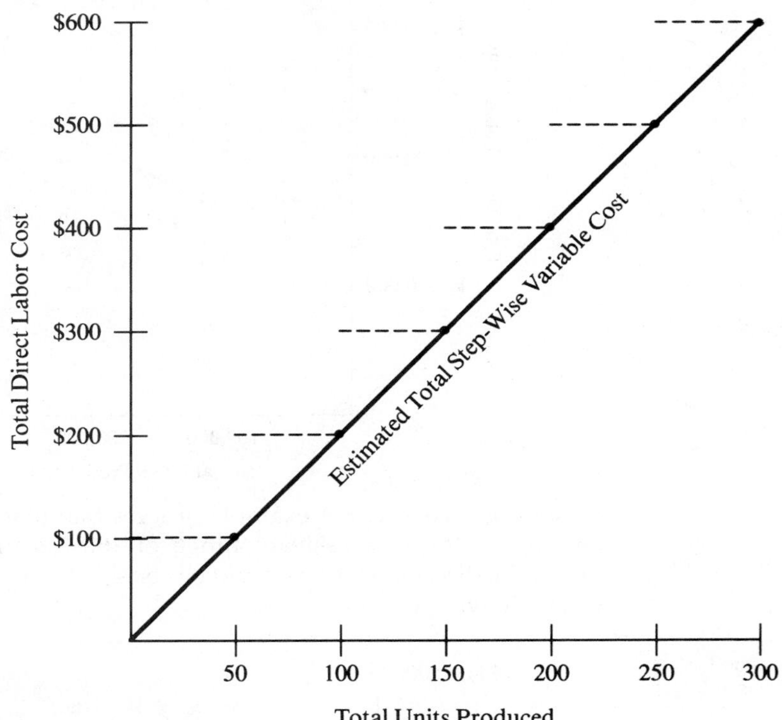

nomenon of changing proportions of costs to changes in an activity base is referred to by economists as the principle of **economies of scale.** This principle recognizes that, when production facilities are limited, some variable costs increase but at a decreasing rate as production increases from a relatively low level. This behavior occurs because, as operations expand, workers learn to be more efficient and division of labor is possible. Therefore, the rate of increase in direct labor costs is not constant. At some point, however, variable costs may begin to increase at an increasing rate, rather than at a constant rate, because of inefficiencies created by such factors as employee fatigue and poor morale.

Graphically, the effect of differing proportions of costs to changes in an activity base is a curvilinear line rather than a straight line. The graph at the top of page 818 illustrates the principle of economies of scale for the direct labor costs of John Manufacturing Inc.

Managerial accountants recognize the curvilinear nature of total costs for wide ranges of production. However, most operating decisions by management focus on a narrow range of relevant activity within which the enterprise is planning to operate. This range of activity is referred to as the **relevant range.** Generally, within the relevant range, variable costs vary so closely to a constant rate that they may be represented by a straight line without a signifi-

Economies of Scale

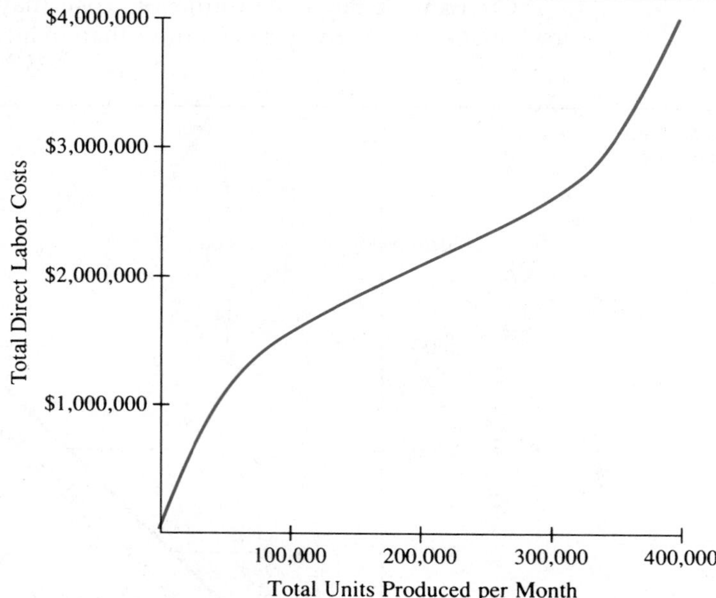

cant loss of accuracy. For example, if John Manufacturing Inc. is considering operating within the relevant range of 100,000 units to 300,000 units per month, the direct labor costs could be considered as linear in nature, as shown in the following graph:

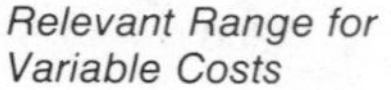

Relevant Range for Variable Costs

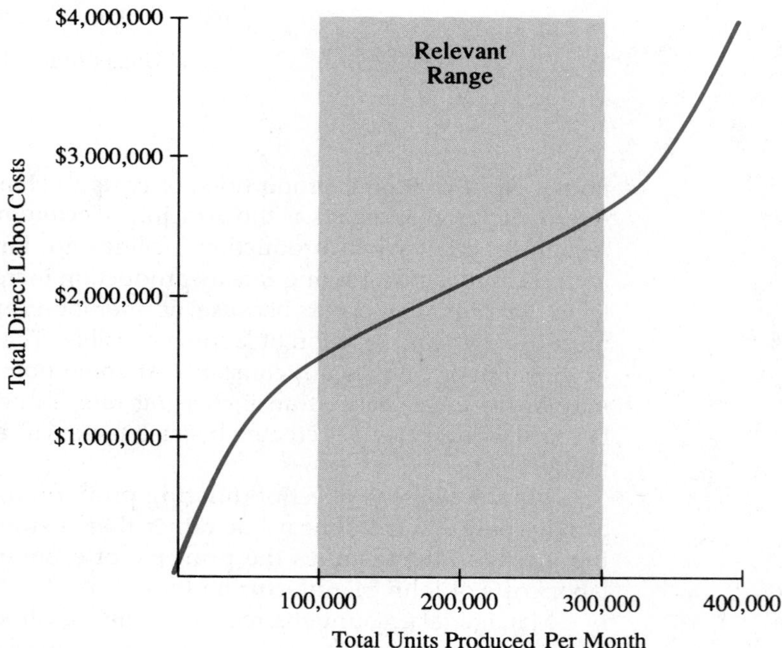

Fixed Costs

Fixed costs are costs that remain constant in total dollar amount as the level of activity changes. Examples of fixed manufacturing costs include staight-line depreciation on factory equipment and buildings, rent on factory plant and equipment, property insurance on factory plant and equipment, and salaries of factory supervisory personnel.

To illustrate, assume that Minton Inc. manufactures, bottles, and distributes La Fleur Perfume at its Los Angeles plant. The production supervisor at the Los Angeles plant is Jane Sovissi, who is paid a salary of $75,000 per year. Sovissi's salary is a fixed cost that does not vary with production. Regardless of whether 50,000, 100,000, or 300,000 bottles are produced, Sovissi will still receive a salary of $75,000.

Although fixed costs remain constant in total dollar amount as the level of production changes, the fixed cost per unit of production changes. As additional units are produced, the total fixed costs are spread over a larger number of units, and hence the fixed cost per unit decreases. This relationship of total fixed cost and fixed cost per unit is illustrated in the following table and graphs for the $75,000 salary of Jane Sovissi:

Number of Bottles of Perfume Produced	Total Salary for Jane Sovissi	Salary per Bottle Produced
50,000 bottles	$75,000	$1.500
100,000	75,000	.750
150,000	75,000	.500
200,000	75,000	.375
250,000	75,000	.300
300,000	75,000	.250

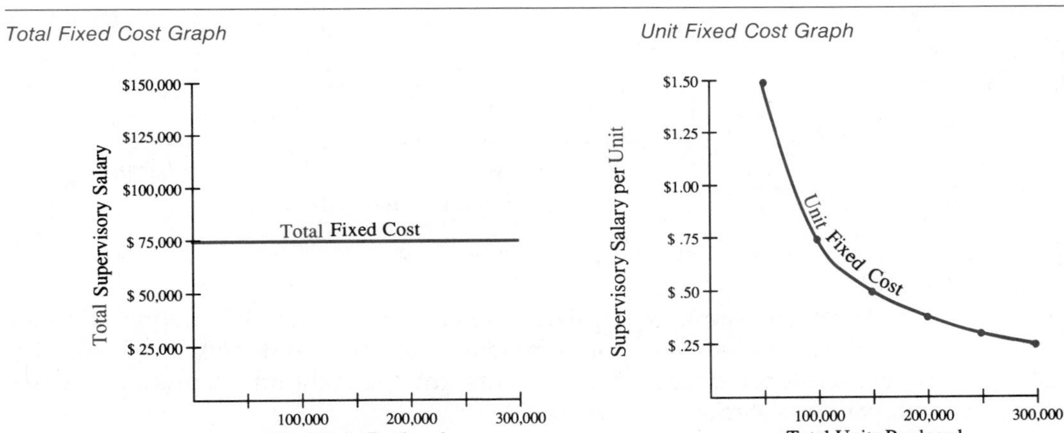

Activity Base for Fixed Costs. Like variable costs, fixed costs are defined relative to an activity base. In most situations, the activity base for fixed costs will be expressed as either units produced, units sold, or sales dollars for a specific time period, normally one year. In the preceding illustration, the activity base was expressed in terms of units of production—bottles of perfume produced.

Step-Wise Fixed Costs. As discussed earlier, many costs behave in a step-wise fashion over a wide range of production. **Step-wise fixed costs** differ from step-wise variable costs in the width of the range of production over which total costs change: the steps are longer for step-wise fixed costs than for step-wise variable costs. For example, a step-wise variable cost might vary with every 50 units produced, while a step-wise fixed cost might vary with every 300,000 units produced.

To illustrate, assume that Minton Inc. can only produce 300,000 bottles of La Fleur Perfume during an 8-hour shift. To produce between 300,000 to 600,000 bottles of perfume, an additional shift has to be added and another production supervisor hired at a salary of $75,000. Likewise, to produce between 600,000 to 900,000 bottles of perfume, yet another production supervisor must be hired. Graphically, the step-wise nature of the production supervisory salary costs is illustrated as follows:

Step-Wise Fixed Costs

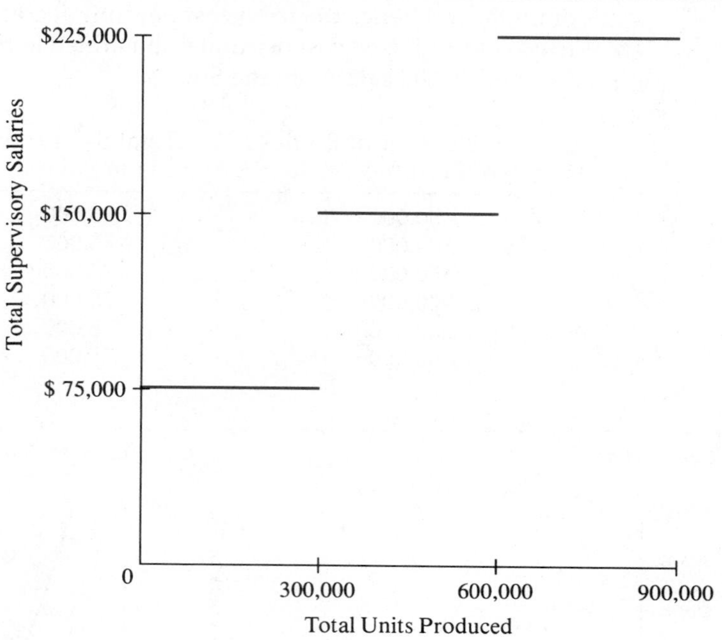

Another example of step-wise fixed costs is straight-line depreciation on machinery. As demand for a product increases and new machines are purchased to produce additional units, total straight-line depreciation costs will vary in a step-wise fashion.

Step-wise fixed costs tend to be long-term in nature and therefore are not easily changed. For this reason, managers should be careful in incurring step-wise fixed costs. Since fixed costs cannot be easily changed, managers often focus on maximizing the usage of existing resources. Later chapters will discuss commonly used methods by which managers evaluate decisions that involve the incurrence of fixed costs.

Relevant Range for Fixed Costs. As discussed in the preceding paragraphs, there exists a relevant range of activity for which management normally focuses its attention for operating purposes. The usefulness of this relevant range for classifying step-wise variable costs was discussed previously. The relevant range is also useful in classifying step-wise fixed costs for management decision-making purposes. To illustrate, if the relevant range of production for Minton Inc. is between 300,000 and 600,000 bottles of perfume, the salary cost of production supervisors is a fixed cost of $150,000, as shown in the following graph:

Relevant Range for Fixed Costs

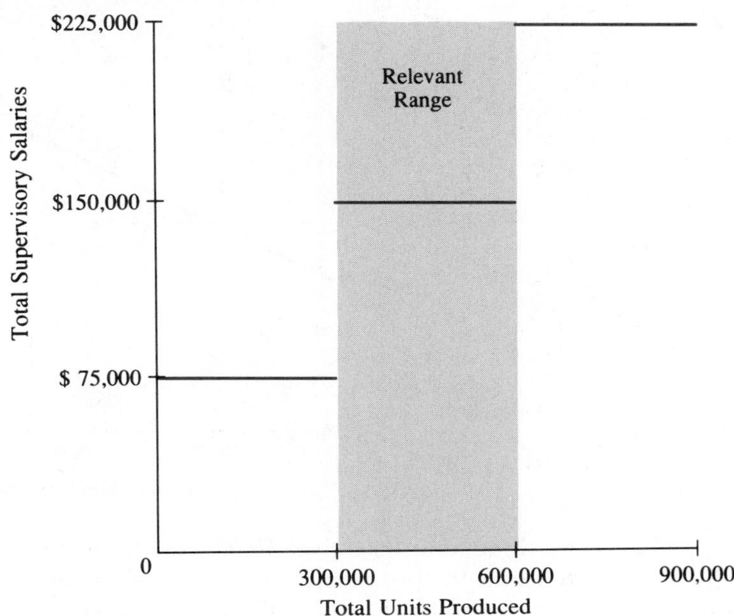

Mixed Costs

A **mixed cost** has characteristics of both a variable and a fixed cost. For example, over one range of the activity base, the mixed cost may remain constant in total amount, and it will therefore be a fixed cost. Over another range of activity, the mixed cost may change in proportion to changes in the activity base, and it will therefore be a variable cost. Mixed costs are sometimes referred to as **semivariable** or **semifixed** costs.

To illustrate, assume that Simpson Inc. manufactures sails, using rented machinery. The rental charges are $20,000 per year plus $1 for each machine hour used. If the machinery is used 20,000 hours, the total rental charge is $40,000 [$20,000 + (20,000 × $1)]. If the machinery is used 30,000 hours, the total rental charge is $50,000 [$20,000 + (30,000 × $1)], and so on. This mixed cost behavior is illustrated graphically at the top of page 822.

In this illustration, which is the most common type of mixed cost behavior, a rental cost of $20,000 will be incurred, even if the machinery is not used. The $20,000 is constant over all levels of production and represents the fixed cost component of the mixed cost. The rental charge of $1 per hour, which represents the variable cost component of the mixed cost, causes the total mixed cost to increase as machine hours are used.

The behavior of mixed costs can vary widely. For example, if the rental charges in the preceding illustration had been $15,000 per year plus $1 for each

Mixed Costs—$20,000 + $1 per Hour

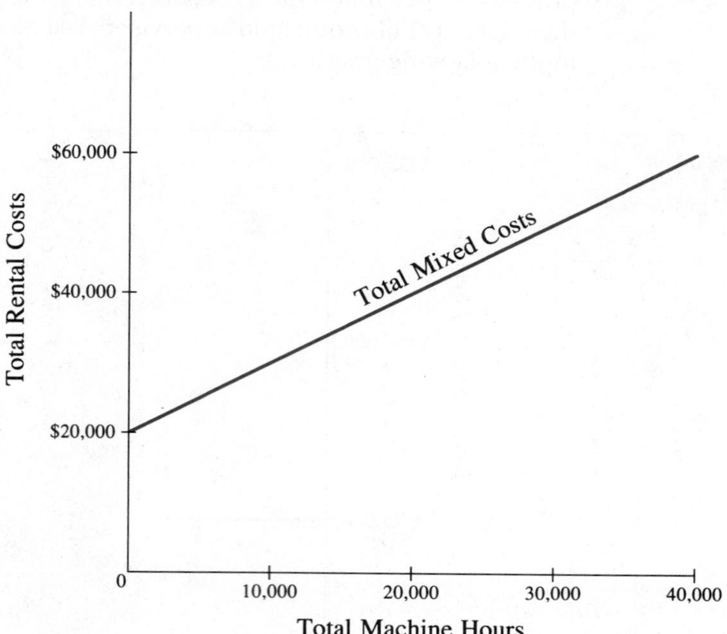

machine hour used over 10,000 hours, the mixed cost graph would appear as follows. In this graph, the fixed cost component is $15,000 and the rental charge of $1 per hour is the variable cost component of the mixed cost. The variable cost component causes the total mixed cost to increase after 10,000 machine hours have been used.

Mixed Costs—$15,000 + $1 per Hour Over 10,000 Hours

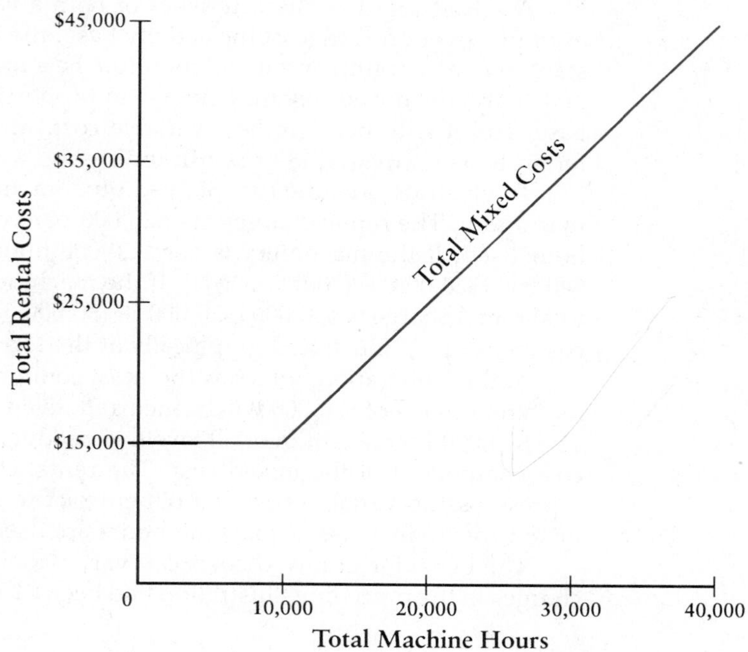

For purposes of analysis, mixed costs can generally be separated into their variable and fixed cost components. The remainder of this chapter describes techniques for such separation, as well as for estimating costs, so that the variable, fixed, and mixed costs can be used by management in decision making.

DISTINGUISHING BETWEEN FIXED AND VARIABLE COSTS

The classification of costs as fixed and variable costs may not be relevant in every situation. In the following excerpt from an article in a British accounting journal, five items that should be considered in distinguishing between fixed and variable costs are identified.

The classification of costs into fixed or variable began, if I remember rightly, in the early 1950s when management accounting really began to take off. It was well suited to the kind of management decisions that had to be taken in the post-war years of industrial expansion. Fixed costs were 'sunk' and need be considered no further except in so far as the plant or buildings concerned would one day have to be replaced. Variable costs were considered to be controllable by line managements and information about variable costs could be used in the improvement of productivity, in pricing decisions and in measurement of divisional performance.

The climate now is different. Since 1959 there have been many changes, of which the following are just a few:

- *companies generally have become more capital intensive.*
- *wages and salaries have increasingly taken on the characteristics of a fixed cost.*
- *product profitability is becoming more important than divisional profitability.*
- *energy cost, which may be neither fixed nor variable, is a higher proportion of total cost.*
- *service industries, which have increased in importance, may need a different approach to cost classification.*
- *contraction and closure is more the order of the day, unfortunately, than expansion and new development.*

In many industries materials have become the only true variable cost. . . . The fixed/variable cost distinction has taken a good battering. Is it then dead—just another chapter in accounting history? I have argued the distinction depends on [the following factors:]

- *Time horizon:*
  how far ahead are you looking?
- *Direction of movement:*
  are you in a situation of expanding or contracting output?
- *Cost center [object]:*
  are you concerned with process, product, department, division, whole company costs, or what?
- *Partly variable costs:*
  are you prepared to study and analyze these one by one?
- *Labor costs:*
  are you aware that some may be fixed, others variable? (not depending solely on whether monthly or weekly paid).

In some companies and some situations, depending . . . on . . . the kind of decisions to be made, it may be safer to abandon the classification fixed/variable altogether and simply assemble ad hoc *the costs which are relevant to the decision. In others, a formal classification may be convenient . . . .*

Source: Edwin Whiting, "Fixed/Variable Cost: Beware!" *Accountancy* (May, 1981), p. 74.

Summary of Cost Behavior Concepts

As indicated in the preceding paragraphs, costs can be classified as variable costs, fixed costs, or mixed costs. Step-wise variable costs and step-wise fixed costs are normally treated as either simple variable costs or fixed costs. Likewise, for purposes of analysis, mixed costs are generally separated into their variable and fixed cost components. The following table summarizes the cost behavior characteristics of variable costs and fixed costs:

Cost	Effect of Changing Activity Level	
	Total Amount	Per Unit Amount
Variable	Increases and decreases proportionately with activity level.	Remains constant regardless of activity level.
Fixed	Remains constant regardless of activity level.	Increases and decreases inversely with activity level.

COST ESTIMATION

OBJECTIVE 2
Describe and illustrate the common methods for estimating costs, including:
High-low method
Scattergraph method
Least squares method.

Although the costs from past operations are known, it is the estimation of future costs that is important for many analyses useful in decision making. In addition, the separation of estimated total costs into fixed and variable cost components is necessary for many decisions. These decisions may involve cost control, product pricing, and production planning, which will be discussed in later chapters. The following paragraphs describe methods of cost estimation, including the high-low method, the scattergraph method, and the least squares method.

High-Low Method

The **high-low method** is used to estimate costs at a desired production level, as well as the variable and fixed components, for either a particular mixed cost or for total costs in general. In this chapter, the examples will use the highest and lowest total costs revealed by past cost patterns. The activity base associated with past cost patterns is usually units of production, although other activity bases, such as machine hours, direct labor hours, or direct labor cost, could be used.

To estimate the variable cost per unit and the fixed cost, the following steps are used:

1. a. The difference between the *total costs* at the highest and lowest levels of production is determined.
   b. The difference between the *total units* produced at the highest and lowest levels of production is determined.
2. Since only the total variable cost will change as the number of units of production changes, the difference in total costs as determined in (1a) is divided by the difference in units produced as determined in (1b) to determine the variable cost per unit.
3. The total variable cost (variable cost per unit × total units produced) at either the highest or the lowest level of production is determined, and the amount is subtracted from the total cost at that level to determine the fixed cost per period.

To illustrate, assume that Sutton Company, which produces sports jerseys, has incurred total costs for the following levels of production during the past 5 months:

	Units Produced	Total Costs
June	175,000 units	$185,000
July	75,000	80,000
August	200,000	210,000
September	325,000	320,000
October	300,000	270,000

The units produced and the total costs at the highest and lowest levels of production and the differences are as follows:

	Units Produced	Total Costs
Highest level	325,000 units	$320,000
Lowest level	75,000	80,000
Differences	250,000 units	$240,000

Since the total fixed cost does not change with changes in volume of production, the $240,000 difference in the total cost represents the change in the total variable cost. Hence, dividing the difference in total costs by the change in production provides an estimate of the variable cost per unit. In this illustration, the variable cost per unit is $.96, as shown in the following computation.

$$\text{Variable Cost per Unit} = \frac{\text{Difference in Total Costs}}{\text{Difference in Production}}$$

$$\text{Variable Cost per Unit} = \frac{\$240{,}000}{250{,}000 \text{ units}} = \$.96 \text{ per unit}$$

The fixed costs will be the same at both the highest and the lowest levels of production. Thus, the fixed cost of $8,000 per month can be estimated by subtracting the estimated total variable cost from the total cost at either the highest or the lowest levels of production, using the total cost equation as follows:

$$\text{Total Cost} = (\text{Variable Cost per Unit} \times \text{Units of Production}) + \text{Fixed Cost}$$

Highest level:

$$\$320{,}000 = (\$.96 \times 325{,}000) + \text{Fixed Cost}$$
$$\$320{,}000 = \$312{,}000 + \text{Fixed Cost}$$
$$\$\ \ 8{,}000 = \text{Fixed Cost}$$

Lowest level:

$$\$\ 80{,}000 = (\$.96 \times 75{,}000) + \text{Fixed Cost}$$
$$\$\ 80{,}000 = \$72{,}000 + \text{Fixed Cost}$$
$$\$\ \ 8{,}000 = \text{Fixed Cost}$$

The variable and fixed cost components of the total cost have now been identified and can be incorporated into the total cost equation:

Total Cost = (Variable Cost per Unit × Units of Production) + Fixed Cost
Total Cost = ($.96 × Units of Production) + $8,000

The cost data and the related total cost for Sutton Company are plotted on the graph below. The graph is constructed in the following manner:

1. Levels of units of production are spread along the horizontal axis. For Sutton Company, it is assumed that a maximum of 400,000 units could be produced per month.
2. The total costs are spread along the vertical axis. For Sutton Company, it is assumed that the total costs could not exceed $400,000 per month.
3. The total cost at the highest and lowest levels of production is then plotted on the graph. For example, the total cost of September's 325,000 units of production would be indicated on the graph by a point representing $320,000. The total cost of July's 75,000 units would be indicated by a point representing $80,000.
4. After the total costs for the highest and lowest levels of production have been plotted on the graph, a straight line (the total cost line) is drawn through the highest and lowest total cost points. The point at which the total cost line intersects the vertical axis represents the estimated fixed cost per month, approximately $8,000. The variable cost per unit, $.96, is represented by the slope of the total cost line. The relevant range on the graph represents the range from which the cost data were gathered.

High-Low Method—Estimated Total Cost Line

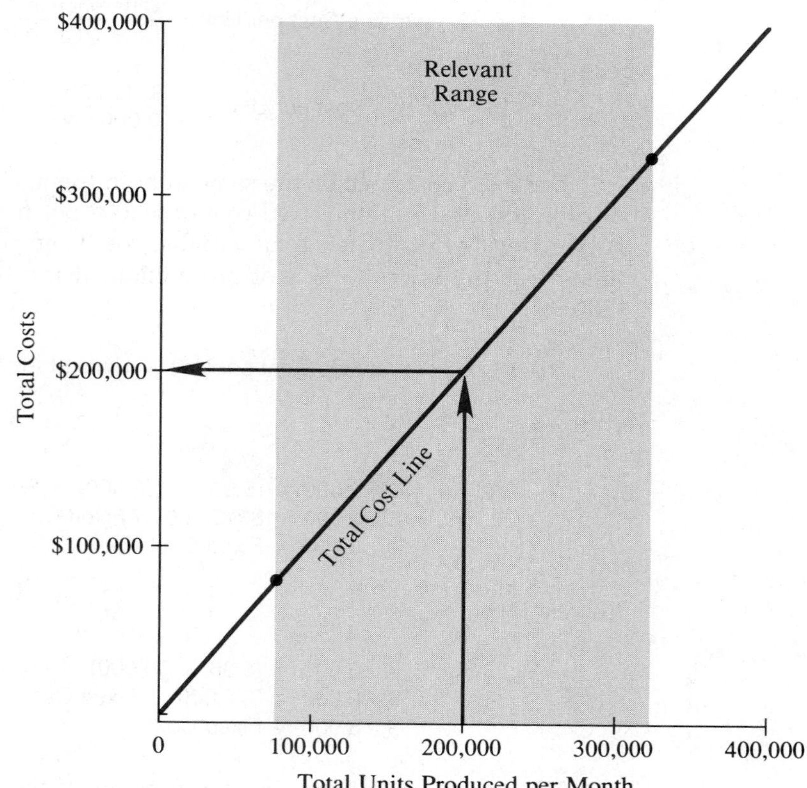

For any level of production within the relevant range, total costs can be estimated using either the graph or the total cost equation. For example, for 200,000 units of production in one month, the estimated total cost would be determined as follows, using the total cost equation:

Total Cost = (\$.96 × 200,000 units) + \$8,000
Total Cost = \$200,000

Alternatively, the total cost can be estimated directly from the graph by locating the total units of production on the horizontal axis, proceeding vertically upward until the total cost line is intersected, and then proceeding horizontally to the left until the vertical axis is intersected. In this way, the estimated total cost of producing 200,000 units is determined to be \$200,000, as shown in the following graph:

High-Low Method—Estimated Total Cost for 200,000 Units of Production

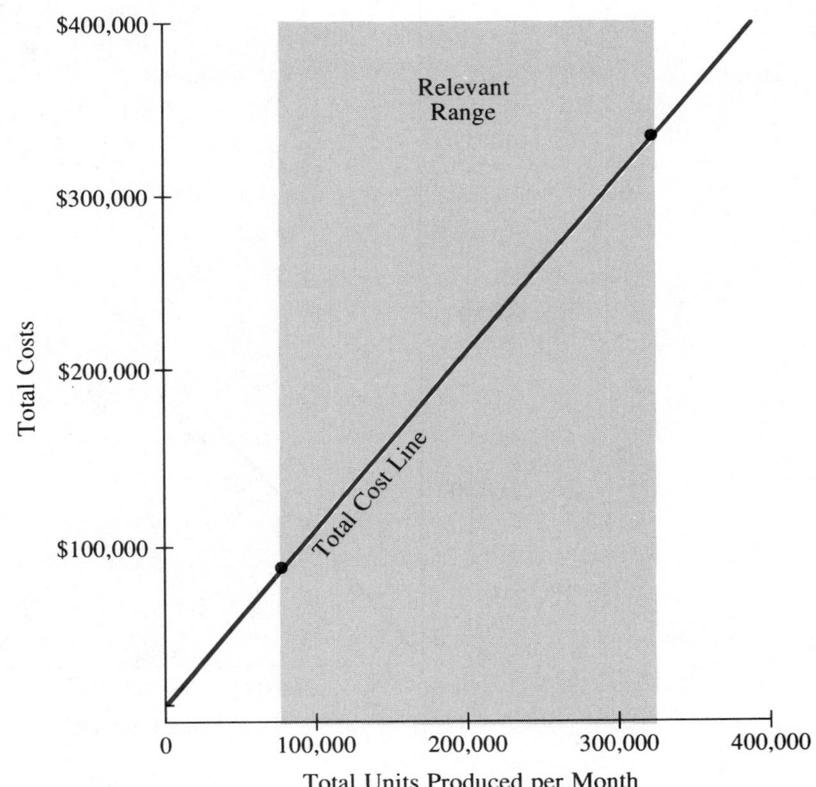

Scattergraph Method

The **scattergraph method** of estimating costs uses a graph format similar to that used for the high-low method. A distinguishing characteristic of the scattergraph method relative to the high-low method is that the scattergraph method uses total costs at all the levels of past production, rather than just the highest and lowest levels. Because the scattergraph method uses all the data available, it tends to be more accurate than the high-low method.

The following cost and production data for Sutton Company, which were used in illustrating the high-low method, are used to illustrate the scattergraph method:

	Units Produced	Total Costs
June	175,000	$185,000
July	75,000	80,000
August	200,000	210,000
September	325,000	320,000
October	300,000	270,000

The following scattergraph was constructed with these data:

Scattergraph—Estimated Total Cost Line

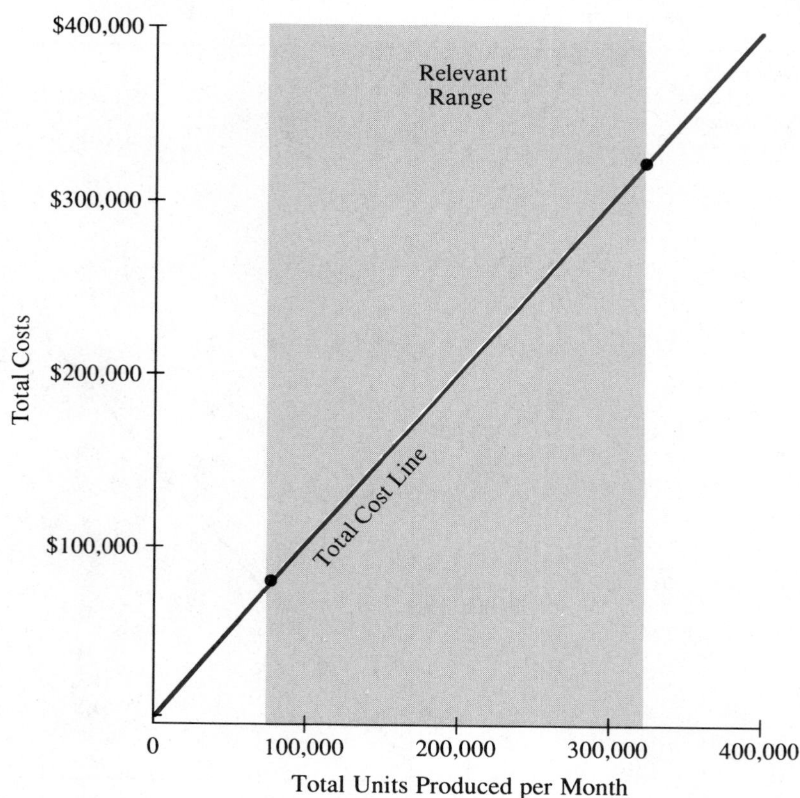

The scattergraph is constructed in the following manner:

1. Levels of units of production are spread along the horizontal axis. For Sutton Company, it is assumed that a maximum of 400,000 units could be produced per month.
2. The total costs are spread along the vertical axis. For Sutton Company, it is assumed that the total costs could not exceed $400,000 per month.
3. The total cost at each past level of production is then plotted on the graph. For example, the total cost of June's 175,000 units of production would be indicated on the graph by a point representing $185,000. The total cost of July's 75,000 units would be indicated by a point representing $80,000.

4. After the total costs for the past levels of production have been plotted on the graph, a straight line representing the total costs is drawn on the graph. *This line is drawn so that the differences between each point and the line are at a minimum in the judgment of the preparer of the graph.*

The scattergraph is simliar to the high-low graph, except for the total cost line. In the high-low method, the total cost line connects the highest and lowest cost points.

From the following scattergraph for Sutton Company, the estimated total costs for various levels of production and the fixed and variable cost components can be determined. The estimated total cost for any level of production within the relevant range can be determined by locating the units of production on the horizontal axis, proceeding vertically upward until the total cost line is intersected, and then proceeding horizontally to the left until the vertical axis is intersected. On the scattergraph for Sutton Company, the estimated total cost for 250,000 units of production is determined to be approximately $240,000.

Scattergraph Method—Estimated Total Cost for 250,000 Units of Production

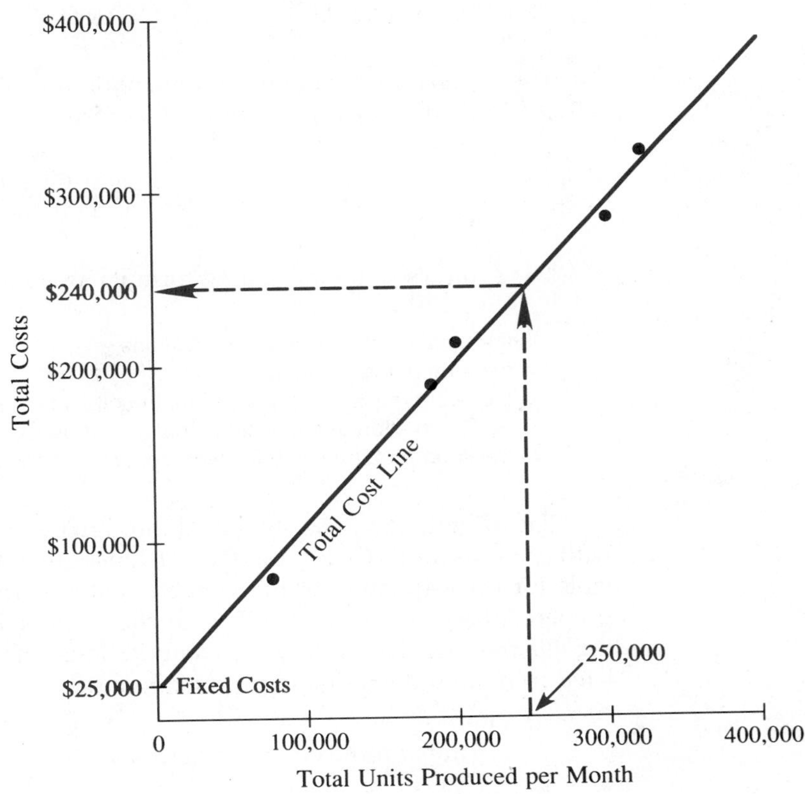

The point at which the total cost line intersects the vertical axis of the scattergraph indicates the estimated fixed cost of production. For Sutton Company, the fixed cost component is approximately $25,000 per month.

The total variable cost for any level of production within the relevant range is the difference between the estimated total cost and the estimated fixed cost. For Sutton Company, the estimated total variable cost for 250,000 units of production is $215,000 ($240,000 − $25,000). The estimated variable cost per unit is $.86 ($215,000 ÷ 250,000 units).

For 200,000 units of production, the estimated total cost would be determined as follows, using the total cost equation:

Total Cost = (Variable Cost per Unit × Units of Production) + Fixed Cost
Total Cost = (\$.86 × Units of Production) + \$25,000
Total Cost = (\$.86 × 200,000 units) + \$25,000
Total Cost = \$197,000

Least Squares Method

While the scattergraph method requires the judgmental drawing of a total cost line through the plotted total cost points, the **least squares method** uses statistics to determine the total cost line. Thus, the resulting estimated total cost line is based on more objective statistical criteria.

The least squares method fits a straight line through the plotted total cost points according to the following total cost equation.

Total Cost = (Variable Cost per Unit × Units of Production) + Fixed Cost

The variable cost per unit component of this equation is estimated statistically, using the following computational formula:

$$\text{Variable Cost per Unit} = \frac{n(\Sigma P_iC_i) - (\Sigma P_i)(\Sigma C_i)}{n(\Sigma P_i^2) - (\Sigma P_i)^2}$$

The symbols in the preceding formula are explained as follows:

n is the number of total cost observations
Σ is the sum of the numbers
P_i is the observed level of production, in units, at period i
C_i is an observation of total cost, in dollars, at period i
P_i^2 is the square of the value P_i, likewise, $(\Sigma P_i)^2$ is the square of the value (ΣP_i)

The formula can be easily solved through the use of a computational table with columns for P_i, C_i, P_i^2, and P_iC_i. To illustrate, the following computational table for the estimation of the variable cost per unit for Sutton Company is prepared, based on the cost and production data that were used in the preceding illustrations. To simplify the computations, the thousands have been deleted from both the cost and production data.

Units Produced (P_i)	Total Costs (C_i)	P_i^2	P_iC_i
175	\$ 185	30,625	\$ 32,375
75	80	5,625	6,000
200	210	40,000	42,000
325	320	105,625	104,000
300	270	90,000	81,000
1,075	\$1,065	271,875	\$265,375
↑ ΣP_i	↑ ΣC_i	↑ ΣP_i^2	↑ ΣP_iC_i

Using the values from the table, the computational formula yields the following results:

$$\text{Variable Cost per Unit} = \frac{n(\Sigma P_iC_i) - (\Sigma P_i)(\Sigma C_i)}{n(\Sigma P_i^2) - (\Sigma P_i)^2}$$

$$\text{Variable Cost per Unit} = \frac{5(\$265,375) - (1,075)(\$1,065)}{5(271,875) - (1,075)^2}$$

$$\text{Variable Cost per Unit} = \frac{\$1,326,875 - \$1,144,875}{1,359,375 - 1,155,625}$$

$$\text{Variable Cost per Unit} = \frac{\$182,000}{203,750} = \$.89 \text{ per unit}$$

The fixed cost component of total cost is estimated statistically, using the following computational forumula:

$$\text{Fixed Cost} = \overline{C} - (\text{Variable Cost per Unit} \times \overline{P})$$

The symbols are explained as follows:

$\overline{C}$ is the average of the monthly total costs
$\overline{P}$ is the average of the monthly units of production

For Sutton Company, the average total cost is \$213,000 (\$1,065,000 ÷ 5), and the average units of production is 215,000 units (1,075,000 units ÷ 5). When these values are substituted into the formula, the fixed cost per month is computed as follows:

$$\text{Fixed Cost} = \$213,000 - (\$.89 \times 215,000 \text{ units})$$
$$\text{Fixed Cost} = \$213,000 - \$191,350$$
$$\text{Fixed Cost} = \$21,650$$

The estimated fixed cost of \$21,650 per month and the variable cost of \$.89 per unit are represented in the total cost equation as follows:

$$\text{Total Cost} = \text{Variable Cost} + \text{Fixed Cost}$$
$$\text{Total Cost} = (\$.89 \times \text{Total Units of Production}) + \$21,650$$

The estimated total cost can be shown graphically by fitting the estimated total cost line to the plotted data, as illustrated on page 832 in the graph of the Sutton Company data. This line, which is sometimes referred to as a **regression line,** is fitted so that the sum of the squares of deviations from each plotted point to the line is smaller (hence, the name *least squares*) than it would be for any other line. Regression lines are discussed in detail in more advanced texts.

For 200,000 units of production in one month, the estimated total cost could be determined by using the graph on the next page or the total cost equation, as follows:

$$\text{Total Cost} = (\$.89 \times 200,000 \text{ units}) + \$21,650$$
$$\text{Total Cost} = \$199,650$$

Least-Squares Method—Estimated Total Cost Line

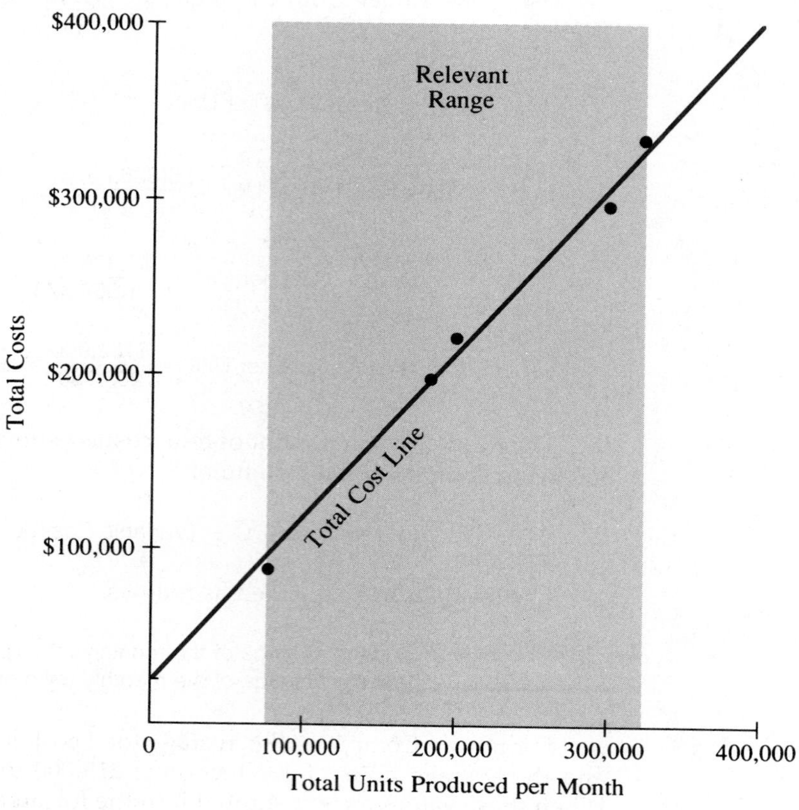

Comparison of Cost Estimation Methods

Each of the three methods described provided different estimates of fixed and variable costs, summarized as follows:

	Variable Cost per Unit	Fixed Cost per Month
High-low method	$.96	$ 8,000
Scattergraph method	.86	25,000
Least squares method	.89	21,650

The cost estimation method that should be used in any given situation depends on such considerations as the cost of gathering data for the estimates and the importance of the accuracy of the estimates. Although the high-low method is the easiest and the least costly to apply, it is also normally the least accurate. The least squares method is generally more accurate, but it is more complex and more costly to use.

In this illustration, the high-low method differs significantly in its estimates of variable and fixed costs, $.96 and $8,000, compared to the variable and fixed cost estimates of the scattergraph and least squares method, $.86 and $25,000, and $.89 and $21,650, respectively. These differences result because the high-low method uses only two cost and production observations to estimate costs for all levels of production. If these two observations are not representative of the normal cost and production patterns for all levels of production, then inaccurate variable and fixed cost estimates may be obtained. To illustrate, if the July production and total cost data for Sutton Company are eliminated because they are seasonal and not typical of normal operations, then the high-low method yields representative estimates which are comparable to the estimates provided by the scattergraph and least squares methods, as shown in the following computations. In these computations, the fixed cost is estimated at the highest level of production.

	Total Units Produced	Total Costs
Highest level	325,000 units	$320,000
Lowest level (excluding July data)	175,000	185,000
Differences	150,000 units	$135,000

$$\text{Variable Cost per Unit} = \frac{\text{Difference in Total Cost}}{\text{Difference in Production}}$$

$$\text{Variable Cost per Unit} = \frac{\$135,000}{150,000 \text{ units}} = \$.90 \text{ per unit}$$

$$\begin{aligned}
\text{Total Cost} &= (\text{Variable Cost per Unit} \times \text{Units of Production}) + \text{Fixed Cost} \\
\$320,000 &= (\$.90 \times 325,000 \text{ units}) + \text{Fixed Cost} \\
\$320,000 &= \$292,500 + \text{Fixed Cost} \\
\$27,500 &= \text{Fixed Cost}
\end{aligned}$$

Care should also be exercised in using the scattergraph and least squares methods. The scattergraph method depends on the judgment of the individual who draws the total cost line through the points on the graph. Different individuals could fit different lines and thereby arrive at different estimates of the total cost. The least squares method is more objective, but it is difficult to use without a computer. Additional complications of the least squares method are described in more advanced texts.

Regardless of which cost estimation method is used, the estimated total cost should be compared periodically with actual costs. Large differences between estimated total costs and actual costs might indicate that the way in which total costs are estimated should be revised. For example, a change in the manufacturing process will likely require the gathering of total cost and production data related to the new process and the estimation of a new total cost equation, using one of the three methods discussed in this section.

OTHER METHODS OF COST ESTIMATION

OBJECTIVE 3
Describe the judgmental and engineering methods of cost estimation.

The preceding paragraphs have described three common methods of cost estimation. Two other methods used in practice include the judgmental method and the engineering method. Each of these methods is briefly discussed in the following paragraphs.

Judgmental Method

The use of the **judgmental method** is viewed by some accountants as an alternative method of cost estimation. Under this method, managers use their experience and past observations of cost-volume relationships to estimate fixed and variable costs. The advantage of this method is its simplicity and its reliance on the seasoned experience of the manager. In some cases, managers use either the high-low, scattergraph, or least-squares method as an initial starting point and then refine the estimates, using experienced judgment. The use of the judgmental method has the further advantage of allowing the manager to incorporate anticipated cost trends into the estimates, rather than relying solely on past cost data. The disadvantage of the judgmental method is its heavy reliance on the judgment of the manager or the accountant who is estimating the costs. If this individual does not exercise good judgment, a significant potential for errors exists. Such errors could have a major effect on related managerial decisions.[1]

Engineering Method

In situations where little or no past cost data are available for use in estimating costs, the **engineering method** may be used to estimate costs. Under this method, industrial engineers provide estimates based on studies of such factors as production methods, materials and labor requirements, equipment needs, and utility demands. The following excerpt taken from a National Association of Accountants Research Report summarizes the use of the engineering method:

> *The industrial engineering approach to determination of how costs should vary with volume proceeds by systematic study of materials, labor, services, and facilities needed at varying volumes. . . . These studies generally make use of . . . results obtained by direct study of the production methods and facilities. Where no past experience is available, as with a new product, plant, or method, this approach can be applied to estimate the changes in cost that will accompany changes in volume.*[2]

CHAPTER REVIEW

KEY POINTS

OBJECTIVE 1 Cost Behavior

Cost behavior refers to the manner in which a cost changes in relation to an activity base. Cost estimation refers to methods used to estimate costs for use in managerial decision making.

Variable costs are costs that vary in total in direct proportion to changes in an activity base. Variable costs remain constant on a per unit basis with changes in the activity base. The relevant activity base for a variable cost depends upon which base is most closely associated with the cost and the decision-making needs of management. In practice, some costs may be classified as variable costs, even though they may not

---

[1] A study sponsored by the National Association of Accountants concluded that managerial judgment is a widely used method of estimating costs. Maryanne M. Mowen, *Accounting for Costs as Fixed and Variable* (National Association of Accountants: Montvale, New Jersey, 1986), p. 19.

[2] National Association of Accountants, *The Analysis of Cost-Volume-Profit Relationships: Research Report No. 16* (New York, 1960).

change in exact proportion to changes in the activity base. Step-wise variable costs change on a step-wise basis with changes in an activity base.

Because variable costs are assumed to change in constant proportion to changes in the activity base, the graph of a variable cost when plotted against the activity base appears as a straight line. In this sense, variable costs are said to be linear in nature. Over a wide range of production, costs often vary in different proportions to changes in an activity base, rather than in a constant proportion. This phenomenon is known as the principle of economies of scale. The narrow range of activity within which an enterprise is planning to operate is referred to as the relevant range. Within the relevant range, variable costs vary so closely to a constant rate that they may be represented by a straight line.

Fixed costs are costs that remain constant in total dollar amount as the level of activity changes. The fixed cost per unit of activity varies. As additional units are produced, the total fixed costs are spread over a larger number of units, and hence the total fixed cost per unit decreases.

Generally, step-wise fixed costs differ from step-wise variable costs in the width of the range of production over which the total costs change. The steps are longer for step-wise fixed costs than for step-wise variable costs. Step-wise fixed costs tend to be long-term in nature and are not easily changed.

A mixed cost has characteristics of both a variable and a fixed cost. For example, over one range of the activity base, a mixed cost may remain constant in total amount, and therefore it will be a fixed cost. Over another range of activity, a mixed cost may change in proportion to changes in the activity base, and it will therefore be a variable cost. Mixed costs are sometimes referred to as semivariable or semifixed costs. For purposes of analysis, mixed costs can generally be separated into their variable or fixed cost components.

The following table summarizes the cost behavior characteristics of variable and fixed costs.

	Effect of Changing Activity Level	
Cost	*Total Amount*	*Per Unit Amount*
Variable	Increases and decreases proportionately with activity level.	Remains constant regardless of activity level.
Fixed	Remains constant regardless of activity level.	Increases and decreases inversely with activity level.

OBJECTIVE 2

Cost Estimation Methods

Cost estimation refers to the methods used to estimate costs for use in managerial decision making. Three commonly used methods for estimating costs are the high-low, scattergraph, and least squares methods.

For either a particular mixed cost or for total costs in general, the high-low method is used to estimate costs at a desired production level, as well as the variable and fixed cost components, by using the highest and the lowest total costs revealed by past cost patterns. To estimate the variable costs per unit and the fixed cost per period, the following steps are used:

1. a. The difference between the total costs at the highest and lowest levels of production is determined.
   b. The difference between the total units produced at the highest and lowest levels of production is determined.

2. The difference in total costs as determined in (1a) is divided by the difference in units produced as determined in (1b) to determine the variable cost per unit.
3. The total variable cost (variable cost per unit × total units produced) at either the highest or the lowest level of production is determined, and the amount is subtracted from the total cost at that level to determine the fixed cost per period.

The estimated total cost line for the high-low method can be plotted on a graph by connecting the highest and the lowest total cost points by a straight line. The point at which the total cost line intersects the vertical axis represents the estimated fixed cost per period. The variable cost per unit is represented by the slope of the total cost line.

The scattergraph method of estimating costs uses a graph format similar to that used for the high-low method. A distinguishing characteristic of the scattergraph method relative to the high-low method is that the scattergraph method uses total costs at all the levels of past production, rather than just the highest and lowest levels.

The scattergraph is constructed using similar procedures as for the high-low graph, except that the total cost line is drawn so that the differences between each plotted point and the line are at a minimum in the judgment of the preparer of the graph.

The least squares method of estimating costs uses statistics to determine the total cost line. The least squares method fits a straight line through the plotted total cost points according to the following total cost equation:

$$\text{Total Cost} = (\text{Variable Cost per Unit} \times \text{Units of Production}) + \text{Fixed Cost}$$

The variable cost per unit component of the equation is estimated statistically, using the following computational formula:

$$\text{Variable Cost per Unit} = \frac{n(\Sigma P_i C_i) - (\Sigma P_i)(\Sigma C_i)}{n(\Sigma P_i^2) - (\Sigma P_i)^2}$$

The fixed cost component of total cost is estimated statistically, using the following computational formula:

$$\text{Fixed Cost} = \overline{C} - (\text{Variable Cost per Unit} \times \overline{P})$$

The high-low method, scattergraph method, and least squares method provide different estimates of fixed and variable costs. The cost estimation method that should be used in any given situation depends upon such considerations as the cost of gathering data for the estimates and the importance of the accuracy of the estimates. Although the high-low method is the easiest and the least costly to apply, it is also normally the least accurate. The least squares method is generally more accurate, but it is more complex and more costly to use.

OBJECTIVE 3

Other Methods of Cost Estimation

Two other methods of cost estimation used in practice include the judgmental method and the engineering method. Under the judgmental method, managers use their experience and past observations to estimate fixed and variable costs. Under the engineering method, industrial engineers estimate fixed and variable costs by studying such factors as production methods, materials and labor requirements, equipment needs, and utility demands.

KEY TERMS

cost behavior 813
cost estimation 813
variable costs 814
step-wise variable costs 815

economies of scale 817
relevant range 817
fixed costs 818
step-wise fixed costs 819
mixed costs 821
semivariable costs 821
high-low method 824
scattergraph method 827
least squares method 830
judgmental method 833
engineering method 834

SELF-EXAMINATION QUESTIONS

Answers at end of chapter.

1. Which of the following statements describes variable costs?
   A. Costs that vary on a per unit basis as the activity base changes
   B. Costs that vary in total in direct proportion to changes in the activity base
   C. Costs that remain constant in total dollar amount as the level of activity changes
   D. Costs that vary on a per unit basis, but remain constant in total as the level of activity changes

2. Which of the following is an example of a mixed cost?
   A. Straight-line depreciation on factory equipment
   B. Direct materials cost
   C. Utility costs of $5,000 per month plus $.50 per kilowatt-hour
   D. Supervisory salaries of $10,000 per month

3. The point at which the total cost line intersects the vertical axis of the scattergraph indicates.
   A. total variable cost
   B. total fixed cost
   C. variable cost per unit
   D. none of the above

4. Which of the following methods of cost estimation always uses statistical formulas to determine the total cost and the variable and fixed cost components?
   A. High-low method
   B. Judgmental method
   C. Least squares method
   D. Scattergraph method

5. Which of the following methods is normally considered the least accurate method of estimating total costs and fixed and variable cost components?
   A. High-low method
   B. Scattergraph method
   C. Least squares method
   D. Engineering method

ILLUSTRATIVE PROBLEM

Hinderman Manufacturing Inc., which began operations in January, 1993, is in the process of estimating variable costs per unit and fixed costs based upon the past year's results. The following production and cost data have been gathered from the accounting and production records for the past 10 months:

	Units Produced	Total Costs
March	80,000	$170,000
April	90,000	190,000
May	100,000	200,000
June	110,000	220,000
July	120,000	224,000
August	115,000	218,000
September	110,000	210,000
October	100,000	205,000
November	110,000	215,000
December	120,000	220,000

January and February cost and production data have been excluded, since operations during these months were in a start-up stage and were not typical.

Instructions:

1. Estimate (a) the variable cost per unit and (b) the fixed cost per month, using the high-low method of cost estimation. Use the cost data for December's production of 120,000 units, rather than the July cost data, since the December costs are more recent.
2. Prepare a least squares computational table for the estimation of variable cost per unit, using the following form. Do not include thousands in the table.

Units Produced (P_i)	Total Costs (C_i)	P_i^2	P_iC_i

3. Determine the estimated variable cost per unit, using the table in (2) and the appropriate least squares formula. Round to the nearest cent.
4. Determine the estimated fixed cost per month, using (2) and (3) and the appropriate least squares formula.
5. Estimate the total cost of 100,000 units of production per month, using (a) the high-low method and (b) the least squares method.

SOLUTION

(1) (a)

	Units Produced	Total Costs
Highest level	120,000	\$220,000
Lowest level	80,000	170,000
Difference	40,000	\$ 50,000

$$\text{Variable Cost per Unit} = \frac{\text{Difference in Total Cost}}{\text{Difference in Production}}$$

$$\text{Variable Cost per Unit} = \frac{\$220{,}000 - \$170{,}000}{120{,}000 \text{ units} - 80{,}000 \text{ units}}$$

$$\text{Variable Cost per Unit} = \frac{\$50{,}000}{40{,}000} = \$1.25 \text{ per unit}$$

(b) The fixed cost per month can be determined by subtracting the estimated total variable cost from the total cost at either the highest or lowest level of production, as follows:

$$\text{Total Cost} = (\text{Variable Cost per Unit} \times \text{Units of Production}) + \text{Fixed Cost}$$

Highest Level:

$$\$220{,}000 = (\$1.25 \times 120{,}000 \text{ units}) + \text{Fixed Cost}$$
$$\$220{,}000 = \$150{,}000 + \text{Fixed Cost}$$
$$\$70{,}000 = \text{Fixed Cost}$$

Lowest Level:

$$\$170{,}000 = (\$1.25 \times 80{,}000 \text{ units}) + \text{Fixed Cost}$$
$$\$170{,}000 = \$100{,}000 + \text{Fixed Cost}$$
$$\$\ 70{,}000 = \text{Fixed Cost}$$

(2)

Units Produced (P_i)	Total Costs (C_i)	P_i^2	P_iC_i
80	$ 170	6,400	$ 13,600
90	190	8,100	17,100
100	200	10,000	20,000
110	220	12,100	24,200
120	224	14,400	26,880
115	218	13,225	25,070
110	210	12,100	23,100
100	205	10,000	20,500
110	215	12,100	23,650
120	220	14,400	26,400
1,055	$2,072	112,825	$220,500

(3) $$\text{Variable Cost per Unit} = \frac{n(\Sigma P_iC_i) - (\Sigma P_i)(\Sigma C_i)}{n(\Sigma P_i^2) - (\Sigma P_i)^2}$$

$$\text{Variable Cost per Unit} = \frac{10(\$220{,}500) - (1{,}055)(\$2{,}072)}{10(112{,}825) - (1{,}055)^2}$$

$$\text{Variable Cost per Unit} = \frac{\$2{,}205{,}000 - \$2{,}185{,}960}{1{,}128{,}250 - 1{,}113{,}025}$$

$$\text{Variable Cost per Unit} = \frac{\$19{,}040}{15{,}225} = \$1.25 \text{ per unit}$$

(4) Fixed Cost = $\overline{C}$ − (Variable Cost per Unit × $\overline{P}$)
$\overline{C}$ = ($2,072,000 ÷ 10) = $207,200
$\overline{P}$ = (1,055,000 units ÷ 10) = 105,500 units
Fixed Cost = $207,200 − ($1.25 × 105,500 units)
Fixed Cost = $207,200 − $131,875
Fixed Cost = $75,325

(5) (a) Total Cost = (Variable Cost per Unit × Units of Production) + Fixed Cost
Total Cost = ($1.25 × 100,000 units) + $70,000
Total Cost = $125,000 + $70,000
Total Cost = $195,000

(b) Total Cost = (Variable Cost per Unit × Units of Production) + Fixed Cost
Total Cost = ($1.25 × 100,000 units) + $75,325
Total Cost = $125,000 + $75,325
Total Cost = $200,325

DISCUSSION QUESTIONS

19–1. Distinguish between cost behavior and cost estimation.

19–2. What are the three most common classifications used for classifying cost behavior?

19–3. Describe how total variable cost and unit variable costs behave with changes in the activity base.

19–4. Which of the following costs would be classified as variable costs for units produced?

(a) Direct labor costs
(b) Straight-line depreciation
(c) Factory supervisor's salary
(d) Electricity costs of $.20 per kilowatt-hour
(e) Insurance premiums on factory plant and equipment of $3,000 per month
(f) Direct materials cost
(g) Oil used in operating factory equipment
(h) Rent of factory building

19–5. Which of the following graphs illustrates how total variable costs behave with changes in total units produced?

(a)

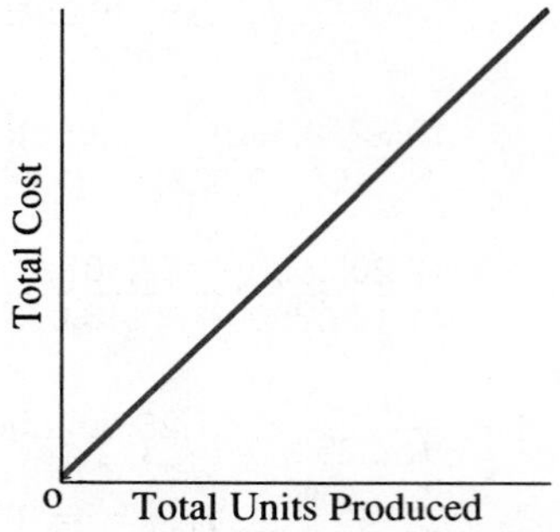

Total Cost
o Total Units Produced

(b)

Total Cost
o Total Units Produced

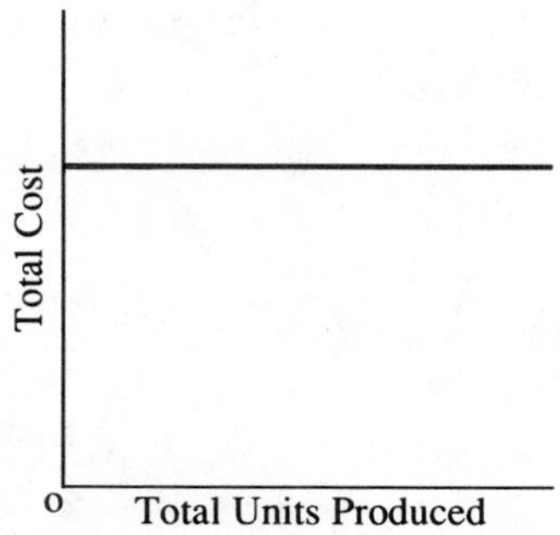

19–6. Which of the following graphs illustrates how unit variable costs behave with changes in total units produced?

(a)

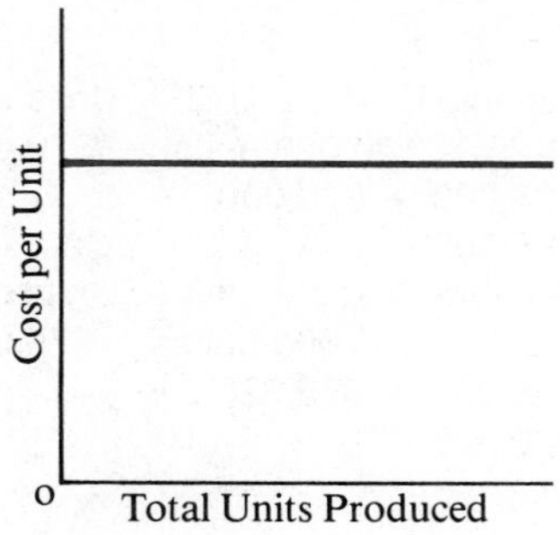

Cost per Unit
o Total Units Produced

(b)

Cost per Unit
o Total Units Produced

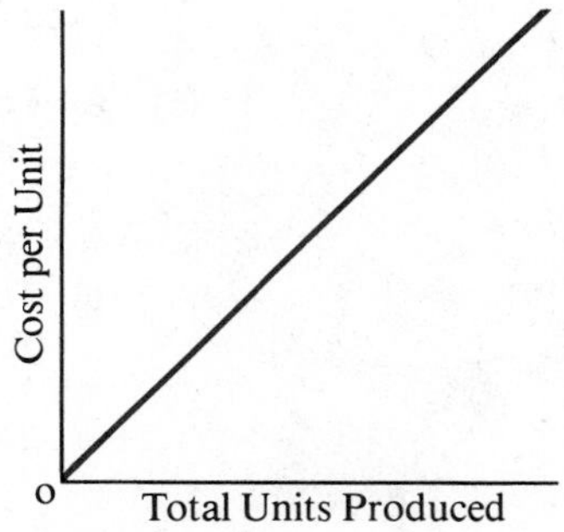

19–7. For Tree Wizard Inc., match each cost in the following table with the activity base most appropriate to it. An activity base may be used more than once.

Cost	Activity Base
(1) Fertilizer	(a) Number of fields
(2) Sales commissions	(b) Number of trees shipped
(3) The cost of water used to water the trees	(c) Number of trees planted in the fields
(4) Dirt for packaging materials for shipping mature trees	(d) Dollar amount of trees planted in the fields
(5) Field managers' salaries	(e) Dollar amount of trees sold

19–8. Which of the following graphs best illustrates the nature of a step-wise cost?

(a)

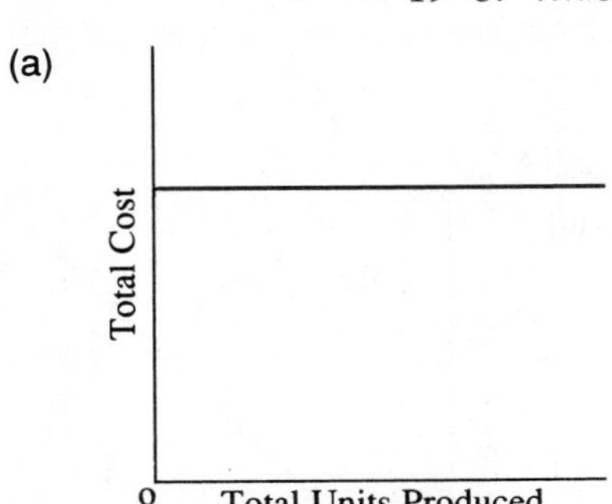

(b)

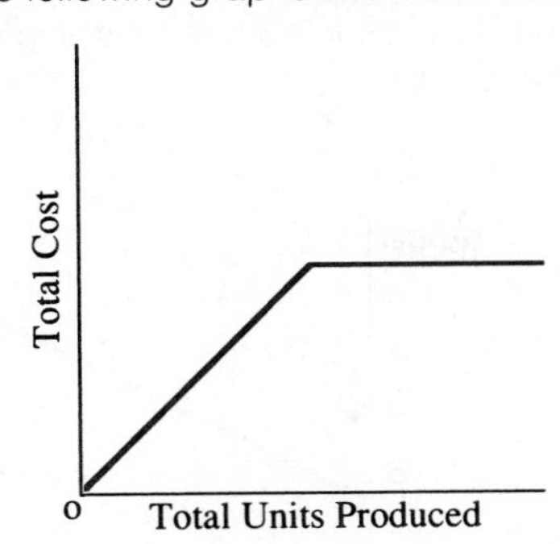

(c)

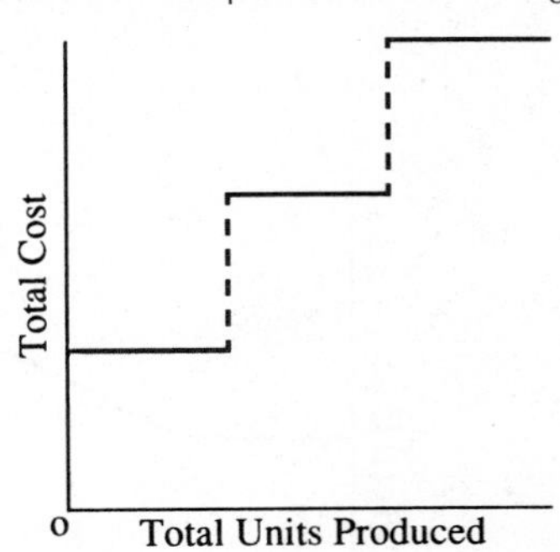

19–9. Why must management exercise added care in planning and scheduling production in order to maximize the efficiency of operations for step-wise costs?

19–10. Does the total cost graph of a variable cost appear as a straight line or as a curvilinear line when plotted against its activity base?

19–11. What term refers to the economic phenomenon of changing proportions of costs to changes in an activity base?

19–12. What term refers to the narrow range of activity within which the enterprise is planning to operate?

19–13. Describe the behavior of (a) total fixed costs and (b) unit fixed costs as the activity base increases.

19–14. Which of the following costs are fixed costs of production?
- (a) Oil and other lubricants used on factory equipment
- (b) Straight-line depreciation on plant and equipment
- (c) Direct materials
- (d) Salary of factory supervisor, $80,000 per year
- (e) Rent of $25,000 per month on factory building
- (f) Electricity used in running machinery, $.08 per kilowatt-hour
- (g) Direct labor
- (h) Property insurance premiums of $5,000 per month on plant and equipment

19–15. Which of the following graphs best illustrates fixed costs per unit as the activity base changes?

(a)

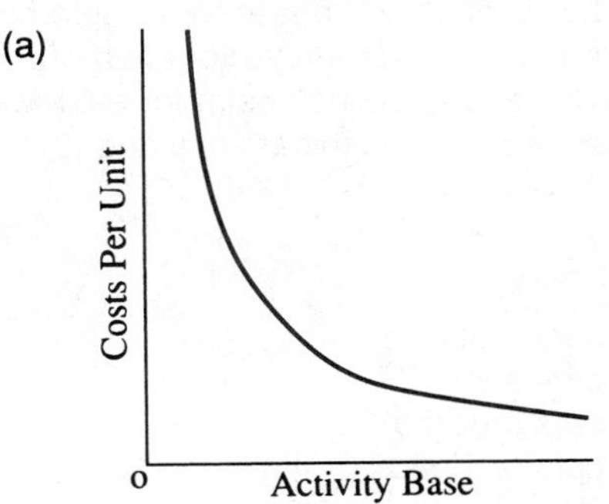

(b)

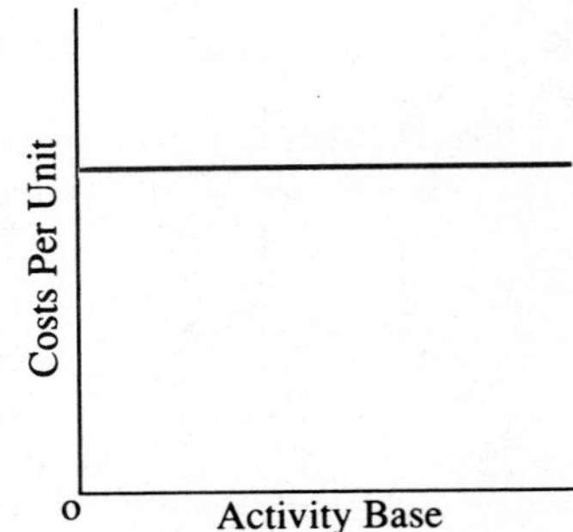

19–16. How do step-wise fixed costs differ from step-wise variable costs?

19–17. What type of cost has both fixed and variable cost characteristics?

19–18. Fate Company rents factory machinery for $10,000 per year plus $.25 per machine hour. Which of the following graphs best illustrates the behavior of the rental costs?

(a)

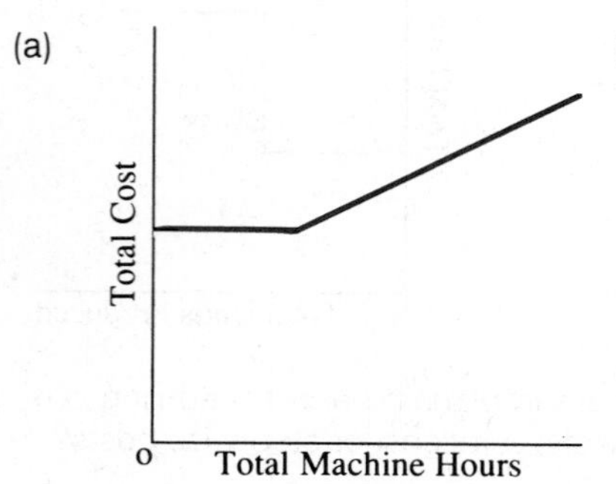

(b)

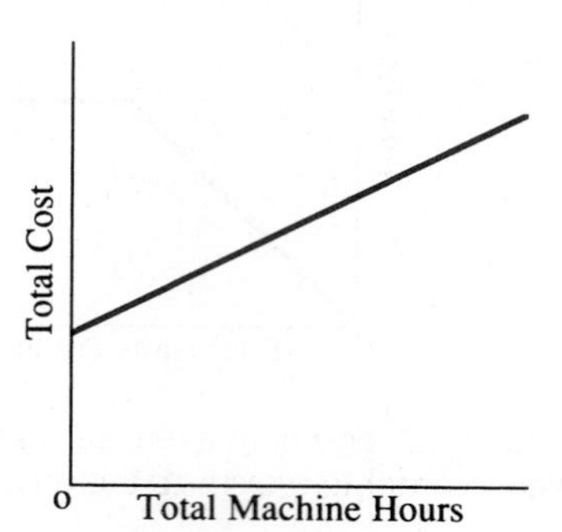

(c)

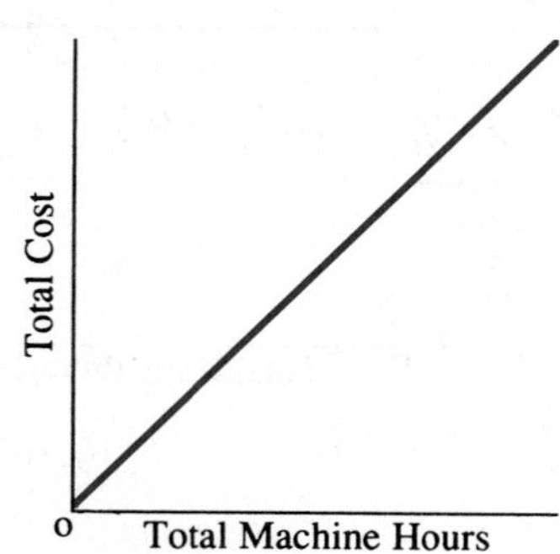

19–19. In applying the high-low method of cost estimation, how is the total fixed cost estimated?

19–20. If the variable cost per unit is $15 and the total fixed cost is $200,000, what is the estimated total cost for the production of 10,000 units?

19–21. Describe how the total cost line is drawn on a scattergraph.

19–22. How is the scattergraph method used to determine the estimated total cost for any level of production?

19–23. Assuming that the least squares method of cost estimation is used to estimate a variable cost per unit of $1, the average of the observed costs is $82,000, and the average of the observed levels of production is 50,000 units, what is the least squares estimate of the total fixed cost?

19–24. What might be indicated by large differences between estimated total costs and actual costs?

19–25. What is the principal disadvantage of using the judgmental method to estimate costs?

19–26. In situations where little or no past cost data are available, what cost estimation method is especially useful to estimate costs?

Real World Focus

19–27. From the following list of activity bases for an automobile dealership, select the base that would be most appropriate for each of these costs: (1) preparation costs (cleaning, oil, and gasoline costs) for each car received, (2) sales persons' commission of 3% for each car sold, and (3) property taxes at the end of the year.

Activity Base

(a) Number of cars received
(b) Number of cars sold
(c) Number of cars ordered
(d) Number of cars on hand
(e) Dollar amount of cars received
(f) Dollar amount of cars sold
(g) Dollar amount of cars ordered
(h) Dollar amount of cars on hand

Ethics Discussion Case

19–28. Alice Gates, who is chief cost accountant for Sanford Industries, has been asked to speak before the local chapter of the Institute of Management Accountants on the topic of "methods of cost estimation." For her speech, Gates plans to discuss and illustrate the cost estimation methods used by Sanford Industries.

Discuss any ethical issues related to Gates' speech.

EXERCISES

Ex. 19–29.
Classification of costs.
OBJ. 1

Following is a list of various costs incurred in producing pencils. With respect to the manufacture and sale of pencils, classify each cost as either variable, fixed, or mixed.

1. Number 2 1/2 lead.
2. Salary of the plant superintendent.
3. Straight-line depreciation on the factory equipment.
4. Red paint for each pencil.
5. Erasers.
6. Property insurance premiums of $1,000 per month plus $.005 for each dollar of property over $2,000,000.
7. Property taxes on factory building and equipment.
8. Hourly wages of machine operators.
9. Pension cost of $.20 per employee hour on the job.
10. Wood costs per pencil.
11. Rent on warehouse of $3,000 per month plus $2 per square foot of storage used.
12. Metal to hold the eraser on the end of the pencil.
13. Electricity costs of $.025 per kilowatt-hour.
14. Janitorial costs of $2,000 per month.
15. Oils used to lubricate machinery.

Ex. 19–30.
Identification of cost graphs.
OBJ. 1

The following cost graphs illustrate various types of cost behavior:

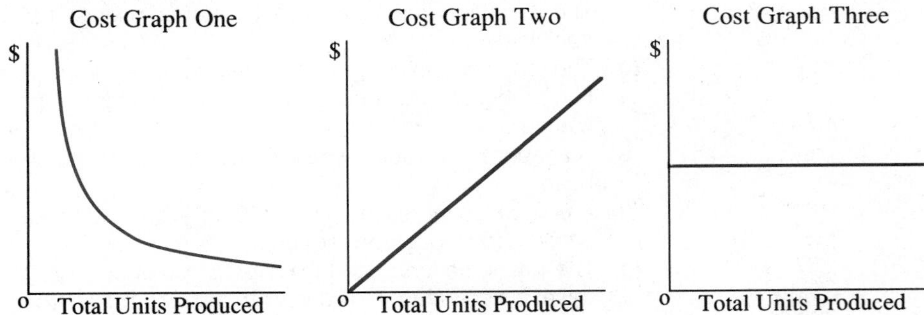

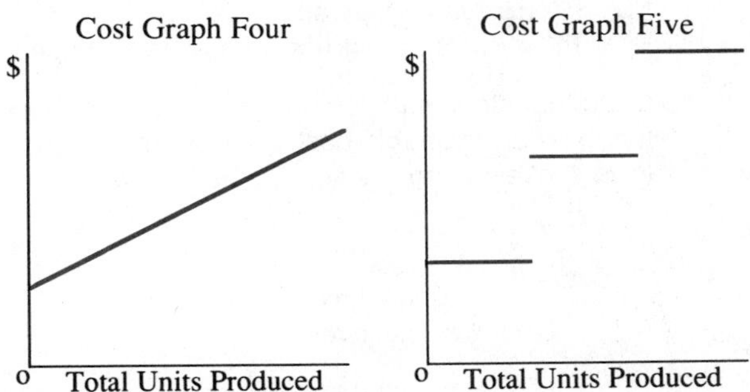

For each of the following costs, identify the cost graph that best illustrates its cost behavior as the number of units produced increases.

(a) Per unit direct labor cost.
(b) Per unit cost of straight-line depreciation on factory equipment.
(c) Electricity costs of $2,000 per month plus $.02 per kilowatt-hour.
(d) Salary of quality control supervisor, $4,000 per month. One quality control supervisor is needed for each 10,000 units produced.
(e) Total direct materials cost.

Ex. 19–31.
Relevant range and computation of fixed and variable costs.
OBJ. 1

Fritz Inc. manufactures tool sets within a relevant range of 50,000 to 150,000 sets a year. Within this range, the following partially completed manufacturing cost schedule has been prepared:

	Tool Sets Produced		
	50,000	100,000	150,000
Total costs:			
Total variable costs	$500,000	(d)	(j)
Total fixed costs	250,000	(e)	(k)
Total costs	$750,000	(f)	(l)
Cost per unit:			
Variable cost per unit	(a)	(g)	(m)
Fixed cost per unit	(b)	(h)	(n)
Total cost per unit	(c)	(i)	(o)

Complete the cost schedule, identifying each cost by the appropriate letter (a) through (o).

Ex. 19–32.
Terminology.
OBJ. 1,2,3.

Choose the appropriate term for completing each of the following sentences.

(a) The term (cost behavior, cost estimation) refers to the manner in which a cost changes as the activity base of the cost changes.
(b) The (high-low, scattergraph) method uses total costs at all levels of past production in estimating costs.
(c) The (least squares, scattergraph) method uses statistics to determine the total cost line.
(d) The (engineering, judgmental) method uses such inputs as studies of production processes, material and labor requirements, and utility demands in estimating costs.
(e) (Variable, Fixed) costs vary in total in direct proportion to changes in an activity base.
(f) A cost which increases by $2,500 for every additional 5,000 units produced is called a (mixed, step-wise) cost.
(g) The phenomenon of changing proportions of costs to changes in an activity base is known as the economic principle of (economies of scale, marginal productivity of inputs).
(h) The range of activity within which the enterprise is planning to operate is the (relevant, tactical) range.
(i) A (mixed, sunk) cost has characteristics of both a variable and a fixed cost.

Ex. 19–33.
Cost estimation, using the high-low method.
OBJ. 2

Dunn Industries has decided to use the high-low method to estimate the total cost and the fixed and variable cost components of the total cost. The data for the highest and lowest levels of production are as follows:

	Units Produced	Total Costs
Highest level	100,000	$370,000
Lowest level	50,000	220,000

(a) Determine the variable cost per unit and the fixed cost.
(b) Based on (a), estimate the total cost for 70,000 units of production.

Ex. 19–34.
Cost estimation, using the scattergraph method.
OBJ. 2

Using data for an 8-month period, a cost accountant for Kessler Company has prepared the following scattergraph as a basis for cost estimation:

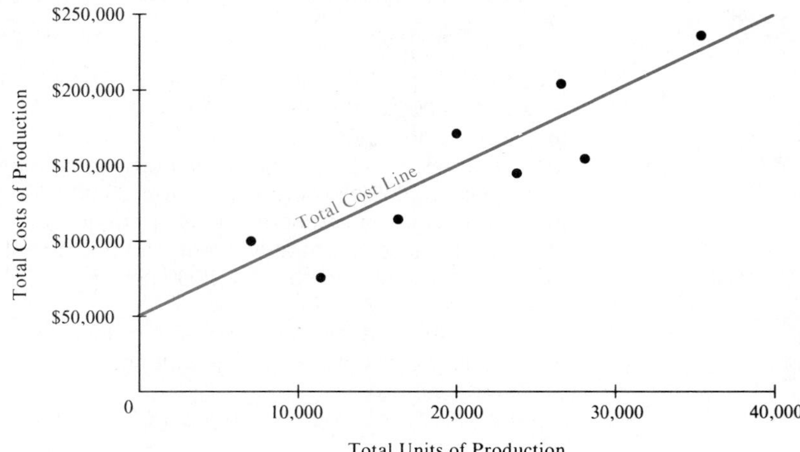

(a) Determine the estimated total fixed cost per month.
(b) Determine the estimated total cost for 30,000 units of production.
(c) Compute the estimated variable cost per unit, based on total cost of producing 30,000 units.

Ex. 19–35.
Cost estimation, using the least squares method.
OBJ. 2

Using data for the first six months of the year, the assistant controller of Winters Company prepared the following table for use in estimating costs:

Total Units Produced (P_i)	Total Costs (C_i)	P_i^2	P_iC_i
120	$100	14,400	$12,000
150	145	22,500	21,750
170	180	28,900	30,600
90	90	8,100	8,100
70	80	4,900	5,600
60	65	3,600	3,900
660	$660	82,400	$81,950

The thousands have been deleted from the table. Thus, 120 units in the table represents 120,000 units of production and $100 represents $100,000.

(a) Determine the estimated variable cost per unit, using the table and the appropriate least squares formula. Round to the nearest cent.
(b) Determine the estimated fixed cost, using the preceding data and the appropriate least squares formula.
(c) Based on (a) and (b), estimate the total cost for 100,000 units of production.

PROBLEMS

Pb. 19–36.
Classification of costs.
OBJ. 1

Helms Inc. manufacturers blue jeans for distribution to several major retail chains. The following costs are incurred in the production and sale of blue jeans:

(a) Blue denim fabric.
(b) Salary of production vice-president.
(c) Rent on experimental equipment, $25,000 per year.

(d) Consulting fee of $50,000 paid to industry specialist for marketing advice.
(e) Janitorial supplies, $2,000 per month.
(f) Salesperon's salary, $12,000 plus 3% of the total sales.
(g) Thread.
(h) Brass buttons.
(i) Legal fees paid to attorneys in defense of the company in a patent infringement suit, $20,000 plus $100 per hour.
(j) Salary of designers.
(k) Insurance premiums on property, plant, and equipment, $10,000 per year plus $3 per $10,000 of insured value over $5,000,000.
(l) Hourly wages of sewing machine operators.
(m) Property taxes on property, plant, and equipment.
(n) Rental costs of warehouse, $2,000 per month plus $1 per square foot of storage used.
(o) Leather for patches identifying each jean style.
(p) Electricity costs of $.07 per kilowatt-hour.
(q) Sewing supplies.
(r) Shipping boxes used to ship orders.
(s) Blue dye.
(t) Straight-line depreciation on sewing machines.

Instructions:

Classify the preceding costs as either fixed, variable, or mixed. Use the following tabular headings and place an X in the appropriate column.

Cost	Fixed Cost	Variable Cost	Mixed Cost

Pb. 19–37.
Identification of cost graphs.
OBJ. 1

The following costs were incurred by Arens Manufacturing Co. in the production of utility trailers:

(a) Aluminum for sides of trailers.
(b) Hourly wages of assemblers, $15 per hour plus time and one half for all hours in excess of 40 per week.
(c) Health insurance costs, $250 per employee plus $.05 per hour worked for first 2,000 hours and $.06 per hour worked for all hours over 2,000.
(d) Maintenance contract for factory equipment: $1,000 for first 1,000 hours, $1,200 for second 1,000 hours, and $1,400 for third 1,000 hours.
(e) Water costs according to the following schedule:

First 1,000 gallons	$.10 per gallon
1,001-3,000 gallons	$.09 per gallon
3,001-5,000 gallons	$.08 per gallon
over 5,000 gallons	$.07 per gallon

(f) Salary of superintendent of production, $75,000 per year.
(g) Rental costs for metal stamping equipment, per machine:

1—100 trailers	$600 per month
101—200 trailers	$500 per month
201—300 trailers	$400 per month

(h) Property taxes paid to city, $5,000, unless 200 trailers are produced, in which case no tax is paid.
(i) Per unit cost of straight-line depreciation.
(j) Electricity costs of $2,000 per month plus $.05 per kilowatt-hour.

(k) Safety chain, where the cost per foot of chain is $.06 per foot for the first 1,000 feet purchased, and $.05 per foot after the purchase of 1,000 feet.

(l) Rental of welding equipment, $1,000 for the first 100 trailers produced plus $7 for each trailer after 100.

Instructions:

For each of the costs, identify the cost graph from the following group of various graphs that best describes the cost behavior as the number of units produced increases. For each graph, the vertical axis represents dollars of cost and the horizontal axis represents units of production.

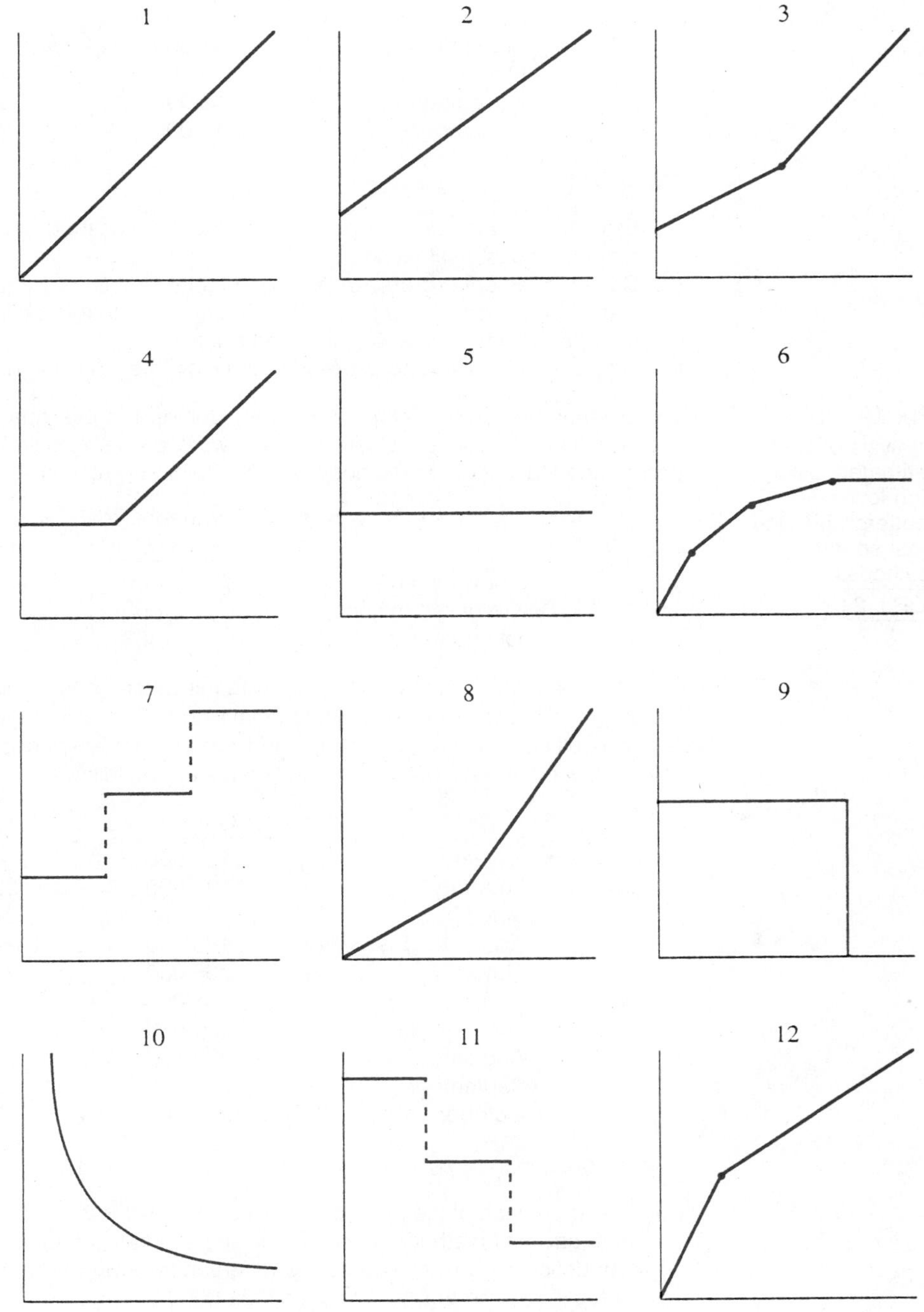

Pb. 19–38.
Cost estimation, using high-low and scattergraph methods.
OBJ. 2

The controller for C.E. Butt Inc. is preparing some preliminary cost projections for the 1993 budget and accumulated the following cost and production data for 1992.

	Units Produced	Total Costs
January	21,000	$42,000
February	20,000	41,500
March	35,000	52,000
April	26,000	46,000
May	48,000	59,000
June	54,000	62,000
July	60,000	65,200
August	45,000	57,000
September	31,000	48,000
October	15,000	40,000
November	12,000	37,000
December	10,000	34,200

Instructions:

(1) Estimate the variable cost per unit and the fixed cost per month using the high-low method of cost estimation.
(2) Construct a scattergraph, including the total cost line.
(3) Based on the scattergraph in (2), estimate the variable cost per unit and the fixed cost per month at 20,000 units of production.
(4) Why are there differences between the estimates in (1) and (3)?

Pb. 19–39.
Analysis of cost estimates, using high-low, scattergraph, and least squares methods.
OBJ. 2

The controller of Curtis Company recently decided to use quantitative techniques for cost estimation purposes. Cost estimates were prepared using the high-low, scattergraph, and least squares methods, with the following results:

	Variable Cost per Unit	Total Fixed Costs
High-low method	$1.00	$45,000
Scattergraph method	1.05	34,500
Least squares method	1.03	38,197

The controller expressed concern with the differences in the estimates, especially the differences between the estimates resulting from the high-low method and the estimates resulting from the scattergraph and least squares-methods. The cost and production data used in developing these estimates are as follows:

	Units Produced	Total Costs
January	135,000	$180,000
February	190,000	232,000
March	200,000	244,000
April	185,000	228,000
May	206,000	248,000
June	197,000	238,000
July	212,000	255,000
August	223,000	272,000
September	218,000	266,000
October	235,000	280,000

Instructions:

(1) Based on each of the preceding cost estimates for the high-low, scattergraph, and least squares methods, (a) compute the estimated total cost for 200,000 units of production, and (b) compute the differences between each of the total cost estimates in (a) and the actual cost of $244,000.

(2) Assuming that the January production and cost data are not typical of normal operations, recompute the variable cost per unit and the total fixed cost, using the high-low method.
(3) Based on (2), recompute the estimated total cost for 200,000 units of production, using the high-low method.
(4) Based on the total cost estimate computed in (3), what is the difference between this estimate and the actual cost of $244,000?
(5) Regardless of which cost estimation method is used, why should the estimated total cost be compared periodically with the actual cost?

Pb. 19–40.
Cost estimation using least squares method.

The management of Andrews Company has decided to use the least squares method for estimating variable costs per unit and fixed costs. The following production and cost data have been gathered from the accounting and production records.

	Units Produced	Total Costs
January	60,000	$160,000
February	70,000	180,000
March	80,000	200,000
April	90,000	220,000
May	100,000	238,000
June	95,000	226,000
July	110,000	260,000
August	120,000	282,000
September	105,000	249,000
October	85,000	212,000

Cost and production data for November and December have been excluded, since operations during these months were not typical because of a strike by the workers.

Instructions:

(1) Prepare a computational table for the estimation of the variable cost per unit, using the following form. Do not include thousands in the table.

Total Units Produced (P_i)	Total Costs (C_i)	P_i^2	P_iC_i

(2) Determine the estimated variable cost per unit, using the table in (1) and the appropriate least squares formula. Round to the nearest cent.
(3) Determine the estimated fixed cost, using (1) and (2) and the appropriate least squares formula.
(4) Estimate the total cost of 80,000 units of production, using the results of (2) and (3).

ALTERNATE PROBLEMS

Pb. 19–36A.
Classification of costs.
OBJ. 1

Taylor and Taylor manufacturers sofas for distribution to several major retail chains. The following costs are incurred in the production and sale of sofas:

(a) Fabric for sofa coverings.
(b) Springs.
(c) Hourly wages of sewing machine operators.
(d) Salary of designers.
(e) Salary of production vice-president.
(f) Rent on experimental equipment, $25 for every sofa produced.
(g) Cartons used to ship sofas.
(h) Rental costs of warehouse, $10,000 per month.
(i) Legal fees paid to attorneys in defense of the company in a patent infringement suit, $10,000 plus $75 per hour.

(j) Property taxes on property, plant, and equipment.
(k) Electricity costs of $.02 per kilowatt-hour.
(l) Consulting fee of $15,000 paid to efficiency specialists.
(m) Janitorial supplies, $10 for each soft produced.
(n) Salesperon's salary, $12,000 plus 5% of the selling price of each sofa sold.
(o) Employer's FICA taxes on controller's salary of $75,000.
(p) Sewing supplies.
(q) Foam rubber for cushion fillings.
(r) Insurance premiums on property, plant, and equipment, $5,000 per year plus $20 per $10,000 of insured value over $8,000,000.
(s) Straight-line depreciation on factory equipment.
(t) Wood for framing the sofas.

Instructions:

Classify the preceding costs as either fixed, variable, or mixed. Use the following tabular headings and place an X in the appropriate column:

Cost	Fixed Cost	Variable Cost	Mixed Cost

Pb. 19–37A.
Identification of cost graphs.
OBJ. 1

The following costs were incurred by Ames Manufacturing Co. in the production of ironing boards:

(a) Wood for top of board.
(b) Hourly wages of assemblers, $15 per hour plus time and one half for all hours in excess of 40 per week.
(c) Property taxes paid to city, $17,500, unless 50,000 ironing boards are produced, in which case no tax is paid.
(d) Water costs according to the following schedule:

First 5,000 gallons	$.28 per gallon
5,001—10,000 gallons	$.25 per gallon
10,001—15,000 gallons	$.23 per gallon
over 15,000 gallons	$.22 per gallon

(e) Maintenance contract for factory equipment; $600 for first 2,000 hours of use, $900 for next 500 hours of use, and $1,200 for remaining hours of use.
(f) Rental of cutting machine according to the following schedule:

1-500 hours of use	$500
501-1,000 hours of use	$400
1,001-2,000 hours of use	$350

(g) Per unit cost of straight-line depreciation.
(h) Electricity costs of $500 per month plus $.03 per kilowatt-hour.
(i) Rental of experimental shipping equipment, $1,000 for first 5,000 shipments and $.04 for each shipment after 5,000.
(j) Special heat-resistant cloth for covering top of board, where the cost per yard is $2 per yard for the first 5,000 yards, and $1.75 per yard thereafter.
(k) Health insurance costs, $250 per employee plus $.015 per hour worked for first 2,000 hours and $.020 per hour worked for all hours over 2,000.
(l) Salary of superintendent of production, $80,000.

Instructions:

For each of the costs, identify the cost graph from the following group of various graphs that best describes the cost behavior as the number of units produced increases. For each graph, the vertical axis represents dollars of cost, and the horizontal axis represents units of production.

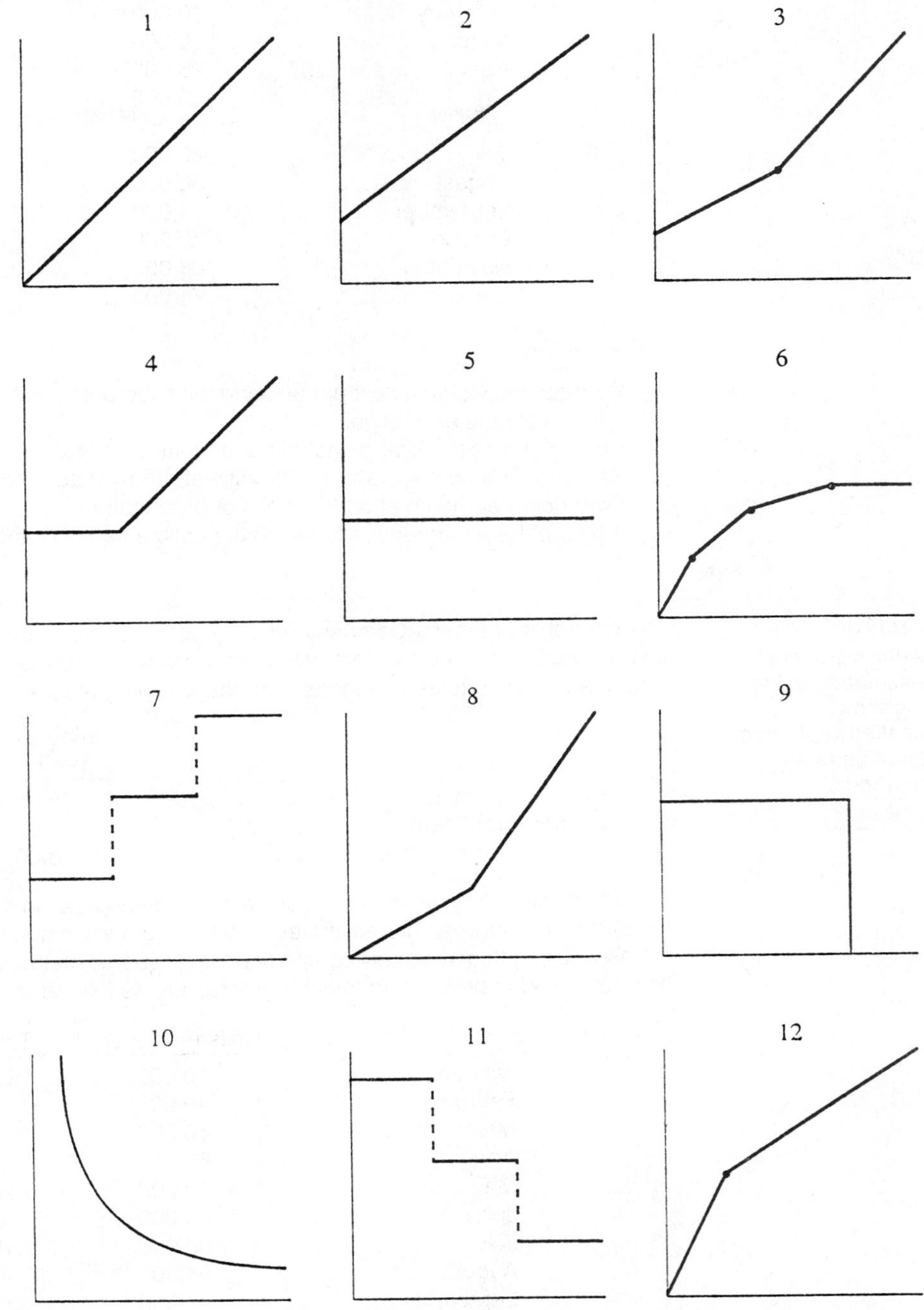

Pb. 19–38A.
Cost estimation, using high-low and scattergraph methods.
OBJ. 2

The controller for Gleason Company is preparing cost projections for the 1993 budget and has accumulated the following cost and production data for 1992:

	Units Produced	Total Costs
January	50,000	$65,000
February	40,000	52,000
March	30,000	44,000
April	25,000	40,000
May	35,000	50,000
June	42,000	54,000
July	20,000	36,000
August	60,000	70,000
September	64,000	72,000
October	70,000	75,000
November	68,000	72,000
December	74,000	76,500

Instructions:

(1) Estimate the variable cost per unit and the fixed cost per month, using the high-low method of cost estimation.
(2) Construct a scattergraph, including the total cost line.
(3) Based on the scattergraph in (2), estimate the variable cost per unit and the total fixed cost per month at 50,000 units of production.
(4) Why are there differences between the estimates in (1) and (3)?

Pb. 19–39A.
Analysis of cost estimates, using high-low, scattergraph, and least squares methods.
OBJ. 2

The controller of Liberty Company recently decided to use quantitative techniques for cost estimation purposes. Cost estimates were prepared using the high-low, scattergraph, and least squares methods, with the following results:

	Variable Cost per Unit	Fixed Costs per Month
High-low method	$8.25	$35,000
Scattergraph method	8.02	60,000
Least squares method	8.00	57,300

The controller expressed concern with the differences in the estimates, especially the difference between the estimates resulting from the high-low method and the estimates resulting from the scattergraph and least squares methods. The cost and production data used in developing these estimates are as follows:

	Units Produced	Total Costs
January	20,000	$200,000
February	40,000	380,000
March	60,000	540,000
April	65,000	600,000
May	50,000	460,000
June	65,000	580,000
July	100,000	860,000
August	94,000	780,000
September	75,000	665,000
October	80,000	700,000

Instructions:

(1) Based on each of the preceding cost estimates for the high-low, scattergraph, and least squares methods, (a) compute the estimated total cost for 75,000 units of production, and (b) compute the differences between each of the total cost estimates in (a) and the actual cost of $667,500.

(2) Assuming that the January production and cost data are not typical of normal operations, recompute the variable cost per unit and the fixed cost per month, using the high-low method.
(3) Based on (2), recompute the estimated total cost for 75,000 units of production, using the high-low method.
(4) Based on the total cost estimate computed in (3), what is the difference between this estimate and the actual cost of $667,500?
(5) Regardless of which cost estimation method is used, why should the estimated total cost be compared periodically with the actual cost?

Pb. 19–40A.
Cost estimation using the least squares method.
OBJ. 2
SPREADSHEET PROBLEM

Rather Company began operations in January, 1992, and has decided to use the least squares method for estimating variable costs per unit and fixed costs. The following production and cost data have been gathered from the accounting and production records for the past 10 months:

	Units Produced	Total Costs
March	110,000	$215,000
April	120,000	220,000
May	100,000	200,000
June..............	110,000	220,000
July	120,000	224,000
August............	115,000	218,000
September	110,000	210,000
October...........	100,000	205,000
November.........	80,000	170,000
December	90,000	190,000

January and February cost and production data have been excluded, since operations during these months were in a start-up stage and were not typical.

Instructions:

(1) Prepare a computational table for the estimation of the variable cost per unit, using the following form. Do not include thousands in the table.

Total Units Produced (P_i)	Total Costs (C_i)	P_i^2	P_iC_i

(2) Determine the estimated variable cost per unit, using the table in (1) and the appropriate least squares formula. Round to the nearest cent.
(3) Determine the estimated fixed cost, using (1) and (2) and the appropriate least squares formula.
(4) Estimate the total cost of 100,000 units of production, using the results of (2) and (3).

MINI-CASE 19

J. C. McBride

J.C. McBride Inc. has recently become concerned with the accuracy of its cost estimates because of large monthly differences between actual and estimated total costs. In the past, the senior cost accountant has used the high-low method to develop estimates of variable costs per unit and fixed costs. These costs estimates are as follows:

Variable cost per unit	$ 3
Fixed cost	20,000

As a new junior cost accountant, the controller has asked you to determine whether the least squares method of cost estimation would provide more accurate estimates. The following twelve-month cost and production data have been gathered as a basis for developing the least squares cost estimates:

	Units Produced	Total Costs
January	60,000	$196,000
February	70,000	220,000
March	80,000	240,000
April	75,000	230,000
May	48,000	165,000
June	40,000	140,000
July	55,000	180,000
August	68,000	212,000
September	62,000	200,000
October	50,000	175,000
November	82,000	245,000
December	90,000	290,000

Instructions:

(1) Prepare a least squares computational table for the estimation of variable cost per unit, using the following form. Do not include thousands in the table.

Total Units Produced (P_i)	Total Costs (C_i)	P_i^2	P_iC_i

(2) Determine the estimated variable cost per unit, using the table in (1) and the appropriate least squares formula. Round to the nearest cent.
(3) Determine the estimated fixed cost, using (1) and (2) and the appropriate least squares formula.
(4) Prepare a table comparing the monthly differences between actual and estimated total costs for the high-low and least squares methods. Use the following headings:

			Total Estimated Costs		Monthly Differences	
Month	Units Produced	Total Actual Costs	High-Low Method	Least Squares Method	High-Low Method	Least Squares Method

(5) Which method is more accurate in estimating total costs? Explain.
(6) Which cost estimation method would you recommend to the controller?

ANSWERS TO SELF-EXAMINATION QUESTIONS

1. B. Variable costs vary in total in direct proportion to changes in the activity base (answer B). Costs that vary on a per unit basis as the activity base changes (answer A) or remain constant in total dollar amount as the level of activity changes (answer C), or both (answer D), are fixed costs.
2. C Mixed costs have characteristics of both variable and fixed costs. Utility costs of $5,000 per month (the fixed component) plus $.50 per kilowatt-hour (the variable

component) (answer C) are a mixed cost. Straight-line depreciation on factory equipment (answer A) and supervisory salaries of $10,000 per month (answer D) are fixed costs. Direct materials cost (answer B) is a variable cost.

3. B The point at which the total cost line intersects the vertical axis of the scattergraph indicates the estimated total fixed cost of production (answer B). The total variable cost (answer A) for any level of production is the difference between the estimated total cost indicated on the scattergraph and the estimated total fixed cost. The estimated variable cost per unit (answer C) can be computed by dividing the total variable cost by the total units of production for a given level of production.
4. C The least squares method (answer C) used statistical formulas to estimate the total cost and the variable and fixed cost components. The high-low method (answer A) uses only data for the highest and lowest levels of production in estimating costs. The scattergraph method (answer D) uses a graph to estimate costs. The judgmental method (answer B) uses experience and past observations of cost-volume relationships to estimate costs. It may also use the high-low, scattergraph, or least squares method as a starting point.
5. A The high-low method (answer A) is normally considered the least accurate method of estimating costs because it uses data for only the highest and lowest levels of production. On the other hand, the scattergraph method (answer B) and the least squares method (answer C) both utilize data for all the observed levels of production. The engineering method (answer D) will provide estimates that are as accurate as the engineering studies upon which the estimates are based.

CHAPTER 20

CHAPTER OBJECTIVES

1 Describe the use of cost-volume-profit analyses in planning operations.

2 Describe and illustrate the use of the contribution margin concept, including the contribution margin ratio and unit contribution margin.

3 Describe and illustrate the mathematical approach to cost-volume-profit analysis.

4 Describe and illustrate the graphic approach to cost-volume-profit analysis.

5 Describe the use of computers in cost-volume-profit analysis.

6 Describe and illustrate the impact of sales mix considerations in cost-volume-profit analysis.

7 Describe and illustrate special cost-volume-profit relationships.

8 Describe the limitations of cost-volume-profit analysis.

COST-VOLUME-PROFIT ANALYSIS

Cost-volume-profit analysis is a commonly used tool that provides management with useful information for decision making. For example, cost-volume-profit analysis may be used in setting selling prices, selecting the mix of products to sell, choosing among alternative marketing stretegies, and analyzing the effects of cost increases or decreases on the profitability of the business enterprise. In the new manufacturing and marketing environment, management must make these kinds of decisions quickly and effectively. As a result, the importance of cost-volume-profit analysis has increased in recent years.[1]

In this chapter, the study of the relationship of costs to volume and profit is based on the cost behavior and cost estimation discussion of Chapter 19. Cost-volume-profit analysis is then applied using the contribution margin concept and in calculating the break-even point, desired profit, sales mix, margin of safety, and operating leverage.

COST-VOLUME-PROFIT RELATIONSHIPS

OBJECTIVE 1
Describe the use of cost-volume-profit analyses in planning operations.

Cost-volume profit analysis is the systematic examination of the interrelationships between selling prices, volume of sales and production, costs, expenses, and profits. This analysis is a complex matter, since these relationships are often affected by forces entirely or partially beyond management's control. For example, the selling price of a product is affected not only by the costs of production, which are generally controllable, but also by changes in consumer trends, which are generally uncontrollable.

Accountants can play an important role in cost-volume-profit analysis by providing management with information on the relative profitability of its various products, the probable effects of changes in selling price, and other variables. Such information can help management improve the relationship between these variables. For example, an analysis of sales and cost data can be

[1] The impact and complexities of the new manufacturing environment on cost-volume-profit analysis is further described and illustrated in Chapter 24.

helpful in determining the level of sales volume necessary for the business to achieve a desired or target profit.

In cost-volume-profit analysis, all costs must be classified into two categories: (1) variable and (2) fixed.[2] As described in Chapter 19, **variable costs** are costs that change, in total, as the volume of activity changes. **Fixed costs** remain constant, in total, as the volume of activity changes. **Mixed costs** sometimes referred to as **semivariable** or **semifixed costs** are costs that have both variable and fixed characteristics. Using the cost estimation methods described in Chapter 19, a mixed cost can generally be separated into its variable and fixed components.

CONTRIBUTION MARGIN CONCEPT

OBJECTIVE 2
Describe and illustrate the use of the contribution margin concept, including the contribution margin ratio and unit contribution margin.

One relationship between cost, volume, and profit that is especially useful in business planning because it gives an insight into the profit potential of a firm is the contribution margin concept. The **contribution margin** is the excess of sales revenues over variable costs and expenses. The deduction of fixed costs and expenses from the contribution margin equals the operating income or loss. To illustrate, the following income statement of Lambert Inc. has been prepared in a contribution margin format:

Contribution Margin Income Statement

Sales	$1,000,000
Variable costs	600,000
Contribution margin	$ 400,000
Fixed costs	300,000
Operating income	$ 100,000

The contribution margin of $400,000 is available to cover the fixed costs of $300,000. Once the fixed costs are covered, any remaining contribution margin adds directly to the operating income of the company.

Contribution Margin Ratio

The contribution margin can also be expressed as a percentage. The **contribution margin ratio** sometimes called the **profit-volume ratio,** indicates the percentage of each sales dollar available to cover the fixed costs and to provide operating income. For Lambert Inc., the contribution margin ratio is 40%, as shown by the following computation:

$$\text{Contribution Margin Ratio} = \frac{\text{Sales} - \text{Variable Costs}}{\text{Sales}}$$

$$\text{Contribution Margin Ratio} = \frac{\$1{,}000{,}000 - \$600{,}000}{\$1{,}000{,}000} = 40\%$$

The contribution margin ratio permits the quick determination of the effect on operating income of an increase or a decrease in sales volume. To

[2] In this chapter, the term "costs" is often used as a convenience to represent both "costs" and "expenses."

illustrate, assume that the management of Lambert Inc. is studying the effect on operating income of adding $80,000 in sales orders. Multiplying the contribution margin ratio (40%) by the change in sales volume ($80,000) indicates an increase in operating income of $32,000 if the additional orders are obtained. The validity of this analysis is illustrated by the following contribution margin income statement of Lambert Inc:

Contribution Margin Income Statement	
Sales	$1,080,000
Variable costs ($1,080,000 × 60%)	648,000
Contribution margin ($1,080,000 × 40%)	$ 432,000
Fixed costs	300,000
Operating income	$ 132,000

Variable costs as a percentage of sales are equal to 100% minus the contribution margin ratio. Thus, in the above income statement, the variable costs are 60% (100%-40%) of sales, or $648,000 ($1,080,000 × 60%). The total contribution margin, $432,000, can also be computed directly by multiplying the sales by the contribution margin ratio ($1,080,000 × 40%).

In using the contribution margin ratio in an analysis, factors other than sales volume, such as the amount of fixed costs, the percentage of variable costs to sales, and the unit sales price, are assumed to remain constant. If these factors are not constant, the effect of any change must be considered in applying the analysis.

The contribution margin ratio is also useful in setting business policy. For example, if the contribution margin ratio of a firm is large and production is at a level below 100% capacity, a comparatively large increase in operating income can be expected from an increase in sales volume. On the other hand, a comparatively large decrease in operating income can be expected from a decline in sales volume. A firm in such a position might decide to devote more effort to additional sales promotion because of the large change in operating income that will result from changes in sales volume. On the other hand, a firm with a small contribution margin ratio will probably want to give more attention to reducing costs and expenses before concentrating large efforts on additional sales promotion.

Unit Contribution Margin

Similar to the contribution margin ratio, the unit contribution margin is also a useful relationship for analyzing the profit potential of proposed projects. The **unit contribution margin** is the dollars available from each unit of sales to cover fixed costs and provide operating profits. For example, if Lambert Inc.'s unit selling price is $20 and its unit variable cost is $12, the unit contribution margin is $8 ($20-$12).

While the contribution margin ratio is most useful when the increase or decrease in sales volume is measured in sales dollars, the unit contribution margin is most useful when the increase or decrease in sales volume is measured in sales units (quantities). To illustrate, assume that Lambert Inc. sold 50,000 units. Its operating income is $100,000, as shown in the following contribution margin income statement:

Contribution Margin Income Statement	
Sales (50,000 units × $20)	$1,000,000
Variable costs (50,000 units × $12)	600,000
Contribution margin (50,000 units × $8)	$ 400,000
Fixed costs	300,000
Operating income	$ 100,000

If Lambert Inc.'s sales could be increased by 15,000 units, from 50,000 units to 65,000 units, its operating income would increase by $120,000 (15,000 units × $8), as shown in the following contribution margin income statement:

Contribution Margin Income Statement	
Sales (65,000 units × $20)	$1,300,000
Variable costs (65,000 units × $12)	780,000
Contribution margin (65,000 units × $8)	$ 520,000
Fixed costs	300,000
Operating income	$ 220,000

Unit contribution margin analyses can provide the useful information for managers. The preceding illustration indicates, for example, that Lambert could spend up to $120,000 to increase sales by 15,000 units. Such expenditures might include special advertising or other product promotions.

MATHEMATICAL APPROACH TO COST-VOLUME-PROFIT ANALYSIS

OBJECTIVE 3
Describe and illustrate the mathematical approach to cost-volume-profit analysis.

Accountants have proposed various approaches for expressing the effect on profits of costs and expenses, along with revenues and volume (cost-volume-profit). The mathematical approach is one approach that is used frequently in practice.

The mathematical approach to cost-volume-profit analysis uses equations (1) to indicate the revenues necessary to achieve the break-even point in operations or (2) to indicate the revenues necessary to achieve a desired or target profit. These equations and their use by management in profit planning are described and illustrated in the paragraphs that follow.

Break-Even Point

The level of operations of an enterprise at which revenues and expired costs are exactly equal is called the **break-even point.** At this level of operations, an enterprise will neither realize an operating income nor incur an operating loss. Break-even analysis can be applied to past periods, but it is most useful when applied to future periods as a guide to business planning, particularly if either an expansion or a curtailment of operations is expected. In such cases, it is concerned with future prospects and future operations and hence relies upon estimates. The reliability of the analysis is greatly influenced by the accuracy of the estimates.

The break-even point can be computed by means of mathematical equations that indicate the relationship between revenue, costs, and volume. To illustrate, assume that the fixed costs for Barker Corporation are estimated to be \$90,000, and variable costs are expected to be 60% of sales. Since the break-even point in sales dollars is that point at which the total sales equals the total costs, it can be computed as follows:

Break-Even Sales (in \$) = Fixed Costs (in \$) + Variable Costs (as % of Break-Even Sales)
S = \$90,000 + 60%S
40%S = \$90,000
S = \$225,000

The validity of the preceding computation is shown in the following income statement:

Sales	\$225,000
Variable costs (\$225,000 × 60%)	135,000
Contribution margin	\$ 90,000
Fixed costs	90,000
Operating income	\$ 0

In practice, the break-even point in sales dollars is often computed by using an equation expressing the relationship between the fixed costs and the contribution margin ratio. The contribution margin ratio for Barker Corporation is 40% (100%—variable costs of 60%), and the break-even point in sales dollars can be computed as follows:

$$\text{Break-Even Sales (Dollars)} = \frac{\text{Fixed Costs}}{\text{Contribution Margin Ratio}}$$

$$\text{Break-Even Sales (Dollars)} = \frac{\$90{,}000}{40\%} = \$225{,}000$$

The break-even point can also be expressed in units. To illustrate, assume the following unit selling price, unit variable cost, and unit contribution margin data for Barker Corporation:

Unit selling price	\$25
Unit variable cost	15
Unit contribution margin	\$10

The break-even point is 9,000 units, which can be computed by dividing the break-even point sales, \$225,000, by the unit selling price, \$25. Alternatively, the break-even units can be computed directly by using the following equation:

$$\text{Break-Even Sales (Units)} = \frac{\text{Fixed Costs}}{\text{Unit Contribution Margin}}$$

$$\text{Break-Even Sales (Units)} = \frac{\$90{,}000}{\$10} = 9{,}000 \text{ units}$$

The computation of the break-even point in dollars emphasizes the contribution margin ratio. The computation of the break-even point in units emphasizes the unit contribution margin. Since unit contribution margin is used most frequently in practice in analyses involving cost-volume-profit, the illustrations in the remainder of this chapter will use the unit contribution margin approach.

The break-even point can be affected by changes in the fixed costs, unit variable costs, and the unit selling price. The effect of each of these factors on the break-even point is briefly described in the following paragraphs.

Effect of Changes in Fixed Costs. Although fixed costs do not change in total with changes in volume of activity, they may change because of other factors, such as changes in property tax rates and salary increases given to factory supervisors. Increases in fixed costs will raise the break-even point. Similarly, decreases in fixed costs will lower the break-even point.

To illustrate, assume that Bishop Co. is evaluating a proposal to budget an additional $100,000 for advertising. Fixed costs (before the additional expenditure of $100,000 is considered) are estimated at $600,000 and the unit contribution margin is $20. The break-even point (before the additional expenditure is considered) is 30,000 units, computed as follows:

$$\text{Break-Even Sales (Units)} = \frac{\text{Fixed Costs}}{\text{Unit Contribution Margin}}$$

$$\text{Break-Even Sales (Units)} = \frac{\$600{,}000}{\$20} = 30{,}000 \text{ units}$$

If the expenditure for advertising is increased by $100,000, the break-even point is raised to 35,000 units, computed as follows:

$$\text{Break-Even Sales (Units)} = \frac{\text{Fixed Costs}}{\text{Unit Contribution Margin}}$$

$$\text{Break-Even Sales (Units)} = \frac{\$700{,}000}{\$20} = 35{,}000 \text{ units}$$

The increased fixed cost of $100,000 increases the break-even point by 5,000 units of sales. The break-even point changes because, for each unit sold, the unit contribution margin of $20 is available to cover fixed costs. An increase in the fixed costs of $100,000 will require an additional 5,000 units ($100,000 ÷ $20) of sales to break even. In other words, an increase in sales of 5,000 units is required in order to generate an additional $100,000 of total contribution margin (5,000 units × $20) to cover the additional fixed costs.

Effect of Changes in Variable Costs. Although unit variable costs do not change with changes in volume of activity, they may change because of other factors, such as changes in the price of direct materials and increases in wages for factory workers providing direct labor. Increases in unit variable costs will raise the break-even point. Similarly, decreases in unit variable costs will lower the break-even point.

To illustrate, assume that Park Co. is evaluating a proposal to pay an additional 2% sales commission to its sales representatives as an incentive to increase sales. Fixed costs are estimated at $840,000, and the unit selling price, unit variable cost, and unit contribution margin before the additional 2% commission is considered are as follows:

Unit selling price	$250
Unit variable cost	145
Unit contribution margin	$105

The break-even point is 8,000 units, computed as follows:

$$\text{Break-Even Sales (Units)} = \frac{\text{Fixed Costs}}{\text{Unit Contribution Margin}}$$

$$\text{Break-Even Sales (Units)} = \frac{\$840{,}000}{\$105} = 8{,}000 \text{ units}$$

If the sales commission proposal is adopted, variable costs will increase by $5 per unit ($250 × 2%). This increase in the variable costs will decrease the unit contribution margin by $5 (from $105 to $100). Thus, the break-even point is raised to 8,400 units, computed as follows:

$$\text{Break-Even Sales (Units)} = \frac{\text{Fixed Costs}}{\text{Unit Contribution Margin}}$$

$$\text{Break-Even Sales (Units)} = \frac{\$840{,}000}{\$100} = 8{,}400 \text{ units}$$

The additional 2% sales commission (a variable cost) increases the break-even point by 400 units. The break-even point changes because, at the original break-even point of 8,000 units, the new unit contribution margin of $100 would only provide $800,000 to cover fixed costs of $840,000. Thus, an additional 400 units of sales will be required in order to provide the additional $40,000 (400 units × $100) contribution margin necessary to break even.

Effect of Changes in the Unit Selling Price. Increases in the unit selling price will lower the break-even point, while decreases in the unit selling price will raise the break-even point. To illustrate, assume that Graham Co. is evaluating a proposal to increase the unit selling price of its product from $50 to $60 and has accumulated the following relevant data:

	Current	Proposed
Unit selling price	$50	$60
Unit variable cost	30	30
Unit contribution margin	$20	$30
Total fixed costs	$600,000	$600,000

The break-even point based on the current selling price is 30,000 units, computed as follows:

$$\text{Break-Even Sales (Units)} = \frac{\text{Fixed Costs}}{\text{Unit Contribution Margin}}$$

$$\text{Break-Even Sales (Units)} = \frac{\$600{,}000}{\$20} = 30{,}000 \text{ units}$$

If the selling price is increased by $10 per unit, the break-even point is decreased to 20,000 units, computed as follows:

$$\text{Break-Even Sales (Units)} = \frac{\text{Fixed Costs}}{\text{Unit Contribution Margin}}$$

$$\text{Break-Even Sales (Units)} = \frac{\$600,000}{\$30} = 20,000 \text{ units}$$

The increase of $10 per unit in the selling price increases the unit contribution margin by $10. Thus, the break-even units decreases by 10,000 units (from 30,000 units to 20,000 units).

Desired Profit

At the break-even point, sales and costs are exactly equal. However, business enterprises do not use the break-even point as their goal for future operations. Rather, they seek to achieve the largest possible volume of sales above the break-even point. By modifying the break-even equation, the sales volume required to earn a desired amount of profit may be estimated. For this purpose, a factor for desired profit is added to the standard break-even formula.

To illustrate, assume that fixed costs are estimated at $200,000, and the desired profit is $100,000. The unit selling price, unit variable cost, and unit contribution margin are as follows:

Unit selling price	$75
Unit variable cost	45
Unit contribution margin	$30

The sales volume necessary to earn the desired profit of $100,000 is 10,000 units, computed as follows:

$$\text{Sales (Units)} = \frac{\text{Fixed Costs + Desired Profit}}{\text{Unit Contribution Margin}}$$

$$\text{Sales (Units)} = \frac{\$200,000 + \$100,000}{\$30} = 10,000 \text{ units}$$

The validity of the preceding computation is shown in the following income statement:

Sales (10,000 units × $75)	$750,000
Variable costs (10,000 units × $45)	450,000
Contribution margin (10,000 units × $30)	$300,000
Fixed costs	200,000
Operating income	$100,000

GRAPHIC APPROACH TO COST-VOLUME-PROFIT ANALYSIS

OBJECTIVE 4
Describe and illustrate the graphic approach to cost-volume-profit analysis.

Cost-volume-profit analysis can be presented graphically as well as in equation form. Many managers prefer the graphic format because the operating profit or loss for any given level of sales can be readily determined, without the necessity of solving an equation. The following paragraphs describe two graphic approaches which managers find useful.

Cost-Volume-Profit (Break-Even) Chart

A **cost-volume-profit chart**, sometimes called a **break-even chart**, is used to assist management in understanding relationships between costs, sales, and operating profit or loss. To illustrate the cost-volume-profit chart, assume that fixed costs are estimated at $100,000 and the unit selling price, unit variable cost, and unit contribution margin are as follows:

Unit selling price	$50
Unit variable cost	30
Unit contribution margin	$20

The following cost-volume-profit chart is based upon the foregoing data:

Cost-Volume-Profit Chart

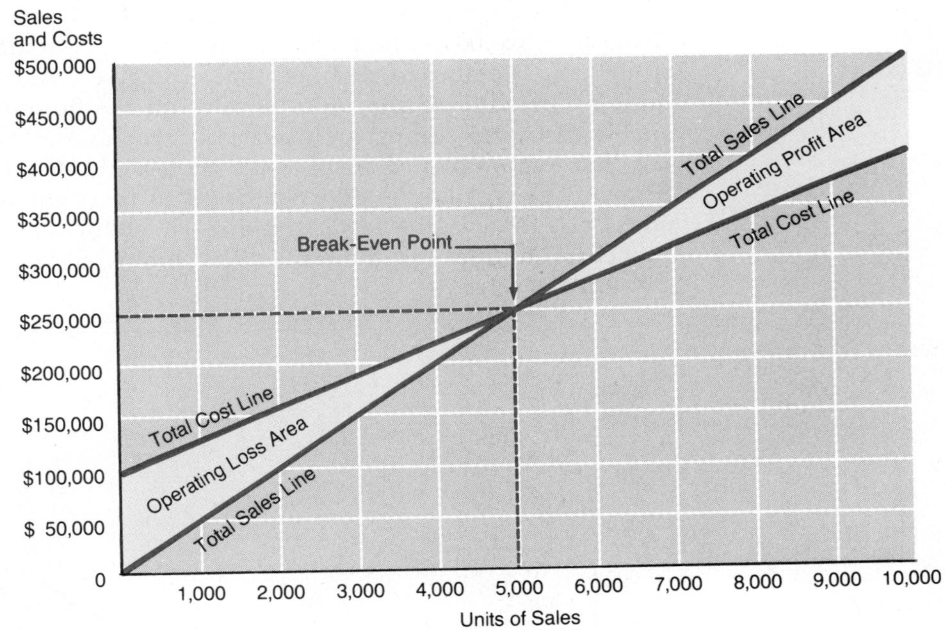

The cost-volume-profit chart is constructed in the following manner:

1. Volume expressed in units of sales is indicated along the horizontal axis. The range of volume shown on the horizontal axis should reflect the relevant range in which the enterprise expects to operate. Dollar amounts representing total sales and costs are indicated along the vertical axis.
2. A sales line is plotted by beginning at zero on the left corner of the graph. A second point is determined by multiplying any units of sales on the horizontal axis by the unit sales price of $50. For example, for 10,000 units of sales, the total sales would be $500,000 (10,000 units × $50). The sales line is drawn upward to the right from zero through the $500,000 point.
3. A cost line is plotted by beginning with total fixed costs, $100,000, on the vertical axis. A second point is determined by multiplying any units of sales on the horizontal axis by the unit variable costs and adding the fixed costs. For example, for 10,000 units of sales, the total estimated costs would be $400,000 [(10,000 units × $30) + $100,000]. The cost line is

drawn upward to the right from $100,000 on the vertical axis through the $400,000 point.

4. Horizontal and vertical lines are drawn at the point of intersection of the sales and cost lines, which is the break-even point, and the areas representing operating profit and operating loss are identified.

In the illustration, the dotted lines drawn from the point of intersection of the total sales line and the total cost line identify the break-even point in total sales dollars and units. In this illustration, the break-even point is $250,000 of sales, which represents a sales volume of 5,000 units. Operating profits will be earned when sales levels are to the right of the break-even point (operating profit area), and operating losses will be incurred when sales levels are to the left of the break-even point (operating loss area).

Changes in the unit selling price, total fixed costs, and unit variable costs can also be analyzed using a cost-volume-profit chart. To illustrate, using the preceding example, assume that a proposal to reduce fixed costs by $20,000 is to be evaluated. In this situation, the total fixed costs would be $80,000 ($100,000 − $20,000). The total cost line should be redrawn, starting at the $80,000 point (total fixed costs) on the vertical axis. A second point is determined by multiplying any units of sales on the horiontal axis by the unit variable costs and adding the fixed costs. For example, for 10,000 units of sales, the total estimated costs would be $380,000 [(10,000 units × $30) + $80,000]. The cost line is drawn upward to the right from $80,000 on the vertical axis through the $380,000 point. The following revised cost-volume-profit chart indicates that the break-even point would decrease to $200,000 or 4,000 units of sales.

Revised Cost-Volume-Profit Chart

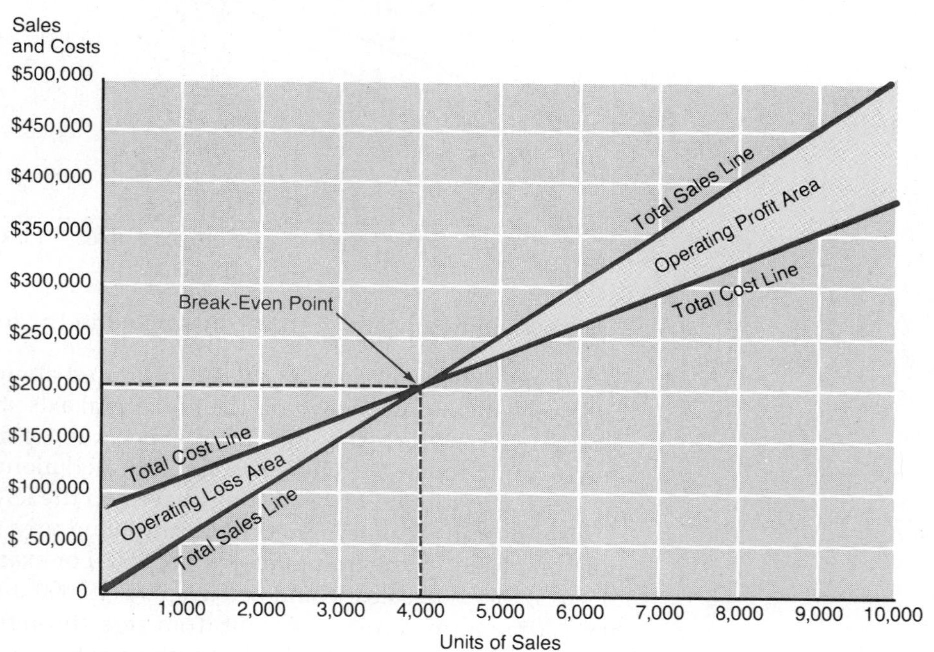

Profit-Volume Chart

Rather than focusing on sales revenues and costs, as was the case for the cost-volume-profit chart, another graphic approach to cost-volume-profit analysis, called the **profit-volume chart** focuses on profitability. On the profit-volume chart, only the difference between total sales revenues and total costs is plotted, which enables management to more easily determine the operating profit (or loss) for various levels of operations.

To illustrate the profit-volume chart, assume the same data as in the preceding illustration for the cost-volume-profit chart. Specifically, assume that fixed costs are $100,000 and the unit selling price, unit variable cost, and unit contribution margin are as follows:

Unit selling price	$50
Unit variable cost	30
Unit contribution margin	$20

The maximum operating loss is equal to the fixed costs of $100,000. Assuming that the maximum unit sales within the relevant range is 10,000 units, the maximum operating profit is $100,000, computed as follows:

Sales (10,000 units × $50)	$500,000
Variable costs (10,000 units × $30)	300,000
Contribution margin (10,000 units × $20)	$200,000
Fixed costs	100,000
Operating profit	$100,000

The following profit-volume chart is based on the foregoing data:

Profit-Volume Chart

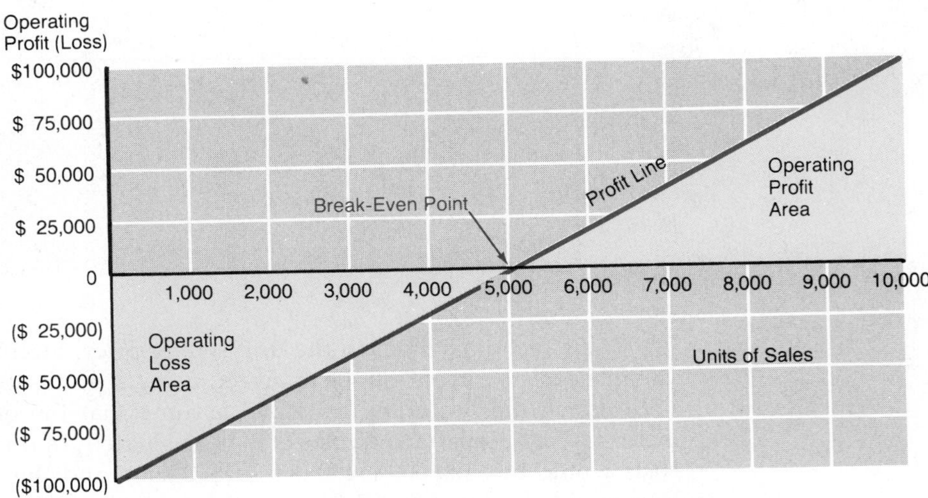

The profit-volume chart is constructed in the following manner:

1. Volume expressed in units of sales is indicated along the horizontal axis. The range of volume shown on the horizontal axis should reflect the relevant range in which the enterprise expects to operate. In this illustration, the maximum number of sales units within the relevant range is assumed to be 10,000 units. Dollar amounts representing operating profits and losses are indicated along the vertical axis.

2. A point representing the maximum operating loss is plotted on the vertical axis at the left. This loss is equal to the total fixed costs at the zero level of sales.
3. A point representing the maximum operating profit within the relevant range is plotted on the right.
4. A diagonal profit line is drawn connecting the maximum operating loss point with the maximum operating profit point.
5. The profit line intersects the horizontal axis at the break-even point expressed in units of sales, and the areas representing operating profit and loss are identified.

In the illustration, the break-even point is 5,000 units of sales, which is equivalent to total sales of $250,000 (5,000 units × $50). Operating profit will be earned when sales levels are to the right of the break-even point (operating profit area), and operating losses will be incurred when sales levels are to the left of the break-even point (operating loss area). For example, at sales of 8,000 units, an operating profit of $60,000 will be earned, as indicated in the following profit-volume chart:

Profit-Volume Chart

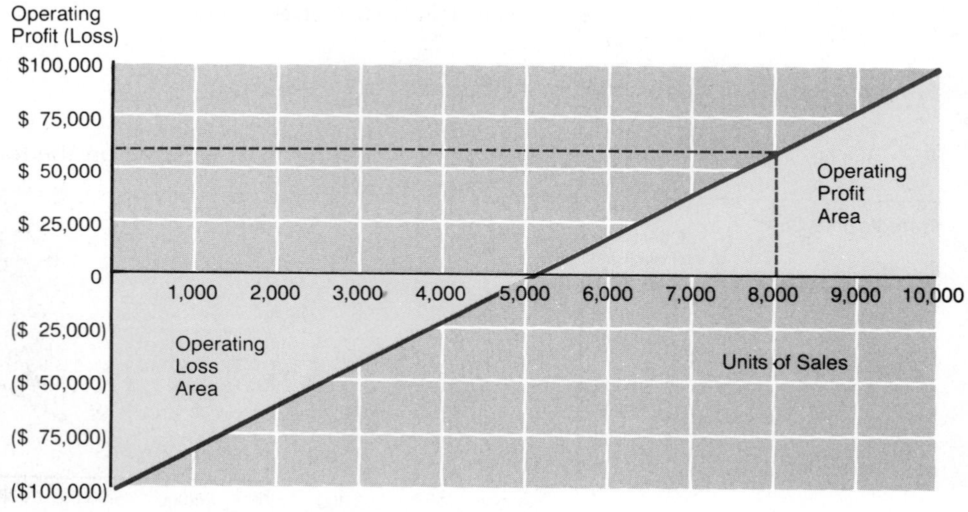

The effect of changes in the unit selling price, total fixed costs, and unit variable costs on profit can be analyzed using a profit-volume chart. To illustrate, using the preceding example, assume that the effect on profit of an increase of $20,000 in fixed costs is to be evaluated. In this case, the total fixed costs would be $120,000 ($100,000 + $20,000), and the maximum operating loss would also be $120,000. If, as in the preceding illustration, the maximum sales within the relevent range is 10,000 units, the maximum operating profit would be $80,000, computed as follows:

Sales (10,000 units × $50)	$500,000
Variable costs (10,000 units × $30)	300,000
Contribution margin (10,000 units × $20)	$200,000
Fixed costs	120,000
Operating profit	$ 80,000

A revised profit-volume chart is constructed by plotting the maximum operating loss and maximum operating profit points and drawing a line between the two points, indicating the revised profit line. The original and the revised profit-volume charts are as follows:

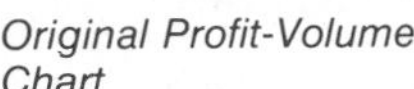

Original Profit-Volume Chart

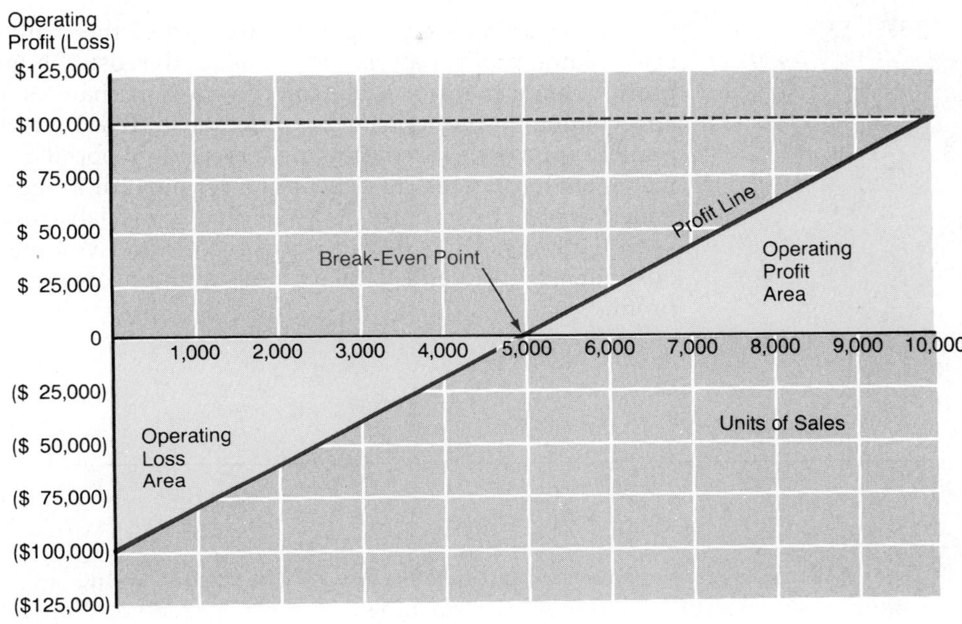

Revised Profit-Volume Chart

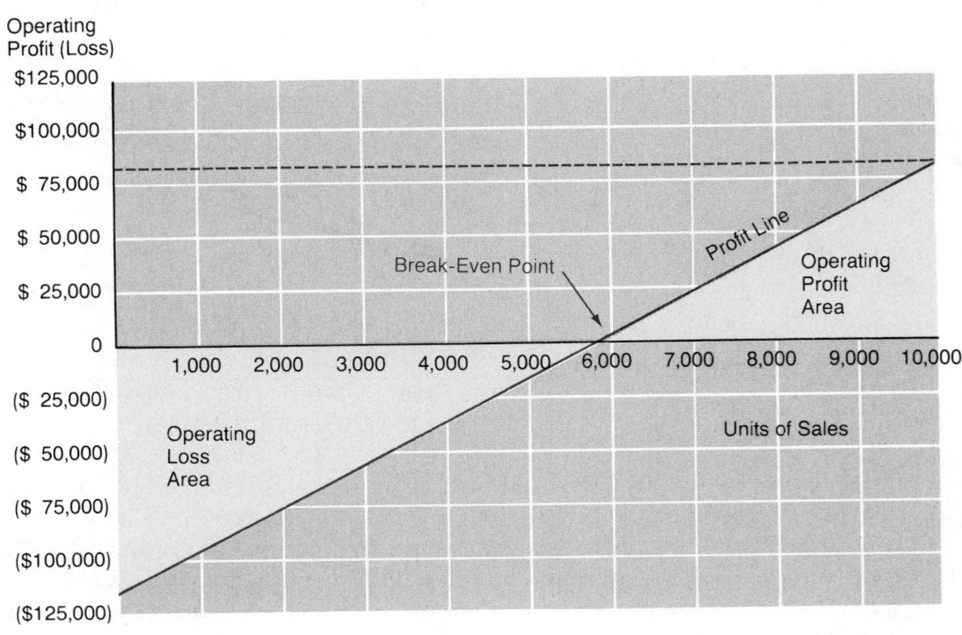

The revised profit-volume chart indicates that the break-even point is 6,000 units of sales, which is equivalent to total sales of $300,000 (6,000 units × $50). Note that the operating loss area of the chart has increased, while the operating profit area has decreased under the proposed change in fixed costs.

USE OF COMPUTERS IN COST-VOLUME-PROFIT ANALYSIS

OBJECTIVE 5
Describe the use of computers in cost-volume-profit analysis.

In the preceding paragraphs, the use of the mathematical approach to cost-volume-profit analysis and the use of the cost-volume-profit chart and the profit-volume chart for analyzing the effect of changes in selling price, costs, and volume on profits have been demonstrated. Both the mathematical and graphic approaches are becoming increasingly popular and easy to use when managers have access to a computer terminal or a microcomputer. With the wide variety of computer software that is available, managers can vary assumptions regarding selling prices, costs, and volume and can instantaneously analyze the effects of each assumption on the break-even point and profit.

BREAK-EVEN ANALYSIS—A CASE STUDY

A break-even analysis based on a multidimensional approach, rather than the traditional two-dimensional approach, was described in an article in *The Journal of Accountancy*. Such an approach is used by The Motor Convoy Inc.'s Chief Financial Officer, who prepared the following break-even chart. The Motor Convoy Inc. is a Georgia-based common carrier operating primarily in the southeastern United States.

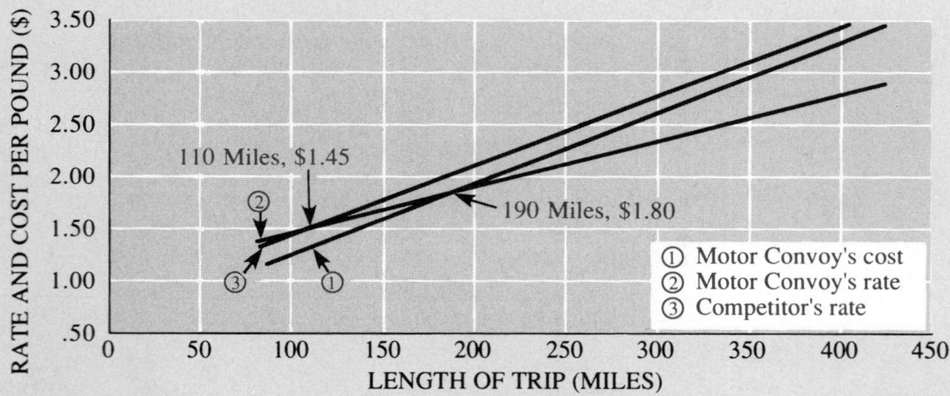

The chart illustrates a typical break-even analysis at The Motor Convoy for a normal load of 2,000 pounds over a relevant range of trips—from about 100 miles to 450 miles. The rate and cost per pound are plotted along the vertical axis, while the length of the trip (in miles) is plotted along the horizontal axis. The rate charged by The Motor Convoy's primary competitor is also graphed, so that the company can assess the effect of competition on developing its operating strategy.

In the above chart, the rate and cost curves are drawn only in the relevant range. The competitor's rate curve is parallel to The

Motor Convoy's cost curve, and both rate curves cross at 110 miles. At this volume, The Motor Convoy's business should be concentrated on trips between 110 miles and 190 miles. On shorter trips, the competition is cheaper than The Motor Convoy, while on longer trips, The Motor Convoy is losing money.

Source: "Multidimensional Break-Even Analysis," *The Journal of Accountancy* (January, 1987), pp. 132-133.

SALES MIX CONSIDERATIONS

OBJECTIVE 6
Describe and illustrate the impact of sales mix considerations in cost-volume-profit analysis.

In most business, more than one product is sold at varying selling prices. In addition, the products often have different unit variable costs, and each product makes a different contribution to profits. Thus, the total business profit, as well as the break-even point, depends upon the proportions in which the products are sold.

Sales mix is the relative distribution of sales among the various products sold by an enterprise. For example, assume that the sales for Cascade Company during the past year, a typical year for the company, are as follows:

Product	Units Sold	Sales Mix
A	8,000	80%
B	2,000	20
	10,000	100%

The sales mix for products A and B can be expressed as a relative percentage, as shown above, or as the ratio of 80:20.

Sales Mix and the Break-Even Point

The break-even point for an enterprise selling two or more products must be calculated on the basis of a specified sales mix. If the sales mix is assumed to be constant, the break-even point and the sales necessary to achieve desired or target levels of operating profit can be computed using the standard calculations.

To illustrate the computation of the break-even point for Cascade Company, assume that fixed costs are $200,000. In addition, assume that the unit selling prices, unit variable costs, unit contribution margins, and sales mix for products A and B are as follows:

Product	Unit Selling Price	Unit Variable Cost	Unit Contribution Margin	Sales Mix
A	$ 90	$70	$20	80%
B	140	95	45	20

To compute the break-even point when several products are sold, it is useful to think of the individual products as components of one overall enterprise product. For Cascade Company, assume that this overall enterprise product is arbitrarily labeled E. The unit selling price of E can be thought of as equal to the total of the unit selling prices of the individual products A and B, multiplied by their respective sales mix percentages. Likewise, the unit variable cost and unit contribution margin of E can be thought of as equal to the total of the unit variable costs and unit contribution margins of products A and B, multiplied by the sales mix percentages. These computations are as follows:

Unit selling price of E: ($90 × .8) + ($140 × .2) = $100
Unit variable cost of E: ($70 × .8) + ($95 × .2) = $75
Unit contribution margin of E: ($20 × .8) + ($45 × .2) = $25

The break-even point of 8,000 units of E can be determined in the normal manner as follows:

$$\text{Break-Even Sales (Units)} = \frac{\text{Fixed Costs}}{\text{Unit Contribution Margin}}$$

$$\text{Break-Even Sales (Units)} = \frac{\$200{,}000}{\$25} = 8{,}000 \text{ units}$$

Since the sales mix for products A and B is 80% and 20% respectively, the break-even quantity of A is 6,400 units (8,000 units × 80%) and B is 1,600 units (8,000 units × 20%). The validity of the preceding analysis can be verified by preparing the following income statement:

Contribution Margin Income Statement

	Product A	Product B	Total
Sales:			
6,400 units × $90	$576,000		$576,000
1,600 units × $140		$224,000	224,000
Total sales	$576,000	$224,000	$800,000
Variable costs:			
6,400 units × $70	$448,000		$448,000
1,600 units × $95		$152,000	152,000
Total variable costs	$448,000	$152,000	$600,000
Contribution margin	$128,000	$ 72,000	$200,000
Fixed costs			200,000
Operating profit			$ 0

The effects of changes in the sales mix on the break-even point can be determined by repeating the preceding analysis, assuming a different sales mix.

Sales Mix and Desired Profit

The sales volume needed to earn an amount of profit when an enterprise sells two or more products can be computed using an approach similar to that described in the previous section. For example, in the preceding illustration, the total sales necessary for Cascade Company to earn an operating profit of $40,000, with the original sales mix of 80% and 20%, is 9,600 units, computed as follows:

$$\text{Sales (Units)} = \frac{\text{Fixed Costs} + \text{Desired Profit}}{\text{Unit Contribution Margin}}$$

$$\text{Sales (Units)} = \frac{\$200{,}000 + \$40{,}000}{\$25} = 9{,}600 \text{ units}$$

Since the sales mix for products A and B is 80% and 20% respectively, the quantity of A to be sold is 7,680 units (9,600 units × 80%) and B is 1,920 units (9,600 units × 20%). The validity of this approach can be verified by preparing the following income statement:

Contribution Margin Income Statement

	Product A	Product B	Total
Sales:			
7,680 units × $90	$691,200		$691,200
1,920 units × $140		$268,800	268,800
Total sales	$691,200	$268,800	$960,000
Variable costs:			
7,680 units × $70	$537,600		$537,600
1,920 units × $95		$182,400	182,400
Total variable costs	$537,600	$182,400	$720,000
Contribution margin	$153,600	$ 86,400	$240,000
Fixed costs			200,000
Operating profit			$ 40,000

SPECIAL COST-VOLUME-PROFIT RELATIONSHIPS

OBJECTIVE 7
Describe and illustrate special cost-volume-profit relationships.

Additional relationships can be developed from the information presented in both the mathematical and graphic approaches to cost-volume-profit analysis. Two of these relationships that are especially useful to management in decision making are discussed in the following paragraphs.

Margin of Safety

The difference between the current sales revenue and the sales at the break-even point is called the **margin of safety.** It represents the possible decrease in sales that may occur before an operating loss results. The margin of safety may be stated in terms of dollars, units, or as a percentage of sales.

To illustrate, assume that sales is $250,000, the unit selling price is $25, and sales at the break-even point amount to $200,000. The margin of safety is $50,000 ($250,000 − $200,000), 2,000 units ($50,000 ÷ $25), or 20%, as shown by the following computation:

$$\text{Margin of Safety} = \frac{\text{Sales} - \text{Sales at Break-Even Point}}{\text{Sales}}$$

$$\text{Margin of Safety} = \frac{\$250{,}000 - \$200{,}000}{\$250{,}000} = 20\%$$

The margin of safety is useful in evaluating past operations and as a guide to business planning. For example, if the margin of safety is low, management should carefully study forecasts of future sales because even a small decline in sales revenue will result in an operating loss.

Operating Leverage

Operating leverage is a measure of the relative mix of an enterprise's variable costs and fixed costs. It is computed by measuring the relationship between contribution margin and operating income, as follows:

$$\text{Operating Leverage} = \frac{\text{Contribution Margin}}{\text{Operating Income}}$$

Since the difference between contribution margin and operating income is fixed costs, companies with large amounts of fixed costs will generally have a high operating leverage. Thus, companies in capital-intensive industries, such as the airline and automotive industries, will generally have a high operating leverage. A low operating leverage is characteristic of companies in industries that are labor-intensive, such as service industries.

Managers can use operating leverage to measure the impact of changes in sales on operating income without preparing formal income statements. A high operating leverage indicates that a small increase in sales will yield a large percentage increase in operating income. In contrast, a low operating leverage indicates that a large increase in sales is necessary to significantly increase operating income. To illustrate, assume the following operating data for Jones Inc. and Wilson Inc.:

	Jones Inc.	Wilson Inc.
Sales	$400,000	$400,000
Variable costs	300,000	300,000
Contribution margin	$100,000	$100,000
Fixed costs	80,000	50,000
Operating income	$ 20,000	$ 50,000

Both companies have the same sales, the same variable costs, and the same contribution margin. Jones Inc. has larger fixed costs than Wilson Inc. and, as a result, a lower operating income and a higher operating leverage. The operating leverage for each company is computed as follows:

Jones Inc.

$$\text{Operating Leverage} = \frac{\$100{,}000}{\$20{,}000} = 5$$

Wilson Inc.

$$\text{Operating Leverage} = \frac{\$100{,}000}{\$50{,}000} = 2$$

Jones Inc.'s operating leverage indicates that, for a given percentage change in sales, operating income will increase 5 times that percentage. In contrast, a percentage change in sales for Wilson Inc. will have only 2 times that percentage impact on operating income. For example, if sales increased by 10% ($40,000) for each company, operating income will increase by 50% (10% × 5) for Jones Inc. and only 20% (10% × 2) for Wilson Inc. The validity of this analysis is shown by the following income statements:

	Jones Inc.	Wilson Inc.
Sales	$440,000	$440,000
Variable costs	330,000	330,000
Contribution margin	$110,000	$110,000
Fixed costs	80,000	50,000
Operating income	$ 30,000	$ 60,000

The management of Jones Inc. knows that even a small increase in sales will generate a large percentage increase in operating income. Thus, they may be motivated to work harder to increase sales. In contrast, the management of Wilson Inc. may concentrate on increasing Wilson's operating leverage through reducing variable costs or changing the cost structure.

LIMITATIONS OF COST-VOLUME-PROFIT ANALYSIS

OBJECTIVE 8
Describe the limitations of cost-volume-profit analysis.

The reliability of cost-volume-profit analysis depends upon the validity of several assumptions. The primary assumptions are briefly described below:

1. In cost-volume-profit analysis, it is assumed that total sales and total costs are linear and can be represented by straight lines. The total sales lines and the total cost lines shown on the cost-volume-profit charts on pages 865-867 illustrate this assumption. Economic theory suggests that in some cases this assumption may not be valid. For example, if an enterprise sells more units, the unit variable costs may decrease because the enterprise may achieve greater operating efficiencies as it produces more units.
2. Cost-volume-profit analysis is performed within a relevant range of operating activity for which the enterprise is planning to operate. Within this range of activity, it is assumed that the productivity and efficiency of operations do not change.
3. Cost-volume-profit analysis assumes that costs can be accurately divided into fixed and variable components. Although this division is sometimes difficult, the methods discussed in Chapter 19 often provide reliable estimates of the fixed and variable cost components of total costs.
4. For companies selling multiple products, it is assumed that the sales mix is constant. The effect of changes in the sales mix on the break-even point and profitability can be assessed by performing separate cost-volume-profit analyses for different sales mixes.
5. Cost-volume-profit analysis assumes that there is no change in the inventory quantities during the period; that is, the quantity of units in the beginning inventory equals the quantity of units in the ending inventory. In other words, the number of units produced during the period equals the number of units sold. When changes in inventory occur, the computations of cost-volume-profit analysis become more complex. These computations are discussed in advanced texts.

The preceding assumptions simplify cost-volume-profit analysis, and since the assumptions are frequently valid for the relevant range of operations under consideration, cost-volume-profit analysis is often used effectively in managerial decision making. In situations where the assumptions are substantially violated, cost-volume-profit analysis must be used cautiously.

CHAPTER REVIEW

KEY POINTS

OBJECTIVE 1

Cost-Volume Profit Relationships

Cost-volume-profit analysis is the systematic examination of the interrelationships between selling prices, volume of sales and production, costs, expenses, and profits. Accountants can play an important role in cost-volume-profit analysis by providing management with information on the relative profitability of its various products, the probable effects of changes in selling price, and other variables.

In cost-volume-profit analysis, costs are subdivided into two categories: (1) variable and (2) fixed. Variable costs are costs that change, in total, as the volume of activity changes. Fixed costs remain constant, in total, as the volume of activity changes. Mixed costs are costs that have both variable and fixed characteristics. For purposes of analysis, mixed costs can generally be separated into variable and fixed components.

OBJECTIVE 2

Contribution Margin Concept

One relationship between cost, volume, and profits that is especially useful in business planning because it gives an insight into the profit potential of a firm is the contribution margin concept. The contribution margin is the excess of sales revenues over variable costs and expenses. The deduction of fixed costs and expenses from the contribution margin equals the operating income or loss.

The contribution margin ratio and unit contribution margin are useful applications of the contribution margin concept. The contribution margin ratio, sometimes called the profit-volume ratio, indicates the percentage of each sales dollar available to cover the fixed costs and to provide operating income. The contribution margin ratio is computed as follows:

$$\text{Contribution Margin Ratio} = \frac{\text{Sales} - \text{Variable Costs}}{\text{Sales}}$$

Similar to the contribution margin ratio, the unit contribution margin is also a useful relationship for analyzing the profit potential of proposed projects. The unit contribution margin is the dollars available from each unit of sales to cover fixed costs and provide operating profits. The unit contribution margin is computed as the unit selling price minus the unit variable cost. While the contribution margin ratio is most useful when the increase or decrease in sales volume is measured in sales dollars, the unit contribution margin is most useful when the increase or decrease in sales volume is measured in sales units (quantities).

OBJECTIVE 3

Mathematical Approach to Cost-Volume-Profit Analysis

The mathematical approach to cost-volume-profit analysis uses equations (1) to indicate the revenues necessary to achieve the break-even point in operations or (2) to indicate the revenues necessary to achieve a desired or target profit. The level of operations of an enterprise at which revenues and expired costs are exactly equal is called the break-even point. The break-even point can be determined in either dollars or units by using one of the following equations:

$$\text{Break-Even Sales (Dollars)} = \text{Fixed Costs} + \text{Variable Costs (as \% of Break-Even Sales)}$$

$$\text{Break-Even Sales (Dollars)} = \frac{\text{Fixed Costs}}{\text{Contribution Margin Ratio}}$$

$$\text{Break-Even Sales (Units)} = \frac{\text{Fixed Costs}}{\text{Unit Contribution Margin}}$$

The computations of the break-even point using the unit contribution margin are used most frequently in practice.

The break-even point is raised by increases in fixed costs, increased in variable costs, or decreases in the unit selling price. The break-even point is lowered by decreases in fixed costs, decreases in variable costs, or increases in the unit selling price. By modifying the break-even equation and adding a factor for desired profit, the sales volume required to earn a desired amount of profit may be estimated.

OBJECTIVE 4

Graphic Approach to Cost-Volume-Profit Analysis

Many managers prefer to use a graphic format for cost-volume-profit analysis because the operating profit or loss for any given level of sales can be readily determined, without the necessity of solving an equation. A cost-volume-profit chart is used to assist management in understanding the relationships between costs, sales, and operating profit or loss. Changes in the unit selling price, total fixed costs, and unit variable costs can also be analyzed using a cost-volume-profit chart. Another graphic approach to cost-volume-profit analysis, called the profit-volume chart, focuses on profitability rather than on sales revenues and costs. The effect of changes in unit selling price, total fixed costs, and unit variable costs on profit can also be analyzed using a profit-volume chart.

OBJECTIVE 5

Use of Computers in Cost-Volume-Profit Analysis

Both the mathematical and graphic approaches to cost-volume-profit analysis are becoming increasing popular and easy to use when managers have access to a computer terminal or a microcomputer. With the wide variety of computer software that is available, managers can vary assumptions regarding selling prices, costs, and volume and can instantaneously analyze the effects of each assumption on the break-even point and profit.

OBJECTIVE 6

Sales Mix Considerations

The break-even point for an enterprise selling two or more products must be calculated on the basis of a specified sales mix. If the sales mix is assumed to be constant, the break-even point can be computed using the standard approaches.

OBJECTIVE 7

Special Cost-Volume-Profit Relationships

The difference between the current sales revenue and the sales at the break-even point is called the margin of safety. The margin of safety is useful in evaluating past operations and as a guide to business planning. Another relationship between costs, volume, and profits that is especially useful in business planning because it gives an insight into the profit potential of a firm is operating leverage. Operating leverage is a measure of the relative mix of an enterprise's variable costs and fixed costs. It is computed by measuring the relationship between contribution margin and operating income, as follows:

$$\text{Operating Leverage} = \frac{\text{Contribution Margin}}{\text{Operating Income}}$$

Managers can use operating leverage to measure the impact of changes in sales on operating income without preparing formal income statements.

OBJECTIVE 8 Limitations of Cost-Volume-Profit Analysis

The reliability of cost-volume-profit analysis depends upon the validity of several assumptions. The primary assumptions are briefly described below:

1. In cost-volume-profit analysis, it is assumed that total sales and total costs are linear and can be represented by straight lines.
2. Cost-volume-profit analysis is performed within a relevant range of operating activity for which the enterprise is planning to operate.
3. Cost-volume-profit analysis assumes that costs can be accurately divided into fixed and variable components.
4. For companies selling multiple products, it is assumed that the sales mix is constant.
5. Cost-volume-profit analysis assumes that there is no change in the inventory quantities during the period.

The preceding assumptions simplify cost-volume-profit analysis, and since the assumptions are frequently valid for the relevant range of operations under consideration, cost-volume-profit analysis is often used effectively in managerial decision making.

KEY TERMS

cost-volume-profit analysis 857
variable costs 858
fixed costs 858
mixed costs 858
contribution margin 858
contribution margin ratio 858
unit contribution margin 859
break-even point 860
cost-volume-profit chart 865
profit-volume chart 867
sales mix 871
margin of safety 873
operating leverage 874

SELF-EXAMINATION QUESTIONS

Answers at end of chapter.

1. Which of the following statements describes variable costs?
   A. Costs that vary on a per unit basis as the activity base changes
   B. Costs that vary in total in direct proportion to changes in the activity base
   C. Costs that remain constant in total dollar amount as the level of activity changes
   D. Costs that vary on a per unit basis, but remain constant in total as the level of activity changes

2. If sales are $500,000, variable costs are $200,000, and fixed costs are $240,000, what is the contribution margin ratio?
   A. 40%
   B. 48%
   C. 60%
   D. none of the above

3. If the unit selling price is $16, the unit variable cost is $12, and fixed costs are $160,000, what are the break-even sales (units)?
   A. 10,000 units
   B. 13,333 units
   C. 40,000 units
   D. none of the above

4. Based on the data presented in Question 3, how many units of sales would be required to realize an operating profit of $20,000?
   A. 11,250 units
   B. 15,000 units
   C. 20,000 units
   D. 45,000 units

5. Based on the following operating data, what is the operating leverage?

Sales	$600,000
Variable costs	240,000
Contribution margin	$360,000
Fixed costs	160,000
Operating income	$200,000

   A. .8
   B. 1.2
   C. 1.8
   D. 4.0

ILLUSTRATIVE PROBLEM

Johnson Inc. expects to maintain the same inventories at the end of the year as at the beginning of the year. The estimated fixed costs for the year are $360,000, and the estimated variable costs per unit are $9. It is expected that 75,000 units will be sold at a price of $15 per unit. Maximum sales within the relevant range are 80,000 units.

Instructions:

1. What is (a) the contribution margin ratio and (b) the unit contribution margin?
2. Determine the break-even point in units.
3. Construct a cost-volume-profit chart, indicating the break-even point.
4. Construct a profit-volume chart, indicating the break-even point.
5. What is the margin of safety?

SOLUTION

(1) (a)

$$\text{Contribution Margin Ratio} = \frac{\text{Sales} - \text{Variable Costs}}{\text{Sales}}$$

$$\text{Contribution Margin Ratio} = \frac{(75{,}000 \text{ units} \times \$15) - (75{,}000 \text{ units} \times \$9)}{(75{,}000 \text{ units} \times \$15)}$$

$$\text{Contribution Margin Ratio} = \frac{\$1{,}125{,}000 - \$675{,}000}{\$1{,}125{,}000} = \frac{\$450{,}000}{\$1{,}125{,}000}$$

$$\text{Contribution Margin Ratio} = 40\%$$

(b)

$$\text{Unit Contribution Margin} = \text{Unit Selling Price} - \text{Unit Variable Costs}$$

$$\text{Unit Contribution Margin} = \$15 - \$9 = \$6$$

(2)

$$\text{Break-Even Sales (Units)} = \frac{\text{Fixed Costs}}{\text{Unit Contribution Margin}}$$

$$\text{Break-Even Sales (Units)} = \frac{\$360{,}000}{\$6} = 60{,}000 \text{ units}$$

(3)

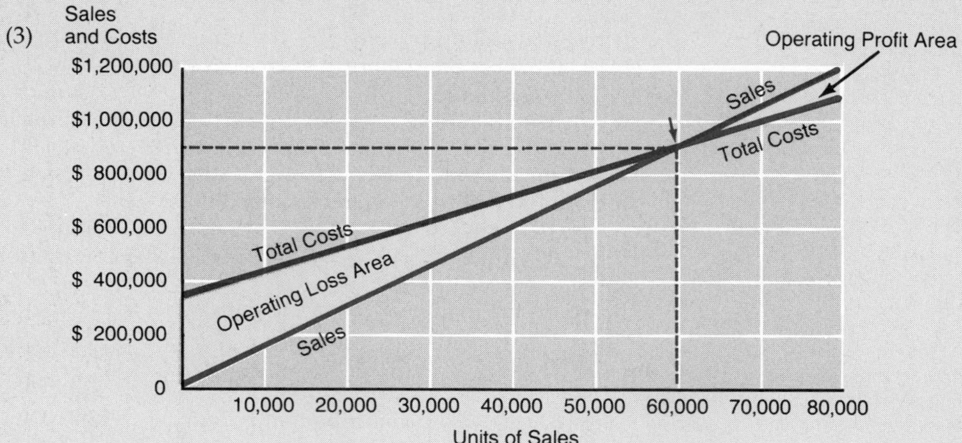

(4)

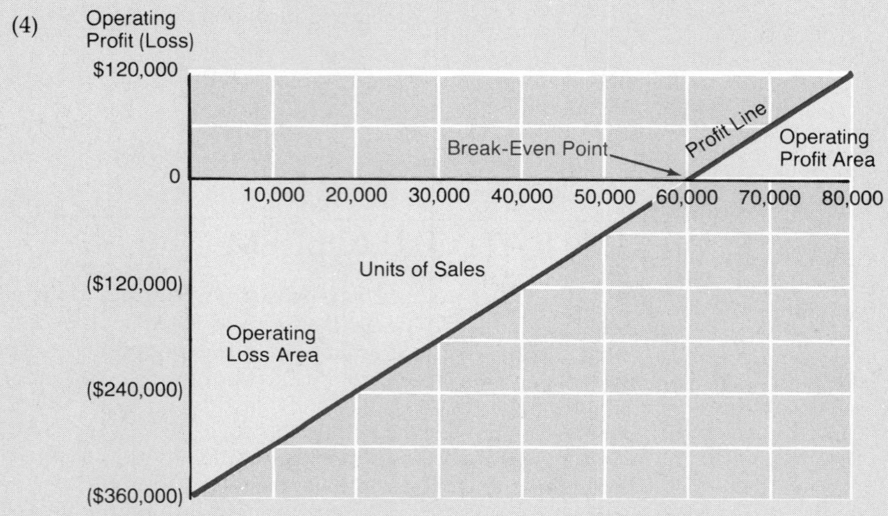

(5) Margin of safety:

Expected sales (75,000 units × $15)	$1,125,000
Break-even point (60,000 units × $15)	900,000
Margin of safety	$ 225,000

or

$$\text{Margin of Safety} = \frac{\text{Sales} - \text{Sales at Break-Even Point}}{\text{Sales}}$$

$$\text{Margin of Safety} = \frac{\$225,000}{\$1,125,000} = 20\%$$

DISCUSSION QUESTIONS

20–1. What is cost-volume-profit analysis?

20–2. How do changes in volume of activity affect (a) total variable costs and (b) total fixed costs?

20–3. What is contribution margin?

20–4. Schrad Inc. had sales of $650,000, variable costs of $390,000, fixed costs of $200,000, and operating income of $60,000. What is Schrad Inc.'s contribution margin?

20–5. Given the data for Schrad Inc. in Question 20–4, what is the contribution margin ratio?

20–6. What ratio indicates the percentage of each sales dollar that is available to cover fixed costs and provide a profit?

20–7. (a) If sales are $400,000 and variable costs are $272,000, what is the contribution margin ratio? (b) What is the contribution margin ratio if variable costs are 55% of sales?

20–8. The management of Geurink Inc. is considering the effect on operating income of an additional $50,000 in sales orders. If Geurink Inc.'s contribution margin ratio is 30%, how much will operating income increase if the sales orders of $50,000 are obtained?

20–9. An examination of the accounting records of Hudson Company disclosed a high contribution margin ratio and production at a level below maximum capacity. Based on this information, suggest a likely means of improving operating profit. Explain.

20–10. What term is used to describe the dollars available from each unit of sales to cover fixed costs and provide operating profits?

20–11. The unit selling price for Casad Inc.'s product is $25 and the unit variable cost is $16. (a) If Casad Inc. sold 40,000 units, what is the total contribution margin? (b) If fixed costs are $100,000, how much would operating income increase if Casad Inc. sells an additional 10,000 units? (c) What is the unit contribution margin for Casad Inc.?

20–12. (a) What is the break-even point? (b) What equation is used in practice to determine the break-even point in sales dollars? (c) What equation is used in practice to determine the break-even point in sales units? (d) Which approach, the contribution margin ratio approach or the unit contribution margin approach, is used most frequently in practice.?

20–13. Sales are $1,000,000, variable costs are $600,000, and fixed costs are $300,000. (a) What is the contribution margin ratio? (b) What is the break-even point in sales dollars?

20–14. Fixed costs are $450,000, the unit selling price is $50, and the unit variable cost is $35. (a) What is the unit contribution margin? (b) What are the break-even sales units?

20–15. If the unit cost of direct materials is decreased, what effect will this change have on the break-even point?

20–16. If insurance rates are increased, what effect will this change in fixed costs have on the break-even point?

20–17. Kernan Inc. is currently selling its product at $60 per unit. The variable cost per unit is $40, and the fixed costs are $180,000. (a) What is the break-even point in sales units? (b) If Kernan Inc. reduced its selling price per unit to $55, would the break-even point increase or decrease? (c) What is the break-even point in sales units if the price is reduced to $55?

20–18. If the unit selling price is $250, the unit variable cost is $200, and the fixed costs are $700,000, what sales in units are required to realize an operating profit of $150,000?

20–19. What is the advantage of presenting cost-volume-profit analysis in the chart form over the equation form?

20–20. Name the following chart and identify the items represented by the letters a through f.

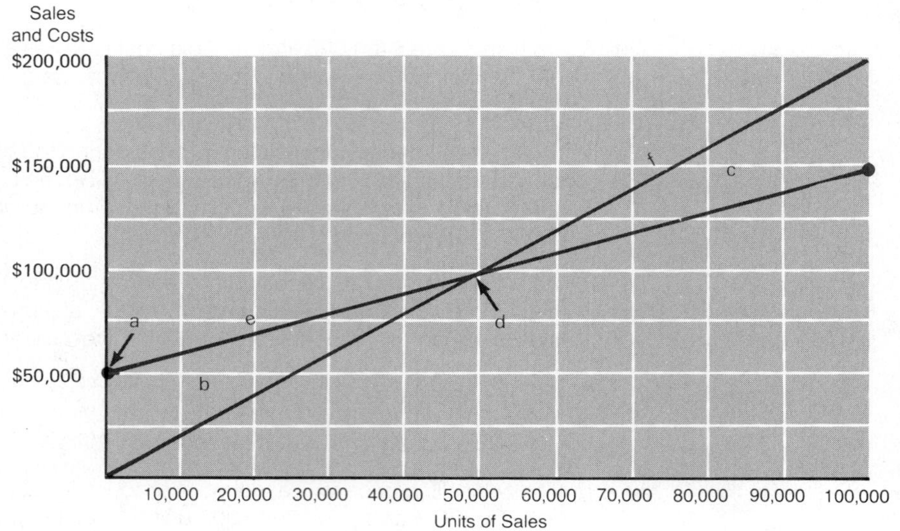

20–21. Name the following chart and identify the items represented by the letters a through f.

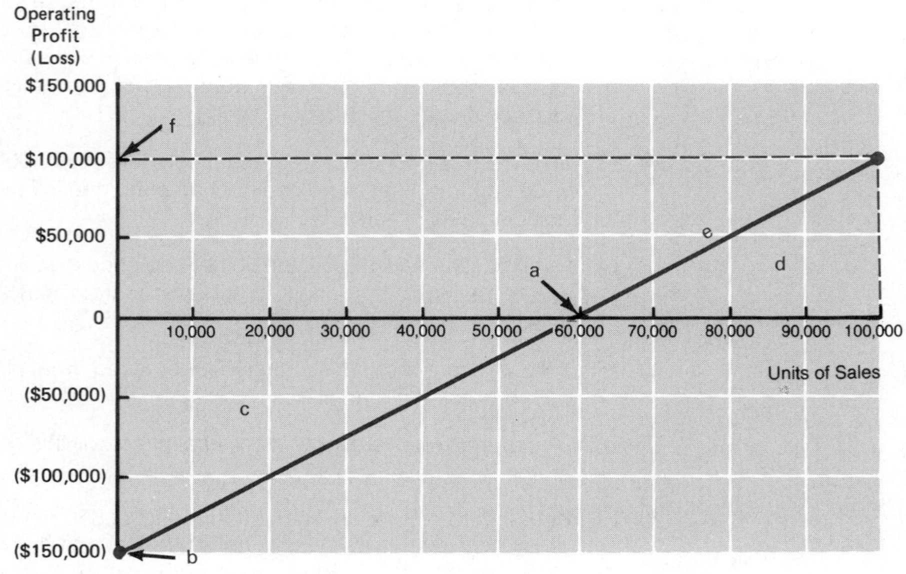

20–22. Both Simmons Company and Pate Company had the same sales, total costs, and operating profit for the current fiscal year, yet Simmons Company had a lower break-even point than Pate Company. Explain the reason for this difference in break-even points.

20–23. (a) What is meant by sales mix? (b) For conventional break-even analysis, is the sales mix assumed to be constant?

20–24. (a) What is meant by the margin of safety? (b) If sales are $900,000, net income is $90,000, and sales at the break-even point are $675,000, what is the margin of safety?

20–25. (a) How is operating leverage computed? (b) What does operating leverage measure?

20–26. Does a high operating leverage indicate that a small increase in sales will yield a large increase or a small increase in operating income?

20–27. Pratt Inc. has an operating leverage of 6 and operating income of $120,000. Sales are expected to increase by 5% next year. (a) What percentage will operating income increase? (b) What would be the expected operating income next year?

20–28. What are five primary limitations of cost-volume-profit analysis?

Real World Focus

20–29. The 1990 annual report of The H.J. Heinz Company indicates that, compared to the previous year, sales was $284,810,000 higher and income from operations was $118,426,000 higher. The H.J. Heinz Company operated above the break-even point in 1990 and 1989. Assuming that fixed costs did not change significantly from the prior year, what is the estimated contribution margin ratio for The H.J. Heinz Company?

Ethics Discussion Case

20–30. William Keller has been controller for Yeltsin Enterprises for 18 years. Recently, Yeltsin Enterprises purchased several microcomputers to be used for analyses such as cost-volume-profit analysis. Keller does not know how to use a microcomputer, and he does not want to learn how to use one. He believes that he can fulfill his responsibilities as controller and adequately evaluate his staff's work without the microcomputer. Discuss any ethical issues related to Keller's refusal to use microcomputers.

EXERCISES

Ex. 20–31. Contribution margin ratio.

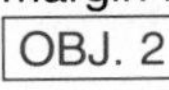

(a) If Snowy Company budgets sales of $1,200,000, fixed costs of $100,000, and variable costs of $816,000, what is the anticipated contribution margin ratio? (b) If the contribution margin ratio for Dallas Company is 36%, sales were $950,000, and fixed costs were $185,000, what was the operating profit?

Ex. 20–32. Contribution margin, contribution margin ratio, break-even sales.

OBJ. 2, 3

Beneventi Inc. sells Product A for $45 per unit, the variable cost per unit is $27, and fixed costs are $252,000. This past year 16,000 units were sold. (a) Prepare a contribution margin income statement for Beneventi Inc. for the past year. (b) Compute the contribution margin ratio. (c) Compute the break-even point in sales dollars.

Ex. 20–33.
Unit contribution margin, break-even sales, and analysis.
OBJ. 2, 3

Based on the data for Beneventi Inc. In Ex. 20–32, (a) compute the unit contribution margin; (b) compute the break-even point in sales units; (c) compute the increase in operating income if next year's sales increase by 5,000 units.

Ex. 20–34.
Break-even sales and sales to realize operating profit.
OBJ. 3

For the current year ending March 31, Andrews Company expects fixed costs of $264,000, a unit variable cost of $134, and a unit selling price of $200. (a) Compute the anticipated break-even sales (units). (b) Compute the sales (units) required to realize an operating profit of $49,500.

Ex. 20–35.
Break-even sales.
OBJ. 3

For the past year, Russell Company had fixed costs of $186,000 and a unit variable cost of $20. All revenues and costs are expected to remain constant for the coming year, except that property taxes are expected to increase by $15,500 during the year. The selling price is $30 per unit. (a) Compute the break-even sales (units) for the past year. (b) Compute the anticipated break-even sales (units) for the coming year.

Ex. 20–36.
Break-even sales.
OBJ. 3

For the current year ending January 31, Pickett Company expects fixed costs of $140,000 and a unit variable cost of $36. For the coming year, a new wage contract will increase the unit variable cost to $37.50. The selling price of $50 per unit is expected to remain the same. (a) Compute the break-even sales (units) for the current year. (b) Compute the anticipated break-even sales (units) for the coming year, assuming that the new wage contract is signed.

Ex. 20–37.
Break-even sales.
OBJ. 3

Currently, the unit selling price of a product is $25, the unit variable cost is $15, and the total fixed costs are $120,000. A proposal is being evaluated to increase the unit selling price to $27. (a) Compute the current break-even sales (units). (b) Compute the anticipated break-even sales (units), assuming that the unit selling price is increased and all costs remain constant.

Ex. 20–38.
Cost-volume-profit chart.
OBJ. 4

For the coming year, Borders Inc. anticipates fixed costs of $400,000, a unit variable cost of $30, and a unit selling price of $50. The maximum sales within the relevant range are $2,000,000. (a) Construct a cost-volume-profit chart. (b) Estimate the break-even sales (dollars) by using the cost-volume-profit chart constructed in (a).

Ex. 20–39.
Profit-volume chart.
OBJ. 4

Using the data for Borders Inc. in Ex. 20–38, (a) determine the maximum possible operating loss; (b) compute the maximum possible operating profit; (c) construct a profit-volume chart; (d) estimate the break-even sales (units) by using the profit-volume chart constructed in (c).

Ex. 20–40.
Sales mix and break-even sales.
OBJ. 6

Scholey Inc. manufacturers and sells two products, C and D. The fixed costs are $364,000, and the sales mix is 80% C and 20% D. The unit selling price, and the unit variable cost for each product is as follows:

Product	Unit Selling Price	Unit Variable Cost
C	$ 50	$ 30
D	150	100

(a) Compute the break-even sales (units) for the enterprise product, E. (b) How many units of each product, C and D, would be sold at the break-even point?

Ex. 20–41.
Margin of safety.
OBJ. 7

(a) If Massey Company, with a break-even point at $680,000 of sales, has actual sales of $850,000, what is the margin of safety expressed (1) in dollars and (2) as a percentage of sales? (b) If the margin of safety for Rogers Company was 20%, fixed costs were $320,000, and variable costs were 75% of sales, what was the amount of actual sales?

Ex. 20–42. **Computation of break-even sales, costs, and operating profit.** OBJ. 3,7 SPREADSHEET PROBLEM

For the past year, Krane Company had sales of $1,500,000, a margin of safety of 18%, and a contribution margin ratio of 36%. Compute (a) break-even sales (dollars), (b) variable costs (c) fixed costs, and (d) operating profit.

Ex. 20–43. **Computation of break-even sales, sales, and operating profit.** OBJ. 3,7

For 1992, a company had sales of $3,000,000 (15,000 units × $200), fixed costs of $750,000, and a contribution margin ratio of 30%. During 1993, the unit variable cost was $140, the fixed costs did not change from the previous year, and the margin of safety was 20%. (a) What was the operating profit for 1992? (b) What were the break-even sales (units) for 1993? (c) What were the break-even sales (dollars) for 1993? (d) What was the amount of sales for 1993? (e) What was the operating profit for 1993?

Ex. 20–44. **Operating leverage.** OBJ. 7

Camlin Inc. and Waite Inc. have the following operating data:

	Camlin Inc.	Waite Inc.
Sales	$500,000	$300,000
Variable costs	250,000	180,000
Contribution margin	$250,000	$120,000
Fixed costs	150,000	80,000
Operating income	$100,000	$ 40,000

(a) Compute the operating leverage for Camlin Inc. and Waite Inc. (b) How much would operating income increase for each company if the sales of each increased by 10%?

Ex. 20–45. **Real world focus.** OBJ. 3, 7

The following income statement data were taken from the 1990 financial statements of General Mills, Inc.:

	(In millions)
Sales	$6,448.3
Cost and expenses:	
Cost of sales	3,485.1
Selling, general, and administrative	2,138.0
Depreciation and amortization	180.1
Interest	32.4
Total costs and expenses	$5,835.6
Operating income	$ 612.7

Assume that the costs have been classified into the following fixed and variable components:

	Fixed	Variable
Cost of sales	20%	80%
Selling, general, and administrative	45%	55%
Depreciation and amortization	100%	0%
Interest	100%	0%

Based on the above data, determine (a) the contribution margin ratio, (b) the break-even sales (dollars), using the contribution margin ratio computed in (a), and (c) the margin of safety expressed in sales dollars and as a percentage of 1990 sales. Round computations to one decimal place.

PROBLEMS

Pb. 20–46.
Break-even sales under present and proposed conditions.
OBJ. 2,3

King Company, operating at full capacity, sold 20,000 units at a price of $300 per unit during 1992. Its income statement for 1992 is as follows:

Sales		$6,000,000
Cost of goods sold		3,600,000
Gross profit		$2,400,000
Operating expenses:		
Selling expenses	$1,275,000	
Administrative expenses	375,000	
Total operating expenses		1,650,000
Operating profit		$ 750,000

The division of costs between fixed and variable is as follows:

	Fixed	Variable
Cost of goods sold	30%	70%
Selling expenses	20%	80%
Administrative expenses	84%	16%

Management is considering a plant expansion program that will permit an increase of $2,100,000 in yearly sales. The expansion will increase fixed costs by $300,000, but will not affect the relationship between sales and variable costs.

Instructions:

(1) Determine for 1992 (a) the total fixed costs and (b) the total variable costs.
(2) Determine the unit variable cost and the unit contribution margin for 1992.
(3) Compute the break-even sales (units) for 1992.
(4) Compute the break-even sales (units) under the proposed program.
(5) Determine the amount of sales (units) that would be necessary under the proposed program to realize the $750,000 of operating profit that was earned in 1992.
(6) Determine the maximum operating profit possible with the expanded plant.
(7) If the proposal is accepted and sales remain at the 1992 level, what will the operating profit or loss be for 1993?
(8) Based on the data given, would you recommend accepting the proposal? Explain.

Pb. 20–47.
Break-even sales and cost-volume-profit chart.
OBJ. 3,4

For the coming year, Adam Company anticipates a unit selling price of $100, a unit variable cost of $75, and fixed costs of $75,000.

Instructions:

(1) Compute the anticipated break-even sales (units).
(2) Compute the sales (units) required to realize an operating profit of $30,000.
(3) Construct a cost-volume-profit chart, assuming maximum sales of 5,000 units within the relevant range.
(4) Determine the probable operating profit (loss) if sales total 4,500 units.

Pb. 20–48.
Break-even point and cost-volume-profit chart.
OBJ. 3,4

Last year, McWhorter Inc. had sales of $800,000, based upon a unit selling price of $200. The variable cost per unit was $120, and fixed costs were $240,000. The maximum sales within McWhorter Inc.'s relevant range of operations is 5,000 units. McWhorter Company is considering a proposal to spend an additional $40,000 on billboard advertising during the current year in an attempt to increase sales and utilize unused capacity.

Instructions:

(1) Construct a cost-volume-profit chart indicating the break-even sales for last year.
(2) Using the cost-volume-profit chart prepared in (1), determine (a) the operating profit

for last year and (b) the maximum operating profit that could have been realized during the year.

(3) Construct a cost-volume-profit chart indicating the break-even sales for the current year, assuming that a noncancellable contract is signed for the additional billboard advertising. No changes are expected in the unit selling price or other costs.

(4) Using the cost-volume-profit chart prepared in (3), determine (a) the operating profit if sales total $800,000 and (b) the maximum operating profit that could be realized during the year.

Pb. 20–49.
Sales mix and break-even sales.
OBJ. 6

Data related to the expected sales of products X and Y for Crowley Company for the current year, which is typical of recent years, are as follows:

Product	Selling Price per Unit	Variable Cost per Unit	Sales Mix
X	$ 50	$30	80%
Y	125	75	20

The estimated fixed costs for the current year are $260,000.

Instructions:

(1) Determine the estimated units of sales of the enterprise product necessary to reach the break-even point for the current year.

(2) Based on the break-even sales (units) in (1), determine the unit sales of both X and Y for the current year.

Pb. 20–50.
Contribution margin, break-even sales, cost-volume-profit chart, margin of safety, and operating leverage.
OBJ. 2,3,4,7

MacNair Company expects to maintain the same inventories at the end of 1992 as at the beginning of the year. The total of all production costs for the year is therefore assumed to be equal to the cost of goods sold. With this in mind, the various department heads were asked to submit estimates of the costs for their departments during 1992. A summary report of these estimates is as follows:

	Estimated Fixed Cost	Estimated Variable Cost (per unit sold)
Production costs:		
Direct materials	—	$15.75
Direct labor	—	25.50
Factory overhead	$100,000	6.20
Selling expenses:		
Sales salaries and commissions	50,000	1.60
Advertising	45,200	—
Travel	31,800	—
Miscellaneous selling expense	7,000	.40
Administrative expenses:		
Office and officers' salaries	45,000	—
Supplies	16,600	.25
Miscellaneous administrative expense	4,400	.30
Total	$300,000	$50.00

It is expected that 8,000 units will be sold at a price of $100 a unit. Maximum sales within the relevant range are 15,000 units.

Instructions:

(1) Prepare an estimated income statement for 1992.
(2) What is the expected contribution margin ratio?
(3) Determine the break-even sales (a) in units and (b) in dollars.
(4) Construct a cost-volume-profit chart, indicating the break-even sales.
(5) What is the expected margin of safety?
(6) Determine the operating leverage.

ALTERNATE PROBLEMS

Pb. 20–46A.
Break-even sales under present and proposed conditions.
OBJ. 2,3

McDermott Inc., operating at full capacity, sold 80,000 units at a price of $100 per unit during 1992. Its income statement for 1992 is as follows:

Sales		$8,000,000
Cost of goods sold		5,000,000
Gross profit		$3,000,000
Operating expenses:		
Selling expenses	$1,000,000	
Administrative expenses	400,000	
Total operating expenses		1,400,000
Operating profit		$1,600,000

The division of costs between fixed and variable is as follows:

	Fixed	Variable
Cost of goods sold	20%	80%
Selling expenses	30%	70%
Administrative expenses	75%	25%

Management is considering a plant expansion program that will permit an increase of $3,000,000 in yearly sales. The expansion will increase fixed costs by $500,000, but will not affect the relationship between sales and variable costs.

Instructions:

(1) Determine for 1992 (a) the total fixed costs and (b) the total variable costs.
(2) Determine the unit variable cost and the unit contribution margin for 1992.
(3) Compute the break-even sales (units) for 1992.
(4) Compute the break-even sales (units) under the proposed program.
(5) Determine the amount of sales (units) that would be necessary under the proposed program to realize the $1,600,000 of operating profit that was earned in 1992.
(6) Determine the maximum operating profit possible with the expanded plant.
(7) If the proposal is accepted and sales remain at the 1992 level, what will the operating profit or loss be for 1993?
(8) Based on the data given, would you recommend accepting the proposal? Explain.

Pb. 20–47A.
Break-even sales and cost-volume-profit chart.
OBJ. 3,4

For the coming year, Melvin Company anticipates a unit selling price of $80, a unit variable cost of $52, and fixed costs of $280,000.

Instructions:

(1) Compute the anticipated break-even sales (units).
(2) Compute the sales (units) required to realize an operating profit of $112,000.
(3) Construct a cost-volume-profit chart, assuming maximum sales of 25,000 units within the relevant range.
(4) Determine the probable operating profit (loss) if sales total 8,750 units.

Pb. 20–48A.
Break-even sales and cost-volume-profit chart.
OBJ. 3,4

Last year, Purcell Company had sales of $900,000, based upon a unit selling price of $100. The variable cost per unit was $55, and fixed costs were $315,000. The maximum sales within Purcell Company's relevant range is 10,000 units. Purcell Company is considering a proposal to spend an additional $45,000 on billboard advertising during the current year in an attempt to increase sales and utilize unused capacity.

Instructions:

(1) Construct a cost-volume-profit chart indicating the break-even sales for last year.
(2) Using the cost-volume-profit chart prepared in (1), determine (a) the operating profit for last year and (b) the maximum operating profit that could have been realized during the year.

(3) Construct a cost-volume-profit chart indicating the break-even sales for the current year, assuming that a noncancellable contract is signed for the additional billboard advertising. No changes are expected in the unit selling price or other costs.
(4) Using the cost-volume-profit chart prepared in (3), determine (a) the operating profit if sales total 9,000 units and (b) the maximum operating profit that could be realized during the year.

Pb. 20–49A.
Sales mix and break-even sales.
OBJ. 6

Data related to the expected sales of products A and B for Finzel Inc. for the current year, which is typical of recent years, are as follows:

Product	Selling Price per Unit	Variable Cost per Unit	Sales Mix
A	$180	$80	25%
B	60	40	75

The estimated fixed costs for the current year are $300,000.

Instructions:

(1) Determine the estimated units of sales of the enterprise product necessary to reach the break-even point for the current year.
(2) Based on the break-even sales (units) in (1), determine the unit sales of both A and B for the current year.

Pb. 20–50A.
Contribution margin, break-even sales, cost-volume-profit chart, margin of safety, and operating leverage.
OBJ. 2,3,4,7

Nexus Company expects to maintain the same inventories at the end of 1992 as at the beginning of the year. The total of all production costs for the year is therefore assumed to be equal to the cost of goods sold. With this in mind, the various department heads were asked to submit estimates of the costs for their departments during 1992. A summary report of these estimates is as follows:

	Estimated Fixed Cost	Estimated Variable Cost (per unit sold)
Production costs:		
Direct materials	—	$3.70
Direct labor	—	6.50
Factory overhead	$150,000	1.20
Selling expenses:		
Sales salaries and commissions	60,000	.30
Advertising	30,000	—
Travel	14,000	—
Miscellaneous selling expense	1,700	.12
Administrative expenses:		
Office and officers' salaries	40,000	—
Supplies	3,300	.16
Miscellaneous administrative expense	1,000	.02
Total	$300,000	$12.00

It is expected that 160,000 units will be sold at a price of $15 a unit. Maximum sales within the relevant range are 200,000 units.

Instructions:

(1) Prepare an estimated income statement for 1992.
(2) What is the expected contribution margin ratio?
(3) Determine the break-even sales (a) in units and (b) in dollars.
(4) Construct a cost-volume-profit chart, indicating the break-even sales.
(5) What is the expected margin of safety?
(6) Determine the operating leverage. Round to one decimal place.

MINI-CASE 20

Owens Company manufactures Product X, which sold for $144 per unit in 1992. For the past several years, sales and operating profit have been declining. On sales of 7,000 units in 1992, the company operated near the break-even sales and used only 40% of its productive capacity. Walter Owens, your father-in-law, is considering several proposals to reverse the trend of declining sales and operating profit, and to more fully use production facilities. One proposal under consideration is to reduce the unit selling price to $120.

Your father-in-law has asked you to aid him in assessing the proposal to reduce the sales price by $24. For this purpose, he provided the following summary of the estimated fixed and variable costs for 1993, which are unchanged from 1992.

Variable costs:		
Production costs		$46.50 per unit
Selling expenses		15.50 per unit
Administrative expenses		10.00 per unit
Fixed costs:		
Production costs	$315,000	
Selling expenses	75,000	
Administrative expenses	60,000	

Instructions:

(1) Determine the break-even sales for 1993 in units, assuming (a) no change in sales price and (b) the proposed sales price.
(2) How much additional sales are necessary for Owens Company to break even in 1993 under the proposal?
(3) Determine the operating profit for 1993, assuming (a) no change in sales price and volume from 1992 and (b) the new sales price and no change in volume from 1992.
(4) Determine the maximum operating profit for 1993, assuming the proposed sales price.
(5) Briefly list factors that you would discuss with your father-in-law in evaluating the proposal.

ANSWERS TO SELF-EXAMINATION QUESTIONS

1. B Variable costs vary in total in direct proportion to changes in the activity base (answer B). Costs that vary on a per unit basis as the activity base changes (answer A) or remain constant in total dollar amount as the level of activity changes (answer C), or both (answer D), are fixed costs.

2. C The contribution margin ratio indicates the percentage of each sales dollar available to cover the fixed costs and provide operating income and is determined as follows:

$$\text{Contribution Margin Ratio} = \frac{\text{Sales} - \text{Variable Costs}}{\text{Sales}}$$

$$\text{Contribution Margin Ratio} = \frac{\$500,000 - \$200,000}{\$500,000} = 60\%$$

3. C The break-even sales of 40,000 units (answer C) is computed as follows:

$$\text{Break-Even Sales (Units)} = \frac{\text{Fixed Costs}}{\text{Unit Contribution Margin}}$$

$$\text{Break-Even Sales (Units)} = \frac{\$160{,}000}{\$4} = 40{,}000 \text{ units}$$

4. D Sales of 45,000 units are required to realize an operating profit of $20,000, computed as follows:

$$\text{Sales (Units)} = \frac{\text{Fixed Costs} + \text{Desired Profit}}{\text{Unit Contribution Margin}}$$

$$\text{Sales (Units)} = \frac{\$160{,}000 + \$20{,}000}{\$4} = 45{,}000 \text{ units}$$

5. C The operating leverage is 1.8, computed as follows:

$$\text{Operating Leverage} = \frac{\text{Contribution Margin}}{\text{Operating Income}}$$

$$\text{Operating Leverage} = \frac{\$360{,}000}{\$200{,}000} = 1.8$$

CHAPTER 21

CHAPTER OBJECTIVES

1 Describe absorption costing and variable costing concepts.

2 Describe and illustrate the reporting of income under variable costing and absorption costing.

3 Describe and illustrate income analysis under variable costing and absorption costing.

4 Describe and illustrate management's use of variable costing and absorption costing for:
- Cost control
- Product pricing
- Production planning
- Sales analysis
- Contribution margin analysis

PROFIT REPORTING FOR MANAGEMENT ANALYSIS

The basic accounting systems used by manufacturers to provide accounting information useful to management in planning and controlling operations were described and illustrated in Chapters 16 and 17. Cost allocation, cost behavior, cost estimation, and cost-volume-profit analysis were discussed in Chapters 18, 19, and 20. In this chapter, two alternate concepts useful to management in interpreting financial results and in planning and controlling operations—absorption costing and variable costing—are described and illustrated. The contribution margin concept, which was introduced in Chapter 20, is further described and illustrated as part of the discussion of variable costing.

ABSORPTION COSTING AND VARIABLE COSTING

OBJECTIVE 1
Describe absorption costing and variable costing concepts.

One of the most important items affecting an enterprise's reported net income is the cost of goods sold. In many cases, the cost of goods sold is larger than all of the other operating expenses combined. In determining the cost of goods sold, either the absorption costing or variable costing concepts can be used.

The cost of manufactured products normally consists of direct materials, direct labor, and factory overhead. For financial reporting purposes, all such costs become a part of the finished goods inventory and remain there as an asset until the goods are sold. This conventional treatment of manufacturing costs is sometimes called **absorption costing** because all costs are "absorbed" into finished goods. Although the concept is necessary in determining historical costs and taxable income, another costing concept may be more useful to management in making decisions.

In **variable costing,** which is also termed **direct costing**, the cost of goods manufactured is composed only of variable costs—those manufacturing costs that increase or decrease as the volume of production rises or falls. These costs are the direct materials, direct labor, and only those factory overhead costs which vary with the rate of production. The remaining factory overhead costs, which are fixed or nonvariable items, are generally related to the productive capacity of the manufacturing plant and are not affected by changes in the quantity of product manufactured. Accordingly, the fixed factory overhead does not become a part of the cost of goods manufactured, but is considered an expense of the period.

The distinction between absorption costing and variable costing is illustrated in the following diagram. Note that the difference between the two costing concepts is in the treatment of the fixed manufacturing costs, which consist of the fixed factory overhead costs.[1]

Absorption Costing Compared with Variable Costing

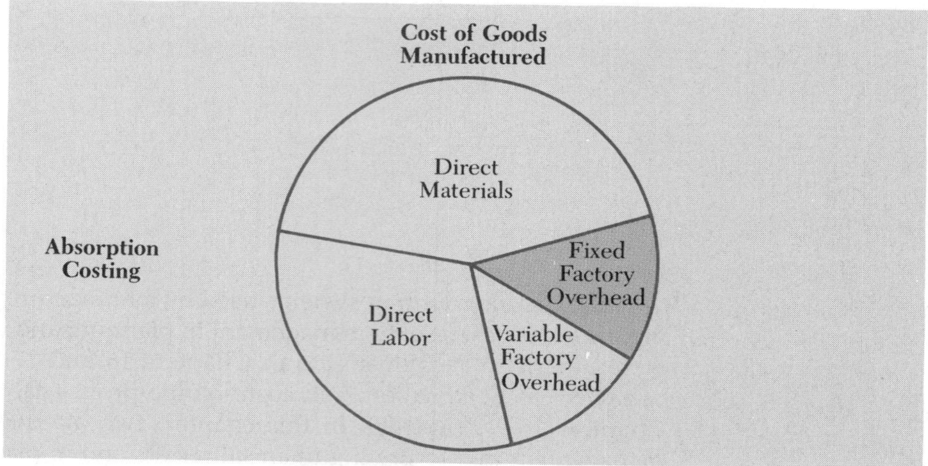

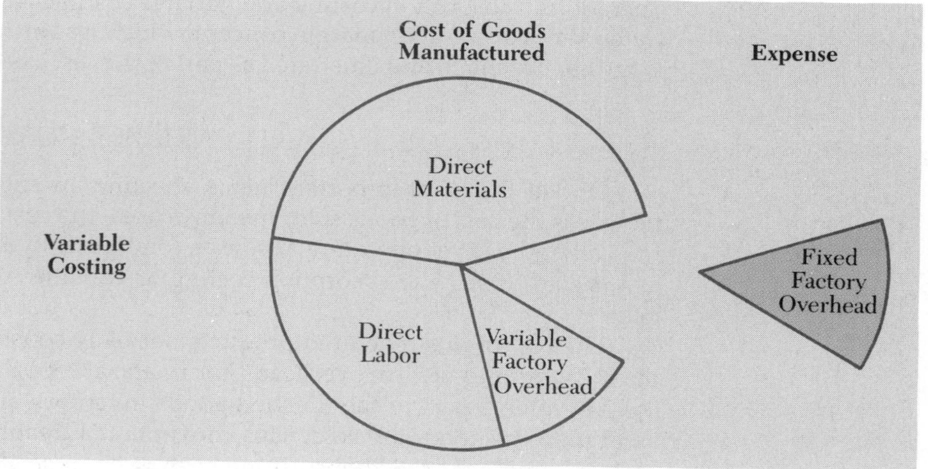

THE INCOME STATEMENT UNDER VARIABLE COSTING AND ABSORPTION COSTING

OBJECTIVE 2
Describe and illustrate the reporting of income under variable costing and absorption costing.

The arrangement of data in the variable costing income statement differs considerably from the format of the conventional absorption costing income statement. Variable costs are presented separately from fixed costs, with significant summarizing amounts inserted at intermediate points. As a basis for illustrating the differences between the two forms, assume that 15,000 units were manufactured and sold at a price of $50 and the costs were as follows:

[1] Some accountants have suggested modifying the traditional concepts of absorption and variable costing presented in this chapter. For further discussion, see advanced texts and H. Thomas Johnson and Robert S. Kaplan, *Relevance Lost*, (Boston: Harvard Business School Press, 1987).

	Total Cost	Number of Units	Unit Cost
Manufacturing costs:			
Variable	$375,000	15,000	$25
Fixed	150,000	15,000	10
Total	$525,000		$35
Selling and administrative expenses:			
Variable ($5 per unit sold)	$ 75,000		
Fixed	50,000		
Total	$125,000		

The two income statements prepared from this information are as follows. The computations in parentheses are shown as an aid to understanding.

Absorption Costing Income Statement

Absorption Costing Income Statement	
Sales (15,000 × $50)	$750,000
Cost of goods sold (15,000 × $35)	525,000
Gross profit	$225,000
Selling and administrative expenses ($75,000 + $50,000)	125,000
Income from operations	$100,000

Variable Costing Income Statement

Variable Costing Income Statement		
Sales (15,000 × $50)		$750,000
Variable cost of goods sold (15,000 × $25)		375,000
Manufacturing margin		$375,000
Variable selling and administrative expenses		75,000
Contribution margin		$300,000
Fixed costs:		
Fixed manufacturing costs	$150,000	
Fixed selling and administrative expenses	50,000	200,000
Income from operations		$100,000

The absorption costing income statement does not distinguish between variable and fixed costs. All manufacturing costs are included in the cost of goods sold. The deduction of the cost of goods sold from sales yields the intermediate amount, gross profit. Deduction of selling and administrative expenses then yields income from operations.

In contrast, the variable costing income statement shows the **contribution margin**, which was defined in Chapter 20 as sales less variable costs and expenses. In the statement illustrated, the variable cost of goods sold, which includes the variable manufacturing costs, is deducted from sales to yield an imtermediate amount, termed the **manufacturing margin**. The variable selling and administrative expenses are deducted from the manufacturing margin to yield the contribution margin. Income from operations is then determined by deducting fixed costs from the contribution margin.

Income Reported When Units Manufactured Equal Units Sold

In the preceding illustration, 15,000 units were manufactured and sold. Both the absorption and the variable costing income statements reported the same income from operations of $100,000. Assuming no other changes, this equality of income will always be the case when the number of units manufactured and the number of units sold are equal. Only when the number of units manufactured and the number of units sold are not equal, which creates a change in the quantity of finished goods in inventory, will the income from operations differ under the two concepts.

Income Reported When Units Manufactured Exceed Units Sold

For any period in which the number of units manufactured exceeds the number of units sold, the operating income reported under the absorption costing concept will be larger than the operating income reported under the variable costing concept. To illustrate, assume that in the preceding example only 12,000 units of the 15,000 units manufactured were sold. The two income statements that result are as follows. Computations are inserted parenthetically as an aid to understanding.

Absorption Costing Income Statement

Absorption Costing Income Statement

Sales (12,000 × $50)		$600,000
Cost of goods sold:		
Cost of goods manufactured (15,000 × $35)	$525,000	
Less ending inventory (3,000 × $35)	105,000	
Cost of goods sold		420,000
Gross profit		$180,000
Selling and administrative expenses [(12,000 × $5) + $50,000]		110,000
Income from operations		$ 70,000

Variable Costing Income Statement

Variable Costing Income Statement

Sales (12,000 × $50)		$600,000
Variable cost of goods sold:		
Variable cost of goods manufactured (15,000 × $25)	$375,000	
Less ending inventory (3,000 × $25)	75,000	
Variable cost of goods sold		300,000
Manufacturing margin		$300,000
Variable selling and administrative expenses		60,000
Contribution margin		$240,000
Fixed costs:		
Fixed manufacturing costs	$150,000	
Fixed selling and administrative expenses	50,000	200,000
Income from operations		$ 40,000

The $30,000 difference in the amount of income from operations ($70,000 – $40,000) is due to the different treatment of the fixed manufacturing costs. The entire amount of the $150,000 of fixed manufacturing costs is included as an expense of the period in the variable costing statement. The ending inventory in the absorption costing statement includes $30,000 (3,000 × $10) of fixed manufacturing costs. This $30,000, by being included in inventory on hand, is thus excluded from the current cost of goods sold and instead is deferred to another period.

Income Reported When Units Manufactured Are Less Than Units Sold

For any period in which the number of units manufactured is less than the number of units sold, the operating income reported under the absorption costing concept will be less than the operating income reported under the variable costing concept. To illustrate, assume that 5,000 units of inventory were on hand at the beginning of a period, 10,000 units were manufactured during the period, and 15,000 units were sold (10,000 units manufactured during the period plus the 5,000 units on hand at the beginning of the period) at $50 per unit. The manufacturing costs and selling and administrative expenses are as follows:

	Total Cost	Number of Units	Unit Cost
Beginning inventory:			
Manufacturing costs:			
Variable	$125,000	5,000	$25
Fixed	50,000	5,000	10
Total	$175,000		$35
Current period:			
Manufacturing costs:			
Variable	$250,000	10,000	$25
Fixed	150,000	10,000	15
Total	$400,000		$40
Selling and administrative expenses:			
Variable ($5 per unit sold)	$ 75,000		
Fixed	50,000		
Total	$125,000		

The two income statements prepared from this information are as follows. Computations are inserted parenthetically as an aid to understanding.

Absorption Costing Income Statement

Absorption Costing Income Statement		
Sales (15,000 × $50)		$750,000
Cost of goods sold:		
Beginning inventory (5,000 × $35)	$175,000	
Cost of goods manufactured (10,000 × $40)	400,000	
Cost of goods sold		575,000
Gross profit		$175,000
Selling and administrative expenses ($75,000 + $50,000)		125,000
Income from operations		$ 50,000

Variable Costing Income Statement

Variable Costing Income Statement		
Sales (15,000 × $50)		$750,000
Variable cost of goods sold:		
Beginning inventory (5,000 × $25)	$125,000	
Variable cost of goods manufactured (10,000 × $25)	250,000	
Variable cost of goods sold		375,000
Manufacturing margin		$375,000
Variable selling and administrative expenses		75,000
Contribution margin		$300,000
Fixed costs:		
Fixed manufacturing costs	$150,000	
Fixed selling and administrative expenses	50,000	200,000
Income from operations		$100,000

The $50,000 difference ($100,000 − $50,000) in the amount of income from operations is attributable to the different treatment of the fixed manufacturing costs. The beginning inventory in the absorption costing income statement includes $50,000 (5,000 units × $10) of fixed manufacturing costs incurred in the preceding period. By being included in the beginning inventory, this $50,000 is included in the cost of goods sold for the current period. Under variable costing, however, this $50,000 was included as an expense in an income statement of a prior period. Therefore, none of it is included as an expense in the current period variable costing income statement.

Comparison of Income Reported Under the Two Concepts

The examples presented in the preceding sections illustrated the effects of the absorption costing and variable costing concepts on reported income from operations when the level of inventory changes during a period. These effects may be summarized as follows:

Units manufactured:	
Equal units sold	Absorption costing income equals variable costing income.
Exceed units sold	Absorption costing income is greater than variable costing income.
Less than units sold	Absorption costing income is less than variable costing income.

INCOME ANALYSIS UNDER VARIABLE COSTING AND ABSORPTION COSTING

OBJECTIVE 3 Describe and illustrate income analysis under variable costing and absorption costing.

As was illustrated in the preceding examples, the operating income reported under the variable costing concept can differ from the operating income reported under the absorption costing concept. This difference results from changes in the quantity of the finished goods inventory, which are caused by differences in the levels of sales and production. In analyzing and evaluating operations, management should therefore be aware of the possible effects of changing inventory levels on operating income reported under the two concepts. To illustrate, assume that the following two proposed production levels are being evaluated by the management of Frand Manufacturing Company:

Proposal 1: 20,000 Units To Be Manufactured

	Total Cost	Number of Units	Unit Cost
Manufacturing costs:			
Variable	$ 700,000	20,000	$35
Fixed	400,000	20,000	20
Total	$1,100,000		$55
Selling and administrative expenses:			
Variable ($5 per unit sold)	$ 100,000		
Fixed	100,000		
Total	$ 200,000		

Proposal 2: 25,000 Units To Be Manufactured

	Total Cost	Number of Units	Unit Cost
Manufacturing costs:			
Variable	$ 875,000	25,000	$35
Fixed	400,000	25,000	16
Total	$1,275,000		$51
Selling and administrative expenses:			
Variable ($5 per unit sold)	$ 100,000		
Fixed	100,000		
Total	$ 200,000		

Frand Manufacturing Company has no beginning inventory and sales are estimated to be 20,000 units at $75 per unit, regardless of production levels. If the company manufactures 20,000 units, which is an amount equal to the estimated sales, income from operations under absorption costing would be $200,000. However, the reported income from operations could be increased by $80,000 by manufacturing 25,000 units and adding 5,000 units to the finished goods inventory. The absorption costing income statements illustrating this effect are as follows:

Absorption Costing Income Statements

Absorption Costing Income Statements

	20,000 Units Manufactured	25,000 Units Manufactured
Sales (20,000 units × $75)	$1,500,000	$1,500,000
Cost of goods sold:		
Cost of goods manufactured:		
(20,000 units × $55)	$1,100,000	
(25,000 units × $51)		$1,275,000
Less ending inventory:		
(5,000 units × $51)		255,000
Cost of goods sold	$1,100,000	$1,020,000
Gross profit	$ 400,000	$ 480,000
Selling and administrative expenses ($100,000 + $100,000)	200,000	200,000
Income from operations	$ 200,000	$ 280,000

The $80,000 increase in operating income would be caused by the allocation of the fixed manufacturing costs of $400,000 over a greater number of units of production. Specifically, an increase in production from 20,000 units to 25,000 units meant that the fixed manufacturing costs per unit decreased from $20 ($400,000 ÷ 20,000 units) to $16 ($400,000 ÷ 25,000 units). Thus, the cost of goods sold when 25,000 units are manufactured would be $4 per unit less, or $80,000 less in total (20,000 units sold times $4). Since the cost of goods sold is less, operating income is $80,000 more when 25,000 units are manufactured rather than 20,000 units.

Under the variable costing concept, income from operations would have been $200,000, regardless of the amount by which units manufactured exceeded sales, because no fixed manufacturing costs are allocated to the units manufactured. To illustrate, the following variable costing income statements are presented for Frand Manufacturing Company for the production of 20,000 units, 25,000 units, and 30,000 units. In each case, the income from operations is $200,000.

Variable Costing Income Statements

Variable Costing Income Statements

	20,000 Units Manufactured	25,000 Units Manufactured	30,000 Units Manufactured
Sales (20,000 units × $75) ..	$1,500,000	$1,500,000	$1,500,000
Variable cost of goods sold:			
Variable cost of goods manufactured:			
(20,000 units × $35)	$ 700,000		
(25,000 units × $35)		$ 875,000	
(30,000 units × $35)			$1,050,000
Less ending inventory:			
(0 units × $35)	0		
(5,000 units × $35)		175,000	
(10,000 units × $35)			350,000
Variable cost of goods sold	$ 700,000	$ 700,000	$ 700,000
Manufacturing margin	$ 800,000	$ 800,000	$ 800,000
Variable selling and administrative expenses ...	100,000	100,000	100,000
Contribution margin	$ 700,000	$ 700,000	$ 700,000
Fixed costs:			
Fixed manufacturing costs .	$ 400,000	$ 400,000	$ 400,000
Fixed selling and administrative expenses .	100,000	100,000	100,000
Total fixed costs	$ 500,000	$ 500,000	$ 500,000
Income from operations	$ 200,000	$ 200,000	$ 200,000

As illustrated, if absorption costing is used, management should be careful in analyzing income from operations when large changes in inventory levels occur. Otherwise, increases or decreases in income from operations due to changes in inventory levels could be misinterpreted to be the result of operating efficiencies or inefficiencies.

BUILDING UP INVENTORY TO "HELP" EARNINGS

In conducting operations, the management of public corporations face a conflict between what is good for the business and what looks good to the public. In an effort to keep the market price of the shares of stock high, the conflict is often resolved by making decisions that look good to Wall Street. As Thomas A. Sanders III, a managing director at Morgan Stanley & Co., stated: "An enormous amount of management time in this country is devoted to managing the market price of the shares [of stock]."

In recent years, many companies have been taken private; that is, all of the shares of stock of a public corporation are acquired by a small group of investors. Frequently these companies are better managed. One reason for this better management is that the manager-owner of a private company need not worry about public perceptions of operations. The following excerpt from an article in *Business Week* illustrates one manager's reaction to a suggestion to "help" earnings by building up inventory accounted for under absorption costing.

Being private . . . eliminates managers' obsession with quarterly earnings and the bad habits that it creates. Shortly after he was brought in to run 12 ITT Corp. divisions that . . . Forstmann Little & Co. bought in 1985, CEO Richard W. Vieser was approached by a couple of the division managers who offered to "help" earnings. How? By using cash to build up inventory, they could show paper profits on increases in inventory value—just as they'd done before. Vieser laid down the law. . . . Don't do anything for mere appearances, especially if it wastes cash. . . .

Source: "When Power Investors Call the Shots." *Business Week* (June 20, 1988), pp. 126-130.

MANAGEMENT'S USE OF VARIABLE COSTING AND ABSORPTION COSTING

OBJECTIVE 4
Describe and illustrate management's use of variable costing and absorption costing for:
Cost control
Product pricing
Production planning
Sales analysis
Contribution margin analysis

Managerial accountants must carefully analyze each situation in evaluating whether variable costing reports or absorption costing reports would be more useful. In many situations, the preparation of reports under both concepts will provide useful insights. Such reports and their advantages and disadvantages are discussed in the following paragraphs.

Cost Control

As discussed in Chapter 15, all costs are controllable in the long run by someone within a business enterprise, but they are not all controllable at the same level of management. For example, plant supervisors, as members of operating management, are responsible for controlling the use of direct materials in their departments. They have no control, however, of the amount of insurance coverage or premium costs related to the buildings housing their departments. For a specific level of management, **controllable costs** are costs that it controls directly, and **noncontrollable costs** are costs that another level of management controls. This distinction, as applied to specific levels of managment, is useful in fixing the responsiblity for incurrence of costs and then for reporting the cost data to those responsible for cost control.

Variable manufacturing costs are controlled at the operating level because the amount of such costs varies with changes in the volume of production. By including only variable manufacturing costs in the cost of the product, variable costing provides a product cost figure that can be controlled by operating management. The fixed factory overhead costs are ordinarily the responsibility of a higher level of managment. When the fixed factory overhead costs are reported as a separate item in the variable costing income statement, they are easier to identify and control than when they are spread among units of product as they are under absorption costing.

As in the case with the fixed and variable manufacturing costs, the control of the variable and fixed operating expenses is usually the responsibility of different levels of management. Under variable costing, the variable selling and administrative expenses are reported in a separate category from the fixed selling and administrative expenses. Because they are reported in this manner, both types of operating expenses are easier to identify and control than is the case under absorption costing, where they are not reported separately.

Product Pricing

Many factors enter into the determination of the selling price of a product. The cost of making the product is clearly significant. Microeconomic theory deduces, from a set of restrictive assumptions, that income is maximized by expanding output to the volume where the revenue realized by the sale of the final unit (marginal revenue) equals the cost of that unit (marginal cost). Although the degree of exactness assumed in economic theory is rarely attainable, the concepts of marginal revenue and marginal cost are useful in setting selling prices.

In the short run, an enterprise is committed to the existing capacity of its manufacturing facilities. The pricing decision should be based upon making the best use of such capacity. The fixed costs and expenses cannot be avoided, but the variable costs and expenses can be eliminated if the company does not manufacture the product. The selling price of a product, therefore, should at least be equal to the variable costs and expenses of making and selling it. Any price above this minimum selling price contributes an amount toward covering fixed costs and expenses and providing operating income. Variable costing procedures yield data that emphasize these relationships.

In the long run, plant capacity can be increased or decreased. If an enterprise is to continue in business, the selling prices of its products must cover all costs and expenses and provide a reasonable operating income. Hence, in establishing pricing policies for the long run, information provided by absorption costing procedures is needed.

The results of a research study sponsored by the National Association of Accountants indicated that the companies studied used absorption costing in making routine pricing decisions. However, these companies regularly used variable costing as a basis for setting prices in many short-run situations.[2]

There are no simple solutions to most pricing problems. Consideration must be given to many factors of varying importance. Accounting can contribute by preparing analyses of various pricing plans for both the short run and the long run.[3]

---

[2] Thomas M. Bruegelmann, Gaile A. Haessly, Michael Schiff, and Clair P. Wolfangel, *The Use of Variable Costing in Pricing Decisions,* National Association of Accountants (Montvale, New Jersey, 1986), p. vii.

[3] Analyses useful for product pricing are further described and illustrated in Chapter 22.

VARIABLE COSTING IN PRICING DECISIONS—TWO CASE STUDIES

A firm may find it profitable to sell its existing products in new markets. For example, consumer products may be targeted for industrial usage, or the firm may decide to expand into national or international markets. Variable costing can aid management in pricing decisions related to such products, as the following case studies illustrate.

Case One

This company is a division of a Fortune 500 firm. The division identified good opportunities in Third World countries for selling its products through distributors. Since there is usually an independent agent acting as an intermediary in arranging sales between the company and the distributors in the United States, dealing with distributors eliminates the commission paid to these agents. In addition, freight costs are lower, since the distributors provide the transportation. The company passes on these cost savings and quotes prices based on variable costs rather than full costs. In this way, the company is able to meet stiff foreign competition.

Case Two

This company is engaged primarily in the manufacture and sale of wire and cable made from nonferrous metals. The company has 25 major product lines. In the initial stages of introducing a product to a new market, price is not a major factor—quality, reliability, and timeliness of delivery are far more important. Hence, in this initial introductory stage, a full cost approach is used to establish the product price. However, once a product has passed the introductory stage and has achieved a good market share, it normally runs into stiff price competition from within the market. It is at this point that variable costing enters into the pricing decision to determine the price floor. If management decides to remain in the market, a price will be set, based upon variable cost, to fight off short-run price wars from competitors.

Source: Thomas M. Bruegelmann, Gaile A. Haessly, Michael Schiff, and Clair P. Wolfangel, *The Use of Variable Costing in Pricing Decisions*, National Association of Accountants (Montvale, New Jersey, 1986), pp. 45-46.

Production Planning

Production planning also has both short-run and long-run implications. In the short run, production is limited to existing capacity, and operating decisions must be made quickly before opportunities are lost. For example, a company manufacturing products with a seasonal demand may have an opportunity to obtain an off-season order that will not interfere with its production schedule nor reduce the sales of its other products. The relevant factors for such a short-run decision are the revenues and the variable costs and expenses. If the revenues from the special order will provide a contribution margin, the order should be accepted because it will increase the company's operating income. For long-run planning, management must also consider the fixed costs and expenses.

Sales Analysis

The primary objective of the marketing and sales functions is to offer the company's products for sale at prices that will result in an adequate amount of income relative to the total assets employed. To evalute these functions properly, management needs information concerning the profitability of various types of products and sales mixes, sales territories, and salespersons. Variable costing can make a significant contribution to management decision making in such areas.

Sales Mix Analysis. Sales mix, sometimes referred to as product mix, is generally defined as the relative distribution of sales among the various products sold. Some products are more profitable than others, and management should concentrate its sales efforts on those that will provide the maximum total operating income.

Sales mix studies are based on assumptions, such as the ability to sell one product in place of another and the ability to convert production facilities to accommodate the manufacture of one product instead of another. Proposed changes in the sales mix often affect only small segments of a company's total operations. In such cases, changes in sales mix may be possible within the limits of existing capacity, and the presentation of cost and revenue data in the variable costing form is useful in achieving the most profitable sales mix.

Two very important factors that should be determined for each product are (1) the production facilities needed for its manufacture and (2) the amount of contribution margin to be gained from its manufacture. If two or more products require equal use of limited production facilities, then managment should concentrate its sales and production efforts on the product or products with the highest contribution margin per unit. The following report, which focuses on product contribution margins, is an example of the type of data needed for an evaluation of sales mix. The enterprise, which manufactures two products and is operating at full capacity, is considering whether to change the emphasis of its advertising and other promotional efforts.

Contribution Margin Statement—Unit of Product

Contribution Margin by Unit of Product
April 15, 19--

	Product A	Product B
Sales price	$6.00	$8.50
Variable cost of goods sold	3.50	5.50
Manufacturing margin	$2.50	$3.00
Variable selling and administrative expenses	1.00	1.00
Contribution margin	$1.50	$2.00

The statement indicates that Product B yields a greater amount of contribution margin per unit than Product A. Therefore, Product B provides the larger contribution to the recovery of fixed costs and expenses and realization of operating income. If the amount of production facilities used for each product is assumed to be equal, it would be desirable to increase the sales of Product B.

If two or more products require unequal use of production resources, managment should concentrate its sales and production efforts on that product or products with the highest contribution margin per unit of resource. For example, assume that in the above illustration, to manufacture Product B requires twice the machine hours required for Product A. Specifically, Product B requires 2 machine hours per unit, while Product A requires only 1 machine hour per unit. Under this assumption, the contribution margin per unit of resource (machine hours) is $1.50 ($1.50 contribution ÷ 1 machine hour) for

Product A and $1 ($2 contribution margin ÷ 2 machine hours) for Product B. Under such circumstances, a change in sales mix designed to increase sales of Product A would be desirable. To illustrate, if 2,000 additional units of Product A (requiring 2,000 machine hours) could be sold in place of 1,000 units of Product B (also requiring 2,000 machine hours), the total company contribution margin would increase by $1,000 as follows:

Additional contribution margin from sale of additional 2,000 units of Product A ($1.50 × 2,000 units)	$3,000
Less contribution margin from forgoing production and sale of 1,000 units of Product B ($2 × 1,000 units)	2,000
Increase in total contribution margin	$1,000

Sales Territory Analysis. An income statement presenting the contribution margin by sales territories is often useful to management in appraising past performance and in directing future sales efforts. The following income statement is prepared in such a format, in abbreviated form:

Contribution Margin Statement—Sales Territories

Contribution Margin Statement by Sales Territory
For Month Ended July 31, 19--

	Territory A	Territory B	Total
Sales	$315,000	$502,500	$817,500
Less variable costs	189,000	251,250	440,250
Contribution margin	$126,000	$251,250	$377,250
Less fixed costs			242,750
Income from operations			$134,500

In addition to the contribution margin, the **contribution margin ratio** (contribution margin divided by sales) for each territory is useful in evaluating sales territories and directing operations toward more profitable activities. For Territory A, the contribution margin ratio is 40% ($126,000 ÷ $315,000), and for Territory B the ratio is 50% ($251,250 ÷ $502,500). Consequently, more profitability could be achieved by efforts to increase the sales of Territory B relative to Territory A.

Salespersons' Analysis. A report to management for use in evaluating the sales performance of each salesperson could include total sales, variable cost of goods sold, variable selling expenses, contribution margin, and contribution margin ratio. Such a report is illustrated as follows:

Salespersons' Analysis

Salespersons' Analysis
For Six Months Ended June 30, 19--

Salesperson	Total Sales	Variable Cost of Goods Sold	Variable Selling Expenses	Contribution Margin	Contribution Margin Ratio
A	$300,000	$180,000	$24,000	$ 96,000	32%
B	250,000	175,000	22,500	52,500	21
C	500,000	375,000	35,000	90,000	18
D	180,000	108,000	18,000	54,000	30
E	460,000	262,200	27,600	170,200	37
F	320,000	208,000	22,400	89,600	28

The preceding report illustrates that the total sales figure is not the only consideration in evaluating a salesperson. For example, although salesperson C has the highest total sales, C's sales are not contributing as much to overall company profits as are the sales of A and E, primarily because C's sales have the lowest contribution margin ratio. Of the six salespersons, E is generating the highest dollar contribution to company profit and is selling the most profitable mix of products, as measured by a contribution margin ratio of 37%.

Other factors should also be considered in evaluating the performance of salespersons. For example, sales growth rates, years of experience, and actual performance compared to budgeted performance may be more important than total sales.

Contribution Margin Analysis

Another use of the contribution margin concept to assist management in planning and controlling operations focuses on differences between planned and actual contribution margins. However, mere knowledge of the differences is insufficient. Management needs information about the causes of the differences. The systematic examination of the differences between planned and actual contribution margin is termed **contribution margin analysis.**

Since contribution margin is the excess of sales over variable costs, a difference between the planned and actual contribution margin can be caused by (1) an increase or decrease in the amount of sales or (2) an increase or decrease in the amount of variable costs. An increase or decrease in either element may in turn be due to (1) an increase or decrease in the number of units sold or (2) an increase or decrease in the unit sales price or unit cost. The effect of these two factors on either sales or variable costs may be stated as follows:

1. **Quantity factor**—the effect of a difference in the number of units sold, assuming no change in unit sales price or unit cost. The quantity factor is computed as the difference between the actual quantity sold and the planned quantity sold, multiplied by the planned unit sales price or unit cost.
2. **Unit price or unit cost factor**—the effect of a difference in unit sales price or unit cost on the number of units sold. The unit price or unit cost factor is computed as the difference between the actual unit price or unit cost and the planned unit price or unit cost, multiplied by the actual quantity sold.

The data at the top of page 907 for Noble Inc. are used as a basis for illustrating contribution margin analysis. For the sake of simplicity, a single commodity is assumed. The amount of detail entering into the analysis would be greater if several different commodities were sold, but the basic principles would not be affected.

The analysis following these data shows that the favorable increase of $25,000 in the contribution margin was due in large part to an increase in the number of units sold. This increase was partially offset by a decrease in the unit sales price and an increase in the unit cost for variable selling and administrative expenses. The decrease in the unit cost for the variable cost of goods sold was an additional favorable result of 1992 operations.

The data presented in the contribution margin analysis report are useful to management in evaluating past performance and in planning future operations. For example, the impact of the $.50 reduction in the unit sales price on the number of units sold and on the total sales for the year is useful informa-

	For Year Ended December 31, 1992		
	Actual	*Planned*	*Difference (Increase or Decrease*)*
Sales	$937,500	$800,000	$137,500
Less:			
Variable cost of goods sold	$425,000	$350,000	$ 75,000
Variable selling and administrative expenses	162,500	125,000	37,500
Total	$587,500	$475,000	$112,500
Contribution margin	$350,000	$325,000	$ 25,000
Number of units sold	125,000	100,000	
Per unit:			
Sales price	$7.50	$8.00	
Variable cost of goods sold	$3.40	$3.50	
Variable selling and administrative expenses	$1.30	$1.25	

Contribution Margin Analysis Report

Noble Inc.
Contribution Margin Analysis
For Year Ended December 31, 1992

Increase in amount of sales attributed to:			
Quantity factor:			
Increase in number of units sold in 1992	25,000		
Planned sales price in 1992	× $8.00	$200,000	
Price factor:			
Decrease in unit sales price in 1992	$.50		
Number of units sold in 1992	×125,000	62,500	
Net increase in amount of sales			$137,500
Increase in amount of variable cost of goods sold attributed to:			
Quantity factor:			
Increase in number of units sold in 1992	25,000		
Planned unit cost in 1992	× $3.50	$ 87,500	
Unit cost factor:			
Decrease in unit cost in 1992	$.10		
Number of units sold in 1992	×125,000	12,500	
Net increase in amount of variable cost of goods sold			75,000
Increase in amount of variable selling and administrative expenses attributed to:			
Quantity factor:			
Increase in number of units sold in 1992	25,000		
Planned unit cost in 1992	× $1.25	$ 31,250	
Unit cost factor:			
Increase in unit cost in 1992	$.05		
Number of units sold in 1992	125,000	6,250	
Net increase in the amount of variable selling and administrative expenses			37,500
Increase in contribution margin			$ 25,000

tion that management can use in determining whether further price reductions might be desirable. The contribution margin analysis report also highlights the impact of changes in unit variable costs and expenses. For example, the $.05 increase in the unit variable selling and administrative expenses might be a result of increased advertising expenditures. If so, the increase in the number of units sold in 1992 could be attributed to both the $.50 price reduction and the increased advertising.

CHAPTER REVIEW

KEY POINTS

OBJECTIVE 1

Absorption Costing and Variable Costing

The costs of manufacturing are direct materials, direct labor, and factory overhead. Under absorption costing, all such costs become part of the cost of goods manufactured. Under variable costing, the cost of goods manufactured is composed of only variable costs—those manufacturing costs that increase or decrease as the volume of production rises or falls. These costs are the direct materials, direct labor, and only those factory overhead costs which vary with the rate of production. The fixed factory overhead costs do not become a part of the cost of goods manufactured, but are considered an expense of the period.

OBJECTIVE 2

The Income Statement Under Variable Costing and Absorption Costing

The arrangement of data in the variable costing income statement differs considerably from the format of the conventional absorption costing income statement. The variable costing income statement includes only the variable manufacturing costs in the cost of goods sold. Deduction of the variable cost of goods sold from sales yields an intermediate amount, termed manufacturing margin. Deduction of the variable selling and administrative expenses yields the contribution margin. The fixed costs are then deducted from the contribution margin to yield income from operations.

A comparison of income reported under the absorption costing and variable costing concepts when the level of inventory changes during the period is summarized in the following table:

Units manufactured:	
Equal units sold	Absorption costing income equals variable costing income.
Exceed units sold	Absorption costing income is greater than variable costing income.
Less than units sold	Absorption costing income is less than variable costing income.

OBJECTIVE 3

Income Analysis Under Variable Costing and Absorption Costing

Management should be aware of the effects of changes in inventory levels on operating income reported under variable costing and absorption costing. If absorption costing is used, increases or decreases in income from operations due to changes in inventory levels could be misinterpreted to be the result of operating efficiencies or inefficiencies.

OBJECTIVE 4

Management's Use of Variable Costing and Absorption Costing

Variable costing is especially useful at the operating level of management because the amount of variable manufacturing costs varies with changes in the volume of production and thus is controllable at this level. The fixed factory overhead costs are ordinarily controllable by a higher level of management.

In the short run, variable costing may be useful in establishing the selling price of a product. This price should be at least equal to the variable costs of making and selling the product. In the long run, however, absorption costing procedures are useful in establishing selling prices, in that all costs and a reasonable amount of operating income must be earned.

Variable costing can make a significant contribution to management decision making in analyzing and evaluating sales. Management should concentrate its sales efforts on those products that will provide the maximum total operating income. Sales mix studies emphasize the contribution margin of each product in evaulating sales territories and directing operations towards more profitable activities. In addition, a salesperson's analysis report may be useful to management in evaluating the sales performance of each salesperson. Such a report emphasizes the contribution of each salesperson to the overall company profit.

Contribution margin analysis is the systematic examination of differences between planned and actual contribution margin. Since contribution margin is the excess of sales over variable costs, a difference between the planned and actual contribution margins can be caused by (1) an increase or decrease in the amount of sales or (2) an increase or decrease in the amount of variable costs. An increase or decrease in either element may in turn be due to (1) an increase or decrease in the number of units sold or (2) an increase or decrease in the unit sales price or unit cost. The effect of these two factors on either sales or variable costs may be stated as follows:

> Quantity factor—the effect of a difference in the number of units sold, assuming no change in unit sales price or unit cost. The quantity factor is computed as the difference between the actual quantity sold and the planned quantity sold, multiplied by the planned unit sales price or unit cost.
>
> Unit price or unit cost factor—the effect of a difference in unit sales price or unit cost on the number of units sold. The unit price or unit cost factor is computed as the difference between the actual unit price or unit cost and the planned unit price or unit cost, multiplied by the actual quantity sold.

KEY TERMS

absorption costing 893
variable costing 893
contribution margin 895
controllable costs 901
noncontrollable costs 901
sales mix 904
contribution margin ratio 905
contribution margin analysis 906

SELF-EXAMINATION QUESTIONS

Answers at end of chapter.

1. The concept that considers the cost of products manufactured to be composed only of those manufacturing costs that vary with the rate of production is known as:
   A. absorption costing
   B. variable costing
   C. replacement cost
   D. none of the above

2. In an income statement prepared under the variable costing concept, the deduction of the variable cost of goods sold from sales yields an intermediate amount referred to as:
   A. gross profit
   B. contribution margin
   C. manufacturing margin
   D. none of the above

3. Sales were $750,000, variable cost of goods sold was $400,000, variable selling and administrative expenses were $90,000, and fixed costs were $200,000. The contribution margin was:
   A. $60,000
   B. $260,000
   C. $350,000
   D. none of the above

4. During a year in which the number of units manufactured exceeded the number of units sold, the operating income reported under the absorption costing concept would be:
   A. larger than the operating income reported under the variable costing concept
   B. smaller than the operating income reported under the variable costing concept
   C. the same as the operating income reported under the variable costing concept
   D. none of the above

5. If actual sales totaled $800,000 for the current year (80,000 units at $10 each) and planned sales were $765,000 (85,000 units at $9 each), the difference between actual and planned sales due to the quantity factor is:
   A. a $50,000 increase
   B. a $35,000 increase
   C. a $45,000 decrease
   D. none of the above

ILLUSTRATIVE PROBLEM

During the current period, McLaughlin Company sold 60,000 units of product at a selling price of $30 per unit. At the beginning of the period, there were 10,000 units in inventory and McLaughlin Company manufactured 50,000 units during the period. The manufacturing costs and selling and administrative expenses were as follows:

	Total Cost	Number of Units	Unit Cost
Beginning inventory:			
Direct materials	$ 67,000	10,000	$ 6.70
Direct labor	155,000	10,000	15.50
Variable factory overhead	18,000	10,000	1.80
Fixed factory overhead	20,000	10,000	2.00
Total	$ 260,000		$26.00
Current period costs:			
Direct materials	$ 350,000	50,000	$ 7.00
Direct labor	810,000	50,000	16.20
Variable factory overhead	90,000	50,000	1.80
Fixed factory overhead	100,000	50,000	2.00
Total	$1,350,000		$27.00
Selling and administrative expenses:			
Variable	$ 65,000		
Fixed	45,000		
Total	$ 110,000		

Instructions:

1. Prepare an income statement based on the absorption costing concept.
2. Prepare an income statement based on the variable costing concept.
3. Explain the reason for the difference in the amount of operating income reported in 1 and 2.

SOLUTION

(1) Absorption Costing Income Statement

Sales (60,000 × $30)		$1,800,000
Cost of goods sold:		
Beginning inventory (10,000 × $26)	$ 260,000	
Cost of goods manufactured (50,000 × $27)	1,350,000	
Cost of goods sold		1,610,000
Gross profit		$ 190,000
Selling and administrative expenses ($65,000 + $45,000)		110,000
Income from operations		$ 80,000

(2) Variable Costing Income Statement

Sales (60,000 × $30)		$1,800,000
Variable cost of goods sold:		
Beginning inventory (10,000 × $24)	$ 240,000	
Variable cost of goods manufactured (50,000 × $25)	1,250,000	
Variable cost of goods sold		1,490,000
Manufacturing margin		$ 310,000
Variable selling and administrative expenses		65,000
Contribution margin		$ 245,000
Fixed costs:		
Fixed manufacturing costs	$ 100,000	
Fixed selling and administrative expenses	45,000	145,000
Income from operations		$ 100,000

(3) The difference of $20,000 ($100,000 − $80,000) in the amount of income from operations is attributable to the different treatment of the fixed manufacturing costs. The beginning inventory in the absorption costing income statement includes $20,000 (10,000 units × $2) of fixed manufacturing costs incurred in the preceding period. This $20,000 was included as an expense in a variable costing income statement of a prior period, however. Therefore, none of it is included as an expense in the current period variable costing income statement.

DISCUSSION QUESTIONS

21–1. What types of costs are customarily included in the cost of manufactured products under (a) the *absorption costing* concept and (b) the *variable costing* concept?

21–2. Which type of manufacturing cost (direct materials, direct labor, variable factory overhead, fixed factory overhead) is included in the cost of goods manufactured under the absorption costing concept but is excluded from the cost of goods manufactured under the variable costing concept?

21–3. At the end of the first year of operations, 1,000 units remained in the finished goods inventory. The unit manufacturing costs during the year were as follows:

Direct materials	$15.00
Direct labor	7.50
Fixed factory overhead	3.00
Variable factory overhead	1.20

What would be the cost of the finished goods inventory reported on the balance sheet under (a) the absorption costing concept and (b) the variable costing concept?

21–4. Which of the following costs would be included in the cost of a manufactured product according to the variable costing concept: (a) direct labor, (b) depreciation on factory building, (c) salary of factory supervisor, (d) electricity purchased to operate factory equipment, (e) property taxes on factory building, (f) rent on factory building, and (g) direct materials?

21–5. In the following equations, based on the variable costing income statement, identify the items designated by **X**:

(a) Net sales − **X** = manufacturing margin
(b) Manufacturing margin − **X** = contribution margin
(c) Contribution margin − **X** = income from operations

21–6. In the variable costing income statement, how are the fixed manufacturing costs reported and how are the fixed selling and administrative expenses reported?

21–7. If the quantity of the ending inventory is larger than that of the beginning inventory, will the amount of income from operations determined by absorption costing be more than or less than the amount determined by variable costing? Explain.

21–8. Since all costs of operating a business are controllable, what is the significance of the term *noncontrollable cost*?

21–9. Discuss how financial data prepared on the basis of variable costing can assist management in the development of short-run pricing policies.

21–10. What term is used to refer to the relative distribution of sales among the various products manufactured?

21–11. A company, operating at full capacity, manufactures two products, with Product H requiring four times the production facilities as Product I. The contribution margin is $100 per unit for Product H and $30 per unit for Product I. How much would the total contribution margin be increased or decreased for the coming year if the sales of Product H could be increased by 5,000 units by changing the emphasis of promotional efforts?

21–12. Explain why rewarding sales personnel on the basis of total sales might not be in the best interests of an enterprise whose goal is to maximize profits.

21–13. Discuss the two factors affecting both sales and variable costs, to which a change in contribution margin can be attributed.

21–14. How is the quantity factor for an increase or decrease in the amount of sales computed in using contribution margin analysis?

21–15. How is the unit cost factor for an increase or decrease in the amount of variable cost of goods sold computed in using contribution margin analysis?

Real World Focus

21–16. Dutch Pantry Inc. operates full-service family restaurants in the eastern states. To assure consistent quality, many of the items served in the restaurants are prepared in a central food processing plant. Classify each of the following costs and expenses of the food processing plant as either variable or fixed:

(a) Garbage collection expense
(b) Salad dressing
(c) Office salaries
(d) Depreciation on equipment (straight-line method)

(e) Cooking oil
(f) Experimental costs
(g) Cleaning supplies
(h) Spices
(i) Water
(j) Property taxes
(k) Electricity

Ethics Discussion Case

21–17. JoAnn Nicholas, assistant controller for Schmidt Enterprises, has been asked to prepare divisional income statements for the past 18 months. The chief executive officer intends to use the monthly statements to analyze the efficiency of each division's operations and to take corrective actions, if necessary. Nicholas did not use the variable costing format but prepared the income statements using the absorption costing format because it indicates generally more favorable operating results for the 18-month period. Discuss whether JoAnn Nicholas is behaving in an ethical manner.

EXERCISES

Ex. 21–18. Income statements under absorption costing and variable costing. OBJ. 2

Northrup Company began operations on May 1 and operated at 100% of capacity during the first month. The following data summarize the results for May:

Sales (24,000 units)		$900,000
Production costs (30,000 units):		
Direct materials	$225,000	
Direct labor	270,000	
Variable factory overhead	75,000	
Fixed factory overhead	45,000	615,000
Selling and administrative expenses:		
Variable selling and administrative expenses	$206,400	
Fixed selling and administrative expenses	41,600	248,000

(a) Prepare an income statement in accordance with the absorption costing concept. (b) Prepare an income statement in accordance with the variable costing concept. (c) What is the reason for the difference in the amount of operating income reported in (a) and (b)?

Ex. 21–19. Cost of goods manufactured, using variable costing and absorption costing. OBJ. 2

On August 31, the end of the first year of operations, Layton Company manufactured 50,000 units and sold 46,000 units. The following income statement was prepared, based on the variable costing concept:

Layton Company
Income Statement
For Year Ended August 31, 19--

Sales		$1,150,000
Variable cost of goods sold:		
Variable cost of goods manufactured	$750,000	
Less ending inventory	60,000	
Variable cost of goods sold		690,000
Manufacturing margin		$ 460,000
Variable selling and administrative expenses		138,000
Contribution margin		$ 322,000
Fixed costs:		
Fixed manufacturing costs	$120,000	
Fixed selling and administrative expenses	92,000	212,000
Income from operations		$ 110,000

Determine the unit cost of goods manufactured, based on (a) the variable costing concept and (b) the absorption costing concept.

Ex. 21–20.
Variable costing income statement.
OBJ. 2

On April 30, the end of the first month of operations, Adams Company prepared the following income statement, based on the absorption costing concept:

Adams Company
Income Statement
For Month Ended April 30, 19--

Sales (9,000 units)		$720,000
Cost of goods sold:		
Cost of goods manufactured	$480,000	
Less ending inventory (1,000 units)	48,000	
Cost of goods sold		432,000
Gross profit		$288,000
Selling and administrative expenses		140,000
Income from operations		$148,000

If the fixed manufacturing costs were $140,000 and the variable selling and administrative expenses were $108,000, prepare an income statement in accordance with the variable costing concept.

Ex. 21–21.
Absorption costing income statement.
OBJ. 2

On November 30, the end of the first month of operations, Cason Company prepared the following income statement, based on the variable costing concept:

Cason Company
Income Statement
For Month Ended November 30, 19--

Sales (15,000 units)		$630,000
Variable cost of goods sold:		
Variable cost of goods manufactured	$450,000	
Less ending inventory (3,000 units)	75,000	
Variable cost of goods sold		375,000
Manufacturing margin		$255,000
Variable selling and administrative expenses		60,000
Contribution margin		$195,000
Fixed costs:		
Fixed manufacturing costs	$ 54,000	
Fixed selling and administrative expenses	22,500	76,500
Income from operations		$118,500

Prepare an income statement with the absorption costing concept.

Ex. 21–22.
Estimated income statements, using absorption and variable costing.
OBJ. 2, 3

Prior to the first month of operations ending July 31, Godwin Company estimated the following operating results:

Sales (8,000 × $30)	$240,000
Manufacturing costs (8,000 units):	
Direct materials	48,000
Direct labor	44,800
Variable factory overhead	30,400
Fixed factory overhead	21,600
Fixed selling and administrative expenses	11,200
Variable selling and administrative expenses	6,400

The company is evaluating a proposal to manufacture 9,000 units instead of 8,000 units. Manufacturing the additional units will not change sales, unit variable manufacturing costs, and fixed factory overhead and total selling and administrative expenses. (a) Prepare an estimated income statement, comparing operating results if 8,000 and 9,000 units are manufactured, in the (1) absorption costing format and (2) variable format. (b) What is the reason for the difference in income from operations reported for the two levels of production by the absorption costing income statement?

Ex. 21–23. Change in sales mix and contribution margin. OBJ. 4

Van DeMark Company manufactures Products F and G and is operating at full capacity. To manufacture Product F requires three times the number of machine hours as required for Product G. Market research indicates that 6,000 additional units of Product G could be sold. The contribution margin by unit of product is as follows:

	Product F	Product G
Sales price	$200	$25
Variable cost of goods sold	120	10
Manufacturing margin	$ 80	$15
Variable selling and administrative expenses	50	6
Contribution margin	$ 30	$ 9

Prepare a tabulation indicating the increase or decrease in total contribution margin if 6,000 additional units of Product G are produced and sold.

Ex. 21–24. Contribution margin analysis—sales. OBJ. 4

The following data for Alens Company are available:

	For Year Ended December 31, 1992		
	Actual	Planned	Difference (Increase or Decrease*)
Sales	$578,000	$600,000	$22,000*
Less:			
Variable cost of goods sold	$292,400	$280,000	$12,400
Variable selling and administrative expenses	149,600	180,000	30,400*
Total	$442,000	$460,000	$18,000*
Contribution margin	$136,000	$140,000	$ 4,000*
Number of units sold	34,000	40,000	
Per unit:			
Sales price	$17.00	$15.00	
Variable cost of goods sold	$8.60	$7.00	
Variable selling and administrative expenses	$4.40	$4.50	

Prepare a contribution analysis of the sales quantity and price factors.

Ex. 21–25. Contribution margin analysis—variable costs. OBJ. 4

Based upon the data in Exercise 21–24, prepare a contribution analysis of the variable costs for Alens Company for the year ended December 31, 1992.

Ex. 21–26. Real world focus. OBJ. 2

The following data were adapted from the income statement of Proctor & Gamble Company for the year ended June 30, 1990:

	In Millions
Net sales	$24,081
Operating costs:	
Cost of products sold	$14,658
Marketing, administrative, and other expenses	7,121
Operating costs	$21,779
Income from operations	$ 2,302

Assume that the variable amount of each category of operating costs is as follows:

Cost of products sold	$ 9,000
Marketing, administrative, and other expenses	5,200

Based on the above data, prepare a variable costing income statement for Proctor & Gamble Company for the year ended June 30, 1990.

PROBLEMS

Pb. 21–27. **Absorption and variable costing income statements.** OBJ. 2, 3

During the first month of operations ended June 30, Mattox Company manufactured 75,000 units, of which 70,000 were sold. Operating data for the month are summarized as follows:

Sales		$840,000
Manufacturing costs:		
Direct materials	$172,500	
Direct labor	180,000	
Variable factory overhead	82,500	
Fixed factory overhead	67,500	502,500
Selling and administrative expenses:		
Variable	$224,000	
Fixed	105,000	329,000

Instructions:

(1) Prepare an income statement based on the absorption costing concept.
(2) Prepare an income statement based on the variable costing concept.
(3) Explain the reason for the difference in the amount of operating income reported in (1) and (2).

Pb. 21–28. **Income statements under absorption costing and variable costing.** OBJ. 2, 3

The demand for Product M, one of numerous products manufactured by Jordan, Inc. has dropped sharply because of recent competition from a similar product. The company's chemists are currently completing tests of various new formulas, and it is anticipated that the manufacture of a superior product can be started on March 1, one month hence. No changes will be needed in the present production facilities to manufacture the new product because only the mixture of the various materials will be changed.

The controller has been asked by the president of the company for advice on whether to continue production during February or to suspend the manufacture of Product M until March 1. The controller has assembled the following pertinent data:

Jordan Inc.
Estimated Income Statement—Product M
For Month Ending January 31, 19--

Sales (80,000 units)	$2,080,000
Cost of goods sold	2,016,000
Gross profit	$ 64,000
Selling and administrative expenses	100,000
Loss from operations	$ 36,000

The estimated production costs and selling and administrative expenses, based on a production of 80,000 units, are as follows:

Direct materials	$14.60 per unit
Direct labor	6.75 per unit
Variable factory overhead	3.10 per unit
Variable selling and administrative expenses	1.00 per unit
Fixed factory overhead	$60,000 for January
Fixed selling and administrative expenses	20,000 for January

Sales for February are expected to drop about 40% below those of the preceding month. No significant changes are anticipated in the production costs or operating expenses. No extra costs will be incurred in discontinuing operations in the portion of the plant associated with Product M. The inventory of Product M at the beginning and end of February is expected to be inconsequential.

Instructions:

(1) Prepare an estimated income statement in absorption costing form for February for Product M, assuming that production continues during the month.
(2) Prepare an estimated income statement in variable costing form for February for Product M, assuming that production continues during the month.
(3) State the estimated operating loss arising from the activities associated with Product M for February if production is temporarily suspended.
(4) Prepare a brief statement of the advice the controller should give.

Pb. 21–29.
Absorption and variable costing income statements for two months and analysis.
OBJ. 2, 3

During the first month of operations ended May 31, Addison Company manufactured 230,000 units, of which 200,000 were sold. Operating data for the month are summarized as follows:

Sales		$2,100,000
Manufacturing costs:		
Direct materials	$552,000	
Direct labor	805,000	
Variable factory overhead	253,000	
Fixed factory overhead	207,000	1,817,000
Selling and administrative expenses:		
Variable	$120,000	
Fixed	75,000	195,000

During June, Addison Company manufactured 170,000 units and sold 200,000 units. Operating data for June are summarized as follows:

Sales		$2,100,000
Manufacturing costs:		
Direct materials	$408,000	
Direct labor	595,000	
Variable factory overhead	187,000	
Fixed factory overhead	207,000	1,397,000
Selling and administrative expenses:		
Variable	$120,000	
Fixed	75,000	195,000

Instructions:

(1) Using the absorption costing concept, prepare income statements for (a) May and (b) June.
(2) Using the variable costing concept, prepare income statements for (a) May and (b) June.
(3) (a) Explain the reason for the differences in the amount of operating income in (1) and (2) for May.
    (b) Explain the reasons for the differences in the amount of operating income in (1) and (2) for June.
(4) Based upon your answers to (1) and (2), did Addison Company operate more profitably in May or in June? Explain.

21-918 **Pb. 21–30.**
Salespersons' report and analysis.
OBJ. 4

Acton Company employs seven salespersons to sell and distribute its product throughout the state. Data taken from reports received from the salespersons during the current year ended June 30 are as follows:

Salesperson	Total Sales	Variable Cost of Goods Sold	Variable Selling Expenses
Barry	$540,000	$351,000	$130,500
Farmer	405,000	251,100	105,300
Griffith	340,000	207,400	71,000
Murray	360,000	226,800	84,600
Owens	225,000	135,000	56,250
Thom	290,000	171,100	67,500
York	250,000	140,000	68,400

Instructions:

(1) Prepare a report for the year, indicating total sales, variable cost of goods sold, variable selling expenses, contribution margin, and contribution margin ratio by salesperson.
(2) Which salesperson generated the highest contribution margin for the year?
(3) Briefly list factors other than contribution margin that should be considered in evaluating the performance of salespersons.

Pb. 21–31.
Variable costing income statement and effect on income of change in operations.
OBJ. 4

Fleming Company manufactures three styles of folding chairs, J, K, and L. The income statement has consistently indicated a net loss for Style K, and management is considering three proposals: (1) continue Style K, (2) discontinue Style K and reduce total output accordingly, or (3) discontinue Style K and conduct an advertising campaign to expand the sales of Style J so that the entire plant capacity can continue to be used.

If Proposal 2 is selected and Style K is discontinued and production curtailed, the annual fixed production costs and fixed operating expenses could be reduced by $45,000 and $30,000 respectively. If proposal 3 is selected, it is anticipated that an additional annual expenditure of $60,000 for advertising Style J would yield an increase of 35% in its sales volume, and that the increased production of Style J would utilize the plant facilities released by the discontinuance of Style K.

The sales and costs have been relatively stable over the past few years, and they are expected to remain so for the foreseeable future. The income statement for the past year ended January 31 is as follows:

	Style			
	J	K	L	Total
Sales	$1,400,000	$400,000	$1,200,000	$3,000,000
Cost of goods sold:				
Variable costs	$ 750,000	$275,000	$ 650,000	$1,675,000
Fixed costs	250,000	85,500	210,000	545,500
Total cost of goods sold	$1,000,000	$360,500	$ 860,000	$2,220,500
Gross profit	$ 400,000	$ 39,500	$ 340,000	$ 779,500
Less operating expenses:				
Variable expenses	$ 130,000	$ 37,800	$ 130,000	$ 297,800
Fixed expenses	72,000	32,000	70,700	174,700
Total operating expenses	$ 202,000	$ 69,800	$ 200,700	$ 472,500
Income from operations	$ 198,000	$ (30,300)	$ 139,300	$ 307,000

Instructions:

(1) Prepare an income statement for the past year in the variable costing format. Use the following headings:

Style			
J	K	L	Total

Data for each style should be reported through contribution margin. The fixed costs should be deducted from the total contribution margin, as reported in the "Total" column, to determine income from operations.

(2) Based on the income statement prepared in (1) and the other data presented above, determine the amount by which total annual operating income would be reduced below its present level if Proposal 2 is accepted.

(3) Prepare an income statement in the variable costing format, indicating the projected annual operating income if Proposal 3 is accepted. Use the following headings:

Style		
J	L	Total

Data for each style should be reported through contribution margin. The fixed costs should be deducted from the total contribution margin as reported in the "Total" column. For purposes of this problem, the additional expenditure of $60,000 for advertising can be added to the fixed operating expenses.

(4) By how much would total annual income increase above its present level if Proposal 3 is accepted? Explain.

Pb. 21–32.
Contribution margin analysis.
OBJ. 4
SPREADSHEET PROBLEM

White Company manufactures only one product. For the year ended December 31, 1992, the contribution margin decreased by $63,000 from the planned level of $210,000. The president of White Company has expressed serious concern about the size of this decrease and has requested a follow-up report.

The following data have been gathered from the accounting records:

	For the Year Ended December 31, 1992		
	Actual	Planned	Difference (Increase or Decrease*)
Sales	$840,000	$780,000	$ 60,000
Less:			
Variable cost of goods sold	$553,000	$480,000	$ 73,000
Variable selling and administrative expenses	140,000	90,000	50,000
Total	$693,000	$570,000	$123,000
Contribution margin	$147,000	$210,000	$ 63,000*
Number of units sold	700,000	600,000	
Per unit:			
Sales price	$1.20	$1.30	
Variable cost of goods sold	$ .79	$ .80	
Variable selling and administrative expenses	$ .20	$ .15	

Instructions:

(1) Prepare a contribution margin analysis report for the year ended December 31, 1992.

(2) At a meeting of the board of directors on January 30, 1993, the president, after reviewing the contribution margin analysis report, made the following comment:

"It looks as if the price decrease of $.10 had the effect of increasing sales. However, we lost control over the variable costs of goods sold and variable selling and administrative expenses. Let's look into these expenses and get them under control! Also, let's consider decreasing the sales price to $1 to increase sales further."

Do you agree with the president's comment? Explain.

ALTERNATE PROBLEMS

Pb. 21–27A.
Absorption and variable costing income statements.
OBJ. 2,3

During the first month of operations ended August 31, Rubin Company manufactured 320,000 units, of which 300,000 were sold. Operating data for the month are summarized as follows:

Sales		$7,500,000
Manufacturing costs:		
Direct materials	$1,600,000	
Direct labor	2,400,000	
Variable factory overhead	576,000	
Fixed factory overhead	384,000	4,960,000
Selling and administrative expenses:		
Variable	$ 720,000	
Fixed	160,000	880,000

Instructions:

(1) Prepare an income statement based on the absorption costing concept.
(2) Prepare an income statement based on the variable costing concept.
(3) Explain the reason for the difference in the amount of operating income reported in (1) and (2).

Pb. 21–28A.
Income statements under absorption costing and variable costing.
OBJ. 2, 3

The demand for Product K, one of numerous products manufactured by Erwin Inc., has dropped sharply because of recent competition from a similar product. The company's chemists are currently completing tests of various new formulas, and it is anticipated that the manufacture of a superior product can be started on November 1, one month hence. No changes will be needed in the present production facilities to manufacture the new product because only the mixture of the various materials will be changed.

The controller has been asked by the president of the company for advice on whether to continue production during October or to suspend the manufacture of Product K until November 1. The controller has assembled the following pertinent data:

Erwin Inc.
Estimated Income Statement—Product K
For Month Ending September 30, 19--

Sales (30,000 units)	$750,000
Cost of goods sold	690,000
Gross profit	$ 60,000
Selling and administrative expenses	92,000
Loss from operations	$ 32,000

The estimated production costs and selling and administrative expenses, based on a production of 30,000 units, are as follows:

Direct materials	$10.80 per unit
Direct labor	7.50 per unit
Variable factory overhead	2.30 per unit
Variable selling and administrative expenses	2.40 per unit
Fixed factory overhead	$72,000 for September
Fixed selling and administrative expenses	20,000 for September

Sales for October are expected to drop about 25% below those of the preceding month. No significant changes are anticipated in the production costs or operating expenses. No extra costs will be incurred in discontinuing operations in the portion of the plant associated with Product K. The inventory of Product K at the beginning and end of October is expected to be inconsequential.

Instructions:

(1) Prepare an estimated income statement in absorption costing form for October for Product K, assuming that production continues during the month.
(2) Prepare an estimated income statement in variable costing form for October for Product K, assuming that production continues during the month.
(3) State the estimated operating loss arising from the activities associated with Product K for October if production is temporarily suspended.
(4) Prepare a brief statement of the advice the controller should give.

Pb. 21–29A.
Absorption and variable costing income statements for two months and analysis.
OBJ. 2, 3

During the first month of operations ended July 31, Barr Company manufactured 115,000 units, of which 100,000 were sold. Operating data for the month are summarized as follows:

Sales		$1,950,000
Manufacturing costs:		
Direct materials	$702,000	
Direct labor	625,000	
Variable factory overhead	283,000	
Fixed factory overhead	207,000	1,817,000
Selling and administrative expenses:		
Variable	$120,000	
Fixed	75,000	195,000

During August, Barr Company manufactured 85,000 units and sold 100,000 units. Operating data for August are summarized as follows:

Sales		$1,950,000
Manufacturing costs:		
Direct materials	$518,500	
Direct labor	470,000	
Variable factory overhead	201,500	
Fixed factory overhead	207,000	1,397,000
Selling and administrative expenses:		
Variable	$120,000	
Fixed	75,000	195,000

Instructions:

(1) Using the absorption costing concept, prepare income statements for (a) July and (b) August.
(2) Using the variable costing concept, prepare income statements for (a) July and (b) August.
(3) (a) Explain the reason for the differences in the amount of operating income in (1) and (2) for July.
(b) Explain the reasons for the differences in the amount of operating income in (1) and (2) for August.
(4) Based upon your answers to (1) and (2), did Barr Company operate more profitably in July or in August? Explain.

21-922

Pb. 21–30A. **Salespersons' report and analysis.** OBJ. 4

Cohen Company employs seven salespersons to sell and distribute its product throughout the state. Data extracted from reports received from the salespersons during the current year ended December 31 are as follows:

Salesperson	Total Sales	Variable Cost of Goods Sold	Variable Selling Expenses
Barry	$900,000	$585,000	$217,500
Farmer	675,000	418,500	175,500
Griffith	560,000	341,600	118,400
Murray	600,000	372,000	141,000
Owens	375,000	225,000	90,000
Thom	480,000	278,400	129,600
York	525,000	315,000	136,500

Instructions:

(1) Prepare a report for the year, indicating total sales, variable cost of goods sold, variable selling expenses, contribution margin, and contribution margin ratio by salesperson.

(2) Which salesperson generated the highest contribution margin for the year?

(3) Briefly list factors other than contribution margin that should be considered in evaluating the performance of salespersons.

Pb. 21–31A. **Variable costing income statement and effect on income of change in operations.** OBJ. 4

A.L. Holt Company manufactures three styles of folding chairs, A, B, and C. The income statement has consistently indicated a net loss for Style B, and management is considering three proposals: (1) continue Style B, (2) discontinue Style B and reduce total output accordingly, or (3) discontinue Style B and conduct an advertising campaign to expand the sales of Style A so that the entire plant capacity can continue to be used.

If Proposal 2 is selected and Style B is discontinued and production curtailed, the annual fixed production costs and fixed operating expenses could be reduced by $21,200 and $13,300 respectively. If Proposal 3 is selected, it is anticipated that an additional annual expenditure of $40,000 for advertising Style A would yield an increase of 40% in its sales volume, and that the increased production of Style A would use the plant facilities released by the discontinuance of Style B.

The sales, costs, and expenses have been relatively stable over the past few years, and they are expected to remain so for the foreseeable future. The income statement for the past year ended June 30 is:

	Style			
	A	B	C	Total
Sales	$650,000	$200,000	$600,000	$1,450,000
Cost of goods sold:				
Variable costs	$370,000	$140,000	$330,000	$ 840,000
Fixed costs	125,000	40,000	120,000	285,000
Total cost of goods sold	$495,000	$180,000	$450,000	$1,125,000
Gross profit	$155,000	$ 20,000	$150,000	$ 325,000
Less operating expenses:				
Variable expenses	$ 64,800	$ 18,900	$ 60,000	$ 143,700
Fixed expenses	36,000	16,000	35,000	87,000
Total operating expenses	$100,800	$ 34,900	$ 95,000	$ 230,700
Income from operations	$ 54,200	$ (14,900)	$ 55,000	$ 94,300

Instructions:

(1) Prepare an income statement for the past year in the variable costing format. Use the following headings:

Style			
A	B	C	Total

Data for each style should be reported through contribution margin. The fixed costs and expenses should be deducted from the total contribution margin, as reported in the "Total" column, to determine income from operations.

(2) Based on the income statement prepared in (1) and the other data presented above, determine the amount by which total annual operating income would be reduced below its present level if Proposal 2 is accepted.

(3) Prepare an income statement in the variable costing format, indicating the projected annual operating income if Proposal 3 is accepted. Use the following headings:

Style		
A	C	Total

Data for each style should be reported through contribution margin. The fixed costs and expenses should be deducted from the total contribution margin as reported in the "Total" column. For purposes of this problem, the additional expenditure of $40,000 for advertising can be added to the fixed operating expenses.

(4) By how much would total annual income increase above its present level if Proposal 3 is accepted? Explain.

Pb. 21–32A.
Contribution margin analysis.
OBJ. 4

Evans Company manufactures only one product. For the year ended December 31, 1992, the contribution margin decreased by $81,000 from the planned level of $225,000. The president of Evans Company has expressed serious concern about the size of this decrease and has requested a follow-up report.

The following data have been gathered from the accounting records:

	For the Year Ended December 31, 1992		
	Actual	Planned	Difference (Increase or Decrease*)
Sales	$1,000,000	$975,000	$ 25,000
Less:			
Variable cost of goods sold	$ 476,000	$450,000	$ 26,000
Variable selling and administrative expenses	380,000	300,000	80,000
Total	$ 856,000	$750,000	$106,000
Contribution margin	$ 144,000	$225,000	$ 81,000*
Number of units sold	80,000	75,000	
Per unit:			
Sales price	$12.50	$13.00	
Variable cost of goods sold	$5.95	$6.00	
Variable selling and administrative expenses	$4.75	$4.00	

Instructions:

(1) Prepare a contribution margin analysis report for the year ended December 31, 1992.

(2) At a meeting of the board of directors on February 10, 1993, the president, after reviewing the contribution margin analysis report, made the following comment:

> "It looks as if the price decrease of $.50 had the effect of increasing sales. However, we lost control over the variable costs of goods sold and variable selling and administrative expenses. Let's look into these expenses and get them under control! Also, let's consider decreasing the sales price to $12 to increase sales further."

Do you agree with the president's comment? Explain.

MINI-CASE 21

Reynolds Company is a family-owned business in which you own 20% of the common stock and your brothers and sisters own the remaining shares. The employment contract of Reynolds' new president, Ellen Edward, stipulates a base salary of $75,000 per year plus 7% of income from operations in excess of $1,000,000. Reynolds uses the absorption costing method of reporting income from operations, which has averaged approximately $1,000,000 for the past several years.

Sales for 1992, Edward's first year as president of Reynolds Company, are estimated at 100,000 units at a selling price of $60 per unit. To maximize the use of Reynolds' productive capacity, Edward has decided to manufacture 150,000 units, rather than the 100,000 units of estimated sales. The beginning inventory at January 1, 1992, is insignificant in amount, and the manufacturing costs and selling and administrative expenses for the production of 100,000 and 150,000 units are as follows:

100,000 Units To Be Manufactured

	Total Cost	Number of Units	Unit Cost
Manufacturing costs:			
Variable	$3,200,000	100,000	$32
Fixed	600,000	100,000	6
Total	$3,800,000		$38
Selling and administrative expenses:			
Variable	$ 900,000		
Fixed	300,000		
Total	$1,200,000		

150,000 Units To Be Manufactured

	Total Cost	Number of Units	Unit Cost
Manufacturing costs:			
Variable	$4,800,000	150,000	$32
Fixed	600,000	150,000	4
Total	$5,400,000		$36
Selling and administrative expenses:			
Variable	$ 900,000		
Fixed	300,000		
Total	$1,200,000		

Instructions:

(1) Prepare absorption costing income statements for the year ending December 31, 1992, based upon sales of 100,000 units and the manufacture of (a) 100,000 units and (b) 150,000 units.

(2) Explain the difference in the income from operations reported in (1).

(3) Compute Edward's total salary for 1992, based on sales of 100,000 units and the manufacture of (a) 100,000 units and (b) 150,000 units.
(4) In addition to maximizing the use of Reynolds Company's productive capacity, why might Edward wish to manufacture 150,000 units rather than 100,000 units?
(5) Can you suggest an alternative way in which Edward's salary could be determined, using a base salary of $75,000 and 7% of income from operations in excess of $1,000,000, so that the salary could not be increased by simply manufacturing more units?

ANSWERS TO SELF-EXAMINATION QUESTIONS

1. B Under the variable costing concept (answer B), the cost of products manufactured is composed of only those manufacturing costs that increase or decrease as the volume of production rises or falls. These costs include direct materials, direct labor, and variable factory overhead. Under the absorption costing concept (answer A), all manufacturing costs become a part of the cost of the products manufactured. The absorption costing concept is required in the determination of historical cost and taxable income. The variable costing concept is often useful to management in making decisions.
2. C In the variable costing income statement, the deduction of the variable cost of goods sold from sales yields the manufacturing margin (answer C). Deduction of the variable selling and administrative expenses from manufacturing margin yields the contribution margin (answer B).
3. B The contribution margin of $260,000 (answer B) is determined by deducting all of the variable costs ($400,000 + $90,000) from sales ($750,000).
4. A In a period in which the number of units manufactured exceeds the number of units sold, the operating income reported under the absorption costing concept is larger than the operating income reported under the variable costing concept (answer A) because a portion of the fixed manufacturing costs are deferred when the absorption costing concept is used. This deferment has the effect of excluding a portion of the fixed manufacturing costs from the current cost of goods sold.
5. C A difference between planned and actual sales can be attributed to (1) a difference in the number of units sold—quanity factory and (2) a difference in the unit price—price factor. The $45,000 decrease (answer C) attributed to the quantity factor is determined as follows:

Decrease in number of units sold	5,000
Planned unit sales price	× $9
Quantity factor—decrease	$45,000

The unit price factor can be determined as follows:

Increase in unit sales price	$1
Actual number of units sold	×80,000
Price factor—increase	$80,000

The increase of $80,000 attributed to the price factor less the decrease of $45,000 attributed to the quantity factor accounts for the $35,000 increase in total sales.

CHAPTER 22

CHAPTER OBJECTIVES

1 Describe and illustrate differential analysis for decisions involving:
   - Leasing or selling
   - Discontinuing an unprofitable segment
   - Making or buying
   - Replacing equipment
   - Processing or selling
   - Accepting business at a special price.

2 Describe and illustrate the setting of normal product selling prices, using the total cost, product cost, and variable cost concepts.

3 Describe the economic theory of product pricing.

DIFFERENTIAL ANALYSIS & PRODUCT PRICING

A primary objective of accounting is to provide management with analyses and reports that will be useful in resolving current problems and planning for the future. The types of analyses and reports depend on the nature of the decisions to be made. However, all decisions require careful consideration of the consequences of alternative courses of action. This chapter discusses differential analysis, which provides management with data on the differences in total revenues and costs associated with alternative actions.

This chapter also describes and illustrates practical approaches frequently used by managers in setting normal product selling prices. The relationship of economic theory to the more practical approaches to product pricing is briefly discussed. Finally, the alternative price strategies used by management during a product's life cycle are discussed.

DIFFERENTIAL ANALYSIS

OBJECTIVE 1
Describe and illustrate differential analysis for decisions involving:
Leasing or selling
Discontinuing an unprofitable segment
Making or buying
Replacing equipment
Processing or selling
Accepting business at a special price

Planning for future operations is chiefly decision making. For some decisions, revenue and cost information drawn from the general ledger and other basic accounting records may be useful. For example, cost data in the absorption costing format may be helpful for long-run planning. However, the revenue and cost data needed to evaluate courses of future operations or to choose among competing alternatives are often not available in the basic accounting records.

The relevant revenue and cost data in the analysis of future possibilities are the differences between the alternatives under consideration. The amounts of such differences are called **differentials,** and the area of accounting concerned with the effect of alternative courses of action on revenues and costs is called **differential analysis.**

Differential revenue is the amount of increase or decrease in revenue expected from a particular course of action as compared with an alternative. To illustrate, assume that certain equipment is being used to manufacture Product M, which provides revenue of $150,000. If the equipment could be used to make Product T, which would provide revenue of $175,000, the differential revenue from making and selling Product T would be $25,000.

Differential cost is the amount of increase or decrease in cost that is expected from a particular course of action as compared with an alternative. For example, if an increase in advertising expenditures from $100,000 to $150,000 is being considered, the differential cost of the action would be $50,000.

The objective of differential analysis is to focus on the relevant revenues and costs related to alternative courses of action. Differential analysis reports thus emphasize the significant factors bearing on the decision, help to clarify the issues, and save the time of the user.

Differential analysis can aid management in making decisions on a variety of alternatives, including (1) whether equipment should be leased or sold, (2) whether to discontinue an unprofitable segment, (3) whether to manufacture or purchase a needed part, (4) whether to replace usable plant assets, (5) whether to process further or sell an intermediate product, and (6) whether to accept additional business at a special price. The following discussion relates to the use of differential analysis in analyzing these alternatives.

Lease or Sell

Management may have a choice between leasing or selling a piece of equipment that is no longer needed in the business. In deciding which option is best, management can use differential analysis. To illustrate, assume that Company A is considering the disposal of equipment that originally cost $200,000 and has been depreciated a total of $120,000 to date. Company A can sell the equipment through a broker for $100,000 less a 6% commission. Alternatively, Company B has tentatively offered to lease the equipment for a number of years for a total of $160,000, after which it would have no residual value. During the period of the lease, Company A would incur repair, insurance, and property tax expenses estimated at $35,000. Company A's analysis of whether to lease or sell the equipment is as follows:

Differential Analysis Report—Lease or Sell

Proposal To Lease or Sell Equipment
June 22, 19--

Differential revenue from alternatives:		
Revenue from lease	$160,000	
Revenue from sale	100,000	
Differential revenue from lease		$60,000
Differential cost of alternatives:		
Repair, insurance, and property tax expenses	$ 35,000	
Commission expense on sale	6,000	
Differential cost of lease		29,000
Net advantage of lease alternative		$31,000

Note that it was not necessary to consider the $80,000 book value ($200,000 − $120,000) of the equipment. The $80,000 is a **sunk cost**, that is, it is a cost that will not be affected by later decisions. In the illustration, the expenditure to acquire the equipment had already been made, and the choice is now between leasing or selling the equipment. The relevant factors to be considered are the differential revenues and differential costs associated with the lease or sell decision. The undepreciated cost of the equipment is irrelevant.

The validity of the foregoing report can be shown by the following conventional analysis:

Lease alternative:			
Revenue from lease		$160,000	
Depreciation expense	$80,000		
Repair, insurance, and property tax expenses	35,000	115,000	
Net gain			$45,000
Sell alternative:			
Sales price		$100,000	
Book value of equipment	$80,000		
Commission expense	6,000	86,000	
Net gain			14,000
Net advantage of lease alternative			$31,000

The alternatives presented in the illustration were relatively uncomplicated. Regardless of the number and complexity of the additional factors that may be involved, the approach to differential analysis remains basically the same. Two factors that often need to be considered are (1) the differential revenue from investing the funds generated by the alternatives and (2) the income tax differential. In the example, there would undoubtedly be a differential advantage to the immediate investment of the $94,000 net proceeds ($100,000 – $6,000) from the sale over the investment of the net proceeds from the lease arrangement, which would become available over a period of years. The income tax differential would be that related to the differences in timing of the income from the alternatives and the differences in the amount of investment income.

Discontinuance of a Segment or Product

When a product or a department, branch, territory, or other segment of an enterprise is generating losses, management should consider eliminating the product or segment. It might be natural to assume (sometimes mistakenly) that the total operating income of the enterprise would be increased if the operating loss could be eliminated. Discontinuance of the product or segment will usually eliminate all of the related variable costs (direct materials, direct labor, sales commissions, etc.). However, if the product or segment represents a relatively small part of the enterprise, the fixed costs (depreciation, insurance, property taxes, etc.) may not be reduced by its discontinuance. It is entirely possible in this situation for the total operating income of a company to be reduced rather than increased by eliminating the product or segment. As a basis for illustrating this type of situation, the income statement at the top of page 930 is presented for the year just ended, which was a normal year.

Because Product A incurs losses annually, management is considering its discontinuance. Discontinuing Product A is assumed to have no effect on fixed costs and expenses. The estimated differential revenue and differential cost related to discontinuing Product A may be assembled in a report such as that shown in the middle of page 930. This report emphasizes the significant factors bearing on the decision.

Instead of an increase in annual operating income to $80,000 (Product B, $40,000; Product C, $40,000) that might seem to be indicated by the income statement, the discontinuance of Product A would reduce operating income to an estimated $54,000 ($69,000 – $15,000). The validity of this conclusion can be shown by the conventional analysis at the bottom of page 930.

Income Statement—Current Operations

Condensed Income Statement
For Year Ended August 31, 19--

	Product A	Product B	Product C	Total
Sales	$100,000	$400,000	$500,000	$1,000,000
Cost of goods sold:				
Variable costs	$ 60,000	$200,000	$220,000	$ 480,000
Fixed costs	20,000	80,000	120,000	220,000
Total cost of goods sold	$ 80,000	$280,000	$340,000	$ 700,000
Gross profit	$ 20,000	$120,000	$160,000	$ 300,000
Operating expenses:				
Variable expenses	$ 25,000	$ 60,000	$ 95,000	$ 180,000
Fixed expenses	6,000	20,000	25,000	51,000
Total operating expenses	$ 31,000	$ 80,000	$120,000	$ 231,000
Income (loss) from operations	$ (11,000)	$ 40,000	$ 40,000	$ 69,000

Differential Analysis Report—Discontinuance of Unprofitable Segment

Proposal To Discontinue Product A
September 29, 19--

Differential revenue from annual sales of product:		
Revenue from sales		$100,000
Differential cost of annual sales of product:		
Variable cost of goods sold	$60,000	
Variable operating expenses	25,000	85,000
Annual differential income from sales of Product A		$ 15,000

Income Statement Comparing Current Operations with Product A Discontinued

Proposal To Discontinue Product A
September 29, 19--

	Current Operations: Product A	Current Operations: Products B and C	Current Operations: Total	Discontinuance of Product A
Sales	$100,000	$900,000	$1,000,000	$900,000
Cost of goods sold:				
Variable costs	$ 60,000	$420,000	$ 480,000	$420,000
Fixed costs	20,000	200,000	220,000	220,000
Total cost of goods sold	$ 80,000	$620,000	$ 700,000	$640,000
Gross profit	$ 20,000	$280,000	$ 300,000	$260,000
Operating expenses:				
Variable expenses	$ 25,000	$155,000	$ 180,000	$155,000
Fixed expenses	6,000	45,000	51,000	51,000
Total operating expenses	$ 31,000	$200,000	$ 231,000	$206,000
Income (loss) from operations	$ (11,000)	$ 80,000	$ 69,000	$ 54,000

In the illustration, only the short-term (one year) effects of discontinuing Product A were considered. In decisions involving the elimination of a product or segment, however, management must also consider the long-term effects. For example, the plant capacity made available by the discontinuance may be eliminated, which would reduce fixed costs, or it may be usable for another purpose. Some employees may have to be laid off and others may have to be relocated and retrained. Also, there may be a decline in sales of more profitable products to customers who were attracted to the firm by a discontinued product.

Make or Buy

The assembly of many parts is often a substantial element in manufacturing operations. Many of the large factory complexes of automobile manufacturers are specifically called assembly plants. Some of the parts of the finished automobile, such as the motor, are produced by the automobile manufacturer, while other parts, such as tires, are often purchased from other manufacturers. Also, in manufacturing the motors, such items as spark plugs and nuts and bolts may be acquired from suppliers in their finished state. When parts or components may be made or purchased, management should evaluate the question of "make or buy" based upon differential costs. For example, if a part is purchased, management has concluded that a savings in cost results from buying the part rather than manufacturing it. "Make or buy" options often arise when a manufacturer has excess productive capacity in the form of unused equipment, space, and labor.

The differential analysis would be similar, whether management is considering making a part that is currently being purchased or purchasing a part that is currently being made. As a basis for illustrating such alternatives, assume that a manufacturer has been purchasing a component, Part X, for $5 a unit. The factory is currently operating at 80% of capacity, and no significant increase in production is anticipated in the near future. The cost of manufacturing Part X, determined by absorption costing methods, is estimated at $1 for direct materials, $2 for direct labor, and $3 for factory overhead (at the predetermined rate of 150% of direct labor cost), or a total of $6. The decision based on a simple comparison of a "make" price of $6 with a "buy" price of $5 is obvious. However, to the extent that unused capacity could be used in manufacturing the part, there would be no increase in the total amount of fixed factory overhead costs. Hence, only the variable factory overhead costs need to be considered. Variable factory overhead costs such as power and maintenance are determined to amount to $1.30. The cost factors to be considered are summarized in the following report:

Differential Analysis Report—Make or Buy

Proposal To Manufacture Part X
February 15, 19--

Purchase price of part		$5.00
Differential cost to manufacture part:		
Direct materials	$1.00	
Direct labor	2.00	
Variable factory overhead	1.30	4.30
Cost reduction from manufacturing Part X		$ .70

Other possible effects of a change in policy should also be considered, such as the possibility that a future increase in volume of production would require the use of the currently idle capacity of 20%. The possible effect of the alternatives on employees and on future business relations with the supplier of the part, who may be providing other essential components, are additional factors that might need study.

Equipment Replacement

The usefulness of plant assets may be impaired long before they are considered to be "worn out." Equipment may no longer be ideally adequate for the purpose for which it is used, but on the other hand it may not have reached the point of complete inadequacy. Similarly, the point in time when equipment becomes obsolete may be difficult to determine. Decisions to replace usable plant assets should be based on studies of relevant costs. The costs to be considered are the alternative future costs of retention as opposed to replacement. The book values of the plant assets being replaced are sunk costs and are irrelevant.

To illustrate some of the factors involved in replacement decisions, assume that an enterprise is considering the disposal of several identical machines having a total book value of $100,000 and an estimated remaining life of five years. The old machines can be sold for $25,000. They can be replaced by a single high-speed machine at a cost of $250,000, with an estimated useful life of five years and no residual value. Analysis of the specifications of the new machine and of accompanying changes in manufacturing methods indicate an estimated annual reduction in variable manufacturing costs from $225,000 to $150,000. No other changes in the manufacturing costs or the operating expenses are expected. The basic data to be considered are summarized in the following report:

Differential Analysis Report—Equipment Replacement

Proposal To Replace Equipment
November 28, 19--

Annual variable costs—present equipment	$225,000	
Annual variable costs—new equipment	150,000	
Annual differential decrease in cost	$ 75,000	
Number of years applicable	× 5	
Total differential decrease in cost	$375,000	
Proceeds from sale of present equipment	25,000	$400,000
Cost of new equipment		250,000
Net differential decrease in cost, 5-year total		$150,000
Annual net differential decrease in cost—new equipment		$ 30,000

Complicating features could be added to the foregoing illustration, such as a disparity between the remaining useful life of the old equipment and the estimated life of the new equipment, or possible improvement in the product due to the new machine, with a resulting increase in selling price or volume of sales. Other factors that should be considered are the time value of money and the alternative uses for the cash outlay needed to obtain the new equipment.[1]

[1] The importance of the time value of money in equipment replacement decisions is described and illustrated in Chapter 23.

The amount of income that would result from the best available alternative to the proposed use of cash or its equivalent is sometimes called **opportunity cost.** If, for example, it is assumed that the cash outlay of $250,000 for the new equipment, less the $25,000 proceeds from the sale of the present equipment, could be used to yield a 10% return, the opportunity cost of the proposal would amount to 10% of $225,000, or $22,500.

The term "opportunity cost" introduces a new concept of "cost." In reality, it is not a cost in any usual sense of the word. Instead, it represents the forgoing of possible income associated with a lost opportunity. Although opportunity cost computations do not appear as a part of historical accounting data, they are unquestionably useful in analyses involving choices between alternative courses of action.

Process or Sell

When a product is manufactured, it progresses through various stages of production. Often a product can be sold at an intermediate stage of production, or it can be processed further and then sold. In deciding whether to sell a product at an intermediate stage or to process it further, the differential revenues that would be provided and the differential costs that would be incurred from further processing must be considered. Since the costs of producing the intermediate product do not change, regardless of whether the intermediate product is sold or processed further, these costs are not differential costs and are not considered.

To illustrate, assume that an enterprise produces Product Y in batches of 4,000 gallons by processing standard quantities of 4,000 gallons of direct materials, which cost $1.20 per gallon. Product Y can be sold without further processing for $2 per gallon. It is possible for the enterprise to process Product Y further to yield Product Z, which can be sold for $5 per gallon. Product Z will require additional processing costs of $5,760 per batch, and 20% of the gallons of Product Y will evaporate during production. The differential revenues and costs to be considered in deciding whether to process Product Y to produce Product Z are summarized in the following report:

Differential Analysis Report—Process or Sell

Proposal To Process Product Y Further
October 1, 19--

Differential revenue from further processing per batch:		
Revenue from sale of Product Z [(4,000 gallons − 800 gallons evaporation) × $5]	$16,000	
Revenue from sale of Product Y (4,000 gallons × $2)	8,000	
Differential revenue		$8,000
Differential cost per batch:		
Additional cost of producing Product Z		5,760
Net advantage of further processing Product Y per batch		$2,240

The net advantage of further processing Product Y into Product Z is $2,240 per batch. Note that the initial cost of producing the intermediate Product Y, $4,800 (4,000 gallons × $1.20), is not considered in deciding whether to process Product Y further. This initial cost will be incurred regardless of whether Product Z is produced.

Acceptance of Business at a Special Price

In determining whether to accept additional business at a special price, management must consider the differential revenue that would be provided and the differential cost that would be incurred. If the company is operating at full capacity, the additional production will increase both fixed and variable production costs. But if the normal production of the company is below full capacity, additional business may be undertaken without increasing fixed production costs. In the latter case, variable manufacturing costs will be the differential cost of the additional production. Thus, variable manufacturing costs are the only manufacturing costs to be considered in making a decision to accept or reject the order. However, if the operating expenses are likely to increase, these differentials must also be considered.

To illustrate, assume that the usual monthly production of an enterprise is 10,000 units of a certain commodity. At this level of operation, which is well below capacity, the manufacturing cost is $20 per unit, composed of variable costs of $12.50 and fixed costs of $7.50. The normal selling price of the product in the domestic market is $30. The manufacturer receives an offer from an exporter for 5,000 units of the product at $18 each. Production can be spread over a three-month period without interfering with normal production or incurring overtime costs. Pricing policies in the domestic market will not be affected. Comparison of a sales price of $18 with the present unit cost of $20 would indicate that this offer should be rejected. However, if attention is limited to the differential cost, which in this case is composed of the variable costs, the conclusion is quite different. The essentials of the analysis are presented in the following brief report:

Differential Analysis Report—Sale at Special Price

Proposal To Sell to Exporter March 10, 19--	
Differential revenue from acceptance of offer:	
Revenue from sale of 5,000 additional units at $18	$90,000
Differential cost of acceptance of offer:	
Variable costs of 5,000 additional units at $12.50	62,500
Gain from acceptance of offer	$27,500

Proposals to sell an increased output in the domestic market at a reduction from the normal price may require additional considerations of a difficult nature. It would clearly be unwise to increase sales volume in one territory by means of a price reduction if sales volume would thereby be jeopardized in other areas. Manufacturers must also exercise care to avoid violations of the Robinson-Patman Act, which prohibits price discrimination within the United States unless the difference in price can be justified by a difference in the cost of serving different customers.

SETTING NORMAL PRODUCT SELLING PRICES

OBJECTIVE 2
Describe and illustrate the setting of normal product selling prices, using the total cost, product cost, and variable cost concepts.

Differential analysis, as illustrated, is useful to management in setting product selling prices for special short-run decisions, such as whether to accept business at a price lower than the normal price. In such situations, the minimum short-run price is set high enough to cover all variable costs. Any price above this minimum price will improve profits in the short run. In the long run, however, the normal selling price must be set high enough to cover all costs and expenses (both fixed and variable) and provide a reasonable amount for profit. Otherwise, the long-run survival of the firm may be jeopardized.

The normal selling price can be viewed as the target selling price which must be achieved in the long run, but which may be deviated from in the short run because of such factors as competition and general market conditions. A practical approach to setting the normal price is the cost-plus approach. Using this approach, managers determine product prices by adding to a "cost" amount a plus, called a **markup**, so that all costs plus a profit are covered in the price.

Three cost concepts commonly used in applying the cost-plus approach are (1) total cost, (2) product cost, and (3) variable cost. Each of these cost concepts is described and illustrated in the following paragraphs.

Total Cost Concept

Using the **total cost concept** of determining the product price, all costs of manufacturing a product plus the selling and administrative expenses are included in the cost amount to which the markup is added. Since all costs and expenses are included in the cost amount, the dollar amount of the markup equals the desired profit.

The first step in applying the total cost concept is to determine the total cost of manufacturing the product. Under the absorption costing system of accounting for manufacturing operations, the costs of direct materials, direct labor, and factory overhead should be available from the accounting records. The next step is to add the estimated selling and administrative expenses to the total cost of manufacturing the product. The cost amount per unit is then computed by dividing the total costs by the total units expected to be produced and sold.

After the cost amount per unit has been determined, the dollar amount of the markup is determined. For this purpose, the markup is expressed as a percentage of cost. This percentage is then multiplied by the cost amount per unit. The dollar amount of the markup is then added to the cost amount per unit to arrive at the selling price.

The markup percentage for the total cost concept is determined by applying the following formula:

$$\text{Markup Percentage} = \frac{\text{Desired Profit}}{\text{Total Costs}}$$

The numerator of the markup percentage formula includes only the desired profit, since all costs and expenses will be covered by the cost amount to which the markup will be added. The denominator of the formula includes the total costs, which are covered by the cost amount.

To illustrate the use of the total cost concept, assume that the costs for Product R of Pellit Co. are as follows:

Variable costs:	
Direct materials	\$ 3.00 per unit
Direct labor	10.00
Factory overhead	1.50
Selling and administrative expenses	1.50
Total	\$16.00 per unit

Fixed costs:	
Factory overhead	$50,000
Selling and administrative expenses	20,000

Pellit Co. desires a profit equal to a 20% rate of return on assets, $800,000 of assets are devoted to producing Product R, and 100,000 units are expected to be produced and sold. The cost amount for Product R is $1,670,000, or $16.70 per unit, computed as follows:

Variable costs ($16.00 × 100,000 units)		$1,600,000
Fixed costs:		
Factory overhead	$50,000	
Selling and administrative expenses	20,000	70,000
Total costs		$1,670,000
Cost amount per unit ($1,670,000 ÷ 100,000 units)		$16.70

The desired profit is $160,000 (20% × $800,000), and the markup percentage for Product R is 9.6% computed as follows:

$$\text{Markup Percentage} = \frac{\text{Desired Profit}}{\text{Total Costs}}$$

$$\text{Markup Percentage} = \frac{\$160{,}000}{\$1{,}670{,}000}$$

$$\text{Markup Percentage} = 9.6\%$$

Based on the cost amount per unit and the markup percentage for Product R, Pellit Co. would price Product R at per unit, as shown in the following computation:

Cost amount per unit	$16.70
Markup ($16.70 × 9.6%)	1.60
Selling price	$18.30

The ability of the selling price of $18.30 to generate the desired profit of $160,000 is shown in the following condensed income statement for Pellit Co.:

Pellit Co.
Income Statement
For Year Ended December 31, 19--

Sales (100,000 units × $18.30)		$1,830,000
Expenses:		
Variable (100,000 units × $16.00)	$1,600,000	
Fixed ($50,000 + $20,000)	70,000	1,670,000
Income from operations		$160,000

The total cost concept of applying the cost-plus approach to product pricing is sometimes used by contractors who sell products to government agencies. In many cases, governement contractors are required by law to be reimbursed for their products on a total-cost-plus-profit basis.

Product Cost Concept

Using the **product cost concept** of determining the product price, only the costs of manufacturing the product, termed the product cost, are included in the cost amount to which the markup is added. Estimated selling expenses, administrative expenses, and profit are covered in the markup. The markup percentage is determined by applying the following formula:

$$\text{Markup Percentage} = \frac{\text{Desired Profit} + \text{Total Selling and Administrative Expenses}}{\text{Total Manufacturing Costs}}$$

The numerator of the markup percentage formula includes the desired profit plus the total selling and administrative expenses. Selling and administrative expenses must be covered by the markup, since they are not covered by the cost amount to which the markup will be added. The denominator of the formula includes the costs of direct materials, direct labor, and factory overhead, which are covered by the cost amount.

To illustrate the use of the product cost concept, assume the same data that were used in the preceding illustration. The cost amount for Pellit Co.'s Product R is $1,500,000 or $15 per unit, computed as follows:

Direct materials ($3 × 100,000 units)		$ 300,000
Direct labor ($10 × 100,000 units)		1,000,000
Factory overhead:		
Variable ($1.50 × 100,000 units)	$150,000	
Fixed	50,000	200,000
Total manufacturing costs		$1,500,000
Cost amount per unit ($1,500,000 ÷ 100,000 units)		$15

The desired profit is $160,000 (20% × $800,000), and the total selling and administrative expenses are $170,000 [(100,000 units × $1.50 per unit) + $20,000]. The markup percentage for Product R is 22%, computed as follows:

$$\text{Markup Percentage} = \frac{\text{Desired Profit} + \text{Total Selling and Administrative Expenses}}{\text{Total Manufacturing Costs}}$$

$$\text{Markup Percentage} = \frac{\$160{,}000 + \$170{,}000}{\$1{,}500{,}000}$$

$$\text{Markup Percentage} = \frac{\$330{,}000}{\$1{,}500{,}000}$$

$$\text{Markup Percentage} = 22\%$$

Based on the cost amount per unit and the markup percentage for Product R, Pellit Co. would price Product R at $18.30 per unit, as shown in the following computation:

Cost amount per unit	$15.00
Markup ($15 × 22%)	3.30
Selling price	$18.30

Variable Cost Concept

Using the **variable cost concept** of determining the product price, only variable costs are included in the cost amount to which the markup is added.

All variable manufacturing costs, as well as variable selling and administrative expenses, are included in the cost amount. Fixed manufacturing costs, fixed selling and administrative expenses, and profit are covered in the markup.

The markup percentage for the variable cost concept is determined by applying the following formula:

$$\text{Markup Percentage} = \frac{\text{Desired Profit} + \text{Total Fixed Costs}}{\text{Total Variable Costs}}$$

The numerator of the markup percentage formula includes the desired profit plus the total fixed manufacturing costs and the total fixed selling and administrative expenses. Fixed manufacturing costs and fixed selling and administrative expenses must be covered by the markup, since they are not covered by the cost amount to which the markup will be added. The denominator of the formula includes the total variable costs, which are covered by the cost amount.

To illustrate the use of the variable cost concept, assume the same data that were used in the two preceding illustrations. The cost amount for Product R is $1,600,000 or $16.00 per unit, computed as follows:

Variable costs:	
Direct materials ($3 × 100,000 units)	$ 300,000
Direct labor ($10 × 100,000 units)	1,000,000
Factory overhead ($1.50 × 100,000 units)	150,000
Selling and administrative expenses ($1.50 × 100,000 units)	150,000
Total variable costs	$1,600,000
Cost amount per unit ($1,600,000 ÷ 100,000 units)	$ 16.00

The desired profit is $160,000 (20% × $800,000), the total fixed manufacturing costs are $50,000, and the total fixed selling and administrative expenses are $20,000. The markup percentage for Product R is 14.4%, computed as follows:

$$\text{Markup Percentage} = \frac{\text{Desired Profit} + \text{Total Fixed Costs}}{\text{Total Variable Costs}}$$

$$\text{Markup Percentage} = \frac{\$160,000 + \$50,000 + \$20,000}{\$1,600,000}$$

$$\text{Markup Percentage} = \frac{\$230,000}{\$1,600,000}$$

$$\text{Markup Percentage} = 14.4\%$$

Based on the cost amount per unit and the markup percentage for Product R, Pellit Co. would price Product R at $18.30 per unit, as shown in the following computation:

Cost amount per unit	$16.00
Markup ($16.00 × 14.4%)	2.30
Selling price	$18.30

The variable cost concept emphasizes the distinction between variable and fixed costs in product pricing. This distinction is similar to the distinction between absorption and variable costing described in Chapter 21.

Choosing a Cost-Plus Approach Cost Concept

The three cost concepts commonly used in applying the cost-plus approach to product pricing are summarized as follows:

Cost Concept	Covered in Cost Amount	Covered in Markup
Total cost	Total costs	Desired profit
Product cost	Total manufacturing costs	Desired profit + Total selling and administrative expenses
Variable cost	Total variable costs	Desired profit + Total fixed costs

For the Pellit Co. illustration, all three cost concepts produced the same selling price ($18.30). In practice, however, the three cost concepts are usually not viewed as alternatives. For some business enterprises one concept is less costly to use than another. In other cases, the decision-making needs of management may require the use of a particular cost concept.

Each cost concept requires different estimates of costs and expenses. Therefore, the cost of gathering data is different for each cost concept. For example, the total cost concept requires the estimation of total costs, but does not require the separate estimation of the selling and administrative expenses and manufacturing costs. Likewise, the variable cost concept requires the estimation of variable and fixed costs, while the total cost and product cost concepts do not. In addition, it is more difficult and more costly for business enterprises with multiple products to trace costs to specific products. Thus, some business enterprises use a cost concept solely on the basis of the cost of gathering the necessary data.

To reduce the costs of gathering data, estimated (standard) costs rather than actual costs may be used with any of the three cost concepts. However, caution should be exercised by management when using estimated costs in applying the cost-plus approach. The estimates should be based on normal (attainable) operating levels and not theoretical (ideal) levels of performance. In product pricing, the use of estimates based on ideal or maximum capacity operating levels might lead to the establishment of product prices which are too low, since the costs of such factors as normal spoilage or normal periods of idle time would not be covered in the price.

The decision-making needs of management is also an important factor in selecting a cost concept for product pricing. For example, managers who frequently make special pricing decisions would likely use the variable cost concept. In contrast, a government defense contractor would likely use the total cost concept.

A variation of the cost concepts discussed in the preceding paragraphs is the **target cost concept**. Under this concept, a product unit cost that will allow the company to compete effectively in the market and earn a normal profit is estimated. The product is then designed, manufactured, and sold to achieve this target cost. In effect, the target cost concept uses external market conditions as a basis for determining the acceptable level of costs, expenses, and prices. In contrast, the three cost concepts discussed in the preceding paragraphs rely primarily upon internal cost data to determine selling prices.[2]

[2]The use of the target cost concept is further discussed in *Cost Management for Today's Advanced Manufacturing*, edited by Callie Berliner and James A. Brimson (Boston: Harvard Business School Press, 1988).

ECONOMIC THEORY OF PRODUCT PRICING

OBJECTIVE 3
Describe the economic theory of product pricing.

In addition to costs, as discussed in the preceding paragraphs, other factors may influence the pricing decision. In considering these factors, which include the general economic conditions of the marketplace, a knowledge of the economic theory underlying product pricing is useful to the managerial accountant. Although the study of **price theory** is generally considered a separate discipline in the area of microeconomics, the following paragraphs present an overview of the economic concepts for explaining pricing behavior.

Maximization of Profits

In microeconomic theory, management's primary objective is assumed to be the maximization of profits. Profits will be maximized at the point at which the difference between total revenues and total costs is the greatest amount. Consequently, microeconomic theory focuses on the behavior of total revenues as price and sales volume vary and the behavior of total costs as production varies.

Revenues

Generally, it is not possible to sell an unlimited number of units of product at the same price. At some point, price reductions will be necessary in order to sell more units. Total revenue may increase as the price is reduced, but there comes a point when further price decreases will reduce total revenue. To illustrate, the following revenue schedule shows the effect on revenue when each $1 reduction in the unit selling price increases the number of units sold:

Revenue Schedule

Price	*Units Sold*	*Total Revenue*	*Marginal Revenue*
$11	1	$11	$11
10	2	20	9
9	3	27	7
8	4	32	5
7	5	35	3
6	6	36	1
5	7	35	−1

In the revenue schedule illustrated, a price reduction from $11 to $10 increases total revenue by $9 (from $11 to $20). This increase (or decrease) in total revenue realized from the sale of an additional unit of product is called the **marginal revenue.** With each successive price reduction from $11 to $6, the total revenue increase is less. Finally, a price reduction from $6 to $5 decreases total revenue by $1.

Costs

As production and sales increase, the total cost increases. The amount by which total cost increases, however, varies as more and more production and sales are squeezed from limited facilities. Economists assume that as the total number of units produced and sold increases from a relatively low level, the total cost increases but in decreasing amounts. This assumption is based on efficiencies created by **economies of scale.** Economies of scale generally imply that, for a given amount of facilities, it is more efficient to produce and sell large quantities than small quantities. At some point, however, the total cost will begin to increase by increasing amounts because of inefficiencies created by such factors as employees getting in each other's way and machine breakdowns caused by heavy use. The increase in total cost from producing and selling an additional unit of product is known as **marginal cost.** To illustrate, the following cost schedule shows the effect on cost when one additional unit is produced and sold:

Cost Schedule

Units Produced and Sold	*Total Cost*	*Marginal Cost*
1	$ 9	$9
2	17	8
3	24	7
4	30	6
5	37	7
6	45	8
7	54	9

In the cost schedule, the cost of producing 1 unit is $9, and for each additional unit the total cost per unit increases by $8, $7, $6, $7, $8, and $9 respectively. The marginal cost of producing and selling the second unit is $8, which is the difference between the total cost of producing and selling 2 units ($17) and the total cost of 1 unit ($9). As production and sales increase from 1 unit to 4 units, the marginal cost decreases from $9 to $6. After the production and sale of 4 units, however, the marginal cost increases from $6 for the fourth unit to $9 for producing and selling the seventh unit.

Product Price Determination

A price-cost combination that maximizes the total profit of an enterprise will occur when marginal revenues and marginal costs are equal. In the illustration, the marginal revenue equals the marginal cost for 3 units of sales and production, as shown in the following table:

Price	Units Produced and Sold	Total Revenue	Marginal Revenue	Total Cost	Marginal Cost
$11	1	$11	$11	$ 9	$9
10	2	20	9	17	8
9	3	27	7	24	7
8	4	32	5	30	6
7	5	35	3	37	7
6	6	36	1	45	8
5	7	35	−1	54	9

For the third unit of sales and production, marginal revenue and marginal cost equal $7. To sell 3 units, the revenue schedule on page 940 indicates that the price should be set at $9 per unit, which will provide total revenue of $27.

The cost schedule on page 941 indicates that the total cost of the 3 units will be $24. Thus, profit will be $3, as follows:

Total revenue (3 units × $9)	$27
Total cost (from cost schedule)	24
Profit	$ 3

The more theoretical economic approach is not often used for product pricing because the data required by this approach are often unavailable. For example, it is difficult to predict the amount that customers will purchase over a range of prices without actually offering the product for sale at those prices. Therefore, since total cost data can be estimated reliably from accounting records, the cost-plus approach to product pricing is frequently used.

Pricing Strategies

Within the constraints of market conditions, managers must decide upon a pricing strategy for a company's various products. The pricing strategy chosen for a product depends upon the factors previously discussed. In addition, the stage in the product's life cycle at which the product is offered for sale has an important effect. The **product life cycle** concept is based on the idea that a

THE ART OF PRICING AIR FARES

One industry in which pricing plays a very significant role is the airline industry. Fare wars and constantly changing fares are commonplace among the major airlines. The fine tuning involved in pricing fares is described in the following excerpt from an article in *The Wall Street Journal*:

The latest round of fare wars . . . has put a spotlight on how carriers use state-of-the-art computer software, complex forecasting techniques and a little intuition to [determine] how many seats at what prices they will offer on any given flight. . . .

Too many wrong projections can lead to huge losses of revenue, or even worse. The inability of People Express to manage its inventory of seats properly, for example, was one of the major causes of its demise.

"It's a sophisticated guessing game," said [the] vice president of pricing and product planning at American Airlines. . . . "You don't want to sell a seat to a guy for $69 when he's willing to pay $400."

With the industry now adopting very low discount but nonrefundable fares, the complex task of managing seat inventory may become easier because airlines will be better able to predict how many people will show up for a flight.

Some airlines have already seen a drop in their no-shows, which means they can overbook less and spare more customers from being bumped. The nonrefundable fares could also enable carriers to sell more discount seats weeks before a flight, rather than putting them on sale at the last minute in an effort to fill up the plane.

American's [pricing] operation illustrates just how complicated the process can be. At the airline's corporate headquarters [in Dallas], 90 yield managers are linked by terminals to five International Business Machines mainframe computers in Tulsa, Okla. The managers monitor and adjust the fare mixes on 1,600 daily flights as well as 528,000 future flights involving nearly 50 million passengers. Their work is hectic: A fare's average life span is two weeks, and industrywide about 200,000 fares change daily.

American and the other airlines base their forecasts largely on historical profiles of each flight. Business travelers, for example, book heavily on many Friday afternoon flights, but often not until the day of departure. The airlines reserve blocks of seats for those frequent fliers. Few, if any, discounts are made available. . . .

For the bargain hunter, finding a discount will increasingly depend on the season, day and time of travel, destination and length of stay. . . .

The table at the top of page 943 indicates the difference between the number of seats sold at each fare for a Wednesday and Friday flight of American Airlines.

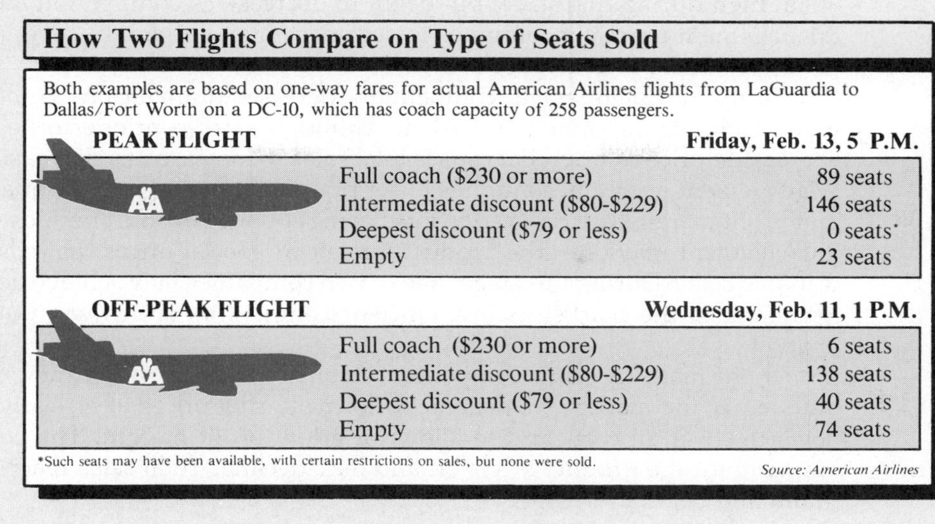

How Two Flights Compare on Type of Seats Sold

Both examples are based on one-way fares for actual American Airlines flights from LaGuardia to Dallas/Fort Worth on a DC-10, which has coach capacity of 258 passengers.

PEAK FLIGHT	Friday, Feb. 13, 5 P.M.
Full coach ($230 or more)	89 seats
Intermediate discount ($80-$229)	146 seats
Deepest discount ($79 or less)	0 seats*
Empty	23 seats

OFF-PEAK FLIGHT	Wednesday, Feb. 11, 1 P.M.
Full coach ($230 or more)	6 seats
Intermediate discount ($80-$229)	138 seats
Deepest discount ($79 or less)	40 seats
Empty	74 seats

*Such seats may have been available, with certain restrictions on sales, but none were sold.

Source: American Airlines

Source: Eric Schmitt, "The Art of Pricing Air Fares," *The Wall Street Journal*, March 4, 1987.

product normally passes through various stages from the time that it is introduced until the time that it disappears from the market.

The normal life cycle for a product is divided into five stages: the introductory stage, the rapid growth stage, the turbulent stage, the maturity stage, and the terminating stage. Graphically, the relationship of these stages to total dollar sales during a product's life cycle can be illustrated as follows:

Product Life Cycle

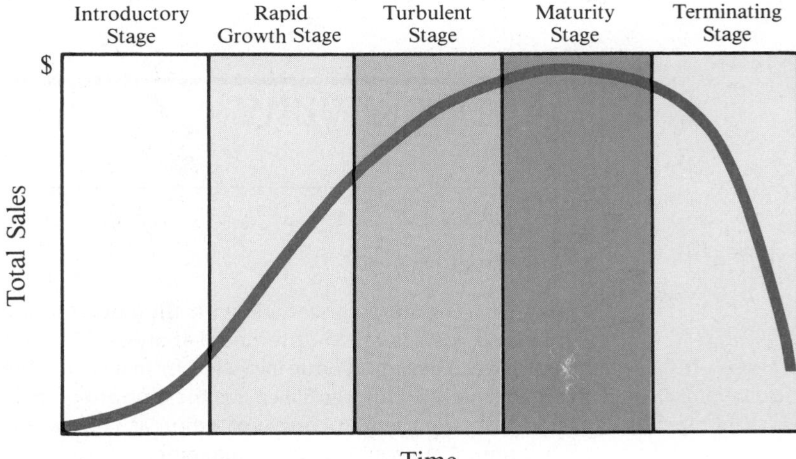

In the introductory stage, the product is new to the market and no direct competition exists. During this stage, management normally spends large amounts on promotional activities in order to develop a market for the product. Since no competition exists, prices are normally set to provide coverage of all costs and to provide high profit margins. Total sales begin low and expand rapidly as more consumers discover the product.

In the rapid growth stage, the product has caught on with consumers and competitors begin to enter the market. Total sales expand rapidly, since the industry cannot meet consumer demand for the product. Prices normally remain high during this stage, but begin to decrease as competition increases. Management normally continues to set prices high enough to cover all costs and provide for a reasonable profit.

In the turbulent stage, competition increases dramatically as more and more competitors enter the market. Although sales continue to be strong, increasing price competition causes total sales to increase at a decreasing rate. Management normally continues to set prices high enough to cover all costs, but profit margins are reduced to meet competition. For short periods of time, management may offer the product for sale at special prices that cover only variable costs. During this stage, one or two companies may achieve dominant positions in the market as less efficient competitors are driven out of the market.

In the maturity stage, competition stabilizes and few, if any, new competitors enter the market. Management normally sets prices at a relatively low level to cover all costs and to allow for a low profit margin. The consumer demand for the product levels off and may decline. Total sales reach a maximum and begin to decline.

In the terminating stage, the strategy of management is to reduce the chance of any losses and to get as much profit out of the remaining product demand as possible. Near the end of this stage, prices are often set to cover only product variable costs in order to reduce the chance that the company will be left with excess inventories after consumer demand has disappeared.

One example of the product life cycle concept is the market for the IBM personal computer during the 1980's. During this period, the price of a standard IBM personal computer decreased from approximately $3,500 in 1980, when it was first introduced, to less than $1,000 in 1990. IBM attempted to prolong the computer's relatively brief life cycle by introducing new enhancements, such as hard disk drives, additional memory, and color monitors.

CHAPTER REVIEW

KEY POINTS

OBJECTIVE 1

Differential Analysis

The area of accounting concerned with the effect of alternative courses of action on revenues and costs is called differential analysis. Differential revenue is the amount of increase or decrease in revenue expected from a particular course of action as compared with an alternative. Differential cost is the amount of increase or decrease in cost that is expected from a particular course of action as compared with an alternative.

Differential analysis can aid management in making decisions on a variety of alternatives, including (1) whether equipment should be leased or sold, (2) whether to discontinue an unprofitable segment, (3) whether to manufacture or purchase a needed part, (4) whether to replace plant assets, (5) whether to process further or sell an intermediate product, and (6) whether to accept additional business at a special price.

OBJECTIVE 2

Setting Normal Product Selling Prices

The normal selling price can be viewed as the target selling price, which must be achieved in the long run but may be deviated from in the short run because of such factors as competition and general market conditions. A practical approach to setting the normal price is the cost-plus approach. Using this approach, managers determine product prices by adding to a "cost" amount a markup, so that all costs plus a profit are covered in the price.

The three cost concepts commonly used in applying the cost-plus approach to product pricing are summarized as follows:

Cost Concept	Covered in Cost Amount	Covered in Markup
Total cost	Total costs	Desired profit
Product cost	Total manufacturing costs	Desired profit + Total selling and administrative expenses
Variable cost	Total variable costs	Desired profit + Total fixed costs

The markup percentage for each cost concept is determined by dividing the amount covered in the markup by the amount covered in the cost.

OBJECTIVE 3

Economic Theory of Product Pricing

The theory underlying product pricing is a separate economic discipline known as price theory. In this theory, management's primary objective is assumed to be the maximization of profits. The increase (decrease) in total revenue realized from the sale of an additional unit of product is called marginal revenue. The increase in total cost from producing and selling an additional unit of product is called marginal cost. The point where marginal revenue and marginal cost are equal is the level of sales and production at which profits are maximized.

The stage in its life cycle at which a product is offered for sale has an important effect on management's choice of a pricing strategy. During the introductory stage, product prices are set to cover all costs and to provide for high profit margins. During the rapid growth stage, product prices remain high, but begin to decrease as new competitors enter the market. During the turbulent stage, profit margins are reduced as prices fall and special prices covering only variable costs may be established for short periods. During the maturity stage, prices remain at low levels as total sales reach a maximum and begin to fall. During the terminating stage, prices may be lowered to cover only variable costs in order to reduce losses and excess inventories.

KEY TERMS

differential analysis 927
differential revenue 927
differential cost 928
sunk cost 928
opportunity cost 933
markup 935
total cost concept 935
product cost concept 937
variable cost concept 937
price theory 940
marginal revenue 940
economies of scale 941
marginal cost 941
product life cycle 942

SELF-EXAMINATION QUESTIONS

Answers at end of chapter.

1. The amount of increase or decrease in cost that is expected from a particular course of action as compared with an alternative is referred to as:
   A. differential cost
   B. replacement cost
   C. sunk cost
   D. none of the above

2. Victor Company is considering the disposal of equipment that was originally purchased for $200,000 and has accumulated depreciation to date of $150,000. The same equipment would cost $310,000 to replace. What is the sunk cost?
   A. $50,000 C. $200,000
   B. $150,000 D. None of the above

3. The amount of income that would result from the best available alternative to a proposed use of cash or its equivalent is referred to as:
   A. actual cost C. opportunity cost
   B. historical cost D. none of the above

4. For which cost concept used in applying the cost-plus approach to product pricing are fixed manufacturing costs, fixed selling and administrative expenses, and desired profit allowed for in the determination of markup?
   A. Total cost C. Variable cost
   B. Product cost D. None of the above

5. According to microeconomic theory, profits of a business enterprise will be maximized at the point where:
   A. marginal revenue equals marginal cost
   B. the change in total revenue is greater than the change in total cost
   C. the change in total cost is greater than the change in total revenue
   D. none of the above

ILLUSTRATIVE PROBLEM

Berry Company recently began production of a new product, M, which required the investment of $2,000,000 in assets. The costs of producing and selling 100,000 units of Product M are estimated as follows:

Variable costs:	
Direct materials	$ 2.40 per unit
Direct labor	6.50
Factory overhead	.90
Selling and administrative expenses	.20
Total	$10.00 per unit
Fixed costs:	
Factory overhead	$ 60,000
Selling and administrative expenses	140,000

Berry Company is currently considering the establishment of a selling price for Product M. The president of Berry Company has decided to use the cost-plus approach to product pricing and has indicated that Product M must earn an 18% rate of return on invested assets.

Instructions:

1. Determine the amount of desired profit from the production and sale of Product M.
2. Assuming that the total cost concept is used, determine (a) the cost amount per unit, (b) the markup percentage, and (c) the selling price of Product M.
3. Assuming that the product cost concept is used, determine (a) the cost amount per unit, (b) the markup percentage, and (c) the selling price of Product M.
4. Assuming that the variable cost concept is used, determine (a) the cost amount per unit, (b) the markup percentage, and (c) the selling price of Product M.
5. Assume that for the current year, the selling price of Product M was $15.60 per unit. To date, 80,000 units have been produced and sold and analysis of the domestic market indicates that 15,000 additional units are expected to be sold during the

remainder of the year. Recently, Berry Company received an offer from Wong Inc. for 4,000 units of Product M at $11.50 each. Wong Inc. will market the units in Korea under its own brand name and no additional selling and administrative expenses associated with the sale will be incurred by Berry Company. The additional business is not expected to affect the domestic sales of Product M and the additional units could be produced during the current year, using existing capacity. (a) Prepare a differential analysis report of the proposed sale to Wong Inc. (b) Based upon the differential analysis report in (a), should the proposal be accepted?

SOLUTION

(1) $360,000 ($2,000,000 × 18%)

(2) (a) Total costs:

Variable ($10 × 100,000 units)	$1,000,000
Fixed ($60,000 + $140,000)	200,000
Total	$1,200,000

Cost amount per unit: $1,200,000 ÷ 100,000 units = $12

(b) $$\text{Markup Percentage} = \frac{\text{Desired Profit}}{\text{Total Costs}}$$

$$\text{Markup Percentage} = \frac{\$360,000}{\$1,200,000}$$

Markup Percentage = 30%

(c)

Cost amount per unit	$12.00
Markup ($12 × 30%)	3.60
Selling price	$15.60

(3) (a) Total manufacturing costs:

Variable ($9.80 × 100,000 units)	$ 980,000
Fixed factory overhead	60,000
Total	$1,040,000

Cost amount per unit: $1,040,000 ÷ 100,000 units = $10.40

(b) $$\text{Markup Percentage} = \frac{\text{Desired Profit} + \text{Total Selling and Administrative Expenses}}{\text{Total Manufacturing Costs}}$$

$$\text{Markup Percentage} = \frac{\$360,000 + \$140,000 + (\$.20 \times 100,000 \text{ units})}{\$1,040,000}$$

$$\text{Markup Percentage} = \frac{\$360,000 + \$140,000 + \$20,000}{\$1,040,000}$$

$$\text{Markup Percentage} = \frac{\$520,000}{\$1,040,000}$$

Markup Percentage = 50%

(c)

Cost amount per unit	$10.40
Markup ($10.40 × 50%)	5.20
Selling price	$15.60

(4) (a) Variable cost amount per unit: $10
Total variable costs: $10 × 100,000 units = $1,000,000

(b) $$\text{Markup Percentage} = \frac{\text{Desired Profit} + \text{Total Fixed Costs}}{\text{Total Variable Costs}}$$

$$\text{Markup Percentage} = \frac{\$360{,}000 + \$60{,}000 + \$140{,}00}{\$1{,}000{,}000}$$

$$\text{Markup Percentage} = \frac{\$560{,}000}{\$1{,}000{,}000}$$

$$\text{Markup Percentage} = 56\%$$

(c)	
Cost amount per unit	$10.00
Markup ($10 × 56%)	5.60
Selling price	$15.60

(5) (a) Proposal To Sell to Wong Inc.

Differential revenue from acceptance of offer:	
Revenue from sale of 4,000 additional units at $11.50	$46,000
Differential cost of acceptance of offer:	
Variable costs of 4,000 additional units at $9.80	39,200
Gain from acceptance of offer	$ 6,800

(b) The proposal should be accepted.

DISCUSSION QUESTIONS

22–1. What term is applied to the type of analysis that emphasizes the difference between the revenues and costs for proposed alternative courses of action?

22–2. Explain the meaning of (a) *differential revenue* and (b) *differential cost.*

22–3. Edmunds Lumber Company incurs a cost of $90 per thousand board feet in processing a certain "rough-cut" lumber, which it sells for $130 per thousand board feet. An alternative is to produce a "finished-cut" at a total processing cost of $115 per thousand board feet, which can be sold for $180 per thousand board feet. What is the amount of (a) the differential revenue and (b) the differential cost associated with the alternative?

22–4. (a) What is meant by *sunk costs*? (b) A company is contemplating replacing an old piece of machinery which cost $450,000 and has $420,000 accumulated depreciation to date. A new machine costs $750,000. What is the sunk cost in this situation?

22–5. The condensed income statement for Hass Company for the current year is as follows:

	Product			
	R	S	T	Total
Sales	$300,000	$120,000	$450,000	$870,000
Less variable costs	160,000	90,000	270,000	520,000
Contribution margin	$140,000	$ 30,000	$180,000	$350,000
Less fixed costs	90,000	75,000	110,000	275,000
Income (loss) from operations	$ 50,000	$ (45,000)	$ 70,000	$ 75,000

Management decided to discontinue the manufacture and sale of Product S. Assuming that the discontinuance will have no effect on the total fixed costs or on the sales of Products R and T, has management made the correct decision? Explain.

22–6. (a) What is meant by *opportunity cost*? (b) Jablow Company is currently earning 12% on $300,000 invested in marketable securities. It proposes to use the $300,000 to acquire plant facilities to manufacture a new product that is expected to add $60,000 annually to net income. What is the opportunity cost involved in the decision to manufacture the new product?

22–7. In the long run, the normal selling price must be set high enough to cover what factors?

22–8. What are three cost concepts commonly used in applying the cost-plus approach to product pricing?

22–9. In using the product cost concept of applying the cost-plus approach to product pricing, what factors are included in the markup?

22–10. The variable cost concept used in applying the cost-plus approach to product pricing includes what costs in the cost amount to which the markup is added?

22–11. In determining the markup percentage for the variable cost concept of applying the cost-plus approach, what is included in the denominator?

22–12. Why might the use of ideal standards in applying the cost-plus approach to product pricing lead to setting product prices which are too low?

22–13. Although the cost-plus approach to product pricing may be used by management as a general guideline, what are some examples of other factors that managers should also consider in setting product prices?

22–14. In microeconomic theory, what is assumed to be management's primary objective for a business enterprise?

22–15. As the terms are used in microeconomic theory, what is meant by (a) marginal revenue and (b) marginal cost?

22–16. If the total revenue for selling 5 units of Product Q is $50 and the total revenue for selling 6 units is $54, what is the marginal revenue associated with selling the sixth unit?

22–17. What does the concept of economies of scale generally imply?

22–18. For a given amount of facilities, why will the total costs begin to increase by increasing amounts at some point?

22–19. According to microeconomic theory, at what point is profit maximized?

22–20. Why is the more theoretical economic approach to product pricing not used as often as the cost-plus approach?

22–21. For the following graph of total sales for a product, identify each stage of the product's life cycle.

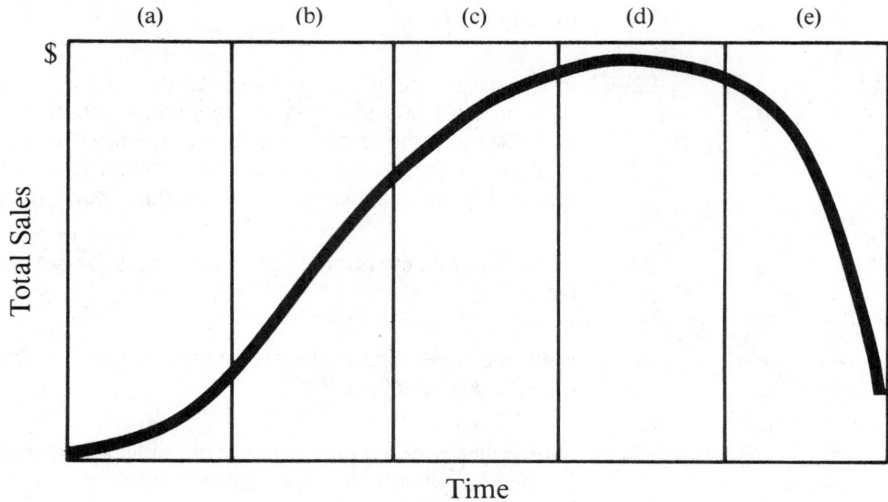

Real World Focus

22–22. In the personal computer hardware market, at what stage in the product life cycle is the 5¼-inch disk drive and at what stage is the 3½-inch drive?

Real World Focus

22–23. In July, 1986, *The Wall Street Journal* reported that the brakes that General Motors produces at its Delco Moraine division for its automobile assembly plants cost up to 15% more to make than they would cost to buy from an outside supplier. The same article reported that Ford Motor Co. and Chrysler Corp. buy almost all their brakes from outside suppliers as far away as Brazil, and these companies save money in the process. The decision of General Motors to produce its brakes internally is an example of what type of decision illustrated in this chapter?

Ethics Discussion Case

22–24. Sarah Gingell is a cost accountant for Norboru Enterprises. Ed Yu, vice-president of marketing, has asked Sarah to meet with representatives of Norboru's major competitor to discuss product cost data. Yu indicates that the sharing of this data will enable Norboru to determine a fair and equitable price for its products.

Would it be ethical for Gingell to attend the meeting and share the relevant cost data?

EXERCISES

Ex. 22–25.
Lease or sell decision.
OBJ. 1

Hayes Corporation is considering selling excess machinery with a book value of $150,000 (original cost of $325,000 less accumulated depreciation of $175,000) for $90,000 less a 10% brokerage commission. Alternatively the machinery can be leased for a total of $115,000 for five years, after which it will have no estimated residual value. During the period of the lease, the costs of repairs, insurance, and property tax expenses expected to be incurred by Hayes Corporation are estimated at $20,000. (a) Prepare a differential analysis report, dated January 4 of the current year, for the lease or sell decision. (b) On the basis of the data presented, would it be advisable to lease or sell the machinery? Explain.

Ex. 22–26. **Differential analysis report for discontinuance of product.** OBJ. 1

A condensed income statement by product line for Alvarez Co. indicated the following for Product K for the past year.

Sales	$300,000
Cost of goods sold	175,000
Gross profit	$125,000
Operating expenses	150,000
Loss from operations	$ (25,000)

It is estimated that 24% of the cost of goods sold represents fixed factory overhead costs and that 20% of operating expenses is fixed. Since Product K is only one of many products, the fixed costs will not be materially affected if the product is discontinued. (a) Prepare a differential analysis report, dated January 7 of the current year, for the proposed discontinuance of Product K. (b) Should Product K be retained? Explain.

Ex. 22–27. **Make or buy decision.** OBJ. 1

LeTrec Company has been purchasing carrying cases for its portable typewriters at a delivered cost of $15 per unit. The company, which is currently operating below full capacity, charges factory overhead to production at the rate of 35% of direct materials cost. The direct materials and direct labor costs per unit to produce comparable carrying cases are expected to be $8 and $5 respectively. If LeTrec Company manufactures the carrying cases, fixed factory overhead costs will not increase and variable factory overhead costs associated with the cases are expected to be 5% of direct materials costs. (a) Prepare a differential analysis report, dated February 3 of the current year, for the make or buy decision. (b) On the basis of the data presented, would it be advisable to make or to continue buying the carrying cases? Explain.

Ex. 22–28. **Differential analysis report for machine replacement.** OBJ. 1 SPREADSHEET PROBLEM

Mortner Company produces a commodity by applying a machine and direct labor to the direct materials. The original cost of the machine is $320,000, the accumulated depreciation is $200,000, its remaining useful life is 8 years, and its salvage value is negligible. On November 4, a proposal was made to replace the present manufacturing procedure with a fully automated machine that will cost $650,000. The automated machine has an estimated useful life of 8 years and no significant salvage value. For use in evaluating the proposal, the accountant accumulated the following annual data on present and proposed operations.

	Present Operations	Proposed Operations
Sales	$1,300,000	$1,300,000
Direct materials	550,000	550,000
Direct labor	250,000	—
Power and maintenance	40,000	100,000
Taxes, insurance, etc.	18,500	25,000
Selling and administrative expenses	110,000	110,000

(a) Prepare a differential analysis report for the proposal to replace the machine. Include in the analysis both the net differential decrease in costs anticipated over the 8 years and the net annual differential decrease in costs anticipated. (b) Based only on the data presented, should the proposal be accepted? (c) What are some of the other factors that should be considered before a final decision is made?

Ex. 22–29. **Decision on acceptance of additional business.** OBJ. 1

OH Company has a plant capacity of 100,000 units, and current production is 75,000 units. Monthly fixed costs are $250,000, and variable costs are $18.50 per unit. The present selling price is $24 per unit. On October 11, the company received an offer from JMC Company for 15,000 units of the product at $20 each. The JMC Company will market the units in a foreign country under its own brand name. The additional business is not expected to affect the regular selling price or quantity of sales of OH Company. (a) Prepare a differential analysis report for the proposed sale to JMC Company. (b) Briefly explain the reason why the acceptance of this additional business will increase operating income. (c) What is the minimum price per unit that would produce a contribution margin?

Ex. 22–30.
Use of absorption costing or variable costing in bidding on contract.
OBJ. 1

Sinclair Company expects to operate at 85% of productive capacity during September. The total manufacturing costs for September for the production of 17,000 grinders are budgeted as follows:

Direct materials	$110,500
Direct labor	34,000
Variable factory overhead	25,500
Fixed factory overhead	40,000
Total manufacturing costs	$210,000

The company has an opportunity to submit a bid for 2,500 grinders to be delivered by September 30 to a government agency. If the contract is obtained, it is anticipated that the additional activity will not interfere with normal production during September or increase the selling or administrative expenses. (a) What is the unit cost below which Sinclair Company should not go in bidding on the government contract? (b) Is a unit cost figure based on absorption costing or one based on variable costing more useful in arriving at a bid on this contract? Explain.

Ex. 22–31.
Total cost concept of product pricing.
OBJ. 2

Milner Inc. uses the total cost concept of applying the cost-plus approach to product pricing. The costs of producing and selling 5,000 units of Product P are as follows:

Variable costs:	
Direct materials	$14.00 per unit
Direct labor	2.80
Factory overhead	1.20
Selling and administrative expenses	3.00
Total	$21.00 per unit
Fixed costs:	
Factory overhead	$30,000
Selling and administrative expenses	15,000

Milner Inc. desires a profit equal to a 15% rate of return on invested assets of $120,000. (a) Determine the amount of desired profit from the production and sale of Product P. (b) Determine the total costs and the cost amount per unit for the production and sale of 5,000 units of Product P. (c) Determine the markup percentage for Product P. (d) Determine the selling price of Product P.

Ex. 22–32.
Product cost concept of product pricing.
OBJ. 2

Based on the data presented in Ex. 22–31, assume that Milner Inc. uses the product cost concept of applying the cost-plus approach to product pricing. (a) Determine the total manufacturing costs and the cost amount per unit for the production and sale of 5,000 units of Product P. (b) Determine the markup percentage for Product P. (c) Determine the selling price of Product P.

Ex. 22–33.
Variable cost concept of product pricing.
OBJ. 2

Based on the data presented in Ex. 22–31, assume that Milner Inc. uses the variable cost concept of applying the cost-plus approach to product pricing. (a) Determine the cost amount per unit for the production and sale of 5,000 units of Product P. (b) Determine the markup percentage for Product P. (c) Determine the selling price of Product P.

Ex. 22–34.
Economic concept of pricing.
OBJ. 3

For the following revenue schedule and cost schedule for Product E, (a) determine the level of sales and production at which marginal cost is equal to marginal revenue, (b) determine the unit sales price at the level of sales determined in (a), and (c) determine the maximum profit for Product E at the level of sales determined in (a).

	Revenue Schedule			Cost Schedule		
Price	Units Sold	Total Revenue	Marginal Revenue	Units Produced and Sold	Total Cost	Marginal Cost
$10	1	$10	$10	1	$ 7	$7
9	2	18	8	2	13	6
8	3	24	6	3	18	5
7	4	28	4	4	22	4
6	5	30	2	5	25	3
5	6	30	0	6	29	4
4	7	28	−2	7	34	5

PROBLEMS

Pb. 22–35.
Differential analysis report involving opportunity costs.
OBJ. 1

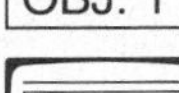

On January 2, Kurowski Company is considering leasing a building and purchasing the necessary equipment to operate a public warehouse. The project would be financed by selling $400,000 of 9% U.S. Treasury bonds that mature in 15 years. The bonds were purchased at face value and are currently selling at face value. The following data have been assembled:

Cost of equipment	$400,000
Life of equipment	15 years
Estimated residual value of equipment	$ 80,000
Yearly costs to operate the warehouse, in addition to depreciation of equipment	$ 28,000
Yearly expected revenues—first 9 years	$120,000
Yearly expected revenues—next 6 years	$ 80,000

Instructions:

(1) Prepare a differential analysis report presenting the differential revenue and the differential cost associated with the proposed operation of the warehouse for the 15 years as compared with present conditions.
(2) Based on the results disclosed by the differential analysis, should the proposal be accepted?
(3) If the proposal is accepted, what is the total estimated income from operation of the warehouse for the 15 years?

Pb. 22–36.
Differential analysis report for machine replacement proposal.
OBJ. 1

Pally Company is considering the replacement of a machine that has been used in its factory for five years. Relevant data associated with the operations of the old machine and the new machine, neither of which has any estimated residual value, are as follows:

Old Machine	
Cost of machine, 15-year life	$ 870,000
Annual depreciation	58,000
Annual manufacturing costs, exclusive of depreciation	320,000
Related annual operating expenses	150,000
Associated annual revenue	2,100,000
Current estimated selling price	500,000

New Machine	
Cost of machine, 10-year life	$1,250,000
Annual depreciation	125,000
Estimated annual manufacturing costs, exclusive of depreciation	200,000

Annual operating expenses and revenue are not expected to be affected by purchase of the new machine.

Instructions:

(1) Prepare a differential analysis report as of May 18 of the current year, comparing operations utilizing the new machine with operations using the present equipment. The analysis should indicate the total net differential decrease or increase in costs that would result over the 10-year period if the new machine is acquired.
(2) List other factors that should be considered before a final decision is reached.

Pb. 22–37.
Differential analysis report for sales promotion proposal.
OBJ. 1

Vaughn Company is planning a one-month campaign for November to promote sales of one of its two products. A total of $50,000 has been budgeted for advertising, contests, redeemable coupons, and other promotional activities. The following data have been assembled for their possible usefulness in deciding which of the products to select for the campaign.

	Product F		Product Q	
Unit selling price		$40		$120
Unit production costs:				
Direct materials	$17		$50	
Direct labor	8		32	
Variable factory overhead	3		7	
Fixed factory overhead	2		2	
Total unit production costs		$30		$ 91
Unit variable operating expenses		5		5
Unit fixed operating expenses		1		4
Total unit costs		$36		$100
Operating income per unit		$ 4		$ 20

No increase in facilities would be necessary to produce and sell the increased output. It is anticipated that 20,000 additional units of Product F or 5,000 aditional units of Product Q could be sold without changing the unit selling price of either product.

Instructions:

(1) Prepare a differential analysis report as of October 7 of the current year, presenting the additional revenue and additional costs anticipated from the promotion of Product F and Product Q.
(2) The sales manager had tentatively decided to promote Product Q, estimating that operating income would be increased by $50,000 ($20 operating income per unit for 5,000 units, less promotion expenses of $50,000). It was also believed that the selection of Product F would increase operating income by only $30,000 ($4 operating income per unit for 20,000 units, less promotion expenses of $50,000). State briefly your reasons for supporting or opposing the tentative decision.

Pb. 22–38.
Differential analysis report for further processing.
OBJ. 1

The managment of Avanti Company is considering whether to process further Product S into Product W. Product W can be sold for $150 per pound, and Product S can be sold without further processing for $80 per pound. Product S is produced in batches of 375 pounds by processing 500 pounds of raw material, which costs $30 per pound. Product W will require additional processing costs of $12 per pound of Product S, and 1.5 pounds of Product S will produce 1 pound of Product W.

Instructions:

(1) Prepare a differential analysis report as of August 15, presenting the differential revenue and differential cost per batch associated with the further processing of Product S to produce Product W.
(2) Briefly report your recommendations.

Pb. 22–39.
Differential analysis report for further processing.
OBJ. 1

Eldridge Refining Inc. refines Product M in batches of 50,000 gallons, which it sells for $5 per gallon. The associated unit costs are currently as follows:

Direct materials	$2.40
Direct labor	1.20
Variable factory overhead	.30
Fixed factory overhead	.15
Sales commissions	.25
Fixed selling and administrative expenses	.08

The company is presently considering a proposal to put Product M through several additional processes to yield Products M and R. Although the company had determined such further processing to be unwise, new processing methods have now been developed. Existing facilities can be used for the additional processing, but since the factory is operating at full 8-hour-day capacity, the processing would have to be performed at night. Additional costs of processing would be $10,000 per batch, and there would be an evaporation loss of 20%, with 45% of the processed material evolving as Product M and 35% as Product R. The selling price of Product R is $9 per gallon. Sales commissions are a uniform percentage based on the sales price.

Instructions:

(1) Prepare a differential analysis report as of December 16, presenting the differential revenue and the differential cost per batch associated with the processing to produce Products M and R, compared with processing to produce Product M only.
(2) Briefly report your recommendations.

Pb. 22–40.
Product pricing using the cost-plus approach concepts; differential analysis report for acceptance of additional business.
OBJ. 1,2

Rowan Company recently began production of a new product, C, which required the investment of $500,000 in assets. The costs of producing and selling 25,000 units of Product C are estimated as follows:

Variable costs per unit:	
Direct materials	$ 5.00
Direct labor	3.25
Factory overhead	1.75
Selling and administrative expenses	2.00
Total	$12.00
Fixed costs:	
Factory overhead	$70,000
Selling and administrative expenses	30,000

Rowan Company is currently considering the establishment of a selling price for Product C. The president of Rowan Company has decided to use the cost-plus approach to product pricing and has indicated that Product C must earn a 16% rate of return on invested assets.

Instructions:

(1) Determine the amount of desired profit from the production and sale of Product C.
(2) Assuming that the total cost concept is used, determine (a) the cost amount per unit, (b) the markup percentage, and (c) the selling price of Product C.
(3) Assuming that the product cost concept is used, determine (a) the cost amount per unit, (b) the markup percentage, and (c) the selling price of Product C. Round to the nearest cent.
(4) Assuming that the variable cost concept is used, determine (a) the cost amount per unit, (b) the markup percentage, and (c) the selling price of Product C.
(5) Comment on any additional considerations that could influence the establishment of the selling price for Product C.

(6) Assume that as of May 1, 22,000 units of Product C have been produced and sold during the current fiscal year. Analysis of the domestic market indicates that 1,500 additional units of Product C are expected to be sold during the remainder of the fiscal year ending June 30, at the normal product price determined under the total cost concept. On May 5, Rowan Company received an offer from Yu Inc. for 1,000 units of Product C at $9.75 each. Yu Inc. will market the units in Japan under its own brand name and no additional selling and administrative expenses associated with the sale will be incurred by Rowan Company. The additional business is not expected to affect the domestic sales of Product C and the additional units could be produced using existing capacity. (a) Prepare a differential analysis report of the proposed sale to Yu Inc. (b) Based upon the differential analysis report in (a), should the proposal be accepted?

ALTERNATE PROBLEMS

Pb.22–35A
Differential analysis report involving opportuntiy costs.
OBJ. 1

On February 1, Runge Company is considering leasing a building and purchasing the necessary equipment to operate a public warehouse. The project would be financed by selling $500,000 of 8% U.S. Treasury bonds that mature in 10 years. The bonds were purchased at face value and are currently selling at face value. The following data have been assembled:

Cost of equipment	$500,000
Life of equipment	10 years
Estimated residual value of equipment	$ 50,000
Yearly costs to operate the warehouse, in addition to depreciation of equipment	$ 30,000
Yearly expected revenues—first 6 years	$120,000
Yearly expected revenues—next 4 years	$ 90,000

Instructions:

(1) Prepare a differential analysis report presenting the differential revenue and the differential cost associated with the proposed operation of the warehouse for the 10 years as compared with present conditions.
(2) Based on the results disclosed by the differential analysis, should the proposal be accepted?
(3) If the proposal is accepted, what is the total estimated income from operation of the warehouse for the 10 years?

Pb. 22–36A.
Differential analysis report for machine replacement proposal.
OBJ. 1

Jost Company is considering the replacement of a machine that has been used in its factory for four years. Relevant data associated with the operations of the old machine and the new machine, neither of which has any residual value, are as follows:

Old Machine	
Cost of machine, 12-year life	$ 600,000
Annual depreciation	50,000
Annual manufacturing costs, exclusive of depreciation	480,000
Related annual operating expenses	220,000
Associated annual revenue	1,200,000
Current estimated selling price	360,000

New Machine	
Cost of machine, 8-year life	$1,500,000
Annual depreciation	187,500
Estimated annual manufacturing costs, exclusive of depreciation	275,000

Annual operating expenses and revenue are not expected to be affected by purchase of the new machine.

Instructions:

(1) Prepare a differential analysis report as of July 20 of the current year, comparing operations utilizing the new machine with operations using the present equipment. The analysis should indicate the total net differential decrease or increase in costs that would result over the 8-year period if the new machine is acquired.
(2) List other factors that should be considered before a final decision is reached.

Pb. 22–37A.
Differential analysis report for sales promotion proposal.
OBJ.1

Bates Company is planning a one-month campaign for May to promote sales of one of its two products. A total of $25,000 has been budgeted for advertising, contests, redeemable coupons, and other promotional activities. The following data have been assembled for their possible usefulness in deciding which of the products to select for the campaign:

	Product A		Product B	
Unit selling price		$50		$60
Unit production costs:				
Direct materials	$15		$16	
Direct labor	9		15	
Variable factory overhead	8		9	
Fixed factory overhead	6		6	
Total unit production costs		$38		$46
Unit variable operating expenses		5		5
Unit fixed operating expenses		3		3
Total unit costs and expenses		$46		$54
Operating income per unit		$ 4		$ 6

No increase in facilities would be necessary to produce and sell the increased output. It is anticipated that 10,000 additional units of Product A or 8,000 additional units of Product B could be sold without changing the unit selling price of either product.

Instructions:

(1) Prepare a differential analysis report as of April 4 of the current year, presenting the additional revenue and additional costs and expenses anticipated from the promotion of Product A and Product B.
(2) The sales manager had tentatively decided to promote Product B, estimating that operating income would be increased by $23,000 ($6 operating income per unit for 8,000 units, less promotion expenses of $25,000). It was also believed that the selection of Product A would increase operating income by only $15,000 ($4 operating income per unit for 10,000 units, less promotion expenses of $25,000). State briefly your reasons for supporting or opposing the tentative decision.

Pb. 22–38A.
Differential analysis report for further processing.
OBJ. 1

The management of Revsine Company is considering whether to process further Product X into Product Y. Product Y can be sold for $60 per pound, and Product X can be sold without further processing for $12 per pound. Product X is produced in batches of 300 pounds by processing 400 pounds of raw material, which costs $7 per pound. Product Y will require additional processing costs of $5 per pound of Product X, and 3 pounds of Product X will produce 1 pound of Product Y.

Instructions:

(1) Prepare a differential analysis report as of October 17, presenting the differential revenue and differential cost per batch associated with the further processing of Product X to produce Product Y.
(2) Briefly report your recommendations.

Pb. 22–39A.
Differential analysis report for further processing.
OBJ. 1

Diaz Refining Inc. refines Product J in batches of 100,000 gallons, which it sells for $5 per gallon. The associated unit costs and expenses are currently as follows:

Direct materials	$2.65
Direct labor	.82
Variable factory overhead	.33
Fixed factory overhead	.22
Sales commissions	.50
Fixed selling and general expenses	.10

The company is presently considering a proposal to put Product J through several additional processes to yield Products J and K. Although the company had determined such further processing to be unwise, new processing methods have now been developed. Existing facilities can be used for the additional processing, but since the factory is operating at full 8-hour-day capacity, the processing would have to be performed at night. Additional costs of processing would be $15,000 per batch, and there would be an evaporation loss of 10%, with 65% of the processed material evolving as Product J and 25% as Product K. The selling price of Product K is $8 per gallon. Sales commissions are a uniform percentage based on the sales price.

Instructions:

(1) Prepare a differential analysis report as of May 5, presenting the differential revenue and the differential cost per batch associated with the processing to produce Products J and K, compared with processing to produce Product J only.
(2) Briefly report your recommendations.

Pb. 22–40A.
Product pricing using the cost-plus approach concepts; differential analysis report for acceptance of additional business.
OBJ. 1, 2

TAC Inc. recently began production of a new product, L, which required the investment of $800,000 in assets. The costs of producing and selling 50,000 units of Product L are estimated as follows:

Variable costs per unit:	
Direct materials	$ 8.40
Direct labor	4.60
Factory overhead	2.00
Selling and administrative expenses	1.00
Total	$16.00
Fixed costs:	
Factory overhead	$150,000
Selling and administrative expenses	50,000

TAC Inc. is currently considering the establishment of a selling price for Product L. The president of TAC Inc. has decided to use the cost-plus approach to product pricing and has indicated that Product L must earn a 10% rate of return on invested assets.

Instructions:

(1) Determine the amount of desired profit from the production and sale of Product L.
(2) Assuming that the total cost concept is used, determine (a) the cost amount per unit, (b) the markup percentage, and (c) the selling price of Product L.
(3) Assuming that the product cost concept is used, determine (a) the cost amount per unit, (b) the markup percentage, and (c) the selling price of Product L.
(4) Assuming that the variable cost concept is used, determine (a) the cost amount per unit, (b) the markup percentage, and (c) the selling price of Product L.
(5) Comment on any additional considerations that could influence the establishment of the selling price of Product L.
(6) Assume that as of September 1, 40,000 units of Product L have been produced and sold during the current year. Analysis of the domestic market indicates that 6,500

additional units are expected to be sold during the remainder of the year at the normal product price determined under the total cost concept. On September 3 TAC Inc. received an offer from DeVoe Company for 3,000 units of Product L at $15.50 each. DeVoe Company will market the units in Canada under its own brand name and no additional selling and administrative expenses associated with the sale will be incurred by TAC Inc. The additional business is not expected to affect the domestic sales of Product L and the additional units could be produced using existing capacity. (a) Prepare a differential analysis report of the proposed sale to DeVoe Company. (b) Based upon the differential analysis report in (a), should the proposal be accepted?

MINI-CASE 22

Your father operates a family-owned automotive dealership. Recently, the city government has requested bids on the purchase of 8 sedans for use by the city police department. Although the city prefers to purchase from local dealerships, state law requires the acceptance of the lowest bid. The past several contracts for automotive purchases have been granted to dealerships from surrounding communities.

The following data were taken from the dealership records for the normal sale of the automobile for which current bids have been requested:

Retail list price of sedan	$14,000
Costs allocated to normal sale:	
Dealer cost from manufacturer	12,000
Fixed overhead	750
Shipping charges from manufacturer	400
Preparation charges	100
Sales commission based on selling price	6%

Your father has asked you to help him in arriving at a "winning" bid price for this contract. In the past, your father has always bid $300 above the total cost (including fixed overhead). No sales commissions will be paid if the bid is accepted, and your father has indicated that the bid price must contribute at least $300 per car to the profits of the dealership.

Instructions:

(1) Do you think that your father has used good bidding procedures for prior contracts? Explain.
(2) What should be the bid price, based upon your father's profit objectives?
(3) Explain why the bid price determined in (2) would not be an acceptable price for normal customers.

ANSWERS TO SELF-EXAMINATION QUESTIONS

1. A Differential cost (answer A) is the amount of increase or decrease in cost that is expected from a particular course of action compared with an alternative. Replacement cost (answer B) is the cost of replacing an asset at current market prices, and sunk cost (answer C) is a past cost that will not be affected by subsequent decisions.
2. A A sunk cost is not affected by later decisions. For Victor Company, the sunk cost is the $50,000 (answer A) book value of the equipment, which is equal to the original cost of $200,000 (answer C) less the accumulated depreciation of $150,000 (answer B).
3. C The amount of income that could have been earned from the best available alternative to a proposed use of cash is called opportunity cost (answer C). Actual cost (answer A) or historical cost (answer B) is the cash or equivalent outlay for goods or services actually acquired.
4. C Under the variable cost concept of product pricing (answer C), fixed manufacturing costs, fixed administrative and selling expenses, and desired profit are allowed for in the determination of the markup. Only desired profit is allowed for in the markup under the total cost concept (answer A). Under the product cost concept (answer B), total selling and administrative expenses and desired profit are allowed for in the determination of the markup.
5. A Microeconomic theory indicates that profits of a business enterprise will be maximized at the point where marginal revenue equals marginal cost (answer A). At lower levels of production and sales, the change in total revenue is greater than the change in total cost (answer B); hence, more profit can be achieved by manufacturing and selling more units. At higher levels of production and sales, the change in total cost is greater than the change in total revenue (answer C); hence, less profit will be achieved by manufacturing and selling more units.

CHAPTER 23

CHAPTER OBJECTIVES

1 Describe the nature and importance of capital investment analysis.

2 Describe and illustrate the following methods of evaluating capital investment proposals:
Average rate of return
Cash payback
Net present value
Internal rate of return.

3 Describe qualitative considerations in capital investment analysis, especially as related to the modern manufacturing environment.

4 Describe factors that complicate capital investment analysis.

5 Describe and illustrate the capital rationing process.

6 Describe the basic concepts for planning and controlling capital investment expenditures.

23

CAPITAL INVESTMENT ANALYSIS

With the accelerated growth of American industry, increasing attention has been given to long-term investment decisions involving property, plant, and equipment. The process by which management plans, evaluates, and controls such investments is called **capital investment analysis,** or **capital budgeting.** This chapter describes analyses useful for making capital investment decisions, which may involve thousands, millions, or even billions of dollars. The similarities and differences between the most commonly used methods of evaluating capital investment proposals, as well as the uses of each method, are emphasized. Qualitative considerations in capital investment analysis are also discussed. Finally, considerations complicating capital investment analyses, the process of allocating available investment funds among competing proposals (capital rationing), and planning and controlling capital expenditures are briefly discussed.

NATURE OF CAPITAL INVESTMENT ANALYSIS

OBJECTIVE 1
Describe the nature and importance of capital investment analysis.

Capital investment expenditures normally involve a long-term commitment of funds and thus affect operations for many years. These expenditures must earn a reasonable rate of return so that the enterprise can meet its obligations to creditors and provide dividends to stockholders. Because capital investment decisions are some of the most important decisions that management makes, the systems and procedures for evaluating, planning, and controlling capital investments must be carefully developed and implemented.

A capital investment program should include a plan for encouraging employees at all levels of an enterprise to submit proposals for capital investments. The plan should provide for communicating to the employees the long-range goals of the enterprise so that useful proposals are submitted. In addition, the plan may provide for rewarding employees whose proposals are implemented. All reasonable proposals should be given serious consideration, and the effects of the economic implications expected from these proposals should be identified.

METHODS OF EVALUATING CAPITAL INVESTMENT PROPOSALS

OBJECTIVE 2
Describe and illustrate the following methods of evaluating capital investment proposals:
Average rate of return
Cash payback
Net present value
Internal rate of return.

The methods of evaluating capital investment proposals can be grouped into two general categories that can be referred to as (1) methods that ignore present value and (2) present value methods. The characteristic that distinguishes one category from the other is the way in which the concept of the time value of money is treated. Both the time value of money and the concept of present value are discussed in more detail later in this chapter. Because cash on hand can be invested to earn more cash while cash to be received in the future cannot, money has a time value. However, the methods that ignore present value do not give consideration to the fact that cash on hand is more valuable than cash to be received in the future. The two methods in this category are (1) the average rate of return method and (2) the cash payback method.

By converting dollars to be received in the future into current dollars, using the concept of present value, the present value methods take into consideration the fact that money has a time value. The two common present value methods used in evaluating capital investment proposals are (1) the net present value method and (2) the internal rate of return method.

Often management will use some combination of the four methods in evaluating the various economic aspects of capital investment proposals. A recent survey of business practices in a variety of industries indicated that 46% of the respondents use the average rate of return method, 71% use the cash payback method, 64% use the net present value method, and 69% use the internal rate of return method.[1]

Each of the methods has both advantages and limitations. In addition, some of the computations can become rather complex. By use of the computer, however, the calculations can be performed easily and quickly. More importantly, the computer can be used in developing models that indicate the effect of changes in key factors on the results of capital investment proposals.

Methods That Ignore Present Value

The average rate of return and the cash payback methods of evaluating capital investment proposals are simple to use and are often used in screening proposals. Management establishes a minimum standard, and proposals not meeting this minimum standard are dropped from further consideration. When several alternative proposals meet the minimum standard, management will often rank the proposals from the most desirable to the least desirable.

The methods that ignore present value may also be useful in evaluating capital investment proposals that have relatively short useful lives. In such situations, the timing of the cash flows is less important and management generally focuses its attention on the amount of income to be earned from the investment and the total net cash flows to be received from the investment.

Average Rate of Return Method. The expected **average rate of return,** sometimes referred to as the **accounting rate of return,** is a measure of the expected profitability of an investment in plant assets. The amount of income

[1] Robert A. Howell, James D. Brown, Stephen R. Soucy, and Allen H. Seed, *Management Accounting in the New Manufacturing Environment* (Montvale, New Jersey: National Association of Accountants and Computer Aided Manufacturing International, 1987).

expected to be earned from the investment is stated as an annual average over the number of years the asset is to be used. The amount of the investment may be considered to be the original cost of the plant asset, or recognition may be given to the effect of depreciation on the amount of the investment. According to the latter view, the investment gradually declines from the original cost to the estimated residual value at the end of its useful life. If straight-line depreciation and no residual value are assumed, the average investment would be equal to one half of the original expenditure.[2]

To illustrate, assume that management is considering the purchase of a certain machine at a cost of $500,000. The machine is expected to have a useful life of 4 years, with no residual value, and its use during the 4 years is expected to yield total income of $200,000. The estimated average annual income is therefore $50,000 ($200,000 ÷ 4), and the average investment is $250,000 [($500,000 + $0 residual value) ÷ 2]. Accordingly, the expected average rate of return on the average investment is 20%, computed as follows:

$$\text{Average Rate of Return} = \frac{\text{Estimated Average Annual Income}}{\text{Average Investment}}$$

$$\text{Average Rate of Return} = \frac{\$200{,}000 \div 4}{(\$500{,}000 + \$0) \div 2}$$

$$\text{Average Rate of Return} = 20\%$$

The expected average rate of return of 20% should be compared with the rate established by management as the minimum reward for the risks involved in the investment. The attractiveness of the proposed purchase of additional equipment is indicated by the difference between the expected rate and the minimum desired rate.

When several alternative capital investment proposals are being considered, the proposals can be ranked by their average rates of return. The higher the average rate of return, the more desirable the proposal. For example, assume that management is considering the following alternative capital investment proposals and has computed the indicated average rates of return:

	Proposal A	Proposal B
Estimated average annual income	$ 30,000	$ 36,000
Average investment	$120,000	$180,000
Average rate of return:		
$30,000 ÷ $120,000	25%	
$36,000 ÷ $180,000		20%

If only the average rate of return is considered, Proposal A, based on its average rate of return of 25%, would be preferred over Proposal B.

The primary advantages of the average rate of return method are its ease of computation and the fact that it emphasizes the amount of income earned over the entire life of the proposal. Its main disadvantage is that it does not directly consider the expected cash flows from the proposal and the timing of these cash flows. These cash flows are important because cash coming from an investment can be reinvested in other income-producing activities. Therefore, the more funds and the sooner the funds become available, the more income that can be generated from their reinvestment.

---

[2] The average investment is the midpoint of the depreciable portion of the cost of the asset. Since a plant asset is never depreciated below its residual value, this midpoint is determined by adding the original cost of the asset to the estimated residual value and dividing by 2.

Cash Payback Method. The expected period of time that will pass between the date of a capital investment and the complete recovery in cash (or equivalent) of the amount invested is called the **cash payback period.** To simplify the analysis, the revenues and the out-of-pocket operating expenses expected to be associated with the operation of the plant assets are assumed to be entirely in the form of cash. The excess of the cash flowing in from revenue over the cash flowing out for expenses is termed **net cash flow.** The time required for the net cash flow to equal the initial outlay for the plant asset is the payback period.

For purposes of illustration, assume that the proposed investment in a plant asset with an 8-year life is $200,000 and that the annual net cash flow is expected to be $40,000. The estimated cash payback period for the investment is 5 years, computed as follows:

$$\frac{\$200{,}000}{\$40{,}000} = \text{5-year cash payback period}$$

In the preceding illustration, the annual net cash flows were equal ($40,000 per year). If these annual net cash flows are not equal, the cash payback period is determined by summing the annual net cash flows until the cumulative sum equals the amount of the proposed investment. To illustrate, assume that for a proposed investment of $400,000, the annual net cash flows and cumulative net cash flows over the proposal's 6-year life are as follows:

Year	Net Cash Flow	Cumulative Net Cash Flow
1	$ 60,000	$ 60,000
2	80,000	140,000
3	105,000	245,000
4	155,000	400,000
5	100,000	500,000
6	90,000	590,000

The cumulative net cash flow at the end of the fourth year equals the amount of the investment, $400,000. Therefore, the payback period is 4 years. If the amount of the proposed investment had been $450,000 in the preceding example, the expected payback would have occurred during the fifth year. If the net cash flows are uniform throughout the period, the cash payback period in this case would be 4½ years.

The cash payback method is widely used in evaluating proposals for expansion and for investment in new projects. A relatively short payback period is desirable, because the sooner the cash is recovered the sooner it becomes available for reinvestment in other projects. In addition, there is likely to be less possibility of loss from changes in economic conditions, obsolescence, and other unavoidable risks when the commitment is short-term. The cash payback concept is also of interest to bankers and other creditors who may be dependent upon net cash flow for the repayment of claims associated with the initial capital investment. The sooner the cash is recovered, the sooner the debt or other liabilities can be paid. Thus, the cash payback method would be especially useful to managers whose primary concern is liquidity.

One of the primary disadvantages of the cash payback method as a basis for decisions is its failure to take into consideration the expected profitability of a proposal. A project with a very short payback period, coupled with relatively poor profitability, would be less desirable than one with a longer payback period but with satisfactory profitability. Another disadvantage of the cash payback method is that the cash flows occurring after the payback period are ignored. A 5-year project with a 3-year payback period and two additional years of substantial cash flows is more desirable than a 3-year project with a 3-year payback period.

Present Value Methods

An investment in plant and equipment may be viewed as the acquisition of a series of future net cash flows composed of two elements: (1) the recovery of the initial investment and (2) income. The period of time over which these net cash flows will be received may be an important factor in determining the value of an investment.

The concept of the time value of money is that any specified amount of cash to be received at some date in the future is not the equivalent of the same amount of cash held at an earlier date. A sum of cash to be received in the future is not as valuable as the same sum on hand today, because cash on hand today can be invested to earn income. For example, $10,000 on hand today would be more valuable than $10,000 to be received a year from today. In other words, if cash can be invested to earn 10% per year, the $10,000 on hand today will accumulate to $11,000 ($10,000 plus $1,000 earnings) by one year from today. The $10,000 on hand today can be referred to as the **present value** amount that is equivalent to $11,000 to be received a year from today.

Net Present Value Method. The **net present value method,** sometimes referred to as the **discounted cash flow method,** uses present value concepts to compute the net present value of the cash flows expected from a proposal. To illustrate, if $1,000 is to be received in one year and if the current rate of earnings is 12%, the present value of the $1,000 is $892.86 ($1,000 ÷ 1.12). If the cash is to be received one year later (two years in all), with the earnings compounded at the end of the first year, the present value amount would be $797.20 ($892.86 ÷ 1.12).

Instead of determining the present value of future cash flows by a series of divisions in the manner just illustrated, it is customary to find the present value of $1 from a table of present values and to multiply it by the amount of the future cash flow. Reference to the following partial table indicates that the present value of $1 to be received two years hence, with earnings at the rate of 12% a year, is .797. Multiplication of .797 by $1,000 yields $797, which is the same amount that was determined in the preceding paragraph by two successive divisions. The small difference is due to rounding the present value factors in the table to three decimal places.[3]

Present Value of $1 at Compound Interest

Year	6%	10%	12%	15%	20%
1	.943	.909	.893	.870	.833
2	.890	.826	.797	.756	.694
3	.840	.751	.712	.658	.579
4	.792	.683	.636	.572	.482
5	.747	.621	.567	.497	.402
6	.705	.564	.507	.432	.335
7	.665	.513	.452	.376	.279
8	.627	.467	.404	.327	.233
9	.592	.424	.361	.284	.194
10	.558	.386	.322	.247	.162

[3]More complete tables of both present values and future values are in Appendix A.

The particular rate of return used in net present value analysis is determined by management, based upon such factors as the nature of the business enterprise and its relative profitability, the purpose of the capital investment, the cost of securing funds for the investment, the minimum desired rate of return, and other related factors. If the net present value of the net cash flow expected from a proposed investment at the selected rate equals or exceeds the amount of the investment, the proposal is desirable. For purposes of illustration, assume a proposal for the acquisition of $200,000 of equipment with an expected useful life of 5 years and a minimum desired rate of return of 10%. The anticipated net cash flow for each of the 5 years and the analysis of the proposal are as follows:

Net Present Value Analysis

Year	Present Value of $1 at 10%	Net Cash Flow	Present Value of Net Cash Flow
1	.909	$ 70,000	$ 63,630
2	.826	60,000	49,560
3	.751	50,000	37,550
4	.683	40,000	27,320
5	.621	40,000	24,840
Total		$260,000	$202,900
Amount to be invested			200,000
Net present value			$ 2,900

The present value of the net cash flow for each year is computed by multiplying the net cash flow for the year by the present value factor of $1 for that year. In the illustration, the net cash flow of $70,000 to be received at the end of year 1 is multiplied by the present value of $1 for 1 year at 10% (.909). Thus, the present value of the $70,000 is $63,630. Likewise, the net cash flow at the end of the second year, $60,000, is multiplied by the present value of $1 for 2 years at 10% (.826) to yield $49,560, and so on. The amount to be invested, $200,000, is then subtracted from the total present value of the net cash flows, $202,900, to determine the net present value, $2,900. The net present value shows that the proposal is expected to recover the investment and provide more than the minimum rate of return of 10%.

When capital investment funds are limited and several alternative investment proposals of the same amount are being considered, the one with the largest net present value is the most desirable. If the alternative proposals involve different amounts of investment, it is useful to prepare a relative ranking of the proposals by using a **present value index**. The present value index for the previous illustration is computed by dividing the total present value of the net cash flow by the amount to be invested, as follows:

$$\text{Present Value Index} = \frac{\text{Total Present Value of Net Cash Flow}}{\text{Amount To Be Invested}}$$

$$\text{Present Value Index} = \frac{\$202,900}{\$200,000}$$

$$\text{Present Value Index} = 1.01$$

To illustrate the ranking of the proposals by use of the present value index, assume that the total present values of the net cash flow and the amounts to be invested for three alternative proposals are as follows:

	Proposal A	Proposal B	Proposal C
Total present value of net cash flow ...	$107,000	$86,400	$93,600
Amount to be invested	100,000	80,000	90,000
Net present value	$ 7,000	$ 6,400	$ 3,600

The present value index for each proposal is as follows:

	Present Value Index
Proposal A	1.07 ($107,000 ÷ $100,000)
Proposal B	1.08 ($ 86,400 ÷ $ 80,000)
Proposal C	1.04 ($ 93,600 ÷ $ 90,000)

The present value indexes indicate that although Proposal A has the largest net present value, it is not as attractive as Proposal B in terms of the amount of present value per dollar invested. Note, however, that Proposal B requires an investment of only $80,000, while Proposal A requires an investment of $100,000. The possible use of the $20,000 if B is selected should be considered before a final decision is made.

The primary advantage of the net present value method is that it gives consideration to the time value of money. A disadvantage of the method is that the computations are more complex than those for the methods that ignore present value. In addition, this method assumes that the cash received from the proposal during its useful life will be reinvested at the rate of return used to compute the present value of the proposal. Because of changing economic conditions, this assumption may not always be reasonable.

Internal Rate of Return Method. The **internal rate of return method,** sometimes called **time-adjusted rate of return method,** uses present value concepts to compute the rate of return from the net cash flows expected from capital investment proposals. Thus, it is similar to the net present value method in that it focuses on the present value of the net cash flows. However, the internal rate of return method starts with the net cash flows and, in a sense, works backwards to determine the rate of return expected from the proposal.

To illustrate the use of the internal rate of return method, assume that management is evaluating a proposal to acquire equipment costing $33,530, which is expected to provide annual net cash flows of $10,000 per year for 5 years. If a rate of return of 12% is assumed, the present value of the net cash flows can be computed using the present value of $1 table on page 966, as follows:

Year	Present Value of $1 at 12%	Net Cash Flow	Present Value of Net Cash Flow
1	.893	$10,000	$ 8,930
2	.797	10,000	7,970
3	.712	10,000	7,120
4	.636	10,000	6,360
5	.567	10,000	5,670
Total		$50,000	$36,050

Since the present value of the net cash flow based on a 12% rate of return, $36,050, is greater than the $33,530 to be invested, the internal rate of return must be greater than 12%. The following analysis indicates that 15% is the rate of return that equates the $33,530 cost of the investment with the present value of the net cash flows:

Year	Present Value of $1 at 15%	Net Cash Flow	Present Value of Net Cash Flow
1	.870	$10,000	$ 8,700
2	.756	10,000	7,560
3	.658	10,000	6,580
4	.572	10,000	5,720
5	.497	10,000	4,970
Total	....	$50,000	$33,530

In the illustration, a rate of 12% was assumed before the internal rate of return of 15% was identified. Such trial and error procedures are tedious and time consuming. When equal annual net cash flows are expected from a proposal, as in the illustration, the computations can be simplified by using a table of the present value of an annuity.[4]

An **annuity** is a series of equal cash flows at fixed intervals. The **present value of an annuity** is the sum of the present values of each cash flow. From another point of view, the present value of an annuity is the amount of cash that would be needed today to yield a series of equal cash flows at fixed intervals in the future. For example, reference to the following table of the present value of an annuity of $1 shows that the present value of cash flows at the end of each of five years, with an internal rate of return of 15% per year, is 3.353. Multiplication of $10,000 by 3.353 yields the same amount ($33,530) that was determined in the preceding illustration by five successive multiplications.

Present Value of an Annuity of $1 at Compound Interest

Year	6%	10%	12%	15%	20%
1	.943	.909	.893	.870	.833
2	1.833	1.736	1.690	1.626	1.528
3	2.673	2.487	2.402	2.283	2.106
4	3.465	3.170	3.037	2.855	2.589
5	4.212	3.791	3.605	3.353	2.991
6	4.917	4.355	4.111	3.785	3.326
7	5.582	4.868	4.564	4.160	3.605
8	6.210	5.335	4.968	4.487	3.837
9	6.802	5.759	5.328	4.772	4.031
10	7.360	6.145	5.650	5.019	4.192

The procedures for using the present value of an annuity of $1 table to determine the internal rate of return are as follows:

1. A present value factor for an annuity of $1 is determined by dividing the amount to be invested by the annual net cash flow, as expressed in the following formula:

$$\text{Present Value Factor for an Annuity of \$1} = \frac{\text{Amount To Be Invested}}{\text{Annual Net Cash Flow}}$$

[4] In the illustration, equal annual net cash flows are assumed, so that attention can be focused on the basic concepts. If the annual net cash flows are not equal, the procedures are more complex, but the basic concepts are not affected. In such cases, computers can be used to perform the computations.

2. The present value factor determined in (1) is located in the present value of an annuity of $1 table by first locating the number of years of expected useful life of the investment in the Year column and then proceeding horizontally across the table until the present value factor determined in (1) is found.
3. The internal rate of return is then identified by the heading of the column in which the present value factor in (2) is located.

To illustrate these procedures, assume that management is considering a proposal to acquire equipment costing $97,360, which is expected to provide equal annual net cash flows of $20,000 for 7 years. The present value factor for an annuity of $1 is 4.868, computed as follows:

$$\text{Present Value Factor for an Annuity of \$1} = \frac{\text{Amount To Be Invested}}{\text{Annual Net Cash Flow}}$$

$$\text{Present Value Factor for an Annuity of \$1} = \frac{\$97{,}360}{\$20{,}000}$$

$$\text{Present Value Factor for an Annuity of \$1} = 4.868$$

For a period of 7 years, the following table for the present value of an annuity of $1 indicates that the factor 4.868 is associated with a percentage of 10%. Thus, 10% is the internal rate of return for this proposal.

Present Value of an Annuity of $1 at Compound Interest

Year	6%	10%	12%
1	9.43	.909	.893
2	1.833	1.736	1.690
3	2.673	2.487	2.402
4	3.465	3.170	3.037
5	4.212	3.791	3.605
6	4.917	4.355	4.111
7	5.582	4.868	4.564
8	6.210	5.335	4.968
9	6.802	5.759	5.328
10	7.360	6.145	5.650

If the minimum acceptable rate of return for similar proposals is 10% or less, then the proposed equipment acquisition should be considered desirable. When several proposals are under consideration, management often ranks the proposals by their internal rates of return, and the proposal with the highest rate is considered the most attractive.

The primary advantage of the internal rate of return method is that the present values of the net cash flows over the entire useful life of the proposal are considered. An additional advantage of the method is that by determining a rate of return for each proposal, all proposals are automatically placed on a common basis for comparison. The primary disadvantage of the internal rate of return method is that the computations are somewhat more complex than for some of the other methods. In addition, like the net present value method, this method assumes that the cash received from a proposal during its useful life will be reinvested at the internal rate of return. Because of changing economic conditions, this assumption may not always be reasonable.

THE INTERNAL RATE OF RETURN METHOD—AN APPLICATION USING THE MICROCOMPUTER

The complexity of using the present value methods of evaluating capital investment proposals can be significantly reduced by using a microcomputer. The following computer program, which was written in the BASIC programming language, computes the internal rate of return for an investment proposal with a series of equal net cash flows:

```
10  INPUT "periods";N: INPUT "investment":I: INPUT "annual net cash flow";C
20  INPUT "guess";G
30  X=(X+G)/100+1:S=I
40  FOR J=1 TO N:S=S+C/X^J:NEXT:X=(X-1)*100
50  IF ABS(Y-X)<=.001 THEN END
60  LPRINT X:Y=X:RESTORE:IF S>0 THEN 30
70  X=X-G:G=G/3:GOTO 30
```

To run this program, the user must have access to the BASIC programming system. The manual accompanying this system will describe the procedures for calling up the system and entering, saving, loading, and running a program. In using the above program, the program steps must be keyboarded exactly as shown. When the program is run, the user will be required to input (1) the number of periods for which the proposed capital investment will yield annual cash inflows, (2) the cost of the investment expressed as a negative initial cash flow, (3) the annual net cash flows, and (4) an initial guess as to the approximate internal rate of return. The initial guess does not necessarily have to be close to the true value, since the computer will estimate the true value regardless of the accuracy of the initial guess. The initial guess only adds efficiency to the estimation process. An example of the use of this computer program for the illustration presented on page 970 is as follows:

```
periods? 7
investment? -97360
annual net cash flow? 20000
guess? 15
  15
  4.999995
  9.999991
  14.99999
  11.66666
  10.55554
  10.18517
  10.06172
  10.02057
  10.00685
  10.00227
  10.00456
  10.00303
```

The program will stop computing the estimated internal rate of return when successive estimates are reasonably close to one another and additional precision is not warranted. In the above example, the approximate internal rate of return is 10%. Note that the difference between the above estimate and the illustration in the text is due to rounding within the computer program.

Note: This program was written for the BASIC programming language using the IBM personal computer.

QUALITATIVE CONSIDERATIONS IN CAPITAL INVESTMENT ANALYSIS

OBJECTIVE 3
Describe qualitative considerations in capital investment analysis, especially as related to the new manufacturing environment.

The methods of evaluating capital investments described and illustrated in the preceding paragraphs emphasize the quantitative aspects of capital investment analysis. For example, in evaluating a proposal to purchase new equipment, the expected net cash inflows are compared with the amount of cash to be invested. However, some benefits of capital investments are qualitative in nature and cannot be readily estimated in dollar terms. If these qualitative considerations are not considered, the quantitative analyses may suggest the rejection of a worthy investment.

Qualitative considerations which may impact upon capital investment analysis include the impact of investment proposals on product quality, manufacturing flexibility, increased employee morale, increased manufacturing productivity, and increased manufacturing control. Many of these qualitative considerations may be as important or more important than the results of quantitative analysis in the new manufacturing environment. This environment is characterized by investments in automated equipment, redesign of the manufacturing process, and implementation of manufacturing systems such as just-in-time manufacturing and computer-integrated manufacturing. The consideration of qualitative factors in capital investment analysis in the modern manufacturing environment is further described and illustrated in Chapter 24.

The possible effect of failing to consider both the quantitative and qualitative aspects of capital investments, and thus to keep abreast of the marketplace, is best summarized by Patrick S. Parker, Chairman of Parker Hannifin Corporation, who stated, "In today's environment, we don't think the numbers really tell the story." Many investments, he indicates, are required just to stay ahead of the competition and to survive.[5]

CAPITAL INVESTMENT IN THE NEW MANUFACTURING ENVIRONMENT

The importance of capital investment analysis in the new manufacturing environment is stressed in the following excerpts from an article in *Management Accounting*. Traditional capital investment methods should be reassessed in light of this new environment, particularly when considering investments in manufacturing automation.

Automation is probably the most evident change in the new manufacturing environment. The objective of automation, besides adding capacity, is to produce high quality goods consistently, quickly, and economically. Effective use of automation can leverage the success achieved through more fundamental efforts aimed at achieving higher quality, lower inventory, streamlined production flow lines, simplified processes, and other major trends in the factory. Thus, automation can enhance the overall competitiveness of a company.

In spite of the obvious advantages of investing in automation, issues central to the invesment decision have changed dramatically over the past 20 years. The new manufacturing environment presents new issues of scope, timing, and uncertainty that require management accountants to reassess the whole capital budgeting process.

The investment decision evaluates whether an investment's returns exceed its costs. While the issue of returns versus costs is still the fundamental question, the nature and risks associated with those investments has changed dramatically in the new manufacturing environment.

. . . Investments are becoming more significant. Stand-alone pieces of equipment, such as robots and computerized numerical control machines, can sell for up to $1 million. Flexible manufacturing systems—a machine or group of machines linked together to perform a series of operations automatically for one or more product lines . . . can cost anywhere from $10 to $50 million. Investments in fully automated factories, such as the IBM Proprinter facility, can cost more than $100 million.

. . . The benefits associated with advanced automation are more indirect and intangible. Where emphasis . . . was previously on direct cost savings, today investments are designed to improve quality, delivery, and customer satisfaction. This new focus requires that management accountants devise new models and methodologies to capture these benefits to establish the value contributed by the investment.

Source: Robert A. Howell and Stephen R. Soucy, "Capital Investment in the New Manufacturing Environment," *Management Accounting* (November, 1987), pp. 26-32.

[5]John F. Towey, "How to Justify Investment in New Technology," *Management Accounting* (July, 1989), p. 55.

FACTORS THAT COMPLICATE CAPITAL INVESTMENT ANALYSIS

OBJECTIVE 4
Describe factors that complicate capital investment analysis.

In the preceding paragraphs, the basic concepts for four widely used methods of evaluating capital investment proposals were discussed. In practice, additional factors may have an impact on the outcome of a capital investment decision. Some of the most important of these factors, which are described in the following paragraphs, are the federal income tax, unequal lives of alternative proposals, the leasing alternative, uncertainty, and changes in price levels.

Income Tax

In many cases, the impact of the federal income tax on capital investment decisions can be very significant. One provision of the Internal Revenue Code (IRC) which should be considered in capital investment analysis is depreciation.

For determining depreciation for federal income tax purposes, useful lives that are much shorter than the actual useful lives can often be used. Also, depreciation can be calculated by methods that approximate the 200 percent declining-balance method. Thus, depreciation for tax purposes often exceeds the depreciation for financial statement purposes in the early years of an asset's use. The tax reduction in these early years is offset by higher taxes as the annual cost recovery allowance decreases, so that accelerated depreciation does not effect a long-run saving in taxes.[6]

Unequal Proposal Lives

In the preceding sections, the discussion of the methods of analyzing capital investment proposals was based on the assumption that alternative proposals had the same useful lives. In practice, however, alternative proposals may have unequal lives. In such cases, the proposals must be made comparable. One widely used method is to adjust the lives of projects with the longest lives to a time period that is equal to the life of the project with the shortest life. In this manner, the useful lives of all proposals are made equal. To illustrate, assume that the net present value method is being used to compare the following two proposals, each of which has an initial investment of $100,000:

	Net Cash Flows	
Year	*Proposal X*	*Proposal Y*
1	$30,000	$30,000
2	30,000	30,000
3	25,000	30,000
4	20,000	30,000
5	15,000	30,000
6	15,000	—
7	10,000	—
8	10,000	—

If the desired rate of return is 10%, each proposal's net present value is determined as follows:

[6] The impact of income taxes on capital investment analysis is further described and illustrated in the appendix at the end of this chapter.

Proposal X

Year	Present Value of $1 at 10%	Net Cash Flow	Present Value of Net Cash Flow
1	.909	$ 30,000	$ 27,270
2	.826	30,000	24,780
3	.751	25,000	18,775
4	.683	20,000	13,660
5	.621	15,000	9,315
6	.564	15,000	8,460
7	.513	10,000	5,130
8	.467	10,000	4,670
Total		$155,000	$112,060
Amount to be invested			100,000
Net present value			$ 12,060

Proposal Y

Year	Present Value of $1 at 10%	Net Cash Flow	Present Value of Net Cash Flow
1	.909	$ 30,000	$ 27,270
2	.826	30,000	24,780
3	.751	30,000	22,530
4	.683	30,000	20,490
5	.621	30,000	18,630
Total		$150,000	$113,700
Amount to be invested			100,000
Net present value			$ 13,700

The two proposals cannot be compared by focusing on the amount of the net present value because Proposal Y has a life of 5 years while Proposal X has a life of 8 years. Proposal X can be adjusted to a 5-year life by assuming that it is to be terminated at the end of 5 years and the asset sold. This assumption requires that the residual value of Proposal X be estimated at the end of 5 years and that this value be considered a cash flow at that date. Both proposals will then cover 5 years, and the results of the net present value analysis can be used to compare the relative attractiveness of the two proposals. For example, assume that Proposal X has an estimated residual value at the end of year 5 of $40,000. For Proposal X, the excess of the present value over the amount to be invested is $18,640 for a 5-year life, as follows:

Proposal X

Year	Present Value of $1 at 10%	Net Cash Flow	Present Value of Net Cash Flow
1	.909	$ 30,000	$ 27,270
2	.826	30,000	24,780
3	.751	25,000	18,775
4	.683	20,000	13,660
5	.621	15,000	9,315
5 (Residual value)	.621	40,000	24,840
Total		$160,000	$118,640
Amount to be invested			100,000
Net present value			$18,640

Since the net present value for Proposal X exceeds that for Proposal Y by $4,940 ($18,640 − $13,700), Proposal X may be viewed as the more attractive of the two proposals.

Lease Versus Capital Investment

Leasing of plant assets has become common in many industries in recent years. Leasing allows an enterprise to acquire the use of plant assets without the necessity of using large amounts of cash to purchase them. In addition, if management believes that a plant asset has a high degree of risk of becoming obsolete before the end of its useful life, then leasing rather than purchasing the asset may be more attractive. By leasing the asset, management reduces the risk of suffering a loss due to obsolescence. Finally, the Internal Revenue Code provisions which allow the lessor (the owner of the asset) to pass tax deductions on to the lessee (the party leasing the asset) have increased the popularity of leasing in recent years. For example, a company that leases for its use a $200,000 plant asset with a life of 8 years for $50,000 per year is permitted to deduct from taxable income the annual lease payments of $50,000.

In many cases, before a final decision is made, management should consider the possibility of leasing assets instead of purchasing them. Ordinarily, leasing assets is more costly than purchasing because the lessor must include in the rental price not only the costs associated with owning the assets but also a profit. Nevertheless, using the methods of evaluating capital investment proposals, management should consider whether or not the profitability and cash flows from the lease alternative with its risks compares favorably to the profitability and cash flows from the purchase alternative with its risks.

Uncertainty

All capital investment analyses rely on factors that are uncertain; that is, the accuracy of the estimates involved, including estimates of expected revenues, expenses, and cash flows, are uncertain. Although the estimates are subject to varying degrees of risk or uncertainty, the long-term nature of capital investments suggests that many of the estimates are likely to involve considerable uncertainty. Errors in one or more of the estimates could lead to incorrect decisions.

Changes in Price Levels

The past three decades, which have been characterized by increasing rather than decreasing price levels, are described as periods of **inflation.** In recent years, the rates of inflation have fluctuated widely, making the estimation of future revenues, expenses, and cash flows more difficult. Therefore, management should consider the expected future price levels and their likely effect on the estimates used in capital investment analyses. Fluctuations in the assumed price levels could significantly affect the analyses.

CAPITAL RATIONING

OBJECTIVE 5
Describe and illustrate the capital rationing process.

Capital rationing refers to the process by which management allocates available investment funds among competing capital investment proposals. Generally, management will use various combinations of the evaluation methods described in this chapter in developing an effective approach to capital rationing.

In capital rationing, an initial screening of alternative proposals is usually performed by establishing minimum standards for the cash payback and the average rate of return methods. The proposals that survive this initial screening are subjected to the more rigorous net present value and internal rate of return methods of analysis. The proposals that survive this final screening are evaluated in terms of qualitative factors, such as employee morale. For example, the acquisition of new, more efficient equipment which eliminates several jobs could lower employee morale to a level that could decrease overall plant productivity.

The final step in the capital rationing process is to rank the proposals according to management's criteria, and to compare the proposals with the funds available to determine which proposals will be funded. The unfunded proposals are reconsidered if funds subsequently become available. The flowchart on page 977 portrays the capital rationing decision process.

PLANNING AND CONTROLLING CAPITAL INVESTMENT EXPENDITURES

OBJECTIVE 6
Describe the basic concepts for planning and controlling capital investment expenditures.

Proposals that are funded in the capital rationing process should be included in the budget to facilitate the planning of operations and the financing of capital expenditures. A capital expenditures budget, which is integrated with the master budget as discussed in Chapter 25, summarizes acquisition decisions for a period typically ranging from one to five years. The following capital expenditures budget was prepared for Hovey Company:

Capital Expenditures Budget

Hovey Company
Capital Expenditures Budget
For Five Years Ending December 31, 1996

Item	1992	1993	1994	1995	1996
Machinery—Department A	$240,000	—	—	$168,000	$216,000
Machinery—Department B	108,000	$156,000	$336,000	120,000	—
Delivery equipment	—	54,000	—	—	36,000
Total	$348,000	$210,000	$336,000	$288,000	$252,000

The capital expenditures budget does not authorize the acquisition of plant assets. Rather, it serves as a planning device to determine the effects of the capital expenditures on operations after management has evaluated the alternative proposals, using the methods described in this chapter. Final authority for capital expenditures must come from the proper level of management. In some corporations, large capital expenditures must be approved by the board of directors.

Once the capital expenditures have been approved, control must be established over the costs of acquiring the assets, including the costs of installation and testing before the assets are placed in service. Throughout this period of acquiring the assets and readying them for use, actual costs should be compared to planned (budgeted) costs. Timely reports should be prepared, so that management can take corrective actions as quickly as possible and thereby minimize cost overruns and operating delays.

Capital Rationing Decision Process

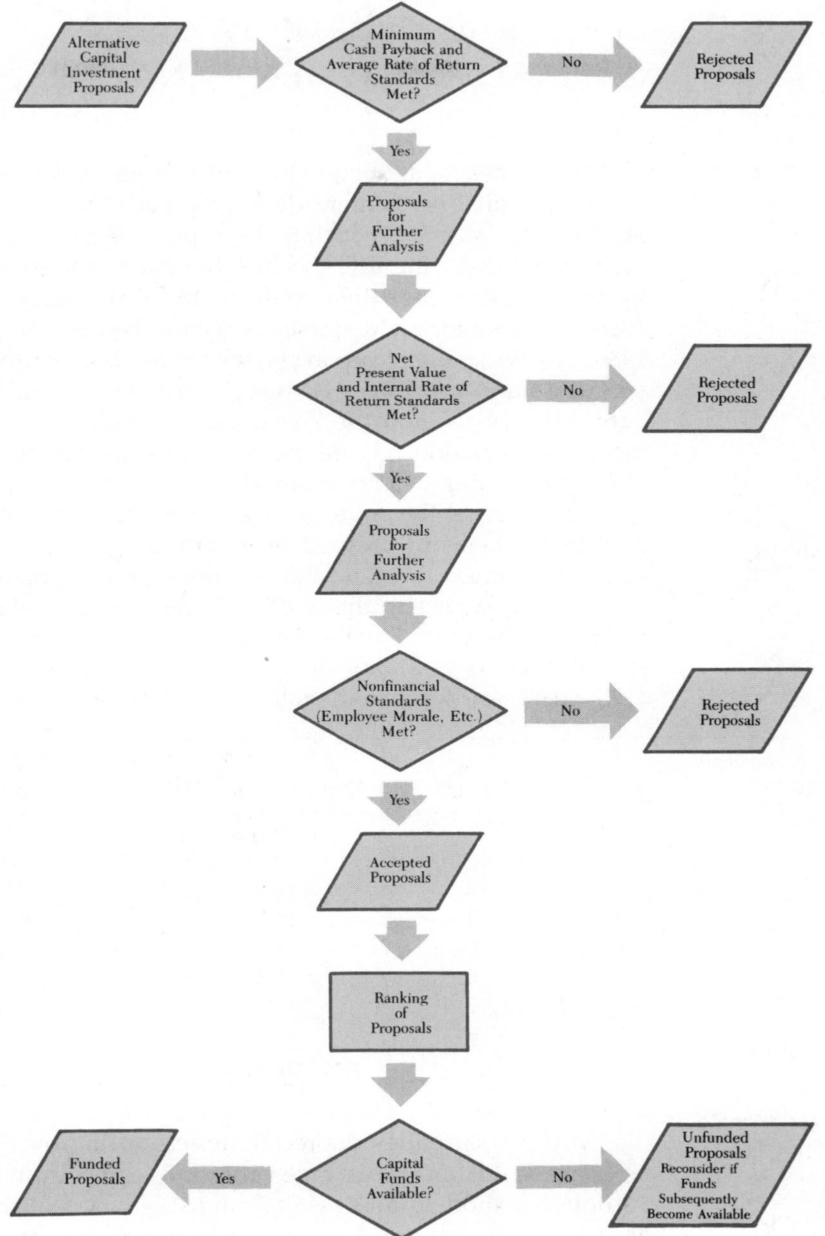

After the assets have been placed in service, attention should be focused on comparisons of actual operating expenses with budgeted operating expenses. Such comparisons provide opportunities for management to follow up on successful expenditures or to terminate or otherwise attempt to salvage failing expenditures.

APPENDIX

IMPACT OF INCOME TAXES ON CAPITAL INVESTMENT ANALYSIS

The allowable deduction for depreciation expense may have a significant effect on capital investment decisions. For determining depreciation, or the *cost recovery deduction*, which is the expensing of the cost of plant assets over their useful lives, the IRC specifies the use of the **Accelerated Cost Recovery System (ACRS). Modified ACRS (MACRS),** under the Tax Reform Act of 1986, provides for eight classes of useful lives for plant assets acquired after 1986. The two most common classes for assets other than real estate are the 5-year class and the 7-year class.[7] The 5-year class includes automobiles and light-duty trucks, and the 7-year class includes most machinery and equipment. Depreciation for these two classes approximates the use of the 200-percent declining-balance method.

The Internal Revenue Service has prescribed methods that result in annual percentages to be used in determining depreciation for each class. In using these rates, salvage value is ignored, and all plant assets are assumed to be placed in service in the middle of the year and taken out of service in the middle of the year. For the 5-year-class assets, for example, depreciation is spread over six years; for the 7-year-class assets, depreciation is spread over eight years, as shown in the following schedule of MACRS depreciation rates:

MACRS Depreciation Rate Schedule

Year	*5-Year-Class Depreciation Rates*	*7-Year-Class Depreciation Rates*
1	20.0%	14.3%
2	32.0	24.5
3	19.2	17.5
4	11.5	12.5
5	11.5	8.9
6	5.8	8.9
7		8.9
8		4.5
	100.0%	100.0%

MACRS simplifies depreciation accounting by eliminating the need to estimate useful life and salvage value and to decide on a depreciation method. Although a short-run tax saving can usually be realized by using the regular MACRS cost recovery allowance, a taxpayer may elect to use a straight-line deduction based on the property classes prescribed under MACRS. The accelerated write-off of depreciable assets provided by MACRS does not, however, effect a long-run net saving in income tax. The tax reduction of the early years of use is offset by higher taxes as the annual cost recovery allowance diminishes.

---

[7] Real estate is classified into 27½-year classes and 31½-year classes and is depreciated by the straight-line method.

To illustrate the potential impact of MACRS depreciation on capital investment decisions, assume that Sierra Company is using the net present value method in evaluating a proposal.[8] The cost of the investment acquired in year 1 is $300,000, with an expected useful life of 5 years, no residual value, and a minimum desired rate of return of 12%. If Sierra Company elects the straight-line method of depreciation, the IRC requires one half of a full year's depreciation to be taken in the first year and one half of a full year's depreciation to be taken in the sixth year. Thus, Sierra Company would deduct the following depreciation amounts during the 5-year life of the asset:

	Depreciation Expense
First year	$30,000 [($300,000 ÷ 5) × 1/2]
Second year	$60,000 ($300,000 ÷ 5)
Third year	$60,000 ($300,000 ÷ 5)
Fourth year	$60,000 ($300,000 ÷ 5)
Fifth year	$60,000 ($300,000 ÷ 5)
Sixth year	$30,000 [($300,000 ÷ 5) × 1/2]

During the six years in which depreciation expense is deducted, the investment is expected to yield annual operating income, before depreciation and income taxes, of $120,000, $100,000, $90,000, $70,000, $60,000, and $30,000, respectively. To simplify the illustration, all revenues and operating expenses except depreciation represent current period cash flows. If the income tax rate is 34%, the annual net aftertax cash flows from acquisition of the asset are as follows:

	Year					
	1	*2*	*3*	*4*	*5*	*6*
Net cash flow before income taxes	$120,000	$100,000	$90,000	$70,000	$60,000	$30,000
Income tax expense*	30,600	13,600	10,200	3,400	0	0
Net cash flow	$ 89,400	$ 86,400	$79,800	$66,600	$60,000	$30,000
*Income tax expense:						
Operating income before depreciation and income taxes	$120,000	$100,000	$90,000	$70,000	$60,000	$30,000
Depreciation expense	30,000	60,000	60,000	60,000	60,000	30,000
Income before income taxes	$ 90,000	$ 40,000	$30,000	$10,000	$ 0	$ 0
Income tax rate	34%	34%	34%	34%	0	0
Income tax expense	$ 30,600	$ 13,600	$10,200	$ 3,400	$ 0	$ 0

Based on the preceding data and using the net present value method, a **$2,899** deficiency of the net present value is computed as follows:

[8] The same general impact of depreciation on capital investment decisions would occur, regardless of which of the four capital investment evaluation methods was used. To simplify the discussion in this chapter, only the net present value method is illustrated.

Year	Present Value of 1 at 12%	Net Cash Flow	Present Value of Net Cash Flow
1	.893	$ 89,400	$ 79,834
2	.797	86,400	68,861
3	.712	79,800	56,818
4	.636	66,600	42,358
5	.567	60,000	34,020
6	.507	30,000	15,210
Total		$412,200	$297,101
Amount to be invested			300,000
Net present value			$ (2,899)

Because the net present value method indicates a deficiency, the decision would be to reject the proposal. However, if the accelerated depreciation provided by the IRC is used, the present value of the acquisition changes significantly and might lead to a different decision. To illustrate, assume that Sierra Company is permitted to deduct depreciation over a 5-year period, beginning with the year the asset is acquired. Using the MACRS percentages shown on page 978, the depreciation for Sierra Company will be as follows:

	Depreciation Expense
First year	$60,000 ($300,000 × 20.0%)
Second year	$96,000 ($300,000 × 32.0%)
Third year	$57,600 ($300,000 × 19.2%)
Fourth year	$34,500 ($300,000 × 11.5%)
Fifth year	$34,500 ($300,000 × 11.5%)
Sixth year	$17,400 ($300,000 × 5.8%)

The annual aftertax net cash flows from the acquisition of the plant asset, including the effect of MACRS depreciation, are as follows:

	Year					
	1	2	3	4	5	6
Net cash flow before income taxes	$120,000	$100,000	$90,000	$70,000	$60,000	$30,000
Income tax expense*	20,400	1,360	11,016	12,070	8,670	4,284
Net cash flow	$ 99,600	$ 98,640	$78,984	$57,930	$51,330	$25,716
*Income tax expense:						
Operating income before depreciation and income taxes	$120,000	$100,000	$90,000	$70,000	$60,000	$30,000
Depreciation expense	60,000	96,000	57,600	34,500	34,500	17,400
Income before income taxes	$ 60,000	$ 4,000	$32,400	$35,500	$25,500	$12,600
Income tax rate	34%	34%	34%	34%	34%	34%
Income tax expense	$ 20,400	$ 1,360	$11,016	$12,070	$ 8,670	$ 4,284

Based on the preceding data and using the net present value method, a **$2,781** net present value is computed as follows:

Year	Present Value of 1 at 12%	Net Cash Flow	Present Value of Net Cash Flow
1	.893	$ 99,600	$ 88,943
2	.797	98,640	78,616
3	.712	78,984	56,237
4	.636	57,930	36,843
5	.567	51,330	29,104
6	.507	25,716	13,038
Total		$412,200	$302,781
Amount to be invested			300,000
Net present value			$ 2,781

The specific dollar effects of tax considerations on the evaluation of capital investment proposals will depend on the deductions and credits allowed by the Internal Revenue Code at the time the capital investment decision is to be made. In this illustration, the net present value method indicates a positive net present value and the decision would be to invest in the asset.

CHAPTER REVIEW

KEY POINTS

OBJECTIVE 1

Nature of Capital Investment Analysis

The process by which management plans, evaluates, and controls investments involving property, plant, and equipment is called capital investment analysis. A capital investment program should include a plan for encouraging employees at all levels of an enterprise to submit proposals for capital investments. All reasonable proposals should be given serious consideration, and the effects of the economic implications expected from these proposals should be identified.

OBJECTIVE 2

Methods of Evaluating Capital Investment Proposals

The methods of evaluating capital investment proposals can be grouped into two general categories: (1) methods that ignore present value and (2) present value methods. The methods that ignore present value include (1) the average rate of return method and (2) the cash payback method. Methods that use present values in evaluating capital investment proposals are (1) the net present value method and (2) the internal rate of return method.

The expected average rate of return is a measure of the expected profitability of an investment in plant assets. When several alternative capital investment proposals are being considered, the proposals can be ranked by their average rates of return. The higher the average rate of return, the more desirable the proposal. The primary advantage of the average rate of return method is its simplicity, and its primary disadvantage is its lack of consideration of expected cash flows from a proposal and the timing of those cash flows.

The cash payback method measures the cash payback period, which is the expected period of time that will pass between the date of a capital investment and the complete recovery in cash (or equivalent) of the amount invested. The cash payback method is especially useful to managers whose primary concern is liquidity. The primary disadvantage of the cash payback method is its failure to take into consideration the expected profitability of a proposal. Another disadvantage of the cash payback method is that the cash flows occurring after the payback period are ignored.

The net present value method uses present value concepts to compute the present value of the cash flows expected from a proposal. When several alternative investment proposals of the same amount are being considered, the one with the largest net present value is the most desirable. If the alternative proposals involve different amounts of investment, it is useful to prepare a ranking of the proposals by using a present value index. The primary advantage of the net present value method is that it gives consideration to the time value of money. A disadvantage of the method is that the computations are more complex than those for the methods that ignore present value. In addition, it assumes that the cash received from the proposal during its useful life will be reinvested at the rate of return used to compute the present value of the proposal.

The internal rate of return method uses present value concepts to compute the rate of return from the net cash flows expected from capital investment proposals. When several proposals are under consideration, management often ranks proposals by their internal rates of return, and the proposal with the highest rate is considered the most attractive. The primary advantage of the internal rate of return method is that the present values of the net cash flows over the entire useful life of the proposal are considered. The primary disadvantage of the internal rate of return method is that the computations are somewhat more complex than for some of the other methods. In addition, like the net present value method, this method assumes that the cash received from a proposal during its useful life will be reinvested at the internal rate of return.

OBJECTIVE 3

Qualitative Considerations in Capital Investment Analysis

Some benefits of capital investment analysis cannot be readily estimated in dollar terms. Such qualitative considerations include product quality, manufacturing flexibility, employee morale, and manufacturing productivity and control.

OBJECTIVE 4

Factors that Complicate Capital Investment Analysis

Factors that may complicate capital investment analysis include the impact of the federal income tax, unequal lives of alternative proposals, the leasing alternative, uncertainty, and changes in price levels.

OBJECTIVE 5

Capital Rationing

Capital rationing refers to the process by which management allocates available investment funds among competing capital investment proposals. In capital rationing, an initial screening of alternative proposals is usually performed by establishing minimum standards for the cash payback and the average rate of return methods. The final step in the capital rationing process is to rank the proposals and to compare the proposals with the funds available to determine which proposals will be funded.

OBJECTIVE 6

Planning and Controlling Capital Investment Expenditures

Proposals that are funded in the capital rationing process should be included in the master budget. Throughout the period of acquiring plant assets and readying them for use, actual costs should be compared to planned costs, and timely reports should be prepared so that management can minimize cost overruns and operating delays.

KEY TERMS

capital investment analysis 962
average rate of return 963
cash payback period 965
present value 966
net present value method 966
present value index 967
internal rate of return method 968
annuity 969
present value of an annuity 969
inflation 975
capital rationing 975

SELF-EXAMINATION QUESTIONS

Answers at end of chapter.

1. Methods of evaluating capital investment proposals that ignore present value include:
   A. average rate of return
   B. cash payback
   C. both A and B
   D. neither A nor B

2. Management is considering a $100,000 investment in a project with a 5-year life and no residual value. If the total income from the project is expected to be $60,000 and recognition is given to the effect of straight-line depreciation on the investment, the average rate of return is:
   A. 12%
   B. 24%
   C. 60%
   D. none of the above

3. As used in the analysis of proposed capital investments, the expected period of time that will elapse between the date of a capital investment and the complete recovery of the amount of cash invested is called:
   A. the average rate of return period
   B. the cash payback period
   C. the net present value period
   D. none of the above

4. Which method of analyzing capital investment proposals determines the total present value of the cash flows expected from the investment and compares this value with the amount to be invested?
   A. Average rate of return
   B. Cash payback
   C. Net present value
   D. Internal rate of return

5. The process by which management allocates available investment funds among competing capital investment proposals is referred to as:
   A. capital rationing
   B. capital expenditure budgeting
   C. leasing
   D. none of the above

ILLUSTRATIVE PROBLEM

The capital investment committee of Bormann Company is currently considering two projects. The estimated operating income and net cash flows expected from each project are as follows:

	Project A		Project B	
Year	Operating Income	Net Cash Flow	Operating Income	Net Cash Flow
1	$ 9,000	$19,000	$ 5,000	$15,000
2	7,000	17,000	6,000	16,000
3	6,000	16,000	8,000	18,000
4	5,000	15,000	7,000	17,000
5	3,000	13,000	4,000	14,000
	$30,000	$80,000	$30,000	$80,000

Each project requires an investment of $50,000. Straight-line depreciation will be used, and no residual value is expected. The committee has selected a rate of 15% for purposes of the net present value analysis.

Instructions:

1. Compute the following:
   a. The average rate of return for each project, giving effect to depreciation on the investment.
   b. The net present value for each project. Use the present value of $1 table appearing in this chapter.
2. Prepare a brief report for the capital investment committee, advising it on the relative merits of the two projects.

SOLUTION

(1) (a) Average annual rate of return for both projects:

$$\frac{\$30,000 \div 5}{(\$50,000 + \$0) \div 2} = 24\%$$

(b) Net present value analysis:

Year	Present Value of $1 at 15%	Net Cash Flow Project A	Net Cash Flow Project B	Present Value of Net Cash Flow Project A	Present Value of Net Cash Flow Project B
1	.870	$19,000	$15,000	$16,530	$13,050
2	.756	17,000	16,000	12,852	12,096
3	.658	16,000	18,000	10,528	11,844
4	.572	15,000	17,000	8,580	9,724
5	.497	13,000	14,000	6,461	6,958
Total		$80,000	$80,000	$54,951	$53,672
Amount to be invested				50,000	50,000
Net present value				$ 4,951	$ 3,672

(2) (a) Both projects offer the same average annual rate of return.
(b) Although both projects exceed the selected rate established for the net present value analysis, Project A offers a larger net present value. Thus, if only one of the two projects can be accepted, Project A would be the more attractive.

DISCUSSION QUESTIONS

23–1. Which two methods of capital investment analysis ignore present value?

23–2. Which two methods of capital investment analysis can be described as present value methods?

23–3. What is the time value of money concept?

23–4. (a) How is the average rate of return computed for capital investment analysis, assuming that consideration is given to the effect of straight-line depreciation on the amount of the investment? (b) If the amount of a 10-year investment is $900,000, the straight-line method of depreciation is used, there is no residual value, and the total income expected from the investment is $810,000, what is the average rate of return?

23–5. What are the principal objections to the use of the average rate of return method in evaluating capital investment proposals?

23–6. (a) As used in analyses of proposed capital investments, what is the cash payback period? (b) Discuss the principal limitations of the cash payback method for evaluating capital investment proposals.

23–7. What is the present value of $8,625 to be received one year from today, assuming an earnings rate of 15%.

23–8. Which method of evaluating capital investment proposals reduces their expected future net cash flows to present values and compares the total present values to the amount of the investment?

23–9. A net present value analysis used to evaluate a proposed equipment acquisition indicated a $12,600 net present value. What is the meaning of the $12,600 as it relates to the desirability of the proposal?

23–10. How is the present value index for a proposal determined?

23–11. What are the major disadvantages of the use of the net present value method of analyzing capital investment proposals?

23–12. What is an annuity?

23–13. What are the major disadvantages of the use of internal rate of return method of analyzing capital investment proposals?

23–14. Give an example of a qualitative factor that should be considered in a capital investment analysis related to the acquisition of automated factory equipment.

23–15. What provision of the Internal Revenue Code is especially important for consideration in analyzing capital investment proposals?

23–16. What method can be used to place two capital investment proposals with unequal useful lives on a comparable basis?

23–17. What are the major advantages of leasing a plant asset rather than purchasing it?

23–18. What is capital rationing?

23–19. Which budget summarizes the acquisition decisions for a period?

Real World Focus

23–20. Boston Metal Products, a small manufacturer in Medford, Mass., was considering the purchase of a robot. The company controller was asked to calculate whether the $200,000 investment made financial sense. Using traditional accounting techniques, the controller concluded that the investment did not meet the financial criteria that had been established. However, the company went ahead and made the investment. What qualitative considerations could Boston Metal Products have used to justify the capital investment in a robot?

Ethics Discussion Case

23–21. Richard Kasner, the controller of Mandelstam Inc., has recently prepared Mandelstam's federal income tax return for the preceding year. In determining depreciation for federal income tax purposes, Kasner used shorter useful lives for several assets than the estimated useful lives used in preparing the company's income statement. In addition, Kasner deducted as expenses several expenditures which were related to depreciable assets acquired during the year. Kasner believes it is highly unlikely that the company's tax return will be audited by the Internal Revenue Service. Discuss whether Kasner behaved in an ethical manner.

EXERCISES

Ex. 23–22.
Average rate of return.
OBJ. 2

The following data are accumulated by Sumner Company in evaluating two competing capital investment proposals:

	Proposal C	Proposal L
Amount of investment	$500,000	$860,000
Useful life	7 years	10 years
Estimated residual value	-0-	-0-
Estimated total income	$332,500	$731,000

Determine the expected average rate of return for each proposal, giving effect to straight-line depreciation on each investment.

Ex. 23–23.
Cash payback period.
OBJ. 2

Noakes Company is evaluating two capital investment proposals, each requiring an investment of $320,000 and each with a 9-year life and expected total net cash flows of $720,000. Proposal 1 is expected to provide equal annual net cash flows of $80,000, and Proposal 2 is expected to have the following unequal annual net cash flows:

Year 1	$145,000
Year 2	90,000
Year 3	85,000
Year 4	85,000
Year 5	75,000
Year 6	70,000
Year 7	60,000
Year 8	55,000
Year 9	55,000

Determine the cash payback period for both proposals.

Ex. 23–24.
Net present value method.
OBJ. 2

The following data are accumulated by Gresham Company in evaluating the purchase of $240,000 of equipment having a 4-year useful life:

	Net Income	Net Cash Flow
Year 1	$40,000	$100,000
Year 2	20,000	80,000
Year 3	6,000	66,000
Year 4	4,000	64,000

(a) Assuming that the desired rate of return is 10%, determine the net present value for the proposal. Use the table of the present value of $1 appearing in this chapter. (b) Would management be likely to look with favor on the proposal? Explain.

Ex. 23–25.
Present value index.
OBJ. 2

Tasker Company has computed the net present value for capital expenditure proposals H and J, using the net present value method. Relevant data related to the computation are as follows:

	Proposal H	Proposal J
Total present value of net cash flow	$189,000	$296,800
Amount to be invested	175,000	280,000
Net present value	$ 14,000	$ 16,800

Determine the present value index for each proposal.

Ex. 23–26.
Average rate of return, cash payback period, net present value method.
OBJ. 2

Freer Company is considering the acquisition of machinery at a cost of $750,000. The machinery has an estimated life of 5 years and no residual value. It is expected to provide yearly income of $37,500 and yearly net cash flows of $187,500. The company's minimum desired rate of return for net present value analysis is 6%. Compute the following:

(a) The average rate of return, giving effect to straight-line depreciation on the investment.
(b) The cash payback period.
(c) The net present value. Use the table of the present value of $1 appearing in this chapter.

Ex. 23–27.
Internal rate of return method.
OBJ. 2

The internal rate of return method is used by Kang Company in analyzing a capital expenditure proposal that involves an investment of $288,400 and annual net cash flows of $80,000 for each of the 7 years of useful life. (a) Determine a present value factor for an annuity of $1 which can be used in determining the internal rate of return. (b) Using the factor determined in (a) and the present value of an annuity of $1 table appearing in this chapter, determine the internal rate of return for the proposal.

Ex. 23–28.
Net present value method and internal rate of return method.
OBJ. 2

Mulvey Inc. is evaluating a proposed expenditure of $158,500 on a 4-year project whose estimated net cash flows are $50,000 for each of the four years.

(a) Compute the net present value using a rate of return of 12%. (b) Based on the analysis prepared in (a), is the rate of return (1) more than 12%, (2) 12%, or (3) less than 12%? Explain. (c) Determine the internal rate of return by computing a present value factor for an annuity of $1 and using the table of the present value of an annuity of $1 presented in the text.

PROBLEMS

Pb. 23–29.
Average rate of return method, net present value method, and analysis.
OBJ. 2

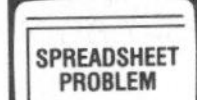

The capital investment budget committee is considering two projects. The estimated operating income and net cash flows from each project are as follows:

	Project S		Project W	
Year	Operating Income	Net Cash Flow	Operating Income	Net Cash Flow
1	$ 50,000	$130,000	$ 40,000	$120,000
2	45,000	125,000	40,000	120,000
3	35,000	115,000	35,000	115,000
4	25,000	105,000	35,000	115,000
5	25,000	105,000	30,000	110,000
Total	$180,000	$580,000	$180,000	$580,000

Each project requires an investment of $400,000. Straight-line depreciation will be used, and no residual value is expected. The committee has selected a rate of 10% for purposes of the net present value analysis.

Instructions:

(1) Compute the following:
  (a) The average rate of return for each project, giving effect to depreciation on the investment.
  (b) The net present value for each project. Use the present value of $1 table appearing in this chapter.
(2) Prepare a brief report for the capital investment committee, advising it on the relative merits of the two projects.

Pb. 23–30.
Cash payback period, net present value method, and analysis.
OBJ. 2

Hemrick Company is considering two projects. The estimated net cash flows from each project are as follows:

Year	Project M	Project N
1	$150,000	$125,000
2	100,000	125,000
3	40,000	70,000
4	40,000	15,000
5	20,000	15,000
Total	$350,000	$350,000

Each project requires an investment of $250,000, with no residual value expected. A rate of 10% has been selected for the net present value analysis.

Instructions:

(1) Compute the following for each project:
  (a) Cash payback period.
  (b) The net present value. Use the present value of $1 table appearing in this chapter.
(2) Prepare a brief report advising management on the relative merits of each of the two projects.

Pb. 23–31.
Net present value method, present value index, and analysis.
OBJ. 2

Joiner Company wishes to evaluate three capital investment projects by using the net present value method. Relevant data related to the projects are summarized as follows:

	Project J	Project K	Project L
Amount to be invested	$500,000	$400,000	$200,000
Annual net cash flows:			
Year 1	320,000	250,000	100,000
Year 2	220,000	200,000	80,000
Year 3	100,000	70,000	40,000

Instructions:

(1) Assuming that the desired rate of return is 10%, prepare a net present value analysis for each project. Use the present value of $1 table appearing in this chapter.
(2) Determine a present value index for each project.
(3) Which project offers the largest amount of present value per dollar of investment? Explain.

Pb. 23–32.
Net present value method, internal rate of return method, and analysis.
OBJ. 2

Management is considering two capital investment projects. The estimated net cash flows from each project are as follows:

Year	Project D	Project E
1	$180,000	$50,000
2	180,000	50,000
3	180,000	50,000
4	180,000	50,000

Project D requires an investment of $513,900, while Project E requires an investment of $129,450.

Instructions:

(1) Compute the following for each project:
  (a) The net present value. Use a rate of 12% and the present value of $1 table appearing in this chapter.
  (b) A present value index.

(2) Determine the internal rate of return for each project by (a) computing a present value factor for an annuity of $1 and (b) using the present value of an annuity of $1 table appearing in this chapter.
(3) What advantage does the internal rate of return method have over the net present value method in comparing projects?

Pb. 23–33.
Evaluation of alternative capital investment decisions.
OBJ. 2,4

The investment committee of Conrad Inc. is evaluating two projects. The projects have different useful lives, but each requires an investment of $165,000. The estimated net cash flows from each project are as follows:

	Net Cash Flows	
Year	Project I	Project II
1	$45,000	$60,000
2	45,000	60,000
3	45,000	60,000
4	45,000	60,000
5	45,000	
6	45,000	

The committee has selected a rate of 15% for purposes of net present value analysis. It also estimates that the residual value at the end of each project's useful life is $0, but at the end of the fourth year, Project I's residual value would be $80,000.

Instructions:

(1) For each project, compute the net present value. Use the present value of $1 table appearing in this chapter. (Ignore the unequal lives of the projects.)
(2) For each project, compute the net present value, assuming that Project I is adjusted to a four-year life for purposes of analysis. Use the present value of $1 table appearing in this chapter.
(3) In reporting to the investment committee, what advice would you give on the relative merits of the two projects?

Pb. 23–34.
Capital rationing decision involving six proposals.
OBJ. 2,5

Shaut Inc. is considering the allocation of a limited amount of capital investment funds among six proposals. The amount of proposed investment, estimated operating income, and net cash flow for each proposal are as follows:

	Investment	Year	Operating Income	Net Cash Flow
Proposal A:	$100,000	1	$20,000	$40,000
		2	10,000	30,000
		3	10,000	30,000
		4	5,000	25,000
		5	5,000	25,000

	Investment	Year	Operating Income	Net Cash Flow
Proposal B:	$500,000	1	$40,000	$140,000
		2	25,000	125,000
		3	20,000	120,000
		4	15,000	115,000
		5	12,500	112,500

	Investment	Year	Operating Income	Net Cash Flow
Proposal C:	$200,000	1	$50,000	$90,000
		2	20,000	60,000
		3	10,000	50,000
		4	5,000	45,000
		5	5,000	45,000

	Investment	Year	Operating Income	Net Cash Flow
Proposal D:	$75,000	1	$3,750	$18,750
		2	3,750	18,750
		3	3,750	18,750
		4	3,750	18,750
		5	3,750	18,750

	Investment	Year	Operating Income	Net Cash Flow
Proposal E:	$50,000	1	$20,000	$30,000
		2	10,000	20,000
		3	4,000	14,000
		4	2,500	12,500
		5	1,000	11,000

	Investment	Year	Operating Income	Net Cash Flow
Proposal F:	$300,000	1	$12,000	$72,000
		2	12,000	72,000
		3	12,000	72,000
		4	12,000	72,000
		5	12,000	72,000

Shaut Inc.'s capital rationing policy requires a minimum cash payback period of 4 years for projects of $100,000 and over, and a minimum cash payback period of 3 years for projects under $100,000. In addition, a minimum average rate of return of 10% is required on all projects. If the preceding minimum standards are met, the net present value method and present value indexes are used to rank the remaining proposals.

Instructions:

(1) Compute the cash payback period for each of the six proposals.
(2) Giving effect to straight-line depreciation on the investments and assuming no estimated residual value, compute the average rate of return for each of the six proposals.
(3) Using the following format, summarize the results of your computations in (1) and (2). By placing a check mark in the appropriate column at the right, indicate which proposals should be accepted for further analysis and which should be rejected.

Proposal	Cash Payback Period	Average Rate of Return	Accept for Further Analysis	Reject
A				
B				
C				
D				
E				
F				

(4) For the proposals accepted for further analysis in (3), compute the net present value. Use a rate of 10% and the present value of $1 table appearing in this chapter.
(5) Compute the present value index for each of the proposals in (4).
(6) Rank the proposals from most attractive to least attractive, based on the present values of net cash flows computed in (4).
(7) Rank the proposals from most attractive to least attractive, based on the present value indexes computed in (5).
(8) Based upon the analyses, comment on the relative attractiveness of the proposals ranked in (6) and (7).

Appendix
Pb. 23–35.
Net present value method and income taxes.

Using the net present value method, the accountant for Farrell Inc. prepared the following analysis of a project expected to be undertaken at the beginning of Year 1:

Year	Present Value of 1 at 10%	Net Cash Flow	Present Value of Net Cash Flow
1	.909	$149,000	$135,441
2	.826	139,600	115,310
3	.751	113,200	85,013
4	.683	100,000	68,300
5	.621	100,000	62,100
6	.564	50,000	28,200
Total		$651,800	$494,364
Amount to be invested			500,000
Net present value			$ (5,636)

A review of the analysis and related items disclosed the following:

(a) The straight-line method was used for computing depreciation, with one half of a year's depreciation taken in the first year and the sixth year.
(b) Operating income (and net cash flow) before depreciation and taxes is expected to be $200,000, $160,000, $120,000, $100,000, $100,000, and $50,000 for the first through sixth years, respectively.
(c) The income tax rate is 34%.

Instructions:

(1) Assuming the use of the straight-line depreciation method with a 5-year life and no residual value, compute the following:
   (a) Amount of depreciation expense for each of the six years covered by the project.
   (b) Income tax expense for each of the six years covered by the project.
   (c) Net cash flow for each of the six years covered by the project. (Note: The net cash flows calculated should agree with those included in the analysis presented in the first paragraph of this problem.)

(2) Compute the following:
   (a) Depreciation expense for each of the six years covered by the project, assuming that the 5-year-class MACRS depreciation rates appearing in this chapter are used.
   (b) Income tax expense for each of the six years, based on the use of MACRS depreciation.
   (c) Net cash flow for each of the six years covered by the project, based on the income tax expense computed in (b).

(Continued)

(d) The net present value, based on the net cash flows determined in (c). Use the present value of $1 table appearing in this chapter and round computations to the nearest dollar.

(3) Should the project be accepted? Explain.

ALTERNATE PROBLEMS

Pb. 23–29A.
Average rate of return method, net present value method, and analysis.
OBJ. 2

The capital investments budget committee is considering two projects. The estimated operating income and net cash flows from each project are as follows:

	Project F		Project K	
Year	Operating Income	Net Cash Flow	Operating Income	Net Cash Flow
1	$ 75,000	$195,000	$ 80,000	$200,000
2	70,000	190,000	60,000	180,000
3	60,000	180,000	60,000	180,000
4	40,000	160,000	60,000	180,000
5	40,000	160,000	25,000	145,000
Total	$285,000	$885,000	$285,000	$885,000

Each project requires an investment of $600,000. Straight-line depreciation will be used, and no residual value is expected. The committee has selected a rate of 15% for purposes of the net present value analysis.

Instructions:

(1) Compute the following:
   (a) The average rate of return for each project, giving effect to depreciation on the investment.
   (b) The net present value for each project. Use the present value of $1 table appearing in this chapter.
(2) Prepare a brief report for the capital investment committee, advising it on the relative merits of the two projects.

Pb. 23–30A.
Cash payback period, net present value method, and analysis.
OBJ. 2

Woburn Company is considering two projects. The estimated net cash flows from each project are as follows:

Year	Project G	Project R
1	$200,000	$190,000
2	175,000	185,000
3	50,000	90,000
4	50,000	30,000
5	50,000	30,000
Total	$525,000	$525,000

Each project requires an investment of $375,000, with no residual value expected. A rate of 15% has been selected for the net present value analysis.

Instructions:

(1) Compute the following for each project:
   (a) Cash payback period.
   (b) The net present value. Use the present value of $1 table appearing in this chapter.
(2) Prepare a brief report advising management on the relative merits of each of the two projects.

Pb. 23–31A.
Net present value method, present value index and analysis.
OBJ. 2

Zarzeski Company wishes to evaluate three capital investment proposals by using the net present value method. Relevant data related to the proposals are summarized as follows:

	Proposal T	Proposal U	Proposal V
Amount to be invested	$750,000	$600,000	$800,000
Annual net cash flows:			
Year 1	400,000	350,000	475,000
Year 2	380,000	320,000	340,000
Year 3	100,000	110,000	220,000

Instructions:

(1) Assuming that the desired rate of return is 12%, prepare a net present value analysis for each proposal. Use the present value of $1 table appearing in this chapter.
(2) Determine a present value index for each proposal.
(3) Which proposal offers the largest amount of present value per dollar of investment? Explain.

Pb. 23–32A.
Net present value method, internal rate of return method, and analysis.
OBJ. 2

Management is considering two capital investment proposals. The estimated net cash flows from each proposal are as follows:

Year	Proposal I	Proposal J
1	$40,000	$120,000
2	40,000	120,000
3	40,000	120,000
4	40,000	120,000

Proposal I requires an investment of $121,480, while Proposal J requires an investment of $380,400.

Instructions:

(1) Compute the following for each proposal:
  (a) The net present value. Use a rate of 6% and the present value of $1 table appearing in this chapter.
  (b) A present value index.
(2) Determine the internal rate of return for each project by (a) computing a present value factor for an annuity of $1 and (b) using the present value of an annuity of $1 table appearing in this chapter.
(3) What advantage does the internal rate of return method have over the net present value method in comparing projects?

Pb. 23–33A.
Evaluation of alternative capital investment decisions.
OBJ. 2,4

The investment committee of Marion Company is evaluating two projects. The projects have different useful lives, but each requires an investment of $150,000. The estimated net cash flows from each project are as follows:

	Net Cash Flows	
Year	Project A	Project B
1	$40,000	$55,000
2	40,000	55,000
3	40,000	55,000
4	40,000	55,000
5	40,000	
6	40,000	

The committee has selected a rate of 15% for purposes of net present value analysis. It also estimates that the residual value at the end of each project's useful life is $0, but at the end of the fourth year, Project A's residual value would be $80,000.

Instructions:

(1) For each project, compute the net present value. Use the present value of $1 table appearing in this chapter. (Ignore the unequal lives of the projects.)
(2) For each project, compute the net present value, assuming that Project A is adjusted to a four-year life for purposes of analysis. Use the present value of $1 table appearing in this chapter.
(3) In reporting to the investment committee, what advice would you give on the relative merits of the two projects?

Pb. 23–34A.
Capital rationing decision involving six proposals.
OBJ. 2,5

Matthews Company is considering the allocation of a limited amount of capital investment funds among six proposals. The amount of proposed investment, estimated operating income, and net cash flow for each proposal are as follows:

	Investment	Year	Operating Income	Net Cash Flow
Proposal A:	$100,000	1	$20,000	$40,000
		2	10,000	30,000
		3	10,000	30,000
		4	5,000	25,000
		5	5,000	25,000

	Investment	Year	Operating Income	Net Cash Flow
Proposal B:	$300,000	1	$25,000	$85,000
		2	15,000	75,000
		3	10,000	70,000
		4	10,000	70,000
		5	5,000	65,000

	Investment	Year	Operating Income	Net Cash Flow
Proposal C:	$200,000	1	$50,000	$90,000
		2	20,000	60,000
		3	10,000	50,000
		4	5,000	45,000
		5	5,000	45,000

	Investment	Year	Operating Income	Net Cash Flow
Proposal D:	$50,000	1	$2,500	$12,500
		2	2,500	12,500
		3	2,500	12,500
		4	2,500	12,500
		5	2,500	12,500

	Investment	Year	Operating Income	Net Cash Flow
Proposal E:	$50,000	1	$20,000	$30,000
		2	10,000	20,000
		3	4,000	14,000
		4	2,500	12,500
		5	1,000	11,000

	Investment	Year	Operating Income	Net Cash Flow
Proposal F:	$500,000	1	$40,000	$140,000
		2	25,000	125,000
		3	17,500	117,500
		4	17,500	117,500
		5	12,500	112,500

Matthews Company's capital rationing policy requires a minimum cash payback period of 4 years for projects of $100,000 and over, and a minimum cash payback period of 3 years for projects under $100,000. In addition, a minimum average rate of return of 10% is required on all projects. If the preceding minimum standards are met, the net present value method and present value indexes are used to rank the remaining proposals.

Instructions:

(1) Compute the cash payback period for each of the six proposals.
(2) Giving effect to straight-line depreciation on the investments and assuming no estimated residual value, compute the average rate of return for each of the six proposals.
(3) Using the following format, summarize the results of your computations in (1) and (2). By placing a check mark in the appropriate column at the right, indicate which proposals should be accepted for further analysis and which should be rejected.

Proposal	Cash Payback Period	Average Rate of Return	Accept for Further Analysis	Reject
A				
B				
C				
D				
E				
F				

(4) For the proposals accepted for further analysis in (3), compute the net present value. Use a rate of 10% and the present value of $1 table appearing in this chapter.
(5) Compute the present value index for each of the proposals in (4).
(6) Rank the proposals from most attractive to least attractive, based on the present values of net cash flows computed in (4).
(7) Rank the proposals from most attractive to least attractive, based on the present value indexes computed in (5).
(8) Based upon the analyses, comment on the relative attractiveness of the proposals ranked in (6) and (7).

Appendix
Pb. 23–35A.
Net present value method and income taxes.

Using the net present value method, the accountant for Martin Inc. prepared the following analysis of a project expected to be undertaken at the beginning of Year 1:

Year	Present Value of 1 at 12%	Net Cash Flow	Present Value of Net Cash Flow
1	.893	$175,400	$156,672
2	.797	139,600	111,261
3	.712	113,200	80,598
4	.636	100,000	63,600
5	.567	100,000	56,700
6	.507	50,000	25,350
Total		$678,200	$494,141
Amount to be invested			500,000
Net present value			$ (5,859)

A review of the analysis and related items disclosed the following:

(a) The straight-line method was used for computing depreciation, with one half of a year's depreciation taken in the first year and the sixth year.
(b) Operating income (and net cash flow) before depreciation and taxes is expected to be $240,000, $160,000, $120,000, $100,000, $100,000, and $50,000 for the first through sixth years, respectively.
(c) The income tax rate is 34%.

Instructions:

(1) Assuming the use of the straight-line depreciation method with a 5-year life and no residual value, compute the following:
 (a) Amount of depreciation expense for each of the six years covered by the project.
 (b) Income tax expense for each of the six years covered by the project.
 (c) Net cash flow for each of the six years covered by the project. (Note: The net cash flows calculated should agree with those included in the analysis presented in the first paragraph of this problem.)
(2) Compute the following:
 (a) Depreciation expense for each of the six years covered by the project, assuming that the 5-year-class MACRS depreciation rates appearing in this chapter are used.
 (b) Income tax expense for each of the six years, based on the use of MACRS depreciation.
 (c) Net cash flow for each of the six years covered by the project, based on the income tax expense computed in (b).
 (d) The net present value, based on the net cash flows determined in (c). Use the present value of $1 table appearing in this chapter and round computations to the nearest dollar.
(3) Should the project be accepted? Explain.

MINI-CASE 23

Your father is considering an investment of $500,000 in either Project B or Project F. In discussing the two projects with an advisor, it was decided that, for the risk involved, a return of 10% on the cash investment would be required. For this purpose, your father estimated the following economic factors for the projects:

	Project B	Project F
Useful life	4 years	4 years
Residual value	-0-	-0-
Net income:		
Year 1	$ 85,000	$ 30,000
2	55,000	30,000
3	25,000	70,000
4	15,000	60,000

Net cash flows:		
Year 1	$210,000	$155,000
2	180,000	155,000
3	150,000	195,000
4	140,000	185,000

Although the average rate of return exceeded 10% on both projects, your father has tentatively decided to invest in Project F because the rate was higher for Project F. Although he doesn't fully understand the importance of cash flow, he has heard others talk about its importance in evaluating investments. In this respect, he noted that the total net cash flow from Project F is $690,000, which exceeds that of Project B by $10,000.

Instructions:

(1) Determine the average rate of return for both projects.
(2) How would you explain the importance of net cash flows in the analysis of investment projects? Include a specific example to demonstrate the importance of net cash flows and their timing to these two projects.

ANSWERS TO SELF-EXAMINATION QUESTIONS

1. C Methods of evaluating capital investment proposals that ignore the time value of money are categorized as methods that ignore present value. This category includes the average rate of return method (answer A) and the cash payback method (answer B).
2. B The average rate of return is 24% (answer B), determined by dividing the expected average annual earnings by the average investment, as follows:

$$\frac{\$60,000 \div 5}{(\$100,000 + \$0) \div 2} = 24\%$$

3. B Of the three methods of analyzing proposals for capital investments, the cash payback period (answer B) refers to the expected period of time required to recover the amount of cash to be invested. The average rate of return (answer A) is a measure of the anticipated profitability of a proposal. The net present value method (answer C) reduces the expected future net cash flows originating from a proposal to their present values.
4. C The net present value method (answer C) uses the concept of present value to determine the total present value of the cash flows expected from a proposal and compares this value with the amount to be invested. The average rate of return method (answer A) and the cash payback method (answer B) ignore present value. The internal rate of return method (answer D) uses the present value concept to determine the internal rate of return expected from the proposal.
5. A Capital rationing (answer A) is the process by which management allocates available investment funds among competing capital investment proposals. Capital expenditure budgeting (answer B) is the process of summarizing the decisions that have been made for the acquisition of plant assets and preparing a capital expenditures budget to reflect these decisions. Leasing (answer C) is an alternative that management should consider before making a final decision on the acquisition of assets.

CHAPTER 24

CHAPTER OBJECTIVES

1 Describe the new manufacturing environment.

2 Describe and illustrate costs related to investing in inventory, including:
   - Opportunity costs
   - Ordering costs
   - Purchase costs
   - Storage costs
   - Costs of interrupting production

3 Describe and illustrate inventory management in a just-in-time manufacturing environment.

4 Describe and illustrate inventory management in a traditional environment, including the use of:
   - Economic order quantity
   - Inventory reorder point
   - Linear programming

5 Describe and illustrate implications of the new manufacturing enviroment environment on analyses, including:
   - Cost-volume-profit analysis
   - Variable costing
   - Differential analysis
   - Capital investment analysis

DECISION MAKING IN THE MODERN MANUFACTURING ENVIRONMENT

A primary objective of managerial accounting is to provide management with information and analyses useful for decision making. To improve the quality of its decisions, management has increased its emphasis on accurate and timely accounting information. The information and type of analysis most appropriate for management's use depends upon the nature of the decision and the environment in which the decision will be made.

In recent years, the manufacturing environment for many companies has changed significantly. Highly automated manufacturing systems, such as computer-integrated manufacturing (CIM) systems, have increased manufacturing flexibility and decreased the amount of time required to manufacture a product. These systems were briefly described in Chapter 15. Activity-based costing (ABC), which was discussed in Chapter 18, more accurately traces manufacturing overhead costs to products in many situations. Just-in-time (JIT) manufacturing systems, which were briefly mentioned in Chapters 15, 17, and 18, have improved productive efficiency and product quality. In this chapter, the characteristics of this new environment are more fully described.

This chapter also discusses the impact of the new manufacturing environment on inventories. The costs related to investing in inventory, as well as inventory management in a just-in-time system and in a traditional manufacturing system are discussed. Finally, the chapter describes and illustrates the use of cost-volume-profit analysis, variable costing, differential analysis, and capital investment analysis in the new manufacturing environment.

CHARACTERISTICS OF THE NEW MANUFACTURING ENVIRONMENT

OBJECTIVE 1
Describe the new manufacturing environment.

To compete effectively in global markets, which are characterized by uncertainty and ever-changing customer needs, manufacturers must produce high-quality products at competitive prices.[1] As a result, the new manufactur-

[1] Concepts and techniques that may be useful in making decisions under uncertainty are described and illustrated in Appendix 2 at the end of this chapter.

ing environment is characterized by an emphasis on manufacturing flexibility and total quality control.

Manufacturing flexibility and quality control may be improved by investing in new technology, such as automated, computer-aided machinery, and by reorganizing the manufacturing process. Because the investment in new technology and automation generally increases manufacturing overhead, it has become increasingly important to accurately trace overhead costs to activities and products. If managers use inaccurate cost information, they may make incorrect decisions. For example, they might set product prices too high or too low, or they might decide to discontinue a profitable product line.

Automated Manufacturing Processes

One of the more visible trends in manufacturing is the increased use of automated machinery to perform routine, repetitive tasks with minimum human involvement in the manufacturing process. Automated machinery can take many forms, including computer-integrated manufacturing (CIM) systems and robots.

The use of automated machinery in the manufacturing process is often justified on the basis of labor and material savings. Other factors, however, such as improved quality control and reduced product development time, are often benefits of the use of automated machinery. For example, with the use of robotics, changes in products can be easily introduced into the manufacturing process by reprogramming robots. This ability to add or modify products quickly allows a company to react to changing market preferences and conditions.

The use of automated machinery increases overhead costs through increases in depreciation, maintenance, repairs, property taxes, and insurance. Automation also reduces the amount of direct labor required in the manufacturing process. Twenty-five years ago, for example, direct labor costs frequently accounted for 40% of production costs. With the use of automated machinery, direct labor costs may now represent no more than 5% of production costs. In such an environment, direct labor costs may be charged to manufacturing overhead rather than accounted for as a separate product cost.

Cost Allocation in the New Manufacturing Environment

As described and illustrated in Chapter 18, some companies have implemented activity-based costing (ABC) in order to more accurately trace manufacturing overhead costs to products. For example, it was recently reported that 11% of United States companies are now using ABC, and 19% are considering its implementation.[2]

Activity-based costing emphasizes the identification of activities that cause the overhead. The allocation of the overhead is then based upon these cost drivers. The accuracy of activity-based costing reduces or eliminates the product cost distortions that are often created by traditional overhead allocation methods.

Activity-based costing also highlights the existence of non-value-adding overhead activities. For example, inspection costs, materials movement costs, and downtime costs might all be traced to activities related to the amount of time required to manufacture a product. This time, which is referred to as **cycle time** or **throughput time,** can be expressed as shown on page 1001.

---

[2] "Eleven Percent of U.S. Companies Adopt ABC—Many More to Follow," *Cost Management Update* (Montvale, New Jersey: National Association of Accountants, January, 1991).

Cycle time = Processing time + Inspection time + Move time + Wait time

The inspection time, move time, and wait time represent non-value-adding activities and related costs, since the product is not being processed (manufactured) during these activities. By identifying the non-value-adding activities and related costs, management can concentrate its efforts on reducing or eliminating these activities and costs. The reduction or elimination of non-value-adding activities also reduces the cycle time, which allows the company to react more quickly to customer needs.

Just-In-Time (JIT) Manufacturing Systems

Just-in-time (JIT) manufacturing systems, sometimes referred to as **flexible flow manufacturing systems,** typically utilize computers and automated machinery such as robots. A JIT system attempts to achieve productive efficiencies and flexibility by reorganizing the traditional production process.

In a traditional production process, a product moves through the process according to functional flows along a continuous production line. That is, the product moves from process to process as each function or step is completed. Each worker is assigned a specific job, which is performed repeatedly as unfinished products are received from the preceding department. In such a process, a product is often said to be "pushed through" production, since each manufacturing department "pushes" the unfinished product to the next stage (department) of manufacturing. For example, a furniture manufacturer might use seven production departments to perform the operating functions necessary to manufacture furniture, as shown in the following diagram:

Traditional Production Line—Furniture Manufacturer

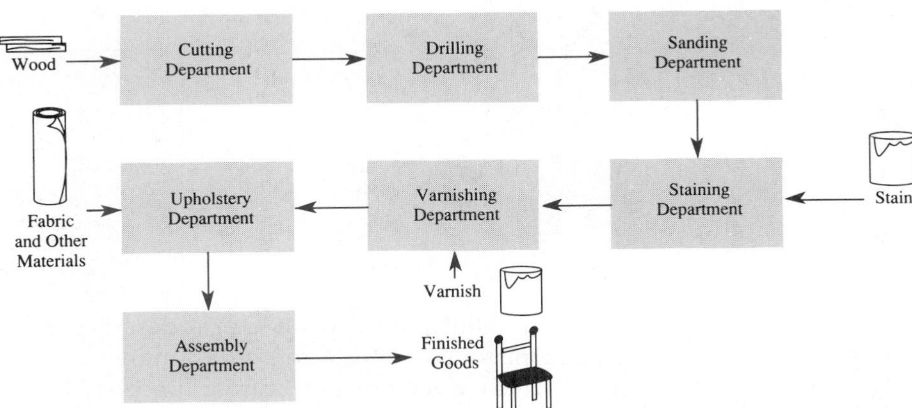

For the furniture maker in the illustration, manufacturing would begin in the Cutting Department, where the wood would be cut to design specifications. Next, the Drilling Department would perform the drilling function, after which the Sanding Department would sand the wood, the Staining Department would stain the furniture, and the Varnishing Department would apply varnish and other protective coatings. Then, the Upholstery Department would add fabric and other materials. Finally, the Assembly Department would assemble the furniture to complete the manufacturing process.

In the traditional production process, production supervisors attempt to enter enough materials into the manufacturing process to keep all the manufacturing departments operating. Some departments, however, may process materials more rapidly than others. In addition, if one department stops production because of machine breakdowns, for example, the preceding departments usually continue production in order to avoid idle time. This unevenness may result in a build-up of work in process between departments. Furthermore, if bottlenecks occur, the entire production line slows or stops because the unfinished product is not passed on to the successive departments.

In a just-in-time manufacturing system, the traditional production process is reorganized by combining processing functions into **work centers**, sometimes referred to as **manufacturing cells**. For example, the seven departments illustrated on page 1001 for the furniture manufacturer might be reorganized into three work centers. As shown in the following diagram, Work Center One would perform the cutting, drilling, and sanding functions; Work Center Two would perform the staining and varnishing functions; and Work Center Three would perform the upholstery and assembly functions.

Just-In-Time Production Line—Furniture Manufacturer

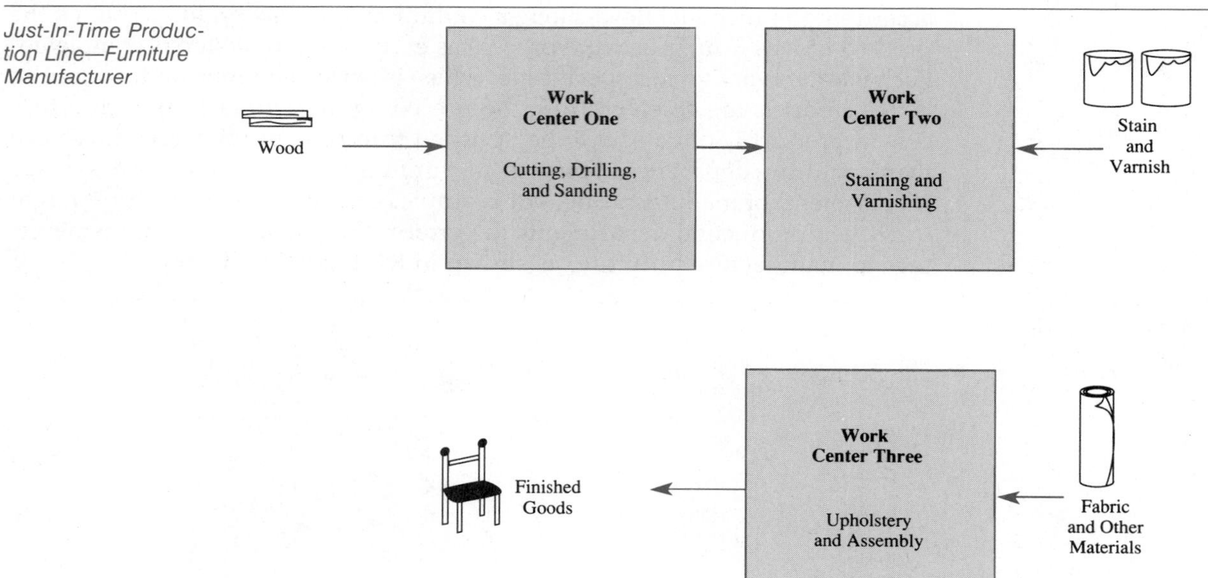

In the traditional production line, as described previously, a worker typically performs only one function on a continous basis. However, in a work center in which several manufacturing functions take place, the workers are often cross-trained to perform more than one function. Research has indicated that workers who perform several manufacturing functions identify better with the end product. This identification creates pride in the products and improves quality and productivity.

The just-in-time reorganization of the manufacturing departments may also result in a reorganization of activities involving services to these departments. Specifically, the service activities may be assigned to individual work centers, rather than to the traditional centralized service departments. For example, each work center may be assigned the responsibility for the repair and maintenance of its machinery and equipment. The acceptance of this responsibility creates an environment in which workers gain a better understanding of the production process and machinery limitations. In turn, workers tend to take better care of the machinery, which decreases repairs and maintenance costs, reduces machine downtime, and improves product quality.

In a just-in-time manufacturing system, the non-value-added activity of moving the product and materials is reduced. The product is often placed on a movable carrier that is centrally located in the work center. After the workers in a work center have completed their activities with the product, the entire carrier and any additional materials are moved to the next work center just-in-time to be completed and to satisfy the demand or need of that work center. In this sense, the product is said to be "pulled through." Each work center is relatively independent of other work centers, and a work center that has idle time may often contract for special jobs outside the company.

In addition to achieving productive efficiencies and flexibility, JIT manufacturing systems emphasize quality control. Because each work center produces only what is demanded or needed by a subsequent work center, any defective part stops production of the product for which that part is needed. In traditional manufacturing systems, inventories are normally large enough to buffer or cushion the discovery of defective parts until the parts can be reworked or replaced. As a result, supporters of JIT manufacturing systems suggest that traditional manufacturing systems often hide manufacturing problems related to poor quality control, machine breakdowns, and poor relationships with suppliers.

Traditional manufacturing systems normally strive for "acceptable" quality limits for production, while JIT manufacturing systems strive for zero defects, or **total quality control (TQC).** Underlying the emphasis on total quality control is a philosophy of continuous improvement in the manufacturing process and the elimination of inefficiencies (such as production of defective parts or products) and waste.

In summary, the primary benefit of just-in-time manufacturing systems is the increased efficiency of operations, which is achieved by eliminating waste and reducing or eliminating non-value-adding activities. At the same time, just-in-time manufacturing systems emphasize continuous improvement in the manufacturing process and the improvement of product quality.[3]

COSTS OF INVESTING IN INVENTORY

OBJECTIVE 2
Describe and illustrate costs related to investing in inventory, including:
Opportunity costs,
Ordering costs,
Purchase costs,
Storage costs,
Costs of interrupting production.

Business enterprises maintain inventories in order to meet production and customer demands. At the same time, however, management attempts to minimize the cost of carrying inventory. The costs of carrying inventory include opportunity costs, the cost of ordering materials, the purchase cost of materials, and storage costs. An additional cost that is influenced by the amount of inventory is the cost of interrupting production due to the lack of inventory. As a basis for understanding inventory management both in new and in traditional manufacturing environments, each of these costs is discussed in the following paragraphs.

Opportunity Costs

To maximize profits, the cost of carrying inventory must be balanced with the opportunity costs related to inventory. The first opportunity cost is the cost of workers' idle time when not enough inventory is carried to continue

---

[3] Concepts of quality control are described in Appendix 1 at the end of this chapter.

the production process, and the completion of other products is delayed. In addition, if not enough inventory is carried to meet customer needs on a timely basis, customers may purchase products from competitors. Thus, the profits that would have been earned are lost.

The second opportunity cost related to inventory is the amount of income that could have been earned on funds invested in inventory. For example, $500,000 invested in inventory precludes the enterprise from investing these funds in other ways. If the $500,000 could have earned an annual rate of return of 10% in other uses, then the opportunity cost of the inventory is $50,000 per year ($500,000 × 10%).

Ordering Costs

Ordering costs include the costs of placing an order, receiving the order, inspecting the materials, verifying supplier invoices, and processing payments. The total annual cost of ordering specific materials will increase as the total number of orders placed increases.

Purchase Cost

The purchase cost is the cost per unit of the materials received, including all costs necessary to obtain the materials once the order has been placed. The total purchase cost includes the total amount billed by the vendor (the cost per unit multiplied by the quantity ordered), as well as the cost of freight and insurance for materials in transit.

Although inventories are usually smaller when materials are purchased in small quantities, additional freight costs may be incurred if shortages arise and rush orders must be shipped by air or special express. Therefore, the total cost of materials is normally decreased by purchasing in large quantities. For example, freight and insurance costs per unit are normally less when large quantities are purchased. In addition, quantity discounts are often obtained for large purchases.

Storage Costs

After materials have been received, costs associated with storing the materials must be incurred. These costs include warehousing costs, such as depreciation, insurance, employee wages, utility costs, inventory taxes, and handling costs. Storage costs are reduced by carrying smaller amounts of inventory.

Costs of Interrupting Production

Additional manufacturing costs may be incurred when production is interrupted because of insufficient inventory. These costs might include overtime to meet production schedules and customer needs, and additional costs of setting up the machinery to process materials. For example, rather than one production run where the machinery is set up once to process a product, another production run may be necessary, with additional setups each time a materials shortage occurs.

INVENTORY MANAGEMENT IN A JUST-IN-TIME MANUFACTURING SYSTEM

OBJECTIVE 3
Describe and illustrate inventory management in a just-in-time manufacturing environment.

The philosophy of just-in-time manufacturing systems, which were described earlier in this chapter, is that materials enter the manufacturing process just in time to be completed and to satisfy the demand of the next work center or the customer. In this sense, materials are said to be "pulled" through the manufacturing process. The five inventory costs that were described previously impact inventory management in such a system.

In a JIT manufacturing system, the opportunity cost associated with lost sales is decreased or eliminated because the time it takes to manufacture a product is reduced. The cycle time is reduced by organizing the production process into work centers, so that the materials movement time between work centers is reduced. The cycle time is also reduced by designing (engineering) flexibility into the manufacturing process. With flexibility, setup times are reduced, and the system can respond quickly to customer needs and demands.

By reducing inventories, JIT manufacturing systems significantly reduce the opportunity cost related to the amount of income that could have been earned on funds invested in inventory. Thus, just-in-time manufacturing systems free up funds for other uses.

In a JIT manufacturing system, management attempts to reduce order costs by entering into long-term purchasing agreements with a few suppliers. By dealing with fewer suppliers, order costs are reduced. Also, the long-term purchasing agreements normally require the suppliers to maintain strict quality control standards. Thus, the need for the enterprise to inspect materials as they are received is eliminated. Some manufacturers have also established computer connections (interfaces) with their suppliers, so that materials can be ordered as they are needed, with little or no human intervention. The materials are delivered directly to the work centers in the quantities required. With this arrangement, most of the traditional receiving department costs can be reduced or eliminated. Finally, the long-term purchasing agreements eliminate or reduce much of the normal paper processing activities (verifying invoices, etc.) associated with traditional systems.

The long-term nature of purchasing agreements with suppliers usually allows just-in-time manufacturers to negotiate favorable prices with suppliers. In many cases, the purchase cost is lower than it would be if large quantities were ordered in order to take advantage of quantity discounts.

Long-term puchasing agreements allow suppliers the financial security of locating warehousing and distribution centers near just-in-time manufacturers. Thus, the purchase cost may also be reduced because the distance necessary to move supplies decreases, and the suppliers' abilities to respond quickly to manufacturing needs increase.

Since inventories are smaller in JIT manufacturing systems, storage costs are reduced or eliminated. Materials are received directly in the work centers, and the costs associated with a central warehouse, including such costs as depreciation, insurance, handling costs, and inventory taxes, can be significantly reduced or eliminated.

Just-in-time manufacturers reduce the costs of interrupting production by entering into the long-term purchasing agreements that were described previously. These agreements guarantee the timely delivery of quality materials. In addition, most just-in-time manufacturers have adopted a total quality control program that emphasizes not only the quality of purchased materials, but also the quality of manufactured components and the final product.

Just-in-time manufacturers often train the workers in each work center to perform preventive maintenance on machinery and equipment. This activity further reduces the possibility of interruptions in the production process due to machine breakdowns.

INVENTORY MANAGEMENT IN A TRADITIONAL MANUFACTURING SYSTEM

OBJECTIVE 4
Describe and illustrate inventory management in a traditional environment, including the use of:
Economic order quantity,
Inventory reorder point,
Linear programming.

Inventory costs are usually more significant in a traditional manufacturing system. However, the primary objective of inventory management in a traditional system is the same as in a JIT manufacturing system. That is, the opportunity cost of lost sales or production must be balanced with the inventory carrying costs in order to minimize total costs.

Some tools are available for aiding in the management of inventory costs. These tools, which include the calculations of the economic order quantity and the inventory reorder point, and the use of linear programming for purchasing decisions, are described in the following paragraphs.

Economic Order Quantity

The quantity of inventory to be ordered that will minimize the total costs of ordering and storing inventory is the **economic order quantity (EOQ).** The economic order quantity addresses the question, "How much should be ordered?"

The annual cost of processing orders for a specified material (cost of placing orders, verifying invoices, processing payments, etc.) increases as the number of orders placed increases. On the other hand, the annual cost of storing the materials (taxes, insurance, occupancy of storage space, etc.) decreases as the number of orders placed increases. The economic order quantity is therefore that quantity that will minimize the combined annual costs of ordering and storing materials.

The combined annual cost incurred in ordering and storing materials can be computed under various assumptions as to the number of orders to be placed during a year. To illustrate, assume the following data for an inventoriable material that is used at the same rate during the year:

Units required during the year	1,200
Ordering cost, per order placed	$10.00
Annual storage cost, per unit	$ .60

If a single order was placed for the entire year's needs, the cost of ordering the 1,200 units would be $10. The average number of units held in inventory during the year would therefore be 600 (1,200 units ÷ 2) and would result in an annual storage cost of $360 (600 units × $.60). The combined order and storage costs for placing only one order during the year would thus be $370 ($10 + $360). If, instead of a single order, two orders were placed during the year, the order cost would be $20 (2 × $10), 600 units would need to be purchased on each order, the average inventory would be 300 units, and the annual storage cost would be $180 (300 units × $.60). Accordingly, the combined order and storage costs for placing two orders during the year would be $200 ($20 + $180). Successive computations will disclose the EOQ when the combined cost reaches its lowest point and starts upward. The following table shows an optimum of 200 units of materials per order, with 6 orders per year, at a combined cost of $120:

Tabulation of Economic Order Quantity

Number of Orders	Number of Units per Order	Average Units in Inventory	Order and Storage Costs: Order Cost	Storage Cost	Combined Cost
1	1,200	600	$10	$360	$370
2	600	300	20	180	200
3	400	200	30	120	150
4	300	150	40	90	130
5	240	120	50	72	122
6	200	100	60	60	120
7	171	86	70	52	122

The economic order quantity may also be determined by a formula based on differential calculus. The formula and its application to the illustration is as follows:

Economic Order Quantity Formula

$$\text{EOQ} = \sqrt{\frac{2 \times \text{Annual Units Required} \times \text{Cost per Order Placed}}{\text{Annual Storage Cost per Unit}}}$$

$$\text{EOQ} = \sqrt{\frac{2 \times 1{,}200 \times \$10}{\$.60}}$$

$$\text{EOQ} = \sqrt{40{,}000}$$

$$\text{EOQ} = 200 \text{ units}$$

Inventory Reorder Point

The **inventory reorder point**, usually expressed in units, is the level to which inventory is allowed to fall before an order for additional inventory is placed. The reorder point adresses the question, "When should the inventory be ordered?"

The inventory reorder point depends on the (1) daily usage of inventory that is expected to be consumed in production or sold, (2) number of production days that it takes to receive an order for inventory, termed the **lead time,** and (3) the **safety stock**, which is the amount of inventory that is available for use when unforeseen circumstances arise, such as delays in receiving ordered inventory as a result of a national truckers' strike. Once the reorder point is reached, the most economical quantity should be ordered.

The inventory reorder point is computed by using the following formula:

Inventory Reorder Point = (Daily Usage × Days of Lead Time) + Safety Stock

To illustrate, assume that Beacon Company, a printing company, estimates daily usage of 3,000 pounds of paper and a lead time of 30 days to receive an order of paper. Beacon Company desires a safety stock of 10,000 pounds. The inventory reorder point for the paper is 100,000 pounds, computed as follows:

Inventory Reorder Point = (Daily Usage × Lead Time) + Safety Stock
Inventory Reorder Point = (3,000 lbs. × 30 days) + 10,000 lbs.
Inventory Reorder Point = 90,000 lbs. + 10,000 lbs.
Inventory Reorder Point = 100,000 lbs.

In this illustration, a safety stock of 10,000 pounds of paper was assumed. This level of safety stock should be established by management after considering many factors, such as the uncertainty in the estimates of daily inventory usage and lead time. If management were 100% certain that estimates of the daily usage and lead time were correct, no safety stock would be required. As the uncertainty in these estimates increases, the amount of safety stock normally increases. In addition, the level of safety stock carried by an enterprise will also depend on the costs of carrying inventory and the costs of being out of inventory when materials are needed for production or sales. If the costs of carrying inventory are low and the costs of being out of inventory are high, then relatively large amounts of safety stock would normally be carried by a business enterprise.

INVENTORY CARDIOGRAM

Henry C. Ekstein, the former chief financial officer of Remington Aluminum, developed an inventory cardiogram for use in controlling inventory. The cardiogram is a graph of inventory levels over time, which portrays the normal inventory usage cycle for a company. For example, the cardiogram indicates when and how many times inventory was overstocked and back ordered, the inventory reorder point, and the safety stock levels. In the following cardiogram, both desired and actual inventory usage are plotted. The reorder point is 275 units, the safety stock is 225 units, and the inventory was back ordered twice during the 12-week period. The economic order quantity is 400 units, indicated by the length of the vertical lines. The vertical lines also indicate the receipt of additional inventory.

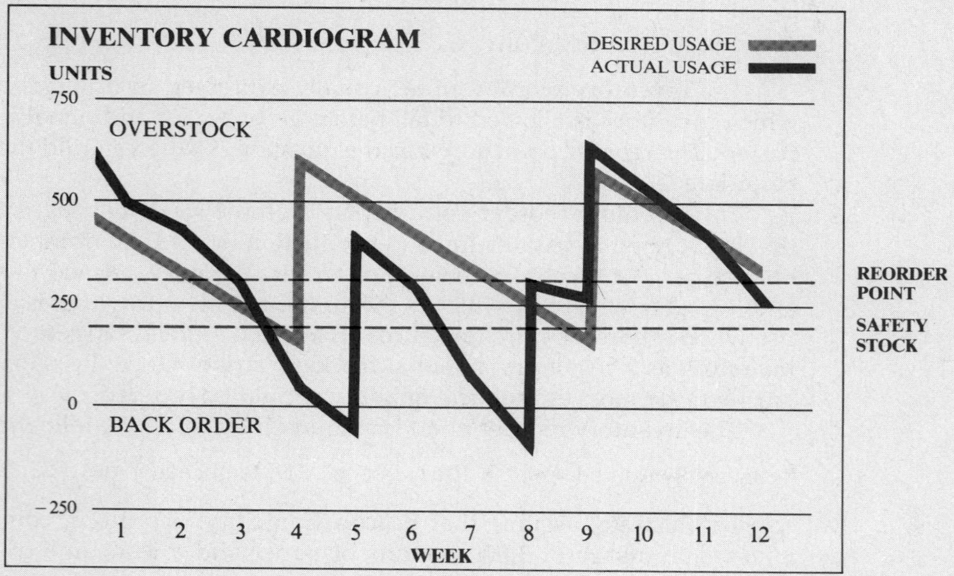

Ekstein believes that the cardiogram is most effective in managing a limited number of inventory items that were previously uncontrolled. "Once you show someone the inventory cardiogram," Ekstein claims, "all of a sudden it makes sense to them—how inventories behave, what the problem is, how many times it occurred over the past year, and what to do about it."

Source: Paul Susca, "Checking the Vital Signs," *CFO* (February, 1986), p. 13.

Linear Programming for Purchasing Decisions

Linear programming is a quantitative method that can provide data for solving a variety of business problems in which management's objective is to minimize costs or maximize profits, subject to several limiting factors. Although a thorough discussion of linear programming is appropriate for more advanced courses, the following simplified illustration demonstrates the way in which linear programming can be applied to determine the most economical purchasing plan. In this situation, management's objective is to minimize the total cost of purchasing materials for several branch locations, subject to the availability of materials from suppliers.

Assume that a manufacturing company purchases Part P for use at both its West Branch and East Branch. Part P is available in limited quantities from two suppliers. The total unit cost price varies considerably for parts acquired from the two suppliers mainly because of differences in transportation charges. The relevant data for the decision regarding the most economical purchase arrangement are summarized in the following diagram:

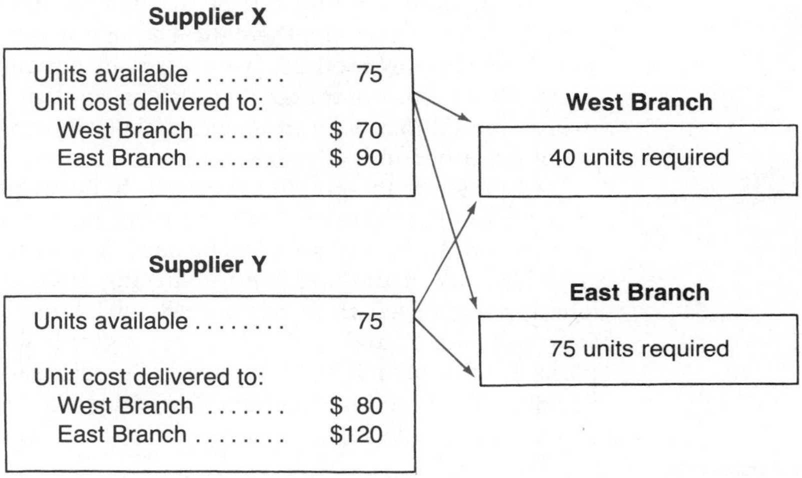

Supplier X

Units available 75
Unit cost delivered to:
West Branch .... $ 70
East Branch .... $ 90

West Branch

40 units required

Supplier Y

Units available 75

Unit cost delivered to:
West Branch .... $ 80
East Branch $120

East Branch

75 units required

It might appear that the most economical course of action would be to purchase (1) the 40 units required by West Branch from Supplier X at $70 a unit, (2) 35 units for East Branch from Supplier X at $90 a unit, and (3) the remaining 40 units required by East Branch from Supplier Y at $120 a unit. If this course of action were followed, the total cost of the parts needed by the two branches would amount to $10,750, as indicated by the following computation:

	Cost of Purchases		
	By West Branch	*By East Branch*	*Total*
From Supplier X:			
40 units at $70	$2,800		$ 2,800
35 units at $90		$3,150	3,150
From Supplier Y:			
40 units at $120		4,800	4,800
Total	$2,800	$7,950	$10,750

Although many different purchasing programs are possible, the most economical course of action would be to purchase (1) the 75 units required by East Branch from Supplier X at $90 a unit and (2) the 40 units required by West Branch from Supplier Y at $80 a unit. If this plan were used, no units would be purchased at the lowest available unit cost, and the total cost of the parts would be $9,950, calculated as follows:

	Cost of Purchases		
	By West Branch	*By East Branch*	*Total*
From Supplier X:			
75 units at $90		$6,750	$6,750
From Supplier Y:			
40 units at $80	$3,200		3,200
Total	$3,200	$6,750	$9,950

Linear programming can be applied to this situation by using either a graphic approach or a mathematical equation approach. This latter approach, called the **simplex method**, uses algebraic equations and is often used more practically with a computer. Because of its complexity and because it is normally covered in advanced managerial accounting texts, the simplex method is not described in this chapter.

To illustrate the graphic approach to linear programming, the preceding facts for the purchase of Part P from Supplier X and Supplier Y by the West Branch and the East Branch will be used. The first step in solving this problem is to place all of the possible purchasing alternatives on a graph. Since the amount purchased from Supplier X will determine the amount purchased from Supplier Y, and vice versa, only a graph showing all possible purchase plans for Supplier X (or Supplier Y) is necessary. The following graph for Supplier X is based on the foregoing data.

Linear Programming Graph—Units Purchased From Supplier X

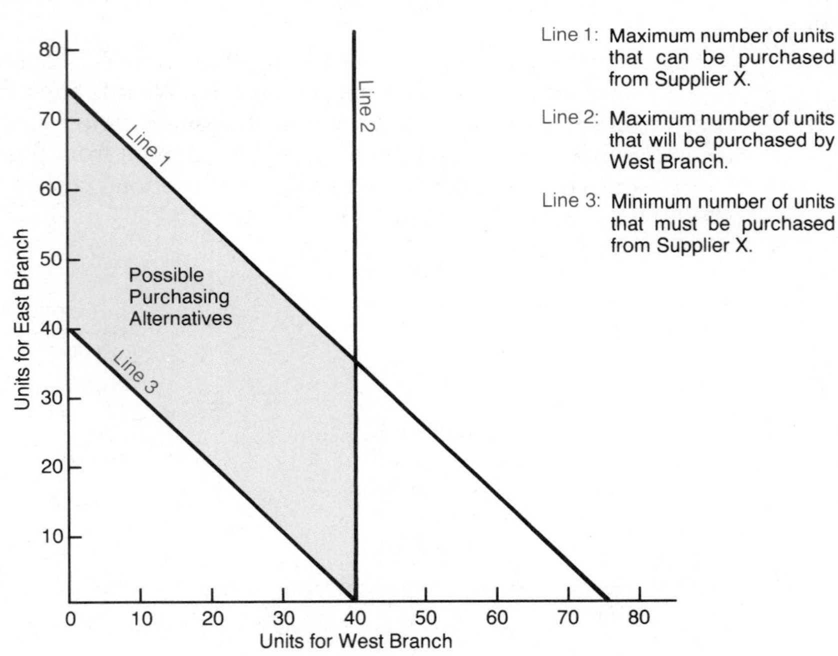

The linear programming graph is constructed in the following manner:

1. Units for the West Branch are plotted on the horizontal axis, and units for the East Branch are plotted on the vertical axis.
2. A point representing the maximum number of units that could be purchased from Supplier X by the West Branch (75 units) is located on the horizontal axis. A point representing the maximum number of units that could be purchased from Supplier X by the East Branch (75 units) is located on the vertical axis.
3. A diagonal line (labeled Line 1) is drawn connecting the points representing the 75 units on the vertical axis with 75 units on the horizontal axis. This line represents the constraint on the maximum number of units (75) that can be purchased from Supplier X by either branch or both branches.
4. The constraint on the number of units that the West Branch would purchase from Supplier X (40) is indicated by a line (labeled Line 2) which is drawn vertically upward from the point of 40 units on the horizontal axis to intersect Line 1.
5. A line (labeled Line 3) is drawn connecting 40 units on the vertical axis with 40 units on the horizontal axis. This line represents the constraint on minimum purchases from Supplier X (115 units required by the branches less 75 units available from each supplier).
6. The area bounded by the vertical axis and Lines 1, 2, and 3 is shaded. This area represents the set of all possible alternatives for purchases from Supplier X.

To illustrate the interpretation of a linear programming graph, assume that the West Branch purchased no units from Supplier X. The East Branch could then purchase between 40 and 75 units from Supplier X. This purchase alternative is indicated on the following graph between points A and B on the vertical axis. On the other hand, if the West Branch purchased 20 units from Supplier X, the East Branch could purchase between 20 and 55 units from Supplier X. This alternative is indicated on the following graph by the colored dotted line connecting points E and F.

Linear Programming Graph—Alternative Purchase Plans

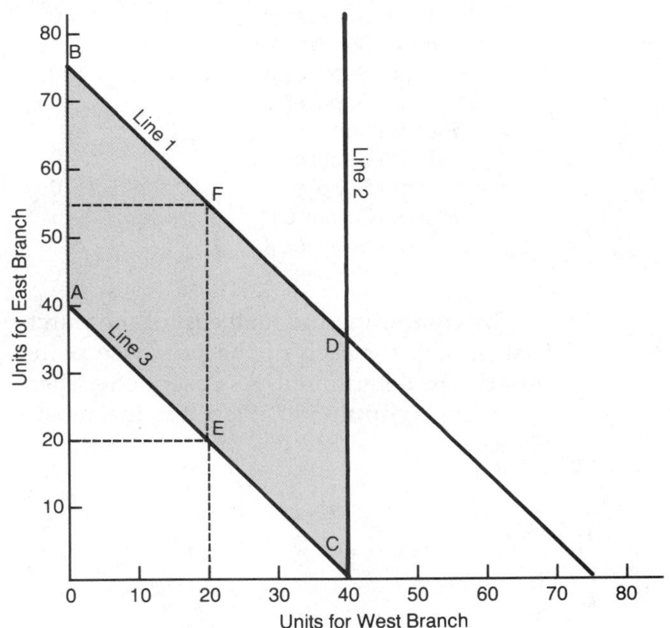

Although any point in the shaded area of the graph is a possible purchasing plan, managers are interested in selecting the most economical plan. According to the mathematical properties of linear programming, an economical purchase plan is located at one of the four points representing the corners of the shaded area of the graph. These corners are labeled A through D on the graph.

Each of the four corners represents the following purchases from Supplier X by the West Branch and the East Branch:

	Purchases by West Branch	Purchases by East Branch
Corner A:		
From Supplier X	0 units	40 units
Corner B:		
From Supplier X	0	75
Corner C:		
From Supplier X	40	0
Corner D:		
From Supplier X	40	35

Since the amount purchased from Supplier X affects the amount purchased from Supplier Y, the four corners identified above can be rewritten in terms of four separate purchase plans. In other words, if only 40 units are purchased from Supplier X and are shipped to the East Branch (Corner A), then the West Branch must obtain its purchases of 40 units from Supplier Y, and the East Branch must obtain an additional 35 units from Supplier Y to fulfill its total needs of 75 units. The four purchase plans represented by the four corners are as follows:

	Purchases by West Branch	Purchases by East Branch
Plan 1 (Corner A):		
From Supplier X.	0 units	40 units
From Supplier Y.	40	35
Plan 2 (Corner B):		
From Supplier X.	0	75
From Supplier Y.	40	0
Plan 3 (Corner C):		
From Supplier X.	40	0
From Supplier Y.	0	75
Plan 4 (Corner D):		
From Supplier X.	40	35
From Supplier Y.	0	40

By computing the total cost of the purchases for the West Branch and the East Branch for each of the purchase plans, the most economical purchase plan can be determined. As described earlier on page 1010 and as shown in the following computation, Plan 2 is the most economical of the four purchase plans.

	Cost of Purchases		
	By West Branch	*By East Branch*	*Total*
Plan 1:			
From Supplier X:			
40 units at $90		$3,600	$ 3,600
From Supplier Y:			
40 units at $80	$3,200		3,200
35 units at $120		4,200	4,200
Total	$3,200	$7,800	$11,000
Plan 2:			
From Supplier X:			
75 units at $90		$6,750	$ 6,750
From Supplier Y:			
40 units at $80	$3,200		3,200
Total	$3,200	$6,750	$ 9,950
Plan 3:			
From Supplier X:			
40 units at $70	$2,800		$ 2,800
From Supplier Y:			
75 units at $120		$9,000	9,000
Total	$2,800	$9,000	$11,800
Plan 4:			
From Supplier X:			
40 units at $70	$2,800		$ 2,800
35 units at $90		$3,150	3,150
From Supplier Y:			
40 units at $120		4,800	4,800
Total	$2,800	$7,950	$10,750

The preceding illustration of the graphic approach to linear programming required the construction of a graph and the consideration of four alternative purchase plans. Although an economical purchasing plan decision could have been determined by trial and error, such an approach can be time-consuming and costly. The trial and error approach could potentially require consideration of a much larger number of possible purchase plans before the most economical plan is found.

IMPLICATIONS OF THE NEW MANUFACTURING ENVIRONMENT FOR ANALYSES

OBJECTIVE 5
Describe and illustrate implications of the new manufacturing environment on analyses.

The new manufacturing environment has been described in previous chapters, beginning with Chapter 15. The following paragraphs describe and illustrate the impact of the new manufacturing environment on cost-volume-profit analysis, variable costing, differential analysis, and capital investment analysis.

Cost-Volume-Profit Analysis

The discussion and illustration of cost-volume-profit analysis in Chapter 20 assumed that all costs could be classified into fixed and variable costs. The activity base used to classify costs as fixed or variable was units produced and sold.[4] As was described and illustrated in Chapter 18, some manufacturing overhead costs may not be caused by or directly related to volume-based cost drivers, such as the number of units produced. Hence, these costs may be misclassified in cost-volume-profit analysis if units produced is used as the only activity base in the analysis.

The use of activity-based costing, as described in Chapter 18, may allow for a more accurate analysis of cost-volume-profit relationships. This accuracy results because the behavior of costs is more correctly described in terms of cost drivers. To illustrate, assume that Shelby Inc.'s product has a unit selling price of $80, a unit variable cost of $30, a unit contribution margin of $50, and fixed costs of $820,000. Using traditional cost-volume-profit analysis, Shelby Inc.'s break-even sales are 16,400 units ($820,000 ÷ $50).

Under activity-based costing, assume that two cost pools are formed, using units produced and production setups as the activity bases (cost drivers). For the units produced cost pool, it is determined that Shelby Inc.'s product has a unit variable cost of $22 per unit, and fixed costs are estimated to be $690,000. The remaining costs can be traced to the production setup cost pool, which includes quality control costs and production setup costs. The quality control and production setup cost pool is allocated on the basis of $1,500 per production setup. For the relevant range of planned production, 120 setups are estimated as being required. Shelby Inc.'s break-even sales under activity-based costing is 15,000 units, computed as follows:

$$\text{Break-Even Sales (Units)} = \frac{\text{Fixed Costs} + \text{Quality Control and Setup Costs}}{\text{Unit Contribution Margin}}$$

$$\text{Break-Even Sales (Units)} = \frac{\$690{,}000 + (\$1{,}500 \times 120 \text{ setups})}{\$80 - \$22}$$

$$\text{Break-Even Sales (Units)} = \frac{\$690{,}000 + \$180{,}000}{\$58} = \frac{\$870{,}000}{\$58} = 15{,}000 \text{ units}$$

The activity-based costing estimate of break-even sales is 1,400 units less (16,400 − 15,000) than the estimate using traditional cost-volume-profit analysis. Thus, to the extent that activity-based costing provides more accurate estimates of how costs behave, cost-volume-profit analysis and management decision making may be improved.

In the new manufacturing environment, direct labor and therefore variable costs are becoming a smaller percentage of the total product cost. In contrast, fixed costs and manufacturing overhead are becoming a larger percentage of total product cost. Thus, accurate cost estimates, such as those derived from activity-based costing, are becoming more and more important in analyses.

Variable Costing

The variable costing income statement described and illustrated in Chapter 21 is still applicable in the new manufacturing environment. However,

---

[4] In cost-volume-profit analysis, the number of units produced is assumed to be equal to the number of units sold. Thus, there is no change in inventories under traditional cost-volume-profit analysis.

activity-based costing can further enhance the use of variable costing for decision making by tracing and presenting fixed costs by individual products in accordance with relevant cost drivers. To illustrate, assume that the management of Casta Inc. is analyzing the profitability of Products X and Y, using the following variable costing income statement:

Variable Costing Income Statement

	Product X	Product Y	Total
Sales	$550,000	$400,000	$950,000
Variable cost of goods sold	355,000	220,000	575,000
Manufacturing margin	$195,000	$180,000	$375,000
Variable selling and admin. exp.	60,000	64,000	124,000
Contribution margin	$135,000	$116,000	$251,000
Fixed costs:			
Fixed manufacturing costs			$170,000
Fixed selling and admin. exp.			51,000
Total fixed costs			$221,000
Income from operations			$ 30,000

After initially reviewing the preceding variable costing income statement, the management of Casta Inc. might conclude that both products are profitable, and therefore both products should be produced and sold. If activity-based costing is used, however, fixed costs can be further traced to their underlying causes (cost drivers). In many cases, these cost drivers will allow the managerial accountant to trace the fixed costs to individual products and thereby assess the product margin. The **product margin** is a measure of the profitability of each product and its contribution to overall enterprise profits. It is determined by deducting the traceable fixed costs from the contribution margin of each product. A variable costing income statement prepared in this format for Casta Inc. is shown at the top of page 1016.

The variable costing income statement on page 1016 indicates that Product X is not contributing to overall company profits, but is actually losing money. In contrast, the traditional variable costing income statement indicated that Product X had the highest contribution margin. Since the traceable fixed costs would be eliminated if Product X is discontinued, the management of Casta Inc. should consider discontinuing Product X. Alternatively, management could consider raising the selling price of Product X or reducing Product X's traceable costs.

The preceding illustration demonstrated the potential value of expanding the traditional variable costing income statement to include product margin. As manufacturing overhead increases as a percentage of product cost, such analyses that report traceable fixed costs will become increasingly important for managerial decision making.

Differential Analysis

The use of activity-based costing allows managers to focus on costs that will change with cost drivers. In addition, a just-in-time manufacturing system increases the traceability of costs to work centers and to individual prod-

Variable Costing Income Statements

	Product X	Product Y	Total
Sales	$550,000	$400,000	$950,000
Variable cost of goods sold	355,000	220,000	575,000
Manufacturing margin	$195,000	$180,000	$375,000
Variable selling and admin. exp.	60,000	64,000	124,000
Contribution margin	$135,000	$116,000	$251,000
Traceable fixed costs:			
Fixed manufacturing costs:			
Maintenance costs	$ 55,000	$ 15,000	$ 70,000
Supervisory costs	25,000	10,000	35,000
Quality control costs	12,000	5,000	17,000
Power costs	10,000	3,000	13,000
Materials handling costs	4,000	1,000	5,000
	$106,000	$ 34,000	$140,000
Fixed selling and admin. expense:			
Advertising expense	$ 18,000	$ 6,000	$ 24,000
Sales salaries	12,000	5,000	17,000
Utilities expense	5,000	2,000	7,000
	$ 35,000	$ 13,000	$ 48,000
Total traceable fixed costs	$141,000	$ 47,000	$188,000
Product margin	$ (6,000)	$ 69,000	$ 63,000
Nontraceable fixed costs:			
Fixed manufacturing costs			$ 30,000
Fixed selling and admin. expense			3,000
Total nontraceable fixed costs			$ 33,000
Income from operations			$ 30,000

ucts. Since management is better able to determine how costs will change with alternative courses of action, differential analysis is improved.

To illustrate, assume that Holte Inc. is currently making a component for Product M and is considering the purchase of the component for $15 per unit. Holte Inc. expects to use 20,000 components a year in the production of Product M. Thus, the cost of purchasing the part is $300,000 ($15 × 20,000 units) per year. The cost of manufacturing the part is $19 per unit, using traditional absorption costing, as shown below:

Direct materials	$ 8
Direct labor	3
Variable manufacturing overhead	1
Fixed manufacturing overhead	7
Total manufacturing cost	$19

The following traditional differential analysis indicates that Holte Inc. should continue manufacturing the component:

Proposal to Purchase Component		
Total cost of purchasing component		$300,000
Differential cost of manufacturing component:		
Direct materials (20,000 units × $8)	$160,000	
Direct labor (20,000 units × $3)	60,000	
Variable manufacturing overhead (20,000 units × $1)	20,000	240,000
Cost savings from manufacture		$ 60,000

To illustrate the potential usefulness of activity-based costing for differential analysis, assume that the fixed manufacturing overhead is composed of the following cost pools and related overhead rates:

Cost Pool	Cost Driver Overhead Rate
Maintenance	$4 per machine hour
Power	$.016 per kilowatt hour
Quality control	$500 per inspection
Setup	$2,500 per production run

The component to Product M uses the following amounts of each cost driver:

Machine hours	3,500
Kilowatt hours	500 000
Inspections	30
Production runs	12

The following differential analysis, based upon activity-based costing, indicates that Holte Inc. should purchase the component:

Proposal to Purchase Component		
Differential cost of manufacturing component:		
Direct materials (20,000 units × $8)	$160,000	
Direct labor (20,000 units × $3)	60,000	
Variable manufacturing overhead (20,000 units × $1)	20,000	
Maintenance (3,500 hrs. × $4)	14,000	
Power (500 000 kwh × $.016)	8,000	
Quality control (30 inspections × $500)	15,000	
Setup (12 setups × $2,500)	30,000	
Total cost of manufacturing component		$307,000
Total cost of purchasing component		300,000
Cost savings from purchasing		$ 7,000

Capital Investment Analysis

As discussed in Chapter 23, traditional capital investment analysis focuses upon the tangible cash flows created from a proposed capital investment. However, intangible benefits such as higher product quality and reliability, greater manufacturing flexibility, and quicker cycle time can have a significant effect on enterprise profitability. Although such intangible benefits can be difficult to estimate, their impact can significantly affect managerial decisions.

To illustrate, assume that Driscoll Inc. is considering the purchase of a robot for $250,000. The robot is not expected to have any significant salvage value at the end of 5 years. Based on the robot's projected cash flows over its 5-year life and a minimum rate of return of 12%, the net present value analysis of the proposal is shown as follows:

Year	Present Value of $1 at 12%	Net Cash Flow	Present Value of Net Cash Flow
1	.893	$ 70,000	$ 62,510
2	.797	60,000	47,820
3	.712	60,000	42,720
4	.636	50,000	31,800
5	.567	40,000	22,680
Total		$280,000	$207,530
Amount to be invested			250,000
Net present value			$ (42,470)

This net present value analysis indicates that the investment should not be made. However, assume that the robot is expected to improve product quality and reliability and reduce the number of rework items and product warranty claims. Although the monetary benefits of reducing rework items and warranty claims may be difficult to estimate, they can have a significant impact on the net present value analysis. For example, assume that the improved quality and reliability of the robot will reduce the cost of rework items and warranty claims by $20,000 per year. The following revised net present value analysis indicates that the investment should be made:

Year	Present Value of $1 at 12%	Revised Net Cash Flow	Present Value of Net Cash Flow
1	.893	$ 90,000	$ 80,370
2	.797	80,000	63,760
3	.712	80,000	56,960
4	.636	70,000	44,520
5	.567	60,000	34,020
Total		$380,000	$279,630
Amount to be invested			250,000
Net present value			$ 29,630

The preceding illustration demonstrates the importance of including estimates of intangible benefits in capital investment analysis. Giving consideration to these benefits is particularly important in the new manufacturing environment, in which companies are increasingly competing on the basis of the quality of their products and their ability to respond quickly to customer needs.

APPENDIX 1 QUALITY CONTROL

The importance of quality control was briefly mentioned in this chapter. In the global marketplace, companies are placing greater emphasis on quality as a competitive tool. This appendix briefly describes quality control concepts, especially as they relate to the new manufacturing environment.

THE NATURE OF QUALITY

The quality of a product is largely determined by the consumers' perceptions of the product's excellence. For example, an automobile that continually requires repairs will generally be perceived by consumers as being of low quality. The quality of a product can be influenced by (1) product design and (2) conformance with manufacturing standards.

Product Design

The starting point for designing quality into a product is to identify consumer expectations. Since consumers will ultimately determine the quality of a product, their expectations are critical to the design process. Many companies believe they know what the consumer wants, but few take the time to ask. If the company is wrong, much time, effort, and money can be wasted doing things the consumer doesn't value, while ignoring those things that the consumer wants.

Once consumer expectations have been identified, the product should be engineered to meet those expectations. This design process should be heavily influenced by the ability to manufacture the product in an efficient and effective manner. One performance measure often used to assess the effectiveness of the engineering function within a company is the number of engineering change orders that are required after a product has been approved for manufacture.

To improve product quality, many companies are designing products that minimize the number of component parts. Experience has generally shown that the fewer the number of components, the fewer the number of defective products, and thus the higher the product quality.

An additional consideration in designing quality into a product is the design of the manufacturing process itself. For example, just-in-time manufacturing systems are designed to facilitate quality control by organizing the manufacturing process into work centers. Research has shown that employees who perform several manufacturing processes within a work center better identify with the end product. This employee identification generates pride in the product and improves product quality and employee productivity.

Conformance with Manufacturing Standards

Once the product has been designed and the manufacturing process approved, quality is normally measured against manufacturing standards. Within traditional manufacturing systems, quality is measured by conforming to acceptable quality limits. For example, quality control charts may be developed, using statistical methods that show desired operating conditions and limits within which production may vary. Production observations outside these limits require investigation and possible corrective action.

In the quality control chart below, the rate of defective units is represented by the vertical axis. The horizontal axis represents 14 samples taken from the production process over a period of time. The upper limit for the rate of defective units is 4%. The actual rates of defective units are plotted on the chart, based on the sample observations. For example, sample observation 3 indicates a rate of defective units of 2%.

Quality Control Chart

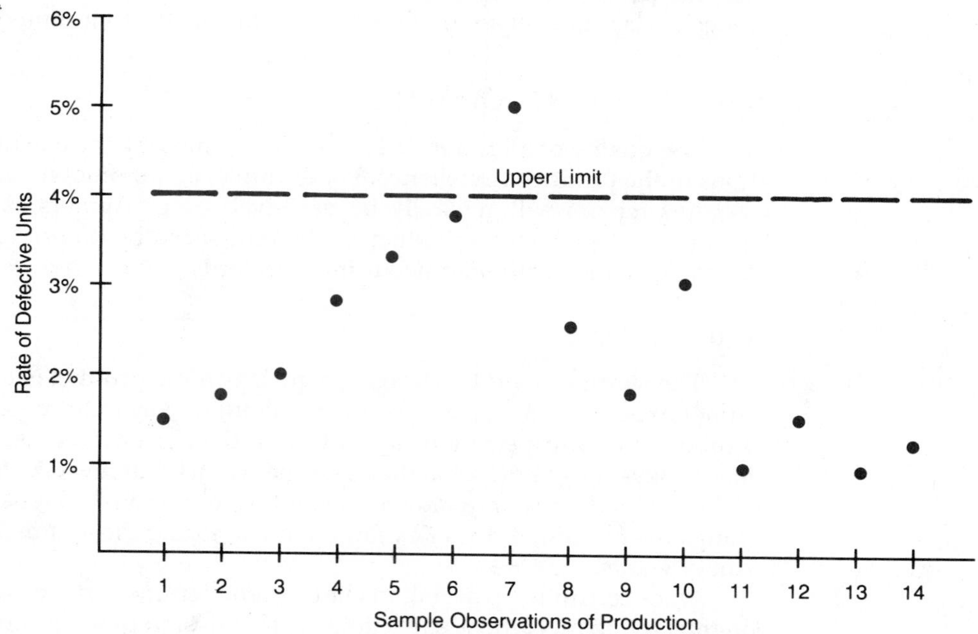

Quality control charts aid managers in determining trends in the rate of defective units and whether the manufacturing process is in control or out of control. For example, in the preceding quality control chart, observations 1-6 indicate increasing rates of defective units, ending with observation 7. At this point, management took corrective action to bring the rate of defective units back into an acceptable range, as indicated by observations 8-14.

In the new manufacturing environment, many companies have implemented total quality control systems. For example, a company that implements a just-in-time manufacturing system must also implement the concept of total quality control. Total quality control systems emphasize zero defects or, in other words, "doing it right the first time." The total quality control concept also emphasizes continued improvement in the manufacturing process.

To improve quality and the manufacturing process, many companies organize workers into quality circles, sometimes referred to as quality control teams. A quality circle is a group of employees who meet periodically to identify and discuss manufacturing concerns and, when appropriate, to suggest and implement solutions to these concerns. The use of quality circles helps to generate greater worker interest and commitment to the manufacturing process and to product quality. The team concept also tends to generate a greater number of suggestions for improving the manufacturing process.

QUALITY CONTROL COSTS

Quality control costs can be classified into four categories: (1) prevention costs, (2) detection costs, (3) internal failure costs, and (4) external failure costs. Each of these costs is briefly described in the following paragraphs.

Prevention Costs

Costs incurred to prevent defects from occurring during the manufacturing process are prevention costs. Thus, the cost of engineering the product and the cost of reorganizing the manufacturing process are classified as prevention costs. Other examples of prevention costs include the cost of training employees, the cost of selecting suppliers, and the cost of quality circles. As prevention costs increase, the number of defects should decrease.

Detection Costs

Costs incurred in detecting and reporting defects in the manufacturing process are detection costs. Thus, the costs of inspecting and testing products for defective units are detection costs. Other examples of detection costs include the cost of preparing and analyzing quality control reports and the cost of field-testing products prior to delivery to consumers. As detection costs increase, the number of defects should decrease.

Internal Failure Costs

Costs incurred after defective units have been detected, such as the cost of reworking defective units, are internal failure costs. Other examples of internal failure costs include the cost of scrap and waste created by defective units, the cost of production downtime because of defective units, the cost of redesigning products, and the costs of retesting and reinspection of defective units. As quality control improves and the number of defective units decreases, internal failure costs will decrease. If no defective units occur, the internal failure costs will be zero.

External Failure Costs

Costs incurred after defective units have been delivered to consumers are external failure costs. Examples of external failure costs include the costs of warranty repairs, recalls, and returns and allowances for defective units, product liability costs, and the cost of lost sales related to defective units. As quality control improves and the number of defective units decreases, external failure costs will decrease.

Summary of Quality Control Costs

Examples of quality control costs for each of the four categories are listed in the following table:

Quality Control Costs

Prevention Costs	Detection Costs
Designing and engineering	Inspecting and testing products
Pilot studies	Monitoring suppliers
Quality circles	Field testing
Vendor selection costs	Preparing quality control reports
Training costs	
Costs of reorganizing the manufacturing process	

Quality Control Costs, continued

Internal Failure Costs	External Failure Costs
Reworking defective units	Product recalls
Scrap and waste from defective units	Warranty repairs
Production downtime due to defective units	Product liability claims
Redesigning products	Returns and allowances from defective units
Reinspecting and retesting defective units	Cost of lost sales from defective units
Disposing of defective units	

MANAGERIAL ACCOUNTING AND QUALITY CONTROL

The role of managerial accounting is to provide information to management for making decisions regarding quality control issues. One example of this information is the traditional quality control chart described in the preceding paragraphs. This chart discloses the existence of defective units or predicts when defective units are likely to occur.

Another example of this information is a report that estimates the total quality control costs based upon prevention costs, detection costs, internal failure costs, and external failure costs. Such a report is valuable to management in deciding the level of quality control to implement. For example, the following graph illustrates the relationship between total quality control costs and the four categories of quality control costs.

Total Quality Control Costs

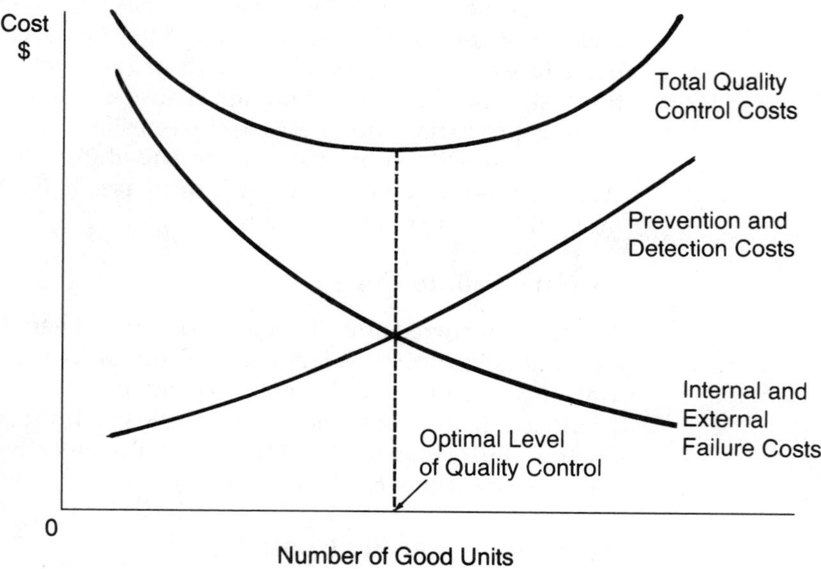

As indicated in the graph, the optimal level of quality control is that level which minimizes the estimated total quality control costs. To reach this level, the trade-off between prevention and detection costs and internal and external failure costs must be recognized. That is, when more effort is given to prevention and detection, internal and external failure costs decrease. Total quality control costs decrease only up to a point, however. Beyond that point, any additional prevention and detection will increase total quality control costs more than will be saved in internal and external failure costs.

APPENDIX 2

DECISION MAKING UNDER UNCERTAINTY

Uncertainty is a characteristic of the environments in which managers must make decisions. The managerial accountant can aid management in making decisions under uncertainty by providing data useful in assessing the chances that future events will occur and the impact of those events. One technique useful for this purpose is the expected value concept.

MANAGERIAL USE OF THE EXPECTED VALUE CONCEPT

The concept of **expected value** involves identifying the possible outcomes from a decision and estimating the likelihood that each outcome will occur. By using the expected value concept, managers can better evaluate the uncertainty of the occurrence of predicted outcomes from decisions.

The likelihood that an outcome will occur from a decision is usually expressed in terms of a probability or chance of occurrence. For example, the probability or chance that, on the flip of a coin, a head will appear is .50 or 50%. Likewise, the probability or chance that the introduction of a new product will be successful might be expressed as .60 or 60%.

The expected value of a decision is the sum of the values that result when the dollar value of each outcome is multiplied by the probability or chance of its occurrence. Thus, expected value can be thought of as an average value.

That is, each possible outcome is weighted by its chance of occurrence to obtain an average expected outcome. For example, assume that you are playing a game in which a coin is flipped. If a head appears, you win \$10,000; if a tail appears, you lose \$6,000. The expected value of this game is \$2,000, computed as follows:

$$\text{Expected Value} = .50(\$10{,}000) + .50(-\$6{,}000)$$
$$\text{Expected Value} = \$5{,}000 - \$3{,}000$$
$$\text{Expected Value} = \$2{,}000$$

If you played the preceding game a large number of times, 50% of the time you would win \$10,000, 50% of the time you would lose \$6,000, and on the average you would win \$2,000 per game. For example, if you played the game twice and won once and lost once, you would have won \$10,000 and lost \$6,000. Hence, you would have net winnings of \$4,000 (\$10,000 − \$6,000). Since you played the game twice, your average winnings would be \$2,000 per game (\$4,000 ÷ 2). Consequently, the expected value of playing the game is \$2,000.

To illustrate the expected value concept within a managerial context, assume that the management of Faxon Company is faced with deciding on a location for a new hotel. The search for the best site has been narrowed to two choices within a large metropolitan area. One site is in the center of the city. The accessibility to the city's business and entertainment district makes this site attractive for conventions. The other location is twenty miles from the center of the city at an intersection of two interstate highways. The site is attractive because of its proximity to the city's international airport. After the hotel is constructed, the management of Faxon Company plans to operate the hotel for one year and then sell the hotel for a profit. Over the past five years, Faxon has successfully constructed and sold four hotels in this fashion.

The estimated profit or loss at each site depends on whether the occupancy rate the first year is high or low. Based on marketing studies, the following profit and loss data have been estimated:

City Site	Profit or Loss	Chance of Occurrence
High occupancy	$1,500,000	70%
Low occupancy	(500,000)	30
Interstate Site	**Profit or Loss**	**Chance of Occurrence**
High occupancy	$1,000,000	60%
Low occupancy	100,000	40

The expected value of each site is computed by weighing each outcome by its chance of occurrence, as follows:

City Site

Expected value = .7($1,500,000) + .3(−$500,000)
Expected value = $1,050,000 − $150,000
Expected value = $900,000

Interstate Site

Expected value = .6($1,000,000) + .4($100,000)
Expected value = $600,000 + $40,000
Expected value = $640,000

Based on the expected values, the city site is more attractive than the interstate site because the city site has a higher expected value. Thus, on the average, the city site is expected to yield a higher profit than the interstate site.

The expected values for the city site and the interstate site of $900,000 and $640,000, respectively, will not actually occur. These values are weighted averages of the estimated profit or loss for each site. For the city site, the estimated outcome will be either a profit of $1,500,000 or a loss of $500,000. Likewise, for the interstate site, the estimated outcome will be either a profit of $1,000,000 or a profit of $100,000.

In the face of uncertainty, expected value is one of the most important pieces of information available to the manager for making a decision. Because expected value is an average concept, however, the range of possible outcomes (the variability of the outcomes) may also be valuable information for management's assessment of the uncertainty surrounding a decision. Although the city site in the preceding illustration has a higher expected value than the interstate site, the city site also has a wider range of possible outcomes (a profit of $1,500,000 or a loss of $500,000) than does the interstate site (a profit of $1,000,000 or $100,000). Consequently, the management of Faxon Company might select the interstate site in order to minimize the variability of the possible outcomes from the site decision. As with many other decisions, management must exercise judgment after weighing all available data and analyses.

The use of the expected value concept by management can be facilitated through the use of decision trees. In addition, the expected value concept may be used by managers in assessing the value of collecting additional information before a decision is made. The remainder of this appendix describes and illustrates the use of decision trees and discusses the value of obtaining additional information.

Decision Trees

Decision trees are graphical representations of decisions, possible outcomes, and chances that outcomes will occur. Decision trees are especially useful to managers who are choosing among alternatives when possible outcomes are dependent on several decisions. For example, if management decides to produce a new product, it must consider whether to offer the product in all consumer markets or only in specific markets, whether to offer special introductory rebates, whether to offer special warranties, and whether and how much to advertise. In this case, the expected profit from producing the new product depends on many decisions, each of which has an effect on the profitability of the new product.

To illustrate the use of decision trees, assume that Lampe Company is considering disposing of unimproved land. If the unimproved land is to be sold as is, its sales price would be \$80,000. If the land is improved, however, there is a 40% chance that it can be rezoned for commercial development and sold for \$120,000 more than the cost incurred in making improvements. There is a 60% chance that the improved land would be rezoned for residential use, in which case the land could be sold to a real estate developer for \$70,000 more than the cost of improvements.

The decision tree for the preceding example can be diagrammed as follows:

Decision Tree—Profit from Sale of Unimproved or Improved Land

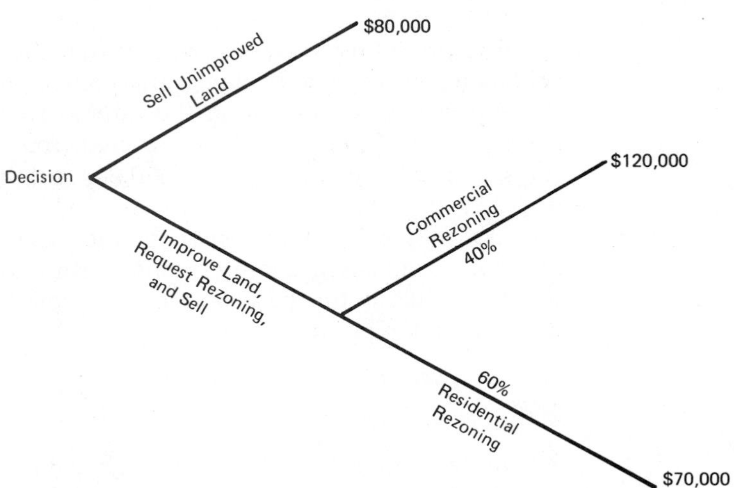

The expected values can be computed directly from the decision tree by tracing back through each branch of the decision tree and multiplying each of the possible outcomes by the chance of its occurrence. For example, the expected value of the land being rezoned for commercial use and sold for \$120,000 is \$48,000 (\$120,000 × .4). The expected value of the residential rezoning is computed in a similar manner and is \$42,000 (\$70,000 × .6). Since there is no uncertainty concerning the selling of the unimproved land for $80,000, the expected value of selling the unimproved land is $80,000. These expected values are summarized in the following decision tree:

Decision Tree with Expected Values—Profit from Sale of Unimproved or Improved Land

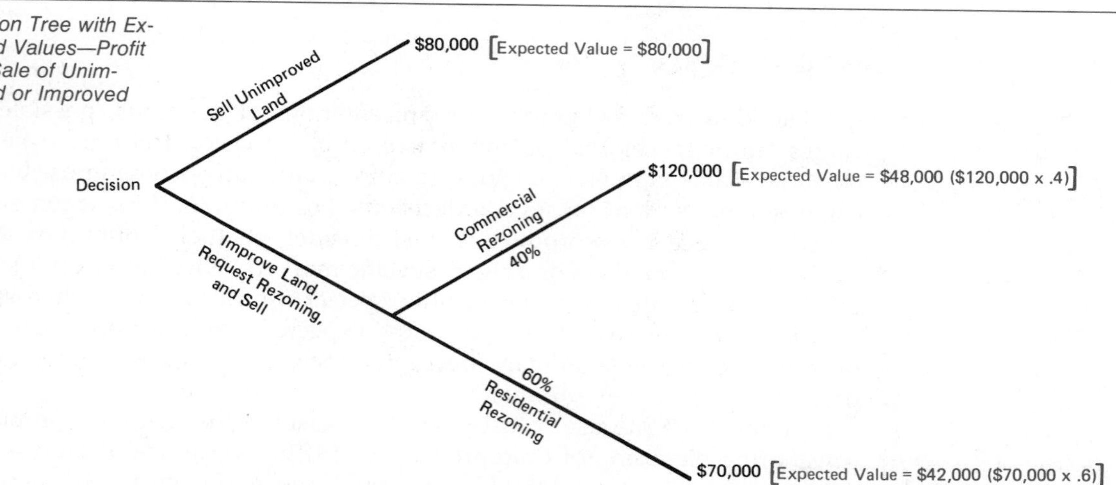

The total expected value of improving the land is equal to the sum of the expected values of the possible outcomes from the land improvement, or $90,000, computed as follows:

Commercial rezoning	$48,000
Residential rezoning	42,000
Total expected value of improving the land	$90,000

The preceding analysis indicates that the land should be improved and sold, since the expected value of this course of action, $90,000, is higher than the expected value of selling the unimproved land, $80,000. Thus, on the average, a profit of $90,000 is expected from improving the land, with the worst possibility being a profit of $70,000 and the best possibility being a profit of $120,000.

Decision trees can be constructed to incorporate a large number of possible courses of action. The preceding illustration was intentionally brief in order to highlight the basic use of decision trees in aiding management's decision making under uncertainty.

Value of Information

In decision making, managers rarely have easy access to all the information they desire. In such cases, management must consider the information available and the value and the cost of seeking additional information relevant to the decision. If the expected value of acquiring additional information exceeds its expected cost, then the additional information should be acquired.

To illustrate, assume that an investment in Proposal A is expected to have a 60% chance of earning net income of $10,000 and a 40% chance of suffering a net loss of $5,000. This situation is diagrammed in the following decision tree:

Decision Tree—Proposal A

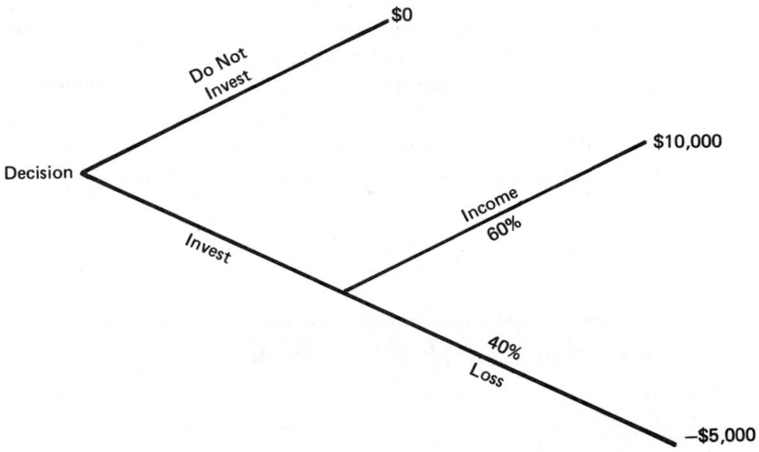

The expected value of investing in Proposal A is equal to the sum of the expected values of the possible outcomes, or $4,000, computed as follows:

Expected value of Proposal A = ($10,000 × .6) + (−$5,000 × .4)
Expected value of Proposal A = $6,000 − $2,000
Expected value of Proposal A = $4,000

Since the expected value of Proposal A is positive, the manager would normally invest in the proposal, even though there is a 40% chance of a loss of $5,000. Assume, however, that the manager could acquire additional information that would indicate with certainty whether Proposal A would earn the $10,000 income or suffer the loss of $5,000. How much would the manager be willing to pay for this additional (perfect) information?

The maximum amount (cost) that would be paid to obtain perfect information concerning a decision is termed the **value of perfect information.** It is the difference between (1) the expected value of a decision based on the perfect information and (2) the expected value of a decision based on existing information. To illustrate, the maximum amount that would be paid to obtain perfect information concerning Proposal A is determined by first computing the expected value of the proposal as if it is known beforehand whether the proposal would be successful or not. If the manager knows that the proposal will be successful, then a decision to invest would be made and income of $10,000 would be earned. If the manager knows that the proposal will be unsuccessful, then a decision not to invest would be made and no income or loss would result. For Proposal A, 60% of the time the perfect information will indicate that the proposal would be successful and therefore income of $10,000 would be earned. Also, 40% of the time the information will indicate that the proposal would be unsuccessful and therefore management would not invest. The expected value of perfect information is equal to the sum of the expected values of the possible outcomes, or $6,000, computed as follows:

Expected value of Proposal A,
based on perfect information = ($10,000 × .6) + ($0 × .4)
Expected value of Proposal A,
based on perfect information = $6,000

The value of perfect information concerning Proposal A is then determined by subtracting $4,000, the expected value of Proposal A, based on existing information, from the $6,000 computed above. Thus, as shown in the following computation, the manager would be willing to pay $2,000 to obtain perfect information concerning Proposal A.

Expected value of Proposal A, based on perfect information	$6,000
Less expected value of Proposal A, based on existing information	4,000
Value of perfect information concerning Proposal A	$2,000

CHAPTER REVIEW

KEY POINTS

OBJECTIVE 1

Characteristics of the New Manufacturing Environment

The new manufacturing environment is characterized by an emphasis on manufacturing flexibility and total quality control. Manufacturing flexibility and quality control may be improved by investing in automated, computer-aided machinery, and by reorganizing the manufacturing process. Because the investment in new technology and automation generally increases manufacturing overhead, it has become increasingly important to accurately trace overhead costs to activities and products. Activity-based costing is being used to reduce or eliminate the product cost distortions that are often created by traditional overhead allocation methods. Activity-based costing also highlights the existence of non-value-adding overhead activities.

OBJECTIVE 2

Investing in Inventory

Business enterprises maintain inventories in order to meet production and customer demands. At the same time, however, management attempts to minimize the cost of carrying inventory and the cost of interrupting production due to lack of inventories. The costs of carrying inventory include opportunity costs, the cost of ordering materials, the purchase cost of materials, and storage costs.

The opportunity costs related to inventory are the cost of workers' idle time when not enough inventory is carried to continue the production process, and the completion of other products is delayed; the profits on sales that are lost when not enough inventory is carried to meet customer needs; and the amount of income that could have been earned on funds invested in inventory.

Ordering costs will increase as the total number of orders placed increases. Purchase costs will increase if shortages arise and rush orders must be shipped at higher freight costs. By purchasing in larger quantities, quantity discounts are often obtained. Storage costs are reduced by carrying smaller amounts of inventory.

Additional manufacturing costs may be incurred when production is interrupted because of insufficient inventory. These costs might include overtime to meet production schedules and customer needs and additional costs of setting up the machinery to process materials.

OBJECTIVE 3

Inventory Management in a Just-in-Time Manufacturing System

In JIT manufacturing systems, materials enter the manufacturing process just in time to be completed and to satisfy the demand of the next work center or the customer. As a result, inventories are reduced to small or insignificant levels. JIT inventory management reduces or eliminates the opportunity costs related to inventory and the ordering costs, purchase costs, storage costs, and costs of interrupting production.

OBJECTIVE 4

Inventory Management in a Traditional Manufacturing System

The primary objective of inventory management in a traditional manufacturing system is the same as in a JIT system. The opportunity cost of lost sales or production must be balanced with the inventory carrying costs in order to minimize total costs.

Some tools that aid in the management of inventory costs are the economic order quantity (EOQ) calculation, the inventory reorder point calculation, and linear programming. The EOQ is the optimum quantity of materials to order that will minimize the costs of ordering and storing the materials. The inventory reorder point is the level to which inventory is allowed to fall before an order for additional inventory is placed. Linear programming can be used to determine the most economical purchasing plan, that is, the plan that minimizes purchase costs.

OBJECTIVE 5

Implications of the New Manufacturing Environment for Analyses

Costs may be misclassified in cost-volume-profit analysis if units produced is used as the only activity base in the analysis. Activity-based costing allows for a more accurate analysis of cost-volume-profit relationships because the behavior costs are more accurately described in terms of cost drivers.

Variable costing is still applicable in the new manufacturing environment. However, activity-based costing can further enhance the use of variable costing for decision making by tracing and presenting fixed costs by individual products in accordance with relevant cost drivers. The profitability of each product and its contribution to overall enterprise profits, referred to as product margin, can then be assessed.

The use of activity-based costing allows managers to better focus on costs that will change with the relevant cost drivers. Since managers are better able to understand how costs will change with alternative courses of action, differential analysis is improved.

Traditional capital investment analysis focuses upon the tangible cash flow created from a proposed capital investment. However, intangible benefits such as higher product quality and reliability, greater manufacturing flexibility, and quicker cycle time can significantly affect an enterprise's profitability. Although such intangible benefits can be difficult to estimate, their impact can affect capital investment decisions.

KEY TERMS

cycle (throughput) time 1000
just-in-time (JIT) manufacturing systems 1001
total quality control (TCQ) 1003
economic order quantity (EOQ) 1006
inventory reorder point 1007
lead time 1007
safety stock 1007
linear programming 1009
product margin 1015

SELF-EXAMINATION QUESTIONS

Answers at end of chapter.

1. Which of the following statements is characteristic of a just-in-time manufacturing system?
   A. It reduces inventories to low or insignificant levels
   B. Materials are received just in time to enter the manufacturing process
   C. It emphasizes total quality control
   D. All of the above

2. In the new manufacturing environment, which of the following activities would be considered a non-value-adding activity of manufacturing this textbook?
   A. Typesetting of the original manuscript
   B. Printing of the textbook
   C. Time spent setting up presses to print the textbook
   D. Binding of the cover to the printed pages

3. Verde Inc. expects to need 2,500 units of Material K, the cost of placing an order is $20 per order, and the storage cost per unit is $.40. What is the economic order quantity for Material K?
   A. 50 units
   B. 100 units
   C. 500 units
   D. 1,250 units

4. Costner Inc., a furniture manufacturer, estimates a daily usage of 5,000 linear feet of oak and a lead time of 7 days to receive an order of oak. Costner Inc. desires a safety stock of 25,000 linear feet of oak. What is the inventory reorder point?
   A. 5,000 linear feet
   B. 30,000 linear feet
   C. 35,000 linear feet
   D. 60,000 linear feet

5. Which of the following analyses does the new manufacturing environment significantly impact?
   A. Cost-volume-profit analysis
   B. Variable costing
   C. Capital investment analysis
   D. All of the above

ILLUSTRATIVE PROBLEM

Colson company has gathered the following data for the materials used in its manufacturing process. The materials are used at a uniform rate throughout the year.

Units required during the year	3,960
Units of safety stock	270
Days of scheduled production	220
Days of lead time to receive an order	20
Ordering cost, per order placed	$ 33
Annual storage cost, per unit	$.15

Instructions:

(1) Complete the following table for "number of orders" of 1 through 6.

Number of Orders	Number of Units per Order	Average Units in Inventory	Order and Storage Costs: Order Cost	Storage Cost	Combined Cost
1	3,960	1,980	$33.00	$297.00	$330.00

(2) Determine the economic order quantity, based on the table completed in (1).

(3) Determine the economic order quantity, using the economic order quantity formula.

(4) Determine the inventory reorder point.

SOLUTION

(1)

Number of Orders	Number of Units per Order	Average Units in Inventory	Order Cost	Storage Cost	Combined Cost
			Order and Storage Costs		
1	3,960	1,980	$ 33.00	$297.00	$330.000
2	1,980	990	66.00	148.50	214.50
3	1,320	660	99.00	99.00	198.00
4	990	495	132.00	74.25	206.25
5	792	396	165.00	59.40	224.40
6	660	330	198.00	49.50	247.50

(2) The table in (1) indicates that the economic order quantity is 1,320 units of materials per order, with 3 orders per year, at a total cost of $198.

(3) $$\text{EOQ} = \sqrt{\frac{2 \times \text{Annual Units Required} \times \text{Cost per Order Placed}}{\text{Annual Storage Cost per Unit}}}$$

$$\text{EOQ} = \sqrt{\frac{2 \times 3{,}960 \times \$33}{\$.15}}$$

$$\text{EOQ} = \sqrt{1{,}742{,}400}$$

$$\text{EOQ} = 1{,}320 \text{ units}$$

(4) Inventory Reorder Point = (Daily Usage × Lead Time) + Safety Stock
Inventory Reorder Point = (18 units* × 20 days) + 270
Inventory Reorder Point = 630 units

*Daily usage = 3,960 units ÷ 220 days = 18 units

DISCUSSION QUESTIONS

24–1. How does the use of automated machinery increase manufacturing overhead costs?

24–2. As direct labor costs decline as a percentage of total product cost, how are some companies accounting for direct labor costs?

24–3. How does activity-based costing generate more accurate product costs than traditional cost methods?

24–4. List some non-value-adding activities that are highlighted by the use of activity-based costing.

24–5. What term is used to refer to the amount of time required to manufacture a product?

24–6. State the mathematical expression for cycle time.

24–7. Describe how a traditional production process is organized.

24–8. What is meant by describing a product as being "pushed through" a traditional production process?

24–9. Why do work in process inventories often build up in a traditional production process?

24–10. Describe how a just-in-time manufacturing system reorganizes traditional production processes.

24–11. Contrast how production workers perform their jobs under a traditional production process and a just-in-time manufacturing system.

24–12. What is an example of a non-value-adding activity that is reduced in a just-in-time manufacturing system?

24–13. What is meant by describing a product as being "pulled through" a just-in-time manufacturing system?

24–14. Contrast quality control in a traditional manufacturing system and a just-in-time manufacturing system.

24–15. What opportunity costs are related to inventory?

24–16. What are the costs of carrying inventory?

24–17. How does just-in-time inventory management reduce order costs?

24–18. Name three traditional tools of inventory management.

24–19. What costs does the economic order quantity minimize?

24–20. What question does the economic order quantity address?

24–21. Based upon the following table, determine the economic order quantity.

Number of Orders	Number of Units per Order	Average Units in Inventory	Order and Storage Costs		
			Order Cost	*Storage Cost*	*Combined Cost*
1	1,200	600	$ 50	$900	$950
2	600	300	100	450	550
3	400	200	150	300	450
4	300	150	200	225	425
5	240	120	250	180	430
6	200	100	300	150	450
7	171	86	350	129	479

24–22. State the mathematical formula for determining the economic order quantity.

24–23. What term is used to describe the level to which inventory is allowed to fall before an order for additional inventory is placed?

24–24. Upon what factors does the inventory reorder point depend?

24–25. What term is used to describe the amount of inventory that is available for use when unforeseen circumstances arise?

24–26. State the formula for computing the inventory reorder point.

24–27. Guerrero Inc. produces personal computers and estimates daily usage of 2,000, 3 1/2-inch disk drives. It takes a lead time of 4 days to receive an order of disk drives, and a safety stock of 6,000 disk drives is desired. What is the inventory reorder point for Guerrero Inc.?

24–28. When would no safety stock be required?

24–29. What quantitative method can provide data for solving a variety of business problems in which management's objective is to minimize costs or maximize profits, subject to several limiting factors?

24–30. What term is used to refer to the mathematical approach to linear programming?

24–31. How does activity-based costing affect cost-volume-profit analysis?

24–32. How does activity-based costing enhance variable costing?

24–33. Define the product margin.

24–34. How does activity-based costing affect differential analysis?

24–35. What are some of the intangible benefits of the new manufacturing environment that affect capital investment analysis?

Real World Focus

24–36. Japan pioneered the development of just-in-time manufacturing systems. In the past several years, many companies in the United States, including General Motors and Ford Motor Company, have implemented just-in-time manufacturing practices. What impact could Japan's smaller geographic size relative to the United States have on its ability to implement JIT manufacturing systems?

Ethics Discussion Case

24–37. Many suppliers who do business with General Motors and other large manufacturing companies depend upon receiving orders from these manufacturers for their survival. For example, a supplier of an engine component for General Motors' automobiles would go out of business if General Motors canceled its orders and switched to another supplier. In implementing a just-in-time manufacturing system, assume that General Motors demands that the supplier build a warehouse near one of its production facilities. In addition, General Motors demands that the supplier implement a total quality control system (subject to review by General Motors' personnel) and invest in a sophisticated bar coding system that would allow General Motors to keep track of all inventory through the use of computer (bar coding) scanners. If the supplier does not comply within one year, General Motors will switch to another supplier. Is it ethical for General Motors to make these demands on its supplier?

EXERCISES

Ex. 24–38.
Economic order quantity.
OBJ. 4

Product T is used at the same rate throughout the year, 8,100 units are required during the year, the cost per order placed is $3, and the storage cost per unit is $1.50. What is the economic order quantity for Product T? Use the formula on page 1007.

Ex. 24–39.
Inventory reorder point.
OBJ. 4

Smith Co. estimates daily usage of 3,000 pounds of Material F, the lead time to receive an order of Material F is 15 days, and a safety stock of 12,000 pounds is desired. What is the inventory reorder point?

Ex. 24–40.
Inventory reorder point.
OBJ. 4

Esquibel Inc., which produces bottled mineral water, estimates daily usage of 10,000, 16-oz. bottles. It normally takes 5 days to receive a shipment of bottles, and Esquibel Inc. desires a safety stock of 80,000 bottles. (a) Determine the inventory reorder point for 16-oz. bottles. (b) Another bottle supplier has a distribution center near Esquibel Inc.'s plant, so that a shipment of bottles could be received in 2 days. In addition, if Esquibel Inc. switches suppliers, it could reduce its desired safety stock to 30,000 bottles. Determine the revised reorder point if Esquibel Inc. switches suppliers. (c) If the average storage cost is $.002 per bottle, the bottles cost $.05 per bottle, and Esquibel Inc. could earn 10% on its funds, how much could Esquibel Inc. save annually by switching suppliers?

Ex. 24–41.
Economic order quantity and inventory reorder point.
OBJ. 4

McKean Company estimates that 2,040 units of Material H will be required during the coming year. The materials will be used at the rate of 20 units per day throughout the 272-day period of budgeted production for the year. Past experience indicates that the annual storage cost is $.30 per unit, the cost to place an order is $34, the lead time to receive an order is 15 days, and the desired amount of safety stock is 700 units. Determine (a) the economic order quantity, (b) the inventory reorder point, and (c) the number of units to be purchased when the inventory reorder point is reached.

Ex. 24–42.
Linear programming for purchasing decisions.
OBJ. 4

Glaser Company purchases Part Q for use at both its Beloit and Racine branches. Part Q is available in limited quantities from two suppliers. The relevant data for determining an economical purchase plan are as follows:

Units required:	
Beloit Branch	100 units
Racine Branch	200 units
Supplier M:	
Total units available	200 units
Unit cost delivered to:	
Beloit Branch	$40 per unit
Racine Branch	$60 per unit
Supplier N:	
Total units available	200 units
Unit cost delivered to:	
Beloit Branch	$50 per unit
Racine Branch	$75 per unit

The following linear programming graph for units purchased from Supplier M has been constructed, based on the above data:

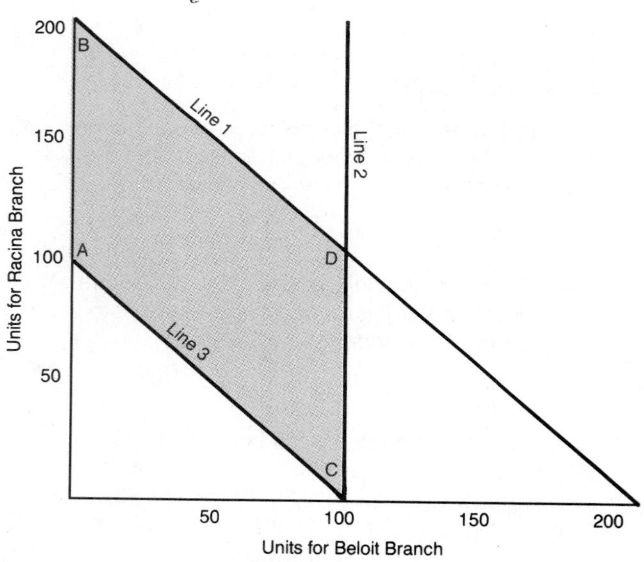

(a) For each of the four corners identified on the above graph by letters A through D, determine the purchases from Supplier M for the Beloit and Racine Branches. Use the same format as shown on page 1012.
(b) For each of the four corners in (a), indicate the units purchased from both Suppliers M and N for the Beloit and Racine Branches. Use the same format as shown on page 1012 and identify Plan 1 with Corner A, Plan 2 with Corner B, Plan 3 with Corner C, and Plan 4 with Corner D.
(c) Determine the most economical purchase plan by computing the total cost of each purchase plan determined in (b).

Ex. 24–43.
Cost-volume-profit analysis and activity-based costing.
OBJ. 5

The controller for DeJarkins Inc. determined that break-even sales were 14,000 units based on the following data:

Unit selling price	$90
Unit variable cost	50
Unit contribution margin	$40
Fixed costs	$560,000

Using activity-based costing, the following two cost pools were formed, with units produced and production setups as the activity bases (cost drivers):

Units produced cost pool:	
Unit variable cost	$30
Fixed costs	$480,000
Production setup cost pool:	
$1,000 per setup	90 setups estimated

Determine the revised break-even sales (units), based upon activity-based costing.

Ex. 24–44.
Differential analysis and activity-based costing.
OBJ. 5

Ortega Inc. is considering the purchase of a component of one of its products for $42 per unit. Ortega Inc. expects to use 25,000 components per year. Traditional differential analysis is as follows:

Absorption cost data:	
Direct materials	$13
Direct labor	7
Variable manufacturing overhead	20
Fixed manufacturing overhead	8
Total manufacturing cost	$48

Proposal To Purchase Component

Total cost of purchasing component		$1,050,000
Differential cost of manufacturing component:		
Direct materials (25,000 units × $13)	$325,000	
Direct labor (25,000 units × $7)	175,000	
Variable manufacturing overhead (25,000 units × $20)	500,000	1,000,000
Cost savings from manufacture		$ 50,000

Based upon activity-based costing, assume that the fixed manufacturing overhead is composed of the following cost pools and related overhead rates:

Cost Pool	Cost Driver Overhead Rate
Maintenance	$3 per machine hour
Power	$.02 per kilowatt hour
Quality control	$300 per inspection
Setup	$900 per production run

The component uses the following amounts of each cost driver:

Machine hours	8,000
Kilowatt hours	400 000
Inspections	40
Production runs	25

Prepare a differential analysis report, based upon activity-based costing.

Ex. 24–45. Effect of intangibles on capital investment analysis. OBJ. 5

Vazquez Inc. is considering the purchase of a robot and has prepared the following net present value analysis:

Year	Present Value of $1 at 12%	Net Cash Flow	Present Value of Net Cash Flow
1	.893	$ 30,000	$ 26,790
2	.797	30,000	23,910
3	.712	25,000	17,800
4	.636	20,000	12,720
5	.567	20,000	11,340
Total		$125,000	$ 92,560
Amount to be invested			100,000
Net present value			$ (7,440)

Assume that the improved quality and reliability of the robot will reduce the cost of rework items and warranty claims by $5,000 per year.

Prepare a revised net present value analysis recognizing the estimated impact of the quality improvement.

Appendix 2 Ex. 24–46. Expected value.

While on vacation in Las Vegas, you are offered the opportunity to play one game of chance in which a die is thrown. The die is numbered one through six, and each number has an equal chance of appearing on any throw of the die. The winnings and losses established for each number on a throw of the die are as follows:

Number	Winnings (Losses)
1	$ 120
2	840
3	(480)
4	(240)
5	(540)
6	1,200

(a) Determine the expected value of playing the game. (b) If the cost of playing the game is $120, would you play? Explain.

Appendix 2 Ex. 24–47. Expected value.

Based on a rumor that a new shopping mall will locate near its office complex, McElroy Company is considering exercising an option to purchase twenty acres of land surrounding its offices. If the shopping mall is constructed, the land should increase substantially in value and be sold for a profit. The chance that the shopping mall will be built near the McElroy Company office complex and the potential profits that could result are as follows:

Outcome	Chance of Occurrence	Profit
Shopping mall locates near office complex	60%	$300,000
Shopping mall locates elsewhere	40	40,000

(a) Determine the expected value of exercising the option and purchasing land. (b) Assuming that exercising the option is one of several investments being considered, briefly discuss how the expected values computed in (a) might be compared with the alternatives.

Appendix 2 Ex. 24–48. Decision tree and expected value.

Sidwell Company is considering whether to offer a new product for sale in the South or in the West. Because of the uncertainty associated with introducing a new product, the decision will be made on the basis of expected annual income. The possible outcomes and chances of occurrence are summarized as follows:

Customer Demand	Southern Region Annual Income	Southern Region Chance of Occurrence	Western Region Annual Income	Western Region Chance of Occurrence
High	$25,000,000	30%	$30,000,000	40%
Moderate	10,000,000	40	6,000,000	20
Low	2,000,000	30	2,000,000	40

(a) To aid management in deciding in which region to offer the new product, prepare a decision tree with expected values. (b) Which region should be selected for the introduction of the new product, based on the expected value concept?

Appendix 2
Ex. 24–49.
Expected value and value of perfect information.

The management of Newsome Company has the opportunity to invest in Proposal E, which is expected to have a 40% chance of earning income of $50,000 and a 60% chance of suffering a loss of $30,000. (a) What is the expected value of Proposal E, based on existing information? (b) What is the expected value of Proposal E, based on perfect information? (c) What is the value of perfect information concerning Proposal E? (d) If the management of Newsome Company could purchase perfect information concerning Proposal E for $10,000, should the perfect information be purchased?

PROBLEMS

Pb. 24–50.
Economic order quantity and inventory reorder point.
OBJ. 4

Daniel Company has recently decided to implement a policy designed to control inventory better. Based on past experience, the following data have been gathered for materials, which are used at a uniform rate throughout the year:

Units required during the year	2,160
Units of safety stock	240
Days of scheduled production	270
Days of lead time to receive an order	20
Ordering cost, per order placed	$ 27
Annual storage cost, per unit	$.40

Instructions:

(1) Complete the following table for "number of orders" of 1 through 6.

Number of Orders	Number of Units per Order	Average Units in Inventory	Order and Storage Cost: Order Cost	Storage Cost	Combined Cost
1	2,160	1,080	$27.00	$432.00	$459.00

(2) Determine the economic order quantity, based on the table completed in (1).
(3) Determine the economic order quantity, using the formula on page 000.
(4) Determine the inventory reorder point.

Pb. 24–51.
Economic order quantity under present and proposed conditions.
OBJ. 4

Based on the data presented in Pb. 24–50, assume that Daniel Company is considering the purchase of new automated storage equipment to facilitate access to materials and to increase storage capacity. In addition, the manager of the Purchasing Department has requested authorization to purchase five microcomputers to expedite the processing of purchase orders.

Instructions:

(1) Assuming that the new storage equipment will increase the annual storage cost from $.40 to $1.60 per unit, determine the economic order quantity for Daniel Company, using the formula on page 1007.
(2) Assuming that the new storage equipment is not purchased and the acquisition of the microcomputer equipment will decrease the cost per order placed from $27.00 to $12.00, determine the economic order quantity, using the formula on page 1007.

(3) Assuming that both the new storage equipment and the microcomputer equipment are purchased, determine the economic order quantity, using the formula on page 1007. As indicated in (1) and (2), the purchase of the storage equipment is expected to increase the storage cost per unit from $.40 to $1.60, and the microcomputer equipment is expected to decrease the cost per order placed from $27.00 to $12.00.

(4) Based on the answers to Pb. 24–50 and (1), (2), and (3) above, what generalization can be made concerning how changes in the cost per order placed and the storage cost per unit affect the economic order quantity?

Pb. 24–52.
Linear programming for purchasing decisions.
OBJ. 4

Schellenberg Company purchases Part V for use at both its Elgin and Pekin Branches. Part V is available in limited quantities from two suppliers. The relevant data are as follows:

Units required:	
Elgin Branch	60
Pekin Branch	100
Supplier K:	
Units available	100
Unit cost delivered to:	
Elgin Branch	$25
Pekin Branch	$50
Supplier L:	
Units available	100
Unit cost delivered to:	
Elgin Branch	$30
Pekin Branch	$70

The new manager of the Purchasing Department of Schellenberg Company has prepared the following purchase plan for the Elgin and Pekin Branches:

	Purchases by Elgin Branch	Purchases by Pekin Branch
From Supplier K	60 units	40 units
From Supplier L	0	60

Instructions:

(1) Construct a linear programming graph for units to be purchased from Supplier K. Plot the units for the Elgin Branch along the horizontal axis.

(2) Identify the four corners at which an economical purchase plan might be identified on the linear programming graph. Label the corners A through D, as shown in the illustration on page 1012.

(3) For each corner in (2), indicate purchases from Suppliers K and L for the Elgin and Pekin branches. Identify Plan 1 with Corner A, Plan 2 with Corner B, Plan 3 with Corner C, and Plan 4 with Corner D.

(4) Determine the most economical purchase plan by computing the total cost of purchases for each plan identified in (3).

(5) Was the Purchasing Department manager's plan the most economical? Explain.

Pb. 24–53.
Cost-volume-profit analysis and activity-based costing.
OBJ. 5

Based upon prior years' data, Nguyen Inc. estimated the following unit selling price, unit variable cost, unit contribution margin, and total fixed costs for the year ending December 31, 1992:

Unit selling price	$120
Unit variable cost	75
Unit contribution margin	$ 45
Fixed costs	$810,000

The preceding cost data were based upon traditional analysis, using units produced as the activity base. Nguyen Inc. has begun implementing activity-based costing and has estimated the following costs, based upon a preliminary study:

Units produced cost pool:	
Unit variable cost	$50
Fixed costs	$630,000
Production setup cost pool:	
$600 per setup	175 setups

Instructions:

(1) Determine the break-even sales (units), using the traditional cost data and units produced as the activity base.
(2) Determine the break-even sales (units), using the activity-based costing estimate.
(3) Discuss why a difference exists between the break-even sales (units) in (1) and (2).

Pb. 24–54.
Variable costing and activity-based costing.
OBJ. 5

Based upon comments from the manufacturing supervisors that the product costs more to produce than it's worth, Sajjan Inc. is considering whether to continue to produce and sell Product S. The controller of Sajjan Inc. has prepared the following variable costing income statement, using the traditional contribution margin format:

Variable Costing Income Statement

	Product S	Other Products	Total
Sales	$180,000	$500,000	$680,000
Variable cost of goods sold	85,000	320,000	405,000
Manufacturing margin	$ 95,000	$180,000	$275,000
Variable selling and admin. exp.	60,000	64,000	124,000
Contribution margin	$ 35,000	$116,000	$151,000
Fixed costs:			
Fixed manufacturing costs			$ 70,000
Fixed selling and admin. exp.			40,000
Total fixed costs			$110,000
Income from operations			$ 41,000

Based upon the preceding variable costing income statement, the controller has recommended that Product S continue to be produced.

At the request of the vice-president of manufacturing, the assistant controller has been asked to prepare a supplemental analysis, based upon interviews with operating personnel. The assistant controller prepared the following list of fixed costs traceable to Product S:

	Product S	Other Products
Fixed manufacturing costs:		
Supervisory cost	$ 7,000	$15,500
Maintenance cost	5,500	9,000
Quality control cost	4,800	6,700
Power cost	2,500	4,300
Materials handling cost	1,200	2,000
	$21,000	$37,500
Fixed selling and admin. expenses:		
Advertising expense	$ 9,000	$12,000
Sales salaries	7,500	6,000
Utilities expense	1,000	1,500
	$17,500	$19,500

Instructions:

(1) Prepare a revised variable costing income statement for Product S.
(2) What are your recommendations for continuing to produce and sell Product S?
(3) What is the primary advantage of using activity-based costing for managerial decision making?
(4) What is the primary disadvantage for using activity-based costing for managerial decision making?

Pb. 24–55.
Effect of intangibles on capital investment analysis.
OBJ 5.

Trice Inc. is considering the purchase of a robot and has prepared the following net present value analysis:

Year	Present Value of $1 at 12%	Net Cash Flow	Present Value of Net Cash Flow
1	.893	$ 60,000	$ 53,580
2	.797	60,000	47,820
3	.712	50,000	35,600
4	.636	50,000	31,800
5	.567	40,000	22,680
Total		$260,000	$191,480
Amount to be invested			200,000
Net present value			$ (8,520)

Assume that the improved quality and reliability of the robot will reduce the cost of rework items and warranty claims by $4,000 per year.

Instruction:

(1) Prepare a revised net present value analysis, recognizing the estimated impact of the quality improvement.
(2) What is the minimum amount of cost savings from the reduction of rework items and warranty claims per year for the net present value of the proposed purchase of the robot to be positive? (Hint: Use the present value of an annuity of $1 of 3.6048.) Round to the nearest dollar.
(3) In addition to the decrease in rework items and warranty claims, what are some examples of other potential intangible benefits from the purchase of robotic equipment?

Appendix 2
Pb. 24–56.
Expected value.

Hudson Science Corporation is considering purchasing the rights to one of two laser patents for purposes of research and development. Patent A has potential developmental applications in the areas of medicine, computer science, pharmacology, and military weaponry. Patent B has potential developmental applications in the areas of mining, automobile manufacturing, telecommunications, and energy. Whichever patent rights are purchased, it is likely that only one of the potential applications will yield research and development results promising enough to market commercially. The estimated profit for each patent application and the estimated chances of occurrence are as follows:

Patent A

Application	Estimated Profit	Chance of Occurrence
Medicine	$ 5,000,000	20%
Computer science	6,500,000	40
Pharmacolocy	8,000,000	30
Military weaponry	12,000,000	10

Patent B

Application	Estimated Profit	Chance of Occurrence
Mining	$ 3,000,000	10%
Automobile manufacturing	5,000,000	30
Telecommunications	9,000,000	40
Energy	15,000,000	20

Instructions:

(1) Determine the expected value of each patent.
(2) Based on the results of (1), which patent rights should be purchased?

Appendix 2
Pb. 24–57.
Expected value and decision tree.

Tatum Mines Inc. is preparing to bid on the purchase of mining rights to one of two plats of federally owned land: Plat #1000 and Plat #1200. Both plats of land are known to contain deposits of uranium; however, the quality of the deposits will not be known until actual mining begins.

Preliminary estimates indicate that, for Plat #1000, there is a 60% chance that the deposit is of high quality and will yield total profits of $30,000,000. There is a 20% chance that the deposit is of moderate quality and will yield total profits of $16,000,000. Finally, there is a 20% chance that the deposit is of low quality and will yield total profits of $4,000,000.

Preliminary estimates indicate that, for Plat #1200, there is a 40% chance that the deposit is of high quality and will yield total profits of $50,000,000. There is a 40% chance that the deposit is of moderate quality and will yield total profits of $10,000,000. Finally, there is a 20% chance that the deposit is of low quality and will yield total profits of $500,000.

Instructions:

(1) Prepare a decision tree with expected values to aid management in deciding on which plat rights to bid.
(2) On which plat rights should the management of Tatum Mines Inc. bid?

ALTERNATE PROBLEMS

Pb. 24–50A.
Economic order quantity and inventory reorder point.
OBJ. 4

Lehman Company has recently decided to implement a policy designed to control inventory better. Based on past experience, the following data have been gathered for materials, which are used at a uniform rate throughout the year:

Units required during the year	3,600
Units of safety stock	100
Days of scheduled production	150
Days of lead time to receive an order	30
Ordering cost, per order placed	$ 30
Annual storage cost, per unit	$ .15

Instructions:

(1) Complete the following table for "number of orders" of 1 through 6.

Number of Orders	Number of Units per Order	Average Units in Inventory	Order and Storage Costs: Order Cost	Storage Cost	Combined Cost
1	3,600	1,800	$30	$270.00	$300.00

(2) Determine the economic order quantity, based on the table completed in (1).
(3) Determine the economic order quantity, using the formula on page 1007.
(4) Determine the inventory reorder point.

Pb. 24–51A.
Economic order quantity under present and proposed conditions.
OBJ. 4

Based on the data presented in Pb. 24–50A, assume that Lehman Company is considering the purchase of new automated storage equipment to facilitate access to materials and to increase storage capacity. In addition, the manager of the Purchasing Department has requested authorization to purchase five microcomputers to expedite the processing of purchase orders.

Instructions:

(1) Assuming that the new storage equipment will increase the annual storage cost from $.15 to $.60 per unit, determine the economic order quantity for Lehman Company, using the formula on page 1007.
(2) Assuming that the new storage equipment is not purchased and the acquisition of the microcomputer equipment will decrease the cost per order placed from $30 to $7.50, determine the economic order quantity, using the formula on page 1007.
(3) Assuming that both the new storage equipment and the microcomputer equipment are purchased, determine the economic order quantity, using the formula on page 1007. As indicated in (1) and (2), the purchase of the storage equipment is expected to increase the storage cost per unit from $.15 to $.60, and the microcomputer equipment is expected to decrease the cost per order placed from $30 to $7.50.
(4) Based on the answers to Pb. 24–50A, and (1), (2), and (3) above, what generalizations can be made concerning how changes in the cost per order placed and the storage cost per unit affect the economic order quantity?

Pb. 24–52A.
Linear programming for purchasing decisions.
OBJ. 4

Hansen Company purchases Part M for use at both its Akron and Tifton branches. Part M is available in limited quantities from two suppliers. The relevant data are as follows:

Units required:	
Akron Branch	200
Tifton Branch	300
Supplier X:	
Units available	300
Unit cost delivered to:	
Akron Branch	$60
Tifton Branch	$80
Supplier Y:	
Units available	300
Unit cost delivered to:	
Akron Branch	$75
Tifton Branch	$70

The manager of the Purchasing Department has prepared the following purchase plan for the Akron and Tifton branches:

(1) Purchase all units for the Akron Branch from Supplier X.
(2) Purchase remaining available units of Supplier X for the Tifton Branch.
(3) Purchase any additional units required by the Tifton Branch from Supplier Y.

Instructions:

(1) Construct a linear programming graph for units to be purchased from Supplier X. Plot the units for the Akron Branch along the horizontal axis.
(2) Identify the four corners at which an economical purchase plan might be identified on the linear programming graph. Label the corners A through D, as shown in the illustration on page 1012.
(3) For each corner in (2), indicate purchases from Suppliers X and Y for the Akron and Tifton branches. Identify Plan 1 with Corner A, Plan 2 with Corner B, Plan 3 with Corner C, and Plan 4 with Corner D.

(4) Determine the most economical purchase plan by computing the total cost of purchases for each plan identified in (3).
(5) Was the Purchasing Department manager's plan the most economical? Explain.

Pb. 24–53A.
Cost-volume-profit analysis and activity-based costing.
OBJ. 5

Based upon prior years' data, Yijun Inc. estimated the following unit selling price, unit variable cost, unit contribution margin, and total fixed costs for the year ending August 31, 1992:

Unit selling price	$90
Unit variable cost	65
Unit contribution margin	$25
Fixed costs	$380,000

The preceding cost data were based upon traditional analysis, using units produced as the activity base. Yijun Inc. has begun implementing activity-based costing and has estimated the following costs, based upon a preliminary study:

Units produced cost pool:	
Unit variable cost	$50
Fixed costs	$340,000
Production setup cost pool:	
$700 per setup	100 setups

Instructions:

(1) Determine the break-even sales (units), using the traditional cost data and units produced as the activity base.
(2) Determine the break-even sales (units), using the activity-based costing estimate.
(3) Discuss why a difference exists between the break-even sales (units) in (1) and (2).

Pb. 24–54A.
Variable costing and activity-based costing.
OBJ. 5

Based upon comments from the manufacturing supervisors that the product costs more to produce than it's worth, LaFrance Inc. is considering whether to continue to produce and sell Product F. The controller of LaFrance Inc. has prepared the following variable costing income statement, using the traditional contribution margin format:

Variable Costing Income Statement

	Product F	Other Products	Total
Sales	$480,000	$700,000	$1,180,000
Variable cost of goods sold	285,000	420,000	705,000
Manufacturing margin	$195,000	$280,000	$ 475,000
Variable selling and admin. exp.	160,000	90,000	250,000
Contribution margin	$ 35,000	$190,000	$ 225,000
Fixed costs:			
Fixed manufacturing costs			$ 130,000
Fixed selling and admin. exp.			45,000
Total fixed costs			$ 175,000
Income from operations			$ 50,000

Based upon the preceding variable costing income statement, the controller has recommended that Product F continue to be produced.

At the request of the vice-president of manufacturing, the assistant controller has been asked to prepare a supplemental analysis based upon interviews with operating personnel. The assistant controller prepared the following list of fixed costs traceable to Product F:

	Product F	Other Products
Fixed manufacturing costs:		
Supervisory cost	$17,000	$25,500
Maintenance cost	10,500	13,200
Quality control cost	8,800	9,700
Power cost	4,500	8,300
Materials handling cost	2,200	5,000
	$43,000	$61,700
Fixed selling and admin. expense:		
Advertising expense	$ 7,000	$ 9,000
Sales salaries	4,500	6,500
Utilities expense	3,000	4,500
	$14,500	$20,000

Instructions:

(1) Prepare a revised variable costing income statement for Product F.
(2) What are your recommendations for continuing to produce and sell Product F?
(3) What is the primary advantage of using activity-based costing for managerial decision making?
(4) What is the primary disadvantage for using activity-based costing for managerial decision making?

Pb. 24–55A. **Effect of intangibles on capital investment analysis.** OBJ 5.

Domingos Inc. is considering the purchase of a robot and has prepared the following net present value analysis:

Year	Present Value of $1 at 12%	Net Cash Flow	Present Value of Net Cash Flow
1	.893	$ 90,000	$ 80,370
2	.797	80,000	63,760
3	.712	70,000	49,840
4	.636	60,000	38,160
5	.567	50,000	28,350
Total		$350,000	$260,480
Amount to be invested			275,000
Net present value			$ (14,520)

Assume that the improved quality and reliability of the robot will reduce the cost of rework items and warranty claims by $10,000 per year.

Instructions:

(1) Prepare a revised net present value analysis, recognizing the estimated impact of the quality improvement.
(2) What is the minimum amount of cost savings from the reduction of rework items and warranty claims per year for the net present value of the proposed purchase of the robot to be positive? (Hint: Use the present value of an annuity of $1 of 3.6048.) Round to the nearest dollar.
(3) In addition to the decrease in rework items and warranty claims, what are some examples of other potential intangible benefits from the purchase of robotic equipment?

Appendix 2 **Pb. 24–56A.** **Expected value.**

International Films Inc. is considering purchasing the rights to one of two autobiographies for the purposes of producing and marketing a motion picture. Each autobiography has the potential for development and sale as one of the following: (1) a cable TV movie, (2) a network (noncable) TV movie, (3) a weekly TV series, or (4) a commercial theater movie. The estimated profit for development and sale of each autobiography and the estimated chances of occurrence are as follows:

Autobiography E

	Estimated Profit	Chance of Occurrence
Cable TV movie	$10,000,000	15%
Network TV movie	8,000,000	30
Weekly TV series	6,000,000	35
Theater movie	12,000,000	20

Autobiography F

	Estimated Profit	Chance of Occurrence
Cable TV movie	$20,000,000	30%
Network TV moive	6,000,000	40
Weekly TV series	2,000,000	10
Theater movie	10,000,000	20

Instructions:

(1) Determine the expected value of each autobiography.
(2) Based on the results of (1), which autobiography rights should be purchased?

Appendix 2
Pb. 24–57A.
Expected value and decision tree.

Davies Mines Inc. is preparing to bid on the purchase of mining rights to one of two plats of federally owned land: Plat #2400 and Plat #3100. Both plats of land are known to contain deposits of coal; however, the quality of the deposits will not be known until actual mining begins.

Preliminary estimates indicate that, for Plat #2400, there is a 60% chance that the deposit is of high quality and will yield total profits of $22,000,000. There is a 25% chance that the deposit is of moderate quality and will yield total profits of $5,000,000. Finally, there is a 15% chance that the deposit is of low quality and will yield total profits of $1,000,000.

Preliminary estimates indicate that, for Plat #3100, there is an 80% chance that the deposit is of high quality and will yield total profits of $16,000,000. There is a 15% chance that the deposit is of moderate quality and will yield total profits of $8,000,000. Finally, there is a 5% chance that the deposit is of low quality and will yield total profits of $2,000,000.

Instructions:

(1) Prepare a decision tree with expected values to aid management in deciding on which plat rights to bid.
(2) On which plat rights should the management of Davies Mines Inc. bid?

MINI-CASE 24

Herfurth Inc., a manufacturer of electronic clocks and timing devices, is considering implementing a just-in-time manufacturing system. The chief executive officer of Herfurth

Inc. read an article on JIT manufacturing in a current business periodical and has requested an analysis of the advantages and disadvantages of JIT manufacturing.

Currently, Herfurth Inc. maintains an average inventory of raw materials, work in process, and finished goods of approximately $1,200,000. The company's current average internal rate of return on capital projects is 22%.

Instructions:

(1) Prepare a list of advantages and disadvantages of implementing a just-in-time manufacturing system for Herfurth Inc.
(2) What is the potential dollar impact of JIT inventory management, assuming that raw materials, work in process, and finished goods inventories will become insignificant in amount?

ANSWERS TO SELF-EXAMINATION QUESTIONS

1. D A just-in-time manufacturing system normally reduces inventories to low or insignificant levels (answer A), materials are received just in time to enter the manufacturing process (answer B), and it emphasizes total quality control (answer C).
2. C Since the textbook is not being produced while the printing presses are being set up for a production run, the time spent setting up the presses (answer C) is considered a non-value-adding activity. The typesetting of the original manuscript (answer A), the printing of the textbook (answer B), and the binding of the cover to the printed pages (answer D) are all a direct part of the manufacturing process and are considered value-adding activities.
3. C The economic order quantity for Material K is 500 units (answer C), computed as follows:

$$\text{EOQ} = \sqrt{\frac{2 \times \text{Annual Units Required} \times \text{Cost per Order Placed}}{\text{Annual Storage Cost per Unit}}}$$

$$\text{EOQ} = \sqrt{\frac{2 \times 2{,}500 \times \$20}{\$.40}} = \sqrt{250{,}000} = 500 \text{ units}$$

4. D The inventory reorder point is 60,000 linear feet of oak (answer D), computed as follows:

Inventory Reorder Point = (Daily Usage × Lead Time) + Safety Stock
Inventory Reorder Point = (5,000 ft. × 7 days) + 25,000 ft.
Inventory Reorder Point = 35,000 ft. + 25,000 ft. = 60,000 ft.

5. D The new manufacturing environment significantly impacts upon cost-volume-profit analysis (answer A), variable costing (answer B), and capital investment analysis (answer C).

PART 7

PLANNING & CONTROL

CHAPTER 25

CHAPTER OBJECTIVES

1 Describe the nature and objectives of budgeting.

2 Describe and illustrate the basic principles of budgeting systems.

3 Describe and illustrate the use of budget performance reports.

4 Describe and illustrate the use of flexible budgets.

5 Describe the use of computerized budgeting systems.

6 Describe the human behavioral aspects of budgeting.

BUDGETING

Effective planning and control are requisites of successful operations. Various uses of accounting data by management in performing these functions have been described and illustrated in earlier chapters. For example, the role of cost accounting in planning production and controlling costs has been discussed and illustrated. This chapter and chapter 26 are devoted to budgeting and standard costs, two additional accounting devices that aid management in planning and controlling the operations of the business.

NATURE AND OBJECTIVES OF BUDGETING

OBJECTIVE 1
Describe the nature and objectives of budgeting.

A **budget** is a formal written statement of management's plans for the future, expressed in financial terms. A budget charts the course of future action. Thus, it serves management's primary functions in the same manner that the architect's blueprints aid the builder and the navigator's flight plan aids the pilot.

A budget, like a blueprint and flight plan, should contain sound, attainable objectives. If the budget is to contain such objectives, planning must be based on careful study, investigation, and research. Management's reliance on data thus obtained lessens the role of guesswork and intuition in managing a business enterprise.

The essentials of budgeting are (1) the establishment of specific goals for future operations and (2) the periodic comparison of actual results with these goals. The establishment of specific goals for future operations encompasses the planning function of management. The periodic comparison of actual results with these goals encompasses the control function of management.

The effectiveness of a budget depends, to some extent, on the business' strategic plan, which is a statement of a company's overall purpose and policy. Strategic planning is viewed as one of the most important factors in the success of a business. For example, in one survey in which the boards of directors of 600 of the 1,000 largest U.S. corporations were asked to identify the most important issues facing them in the future, the results were as follows:[1]

Issue	Ranking as No. 1 in Importance
Strategic planning	44%
Financial results	37
Managerial succession	17
Other	2

Although budgets are commonly associated with profit-making enterprises, they play an important role in operating most units of government, ranging from rural school districts and small villages to gigantic agencies of the federal government. They are also an important part of the operations of churches, hospitals, and other nonprofit institutions. Individuals and family units often use budgeting techniques as an aid to careful management of resources. In this chapter, the principles of budgeting are discussed in the context of profit-making enterprises.

BUDGETING SYSTEMS

OBJECTIVE 2
Describe and illustrate the basic principles of budgeting systems.

The details of budgeting systems are affected by the type and degree of complexity of a particular company, the amount of its revenues, the relative importance of its various divisions, and many other factors. A budgeting system used by a large manufacturer of automobiles would obviously differ in many ways from a system designed for a small manufacturer of paper products. The differences between a system designed for factory operations of any type and a service enterprise such as an accounting firm would be even more significant.

Budgets of operating activities usually include the fiscal year of an enterprise. A year is short enough to make possible fairly dependable estimates of future operations, and yet long enough to make it possible to view the future in a reasonably broad context. However, to achieve effective control, the annual budgets must be subdivided into shorter time periods, such as quarters of the year, months, or weeks. It is also necessary to review the budgets from time to time and make any changes that become necessary as a result of unforeseen changes in general business conditions, in the particular industry, or in the individual enterprise.

A frequent variant of fiscal-year budgeting, sometimes called **continuous budgeting,** provides for maintenance of a twelve-month projection into the future. At the end of each time interval used, the twelve-month budget is revised by removing the data for the period just ended and adding the newly estimated budget data for the same period next year.

The development of budgets for the next fiscal year usually begins several months prior to the end of the current year. The responsibility for their development is ordinarily assigned to a committee made up of the budget director and such high-level executives as the controller, treasurer, production manager, and sales manager. The process is started by requesting estimates of sales, production, and other operating data from the various administrative units concerned. It is important that all levels of management and all departments participate in the preparation and submission of budget estimates. The

[1] Deloitte Haskins & Sells, "Major Issues Facing Boards of Directors," *DH + S Review* (September 2, 1985), p. 6.

involvement of all supervisory personnel fosters cooperation both within and among departments and also heightens awareness of each department's importance in the overall processes of the company. All levels of management are thus encouraged to set goals and to control operations in a manner that strengthens the possibilities of achieving the goals.

The process of developing budget estimates differs among enterprises. One method is to require all levels of management to start from zero and estimate sales, production, and other operating data as though operations were being started for the first time. Although this concept, called **zero-base budgeting,** has received a considerable amount of attention in regard to budgeting for governmental units, it can also be useful to commercial enterprises. Another method of developing estimates is for each level of management to modify last year's budgeted amounts in light of last year's operating results and expected changes for the coming year.

The various estimates received by the budget committee are revised, reviewed, coordinated, cross-referenced, and finally put together to form the **master budget.** The estimates submitted should not be substantially revised by the committee without first giving the originators an opportunity to defend their proposals. After agreement has been reached and the master budget has been adopted by the budget committee, copies of the pertinent sections are distributed to the proper personnel in the chain of accountability. Periodic reports comparing actual results with the budget should likewise be distributed to all supervisory personnel.

As a framework for describing and illustrating budgeting, a small manufacturing enterprise, Kennedy Company, will be assumed. The major parts of Kennedy Company's master budget are as follows:

Components of Master Budget

- Budgeted income statement
  - Sales budget
  - Cost of goods sold budget
    - Production budget
    - Direct materials purchases budget
    - Direct labor cost budget
    - Factory overhead cost budget
  - Operating expenses budget
- Budgeted balance sheet
  - Capital expenditures budget
  - Cash budget

Sales Budget

The first budget to be prepared is usually the sales budget. An estimate of the dollar volume of sales revenue serves as the foundation upon which the other budgets are based. Sales volume will have a significant effect on all of the factors entering into the determination of operating income.

The sales budget ordinarily indicates (1) the quantity of forecasted sales for each product and (2) the expected unit selling price of each product. These data are often classified by areas and/or sales representatives.

In forecasting the quantity of each product expected to be sold, the starting point is generally past sales volumes. These amounts are revised for various factors expected to affect future sales, such as a backlog of unfilled sales orders, planned advertising and promotion, expected industry and general economic conditions, productive capacity, projected pricing policy, and market research study findings. Statistical analysis can be used in this process to evaluate the effect of these factors on past sales volume. Such analysis can provide a mathematical association between past sales and the several variables expected to affect future sales.

Once the forecast of sales volume is completed, the anticipated sales revenue is then determined by multiplying the volume of forecasted sales by the expected unit sales price, as shown in the following sales budget for Kennedy Company:

Sales Budget

Kennedy Company
Sales Budget
For Year Ending December 31, 19--

Product and Area	Unit Sales Volume	Unit Selling Price	Total Sales
Product X:			
Area A	208,000	$ 9.90	$2,059,200
Area B	162,000	9.90	1,603,800
Area C	158,000	9.90	1,564,200
Total	528,000		$5,227,200
Product Y:			
Area A	111,600	$16.50	$1,841,400
Area B	78,800	16.50	1,300,200
Area C	89,600	16.50	1,478,400
Total	280,000		$4,620,000
Total revenue from sales			$9,847,200

Frequent comparisons of actual sales with the budgeted volume, by product, area, and/or sales representative, will show differences between the two. Management is then able to investigate the probable cause of the significant differences and consider corrective action.

Production Budget

The production needs must be carefully coordinated with the sales budget to assure that production and sales are kept in balance during the period. The number of units of each commodity expected to be manufactured to meet budgeted sales and inventory requirements is set forth in the production budget. The budgeted volume of production is based on the sum of (1) the expected sales volume and (2) the desired year-end inventory, less (3) the inventory expected to be available at the beginning of the year. A production budget for Kennedy Company is illustrated as follows:

Production Budget

Kennedy Company
Production Budget
For Year Ending December 31, 19--

	Units	
Sales	528,000	280,000
Plus desired ending inventory, December 31, 19--	80,000	60,000
Total	608,000	340,000
Less estimated beginning inventory, January 1, 19--	88,000	48,000
Total production	520,000	292,000

Direct Materials Purchases Budget

The production needs shown by the production budget, combined with data on direct materials needed, provide the data for the direct materials purchases budget. The quantities of direct materials purchases necessary to meet production needs is based on the sum of (1) the materials expected to be needed to meet production requirements and (2) the desired year-end inventory, less (3) the inventory expected to be available at the beginning of the year. The quantities of direct materials required are then multiplied by the expected unit purchase price to determine the total cost of direct materials purchases.

In Kennedy Company's production operations, materials A and C are required for Product X, and materials A, B, and C are required for Product Y. A direct materials purchases budget for Kennedy Company is illustrated as follows:

Direct Materials Purchases Budget

Kennedy Company
Direct Materials Purchases Budget
For Year Ending December 31, 19--

	Direct Materials		
	A	B	C
Units required for production:			
Product X	390,000	—	520,000
Product Y	146,000	292,000	294,200
Plus desired ending inventory, Dec. 31, 19--	80,000	40,000	120,000
Total	616,000	332,000	934,200
Less estimated beginning inventory, Jan. 1, 19--	103,000	44,000	114,200
Total units to be purchased	513,000	288,000	820,000
Unit price	$ .60	$ 1.70	$ 1.00
Total direct materials purchases	$307,800	$489,600	$820,000

The timing of the direct materials purchases requires close coordination between the purchasing and production departments so that inventory levels can be maintained within reasonable limits.

Direct Labor Cost Budget

The needs indicated by the production budget provide the starting point for the preparation of the direct labor cost budget. The direct labor hours necessary to meet production needs are multiplied by the estimated hourly rate to yield the total direct labor cost. In Kennedy Company's operations, Products X and Y are produced in Departments 1 and 2. A direct labor cost budget is illustrated as follows:

Direct Labor Cost Budget

Kennedy Company
Direct Labor Cost Budget
For Year Ending December 31, 19--

	Department 1	Department 2
Hours required for production:		
Product X	50,000	41,600
Product Y	31,200	46,720
Total	81,200	88,320
Hourly rate	$15	$20
Total direct labor cost	$1,218,000	$1,766,400

The direct labor requirements must be carefully coordinated with available labor time to assure that sufficient labor will be available to meet production needs. Efficient manufacturing operations minimize idle time and labor shortages.

Factory Overhead Cost Budget

The factory overhead costs estimated to be necessary to meet production needs are presented in the factory overhead cost budget. For use as part of the master budget, the factory overhead cost budget usually presents the total estimated cost for each item of factory overhead. A factory overhead cost budget for Kennedy Company is illustrated as follows:

Factory Overhead Cost Budget

Kennedy Company
Factory Overhead Cost Budget
For Year Ending December 31, 19--

Indirect factory wages	$ 732,800
Supervisory salaries	360,000
Power and light	306,000
Depreciation of plant and equipment	288,000
Indirect materials	182,800
Maintenance	140,280
Insurance and property taxes	79,200
Total factory overhead cost	$2,089,080

Supplemental schedules are often prepared to present the factory overhead cost for each individual department. Such schedules enable department supervisors to direct attention to those costs for which each is solely responsible. They also aid the production manager in evaluating performance in each department.

Cost of Goods Sold Budget

The budget for the cost of goods sold is prepared by combining data on estimated inventories with the relevant estimates of quantities and costs in the budgets for (1) direct materials purchases, (2) direct labor costs, and (3) factory overhead costs. A cost of goods sold budget for Kennedy Company is illustrated as follows:

Cost of Goods Sold Budget

Kennedy Company
Cost of Goods Sold Budget
For Year Ending December 31, 19--

Finished goods inventory, January 1, 19--			$1,095,600
Work in process inventory, January 1, 19--		$ 214,400	
Direct materials:			
Direct materials inventory, January 1, 19--	$ 250,800		
Direct materials purchases	1,617,400		
Cost of direct materials available for use	$1,868,200		
Less direct materials inventory, December 31, 19--	236,000		
Cost of direct materials placed in production	$1,632,200		
Direct labor	2,984,400		
Factory overhead	2,089,080		
Total manufacturing costs		6,705,680	
Total work in process during period		$6,920,080	
Less work in process inventory, December 31, 19--		220,000	
Cost of goods manufactured			6,700,080
Cost of finished goods available for sale			$7,795,680
Less finished goods inventory, December 31, 19--			1,195,000
Cost of goods sold			$6,600,680

Operating Expenses Budget

Based on past experiences, which are adjusted for future expectations, the estimated selling and administrative expenses are set forth in the operating expenses budget. For use as part of the master budget, the operating expenses budget ordinarily presents the expenses by nature or type of expenditure, such as sales salaries, rent, insurance, and advertising. An operating expenses budget for Kennedy Company is illustrated at the top of page 1056.

Detailed supplemental schedules based on departmental responsibility are often prepared for major items in the operating expenses budget. The advertising expense schedule, for example, should include such details as the advertising media to be used (newspaper, direct mail, television), quantities (column inches, number of pieces, minutes), cost per unit, frequency of use, and sectional totals. A realistic budget is prepared through careful attention to details, and effective control is achieved through assignment of responsibility to departmental supervisors.

Operating Expenses Budget

Kennedy Company Operating Expenses Budget For Year Ending December 31, 19--		
Selling expenses:		
Sales salaries expense	$595,000	
Advertising expense	360,000	
Travel expense	115,000	
Telephone expense—selling	95,000	
Miscellaneous selling expense	25,000	
Total selling expenses		$1,190,000
Administrative expenses:		
Officers' salaries expense	$360,000	
Office salaries expense	105,000	
Heating and lighting expense	75,000	
Taxes expense	60,000	
Depreciation expense—office equipment	27,000	
Telephone expense—administrative	18,000	
Insurance expense	17,500	
Office supplies expense	7,500	
Miscellaneous administrative expense	25,000	
Total administrative expenses		695,000
Total operating expenses		$1,885,000

Budgeted Income Statement

A budgeted income statement can usually be prepared from the estimated data presented in the budgets for sales, cost of goods sold, and operating expenses, with the addition of data on other income, other expense, and income tax. A budgeted income statement for Kennedy Company is illustrated as follows:

Budgeted Income Statement

Kennedy Company Budgeted Income Statement For Year Ending December 31, 19--		
Revenue from sales		$9,847,200
Cost of goods sold		6,600,680
Gross profit		$3,246,520
Operating expenses:		
Selling expenses	$1,190,000	
Administrative expenses	695,000	
Total operating expenses		1,885,000
Income from operations		$1,361,520
Other income:		
Interest income	$ 98,000	
Other expense:		
Interest expense	90,000	8,000
Income before income tax		$1,369,520
Income tax		610,000
Net income		$ 759,520

The budgeted income statement brings together in condensed form the projection of all profit-making phases of operations and enables management to weigh the effects of the individual budgets on the profit plan for the year. If the budgeted net income in relationship to sales or to stockholders' equity is disappointingly low, additional review of all factors involved should be undertaken in an attempt to improve the plans.

Capital Expenditures Budget

The **capital expenditures budget** summarizes future plans for acquisition of plant facilities and equipment. Substantial expenditures may be needed to replace machinery and other plant assets as they wear out, become obsolete, or for other reasons fall below minimum standards of efficiency. In addition, an expansion of plant facilities may be planned to keep pace with increasing demand for a company's product or to provide for additions to the product line.

The useful life of many plant assets extends over relatively long periods of time, and the amount of the expenditures for such assets usually changes a great deal from year to year. The customary practice, therefore, is to project the plans for a number of years into the future in preparing the capital expenditures budget. A five-year capital expenditures budget is illustrated as follows:

Capital Expenditures Budget

Kennedy Company
Capital Expenditures Budget
For Five Years Ending December 31, 1996

Item	1992	1993	1994	1995	1996
Machinery—Department 1	$400,000			$280,000	$360,000
Machinery—Department 2	180,000	$260,000	$560,000	200,000	
Office equipment		90,000			60,000
Total	$580,000	$350,000	$560,000	$480,000	$420,000

The various proposals recognized in the capital expenditures budget must be considered in preparing certain operating budgets. For example, the expected amount of depreciation on new equipment to be acquired in the current year must be taken into consideration when the budgets for factory overhead and operating expenses are prepared. The manner in which the proposed expenditures are to be financed will also affect the cash budget.

Cash Budget

The cash budget presents the expected inflow and outflow of cash for a day, week, month, or longer period. Receipts are classified by source and disbursements by purpose. The expected cash balance at the end of the period is then compared with the amount established as the minimum balance and the difference is the anticipated excess or deficiency for the period.

The minimum cash balance represents a safety buffer for mistakes in cash planning and for emergencies. However, the amount stated as the minimum balance need not remain fixed. It should perhaps be larger during periods of "peak" business activity than during the "slow" season. In addition, for effective cash management, much of the minimum cash balance can often be deposited in interest-bearing accounts.

The interrelationship of the cash budget with other budgets may be seen from the following illustration. Data from the sales budget, the various budgets for manufacturing costs and operating expenses, and the capital expenditures budget affect the cash budget. Consideration must also be given to dividend policies, plans for equity or long-term debt financing, and other projected plans that will affect cash.

Cash Budget

Kennedy Company
Cash Budget
For Three Months Ending March 31, 19--

	January	February	March
Estimated cash receipts from:			
Cash sales	$168,000	$185,000	$ 115,000
Collections of accounts receivable	699,000	712,800	572,000
Other sources (issuance of securities, interest, etc.)	—	—	27,000
Total cash receipts	$867,000	$897,800	$ 714,000
Estimated cash disbursements for:			
Manufacturing costs	$541,200	$557,000	$ 536,000
Operating expenses	150,200	151,200	140,800
Capital expenditures	—	144,000	80,000
Other purposes (notes, income tax, etc.)	47,000	20,000	160,000
Total cash disbursements	$738,400	$872,200	$ 916,800
Cash increase (decrease)	$128,600	$ 25,600	$(202,800)
Cash balance at beginning of month	280,000	408,600	434,200
Cash balance at end of month	$408,600	$434,200	$ 231,400
Minimum cash balance	300,000	300,000	300,000
Excess (deficiency)	$108,600	$134,200	$ (68,600)

In some cases, it is useful to present supplemental schedules to indicate the details of some of the amounts in the cash budget. For example, the following schedule illustrates the determination of the estimated cash receipts aris-

Schedule of Collections of Accounts Receivable

Kennedy Company
Schedule of Collections of Accounts Receivable
For three Months Ending March 31, 19--

	January	February	March
January 1 balance	$295,800		
January sales on account (80% × $840,000):			
Collected in January (60% × $672,000)	403,200		
Collected in February (40% × $672,000)		$268,800	
February sales on account (80% × $925,000):			
Collected in February (60% × $740,000)		444,000	
Collected in March (40% × $740,000)			$296,000
March sales on account (80% × $575,000):			
Collected in March (60% × $460,000)			276,000
Totals	$699,000	$712,800	$572,000

ing from collections of accounts receivable. For the illustration, it is assumed that the accounts receivable balance was $295,800 on January 1, and sales for each of the three months ending March 31 are $840,000, $925,000, and $575,000, respectively. Kennedy Company expects to sell 20% of its merchandise for cash. Of the sales on account, 60% are expected to be collected in the month of the sale and the remainder in the following month.

The importance of accurate cash budgeting can scarcely be overemphasized. An unanticipated lack of cash can result in loss of discounts, unfavorable borrowing terms on loans, and damage to the credit rating. On the other hand, excess cash can be used to reduce loans or purchase investments in readily marketable income-producing securities. Reference to the Kennedy Company cash budget shows excess cash during January and February and a deficiency during March.

GETTING THE MOST OUT OF YOUR CASH

Most businesses could reduce their interest expenses if they would improve their management of cash. The goal of cash management is to use the company's money to maximize earnings while paying all liabilities and maintaining adequate liquidity. Accelerating collections, delaying disbursements, and getting the needed information about the cash status are the foundation of effective cash management.

One of the most efficient cash management tools is the wire transfer, which is the safest and fastest way to move a large sum of money quickly. It is used by having your customers who monthly pay you large amounts wire the money directly to your bank.

Another efficient cash management tool is the lockbox, which is a system that has your customers mail their remittance checks directly to a post office box in the name of your company. You authorize your bank to collect the customers' payments, and each item is deposited directly to the bank, according to your instructions. A lockbox greatly accelerates the transformation of your receivables into cash, and it eliminates delays from mail and processing.

If your company is borrowing from a bank and not using its cash as effectively as it can, your company is losing interest every day. If the money is not needed on a day-by-day basis, you should invest the excess money in overnight, one- or two-week or 30-day instruments. If you are required to keep a compensating balance, monitor the account so that you do not keep more than the required amount.

Every morning, through phone calls or through a third party, you can receive information on your previous night's bank balances, credits, and disbursements in order to determine what you have available for investments that day. You can arrange for your bank to transfer the money out of your account and into investments every day.

Source: Allen E. Fishman, "Getting the Most Out of Your Cash," *St. Louis Post-Dispatch* (May 5, 1986), p. 14A.

Budgeted Balance Sheet

The budgeted balance sheet presents estimated details of the financial condition at the end of a budget period, assuming that all budgeted operating and financing plans are fulfilled. It need not differ in form and arrangement from a balance sheet based on actual data in the accounts and hence is not illustrated. If the budgeted balance sheet shows weaknesses in financial position, such as an abnormally large amount of current liabilities in relation to current assets, or excessive long-term debt in relation to stockholders' equity, the relevant factors should be given further study so that corrective action may be taken.

BUDGET PERFORMANCE REPORTS

OBJECTIVE 3
Describe and illustrate the use of budget performance reports.

A **budget performance report** comparing actual results with the budgeted figures should be prepared periodically for each budget. This "feedback" enables management to determine the cause of significant differences and to seek means of preventing their recurrence. If corrective action cannot be taken because of changed conditions that have occurred since the budget was prepared, future budget figures should be revised accordingly.

A budget performance report for Kennedy Company is illustrated as follows:

Budget Performance Report

Kennedy Company
Budget Performance Report—Factory Overhead Cost, Department 1
For Month Ended June 30, 19--

	Budget	Actual	Over	Under
Indirect factory wages	$30,200	$30,400	$200	
Supervisory salaries	15,000	15,000		
Power and light	12,800	12,750		$ 50
Depreciation of plant and equipment	12,000	12,000		
Indirect materials	7,600	8,250	650	
Maintenance	5,800	5,700		100
Insurance and property taxes	3,300	3,300		
	$86,700	$87,400	$850	$150

The amounts reported in the "Budget" column were obtained from supplemental schedules accompanying the master budget. The amounts in the "Actual" column are the costs actually incurred. The last two columns show the amounts by which actual costs exceeded or were below budgeted figures. As shown in the illustration, there were differences between the actual and budgeted amounts for some of the items of overhead cost. The cause of the significant difference in indirect materials cost should be investigated, and an attempt to find means of corrective action should be made. For example, if the difference in indirect materials cost were found to be caused by a marketwide increase in the price of materials used, a corrective action may not be possible. On the other hand, if the difference resulted from the inefficient use of materials in the production process, it may be possible to eliminate the inefficiency and effect a savings in future indirect materials costs.

FLEXIBLE BUDGETS

OBJECTIVE 4
Describe and illustrate the use of flexible budgets.

In the discussion of budget systems, it has been assumed that the amount of sales and the level of manufacturing activity achieved during a period approximated the goals established in the budgets. When substantial changes in expectations occur during a budget period, the budgets should be revised to give effect to such changes. Otherwise, they will be of questionable value as incentives and instruments for controlling costs and expenses.

The effect of changes in volume of activity can be "built in" to the budget system by what is termed a flexible budget. A **flexible budget** is in reality a series of budgets for varying rates of activity. To illustrate, assume that because of extreme variations in demand and other uncontrollable factors, the output of a particular manufacturing enterprise fluctuates widely from month to month. In such circumstances, the total factory overhead costs incurred during periods of high activity are certain to be greater than during periods of low activity. It is equally certain, however, that fluctuations in total factory overhead costs will not be exactly proportionate to the volume of production. For example, if $100,000 of factory overhead costs are usually incurred during a month in which production totals 10,000 units, the factory overhead for a month in which only 5,000 units are produced would unquestionably be more than $50,000.

Although there are many approaches to the preparation of a flexible budget, the first step is to identify the fixed and variable components of the various factory overhead and operating expenses being budgeted. The costs and expenses can then be presented in variable and fixed categories. For example, in the following flexible budget for factory overhead cost for one department and one product, "electric power" is broken down into its fixed and variable cost components for three different levels of production. The fixed portion is $10,000 for all levels of production. The variable portion is $30,000 for 10,000 units of product, $27,000 ($30,000 × 9,000 ÷ 10,000) for 9,000 units of product, and $24,000 ($30,000 × 8,000 ÷ 10,000) for 8,000 units of product.

Flexible Budget for Factory Overhead Cost

Colter Manufacturing Company
Monthly Factory Overhead Cost Budget

Units of product	8,000	9,000	10,000
Variable cost:			
Indirect factory wages	$ 32,000	$ 36,000	$ 40,000
Electric power	24,000	27,000	30,000
Indirect materials	12,000	13,500	15,000
Total variable cost	$ 68,000	$ 76,500	$ 85,000
Fixed cost:			
Supervisory salaries	$ 40,000	$ 40,000	$ 40,000
Depreciation of plant and equipment	25,000	25,000	25,000
Property taxes	15,000	15,000	15,000
Insurance	12,000	12,000	12,000
Electric power	10,000	10,000	10,000
Total fixed cost	$102,000	$102,000	$102,000
Total factory overhead cost	$170,000	$178,500	$187,000

In practice, the number of production levels and the interval between levels in a flexible budget will vary with the range of production volume. For example, instead of budgeting for 8,000, 9,000, and 10,000 units of product, it might be necessary to provide for levels, at intervals of 500, from 6,000 to 12,000 units. Alternative bases, such as machine hours or direct labor hours, may also be used in measuring the volume of activity.

In preparing budget performance reports, the actual results would be compared with the flexible budget figures for the level of operations achieved. For example, if Colter Manufacturing Company manufactured 10,000 units during a month, the budget figures reported in the budget performance report would be those appearing in the "10,000 units" column of Colter's flexible budget.

COMPUTERIZED BUDGETING SYSTEMS

OBJECTIVE 5
Describe the use of computerized budgeting systems.

Many firms use computers in the budgeting process. Computers can not only speed up the budgeting process, but they can also reduce the cost of budget preparation when large quantities of data need to be processed. Computers are especially useful in preparing flexible budgets and in continuous budgeting. Budget performance reports can also be prepared on a timely basis by the use of the computer.

By using the computerized simulation models, which are mathematical statements of the relationships among various operating activities, management can determine the impact of various operating alternatives on the master budget. For example, if management wishes to evaluate the impact of a proposed change in direct labor wage rates, the computer can quickly provide a revised master budget that reflects the new rates. If management wishes to evaluate a proposal to add a new product line, the computer can quickly update current budgeted data and indicate the effect of the proposal on the master budget.

BUDGETING AND HUMAN BEHAVIOR

OBJECTIVE 6
Describe the human behavioral aspects of budgeting.

In the budgeting process, overall goals of the business as well as specific goals for individual units within the business are established. Significant human behavior problems can develop if managers view these goals as unrealistic or unachievable. In such a case, managers may become discouraged as well as uncommitted to the achievement of the goals. As a result, the budget becomes less effective as a tool for planning and controlling operations. On the other hand, goals set within a range that managers consider attainable are likely to inspire managers to achieve the goals. Therefore, it is important that all levels of management be involved in establishing the goals which they will be expected to achieve. In such an environment, the budget is a planning tool that will favorably affect human behavior and increase the possibility of achieving the goals.

Human behavior problems can also arise when the budgeted and actual results are compared in budget performance reports. These problems can be minimized if budgets are revised when substantial changes in expectations occur during a budget period. Otherwise, the budgets will be of questionable value as incentives and instruments for controlling costs and expenses.

CHAPTER REVIEW

KEY POINTS

OBJECTIVE 1

Nature and Objectives of Budgeting

The essentials of budgeting are (1) the establishment of specific goals for future operations and (2) the periodic comparison of actual results with these goals. The establishment of specific goals for future operations encompasses the planning function of management. The periodic comparison of actual results with these goals encompasses the control function of management.

OBJECTIVE 2

Budgeting Systems

Although budgets may be prepared for quarters of the year, months, or weeks, budgets of operating activities usually include the fiscal year of an enterprise. A variant of fiscal-year budgeting, continuous budgeting, provides for maintenance of a twelve-month projection into the future.

All levels of management should be encouraged to participate in the budgeting process. Usually a budget committee has final responsibility for preparation of the master budget.

The sales budget is usually the first component of the master budget that is prepared. The production budget sets forth the number of units of each commodity expected to be manufactured to meet budgeted sales and inventory requirements. The direct materials purchases budget is based on the needs shown by the production budget. The production budget also serves as a starting point for the preparation of the direct labor cost budget and factory overhead cost budget. The cost of goods sold budget is prepared by combining data on estimated inventories with the relevant estimates of quantities and costs in the budgets for (1) direct materials purchases, (2) direct labor costs, and (3) factory overhead costs. After the operating expenses budget is prepared, the budgeted income statement can be prepared.

The capital expenditures budget summarizes future plans for the acquisition of plant facilities and equipment, while the cash budget represents the expected inflow and outflow of cash for a day, week, month, or a longer period. The budgeted balance sheet presents estimated details of financial condition at the end of a budget period, assuming that all the budgeted operating and financing plans are fulfilled.

OBJECTIVE 3

Budget Performance Reports

A budget performance report provides feedback to management by reporting actual results compared with budgeted figures. Significant differences can then be investigated and corrective action taken.

OBJECTIVE 4

Flexible Budgets

Through the use of flexible budgets, the effect of changes in volume of activity can be built into the budgetary system. The preparation of flexible budgets requires the separation of costs and expenses into fixed and variable components. The use of flexible budgets facilitates the preparation of budget performance reports based on the actual level of operations achieved.

OBJECTIVE 5

Computerized Budgeting Systems

Computers can be useful in speeding up the budgetary process and in preparing timely budget performance reports. In addition, through the use of simulation models, management can determine the impact of operating alternatives on the various budgets.

OBJECTIVE 6

Budgeting and Human Behavior

Significant human behavior problems can develop if managers view a budget as unrealistic or unachievable. Human behavior problems can also arise when budgeted and actual results are compared. These problems can be minimized if managers are involved in establishing budgets initially and budgets are revised for changes and expectations that occur during a budget period.

KEY TERMS

budget 1049
continuous budgeting 1050
zero-base budgeting 1051
master budget 1051
capital expenditures budget 1057
budget performance report 1060
flexible budget 1060

SELF-EXAMINATION QUESTIONS

Answers at end of chapter.

1. Budgeting of operating activities to provide at all times for maintenance of a twelve-month project into the future is called:
   A. fixed budgeting C. continuous budgeting
   B. variable budgeting D. none of the above

2. The total estimated units of sales for the coming year is 250,000. If the estimated inventory at the beginning of the year is 22,500 units and the desired inventory at the end of the year is 30,000 units, the total production indicated in the production budget is:
   A. 242,500 units C. 280,000 units
   B. 257,500 units D. 302,500 units

3. The budget that summarizes future plans for acquisition of plant facilities and equipment is the:
   A. cash budget C. capital expenditures budget
   B. sales budget D. none of the above

4. A report comparing actual results with the budget figures is called a:
   A. budget report C. flexible budget report
   B. budget performance report D. none of the above

5. The system that "builds in" the effect of fluctuations in volume of activity into the various budgets is termed:
   A. budget performance reporting C. flexible budgeting
   B. continuous budgeting D. none of the above

ILLUSTRATIVE PROBLEM

Partin Company prepared the following factory overhead cost budget for the Finishing Department for June of the current year:

Partin Company
Factory Overhead Cost Budget—Finishing Department
For Month Ending June 30, 19--

Machine hours budgeted		9,000
Variable cost:		
Indirect factory wages	$9,450	
Indirect materials	6,750	
Power and light	5,400	
Total variable cost		$21,600
Fixed cost:		
Supervisory salaries	$8,000	
Indirect factory wages	3,300	
Depreciation of plant and equipment	3,100	
Insurance	1,500	
Power and light	1,200	
Property taxes	900	
Total fixed cost		18,000
Total factory overhead cost		$39,600

Instructions:

1. Prepare a flexible budget for the month of July, indicating capacities of 8,000, 9,000, 10,000, and 11,000 machine hours.

2. Prepare a budget performance report for July. The Finishing Department was operated for 8,000 machine hours and the following factory overhead costs were incurred:

Indirect factory wages	$11,500
Supervisory salaries	8,000
Power and light	6,350
Indirect materials	6,050
Depreciation of plant and equipment	3,100
Insurance	1,500
Property taxes	900
Total factory overhead costs incurred	$37,400

SOLUTION

(1)

Partin Company
Factory Overhead Cost Budget—Finishing Department
For Month Ending July 31, 19--

Machine hours	8,000	9,000	10,000	11,000
Budgeted factory overhead:				
Variable cost:				
Indirect factory wages	$ 8,400	$ 9,450	$10,500	$11,550
Indirect materials	6,000	6,750	7,500	8,250
Power and light	4,800	5,400	6,000	6,600
Total variable cost	$19,200	$21,600	$24,000	$26,400
Fixed cost:				
Supervisory salaries	$ 8,000	$ 8,000	$ 8,000	$ 8,000
Indirect factory wages	3,300	3,300	3,300	3,300
Depreciation of plant and equipment	3,100	3,100	3,100	3,100
Insurance	1,500	1,500	1,500	1,500
Power and light	1,200	1,200	1,200	1,200
Property taxes	900	900	900	900
Total fixed cost	$18,000	$18,000	$18,000	$18,000
Total factory overhead cost	$37,200	$39,600	$42,000	$44,400

(2)

Partin Company
Budget Performance Report—Finishing Department
For Month Ended July 31, 19--

	Budget	Actual	Over	Under
Variable cost:				
Indirect factory wages	$ 8,400	$ 8,200		$ 200
Indirect materials	6,000	6,050	$ 50	
Power and light	4,800	5,150	350	
Total variable cost	$19,200	$19,400		
Fixed cost:				
Supervisory salaries	$ 8,000	$ 8,000		
Indirect factory wages	3,300	3,300		
Depreciation of plant and equipment	3,100	3,100		
Insurance	1,500	1,500		
Power and light	1,200	1,200		
Property taxes	900	900		
Total fixed cost	$18,000	$18,000		
Total factory overhead cost	$37,200	$37,400	$400	$ 200

DISCUSSION QUESTIONS

25–1. What is a budget?

25–2. (a) Name the two basic functions of management in which accounting is involved. (b) How does a budget aid management in the discharge of these basic functions?

25–3. What is meant by *continuous budgeting*?

25–4. Why should all levels of management and all departments participate in the preparation and submission of budget estimates?

25–5. Which budgetary concept requires all levels of managment to start from zero and estimate sales, production, and other operating data as though the operations were being initiated for the first time?

25–6. Why should the production requirements as set forth in the production budget be carefully coordinated with the sales budget?

25–7. Why should the timing of direct materials puchases be closely coordinated with the production budget?

25–8. Merriam Inc., which estimates that 130,000 units will be sold during the current year, desires an ending inventory of 15,000 units. If 12,500 units are in the beginning inventory, what is the estimated production for the current year?

25–9. What are the three budgets from which data on relevant estimates of quantities and costs are combined with data on estimated inventories in preparing the budget for the cost of goods sold?

25–10. What is a capital expenditures budget?

25–11. (a) Discuss the purpose of the cash budget. (b) If the cash for the first quarter of the fiscal year indicates excess cash at the end of each of the first two months, how might the excess cash be used?

25–12. What is a budget performance report?

25–13. What is a flexible budget?

25–14. Owens Corporation uses flexible budgets. For each of the following variable operating expenses, indicate whether there has been a saving or an excess of expenses, assuming that actual sales were $800,000.

Expense Item	Actual Amount	Budget Allowance Based on Sales
Factory supplies expense	$ 8,250	1%
Uncollectible accounts expense	21,750	3%

25–15. How can computerized budgeting systems aid firms in the budgeting process?

25–16. Briefly discuss the type of human behavior problem that might arise if goals used in developing budgets are unrealistic or unachievable.

Real World Focus

25–17. During the ten-year period, 1978—1987, the ratio of cost of sales to net sales for PepsiCo Inc. decreased from 48.4% to 38.8%. During this same period, the net sales of PepsiCo increased by almost 400%. As sales increase, why would management normally expect the ratio of cost of sales to net sales to decrease?

Ethics Discussion Case

25–18. Jan Himmel, a cost accounting clerk for Icahn Inc., has been assigned the task of preparing the first draft of the cost of goods sold and related budgets for the manufacturing operations. Himmel has received budget estimates for the forthcoming year from the various production supervisors. Because she thinks that the production supervisors probably over-estimated their costs in order to have some cushion for possible production problems, she decided to cut all the supervisors' estimates by 15%.

Discuss whether Jan Himmel behaved in an ethical manner by cutting all the budget estimates by 15%.

EXERCISES

Ex. 25–19.
Sales and production budgets.
OBJ. 2

Coker Company manufactures two models of humidifiers, H10 and H20. Based on the following production and sales data for April of the current year, prepare (a) a sales budget and (b) a production budget.

	H10	H20
Estimated inventory (units), April 1	54,700	13,100
Desired inventory (units), April 30	65,000	10,000
Expected sales volume (units):		
Northern Region	100,000	50,000
Southern Region	80,000	20,000
Unit sales price	$8.50	$11.40

Ex. 25–20.
Professional fees budget.
OBJ. 2

Mitchell and Momper, CPAs, offer three types of services to clients: auditing, tax, and computer installation. Based upon past experience and projected growth, the following billable hours have been estimated for the year ending December 31, 1992:

	Billable Hours
Audit Department:	
Staff	18,000
Partners	6,000
Tax Department:	
Staff	15,000
Partners	3,000
Computer Installation:	
Staff	12,000
Partners	2,000

The average billing rate for staff is $40 per hour, and the average billing rate for partners is $80 per hour.

Prepare a professional fees budget for Mitchell and Momper, CPAs, for the year ending December 31, 1992, using the following columnar headings and showing the estimated professional fees by type of service rendered:

Billable Hours	Hourly Rate	Total Revenue

Ex. 25–21.
Direct labor cost budget.
OBJ. 2

Based upon the data in Ex. 25–20 and assuming that the average compensation per hour for staff and partners is $25 and $50 respectively, prepare a direct labor cost budget for Mitchell and Momper, CPAs, for the year ending December 31, 1992. Use the following columnar headings:

Billable Hours Required	
Staff	Partners

Ex. 25–22.
Schedule of cash collections of accounts receivable.
OBJ. 2

McNeely Company was organized on September 1 of the current year. Projected sales for each of the first three months of operations are as follows:

September	$240,000
October	300,000
November	420,000

The company expects to sell 20% of its merchandise for cash. Of sales on account, 70% are expected to be collected in the month of the sale, 25% in the month following the sale, and the remainder in the following month. Prepare a schedule indicating cash collections of accounts receivable for September, October, and November.

Ex. 25–23.
Schedule of cash disbursements.
OBJ. 2

Sussex Company was organized on March 31 of the current year. Projected operating expenses for each of the first three months of operations are as follows:

April	$156,800
May	195,200
June	217,600

Depreciation, insurance, and property taxes represent $28,800 of the estimated monthly operating expenses. Insurance was paid on March 31, and property taxes will be paid in November. Three fourths of the remainder of the operating expenses are expected to be paid in the month in which they are incurred, with the balance to be paid in the following month. Prepare a schedule indicating cash disbursements for operating expenses for April, May, and June.

Ex. 25–24.
Flexible budget for operating expenses.
OBJ. 4

Wang Company uses flexible budgets that are based on the following data:

Sales commissions	4% of sales
Advertising expense	$20,000 for $400,000 of sales
	$30,000 for $500,000 of sales
	$40,000 for $600,000 of sales
Miscellaneous selling expense	$3,000 plus 3/4% of sales
Office salaries expense	$35,000
Office supplies expense	3% of sales
Miscellaneous administrative expense	$600 plus 1/2% of sales

Prepare a flexible operating expenses budget for July of the current year for sales volumes of $400,000, $500,000, and $600,000.

Ex. 25–25.
Budget performance report.
OBJ. 3

The operating expenses incurred during July of the current year by Wang Company were as follows:

Sales commissions	$21,250
Advertising expense	29,100
Miscellaneous selling expense	7,000
Office salaries expense	35,000
Office supplies expense	15,300
Miscellaneous administrative expense	3,000

Assuming that the total sales for July were $500,000, prepare a budget performance report for operating expenses on the basis of the data presented above and in Ex. 25–24.

Ex. 25–26. **Flexible factory overhead cost budget.** OBJ. 4

Tudor Company prepared the following factory overhead cost budget for Department C for March of the current year, during which it expected to manufacture 20,000 units:

Variable cost:		
Indirect factory	$20,000	
Power and light	12,500	
Indirect materials	5,000	
Total variable cost		$37,500
Fixed cost:		
Supervisory salaries	$12,500	
Depreciation of plant and equipment	4,000	
Insurance and property taxes	2,000	
Total fixed cost		18,500
Total factory overhead cost		$56,000

Assuming that the estimated costs in March are applicable to April operations, prepare a flexible factory overhead cost budget for Department C for April for 18,000, 20,000, and 22,000 units of product.

Ex. 25–27. **Budget performance report.** OBJ. 3

During April, Tudor Company manufactured 22,000 units, and the factory overhead costs incurred in Department C were: indirect factory wages, $21,700; power and light, $14,000; indirect materials, $5,600; supervisory salaries, $12,500; depreciation of plant and equipment, $4,000; and insurance and property taxes, $2,000.

Prepare a budget performance report for Department C for April. To be useful for cost control, the budgeted amounts should be based on the data for 22,000 units, as revealed in Ex. 25–26.

PROBLEMS

Pb. 25–28. **Forecast sales volume and sales budget.** OBJ. 2

Rosa Company prepared the following sales budget for the current year:

Rosa Company
Sales Budget
For Year Ending December 31, 1992

Product and Area	Unit Sales Volume	Unit Selling Price	Total Sales
Product A:			
East	20,000	$25.00	$ 500,000
Central	15,000	25.00	375,000
West	30,000	25.00	750,000
Total	65,000		$1,625,000
Product B:			
East	15,000	$20.00	$300,000
Central	12,000	20.00	240,000
West	20,000	20.00	400,000
Total	47,000		$ 940,000
Total revenue from sales			$2,565,000

At the end of September, 1992, the following unit sales data were reported for the first nine months of the year:

	Unit Sales	
	Product A	Product B
East	14,100	11,475
Central	11,700	9,270
West	21,600	14,250

For the year ending December 31, 1993, unit sales are expected to follow the patterns established during the first nine months of the year ending December 31, 1992. The unit selling price for Product A is not expected to change, and the unit selling price for Product B is expected to be increased to $21, effective January 1, 1993.

Instructions:

(1) Compute the increase or decrease of actual *unit* sales for the nine months ended September 30, 1992, over expectations for this nine-month period. Since sales have historically occurred evenly throughout the year, budgeted sales for the first nine months of a year would be 75% of the year's budgeted sales. Comparison of this amount with actual sales will indicate the percentage increase or decrease of actual sales for the nine months over budgeted sales for the nine months. (Round percent changes to the nearest whole percent.) Place your answers in a columnar table with the following format:

	Unit Budgeted Sales		Actual Sales	Increase (Decrease)	
	Year	Nine Months	for Nine Months	Amount	Percent
Product A					
East					
Central					
West					
Product B					
East					
Central					
West					

(2) Assuming that the trend of sales indicated in (1) is to continue in 1993, compute the unit sales volume to be used for preparing the sales budget for the year ending December 31, 1993. Place your answers in a columnar table with the following format:

	1992 Budgeted Units	Percentage Increase (Decrease)	1993 Budgeted Units
Product A			
East			
Central			
West			
Product B			
East			
Central			
West			

(3) Prepare a sales budget for the year ending December 31, 1993.

Pb. 25–29.
Sales, production, direct materials, and direct labor budgets.
OBJ. 2

The budget director of DeBow Company requests estimates of sales, production, and other operating data from the various administrative units every month. Selected information concerning sales and production for April of the current year are summarized as follows:

(a) Estimated sales for April by sales territory:

Northeast:
- Product E: 12,000 units at $50 per unit
- Product F: 10,000 units at $70 per unit

Southeast:
- Product E: 9,000 units at $50 per unit
- Product F: 13,500 units at $70 per unit

Southwest:
Product E: 19,000 units at $50 per unit
Product F: 21,500 units at $70 per unit

(b) Estimated inventories at April 1:
Direct materials:
Material P: 8,500 lbs. Material R: 7,000 lbs.
Material Q: 18,000 lbs. Material S: 6,500 lbs.
Finished products:
Product E: 7,500 units Product F: 8,000 units

(c) Desired inventories at April 30:
Direct materials:
Material P: 9,000 lbs. Material R: 8,000 lbs.
Material Q: 16,500 lbs. Material S: 6,000 lbs.
Finished Products:
Product E: 9,100 units Product F: 10,500 units

(d) Direct materials used in production:
In manufacture of Product E:
Material P: 2.4 lbs. per unit of product
Material Q: 1.2 lbs. per unit of product
Material R: .9 lbs. per unit of product
In manufacture of Product F:
Material Q: 1.8 lbs. per unit of product
Material R: 1.0 lbs. per unit of product
Material S: 1.3 lbs. per unit of product

(e) Anticipated purchase price for direct materials:
Material P: $1.50 per lb. Material R: $5.00 per lb.
Material Q: $ .75 per lb. Material S: $2.60 per lb.

(f) Direct labor requirements:
Product E:
Department 20: 2.0 hours at $12 per hour
Department 30: .5 hours at $10 per hour
Product F:
Department 10: 1.8 hours at $16 per hour
Department 20: 1.2 hours at $12 per hour

Instructions:

(1) Prepare a sales budget for April.
(2) Prepare a production budget for April.
(3) Prepare a direct materials purchases budget for April.
(4) Prepare a direct labor cost budget for April.

Pb. 25–30.
Budgeted income statement and supporting budgets.
OBJ. 2

The budget director of Gear Inc., with the assistance of the controller, treasurer, production manager, and sales manager, has gathered the following data for use in developing the budgeted income statement for May:

(a) Estimated sales for May:
Product H: 40,000 units at $75 per unit
Product I: 60,000 units at $60 per unit

(b) Estimated inventories at May 1:
Direct materials:
Material A: 8,500 lbs.
Material B: 11,200 lbs.
Material C: 10,000 lbs.
Finished products:
Product H: 5,000 units at $50 per unit
Product I: 7,500 units at $36 per unit

25-1072 (c) Desired inventories at May 31:

Direct materials:
- Material A: 10,000 lbs.
- Material B: 12,000 lbs.
- Material C: 8,000 lbs.

Finished products:
- Product H: 4,500 units at $50 per unit
- Product I: 8,000 units at $36 per unit

(d) Direct materials used in production:

In manufacture of Product H:
- Material A: .8 lbs. per unit of product
- Material B: 1.2 lbs. per unit of product

In manufacture of Product I:
- Material B: 1.4 lbs. per unit of product
- Material C: 2.0 lbs. per unit of product

(e) Anticipated cost of purchases and beginning and ending inventory of direct materials:
- Material A: $15.50 per lb.
- Material B: 2.00 per lb.
- Material C: 7.20 per lb.

(f) Direct labor requirements:

Product H:
- Department 100: 1.5 hours at $18 per hour
- Department 200: .6 hours at $10 per hour

Product I:
- Department 200: .8 hours at $10 per hour
- Department 300: .2 hours at $9 per hour

(g) Estimated factory overhead costs for May:

Indirect factory wages	$225,000
Depreciation of plant and equipment	110,000
Supervisory salaries	50,000
Power and light	36,000
Indirect materials	32,000
Maintenance	15,000
Insurance and property taxes	7,000

(h) Estimated operating expenses for May:

Sales salaries expense	$381,000
Officers' salaries expense	270,000
Advertising expense	250,000
Office salaries expense	125,000
Depreciation expense—office equipment	80,000
Telephone expense—selling	37,200
Telephone expense—administrative	21,400
Travel expense—selling	13,250
Travel expense—administrative	7,750
Office supplies expense	3,350
Miscellaneous selling expense	8,000
Miscellaneous administrative expense	6,000

(i) Estimated other income and expense for May:

Interest income	$200,000
Interest expense	150,000

(j) Estimated tax rate: 40%.

Instructions:

(1) Prepare a sales budget for May.
(2) Prepare a production budget for May.
(3) Prepare a direct materials purchases budget for May.
(4) Prepare a direct labor cost budget for May.
(5) Prepare a factory overhead cost budget for May.
(6) Prepare a cost of goods sold budget for May. Work in process at the beginning of May is estimated to be $80,000, and work in process at the end of May is estimated to be $65,000.
(7) Prepare an operating expenses budget for May. Classify the expenses as either selling or administrative expenses.
(8) Prepare a budgeted income statement for May.

Pb. 25–31.
Cash budget.
OBJ. 2

The treasurer of Brady Company instructs you to prepare a monthly cash budget for the next three months. You are presented with the following budget information:

	May	June	July
Sales	$120,000	$180,000	$200,000
Manufacturing costs	70,000	110,000	125,000
Operating expenses	20,000	27,000	30,000
Capital expenditures	—	18,000	—

The company expects to sell about 25% of its merchandise for cash. Of sales on account, 60% are expected to be collected in full in the month following the sale and the remainder the following month. Depreciation, insurance, and property taxes represent $10,000 of the estimated monthly manufacturing costs and $4,000 of the probable monthly operating expenses. Insurance and property taxes are paid in February and October respectively. Of the remainder of the manufacturing costs and operating expenses, 60% are expected to be paid in the month in which they are incurred and the balance in the following month.

Current assets as of May 1 are composed of cash of $15,000, marketable securities of $25,000, and accounts receivable of $90,000 ($60,000 from April sales and $30,000 from March sales). Current liabilities as of May 1 are composed of a $20,000, 9%, 120-day note payable due June 10, $38,000 of accounts payable incurred in April for manufacturing costs, and accrued liabilities of $6,000 incurred in April for operating expenses.

It is expected that $5,000 in dividends will be received in May. An estimated income tax payment of $3,500 will be made in June. Brady Company's regular quarterly dividend of $1,000 is expected to be declared in June and paid in July. Management desires to maintain a minimum cash balance of $20,000.

Instructions:

(1) Prepare a monthly cash budget for May, June, and July.
(2) On the basis of the cash budget prepared in (1), what recommendation should be made to the treasurer?

Pb. 25–32.
Budgeted income statement and balance sheet.
OBJ. 2

As a preliminary to requesting budget estimates of sales, costs, and expenses for the fiscal year beginning January 1, 1992, the following tentative trial balance as of December 31 of the preceding year is prepared by the accounting department of Crymes Company:

25-1074

Cash	41,000	
Accounts Receivable	54,000	
Finished Goods	90,000	
Work in Process	47,200	
Materials	31,300	
Prepaid Expenses	6,100	
Plant and Equipment	480,400	
Accumulated Depreciation—Plant and Equipment		192,000
Accounts Payable		60,000
Notes Payable		40,000
Common Stock, $20 par		100,000
Retained Earnings		358,000
	750,000	750,000

Factory output and sales for 1992 are expected to total 50,000 units of product, which are to be sold at $24 per unit. The quantities and costs of the inventories (lifo method) at December 31, 1992, are expected to remain unchanged from the balances at the beginning of the year.

Budget estimates of manufacturing costs and operating expenses for the year are summarized as follows:

	Estimated Costs and Expenses	
	Fixed (Total for Year)	Variable (Per Unit Sold)
Cost of goods manufactured and sold:		
Direct materials	—	$7.10
Direct labor	—	3.90
Factory overhead:		
Depreciation of plant and equipment	$15,000	—
Other factory overhead	10,000	1.75
Selling expenses:		
Sales salaries and commissions	25,000	.80
Advertising	20,000	—
Miscellaneous selling expense	2,000	.18
Administrative expenses:		
Office and officers' salaries	30,000	.20
Supplies	1,000	.05
Miscellaneous administrative expense	500	.02

Balances of accounts receivable, prepaid expenses, and accounts payable at the end of the year are expected to differ from the beginning balances by only inconsequential amounts.

For purposes of this problem, assume that federal income tax of $160,000 on 1992 taxable income will be paid during 1992. Regular quarterly cash dividends of $.15 a share are expected to be declared and paid in March, June, September, and December. It is anticipated that plant and equipment will be purchased for $250,000 cash in November.

Instructions:

(1) Prepare a budgeted income statement for 1992.
(2) Prepare a budgeted balance sheet as of December 31, 1992.

Pb. 25–33. **Flexible factory overhead cost budget and budget performance report.** OBJ. 3,4

Kenon Inc. prepared the following factory overhead cost budget for May of the current year for 10,000 units of product:

Kenon Inc.
Factory Overhead Cost Budget
For Month Ending May 31, 19--

Variable cost:		
Indirect factory wages	$40,000	
Indirect materials	25,000	
Power and light	13,200	
Total variable cost		$78,200
Fixed cost:		
Supervisory salaries	$16,200	
Indirect factory wages	15,300	
Depreciation of plant and equipment	12,000	
Insurance	7,100	
Power and light	6,750	
Property taxes	2,250	
Total fixed cost		59,600
Total factory overhead cost		$137,800

The following factory overhead costs were incurred in producing 9,000 units in May:

Indirect factory wages	$52,000
Indirect materials	22,350
Power and light	18,450
Supervisory salaries	16,200
Depreciation of plant and equipment	12,000
Insurance	7,100
Property taxes	2,250
Total factory overhead cost incurred	$130,350

Instructions:

(1) Prepare a flexible factory overhead cost budget for May, indicating capacities of 7,000, 8,000, 9,000, and 10,000 units of product.
(2) Prepare a budget performance report for May.

ALTERNATE PROBLEMS

Pb. 25–28A. **Forecast sales volume and sales budget.** OBJ. 2

Morhaim Company prepared the sales budget shown at the top of page 1076 for the current year.

At the end of September, 1992, the following unit sales data were reported for the first nine months of the year:

	Unit Sales	
	Product E	Product F
East	14,550	39,750
Central	22,950	44,100
West	28,800	64,800

For the year ending December 31, 1993, unit sales are expected to follow the patterns established during the first nine months of the year ending December 31, 1992. The unit selling price for Product E is expected to be increased to $30, effective January 1, 1993, and the unit selling price for Product F is expected to be increased to $17.

25-1076

Morhaim Company
Sales Budget
For Year Ending December 31, 1992

Product and Area	Unit Sales Volume	Unit Selling Price	Total Sales
Product E:			
East	20,000	$28.00	$ 560,000
Central	30,000	28.00	840,000
West	40,000	28.00	1,120,000
Total	90,000		$2,520,000
Product F:			
East	50,000	$15.00	$ 750,000
Central	60,000	15.00	900,000
West	80,000	15.00	1,200,000
Total	190,000		$2,850,000
Total revenue from sales			$5,370,000

Instructions:

(1) Compute the increase or decrease of actual *unit* sales for the nine months ended September 30, 1992, over expectations for this nine-month period. Since sales have historically occurred evenly throughout the year, budgeted sales for the first nine months of a year would be 75% of the year's budgeted sales. Comparison of this amount with actual sales will indicate the percentage increase or decrease of actual sales for the nine months over budgeted sales for the nine months. Place your answers in a columnar table with the following format:

	Unit Budgeted Sales		Actual Sales	Increase (Decrease)	
	Year	Nine Months	for Nine Months	Amount	Percent
Product E					
East					
Central					
West					
Product F					
East					
Central					
West					

(2) Assuming that the trend of sales indicated in (1) is to continue in 1993, compute the unit sales volume to be used for preparing the sales budget for the year ending December 31, 1993. Place your answers in a columnar table with the following format:

	1992 Budgeted Units	Percentage Increase (Decrease)	1993 Budgeted Units
Product E			
East			
Central			
West			
Product F			
East			
Central			
West			

(3) Prepare a sales budget for the year ending December 31, 1993.

Pb. 25–29A. **Sales, production, direct materials, and direct labor budgets.**

OBJ. 2

The budget director of Kotch Company requests estimates of sales, production, and other operating data from the various administrative units every month. Selected information concerning sales and production for May of the current year are summarized as follows:

(a) Estimated sales for May by sales territory:
  Northeast:
    Product E: 5,000 units at $120 per unit
    Product F: 40,000 units at $ 40 per unit
  Southeast:
    Product E: 6,000 units at $120 per unit
    Product F: 36,000 units at $ 40 per unit
  Southwest:
    Product E: 3,000 units at $120 per unit
    Product F: 50,000 units at $ 40 per unit

(b) Estimated inventories at May 1:
  Direct materials:
    Material W: 18,200 lbs. Material Y: 7,700 lbs.
    Material X: 4,600 lbs. Material Z: 13,250 lbs.
  Finished products:
    Product E: 2,000 units Product F: 11,000 units

(c) Desired inventories at May 31:
  Direct materials:
    Material W: 20,000 lbs. Material Y: 8,000 lbs.
    Material X: 5,000 lbs. Material Z: 14,000 lbs.
  Finished products:
    Product E: 1,500 units Product F: 12,000 units

(d) Direct materials used in production:
  In manufacture of Product E:
    Material X: 3.6 lbs. per unit of product
    Material Y: 1.4 lbs. per unit of product
    Material Z: .5 lbs. per unit of product
  In manufacture of Product F:
    Material W: 1.6 lbs. per unit of product
    Material Y: .4 lbs. per unit of product
    Material Z: 1.0 lb. per unit of product

(e) Anticipated purchase price for direct materials:
    Material W: $10.00 per lb. Material Y: $2.50 per lb.
    Material X: $ .30 per lb. Material Z: $ .80 per lb.

(f) Direct labor requirements:
  Product E:
    Department 20: 3.2 hours at $15 per hour
    Department 30: .4 hours at $12 per hour
  Product F:
    Department 10: .2 hours at $9 per hour
    Department 20: .1 hours at $15 per hour

Instructions:

(1) Prepare a sales budget for May.
(2) Prepare a production budget for May.
(3) Prepare a direct materials purchases budget for May.
(4) Prepare a direct labor cost budget for May.

25-1078

Pb. 25–30A.
Budgeted income statement and supporting budgets.
OBJ. 2

The budget director of Gonzales Inc., with the assistance of the controller, treasurer, production manager, and sales manager, has gathered the following data for use in developing the budgeted income statement for June:

(a) Estimated sales for June:
  Product G: 100,000 units at $50 per unit
  Product H: 20,000 units at $15 per unit

(b) Estimated inventories at June 1:

Direct materials:	Finished products:
Material A: 15,800 lbs.	Product G: 9,000 units at $34 per unit
Material B: 9,500 lbs.	Product H: 3,000 units at $11 per unit

(c) Desired inventories at June 30:

Direct materials:	Finished products:
Material A: 18,000 lbs.	Product G: 11,000 units at $34 per unit
Material B: 9,000 lbs.	Product H: 1,500 units at $11 per unit

(d) Direct materials used in production:
  In manufacture of Product G:
    Material A: 1.5 lbs. per unit of product
    Material B: .7 lbs. per unit of product
  In manufacture of Product H:
    Material B: .8 lbs. per unit of product

(e) Anticipated cost of purchases and beginning and ending inventory of direct materials:
    Material A: $7 per lb.
    Material B: $4 per lb.

(f) Direct labor requirements:
  Product G:
    Department 100: 1.2 hours at $12 per hour
    Department 200: .1 hours at $8 per hour
  Product H:
    Department 200: .2 hours at $8 per hour
    Department 300: .5 hours at $9 per hour

(g) Estimated factory overhead costs for June:

Indirect factory wages	$150,000
Depreciation of plant and equipment	110,000
Supervisory salaries	90,000
Power and light	80,000
Indirect materials	40,000
Maintenance	25,000
Insurance and property taxes	15,000

(h) Estimated operating expenses for June:

Sales salaries expense	$230,000
Officers' salaries expense	150,000
Advertising expense	110,000
Office salaries expense	70,000
Depreciation expense—office equipment	42,000
Telephone expense—selling	24,000
Telephone expense—administrative	10,000
Travel expense—selling	7,500
Travel expense—administrative	6,500
Office supplies expense	3,000
Miscellaneous selling expense	2,000
Miscellaneous administrative expense	1,000

(i) Estimated other income and expense for June:

Interest income	$100,000
Interest expense	90,000

(j) Estimated tax rate: 40%.

Instructions:

(1) Prepare a sales budget for June.
(2) Prepare a production budget for June.
(3) Prepare a direct materials purchases budget for June.
(4) Prepare a direct labor cost budget for June.
(5) Prepare a factory overhead cost budget for June.
(6) Prepare a cost of goods sold budget for June. Work in process at the beginning of June is estimated to be $28,500, and work in process at the end of June is estimated to be $29,000.
(7) Prepare an operating expenses budget for June. Classify the expenses as either selling or administrative expenses.
(8) Prepare a budgeted income statement for June.

Pb. 25–31A.
Cash budget.
OBJ. 2

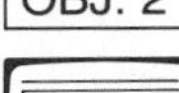

The treasurer of Grayson Company instructs you to prepare a monthly cash budget for the next three months. You are presented with the following budget information:

	July	August	September
Sales	$300,000	$250,000	$400,000
Manufacturing costs	200,000	130,000	250,000
Operating expenses	40,000	25,000	60,000
Capital expenditures	—	240,000	—

The company expects to sell about 20% of its merchandise for cash. Of sales on account, 75% are expected to be collected in full in the month following the sale and the remainder the following month. Depreciation, insurance, and property taxes represent $25,000 of the estimated monthly manufacturing costs and $4,000 of the probable monthly operating expenses. Insurance and property taxes are paid in December. Of the remainder of the manufacturing costs and operating expenses, 60% are expected to be paid in the month in which they are incurred and the balance in the following month.

Current assets as of July 1 are composed of cash of $35,100, marketable securities of $20,000 and accounts receivable of $282,000 ($210,000 from June sales and $72,000 from May sales). Current liabilities as of July 1 are composed of a $70,000, 15%, 180-day note payable due September 15, $42,000 of accounts payable incurred in June for manufacturing costs, and accrued liabilities of $10,300 incurred in June for operating expenses.

It is expected that $5,000 in dividends will be received in August. An estimated income tax payment of $8,000 will be made in September. Grayson Company's regular semiannual dividend of $10,000 is expected to be declared in August and paid in September. Management desires to maintain a minimum cash balance of $30,000.

Instructions:

(1) Prepare a monthly cash budget for July, August, and September.
(2) On the basis of the cash budget prepared in (1), what recommendation should be made to the treasurer?

Pb. 25–32A.
Budgeted income statement and balance sheet.
OBJ. 2

As a preliminary to requesting budget estimates of sales, costs, and expenses for the fiscal year beginning January 1, 1993, the following tentative trial balance as of December 31 of the preceding year is prepared by the accounting department of Mayberry Company.

25-
1080

Cash	39,000	
Accounts Receivable	60,000	
Finished Goods	90,000	
Work in Process	47,200	
Materials	31,300	
Prepaid Expenses	7,500	
Plant and Equipment	460,000	
Accumulated Depreciation—Plant and Equipment		300,000
Accounts Payable		75,000
Notes Payable		50,000
Common Stock, $20 par		200,000
Retained Earnings		110,000
	735,000	735,000

Factory output and sales for 1993 are expected to total 30,000 units of product, which are to be sold at $33 per unit. The quantities and costs of the inventories (lifo method) at December 31, 1993, are expected to remain unchanged from the balances at the beginning of the year.

Budget estimates of manufacturing costs and operating expenses for the year are summarized as follows:

	Estimated Costs and Expenses	
	Fixed (Total for Year)	Variable (Per Unit Sold)
Cost of goods manufactured and sold:		
Direct materials	—	$9.05
Direct labor	—	6.90
Factory overhead:		
Depreciation of plant and equipment	$15,000	—
Other factory overhead	10,000	2.85
Selling expenses:		
Sales salaries and commissions	40,000	1.00
Advertising	15,000	—
Miscellaneous selling expense	2,000	.30
Administrative expenses:		
Office and officers' salaries	34,000	.20
Supplies	2,600	.03
Miscellaneous administrative expense	900	.02

Balances of accounts receivable, prepaid expenses, and accounts payable at the end of the year are expected to differ from the beginning balances by only inconsequential amounts.

For purposes of this problem, assume that federal income tax of $84,500 on 1993 taxable income will be paid during 1993. Regular quarterly cash dividends of $1.25 a share are expected to be declared and paid in March, June, September, and December. It is anticipated that plant and equipment will be purchased for $125,000 cash in May.

Instructions:

(1) Prepare a budgeted income statement for 1993.
(2) Prepare a budgeted balance sheet as of December 31, 1993.

Pb. 25–33A.
Flexible factory overhead cost budget and budget performance report.
OBJ. 3,4

Maxwell Inc. prepared the following factory overhead cost budget for April of the current year for 20,000 units of product:

Maxwell Inc.
Factory Overhead Cost Budget
For Month Ending April 30, 19--

Variable cost:		
Indirect factory wages	$40,000	
Indirect materials	22,500	
Power and light	15,000	
Total variable cost		$ 77,500
Fixed cost:		
Supervisory salaries	$35,000	
Indirect factory wages	11,250	
Depreciation of plant and equipment	9,150	
Insurance	7,500	
Power and light	7,000	
Property taxes	4,500	
Total fixed cost		74,400
Total factory overhead cost		$151,900

The following factory overhead costs were incurred in producing 21,000 units in April:

Indirect factory wages	$ 54,050
Supervisory salaries	35,000
Indirect materials	23,100
Power and light	22,325
Depreciation of plant and equipment	9,150
Insurance	7,500
Property taxes	4,500
Total factory overhead cost incurred	$155,625

Instructions:

(1) Prepare a flexible factory overhead cost budget for April, indicating capacities of 19,000, 20,000, 21,000, and 22,000 units of product.
(2) Prepare a budget performance report for April.

MINI-CASE 25

Your father is president and chief operating officer of Barnes Manufacturing Company and has hired you as a summer intern to assist the controller. The controller has asked you to visit with the production supervisor of the Polishing Department and evaluate the supervisor's concern with the budgeting process. After this evaluation, you are to meet with the controller to discuss suggestions for improving the budgeting process.

This morning, you met with the supervisor, who expressed dissatisfaction with the budgets and budget performance reports prepared for the factory overhead costs for the Polishing Department. Specifically, March's budget performance report was mentioned as an example. The supervisor indicated that this report is not useful in evaluating the efficiency of the department, because most of the overages for the individual factory overhead items are not caused by inefficiencies, but by variations in the volume of activity between actual and budget. Although you were not provided with a copy of the budget for March, the supervisor indicated that it is standard practice for the plant manager to prepare a budget based on the production of 10,000 units. Actual production varies widely, however, with approximately 12,000 to 15,000 units being produced each month for the past several months. You are provided with the following budget performance report for March of the current year, when actual production was 15,000 units. All of the overages relate to variable costs, and the other costs are fixed.

Barnes Manufacturing Company
Budget Performance Report—Factory Overhead Cost, Polishing Department
For Month Ended March 31, 19--

	Budget	Actual	Over	Under
Indirect factory wages	$28,000	$ 41,700	$13,700	
Electric power	17,800	27,000	9,200	
Supervisory salaries	16,000	16,000		
Depreciation of plant assets	12,000	12,000		
Indirect materials	8,200	12,400	4,200	
Insurance and property taxes	4,000	4,000		
	$86,000	$113,100	$27,100	$0

In your discussion, you learned that the department supervisor has little faith in the budgeting process. The supervisor views the budgets as worthless and the budget performance reports as a waste of time, because they require an explanation of the budget overages, which, for the most part, are not departmentally controlled.

Instructions:

Prepare a list of suggestions for improving the budgeting process. Include any reports that you might find useful when you meet with the controller to discuss your suggestions.

ANSWERS TO SELF-EXAMINATION QUESTIONS

1. C Continuous budgeting (answer C) is a type of budgeting that continually provides for maintenance of a twelve-month projection into the future.
2. B The total production indicated in the production budget is 257,500 units (answer B), which is computed as follows:

Sales	250,000 units
Plus desired ending inventory	30,000 units
Total	280,000 units
Less estimated beginning inventory	22,500 units
Total production	257,500 units

3. C The capital expenditures budget (answer C) summarizes the plans for the acquisition of plant facilities and equipment for a number of years into the future. The cash budget (answer A) presents the expected inflow and outflow of cash for a budget period, and the sales budget (answer B) presents the expected sales for the budget period.
4. B A budget performance report (answer B) compares actual results with budgeted figures.
5. C Flexible budgeting (answer C) provides a series of budgets for varying rates of activity and thereby builds into the budgeting system the effect of fluctuations in volume of activity. Budget performance reporting (answer A) is a system of reports that compares actual results with budgeted figures. Continuous budgeting (answer B) is a variant of fiscal-year budgeting that provides for continuous twelve-month projections into the future. This is achieved by periodically deleting from the current budget the data for the elapsed period and adding newly estimated budget data for the same period next year.

CHAPTER 26

CHAPTER OBJECTIVES

1 Describe the use of standard costs in planning and controlling operations.

2 Describe and illustrate the use of variance analysis for direct materials, direct labor, and factory overhead.

3 Describe and illustrate how standards may be included in the accounts of a manufacturing enterprise.

4 Describe the importance of periodic review and revision of standards.

5 Describe the use of standards for nonmanufacturing expenses.

STANDARD COST SYSTEMS

The preceding chapter focused on the use of budgets as an aid to management in planning and controlling the operations of a business. This chapter will focus on standard cost systems and variance analysis, which can also be used by management in planning and controlling operations.

THE NATURE AND OBJECTIVES OF STANDARDS

OBJECTIVE 1
Describe the use of standard costs in planning and controlling operations.

Standards are used to measure and evaluate performance in many areas of life. For example, colleges and universities set standards for graduation, such as a C average. They may establish a B+ average for graduation with honors. Golfers use par as a standard in evaluating their play on the golf course. In each of these cases, the predetermined standard is used to measure and evaluate an individual's performance. In a like manner, business enterprises may use carefully predetermined standards to evaluate and control operations.

Service, merchandising, and manufacturing enterprises can all use standards. For example, an automobile repair garage may use a *standard* amount of time, as expressed in service manuals, as the basis for computing the labor charges for automobile repairs and measuring the performance of the mechanic. The driver of a truck delivering merchandise may be expected to make a *standard* number of deliveries each day. The widest use of standards is by manufacturing enterprises, which establish standard costs for the three categories of manufacturing costs: direct materials, direct labor, and factory overhead.

Accounting systems that use standards for each element of manufacturing cost entering into the finished product are sometimes called **standard cost systems**. Such systems enable management to determine how much a product should cost **(standard)**, how much it does cost (actual), and the causes of any difference **(variance)** between the two. Standard costs thus serve as a device for measuring efficiency. If the actual costs are compared with the standard costs, unfavorable conditions can be determined and corrective actions taken.

Thus, management has a device for controlling costs and motivating employees to become more cost conscious.

Setting Standards

The starting point in setting standards is often a review of past operations. In this review, management and the managerial accountant rely on their knowledge and judgment of past processes and costs to estimate the costs to produce a unit of product. However, standards should not be merely an extension of past costs. Inefficiencies may be reflected in past costs, and these inefficiencies should be considered in determining what the costs should be (standards). In addition, changes in technology, machinery, production methods, and economic conditions must be considered.

The setting of standards is both an art and a science. Although the standard-setting process varies among enterprises, it often requires the joint efforts of accountants, engineers, personnel administrators, and other management personnel. The managerial accountant plays an important role by expressing the results of judgments and studies in terms of dollars and subsequently reporting how actual results compare with these standards. Engineers contribute to the standard-setting process by studying the requirements of the product and the production process. For example, direct materials requirements can be determined by studying such factors as the materials specifications for the product and the normal spoilage in production. Time and motion studies may be used to determine the length of time required for each of the various manufacturing operations. Engineering studies may also be used to determine standards for some of the elements of factory overhead, such as the amount of power needed to operate machinery.

THE DEVELOPMENT OF STANDARD COSTS

An example of a company that uses standard costs is Dutch Pantry Inc., which operates 53 family restaurants in 12 eastern states. To assure consistent quality in the items served in these restaurants, much of the food preparation is done in a central commissary. Because the commissary produces more than 150 different items, it uses a standard cost system based on the production of a batch of product. This system allows the costs for the many products to flow through the various operations involved in food preparation.

The food processing activity of the central commissary consists of the following operations:

Spice room	Trim	Meat/broth	Bulk pack
Butcher shop	Weigh	Cooking kettles	Salad dressing
Pan/stuffing	Pop-out	Frying	Case packing
Bake/roast	Sure flow	Slicing	Warehouse

As production passes through each of these operations, the various elements of cost are incurred. How standard costs are developed for Dutch Pantry's raw materials, ingredients, packaging, and direct labor is described in the following excerpts from an article in *Management Accounting:*

. . .The standard costs of raw materials, ingredients and packaging are calculated by the use of a Recipe Sheet. . . , which is actually a bill of materials for a batch of the product. For costing purposes, the recipes are input to a computer program called the Recipe Master List. All costs are calculated on a hundred weight (CWT) basis. . . .

The standard costs of the component items are updated monthly on the Inventory Master Listing. At the same time, the updated costs are input to the Recipe Master List. This permits a timely revision of the costs of the finished products for changes in the standards of any components.

Direct labor dollars are [incurred in] production [as] the product passes through [the various operations.] A labor grid is prepared for each product. This grid lists the various [operations] for the product and the number of workers required to staff each [operation]. The various worker classifications and hourly rates are used to calculate a weighted-average cost per hour for direct labor.

Next, a standard poundage of product processed per hour is developed for each [operation]. A weighted average of the actual production runs from the prior year is used for this calculation. The direct labor cost per CWT is recorded on the product rate master (report) by [operation]. . . .

[Finally, the] budgeted direct labor dollars for the warehouse are divided by the forecasted quantity of production (cases). The result is the warehousing cost per case. . . .

Source: Dennis M. Boll, "How Dutch Pantry Accounts for Standard Costs," *Management Accounting* (December, 1982), pp. 32–35.

Types of Standards

Implicit in the use of standards is the concept of an acceptable level of production efficiency. One of the major objectives in selecting this performance level is to motivate workers to expend the efforts necessary to achieve the most efficient operations.

Standards that are too high, that is, standards that are unrealistic, may have a negative impact on performance because workers may become frustrated with their inability to meet the standards and, therefore, may not be motivated to do their best. Such standards represent levels of performance that can be achieved only under perfect operating conditions, such as no idle time, no machine breakdowns, and no materials spoilage. Such standards, often called **theoretical standards** or **ideal standards,** are not widely used.

Standards that are too low might not motivate employees to perform at their best because the standard level of performance can be reached too easily. As a result, productivity may be lower than that which could be achieved.

Most companies use **currently attainable standards** (sometimes called **normal standards**), which represent levels of operation that can be attained with reasonable effort. Such currently attainable standards allow for reasonable production problems and errors, such as normal materials spoilage and machinery downtime for maintenance. When reasonable standards are used, employees often become cost conscious and expend their best efforts to achieve the best possible results at the lowest possible cost. Also, if employees are given bonuses for exceeding normal standards, the standards may be even more effective in motivating employees to perform at their best.

VARIANCES FROM STANDARDS

OBJECTIVE 2
Describe and illustrate the use of variance analysis for direct materials, direct labor, and factory overhead.

One of the primary purposes of a standard cost system is to facilitate control over costs by comparing actual costs with standard costs. Control is achieved by the action of management in investigating significant deviations of performance from standards and taking corrective action. Differences between the standard costs of a department or product and the actual costs incurred are termed **variances**. If the actual cost incurred is less than the standard cost, the variance is favorable. If the actual cost exceeds the standard cost, the variance is unfavorable. When actual costs are compared with standard costs, only the "exceptions" or significant variances are reported to the person responsible for cost control. This reporting by the "principle of exceptions" enables the one responsible for cost control to concentrate on the cause and correction of the variances.

When manufacturing operations are automated, standard cost data can be integrated with the computer that directs operations. Variances can then be detected and reported automatically by the computer system, and adjustments can be made to operations in progress.

The total variance for a certain period is usually made up of several variances, some of which may be favorable and some unfavorable. There may be variances from standards in direct materials costs, in direct labor costs, and in factory overhead costs. Illustrations and analyses of these variances for Mayer Company, a manufacturing enterprise, are presented in the following paragraphs. For illustrative purposes, it is assumed that only one type of direct material is used, that there is a single processing department, and that Product X is the only commodity manufactured by the enterprise. The standard costs for direct materials, direct labor, and factory overhead for a unit of Product X are as follows:

Direct materials:	
2 pounds at $1 per pound	$ 2.00
Direct labor:	
.4 hour at $16 per hour.......................	6.40
Factory overhead:	
.4 hour at $8.40 per hour	3.36
Total per unit	$11.76

Direct Materials Cost Variance

Two major factors enter into the determination of standards for direct materials cost: (1) the quantity (usage) standard and (2) the price standard. If the actual quantity of direct materials used in producing a commodity differs from the standard quantity, there is a **quantity variance**. If the actual unit price of the materials differs from the standard price, there is a **price variance**. To illustrate, assume that the standard direct materials cost of producing 10,000 units of Product X and the direct materials cost actually incurred during June were as follows:

Actual: 20,600 pounds at $1.04	$21,424
Standard: 20,000 pounds (10,000 units × 2 lbs. per unit) at $1.00 ...	20,000

The unfavorable variance of $1,424 resulted in part from an excess usage of 600 pounds of direct materials and in part from an excess cost of $.04 per pound. The analysis of the direct materials cost variance is as follows:

Direct Materials Cost Variance

Quantity variance:			
Actual quantity	20,600 pounds		
Standard quantity	20,000 pounds		
Variance—unfavorable ...	600 pounds	× standard price, $1	$ 600
Price variance:			
Actual price	$1.04 per pound		
Standard price	1.00 per pound		
Variance—unfavorable ..	$ .04 per pound	× actual quantity, 20,600 ..	824
Total direct materials cost variance—unfavorable			$1,424

Direct Materials Quantity Variance. The direct materials quantity variance is the difference between the actual quantity used and the standard quantity, multiplied by the standard price per unit. If the standard quantity exceeds the actual quantity used, the variance is favorable. If the actual quantity of materials used exceeds the standard quantity, the variance is unfavorable, as shown for Mayer Company in the following illustration:

Direct Materials Quantity Variance

Direct Materials Quantity Variance	=	Actual Quantity Used − Standard Quantity	×	Standard Price per Unit
Quantity variance	=	(20,600 pounds − 20,000 pounds)	×	$1.00 per pound
Quantity variance	=	600 pounds	×	$1.00 per pound
Quantity variance	=	$600 unfavorable		

Direct Materials Price Variance. The direct materials price variance is the difference between the actual price per unit and the standard price per unit, multiplied by the actual quantity used. If the standard price per unit exceeds the actual price per unit, the variance is favorable. If the actual price per unit exceeds the standard price per unit, the variance is unfavorable, as shown for Mayer Company in the following illustration:

Direct Materials Price Variance

Direct Materials Price Variance	=	Actual Price Per Unit − Standard Price	×	Actual Quantity Used
Price variance	=	($1.04 per pound − $1.00 per pound)	×	20,600 pounds
Price variance	=	$.04 per pound	×	20,600 pounds
Price variance	=	$824 unfavorable		

Reporting Direct Materials Cost Variance. The physical quantity and the dollar amount of the quantity variance should be reported to the factory superintendent and other personnel responsible for production. If excessive amounts of direct materials were used because of the malfunction of equipment or some other failure within the production department, those responsible should correct the situation. However, an unfavorable direct materials quantity variance is not necessarily the result of inefficiency within the production department. If the excess usage of 600 pounds of materials in the example above had been caused by inferior materials, the purchasing department should be held responsible.

The unit price and the total amount of the materials price variance should be reported to the purchasing department, which may or may not be able to control this variance. If materials of the same quality could have been purchased from another supplier at the standard price, the variance was controllable. On the other hand, if the variance resulted from a marketwide price increase, the variance was not subject to control.

Direct Labor Cost Variance

As in the case of direct materials, two major factors enter into the determination of standards for direct labor cost: (1) the time (usage or efficiency) standard and (2) the rate (price or wage) standard. If the actual direct labor hours spent producing a product differ from the standard hours, there is a **time variance**. If the wage rate paid differs from the standard rate, there is a **rate variance**. The standard cost and the actual cost of direct labor in the production of 10,000 units of Product X during June are assumed to be as follows:

Actual:	3,950 hours at $16.40	$64,780
Standard:	4,000 hours (10,000 units × .4 hr. per unit) at $16.00	64,000

The unfavorable direct labor variance of $780 is made up of a favorable time variance and an unfavorable rate variance, determined as follows:

Direct Labor Cost Variance

Time variance:		
Actual time	3,950 hours	
Standard time	4,000 hours	
Variance—favorable	−50 hours × standard rate, $16	$ 800
Rate variance:		
Actual rate	$16.40 per hour	
Standard rate	16.00 per hour	
Variance—unfavorable	$ .40 per hour × actual time, 3,950 hours	1,580
Total direct labor cost variance—unfavorable		$ 780

Direct Labor Time Variance. The direct labor time variance is the difference between the actual hours worked and the standard hours, multiplied by the standard rate per hour. If the actual hours worked exceed the standard hours, the variance is unfavorable. If the actual hours worked are less than the standard hours, the variance is favorable, as shown for Mayer Company in the following illustration:

Direct Labor Time Variance

Direct Labor Time Variance	=	Actual Hours Worked − Standard Hours	×	Standard Rate per Hour
Time variance	=	(3,950 hours − 4,000 hours)	×	$16 per hour
Time variance	=	−50 hours	×	$16 per hour
Time variance	=	$800 favorable		

In the illustration, when the standard hours (4,000) are subtracted from the actual hours worked (3,950), the difference is "−50 hours." The minus sign indicates that the variance of 50 hours, or $800 (50 hours × $16), is favorable.

Direct Labor Rate Variance. The direct labor rate variance is the difference between the actual rate per hour and the standard rate per hour, multiplied by the actual hours worked. If the standard rate per hour exceeds the actual rate per hour, the variance is favorable. If the actual rate per hour exceeds the standard rate per hour, the variance is unfavorable, as shown for Mayer Company in the following illustration:

Direct Labor Rate Variance

Direct Labor Rate Variance	=	Actual Rate per Hour − Standard Rate	×	Actual Hours Worked
Rate variance	=	($16.40 per hour − $16.00 per hour)	×	3,950 hours
Rate variance	=	$.40 per hour	×	3,950 hours
Rate variance	=	$1,580 unfavorable		

Reporting Direct Labor Cost Variance. The control of direct labor cost is often in the hands of production supervisors. To aid them, periodic reports analyzing the cause of any direct labor variance may be prepared. A comparison of standard direct labor hours and actual direct labor hours will provide the basis for an investigation into the efficiency of direct labor (time variance).

A comparison of the rates paid for direct labor with the standard rates highlights the efficiency of the supervisors or the personnel department in scheduling and selecting the proper level of direct labor for production (rate variance).

Factory Overhead Cost Variance

Some of the difficulties encountered in allocating factory overhead costs among products manufactured have been considered in Chapters 16 and 18. These difficulties stem from the great variety of costs that are included in factory overhead and their nature as indirect costs. For the same reasons, the procedures used in determining standards and variances for factory overhead cost are more complex than those used for direct materials cost and direct labor cost.

A flexible budget may be used to establish the standard factory overhead rate and to aid in determining subsequent variations from standard. The standard rate is determined by dividing the standard factory overhead costs by the standard amount of productive activity, generally expressed in terms of a cost driver or an activity base, such as machine hours, direct labor hours, or direct labor cost. A flexible budget showing the standard factory overhead rate for a month is as follows:

Factory Overhead Cost Budget Indicating Standard Factory Overhead Rate

Mayer Company
Factory Overhead Cost Budget
For Month Ending June 30, 19--

Percent of productive capacity	80%	90%	100%	110%
Machine hours	4,000	4,500	5,000	5,500
Budgeted factory overhead:				
Variable costs:				
Indirect factory wages	$12,800	$14,400	$16,000	$17,600
Power and light	5,600	6,300	7,000	7,700
Indirect materials	3,200	3,600	4,000	4,400
Maintenance	2,400	2,700	3,000	3,300
Total variable cost	$24,000	$27,000	$30,000	$33,000
Fixed costs:				
Supervisory salaries	$ 5,500	$ 5,500	$ 5,500	$ 5,500
Depreciation of plant and equipment	4,500	4,500	4,500	4,500
Insurance and property taxes	2,000	2,000	2,000	2,000
Total fixed cost	$12,000	$12,000	$12,000	$12,000
Total factory overhead cost	$36,000	$39,000	$42,000	$45,000

Factory overhead rate per machine hour ($42,000 ÷ 5,000) . . . $8.40

In this illustration, the standard factory overhead cost rate is determined on the basis of the projected factory overhead costs at 100% of productive capacity, where this level of capacity represents the general expectation of business activity under normal operating conditions. The standard rate is $8.40 per machine hour, that can be subdivided into $6 per hour for variable factory overhead ($30,000 ÷ 5,000 hours) and $2.40 per hour for fixed factory overhead ($12,000 ÷ 5,000 hours).

Variances from standard for factory overhead cost result (1) from operating at a level above or below 100% of capacity and (2) from incurring a total amount of factory overhead cost greater or less than the amount budgeted for the level of operations achieved. The first factor results in the **volume variance**, which is a measure of the penalty of operating at less than 100% of productive capacity or the benefit from operating at a level above 100% of productive capacity. The second factor results in the **controllable variance** which is the difference between the actual amount of factory overhead incurred and the amount of factory overhead budgeted for the level of production achieved during the period. To illustrate, assume that the actual cost and standard cost of factory overhead for Mayer Company's production of 10,000 units of Product X during June were as follows:

Actual:	Variable factory overhead	$24,600	
	Fixed factory overhead	12,000	$36,600
Standard:	4,000 hours (10,000 units × .4) at $8.40		33,600

The unfavorable factory overhead cost variance of $3,000 is made up of a volume variance and a controllable variance, determined as follows:

Factory Overhead Cost Variance

Volume variance:		
Productive capacity of 100%	5,000 hours	
Standard for amount produced	4,000 hours	
Productive capacity not used	1,000 hours	
Standard fixed factory overhead cost rate	× $2.40	
Variance—unfavorable		$2,400
Controllable variance:		
Actual factory overhead cost incurred	$36,600	
Budgeted factory overhead for standard product produced	36,000	
Variance—unfavorable		600
Total factory overhead cost variance—unfavorable		$3,000

Factory Overhead Volume Variance. The factory overhead volume variance is the difference between the productive capacity at 100% and the standard productive capacity, multiplied by the standard fixed factory overhead rate. If the standard capacity for the amount produced exceeds the productive capacity at 100%, the variance is favorable. If the productive capacity at 100% exceeds the standard capacity for the amount produced, the variance is unfavorable, as shown for Mayer Company in the following illustration:

Factory Overhead Volume Variance

Factory Overhead Volume Variance	=	Productive Capacity at 100% − Standard Capacity for Amount Produced	× Standard Fixed Factory Overhead Rate
Volume variance	=	(5,000 hours − 4,000 hours)	× $2.40 per hour
Volume variance	=	1,000 hours	× $2.40 per hour
Volume variance	=	$2,400 unfavorable	

In the illustration, the unfavorable volume variance of $2,400 can be viewed as the cost of the available but unused productive capacity (1,000 hours). It should also be noted that the variable portion of the factory overhead cost rate was ignored in determining the volume variance. Variable factory overhead costs vary with the level of production. Thus, a curtailment of production should be accompanied by a comparable reduction of such costs. On the other hand, fixed factory overhead costs are not affected by changes in the volume of production. The fixed factory overhead costs represent the costs of providing the capacity for production, and the volume variance measures the amount of the fixed factory overhead cost due to the variance between capacity used and 100% of capacity.

The idle time that resulted in a volume variance may be due to such factors as failure to maintain an even flow of work, machine breakdowns or repairs causing work stoppages, and failure to obtain enough sales orders to keep the factory operating at full capacity. Management should determine the causes of the idle time and should take corrective action. A volume variance caused by failure of supervisors to maintain an even flow of work, for example, can be remedied. Volume variances caused by lack of sales orders may be corrected through increased advertising or other sales effort, or it may be advisable to develop other means of using the excess plant capacity.

Factory Overhead Controllable Variance. The factory overhead controllable variance is the difference between the actual factory overhead and the budgeted factory overhead for the standard amount produced. If the budgeted factory overhead for the standard amount produced exceeds the actual factory overhead, the variance is favorable. If the actual factory overhead exceeds the budgeted factory overhead for the standard amount produced, the variance is unfavorable. For Mayer Company, the standard hours for the amount produced during June was 4,000 (80% of productive capacity). Therefore, the factory overhead budgeted at this level of production, according to the budget on page 1091 was $36,000. When this budgeted factory overhead is compared with the actual factory overhead, as shown in the following illustration for Mayer Company, an unfavorable variance results.

Factory Overhead Controllable Variance

Factory Overhead Controllable Variance	=	Actual Factory Overhead	–	Budgeted Factory Overhead for Standard Amount Produced
Controllable variance	=	$36,600	–	$36,000
Controllable variance	=	$600 unfavorable		

The amount and the direction of the controllable variance show the degree of efficiency in keeping the factory overhead cost within the limits established by the budget. Most of the controllable variance is related to the cost of the variable factory overhead items because generally there is little or no variation in the costs incurred for the fixed factory overhead items. Therefore, responsibility for the control of this variance generally rests with department supervisors.

Reporting Factory Overhead Cost Variance. The best means of presenting standard factory overhead cost variance data is through a factory overhead cost variance report. Such a report, illustrated on page 1094, can present both the controllable variance and the volume variance in a format that pinpoints the causes of the variances and aids in placing the responsibility for control.

The variance in many of the individual cost items in factory overhead can be subdivided into quantity and price variances, as were the variances in direct materials and direct labor. For example, the indirect factory wages variance may include both time and rate variances, and the indirect materials variance may be made up of both a quantity variance and a price variance.

Factory Overhead Cost Variance Report

Mayer Company
Factory Overhead Cost Variance Report
For Month Ended June 30, 19--

			Variances	
Productive capacity for the month				5,000 hours
Actual production for the month				4,000 hours
	Budget	Actual	Favorable	Unfavorable
Variable costs:				
Indirect factory wages	$12,800	$13,020		$ 220
Power and light	5,600	5,550	$50	
Indirect materials	3,200	3,630		430
Maintenance	2,400	2,400		
Total variable cost	$24,000	$24,600		
Fixed costs:				
Supervisory salaries	$ 5,500	$ 5,500		
Depreciation of plant and equipment	4,500	4,500		
Insurance and property taxes	2,000	2,000		
Total fixed cost	$12,000	$12,000		
Total factory overhead cost	$36,000	$36,600		
Total controllable variances			$50	$ 650
Net controllable variance—unfavorable				$ 600
Volume variance—unfavorable:				
Idle hours at the standard rate for fixed factory overhead—1,000 × $2.40				2,400
Total factory overhead cost variance—unfavorable				$3,000

STANDARDS IN THE ACCOUNTS

OBJECTIVE 3
Describe and illustrate how standards may be included in the accounts of a manufacturing enterprise.

Although standard costs can be used solely as a statistical device apart from the ledger, it is generally considered preferable to incorporate them in the accounts. One approach, when this plan is used, is to identify the variances in the accounts at the time the manufacturing costs are recorded in the accounts. To illustrate, assume that Marin Corporation purchased, on account, 10,000 pounds of direct materials at $1 per pound, when the standard price was $.95 per pound. The entry to record the purchase and the unfavorable direct materials price variance is as follows:

Materials	9,500	
Direct Materials Price Variance	500	
Accounts Payable		10,000

The materials account is debited for the 10,000 pounds at the standard price of $.95 per pound. The unfavorable direct materials price variance is $500 [($1.00 actual price per pound − $.95 standard price per pound) × 10,000 pounds purchased] and is recorded by a debit to Direct Materials Price Variance. Accounts Payable is credited for the actual amount owed, $10,000 (10,000 pounds at $1 per pound). If the variance had been favorable, Direct Materials Price Variance would have been credited for the amount of the variance.

The accounts affected by the purchase of direct materials would appear as follows:

ACCOUNT MATERIALS — ACCOUNT NO.

Date	Item	Debit	Credit	Balance Debit	Balance Credit
	Purchased	9,500		9,500	

ACCOUNT DIRECT MATERIALS PRICE VARIANCE — ACCOUNT NO.

Date	Item	Debit	Credit	Balance Debit	Balance Credit
	Purchased	500		500	

ACCOUNT ACCOUNTS PAYABLE — ACCOUNT NO.

Date	Item	Debit	Credit	Balance Debit	Balance Credit
	Actual cost		10,000		10,000

Variances in other manufacturing costs are recorded in a manner similar to the direct materials price variance. For example, if Marin Corporation used 4,900 pounds of direct materials to produce a product with a standard of 5,000 pounds, the entry to record the variance and the materials used would be as follows:

Work in Process	4,750	
Materials		4,655
Direct Materials Quantity Variance		95

The accounts affected by the use of direct materials would appear as follows:

ACCOUNT MATERIALS — ACCOUNT NO.

Date	Item	Debit	Credit	Balance Debit	Balance Credit
	Purchased	9,500		9,500	
	Used		4,655	4,845	

ACCOUNT DIRECT MATERIALS QUANTITY VARIANCE — ACCOUNT NO.

Date	Item	Debit	Credit	Balance Debit	Balance Credit
	Used		95		95

ACCOUNT WORK IN PROCESS — ACCOUNT NO.

Date	Item	Debit	Credit	Balance Debit	Balance Credit
	Direct materials (actual)	4,750		4,750	

The work in process account is debited for the standard price of the standard amount of direct materials required, \$4,750 (5,000 pounds × \$.95). Materials is credited for the actual amount of materials used at the standard price,

$4,655 (4,900 pounds × $.95). The favorable direct materials quantity variance of $95 [(5,000 standard pounds − 4,900 actual pounds) × $.95 standard price per pound] is credited to Direct Materials Quantity Variance. If the variance had been unfavorable, Direct Materials Quantity Variance would have been debited for the amount of the variance.

For Marin Corporation, the entries for direct labor, factory overhead, and other variances are recorded in a manner similar to the entries for direct materials. The work in process account is debited for the standard costs of direct labor and factory overhead as well as direct materials. Likewise, the work in process account is credited for the standard cost of the product completed and transfered to the finished goods account.

In a given period, it is possible to have both favorable and unfavorable variances. For example, if a favorable variance has been recorded, such as the direct materials quantity variance for Marin Corporation, and unfavorable direct materials quantity variances occur later in the period, the unfavorable variances would be recorded as debits in the direct materials quantity variance account. Analyses of this account may provide management with insights for controlling direct materials usage.

Another means of incorporating standards in the accounts is to debit the work in process account for the actual cost of direct materials, direct labor, and factory overhead entering into production. The same account is credited for the standard cost of the product completed and transferred to the finished goods account. The balance remaining in the work in process account is then made up of the ending inventory of work in process and the variances of actual cost from standard cost. In the following illustrative accounts for Mayer Company, there is assumed to be no ending inventory of work in process:

Standard Costs in Accounts

ACCOUNT WORK IN PROCESS — ACCOUNT NO.

Date		Item	Debit	Credit	Balance Debit	Balance Credit
June	30	Direct materials (actual)	21,424		21,424	
	30	Direct labor (actual)	64,780		86,204	
	30	Factory overhead (actual)	36,600		122,804	
	30	Units finished (standard)		117,600		
	30	Balance (variances)			5,204	

ACCOUNT FINISHED GOODS — ACCOUNT NO.

Date		Item	Debit	Credit	Balance Debit	Balance Credit
June	1	Inventory (standard)			88,800	
	30	Units finished (standard)	117,600		206,400	
	30	Units sold (standard)		113,500	92,900	

The balance in the work in process account is the sum of the variances between the standard and actual costs. In the illustration, the debit balance of $5,204 indicates a net unfavorable variance. If the balance had been a credit, it would have indicated a net favorable variance.

Variances from standard costs are usually not reported to stockholders and others outside of management. If standards are recorded in the accounts, however, it is customary to disclose the variances on income statements prepared for management. An interim monthly income statement prepared for Mayer Company's internal use is illustrated as follows:

Variances from Standards in Income Statement

Mayer Company Income Statement For Month Ended June 30, 19--			
Sales			$190,000
Cost of goods sold—at standard			111,720
Gross profit—at standard			$ 78,280
	Favorable	Unfavorable	
Less variances from standard cost:			
Direct materials quantity		$ 600	
Direct materials price		824	
Direct labor time	$800		
Direct labor rate		1,580	
Factory overhead volume		2,400	
Factory overhead controllable		600	5,204
Gross profit			$ 73,076
Operating expenses:			
Selling expenses		$22,500	
Administrative expenses		19,225	41,725
Income before income tax			$ 31,351

At the end of the fiscal year, the variances from standard are usually transferred to the cost of goods sold account. However, if the variances are significant or if many of the products manufactured are still on hand, the variances should be allocated to the work in process, finished goods, and cost of goods sold accounts. The result of such an allocation is to convert these account balances from standard cost to actual cost.

REVISION OF STANDARDS

OBJECTIVE 4
Describe the importance of periodic review and revision of standards.

Standard costs should be continuously reviewed, and when they no longer represent the conditions that were present when the standards were set, they should be changed. Standards should not be revised merely because they differ from actual costs, but because they no longer reflect the conditions that they were intended to measure. For example, the direct labor cost standard would not be revised simply because workers were unable to meet properly determined standards. On the other hand, standards should be revised when prices, product designs, labor rates, manufacturing methods, or other circumstances change to such an extent that the current standards no longer represent a useful measure of performance.

STANDARDS FOR NONMANUFACTURING EXPENSES

OBJECTIVE 5
Describe the use of standards for nonmanufacturing expenses.

The use of standards for nonmanufacturing expenses is not as common as the use of standards for manufacturing costs. This difference in the use of standards is due in part to the fact that nonmanufacturing expenses are, in many cases, not nearly as large as the manufacturing costs. Another major reason is that while many manufacturing operations are repetitive and thus subject to the determination of a per unit cost of output, many nonmanufacturing expenses do not lend themselves to such measurement. In many cases, for example, the costs associated with an assembly line can be measured and related to a uniform product unit. On the other hand, the expenses associated with the work of the office manager are not easily related to any unit of output.

When nonmanufacturing activities are repetitive and generate a somewhat homogeneous product, the concept of standards can be applied. In these cases, the process of estimating and using standards can be similar to that described for a manufactured product. For example, standards can be applied to the work of office personnel who process sales orders, and a standard unit expense for processing a sales order could be determined. The variance between the actual cost of processing a sales order with the standard expense can then be evaluated by management and corrective action taken.

In practice, standards are not widely used for nonmanufacturing expenses. Instead, these expenses are generally controlled by the use of budgets and budget performance reports, as discussed in Chapter 25. However, the use of standards appears to be gaining in acceptance as more attention is being given to the nonmanufacturing expenses by the managerial accountant.

CHAPTER REVIEW

KEY POINTS

OBJECTIVE 1

The Nature and Objectives of Standards

Accounting systems that use standards for each element of manufacturing cost entering into the finished product are called standard cost systems. Such systems enable management to determine how much a product should cost (standard), how much it does cost (actual), and the causes of any difference (variance) between the two. Standard costs thus serve as a device for measuring efficiency.

The setting of standards is both an art and a science. Although the standard-setting process varies among enterprises, it often requires the joint efforts of accountants, engineers, personnel administrators, and other management personnel. Standards that represent levels of performance that can be achieved only under perfect operating conditions, such as no idle time, no machine breakdowns, and no materials spoilage, are called theoretical standards or ideal standards. Standards that represent levels of operation that can be attained with reasonable effort are called currently attainable standards or normal standards.

OBJECTIVE 2

Variances from Standards

One of the primary purposes of a standard cost system is to facilitate control over costs by comparing actual costs with standard costs and thus determining variances. The two major variances for direct materials cost are the (1) direct materials quantity variance and (2) direct materials price variance. The two major variances for direct labor costs are the (1) direct labor time variance and (2) direct labor rate variance. The two major variances for factory overhead costs are the (1) factory overhead volume variance and (2) factory overhead controllable variance.

OBJECTIVE 3

Standards in the Accounts

It is generally preferable to incorporate standards in the accounts. One approach is to identify the variances in the accounts at the time the manufacturing costs are recorded in the accounts. Under this approach, the work in process account is debited for the standard costs of direct materials, direct labor, and factory overhead. Likewise, the work in process account is credited for the standard cost of the product completed and transferred to the finished goods account.

Another approach to incorporating standards in the accounts is to debit the work in process account for the actual costs of direct materials, direct labor, and factory overhead entering into production. The same account is then credited for the standard costs of the product completed and transferred to the finished goods account. Thus, the variances of actual costs from standard costs are isolated along with the ending inventory in the work in process account. At the end of the fiscal year, the variances are usually transferred to the cost of goods sold account.

Variances from standard costs are usually not reported to stockholders and others outside management. If standards are recorded in the accounts, however, it is customary to disclose the variances on interim income statements prepared for management. At the end of the year, the variances from standard are usually transferred to the cost of goods sold account. However, if the variances are significant or if many of the products manufactured are still on hand, the variances should be allocated to the work in process, finished goods, and cost of goods sold accounts.

OBJECTIVE 4

Revision of Standards

Established standards should be continually reviewed. If the standards no longer represent present conditions, they should be revised.

OBJECTIVE 5

Standards for Nonmanufacturing Expenses

The use of standards for nonmanufacturing expenses is not as common as the use of standards for manufacturing costs. When nonmanufacturing activities are repetitive and generate a somewhat homogeneous product, the concept of standards can be applied. In these cases, the process of estimating and using standards is similar to that described for a manufactured product.

KEY TERMS

standard cost systems 1085
standard costs 1085
variances 1085
theoretical standards 1087
currently attainable standards 1087
direct materials quantity variance 1088
direct materials price variance 1088
direct labor time variance 1089
direct labor rate variance 1089
factory overhead volume variance 1092
factory overhead controllable variance 1092

SELF-EXAMINATION QUESTIONS

Answers at end of chapter.

1. The actual and standard direct materials costs for producing a specified quantity of product are as follows:

Actual:	51,000 pounds at $5.05	$257,550
Standard:	50,000 pounds at $5.00	250,000

The direct materials price variance is:

A. $2,500 unfavorable
B. $2,550 unfavorable
C. $7,550 unfavorable
D. none of the above

2. The actual and standard direct labor costs for producing a specified quantity of product are as follows:

Actual:	990 hours at $10.90	$10,791
Standard:	1,000 hours at $11.00	11,000

The direct labor cost time variance is:

A. $99 favorable
B. $99 unfavorable
C. $110 favorable
D. $110 unfavorable

3. The actual and standard factory overhead costs for producing a specified quantity of product are as follows:

Actual:	Variable factory overhead	$72,500	
	Fixed factory overhead	40,000	$112,500
Standard:	19,000 hours at $6		
	($4 variable and $2 fixed)		114,000

If 1,000 hours of productive capacity were unused, the factory overhead volume variance would be:

A. $1,500 favorable
B. $2,000 unfavorable
C. $4,000 unfavorable
D. none of the above

4. Based on the data in Question 3, the factory overhead controllable variance would be:

A. $3,500 favorable
B. $3,500 unfavorable
C. $1,500 favorable
D. none of the above

5. Variances from standard costs are reported on interim income statements as:

A. selling expenses
B. administrative expenses
C. other expenses
D. none of the above

ILLUSTRATIVE PROBLEM

Wolfram Inc. manufactures Product S for distribution nationally. The standard costs and actual costs for direct materials, direct labor, and factory overhead incurred for the manufacture of 1,000 units of Product S were as follows:

	Standard Costs	Actual Costs
Direct materials...........	1,000 pounds at $75	980 pounds at $75.50
Direct labor	12,500 hours at $9	12,600 hours at $8.95
Factory overhead	Rates per machine hour, based on 100% of capacity of 15,000 machine hours:	
	Variable cost, $3.50	$44,150 variable cost
	Fixed cost, $1.00	$15,000 fixed cost

Instructions:

1. Determine the quantity variance, price variance, and total direct materials cost variance for Product S.
2. Determine the time variance, rate variance, and total direct labor cost variance for Product S.
3. Determine the volume variance, controllable variance, and total factory overhead cost variance for Product S.

SOLUTION

(1) Direct Materials Cost Variance

Quantity variance:		
Actual quantity	980 pounds	
Standard quantity	1,000 pounds	
Variance—favorable ..	20 pounds × standard price, $75.....	$1,500
Price variance:		
Actual price	$75.50 per pound	
Standard price	75.00 per pound	
Variance—unfavorable	$ .50 per pound × actual quantity, 980 ..	490
Total direct materials cost variance—favorable		$1,010

(2) Direct Labor Cost Variance

Time variance:		
Actual time	12,600 hours	
Standard time	12,500 hours	
Variance—unfavorable	100 hours × standard rate, $9	$ 900
Rate variance:		
Actual rate.............	$8.95	
Standard rate	9.00	
Variance—favorable ..	–$ .05 per hour × actual time, 12,600	$ 630
Total direct labor cost variance—unfavorable		$ 270

(3) Factory Overhead Cost Variance

Volume variance:		
Productive capacity of 100%	15,000 hours	
Standard for amount produced	12,500 hours	
Productive capacity not used	2,500 hours	
Standard fixed factory overhead cost rate	× $1	
Variance—unfavorable		$2,500
Controllable variance:		
Actual factory overhead cost incurred	$59,150	
Budgeted factory overhead for 12,500 hours	58,750	
Variance—unfavorable		400
Total factory overhead cost variance—unfavorable		$2,900

DISCUSSION QUESTIONS

26–1. What are the basic objectives in the use of standard costs?

26–2. (a) Describe theoretical (ideal) standards and discuss the possible impact of theoretical standards on worker performance. (b) Describe currently attainable (normal) standards and discuss the possible impact of currently attainable standards on worker performance.

26–3. How can standards be used by management to achieve control over costs?

26–4. As the term is used in reference to standard costs, what is a *variance*?

26–5. What is meant by reporting by the "principle of exceptions" as the term is used in reference to cost control?

26–6. (a) What are the two variances between actual cost and standard cost for direct materials? (b) Discuss some possible causes of these variances.

26–7. The materials cost variance report for Nickols Inc. indicates a large favorable materials price variance and a significant unfavorable materials quantity variance. What might have caused these offsetting variances?

26–8. (a) What are the two variances between actual cost and standard cost for direct labor? (b) Who generally has control over the direct labor cost?

26–9. A new assistant controller recently was heard to remark: "All the assembly workers in this plant are covered by union contracts, so there should be no labor variances." Was the controller's remark correct? Discuss.

26–10. (a) Describe the two variances between actual costs and standard costs for factory overhead. (b) What is a factory overhead cost variance report?

26–11. If variances are recorded in the accounts at the time the manufacturing costs are incurred, what does a debit balance in Direct Materials Price Variance represent?

26–12. If variances are recorded in the accounts at the time the manufacturing costs are incurred, what does a credit balance in Direct Materials Quantity Variance represent?

26–13. If standards are recorded in the accounts and Work in Process is debited for the actual manufacturing costs and credited for the standard cost of products produced, what does the balance in Work in Process represent?

26–14. Are variances from standard costs usually reported in financial statements issued to stockholders and others outside the firm?

26–15. Assuming that the variances from standards are not significant at the end of the period, to what account are they transferred?

26–16. How often should standards be revised?

26–17. Are standards for nonmanufacturing expenses as widely used as standards for manufacturing costs?

Real World Focus

26–18 Concrete Pipe & Products Co. Inc. manufacturers concrete pipe in its operations in Richmond, Virginia. The primary materials used in producing concrete are cement, sand, and gravel. The costs for a batch of concrete weighing 13,250 pounds are as follows:

	Pounds per batch	Price per pound
Cement	2,350	$.03000
Sand	6,700	.00205
Gravel	4,200	.00270
	13,250	

Assuming 5% waste, compute the standard cost per pound for concrete. Use the following tabular headings for organizing the computations:

	Pounds per batch	Price per pound	Batch cost	5% waste	Total batch cost	Cost per pound
Cement	2,350	$.03000				
Sand	6,700	.00205				
Gravel	4,200	.00270				
	13,250					

Ethics Discussion Case

26–19. Ann Santos, chief cost accountant for W. L. Weeks Company, has been assigned the task of reviewing the current standard costs. After studying the results of time and motion studies conducted by an independent engineering firm, she proposed changing the current standards. She explained that manufacturing methods recently had been changed and the current standards no longer represented a useful measure of performance. Frank Wilson, production supervisor, objected to the new standards because his workers would be held to a higher standard than the current standards.

Discuss whether Ann Santos behaved in an ethical manner by proposing the new standards.

EXERCISES

Ex. 26–20. Direct materials variances. OBJ. 2

The following data related to the direct materials cost for the production of 50,000 units of product:

Actual:	87,500 pounds at $3.40	$297,500
Standard:	90,000 pounds at $3.20	288,000

Determine the quantity variance, price variance, and total direct materials cost variance.

Ex. 26–21. Standard direct materials cost per unit from variance data. OBJ. 2

The following data relating to direct materials cost for August of the current year are taken from the records of Hammar Company:

Quantity of direct materials used	17,760 pounds
Unit cost of direct materials	$3.50 per pound
Units of finished product manufactured	15,000 units
Standard direct materials per unit of finished product	1.2 pounds
Direct materials quantity variance—favorable	$720
Direct materials price variance—unfavorable	$8,880

Determine the standard direct materials cost per unit of finished product, assuming that there was no inventory of work in process at either the beginning or the end of the month. Present your computations.

Ex. 26–22. Direct labor variances. OBJ. 2

The following data relate to direct labor cost for the production of 25,000 units of product:

Actual:	61,200 hours at $13.25	$810,900
Standard:	60,000 hours at $13.50	810,000

Determine the time variance, rate variance, and total direct labor cost variance.

Ex. 26–23. Factory overhead cost variances. OBJ. 2

The following data relate to factory overhead cost for the production of 75,000 units of product:

Actual:	Variable factory overhead	$127,500
	Fixed factory overhead	98,000
Standard:	30,000 hours at $7	210,000

If productive capacity of 100% was 35,000 hours and the factory overhead costs budgeted at the level of 30,000 standards hours was $224,000, determine the volume variance, controllable variance, and total factory overhead cost variance. The fixed factory overhead rate was $2.80 per hour.

Ex. 26–24. Flexible budget. OBJ. 2

Stevens Company prepared the following factory overhead cost budget for Department G for April of the current year, when the company expected to operate at 4,500 machine hours:

Variable cost:		
Indirect factory wages	$21,600	
Power and light	12,600	
Indirect materials	7,380	
Total variable cost		$41,580
Fixed cost:		
Supervisory salaries	$15,000	
Depreciation of plant and equipment	10,700	
Insurance and property taxes	4,000	
Total fixed cost		29,700
Total factory overhead cost		$71,280

Stevens Company has decided to install a standard cost system and has determined that productive capacity is 5,000 machine hours. Prepare a flexible budget indicating production levels of 4,000, 4,500, and 5,000 machine hours and showing the standard factory overhead rate.

Ex. 26–25.
Entries for recording standards in accounts.
OBJ. 3

Appes Manufacturing Company incorporates standards in the accounts and identifies variances at the time the manufacturing costs are incurred. Prepare entries to record the following transactions:

(a) Purchased 500 units of direct material A at $25.20 per unit. The standard price is $25 per unit.
(b) Used 190 units of direct material A in the process of manufacturing 50 units of finished product. Four units of material A are required, at standard, to produce a finished unit.

Ex. 26–26.
Income statement indicating standard cost variances.
OBJ. 3

The following data were taken from the records of Comer Company for January of the current year:

Administrative expenses	$ 62,500
Cost of goods sold (at standard)	975,000
Direct materials quantity variance—favorable	6,400
Direct materials price variance—favorable	3,300
Direct labor time variance—unfavorable	8,175
Direct labor rate variance—unfavorable	2,250
Factory overhead volume variance—unfavorable	25,000
Factory overhead controllable variance—favorable	4,000
Sales	1,250,000
Selling expenses	105,000

Prepare an income statement for presentation to management.

PROBLEMS

Pb. 26–27.
Direct materials, direct labor, and factory overhead cost variance analysis.
OBJ. 2

Standard costs and actual costs for direct materials, direct labor, and factory overhead incurred for the manufacture of 8,000 units of product were as follows:

	Standard Costs	Actual Costs
Direct materials	14,400 pounds at $7.50	14,600 pounds at $7.95
Direct labor	5,600 hours at $15	5,250 hours at $15.80
Factory overhead	Rates per machine hour, based on 100% of capacity of 20,000 machine hours:	
	Variable cost, $3.70	$60,100 variable cost
	Fixed cost, $2.50	$50,000 fixed cost

Two machine hours are required per unit.

Instructions:

Determine (a) the quantity variance, price variance, and total direct materials cost variance; (b) the time variance, rate variance, and total direct labor cost variance; and (c) the volume variance, controllable variance, and total factory overhead cost variance.

Pb. 26–28.
Standard factory overhead variance report.
OBJ. 2

Martino Inc. prepared the following factory overhead cost budget for Department A for May of the current year. The company expected to operate the department at 100% of capacity of 600 hours.

Variable costs:		
Indirect factory wages	$24,000	
Power and light	6,000	
Indirect materials	4,500	
Total variable cost		$34,500
Fixed costs:		
Supervisory salaries	$18,000	
Depreciation of plant and equipment	8,500	
Insurance and property taxes	3,500	
Total fixed cost		30,000
Total factory overhead cost		$64,500

During May, the department operated at 540 hours, and the factory overhead costs incurred were: indirect factory wages, $22,100; power and light, $4,990, indirect materials, $4,610; supervisory salaries, $18,000; depreciation of plant and equipment, $8,500; and insurance and property taxes, $3,500.

Instructions:

Prepare a standard factory overhead variance report for May. To be useful for cost control, the budgeted amounts should be based on 540 hours.

Pb. 26–29.
Flexible factory overhead cost budget and variance report.
OBJ. 2

Webster Inc. prepared the following factory overhead cost budget for the Polishing Department for July of the current year:

Webster Inc.
Factory Overhead Cost Budget—Polishing Department
For Month Ending July 31, 19--

Machine hours:		
Productive capacity of 100%		10,000
Hours budgeted		11,500
Variable cost:		
Indirect factory wages	$7,475	
Indirect materials	3,680	
Power and light	2,875	
Total variable cost		$14,030
Fixed cost:		
Supervisory salaries	$5,500	
Indirect factory wages	3,100	
Depreciation of plant and equipment	2,090	
Insurance	1,260	
Power and light	1,120	
Property taxes	730	
Total fixed cost		13,800
Total factory overhead cost		$27,830

During July, the Polishing Department was operated for 11,500 machine hours, and the following factory overhead costs were incurred:

Indirect factory wages	$10,700
Supervisory salaries	5,500
Power and light	4,100
Indirect materials	3,500
Depreciation of plant and equipment	2,090
Insurance	1,260
Property taxes	730
Total factory overhead cost incurred	$27,880

Instructions:

(1) Prepare a flexible budget for July, indicating capacities of 7,000, 8,500, 10,000, and 11,500 hours and the determination of a standard factory overhead rate per machine hour.
(2) Prepare a standard factory overhead cost variance report for July.

Pb. 26–30.
Entries and standard cost variance analysis.
OBJ. 3

Alexander Inc. maintains perpetual inventory accounts for materials, work in process, and finished goods and uses a standard cost system based on the following data:

	Standard Cost per Unit
Direct materials: 5 kilograms at $1.80 per kg	$ 9
Direct labor: 3/4 hour at $20 per hour	15
Factory overhead: $8.00 per direct labor hour	6
Total	$30

There was no inventory of work in process at the beginning or end of November, the first month of the current fiscal year. The transactions relating to production completed during November are summarized as follows:

(a) Materials purchased on account, $130,700.
(b) Direct materials used, $108,240. This represented 61,500 kilograms at $1.76 per kilogram.
(c) Direct labor paid, $182,310. This represented 8,850 hours at $20.60 per hour. There were no accruals at either the beginning or the end of the period.
(d) Factory overhead incurred during the month was composed of depreciation on plant and equipment, $24,500; indirect labor, $18,500; insurance, $12,000; and miscellaneous factory costs, $9,500. The indirect labor and miscellaneous factory costs were paid during the period, and the insurance represents an expiration of prepaid insurance. Of the total factory overhead of $64,500, fixed costs amounted to $30,000, and variable costs were $34,500.
(e) Goods finished during the period, 12,000 units.

Instructions:

(1) Prepare entries to record the transactions, assuming that the work in process account is debited for actual production costs and credited with standard costs for goods finished.
(2) Prepare a T account for Work in Process and post to the account, using the identifying letters as dates.
(3) Prepare schedules of variances for direct materials cost, direct labor cost, and factory overhead cost. Productive capacity for the plant is 10,000 direct labor hours.
(4) Total the amount of the standard cost variances and compare this total with the balance of the work in process account.

Pb. 26–31.
Income statement indicating standard cost variances.
OBJ. 3

The following data were taken from the records of Comer Company for January of the current year:

Administrative expenses	$ 40,000
Cost of goods sold (at standard)	775,000
Direct materials quantity variance—favorable	3,100
Direct materials price variance—favorable	1,500
Direct labor time variance—unfavorable	4,000
Direct labor rate variance—unfavorable	2,200
Factory overhead volume variance—unfavorable	15,000
Factory overhead controllable variance—favorable	4,000
Interest expense	1,900
Sales	950,000
Selling expenses	71,500

Prepare an income statement for presentation to management.

ALTERNATE PROBLEMS

Pb. 26–27A.
Direct materials, direct labor, and factory overhead cost variance analysis.
OBJ. 2

Standard costs and actual costs for direct materials, direct labor, and factory overhead incurred for the manufacture of 12,000 units of product were as follows:

	Standard Costs	Actual Costs
Direct materials	9,000 pounds at $23	9,250 pounds at $22.20
Direct labor	3,000 hours at $18	2,800 hours at $18.50
Factory overhead	Rates per machine hour, based on 100% of capacity of 50,000 machine hours:	
	Variable cost, $2.60	$130,000 variable cost
	Fixed cost, $1.80	$90,000 fixed cost

Four machine hours are required per unit.

Instructions:

Determine (a) the quantity variance, price variance, and total direct materials cost variance; (b) the time variance, rate variance, and total direct labor cost variance; and (c) the volume variance, controllable variance, and total factory overhead cost variance.

Pb. 26–28A.
Standard factory overhead variance report.
OBJ. 2

Conrad Company prepared the following factory overhead cost budget for Department C for June of the current year. The company expected to operate the department at 100% of capacity of 500 hours.

Variable costs:		
Indirect factory wages	$25,000	
Power and light	12,000	
Indirect materials	7,500	
Total variable cost		$44,500
Fixed costs:		
Supervisory salaries	$12,000	
Depreciation of plant and equipment	10,000	
Insurance and property taxes	3,500	
Total fixed cost		25,500
Total factory overhead cost		$70,000

During June, the department operated at 450 hours, and the factory overhead costs incurred were: indirect factory wages, $23,350; power and light, $10,000; indirect materials, $7,310; supervisory salaries $12,000; depreciation of plant and equipment, $10,000; and insurance ad property taxes, $3,500.

Instructions:

Prepare a standard factory overhead variance report for June. To be useful for cost control, the budgeted amounts should be based on 450 hours.

Pb. 26–29A.
Flexible factory overhead cost budget and variance report.
OBJ. 2

Zuber Company prepared the following factory overhead cost budget for the Painting Department for March of the current year:

Zuber Company
Factory Overhead Cost Budget—Painting Department
For Month Ending March 31, 19--

Machine hours:		
Productive capacity of 100%		70,000
Hours budgeted		56,000
Variable cost:		
Indirect factory wages	$84,000	
Indirect materials	33,600	
Power and light	16,800	
Total variable cost		$134,400
Fixed cost:		
Supervisory salaries	$63,000	
Indirect factory wages	43,400	
Depreciation of plant and equipment	26,250	
Insurance	21,700	
Power and light	14,350	
Property taxes	13,300	
Total fixed cost		182,000
Total factory overhead cost		$316,400

During March, the Painting Department was operated for 56,000 machine hours, and the following factory overhead costs were incurred:

Indirect factory wages	$133,000
Supervisory salaries	63,000
Indirect materials	32,900
Power and light	32,000
Depreciation of plant and equipment	26,250
Insurance	21,700
Property taxes	13,300
Total factory overhead cost incurred	$322,150

Instructions:

(1) Prepare a flexible budget for March, indicating capacities of 49,000, 56,000, 63,000, and 70,000 hours and the determination of a standard factory overhead rate per machine hour.
(2) Prepare a standard factory overhead cost variance report for March.

Pb. 26–30A.
Entries and standard cost variance analysis.
OBJ. 3

Johns Inc. maintains perpetual inventory accounts for materials, work in process, and finished goods and uses a standard cost system based on the following data:

	Standard Cost per Unit
Direct materials: 6 kilograms at $2.80 per kg	$16.80
Direct labor: 1 hour at $18 per hour	18.00
Factory overhead: $3.10 per machine hour	6.20
Total	$41.00

Each unit of product uses a standard of 2 machine hours. There was no inventory of work in process at the beginning or end of March, the first month of the current fiscal year. The transactions relating to production completed during March are summarized as follows:

(a) Materials purchased on account, $98,300.
(b) Direct materials used, $93,000. The amount represented 31 000 kilograms at $3.00 per kilogram.
(c) Direct labor paid, $88,690. This amount represented 4,900 hours at $18.10 per hour. There were no accruals at either the beginning or the end of the period.
(d) Factory overhead incurred during the month was composed of depreciation on plant and equipment, $14,300; indirect labor, $12,700; insurance, $4,960; and miscellaneous factory costs, $2,940. The indirect labor and miscellaneous factory costs were paid during the period, and the insurance represents an expiration of prepaid insurance. Of the total factory overhead of $34,900, fixed costs amounted to $18,000, and variable costs were $16,900.
(e) Goods finished during the period, 5,000 units.

Instructions:

(1) Prepare entries to record the transactions, assuming that the work in process account is debited for actual production costs and credited with standard costs for goods finished.
(2) Prepare a T account for Work in Process and post to the account, using the identifying letters as dates.
(3) Prepare schedules of variances for direct materials cost, direct labor cost, and factory overhead cost. Productive capacity for the plant is 15,000 machine hours.
(4) Total the amount of the standard cost variances and compare this total with the balance of the work in process account.

Pb. 26–31A.
Income statement indicating standard cost variances.
OBJ. 3

The following data were taken from the records of Perez Company for May of the current year:

Interest expense	$ 2,500
Cost of goods sold (at standard)	550,000
Direct materials quantity variance—favorable	1,750
Direct materials price variance—unfavorable	1,900
Direct labor time variance—unfavorable	3,270
Direct labor rate variance—favorable	960
Factory overhead volume variance—unfavorable	10,000
Factory overhead controllable variance—favorable	450
Administrative expenses	28,000
Sales	660,000
Selling expenses	37,500

Instructions:

Prepare an income statement for presentation to management.

MINI-CASE 26

Pall Company

Pall Company operates a plant in Decatur, Illinois, where you have been assigned as the new cost analyst. To familiarize yourself with your new responsibilities, you have gathered the following cost variance data for July. During July, 17,000 units of product were manufactured.

Factory Overhead Cost Variance Report

Productive capacity for the month (100%)	10,000 hours
Standard for amount produced during month	8,500 hours

	Budget	Actual	Variances Favorable	Variances Unfavorable
Variable costs:				
Indirect factory wages	$27,200	$27,700		$ 500
Power and light	17,850	18,200		350
Indirect materials	10,200	10,000	$200	
Maintenance	4,250	4,100	150	
Total variable cost	$59,500	$60,000		
Fixed costs:				
Supervisory salaries	$25,000	$25,000		
Depreciation of plant and equipment	10,000	10,000		
Insurance and property taxes	3,000	3,000		
Total fixed cost	$38,000	$38,000		
Total factory overhead cost	$97,500	$98,000		
Total controllable variances			$350	$ 850

Net controllable variance—unfavorable	$ 500
Volume variance—unfavorable:	
Idle hours at the standard rate for fixed factory overhead − 1,500 × $3.80	5,700
Total factory overhead cost variance—unfavorable	$6,200

Direct Materials Cost Variance

Quantity variance:			
Actual quantity	20,500 pounds		
Standard quantity	20,400 pounds		
Variance—unfavorable	100 pounds × standard price, $4.50		$ 450
Price variance:			
Actual price	$4.80 per pound		
Standard price	4.50 per pound		
Variance—unfavorable	$ .30 per pound × actual quantity, 20,500		6,150
Total direct materials cost variance—unfavorable			$6,600

Direct Labor Cost Variance

Time variance:		
Actual time	8,750 hours	
Standard time	8,500 hours	
Variance—unfavorable	250 hours × standard rate, $24	$6,000
Rate variance:		
Actual rate	$23.50 per hour	
Standard rate	24.00 per hour	
Variance—favorable . . . −$	.50 per hour × actual hours, 8,750	4,375
Total direct labor cost—unfavorable		$1,625

After your review of the July cost variance data, you arranged a meeting with the factory superintendent to discuss manufacturing operations. During this meeting, the factory superintendent made the following comment:

> *"Why do you have to compute a factory overhead volume variance? I don't have any control over the level of operations. I can only control costs for the level of production at which I am told to operate. Why not just eliminate the volume variance from the factory overhead cost variance report?"*

You next discussed the direct materials variance analyses with the purchasing department manager, who made the following comment:

> *"The materials price variance is computed incorrectly. The computations should be actual price minus standard price times the standard quantity of materials for the amount produced. By multiplying the difference in the actual and standard price by the actual quantity of materials used, my department is being penalized for the inefficiencies of the production department."*

During August the standard costs were not changed, productive capacity was 10,000 hours, and the following data were taken from the records for the production of 18,000 units of product:

Quantity of direct materials used	21,800 pounds
Cost of direct materials	$4.84 per pound
Quantity of direct labor used	9,300 hours
Cost of direct labor	$23.20 per hour
Factory overhead costs:	
Indirect factory wages	$30,000
Supervisory salaries	25,000
Power and light	19,400
Indirect materials	10,600
Depreciation of plant and equipment	10,000
Maintenance	4,350
Insurance and property taxes	3,000

Instructions:

(1) Prepare a factory overhead cost variance report for August.
(2) Determine (a) the quantity variance, price variance, and total direct materials cost variance, and (b) the time variance, rate variance, and total direct labor cost variance for August.
(3) Based upon the cost variances for July and August, what areas of operations would you investigate and why?
(4) How would you respond to the comments of the factory superintendent?
(5) How would you respond to the comments of the manager of the purchasing department?

ANSWERS TO SELF-EXAMINATION QUESTIONS

1. B The unfavorable direct materials price variance of $2,550 (answer B) is determined as follows:

Actual price	$5.05 per pound
Standard price	5.00 per pound
Price variance—unfavorable	$ .05 per pound

$.05 × 51,000 actual quantity = $2,550

2. C The favorable direct labor cost time variance of $110 (answer C) is determined as follows:

Actual time	990 hours
Standard time	1,000 hours
Time variance—favorable	− 10 hours
10 hours × $11 standard	$110

3. B The unfavorable factory overhead volume variance of $2,000 (answer B) is determined as follows:

Productive capacity not used	1,000 hours
Standard fixed factory overhead cost rate	× $2
Factory overhead volume variance—unfavorable	$2,000

4. A The favorable factory overhead controllable variance of $3,500 (answer A) is determined as follows:

Actual factory overhead cost incurred	$112,500
Budgeted factory overhead for standard product produced [(19,000 hours at $4 variable) + (20,000 hours at $2 fixed)]	116,000
Factory overhead controllable variance—favorable	$ 3,500

5. D Since variances from standard costs represent the differences between the standard cost of manufacturing a product and the actual costs incurred, the variances relate to the product. Therefore, they should be reported on interim income statements as an adjustment to gross profit—at standard.

CHAPTER 27

CHAPTER OBJECTIVES

1 Describe the nature of centralized and decentralized operations.

2 Describe the three types of responsibility centers.

3 Describe and illustrate responsibility accounting for cost centers.

4 Describe and illustrate responsibility accounting for profit centers.

5 Describe and illustrate responsibility accounting for investment centers.

6 Describe and illustrate the use of transfer prices among decentralized segments of a business enterprise.

27

ACCOUNTING FOR DECENTRALIZED OPERATIONS; TRANSFER PRICING

In a small business, virtually all plans and decisions can be made by one individual. As a business grows or its operations become more diverse, it becomes difficult, if not impossible, for one individual to perform these functions. For example, the responsibility for planning and controlling operations is clear in a one-person real estate agency. If the agency expands by opening an office in a distant city, some of the authority and responsibility for planning and decision making in a given area of operations might be delegated to others. In other words, if centralized operations become unwieldy as a business grows, the need to delegate responsibility for portions of operations arises. This delegation of responsibility and separation of the business into distinct organizational units for management purposes is termed **decentralization**. In a decentralized business, an important function of the managerial accountant is to assist individual managers in evaluating and controlling their areas of responsibility or responsibility centers.

A term frequently applied to the process of measuring and reporting operating data by responsibility centers is **responsibility accounting**. Some of the concepts useful in responsibility accounting were presented in preceding chapters. For example, in discussing budgetary control of operations, the use of the master budget, budgets for various departments, and budget performance reports in controlling operations by areas of responsibility were discussed. In this chapter, the concept of responsibility accounting as it relates to three types of responsibility centers is described and illustrated. In addition, the pricing of products or services that are transferred between decentralized segments of a company is discussed and illustrated.

CENTRALIZED AND DECENTRALIZED OPERATIONS

OBJECTIVE 1
Describe the nature of centralized and decentralized operations.

A completely centralized business organization is one in which all major planning and operating decisions are made by the top echelon of management. For example, a one-person, owner-manager-operated business is centralized because all plans and decisions are made by one person. In a small owner-manager-operated business, centralization may be desirable, since the owner-manager's close supervision ensures that the business will be operated in conformity with the manager's wishes and desires.

In a decentralized business organization, responsibility for planning and controlling operations is delegated among managers. These managers have the authority to make decisions without first seeking the approval of higher management. The level of decentralization varies significantly, and there is no one best level of decentralization for all businesses. In some companies, for example, plant managers have authority over all plant operations, including plant asset acquisitions and retirements. In other companies, a plant manager may only have authority for scheduling production and for controlling the costs of direct materials, direct labor, and factory overhead. The proper level of decentralization for a company depends on the advantages and disadvantages of decentralization as they apply to a company's specific, unique circumstances.

Advantages of Decentralization

As a business grows, it becomes more difficult for top management to maintain close daily contact with all operations. Hence, a top management that delegates authority in such circumstances has a better chance of sound decisions being made, and the managers closest to the operations may anticipate and react to operating information more quickly. In addition, as a company diversifies into a wide range of products and services, it becomes more difficult for top management to maintain operating expertise in all product lines and services. In such cases, decentralization allows managers to concentrate on acquiring expertise in their areas of responsibility. For example, in a company that maintains diversified operations in oil refining, banking, and the manufacture of office equipment, individual managers could become "expert" in the area of their responsibility.

The delegation of responsibility for day-to-day operations from top management to middle management frees top management to concentrate more on strategic planning. **Strategic planning** is the process of establishing long-term goals for an enterprise and developing plans to achieve these goals. For example, a goal to expand an enterprise's product line into new markets and to plan to finance this expansion through the issuance of long-term debt rather than additional common stock are examples of strategic planning decisions. As the business environment becomes more complex and as companies grow, strategic planning assumes an increasingly important role in the long-run success of a company.

Decentralized decision making provides excellent training for managers, which may be a factor in enabling a company to retain quality managers. Since the art of management can best be acquired through experience, the delegation of responsibility enables managers to acquire and develop managerial expertise early in their careers. Also, the operating personnel may be more creative in suggesting operating improvements, since personnel in a decentralized company tend to identify closely with the operations for which they are responsible.

The delegation of responsibility also serves as a positive reinforcement for managers, in that they may view such delegation as an indication of top management's confidence in their abilities. Thus, manager morale tends to increase because managers feel that they have more control over factors affecting their careers and their performance evaluation.

Disadvantages of Decentralization

The primary disadvantage of decentralized operations is that decisions made by one manager may affect other managers in such a way that the profitability of the entire company may suffer. For example, two managers competing in a common product market may engage in price cutting to win customers. As a result, the overall company profits may be less than the profits that could have been if the price cutting had not occurred.

Other potential disadvantages of decentralized operations may be the duplication of various assets and costs in the operating division. For example, each manager of a product line might have a separate sales force and administrative office staff, but centralization of these personnel could save money. Likewise, the costs of gathering and processing operating information in a decentralized operation might be greater than if such information were gathered and processed centrally.

THINKING SMALL

One company that experienced positive results from decentralizing was NCR (formerly National Cash Register Co.), a Dayton-based multinational electronics and computer manufacturing corporation. In 1979, NCR was a troubled company. Management began to examine NCR's problems and to reevaluate the company's structure, which appeared to be inhibiting NCR's ability to innovate and adapt. Additional background and the results of NCR's changes were reported in *Inc.* as follows:

As part of this reevaluation process, NCR commissioned the McKinsey & Co. consulting group to study the attributes of a number of highly successful companies. The researchers looked at such corporations as Sperry, IBM, and Hewlett-Packard, to determine what they had done that might be applied to NCR.

Using this study as background, NCR developed a plan for restructuring itself. Analyzing the path of a product from idea to implementation, it discovered some obvious impediments. The development, production, and marketing of a new product involved three separate divisions. This cumbersome system created opportunities for false starts and misinterpreting . . . the market. . . . It took a long time to get a product through this entire process, and sometimes products got lost in translation. . . .

So NCR proceeded to break up its product-management organization and move the parts to units that would develop, manufacture, and market products. In consulting jargon, this is called shifting from a "functional" to a "divisional" organization, and it has been done many times before in other industries. . . .

These changes transformed NCR Corp. from a highly centralized operation into a series of stand-alone [or decentralized] units. Today there is no requirement that one unit buy components from another NCR unit if it can find better or cheaper products outside the company. Moreover, based upon the nature of their products, the different divisions make their own decisions about how they want to structure themselves with regard to such activities as marketing.

Source: Eugene Linden, "Let a Thousand Flowers Bloom," *Inc.* (April, 1984), pp. 64-76.

TYPES OF RESPONSIBILITY CENTERS

OBJECTIVE 2
Describe the three types of responsibility centers.

Responsibility centers can be classified by the scope of responsibility assigned and the decision-making authority given to individual managers. The three common types of responsibility centers are referred to as cost centers, profit centers, and investment centers. Each of these types of responsibility centers is briefly described in the following paragraphs. Responsibility accounting for each type is then discussed and illustrated.

Cost Centers

In a **cost center** the department or division manager has responsibility for the control of costs incurred and the authority to make decisions that affect these costs. For example, the marketing manager has responsibility for the costs of the Marketing Department, and the supervisor of the Power Department has responsibility for the costs incurred in providing power. The department manager does not make decisions concerning sales of the cost center's output, nor does the department manager have control over the plant assets available to the cost center.

Cost centers are the most widely used type of responsibility center, because the organization and operation of most businesses allow for an easy identification of areas where managers can be assigned responsibility for and authority over costs. Cost centers may vary in size from a small department with a few employees to an entire manufacturing plant. In addition, cost centers may exist within other cost centers. For example, a manager of a manufacturing plant organized as a cost center may treat individual departments within the plant as separate cost centers, with the department managers reporting directly to the plant manager.

Profit Centers

In a **profit center** the manager has the responsibility and the authority to make decisions that affect both costs and revenues (and thus profits) for the department or division. For example, a retail department store might decentralize its operations by product line. The manager of each product line would have responsibility for the cost of merchandise and decisions regarding revenues, such as the determination of sales prices. The manager of a profit center does not make decisions concerning the plant assets available to the center. For example, the manager of the Sporting Goods Department does not make the decision to expand the available floor space for the department.

Profit centers are widely used in businesses in which individual departments or divisions sell products or services to those outside the company. A partial organization chart for a department store decentralized by retail departments as profit centers is as follows:

Partial Organization Chart for Department Store with Profit Centers

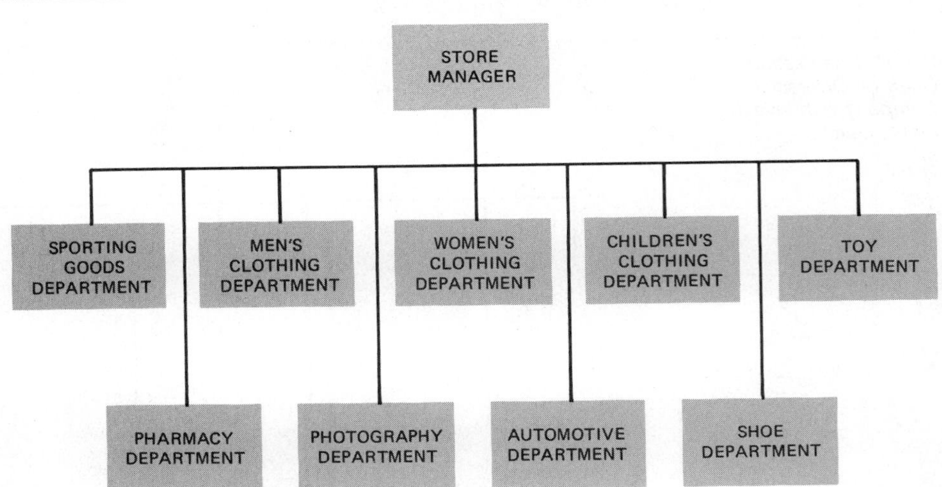

Occasionally, profit centers are established when the center's product or service is consumed entirely within the company. For example, a Repairs and Maintenance Department of a manufacturing plant could be treated as a profit center if its manager were allowed to bill other departments, such as the various production departments, for services rendered. Likewise, the Data Processing Department of a company might bill each of the company's administrative and operating units for computing services.

In a sense, a profit center may be viewed as a business within a business. While the primary concern of a cost center manager is the control of costs, the profit center is concerned with both revenues and costs.

Profit centers are often viewed as an excellent training assignment for new managers. For example, Lester B. Korn, Chairman and Chief Executive Officer of Korn/Ferry International, recently offered the following strategy for young executives en route to top management positions:

> *Get Profit-Center Responsibility—Obtain a position where you can prove yourself as both a specialist with particular expertise and a generalist who can exercise leadership, authority, and inspire enthusiasm among colleagues and subordinates.*

Investment Centers

In an **investment center,** the manager has the responsibility and the authority to make decisions that affect not only costs and revenues, but also the plant assets available to the center. For example, a plant manager sets selling prices of products and establishes controls over costs. In addition, the plant manager could, within general constraints established by top management, expand production facilities through equipment acquisitions and retirements.

The manager of an investment center has more authority and responsibility than the manager of either a cost center or a profit center. The manager of an investment center occupies a position similar to that of a chief operating officer or president of a separate company. As such, an investment center manager is evaluated in much the same way as a manager of a separate company is evaluated.

Investment centers are widely used in highly diversified companies. A partial organizational chart for a diversified company with divisions organized as investment centers is as follows:

Partial Organization Chart for Diversified Company with Investment Centers

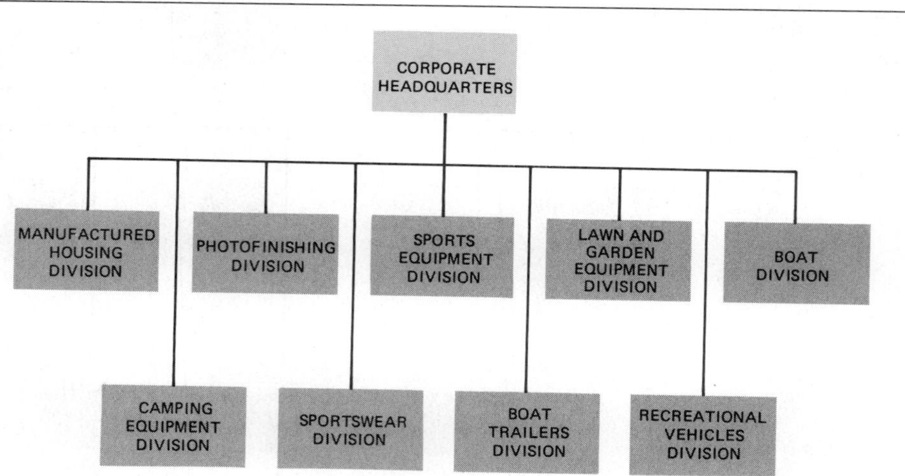

Since managers of cost centers have responsibility for and authority to make decisions regarding costs, responsibility accounting for cost centers focuses on costs. The primary accounting tools appropriate for controlling and reporting costs are budgets and standard costs, which were described and illustrated in Chapters 25 and 26. Responsibility accounting for a cost center which uses budgeting to assist in the control of costs will be illustrated in this chapter. The basic concepts of responsibility accounting, as illustrated, are equally applicable to cost centers that use standard cost systems to aid in cost control.

For purposes of illustration, assume that the responsibility for the manufacturing operations of an enterprise is as represented in the following organization chart:

Organization Chart Depicting Management Responsibility for Production

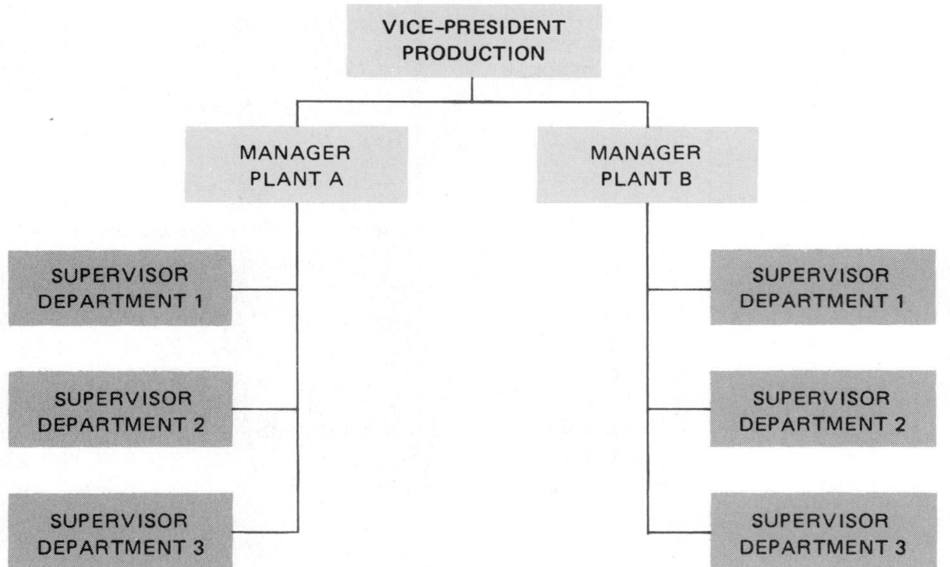

Within the organizational structure illustrated, there are three levels of cost centers. At the operating level, each department is a cost center, with the department supervisors responsible for controlling costs within their departments. At the next level of the organization, each plant is a cost center, with each plant manager responsible for controlling plant administrative costs as well as supervising the control of costs in the plant departments. Finally, at the top level, the office of the vice-president of production is a cost center with responsibility for controlling the administrative costs of the office as well as supervising the control of costs in each plant.

Managerial accounting reports aid each level of management in carrying out its assigned responsibilities for the control of costs. To illustrate, the budget performance reports shown on page 1120 are part of a responsibility accounting system for the enterprise.

The budget performance reports for the plant managers contain summarized data on the budgeted and actual costs for the departments under their jurisdiction. These reports enable them to identify the department supervisors responsible for significant variances. The report for the vice-president in

Budget Performance Report—
Vice-President, Operations
For Month Ended October 31, 19--

	Budget	Actual	Over	Under
Administration	$ 19,500	$ 19,700	$ 200	
Plant A	467,475	470,330	2,855	
Plant B	395,225	394,300		$925
	$882,200	$884,330	$3,055	$925

Budget Performance Report—Manager, Plant A
For Month Ended October 31, 19--

	Budget	Actual	Over	Under
Administration	$ 17,500	$ 17,350		$150
Department 1	109,725	111,280	$1,555	
Department 2	190,500	192,600	2,100	
Department 3	149,750	149,100		650
	$467,475	$470,330	$3,655	$800

Budget Performance Report—
Supervisor, Department 1-Plant A
For Month Ended October 31, 19--

	Budget	Actual	Over	Under
Factory wages	$ 58,100	$ 58,000		$100
Materials	32,500	34,225	$1,725	
Supervisory salaries	6,400	6,400		
Power and light	5,750	5,690		60
Depreciation of plant and equipment	4,000	4,000		
Maintenance	2,000	1,990		10
Insurance and property taxes	975	975		
	$109,725	$111,280	$1,725	$170

charge of operations summarizes the data by plant. The persons responsible for plant operations can thus be held accountable for significant variations from predetermined objectives.

The amount of detail presented in the budget performance report depends upon the level of management to which the report is directed. The reports prepared for the department supervisors present details of the budgeted and actual manufacturing costs for their departments. Each supervisor can then concentrate on the individual items that resulted in significant variations. In the illustration, the budget performance report for Department 1-Plant A indicates a significant variation between the budgeted and actual amounts for materials. A supplemental report, such as the following materials scrap report, would indicate the cause of a significant part of the variation and would aid the supervisor in taking corrective action. Other examples of supplemental reports are reports on factory wages and the cost of idle time.

Scrap Report

Materials Scrap Report—Department 1-Plant A
For Month Ended October 31, 19--

Material No.	*Units Spoiled*	*Unit Cost*	*Dollar Loss*	*Remarks*
A392	50	$3.10	$ 155.00	Machine malfunction
C417	76	.80	60.80	Inexperienced employee
G118	5	1.10	5.50	
J510	120	8.25	990.00	Substandard materials
K277	2	1.50	3.00	
P719	7	2.10	14.70	
V112	22	4.25	93.50	Machine malfunction
			$1,322.50	

RESPONSIBILITY ACCOUNTING FOR PROFIT CENTERS

OBJECTIVE 4
Describe and illustrate responsibility accounting for profit centers.

Since managers of profit centers have responsibility for and authority to make decisions regarding expenses and revenues, responsibility accounting reports for profit centers are normally in the form of income statements. These income statements usually include a breakdown of revenues and expenses by the department responsible for their incurrence, and identify contributions made by each department to overall company profit. Alternatively, some companies use traditional income statement formats that report gross profit or operating income by department.

Since profit centers are widely used by merchandising enterprises, such as department stores, a merchandising enterprise is used as the basis for the following discussion and illustration of responsibility accounting for profit centers. Although the degree to which profit centers are used by a merchandising enterprise varies, profit centers are typically established for each major retail department. The enterprise in the illustrations, Harris Company, has established Departments A and B as profit centers.

Departmental Margin

The departmental margin approach to responsibility accounting for profit centers emphasizes the contribution of each department to overall company net income. This contribution to overall company net income is termed **departmental margin**.

Prior to preparing an income statement and using the departmental margin approach, it is necessary to differentiate between operating expenses that are direct and those that are indirect. As discussed in Chapter 15, expenses or costs are classified as direct or indirect by identifying a cost object to which the expenses can (**direct**) or cannot (**indirect**) be traced. For purposes of profit center reporting, the cost objects are individual departments. Operating expenses directly traceable to or incurred for the sole benefit of a specific department (cost object) are usually subject to the control of the department manager. Indirect operating expenses are incurred for the benefit of the entire enterprise and are thus not subject to the control of individual department managers.

The details of departmental sales and the cost of goods sold are presented on the departmental income statement in the usual manner. The direct expenses of each department are then deducted from the related departmental gross profit, yielding balances that are identified as the departmental margin. The remaining expenses, including the indirect operating expenses, are not departmentalized. They are reported separately below the total departmental margin.

An income statement in the departmental margin format for Harris Company is presented below. The expenses identified as "direct" are sales salaries, property tax, uncollectible accounts, insurance, depreciation, and the newspaper advertising portion of advertising. The billboard portion of advertising, which is for the benefit of the business as a whole, as well as officers' and office salaries, and the remaining operating expenses, are identified as "indirect."

Income Statement Departmentalized through Departmental Margin

Harris Company
Income Statement
For Year Ended December 31, 19--

	Department A		Department B		Total	
Net sales		$614,700		$262,900		$877,600
Cost of goods sold		323,350		180,750		504,100
Gross profit		$291,350		$ 82,150		$373,500
Direct departmental expenses:						
Sales salaries expense	$54,000		$30,900		$84,900	
Advertising expense	9,100		4,900		14,000	
Property tax expense	3,740		3,060		6,800	
Uncollectible accounts expense	3,220		1,380		4,600	
Depreciation expense—store equipment	2,640		1,760		4,400	
Insurance expense	2,145		1,755		3,900	
Total direct departmental expenses		74,845		43,755		118,600
Departmental margin		$216,505		$ 38,395		$254,900
Indirect expenses:						
Officers' salaries expense					$52,000	
Office salaries expense					17,600	
Rent expense					15,400	
Heating and lighting expense					5,100	
Advertising expense					5,000	
Miscellaneous selling expense					4,700	
Miscellaneous administrative expense					4,800	
Total indirect expenses						104,600
Income from operations						$150,300
Other expense:						
Interest expense						2,500
Income before income tax						$147,800
Income tax						64,444
Net income						$ 83,356

With departmental margin income statements, the manager of each department can be held responsible for operating expenses traceable to the department. A reduction in the direct expenses of a department will have a favorable effect on that department's contribution to the net income of the enterprise.

The departmental margin income statement may also be useful to management in making plans for future operations. For example, this type of analysis can be used when the discontinuance of a certain operation or department is being considered. If a specific department yields a departmental margin, it generally should be retained, even though the allocation of the indirect operating expenses would result in a net loss for that department. This observation is based upon the assumption that the department in question represents a relatively small segment of the enterprise. Its termination, therefore, would not cause any significant reduction in the amount of indirect expenses.

Gross Profit by Departments

Some companies prefer to use traditional income statements for purposes of responsibility accounting for profit centers. These income statements report revenues and expenses by departments through either gross profit or operating income. An income statement showing gross profit by departments for Harris Company appears on pages 1124 and 1125. For illustrative purposes, the operating expenses are shown in condensed form. Usually they would be listed in detail.

For a merchandising enterprise, the gross profit is one of the most significant figures in the income statement. Since the sales and the cost of goods sold are both controlled by departmental management, the reporting of gross profit by departments is useful in cost analysis and control. In addition, such reports aid management in directing its efforts toward obtaining a mix of sales that will maximize profits. For example, after studying the reports, management may decide to change sales or purchases policies to achieve a higher gross profit for each department. Caution must be exercised in the use of such reports to insure that proposed changes affecting gross profit do not have an adverse effect on net income. A change that increases gross profit could result in an even greater increase in operating expenses and thereby decrease net income.

Operating Income by Departments

Departmental reporting may be extended to operating income. In such cases, each department must be assigned not only the related revenues and the cost of goods sold (as in the income statement on pages 1124 and 1125), but also that part of operating expenses incurred for its benefit. Some of these expenses may be easily identified with and traced to the department benefited. For example, if each salesperson is restricted to a certain sales department, the sales salaries may be assigned to the proper departmental salary accounts each time the payroll is prepared. On the other hand, the salaries of company officers, executives, and office personnel are not identifiable with specific sales departments and must therefore be allocated if an equitable and reasonable basis for allocation exists.

When operating expenses are allocated, they should be apportioned to the respective departments as nearly as possible in accordance with the cost of services rendered to them. Determining the amount of an expense chargeable

Income Statement Departmentalized through Gross Profit

Harris
Income
For Year Ended

	Department A		
Revenue from sales:			
Sales		$630,000	
Less sales returns and allowances		15,300	
Net sales			$614,700
Cost of goods sold:			
Inventories, January 1, 19--		$ 80,150	
Purchases	$334,550		
Less purchases discounts	6,200	328,350	
Goods available for sale		$408,500	
Less inventories, December 31, 19--		85,150	
Cost of goods sold			323,350
Gross profit			$291,350
Operating expenses:			
Selling expenses			
Administrative expenses			
Total operating expenses			
Income from operations			
Other expense:			
Interest expense			
Income before income tax			
Income tax			
Net income			

to each department is not always a simple matter. In the first place, it requires the exercise of judgment; and accountants of equal ability may well differ in their opinions as to the proper basis for the apportionment of operating expenses. Second, the cost of collecting data for use in making an apportionment must be kept within reasonable bounds. Consequently, information that is readily available and is substantially reliable may be used instead of more accurate information that would be more costly to collect.

To illustrate the operating income approach to responsibility accounting for profit centers, assume that Harris Company extends its departmental reporting through income from operations. The company's operating expenses for the year and the methods used in apportioning them are presented in the paragraphs that follow.

Sales Salaries Expense is apportioned to the two departments according to the distributions shown in the payroll records. Of the $84,900 total in the account, $54,000 is chargeable to Department A and $30,900 is chargeable to Department B.

Advertising Expense, covering billboard advertising and newspaper advertising, is apportioned according to the amount of advertising incurred for each department. The billboard advertising totaling $5,000 emphasizes the name and the location of the company. This expense is allocated on the basis

Company
Statement
December 31, 19--

Department B			Total		
	$270,000			$900,000	
	7,100			22,400	
		$262,900			$877,600
	$ 61,750			$141,900	
$200,350			$534,900		
2,400	197,950		8,600	526,300	
	$259,700			$668,200	
	78,950			164,100	
		180,750			504,100
		$ 82,150			$373,500
				$113,000	
				110,200	
					223,200
					$150,300
					2,500
					$147,800
					64,444
					$ 83,356

of gross sales, the assumption being that this basis represents a fair allocation of billboard advertising to each department. Analysis of the newspaper space costing $14,000 indicates that 65% of the space was devoted to Department A and 35% to Department B. The computations of the apportionment of the total advertising expense are as follows:

	Total		Department A		Department B	
Sales—dollars	$900,000		$630,000		$270,000	
Sales—percent	100%		70%		30%	
Bilboard advertising		$ 5,000		$ 3,500		$1,500
Newspaper space—percent	100%		65%		35%	
Newspaper advertising		14,000		9,100		4,900
Advertising expense		$19,000		$12,600		$6,400

Depreciation Expense—Store Equipment is apportioned according to the average cost of the equipment in each of the two departments. The computations for the apportionment of the depreciation expense are as follows:

	Total	Department A	Department B
Cost of store equipment:			
January 1	$28,300	$16,400	$11,900
December 31	31,700	19,600	12,100
Total	$60,000	$36,000	$24,000
Average	$30,000	$18,000	$12,000
Percent	100%	60%	40%
Depreciation expense	$ 4,400	$ 2,640	$ 1,760

Officers' Salaries Expense and **Office Salaries Expense** are apportioned on the basis of the relative amount of time devoted to each department by the officers and by the office personnel. Obviously, this can be only an approximation. The number of sales transactions may have some bearing on the matter, as may billing and collection procedures and other factors such as promotional campaigns that might vary from period to period. Of the total officers' salaries of $52,000 and office salaries of $17,600, it is estimated that 60%, or $31,200 and $10,560 respectively, is chargeable to Department A and that 40%, or $20,800 and $7,040 respectively, is chargeable to Department B.

Rent Expense and **Heating and Lighting Expense** are usually apportioned on the basis of floor space devoted to each department. In apportioning rent expense for a multistory building, differences in the value of the various floors and locations may be taken into account. For example, the space near the main entrance of a department store is more valuable than the same amount of floor space located far from the elevator on the sixth floor. For Harris Company, rent expense is apportioned on the basis of floor space used because there is no significant difference in the value of the floor areas used by each department. In allocating heating and lighting expense, it is assumed that the number of lights, their wattage, and the extent of use are uniform throughout the sales departments. If there are major variations and the total lighting expense is material, further analysis and separate apportionment may be advisable. The rent expense and the heating and lighting expense are apportioned as follows:

	Total	Department A	Department B
Floor space, square feet	160,000	104,000	56,000
Percent	100%	65%	35%
Rent expense	$15,400	$10,010	$5,390
Heating and lighting expense	$ 5,100	$ 3,315	$1,785

Property Tax Expense and **Insurance Expense** are related primarily to the cost of the inventories and the store equipment. Although the cost of these assets may differ from their assessed value for tax purposes and their value for insurance purposes, the cost is most readily available and is considered to be satisfactory as a basis for apportioning these expenses. The computations of the apportionment of the personal property tax expense and the insurance expense are as follows:

	Total	Department A	Department B
Inventories:			
January 1	$141,900	$ 80,150	$ 61,750
December 31	164,100	85,150	78,950
Total	$306,000	$165,300	$140,700
Average	$153,000	$ 82,650	$ 70,350
Average cost of store equipment (computed previously)	30,000	18,000	12,000
Total	$183,000	$100,650	$ 82,350
Percent	100%	55%	45%
Property tax expense	$ 6,800	$ 3,740	$ 3,060
Insurance expense	$ 3,900	$ 2,145	$ 1,755

Uncollectible Accounts Expense, Miscellaneous Selling Expense, and **Miscellaneous Administrative Expense** are apportioned on the basis of gross sales. Although the uncollectible accounts expense may be apportioned on the basis of an analysis of accounts receivable written off, it is assumed that the expense is closely related to gross sales. The miscellaneous selling and administrative expenses are apportioned on the basis of gross sales, which are assumed to be a reasonable measure of the benefit to each department. The computation of the apportionment is as follows:

	Total	Department A	Department B
Sales	$900,000	$630,000	$270,000
Percent	100%	70%	30%
Uncollectible accounts expense	$ 4,600	$ 3,220	$ 1,380
Miscellaneous selling expense	$ 4,700	$ 3,290	$ 1,410
Miscellaneous administrative expense	$ 4,800	$ 3,360	$ 1,440

An income statement presenting income from operations by departments for Harris Company appears on pages 1128 and 1129. The amounts for sales and the cost of goods sold are presented in condensed form. Details could be reported, if desired, in the manner illustrated on pages 1124 and 1125.

In a research study, 85% of the companies surveyed indicated that they allocate some operating expenses to profit centers (departments) using methods that were illustrated in the preceding paragraphs.[1] Caution should be used, however, in relying on income statements departmentalized through income from operations, since the allocation of many indirect operating expenses involves a high degree of judgment. In addition, the reporting of operating income by departments may be misleading, since the departments are not independent operating units. The departments are segments of a business

[1] James M. Fremgen and Shu S. Liao, *The Allocation of Corporate Indirect Costs* (New York: National Association of Accountants, 1981), pp. 33–34.

Income Statement Departmentalized through Income from Operations

Harris
Income
For Year Ended

	Department A		
Net sales	....	....	$614,700
Cost of goods sold	....	....	323,350
Gross profit	....	....	$291,350
Operating expenses:			
Selling expenses:			
Sales salaries expense	$ 54,000	....	....
Advertising expense	12,600	....	....
Depreciation expense—store equipment	2,640	....	....
Miscellaneous selling expense	3,290	....	....
Total selling expenses	....	$ 72,530	....
Administrative expenses:			
Officers' salaries expense	$ 31,200	....	....
Office salaries expense	10,560	....	....
Rent expense	10,010	....	....
Property tax expense	3,740	....	....
Heating and lighting expense	3,315	....	....
Uncollectible accounts expense	3,220	....	....
Insurance expense	2,145	....	....
Miscellaneous administrative expense	3,360	....	....
Total administrative expenses	....	67,550	....
Total operating expenses	....	....	140,080
Income (loss) from operations	....	....	$151,270
Other expense:			
Interest expense	....	....	....
Income before income tax	....	....	....
Income tax	....	....	....
Net income	....	....	....

enterprise, and no single department of a business can earn an income independently. For Harris Company, the departmental margin of $38,395 for Department B, as shown on page 1122, is more reliable for management's use in making decisions than is the $970 loss from operations in the income statement for Department B.

RESPONSIBILITY ACCOUNTING FOR INVESTMENT CENTERS

OBJECTIVE 5
Describe and illustrate responsibility accounting for investment centers.

Since investment center managers have responsibility for revenues and expenses, operating income is an essential part of investment center reporting. In addition, because the investment center manager also has responsibility for the assets invested in the center, two additional measures of performance are often used. These additional measures are the rate of return on investment and residual income. In practice, most companies use a variety of performance measures. For example, a survey of manufacturers found that 70% of the respondents used operating income as a percent of sales, 62% used rate of return on investment, and 13% used residual income as performance

Company
Statement
December 31, 19--

Department B			Total		
		$262,900			$877,600
		180,750			504,100
		$ 82,150			$373,500
$ 30,900			$ 84,900		
6,400			19,000		
1,760			4,400		
1,410			4,700		
	$ 40,470			$113,000	
$ 20,800			$ 52,000		
7,040			17,600		
5,390			15,400		
3,060			6,800		
1,785			5,100		
1,380			4,600		
1,755			3,900		
1,440			4,800		
	42,650			110,200	
		83,120			223,200
		$ (970)			$150,300
					2,500
					$147,800
					64,444
					$ 83,356

measures in setting enterprise goals.[2] The following paragraphs focus on these performance measures for investment centers. Each of these performance measures is described and illustrated for Waller Company, a diversified company with three operating divisions, A, B, and C.

Operating Income

Because investment centers are evaluated as if they were separate companies, traditional financial statements are normally prepared for each center. For purposes of assessing profitability, operating income is the focal point of analysis. Since the determination of operating income for responsibility centers was described and illustrated in the preceding paragraphs, only condensed divisional income statements will be used for illustrative purposes. The condensed divisional income statements for Waller Company are as follows:

[2] Robert A. Howell, James D. Brown, Stephen R. Soucy, and Allen H. Seed, *Management Accounting in the New Manufacturing Environment* (Montvale, New Jersey: National Association of Accountants, 1987).

Waller Company
Divisional Income Statements
For Year Ended December 31, 19--

	Division A	Division B	Division C
Sales	$560,000	$672,000	$750,000
Cost of goods sold	336,000	470,400	562,500
Gross profit	$224,000	$201,600	$187,500
Operating expenses	154,000	117,600	112,500
Operating income	$ 70,000	$ 84,000	$ 75,000

Based on the amount of divisional operating income, Division B is the most profitable of Waller Company's divisions, with income from operations of $84,000. Divisions A and C are less profitable, with Division C reporting $5,000 more operating income than Division A.

Although operating income is a useful measure of investment center profitability, it does not reflect the amount of investment in assets committed to each center. For example, if the amount of assets invested in Division B is twice that of the other divisions, then Division B is the least profitable of the divisions in terms of the rate of return on investment. Since investment center managers also control the amount of assets invested in their centers, they should be held accountable for the use of invested assets.

Rate of Return on Investment

One of the most widely used measures of divisional performance for investment centers is the **rate of return on investment (ROI)** or **rate of return on assets.** This rate is computed as follows:

$$\text{Rate of Return on Investment (ROI)} = \frac{\text{Operating Income}}{\text{Invested Assets}}$$

The rate of return on investment is useful because the three factors subject to control by divisional managers (revenues, expenses, and invested assets) are considered in its computation. By measuring profitability relative to the amount of assets invested in each division, the rate of return on investment can be used to compare divisions. The higher the rate of return on investment, the more effectively the division is utilizing its assets in generating income. To illustrate, the rate of return on investment for each division of Waller Company, based on the book value of invested assets, is as follows:

	Operating Income	Invested Assets	Rate of Return on Investment
Division A	$70,000	$350,000	20%
Division B	84,000	700,000	12
Division C	75,000	500,000	15

Although Division B generated the largest operating income, its rate of return on investment (12%) is the lowest. Hence, relative to the assets invested, Division B is the least profitable division. In comparison, the rates of return on investment of Divisions A and C are 20% and 15% respectively. These differences in the rates of return on investment may be analyzed by restating the expression for the rate of return on investment in expanded form, as follows:

$$\text{Rate of Return on Investment (ROI)} = \frac{\text{Operating Income}}{\text{Sales}} \times \frac{\text{Sales}}{\text{Invested Assets}}$$

In the expanded form, the rate of return on investment is the product of two factors: (1) the ratio of operating income to sales, often termed the **profit margin,** and (2) the ratio of sales to invested assets, often termed the **investment turnover.** As shown in the following computation, the use of this expanded expression yields the same rate of return for Division A, 20%, as the previous expression for the rate of return on investment:

$$\text{Rate of Return on Investment (ROI)} = \frac{\text{Operating Income}}{\text{Sales}} \times \frac{\text{Sales}}{\text{Invested Assets}}$$

$$\text{ROI} = \frac{\$70{,}000}{\$560{,}000} \times \frac{\$560{,}000}{\$350{,}000}$$

$$\text{ROI} = 12.5\% \times 1.6$$

$$\text{ROI} = 20\%$$

The expanded expression for the rate of return on investment is useful in management's evaluation and control of decentralized operations because the profit margin and the investment turnover focus on the underlying operating relationships of each division. The profit margin component focuses on profitability by indicating the rate of profit earned on each sales dollar. When efforts are aimed at increasing a division's profit margin by changing the division's sales mix, for example, the division's rate of return on investment may increase.

The investment turnover component focuses on efficiency in the use of assets and indicates the rate at which sales are being generated for each dollar of invested assets. The more sales per dollar invested, the greater the efficiency in the use of the assets. When efforts are aimed at increasing a division's investment turnover through special sales promotions, for example, the division's rate of return on investment may increase.

The rate of return on investment, using the expanded expression for each division of Waller Company, is summarized as follows:

$$\text{Rate of Return on Investment (ROI)} = \text{Profit Margin} \times \text{Investment Turnover}$$

$$\text{ROI} = \frac{\text{Operating Income}}{\text{Sales}} \times \frac{\text{Sales}}{\text{Invested Assets}}$$

Division A:

$$\text{ROI} = \frac{\$70{,}000}{\$560{,}000} \times \frac{\$560{,}000}{\$350{,}000}$$

$$\text{ROI} = 12.5\% \times 1.6$$

$$\text{ROI} = 20\%$$

Division B:

$$\text{ROI} = \frac{\$84{,}000}{\$672{,}000} \times \frac{\$672{,}000}{\$700{,}000}$$

$$\text{ROI} = 12.5\% \times .96$$

$$\text{ROI} = 12\%$$

$$\text{ROI} = \frac{\text{Operating Income}}{\text{Sales}} \times \frac{\text{Sales}}{\text{Invested Assets}}$$

$$\text{Division C:} \quad \text{ROI} = \frac{\$75{,}000}{\$750{,}000} \times \frac{\$750{,}000}{\$500{,}000}$$

$$\text{ROI} = 10\% \times 1.5$$

$$\text{ROI} = 15\%$$

Although Divisions A and B have the same profit margins, Division A's investment turnover is larger than that of Division B (1.6 to .96). Thus, by more efficiently utilizing its invested assets, Division A's rate of return on investment is higher than Division B's. Division C's profit margin of 10% and investment turnover of 1.5 are lower than the corresponding factors for Division A. The product of these factors results in a return on investment of 15% for Division C, as compared to 20% for Division A.

To determine possible ways of increasing the rate of return on investment, the profit margin and investment turnover for a division should be analyzed. For example, if Division A is in a highly competitive industry where the profit margin cannot be easily increased, the division manager should concentrate on increasing the investment turnover. To illustrate, assume that sales of Division A could be increased by $56,000 through changes in advertising expenditures. The cost of goods sold is expected to be 60% of sales, and operating expenses will increase to $169,400. If the advertising changes are undertaken, Division A's operating income would increase from $70,000 to $77,000, as shown in the following condensed income statement:

Sales ($560,000 + $56,000)	$616,000
Cost of goods sold ($616,000 × 60%)	369,600
Gross profit	$246,400
Operating expenses	169,400
Operating income	$ 77,000

The rate of return on investment for Division A, using the expanded expression, is recomputed as follows:

$$\text{Rate of Return on Investment (ROI)} = \frac{\text{Operating Income}}{\text{Sales}} \times \frac{\text{Sales}}{\text{Invested Assets}}$$

$$\text{ROI} = \frac{\$77{,}000}{\$616{,}000} \times \frac{\$616{,}000}{\$350{,}000}$$

$$\text{ROI} = 12.5\% \times 1.76$$

$$\text{ROI} = 22\%$$

Although Division A's profit margin remains the same (12.5%), the division's investment turnover has increased from 1.6 to 1.76, an increase of 10% (.16 ÷ 1.6). The 10% increase in investment turnover has the effect of also increasing the rate of return on investment by 10% (from 20% to 22%).

The major advantage of the use of the rate of return on investment instead of operating income as a divisional performance measure is that the amount of divisional investment is directly considered. Thus, divisional performances can be compared, even though the sizes of the divisions may vary significantly.

In addition to its use as a performance measure, the rate of return on investment can assist management in other ways. For example, in considering a decision to expand the operations of Waller Company, management should consider giving priority to Division A because it earns the highest rate of return on investment. If the current rates of return on investment can be maintained in the future, an investment in Division A will return 20 cents (20%) on each dollar invested, while investments in Divisions B and C will return only 12 cents and 15 cents respectively.

A major disadvantage of the rate of return on investment as a performance measure is that it may lead divisional managers to reject new investment proposals, even though the rate of return on these investments exceeds the minimum considered acceptable by the company. For example, a division might have an overall rate of return on investment of 25%, and the company might have an overall rate of return on investment of 15%. If the division accepts a new investment that would earn a 20% rate of return on investment, the overall rate of return for the division would decrease, but the overall rate of return for the company as a whole would increase. Thus, the division manager might reject the proposal, even though its acceptance would be in the best interests of the company.

Residual Income

In the previous illustration for Waller Company, two measures of evaluating divisional performance were discussed and illustrated. The advantages and disadvantages of both measures were also discussed. An additional measure, residual income, is useful in overcoming some of the disadvantages associated with the operating income and rate of return on investment measures.

Residual income is the excess of divisional operating income over a minimum amount of desired operating income. The minimum amount of desired divisional operating income is set by top management by establishing a minimum rate of return for the invested assets and then multiplying this rate by the amount of divisional assets. To illustrate, assume that the top management of Waller Company has established 10% as the minimum rate of return on divisional assets. The residual incomes for Divisions A, B, and C are computed as follows:

Residual Income by Division

	Division A	Division B	Division C
Divisional operating income	$70,000	$84,000	$75,000
Minimum amount of divisional operating income:			
$350,000 × 10%	35,000		
$700,000 × 10%		70,000	
$500,000 × 10%			50,000
Residual income	$35,000	$14,000	$25,000

The major advantage of residual income as a performance measure is that it gives consideration not only to a minimum rate of return on investment, but also to the total magnitude of the operating income earned by each division. For example, Division A has more residual income than the other divisions of Waller Company, even though it has the least operating income. Also, Division C earns $11,000 more residual income than Division B, even though Division B generates more operating income than Division C. The reason for this difference is that Division B has $200,000 more assets than Division C. Hence, Division B's operating income is reduced by $20,000 ($200,000 × 10%) more than Division C's operating income in determining residual income.

TRANSFER PRICING

OBJECTIVE 6
Describe and illustrate the use of transfer prices among decentralized segments of a business enterprise.

The use of responsibility accounting and reporting in measuring performance in decentralized companies can be important in motivating managers to achieve common profit goals. However, when decentralized units transfer products or render services to each other, the **transfer price**—the price to charge for the products or services—becomes an issue. Since transfer prices affect the revenues and expenses of both the receiving unit and the unit providing the product or service, transfer prices affect the performance measures used for evaluating divisional performance.

The objective of transfer pricing is to encourage each divisional manager to transfer goods and services between divisions if overall company income can be increased by doing so. As will be illustrated, however, transfer prices may be misused to the detriment of overall company income.

The following paragraphs describe and illustrate various approaches to establishing transfer prices, the effect of transfer prices on the evaluation of decentralized performance, and their potential impact on overall company income. Three commonly used approaches are (1) the market price approach, (2) the negotiated price approach, and (3) the cost price approach.[3]

Although transfer prices may apply when decentralized units are organized as cost or profit centers, a diversified company (Wilson Company) with two operating divisions (M and N) organized as investment centers will be used for the illustrations in the remainder of this chapter. Condensed income statements for Wilson Company's divisions, assuming there are no intracompany transfers, are as follows:

Wilson Company
Divisional Income Statements
For Year Ended December 31, 19--

	Division M	Division N	Total
Sales:			
50,000 units × $20 per unit	$1,000,000		$1,000,000
20,000 units × $40 per unit		$800,000	800,000
			$1,800,000
Expenses:			
Variable:			
50,000 units × $10 per unit	$ 500,000		$ 500,000
20,000 units × $30* per unit		$600,000	600,000
Fixed	300,000	100,000	400,000
Total expenses	$ 800,000	$700,000	$1,500,000
Operating income	$ 200,000	$100,000	$ 300,000

*$20 of the $30 per unit represents materials costs, and the remaining $10 per unit represents other expenses incurred within Division N.

[3] The discussion highlights the essential concepts of transfer pricing. More in-depth discussion of transfer pricing can be found in advanced texts.

Market Price Approach

Under the **market price approach,** the transfer price is the price at which the product or service transferred could be sold to outside buyers. If an outside market exists for the product or service transferred, then the current market price at which the purchasing division could buy the product or service outside the company would seem to be a reasonable transfer price for intracompany transfers. However, the appropriateness of the market price approach depends on whether the division supplying the product or service is operating at full capacity and can sell all it produces.

To illustrate, assume that materials used by Wilson Company in producing Division N's product are currently purchased from an outside supplier at $20 per unit. The same materials are produced by Division M. If Division M is operating at full capacity of 50,000 units and can sell all it produces to either Division N or to outside buyers, then the use of a transfer price of $20 per unit (the market price) has no effect on the income of Division M or total company income. Division M will earn revenues of $20 per unit on all its production and sales, regardless of who buys its product, and Division N will pay $20 per unit, regardless of whether it purchases the materials from Division M or from an outside supplier. In this situation, the use of the market price as the transfer price is appropriate. The condensed divisional income statements for Wilson Company under such circumstances would be as shown on page 1134.

If unused capacity exists in the supplying division, the use of the market price approach may not lead to the maximization of total company income. To illustrate, assume that Division M has unused capacity of 20,000 units and it can continue to sell only 50,000 units to outside buyers. In this situation, the transfer price should be set to motivate the manager of Division N to purchase from Division M if the variable cost per unit of product of Division M is less than the market price. If the variable costs are less than $20 per unit but the transfer price is set equal to the market price of $20, then the manager of Division N is indifferent as to whether materials are purchased from Division M or from outside suppliers, since the cost per unit to Division N would be the same, $20. However, Division N's purchase of 20,000 units of materials from outside suppliers at a cost of $20 per unit would not maximize overall company income, since this market price per unit is greater than the unit variable expenses of Division M, $10. Hence, the intracompany transfer could save the company the difference between the market price per unit and Division M's unit variable expenses. This savings of $10 per unit would add $200,000 (20,000 units × $10) to overall company income.

Negotiated Price Approach

In the previous illustration, the manager of Division N should be encouraged to purchase from Division M by establishing a transfer price at an amount less than the market price of $20 per unit. Division N's materials cost per unit would thus decrease, and its operating income would increase. In such situations, the negotiated price approach can be used to establish an appropriate transfer price.

The **negotiated price approach** allows the managers of decentralized units to agree (negotiate) among themselves as to the proper transfer price. If agreement cannot be reached among the division managers, the company's top management may have to intervene to set the transfer price. To illustrate, assume that Wilson Company's division managers agree to a transfer price of

$15 for Division M's product. By purchasing from Division M, Division N would then report $5 per unit less materials cost. At the same time, Division M would increase its sales to a total of 70,000 units (50,000 units to outside buyers and 20,000 units to Division N). The effect of increasing Division M's sales by $300,000 (20,000 units × $15 per unit) is to increase its income by $100,000 ($300,000 sales − $200,000 variable expenses). The effect of reducing Division N's materials cost by $100,000 (20,000 units × $5 per unit) is to increase its income by $100,000. Therefore, Wilson Company's income is increased by $200,000 ($100,000 reported by Division M and $100,000 reported by Division N), as shown in the following condensed income statements:

Wilson Company
Divisional Income Statements
For Year Ended December 31, 19--

	Division M	Division N	Total
Sales:			
50,000 units × $20 per unit	$1,000,000		$1,000,000
20,000 units × $15 per unit	300,000		300,000
20,000 units × $40 per unit		$800,000	800,000
	$1,300,000	$800,000	$2,100,000
Expenses:			
Variable:			
70,000 units × $10 per unit	$ 700,000		$ 700,000
20,000 units × $25* per unit		$500,000	500,000
Fixed	300,000	100,000	400,000
Total expenses	$1,000,000	$600,000	$1,600,000
Operating income	$ 300,000	$200,000	$ 500,000

*$10 per unit of the $25 is incurred solely within Division N, and $15 per unit represents the transfer price per unit from Division M.

In the Wilson Company illustration, any transfer price less than the market price of $20 but greater than Division M's unit variable expenses of $10 would increase each division's income and would increase overall company income by $200,000. By establishing a range of $20 to $10 for the negotiated transfer price, each division manager will have an incentive to negotiate the intracompany transfer of the materials. For example, a transfer price of $18 would increase Division M's income by $160,000 (from $200,000 to $360,000) and Division N's income by $40,000 (from $100,000 to $140,000). Overall company income would still be increased by $200,000 (from $300,000 to $500,000), as shown in the condensed income statements on page 1137.

Cost Price Approach

Under the **cost price approach,** cost is used as the basis for setting transfer prices. With this approach, a variety of cost concepts may be used. For example, cost may refer to either total product cost per unit or variable product cost per unit. If total product cost per unit is used, direct materials, direct labor, and factory overhead are included in the transfer price. If variable product cost per unit is used, the fixed factory overhead component of total product cost is excluded from the transfer price.

Wilson Company
Divisional Income Statements
For Year Ended December 31 19--

	Division M	Division N	Total
Sales:			
50,000 units × $20 per unit	$1,000,000		$1,000,000
20,000 units × $18 per unit	360,000		360,000
20,000 units × $40 per unit		$800,000	800,000
	$1,360,000	$800,000	$2,160,000
Expenses:			
Variable:			
70,000 units × $10 per unit	$ 700,000		$ 700,000
20,000 units × $28* per unit		$560,000	560,000
Fixed	300,000	100,000	400,000
Total expenses	$1,000,000	$660,000	$1,660,000
Operating income	$ 360,000	$140,000	$ 500,000

*$10 per unit of the $28 is incurred solely within Division N, and $18 per unit represents the transfer price per unit from Division M.

Either actual costs or standard (budgeted) costs may be used in applying the cost price approach. If actual costs are used, inefficiencies of the producing division are transferred to the purchasing division, and thus there is little incentive for the producing division to control costs carefully. For this reason, most companies use standard costs in the cost price approach, so that differences between actual and standard costs are isolated in the producing divisions for cost control purposes.

When division managers have responsibility for only costs incurred in their divisions, the cost price approach to transfer pricing is frequently used. However, many accountants argue that the cost price approach is inappropriate for decentralized operations organized as profit or investment centers. In profit and investment centers, division managers have responsibility for both revenues and expenses. The use of cost as a transfer price, however, ignores the supplying division manager's responsibility over revenues. When a supplying division's sales are all intracompany transfers, for example, the use of the cost price approach would prevent the supplying division from reporting any operating income. A cost-based transfer price would therefore not motivate the division manager to make intracompany transfers, even though they are in the best interests of the company.

TRANSFER PRICING FOR AN AUTOMOBILE DEALERSHIP—A CASE ANALYSIS

The importance of developing appropriate transfer prices can be demonstrated by the following case, which was reported in *Management Accounting*. The case is based on an actual company, an automobile dealership that is one of the largest volume import dealers in the state of Pennsylvania.

... With sales expected to exceed 1,000 new units in [the] calendar year, ... the dealership

serves as a leader in the field. Dollar sales of new units will top $9 million by calendar year-end. In addition to the sales department, the dealership also has separate parts and service departments. [The sales department] is a major customer of both [the] service and parts [departments] . . . .

[The transfer prices for floormats, rustproofing, paint protection, AM-FM stereo cassettes, and air conditioning transferred from the parts and service departments to the sales department were determined as follows:]

Item	Cost*	Markup	Transfer Price
Deluxe floormats . . .	$ 27.49	27%	$ 35.00
Rustproofing	25.54	135	60.00
Paint protection	25.54	135	60.00
AM-FM stereo cassette	225.60	13	255.00
A/C	484.70	34	650.00

*Includes installation costs.

All of the above prices were set by the dealer-owner in conjunction with his service manager and parts manager with the implied intention of giving these departments a share of the sales department's profit. These prices are not retail prices, nor are they legitimate wholesale prices; they are simply arbitrary transfer prices.

[The above transfer prices illustrate] the haphazard method by which [the sales department] is charged for goods from the two supporting departments. Notice that floormats are charged to sales at approximately a 27% mark-up on cost, rustproofing and paint protection at 135% mark-up, and air conditioning at 34% mark-up. The lowest mark-up occurs on radios, a mere 13% increase. . . .

Because of perceived excess charges, the frustrated sales manager looked outside the company for the products and services he needed. After minimal investigation he found a subcontractor willing to supply comparable performance radios and air conditioners at considerable savings. He was able to and did buy radios for $227.00 installed and air conditioners for $525.00 installed. This practice continued for approximately two years. During this period the sales manager was noticeably ecstatic over his increased bonuses, while the parts and service managers were long-faced and moody due to declining profits. In this period 618 air conditioners and 267 AM-FM stereo cassettes were sold by the sales department. Of these, 112 air conditioners and three stereo cassettes were purchased internally. Although the sales department saved $63,250.00 (506 units @ $125.00 savings) on air conditioners, and [$7,392.00 (264 units @ $28.00 savings)] on cassette radios, the company as a whole lost money. By buying 506 air conditioners from a third party the company lost $20,391.80 [506 units × ($525.00 price paid − $484.70 cost to internally install)]. By purchasing 264 AM-FM stereo cassettes from an outsider the company gave up $369.60 [264 units × ($227.00 price paid − $225.60 cost to internally install)]. Total company losses totalled $20,761.40.

After two years the dealer-owner realized the extent of his lost profits and immediately called all three managers together in conference to discuss the problem. . . . After several days of negotiation, . . . the parties settled on what they believed were fair and reasonable transfer prices for the products involved as well as all other products sold internally to the sales department. . . .

Source: Joseph A. Scarpo, Jr., "Auto Dealers Lag in Transfer Pricing," *Management Accounting* (July, 1984), pp. 54–56.

CHAPTER REVIEW

KEY POINTS

OBJECTIVE 1 Centralized and Decentralized Operations

Responsibility accounting is the process of measuring and reporting operating data to management by areas of responsibility. In a centralized business organization, all major planning and operating decisions are made by the top echelon of management. In a decentralized business organization, the responsibility for planning and controlling operations is delegated among managers who have authority to make decisions without first seeking the approval of higher management. In a decentralized organization, an important function of the managerial accountant is to assist managers in the process of measuring and reporting data by their areas of responsibility or responsibility centers.

OBJECTIVE 2

Types of Responsibility Centers

Responsibility centers can be classified by the scope of the responsibility assigned and the decision-making authority given to individual managers. In a cost center, the manager has the responsibility for the control of costs incurred and the authority to make decisions that affect those costs. In a profit center, the manager has the responsibility and the authority to make decisions that affect both costs and revenue (and thus profits) for the department or division. In an investment center, the manager has the responsibility and the authority to make decisions that affect not only costs and revenues, but also the plant assets available to the center.

OBJECTIVE 3

Responsibility Accounting for Cost Centers

Since managers of cost centers have responsibility for and authority to make decisions regarding costs, responsibility accounting for cost centers focuses on costs. The primary accounting tools for planning and controlling costs for a cost center are budgets and standard costs.

OBJECTIVE 4

Responsibility Accounting for Profit Centers

Since managers of profit centers have responsibility for and authority to make decisions regarding expenses and revenues, responsibility accounting reports for profit centers are normally in the form of income statements. Some accountants advocate the preparation of departmental income statements based upon departmental margin. Departmental margin is determined by deducting the direct expenses of each department from departmental gross profit. The remaining expenses are not allocated to a department, but are reported in the income statement separately below the total departmental margin. A company may prefer to use traditional income statements for profit centers. One such statement determines gross profit by departments. Departmental reporting may be extended to operating income, in which case the operating expenses incurred by the company must be allocated to the departments. These expenses are usually allocated on the basis of the departmental benefit received from the expenditure.

OBJECTIVE 5

Responsibility Accounting for Investment Centers

Because investment centers are evaluated as if they were separate companies, traditional financial statements which report operating income are normally prepared for each center. A measure of performance for investment centers is the rate of return on investment. The rate of return on investment is computed by dividing operating income by invested assets. In addition, the rate of return on investment may be considered as the product of two factors: (1) the profit margin and (2) the investment turnover. An additional measure of investment center performance, residual income, is the excess of divisional operating income over a minimum amount of desired operating income.

OBJECTIVE 6

Transfer Pricing

The transfer price is the price charged by a unit for products or services provided to another unit in a decentralized company. The objective of transfer pricing is to encourage each divisional manager to transfer goods and services between divisions if overall company income can be increased by doing so. Three commonly used approaches to establishing transfer prices are (1) the market price approach, (2) the negotiated price approach, and (3) the cost price approach.

Under the market price approach to transfer pricing, the transfer price is set at the price at which the product or services transferred between units could be sold to outside buyers. Under the negotiated price approach, the transfer price is the price agreed to (negotiated) among the managers of the decentralized units. Under the cost price approach, cost is used as the basis for setting transfer prices. The cost may be either total product cost per unit or variable product cost per unit, and most companies use the standard cost rather than the actual cost.

KEY TERMS

decentralization 1114
responsibility accounting 1114
strategic planning 1115
cost center 1117
profit center 1117
investment center 1118
departmental margin 1121
direct expense 1121
indirect expense 1121
rate of return on investment (ROI) 1130
profit margin 1131
investment turnover 1131
residual income 1133
transfer price 1134
market price approach 1135
negotiated price approach 1135
cost price approach 1136

SELF-EXAMINATION QUESTIONS

Answers at end of chapter.

1. When the manager has the responsibility for and authority to make decisions that affect costs and revenues, but no responsibility for or authority over assets invested in the department, the department is referred to as:
   A. a cost center
   B. a profit center
   C. an investment center
   D. none of the above

2. The term used to describe the excess of departmental gross profit over direct departmental expenses is:
   A. income from operations
   B. net income
   C. departmental margin
   D. none of the above

3. Division A of Kern Co. has sales of $350,000, cost of goods sold of $200,000, operating expenses of $30,000, and invested assets of $600,000. What is the rate of return on investment for Division A?
   A. 20%
   B. 25%
   C. 40%
   D. None of the above

4. Division L of Liddy Co. has a rate of return on investment of 24% and an investment turnover of 1.6. What is the profit margin?
   A. 6%
   B. 15%
   C. 24%
   D. None of the above

5. Which approach to transfer pricing uses the price at which the product or service transferred could be sold to outside buyers?
   A. Cost price approach
   B. Negotiated price approach
   C. Market price approach
   D. None of the above

ILLUSTRATIVE PROBLEM

Reese Company has two divisions, A and B. Invested assets and condensed income statement data for each division for the past year ended December 31 are as follows:

	Division A	Division B
Sales	$3,125,000	$5,100,000
Cost of goods sold	2,500,000	4,000,000
Operating expenses	150,000	590,000
Invested assets	2,500,000	3,000,000

Instructions:

1. Prepare condensed income statements for the past year for each division.
2. Using the expanded expression, determine the profit margin, investment turnover, and rate of return on investment for each division.
3. If management desires a minimum rate of return of 12%, determine the residual income for each division.

SOLUTION

(1)

Reese Company
Divisional Income Statements
For Year Ended December 31, 19--

	Division A	Division B
Sales	$3,125,000	$5,100,000
Cost of goods sold	2,500,000	4,000,000
Gross profit	$ 625,000	$1,100,000
Operating expenses	150,000	590,000
Operating income	$ 475,000	$ 510,000

(2)

Rate of Return on Investment (ROI) = Profit Margin × Investment Turnover

$$\text{ROI} = \frac{\text{Operating Income}}{\text{Sales}} \times \frac{\text{Sales}}{\text{Invested Assets}}$$

$$\text{Division A: ROI} = \frac{\$475{,}000}{\$3{,}125{,}000} \times \frac{\$3{,}125{,}000}{\$2{,}500{,}000}$$

$$\text{ROI} = 15.2\% \times 1.25$$

$$\text{ROI} = 19\%$$

$$\text{Division B: ROI} = \frac{\$510{,}000}{\$5{,}100{,}000} \times \frac{\$5{,}100{,}000}{\$3{,}000{,}000}$$

$$\text{ROI} = 10\% \times 1.7$$

$$\text{ROI} = 17\%$$

(3) Division A: $175,000 ($475,000 − $300,000)
Division B: $150,000 ($510,000 − $360,000)

DISCUSSION QUESTIONS

27–1. What is responsibility accounting?

27–2. Name three common types of responsibility centers for decentralized operations.

27–3. Differentiate between a cost center and a profit center.

27–4. Differentiate between a profit center and an investment center.

27–5. In what major respect would budget performance reports prepared for the use of plant managers of a manufacturing enterprise with cost centers differ from those prepared for the use of the various department supervisors who report to the plant managers?

27–6. Indicate whether each of the following operating expenses incurred by an individual department within a merchandising enterprise is a direct or an indirect expense:

(a) Depreciation of store equipment
(b) General manager's salary
(c) Heating and lighting expense
(d) Insurance expense on building
(e) Sales commissions
(f) Uncollectible accounts expense

27–7. What term is applied to the dollar amount representing the excess of departmental gross profit over direct departmental expenses?

27–8. Recent income statements departmentalized through income from operations report operating losses for Department E, a relatively minor segment of the business. Management studies indicate that discontinuance of Department E would not affect sales of other departments or the volume of indirect expenses. Under what circumstances would the discontinuance of Department E result in a decrease of net income of the enterprise?

27–9. The newly appointed manager of the Clothing Department in a department store is studying the income statements presenting gross profit by departments in an attempt to adjust operations to achieve the highest possible gross profit for the department. (a) Suggest ways in which an income statement departmentalized through gross profit can be used in achieving this goal. (b) Suggest reasons why caution must be exercised in using such statements.

27–10. For each of the following types of expenses, select the allocation basis listed that is most appropriate for use in arriving at operating income by departments:

Expense:	Basis of allocation:
(a) Advertising expense	(1) Cost of inventory and equipment
(b) Rent expense	(2) Departmental sales
(c) Property tax expense	(3) Time devoted to departments
(d) Sales salaries	(4) Physical space occupied

27–11. Describe an appropriate basis for apportioning Officers' Salaries Expense among departments for purposes of the income statement departmentalized through income from operations.

27–12. Name three performance measures useful in evaluating investment centers.

27–13. What is the major shortcoming of using operating income as a performance measure for investment centers?

27–14. Why should the factors under the control of the investment center manager (revenues, expenses, and invested assets) be considered in the computation of the rate of return on investment?

27–15. Wenstrup Co. has $500,000 invested in Division Q, which earned $90,000 of operating income. What is the rate of return on investment for Division Q?

27–16. If Wenstrup Co. in Question 27–15 had sales of $1,500,000, what is (a) the profit margin and (b) the investment turnover for Division Q?

27–17. What are two ways of expressing the rate of return on investment?

27–18. In evaluating investment centers, what does multiplying the profit margin by the investment turnover equal?

27–19. In a decentralized company in which the divisions are organized as investment centers, how could a division be considered the least profitable, even though it earned the largest amount of operating income?

27–20. Which component of the rate of return on investment (profit margin factor or investment turnover factor) focuses on efficiency in the use of assets and indicates the rate at which sales are generated for each dollar of invested assets?

27–21. Division D of Shaut Co. has a rate of return on investment of 10%. (a) If Division D increases its investment turnover by 40%, what would be the new rate of return on investment? (b) If Division D also increases its profit margin from 6% to 9%, what would be the new rate of return on investment?

27–22. How does the use of the rate of return on investment facilitate comparability of divisions of decentralized companies?

27–23. The rates of return on investment for Sauter Co.'s three divisions, A, B, and C, are 25%, 20%, and 17%, respectively. In expanding operations, which of Sauter Co.'s divisions should be given priority? Explain.

27–24. What term is used to describe the excess of divisional operating income over a minimum amount of desired operating income?

27–25. Division L of Jaffe Co. reported operating income of $350,000, based on invested assets of $1,600,000. If the minimum rate of return on divisional investments is 20%, what is the residual income for Division L?

27–26. What is the objective of transfer pricing?

27–27. What approach uses as the transfer price the price at which the product or service transferred could be sold to outside buyers?

27–28. When is the negotiated price approach preferred over the market price approach in setting transfer prices?

27–29. If division managers cannot agree among themselves on a transfer price when using the negotiated price approach, how is the transfer price established?

27–30. When using the negotiated price approach to transfer pricing, within what range should the transfer price be established?

Real World Focus

27–31. Tandy Corporation's annual report for the year ended June 30, 1990, reports a profit margin of 6.5% and an investment turnover rate of 1.39. (a) What was the rate of return on investment for the year ended June 30, 1990? (b) If the investment turnover rate does not change for the year ended June 30, 1991, what must the profit margin be to earn a rate of return on investment of 12%? (Round to the nearest tenth of one percent.)

Ethics Discussion Case

27–32. Vernon Baxter, the assistant controller for Loucks Enterprises, prepares responsibility accounting reports for the various divisions of the company. On December 20th, a case of wine with a card wishing "Merry Christmas" from John Potts, manager of the beverage division, was delivered to Baxter's home. Baxter accepted the wine and sent a note of thanks to Potts. Discuss whether Baxter behaved in an ethical manner.

EXERCISES

Ex. 27–33.
Budget performance report.
OBJ. 3

The budget for Department R of Elgin Plant for the current month ended June 30 is as follows:

Factory wages	$250,000
Materials	220,000
Power and light	75,000
Supervisory salaries	55,000
Depreciation of plant and equipment	30,000
Maintenance	27,500
Insurance and property taxes	17,500

During June, the costs incurred in Department R of Elgin Plant were as follows: factory wages, $261,300; materials, $219,100; power and light, $75,100; supervisory salaries, $55,000; depreciation of plant and equipment, $30,000; maintenance, $27,650; insurance and property taxes, $17,500. (a) Prepare a budget performance report for the supervisor of Department R, Elgin Plant, for the month of June. (b) For what significant variations in costs might the supervisor be expected to request supplemental reports?

Ex. 27–34.
Departmental income statement.
OBJ. 4
SPREADSHEET PROBLEM

The following data were summarized from the accounting records for Ricks Company for the current year ended August 31:

Cost of goods sold:	
Department P	$250,200
Department Q	355,500
Direct expenses:	
Department P	132,000
Department Q	178,800
Income tax	54,000
Indirect expenses	115,500
Interest income	24,000
Net sales:	
Department P	492,600
Department Q	699,400

Prepare an income statement departmentalized through departmental margin.

Ex. 27–35.
Decision on discontinuance of department.
OBJ. 4

A portion of an income statement in condensed form, departmentalized through loss from operations for the year just ended, is as follows:

	Department G
Net sales	$226,600
Cost of goods sold	179,700
Gross profit	$ 46,900
Operating expenses	63,000
Loss from operations	$(16,100)

The operating expenses of Dept. G include $30,000 for indirect expenses. It is believed that the discontinuance of Department G would not affect the sales of the other departments nor reduce the indirect expenses of the enterprise. Based on this information, determine the increase or decrease in income from operations of the enterprise if Department G had been discontinued prior to the year just ended.

Ex. 27–36.
Apportionment of depreciation and property tax expense to departments.
OBJ. 4

In income statements prepared for Wong Company, depreciation expense on equipment is apportioned on the basis of the average cost of the equipment, and property tax expense is apportioned on the basis of the combined total of the average cost of the equipment and the average cost of the inventories. Depreciation expense on equipment amounted to $300,000, and property tax expense amounted to $45,000 for the year. Determine the apportionment of the depreciation expense and the property tax expense, based on the following data:

	Average Cost	
Departments	Equipment	Inventories
Service:		
S1	$ 420,000	
S2	280,000	
Sales:		
R10	840,000	$ 70,000
R11	560,000	140,000
R12	700,000	490,000
Total	$2,800,000	$700,000

Ex. 27–37.
Rate of return on investment.
OBJ. 5

The operating income and the amount of invested assets in each division of Karsten Company are as follows:

	Operating Income	Invested Assets
Division H	$151,200	$ 840,000
Division I	180,000	1,200,000
Division J	107,800	490,000

(a) Compute the rate of return on investment for each division. (b) Which division is the most profitable per dollar invested?

Ex. 27–38.
Residual income.
OBJ. 5

Based on the data in Ex. 27–37, assume that management has established a minimum rate of return for invested assets of 12%. (a) Determine the residual income for each division. (b) Based on residual income, which of the divisions is the most profitable?

Ex. 27–39.
Determination of missing items for computations of rate of return on investment.
OBJ. 5

One item is omitted from each of the following computations of the rate of return on investment:

Rate of Return on Investment	=	Profit Margin	×	Investment Turnover
18%		15%		(a)
(b)		18%		1.5
20%		(c)		2.5
17%		10%		(d)
(e)		25%		.6

Determine the missing items, identifying each by the appropriate letter.

Ex. 27–40.
Profit margin, investment turnover, and rate of return on investment.
OBJ. 5

The condensed income statement for Division G of Dunlop Company is as follows:

Sales	$1,500,000
Cost of goods sold	900,000
Gross profit	$ 600,000
Operating expenses	330,000
Operating income	$ 270,000

The manager of Division G is considering ways to increase the rate of return on investment. (a) Using the expanded expression, determine the profit margin, investment turnover, and rate of return on investment of Division G, assuming that $1,250,000 of assets have been invested in Division G. (b) If expenses could be reduced by $30,000 without decreasing sales, what would be the impact on the profit margin, investment turnover, and rate of return on investment for Division G?

Ex. 27–41.
Determination of missing items for computations of rate of return on investment and residual income.
OBJ. 5

One or more items is missing from the following tabulation of rate of return on investment and residual income:

Invested Assets	Operating Income	Rate of Return on Investment	Minimum Rate of Return	Minimum Amount of Operating Income	Residual Income
$ 900,000	$153,000	(a)	15%	(b)	(c)
$ 500,000	(d)	18%	(e)	$55,000	$35,000
$1,200,000	(f)	(g)	(h)	$96,000	$60,000
$ 750,000	$120,000	(i)	9%	(j)	(k)

Determine the missing items, identifying each item by the appropriate letter.

Ex. 27–42.
Decision on transfer pricing.
OBJ. 6

Materials used by Snead Company in producing Division R's product are currently purchased from outside suppliers at a cost of $40 per unit. However, the same materials are available from Division W. Division W has unused capacity and can produce the materials needed by Division R at a variable cost of $25 per unit. (a) If a transfer price of $32 per unit is established and 50,000 units of material are transferred, with no reduction in Division W's current sales, how much would Snead Company's total operating income increase? (b) How much would operating income of Division R increase? (c) How much would the operating income of Division W increase?

Ex. 27–43.
Division on transfer pricing.
OBJ. 6

Based on the Snead Company data in Ex. 27–42, assume that a transfer price of $30 has been established and 50,000 units of materials are transferred, with no reduction in Division W's current sales. (a) How much would Snead Company's total operating income increase? (b) How much would Division R's operating income increase? (c) How much would Division W's operating income increase? (d) If the negotiated price approach is used, what would be the range of acceptable transfer prices?

PROBLEMS

Pb. 27–44.
Decision on discontinuance of department.
OBJ. 4

E. E. Eden Company is considering discontinuance of one of its ten departments. If operations in Department J are discontinued, it is estimated that the indirect operating expenses and the level of operations in the other departments will not be affected.

Data from the income statement for the past year ended December 31, which is considered to be a typical year, are as follows:

	Department J		Other Departments	
Sales	$44,000			$765,000
Cost of goods sold	23,500			420,750
Gross profit	$20,500			$344,250
Operating expenses:				
Direct expenses	$16,500		$192,500	
Indirect expenses	9,000	25,500	99,000	291,500
Income (loss) before income tax		$ (5,000)		$52,750

Instructions:

(1) Prepare an estimated income statement for the current year ending December 31, assuming the discontinuance of Department J.
(2) On the basis of the data presented, would it be advisable to retain Department J?

Pb. 27–45. Departmental income statement through departmental margin. OBJ. 4

Lakeshore Fashions has 20 departments. Those with the least sales volume are Department 10 and Department 16, which were established about twenty months ago on a trial basis. The board of directors believes that it is now time to consider the retention or the termination of these two departments. The following adjusted trial balance as of August 31, the end of the first month of the current fiscal year, is severely condensed. August is considered to be a typical month. The income tax accrual has no bearing on the decision and is excluded from consideration.

Lakeshore Fashions
Trial Balance
August 31, 19--

Current Assets	236,200	
Plant Assets	672,400	
Accumulated Depreciation—Plant Assets		168,100
Current Liabilities		118,100
Common Stock		200,000
Retained Earnings		403,304
Cash Dividends	30,000	
Sales—Department 10		32,500
Sales—Department 16		21,400
Sales—Other Departments		948,600
Cost of Goods Sold—Department 10	21,125	
Cost of Goods Sold—Department 16	14,980	
Cost of Goods Sold—Other Departments	569,160	
Direct Expenses—Department 10	8,125	
Direct Expenses—Department 16	7,490	
Direct Expenses—Other Departments	227,664	
Indirect Expenses	94,860	
Interest Expense	10,000	
	1,892,004	1,892,004

Instructions:

(1) Prepare an income statement for August, departmentalized through departmental margin.
(2) State your recommendations concerning the retention of Departments 10 and 16, giving reasons.

Pb. 27–46.
Departmental income statement through departmental margin.
OBJ. 4

Moffett Corporation consists of two departments, S and T. The bases to be used in apportioning expenses between the two departments, together with other essential data, are as follows:

Sales salaries and commissions expense—basic salary plus 6% of sales. Basic salaries for Department S, $80,000; Department T, $36,000.
Advertising expense for brochures—usage within each department advertising specific products: Department S, $13,000; Department T, $8,000.
Depreciation expense—average cost of store equipment: Department S, $122,500; Department T, $52,500.
Insurance expense—average cost of store equipment plus average cost of inventories. Average cost of inventories was $42,500 for Department S and $82,500 for Department T.
Uncollectible accounts expense—.3% of sales. Departmental managers are responsible for the granting of credit on the sales made by their respective departments.

The following data are obtained from the ledger on October 31, the end of the current fiscal year:

Sales—Department S		1,250,000
Sales—Department T		450,000
Cost of Goods Sold—Department S	750,000	
Cost of Goods Sold—Department T	300,000	
Sales Salaries and Commissions Expense	218,000	
Advertising Expense	21,000	
Depreciation Expense—Store Equipment	18,000	
Miscellaneous Selling Expense	4,000	
Administrative Salaries Expense	60,000	
Rent Expense	35,000	
Utilities Expense	11,250	
Insurance Expense	10,000	
Uncollectible Accounts Expense	5,100	
Miscellaneous Administrative Expense	1,500	
Interest Income		15,000
Income Tax	110,700	

Instructions:

(1) Prepare an income statement departmentalized through departmental margin.
(2) Determine the rate of gross profit for each department.
(3) Determine the rate of departmental margin to sales for each department.

Pb. 27–47.
Departmental income statement through income from operations.
OBJ. 4

Goldblum Appliances operates two sales departments—Department H for small appliances, such as radios and televisions, and Department I for large apliances, such as refrigerators and washing machines. The trial balance on page 1149 was prepared as of March 31, the end of the current fiscal year, after all adjustments were recorded and posted.

Inventories at the end of the year were as follows: Department H, $18,200; Department I, $64,300.

The bases to be used in apportioning expenses, together with other essential information, are as follows:

Sales salaries expense—payroll records: Department H, $17,700; Department I, $33,100.
Advertising expense—usage: Department H, $6,300; Department I, $11,700.
Depreciation expense—average cost of equipment. Equipment balances at beginning of year: Department H, $30,000; Department I, $45,000. Equipment balances at end of year: Department H, $37,200; Department I, $47,800.

Store supplies expense—requisitions: Department H, $870; Department I, $1,530.
Office salaries expense—Department H, 45%; Department I, 55%.
Rent expense and heating and lighting expense—floor space: Department H, 11,100 sq. ft.; Department I, 18,900 sq. ft.
Property tax expense and insurance expense—average cost of equipment plus average cost of inventories.
Uncollectible accounts expense, miscellaneous selling expense, and miscellaneous administrative expense—volume of gross sales.

Account	Debit	Credit
Cash	39,260	
Accounts Receivable	90,100	
Inventories—Department H	23,400	
Inventories—Department I	74,100	
Prepaid Insurance	2,040	
Store Supplies	2,000	
Store Equipment	85,000	
Accumulated Depreciation—Store Equipment		19,100
Accounts Payable		15,900
Income Tax Payable		11,300
Common Stock		100,000
Retained Earnings		21,200
Cash Dividends	5,200	
Sales—Department H		420,000
Sales—Department I		780,000
Sales Returns and Allowances—Department H	3,800	
Sales Returns and Allowances—Department I	6,200	
Purchases—Department H	252,000	
Purchases—Department I	507,000	
Sales Salaries Expense	50,800	
Advertising Expense	18,000	
Depreciation Expense—Store Equipment	9,500	
Store Supplies Expense	2,400	
Miscellaneous Selling Expense	2,800	
Office Salaries Expense	50,000	
Rent Expense	18,000	
Heating and Lighting Expense	15,000	
Property Tax Expense	6,000	
Insurance Expense	3,000	
Uncollectible Accounts Expense	2,400	
Miscellaneous Administrative Expense	2,200	
Interest Expense	5,000	
Income Tax	92,300	
	1,367,500	1,367,500

Instructions:

Prepare an income statement departmentalized through income from operations.

Pb. 27–48.
Divisional income statements and rate of return on investment analysis.
OBJ. 5
SPREADSHEET PROBLEM

Lambert Company is a diversified company with three operating divisions organized as investment centers. Condensed data taken from the records of the three divisions for the year ended March 31 are as follows:

	Division P	Division Q	Division R
Sales	$1,050,000	$2,250,000	$1,800,000
Cost of goods sold	630,000	1,800,000	1,350,000
Operating expenses	336,000	247,500	261,000
Invested assets	750,000	1,500,000	1,125,000

The management of Lambert Company is evaluating each division as a basis for planning a future expansion of operations.

Instructions:

(1) Prepare condensed divisional income statements for Divisions P, Q, and R.
(2) Using the expanded expression, compute the profit margin, investment turnover, and rate of return on investment for each division.
(3) If available funds permit the expansion of operations of only one division, which of the divisions would you recommend for expansion, based on (1) and (2)?

Pb. 27–49.
Effect of proposals on divisional performance.
OBJ. 5

A condensed income statement for Division J of Siegel Company for the year ended January 31 is as follows:

Sales	$3,200,000
Cost of goods sold	2,000,000
Gross profit	$1,200,000
Operating expenses	880,000
Operating income	$ 320,000

The president of Siegel Company is concerned with Division J's rate of return on invested assets of $2,000,000, and has indicated that the division's rate of return on investment must be increased to at least 18% by the end of the next year if operations are to continue. The division manager is considering the following three proposals:

Proposal 1: Transfer equipment with a book value of $400,000 to other divisions at no gain or loss and lease similar equipment. The annual lease payments would exceed the amount of depreciation expense on the old equipment by $48,000. This increase in expense would be included as part of the cost of goods sold. Sales would remain unchanged.

Proposal 2: Reduce invested assets by discontinuing a product line. This action would eliminate sales of $1,325,000, cost of goods sold of $1,060,000, and operating expenses of $207,500. Assets of $500,000 would be transferred to other divisions at no gain or loss.

Proposal 3: Purchase new and more efficient machinery and thereby reduce the cost of goods sold by $153,600. Sales would remain unchanged, and the old machinery, which has no remaining book value, would be scrapped at no gain or loss. The new machinery would increase invested assets by $560,000 for the year.

Instructions:

(1) Using the expanded expression, determine the profit margin, investment turnover, and rate of return on investment for Division J for the past year.
(2) Prepare condensed estimated income statements for Division J for each proposal.
(3) Using the expanded expression, determine the profit margin, investment turnover, and rate of return on investment for Division J under each proposal.
(4) Which of the three proposals would meet the required 18% rate of return on investment?
(5) If Division J were in an industry where the profit margin could not be increased, how much would the investment turnover have to increase to meet the president's required 18% rate of return on investment?

Pb. 27–50. **Determination of missing items from computations.** OBJ. 5

Data for Divisions R, S, T, U, and V of Van Spyk Company are as follows:

	Sales	Operating Income	Invested Assets	Rate of Return on Investment	Profit Margin	Investment Turnover
Division R	$ 660,000	$ 99,000	$ 550,000	(a)	(b)	(c)
Division S	$1,120,000	(d)	$ 800,000	21%	(e)	(f)
Division T	(g)	$180,000	(h)	(i)	12%	1.25
Division U	$1,210,000	(j)	(k)	22%	20%	(l)
Division V	(m)	$300,000	$1,200,000	(n)	(o)	2.5

Instructions:

(1) Determine the missing items, identifying each by letters (a) through (o).
(2) Determine the residual income for each division, assuming that the minimum rate of return established by management is 15%.
(3) Which division is the most profitable?

Pb. 27–51. **Divisional performance analysis and evaluation.** OBJ. 5

The vice-president of operations of Argo Company is evaluating the performance of two divisions organized as investment centers. Division B has the highest rate of return on investment, but generates the smallest amount of operating income. Division C generates the largest operating income, but has the lowest rate of return on investment. Invested assets and condensed income statement data for the past year for each division are as follows:

	Division B	Division C
Sales	$2,160,000	$3,000,000
Cost of goods sold	1,620,000	1,875,000
Operating expenses	172,800	735,000
Invested assets	1,800,000	2,000,000

Instructions:

(1) Prepare condensed divisional income statements for each division for the year ended January 31.
(2) Using the expanded expression, determine the profit margin, investment turnover, and rate of return on investment for each division.
(3) If management desires a minimum rate of return of 15%, determine the residual income for each division.
(4) Discuss the evaluation of Divisions B and C, using the performance measures determined in (1), (2), and (3).

Pb. 27–52. **Divisional performance analysis and evaluation.** OBJ. 5

The vice-president of operations of Bristol Inc. recently resigned, and the president is considering which one of two division managers to promote to the vacated position. Both division managers have been with the company approximately ten years. Operating data for each division for the past three years are as follows:

	1993	1992	1991
Division P:			
Sales	$ 2,500,000	$ 1,800,000	$ 950,000
Cost of goods sold	1,500,000	1,000,000	570,000
Gross profit	$ 1,000,000	$ 800,000	$ 380,000
Operating expenses	750,000	638,000	304,000
Operating income	$ 250,000	$ 162,000	$ 76,000
Invested assets	$ 1,000,000	$ 900,000	$ 500,000
Total industry sales	$12,500,000	$12,000,000	$9,500,000

	1993	1992	1991
Division Q:			
Sales	$ 2,100,000	$ 2,000,000	$1,575,000
Cost of goods sold	1,500,000	1,400,000	1,100,000
Gross profit	$ 600,000	$ 600,000	$ 475,000
Operating expenses	432,000	430,000	317,500
Operating income	$ 168,000	$ 170,000	$ 157,500
Invested assets	$ 1,200,000	$ 1,000,000	$ 750,000
Total industry sales	$14,000,000	$10,000,000	$6,300,000

Instructions:

(1) For each division for each of the three years, use the expanded expression to determine the profit margin, investment turnover, and rate of return on investment.
(2) Assuming that 12% has been established as a minimum rate of return, determine the residual income for each division for each of the three years.
(3) Determine each division's market share (division sales divided by total industry sales) for each of the three years.
(4) Based on (1), (2), and (3), which division manager would you recommend for promotion to vice-president of operations?
(5) What other factors should be considered in the promotion decision?

Pb. 27–53.
Transfer pricing.
OBJ. 6

Demars Company is diversified, with two operating divisions, X and Y. Condensed divisional income statements, which involve no intracompany transfers and which include a breakdown of expenses into variable and fixed components, are as follows:

Demars Company
Divisional Income Statements
For Year Ended December 31, 19--

	Division X	Division Y	Total
Sales:			
150,000 units × \$60 per unit	\$9,000,000		\$ 9,000,000
50,000 units × \$80 per unit		\$4,000,000	4,000,000
			\$13,000,000
Expenses:			
Variable:			
150,000 units × \$30 per unit	\$4,500,000		\$ 4,500,000
50,000 units × \$50* per unit		\$2,500,000	2,500,000
Fixed	3,000,000	1,000,000	4,000,000
Total expenses	\$7,500,000	\$3,500,000	\$11,000,000
Operating income	\$1,500,000	\$ 500,000	\$ 2,000,000

*\$40 of the \$50 per unit represents materials costs, and the remaining \$10 per unit represents other expenses incurred within Division Y.

Division X is operating at three fourths of capacity of 200,000 units. Materials used in producing Division Y's product are currently purchased from outside suppliers at a price of \$40 per unit. The materials used by Division Y are produced by Division X. Except for the possible transfer of materials between divisions, no changes are expected in sales and expenses.

Instructions:

(1) Would the market price of \$40 per unit be an appropriate transfer price for Demars Company? Explain.

(2) If Division Y purchases 50,000 units from Division X and a transfer price of $35 per unit is negotiated between the managers of Divisions X and Y, how much would the operating income of each division and total company operating income increase?
(3) Prepare condensed divisional income statements for Demars Company, based on the data in (2).
(4) If a transfer price of $34 per unit is negotiated, how much would the operating income of each division and total company income increase?
(5) (a) What is the range of possible negotiated transfer prices that would be acceptable for Demars Company?
(b) Assuming that the division managers of X and Y cannot agree on a transfer price, what price would you suggest as the transfer price?

ALTERNATE PROBLEMS

Pb. 27–44A. Decision on discontinuance of departments. OBJ. 4

C. M. Lyle Company is considering discontinuance of one of its fourteen departments. If operations in Department 6 are discontinued, it is estimated that the indirect operating expenses and the level of operations in the other departments will not be affected.

Data from the income statement for the past year ended August 31, which is considered to be a typical year, are as follows:

	Department 6		Other Departments	
Sales		$68,000		$981,000
Cost of goods sold		44,200		588,600
Gross profit		$23,800		$392,400
Operating expenses:				
Direct expenses	$18,400		$208,000	
Indirect expenses	9,500	27,900	114,000	322,000
Income (loss) before income tax		$ (4,100)		$ 70,400

Instructions:

(1) Prepare an estimated income statement for the current year ending August 31, assuming the discontinuance of Department 6.
(2) On the basis of the data presented, would it be advisable to retain Department 6?

Pb. 27–45A. Department income statement through departmental margin. OBJ. 4

Ross Department Store has 18 departments. Those with the least sales volume are Department 16 and Department 17, which were established about a year ago on a trial basis. The board of directors feels that it is now time to consider the retention or the termination of these two departments. The following adjusted trial balance as of May 31, the end of the first month of the current fiscal year, is severely condensed. May is considered to be a typical month. The income tax accrual has no bearing on the decision and is excluded from consideration.

Ross Department Store
Trial Balance
May 31, 19--

Current Assets	333,200	
Plant Assets	642,700	
Accumulated Depreciation—Plant Assets		252,810
Current Liabilities		190,920
Common Stock		100,000
Retained Earnings		291,860
Cash Dividends	15,000	
Sales—Department 16		31,900
Sales—Department 17		24,200
Sales—Other Departments		861,500
Cost of Goods Sold—Department 16	22,330	
Cost of Goods Sold—Department 17	15,730	
Cost of Goods Sold—Other Departments	516,900	
Direct Expenses—Department 16	11,450	
Direct Expenses—Department 17	4,820	
Direct Expenses—Other Departments	126,760	
Indirect Expenses	58,300	
Interest Expense	6,000	
	1,753,190	1,753,190

Instructions:

(1) Prepare an income statement for May, departmentalized through departmental margin.
(2) State your recommendations concerning the retention of Departments 16 and 17, giving reasons.

Pb. 27–46A.
Departmental income statement through departmental margin.
OBJ. 4

Wilson Corporation consists of two departments, J and M. The bases to be used in apportioning expenses between the two departments, together with other essential data, are as follows:

Sales salaries and commissions expense—basic salary plus 6% of sales. Basic salaries for Department A, $54,600; Department B, $26,520.
Advertising expense for brochures distributed within each department advertising specific products—usage: Department A, $12,745; Department B, $6,090.
Depreciation expense—average cost of store equipment: Department A, $78,300; Department B, $56,700.
Insurance expense—average cost of store equipment plus average cost of merchandise inventory. Average cost of merchandise inventory was $58,100 for Department A and $26,900 for Department B.
Uncollectible accounts expense—3/8% of sales. Departmental managers are responsible for the granting of credit on the sales made by their respective departments.

The following data are obtained from the ledger on April 30, the end of the current fiscal year:

Sales—Department A		740,000
Sales—Department B		296,000
Cost of Goods Sold—Department A	495,800	
Cost of Goods Sold—Department B	192,400	
Sales Salaries and Commissions Expense	143,280	
Advertising Expense	18,835	
Depreciation Expense—Store Equipment	12,500	
Miscellaneous Selling Expense	2,020	

Administrative Salaries Expense	43,850	
Rent Expense	24,000	
Utilities Expense	14,620	
Insurance Expense	6,500	
Uncollectible Accounts Expense	3,885	
Miscellaneous General Expense	710	
Interest Income		4,400
Income Tax	17,750	

Instructions:

(1) Prepare an income statement departmentalized through departmental margin.
(2) Determine the rate of gross profit for each department.
(3) Determine the rate of departmental margin to sales for each department.

Pb. 27–47A.
Departmental income statement through income from operations.
OBJ. 4

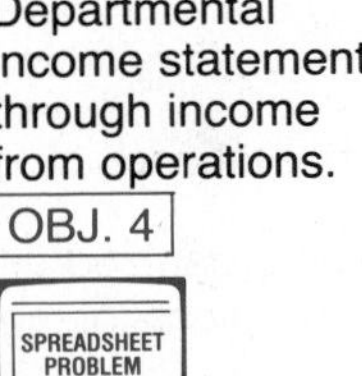

Smolinski Co. operates two sales departments—Department K for sporting goods and Department W for camping equipment. The following trial balance was prepared as of April 30, the end of the current fiscal year, after all adjustments were recorded and posted:

Cash	29,600	
Accounts Receivable	64,200	
Inventories—Department K	41,400	
Inventories—Department W	17,600	
Prepaid Insurance	2,250	
Store Supplies	2,150	
Store Equipment	128,400	
Accumulated Depreciation—Store Equipment		33,300
Accounts Payable		25,900
Income Tax Payable		6,550
Common Stock		100,000
Retained Earnings		77,250
Cash Dividends	13,000	
Sales—Department K		450,000
Sales—Department W		150,000
Sales Returns and Allowances—Department K	4,000	
Sales Returns and Allowances—Department W	2,200	
Purchases—Department K	200,000	
Purchases—Department W	108,000	
Sales Salaries Expense	80,000	
Advertising Expense	16,500	
Depreciation Expense—Store Equipment	10,000	
Store Supplies Expense	5,400	
Miscellaneous Selling Expense	4,100	
Office Salaries Expense	45,000	
Rent Expense	15,000	
Heating and Lighting Expense	9,000	
Property Tax Expense	4,800	
Insurance Expense	4,200	
Uncollectible Accounts Expense	3,400	
Miscellaneous Administrative Expense	1,600	
Interest Expense	5,000	
Income Tax	26,200	
	843,000	843,000

Inventories at the end of the year were as follows: Department K, $36,400; Department W, $20,600.

The bases to be used in apportioning expenses, together with other essential information, are as follows:

Sales salaries expense—payroll records: Department K, $50,000; Department W, $30,000.
Advertising expense—usage: Department K, $10,800; Department W, $5,700.
Depreciation expense—average cost of equipment. Balances of equipment at beginning of year: Department K, $71,600; Department W, $40,000. Balances at end of year: Department K, $82,000; Department W, $46,400.
Store supplies expense—requisitions: Department K, $3,600; Department W, $1,800.
Office salaries expense—Department K, 70%; Department W, 30%.
Rent expense and heating and lighting expense—floor space: Department K, 17,400 sq. ft.; Department W, 12,600 sq. ft.
Property tax expense and insurance expense—average cost of equipment plus average cost of inventories.
Uncollectible accounts expense, miscellaneous selling expense, and miscellaneous administrative expense—volume of gross sales.

Instructions:

Prepare an income statement departmentalized through income from operations.

Pb. 27–48A.
Divisional income statements and rate of return on investment analysis.
OBJ. 5

Colton Company is a diversified company with three operating divisions organized as investment centers. Condensed data taken from the records of the three divisions for the year ended July 31 are as follows:

	Division X	Division Y	Division Z
Sales	$1,250,000	$750,000	$2,250,000
Cost of goods sold	800,000	550,000	1,575,000
Operating expenses	300,000	80,000	405,000
Invested assets	1,000,000	600,000	1,500,000

The management of Colton Company is evaluating each division as a basis for planning a future expansion of operations.

Instructions:

(1) Prepare condensed divisional income statements for Divisions X, Y, and Z.
(2) Using the expanded expression, compute the profit margin, investment turnover, and rate of return on investment for each division.
(3) If available funds permit the expansion of operations of only one division, which of the divisions would you recommend for expansion, based on (1) and (2)?

Pb. 27–49A.
Effect of proposals on divisional performance.
OBJ. 5

A condensed income statement for Division H of Searcy Company for the year ended October 31 is as follows:

Sales	$1,500,000
Cost of goods sold	1,050,000
Gross profit	$ 450,000
Operating expenses	270,000
Operating income	$ 180,000

The president of Searcy Company is concerned with Division H's low rate of return on invested assets of $1,200,000, and has indicated that the division's rate of return on investment must be increased to at least 18% by the end of the next year if operations are to continue. The division manager is considering the following three proposals:

Proposal 1: Reduce invested assets by discontinuing a product line. This would eliminate sales of $200,000, cost of goods sold of $140,000, and operating expenses of $49,000. Assets of $160,000 would be transferred to other divisions at no gain or loss.

Proposal 2: Purchase new and more efficient machinery and thereby reduce the cost of goods sold by $93,000. Sales would remain unchanged, and the old machinery, which has no remaining book value, would be scrapped at no gain or loss. The new machinery would increase invested assets by $300,000 for the year.

Proposal 3: Transfer equipment with a book value of $200,000 to other divisions at no gain or loss and lease similar equipment. The annual lease payments would exceed the amount of depreciation expense on the old equipment by $6,000. This increase in expense would be included as part of the cost of goods sold. Sales would remain unchanged.

Instructions:

(1) Using the expanded expression, determine the profit margin, investment turnover, and rate of return on investment for Division H for the past year.
(2) Prepare condensed estimated income statements for Division H for each proposal.
(3) Using the expanded expression, determine the profit margin, investment turnover, and rate of return on investment for Division H under each proposal.
(4) Which of the three proposals would meet the required 18% rate of return on investment?
(5) If Division H were in a highly competitive industry where the profit margin and sales could not be increased, how much would invested assets have to be reduced to meet the president's required 18% rate of return on investment?

Pb. 27–50A.
Determination of missing items from computations.
OBJ. 5

Data for Divisions G, H, I, J, and K of Beacon Company are as follows:

	Sales	Operating Income	Invested Assets	Rate of Return on Investment	Profit Margin	Investment Turnover
Division G	$ 800,000	$128,000	$640,000	(a)	(b)	(c)
Division H	(d)	(e)	$750,000	14%	(f)	1.75
Division I	$1,800,000	(g)	(h)	(i)	12%	1.50
Division J	$ 650,000	(j)	(k)	(l)	10%	1.3
Division K	(m)	$120,000	(n)	25%	12.5%	(o)

Instructions:

(1) Determine the missing items, identifying each by letters (a) through (o).
(2) Determine the residual income for each division, assuming that the minimum rate of return established by management is 12%.
(3) Which division is the most profitable?

Pb. 27–51A.
Divisional performance analysis and evaluation.
OBJ. 5

The vice-president of operations of DeRoma Company is evaluating the performance of two divisions organized as investment centers. Division W generates the largest amount of operating income, but has the lowest rate of return on investment. Division S has the highest rate of return on investment, but generates the smallest operating income. Invested assets and condensed income statement data for the past year for each division are as follows:

	Division S	Division W
Sales	$18,750,000	$16,000,000
Cost of goods sold	14,000,000	12,000,000
Operating expenses	3,250,000	2,480,000
Invested assets	7,500,000	8,000,000

Instructions:

(1) Prepare condensed divisional income statements for each division for the year ended August 31.
(2) Using the expanded expression, determine the profit margin, investment turnover, and rate of return on investment for each division.
(3) If management desires a minimum rate of return of 16%, determine the residual income for each division.
(4) Discuss the evaluation of Divisions S and W, using the performance measures determined in (1), (2), and (3).

Pb. 27–52A.
Divisional performance analysis and evaluation.
OBJ. 5

The vice-president of operations of Swann Inc. recently resigned, and the president is considering which one of two division managers to promote to the vacated position. Both division managers have been with the company approximately ten years. Operating data for each division for the past three years are as follows:

	1993	1992	1991
Division A:			
Sales	$ 770,000	$ 650,000	$ 600,000
Cost of goods sold	462,000	390,000	360,000
Gross profit	$ 308,000	$ 260,000	$ 240,000
Operating expenses	200,200	175,500	163,200
Operating income	$ 107,800	$ 84,500	$ 76,800
Invested assets	$ 550,000	$ 500,000	$ 480,000
Total industry sales	$5,500,000	$5,200,000	$5,000,000
Division B:			
Sales	$ 966,000	$ 840,000	$ 750,000
Cost of goods sold	670,000	588,000	525,000
Gross profit	$ 296,000	$ 252,000	$ 225,000
Operating expenses	151,100	117,600	105,000
Operating income	$ 144,900	$ 134,400	$ 120,000
Invested assets	$ 700,000	$ 600,000	$ 500,000
Total industry sales	$6,440,000	$4,800,000	$3,750,000

Instructions:

(1) For each division for each of the three years, use the expanded expression to determine the profit margin, investment turnover, and rate of return on investment.
(2) Assuming that 15% has been established as a minimum rate of return, determine the residual income for each division for each of the three years.
(3) Determine each division's market share (division sales divided by total industry sales) for each of the three years.
(4) Based on (1), (2), and (3), which division manager would you recommend for promotion to vice-president of operations?
(5) What other factors should be considered in the promotion decision?

Pb. 27–53A.
Transfer pricing.
OBJ. 6

Grant Company is diversified, with two operating divisions, F and G. Condensed divisional income statements, which involve no intracompany transfers and which include a breakdown of expenses into variable and fixed components, are as follows:

Grant Company 27-1159
Divisional Income Statements
For Year Ended December 31, 19--

	Division F	Division G	Total
Sales:			
120,000 units × \$40 per unit........	\$4,800,000		\$4,800,000
40,000 units × \$50 per unit.........		\$2,000,000	2,000,000
			\$6,800,000
Expenses:			
Variable:			
120,000 units × \$24 per unit......	\$2,880,000		\$2,880,000
40,000 units × \$32* per unit......		\$1,280,000	1,280,000
Fixed............................	920,000	520,000	1,440,000
Total expenses..................	\$3,800,000	\$1,800,000	\$5,600,000
Operating income	\$1,000,000	\$ 200,000	\$1,200,000

*\$28 of the \$32 per unit represents materials costs, and the remaining \$4 per unit represents other expenses incurred within Division G.

Division F is operating at two thirds of its capacity of 180,000 units. Materials used in producing Division G's product are currently purchased from outside suppliers at a price of \$28 per unit. The materials used by Division G are produced by Division F. Except for the possible transfer of materials between divisions, no changes are expected in sales and expenses.

Instructions:

(1) Would the market price of \$28 per unit be an appropriate transfer price for Grant Company? Explain.
(2) If Division G purchases 40,000 units from Division F and a transfer price of \$26 per unit is negotiated between the managers of Divisions F and G, how much would the operating income of each division and total company operating income increase?
(3) Prepare condensed divisional income statements for Grant Company, based on the data in (2).
(4) If a transfer price of \$27 per unit had been negotiated, how much would the operating income of each division and total company income have increased?
(5) (a) What is the range of possible negotiated transfer prices that would be acceptable for Grant Company?
    (b) If the division managers of F and G cannot agree on a transfer price, what price would you suggest as the transfer price?

MINI-CASE 27

Your father is the president of Newman Company, a privately held, diversified company with five separate divisions organized as investment centers. A condensed income statement for the Carpet Division for the past year is as follows:

Newman Company—Carpet Division
Income Statement
For Year Ended December 31, 19--

Sales	$12,000,000
Cost of goods sold	7,800,000
Gross profit	$ 4,200,000
Operating expenses	2,520,000
Operating income	$ 1,680,000

The manager of the Carpet Division was recently presented with the opportunity to add an additional product line, which would require invested assets of $2,000,000. A projected income statement for the new product line is as follows:

New Product Line
Projected Income Statement
For Year Ended December 31, 19--

Sales	$ 2,500,000
Cost of goods sold	1,500,000
Gross profit	$ 1,000,000
Operating expenses	680,000
Operating income	$ 320,000

The Carpet Division currently has $8,000,000 in invested assets, and Newman Company's overall rate of return on investment, including all divisions, is 12%. Each division manager is evaluated on the basis of divisional rate of return on investment, and a bonus equal to $5,000 for each percentage point by which the division's rate of return on investment exceeds the company average is awarded each year.

Your father is concerned that the manager of the Carpet Division rejected the addition of the new product line, when all estimates indicated that the product line would be profitable and would increase overall company income. You have been asked to analyze the possible reasons why the Carpet Division manager rejected the new product line.

Instructions:

(1) Determine the rate of return on investment for the Carpet Division for the past year.
(2) Determine the Carpet Division manager's bonus for the past year.
(3) Determine the estimated rate of return on investment for the new product line.
(4) Why might the manager of the Carpet Division decide to reject the new product line?
(5) Can you suggest an alternative performance measure for motivating division managers to accept new investment opportunities that would increase the overall company income and rate of return on investment?

ANSWERS TO SELF-EXAMINATION QUESTIONS

1. B The manager of a profit center (answer B) has responsibility for and authority over costs and revenues. If the manager has responsibility and authority for only costs, the department is referred to as a cost center (answer A). If the responsibility and authority extend to the investment in assets as well as costs and revenues, it is referred to as an investment center (answer C).

2. C When the departmental margin approach to income reporting is employed, the direct departmental expenses for each department are deducted from the gross profit for each department to yield departmental margin for each department (answer C). The indirect expenses are deducted from the total departmental margin to yield income from operations (answer A). The final total income is identified as net income (answer B).
3. A The rate of return on investment for Division A is 20% (answer A), computed as follows:

$$\text{Rate of Return on Investment (ROI)} = \frac{\text{Operating Income}}{\text{Invested Assets}}$$

$$\text{ROI} = \frac{\$350{,}000 - \$200{,}000 - \$30{,}000}{\$600{,}000}$$

$$\text{ROI} = \frac{\$120{,}000}{\$600{,}000}$$

$$\text{ROI} = 20\%$$

4. B The profit margin for Division L of Liddy Co. is 15% (answer B), computed as follows:

$$\text{Rate of Return on Investment (ROI)} = \text{Profit Margin} \times \text{Investment Turnover}$$

$$24\% = \text{Profit Margin} \times 1.6$$

$$15\% = \text{Profit Margin}$$

5. C The market price approach (answer C) to transfer pricing uses the price at which the product or service transferred could be sold to outside buyers as the transfer price. The cost price approach (answer A) uses cost as the basis for setting transfer prices. The negotiated price approach (answer B) allows managers of decentralized units to agree (negotiate) among themselves as to the proper transfer price.

CHAPTER 28

CHAPTER OBJECTIVES

1 Describe basic financial statement analytical procedures.

2 Describe the focus of financial statement analyses.

3 Describe and illustrate the application of financial statement analysis in assessing solvency.

4 Describe and illustrate the application of financial statement analysis in assessing profitability.

5 Summarize and describe how analytical measures can be used in appraising the present performance of an enterprise and in forecasting its future.

6 Identify and illustrate the content of corporate annual reports.

7 Describe the content of interim financial reports.

FINANCIAL STATEMENT ANALYSIS & ANNUAL REPORTS

One of the primary objectives of accounting is to provide useful data to management for directing operations. In providing data to assist management, the accountant relies on a variety of concepts and techniques. Many of these concepts and techniques, such as budgeting, standard costs, differential analysis, break-even analysis, and variable costing, were discussed in preceding chapters. Also discussed were the basic financial statements which are used to assess the effectiveness of past management decisions in planning and controlling operations. In addition, management recognizes that the evaluation of past operations, as revealed by the analysis of the basic statements, represents a good starting point in planning future operations. Management uses financial statement analysis, therefore, as an important means of assessing past performance and in forecasting and planning future performance.

In this chapter, management's use of analyses of the data reported in the basic financial statements is presented. In addition, the annual reports and the interim reports that are issued by corporations are discussed. These reports often contain some financial analyses as well as much of the basic information used by outsiders in evaluating management's performance.

BASIC ANALYTICAL PROCEDURES

OBJECTIVE 1
Describe basic financial statement analytical procedures.

The analytical measures obtained from financial statements are usually expressed as ratios or percentages. For example, the relationship of $150,000 to $100,000 ($150,000/$100,000 or $150,000:$100,000) may be expressed as 1.5, 1.5:1, or 150%. This ease of computation and simplicity of form for expressing financial relationships are major reasons for the widespread use of ratios and percentages in financial analysis.

Analytical procedures may be used to compare the amount of specific items on a current statement with the corresponding amounts on earlier statements. For example, in comparing cash of $150,000 on the current balance sheet with cash of $100,000 on the balance sheet of a year earlier, the current amount may be expressed as 1.5 or 150% of the earlier amount. The relationship may also be expressed in terms of change, that is, the increase of $50,000 may be stated as a 50% increase.

Analytical procedures are also widely used to show the relationships of individual terms to each other and of individual items to totals on a single statement. To illustrate, assume that included in the total of $1,000,000 of assets on a balance sheet are cash of $50,000 and inventories of $250,000. In relative terms, the cash balance is 5% of total assets and the inventories represent 25% of total assets. Individual items in the current asset group could also be related to total current assets. Assuming that the total of current assets in the example is $500,000, cash represents 10% of the total and inventories represent 50% of the total.

Increases or decreases in items may be expressed in percentage terms only when the base figure is positive. If the base figure is zero or a negative value, the amount of change cannot be expressed as a percentage. For example, if comparative balance sheets indicate no liability for notes payable on the first, or base, date and a liability of $10,000 on the later date, the increase of $10,000 cannot be stated as a percent of zero. Similarly, if a net loss of $10,000 in a particular year is followed by a net income of $5,000 in the next year, the increase of $15,000 cannot be stated as a percent of the loss of the base year.

In the following discussion and illustrations of analytical procedures, the basic significance of the various measures will be emphasized. The measures developed are not ends in themselves; they are only guides to the evaluation of financial and operating data. Many other factors, such as trends in the industry, changes in price levels, and general economic conditions and prospects, may also need consideration in order to arrive at sound conclusions.

Horizontal Analysis

The percentage analysis of increases and decreases in corresponding items in comparative financial statements is called **horizontal analysis.** The amount of each item on the most recent statement is compared with the corresponding item on one or more earlier statements. The increase or decrease in the amount of the item is then listed, together with the percent of increase or decrease. When the comparison is made between two statements, the earlier statement is used as the base. If the analysis includes three or more statements, there are two alternatives in the selection of the base: the earliest date or period may be used as the basis for comparing all later dates or periods, or each statement may be compared with the immediately preceding statement. The two alternatives are illustrated as follows:

BASE: EARLIEST YEAR

				Increase (Decrease*)			
				1992–93		1992–94	
Item	1992	1993	1994	Amount	Percent	Amount	Percent
A	$100,000	$150,000	$200,000	$ 50,000	50%	$100,000	100%
B	100,000	200,000	150,000	100,000	100%	50,000	50%

BASE: PRECEDING YEAR

				Increase (Decrease*)			
				1992–93		1993–94	
Item	1992	1993	1994	Amount	Percent	Amount	Percent
A	$100,000	$150,000	$200,000	$ 50,000	50%	$50,000	33%
B	100,000	200,000	150,000	100,000	100%	50,000*	25%*

Comparison of the amounts in the last two columns of the first analysis with the amounts in the corresponding columns of the second analysis reveals the effect of the base year on the direction of change and the amount and percent of change.

A condensed comparative balance sheet for two years, with horizontal analysis, is illustrated as follows:

Comparative Balance Sheet—Horizontal Analysis

Marlea Company
Comparative Balance Sheet
December 31, 1992 and 1991

	1992	1991	Increase (Decrease*) Amount	Increase (Decrease*) Percent
Assets				
Current assets	$ 550,000	$ 533,000	$ 17,000	3.2%
Long-term investments	95,000	177,500	82,500*	46.5%*
Plant assets (net)	444,500	470,000	25,500*	5.4%*
Intangible assets	50,000	50,000	—	
Total assets	$1,139,500	$1,230,500	$ 91,000*	7.4%*
Liabilities				
Current liabilities	$ 210,000	$ 243,000	$ 33,000*	13.6%*
Long-term liabilities	100,000	200,000	100,000*	50.0%*
Total liabilities	$ 310,000	$ 443,000	$133,000*	30.0%*
Stockholders' Equity				
Preferred 6% stock, $100 par	$ 150,000	$ 150,000	—	—
Common stock, $10 par	500,000	500,000	—	—
Retained earnings	179,500	137,500	$ 42,000	30.5%
Total stockholders' equity	$ 829,500	$ 787,500	$ 42,000	5.3%
Total liabilities and stockholders' equity	$1,139,500	$1,230,500	$ 91,000*	7.4%*

The significance of the various increases and decreases in the items shown cannot be fully determined without additional information. Although total assets at the end of 1992 were $91,000 (7.4%) less than at the beginning of the year, liabilities were reduced by $133,000 (30%) and stockholders' equity increased $42,000 (5.3%). It would appear that the reduction of $100,000 in long-term liabilities was accomplished, for the most part, through the sale of long-term investments.

The foregoing balance sheet may be expanded to include the details of the various categories of assets and liabilities, or the details may be presented in separate schedules. Opinions differ as to which method presents the clearer picture. A supporting schedule with horizontal analysis is illustrated by the comparative schedule of current assets on page 166.

The reduction in accounts receivable may have come about through changes in credit terms or improved collection policies. Similarly, a reduction in inventories during a period of increased sales probably indicates an improvement in the management of inventories.

Comparative Schedule of Current Assets—Horizontal Analysis

Marlea Company
Comparative Schedule of Current Assets
December 31, 1992 and 1991

	1992	1991	Increase (Decrease*) Amount	Percent
Cash	$ 90,500	$ 64,700	$25,800	39.9%
Marketable securities	75,000	60,000	15,000	25.0%
Accounts receivable (net)	115,000	120,000	5,000*	4.2%*
Inventories	264,000	283,000	19,000*	6.7%*
Prepaid expenses	5,500	5,300	200	3.8%
Total current assets	$550,000	$533,000	$17,000	3.2%

The changes in the current assets would appear to be favorable, particularly in view of the 24.8% increase in net sales, shown below in the comparative income statement with horizontal analysis.

Comparative Income Statement—Horizontal Analysis

Marlea Company
Comparative Income Statement
For Years Ended December 31, 1992 and 1991

	1992	1991	Increase (Decrease*) Amount	Percent
Sales	$1,530,500	$1,234,000	$296,500	24.0%
Sales returns and allowances	32,500	34,000	1,500*	4.4%*
Net sales	$1,498,000	$1,200,000	$298,000	24.8%
Cost of goods sold	1,043,000	820,000	223,000	27.2%
Gross profit	$ 455,000	$ 380,000	$ 75,000	19.7%
Selling expenses	$ 191,000	$ 147,000	$ 44,000	29.9%
Administrative expenses	104,000	97,400	6,600	6.8%
Total operating expenses	$ 295,000	$ 244,400	$ 50,600	20.7%
Operating income	$ 160,000	$ 135,600	$ 24,400	18.0%
Other income	8,500	11,000	2,500*	22.7%*
	$ 168,500	$ 146,600	$ 21,900	14.9%
Other expense	6,000	12,000	6,000*	50.0%*
Income before income tax	$ 162,500	$ 134,600	$ 27,900	20.7%
Income tax	71,500	58,100	13,400	23.1%
Net income	$ 91,000	$ 76,500	$ 14,500	19.0%

An increase in net sales, considered alone, is not necessarily favorable. The increase in Marlea Company's net sales was accompanied by a somewhat greater percentage increase in the cost of goods (merchandise) sold, which indicates a narrowing of the gross profit margin. Selling expenses increased markedly and administrative expenses increases slightly, making an overall increase in operating expenses of 20.7%, as contrasted with a 19.7% increase in gross profit.

Although the increase in operating income and in the final net income figure is favorable, it would be incorrect for management to conclude that its operations were at maximum efficiency. A study of the expenses and additional analysis and comparisons of individual expense accounts should be made.

The income statement illustrated is in condensed form. Such a condensed statement usually provides enough information for all interested groups except management. If desired, the statement may be expanded or supplemental schedules may be prepared to present details of the cost of goods sold, selling expenses, administrative expenses, other income, and other expense.

A comparative retained earnings statement with horizontal analysis is illustrated as follows:

Comparative Retained Earnings Statement—Horizontal Analysis

Marlea Company
Comparative Retained Earnings Statement
For Years Ended December 31, 1992 and 1991

	1992	1991	Increase (Decrease*) Amount	Percent
Retained earnings,				
January 1	$137,500	$100,000	$37,500	37.5%
Net income for year	91,000	76,500	14,500	19.0%
Total	$228,500	$176,500	$52,000	29.5%
Dividends:				
On preferred stock	$ 9,000	$ 9,000	—	—
On common stock	40,000	30,000	$10,000	33.3%
Total	$ 49,000	$ 39,000	$10,000	25.6%
Retained earnings,				
December 31	$179,500	$137,500	$42,000	30.5%

Examination of the statement reveals an increase of 30.5% in retained earnings for the year. The increase was attributable to the retention of $42,000 of the net income for the year ($91,000 net income — $49,000 dividends paid).

Vertical Analysis

Percentage analysis may also be used to show the relationship of the component parts to the total in a single statement. This type of analysis is called **vertical analysis.** As in horizontal analysis, the statements may be prepared in either detailed or condensed form. In the latter case, additional details of the changes in the various categories may be presented in supporting schedules. If such schedules are prepared, the percentage analysis may be based on either the total of the schedule or the balance sheet total. Although vertical analysis is confined within each individual statement, the significance of both the amounts and the percentages is increased by preparing comparative statements.

In vertical analysis of the balance sheet, each asset item is stated as a percent of total assets, and each liability and stockholders' equity item is stated as a percent of total liabilities and stockholders' equity. A condensed comparative balance sheet with vertical analysis is illustrated at the top of page 1168.

The major relative changes in Marlea Company's assets were in the current asset and long-term investment groups. In the lower half of the balance sheet, the greatest relative change was in long-term liabilities and retained earnings. Stockholders' equity increased from 64% of total liabilities and stockholders' equity at the end of 1991 to 72.8% at the end of 1992, with a corresponding decrease in the claims of creditors.

Comparative Balance Sheet—Vertical Analysis

Marlea Company
Comparative Balance Sheet
December 31, 1992 and 1991

	1992		1991	
	Amount	Percent	Amount	Percent
Assets				
Current assets	$ 550,000	48.3%	$ 533,000	43.3%
Long-term investments	95,000	8.3	177,500	14.4
Plant assets (net)	444,500	39.0	470,000	38.2
Intangible assets	50,000	4.4	50,000	4.1
Total assets	$1,139,500	100.0%	$1,230,500	100.0%
Liabilities				
Current liabilities	$ 210,000	18.4%	$ 243,000	19.7%
Long-term liabilities	100,000	8.8	200,000	16.3
Total liabilities	$ 310,000	27.2%	$ 443,000	36.0%
Stockholders' Equity				
Preferred 6% stock, $100 par	$ 150,000	13.2%	$ 150,000	12.2%
Common stock, $10 par	500,000	43.9	500,000	40.6
Retained earnings	179,500	15.7	137,500	11.2
Total stockholders' equity	$ 829,500	72.8%	$ 787,500	64.0%
Total liabilities and stockholders' equity	$1,139,500	100.0%	$1,230,500	100.0%

In vertical analysis of the income statement, each item is stated as a percent of net sales. A condensed comparative income statement with vertical analysis is illustrated as follows:

Comparative Income Statement—Vertical Analysis

Marlea Company
Comparative Income Statement
For Years Ended December 31, 1992 and 1991

	1992		1991	
	Amount	Percent	Amount	Percent
Sales	$1,530,500	102.2%	$1,234,000	102.8%
Sales returns and allowances	32,500	2.2	34,000	2.8
Net sales	$1,498,000	100.0%	$1,200,000	100.0%
Cost of goods sold	1,043,000	69.6	820,000	68.3
Gross profit	$ 455,000	30.4%	$ 380,000	31.7%
Selling expenses	$ 191,000	12.8%	$ 147,000	12.3%
Administrative expenses	104,000	6.9	97,400	8.1
Total operating expenses	$ 295,000	19.7%	$ 244,400	20.4%
Operating income	$ 160,000	10.7%	$ 135,600	11.3%
Other income	8,500	.6	11,000	.9
	$ 168,500	11.3%	$ 146,600	12.2%
Other expense	6,000	.4	12,000	1.0
Income before income tax	$ 162,500	10.9%	$ 134,600	11.2%
Income tax	71,500	4.8	58,100	4.8
Net income	$ 91,000	6.1%	$ 76,500	6.4%

Care must be used in judging the significance of differences between percentages for the two years. For example, the decline of the gross profit rate from 31.7% in 1991 to 30.4% in 1992 is only 1.3 percentage points. In terms of dollars of potential gross profit, however, it represents a decline of approximately \$19,500 (1.3% × \$1,498,000).

Common-Size Statements

Horizontal and vertical analyses with both dollar and percentage figures are helpful in disclosing relationships and trends in financial condition and operations of individual enterprises. Vertical analysis with both dollar and percentage figures is also useful in comparing one company with another or with industry averages. Such comparisons may be made easier by the use of **common-size statements,** in which all items are expressed only in relative terms.

Common-size statements may be prepared in order to compare percentages of a current period with past periods, to compare individual businesses, or to compare one business with industry percentages published by trade associations and financial information services. A comparative common-size income statement for two enterprises is illustrated as follows:

Common-Size Income Statement

Marlea Company and Gram Corporation
Condensed Common-Size Income Statement
For Year Ended December 31, 1992

	Marlea Company	Gram Corporation
Sales	102.2%	102.3%
Sales returns and allowances	2.2	2.3
Net sales	100.0%	100.0%
Cost of goods sold	69.6	70.0
Gross profit	30.4%	30.0%
Selling expenses	12.8%	11.5%
Administrative expenses	6.9	4.1
Total operating expenses	19.7%	15.6%
Operating income	10.7%	14.4%
Other income	.6	.6
	11.3%	15.0%
Other expense	.4	.5
Income before income tax	10.9%	14.5%
Income tax	4.8	5.5
Net income	6.1%	9.0%

Examination of the statement reveals that although Marlea Company has a slightly higher rate of gross profit than Gram Corporation, the advantage is more than offset by its higher percentage of both selling and administrative expenses. As a consequence, the operating income of Marlea Company is 10.7% of net sales as compared with 14.4% for Gram Corporation, an unfavorable difference of 3.7 percentage points.

Other Analytical Measures

In addition to the percentage analyses previously discussed, there are a number of other relationships that may be expressed in ratios and percentages. The items used in the measures are taken from the financial statements of the current period and hence are a further development of vertical analysis. Comparison of the items with corresponding measures of earlier periods is an extension of horizontal analysis.

FOCUS OF FINANCIAL STATEMENT ANALYSES

OBJECTIVE 2
Describe the focus of financial statement analyses.

Certain aspects of financial condition or of operations are of greater importance to management than are other aspects. However, management is especially interested in the ability of a business to pay its debts as they come due and to earn a reasonable amount of income. These two aspects of the status of an enterprise are called factors of **solvency** and **profitability.** An enterprise that cannot meet its obligations to its creditors on a timely basis may experience difficulty in obtaining credit, which may lead to a decline in its profitability, and it may even be forced into bankruptcy. Similarly, an enterprise whose earnings are less than those of its competitors is likely to be at a disadvantage in obtaining credit or new capital from stockholders. In addition to this interrelationship between solvency and profitability, it is important to recognize that analyses of historical data are useful in assessing the past performance of an enterprise and in forecasting its future performance. Also, the results of financial analyses may be even more useful when they are compared with those of competing enterprises and with industry averages.

The various types of financial analyses useful in evaluating the solvency and profitability of an enterprise are discussed in the following paragraphs. The examples are based on the illustrative statements presented earlier. In a few instances, data from a company's statements of the preceding year and from other sources are also used.

SOLVENCY ANALYSIS

OBJECTIVE 3
Describe and illustrate the application of financial statement analysis in assessing solvency.

Solvency is the ability of a business to meet its financial obligations as they come due. Solvency analysis, therefore, focuses mainly on balance sheet relationships that indicate the ability to liquidate current and noncurrent liabilities. Major analyses used in assessing solvency include (1) current position analysis, (2) accounts receivable analysis, (3) inventory analysis, (4) the ratio of plant assets to long-term liabilities, (5) the ratio of stockholders' equity to liabilities, and (6) the number of times interest charges are earned.

Current Position Analysis

To be useful, ratios relating to a firm's solvency must show the firm's ability to liquidate its liabilities. The use of ratios showing the ability to liquidate current liabilities is called **current position analysis** and is of particular interest to short-term creditors.

Working Capital. The excess of the current assets of an enterprise over its current liabilities at a certain moment of time is called **working capital.** The amount of working capital is often used in evaluating a company's ability to meet currently maturing obligations. Although useful for making intraperiod comparisons for a company, these absolute amounts are difficult to use in comparing companies of different sizes or in comparing such amounts with industry figures. For example, working capital of $250,000 may be very adequate for a small building contractor specializing in residential construction, but it may be completely inadequate for a large building contractor specializing in industrial and commercial construction.

Current Ratio. Another means of expressing the relationship between current assets and current liabilities is through the **current ratio,** sometimes referred to as the **working capital ratio** or **bankers' ratio.** The ratio is computed by dividing the total of current assets by the total of current liabilities. The determination of working capital and the current ratio for Marlea Company is illustrated as follows:

	1992	1991
Current assets	$550,000	$533,000
Current liabilities	210,000	243,000
Working capital	$340,000	$290,000
Current ratio	2.6:1	2.2:1

The current ratio is a more dependable indication of solvency than is working capital. To illustrate, assume that as of December 31, 1992, the working capital of a competing corporation is much greater than $340,000, but its current ratio is only 1.3:1. Considering these factors alone, Marlea Company, with its current ratio of 2.6:1, is in a more favorable position to obtain short-term credit than the corporation with the greater amount of working capital.

Acid-Test Ratio. The amount of working capital and the current ratio are two solvency measures that indicate a company's ability to meet currently maturing obligations. However, these two measures do not take into account the composition of the current assets. To illustrate the significance of this additional factor, the current position data for Marlea Company and Wilson Corporation as of December 31, 1992, are as follows:

	Marlea Company	Wilson Corporation
Current assets:		
Cash	$90,500	$45,500
Marketable securities	75,000	25,000
Accounts receivable (net)	115,000	90,000
Inventories	264,000	380,000
Prepaid expenses	5,500	9,500
Total current assets	$550,000	$550,000
Current liabilities	210,000	210,000
Working capital	$340,000	$340,000
Current ratio	2.6:1	2.6:1

Both companies have working capital of $340,000 and a current ratio of 2.6:1. But the ability of each company to meet its currently maturing debts is vastly different. Wilson Corporation has more of its current assets in inventories, which must be sold and the receivables collected before the current liabilities can be paid in full. A considerable amount of time may be required to convert these inventories into cash. Declines in market prices and a reduction in demand could also impair the ability to pay current liabilities. Conversely, Marlea Company has enough cash and current assets (marketable securities and accounts receivable) which can generally be converted to cash rather quickly to meet its current liabilities.

A ratio that measures the "instant" debt-paying ability of a company is called the **acid-test ratio** or **quick ratio.** It is the ratio of the total **quick assets,** which are the cash, the marketable securities, and the receivables, to the total current liabilities. The acid-test ratio data for Marlea Company are as follows:

	1992	1991
Quick assets:		
Cash	$90,500	$64,700
Marketable securities	75,000	60,000
Accounts receivable (net)	115,000	120,000
Total	$280,500	$244,700
Current liabilities	$210,000	$243,000
Acid-test ratio	1.3:1	1.0:1

A thorough analysis of a firm's current position would include the determination of the amount of working capital, the current ratio, and the acid-test ratio. The current and acid-test ratios are most useful when viewed together and when compared with similar ratios for previous periods and with those of other firms in the industry.

Accounts Receivable Analysis

The size and composition of accounts receivable change continually during business operations. The amount is increased by sales on account and reduced by collections. Firms that grant long credit terms tend to have relatively greater amounts tied up in accounts receivable than those granting short credit terms. Increases or decreases in the volume of sales also affect the amount of outstanding accounts receivable.

Accounts receivable yield no revenue, hence it is desirable to keep the amount invested in them at a minimum. The cash made available by prompt collection of receivables improves solvency and may be used for purchases of merchandise in larger quantities at a lower price, for payment of dividends to stockholders, or for other purposes. Prompt collection also lessens the risk of loss from uncollectible accounts.

Accounts Receivable Turnover. The relationship between credit sales and accounts receivable may be stated as the **accounts receivable turnover.** It is computed by dividing net sales on account by the average net accounts receivable. It is preferable to base the average on monthly balances, which gives effect to seasonal changes. When such data are not available, it is necessary to use the average of the balances at the beginning and the end of the year. If there are trade notes receivable as well as accounts, the two should be combined. The accounts receivable turnover data for Marlea Company are as follows. All sales were made on account.

	1992	1991
Net sales on account	$1,498,000	$1,200,000
Accounts receivable (net):		
Beginning of year	$ 120,000	$ 140,000
End of year	115,000	120,000
Total	$ 235,000	$ 260,000
Average	$ 117,500	$ 130,000
Accounts receivable turnover	12.7	9.2

The increase in the accounts receivable turnover for 1992 indicates that there has been an acceleration in the collection of receivables, due perhaps to improvement in either the granting of credit or the collection practices used, or both.

Number of Days' Sales in Receivables. Another means of expressing the relationship between credit sales and accounts receivable is the **number of days' sales in receivables**. This measure is determined by dividing the net accounts receivable at the end of the year by the average daily sales on account (net sales on account divided by 365), illustrated as follows for Marlea Company:

	1992	1991
Accounts receivable (net), end of year	$ 115,000	$ 120,000
Net sales on account	$1,498,000	$1,200,000
Average daily sales on account	$ 4,104	$ 3,288
Number of days' sales in receivables	28.0	36.5

The number of days' sales in receivables gives a rough measure of the length of time the accounts receivable have been outstanding. A comparison of this measure with the credit terms, with figures for comparable firms in the same industry, and with figures of Marlea Company for prior years will help reveal the efficiency in collecting receivables and the trends in the management of credit.

Inventory Analysis

Although an enterprise must maintain sufficient inventory quantities to meet the demands of its operations, it is desirable to keep the amount invested in inventory to a minimum. Inventories in excess of the needs of business reduce solvency by tying up funds. Excess inventories may also cause increases in the amount of insurance, property taxes, storage, and other related expenses, further reducing funds that could be used to better advantage. There is also added risk of loss through price declines and deterioration or obsolescence of the inventory.

Inventory Turnover. The relationship between the volume of goods (merchandise) sold and inventory may be stated as the **inventory turnover**. It is computed by dividing the cost of goods sold by the average inventory. If monthly data are not available, it is necessary to use the average of the inventories at the beginning and the end of the year. The inventory turnover data for Marlea Company are as follows:

	1992	1991
Cost of goods sold	$1,043,000	$820,000
Inventories:		
Beginning of year	$283,000	$311,000
End of year	264,000	283,000
Total	$ 547,000	$594,000
Average	$ 273,500	$297,000
Inventory turnover	3.8	2.8

The improvement in the turnover resulted from an increase in the cost of goods sold, combined with a decrease in average inventory. The variation in types of inventories is too great to permit any broad generalizations as to what is a satisfactory turnover. For example, a firm selling food should have a much higher turnover than one selling furniture or jewelry, and the perishable foods department of a supermarket should have a higher turnover than the soaps and cleansers department. However, for each business or each department within a business, there is a reasonable turnover rate. A turnover below this rate means that the company or the department is incurring extra expenses such as those for administration and storage, is increasing its risk of loss because of obsolescence and adverse price changes, is incurring interest charges in excess of those considered necessary, and is failing to free funds for other uses.

Number of Days' Sales in Inventory. Another means of expressing the relationship between the cost of goods sold and inventory is the **number of days' sales in inventory.** This measure is determined by dividing the inventories at the end of the year by the average daily cost of goods sold (cost of goods sold divided by 365), illustrated as follows for Marlea Company:

	1992	1991
Inventories, end of year	$ 264,000	$283,000
Cost of goods sold	$1,043,000	$820,000
Average daily cost of goods sold	$ 2,858	$ 2,247
Number of days' sales in inventory	92.4	125.9

The number of days' sales in inventory gives a rough measure of the length of time it takes to acquire, sell, and then replace the average inventory. Although there was a substantial improvement in the second year, comparison of the measure with those of earlier years and of comparable firms is an essential element in judging the effectiveness of Marlea Company's inventory control.

As with many attempts to analyze financial data, it is possible to determine more than one measure to express the relationship between the cost of goods sold and inventory. Both the inventory turnover and number of days' sales in inventory are useful for evaluating the efficiency in the management of inventory. Whether both measures are used or whether one measure is preferred over the other is a matter for the individual analyst to decide.

Ratio of Plant Assets to Long-Term Liabilities

Long-term notes and bonds are often secured by mortgages on plant assets. *The* **ratio of total plant assets to long-term liabilities** *provides a solvency measure that shows the margin of safety of the noteholders or bondholders. It also gives an indication of the potential ability of the enterprise to borrow additional funds on a long-term basis.* The ratio of plant assets to long-term liabilities of Marlea Company is as follows:

	1992	1991
Plant assets (net)	$444,500	$470,000
Long-term liabilities	$100,000	$200,000
Ratio of plant assets to long-term liabilities	4.4:1	2.4:1

The marked increase in the ratio at the end of 1992 was mainly due to the liquidation of one half of Marlea Company's long-term liabilities. If the company should need to borrow additional funds on a long-term basis, it is in a stronger position to do so.

Ratio of Stockholders' Equity to Liabilities

Claims against the total assets of an enterprise are divided into two basic groups, those of the creditors and those of the owners. *The relationship between the total claims of the creditors and owners provides a solvency measure that indicates the margin of safety for the creditors and the ability of the enterprise to withstand adverse business conditions.* If the claims of the creditors are large in proportion to the equity of the stockholders, there are likely to be substantial charges for interest payments. If earnings decline to the point where the company is unable to meet its interest payments, control of the business may pass to the creditors.

The relationship between stockholder and creditor equity is shown in the vertical analysis of the balance sheet. For example, the balance sheet of Marlea Company presented on page 1168 indicates that on December 31, 1992, stockholders' equity represented 72.8% and liabilities represented 27.2% of the sum of the liabilities and stockholders' equity (100.0%). Instead of expressing each item as a percent of the total, the relationship may be expressed as a ratio of one to the other, as follows:

	1992	1991
Total stockholders' equity	$829,500	$787,500
Total liabilities	$310,000	$443,000
Ratio of stockholders' equity to liabilities	2.7:1	1.8:1

The balance sheet of Marlea Company shows that the major factor affecting the change in the ratio was the $100,000 reduction in long-term liabilities during 1992. The ratio at both dates shows a large margin of safety for the creditors.

Number of Times Interest Charges Earned

Some corporations, such as public utilities, have a high ratio of debt to stockholders' equity. In analyzing such corporations, it is customary to express *the solvency measure that shows the relative risk of the debtholders in terms of the* **number of times the interest charges are earned** during the year. The higher the ratio, the greater the assurance of continued interest payments in case of decreased earnings. *The measure also provides an indication of general financial strength,* which is of concern to stockholders and employees, as well as to creditors.

In the following data, the amount available to meet interest charges is not affected by taxes on income because interest is deductible in determining taxable income.

	1992	1991
Income before income tax	$ 900,000	$ 800,000
Add interest charges	300,000	250,000
Amount available to meet interest charges	$1,200,000	$1,050,000
Number of times interest charges earned	4	4.2

Analyses like the above can be applied to dividends on preferred stock. In such cases, net income would be divided by the amount of preferred dividends to yield the number of times preferred dividends were earned. This measure gives an indication of the relative assurance of continued dividend payments to preferred stockholders.

FINANCIAL ANALYSES FOR STOCK INVESTORS

In a faltering economy, stock investors look to financial analyses to assist them in avoiding losses in their portfolios. The type of analyses useful in such circumstances is addressed in the following excerpts from an article in *The Wall Street Journal*:

Baruch Lev, an accounting professor at the University of California at Berkeley, has tested several gauges that analysts typically use, to see which of them are best in measuring a company's earnings potential, and in predicting its stock performance.

The most important items on financial statements, he says, are trends in inventory, accounts receivable and order backlogs. . . .

In particular, investors should look at how companies' inventories of finished goods track their sales. If inventories are rising faster than sales, "It's a bad signal, because it shows the company is having difficulty selling its product, and suggests a hit to future earnings as a result of management's efforts to get rid of those inventories," he says.

For similar reasons, he says, it pays to watch accounts receivable, or IOUs from customers that have received goods but not yet paid for them. If these are rising faster than sales, not only can this signal trouble with sales but may show vulnerability to customer defaults.

Mr. Lev also advises comparing the percentage change in a company's order backlog to the percentage change in its sales. . . . If the order backlog is growing faster than sales, this is a good sign for investors, but if it is lagging, this spells trouble.

Companies aren't required to report their order backlogs, however. If a particular company doesn't do this, Mr. Lev says, check the trend in its gross operating margins compared with its sales trend. If margin growth lags behind sales growth, this can mean future earnings are on shaky footing; if margin growth is outpacing sales growth, this can be a sign of strength.

If long-term debt as a percentage of a company's equity is high, relative to other companies in the same industry or the market as a whole, this means the company doesn't have much of a buffer against lean times. . . . By contrast, a large cash position is a big plus, not only for safety but also because it indicates the company is in a position to take advantage of competitors' problems. . . .

Source: Barbara Donnelly, "Future Signposts Lie Behind Balance-Sheet Cosmetics." *The Wall Street Journal* (December 7, 1990), p. C-1.

PROFITABILITY ANALYSIS

OBJECTIVE 4
Describe and illustrate the application of financial statement analysis in assessing profitability.

Profitability is the ability of an entity to earn income. It can be assessed by computing various relevant measures, including (1) the ratio of net sales to assets, (2) the rate earned on total assets, (3) the rate earned on stockholders' equity, (4) the rate earned on common stockholders' equity, (5) earnings per share on common stock, (6) the price-earnings ratio, and (7) dividend yield.

Ratio of Net Sales to Assets

The **ratio of net sales to assets** *is a profitability measure that shows how effectively a firm utilizes its assets.* Assume that two competing enterprises have equal amounts of assets, but the amount of the sales of one is double the amount of the sales of the other. Obviously, the former is making better use of its assets. In computing the ratio, any long-term investments should be excluded from total assets because they are wholly unrelated to sales of goods or services. Assets used in determining the ratio may be the total at the end of the year, the average at the beginning and the end of the year, or the average of the monthly totals. The basic data and the ratio of net sales to assets for Marlea Company are as follows:

	1992	1991
Net sales	$1,498,000	$1,200,000
Total assets (excluding long-term investments):		
Beginning of year	$1,053,000	$1,010,000
End of year	1,044,500	1,053,000
Total	$2,097,500	$2,063,000
Average	$1,048,750	$1,031,500
Ratio of net sales to assets	1.4:1	1.2:1

The ratio improved to a minor degree in 1992, largely due to the increased sales volume. A comparison of the ratio with those of other enterprises in the same industry would be helpful in assessing Marlea Company's effectiveness in the utilization of assets.

Rate Earned on Total Assets

The **rate earned on total assets** *is a measure of the profitability of the assets, without regard to the equity of creditors and stockholders in the assets.* The rate is therefore not affected by differences in methods of financing an enterprise.

The rate earned on total assets is derived by adding interest expense to net income and dividing this sum by the average of total assets. By adding interest expense to net income, the profitability of the assets is determined without considering the means of financing the acquisition of the assets. The rate earned by Marlea Company on total assets is determined as follows:

	1992	1991
Net income	$ 91,000	$ 76,500
Plus interest expense	6,000	12,000
Total	$ 97,000	$ 88,500
Total assets:		
Beginning of year	$1,230,500	$1,187,500
End of year	1,139,500	1,230,500
Total	$2,370,000	$2,418,000
Average	$1,185,000	$1,209,000
Rate earned on total assets	8.2%	7.3%

The rate earned on total assets of Marlea Company for 1992 indicates an improvement over that for 1991. A comparison with other companies and with industry averages would also be useful in evaluating the effectiveness of management performance.

It is sometimes preferable to determine the rate of operating income (income before nonoperating income, nonoperating expense, extraordinary items, and income tax) to total assets. If nonoperating income is not considered, the investments yielding such income should be excluded from the assets. The use of income before income tax eliminates the effect of changes in the tax structure on the rate of earnings. When considering published data on rates earned on assets, the reader should note the exact nature of the measure.

Rate Earned on Stockholders' Equity

Another relative measure of profitability is obtained by dividing net income by the total stockholders' equity. In contrast to the rate earned on total assets, **the rate earned on stockholders' equity** *emphasizes the income yield in relationship to the amount invested by the stockholders.*

The amount of the total stockholders' equity throughout the year varies for several reasons—the issuance of additional stock, the retirement of a class of stock, the payment of dividends, and the gradual accrual of net income. If monthly figures are not available, the average of the stockholders' equity at the beginning and the end of the year is used, as in the following illustration:

	1992	1991
Net income	$ 91,000	$ 76,500
Stockholders' equity:		
Beginning of year	$ 787,500	$ 750,000
End of year	829,500	787,500
Total	$1,617,000	$1,537,500
Average	$ 808,500	$ 768,750
Rate earned on stockholders' equity	11.3%	10.0%

The rate earned by a thriving enterprise on the equity of its stockholders is usually higher than the rate earned on total assets. The reason for the difference is that the amount earned on assets acquired through the use of funds provided by creditors is more than the interest charges paid to creditors. This tendency of the rate on stockholders' equity to vary disproportionately from the rate on total assets is sometimes called **leverage.** Marlea Company's rate on stockholders' equity for 1992, 11.3%, compares favorably with the rate of 8.2% earned on total assets, as reported on the preceding page. The leverage factor of 3.1% (11.3% − 8.2%) for 1992 also compares favorably with the 2.7% (10.0% − 7.3%) differential for the preceding year. These leverage factors for Marlea Company are illustrated graphically in the following chart.

Chart of Rate Earned on Stockholders' Equity and Total Assets

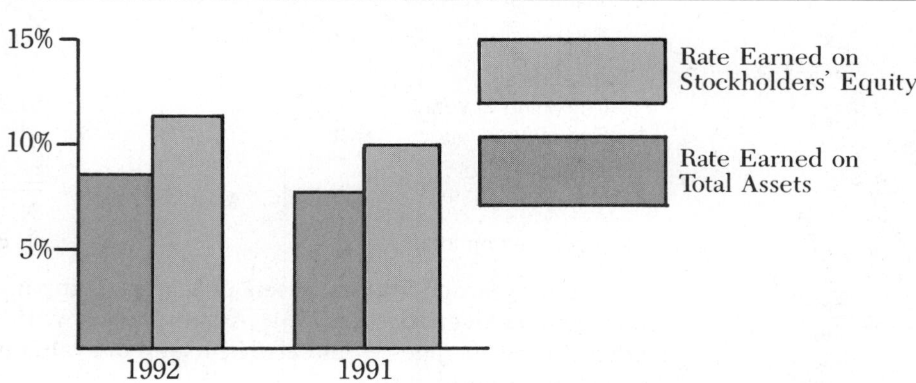

Rate Earned on Common Stockholders' Equity

When a corporation has both preferred and common stock outstanding, the holders of the common stock have the residual claim on earnings. The **rate earned on common stockholders' equity** is the net income less preferred dividend requirements for the period, stated as a percent of the average equity of the common stockholders.

Marlea Company has $150,000 of 6% nonparticipating preferred stock outstanding at both balance sheet dates, hence annual preferred dividends amount to $9,000. The common stockholders' equity is the total stockholders' equity, including retained earnings, reduced by the par of the preferred stock ($150,000). The basic data and the rate earned on common stockholders' equity are as follows:

	1992	1991
Net income	$ 91,000	$ 76,500
Preferred dividends	9,000	9,000
Remainder—identified with common stock	$ 82,000	$ 67,500
Common stockholders' equity:		
Beginning of year	$ 637,500	$ 600,000
End of year	679,500	637,500
Total	$1,317,000	$1,237,500
Average	$ 658,500	$ 618,750
Rate earned on common stockholders' equity	12.5%	10.9%

The rate earned on common stockholders' equity differs from the rates earned by Marlea Company on total assets and total stockholders' equity. This situation will occur if there are borrowed funds and if there is preferred stock outstanding, which rank ahead of the common shares in their claim on earnings. Thus the concept of leverage, as discussed in the preceding section, can be applied to the use of funds from the sale of preferred stock as well as from borrowing. Funds from both sources can be used in an attempt to increase the return on common stockholders' equity.

Earnings per Share on Common Stock

One of the profitability measures most commonly quoted by the financial press and included in the income statement in corporate annual reports is **earnings per share on common stock.** If a company has issued only one class of stock, the earnings per share are determined by dividing net income by the number of shares of stock outstanding. If there are both preferred and common stock outstanding, the net income must first be reduced by the amount necessary to meet the preferred dividend requirements.

Any changes in the number of shares outstanding during the year, such as would result from stock dividends or stock splits, should be disclosed in quoting earnings per share on common stock. Also, the income per share before any nonrecurring (extraordinary, etc.) items in the income statement, as discussed in Chapter 11, should be reported along with net income per share. In addition, if there are convertible bonds or convertible preferred stock outstanding, also discussed in Chapter 11, the amount reported as net income per share should be stated without considering the conversion privilege, followed by net income per share assuming conversion had occurred.

The data on the earnings per share of common stock for Marlea Company are as follows:

	1992	1991
Net income	$91,000	$76,500
Preferred dividends	9,000	9,000
Remainder—identified with common stock	$82,000	$67,500
Shares of common stock outstanding	50,000	50,000
Earnings per share on common stock	$1.64	$1.35

Since earnings form the primary basis for dividends, earnings per share and dividends per share on common stock are commonly used by investors in weighing the merits of alternative investment opportunities. Earnings per share data can be presented in conjunction with dividends per share data to indicate the relationship between earnings and dividends and the extent to which the corporation is retaining its earnings for use in the business. The following chart shows this relationship for Marlea Company:

Chart of Earnings and Dividends per Share of Common Stock

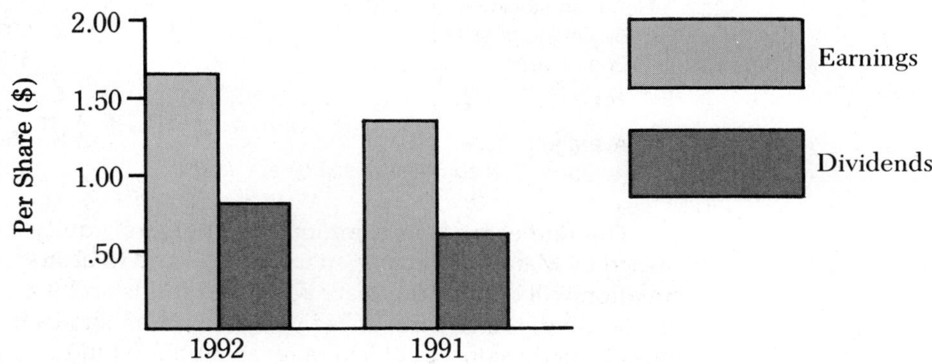

Price-Earnings Ratio

A profitability measure commonly quoted by the financial press is the **price-earnings (P/E) ratio** on common stock. *The price-earnings ratio is used as an indicator of a firm's future earnings prospects.* It is computed by dividing the market price per share of common stock at a specific date by the annual earnings per share. Assuming market prices per common share of 20 1/2 at the end of 1992 and 13 1/2 at the end of 1991, the price-earnings ratio on common stock of Marlea Company is as follows:

	1992	1991
Market price per share of common stock	$20.50	$13.50
Earnings per share on common stock	$ 1.64	$ 1.35
Price-earnings ratio on common stock	12.5	10.0

The price-earnings ratio indicates that a share of common stock of Marlea Company was selling for 12.5 and 10 times the amount of earnings per share at the end of 1992 and 1991 respectively.

Dividend Yield

The **dividend yield** on common stock is a profitability measure that shows the rate of return to common stockholders in terms of cash dividend distributions. It is of special interest to investors whose main investment objective is to receive a current return on the investment rather than an increase in the market price of the investment. The dividend yield is computed by dividing the annual dividends paid per share of common stock by the market price per share at a specific date. Assuming dividends of $.80 and $.60 per common share and market prices per common share of 20 1/2 and 13 1/2 at the end of 1992 and 1991 respectively, the dividend yield on common stock of Marlea Company is as follows:

	1992	1991
Dividends per share of common stock	$ .80	$ .60
Market price per share of common stock	$20.50	$13.50
Dividend yield on common stock	3.9%	4.4%

SUMMARY OF ANALYTICAL MEASURES

OBJECTIVE 5
Summarize and describe how analytical measures can be used in appraising the present performance of an enterprise and in forecasting its future.

The analytical measures that have been discussed and illustrated are representative of many that can be developed for a medium-size merchandising enterprise. Some of them might well be omitted in analyzing a specific firm, or additional measures could be developed. The type of business activity, the capital structure, and the size of the enterprise usually affect the measures used.

Percentage analyses, ratios, turnovers, and other measures of financial position and operating results are useful analytical devices. They are helpful in appraising the present performance of an enterprise and in forecasting its future. They are not, however, a substitute for sound judgment, nor do they provide definitive guides to action. In selecting and interpreting analytical indexes, proper consideration should be given to any conditions peculiar to the enterprise or to the industry of which the enterprise is a part. The possible influence of the general economic and business environment should also be weighed.

To determine trends, the interrelationship of the measures used in appraising a certain enterprise should be carefully studied, as should comparable indexes of earlier fiscal periods. Data from competing enterprises may also be compared in order to determine the relative efficiency of the firm being analyzed. In making such comparisons, however, it is essential to consider the potential effects of any significant differences in the accounting methods used by the enterprises.

The following presentation is a summary of the method of computation and use of the analytical measures discussed in this chapter:

	Method of Computation	Use
Solvency measures		
Working capital	Current assets − current liabilities	**To indicate the ability to meet currently maturing obligations**
Current ratio	$\frac{\text{Current assets}}{\text{Current liabilities}}$	
Acid-test ratio	$\frac{\text{Quick assets}}{\text{Current liabilities}}$	**To indicate instant debt-paying ability**
Accounts receivable turnover	$\frac{\text{Net sales on account}}{\text{Average accounts receivable}}$	**To assess the efficiency in collecting receivables and in the management of credit**
Number of days' sales in receivables	$\frac{\text{Accounts receivable, end of year}}{\text{Average daily sales on account}}$	

	Method of Computation	Use
Solvency measures		
Inventory turnover	$\frac{\text{Cost of goods sold}}{\text{Average inventory}}$	To assess the efficiency in the management of inventory
Number of days' sales in inventory	$\frac{\text{Inventory, end of year}}{\text{Average daily cost of goods sold}}$	
Ratio of plant assets to long-term liabilities	$\frac{\text{Plant assets (net)}}{\text{Long-term liabilities}}$	To indicate the margin of safety to long-term creditors
Ratio of stockholders' equity to liabilities	$\frac{\text{Total stockholders' equity}}{\text{Total liabilities}}$	To indicate the margin of safety to creditors
Number of times interest charges earned	$\frac{\text{Income before income tax} + \text{interest expense}}{\text{Interest expense}}$	To assess the risk to debtholders in terms of number of times interest charges were earned
Profitability measures		
Ratio of net sales to assets	$\frac{\text{Net sales}}{\text{Average total assets (excluding long-term investments)}}$	To assess the effectiveness in the use of assets
Rate earned on total assets	$\frac{\text{Net income} + \text{interest expense}}{\text{Average total assets}}$	To assess the profitability of the assets
Rate earned on stockholders' equity	$\frac{\text{Net income}}{\text{Average stockholders' equity}}$	To assess the profitability of the investment by stockholders
Rate earned on common stockholders' equity	$\frac{\text{Net income} - \text{preferred dividends}}{\text{Average common stockholders' equity}}$	To assess the profitability of the investment by common stockholders
Earnings per share on common stock	$\frac{\text{Net income} - \text{preferred dividends}}{\text{Shares of common stock outstanding}}$	
Dividends per share of common stock	$\frac{\text{Dividends}}{\text{Shares of common stock outstanding}}$	To indicate the extent to which earnings are being distributed to common stockholders
Price-earnings ratio	$\frac{\text{Market price per share of common stock}}{\text{Earnings per share on common stock}}$	To indicate future earnings prospects, based on the relationship between market value of common stock and earnings
Dividend yield	$\frac{\text{Dividends per common share}}{\text{Market price per common share}}$	To indicate the rate of return to common stockholders in terms of dividends

PERCEPTIONS OF FINANCIAL RATIOS

Financial statements serve as the primary financial reporting mechanism of an entity, both internally and externally. An analysis of the financial information communicated by these statements should include the computation and interpretation of financial ratios.

A survey of the views of financial executives on important issues relating to financial ratios indicated that financial ratios are an important tool in analyzing the financial results of a company and in managing a company. In addition, 93 of the 100 respondents to the survey indicated that their firms use financial ratios as part of their corporate objectives. The ratios most significant to the respondents are those that measure the ability of the firm to earn a profit.

Source: Charles H. Gibson, "How Industry Perceives Financial Ratios," *Management Accounting* (April, 1982), pp. 13–19.

Financial ratios are often more useful when they are compared with similar ratios of other companies or groups of companies. For this purpose, average ratios for many industries are compiled by various financial services and trade associations. In this process, however, it should be remembered that averages are just that—averages—and care should be taken in their use. The danger in interpreting averages was graphically illustrated by Eldon Grimm, a Wall Street analyst who said: "A statistician is an individual who has his head in the refrigerator, his feet in the oven and on the average feels comfortable."

Source: "Twenty-Five Years Ago in *Forbes*" *Forbes* (August 16, 1982), p. 107.

CORPORATE ANNUAL REPORTS

OBJECTIVE 6
Identify and illustrate the content of corporate annual reports.

Corporations ordinarily issue to their stockholders and other interested parties annual reports summarizing activities of the past year and any significant plans for the future. Although there are many differences in the form and sequence of the major sections of annual reports, one section is always devoted to the financial statements, including the accompanying notes. In addition, annual reports usually include (a) selected data referred to as financial highlights, (b) a letter from the president of the corporation, which is sometimes also signed by the chairperson of the board of directors, (c) the independent auditors' report, (d) the management report, and (e) a five- or ten-year historical summary of financial data. As a way to strengthen the relationship with stockholders, many corporations also include pictures of their products and officers or other materials. The following subsections describe the portions of annual reports commonly related to financial matters, with the exception of the principal financial statements, examples of which appear in Appendix H.

Financial Highlights

This section, sometimes called *Results in Brief*, typically summarizes the major financial results for the last year or two. It is usually presented on the first one or two pages of the annual report. Such items as sales, income before income taxes, net income, net income per common share, cash dividends, cash dividends per common share, and the amount of capital expenditures are typically presented. An example of a financial highlights section from a corporation's annual report is on page 1184.

There are many variations in format and content of the financial highlights section of the annual report. In addition to the selected income statement data, information about the financial position at year end, such as the amount of working capital, total assets, long-term debt, and stockholders' equity, is often provided. Other year-end data often reported are the number of common and preferred shares outstanding, number of common and preferred stockholders, and number of employees.

Financial Highlights Section

FINANCIAL HIGHLIGHTS
(Dollars in thousands except per share amounts)

For the Year	Current Year	Preceding Year
Sales	$1,336,750	$ 876,400
Income before income tax	149,550	90,770
Net income	105,120	66,190
Per common share	4.03	2.62
Dividends declared on common stock	34,990	33,150
Per common share	1.48	1.40
Capital expenditures and investments	265,120	157,050
At Year-End		
Working capital	$ 415,410	$ 423,780
Total assets	1,712,170	1,457,240
Long-term debt	440,680	457,350
Stockholders' equity	840,350	692,950

President's Letter

A letter by the president to the stockholders, discussing such items as reasons for an increase or decrease in net income, changes in existing plant or purchase or construction of new plants, significant new financing commitments, attention given to social responsibility issues, and future prospects, is also found in most annual reports. A condensed version of a president's letter adapted from a corporation's annual report is on page 1185.

During recent years, corporate enterprises have become increasingly active in accepting environmental and other social responsibilities. In addition to the brief discussion that may be contained in the president's letter, a more detailed analysis of the company's social concerns may be included elsewhere in the annual report. Knowledgeable investors recognize that the failure of a business enterprise to meet acceptable social norms can have long-run unfavorable implications. In the near future, an important function of accounting may be to assist management in developing a statement covering the social responsibilities of corporate enterprises and what management is doing about them.

Independent Auditors' Report

Before issuing annual statements, all publicly held corporations, as well as many other corporations, engage independent public accountants, usually CPAs, to conduct an *examination* of the financial statements. Such an examination is for the purpose of adding credibility to the statements that have been prepared by management. Upon completion of the examination, which for large corporations may engage many accountants for several weeks or longer, an **independent auditors' report** is prepared. This report accompanies the financial statements. A typical report includes three paragraphs: (1) an introductory paragraph identifying the financial statements being audited, (2) a

President's Letter Section

To the Stockholders:

FISCAL YEAR REVIEWED

The record net income in this fiscal year resulted from very strong product demand experienced for about two thirds of the fiscal year, more complete utilization of plants, and a continued improvement in sales mix. Income was strong both domestically and internationally during this period.

PLANT EXPANSION CONTINUES

Capital expenditures during the year were $14.5 million. Expansions were in progress or completed at all locations. Portions of the Company's major new expansion at one of its West Coast plants came on stream in March of this year and will provide much needed capacity in existing and new product areas. Capital expenditures will be somewhat less during next year.

ENVIRONMENTAL CONCERN

The Company recognizes its responsibility to provide a safe and healthy environment at each of its plants. The Company expects to spend approximately $1 million in the forthcoming year to help continue its position as a constructive corporate citizen.

OUTLOOK

During the past 10 years the Company's net income and sales have more than tripled. Net income increased from $3.1 million to $10.7 million, and sales from $45 million to $181 million.

The Company's employees are proud of this record and are determined to carry the momentum into the future. The current economic slowdown makes results for the new fiscal year difficult to predict. However, we are confident and enthusiastic about the Company's prospects for continued growth over the longer term.

Respectfully submitted,

Frances B. Davis

Frances B. Davis
President

March 24, 1992

"scope" paragraph describing the nature of the audit, and (3) an "opinion" paragraph presenting the auditor's opinion as to the fairness of the statements.[1] The wording of the report on page 1186 for J.C. Penney Company, Inc. conforms with general usage.

In most instances, the auditors can render a report such as the one illustrated, which may be said to be "unqualified." However, it is possible that accounting methods used by a client do not conform with generally accepted accounting principles. In such cases, a "qualified" opinion must be rendered and the exception briefly described. If the effect of the departure from accepted principles is sufficiently material, an "adverse" or negative opinion

---

[1] *Statements on Auditing Standards No. 58*, "Reports on Audited Financial Statements," (New York: American Institute of Certified Public Accountants, 1988), par. 8.

Independent Auditors' Report Section

Independent Auditors' Report

To the Stockholders and Board of Directors
of J.C. Penney Company, Inc.:

We have audited the accompanying consolidated balance sheets of J.C. Penney Company, Inc. and Subsidiaries as of January 26, 1991, January 27, 1990, and January 28, 1989, and the related consolidated statements of income, reinvested earnings, and cash flows, appearing on pages 19 through 21 and pages 25 through 36, for the years then ended. These consolidated financial statements are the responsibility of the Company's management. Our responsibility is to express an opinion on these consolidated financial statements based on our audits.

We conducted our audits in accordance with generally accepted auditing standards. Those standards require that we plan and perform the audit to obtain reasonable assurance about whether the financial statements are free of material misstatement. An audit includes examining, on a test basis, evidence supporting the amounts and disclosures in the financial statements. An audit also includes assessing the accounting principles used and significant estimates made by management, as well as evaluating the overall financial statement presentation. We believe that our audits provide a reasonable basis for our opinion.

In our opinion, the consolidated financial statements referred to above present fairly, in all material respects, the financial position of J.C. Penney Company, Inc. and Subsidiaries as of January 26, 1991, January 27, 1990, and January 28, 1989, and the results of their operations and their cash flows for the years then ended in conformity with generally accepted accounting principles.

KPMG Peat Marwick

KPMG Peat Marwick
1601 Elm Street, Dallas, Texas 75201
February 28, 1991

must be issued and the exception described. In rare circumstances, the auditors may be unable to perform sufficient auditing procedures to enable them to reach a conclusion as to the fairness of the financial statements. In such circumstances, the auditors must issue a "disclaimer" and briefly describe the reasons for their failure to be able to reach a decision as to the fairness of the statements.

Professional accountants cannot disregard their responsibility in attesting to the fairness of financial statements without seriously jeopardizing their reputations. This responsibility is described as follows:

> *The report shall either contain an expression of opinion regarding the financial statements, taken as a whole, or an assertion to the effect that an opinion cannot be expressed. When an overall opinion cannot be expressed, the reasons therefor should be stated. In all cases where an auditor's name is associated with financial statements, the report should contain a clear-cut indication of the character of the auditor's examination, if any, and the degree of responsibility he is taking.*[2]

---

[2] *Ibid.*, par. 4.

Management Report

Responsibility for the accounting system and the resultant financial statements rests mainly with the principal officers of a corporation. In the **management report,** the chief financial officer or other representative of management (1) states that the financial statements are management's responsibility and that they have been prepared according to generally accepted accounting principles, (2) presents management's assessment of the company's internal accounting control system, and (3) comments on any other pertinent matters related to the accounting system, the financial statements, and the examination by the independent auditor.

Although the concept of a management report is relatively new, an increasing number of corporations are including such a report in the annual report. An example of such a report taken from the 1990 annual report for Sears, Roebuck and Co. is shown below.

Management Report Section

The financial statements, including the financial analysis and all other information in this annual report, were prepared by management which is responsible for their integrity and objectivity. Management believes the financial statements, which require the use of certain estimates and judgments, fairly and accurately reflect the company's financial position and operating results, in accordance with generally accepted accounting principles. All financial information in this annual report is consistent with the financial statements.

Management maintains a system of internal controls which it believes provides reasonable assurance that, in all material respects, assets are maintained and accounted for in accordance with management's authorizations and transactions are recorded accurately in the books and records. The concept of reasonable assurance is based on the premise that the cost of internal controls should not exceed the benefits derived. To assure the effectiveness of the internal control system, the organizational structure provides for defined lines of responsibility and delegation of authority. The company's formally stated and communicated policies demand of employees high ethical standards in their conduct of its business. These policies address, among other things, potential conflicts of interest; compliance with all domestic and foreign laws, including those related to financial disclosure; and the confidentiality of proprietary information. As a further enhancement of the above, the company's comprehensive internal audit program is designed for continual evaluation of the adequacy and effectiveness of its internal controls and measures adherence to established policies and procedures.

Deloitte & Touche, independent certified public accountants, have audited the financial statements of the company and their report is presented below. Their audit also includes a study and evaluation of the company's control environment, accounting systems and control procedures. The independent accountants and internal auditors advise management of the results of their reviews, and make recommendations to improve the system of internal controls. Management evaluates the audit recommendations and takes appropriate action.

The Audit Committee of the Board of Directors is comprised entirely of directors who are not employees of the company. The committee reviews audit plans, internal controls, financial reports and related matters and meets regularly with the company's management, internal auditors and independent accountants. The independent accountants and the internal auditors advise the committee of any significant matters resulting from their audits of our financial statements and internal controls and have free access to the committee without management being present.

Edward A. Brennan
Chairman, President
and Chief Executive Officer

James M. Denny
Senior Vice President and
Chief Financial Officer

John S. Vivian
Vice President and
Corporate Comptroller

Historical Summary

This section, for which there are many variations in title, reports selected financial and operating data of past periods, usually for five or ten years. It is usually presented in close proximity to the financial statements for the current year, and the types of data reported are varied. An example of a portion of such a report is shown below.

Historical Summary Section

Five-Year Consolidated Financial and Statistical Summary
For Years Ended December 31
(Dollar amounts in millions except for per share data)

For the Year	1992	1991	1988
Net sales	$1,759.7	$1,550.1	$997.4
Gross profit	453.5	402.8	270.8
Percent to net sales	25.8%	26.0%	27.2%
Interest expense	33.9	21.3	15.0
Income before income tax	172.7	163.4	87.5
Income tax	82.8	77.8	40.2
Net income	89.9	85.6	47.3
Percent to net sales	5.1%	5.5%	4.7%
Per common share:			
Net income	5.19	4.84	2.54
Dividends	1.80	1.65	1.40
Return on stockholders' equity	15.9%	16.4%	11.2%
Common share market price:			
High	31	41½	40⅝
Low	18	22⅜	22¼
Depreciation and amortization	43.3	41.0	23.6
Capital expenditures	98.5	72.1	55.5
At Year End			
Working capital	$ 443.9	$ 434.8	$ 254.6
Plant assets—gross	704.7	620.3	453.7
Plant assets—net	420.0	362.7	263.4
Stockholders' equity	594.3	536.9	447.6
Stockholders' equity per common share	33.07	29.69	23.02
Number of holders of common shares	39,503	39,275	43,852
Number of employees	50,225	50,134	42,826

Segment of a Business

Many companies diversify their operations; that is, they are involved in more than one type of business activity. These companies may also operate in foreign markets. The individual segments of such diversified companies ordinarily experience differing rates of profitability, degrees of risk, and opportunities for growth. To help financial statement users in assessing past performance and future potential of diversified companies, financial statements should disclose such information as the enterprise's operations in different industries, its foreign markets, and its major customers. The required information for each significant reporting segment includes the following: revenue, income from operations, and identifiable assets associated with the segment.[3] An example of financial reporting for segments of a business is illustrated by the following note adapted from the 1990 financial statements of IBM Corporation.

Revenue by Industry Segments and Classes of Similar Products or Services

	Consolidated		
	1990	1989†	1988
(Dollars in millions)			
Information technology:			
Processors*	$16,433	$16,236	$15,077
Workstations:			
Personal systems*	9,644	8,409	6,934
Other workstations	4,312	4,169	4,550
Peripherals	13,190	11,458	11,280
Software	9,952	8,424	7,927
Maintenance services	7,768	7,070	7,347
Other	5,791	4,938	4,470
	67,090	60,704	57,585
Federal systems	1,928	2,006	2,065
Other business	—	—	31
Total	$69,018	$62,710	$59,681

†Reclassified to conform with 1990 presentation.
*Excludes peripheral functions not embedded, software and maintenance.

Supplemental Data on the Effects of Price-Level Changes

Financial statements are expressed in terms of money. Because money changes in value as prices change, changing price levels will affect financial reporting. The means of disclosing the effects of these changing prices on financial reporting have been the subject of much experimentation by the accounting profession. Currently there are two widely discussed possibilities for supplementing conventional statements and thus resolving financial reporting problems created by changing price levels: (1) supplemental financial data based on current costs, and (2) supplemental financial data based on constant dollars. The discussion in the following sections is confined to the basic concepts and problems of these recommendations.

Current Cost Data. Current cost is the amount of cash that would have to be paid currently to acquire assets of the same age and in the same condition as existing assets. When current costs are used as the basis for financial reporting, assets, liabilities, and owner's equity are stated at current values, and expenses are stated at the current cost of doing business. The use of current costs permits the identification of gains and losses that result from holding assets during periods of changes in price levels. To illustrate, assume that a firm acquired land at the beginning of the fiscal year for $50,000 and that at the end of the year its current cost (value) is $60,000. The land could be reported at its current cost of $60,000, and the $10,000 increase in value could be reported as an unrealized gain from holding the land.

[3] *Statement of Financial Accounting Standards, No. 14,* "Financial Reporting for Segments of a Business Enterprise" (Stamford: Financial Accounting Standards Board, 1976). Nonpublic corporations are exempted from this requirement by *Statement of Financial Accounting Standards, No. 21,* "Suspension of the Reporting of Earnings per Share and Segment Information by Nonpublic Enterprises" (Stamford: Financial Accounting Standards Board, 1978).

The major disadvantage in the use of current costs is the absence of established standards and procedures for determining such costs. However, many accountants believe that adequate standards and procedures will evolve through experimentation with actual applications.

Constant Dollar Data. Constant dollar data, also known as general price-level data, are historical costs that have been converted to constant dollars through the use of a price-level index. In this manner, financial statement elements are reported in dollars, each of which has the same (that is, constant) general purchasing power.

A **price-level index** is the ratio of the total cost of a group of commodities prevailing at a particular time to the total cost of the same group of commodities at an earlier base time. The total cost of the commodities at the base time is assigned a value of 100 and the price-level indexes for all later times are expressed as a ratio to 100. For example, assume that the cost of a selected group of commodities amounted to $12,000 at a particular time and $13,200 today. The price index for the earlier, or base, time becomes 100 and the current price index is 110 [(13,200 ÷ 12,000) × 100].

A general price-level index may be used to determine the effect of changes in price levels on certain financial statement items. To illustrate, assume a price index of 120 at the time of purchase of a plot of land for $10,000 and a current price index of 150. The **constant dollar equivalent** of the original cost of $10,000 may be computed as follows:

$$\frac{\text{Current Price Index}}{\text{Price Index at Date of Purchase}} \times \text{Original Cost} = \text{Constant Dollar Equivalent}$$

$$\frac{150}{120} \times \$10{,}000 = \$12{,}500$$

Current Annual Reporting Requirements for Price-Level Changes. In 1979, the Financial Accounting Standards Board undertook an experimental program for reporting the effects of changing prices by requiring approximately 1,300 large, publicly held enterprises to disclose certain current cost information and constant dollar information annually as supplemental data. In 1984, after reviewing the experiences with these 1979 disclosure requirements, the FASB concluded that current cost information was more useful than constant dollar information as a supplement to the basic financial statements. In 1986, the FASB eliminated the requirement to disclose the effects of changing prices, but encouraged companies to disclose such information voluntarily.[4]

Other Information

The preceding paragraphs described the most commonly presented sections of annual reports related to financial matters. Some annual reports may include other financial information, such as forecasts which indicate financial plans and expectations for the year ahead.

---

[4] *Statement of Financial Accounting Standards, No. 89,* "Financial Reporting and Changing Prices" (Stamford: Financial Accounting Standards Board, 1986).

INTERIM FINANCIAL REPORTS

OBJECTIVE 7
Describe the content of interim financial reports.

Corporate enterprises customarily issue interim financial reports to their stockholders. Corporations that are listed on a stock exchange or file reports with the Securities and Exchange Commission or other regulatory agencies are required to submit interim reports, usually on a quarterly basis. Such reports often have a significant influence on the valuation of a corporation's equity securities on stock exchanges.

Interim reports of an enterprise should disclose such information as gross revenue, costs and expenses, provision for income taxes, extraordinary or infrequently occurring items, net income, earnings per share, contingent items, and cash flow.[5] The particular accounting principles used on an annual basis, such as depreciation methods and inventory cost flow assumptions, are usually followed in preparing interim statements. However, if changes in accounting principles occur before the end of a fiscal year, there are detailed guidelines for their disclosure.[6]

Much of the value of interim financial reports to the investing public is based on their timeliness. Lengthy delays between the end of a quarter and the issuance of reports would usually reduce their value greatly. This is one of the reasons that interim reports are usually not audited by independent CPAs. In some cases, the interim reports are subjected to a "limited review" by the CPA and a report on this limited review is issued.

CHAPTER REVIEW

KEY POINTS

OBJECTIVE 1

Basic Analytical Procedures

The analytical measures obtained from financial statements are usually expressed as ratios or percentages. The basic measures developed through the use of analytical procedures are not ends in themselves. They are only guides to the evaluation of financial and operating data. Many other factors, such as trends in the industry, changes in price levels, and general economic conditions and prospects, may also need consideration in order to arrive at sound conclusions.

The percentage analysis of increases and decreases in corresponding items in comparative financial statements is called horizontal analysis. Percentage analysis may also be used to show the relationship of the component parts to the total in a single statement. This type of analysis is called vertical analysis. Although vertical analysis is confined within each individual statement, the significance of both the amounts and the percentages is increased by preparing comparative statements. Vertical analysis with both dollar and percentage figures is also useful in comparing one company with another or with industry averages. Such comparisons may be made easier by the use of common-size statements, in which all items are expressed only in relative terms.

[5] *Opinions of the Accounting Principles Board, No. 28,* "Interim Financial Reporting" (New York: American Institute of Certified Public Accountants, 1973).

[6] *Statement of Financial Accounting Standards, No. 3,* "Reporting Accounting Changes in Interim Financial Statements" (Stamford: Financial Accounting Standards Board, 1974).

OBJECTIVE 2

Focus of Financial Statement Analyses

Users of financial statements are especially interested in solvency and profitability. Analyses of historical data in financial statements are useful in assessing the past performance of an enterprise and in forecasting its future performance, especially when the results of the analyses are compared with those of competing enterprises and with industry averages.

OBJECTIVE 3

Solvency Analysis

Solvency is the ability of a business to meet its financial obligations as they come due. Solvency analysis, therefore, focuses mainly on balance sheet relationships that indicate the ability to liquidate liabilities. Major analyses used in assessing solvency include (1) current position analysis, (2) accounts receivable analysis, (3) inventory analysis, (4) the ratio of plant assets to long-term liabilities, (5) the ratio of stockholders' equity to liabilities, and (6) the number of times interest charges are earned.

Current position analysis includes the assessment of working capital, the current ratio, and the acid-test ratio. Accounts receivable analysis includes the assessment of accounts receivable turnover and number of days' sales in receivables. Inventory analysis includes the assessment of inventory turnover and number of days' sales in inventory. The ratio of plant assets to long-term liabilities shows the margin of safety for the creditors. The ratio of stockholders' equity to liabilities indicates the margin of safety for the creditors and the ability of the enterprise to withstand adverse business conditions. The number of times interest charges are earned indicates the relative risk of the debtholders continuing to receive interest payments.

OBJECTIVE 4

Profitability Analysis

Profitability is the ability of an entity to earn income. It can be assessed by computing various relevant measures, including (1) the ratio of net sales to assets, (2) the rate earned on total assets, (3) the rate earned on stockholders' equity, (4) the rate earned on common stockholders' equity, (5) earnings per share on common stock, (6) the price-earnings ratio, and (7) dividend yield.

OBJECTIVE 5

Summary of Analytical Measures

The type of business activity, the capital structure, and the size of the enterprise usually affect the measures used in financial statement analysis. These analytical measures, however, are not a substitute for sound judgment, nor do they provide definitive guides to action. In selecting and interpreting analytical indexes, proper consideration should be given to any conditions peculiar to the enterprise or to the industry of which the enterprise is a part.

OBJECTIVE 6

Corporate Annual Reports

Corporations ordinarily issue to their stockholders and other interested parties annual reports summarizing activities of the past year and any significant plans for the future. These reports normally include the financial highlights section, the president's letter, the independent auditors' report, the management report, and a historical summary of operations. Reporting of segments and supplementary data on the effects of price-level changes may also be included.

OBJECTIVE 7

Interim Financial Reports

Corporations customarily issue interim financial reports to their stockholders. Interim reports disclose such information as gross revenue, expenses, net income, and cash flows, following the accounting principles that are used on an annual basis.

KEY TERMS

horizontal analysis 1164
vertical analysis 1167
common-size statements 1169
solvency 1170
working capital 1170
current ratio 1171
acid-test ratio 1172
quick assets 1172
accounts receivable turnover 1172
number of days' sales in receivables 1173
inventory turnover 1173
number of days' sales in inventory 1174
profitability 1176
rate earned on total assets 1177
rate earned on stockholders' equity 1177
leverage 1178
rate earned on common stockholders' equity 1178
earnings per share on common stock 1179
price-earnings (P/E) ratio 1180
current cost 1189
constant dollar 1190
price-level index 1190

SELF-EXAMINATION QUESTIONS

Answers at end of chapter.

1. What type of analysis is indicated by the following?

	Amount	Percent
Current assets	$100,000	20%
Plant assets	400,000	80
Total assets	$500,000	100%

A. Vertical analysis
B. Horizontal analysis
C. Current position analysis
D. None of the above

2. Which of the following measures is useful as an indication of the ability of a firm to liquidate current liabilities?
A. Working capital
B. Current ratio
C. Acid-test ratio
D. All of the above

3. The ratio determined by dividing total current assets by total current liabilities is:
A. current ratio
B. working capital ratio
C. bankers' ratio
D. all of the above

4. The ratio of the quick assets to current liabilities, which indicates the "instant" debt-paying ability of a firm, is:
A. current ratio
B. working capital ratio
C. acid-test ratio
D. none of the above

5. A measure useful in evaluating the efficiency in the management of inventories is:
A. inventory turnover
B. number of days' sales in inventory
C. both A and B
D. none of the above

ILLUSTRATIVE PROBLEM

Fleming Inc.'s comparative financial statements for the years ending December 31, 1992 and 1991, are as follows. The market price of Fleming Inc.'s common stock was $30 on December 31, 1991, and $25 on December 31, 1992.

28-
1194

Fleming Inc.
Comparative Income Statement
For Years Ended December 31, 1992 and 1991

	1992	1991
Sales (all on account)	$5,125,000	$3,257,600
Sales returns and allowances	125,000	57,600
Net sales	$5,000,000	$3,200,000
Cost of goods sold	3,400,000	2,080,000
Gross profit	$1,600,000	$1,120,000
Selling expenses	$ 650,000	$ 464,000
Administrative expenses	325,000	224,000
Total operating expenses	$ 975,000	$ 688,000
Operating income	$ 625,000	$ 432,000
Other income	25,000	19,200
	$ 650,000	$ 451,200
Other expense (interest)	105,000	64,000
Income before income tax	$ 545,000	$ 387,200
Income tax	300,000	176,000
Net income	$ 245,000	$ 211,200

Fleming Inc.
Comparative Retained Earnings Statement
For Years Ended December 31, 1992 and 1991

	1992	1991
Retained earnings, January 1	$ 723,000	$ 581,800
Add net income for year	245,000	211,200
Total	$ 968,000	$ 793,000
Deduct dividends:		
On preferred stock	$ 40,000	$ 40,000
On common stock	45,000	30,000
Total	$ 85,000	$ 70,000
Retained earnings, December 31	$ 883,000	$ 723,000

Fleming Inc.
Comparative Balance Sheet
December 31, 1992 and 1991

Assets	1992	1991
Current assets:		
Cash	$ 175,000	$ 125,000
Marketable securities	150,000	50,000
Accounts receivable (net)	425,000	325,000
Inventories	720,000	480,000
Prepaid expenses	30,000	20,000
Total current assets	$1,500,000	$1,000,000
Long-term investments	250,000	225,000
Plant assets	2,093,000	1,948,000
Total assets	$3,843,000	$3,173,000

Liabilities		
Current liabilities	$ 750,000	$ 650,000
Long-term liabilities:		
Mortgage note payable, 10%, due 2001	$ 410,000	—
Bonds payable, 8%, due 2003	800,000	$ 800,000
Total long-term liabilities	$1,210,000	$ 800,000
Total liabilities	$1,960,000	$1,450,000
Stockholders' Equity		
Preferred 8% stock, $100 par	$ 500,000	$ 500,000
Common stock, $10 par	500,000	500,000
Retained earnings	883,000	723,000
Total stockholders' equity	$1,883,000	$1,723,000
Total liabilities and stockholders' equity	$3,843,000	$3,173,000

Instructions:

Determine the following measures for 1992:

(1) Working capital
(2) Current ratio
(3) Acid-test ratio
(4) Accounts receivable turnover
(5) Number of days' sales in receivables
(6) Inventory turnover
(7) Number of days' sales in inventory
(8) Ratio of plant assets to long-term liabilities
(9) Ratio of stockholders' equity to liabilities
(10) Number of times interest charges earned
(11) Number of times preferred dividends earned
(12) Ratio of net sales to assets
(13) Rate earned on total assets
(14) Rate earned on stockholders' equity
(15) Rate earned on common stockholders' equity
(16) Earnings per share on common stock
(17) Price-earnings ratio
(18) Dividend yield

SOLUTION

(1) Working capital: $750,000
$1,500,000 − $750,000

(2) Current ratio: 2.0:1
$1,500,000 ÷ $750,000

(3) Acid-test ratio: 1.0:1
$750,000 ÷ $750,000

(4) Accounts receivable turnover: 13.3

$$\$5{,}000{,}000 \div \frac{\$425{,}000 + \$325{,}000}{2}$$

(5) Number of days' sales in receivables: 31 days
$5,000,000 ÷ 365 = $13,699
$425,000 ÷ $13,699

(6) Inventory turnover: 5.7

$$\$3{,}400{,}000 \div \frac{\$720{,}000 + \$480{,}000}{2}$$

(7) Number of days' sales in inventory: 77.3 days
$3,400,000 ÷ 365 = $9,315
$720,000 ÷ $9,315

(8) Ratio of plant assets to long-term liabilities: 1.7:1
$2,093,000 ÷ $1,210,000

(9) Ratio of stockholders' equity to liabilities: 1.0:1
$1,883,000 ÷ $1,960,000

(10) Number of times interest charges earned: 6.2
($545,000 + $105,000) ÷ $105,000

(11) Number of times preferred dividends earned: 6.1
$245,000 ÷ $40,000

(12) Ratio of net sales to assets: 1.5:1

$$\$5{,}000{,}000 \div \frac{\$3{,}593{,}000 + \$2{,}948{,}000}{2}$$

(13) Rate earned on total assets: 10.0%

$$(\$245{,}000 + \$105{,}000) \div \frac{\$3{,}843{,}000 + \$3{,}173{,}000}{2}$$

(14) Rate earned on stockholders' equity: 13.6%

$$\$245{,}000 \div \frac{\$1{,}883{,}000 + \$1{,}723{,}000}{2}$$

(15) Rate earned on common stockholders' equity: 15.7%

$$(\$245{,}000 - \$40{,}000) \div \frac{\$1{,}383{,}000 + \$1{,}223{,}000}{2}$$

(16) Earnings per share on common stock: $4.10
($245,000 − $40,000) ÷ 50,000

(17) Price-earnings ratio: 6.1
$25 ÷ $4.10

(18) Dividend yield: 3.6%

$$\frac{(\$45{,}000 \div 50{,}000 \text{ shares})}{\$25}$$

DISCUSSION QUESTIONS

28–1. Using the following data taken from a comparative balance sheet, illustrate (a) horizontal analysis and (b) vertical analysis.

	Current Year	Preceding Year
Accounts payable	$270,000	$200,000
Total current liabilities	900,000	800,000

28–2. What is the advantage of using comparative statements for financial analysis rather than statements for a single date or period?

28–3. The current year's amount of net income (after income tax) is 15% larger than that of the preceding year. Does this indicate an improved operating performance? Discuss.

28–4. What are common-size financial statements?

28–5. In the analysis of the financial status of an enterprise, what is meant by *solvency* and *profitability*?

28–6. (a) Name the major ratios useful in assessing solvency and profitability.
(b) Why is it important not to rely on only one ratio or measure in assessing the solvency or profitability of an enterprise?

28–7. Identify the measure of current position analysis described by each of the following: (a) the excess of the current assets over current liabilities, (b) the ratio of current assets to current liabilities, (c) the ratio of quick assets to current liabilities.

28–8. Selected condensed data taken from the balance sheet of North Corporation at April 30, the end of the current fiscal year, are as follows:

Cash, marketable securities, and receivables	$520,000
Other current assets	180,000
Total current assets	$700,000
Current liabilities	$400,000

At April 30, what are (a) the working capital, (b) the current ratio, and (c) the acid-test ratio?

28–9. For Rawlins Company, the working capital at the end of the current year is $30,000 greater than the working capital at the end of the preceding year, reported as follows:

	Current Year	Preceding Year
Current assets:		
Cash, marketable securities, and receivables	$330,000	$240,000
Inventories	150,000	110,000
Total current assets	$480,000	$350,000
Current liabilities	300,000	200,000
Working capital	$180,000	$150,000

Has Rawlins' current position improved? Explain.

28–10. A company that grants terms of n/45 on all sales has an accounts receivable turnover for the year, based on monthly averages, of 5. Is this a satisfactory turnover? Discuss.

28–11. What does an increase in the number of days' sales in receivables ordinarily indicate about the credit and collection policy of the firm?

28–12. (a) Why is it advantageous to have a high inventory turnover? (b) Is it possible for the inventory turnover to be too high? Discuss. (c) Is it possible to have a high inventory turnover and a high number of days' sales in inventory? Discuss.

28–13. What does the following data taken from a comparative balance sheet indicate about the company's current ability to borrow additional funds on a long-term basis as compared to the preceding year?

	Current Year	Preceding Year
Plant assets (net)	$2,100,000	$1,250,000
Long-term liabilities	750,000	500,000

28–14. What does an increase in the ratio of stockholders' equity to liabilities indicate about the margin of safety for the firm's creditors and the ability of the firm to withstand adverse business conditions?

28–15. In computing the ratio of net sales to assets, why are long-term investments excluded in determining the amount of the total assets?

28–16. In determining the number of times interest charges are earned, why are interest charges added to income before income tax?

28–17. In determining the rate earned on total assets, why is interest expense added to net income before dividing by total assets?

28–18. (a) Why is the rate earned on stockholders' equity by a thriving enterprise ordinarily higher than the rate earned on total assets?
(b) Should the rate earned on common stockholders' equity normally be higher or lower than the rate earned on total stockholders' equity? Explain.

28–19. The net income (after income tax) of Smith Company was $4.20 per common share in the latest year and $8 per common share for the preceding year. At the beginning of the latest year, the number of shares outstanding was doubled by a stock split. There were no other changes in the amount of stock outstanding. What were the earnings per share in the preceding year, adjusted to place them on a comparable basis with the latest year?

28–20. The price-earnings ratio for the common stock of Orlando Company was 18 at December 31, the end of the current fiscal year. What does the ratio indicate about the selling price of the common stock in relation to current earnings?

28–21. Why would the dividend yield differ significantly from the rate earned on common stockholders' equity?

28–22. Favorable business conditions may bring about certain seemingly unfavorable ratios, and unfavorable business operations may result in apparently favorable ratios. For example, Arron Company increased its sales and net income substantially for the current year, yet the current ratio at the end of the year is lower than at the beginning of the year. Discuss some possible causes of the apparent weakening of the current position while sales and net income have increased substantially.

28–23. (a) The typical independent auditors' report expressing an unqualified opinion consists of three paragraphs. What is reported in each paragraph? (b) Under what condition does an auditor give a qualified opinion?

28–24. Conventional financial statements do not give recognition to the instability of the purchasing power of the dollar. How can the effect of the fluctuating dollar on business operations be presented to the users of the financial statements?

28–25. What is the current cost of an asset?

28–26. If land was purchased for $50,000 when the general price-level index was 200, and the general price-level index has risen to 240, what is the constant dollar equivalent of the original cost of the land?

Real World Focus

28–27. The "Your Money Matters" column in the December 17, 1990 issue of *The Wall Street Journal* states that "trends in inventory [and] accounts receivable [are] strong indicators . . . in measuring a company's earnings potential, and predicting its stock performance." What measures mentioned in the text, are useful in (a) accounts receivable analysis, (b) inventory analysis?

Real World Focus

28–28. The rate of return on total assets based upon Fay's Incorporated's 1990 annual report is 9.1%. The rate of return on stockholders' equity for the same period is 16.4%. What is the explanation for the difference in the two rates?

Ethics Discussion Case

28–29. Debra Lowery, president of Logan Equipment Co., prepared a draft of the "President's Letter" to be included with Logan Equipment Co.'s 1992 annual report. The letter mentions a 15% increase in sales and a recent expansion of plant facilities, but fails to mention the net loss of $250,000 for the year.

You have been asked to review the letter for inclusion in the annual report. How would you respond to the omission of the net loss of $250,000? Specifically, is such an action ethical?

EXERCISES

Ex. 28–30.
Vertical analysis of income statement.
OBJ. 1

Revenue and expense data for W.E. Corbett Company are as follows:

	1992	1991
Sales	$1,000,000	$750,000
Cost of goods sold	600,000	420,000
Selling expenses	160,000	127,500
Administrative expenses	80,000	67,500
Income tax	50,000	30,000

(a) Prepare an income statement in comparative form, stating each item for both 1992 and 1991 as a percent of sales.
(b) Comment on the significant changes disclosed by the comparative income statement.

Ex. 28–31.
Horizontal analysis of balance sheet.
OBJ. 1

Balance sheet data for Higgins Company on December 31, the end of the fiscai year, are as follows:

	1992	1991
Current assets	$436,000	$400,000
Plant assets	637,000	650,000
Intangible assets	66,500	70,000
Current liabilities	115,000	100,000
Long-term liabilities	357,200	380,000
Common stock	500,000	500,000
Retained earnings	167,300	140,000

Prepare a comparative balance sheet with horizontal analysis, indicating the increase (decrease) for 1992 when compared with 1991.

Ex. 28–32.
Current position analysis.
OBJ. 3

The following data were abstracted from the balance sheet of Laskey Company:

	Current Year	Preceding Year
Cash	$202,800	$180,000
Marketable securities	112,000	80,000
Accounts and notes receivable (net)	285,200	260,000
Inventories	485,000	422,400
Prepaid expenses	15,000	17,600
Accounts and notes payable (short-term)	420,000	350,500
Accrued liabilities	80,000	49,500

(a) Determine for each year (1) the working capital, (2) the current ratio, and (3) the acid-test ratio. (Present figures used in your computations.)
(b) What conclusions can be drawn from these data as to the company's ability to meet its currently maturing debts?

Ex. 28–33.
Accounts receivable analysis.
OBJ. 3

The following data are taken from the financial statements for Owen Company.

	Current Year	Preceding Year
Accounts receivable, end of year	$ 496,500	$ 463,800
Monthly average accounts receivable (net)	485,000	450,000
Net sales on account	5,335,000	4,050,000

Terms of all sales are 1/10, n/45.

(a) Determine for each year (1) the accounts receivable turnover and (2) the number of days' sales in receivables.
(b) What conclusions can be drawn from these data concerning the composition of the accounts receivable?

Ex. 28–34.
Inventory analysis.
OBJ. 3

The following data were abstracted from the income statement of Caball Corporation:

	Current Year	Preceding Year
Sales	$3,210,000	$3,120,000
Beginning inventories	490,000	418,500
Purchases	2,270,000	2,330,500
Ending inventories	510,000	486,500

(a) Determine for each year (1) the inventory turnover and (2) the number of days' sales in inventory.
(b) What conclusions can be drawn from these data concerning the composition of the inventories?

Ex. 28–35.
Six measures of solvency or profitability.
OBJ. 3,4

The following data were taken from the financial statements of Roger Clemens and Co. for the current fiscal year:

Plant assets (net)			$1,500,000
Liabilities:			
Current liabilities			$ 250,000
Mortgage note payable, 8%, issued 1985, due 1999			750,000
Total liabilities			$1,000,000
Stockholders' equity:			
Preferred 5% stock, $100 par, cumulative, nonparticipating (no change during year)			$ 300,000
Common stock, $10 par (no change during year)			1,200,000
Retained earnings:			
Balance, beginning of year	$865,000		
Net income	230,000	$1,095,000	
Preferred dividends	$ 15,000		
Common dividends	80,000	95,000	
Balance, end of year			1,000,000
Total stockholders' equity			$2,500,000
Net sales			$4,800,000
Interest expense			60,000

Assuming that long-term investments totaled $250,000 throughout the year and that total assets were $3,000,000 at the beginning of the year, determine the following, presenting figures used in your computations: (a) ratio of plant assets to long-term liabilities, (b) ratio of stockholders' equity to liabilities, (c) ratio of net sales to assets, (d) rate earned on total assets, (e) rate earned on stockholders' equity, (f) rate earned on common stockholders' equity.

Ex. 28–36.
Five measures of solvency or profitability.
OBJ. 3,4

The balance sheet for Laudner Corporation at the end of the current fiscal year indicated the following:

Bonds payable, 10% (issued in 1978, due in 1998)	$3,000,000
Preferred 6% stock, $100 par	1,000,000
Common stock, $100 par	5,000,000

Income before income tax was $750,000, and income taxes were $270,000 for the current year. Cash dividends paid on common stock during the current year totaled

$262,500. The common stock was selling for $105 per share at the end of the year. Determine each of the following: (a) number of times bond interest charges were earned, (b) number of times preferred dividends were earned, (c) earnings per share on common stock, (d) price-earnings ratio, and (e) dividend yield.

Ex. 28–37.
Earnings per share.
OBJ. 4

The net income reported on the income statement of Martinez and Co. was $1,475,000. There were 250,000 shares of $20 par common stock and 30,000 shares of $6 cumulative preferred stock outstanding throughout the current year. The income statement included two extraordinary items: a $400,000 gain from condemnation of land and a $250,000 loss arising from flood damage, both after applicable income tax. Determine the per share figures for common stock for (a) income before extraordinary items and (b) net income.

Ex. 28–38.
Effect of price-level change on investment in land.
OBJ. 6

Several years ago, Doran Company purchased land as a future building site for $40,000. The price-level index at that time was 120. On July 19 of the current year, when the price-level index was 156, the land was sold for $61,500.

(a) Determine the amount of the gain that would be realized according to conventional accounting.
(b) Indicate the amount of the gain that may be (1) attributed to the change in purchasing power and (2) considered a true gain in terms of current dollars.

Ex. 28–39.
Real world focus.
OBJ. 1

The following comparative income statement (in thousands of dollars) for the years ending December 31, 1990 and 1989, was adapted from the 1990 annual report of William Wrigley Jr. Company:

	1990	1989
Revenues	$1,123,508	$1,010,702
Costs and expenses:		
Cost of sales	$ 508,957	$ 451,773
Selling, distribution, and administrative	425,175	387,677
Interest	1,117	826
Total costs and expenses	$ 935,249	$ 840,276
Earnings before income taxes	$ 188,259	$ 170,426
Income taxes	70,897	64,277
Net earnings	$ 117,362	$ 106,149

(a) Prepare a comparative income statement for 1990 and 1989 in vertical form, stating each item as a percent of revenues. (b) Based upon (a), which 1990 income statement item(s) might warrant additional investigation?

PROBLEMS

Pb. 28–40.
Horizontal analysis for income statement.
OBJ. 1

For 1992, Gedman Company reported its most significant increase in net income in years. At the end of the year, Sue Gedman, the president, is presented with the following condensed comparative income statement:

28-
1202

Gedman Company
Comparative Income Statement
For Years Ended December 31, 1992 and 1991

	1992	1991
Sales	$741,600	$612,000
Sales returns and allowances	21,600	12,000
Net sales	$720,000	$600,000
Cost of goods sold	442,800	360,000
Gross profit	$277,200	$240,000
Selling expenses	$ 94,300	$115,000
Administrative expenses	61,000	50,000
Total operating expenses	$155,300	$165,000
Operating income	$121,900	$ 75,000
Other income	1,500	2,000
Income before income tax	$123,400	$ 77,000
Income tax	31,000	15,400
Net income	$ 92,400	$ 61,600

Instructions:

(1) Prepare a comparative income statement with horizontal analysis for the two-year period, using 1991 as the base year.
(2) To the extent the data permit, comment on the significant relationships revealed by the horizontal analysis prepared in (1).

Pb. 28–41.
Vertical analysis for income statement.
OBJ. 1

For 1992, Evans Company initiated an extensive sales promotion campaign that included the expenditure of an additional $30,000 for advertising. At the end of the year, Rob Evans, the president, is presented with the following condensed comparative income statement:

Evans Company
Comparative Income Statement
For Years Ended December 31, 1992 and 1991

	1992	1991
Sales	$515,000	$354,200
Sales returns and allowances	15,000	4,200
Net sales	$500,000	$350,000
Cost of goods sold	330,000	221,900
Gross profit	$170,000	$128,100
Selling expenses	$ 93,000	$ 56,000
Administrative expenses	24,000	17,500
Total operating expenses	$117,000	$ 73,500
Operating income	$ 53,000	$ 54,600
Other income	6,000	3,500
Income before income tax	$ 59,000	$ 58,100
Income tax	11,000	10,850
Net income	$ 48,000	$ 47,250

Instructions:

(1) Prepare a comparative income statement for the two-year period, presenting an analysis of each item in relationship to net sales for each of the years.
(2) To the extent the data permit, comment on the significant relationships revealed by the vertical analysis prepared in (1).

Pb. 28–42.
Common-size income statement.
OBJ. 1

Revenue and expense data for the current calendar year for Greenwell Publishing Company and for the publishing industry are as follows. The Greenwell Publishing Company data are expressed in dollars; the publishing industry averages are expressed in percentages.

	Greenwell Publishing Company	Publishing Industry Average
Sales	$7,056,000	100.5%
Sales returns and allowances	56,000	.5%
Cost of goods sold	4,760,000	64.8%
Selling expenses	735,000	9.9%
Administrative expenses	301,000	8.9%
Other income	49,000	.6%
Other expense	91,000	1.2%
Income tax	483,000	6.8%

Instructions:

(1) Prepare a common-size income statement comparing the results of operations for Greenwell Publishing Company with the industry average.
(2) As far as the data permit, comment on significant relationships revealed by the comparisons.

Pb. 28–43.
Effect of transactions on current position analysis.
OBJ. 3

Data pertaining to the current position of C. Dykstra Inc. are as follows:

Cash	$ 11,600
Marketable securities	40,000
Accounts and notes receivable (net)	58,400
Inventories	101,100
Prepaid expenses	8,900
Accounts payable	43,500
Notes payable (short-term)	50,000
Accrued liabilities	6,500

Instructions:

(1) Compute (a) the working capital, (b) the current ratio, and (c) the acid-test ratio.
(2) List the following captions on a sheet of paper:

Transaction	Working Capital	Current Ratio	Acid-Test Ratio

Compute the working capital, the current ratio, and the acid-test ratio after each of the following transactions, and record the results in the appropriate columns. Consider each transaction separately and assume that only that transaction affects the data given above.

(a) Paid accounts payable, $20,000.
(b) Sold marketable securities, $40,000.
(c) Purchased goods on account, $30,000.
(d) Paid short-term notes payable, $50,000.
(e) Declared a cash dividend, $20,000.
(f) Declared a common stock dividend on common stock, $48,500.
(g) Borrowed cash from bank on a long-term note, $100,000.
(h) Received cash on account, $15,000.
(i) Issued additional shares of stock for cash, $80,000.
(j) Paid cash for office supplies, $6,000.

28-1204 **Pb. 28–44.**

Effect of errors on current position analysis.

OBJ. 3

Prior to approving an application for a short-term loan, Toccoa National Bank required that Harvey Company provide evidence of working capital of at least $200,000, a current ratio of at least 1.8:1, and an acid-test ratio of at least 1.0:1. The chief accountant of Harvey Company compiled the following data pertaining to the current position:

Harvey Company
Schedule of Current Assets and Current Liabilities
December 31, 1992

Current assets:	
Cash	$ 36,250
Marketable securities	75,000
Accounts receivable	115,250
Notes receivable	70,000
Interest receivable	3,500
Inventories	192,620
Supplies	7,380
Total current assets	$500,000
Current liabilities:	
Accounts payable	$200,000
Notes payable	50,000
Total current liabilities	$250,000

Instructions:

(1) Compute (a) the working capital, (b) the current ratio, and (c) the acid-test ratio.

(2) At the request of the bank, a firm of independent auditors was retained to examine data submitted with the loan application. This examination disclosed several errors. Prepare correcting entries for each of the following errors:

(a) A canceled check indicates that a bill for $25,000 for repairs on factory equipment had not been recorded in the accounts.

(b) Accounts receivable of $15,250 are uncollectible and should be immediately written off. In addition, it was estimated that of the remaining receivables, 4% would eventually become uncollectible. An allowance should be made for these future uncollectible accounts.

(c) Six months' interest had been accrued on the $70,000, 10%, six-month note receivable dated October 1, 1992.

(d) Supplies on hand at December 31, 1992, total $1,380.

(e) The marketable securities portfolio includes $50,000 of Oliver Company stock that is held as a long-term investment.

(f) The notes payable account consists of an 18%, 120-day note dated November 1, 1992. No interest had been accrued on the note.

(g) Accrued wages as of December 31, 1992, totaled $20,000.

(h) Rental Income had been credited upon receipt of $28,000, which was the full amount of a year's rent for warehouse space leased to F.H. Smith Inc., effective July 1, 1992.

(i) The purchase of inventory shipped FOB shipping point on December 30, 1992, was not recorded until it was received on January 4, 1993, $22,000.

(3) Giving effect to each of the preceding errors separately and assuming that only that error affects the current position of Harvey Company, compute (a) the working capital, (b) the current ratio, and (c) the acid-test ratio. Use the following column headings for recording your answers:

Error	Working Capital	Current Ratio	Acid-Test Ratio

(4) Prepare a revised schedule of working capital as of December 31, 1992, and recompute the current ratio and the acid-test ratio, giving effect to the corrections of all of the preceding errors.

(5) Discuss the action you would recommend that the bank take regarding the pending loan application.

Pb. 28–45.
Eighteen measures of solvency and profitability.
OBJ. 3,4

The comparative financial statements of F.I. Brady Company are as folllows. The market price of F.I. Brady Company's common stock was $20.30 on December 31, 1991, and $28.40 on December 31, 1992.

F.I. Brady Company
Comparative Income Statement
For Years Ended December 31, 1992 and 1991

	1992	1991
Sales (all on account)	$5,145,000	$4,120,000
Sales returns and allowances	145,000	120,000
Net sales	$5,000,000	$4,000,000
Cost of goods sold	3,000,000	2,360,000
Gross profit	$2,000,000	$1,640,000
Selling expenses	$ 450,000	$ 400,000
Administrative expenses	220,000	180,000
Total operating expenses	$ 670,000	$ 580,000
Operating income	$1,330,000	$1,060,000
Other income	30,000	40,000
	$1,360,000	$1,100,000
Other expense (interest)	260,000	200,000
Income before income tax	$1,100,000	$ 900,000
Income tax	340,000	270,000
Net income	$ 760,000	$ 630,000

F.I. Brady Company
Comparative Retained Earnings Statement
For Years Ended December 31, 1992 and 1991

	1992	1991
Retained earnings, January 1	$1,130,000	$ 750,000
Add net income for year	760,000	630,000
Total	$1,890,000	$1,380,000
Deduct dividends:		
On preferred stock	$ 50,000	$ 50,000
On common stock	240,000	200,000
Total	$ 290,000	$ 250,000
Retained earnings, December 31	$1,600,000	$1,130,000

F.I. Brady Company
Comparative Balance Sheet
December 31, 1992 and 1991

Assets	1992	1991
Current assets:		
Cash	$ 187,500	$ 287,500
Marketable securities	250,000	200,000
Accounts receivable (net)	362,500	262,500
Inventories	880,000	710,000
Prepaid expenses	80,000	115,000
Total current assets	$1,760,000	$1,575,000
Long-term investments	1,000,000	1,000,000
Plant assets	6,140,000	5,305,000
Total assets	$8,900,000	$7,880,000

Liabilities		
Current liabilities	$ 800,000	$ 750,000
Long-term liabilities:		
Mortgage note payable, 12%, due 2002	$ 500,000	—
Bonds payable, 10%, due 2005	2,000,000	$2,000,000
Total long-term liabilities	$2,500,000	$2,000,000
Total liabilities	$3,300,000	$2,750,000
Stockholders' Equity		
Preferred $5 stock, $100 par	$1,000,000	$1,000,000
Common stock, $15 par	3,000,000	3,000,000
Retained earnings	1,600,000	1,130,000
Total stockholders' equity	$5,600,000	$5,130,000
Total liabilities and stockholders' equity	$8,900,000	$7,880,000

Instructions:

Determine the following measures for 1992, presenting the figures used in your computations:

(1) Working capital.
(2) Current ratio.
(3) Acid-test ratio.
(4) Accounts receivable turnover.
(5) Number of days' sales in receivables.
(6) Inventory turnover.
(7) Number of days' sales in inventory.
(8) Ratio of plant assets to long-term liabilities.
(9) Ratio of stockholders' equity to liabilities.
(10) Number of times interest charges earned.
(11) Number of times preferred dividends earned.
(12) Ratio of net sales to assets.
(13) Rate earned on total assets.
(14) Rate earned on stockholders' equity.
(15) Rate earned on common stockholders' equity.
(16) Earnings per share on common stock.
(17) Price-earnings ratio.
(18) Dividend yield.

Pb. 28–46.
Report on detailed financial analysis.
OBJ. 3,4,5

B. O'Neil is considering making a substantial investment in F.I. Brady Company. The company's comparative financial statements for 1992 and 1991 are given in Pb. 28–45. To assist in the evaluation of the company, O'Neil secured the following additional data taken from the balance sheet at December 31, 1990:

Accounts receivable (net)	$ 250,000
Inventories	670,000
Long-term investments	800,000
Total assets	6,800,000
Total stockholders' equity (preferred and common stock outstanding same as in 1991)	4,750,000

Instructions:

Prepare a report for O'Neil, based on an analysis of the financial data presented. In preparing your report, include all ratios and other data that will be useful in arriving at a decision regarding the investment.

ALTERNATE PROBLEMS

Pb. 28–40A.
Horizontal analysis for income statement.
OBJ. 1

For 1992, Getz Company reported its most significant increase in net income in years. At the end of the year, Jane Getz, the president, is presented with the following condensed comparative income statement:

Getz Company
Comparative Income Statement
For Years Ended December 31, 1992 and 1991

	1992	1991
Sales	$907,200	$803,200
Sales returns and allowances	7,200	3,200
Net sales	$900,000	$800,000
Cost of goods sold	557,000	488,000
Gross profit	$343,000	$312,000
Selling expenses	$108,000	$136,000
Administrative expenses	81,000	65,000
Total operating expenses	$189,000	$201,000
Operating income	$154,000	$111,000
Other income	2,000	1,000
Income before income tax	$156,000	$112,000
Income tax	58,000	42,000
Net income	$ 98,000	$ 70,000

Instructions:

(1) Prepare a comparative income statement with horizontal analysis for the two-year period, using 1991 as the base year.
(2) To the extent the data permit, comment on the significant relationships revealed by the horizontal analysis prepared in (1).

Pb. 28–41A.
Vertical analysis for income statement.
OBJ. 1

For 1992, Boggs Company initiated an extensive sales promotion campaign that included the expenditure of an additional $50,000 for advertising. At the end of the year, Karl Boggs, the president, is presented with the following condensed comparative income statement:

Boggs Company
Comparative Income Statement
For Years Ended December 31, 1992 and 1991

	1992	1991
Sales	$947,200	$760,500
Sales returns and allowances	22,200	10,500
Net sales	$925,000	$750,000
Cost of goods sold	593,850	495,000
Gross profit	$331,150	$255,000
Selling expenses	$203,500	$135,000
Administrative expenses	27,750	42,000
Total operating expenses	$231,250	$177,000
Operating income	$ 99,900	$ 78,000
Other expense	1,850	3,000
Income before income tax	$ 98,050	$ 75,000
Income tax	24,050	18,000
Net income	$ 74,000	$ 57,000

Instructions:

(1) Prepare a comparative income statement for the two-year period, presenting an analysis of each item in relationship to net sales for each of the years.
(2) To the extent the data permit, comment on the significant relationships revealed by the vertical analysis prepared in (1).

Pb. 28–42A.
Common-size income statement.
OBJ. 1

Revenue and expense data for the current calendar year for Harpo Publishing Company and for the publishing industry are as follows. The Harpo Publishing Company data are expressed in dollars; the publishing industry averages are expressed in percentages.

	Harpo Publishing Company	Publishing Industry Average
Sales	$8,072,000	100.5%
Sales returns and allowances	72,000	.5
Cost of goods sold	5,760,000	69.0
Selling expenses	656,000	9.0
Administrative expenses	496,000	8.2
Other income	48,000	.6
Other expense	104,000	1.4
Income tax	384,000	5.0

Instructions:

(1) Prepare a common-size income statement comparing the results of operations for Harpo Publishing Company with the industry average.
(2) As far as the data permit, comment on significant relationships revealed by the comparisons.

Pb. 28–43A.
Effect of transactions on current position analysis.
OBJ. 3

Data pertaining to the current position of Jeffries Company are as follows:

Cash	$125,500
Marketable securities	70,000
Accounts and notes receivable (net)	224,500
Inventories	348,600
Prepaid expenses	36,400
Accounts payable	196,000
Notes payable (short-term)	105,000
Accrued liabilities	49,000

Instructions:

(1) Compute (a) the working capital, (b) the current ratio, and (c) the acid-test ratio.
(2) List the following captions on a sheet of paper:

Transaction	Working Capital	Current Ratio	Acid-Test Ratio

Compute the working capital, the current ratio, and the acid-test ratio after each of the following transactions, and record the results in the appropriate columns. Consider each transaction separately and assume that only that transaction affects the data given above.

(a) Declared a cash dividend, $75,000.
(b) Issued additional shares of stock for cash, $245,000.
(c) Purchased goods on account, $45,000.
(d) Paid accounts payable, $30,000.
(e) Borrowed cash from bank on a long-term note, $100,000.
(f) Paid cash for office supplies, $18,000.
(g) Received cash on account, $24,800.
(h) Paid short-term notes payable, $80,000.
(i) Declared a common stock dividend on common stock, $150,000.
(j) Sold marketable securities, $70,000.

Pb. 28–44A.

Effect of errors on current position analysis.

OBJ. 3

Prior to approving an application for a short-term loan, Citizens National Bank required that Fite Company provide evidence of working capital of at least $300,000, a current ratio of at least 1.5:1, and an acid-test ratio of at least 1.0:1. The chief accountant of Fite Company compiled the following data pertaining to the current position:

Fite Company
Schedule of Current Assets and Current Liabilities
December 31, 1992

Current assets:	
Cash	$115,250
Marketable securities	101,250
Accounts receivable	330,500
Notes receivable	50,000
Interest receivable	3,000
Inventories	179,250
Supplies	20,750
Total current assets	$800,000
Current liabilities:	
Accounts payable	$325,000
Notes payable	75,000
Total current liabilities	$400,000

Instructions:

(1) Compute (a) the working capital, (b) the current ratio, and (c) the acid-test ratio.

(2) At the request of the bank, a firm of independent auditors was retained to examine data submitted with the loan application. This examination disclosed several errors. Prepare correcting entries for each of the following errors:

(a) A canceled check indicates that a bill for $25,000 for repairs on factory equipment had not been recorded in the accounts.

(b) Accounts receivable of $30,500 are uncollectible and should be immediately written off. In addition, it was estimated that of the remaining receivables, 5% would eventually become uncollectible. An allowance should be made for these future uncollectible accounts.

(c) Six months' interest had been accrued on the $50,000, 12%, six-month note receivable dated October 1, 1992.

(d) Supplies on hand at December 31, 1992, total $9,750.

(e) The marketable securities portfolio includes $50,000 of Porter Company stock that is held as a long-term investment.

(f) The notes payable account consists of a 12%, 90-day note dated November 1, 1992. No interest had been accrued on the note.

(g) Accrued wages as of December 31, 1992, totaled $30,000.

(h) Rental income had been credited upon receipt of $72,000, which was the full amount of a year's rent for warehouse space leased to C. Pena and Son, effective July 1, 1992.

(3) Giving effect to each of the preceding errors separately and assuming that only that error affects the current position of Fite Company, compute (a) the working capital, (b) the current ratio, and (c) the acid-test ratio. Use the following column headings for recording your answers:

Error	Working Capital	Current Ratio	Acid-Test Ratio

(4) Prepare a revised schedule of working capital as of December 31, 1992, and recompute the current ratio and the acid-test ratio, giving effect to the corrections of all the preceding errors.

(5) Discuss the action you would recommend that the bank take regarding the pending loan application.

Pb. 28–45A. **Eighteen measures of solvency and profitability.**
OBJ. 3,4

The comparative financial statements of R.J. Combs Inc. are as follows. The market price of R.J. Combs Inc.'s common stock was $54 on December 31, 1991, and $50.40 on December 31, 1992.

R.J. Combs Inc.
Comparative Income Statement
For Years Ended December 31, 1992 and 1991

	1992	1991
Sales (all on account)	$7,517,400	$6,419,200
Sales returns and allowances	37,400	19,200
Net sales	$7,480,000	$6,400,000
Cost of goods sold	4,800,000	3,840,000
Gross profit	$2,680,000	$2,560,000
Selling expenses	$1,280,000	$ 985,600
Administrative expenses	540,000	526,400
Total operating expenses	$1,820,000	$1,512,000
Operating income	$ 860,000	$1,048,000
Other income	140,000	112,000
	$1,000,000	$1,160,000
Other expense (interest)	200,000	180,000
Income before income tax	$ 800,000	$ 980,000
Income tax	320,000	400,000
Net income	$ 480,000	$ 580,000

R.J. Combs Inc.
Comparative Retained Earnings Statement
For Years Ended December 31, 1992 and 1991

	1992	1991
Retained earnings, January 1	$2,416,000	$1,936,000
Add net income for year	480,000	580,000
Total	$2,896,000	$2,516,000
Deduct dividends:		
On preferred stock	$ 30,000	$ 30,000
On common stock	50,000	70,000
Total	$ 80,000	$ 100,000
Retained earnings, December 31	$2,816,000	$2,416,000

R.J. Combs Inc.
Comparative Balance Sheet
December 31, 1992 and 1991

Assets	1992	1991
Current assets:		
Cash	$ 130,000	$ 120,000
Marketable securities	200,000	150,000
Accounts receivable (net)	440,000	400,000
Inventories	769,600	674,800
Prepaid expenses	70,400	35,200
Total current assets	$1,610,000	$1,380,000
Long-term investments	300,000	250,000
Plant assets	4,506,000	4,086,000
Total assets	$6,416,000	$5,716,000

Liabilities		
Current liabilities	$ 700,000	$ 600,000
Long-term liabilities:		
Mortgage note payable, 10%, due 1992	$ 200,000	—
Bonds payable, 15%, due 2007	1,200,000	$1,200,000
Total long-term liabilities	$1,400,000	$1,200,000
Total liabilities	$2,100,000	$1,800,000
Stockholders' Equity		
Preferred 6% stock, $50 par	$ 500,000	$ 500,000
Common stock, $20 par	1,000,000	1,000,000
Retained earnings	2,816,000	2,416,000
Total stockholders' equity	$4,316,000	$3,916,000
Total liabilities and stockholders' equity	$6,416,000	$5,716,000

Instructions:

Determine the following measures for 1992, presenting the figures used in your computations:

(1) Working capital.
(2) Current ratio.
(3) Acid-test ratio.
(4) Accounts receivable turnover.
(5) Number of days' sales in receivables.
(6) Inventory turnover.
(7) Number of days' sales in inventory.
(8) Ratio of plant assets to long-term liabilities.
(9) Ratio of stockholders' equity to liabilities.
(10) Number of times interest charges earned.
(11) Number of times preferred dividends earned.
(12) Ratio of net sales to assets.
(13) Rate earned on total assets.
(14) Rate earned on stockholders' equity.
(15) Rate earned on common stockholders' equity.
(16) Earnings per share on common stock.
(17) Price-earnings ratio.
(18) Dividend yield.

Pb. 28–46A.
Report on detailed financial analysis.
OBJ. 3,4,5

Ann Raines is considering making a substantial investment in R.J. Combs Inc. The company's comparative financial statements for 1992 and 1991 are given in Pb. 28–45A. To assist in the evaluation of the company, Raines secured the following additional data taken from the balance sheet at December 31, 1990:

Accounts receivable (net)	$ 350,000
Inventories	654,800
Long-term investments	250,000
Total assets	5,284,000
Total stockholders' equity (preferred and common stock outstanding same as in 1991)	3,684,000

Instructions:

Prepare a report for Raines, based on an analysis of the financial data presented. In preparing your report, include all ratios and other data that will be useful in arriving at a decision regarding the investment.

MINI-CASE 28

You and your sister are both presidents of companies in the same industry, RST Inc. and CDP Inc., respectively. Both companies were originally operated as a single-family business; but, shortly after your father's death in 1978, the business was divided into two companies. Your sister took over CDP Inc., located in St. Paul while you took over RST Inc., located in Des Moines.

During a recent family reunion, your sister referred to the much larger rate of return to her stockholders than was the case in your company and suggested that you consider rearranging the method of financing your corporation. The difference is highlighted by the following chart, which compares the rates earned on the stockholders' equity and the assets of the two companies:

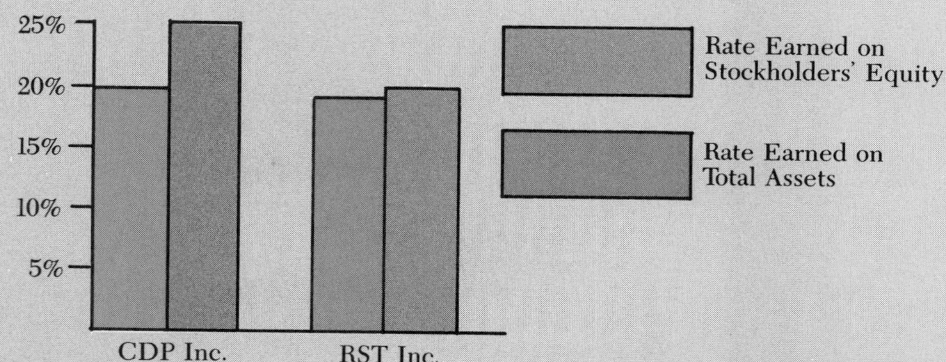

Since 1978, the growth in your sister's company has been financed largely through borrowing and yours largely through the issuance of additional common stock. Both companies have about the same volume of sales, gross profit, operating income, and total assets.

The income statements for the year ended December 31, 1992, and the balance sheets at December 31, 1992, for both companies are shown on the next page.

In addition to the 1992 financial statements, the following data were taken from the balance sheet at December 31, 1991:

	CDP Inc.	RST Inc.
Total assets	$ 960,000	$1,030,000
Total stockholders' equity	500,000	900,000

Income Statements

	CDP Inc.	RST Inc.
Sales	$2,435,400	$2,343,000
Sales returns and allowances	35,400	27,000
Net sales	$2,400,000	$2,316,000
Cost of goods sold	1,470,000	1,416,000
Gross profit	$ 930,000	$ 900,000
Selling expenses	$ 400,000	$ 366,700
Administrative expenses	235,000	210,300
Total operating expenses	$ 635,000	$ 577,000
Operating income	$ 295,000	$ 323,000
Interest expense	40,000	12,000
Income before income tax	$ 255,000	$ 311,000
Income tax	100,000	124,000
Net income	$ 155,000	$ 187,000

Balance Sheets

Assets	CDP Inc.	RST Inc.
Current assets	$ 75,000	$ 78,000
Plant assets (net)	930,000	972,000
Intangible assets	15,000	30,000
Total assets	$1,020,000	$1,080,000
Liabilities		
Current liabilities	$ 30,000	$ 48,000
Long-term liabilities	400,000	100,000
Total liabilities	$ 430,000	$ 148,000
Stockholders' Equity		
Common stock ($10 par)	$ 100,000	$ 450,000
Retained earnings	490,000	482,000
Total stockholders' equity	$ 590,000	$ 932,000
Total liabilities and stockholders' equity	$1,020,000	$1,080,000

Instructions:

(1) Determine for 1992 the following ratios and other measures for both companies.
  (a) Ratio of plant assets to long-term liabilities.
  (b) Ratio of stockholders' equity to liabilities.
  (c) Ratio of net sales to assets.
  (d) Rate earned on total assets.
  (e) Rate earned on stockholders' equity.

(2) For both CDP Inc. and RST Inc., the rate earned on stockholders' equity is greater than the rate earned on total assets. Explain.

(3) Why is the rate of return on stockholders' equity for CDP Inc. approximately 25% greater than for RST Inc.?

(4) Comment on your sister's suggestion for rearranging the financing of RST Inc.

ANSWERS TO SELF-EXAMINATION QUESTIONS

1. A Percentage analysis indicating the relationship of the component parts to the total in a financial statement, such as the relationship of current assets to total assets (20% to 100%) in the question, is called vertical analysis (answer A). Percentage analysis of increases and decreases in corresponding items in comparative financial statements is called horizontal analysis (answer B). An example of horizontal analysis would be the presentation of the amount of current assets in the preceding balance sheet along with the amount of current assets at the end of the current year, with the increase or decrease in current assets between the periods expressed as a percentage. Current position analysis (answer C), relates to analysis of various current asset and current liability items.
2. D Various solvency measures, categorized as current position analysis, indicate a firm's ability to meet currently maturing obligations. Each measure contributes in the analysis of a firm's current position and is most useful when viewed with other measures and when compared with similar measures for other periods and for other firms. Working capital (answer A) is the excess of current assets over current liabilities; the current ratio (answer B) is the ratio of current assets to current liabilities; and the acid-test ratio (answer C) is the ratio of the sum of cash, receivables, and marketable securities to current liabilities.
3. D The ratio of current assets to current liabilities is usually referred to as the current ratio (answer A) and is sometimes referred to as the working capital ratio (answer B) or bankers' ratio (answer C).
4. C The ratio of the sum of cash, receivables, and marketable securities (sometimes called quick assets) to current liabilities is called the acid-test ratio (answer C) or quick ratio. The current ratio (answer A) and working capital ratio (answer B) are two terms that describe the ratio of current assets to current liabilities.
5. C As with many attempts at analyzing financial data, it is possible to determine more than one measure that is useful for evaluating the efficiency in the management of inventories. Both the inventory turnover (answer A), which is determined by dividing the cost of goods sold by the average inventory, and the number of days' sales in inventory (answer B), which is determined by dividing the inventories at the end of the year by the average daily cost of goods sold, express the relationship between the cost of goods sold and inventory.

APPENDIX A: INTEREST TABLES

The following present value and future value tables contain factors carried to six decimal places for interest rates of 5% to 14% for 50 periods.

Present Value of 1 at Compound Interest Due in *n* Periods: $p_{\overline{n}|i} = \frac{1}{(1+i)^n}$

n \ i	5%	5.5%	6%	6.5%	7%	8%	9%	10%	11%	12%	13%	14%
1	0.952381	0.94787	0.943396	0.93897	0.934580	0.925926	0.917431	0.909091	0.90090	0.892857	0.88496	0.87719
2	0.907029	0.89845	0.889996	0.88166	0.873439	0.857339	0.841680	0.826446	0.81162	0.797194	0.78315	0.76947
3	0.863838	0.85161	0.839619	0.82785	0.816298	0.793832	0.772183	0.751315	0.73119	0.711780	0.69305	0.67497
4	0.822702	0.80722	0.792094	0.77732	0.762895	0.735030	0.708425	0.683013	0.65873	0.635518	0.61332	0.59208
5	0.783526	0.76513	0.747258	0.72988	0.712986	0.680583	0.649931	0.620921	0.59345	0.567427	0.54276	0.51937
6	0.746215	0.72525	0.704961	0.68533	0.666342	0.630170	0.596267	0.564474	0.53464	0.506631	0.48032	0.45559
7	0.710681	0.68744	0.665057	0.64351	0.622750	0.583490	0.547034	0.513158	0.48166	0.452349	0.42506	0.39964
8	0.676839	0.65160	0.627412	0.60423	0.582009	0.540269	0.501866	0.466507	0.43393	0.403883	0.37616	0.35056
9	0.644609	0.61763	0.591898	0.56735	0.543934	0.500249	0.460428	0.424098	0.39092	0.360610	0.33288	0.30751
10	0.613913	0.58543	0.558395	0.53273	0.508349	0.463193	0.422411	0.385543	0.35218	0.321973	0.29459	0.26974
11	0.584679	0.55491	0.526788	0.50021	0.475093	0.428883	0.387533	0.350494	0.31728	0.287476	0.26070	0.23662
12	0.556837	0.52598	0.496969	0.46968	0.444012	0.397114	0.355535	0.318631	0.28584	0.256675	0.23071	0.20756
13	0.530321	0.49856	0.468839	0.44102	0.414964	0.367698	0.326179	0.289664	0.25751	0.229174	0.20416	0.18207
14	0.505068	0.47257	0.442301	0.41410	0.387817	0.340461	0.299246	0.263331	0.23199	0.204620	0.18068	0.15971
15	0.481017	0.44793	0.417265	0.38883	0.362446	0.315242	0.274538	0.239392	0.20900	0.182696	0.15989	0.14010
16	0.458112	0.42458	0.393646	0.36510	0.338735	0.291890	0.251870	0.217629	0.18829	0.163122	0.14150	0.12289
17	0.436297	0.40245	0.371364	0.34281	0.316574	0.270269	0.231073	0.197845	0.16963	0.145644	0.12522	0.10780
18	0.415521	0.38147	0.350344	0.32189	0.295864	0.250249	0.211994	0.179859	0.15282	0.130040	0.11081	0.09456
19	0.395734	0.36158	0.330513	0.30224	0.276508	0.231712	0.194490	0.163508	0.13768	0.116107	0.09806	0.08295
20	0.376889	0.34273	0.311805	0.28380	0.258419	0.214548	0.178431	0.148644	0.12403	0.103667	0.08678	0.07276
21	0.358942	0.32486	0.294155	0.26648	0.241513	0.198656	0.163698	0.135131	0.11174	0.092560	0.07680	0.06383
22	0.341850	0.30793	0.277505	0.25021	0.225713	0.183941	0.150182	0.122846	0.10067	0.082643	0.06796	0.05599
23	0.325571	0.29187	0.261797	0.23494	0.210947	0.170315	0.137781	0.111678	0.09069	0.073788	0.06014	0.04911
24	0.310068	0.27666	0.246979	0.22060	0.197147	0.157699	0.126405	0.101526	0.08170	0.065882	0.05323	0.04308
25	0.295303	0.26223	0.232999	0.20714	0.184249	0.146018	0.115968	0.092296	0.07361	0.058823	0.04710	0.03779
26	0.281241	0.24856	0.219810	0.19450	0.172195	0.135202	0.106393	0.083905	0.06631	0.052521	0.04168	0.03315
27	0.267848	0.23560	0.207368	0.18263	0.160930	0.125187	0.097608	0.076278	0.05974	0.046894	0.03689	0.02908
28	0.255094	0.22332	0.195630	0.17148	0.150402	0.115914	0.089548	0.069343	0.05382	0.041869	0.03264	0.02551
29	0.242946	0.21168	0.184557	0.16101	0.140563	0.107328	0.082155	0.063039	0.04849	0.037383	0.02889	0.02237
30	0.231377	0.20064	0.174110	0.15119	0.131367	0.099377	0.075371	0.057309	0.04368	0.033378	0.02557	0.01963
31	0.220359	0.19018	0.164255	0.14196	0.122773	0.092016	0.069148	0.052099	0.03935	0.029802	0.02262	0.01722
32	0.209866	0.18027	0.154957	0.13329	0.114741	0.085200	0.063438	0.047362	0.03545	0.026609	0.02002	0.01510
33	0.199873	0.17087	0.146186	0.12516	0.107235	0.078889	0.058200	0.043057	0.03194	0.023758	0.01772	0.01325
34	0.190355	0.16196	0.137912	0.11752	0.100219	0.073045	0.053395	0.039143	0.02878	0.021212	0.01568	0.01162
35	0.181290	0.15352	0.130105	0.11035	0.093663	0.067635	0.048986	0.035584	0.02592	0.018940	0.01388	0.01019
40	0.142046	0.11746	0.097222	0.08054	0.066780	0.046031	0.031838	0.022095	0.01538	0.010747	0.00753	0.00529
45	0.111297	0.08988	0.072650	0.05879	0.047613	0.031328	0.020692	0.013719	0.00913	0.006098	0.00409	0.00275
50	0.087204	0.06877	0.054288	0.04291	0.033948	0.021321	0.013449	0.008519	0.00542	0.003460	0.00222	0.00143

Present Value of Ordinary Annuity of 1 per Period: $P_{\overline{n}|i} = \dfrac{1 - \dfrac{1}{(1+i)^n}}{i}$

n \ i	5%	5.5%	6%	6.5%	7%	8%	9%	10%	11%	12%	13%	14%
1	0.952381	0.94787	0.943396	0.93897	0.934579	0.925926	0.917431	0.909091	0.90090	0.892857	0.88496	0.87719
2	1.859410	1.84632	1.833393	1.82063	1.808018	1.783265	1.759111	1.735537	1.71252	1.690051	1.66810	1.64666
3	2.723248	2.69793	2.673012	2.64848	2.624316	2.577097	2.531295	2.486852	2.44371	2.401831	2.36115	2.32163
4	3.545951	3.50515	3.465106	3.42580	3.387211	3.312127	3.239720	3.169865	3.10245	3.037349	2.97447	2.91371
5	4.329477	4.27028	4.212364	4.15568	4.100197	3.992710	3.889651	3.790787	3.69590	3.604776	3.51723	3.43308
6	5.075692	4.99553	4.917324	4.84101	4.766540	4.622880	4.485919	4.355261	4.23054	4.111407	3.99755	3.88867
7	5.786373	5.68297	5.582381	5.48452	5.389289	5.206370	5.032953	4.868419	4.71220	4.563757	4.42261	4.28830
8	6.463213	6.33457	6.209794	6.08875	5.971299	5.746639	5.534819	5.334926	5.14612	4.967640	4.79677	4.63886
9	7.107822	6.95220	6.801692	6.65610	6.515232	6.246888	5.995247	5.759024	5.53705	5.328250	5.13166	4.94637
10	7.721735	7.53763	7.360087	7.18883	7.023582	6.710081	6.417658	6.144567	5.88923	5.650223	5.42624	5.21612
11	8.306414	8.09254	7.886875	7.68904	7.498674	7.138964	6.805191	6.495061	6.20652	5.937699	5.68694	5.45273
12	8.863252	8.61852	8.383844	8.15873	7.942686	7.536078	7.160725	6.813692	6.49236	6.194374	5.91765	5.66029
13	9.393573	9.11708	8.852683	8.59974	8.357651	7.903776	7.486904	7.103356	6.74987	6.423548	6.12181	5.84236
14	9.898641	9.58965	9.294984	9.01384	8.745468	8.224237	7.786150	7.366687	6.96187	6.628168	6.30249	6.00207
15	10.379658	10.03758	9.712249	9.40267	9.107914	8.559479	8.060688	7.606080	7.19087	6.810864	6.46238	6.14217
16	10.837770	10.46216	10.105895	9.76776	9.446649	8.851369	8.312558	7.823709	7.37916	6.973986	6.60388	6.26506
17	11.274066	10.86461	10.477260	10.11058	9.763223	9.121638	8.543631	8.021553	7.54879	7.119630	6.72909	6.37286
18	11.689587	11.24607	10.827603	10.43247	10.059087	9.371887	8.755625	8.201412	7.70162	7.249670	6.83991	6.46742
19	12.085321	11.60765	11.158116	10.73471	10.335595	9.603599	8.950115	8.364920	7.83929	7.365777	6.93797	6.55037
20	12.462210	11.95038	11.469921	11.01851	10.594014	9.818147	9.128546	8.513564	7.96333	7.469444	7.02475	6.62313
21	12.821153	12.27524	11.764077	11.28498	10.835527	10.016803	9.292244	8.648694	8.07507	7.562003	7.10155	6.68696
22	13.163003	12.58317	12.041582	11.53520	11.061241	10.200744	9.442425	8.771540	8.17574	7.644646	7.16951	6.74294
23	13.488574	12.87504	12.303379	11.77014	11.272187	10.371059	9.580207	8.883218	8.26643	7.718434	7.22966	6.79206
24	13.798642	13.15170	12.550358	11.99074	11.469334	10.528758	9.706612	8.984744	8.34814	7.784316	7.28288	6.83514
25	14.093945	13.41393	12.783356	12.19788	11.653583	10.674776	9.822580	9.077040	8.42174	7.843139	7.32998	6.87293
26	14.375185	13.66250	13.003166	12.39237	11.825779	10.809978	9.928972	9.160945	8.48806	7.895660	7.37167	6.90608
27	14.643034	13.89810	13.210534	12.57500	11.986709	10.935165	10.026580	9.237223	8.54780	7.942554	7.40856	6.93515
28	14.898127	14.12142	13.406164	12.74648	12.137111	11.051078	10.116128	9.306567	8.60162	7.984423	7.44120	6.96066
29	15.141074	14.33310	13.590721	12.90749	12.277674	11.158406	10.198283	9.369606	8.65011	8.021806	7.47009	6.98304
30	15.372451	14.53375	13.764831	13.05868	12.409041	11.257783	10.273654	9.426914	8.69379	8.055184	7.49565	7.00266
31	15.592811	14.72393	13.929086	13.20063	12.531814	11.349799	10.342802	9.479013	8.73315	8.084986	7.51828	7.01988
32	15.802677	14.90420	14.084043	13.33393	12.646555	11.434999	10.406240	9.526376	8.76860	8.111594	7.53830	7.03498
33	16.002549	15.07507	14.230230	13.45909	12.753790	11.513888	10.464441	9.569432	8.80054	8.135352	7.55602	7.04823
34	16.192904	15.23703	14.368141	13.57661	12.854009	11.586934	10.517835	9.608575	8.82932	8.156564	7.57170	7.05985
35	16.374194	15.39055	14.498246	13.68696	12.947672	11.654568	10.566821	9.644159	8.85524	8.175504	7.58557	7.07005
40	17.159086	16.04612	15.046297	14.14553	13.331709	11.924613	10.757360	9.779051	8.95105	8.243777	7.63438	7.10504
45	17.774070	16.54773	15.455832	14.48023	13.605522	12.108402	10.881197	9.862808	9.00791	8.282516	7.66086	7.12322
50	18.255925	16.93152	15.761861	14.72452	13.800746	12.233485	10.961683	9.914814	9.04165	8.304498	7.67524	7.13266

Future Amount of 1 at Compound Interest Due in *n* Periods: $a_{\overline{n}|i} = (1 + i)^n$

n \ i	5%	5.5%	6%	6.5%	7%	8%	9%	10%	11%	12%	13%	14%
1	1.050000	1.05500	1.060000	1.06500	1.070000	1.080000	1.090000	1.100000	1.11000	1.120000	1.13000	1.14000
2	1.102500	1.11303	1.123600	1.13423	1.144900	1.166400	1.188100	1.210000	1.23210	1.254400	1.27690	1.29960
3	1.157625	1.17424	1.191016	1.20795	1.225043	1.259712	1.295029	1.331000	1.36763	1.404928	1.44290	1.48154
4	1.215506	1.23882	1.262477	1.28647	1.310796	1.360489	1.411582	1.464100	1.51807	1.573519	1.63047	1.68896
5	1.276282	1.30696	1.338226	1.37009	1.402552	1.469328	1.538624	1.610510	1.68506	1.762342	1.84244	1.92541
6	1.340096	1.37884	1.418519	1.45914	1.500730	1.586874	1.677100	1.771561	1.87041	1.973823	2.08195	2.19497
7	1.407100	1.45468	1.503630	1.55399	1.605781	1.713824	1.828039	1.948717	2.07616	2.210681	2.35261	2.50227
8	1.543469	1.53469	1.593848	1.65500	1.718186	1.850930	1.992563	2.143589	2.30454	2.475963	2.65844	2.85259
9	1.551328	1.61909	1.689479	1.76257	1.838459	1.999005	2.171893	2.357948	2.55804	2.773079	3.00404	3.25195
10	1.628895	1.70814	1.790848	1.87714	1.967151	2.158925	2.367364	2.593742	2.83942	3.105848	3.39457	3.70722
11	1.710339	1.80209	1.898299	1.99915	2.104852	2.331639	2.580426	2.853117	3.15176	3.478550	3.83586	4.22623
12	1.795856	1.90121	2.012196	2.12910	2.252192	2.518170	2.812665	3.138428	3.49845	3.895976	4.33452	4.81790
13	1.885649	2.00577	2.132928	2.26749	2.409845	2.719624	3.065805	3.452271	3.88328	4.363493	4.89801	5.49241
14	1.979932	2.11609	2.260904	2.41487	2.578534	2.937194	3.341727	3.797498	4.31044	4.887112	5.53475	6.26135
15	2.078928	2.23248	2.396558	2.57184	2.759032	3.172169	3.642482	4.177248	4.78459	5.473566	6.25427	7.13794
16	2.182875	2.35526	2.540352	2.73901	2.952164	3.425943	3.970306	4.594973	5.31089	6.130394	7.06733	8.13725
17	2.292018	2.48480	2.692773	2.91705	3.158815	3.700018	4.327633	5.054470	5.89509	6.866041	7.98608	9.27646
18	2.406619	2.62147	2.854339	3.10665	3.379932	3.996019	4.717120	5.559917	6.54355	7.689966	9.02427	10.57517
19	2.526950	2.76565	3.025600	3.30859	3.616528	4.315701	5.141661	6.115909	7.26334	8.612762	10.19742	12.05569
20	2.653298	2.91776	3.207135	3.52365	3.869684	4.660957	5.604411	6.727500	8.06231	9.646293	11.52309	13.74349
21	2.785963	3.07823	3.399564	3.75268	4.140562	5.033834	6.108808	7.400250	8.94917	10.803848	13.02109	15.66758
22	2.925261	3.24754	3.603537	3.99661	4.430402	5.436540	6.658600	8.140275	9.93357	12.100310	14.71383	17.86104
23	3.071524	3.42615	3.819750	4.25639	4.740530	5.871464	7.257874	8.954302	11.02627	13.552347	16.62663	20.36158
24	3.225100	3.61459	4.048935	4.53305	5.072367	6.341181	7.911083	9.849733	12.23916	15.178629	18.78809	23.21221
25	3.386355	3.81339	4.291871	4.82770	5.427433	6.848475	8.623081	10.834706	13.58546	17.000064	21.23054	26.46192
26	3.555673	4.02313	4.549383	5.14150	5.807353	7.396353	9.399158	11.918177	15.07986	19.040072	23.99051	30.16658
27	3.733456	4.24440	4.822346	5.47570	6.213868	7.988061	10.245082	13.109994	16.73865	21.324881	27.10928	34.38991
28	3.920129	4.47784	5.111687	5.83162	6.648838	8.627106	11.167140	14.420994	18.57990	23.883866	30.63349	39.20449
29	4.116136	4.72412	5.418388	6.21067	7.114257	9.317275	12.172182	15.863093	20.62369	26.749930	34.61584	44.69312
30	4.321942	4.98395	5.743491	6.61437	7.612255	10.062657	13.267678	17.449402	22.89230	29.959922	39.11590	50.95016
31	4.538039	5.25807	6.088101	7.04430	8.145113	10.867669	14.461770	19.194342	25.41045	33.555113	44.20096	58.08318
32	4.764941	5.54726	6.453387	7.50218	8.715271	11.737083	15.763329	21.113777	28.20560	37.581726	49.94709	66.21483
33	5.003189	5.85236	6.840590	7.98982	9.325340	12.676050	17.182028	23.225154	31.30821	42.091533	56.44021	75.48490
34	5.253348	6.17424	7.251025	8.50916	9.978114	13.690134	18.728411	25.547670	34.75212	47.142517	63.77744	86.05279
35	5.516015	6.51383	7.686087	9.06225	10.676581	14.785344	20.413968	28.102437	38.57485	52.799620	72.06851	98.10018
40	7.039989	8.51331	10.285718	12.41607	14.974458	21.724521	31.409420	45.259256	65.00087	93.050970	132.78155	188.88351
45	8.985008	11.12655	13.764611	17.01110	21.002452	31.920449	48.327286	72.890484	109.53024	163.987604	244.64140	363.67907
50	11.467400	14.54196	18.420154	23.30668	29.457025	46.901613	74.357520	117.390853	184.56483	289.002190	450.73593	700.23299

Future Amount of Ordinary Annuity of 1 per Period: $A_{\overline{n}|i} = \frac{(1+i)^n - 1}{i}$

n \ i	5%	5.5%	6%	6.5%	7%	8%	9%	10%	11%	12%	13%	14%
1	1.000000	1.00000	1.000000	1.00000	1.000000	1.000000	1.000000	1.000000	1.00000	1.000000	1.00000	1.00000
2	2.050000	2.05500	2.060000	2.06500	2.070000	2.080000	2.090000	2.100000	2.11000	2.120000	2.13000	2.14000
3	3.152500	3.16802	3.183600	3.19922	3.214900	3.246400	3.278100	3.310000	3.34210	3.374400	3.40690	3.43960
4	4.310125	4.34227	4.374616	4.40717	4.439943	4.506112	4.573129	4.641000	4.70973	4.779328	4.84980	4.92114
5	5.525631	5.58109	5.637093	5.69364	5.750740	5.866601	5.984711	6.105100	6.22780	6.352847	6.48027	6.61010
6	6.801913	6.88805	6.975319	7.06373	7.153291	7.335929	7.523335	7.715610	7.91286	8.115189	8.32271	8.53552
7	8.142008	8.26689	8.393838	8.52287	8.654021	8.922803	9.200435	9.487171	9.78327	10.089012	10.40466	10.73049
8	9.549109	9.72157	9.897468	10.07686	10.259803	10.636628	11.028474	11.435888	11.85943	12.299693	12.75726	13.23276
9	11.026564	11.25626	11.491316	11.73185	11.977989	12.487558	13.021036	13.579477	14.16397	14.775656	15.41571	16.08535
10	12.577893	12.87535	13.180795	13.49442	13.816448	14.486562	15.192930	15.937425	16.72201	17.548735	18.41975	19.33730
11	14.206787	14.58350	14.971643	15.37156	15.783599	16.645487	17.560293	18.531167	19.56143	20.654583	21.81432	23.04452
12	15.917127	16.38559	16.869941	17.37071	17.888451	18.977126	20.140720	21.384284	22.71319	24.133133	25.65018	27.27075
13	17.712983	18.28680	18.882138	19.49981	20.140643	21.495297	22.953385	24.522712	26.21164	28.029109	29.98470	32.08865
14	19.598632	20.29257	21.015066	21.76730	22.550488	24.214920	26.019189	27.974983	30.09492	32.392602	34.88271	37.58107
15	21.578564	22.40866	23.275970	24.18217	25.129022	27.152114	29.360916	31.772482	34.40536	37.279715	40.41746	43.84241
16	23.657492	24.64114	25.672528	26.75401	27.888054	30.324283	33.003399	35.949730	39.18995	42.753280	46.67173	50.98035
17	25.840366	26.99640	28.212880	29.49302	30.840217	33.750226	36.973705	40.544703	44.50084	48.883674	53.73906	59.11760
18	28.132385	29.48120	30.905653	32.41007	33.999033	37.450244	41.301338	45.599173	50.39594	55.749715	61.72514	68.39407
19	30.539004	32.10267	33.759992	35.51672	37.378965	41.446263	46.018458	51.159090	56.93949	63.439681	70.74941	78.96923
20	33.065954	34.86832	36.785591	38.82531	40.995492	45.761964	51.160120	57.274999	64.20283	72.052442	80.94683	91.02493
21	35.719252	37.78608	39.992727	42.34895	44.865177	50.422921	56.764530	64.002499	72.26514	81.698736	92.46992	104.76842
22	38.505214	40.86431	43.392290	46.10164	49.005739	55.456755	62.873338	71.402749	81.21431	92.502584	105.49101	120.43600
23	41.430475	44.11185	46.995828	50.09824	53.436141	60.893296	69.531939	79.543024	91.14788	104.602894	120.20484	138.29704
24	44.501999	47.53800	50.815577	54.35463	58.176671	66.764759	76.789813	88.497327	102.17415	118.155241	136.83147	158.65862
25	47.727099	51.15259	54.864512	58.88768	63.249038	73.105940	84.700896	98.347059	114.41331	133.333870	155.61956	181.87083
26	51.113454	54.96598	59.156383	63.71538	68.676470	79.954415	93.323977	109.181765	127.99877	150.333934	176.85010	208.33274
27	54.669126	58.98911	63.705766	68.85688	74.483823	87.350768	102.723135	121.099942	143.07864	169.374007	200.84061	238.49933
28	58.402583	63.23351	68.528112	74.33257	80.697691	95.338830	112.968217	134.209936	159.81729	190.698887	227.94989	272.88923
29	62.322712	67.71135	73.629798	80.16419	87.346529	103.965936	124.135356	148.630930	178.39719	214.582754	258.58338	312.09373
30	66.438848	72.43548	79.058186	86.37486	94.460786	113.283211	136.307539	164.494023	199.02088	241.332684	293.19922	356.78685
31	70.760790	77.41943	84.801677	92.98923	102.073041	123.345868	149.575217	181.943425	221.91317	271.292606	332.31511	407.73701
32	75.298829	82.67750	90.889778	100.03353	110.218154	134.213537	164.036987	201.137767	247.32362	304.847719	376.51608	465.82019
33	80.063771	88.22476	97.343165	107.53571	118.933425	145.950620	179.800315	222.251544	275.52922	342.429446	426.46317	532.03501
34	85.066959	94.07712	104.183755	115.52553	128.258765	158.626670	196.982344	245.476699	306.83744	384.520979	482.90338	607.51991
35	90.320307	100.25136	111.434780	124.03469	138.236878	172.316804	215.710755	271.024368	341.58955	431.663496	546.68082	693.57270
40	120.799774	136.60561	154.761966	175.63192	199.635112	259.056519	337.882445	442.592556	581.82607	767.091420	1013.70424	1342.02510
45	159.700156	184.11917	212.743514	246.32459	285.749311	386.505617	525.858734	718.904837	986.63856	1358.230032	1874.16463	2590.56480
50	209.347996	246.21748	290.335905	343.17967	406.528929	573.770156	815.083556	1163.908529	1668.77115	2400.018249	3459.50712	4994.52135

APPENDIX B: CODES OF PROFESSIONAL ETHICS FOR ACCOUNTANTS

In recent years, governments, businesses, and the public have given increased attention to ethical conduct. They have insisted upon a level of human behavior that goes beyond that required by laws and regulations. Thus many businesses, as well as professional groups (such as accountants) and governmental organizations, have established standards of ethical conduct. This text emphasizes the ethical conduct of accountants, who serve various business interests as well as the public.

This appendix sets forth the standards of professional conduct expected of accountants in public accounting and private accounting. For accountants employed in public accounting, the American Institute of Certified Public Accountants' *Code of Professional Conduct* is presented.[1] For accountants employed in private accounting, the National Association of Accountants' *Standards of Ethical Conduct for Management Accountants* is presented as a guide to professional conduct.[2]

Supplementing the codes of professional ethics are ethics discussion cases that appear at the end of each chapter. These cases represent "real world" examples of ethical issues facing accountants. It should be noted that codes of professional ethics are general guides to good behavior and their application to specific situations often requires the exercise of professional judgment. In some cases, the line between right and wrong may be quite fine, and reasonable people may disagree. In addition, business is dynamic and everchanging, and what society considers to be acceptable behavior changes from time to time.

---

[1]*Code of Professional Conduct* (New York: American Institute of Certified Public Accountants, 1988), pp. 3–8.

[2]*Statements on Management Accounting, No. 1C,* "Standards of Ethical Conduct for Management Accountants" (New York: National Association of Accountants, 1983), pp. 1–2.

Code of Professional Conduct

as adopted January 12, 1988

Composition, Applicability, and Compliance

The Code of Professional Conduct of the American Institute of Certified Public Accountants consists of two sections — (1) the Principles and (2) the Rules. The Principles provide the framework for the Rules, which govern the performance of professional services by members. The Council of the American Institute of Certified Public Accountants is authorized to designate bodies to promulgate technical standards under the Rules, and the bylaws require adherence to those Rules and standards.

The Code of Professional Conduct was adopted by the membership to provide guidance and rules to all members — those in public practice, in industry, in government, and in education — in the performance of their professional responsibilities.

Compliance with the Code of Professional Conduct, as with all standards in an open society, depends primarily on members' understanding and voluntary actions, secondarily on reinforcement by peers and public opinion, and ultimately on disciplinary proceedings, when necessary, against members who fail to comply with the Rules.

Section I — Principles

Preamble

Membership in the American Institute of Certified Public Accountants is voluntary. By accepting membership, a certified public accountant assumes an obligation of self-discipline above and beyond the requirements of laws and regulations.

These Principles of the Code of Professional Conduct of the American Institute of Certified Public Accountants express the profession's recognition of its responsibilities to the public, to clients, and to colleagues. They guide members in the performance of their professional responsibilities and express the basic tenets of ethical and professional conduct. The Principles call for an unswerving commitment to honorable behavior, even at the sacrifice of personal advantage.

Article I

Responsibilities

In carrying out their responsibilities as professionals, members should exercise sensitive professional and moral judgments in all their activities.

As professionals, certified public accountants perform an essential role in society. Consistent with that role, members of the American Institute of Certified Public Accountants have responsibilities to all those who use their professional services. Members also have a continuing responsibility to cooperate with each other to improve the art of accounting, maintain the public's confidence, and carry out the profession's special responsibilities for self-governance. The collective efforts of all members are required to maintain and enhance the traditions of the profession.

Article II

The Public Interest

Members should accept the obligation to act in a way that will serve the public interest, honor the public trust, and demonstrate commitment to professionalism.

A distinguishing mark of a profession is acceptance of its responsibility to the public. The accounting profession's public consists of clients, credit grantors, governments, employers, investors, the business and financial community, and others who rely on the objectivity and integrity of certified public accountants to maintain the orderly functioning of commerce. This reliance imposes a public interest responsibility on certified public accountants. The public interest is defined as the collective well-being of the community of people and institutions the profession serves.

In discharging their professional responsibilities, members may encounter conflicting pressures from among each of those groups. In resolving those conflicts, members should act with integrity, guided by the precept that when members fulfill their responsibility to the public, clients' and employers' interests are best served.

Those who rely on certified public accountants expect them to discharge their responsibilities with integrity, objectivity, due professional care, and a genuine interest in serving the public. They are expected to provide quality services, enter into fee arrangements, and offer a range of services — all in a manner that demonstrates a level of professionalism consistent with these Principles of the Code of Professional Conduct.

All who accept membership in the American Institute of Certified Public Accountants commit themselves to honor the public trust. In return for the faith that the public reposes in them, members should seek continually to demonstrate their dedication to professional excellence.

Article III

Integrity

To maintain and broaden public confidence, members should perform all professional responsibilities with the highest sense of integrity.

Integrity is an element of character fundamental to professional recognition. It is the quality from which the public trust derives and the benchmark against which a member must ultimately test all decisions.

Integrity requires a member to be, among other things, honest and candid within the constraints of client confidentiality. Service and the public trust should not be subordinated to personal gain and advantage. Integrity can accommodate the inadvertent error and the honest difference of opinion; it cannot accommodate deceit or subordination of principle.

Integrity is measured in terms of what is right and just. In the absence of specific rules, standards, or guidance, or in the face of conflicting opinions, a member should test decisions and deeds by asking: "Am I doing what a person of integrity would do? Have I retained my integrity?" Integrity requires a member to observe both the form and the spirit of technical and ethical standards; circumvention of those standards constitutes subordination of judgment.

Integrity also requires a member to observe the principles of objectivity and independence and of due care.

Article IV

Objectivity and Independence

A member should maintain objectivity and be free of conflicts of interest in discharging professional responsibilities. A member in public practice should be independent in fact and appearance when providing auditing and other attestation services.

Objectivity is a state of mind, a quality that lends value to a member's services. It is a distinguishing feature of the profession. The principle of objectivity imposes the obligation to be impartial, intellectually honest, and free of conflicts of interest. Independence precludes relationships that may appear to impair a member's objectivity in rendering attestation services.

Members often serve multiple interests in many different capacities and must demonstrate their objectivity in varying circumstances. Members in public practice render attest, tax, and management advisory services. Other members prepare financial statements in the employment of others, perform internal auditing services, and serve in financial and management capacities in industry, education, and government. They also educate and train those who aspire to admission into the profession. Regardless of service or capacity, members should protect the integrity of their work, maintain objectivity, and avoid any subordination of their judgment.

For a member in public practice, the maintenance of objectivity and independence requires a continuing assessment of client relationships and public responsibility. Such a member who provides auditing and other attestation services should be independent in fact and appearance. In providing all other services, a member should maintain objectivity and avoid conflicts of interest.

Although members not in public practice cannot maintain the appearance of independence, they nevertheless have the responsibility to maintain objectivity in rendering professional services. Members employed by others to prepare financial statements or to perform auditing, tax, or consulting services are charged with the same responsibility for objectivity as members in public practice and must be scrupulous in their application of generally accepted accounting principles and candid in all their dealings with members in public practice.

Article V

Due Care

A member should observe the profession's technical and ethical standards, strive continually to improve competence and the quality of services, and discharge professional responsibility to the best of the member's ability.

The quest for excellence is the essence of due care. Due care requires a member to discharge professional responsibilities with competence and diligence. It imposes the obligation to perform professional services to the best of a member's ability with concern for the best interest of those for whom the services are performed and consistent with the profession's responsibility to the public.

Competence is derived from a synthesis of education and experience. It begins with a mastery of the common body of knowledge required for designation as a certified public accountant. The maintenance of competence requires a commitment of learning and professional improvement that must continue throughout a member's professional life. It is a member's individual responsibility. In all engagements and in all responsibilities, each member should undertake to achieve a level of competence that will assure that the quality of the member's services meets the high level of professionalism required by these Principles.

Competence represents the attainment and maintenance of a level of understanding and knowledge that enables a member to render services with facility and acumen. It also establishes the limitations of a member's capabilities by dictating that consultation or referral may be required when a professional engagement exceeds the personal competence of a member or a member's firm. Each member is responsible for assessing his or her own competence—of evaluating whether education, experience, and judgment are adequate for the responsibility to be assumed.

Members should be diligent in discharging responsibilities to clients, employers, and the public. Diligence imposes the responsibility to render services promptly and carefully, to be thorough, and to observe applicable technical and ethical standards.

Due care requires a member to plan and supervise adequately any professional activity for which he or she is responsible.

Article VI

Scope and Nature of Services

A member in public practice should observe the Principles of the Code of Professional Conduct in determining the scope and nature of services to be provided.

The public interest aspect of certified public accountants' services requires that such services be consistent with acceptable professional behavior for certified public accountants. Integrity requires that service and the public trust not be subordinated to personal gain and advantage. Objectivity and independence require that members be free from conflicts of interest in discharging professional responsibilities. Due care requires that services be provided with competence and diligence.

Each of these Principles should be considered by members in determining whether or not to provide specific services in individual circumstances. In some instances, they may represent an overall constraint on the nonaudit services that might be offered to a specific client. No hard-and-fast rules can be developed to help members reach these judgments, but they must be satisfied that they are meeting the spirit of the Principles in this regard.

In order to accomplish this, members should:

- Practice in firms that have in place internal quality-control procedures to ensure that services are competently delivered and adequately supervised.
- Determine, in their individual judgments, whether the scope and nature of other services provided to an audit client would create a conflict of interest in the performance of the audit function for that client.
- Assess, in their individual judgments, whether an activity is consistent with their role as professionals (for example, Is such activity a reasonable extension or variation of existing services offered by the member or others in the profession?).

Standards of Ethical Conduct for Management Accountants

Management accountants have an obligation to the organizations they serve, their profession, the public, and themselves to maintain the highest standards of ethical conduct. In recognition of this obligation, the Institute of Management Accountants (formerly the National Association of Accountants) has promulgated the following standards of ethical conduct for management accountants. Adherence to these standards is integral to achieving the *Objectives of Management Accounting*.[1] Management accountants shall not commit acts contrary to these standards nor shall they condone the commission of such acts by others within their organizations.

Competence

Management accountants have a responsibility to:

- Maintain an appropriate level of professional competence by ongoing development of their knowledge and skills.
- Perform their professional duties in accordance with relevant laws, regulations, and technical standards.

---

[1] National Association of Accountants, *Statements on Management Accounting: Objectives of Management Accounting,* Statement No. 1B, New York, N.Y., June 17, 1982.

- Prepare complete and clear reports and recommendations after appropriate analyses of relevant and reliable information.

Confidentiality

Management accountants have a responsibility to:

- Refrain from disclosing confidential information acquired in the course of their work except when authorized, unless legally obligated to do so.
- Inform subordinates as appropriate regarding the confidentiality of information acquired in the course of their work and monitor their activities to assure the maintenance of that confidentiality.
- Refrain from using or appearing to use confidential information acquired in the course of their work for unethical or illegal advantage either personally or through third parties.

Integrity

Management accountants have a responsibility to:

- Avoid actual or apparent conflicts of interest and advise all appropriate parties of any potential conflict.
- Refrain from engaging in any activity that would prejudice their ability to carry out their duties ethically.
- Refuse any gift, favor, or hospitality that would influence or would appear to influence their actions.
- Refrain from either actively or passively subverting the attainment of the organization's legitimate and ethical objectives.
- Recognize and communicate professional limitations or other constraints that would preclude responsible judgment or successful performance of an activity.
- Communicate unfavorable as well as favorable information and professional judgments or opinions.
- Refrain from engaging in or supporting any activity that would discredit the profession.

Objectivity

Management accountants have a reponsibility to:

- Communicate information fairly and objectively.
- Disclose fully all relevant information that could reasonably be expected to influence an intended user's understanding of the reports, comments, and recommendations presented. □

APPENDIX C: ALTERNATIVE METHOD OF RECORDING PREPAID EXPENSES

In Chapter 3, prepaid expenses were debited to an asset account at the time of payment. As an alternative, prepaid expenses may be debited to an expense account at the time of payment.

To illustrate the alternative methods of recording prepaid expenses, assume that premiums on insurance policies acquired during the first year of operation were $2,034. Also, assume that $906 of the premiums had expired during the year, leaving $1,128 as unexpired premiums, computed as follows:

Premiums on insurance policies aquired during the year	$2,034
Premiums expired during the year	906
Unexpired premiums at the end of year	$1,128

Based on these data, the entries under the alternative methods can be summarized as follows:

Systems of Recording Prepaid Expenses

Prepaid Expense Recorded Initially as Asset			**Prepaid Expense** Recorded Initially as Expense		
Initial entries (to record initial expenditures):			Initial entries (to record initial expenditures):		
Prepaid Insurance	1,250		Insurance Expense	1,250	
Cash.		1,250	Cash.		1,250
~~			~~~		
Prepaid Insurance	180		Insurance Expense	180	
Cash.		180	Cash.		180
Adjusting entry (to transfer amount **used** to appropriate **expense** account):			Adjusting entry (to transfer amount **unused** to the appropriate **asset** account):		
Insurance Expense	906		Prepaid Insurance	1,128	
Prepaid Insurance		906	Insurance Expense		1,128

After the entries to record the prepaid insurance initially as an asset have been posted, the prepaid insurance and insurance expense accounts appear as follows:

Prepaid Expense Recorded as Asset

ACCOUNT PREPAID INSURANCE ACCOUNT NO. 118

Date		Item	Debit	Credit	Balance	
					Debit	Credit
1992						
Jan.	3		1,250		1,250	
Mar.	18		225		1,475	
Aug.	26		379		1,854	
Nov.	11		180		2,034	
Dec.	31	Adjusting		906	1,128	

ACCOUNT INSURANCE EXPENSE ACCOUNT NO. 716

Date		Item	Debit	Credit	Balance	
					Debit	Credit
1992						
Dec.	31	Adjusting	906		906	

After the entries to record prepaid insurance initially as an expense have been posted, the prepaid insurance and the insurance expense accounts appear as follows:

Prepaid Expense Recorded as Expense

ACCOUNT PREPAID INSURANCE ACCOUNT NO. 118

Date		Item	Debit	Credit	Balance	
					Debit	Credit
1992						
Dec.	31	Adjusting	1,128		1,128	

ACCOUNT INSURANCE EXPENSE ACCOUNT NO. 716

Date		Item	Debit	Credit	Balance	
					Debit	Credit
1992						
Jan.	3		1,250		1,250	
Mar.	18		225		1,475	
Aug.	26		379		1,854	
Nov.	11		180		2,034	
Dec.	31	Adjusting		1,128	906	

Either of the two systems of recording prepaid expenses may be used for all of the prepaid expenses of an enterprise, or one system may be used for some kinds of prepaid expenses and the other system for other kinds. Initial debits to the asset account seem to be logical for prepayments of insurance, which are usually for periods of from one to three years. On the other hand, interest charges on notes payable are usually for short periods. Some charges may be recorded when a note is issued; other charges may be recorded when a note is paid; and few, if any, of the debits for interest may require adjustment at the end of the period. It therefore seems logical to record all interest charges initially by debiting the expense account rather than the asset account.[1]

[1] Notes payable and related interest charges are discussed in more detail in Chapter 9.

As indicated in the illustration, the amounts reported as expenses in the income statement and as assets on the balance sheet will be the same regardless of the method used. To avoid confusion, the method adopted by an enterprise for each kind of prepaid expense should be followed consistently from year to year.

EXERCISES

Ex. C–1.
Adjusting entries for office supplies.

The office supplies purchased during the year total $5,450, and the inventory at the end of the year is $1,530.

(a) Set up T accounts for Office Supplies and Office Supplies Expense, and record the following directly in the accounts, employing the system of initially recording supplies as an asset (identify each entry by number): (1) purchases for the period; (2) adjusting entry at the end of the period.

(b) Set up T accounts for Office Supplies and Office Supplies Expense, and record the following directly in the accounts, employing the system of initially recording supplies as an expense (identify each entry by number): (1) purchases for the period; (2) adjusting entry at the end of the period.

Ex. C–2.
Adjusting entries for prepaid insurance.

During the first year of operations, insurance premiums of $4,500 were paid. At the end of the year, unexpired premiums totaled $2,000. Journalize the adjusting entry at the end of the year assuming (a) prepaid expenses were initially recorded as assets and (b) prepaid expenses were initially recorded as expenses.

APPENDIX D: ALTERNATIVE METHOD OF RECORDING UNEARNED REVENUE

In Chapter 4, unearned revenues were credited to a liability account at the time of receipt. As an alternative, unearned revenues may be credited to a revenue account at the time of receipt.

As a basis for illustrating the two methods of recording revenues received in advance, assume that on October 1 a business rents a portion of its building for a period of one year, receiving $7,200 in payment for the entire term of the lease. On December 31, the end of the fiscal year, $1,800 (1/4 of $7,200) has been earned and $5,400 (3/4 of $7,200) has not yet been earned.

Based on these data, the entries under the alternative methods can be summarized as follows:

Systems of Recording Unearned Revenue

Unearned Revenue Recorded Initially as Liability			**Unearned Revenue** Recorded Initially as Revenue		
Initial entry (to record initial receipt):			Initial entry (to record initial receipt):		
Cash.	7,200		Cash.	7,200	
Unearned Rent.		7,200	Rent Income		7,200
Adjusting entry (to transfer amount **earned** to appropriate **revenue** account):			Adjusting entry (to transfer amount **unearned** to appropriate **liability** account):		
Unearned Rent.	1,800		Rent Income	5,400	
Rent Income		1,800	Unearned Rent.		5,400

After the entries to record unearned revenue initially as a liability have been posted, the unearned rent account and the rent income account appear as follows:

Unearned Revenue Recorded as Liability

ACCOUNT UNEARNED RENT — ACCOUNT NO. 218

Date		Item	Debit	Credit	Balance Debit	Balance Credit
1992						
Oct.	1			7,200		7,200
Dec.	31	Adjusting	1,800			5,400

ACCOUNT RENT INCOME ACCOUNT NO. 812

Date		Item	Debit	Credit	Balance	
					Debit	Credit
1992						
Dec.	31	Adjusting		1,800		1,800

After the entries to record unearned revenue initially as revenue have been posted, the unearned rent account and the rent income account appear as follows:

Unearned Revenue Recorded as Revenue

ACCOUNT UNEARNED RENT ACCOUNT NO. 218

Date		Item	Debit	Credit	Balance	
					Debit	Credit
1992						
Dec.	31	Adjusting		5,400		5,400

ACCOUNT RENT INCOME ACCOUNT NO. 812

Date		Item	Debit	Credit	Balance	
					Debit	Credit
1992						
Oct.	1			7,200		7,200
Dec.	31	Adjusting	5,400			1,800

Either of the two methods may be used for all revenues received in advance, or the first method may be used for advance receipts of some kinds of revenue and the second method for other kinds. The results obtained are the same under both methods, but to avoid confusion the system used should be followed consistently from year to year.

EXERCISES

Ex. D–1.
Adjusting entries for advertising revenue.

The advertising revenues received during the year total $280,000, and the unearned advertising revenue at the end of the year is $40,000.

(a) Set up T accounts for Unearned Advertising Revenue and Advertising Revenue and record the following directly in the accounts, employing the system of initially recording advertising fees as a liability (identify each entry by number): (1) revenues received during the period; (2) adjusting entry at the end of the period.

(b) Set up T accounts for Unearned Advertising Revenue and Advertising Revenue and record the following directly in the accounts, employing the system of initially recording advertising fees as a revenue (identify each entry by number): (1) revenues received during the period; (2) adjusting entry at the end of the period.

Ex. D–2.
Year-end entries for deferred revenues.

In their first year of operations, Easterly Publishing Co. received $600,000 from advertising contracts and $975,000 from magazine subscriptions, crediting the two amounts to Unearned Advertising Revenue and Circulation Revenue, respectively. At the end of the year, the unearned advertising revenue amounts to $125,000, and the unearned circulation revenue amounts to $250,000. Present the adjusting entries that should be made at the end of the year.

APPENDIX E: ALTERNATIVE METHOD OF RECORDING MERCHANDISE INVENTORIES

The recording of merchandise inventory at the end of the accounting period is described and illustrated in Chapter 4. The alternative method presented in this appendix classifies the entries for the beginning and the ending merchandise inventories as *adjusting* entries instead of *closing* entries. The difference in viewpoint has a minor effect on the work sheet, the sequence of entries in the journal, and the income summary account. It does not alter the financial statements in any way. The data for Cox Co. presented in Chapter 4 is used for the illustrations in this appendix.

MERCHANDISE INVENTORY ADJUSTMENTS

At the end of the period it is necessary to remove from Merchandise Inventory the amount representing the inventory at the beginning of the period and to replace it with the amount representing the inventory at the end of the period. This can be accomplished by two adjusting entries. The first entry transfers the beginning inventory to Income Summary. Since this beginning inventory is part of the cost of merchandise sold, it is debited to Income Summary. It is also a subtraction from the asset account, Merchandise Inventory, and hence is credited to that account. The first adjusting entry for Cox Co. is as follows:

Dec. 31	Income Summary	59,700	
	Merchandise Inventory		59,700

The second adjusting entry debits the cost of the merchandise inventory at the end of the period to the asset account, Merchandise Inventory. The credit portion of the entry effects a deduction of the unsold merchandise from the total cost of the merchandise available for sale during the period. The second adjusting entry for Cox Co. is as follows:

Dec. 31	Merchandise Inventory	62,150	
	Income Summary		62,150

The effect of the two inventory adjustments is indicated by the following T accounts for Merchandise Inventory and Income Summary:

Merchandise Inventory

Dec. 31, 1991	59,700	Dec. 31, 1991	59,700
Dec. 31, 1992	62,150		

Income Summary

Dec. 31, 1992	59,700	Dec. 31, 1992	62,150

In the accounts, the inventory of $59,700 at the end of the preceding year (December 31, 1991), which is the beginning of the current year, has been transferred to Income Summary as a part of the cost of merchandise available for sale. It is replaced by a debit of $62,150, the merchandise inventory at the end of the current year (December 31, 1992). The credit of the same amount to Income Summary is a deduction from the cost of merchandise available for sale.

WORK SHEET

All adjustments are recorded in the Adjustments columns of the work sheet in the same manner as was illustrated on pages 158-162, except that by this method entries are required in the Adjustments columns for merchandise inventory. The balances are then extended to the Income Statement and Balance Sheet columns, and the work sheet is completed. An exception to the usual practice of extending only the account balances should be noted. Both the debit and credit amounts for Income Summary are extended to the Income Statement columns. Since both the amount of the debit adjustment (beginning inventory of $59,700) and the amount of the credit adjustment (ending inventory of $62,150) may be reported on the income statement, there is no need to determine the difference between the two amounts. A work sheet for Cox Co. employing this alternative procedure is illustrated on page E-3. Note that the Income Statement and Balance Sheet columns, including column totals and the amount of net income, are the same as those on the work sheet on pages 160 and 161.

Cox Co.
Work Sheet
For Year Ended December 31, 1992

ACCOUNT TITLE	TRIAL BALANCE		ADJUSTMENTS		INCOME STATEMENT		BALANCE SHEET	
	DEBIT	CREDIT	DEBIT	CREDIT	DEBIT	CREDIT	DEBIT	CREDIT
Cash	62,950						62,950	
Notes Receivable	40,000						40,000	
Accounts Receivable	60,880						60,880	
Interest Receivable			(h) 200				200	
Merchandise Inventory	59,700		(b) 62,150	(a) 59,700			62,150	
Office Supplies	1,090			(c) 610			480	
Prepaid Insurance	4,560			(d) 1,910			2,650	
Store Equipment	27,100						27,100	
Accumulated Depreciation — Store Equipment		2,600		(e) 3,100				5,700
Office Equipment	15,570						15,570	
Accumulated Depreciation — Office Equipment		2,230		(f) 2,490				4,720
Accounts Payable		22,420						22,420
Salaries Payable				(g) 1,140				1,140
Unearned Rent		2,400	(i) 600					1,800
Notes Payable		25,000						25,000
Capital Stock		100,000						100,000
Retained Earnings		53,800						53,800
Dividends	18,000						18,000	
Income Summary			(a) 59,700	(b) 62,150	59,700	62,150		
Sales		720,185				720,185		
Sales Returns and Allowances	6,140				6,140			
Sales Discounts	5,790				5,790			
Purchases	521,980				521,980			
Purchases Returns and Allowances		9,100				9,100		
Purchases Discounts		2,525				2,525		
Transportation In	17,400				17,400			
Sales Salaries Expense	59,250		(g) 780		60,030			
Advertising Expense	10,860				10,860			
Depreciation Expense — Store Equipment			(e) 3,100		3,100			
Miscellaneous Selling Expense	630				630			
Office Salaries Expense	20,660		(g) 360		21,020			
Rent Expense	8,100				8,100			
Depreciation Expense — Office Equipment			(f) 2,490		2,490			
Insurance Expense			(d) 1,910		1,910			
Office Supplies Expense			(c) 610		610			
Miscellaneous Administrative Expense	760				760			
Rent Income				(i) 600		600		
Interest Income		3,600		(h) 200		3,800		
Interest Expense	2,440				2,440			
	943,860	943,860	131,900	131,900	722,960	798,360	289,980	214,580
Net Income					75,400			75,400
					798,360	798,360	289,980	289,980

ADJUSTING ENTRIES

The adjusting entries made from the alternative work sheet are illustrated as follows. They are exactly the same as those illustrated on pages 160 and 161, except for the inclusion of adjustments for inventory.

Adjusting Entries

JOURNAL PAGE

DATE		DESCRIPTION	POST. REF.	DEBIT	CREDIT
		Adjusting Entries			
1992 Dec.	31	Income Summary		59,700.00	
		Merchandise Inventory			59,700.00
	31	Merchandise Inventory		62,150.00	
		Income Summary			62,150.00
	31	Office Supplies Expense		610.00	
		Office Supplies			610.00
	31	Insurance Expense		1,910.00	
		Prepaid Insurance			1,910.00
	31	Depreciation Expense—Store Equip.		3,100.00	
		Accumulated Depr.—Store Equip.			3,100.00
	31	Depreciation Expense—Office Equip.		2,490.00	
		Accumulated Depr.—Office Equip.			2,490.00
	31	Sales Salaries Expense		780.00	
		Office Salaries Expense		360.00	
		Salaries Payable			1,140.00
	31	Interest Receivable		200.00	
		Interest Income			200.00
	31	Unearned Rent		600.00	
		Rent Income			600.00

CLOSING ENTRIES

All accounts with balances in the Income Statement Credit column of the work sheet, with the exception of the amount for Income Summary, which represents the ending merchandise inventory balance, are closed in one compound journal entry by debiting each account and crediting Income Summary. All accounts with balances in the Income Statement Debit column, with the exception of the amount for Income Summary, which represents the beginning merchandise inventory balance, are closed in one entry by debiting Income Summary and crediting each account. The Income Summary and the dividends accounts are then closed to the retained earnings account. All of the closing entries for the alternative procedure for Cox Co. are as follows:

Closing Entries

JOURNAL PAGE

DATE		DESCRIPTION	POST. REF.	DEBIT	CREDIT
		Closing Entries			
1992 Dec.	31	Sales		720,185 00	
		Purchases Returns and Allowances		9,100 00	
		Purchases Discounts		2,525 00	
		Interest Income		3,800 00	
		Rent Income		600 00	
		Income Summary			736,210 00
	31	Income Summary		663,260 00	
		Sales Returns and Allowances			6,140 00
		Sales Discounts			5,790 00
		Purchases			521,980 00
		Transportation In			17,400 00
		Sales Salaries Expense			60,030 00
		Advertising Expense			10,860 00
		Depreciation Exp.—Store Equip.			3,100 00
		Miscellaneous Selling Expense			630 00
		Office Salaries Expense			21,020 00
		Rent Expense			8,100 00
		Depreciation Exp.—Office Equip.			2,490 00
		Insurance Expense			1,910 00
		Office Supplies Expense			610 00
		Miscellaneous Administrative Exp.			760 00
		Interest Expense			2,440 00
	31	Income Summary		75,400 00	
		Retained Earnings			75,400 00
	31	Retained Earnings		18,000 00	
		Dividends			18,000 00

The income summary account, as it will appear after the merchandise inventory adjustments and the closing entries have been posted, is as follows. Each item in the account is identified as an aid to understanding. Such notations are not an essential part of the posting procedure.

Income Summary

ACCOUNT Income Summary ACCOUNT NO.

DATE		ITEM	POST. REF.	DEBIT	CREDIT	BALANCE DEBIT	BALANCE CREDIT
1992 Dec.	31	Mer. inv., Jan. 1		59,700 00		59,700 00	
	31	Mer. inv., Dec. 31			62,150 00		2,450 00
	31	Revenue, etc.			736,210 00		738,660 00
	31	Expense, etc.		663,260 00			75,400 00
	31	Net income		75,400 00		—	—

APPENDIX F: SPECIAL JOURNALS & SUBSIDIARY LEDGERS

A manual accounting system is used in the text because such a system enables the student to focus most easily on the basic principles of accounting. In practice, when the manual system is used, it is often modified somewhat in order to process accounting data more effectively. One such modification is discussed in this appendix.

In the text, all transactions initially were recorded in a two-column journal, then posted individually to the appropriate accounts in the ledger. Applying such detailed procedures to a large number of transactions that are often repeated is impractical. For example, if many credit sales are made, each of these transactions would require an entry debiting Accounts Receivable and crediting Sales. In addition, the accounts receivable account in the ledger would include receivables from a large number of customers. In such cases, special journals can be used to record like kinds of transactions, and subsidiary ledgers can be used for accounts with a common characteristic.

Special Journals

One of the simplest methods of processing data more efficiently in a manual accounting system is to expand the two-column journal to a **multicolumn** journal. Each amount column included in a multicolumn journal is restricted to the recording of transactions affecting a certain account. For example, a special column could be used only for recording debits to the cash account and another special column could be used only for recording credits to the cash account. The addition of the two special columns would eliminate the writing of "Cash" in the journal for every receipt and payment of cash. Furthermore, there would be no need to post each individual debit and credit to the cash account. Instead, the "Cash Dr." and "Cash Cr." columns could be totaled periodically and only the totals posted, yielding additional economies. In a similar manner, special columns could be added for recording credits to Sales, debits and credits to Accounts Receivable and Accounts Payable, and for other entries that are repeated. Although there is no exact number of columns that may be effectively used in a multicolumn journal, there is a maximum number beyond which the journal would become unmanageable. Also, the possibilities of errors in recording become greater as the number of columns and the width of the page increase.

An all-purpose multicolumn journal usually is satisfactory for a small business enterprise that needs the services of only one accountant. If the number of transactions is enough to require two or more accountants, the use of a single journal usually is not efficient. The next logical development in expanding the system is to replace an all-purpose journal with a number of **special journals**, each designed to record a single kind of transaction. Special journals would be needed only for the kinds of transactions that occur frequently. Since most enterprises have many transactions in which cash is received and many in which cash is paid out, it is common practice to use a special journal for recording cash receipts and another special journal for recording cash payments. An enterprise that sells services or merchandise to customers on account might use a special journal designed for recording only such transactions. On the other hand, a business that does not give credit would have no need for such a journal.

The transactions that occur most often in a medium-size merchandising firm and the special journals in which they are recorded are as follows:

Transaction		Journal
Purchase of merchandise or other items *on account*	recorded in	Purchases journal
Payments of cash for *any* purpose	recorded in	Cash payments journal
Sale of merchandise *on account*	recorded in	Sales journal
Receipt of cash from *any* source	recorded in	Cash receipts journal

Sometimes the business documents evidencing purchases and sales transactions are used as special journals. When there are a large number of such transactions on a credit basis, the use of this procedure may result in a substantial savings in record keeping expenses and a reduction of record keeping errors.

The two-column form illustrated in earlier chapters can be used for miscellaneous entries, such as adjusting and closing entries, that do not "fit" in any of the special journals. The two-column form commonly is called the **general journal** or simply the **journal.**

Subsidiary Ledgers

As the number of purchases and sales on account increase, the need for maintaining a separate account for each creditor and debtor is clear. If such accounts are numerous, their inclusion in the same ledger with all other accounts would cause the ledger to become unmanageable. The chance of posting errors would also be increased and the preparation of the trial balance and the financial statements wouid be delayed.

When there are a large number of individual accounts with a common characteristic, it is common to place them in a separate ledger called a **subsidiary ledger.** The principal ledger, which contains all of the balance sheet and income statement accounts, is then called the **general ledger.** Each subsidiary ledger is represented in the general ledger by a summarizing account, called a **controlling account.** The sum of the balances of the accounts in a subsidiary ledger must agree with the balance of the related controlling account. Thus, a subsidiary ledger may be said to be *controlled* by its controlling account.

The individual accounts with creditors are arranged in alphabetical order in a subsidiary ledger called the **accounts payable ledger** or **creditors ledger.** The related controlling account in the general ledger is Accounts Payable.

The subsidiary ledger for credit customers is needed for most business enterprises. This ledger containing the individual accounts is called the **accounts receivable ledger** or **customers ledger.** The controlling account in the general ledger that summarizes the debits and credits to the individual customers accounts is Accounts Receivable.

Purchases Journal

Property most frequently purchased on account by a merchandising concern is of the following types: (1) merchandise for resale to customers, (2) supplies for use in conducting the business, and (3) equipment and other plant assets. Because of the variety of items acquired on credit terms, the **purchases journal** should be designed to allow for the recording of everything purchased on account. The form of purchases journal used by Kannon Corporation is illustrated below.

For each transaction recorded in the purchases journal, the credit is entered in the Accounts Payable Cr. column. The next three amount columns are used for accumulating debits to the particular accounts most frequently affected. Invoice amounts for merchandise purchased for sale to customers are recorded in the Purchases Dr. column. The purpose of the Store Supplies Dr. and Office Supplies Dr. columns is readily apparent. If supplies of these two categories were purchased only once in a while, the two columns could be omitted from the journal.

The final set of columns, under the main heading Sundry Accounts Dr., is used to record acquisitions, on account, of items not provided for in the special debit columns. The title of the account to be debited is entered in the Account column and the amount is entered in the Amount column. A separate posting reference column is provided for this section of the purchases journal.

Purchases Journal

PAGE 19 PURCHASES

	DATE		ACCOUNT CREDITED	POST. REF.	ACCOUNTS PAYABLE CR.
1	1992 Oct.	2	Video Co.	✓	5,724 00
2		3	Marsh Inc.	✓	7,406 00
3		9	Parker Supply Co.	✓	257 00
4		11	Marsh Inc.	✓	3,208 00
5		16	Dunlap Corporation	✓	3,593 00
6		17	Robinson Supply	✓	1,500 00
7		20	Walton Co.	✓	15,125 00
8		23	Parker Supply Co.	✓	132 00
9		27	Dunlap Corporation	✓	6,375 00
10		31			43,320 00
11					(211)

Posting the Purchases Journal. The special journals used in recording most of the transactions affecting creditors accounts are designed to allow the posting of individual transactions to the accounts payable ledger and a single monthly total to Accounts Payable. The basic techniques of posting credits from a purchases journal to an accounts payable ledger and the controlling account are shown in the following flowchart:

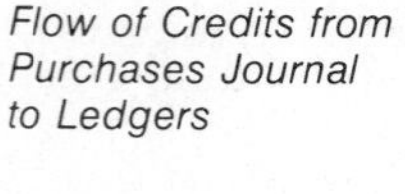
Flow of Credits from Purchases Journal to Ledgers

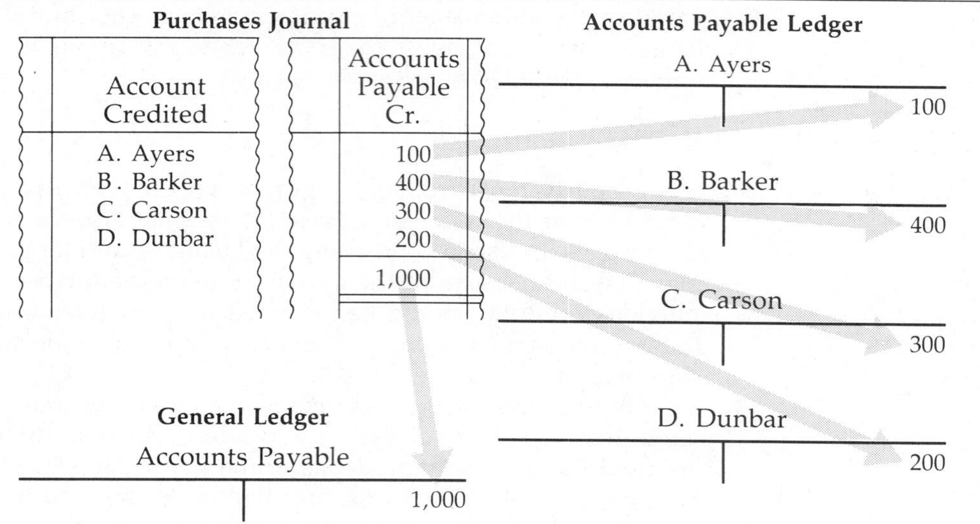

The individual credits of $100, $400, $300, and $200 to Ayers, Barker, Carson, and Dunbar, respectively are posted to their accounts in the accounts payable ledger. The sum of the credits to the four individual accounts in the subsidiary ledger is posted as a single $1,000 credit to Accounts Payable, the controlling account in the general ledger.

The source of the entries posted to the subsidiary and general ledgers is indicated in the posting reference column of each account by inserting the

JOURNAL PAGE 19

Purchases Dr.	Store Supplies Dr.	Office Supplies Dr.	Sundry Accounts Dr. Account	Post. Ref.	Amount	
5,724 00						1
7,406 00						2
	131 00	126 00				3
3,208 00						4
3,593 00						5
1,500 00						6
			Store Equipment	121	15,125 00	7
	75 00	57 00				8
6,375 00						9
27,806 00	206 00	183 00			15,125 00	10
(511)	(115)	(116)			(✓)	11

letter "P" and the page number of the purchases journal. An account in the accounts payable ledger of Kannon Corporation is presented as an example.

An Account in the Accounts Payable Ledger

NAME Robinson Supply

ADDRESS 3800 Mission Street, San Francisco, CA 94110-1732

DATE		ITEM	POST. REF.	DEBIT	CREDIT	BALANCE
1992 Oct.	17		P19		1 500 00	1 500 00

Since the balances in the creditors accounts are usually credit balances, a three-column account form is used instead of the four-column account form illustrated earlier. When a creditor's account is overpaid and a debit balance occurs, that fact should be indicated by an asterisk or parentheses in the Balance column. When an account's balance is zero, a line may be drawn in the Balance column.

The creditors accounts in the subsidiary ledger are not numbered, because the order changes each time a new account is inserted alphabetically or an old account is removed. Thus, instead of a number, a check mark (✓) is inserted in the posting reference column of the purchases journal after a credit is posted.

The amounts in the Sundry Accounts Dr. column of the purchases journal are posted to the appropriate accounts in the general ledger and the posting reference ("P" and page number) are inserted in the accounts. As each amount is posted, the related general ledger account number is inserted in the posting reference column of the Sundry Accounts section.

At the end of each month, the purchases journal is totaled and ruled in the manner illustrated on pages F-3 and F-4. Before posting the totals to the general ledger, the sum of the totals of the four debit columns should be compared with the total of the credit column to prove their equality.

The totals of the four special columns are posted to the appropriate general ledger accounts in the usual manner, with the related account numbers inserted below the columnar totals. Because each amount in the Sundry Accounts Dr. column was posted individually, a check mark is placed below the $15,125 total to show that no further action is needed.

Two of the general ledger accounts to which postings were made are presented as examples. The debit posting to Store Equipment was from the Sundry Accounts Dr. column; the credit posting to Accounts Payable was from the total of the Accounts Payable Cr. column.

General Ledger Accounts after Posting from Purchases Journal

ACCOUNT Store Equipment — ACCOUNT NO. 121

DATE		ITEM	POST. REF.	DEBIT	CREDIT	BALANCE	
						DEBIT	CREDIT
1992 Oct.	1	Balance	✓			11 975 00	
	20		P19	15 125 00		27 100 00	

ACCOUNT Accounts Payable — ACCOUNT NO. 211

DATE		ITEM	POST. REF.	DEBIT	CREDIT	BALANCE	
						DEBIT	CREDIT
1992 Oct.	1	Balance	✓				21 975 00
	31		P19		43 320 00		65 295 00

The flow of data from the purchases journal of Kannon Corporation to its two related ledgers is presented graphically in the diagram below. Two procedures revealed by the flow diagram should be given special attention:

1. Postings are made from the purchases journal to both (a) accounts in the subsidiary ledger and (b) accounts in the general ledger.
2. The sum of the postings to individual accounts payable in the subsidiary ledger equals the columnar total posted to Accounts Payable (controlling account) in the general ledger.

Flow of Data from Purchases Journal to Ledgers

Purchases Journal

Account Credited	P. R.	Accts. Payable Cr.	Purchases Dr.	Store Sup. Dr.	Office Sup. Dr.	Sundry Accounts Debit: Account	P. R.	Amount
Video Co.	✓	5,724	5,724					
Marsh Inc.	✓	7,406	7,406					
Parker Supply Co.	✓	257		131	126			
Walton Co.	✓	15,125				Store Equip.	121	15,125
Parker Supply Co.	✓	132		75	57			
Dunlap Corporation	✓	6,375	6,375					
		43,320	27,806	206	183			15,125

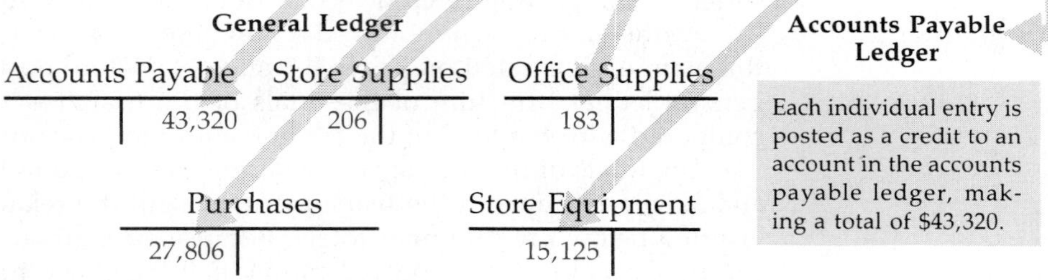

General Ledger

Account	Debit	Credit
Accounts Payable		43,320
Store Supplies	206	
Office Supplies	183	
Purchases	27,806	
Store Equipment	15,125	

Accounts Payable Ledger

Each individual entry is posted as a credit to an account in the accounts payable ledger, making a total of $43,320.

Purchases Returns and Allowances. When merchandise purchased is returned or a price adjustment is granted, an entry is made in the general journal according to the principles described in Chapter 2. To illustrate, assume that during October, Kannon Corporation issued a debit memorandum for a return of merchandise. The entry may be recorded in a two-column general journal, as follows:

General Journal Entry for Returns and Allowances

JOURNAL — PAGE 18

	DATE		DESCRIPTION	POST. REF.	DEBIT	CREDIT	
17	Oct.	20	Accounts Payable—Dunlap Corp.	211/✓	97 50		17
18			Purchases Returns and Allowances	512		97 50	18
19			Debit Memo No. 20.				19

The debit portion of the entry is posted to the accounts payable account in the general ledger (No. 211) and also to the creditor's account in the subsidiary ledger (✓). The need for posting the debits to two different accounts is indicated, at the time these entries are journalized, by drawing a *diagonal line* in the posting reference column. The account number and check mark are inserted, in the usual manner, at the time the entry is posted.

After the entry has been recorded, the memorandum is attached to the related unpaid invoice. If the invoice had been paid before the return or allowance was granted, the settlement might be a cash refund.

If goods other than merchandise are returned or a price adjustment is granted, the account to which the goods were first debited should be credited. For example, if a purchase of office equipment is returned, the credit would be to Office Equipment rather than Purchases Returns and Allowances.

Cash Payments Journal

The standards for determining the special columns to be provided in the **cash payments journal** are the same as for the purchases journal, namely, the kind of transactions to be recorded and the frequency of their occurrence. It is necessary to have a Cash Cr. column. Payments to creditors on account happen often enough to require columns for Accounts Payable Dr. and Purchases Discounts Cr. The cash payments journal illustrated below has these three columns and an additional column for Sundry Accounts Dr.

Cash Payments Journal after Posting

CASH PAYMENTS JOURNAL — PAGE 16

	DATE	CK. NO.	ACCOUNT DEBITED	POST. REF.	SUNDRY ACCOUNTS DR.	ACCOUNTS PAYABLE DR.	PURCHASES DISCOUNTS CR.	CASH CR.	
1	1992 Oct. 2	312	Purchases	511	1275 00			1275 00	1
2	4	313	Store Equipment	121	350 00			350 00	2
3	12	314	Marsh Inc.	✓		7406 00	74 06	7331 94	3
4	12	315	Sales Salaries Exp.	611	2560 00			2560 00	4
5	12	316	Office Salaries Exp.	711	880 00			880 00	5
6	14	317	Misc. Adm. Exp.	719	56 40			56 40	6
7	16	318	Prepaid Insurance	117	984 00			984 00	7
8	20	319	Marsh Inc.	✓		3208 00	32 08	3175 92	8
9	20	320	Heath Co.	✓		4850 00		4850 00	9
10	21	321	Sales Ret. & Allow.	412	462 00			462 00	10
11	23	322	Robinson Supply	✓		1500 00	30 00	1470 00	11
12	23	323	Video Co.	✓		7600 00		7600 00	12
13	23	324	Rent Expense	712	789 20			789 20	13
14	24	325	Walton Co.	✓		9525 00		9525 00	14
15	26	326	Sales Salaries Exp.	611	2560 00			2560 00	15
16	26	327	Office Salaries Exp.	711	880 00			880 00	16
17	26	328	Advertising Expense	612	786 00			786 00	17
18	27	329	Misc. Selling Exp.	619	41 50			41 50	18
19	28	330	Office Equipment	123	900 00			900 00	19
20	31				12524 10	34089 00	136 14	46476 96	20
21					(✓)	(211)	(513)	(111)	21

All payments by Kannon Corporation are made by check. As each transaction is recorded in the cash payments journal, the related check number is entered in the column at the right of the Date column. The check numbers provide a convenient cross-reference, and their use also is helpful in controlling cash payments.

The Sundry Accounts Dr. column is used to record debits to any account for which there is no special column. On October 2, for example, Kannon Corporation paid $1,275 for a cash purchase of merchandise. The transaction was recorded by writing "Purchases" in the space provided and $1,275 in the Sundry Accounts Dr. and the Cash Cr. columns. The posting reference (511) was inserted later, at the time the debit was posted.

Debits to creditors accounts for invoices paid are recorded in the Accounts Payable Dr. column and credits for the amounts paid are recorded in the Cash Cr. column. If a discount is taken, the debit to the account payable will, of course, differ from the amount of the payment. Cash discounts taken on merchandise purchased for resale are recorded in the Purchases Discounts Cr. column.

At frequent intervals during the month, the amounts entered in the Accounts Payable Dr. column are posted to the creditors accounts in the accounts payable ledger. After each posting, "CP" and the page number of the journal are inserted in the posting reference column of the account. Check marks are placed in the posting reference column of the cash payments journal to indicate that the amounts have been posted. The items in the Sundry Accounts Dr. column are also posted to the appropriate accounts in the general ledger at frequent intervals. The posting is indicated by writing the account numbers in the posting reference column of the cash payments journal. At the end of the month, each of the amount columns in the cash payments journal is totaled, the sum of the two debit totals is compared with the sum of the two credit totals to determine their equality, and the journal is ruled.

A check mark is placed below the total of the Sundry Accounts Dr. column to indicate that it is not posted. As each of the totals of the other three columns is posted to a general ledger account, the proper account numbers are inserted below the column totals.

Accounts Payable Control and Subsidiary Ledger

During October, the following postings were made to Accounts Payable in the general ledger of Kannon Corporation:

Credits to Accounts Payable

Oct. 31	Total purchases on account (purchases journal)	$43,320.00

Debits to Accounts Payable

Oct. 20	A return of merchandise (general journal)	97.50
31	Total cash payments on account (cash payments journal)	34,089.00

The accounts payable controlling account and the subsidiary accounts payable ledger of Kannon Corporation as of October 31 are presented below and on pages F-9 and F-10.

GENERAL LEDGER

Accounts Payable Account in the General Ledger at the End of the Month

ACCOUNT Accounts Payable — ACCOUNT NO. 211

DATE		ITEM	POST. REF.	DEBIT	CREDIT	BALANCE DEBIT	BALANCE CREDIT
1992 Oct.	1	Balance	✓				21,975.00
	20		J18	97.50			21,877.50
	31		P19		43,320.00		65,197.50
	31		CP16	34,089.00			31,108.50

ACCOUNTS PAYABLE LEDGER

Accounts Payable Ledger at the End of the Month

NAME Dunlap Corporation
ADDRESS 521 Scottsdale Blvd., Phoenix, AZ 85004-1100

DATE		ITEM	POST. REF.	DEBIT	CREDIT	BALANCE
1992 Oct.	16		P19		3,593.00	3,593.00
	20		J18	97.50		3,495.50
	27		P19		6,375.00	9,870.50

NAME Heath Co.
ADDRESS 9950 Ridge Ave., Los Angeles, CA 90048-3694

DATE		ITEM	POST. REF.	DEBIT	CREDIT	BALANCE
1992 Sept.	21		P18		4,850.00	4,850.00
Oct.	20		CP16	4,850.00		—

NAME Marsh Inc.
ADDRESS 650 Wilson, Portland, OR 97209-1406

DATE		ITEM	POST. REF.	DEBIT	CREDIT	BALANCE
1992 Oct.	3		P19		7,406.00	7,406.00
	11		P19		3,208.00	10,614.00
	12		CP16	7,406.00		3,208.00
	20		CP16	3,208.00		—

NAME Parker Supply Co.
ADDRESS 142 West 8th, Los Angeles, CA 90014-1225

DATE		ITEM	POST. REF.	DEBIT	CREDIT	BALANCE
1992 Oct.	9		P19		257.00	257.00
	23		P19		132.00	389.00

NAME Robinson Supply
ADDRESS 3800 Mission Street, San Francisco, CA 94110-1732

DATE		ITEM	POST. REF.	DEBIT	CREDIT	BALANCE
1992 Oct.	17		P19		1,500.00	1,500.00
	23		CP16	1,500.00		—

NAME Video Co.
ADDRESS 1200 Capital Ave., Sacramento, CA 95814-1048

DATE		ITEM	POST. REF.	DEBIT	CREDIT	BALANCE
1992 Sept.	25		P18		7,600.00	7,600.00
Oct.	2		P19		5,724.00	13,324.00
	23		CP16	7,600.00		5,724.00

Accounts Payable Ledger at the End of the Month—Concluded

NAME Walton Co.

ADDRESS 9554 W. Colorado Blvd., Pasadena, CA 91107-1318

DATE		ITEM	POST. REF.	DEBIT	CREDIT	BALANCE
1992 Sept.	28		P18		9,525 00	9,525 00
Oct.	20		P19		15,125 00	24,650 00
	24		CP16	9,525 00		15,125 00

After all posting has been completed for the month, the sum of the balances in the accounts payable ledger should be compared with the balance of the accounts payable account in the general ledger. If the controlling account and the subsidiary ledger do not agree, the error or errors must be located and corrected. The balances of the individual creditors accounts may be summarized on a calculator tape, or a schedule such as the following may be prepared. The total of the schedule, $31,108.50, agrees with the balance of the accounts payable account shown on page F-8.

Schedule of Accounts Payable

Kannon Corporation
Schedule of Accounts Payable
October 31, 1992

Dunlap Corporation	$ 9,870.50
Parker Supply Co.	389.00
Video Co.	5,724.00
Walton Co.	15,125.00
Total accounts payable	$31,108.50

Sales Journal

The **sales journal** is used only for recording *sales of merchandise on account;* sales of merchandise for cash are recorded in the cash receipts journal. Sales of nonmerchandise assets are recorded in the cash receipts journal or the general journal, depending upon whether the sale was made for cash or on account. The sales journal of Kannon Corporation for October is as follows:

Sales Journal after Posting

SALES JOURNAL — PAGE 35

	DATE		INVOICE NO.	ACCOUNT DEBITED	POST. REF.	ACCTS. REC. DR. SALES CR.	
1	1992 Oct.	2	615	Barnes Inc.	✓	9,350 00	1
2		3	616	Standard Supply Co.	✓	1,604 00	2
3		5	617	David T. Mattox	✓	15,305 00	3
4		9	618	Barnes Inc.	✓	1,396 00	4
5		10	619	Adler Company	✓	6,750 00	5
6		17	620	Hamilton Inc.	✓	7,865 00	6
7		23	621	Cooper & Co.	✓	1,502 00	7
8		26	622	Tracy & Lee Inc.	✓	3,260 00	8
9		27	623	Standard Supply Co.	✓	1,908 00	9
10		31				48,940 00	10
11						(113) (411)	11

Details of the first sale recorded by Kannon Corporation in October are taken from Invoice No. 615. The customer is Barnes Inc. and the invoice total is $9,350. Since the amount of the debit to Accounts Receivable is the same as the credit to Sales, a single amount column in the sales journal is sufficient. However, if sales are subject to a sales tax, a special column may be added to the sales journal for recording the credit to Sales Tax Payable.

Posting the Sales Journal. The principles used in posting the sales journal compare to those used in posting the purchases journal. The source of the entry being posted is shown in the posting reference column of an account by the letter "S" and the proper page number. A customer's account with a posting from the sales journal is as follows:

An Account in the Accounts Receivable Ledger

NAME Adler Company

ADDRESS 7608 Melton Ave., Los Angeles, CA 90025-3942

DATE		ITEM	POST. REF.	DEBIT	CREDIT	BALANCE
1992 Oct.	10		S35	6 7 5 0 00		6 7 5 0 00

As each debit to a customer's account is posted, a check mark (✓) is inserted in the posting reference column of the sales journal. At the end of each month, the amount column of the sales journal is added, the journal is ruled, and the total is posted as a debit to Accounts Receivable and a credit to Sales. The respective account numbers are then inserted below the total to indicate that the posting is completed.

Sales Returns and Allowances. When merchandise sold is returned or a price adjustment is granted, an entry is made in the general journal according to the principles described in Chapter 4. During October, Kannon Corporation issued a credit memorandum and prepared the following entry in a two-column general journal:

General Journal Entry for Sales Returns and Allowances

JOURNAL PAGE 18

	DATE		DESCRIPTION	POST. REF.	DEBIT	CREDIT	
1	1992 Oct.	13	Sales Returns and Allowances	412	2 2 5 00		1
2			Accounts Receivable—				2
3			Adler Company	113/✓		2 2 5 00	3
4			Credit Memo No. 32				4

Note the *diagonal line* and *double posting* in the entry to record the credit memorandum. The diagonal line is placed in the posting reference column *at the time the entry is recorded in the general journal.*

If a cash refund is made because of merchandise returned or for an allowance, Sales Returns and Allowances is debited and Cash is credited. The entry would be recorded in the cash payments journal.

Cash Receipts Journal

All transactions that increase the amount of cash are recorded in a **cash receipts journal**. In a typical merchandising business, the most frequent sources of cash receipts are likely to be cash sales and collections from customers on account.

The cash receipts journal has a special column entitled Cash Dr. The frequency of the various kinds of transactions in which cash is received determines the titles of the other columns. The cash receipts journal of Kannon Corporation for October is as follows:

Cash Receipts Journal after Posting

CASH RECEIPTS JOURNAL — PAGE 14

DATE		ACCOUNT CREDITED	POST. REF.	SUNDRY ACCOUNTS CR.	SALES CR.	ACCOUNTS REC. CR.	SALES DISCOUNTS DR.	CASH DR.
1992 Oct.	2	Notes Receivable	112	2400 00				2544 00
		Interest Income	812	144 00				
	5	Barnes Inc.	✓			5800 00	116 00	5684 00
	6	Fogarty & Jacobs	✓			2625 00	52 50	2572 50
	7	Sales	✓		3700 00			3700 00
	10	David T. Mattox	✓			600 00	12 00	588 00
	13	Standard Supply Co.	✓			1604 00	32 08	1571 92
	14	Sales	✓		1632 00			1632 00
	17	Adler Company	✓			6525 00	130 50	6394 50
	19	Hamilton Inc.	✓			4850 00		4850 00
	21	Sales	✓		1920 30			1920 30
	23	Purchases Returns						
		and Allowances	512	86 20				86 20
	24	Wallace Corporation	✓			2200 00		2200 00
	27	Hamilton Inc.	✓			7865 00	157 30	7707 70
	28	Sales	✓		2086 00			2086 00
	31	Sales	✓		2423 40			2423 40
	31			2630 20	11761 70	32069 00	500 38	45960 52
				(✓)	(411)	(113)	(413)	(111)

The Sundry Accounts Cr. column is used for recording credits to any account for which there is no special column. For example, as of October 2, in the illustration, the receipt of $2,544 in payment of an interest-bearing note was recorded by a credit to Notes Receivable of $2,400 and a credit to Interest Income of $144. Both amounts were entered in the Sundry Accounts Cr. column. The posting references for the credits were inserted at the time the amounts were posted.

The Sales Cr. column is used for recording sales of merchandise for cash. Each individual sale is recorded on a cash register, and the totals thus accumulated are recorded in the cash receipts journal daily, weekly, or at other regular intervals. This is illustrated by the entry of October 7 recording weekly sales and cash receipts of $3,700. Since the total of the Sales Cr. column will be posted at the end of the month, a check mark is inserted in the posting reference column to show that the $3,700 item needs no further attention.

Credits to customers accounts for payments of invoices are recorded in the Accounts Receivable Cr. column. The amount of the cash discount granted, if any, is recorded in the Sales Discounts Dr. column, and the amount of cash actually received is recorded in the Cash Dr. column. The entry on October 5 illustrates the use of these columns. Cash in the amount of $5,684 was received from Barnes Inc. in payment of its account of $5,800, the cash discount being 2% of $5,800 or $116.

Each amount in the Sundry Accounts Cr. column of the cash receipts journal is posted to the proper account in the general ledger at frequent intervals during the month. The posting is indicated by inserting the account number in the posting reference column. At regular intervals the amounts in the Accounts Receivable Cr. column are posted to the customers accounts in the subsidiary ledger, and "CR" and the proper page number are inserted in the posting reference columns of the accounts. Check marks are placed in the posting reference column of the journal to show that the amounts have been posted. None of the individual amounts in the remaining three columns of the cash receipts journal are posted.

At the end of the month, all of the amount columns are totaled, the equality of the debits and credits is proved, and the journal is ruled. Because each amount in the Sundry Accounts Cr. column has been posted individually to a general ledger account, a check mark is inserted below the column total to indicate that no further action is needed. The totals of the other four columns are posted to the proper accounts in the general ledger and their account numbers are inserted below the totals to show that the posting has been completed.

The flow of data from the cash receipts journal to the ledgers of Kannon Corporation is illustrated in the following diagram:

Flow of Data from Cash Receipts Journal to Ledgers

Cash Receipts Journal

Account Credited	P. R.	Sundry Accounts Cr.	Sales Cr.	Accounts Receivable Cr.	Sales Discounts Dr.	Cash Dr.
Notes Receivable	112	2,400.00				2,544.00
Interest Income	811	144.00				
Barnes Inc.	✓			5,800.00	116.00	5,684.00
Fogarty & Jacobs	✓			2,625.00	52.50	2,572.50
Sales	✓		3,700.00			3,700.00
David T. Mattox	✓			600.00	12.00	588.00
Sales	✓		2,423.40			2,423.40
		2,630.20	11,761.70	32,069.00	500.38	45,960.52

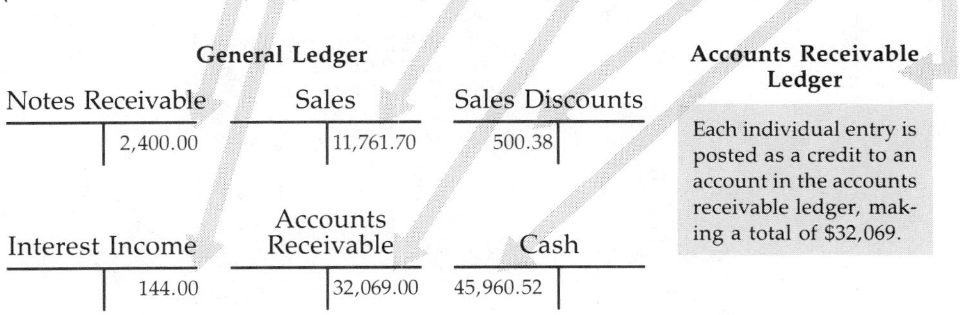

General Ledger

Account	Debit	Credit
Notes Receivable		2,400.00
Sales		11,761.70
Sales Discounts	500.38	
Interest Income		144.00
Accounts Receivable		32,069.00
Cash	45,960.52	

Accounts Receivable Ledger

Each individual entry is posted as a credit to an account in the accounts receivable ledger, making a total of $32,069.

Accounts Receivable Control and Subsidiary Ledger

During October, the following postings were made to Accounts Receivable in the general ledger of Kannon Corporation:

Debits

Oct. 31	Total sales on account (sales journal)	$48,940.00

Credits

Oct. 13	A sales return (general journal)	225.00
Oct. 31	Total cash received on account (cash receipts journal)	32,069.00

The accounts receivable controlling account of Kannon Corporation as of October 31 is as follows:

Accounts Receivable Account in the General Ledger at the End of the Month

GENERAL LEDGER

ACCOUNT Accounts Receivable ACCOUNT NO. 113

DATE		ITEM	POST. REF.	DEBIT	CREDIT	BALANCE DEBIT	BALANCE CREDIT
1992 Oct.	1	Balance	✓			17 260 00	
	13		J18		225 00	17 035 00	
	31		S35	48 940 00		65 975 00	
	31		CR14		32 069 00	33 906 00	

The posting procedures and determination of the balances of the accounts in the accounts receivable ledger and the preparation of the schedule of accounts receivable are comparable to those for accounts payable and are therefore not illustrated.

PROBLEMS

Pb. F–1.
Determination of proper special journals to use.

For the past few years, your aunt has operated a small jewelry store, Reed Jewelers. Its current annual revenues are approximately $525,000. Because the company's accountant has been taking more and more time each month to record all transactions in a two-column journal and to prepare the financial statements, your aunt is considering improving the company's accounting system by adding special journals and subsidiary ledgers. Your aunt has asked you to help her with this project. She has compiled the following information:

(1)

Type of Transaction	Estimated Frequency per Month
Purchases of merchandise on account	100
Sales on account	225
Cash receipts from customers on account	210
Daily cash register summaries of cash sales	25
Purchases of merchandise for cash	20
Purchases of office supplies on account	5
Purchases of store supplies on account	5
Cash payments for utilities expenses	4
Cash purchases of office supplies	4
Cash purchases of store supplies	4

(2) For merchandise purchases of high dollar-value items, Reed Jewelers issues notes payable at current interest rates to vendors. These notes are issued because many of the high-value items may not sell immediately and the issuance of the notes reduces the need to maintain large balances of cash or assets that can be readily converted to cash. Notes are issued to approximately 10% of the purchases on account.

(3) All purchases discounts are taken when available.

(4) A sales discount of 1/10, n/30 is offered to all credit customers.

(5) A local sales tax of 6% is collected on all intrastate sales of merchandise.

(6) Monthly financial statements are prepared.

Instructions:

(1) Based upon the preceding description of Reed Jewelers, indicate which special journals you would recommend as part of Reed Jewelers' accounting system.
(2) Assume that your aunt has decided to use a sales journal and a purchases journal. Design the format for each journal, giving special consideration to the needs of Reed Jewelers.
(3) Which subsidiary ledgers would you recommend for Reed Jewelers?

Pb. F–2.
Purchases and purchases returns, accounts payable account, and accounts payable ledger.

Purchases on account and related returns and allowances completed by Gladen Co. during May of the current year are as follows:

May 1. Purchased merchandise on account from Vero Co., $5,775.20.
3. Purchased merchandise on account from Lane Corp., $11,552.50.
4. Received a credit memorandum from Vero Co. for merchandise returned, $200.
8. Purchased office supplies on account from Tyler Supply, $175.30.
12. Purchased merchandise on account from Vero Co., $4,370.50.
13. Purchased office equipment on account from Foster Equipment Co., $11,900.
15. Purchased merchandise on account from James Co., $3,100.
18. Received a credit memorandum from Tyler Supply for office supplies returned, $22.50.
19. Purchased merchandise on account from Ames Co., $2,500.
23. Purchased store supplies on account from Tyler Supply, $325.
26. Received a credit memorandum from Lane Corp. as an allowance for damaged merchandise, $500.
26. Purchased merchandise on account from James Co., $475.15.
30. Purchased office supplies on account from Tyler Supply, $375.10.

Instructions:

(1) Open the following accounts in the general ledger and enter the balances as of May 1:

114	Store Supplies	$ 572.50
115	Office Supplies	319.50
122	Office Equipment	33,500.00
211	Accounts Payable	11,855.10
511	Purchases	107,313.30
512	Purchases Returns and Allowances	3,050.25

(2) Open the following accounts in the accounts payable ledger and enter the balances in the balance columns as of May 1: Ames Co., $3,150; Foster Equipment Co.; James Co., $3,220.75; Lane Corp., $5,484.35; Tyler Supply; Vero Co.
(3) Record the transactions for May, posting to the creditors accounts in the accounts payable ledger immediately after each entry. Use a purchases journal, similar to the one illustrated on pages F-3 and F-4, and a two-column general journal.
(4) Post the general journal and the purchases journal to the accounts in the general ledger.
(5) (a) What is the sum of the balances in the subsidiary ledger at May 31?
(b) What is the balance of the controlling account at May 31?

Pb. F–3.
Purchases and cash payments journals; accounts payable and general ledgers.

Ashe Co. was established on March 16 of the current year. Transactions related to purchases, returns and allowances, and cash payments during the remainder of March are as follows:

Mar. 16. Issued Check No. 1 in payment of rent for the remainder of March, $2,250.
17. Purchased store equipment on account from Midtown Co., $7,750.
18. Purchased merchandise on account from Carter Clothing, $3,250.

Mar. 19. Issued Check No. 2 in payment of store supplies, $210, and office supplies, $125.
20. Purchased merchandise on account from Norris Clothing Co., $6,420.
21. Purchased merchandise on account from Agassi Co., $4,900.
22. Received a credit memorandum from Norris Clothing Co. for returned merchandise, $720.
Post the journals to the accounts payable ledger.
24. Issued Check No. 3 to Midtown Co. in payment of invoice of $7,750.
25. Received a credit memorandum from Agassi Co. for defective merchandise, $600.
26. Issued Check No. 4 to Carter Clothing in payment of invoice of $3,250, less 2% discount.
28. Issued Check No. 5 to a cash customer for merchandise returned, $90.
28. Issued Check No. 6 to Norris Clothing Co. in payment of the balance owed, less 2% discount.
28. Purchased merchandise on account from Agassi Co., $7,100.
Post the journals to the accounts payable ledger.
30. Purchased the following from Midtown Co. on account: store supplies, $110; office supplies, $42; office equipment, $3,450.
30. Issued Check No. 7 to Agassi Co. in payment of invoice of $4,900, less the credit of $600 and 1% discount.
30. Purchased merchandise on account from Carter Clothing, $2,150.
31. Issued Check No. 8 in payment of store supplies, $170.
31. Issued Check No. 9 in payment of sales salaries, $2,200.
31. Received a credit memorandum from Midtown Co. for defect in office equipment, $125.
Post the journals to the accounts payable ledger.

Instructions:

(1) Open the following accounts in the general ledger, using the account numbers indicated:

111	Cash	412	Sales Returns and Allowances
116	Store Supplies	511	Purchases
117	Office Supplies	512	Purchases Returns and Allowances
121	Store Equipment	513	Purchases Discounts
122	Office Equipment	611	Sales Salaries Expense
211	Accounts Payable	712	Rent Expense

(2) Open the following accounts in the accounts payable ledger: Agassi Co.; Carter Clothing; Midtown Co.; Norris Clothing Co.

(3) Record the transactions for March, using a purchases journal similar to the one illustrated on pages F-3 and F-4, a cash payments journal similar to the one illustrated on page F-7, and a two-column general journal. Post to the accounts payable ledger at the points indicated in the narrative of transactions.

(4) Post the appropriate individual entries to the general ledger (Sundry Accounts columns of the purchases journal and the cash payments journal; both columns of the general journal).

(5) Total each of the columns of the purchases journal and the cash payments journal and post the appropriate totals to the general ledger. (Because the problem does not include transactions related to cash receipts, the cash account in the ledger will have a credit balance.)

(6) Prepare a schedule of accounts payable.

Pb. F–4.
Sales journal; accounts receivable and general ledgers.

SKL Company was established on May 12 of the current year. Its sales of merchandise on account and related returns and allowances during the remainder of the month are as follows. Terms of all sales were 2/10, n/30, FOB destination.

May 15. Sold merchandise on account to Downs Co., Invoice No. 1, $2,000.
20. Sold merchandise on account to Reese Inc., Invoice No. 2, $2,750.

May 22. Sold merchandise on account to Innis Co., Invoice No. 3, $3,375.
23. Issued Credit Memorandum No. 1 for $250 to Downs Co. for merchandise returned.
27. Sold merchandise on account to D. L. Victor Co., Invoice No. 4, $3,000.
28. Sold merchandise on account to Unisac Inc., Invoice No. 5, $500.
28. Issued Credit Memorandum No. 2 for $150 to Reese Inc. for merchandise returned.
30. Sold merchandise on account to Reese Inc., Invoice No. 6, $1,925.
30. Issued Credit Memorandum No. 3 for $75 to D. L. Victor Co. for damages to merchandise caused by faulty packing.
31. Sold merchandise on account to Innis Co., Invoice No. 7, $1,495.

Instructions:

(1) Open the following accounts in the general ledger, using the account numbers indicated: Accounts Receivable, 113; Sales, 411; Sales Returns and Allowances, 412.
(2) Open the following accounts in the accounts receivable ledger: Downs Co.; Innis Co.; Reese Inc.; Unisac Inc.; D. L. Victor Co.
(3) Record the transactions for May, posting to the customers accounts in the accounts receivable ledger and inserting the balance immediately after recording each entry. Use a sales journal, similar to the one illustrated on page F-10, and a two-column general journal.
(4) Post the general journal and the sales journal to the three accounts opened in the general ledger, inserting the account balances only after the last postings.
(5) (a) What is the sum of the balances of the accounts in the subsidiary ledger at May 31?
(b) What is the balance of the controlling account at May 31?

If the working papers correlating with the textbook are not used, omit Pb. F-5.

Pb. F–5.
Sales and cash receipts journals; accounts receivable and general ledgers.

Three journals, the accounts receivable ledger, and portions of the general ledger of Larkin Company are presented in the working papers. Sales invoices and credit memorandums were entered in the journals by an assistant. Terms of sales on account are 1/10, n/30, FOB shipping point. Transactions in which cash and notes receivable were received during July are as follows:

July 3. Received $5,445 from G. L. Powell Co. in payment of June 23 invoice, less discount.
6. Received $25,500 in payment of $25,000 note receivable and interest of $500.
Post transactions of July 2, 3, and 6 to accounts receivable ledger.
7. Received $6,930 from Marion Rau Co. in payment of June 29 invoice, less discount.
10. Received $2,200 from W. A. Edwards Co. in payment of June 10 invoice, no discount.
15. Cash sales for first half of July totaled $16,250.
Post transactions of July 7, 10, 12, and 15 to accounts receivable ledger.
19. Received $800 refund for return of defective equipment purchased for cash in June.
20. Received $3,168 from G. L. Powell Co. in payment of balance due on July 10 invoice, less discount.
22. Received $5,445 from W. A. Edwards Co. in payment of July 12 invoice, less discount.
Post transactions of July 17, 20, 22, and 23 to accounts receivable ledger.
28. Received $50 for sale of office supplies at cost.
31. Received $1,250 cash and a $2,500 note receivable from Bob Harris and Son in settlement of the balance due on the invoice of July 2, no discount. (Record receipt of note in the general journal.)

July 31. Cash sales for the second half of July totaled $16,100.
Post transactions of July 27, 28, 30, and 31 to accounts receivable ledger.

Instructions:

(1) Record the cash receipts in the cash receipts journal and the note in the general journal. Before recording a receipt of cash on account, determine the balance of the customer's account. Post the entries from the three journals, in date sequence, to the accounts receivable ledger in accordance with the instructions in the narrative of transactions. Insert the new balance after each posting to an account.
(2) Post the appropriate individual entries from the cash receipts journal and the general journal to the general ledger.
(3) Total each of the columns of the sales journal and the cash receipts journal and post the appropriate totals to the general ledger. Insert the balance of each account after the last posting.
(4) Prepare a schedule of the accounts receivable as of July 31 and compare the total with the balance of the controlling account.

Pb. F–6.
Sales and cash receipts journals; accounts receivable and general ledgers.

Transactions related to sales and cash receipts completed by Menter Company during the period June 16–30 of the current year are as follows. The terms of all sales on account are 1/10, n/30, FOB shipping point.

June 16. Issued Invoice No. 808 to Thomas Co., $7,250.
16. Received cash from T. A. Davis Co. for the balance owed on its account, less discount.
17. Issued Invoice No. 809 to Jackson Co., $3,500.
18. Issued Invoice No. 810 to R. D. Reed Inc., $5,100.
Post all journals to the accounts receivable ledger.
21. Received cash from Jackson Co. for the balance owed on June 16, no discount.
22. Issued Credit Memorandum No. 55 to Thomas Co., $250.
24. Issued Invoice No. 811 to Jackson Co., $7,000.
24. Received $1,050 in payment of a $1,000 note receivable and interest of $50.
Post all journals to the accounts receivable ledger.
25. Received cash from Thomas Co. for the balance due on invoice of June 16, less discount.
27. Received cash from Jackson Co. for invoice of June 17, less discount.
29. Issued Invoice No. 812 to T. A. Davis Co., $8,000.
30. Recorded cash sales for the second half of the month, $11,750.
30. Issued Credit Memorandum No. 56 to T. A. Davis Co., $150.
Post all journals to the accounts receivable ledger.

Instructions:

(1) Open the following accounts in the general ledger, inserting the balances indicated, as of June 1:

111	Cash	$19,222
112	Notes Receivable	7,500
113	Accounts Receivable	14,650
411	Sales	—
412	Sales Returns and Allowances	—
413	Sales Discounts	—
811	Interest Income	—

(2) Open the following accounts in the accounts receivable ledger, inserting the balances indicated, as of June 16: T. A. Davis Co., $7,400; Jackson Co., $9,925; R. D. Reed Inc.; Thomas Co.

(3) In a sales journal similar to the one illustrated on page F-10 and a cash receipts journal similar to the one illustrated on page F-12, insert "June 16 Total(s) Forwarded" on the first line of the Account Debited or Account Credited column, "✓" in the Post. Ref. column, and the following dollar figures in the respective amount columns:

Sales journal: 25,350
Cash receipts journal: 3,442; 13,420; 22,675; 185; 39,352.

(4) Using the two special journals and a two-column general journal, record the transactions for the remainder of June. Post to the accounts receivable ledger and insert the balances at the points indicated in the narrative of transactions. *Determine the balance in the customer's account before recording a cash receipt.*
(5) Total each of the columns of the special journals and post the individual entries and totals to the general ledger. Insert account balances after the last posting.
(6) Determine that the subsidiary ledger agrees with the controlling account in the general ledger.

Pb. F–7.
All journals and general ledger; trial balance.

The transactions completed by F. C. Marr Co. during July, the first month of the current fiscal year, were as follows:

July 1. Issued Check No. 830 for July rent, $2,500.
3. Purchased equipment on account from Olin Co., $5,800.
3. Purchased merchandise on account from Polk Inc., $3,950.
6. Issued Invoice No. 922 to Wallace Co., $2,125.
7. Received check for $4,950 from Dunn Corp. in payment of $5,000 invoice, less discount.
7. Issued Check No. 831 for miscellaneous selling expense, $225.
8. Received credit memorandum from Polk Inc. for returned merchandise, $450.
8. Issued Invoice No. 923 to Green Co., $6,000.
9. Issued Check No. 832 to Engles Co. in payment of $7,500 invoice, less 2% discount.
9. Received check for $9,405 from Baker Manufacturing Co. in payment of $9,500 invoice, less discount.
10. Issued Check No. 833 to Davis Enterprises in payment of $4,250 invoice, no discount.
12. Issued Invoice No. 924 to Dunn Corp., $3,500.
12. Issued Check No. 834 for $930 to Ross Corp. in payment of account, no discount.
12. Received check for $775 from Wallace Co. on account, no discount.
14. Issued credit memorandum to Dunn Corp. for damaged merchandise, $500.
15. Issued Check No. 835 for $3,465 to Polk Inc. in payment of $3,500 balance, less 1% discount.
15. Issued Check No. 836 for $2,250 for cash purchase of merchandise.
15. Cash sales for July 1–15, $19,650.
18. Purchased merchandise on account from Davis Enterprises, $6,420.
18. Received check for return of merchandise that had been purchased for cash, $110.
19. Issued Check No. 837 for miscellaneous administrative expense, $175.
21. Purchased the following on account from Cass Supply Inc.: store supplies, $225; office supplies, $195.
23. Issued Check No. 838 in payment of advertising expense, $850.
23. Issued Invoice No. 925 to Baker Manufacturing Co., $1,950.
24. Purchased the following on account from Engles Co.: merchandise, $4,170; store supplies, $130.
25. Issued Invoice No. 926 to Gnatt Corp., $4,600.
25. Received check for $2,970 from Dunn Corp. in payment of $3,000 balance, less discount.

July 29. Issued Check No. 839 for $5,800 to Olin Co. in payment of invoice of July 3, no discount.

30. Issued Check No. 840 in payment of dividends, $3,000.

31. Issued Check No. 841 for monthly salaries as follows: sales salaries, $11,100; office salaries, $4,500.

31. Cash sales for July 16–31, $26,150.

31. Issued Check No. 842 in payment of transportation charges for merchandise purchased during the month, $350.

Instructions:

(1) Open the following accounts in the general ledger, entering the balances indicated as of July 1:

111	Cash	$11,350
113	Accounts Receivable	15,275
114	Merchandise Inventory	31,450
115	Store Supplies	745
116	Office Supplies	410
117	Prepaid Insurance	2,100
121	Equipment	47,250
122	Accumulated Depreciation	22,250
211	Accounts Payable	12,680
311	Capital Stock	50,000
312	Retained Earnings	23,650
313	Dividends	—
411	Sales	—
412	Sales Returns and Allowances	—
413	Sales Discounts	—
511	Purchases	—
512	Purchases Returns and Allowances	—
513	Purchases Discounts	—
514	Transportation In	—
611	Sales Salaries Expense	—
612	Advertising Expense	—
619	Miscellaneous Selling Expense	—
711	Office Salaries Expense	—
712	Rent Expense	—
719	Miscellaneous Administrative Expense	—

(2) Record the transactions for July, using a purchases journal (as on pages F-3 and F-4), a sales journal (as on page F-10), a cash payments journal (as on page F-7), a cash receipts journal (as on page F-12), and a two-column general journal. The terms of all sales on account are FOB shipping point, 1/10, n/30. Assume that an assistant makes daily postings to the individual accounts in the accounts payable ledger and the accounts receivable ledger.

(3) Post the appropriate individual entries to the general ledger.

(4) Total each of the columns of the special journals and post the appropriate totals to the general ledger; insert the account balances.

(5) Prepare a trial balance.

(6) Balances of the accounts in the subsidiary ledgers as of July 31 are as follows:

Accounts receivable: 1,950; 6,000; 4,600; 2,125.
Accounts payable: 420; 6,420; 4,300.

Verify the agreement of the subsidiary ledgers with their respective controlling accounts.

APPENDIX G: INCOME TAXES

The federal government and more than three-fourths of the states levy an income tax. In addition, some of the states permit municipalities or other political subdivisions to levy income taxes. In operating a business or determining one's personal income tax, it is only good management to plan to keep these taxes to a minimum. This idea was expressed by Judge Learned Hand in *Newman* [35 AFTR 857], as follows:

> *Over and over again courts have said that there is nothing sinister in so arranging one's affairs as to keep taxes as low as possible. Everybody does so, rich or poor; and all do right, for nobody owes any public duty to pay more than the law demands; taxes are enforced exactions, not voluntary contributions. To demand more in the name of morals is mere cant.*

An understanding of any but the simplest aspects of income taxes is almost impossible without some knowledge of accounting concepts. Conversely, an understanding of the basic concepts of income taxes enable an individual or business to minimize taxes. In many cases, this understanding of the basic concepts leads one to seek the advice and assistance of professional accountants who specialize in determining the tax or developing plans to minimize the tax.

The explanations and illustrations of the federal system presented in this appendix are illustrative of the nature of income taxes. They are brief and relatively free of the many complexities encountered in actual practice. In addition, it should be noted that the federal tax laws are often changed, and that major tax bills have been enacted on the average of every 18 months since the original tax law was passed in 1913. The tax law upon which this discussion is based is the Tax Reform Act of 1986 (as amended by the Revenue Act of 1987, the Technical and Miscellaneous Revenue Act of 1988, and the Omnibus Budget Reconciliation Act of 1990). The current tax law and the current tax rates should be examined before tax-related decisions are made.

FEDERAL INCOME TAX SYSTEM

The present system of federal income tax began with the Revenue Act of 1913, which was enacted soon after the ratification of the Sixteenth Amendment to the Constitution. All current income tax statutes, as well as other federal tax laws, are now codified in the Internal Revenue Code (IRC).

The Treasury Department is charged with responsibility in federal tax matters. The division of the Department concerned specifically with enforcement and collection of the income tax is the Internal Revenue Service (IRS), headed by the Commissioner of Internal Revenue. Interpretations of the law and directives formulated according to express provisions of the IRC are issued in various forms. The most important and comprehensive are the "Regulations," which extend to more than two thousand pages.

The data required for the determination of income tax liability are supplied by the taxpayer on official forms and supporting schedules that are referred to collectively as a tax return. Failure to receive the forms from the IRS or failure to maintain adequate records does not relieve taxpayers of their legal obligations to file annual tax returns. Willful failure to comply with the income tax laws may result in the imposition of severe civil and criminal penalties.

Taxpayers alleged by the IRS to be deficient in reporting or paying their tax may, if they disagree with the determination, present their case in informal conferences at district and regional levels. Unresolved disputes may be taken to the federal courts for settlement. The taxpayer may seek relief in the Tax Court or may pay the disputed amount and sue to recover it.

The income tax is not imposed upon business units as such, but upon taxable entities. The principal taxable entities are individuals, corporations, estates, and trusts. Business enterprises organized as sole proprietorships are not taxable entities. The revenues and expenses of such business enterprises are reported in the individual tax returns of the owners. Partnerships are not taxable entities but are required to report on an informational return the details of their revenues, expenses, and allocation to partners. The partners then report on their individual tax returns the amount of net income and other special items allocated to them on the partnership return.

Corporations engaged in business for profit generally are treated as distinct taxable entities. However, it is possible for two or more corporations with common ownership to join in filing a consolidated return. Subchapter S of the IRC also permits a nonpublic corporation that conforms to specified requirements to elect to be treated in a manner similar to a partnership. The effect of the election is to tax the shareholders on their distributive shares of the net income instead of taxing the corporation.

ACCOUNTING METHODS

Although neither the IRC nor the Regulations provide uniform systems of accounting for use by all taxpayers, detailed procedures are prescribed in certain cases. In addition, the IRS has the authority to prescribe accounting methods where those used by a taxpayer fail to yield a fair determination of taxable income. In general, taxpayers have the option of using either the cash basis or the accrual basis.

Cash Basis

Because of its greater simplicity, the cash basis of determining taxable income is usually used by individuals whose sources of of income are limited to salary, dividends, and interest. Professional and other service enterprises (e.g., physicians, attorneys, insurance agencies) also ordinarily use the cash basis in determining taxable income. One of the advantages is that the fees charged to clients or customers are not considered to be earned until payment is received. Similarly, it is not necessary to accrue expenses incurred but not paid within the tax year. It is not permissible, however, to treat the entire cost of long-lived assets as an expense of the period in which the cash payment is made.[1] Deductions for depreciation on equipment and buildings used by business purposes may be claimed in the same manner as under the accrual basis, regardless of when payment is made.

Recognition of revenue according to the cash basis is not always contingent upon the actual receipt of cash. In some cases, revenue is said to be constructively received at the time it becomes available to the taxpayer, regardless of when it is actually converted to cash. For example, a check for services rendered which is received before the end of a taxable year is income of that year, even though the check is not deposited or cashed until the following year. Other examples of constructive receipt are bond interest coupons due within the taxable year and interest credited to a savings account as of the last day of the taxable year.

Accrual Basis

For businesses in which production or trading in merchandise is an important factor, purchases and sales must be accounted for on the accrual basis. Thus, revenues from sales must be reported in the year in which the goods are sold, regardless of when the cash is received. Similarly, the cost of goods purchased must be reported in the year in which the liabilities are incurred, regardless of when payment is made. The usual adjustments must also be made for the beginning and ending inventories in order to determine the cost of goods sold and the gross profit. However, enterprises are not required to extend the accrual basis to every other phase of their operations. A mixture of cash and accrual methods of accounting is permissible, if it yields reasonable results and is used consistently from year to year.

INCOME TAX ON INDIVIDUALS

Methods of accounting in general, as well as many of the regulations affecting the determination of net business or professional income, are not affected by the legal nature or the organizational structure of the taxpayer. On the other hand, the tax base and the tax rate structure for individuals differ markedly from those which apply to corporations.

The individual's tax base, upon which the amount of income tax is determined, is called taxable income. Taxable income is gross income less certain deductions as specified by the IRC. It is determined as follows:

Determination of Taxable Income for Individuals

GROSS INCOME
minus
DEDUCTIONS FROM GROSS INCOME
equals
ADJUSTED GROSS INCOME
minus
ITEMIZED DEDUCTIONS AND EXEMPTIONS
equals
TAXABLE INCOME

[1] The current tax law allows small businesses to write off as an expense as much as $10,000 of annual equipment purchases.

The basic concepts underlying the determination of taxable income are discussed in the paragraphs that follow.

Gross Income

Items of gross income subject to tax are sometimes called taxable gross income. Some of the taxable and nontaxable items of gross income of individuals are as follows:

Partial List of Taxable and Nontaxable Gross Income Items

TAXABLE ITEMS	NONTAXABLE ITEMS
Wages and other remuneration from employer.	All or portions of federal old-age pension benefits, depending on amounts of other income.
Tips and gratuities for services rendered.	Value of property received as a gift.
Cash dividends.	Value of property received by bequest, devise, or inheritance.
Rents and royalties.	Life insurance proceeds received because of death of insured.
Income from a business or profession.	Interest on most obligations of a state or political subdivision.
Gains from the sale of real estate, securities, and other property.	Scholarships for tuition and fees.
Distributive share of partnership income.	Compensation for injuries or for damages related to personal or family rights.
Income from an estate or trust.	Worker's compensation insurance for sickness or injury.
Prizes won in contests.	
Gambling winnings.	
Jury fees.	
Gains from illegal transactions.	
Unemployment compensation.	

Deductions from Gross Income

Business expenses and other expenses related to earning revenue are deductible in full or in part from gross income to yield adjusted gross income. For example, ordinary and necessary expenses incurred in the operations of a sole proprietorship are deductible from gross income. Also, expenses that are directly connected with earning rent or royalty income are allowable as deductions from gross income.

A self-employed individual may establish a qualified retirement fund (called a Keogh plan) and deduct the annual contribution from gross income in determining adjusted gross income. Also, certain employees may deduct contributions to plans provided by employers (called 401K plans), and low- and middle-income workers can deduct contributions to individual retirement accounts (called IRAs). The IRC and related regulations state many limitations on the amount of such deductions from gross income.

Adjusted Gross Income

The expenses described in the preceding section are deducted from an amount of related gross income. The resulting figure is the adjusted gross income. The amount of adjusted gross income is used in determining the amount of some of the deductions described in the following section. For example, the medical deduction is limited to the portion of total medical expenses which exceed 7 1/2% of adjusted gross income.

Itemized Deductions, the Standard Deduction, and Exemptions

After the amount of adjusted gross income of an individual is determined, two categories of deductions are subtracted to yield taxable income: (1) itemized deductions or the standard deduction and (2) exemptions. These two deductions from adjusted gross income are described in the following paragraphs.

Itemized Deductions. Certain specified expenditures and losses may be *itemized* and deducted from adjusted gross income. The most common deductions available to individuals who itemize deductions are described in the paragraphs that follow.[2]

Charitable Contributions. Contributions made by an individual to domestic organizations created exclusively for religious, charitable, scientific, literary, or educational purposes, or for the prevention of cruelty to children or animals are deductible, provided the organization is not-for-profit and does not devote a substantial part of its activities to influencing legislation. Contributions to domestic governmental units and to organizations of war veterans also are deductible.

The limitation on the amount of qualified contributions that may be deducted ranges from 20% of adjusted gross income for contributions to private foundations to 50% of adjusted gross income for contributions to public charities, with 50% being the overall maximum. There are other intermediate limitations related to contributions of various types of property other than cash.

Interest Expense. Interest expense on indebtedness for the taxpayer's principal and second residences is deductible, subject to certain limitations. Interest expense on indebtedness used for investment purposes is fully deductible up to an amount equal to investment income.

Taxes. Most of the taxes levied by the federal government are *not* deductible from adjusted gross income. Some of the taxes of a nonbusiness or personal nature levied by states or their political subdivisions are deductible from adjusted gross income. The common deductible state and local taxes are real estate, personal property, and income taxes.

Medical Expenses. Amounts paid for prescription drugs and insulin and other medical expenses are generally deductible to the extent they exceed 7 1/2% of adjusted gross income. Other medical expenses deductible in total or in part include medical care insurance, doctors' fees, hospital expenses, etc.

Standard Deduction. As an alternative to itemizing deductions, the taxpayer may take a standard deduction. The amount of the deduction depends upon whether the taxpayer is filing as a single taxpayer, as a head of household, or with a spouse (joint return). The amount of the standard deduction is adjusted annually for inflation.

Exemptions. In general, each taxpayer is entitled to a personal exemption.[3] An additional exemption is allowed for each dependent. The amount of the personal exemption is adjusted annually for inflation.

Taxable Income and Determination of Income Tax

After the taxable income is determined, the taxpayer uses various tax rate schedules to determine the amount of the income tax. For example, the individual tax rates for a single taxpayer are as follows for 1991:

Taxable Income	Tax Rate[4]
\$0–\$20,350	15%
\$20,350–\$49,300	28%
Over \$49,300	31%

[2]For certain high-income taxpayers, the itemized deductions (except for medical expenses) are limited.

[3]For certain high-income taxpayers, the personal exemption is phased out.

[4]Capital gains are subject to a maximum tax rate of 28%. Such gains result from the sale of capital assets, most commonly stocks and bonds.

To illustrate the use of the tax rate schedules, assume that a single taxpayer has taxable income of $59,300. The tax is determined as follows:

Individual Tax Rates—Single Taxpayer

Tax on $20,350 at 15%	$ 3,053 (rounded)
Tax on $28,950 ($49,300 − $20,350) at 28% ..	8,106
Tax on $10,000 ($59,300 − $49,300) at 31% ..	3,100
Total on $59,300	$14,259

Credits Against the Tax

After the amount of the income tax has been determined, the tax may be reduced on a dollar-for-dollar basis by the amount of various credits. These credits are therefore quite different from deductions and exemptions, which are reductions of the income subject to tax. The most common credits are described in the paragraphs that follow.

Credit for the Elderly. Some elderly taxpayers receive nontaxable retirement income, while others receive taxable retirement income. The credit for the elderly is an attempt to overcome this perceived inequity. The formula for determining the credit is complex and the IRC should be consulted for the details.

Child and Disabled Dependent Care Expenses Credit. Taxpayers who maintain a household are allowed a tax credit for expenses, including household expenses, involved in the care of a dependent child under age 15 or a physically or mentally incapacitated dependent or spouse, provided the expenses were incurred to enable the taxpayer to be gainfully employed. The amount of the credit is on a sliding scale, depending on the amount of adjusted gross income and the number of dependents.

Earned Income Credit. This credit against the tax is available to low-income workers who maintain a household for at least one of their dependent children and who have earned income (wages and self-employment income). Unlike the other credits, which cannot exceed the amount of the tax before applying the credit, if the earned income credit reduces the tax liability below zero, the negative amount is paid to the taxpayer. For example, if a worker's tax liability before applying the credit is $150 and the earned income credit is $375, the taxpayer will receive a direct payment of $225. Direct payments of tax revenues to individuals who have no liability for federal income tax is a concept with significant socioeconomic implications. The concept is often called a "negative income tax."

Filing Returns; Payment of Tax

The income tax withheld from an employee's earnings by an employer represents current payments on account. An individual whose income is not subject to withholding, or only partially so, or an individual whose income is fairly large must estimate the income tax in advance. The estimated tax for the year, after deducting the estimated amount to be withheld and any credit for overpayment form prior years, must be paid currently, usually in quarterly installments.

Annual income tax returns must be filed at the appropriate Internal Revenue Service office within 3 1/2 months following the end of the taxpayer's taxable year. Any balance owed must accompany the return. If there has been an overpayment of the tax liability, the taxpayer may request that the overpayment be refunded or credited against the estimated tax for the following year.

INCOME TAX ON CORPORATIONS

The taxable income of a corporation is determined, in general by deducting its ordinary business expenses from the total amount of its includable gross income. The corporate tax rates, in general, are as follows for 1991:

Corporate Income Tax Rates

Taxable Income	Tax Rate[5]
$0–$50,000	15%
$50,000–$75,000	25%
Over $75,000	34%

TAX PLANNING TO MINIMIZE INCOME TAXES

There are various legal means of minimizing or reducing federal income taxes, some of which are of broader applicability than others. Much depends upon the volume and the source of a taxpayer's gross income, the nature of the expenses and other deductions, and the accounting methods used. Examples of means to minimize income taxes are presented in the following paragraphs.

Alternative Accounting Principles

There are many cases in which an enterprise may choose from among two or more optional accounting principles in determining the amount of its taxable income. The particular principle chosen may have an effect on the amount of income tax, not only in the year in which the choice is made but also in later years. To illustrate, the tax law generally permits an enterprise to choose its method of determining the cost of inventory. Two widely used methods are fifo (first-in, first-out) and lifo (last-in, first-out). The more traditional method is fifo, while the more widely used method is lifo. The method chosen may have a significant effect on income and the tax on income in periods of changing price levels.

Under fifo, the first goods purchased during a year are assumed to be the first goods sold. During a period of rising prices, the first goods purchased are the least costly. If the least costly goods are sold, they are charged against revenue, and the most costly goods are included in inventory. Under lifo, however, the last goods purchased during a year are assumed to be the first goods sold. During a period of rising prices, the last goods purchased are the most costly. If the most costly goods are sold, they are charged against revenue, and the least costly goods are included in inventory. Thus, in periods of rising prices, lifo results in higher cost of goods sold, lower income, and lower taxes than fifo. During periods of declining prices, lifo results in lower cost of goods sold, higher income, and higher taxes than fifo.

In times of inflation, which has been the long-term trend in the United States since World War II, the use of lifo not only results in a lower annual income tax, but it also permits the taxpayer to retain more funds, by lowering tax payments, to replace goods sold with higher-priced goods. Clearly this advantage is one of the most important reasons for lifo's popularity.

---

[5] The benefits of the initial 15% and 25% tax rates are phased out for companies whose income exceeds $100,000. For those companies, a 5% tax on income over $100,000 would be added until the tax is equal to a flat rate of 34%.

Use of Corporate Debt

If a corporation is in need of relatively permanent funds, it generally considers borrowing money on a long-term basis or issuing stock. Since interest on debt is a deductible expense in determining taxable income and dividends paid in stock are not, this impact on income tax is one of the important factors to consider in evaluating the two methods of financing. To illustrate, assume that a corporation which expects a tax rate of 34% is considering issuing (1) $1,000,000 of 10% bonds or (2) $1,000,000 of 10% cumulative preferred stock. If the bonds are issued, the deduction of the yearly $100,000 of interest in determining taxable income results in an annual net borrowing cost of $66,000 ($100,000 less tax savings of 34% of $100,000). If the preferred stock is issued, the dividends are not deductible in determining taxable income and the net annual outlay for this method of financing is $100,000. Thus, issuing bonds instead of preferred stock reduced the annual financing expenditure by $34,000 ($100,000 − $66,000).

Nontaxable Investment Income

Interest on bonds issued by a state or political subdivision is exempt from the federal income tax. To illustrate, the following table compares the income after tax on a $100,000 investment in a 10% industrial bond and a $100,000 investment in an 8% municipal bond for a corporation with a tax rate of 34%.

	Taxable 10% Industrial Bond	Nontaxable 8% Municipal Bond
Income	$10,000	$8,000
Tax (34% of $10,000)	3,400	—
Income after tax	$ 6,600	$8,000

Although the interest rate on the municiple bond (8%) is less than the rate on the industrial bond (10%), the aftertax income is larger from the investment in the municipal bond.

GENERAL IMPACT OF INCOME TAXES

The foregoing description of the federal income tax system and discussion of tax minimization demonstrates the importance of income taxes to individuals and to business enterprises. Many accountants, in both private and public practice, devote their entire attention to tax planning for their employers or their clients. The statutes and the administrative regulations, which are often changed, must be studied continuously by anyone who engages in this phase of accounting.

DISCUSSION QUESTIONS

G–1. (a) Does the failure to receive tax forms from the IRS qualify as a legitimate means of tax avoidance? (b) Does the failure to maintain adequate records qualify as a legitimate means of tax avoidance?

G–2. (a) What are the principle taxable entities subject to the federal income tax? (b) How is the income of a sole proprietorship taxed?

G–3. Describe briefly the system employed in subjecting the income of partnerships to the federal income tax.

G–4. The adjusted gross income of a sole proprietorship for the year was $75,000, of which the owner withdrew $48,000. What amount of income from the business enterprise must be reported on the owner's income tax return?

G–5. Do corporations electing partnership treatment (Subchapter S) pay federal income tax? Discuss.

G–6. Which of the two methods of accounting, cash or accrual, is more commonly used by individual taxpayers?

G–7. Describe constructive receipt of gross income as it applies to (a) a salary check received from an employer, (b) interest credited to a savings account, and (c) bond interest coupons.

G–8. Arrange the following items in their proper sequence for the determination of taxable income of an individual.
(a) Adjusted gross income
(b) Taxable income
(c) Itemized deductions and exemptions
(d) Gross income
(e) Expenses related to business or specified revenue

G–9. Which inventory method (lifo or fifo) would result in the lower income tax during a period of rising prices? Explain.

EXERCISES

Ex. G–10.
Determination of income using cash method and accrual method.

Janet Long, MD, opened her office after graduation from medical school in early January of the current year. On December 30, the accounting records indicated the following for the current year to date:

	Total	Cash Received	Cash Paid
Fees earned	$113,000	$95,000	—
Lease of office and equipment	30,000	—	$27,500
Medical assistant salary	24,000	—	22,000
Medical supplies, utilities, etc.	9,500	—	8,700

(a) Determine the amount of net income Long would report from her practice for the current year under the (a) cash method and (b) accrual method.
(b) List the advantages of using the cash method rather than the accrual method in accounting for Long's practice.
(c) What is the principal advantage of using the accrual method rather than the cash method in accounting for Long's practice?

Ex. G–11.
Determination of corporation income tax.

During the current year, three corporations realized the following taxable income:

Corporation X	$90,000
Corporation Y	10,000
Corporation Z	60,000

Using the tax rates indicated in the chapter, determine the amount of income tax owed by each corporation.

Ex. G–12.
Effects of using fifo and lifo for inventory costing.

A-1 Limousine Sales sold 30 limousines for $25,000 each during the first year of operations. Data related to purchases during the year are as follows:

	Quantity	Unit Cost
January 5	5	$20,000
March 15	7	20,500
June 30	9	20,750
September 3	10	20,800
November 10	5	20,900

Sales of limousines are the company's only source of income, and operating expenses for the current year are $52,500.

(a) Determine the net income for the current year, using the fifo (first-in, first-out) inventory method.
(b) Determine the net income for the current year, using the lifo (last-in, first-out) inventory method.
(c) Which method of inventory costing, fifo or lifo, would you recommend for tax purposes? Discuss.

Ex. G–13.
Effects of corporation income tax on two financing plans.

The board of directors of Wayne Inc. is planning an expansion of plant facilities expected to cost $2,500,000. The board is undecided about the method of financing this expansion and is considering two plans:

Plan 1. Issue 25,000 shares of $100, 9% cumulative preferred stock at par.
Plan 2. Issue $2,500,000 of 20-year, 11% bonds at face amount.

The condensed balance sheet of the corporation at the end of the most recent fiscal year is as follows:

Wayne Inc.
Balance Sheet
December 31, 19--

Assets		Liabilities and Stockholders' Equity	
Current assets	$1,400,000	Current liabilities	$1,140,000
Plant assets	4,600,000	Common stock, $25 par . . .	2,500,000
		Paid-in capital in excess of par	1,000,000
		Retained earnings	1,360,000
Total assets	$6,000,000	Total liabilities and stockholders' equity	$6,000,000

Net income has remained relatively constant over the past several years. As a result of the expansion program, yearly income after tax but before bond interest and related income tax is expected to increase to $475,000.

(a) Prepare a tabulation indicating the net annual outlay (dividends and interest after tax) for financing under each plan. (Use the 34% income tax rate indicated in the chapter.)
(b) List factors other than the net cost of financing that the board should consider in evaluating the two plans.

APPENDIX H: SPECIMEN FINANCIAL STATEMENTS

This appendix contains selected statements and notes for real companies.

Pages H-4 through H-16 contain the complete financial statements for Bob Evans Farms, Inc.

Consolidated Statements of Income

Coca-Cola Enterprises Inc.

(In thousands except per share data)	Fiscal Year		
	1988	1987	1986
Net Operating Revenues	$3,874,445	$3,329,134	$1,951,008
Cost of sales (includes purchases from The Coca-Cola Company of approximately $759,400 in 1988, $652,800 in 1987 and $392,400 in 1986)	2,268,038	1,916,724	1,137,720
Gross Profit	1,606,407	1,412,410	813,288
Selling, administrative and general expenses	1,225,238	1,075,290	645,218
Provision for restructuring	27,000	–	–
Operating Income	354,169	337,120	168,070
Interest income	8,505	11,566	6,327
Interest expense	210,936	171,466	82,526
Other income (deductions) - net	12,183	(4,445)	(7,101)
Gain on sale of bottling operation	103,800	–	–
Income Before Income Taxes	267,721	172,775	84,770
Provision for income taxes	115,120	84,403	56,978
Net Income	152,601	88,372	27,792
Preferred stock dividend requirements	9,882	–	–
Net Income Available to Common Shareholders	$ 142,719	$ 88,372	$ 27,792
Average Common Shares Outstanding	138,755	140,036	76,705
Net Income Per Common Share	$ 1.03	$ 0.63	$ 0.36

Consolidated Balance Sheets

Coca-Cola Enterprises Inc.

(In thousands except share data)	December 30, 1988	January 1, 1988
Assets		
Current		
Cash and cash equivalents, at cost (approximates market)	$ 162	$ 11,297
Trade accounts receivable, less allowances of $8,766 in 1988 and $6,140 in 1987	293,890	262,508
Inventories	124,852	117,724
Prepaid expenses and other assets	69,558	60,462
Total Current Assets	488,462	451,991
Investments and Other Long-Term Assets	65,674	68,949
Property, Plant and Equipment		
Land	135,293	124,831
Buildings and improvements	436,322	365,607
Machinery and equipment	1,124,981	943,917
Containers	41,374	63,044
	1,737,970	1,497,399
Less allowances for depreciation	558,233	459,265
	1,179,737	1,038,134
Goodwill and Other Intangible Assets	2,935,334	2,690,950
	$4,669,207	$4,250,024

	December 30, 1988	January 1, 1988
Liabilities and Shareholders' Equity		
Current		
Accounts payable and accrued expenses	$ 399,777	$ 376,448
Accounts payable to The Coca-Cola Company	1,849	31,475
Current maturities of long-term debt	148,495	66,091
Total Current Liabilities	550,121	474,014
Long-Term Debt	2,062,022	2,091,089
Deferred Income Taxes	221,543	152,992
Other Long-Term Obligations	27,144	5,782
Shareholders' Equity		
Preferred stock, $1 par value Authorized – 100,000,000 shares; Issued and outstanding – 2,500 shares, at aggregate liquidation preference	250,000	–
Common stock, $1 par value Authorized – 500,000,000 shares; Issued – 140,260,000 shares	140,260	140,260
Paid-in capital	1,260,814	1,264,965
Reinvested earnings	264,394	127,513
Common stock in treasury, at cost (7,378,835 shares at December 30, 1988 and 471,800 shares at January 1, 1988)	(107,091)	(6,591)
	1,808,377	1,526,147
	$4,669,207	$4,250,024

Consolidated Balance Sheets

Bob Evans Farms, Inc. and Subsidiaries

Assets	April 26, 1991	April 27, 1990
Current Assets		
Cash	$ 6,341,000	$ 4,307,000
Investments	18,886,000	11,064,000
Accounts receivable	11,103,000	6,141,000
Inventories	7,155,000	7,198,000
Prepaid expenses	2,760,000	2,402,000
Total Current Assets	46,245,000	31,112,000
Property, Plant and Equipment, at cost		
Buildings	167,879,000	156,013,000
Machinery and equipment	80,673,000	76,042,000
Other	13,284,000	11,857,000
	261,836,000	243,912,000
Less accumulated depreciation	107,084,000	93,198,000
	154,752,000	150,714,000
Land	77,031,000	71,955,000
Construction in progress	3,146,000	2,146,000
Net Property, Plant and Equipment	234,929,000	224,815,000
Other Assets	2,739,000	1,214,000
Cost in Excess of Net Assets Acquired — Note A	3,341,000	3,502,000
	$287,254,000	$260,643,000

Liabilities and Stockholders' Equity		
Current Liabilities		
Accounts payable	$ 6,902,000	$ 7,248,000
Dividends payable	2,032,000	2,061,000
Federal and state income tax	6,956,000	4,872,000
Accrued wages and related liabilities	9,697,000	9,460,000
Other accrued expenses	12,490,000	9,498,000
Current portion of long-term debt	400,000	400,000
Total Current Liabilities	38,477,000	33,539,000
Long-Term Liabilities		
Long-term debt — Note B	1,600,000	2,000,000
Deferred income taxes	5,351,000	5,650,000
Total Long-Term Liabilities	6,951,000	7,650,000
Stockholders' Equity — Note E		
Common stock, $.01 par value		
Authorized 50,000,000 shares; issued 32,189,459 shares in 1991 and 1990	322,000	322,000
Capital in excess of par value	142,885,000	143,253,000
Retained earnings	110,723,000	82,991,000
	253,930,000	226,566,000
Less treasury stock 927,621 shares in 1991 and 518,516 shares in 1990, at cost	12,104,000	7,112,000
Total Stockholders' Equity	241,826,000	219,454,000
	$287,254,000	$260,643,000

Consolidated Statements of Income

Bob Evans Farms, Inc. and Subsidiaries

Years Ended April 26, 1991, April 27, 1990, and April 28, 1989	1991	1990	1989
Sales	$501,305,000	$454,339,000	$419,529,000
Cost of goods sold	388,334,000	357,687,000	319,450,000
	112,971,000	96,652,000	100,079,000
Selling and administrative expenses	60,283,000	54,743,000	53,019,000
	52,688,000	41,909,000	47,060,000
Other income, net	1,194,000	2,137,000	1,694,000
Income Before Income Taxes	53,882,000	44,046,000	48,754,000
Provisions for income taxes — Note C			
Federal			
Currently payable	18,400,000	13,757,000	14,910,000
Deferred	(1,625,000)	(154,000)	390,000
	16,775,000	13,603,000	15,300,000
State	3,472,000	2,698,000	2,791,000
	20,247,000	16,301,000	18,091,000
Net Income Before Extraordinary Gain	33,635,000	27,745,000	30,663,000
Extraordinary gain (net of tax effect of $1,326,000) — Note G	2,250,000	—	—
Net Income	$ 35,885,000	$ 27,745,000	$ 30,663,000
Net income per share before extraordinary gain	$1.07	$.87	$.95
Net income per share after extraordinary gain	$1.14	$.87	$.95

Consolidated Statements of Stockholders' Equity

Bob Evans Farms, Inc. and Subsidiaries

Years Ended April 26, 1991, April 27, 1990, and April 28, 1989

	Common Stock		Capital in Excess of Par Value	Retained Earnings	Treasury Stock	Total Stockholders' Equity
	Shares	Par Value				
Balances at 4/29/88	29,277,478	$293,000	$ 98,666,000	$ 84,852,000	$ (1,606,000)	$182,205,000
Net income				30,663,000		30,663,000
Dividends declared of $.23 per share				(7,297,000)		(7,297,000)
Purchase of treasury stock					(799,000)	(799,000)
Distribution of treasury stock due to exercise of stock options and payment of employee bonuses			(50,000)		471,000	421,000
Balances at 4/28/89	29,277,478	293,000	98,616,000	108,218,000	(1,934,000)	205,193,000
Net income				27,745,000		27,745,000
Dividends declared of $.25 per share				(8,200,000)		(8,200,000)
Purchase of treasury stock					(5,690,000)	(5,690,000)
Distribution of treasury stock due to exercise of stock options and payment of employee bonuses			(106,000)		512,000	406,000
Adjust par for stock dividend — Note E	2,911,981	29,000	44,743,000	(44,772,000)		
Balances at 4/27/90	32,189,459	322,000	143,253,000	82,991,000	(7,112,000)	219,454,000
Net income				35,885,000		35,885,000
Dividends declared of $.26 per share				(8,153,000)		(8,153,000)
Purchase of treasury stock					(7,368,000)	(7,368,000)
Distribution of treasury stock due to exercise of stock options and payment of employee bonuses			(368,000)		2,376,000	2,008,000
Balances at 4/26/91	32,189,459	$322,000	$142,885,000	$110,723,000	$(12,104,000)	$241,826,000

Consolidated Statements of Cash Flows

Bob Evans Farms, Inc. and Subsidiaries

For The Years Ended April 26, 1991, April 27, 1990, and April 28, 1989	1991	1990	1989
Operating Activities:			
Net income before extraordinary gain	$33,635,000	$27,745,000	$30,663,000
Adjustments to reconcile net income to net cash provided by operating activities:			
Depreciation and amortization	17,409,000	17,009,000	16,761,000
Deferred federal income taxes	(299,000)	(154,000)	390,000
Loss (gain) on sale of property and equipment	638,000	(918,000)	(717,000)
Cash provided by (used for) current assets and current liabilities:			
Accounts receivable	(4,962,000)	(902,000)	560,000
Inventories	43,000	(443,000)	(29,000)
Prepaid expenses	(358,000)	(114,000)	(341,000)
Accounts payable	(346,000)	595,000	225,000
Federal and state income taxes	2,084,000	(380,000)	574,000
Accrued wages and related liabilities	237,000	(574,000)	711,000
Other accrued expenses	2,992,000	2,931,000	118,000
Net Cash Provided by Operating Activities Excluding Extraordinary Gain	51,073,000	44,795,000	48,915,000
Extraordinary Gain	2,250,000	–	–
Net Cash Provided by Operating Activities	53,323,000	44,795,000	48,915,000
Investing Activities:			
Purchase of property, plant and equipment	(28,557,000)	(32,819,000)	(37,813,000)
Proceeds from sale of investments	51,979,000	36,129,000	2,882,000
Purchase of investments	(59,801,000)	(37,953,000)	(11,000,000)
Proceeds from sales of property, plant and equipment	557,000	3,473,000	6,328,000
Other	(1,525,000)	(183,000)	290,000
Net Cash Used in Investing Activities	(37,347,000)	(31,353,000)	(39,313,000)
Financing Activities:			
Cash dividends paid	(8,182,000)	(8,034,000)	(7,153,000)
Short-term line of credit:			
Proceeds	–	–	25,900,000
Principal payments	–	–	(25,900,000)
Purchase of treasury stock	(7,368,000)	(5,690,000)	(799,000)
Principal payments on long-term debt	(400,000)	(400,000)	(400,000)
Distribution of treasury stock and issuance of common stock due to the exercise of stock options and employee bonuses	2,008,000	406,000	421,000
Net Cash Used in Financing Activities	(13,942,000)	(13,718,000)	(7,931,000)
Increase (Decrease) in cash	2,034,000	(276,000)	1,671,000
Cash at the beginning of the year	4,307,000	4,583,000	2,912,000
Cash at the end of the year	$ 6,341,000	$ 4,307,000	$ 4,583,000

Notes to Consolidated Financial Statements

Bob Evans Farms, Inc. and Subsidiaries • April 26, 1991

Note A — Summary of Significant Accounting Policies

Principles of Consolidation: The consolidated financial statements include the accounts of the company and its wholly owned subsidiaries. Intercompany accounts and transactions have been eliminated.

Fiscal Year: The company's fiscal year ends on the last Friday in April. References herein to 1991, 1990 and 1989 refer to fiscal years ended April 26, 1991, April 27, 1990, and April 28, 1989, respectively.

Investments: The company records investments at cost, which approximates market.

Property, Plant and Equipment: The company calculates depreciation on the declining-balance and straight-line methods in amounts adequate to amortize costs over the assets' estimated useful lives.

Inventories: The company values inventories at the lower of first-in, first-out, cost or market.

Cost in Excess of Net Assets Acquired: The cost in excess of net assets acquired is being amortized over 25 years using the straight-line method. Accumulated amortization at April 26, 1991, and April 27, 1990, was $686,000 and $525,000, respectively.

Pre-opening Expenses: Expenditures related to the opening of new restaurants, other than those for capital assets, are charged to expense when incurred.

Net Income Per Share: The company calculates net income per share based upon the weighted average number of common shares outstanding during the year. Weighted average number of common shares outstanding for 1991, 1990 and 1989, were 31,358,000, 31,987,000 and 32,112,000, respectively. Outstanding stock options do not have a material dilutive effect.

Note B — Credit Arrangements

The company has arrangements with certain banks from which it may borrow up to $22,250,000. The arrangements are reviewed annually for renewal. During 1991 and 1990, these credit arrangements were not used. For 1989, the maximum amount outstanding under this arrangement was $8,800,000. The average amount outstanding during 1989 was $2,057,000 with a weighted average interest rate of 9.3%.

Long-term debt consists of industrial revenue bonds payable in annual installments of $400,000 through Dec. 1, 1995, plus accrued interest at 8.3%. The bonds are secured by certain fixed assets and contain various restrictive covenants which include requirements to maintain certain financial ratios.

Total interest expense of $226,000, $292,000 and $476,000 incurred during 1991, 1990 and 1989, respectively, was capitalized in connection with the company's restaurant construction activities.

Notes to Consolidated Financial Statements

Bob Evans Farms, Inc. and Subsidiaries • April 26, 1991

Note C—Income Taxes

Deferred taxes result from timing differences in the recognition of revenues and expenses for tax and financial statement purposes. The sources and the tax effect of the major timing differences follow:

	1991	1990	1989
Depreciation and amortization	$ 747,000	$ (559,000)	$ (726,000)
Employee benefits expense	597,000	906,000	336,000
Miscellaneous items	281,000	(193,000)	—
	$1,625,000	$ 154,000	$ (390,000)

The company's provisions for income taxes differ from the amounts computed by applying the federal statutory rate due to the following:

	1991	1990	1989
Expected tax	$18,320,000	$14,976,000	$16,576,000
State income tax (net)	2,292,000	1,781,000	1,842,000
Tax-free interest income	(232,000)	(203,000)	(32,000)
Targeted jobs credit (net)	(462,000)	(481,000)	(521,000)
Other	329,000	228,000	226,000
Provision for income taxes	$20,247,000	$16,301,000	$18,091,000

Taxes paid during 1991, 1990 and 1989 were $19,792,000, $17,678,000 and $18,056,000, respectively.

On Dec. 30, 1987, the Financial Accounting Standards Board issued Statement of Financial Accounting Standards No. 96, "Accounting for Income Taxes." The company does not intend to adopt this new method of accounting for income taxes until May 1, 1992, (i.e., fiscal 1993). Although the company has not completed all of the complex analyses required to estimate the impact of the new statement, Statement 96 is not expected to have a significant impact on the company's financial position.

Note D—Leases

Rental expense approximated $1,284,000 in 1991, $1,243,000 in 1990 and $1,103,000 in 1989. The company has no significant agreements involving contingent rentals or sub-leases.

Most of the operating leases contain one of the following options: (a) the company can, after the initial lease term, purchase the property at the then fair value of the property, or (b) the company can, at the end of the initial lease term, renew its lease at the then fair rental value for the periods of five to 10 years. In most cases, management expects that, in the normal course of business, leases will be renewed or replaced by other leases.

The future minimum rental payments required under operating land leases that have remaining non-cancelable lease terms in excess of one year are as follows: $894,000 in 1992, $835,000 in 1993, $796,000 in 1994, $801,000 in 1995, $803,000 in 1996 and $7,783,000 through 2028.

Notes to Consolidated Financial Statements

Bob Evans Farms, Inc. and Subsidiaries • April 26, 1991

Note E—Stockholders' Equity

On Aug. 14, 1989, the board of directors authorized a 10% stock dividend on the company's issued and outstanding common stock as of Sept. 8, 1989. All net income per share data and cash dividends per share amounts have been adjusted for this stock dividend.

The company has employee stock option plans adopted June 12, 1975 (1975 Plan), June 20, 1985 (1985 Plan), and May 14, 1987 (1987 Plan), and a non-employee directors stock option plan adopted June 16, 1989 (1989 Plan). Among other things, the plans provide that the option price shall be the fair market value of the stock at the date of grant. Options may be granted for a period of up to five years under the 1975 Plan, for a period of up to 10 years under the 1985 Plan and the 1987 Plan, and until all available shares reserved have been issued or until the board determines that the plan shall terminate under the 1989 Plan. Options granted under the plans become exercisable at the rate of 20% per year beginning at the date of grant. As of April 26, 1991, options for 425,293 shares were outstanding, and options for 212,721 shares were exercisable at prices ranging from $11.50 to $17.82 per share.

During 1991, 1990 and 1989, options of 147,974, 13,445 and 21,258 shares respectively, were exercised at prices ranging from $9.52 to $17.82 per share. At April 26, 1991, 596,175 shares were reserved for issuance under the plans.

Note F—Profit-Sharing Plan

Effective May 1, 1990, the company's non-contributory profit-sharing plan was amended to permit participants to make contributions to the plan. The plan covers substantially all employees with at least one year of service.

The annual contribution to the plan is at the discretion of the company's board of directors. The company's expense related to contributions to the plan in 1991, 1990 and 1989 was $1,985,000, $1,597,000 and $1,709,000, respectively.

Note G—Extraordinary Gain—Gallipolis Plant Fire, December 1990

In December 1990, a fire nearly destroyed the company's sausage production plant in Gallipolis, Ohio. The loss was insured, and as a result, the company reported an estimated gain of $2,250,000 ($1,500,000 in the third quarter and $750,000 in the fourth quarter) based upon the expected insurance settlement. These amounts were net of deferred taxes of $1,326,000. The building and equipment were insured at replacement cost. Accounts receivable at April 26, 1991, included $4,350,000 related to the expected insurance settlement.

Note H—Commitments and Contingencies

At April 26, 1991, the company had contractual commitments for restaurant construction, plant equipment additions and the purchase of land approximating $7,800,000.

The company is from time to time involved in a number of claims and litigation considered normal in the course of business. Various lawsuits and assessments, among them employment discrimination, product liability, workers' compensation claims and tax assessments, are in litigation or pending litigation. While it is not feasible to predict the outcome of these actions, in the opinion of the company, these actions should not ultimately have a material adverse effect on the financial position of the company.

Notes to Consolidated Financial Statements

Bob Evans Farms, Inc. and Subsidiaries • April 26, 1991

Note I—Industry Segments

The company's operations include the processing and sale of food products (previously referred to as the sausage segment) and restaurant operations. The revenues from these segments include both sales to unaffiliated customers and intersegment sales, which are accounted for on a basis consistent with sales to unaffiliated customers. Intersegment sales and other intersegment transactions have been eliminated in the financial statements.

Operating profit is total revenues less operating expenses. General corporate revenue, interest income, interest expense and income taxes have not been added or deducted in computing operating profit by segment. Identifiable assets by segment are those assets that are used in the company's operations in each segment. General corporate assets consist of temporary investments.

Information on the company's industry segments is summarized as follows:

Fiscal Year	1991	1990	1989
Sales and Other Income			
Food products	$166,594,000	$151,191,000	$145,300,000
Restaurant operations	358,248,000	322,266,000	293,531,000
	524,842,000	473,457,000	438,831,000
Intersegment sales of food products	(23,537,000)	(19,118,000)	(19,302,000)
	501,305,000	454,339,000	419,529,000
General corporate revenue	1,194,000	2,137,000	1,694,000
Total	$502,499,000	$456,476,000	$421,223,000
Operating Profit			
Food products	$ 10,567,000	$ 6,824,000	$ 14,584,000
Restaurant operations	42,121,000	35,085,000	32,476,000
General corporate revenue	1,194,000	2,137,000	1,694,000
Total	$ 53,882,000	$ 44,046,000	$ 48,754,000
Depreciation and Amortization Expense			
Food products	$ 4,476,000	$ 4,518,000	$ 4,487,000
Restaurant operations	12,933,000	12,491,000	12,274,000
Total	$ 17,409,000	$ 17,009,000	$ 16,761,000
Capital Expenditures			
Food products	$ 4,419,000	$ 4,453,000	$ 4,886,000
Restaurant operations	24,138,000	28,366,000	32,927,000
Total	$ 28,557,000	$ 32,819,000	$ 37,813,000
Identifiable Assets			
Food products	$ 54,049,000	$ 48,683,000	$ 47,155,000
Restaurant operations	214,319,000	200,896,000	187,803,000
	268,368,000	249,579,000	234,958,000
General corporate assets	18,886,000	11,064,000	9,240,000
Total	$287,254,000	$260,643,000	$244,198,000

Notes to Consolidated Financial Statements

Bob Evans Farms, Inc. and Subsidiaries • April 26, 1991

Note J—Quarterly Financial Data (Unaudited)

	Sales	Cost of Goods Sold	Net Income Before Extraordinary Gain	Net Income Per Share Before Extraordinary Gain	Net Income
Fiscal Year 1991					
First Quarter	$122,778,000	$96,151,000	$7,663,000	$.24	$ 7,663,000
Second Quarter	127,293,000	98,105,000	8,792,000	.28	8,792,000
Third Quarter	126,404,000	96,619,000	8,735,000	.28	10,235,000
Fourth Quarter	124,830,000	97,459,000	8,445,000	.27	9,195,000
Fiscal Year 1990					
First Quarter	$108,336,000	$83,129,000	$7,574,000	$.24	$ 7,574,000
Second Quarter	114,580,000	88,637,000	7,646,000	.23	7,646,000
Third Quarter	114,626,000	91,522,000	5,928,000	.19	5,928,000
Fourth Quarter	116,797,000	94,399,000	6,597,000	.21	6,597,000
Fiscal Year 1989					
First Quarter	$101,274,000	$76,689,000	$7,479,000	$.23	$ 7,479,000
Second Quarter	107,939,000	81,657,000	8,100,000	.25	8,100,000
Third Quarter	105,676,000	79,771,000	8,070,000	.25	8,070,000
Fourth Quarter	104,640,000	81,333,000	7,014,000	.22	7,014,000

Auditors' Report

Bob Evans Farms, Inc. and Subsidiaries

Report of Ernst & Young, Independent Auditors

Board of Directors
Bob Evans Farms, Inc.
Columbus, Ohio

We have audited the accompanying consolidated balance sheets of Bob Evans Farms, Inc. and Subsidiaries as of April 26, 1991, and April 27, 1990, and the related consolidated statements of income, shareholders' equity, and cash flows for each of the three years in the period ended April 26, 1991. These financial statements are the responsibility of the company's management. Our responsibility is to express an opinion on these financial statements based on our audits.

We conducted our audits in accordance with generally accepted auditing standards. Those standards require that we plan and perform the audit to obtain reasonable assurance about whether the financial statements are free of material misstatement. An audit includes examining, on a test basis, evidence supporting the amounts and disclosures in the financial statements. An audit also includes assessing the accounting principles used and significant estimates made by management, as well as evaluating the overall financial statement presentation. We believe that our audits provide a reasonable basis for our opinion.

In our opinion, the financial statements referred to above present fairly, in all material respects, the consolidated financial position of Bob Evans Farms, Inc. and Subsidiaries at April 26, 1991, and April 27, 1990, and the consolidated results of their operations and their cash flows for each of the three years in the period ended April 26, 1991, in conformity with generally accepted accounting principles.

Ernst + Young

Columbus, Ohio
May 24, 1991

Management's Discussion and Analysis of Selected Financial Information

Bob Evans Farms, Inc. and Subsidiaries

Sales

Total sales for Bob Evans Farms, Inc. and Subsidiaries increased 10% in 1991 over 1990. This compares with an 8% increase in 1990 over 1989.

Restaurant sales increased 11% in 1991 compared to 1990. This increase was due mainly to more restaurants in operation (255 open at the end of 1991 compared to 241 open at the end of 1990) and a 4% weighted average menu price increase. Core stores (restaurants open for a full 12 months in both fiscal years) had no increase in comparable sales after subtracting the menu price increase. The remaining 7% increase in restaurant sales was attributable to new restaurants and restaurants without a full-year comparison.

Restaurant sales increased 10% in 1990 compared to 1989. This increase was due mainly to more restaurants in operation (241 open at the end of 1990 compared to 222 open at the end of 1989) and a 4% weighted average menu price increase. Restaurants which were open for a full 12 months during both fiscal years had a 4% increase in sales. After subtracting the menu price increase, core store comparable sales were the same in 1990 compared to 1989. New restaurants and restaurants without a full year comparison accounted for the remaining 6% increase in restaurant sales.

Food products segment sales, which currently consist principally of sausage products, increased 8% in 1991 compared to 1990. The increase in sales was attributable to higher wholesale prices being charged this year compared to last year. Pounds sold decreased 6% in 1991 compared to 1990 primarily due to higher wholesale prices as well as a general decline in consumption of sausage products. While the company has experienced a decrease in number of pounds sold, it has maintained its market share.

No new geographical markets were opened during fiscal year 1991, and in January 1991, the company discontinued its two retail sales routes in the Memphis, Tenn., market because of low sales. The food products segment is continually testing and researching a variety of new products for existing retail markets as well as institutional and foodservice customers. New products which have been successfully introduced in five retail markets at fiscal year end are the Bob Evans Burritos. Early sales are meeting the company's expectations, and the company plans to continue to introduce these new products in all of its market territory during the coming year.

In the food products segment, sales increased 5% in 1990 compared to 1989. This increase was due mainly to higher wholesale prices being charged for sausage sold in 1990 compared to 1989. Total pounds sold increased slightly in 1990 compared to 1989. The Richmond/Norfolk, Va., market was opened in October 1989.

Cost of Goods Sold

Cost of goods sold was 77% of sales in 1991, and increased 9% over the cost of goods sold in 1990. Cost of goods sold in the restaurant segment increased 9% in 1991 over the prior year due mainly to new restaurants in operation and restaurants opened in the prior year with a full year of operations. The food products segment had a 9% increase in cost of goods sold. This was the result of higher live hog costs in 1991 (during which the average live hog cost was $50.36 per hundredweight), compared to 1990 (during which the average cost of live hogs was $42.13 per hundredweight).

Cost of goods sold was 79% of sales in 1990, and increased 12% over the cost of goods sold in 1989. In the restaurant segment increases were mainly due to the addition of 19 new restaurants. In the food products segment increases were due to higher live hog costs in 1990 (during which the average live hog cost was $42.13 per hundredweight), compared to 1989 (during which the average live hog cost was $34.85 per hundredweight).

Selling and Administrative Expenses

Selling and administrative expenses for 1991, 1990 and 1989 were 12%, 12% and 13% respectively, of sales.

Selling and administrative expenses increased 10% in 1991 compared to 1990. This increase resulted mainly from increases in wages and fringe benefit expenses in the restaurant segment due to more restaurants in operation. Increases in the food products segment were due to increases in wages and fringe benefit expenses as well as increases in direct advertising expense.

Selling and administrative expenses increased 3% in 1990 compared to 1989. This increase was mainly due to increases in the restaurant segment, specifically administrative wages and fringe benefit expense and training and development costs. Food products segment selling and administrative expenses were nearly the same in 1990 as they were in 1989.

Other Income

Other income decreased 44% in 1991 compared to 1990. This decrease was due to a decrease in other income

Management's Discussion and Analysis of Selected Financial Information

Bob Evans Farms, Inc. and Subsidiaries

Other income decreased 44% in 1991 compared to 1990. This decrease was due to a decrease in other income in the fourth quarter of 1991 compared to 1990 due to gains received on a one-time basis in 1990 related to the sale of excess parcels of land in the restaurant segment. Also, during the fourth quarter of fiscal year 1991, a loss reserve of $450,000 was established in anticipation of the May 13, 1991, closing of two restaurants located in Villa Park, Ill., and Clearwater, Fla.

Other income increased 26% in 1990 compared to 1989. This increase was due to income generated from gains from the sale of excess parcels of land in the restaurant segment. Interest income was also higher in 1990 compared to 1989 due to an increase in the amount of investments held by the company.

Interest expense in 1991, 1990 and 1989 was capitalized in connection with the company's restaurant construction activities.

Taxes

The effective federal and state income tax rates applicable to the company in 1991, 1990 and 1989 were 37.6%, 37.0% and 37.1%, respectively.

On Dec. 30, 1987, the Financial Accounting Standards Board issued Statement of Financial Accounting Standards No. 96 "Accounting for Income Taxes." The company does not intend to adopt this new method of accounting for income taxes until May 1, 1992 (i.e., fiscal 1993). Although the company has not completed all of the complex analyses required to estimate the impact of the new statement, Statement 96 is not expected to have a significant impact on the company's financial position.

Net Income

The company's net income before extraordinary gain increased 21% in 1991 compared to 1990. In the restaurant segment, net income before extraordinary gain increased 15% over 1990. This increase resulted from more restaurants in operation and better profit margins in comparable restaurants in 1991 compared to 1990. Food products segment net income before extraordinary gain increased 42% over the same period a year ago. This is the direct result of better pre-tax profit margins on sausage sold due to increases in the wholesale price of sausage products. The company recorded an extraordinary gain with an after-tax benefit of $2,250,000 or $.07 per share based upon expected insurance proceeds related to the Gallipolis plant fire. The expected insurance proceeds have been included in accounts receivable on the company's balance sheets. (See Note G in Notes to Consolidated Financial Statements.)

The company's net income decreased 10% in 1990 compared to 1989. The food products segment accounted for all of the decrease, which was attributable to the high cost of live hogs in 1990. The high cost of live hogs had a dramatic effect on both operating margins and profitability in the food products segment, and for the year, food products segment net income declined 43% compared to 1989. Restaurant segment net income increased 8% in 1990 compared to 1989. This increase was due to more restaurants in operation during 1990 compared to 1989.

Liquidity and Capital Resources

The company continues to maintain a strong financial position and relies on cash and short-term investments as a principal source of liquidity. Cash generated from both the restaurant and food products segments is used to satisfy working capital needs and to fund capital expenditures. Cash and short-term investments totaled $25.2 million in 1991 and $15.4 million in 1990.

The company has available lines of credit aggregating $22,250,000. At April 26, 1991, no amounts were outstanding under such arrangements.

At April 26, 1991, the company had contractual commitments for restaurant construction, plant equipment additions and purchases of land approximating $7,800,000. The company estimates that total capital expenditures for fiscal year 1992 will be approximately $44,000,000 and that depreciation expense will be $18,500,000. The company plans to build and open 20 additional restaurants and build a new food processing facility. It is anticipated that financing for all capital expenditures will be with internally generated funds.

On Aug. 14, 1989, the board of directors declared a 10% stock dividend on all of the company's issued and outstanding common stock. After the stock dividend, the board maintained the annual dividend rate of $.26 per share on the shares outstanding. This resulted in a 10% increase in dividend payout. Dividends paid during 1991 represented 24% of 1991 earnings before extraordinary gain.

The company anticipates that funds necessary for capital expenditures and working capital during 1992 will be generated internally. Available bank lines of credit may be used for short-term cash needs when required. Long-term sources of credit should not be needed during 1992.

Management's Outlook

Bob Evans Farms, Inc. and Subsidiaries

Food Products Segment

The food products segment, renamed in 1991 from the former sausage segment, continues to operate our base wholesale sausage business. Management is aware of the general decline in the consumption of pork sausage and plans to continue to develop and introduce a variety of new food products to meet consumer trends and demands. In addition, the company is putting a new emphasis on developing food products for the institutional and food-service business.

Management is unaware of any other uncertainties in the food products segment that would cause the company's reported financial information not to be indicative of future operating results, other than the cyclical nature of the live hog market.

Restaurant Segment

In the restaurant segment, management is unaware of uncertainties that would cause the reported financial information not to be indicative of future operating results. Competition for customer growth is as intense as it has ever been. In an effort to expand our restaurant business, the Bob Evans General Store and Restaurant was opened in the fourth quarter of 1991. Early indications of the performance of the General Store and Restaurant are positive and the company plans to build five more General Store and Restaurants in 1992. Announced also in the fourth quarter of 1991 were plans to build and operate a new restaurant called Cantina del Rio, serving authentic Southwestern foods in a Mexican atmosphere. This new concept is in the final development stages and the first Cantina del Rio should open during the latter part of fiscal year 1992. Management believes the General Store and Restaurant and Cantina del Rio will provide viable growth avenues for the restaurant segment in the future.

During 1991, the company built and opened a second generation prototype restaurant in Indianapolis. This new prototype building was designed to more efficiently serve customers and ensure their comfort by relocating the restrooms, enlarging the foyer and non-smoking seating area, and streamlining kitchen operations and carry-out services. The company plans to build and use the new prototype building design in future expansion, while maintaining our current 255 restaurants, the core of our business and fundamental to our success.

Wages will be impacted by the recent increase in the minimum wage rate. Cost of fringe benefits, particularly workers' compensation expense continue to increase. The company has implemented various cost sharing and cost prevention programs to help offset these increased costs. The recruiting and training of qualified personnel is a challenge in the restaurant segment. Programs to reduce turnover appear to be working and will continue to be important to the restaurant segment in the future.

GLOSSARY

A

Absorption costing. The concept that considers the cost of manufactured products to be composed of direct materials, direct labor, and factory overhead. (893)

Accelerated depreciation method. A depreciation method that provides for a high depreciation charge in the first year of use of an asset and gradually declining periodic charges thereafter. (336)

Account. The form used to record additions and deductions for each individual asset, liability, owner's equity, revenue, and expense. (53)

Account form of balance sheet. A balance sheet with assets on the left-hand side and liabilities and owner's equity on the right-hand side. (28, 167)

Accounting. The process of identifying, measuring, and communicating economic information to permit informed judgments and decisions by users of the information. (12)

Accounting cycle. The sequence of principle accounting procedures employed to process transactions during a fiscal period. (122)

Accounting equation. The expression of the relationship between assets, liabilities, and owner's equity; most commonly stated as Assets = Liabilities + Owner's Equity. (20)

Accounting system. The system that provides the information for use in conducting the affairs of the business and reporting to owners, creditors, and other interested parties. (217)

Account payable. A liability created by a purchase made on credit. (21)

Account receivable. A claim against a customer for sales made on credit. (22)

Accounts payable ledger. The subsidiary ledger containing the individual accounts with suppliers (creditors). (F-3)

Accounts receivable ledger. The subsidiary ledger containing the individual accounts with customers (debtors). (F-3)

Accounts receivable turnover. The relationship between credit sales and accounts receivable, computed by dividing net sales on account by the average net accounts receivable. (1172)

Accrual basis. Revenues are recognized in the period earned and expenses are recognized in the period incurred in the process of generating revenues. (101)

Accrued asset (accrued revenue) or accrued liability (accrued expense). An asset (revenue) or a liability (expense) that gradually increases with the passage of time and that is recorded at the end of the accounting period by an adjusting entry. (106, 158)

Accumulated depreciation account. The contra asset account used to accumulate the depreciation recognized to date on plant assets. (105)

Acid-test ratio. The ratio of the sum of cash, receivables, and marketable securities to current liabilities. (1172)

Activity-based costing. A cost allocation method that initially assigns costs to activities and then to products. (782)

Adequate disclosure. The concept that financial statements and their accompanying footnotes should contain all of the pertinent data believed essential to the reader's understanding of an enterprise's financial status. (163)

Adjusting entry. An entry required at the end of an accounting period to record an internal transaction and to bring the ledger up to date. (103)

Administrative expense. An expense incurred in the administration or general operations of the business. (164)

Aging the receivables. The process of analyzing the accounts receivable and classifying them according to various age groupings, with the due date being the base point for determining age. (265)

Allowance method. The method of accounting for uncollectible receivables, by which advance provision for the uncollectibles is made. (262)

American Institute of Certified Public Accountants (AICPA). The national professional organization of CPAs. (15)

Amortization. The periodic expense attributed to the decline in usefulness of an intangible asset or the allocation of bond premium or discount over the life of a bond issue. (349)

Annuity. A series of equal cash flows at fixed intervals. (508, 982)

Appropriation of retained earnings. The amount of a corporation's retained earnings that has been restricted and therefore is not available for distribution to shareholders as dividends. (471)

Articles of partnership. The formal written contract creating a partnership. (419)

Asset. Property owned by a business enterprise. (20)

Average cost method. (a) The method of inventory costing for a merchandising enterprise that is based on the assumption that costs should be charged against revenue in accordance with the weighted average unit costs of the commodities sold. (b) A method of determining manufactured products costs in which all costs incurred in manufacturing the goods completed during a period are averaged, and this average is used in determining the unit product cost of the goods completed during the period and the work in process at the end of the period. (297, 745)

Average rate of return. A method of evaluating capital investment proposals that focuses on the expected profitability of the investment. (963)

B

Balance of an account. The amount of difference between the debits and the credits that have been entered into an account (55).

Balance sheet. A financial statement listing the assets, liabilities, and owner's equity of a business entity as of a specific date. (25)

Bank reconciliation. The method of analysis that details the items that are responsible for the difference between the cash balance reported in the bank statement and the balance of the cash account in the ledger. (226)

Betterments. Expenditures that increase operating efficiency or capacity for the remaining useful life of a plant asset. (342)

Bond. A form of interest-bearing note employed by corporations to borrow on a long-term basis. (503)

Bond indenture. The contract between a corporation issuing bonds and the bondholders. (505)

Book value of an asset. The cost of an asset less the balance of any related contra asset account. (106)

Boot. The balance owed the supplier when an old asset is traded for a new asset. (346)

Break-even point. The level of operations of an enterprise at which revenues and expired costs are equal. (860)

Budget. A formal written statement of management's plans for the future, expressed in financial terms. (1049)

Budget performance report. A report comparing actual results with budget figures. (1060)

Budgeted cost. Carefully estimated costs which management plans to incur. (772)

Business entity concept. The concept that assumes that accounting applies to individual economic units and that each unit is separate and distinct from the persons who supply its asset. (17)

Business transaction. The occurrence of an event or of a condition that must be recorded in the accounting records. (19)

By-product. A product resulting from a manufacturing process and having little value in relation to the principal product or joint products. (737)

C

Capital. The rights (equity) of the owners in a business enterprise. (422)

Capital expenditure. A cost that adds to the utility of an asset for more than one accounting period. (342)

Capital expenditures budget. The budget summarizing future plans for acquisition of plant facilities and equipment. (1057)

Capital investment analysis. The process by which management plans, evaluates, and controls long-term capital investments involving property, plant, and equipment. (962)

Capital lease. A lease which includes one or more of four provision that result in treating the leased asset as a purchased asset in the accounts. (347)

Capital rationing. The process by which management allocates available investment funds among competing capital investment proposals. (975)

Capital stock. Shares of ownership of a corporation. (20, 423)

Carrying amount. The amount at which a temporary or a long-term investment or a long-term liability is reported on the balance sheet; also called basis or book value. (269, 511)

Cash basis. Revenue is recognized in the period cash is received, and expenses are recognized in period cash is paid. (101)

Cash discount. The deduction allowable if an invoice is paid by a specified date. (149)

Cash dividend. A cash distribution of earnings by a corporation to its shareholders. (474)

Cash flows from financing activities. The section of the statement of cash flows in which is reported the transactions involving cash receipts from the issuance of equity and debt securities; and cash payments for dividends, repurchase of equity securities, and redemption of debt securities. (593)

Cash flows from investing activities. The section of the statement of cash flows in which is reported the activities involving cash receipts from the sale of investments, plant assets, and other noncurrent assets; and cash payments for the acquisition of investments, plant assets, and other noncurrent assets. (593)

Cash flows from operating activities. The section of the statement of cash flows in which is reported the cash transactions that entered into the determination of net income. (593)

Cash payback period. The expected period of time that will elapse between the date of a capital expenditure and the complete recovery in cash (or equivalent) of the amount invested. (965)

Cash payments journal. The journal in which all cash payments are recorded. (F-7)

Cash receipts journal. The journal in which all cash receipts are recorded. (F-11)

Certified Public Accountant (CPA). An accountant who meets state licensing requirements for engaging in the practice of public accounting as a CPA. (6)

Chart of accounts. A listing of all the accounts used by a business enterprise. (54)

Closing entry. An entry necessary to eliminate the balance of a temporary account in preparation for the following accounting period. (117)

Codes of professional conduct. Standards of conduct established by professional organizations of CPAs to guide CPAs in the conduct of their practices. (16)

Common-size statement. A financial statement in which all items are expressed only in relative terms. (1169)

Common stock. The basic ownership class of corporate capital stock. (423)

Completed-contract method. The method that recognizes revenue from long-term construction contracts when the project is completed. (310)

Composite-rate depreciation method. A method of depreciation based on the use of a single rate that applies to entire groups of assets. (341)

Consistency. The concept that assumes that the same generally accepted accounting principles have been applied in the preparation of successive financial statements. (466)

Consolidated statement. A financial statement resulting from combining parent and subsidiary company statements. (547)

Consolidation. The creation of a new corporation by the transfer of assets and liabilities from two or more existing corporations. (545)

Constant dollar. Historical costs that have been converted into dollars of constant value through the use of a price-level index. (1190)

Contingent liability. A potential obligation that will materialize only if certain events occur in the future. (260, 374)

Continuous budgeting. A method of budgeting that provides for maintenance of a twelve-month projection into the future. (1050)

Contra account. An account that is offset against another account. (105)

Contract rate of interest. The interest rate specified on a bond. (508)

Contribution margin. Sales less variable cost of goods sold and variable selling and administrative expenses. (858, 895)

Contribution margin analysis. The systematic examination of the differences between planned and actual contribution margin. (906)

Contribution margin ratio. The percentage of each sales dollar that is available to cover the fixed expenses and provide an operating income. (858, 905)

Controllable cost. For a specific level of management, a cost that can be directly controlled. (658, 901)

Controller. The chief managerial accountant of an organization. (653)

Controlling. The process by which managers attempt to achieve the goals identified in an enterprise's strategic and operational plans. (650)

Controlling account. The account in the general ledger that summarizes the balances of a subsidiary ledger. (217)

Conversion costs. The combination of direct labor and factory overhead costs. (662, 731)

Corporation. A separate legal entity that is organized in accordance with state or federal statutes and in which ownership is divided into shares of stock. (18)

Cost accounting system. An accounting system which uses the perpetual system of inventory accounting for the three manufacturing inventories: direct materials, work in process, and finished goods. (693)

Cost allocation. The assignment of costs to a cost object. (769)

Cost behavior. The manner in which a cost changes in relation to its activity base. (813)

Cost center. A decentralized unit in which the department or division manager has responsibility for control of costs incurred and the authority to make decisions that affect these costs. (1117)

Cost driver. An activity measure overhead cost. (698, 791)

Cost estimation. The method or methods used to estimate costs for use in managerial decision making. (813)

Cost ledger. A subsidiary ledger employed in a job order cost system and which contains an account for each job order. (701)

Cost method. A method of accounting for an investment in stock, by which the investor recognizes as income its share of cash dividends of the investee. (542)

Cost object. The object or segment of operations to which costs are related such as a product or department. (657, 791)

Cost of goods sold. The cost of the manufactured product sold. (164, 668)

Cost of merchandise sold. The cost of the merchandise purchased and sold. (157)

Cost of production report. A report prepared periodically by a processing department, summarizing (1) the units for which the department is accountable and the disposition of these units and (2) the costs charged to the department and the allocation of these costs. (735)

Cost price approach. An approach to transfer pricing that uses cost as the basis for setting the transfer price. (1136)

Cost principle. The principle that assumes that the monetary record for properties and services purchased by a business should be maintained in terms of cost. (18)

Costs. The disbursement of cash (or the commitment to pay cash in the future) for the purpose of generating revenues. (656)

Cost-volume-profit analysis. The systematic examination of the interrelationships between selling prices, volume of sales and production, costs, expenses, and profits. (857)

Cost-volume-profit chart. A chart used to assist management in understanding the relationships between costs, expenses, sales, and operating profit or loss. (865)

Credit. (1) The right side of an account; (2) the amount entered on the right side of an account; (3) to enter an amount on the right side of an account. (55)

Credit memorandum. The form issued by a seller to inform a debtor that a credit has been posted to the debtor's account receivable. (150)

Cumulative preferred stock. Preferred stock that is entitled to current and past dividends before dividends may be paid on common stock. (425)

Current asset. Cash or another asset that may reasonably be expected to be realized in cash or sold or consumed, usually within a year or less, through the normal operations of a business. (115)

Current cost. The amount of cash that would have to be paid currently to acquire assets of the same age and in the same condition as existing assets. (1189)

Current liability. A liability that will be due within a short time (usually one year or less) and that is to be paid out of current assets. (116)

Current ratio. The ratio of current assets to current liabilities. (1171)

Currently attainable standards. Standards which represent levels of operation that can be attained with reasonable effort. (1087)

Cycle time. The time required to manufacture a product. Sometimes referred to as throughput time. (665, 1000)

D

Data base. The entire amount of data needed by an enterprise. (217)

Debit. (1) The left side of an account; (2) the amount entered on the left side of an account; (3) to enter an amount on the left side of an account. (55)

Debit memorandum. The form issued by a buyer to inform a creditor that a debit has been posted to the creditor's account payable. (150)

Debt security. A bond or a note payable. (519)

Decentralization. The separation of a business into more manageable units. (1114)

Decision making. The process by which managers determine to follow one course of action as opposed to an alternative. (650)

Declining-balance depreciation method. A method of depreciation that provides declining periodic depreciation charges to expense over the estimated life of an asset. (334)

Deficit. A debit balance in the retained earnings account. (422)

Departmental margin. Departmental gross profit less direct departmental expenses. (1121)

Depletion. The cost of metal ores and other minerals removed from the earth. (348)

Depreciation. The decrease in usefulness of all plant assets except land. (105, 331)

Differential analysis. The area of accounting concerned with the effect of alternative courses of action on revenues and costs. (927)

Differential cost. The amount of increase or decrease in cost that is expected from a particular course of action compared with an alternative. (658)

Differential revenue. The amount of increase or decrease in revenue expected from a particular course of action as compared with an alternative. (927)

Direct cost. A cost that can be traced directly to a cost object. (657)

Direct expense. An expense directly traceable to or incurred for the sole benefit of a specific department and ordinarily subject to the control of the department manager. (1121)

Direct labor cost. Wages of factory workers who convert materials into a finished product. (310, 661)

Direct labor rate variance. The cost associated with the difference between the standard rate and the actual rate paid for direct labor used in producing a commodity. (1089)

Direct labor time variance. The cost associated with the difference between the standard hours and actual hours of direct labor spent producing a commodity. (1089)

Direct materials cost. The cost of materials that enter directly into the finished product. (310)

Direct materials inventory. The cost of direct materials which have not yet entered into the manufacturing process. (661)

Direct materials price variance. The cost associated with the difference between the standard price and the actual price of direct materials used in producing a commodity. (1088)

Direct materials quantity variance. The cost associated with the difference between the standard quantity and the actual quantity of direct materials used in producing a commodity. (1088)

Direct method. (a) A method of reporting the cash flows from operating activities as the difference between the operating cash receipts and the operating cash payments. (b) A method of allocating service department costs. (594, 791)

Direct write-off method. A method of accounting for uncollectible receivables, whereby an expense is recognized only when specific accounts are judged to be uncollectible. (262)

Directing. The process by which managers, given their assigned level of responsibilities, run day-to-day operations. (650)

Discontinued operations. The operations of a business segment that has been disposed of. (465)

Discount. (a) The interest deducted from the maturity value of a note; (b) excess of par value of stock over its sales price; (c) excess of the face amount of bonds over their issue price. (259, 395, 426, 508)

Discount rate. The rate used in computing the interest to be deducted from the maturity value of a note. (388)

Discretionary cost. A cost that is not essential to short-term operations. (659)

Dishonored note receivable. A note which the maker fails to pay on the due date. (261)

Dividend. A distribution of earnings of a corporation to its owners (stockholders). (23, 473)

Double-entry accounting. A system for recording transactions based on recording increases and decreases in accounts so that debits always equal credits. (57)

E

Earnings per share (EPS) on common stock. The profitability ratio of net income available to common shareholders to the number of common shares outstanding. (469, 1179)

Economic order quantity (EOQ). The optimum quantity of specified inventoriable materials to be ordered at one time. (1006)

Economies of scale. An economic concept that recognizes that over a wide range of production, costs vary in differing proportions to changes in an activity base. When production facilities are limited, costs tend to increase but at a decreasing rate as production increases from a relatively low level. (817, 941)

Effective rate of interest. The market rate of interest at the time bonds are issued. (508)

Electronic funds transfer (EFT). A payment system that uses computerized electronic impulses rather than paper (money, checks, etc.) to effect a cash transaction. (235)

Employee's earnings record. A detailed record of each employee's earnings. (382)

Engineering method. A cost estimation method in which engineers estimate total cost, as well as variable and fixed components, based on studies of such factors as production methods, materials and labor requirements, equipment needs, and utility demands. (834)

Equity. The right or claim to the properties of a business enterprise. (20)

Equity method. A method of accounting for investments in common stock, by which the investment account is adjusted for the investor's share of periodic net income and property dividends of the investee. (542)

Equity per share. The ratio of stockholders' equity to the related number of shares of stock outstanding. (431)

Equity security. Preferred or common stock. (541)

Equivalent units of production. The number of units that could have been manufactured from start to finish during a period. (733)

Ethics. Moral principals that guide the conduct of individuals (654).

Exchange rate. The rate at which one unit of currency can be converted into another currency. (560)

Expected value. A concept useful for managers in decision making which involves identifying the possible outcomes from a decision and estimating the likelihood that each outcome will occur. (1023)

Expense. The amount of assets consumed or services used in the process of earning revenue. (22)

Extraordinary item. An event or transaction that is unusual and infrequent. (466)

Extraordinary repairs. Expenditures that increase the useful life of an asset beyond the original estimate. (343)

F

Factory overhead cost. All of the costs of operating the factory except for direct materials and direct labor. (310, 661)

Factory overhead controllable variance. The difference between the actual amount of factory overhead cost incurred and the amount of factory overhead budgeted for the level of operations achieved. (1092)

Factory overhead volume variance. The cost or benefit associated with operating at a level above or below 100% of productive capacity. (1092)

FICA tax. Federal Insurance Contributions Act tax used to finance federal programs for old-age and disability benefits and health insurance for the aged. (377)

Financial accounting. The branch of accounting that is concerned with the recording of transactions using generally accepted accounting principles (GAAP) for a business enterprise or other economic unit and with a periodic preparation of various statements from such records. (12, 647)

Financial Accounting Standards Board (FASB). The current authoritative body for the development of accounting principles for all entities except state and municipal governments. (15)

Finished goods inventory. The cost of finished products on hand that have not been sold. (310)

Finished goods ledger. The subsidiary ledger that contains the individual accounts for each kind of commodity produced. (703)

First-in, first-out (fifo) method. (a) A method of inventory costing based on the assumption that the costs of merchandise sold should be charged against revenue in the order in which the costs were incurred. (b) A method of determining costs of goods manufactured in which the beginning work in process inventory costs are kept separate from the costs incurred during the period and these costs are assigned to the goods manufactured in the order incurred. (295, 745)

Fiscal year. The annual accounting period adopted by an enterprise. (100)

Fixed expense (cost). An expense (cost) that tends to remain constant in amount regardless of variations in volume of activity. (659, 818, 878)

Flexible budget. A series of budgets for varying rates of activity. (1060)

FOB destination. Terms of agreement between buyer and seller, whereby ownership passes when merchandise is received by the buyer, and the seller absorbs the transportation costs. (155)

FOB shipping point. Terms of agreement between buyer and seller, whereby ownership passes when merchandise is delivered to the shipper, and the buyer absorbs the transportation costs. (154)

Funded. An appropriation of retained earnings accompanied by a segregation of cash or marketable securities. (472)

Future value. The amount that will accumulate at some future date as a result of an investment or a series of investments. (514)

G-H

General accounting system. An accounting system which extends the periodic system of inventory accounting used by merchandising enterprises to the three manufacturing inventories: direct materials, work in process, and finished goods. (693)

General journal. The two-column form used to record journal entries that do not "fit" in any special journals. (F-2)

General ledger. The principal ledger, when used in conjunction with subsidiary ledgers, that contains all of the balance sheet and income statement accounts. (217)

Generally accepted accounting principles (GAAP). Generally accepted guidelines for the preparation of financial statements. (12)

Going concern concept. The concept that assumes that a business entity has a reasonable expectation of continuing in business at a profit for an indefinite period of time. (99)

Goodwill. An intangible asset that attaches to a business as a result of such favorable factors as location, product superiority, reputation, and managerial skills. (350)

Governmental Accounting Standards Board (GASB). The current authoritative body for the development of accounting principles for state and municipal governments. (15)

Gross pay. The total earnings of an employee for a payroll period. (377)

Gross profit. The excess of net revenue from sales over the cost of merchandise sold. (164, 377)

Gross profit method. A means of estimating inventory on hand without the need for a physical count. (309)

High-low method. A technique that uses the highest and lowest total costs as a basis for estimating the variable cost per unit and fixed cost component of a mixed cost. (824)

Horizontal analysis. The percentage of increases and decreases in corresponding items in comparative financial statements. (1164)

I

Income from operations. The excess of gross profit over total operating expenses. (164)

Income statement. A summary of the revenues and expenses of a business entity for a specific period of time. (25)

Income summary account. The account used in the closing process for summarizing the revenue and expense accounts. (117)

Indirect cost. A cost that cannot be traced directly to a cost object. (657)

Indirect expense. An expense that is incurred for an entire business enterprise as a unit and that is not subject to the control of individual department managers. (1121)

Indirect method. A method of reporting the cash flows from operating activities as the net income from operations adjusted for all deferrals of past cash receipts and payments and all accruals of expected future cash receipts and payments. (594)

Inflation. A period when prices in general are rising and the purchasing power of money is declining. (975)

Installment method. The method of recognizing revenue, whereby each receipt of cash from installment sales is considered to be composed of partial payment of cost of merchandise sold and gross profit. (268)

Intangible asset. A long-lived asset that is useful in the operations of an enterprise, is not held for sale, and is without physical qualities. (330)

Interim statements. A financial statement issued for a period covering less than a fiscal year. (1191)

Internal controls. The detailed procedures adopted by an enterprise to control its operations. (218)

Internal rate of return method. A method of analysis of proposed capital investments that focuses on using present value concepts to compute the rate of return from the net cash flows expected from the investment. (968)

Internal Revenue Service (IRS). The branch of the U.S. Treasury Department concerned with enforcement and collection of the income tax. (16)

Inventory reorder point. The level to which inventory is allowed to fall before an order for additional inventory is placed. (1007)

Inventory turnover. The relationship between the volume of goods sold and inventory, computed by dividing the cost of goods sold by the average inventory. (1131, 1173)

Investment center. A decentralized unit in which the manager has the responsibility and authority to make decisions that affect not only costs and revenues, but also the plant assets available to the center. (1118)

Investment turnover. A component of the rate of return on investment, computed as the ratio of sales to invested assets. (1131)

Invoice. The bill provided by the seller (who refers to it as a sales invoice) to a buyer (who refers to its as a purchase invoice) for item purchased. (149)

J

Job cost sheet. An account in the cost ledger in which the costs charged to a particular job order are recorded. (701)

Job order cost system. A type of cost system that provides for a separate record of the cost of each particular quantity of product that passes through the factory. (693)

Joint cost. The cost common to the manufacture of two or more products (joint products). (737)

Joint products. Two or more commodities of significant value produced from a single principal direct material. (737)

Journal. The initial record in which the effects of a transaction on accounts are recorded. (55)

Journalizing. The process of recording a transaction in a journal. (56)

Judgmental method. A cost estimation method in which managers estimate total cost, as well as variable and fixed components, using experience and past observations of cost-volume-relationships. (833)

Just-in-time manufacturing system. A system of manufacturing in which a primary emphasis is on the manufacture of products only as they are needed by the next stage of production or by the marketplace. (664, 1001)

L

Last-in, first-out (lifo) method. A method of inventory costing based on the assumption that the most recent merchandise costs incurred should be charged against revenue. (296)

Lead time. The time, usually expressed in days, that it takes to receive an order for inventory. (1007)

Least squares method. A cost estimation method that uses statistics to estimate total cost and the fixed and variable cost components. (830)

Ledger. The group of accounts used by an enterprise. (53)

Leverage. The tendency of the rate earned on stockholders' equity to vary from the rate earned on total assets because the amount earned on assets acquired through the use of funds provided by creditors varies from the interest paid to these creditors. (1178)

Liability. A debt of a business enterprise. (20)

Linear programming. A quantitative method that can be used in providing data for solving a variety of business problems in which management's objective is to minimize cost or maximize profits, subject to several limiting factors. (1009)

Liquidating dividend. A distribution out of paid-in capital when a corporation permanently reduces its operations or winds up its affairs completely. (477)

Liquidation. The winding-up process when a partnership goes out of business. (477)

Long-term investment. An investment that is not intended to be a ready source of cash in the normal operations of a business and that is listed in the "investments" section of the balance sheet. (519)

Long-term liability. A liability that is not due for a comparatively long time (usually more than one year). (116)

Lower of cost or market. A method of costing inventory or valuing temporary investments that carries those assets at the lower of their cost or current market prices. (305)

M

Management. Individuals who are charged with the responsibility of directing the operations of enterprises. (647)

Management by exception. The philosophy of managing which involves monitoring the operating results of implemented plans and comparing the expected results with the actual results. This feedback allows management to isolate significant variations for further investigation and possible remedial action. (650)

Management process. The four basic functions of (1) planning, (2) organizing and directing, (3) controlling, and (4) decision making used in managing an organization. (647)

Managerial accounting. The branch of accounting that uses both historical and estimated data in providing information which management uses in conducting daily operations and in planning future operations. (13,647)

Manufacturing margin. Sales less variable cost of goods sold. (895)

Marginal cost. The increase in total cost of producing and selling an additional unit of product. (941)

Marginal revenue. The increase in total revenue realized from the sale of an additional unit of product. (940)

Margin of safety. The difference between current sales revenue and the sales at the break-even point. (873)

Market price approach. An approach to transfer pricing that uses the price at which the product or service transferred could be sold to outside buyers as the transfer price. (1135)

Marketable security. An investment in a security that can be readily sold when cash is needed. (268)

Market (sales) value method. A method of allocating joint costs among products according to their relative sales values. (745)

Markup. An amount which is added to a "cost" amount to determine product price. (935)

Master budget. The comprehensive budget plan encompassing all the individual budgets related to sales, cost of goods sold, operating expenses, capital expenditures, and cash. (1051)

Matching. The principle of accounting that all revenues should be matched with the expenses incurred in earning those revenues during a period of time. (27, 101)

Materiality. The concept that recognizes the practicality of ignoring small or insignificant deviations from generally accepted accounting principles. (69)

Materials. Goods in the state in which they were acquired for use in manufacturing operations. (310)

Materials ledger. The subsidiary ledger containing the individual accounts for each type of material. (695)

Materials requisition. The form used by the appropriate manufacturing department to authorize the issuance of materials from the storeroom. (696)

Maturity value. The amount due at the maturity or due date of a note. (258)

Merchandise inventory. Merchandise on hand and available for sale. (289)

Merger. The fusion of two corporation by the acquisition of the properties of one corporation by another, with the dissolution of one of the corporations. (545)

Minority interest. The portion of a subsidiary corporation's capital stock that is not owned by the parent corporation. (551)

Mixed cost. A cost with both variable and fixed characteristics, sometimes referred to as semivariable or semifixed cost. (660, 821, 878)

Modified Accelerated Cost Recovery System (MACRS). The system described in the Internal Revenue Code for determining depreciation (cost recovery) of plant asset acquisitions. (337)

Multiple-step income statement. An income statement with numerous sections and subsections with several intermediate balances before net income. (163)

N

Natural business year. A year that ends when a business's activities have reached the lowest point in its annual operating cycle. (100)

Negotiated price approach. An approach to transfer pricing that allows the managers of decentralized units to agree (negotiate) among themselves as to the proper transfer price. (1135)

Net income. The final figure in the income statement when revenues exceed expenses. (25, 166)

Net loss. The final figure in the income statement when expenses exceed revenues. (25, 166)

Net pay. Gross pay less payroll deductions; the amount the employer is obligated to pay the employee. (377)

Net present value method. A method of analysis of proposed capital investments that focuses on the present value of the cash flows expected from the investment. (966)

Net realizable value. The amount at which merchandise that can be sold only at prices below cost should be valued, determined as the estimated selling price less any direct cost of disposition. (307)

Nominal account. A revenue or expense account periodically closed to the income summary account; a temporary owner's equity account. (59)

Noncontrollable cost. For a specific level of management, a cost that cannot be directly controlled. (658, 901)

Note payable. A written promise to pay, representing an amount owed by a business. (56)

Note receivable. A written promise to pay, representing an amount to be received by a business. (254)

Number of days' sales in inventory. The relationship between the volume of sales and inventory, computed by dividing the inventory at the end of the year by the average daily cost of goods sold. (1174)

Number of days' sales in receivables. The relationship between credit sales and accounts receivable, computed by dividing the net accounts receivable at the end of the year by the average daily sales on account. (1173)

O

Operational planning. The development of short-term plans to achieve goals identified in an enterprise's strategic plan. Sometimes referred to as tactical planning. (648)

Operating lease. A lease which does not meet the criteria for a capital lease, and thus which is accounted for as an operating expense, so that neither future lease obligations nor future rights to use the leased asset as recognized in the accounts. (348)

Operating leverage. The ratio determined by dividing contribution margin by operating income. (874)

Operation costing. A hybrid system that combines features of job order and process cost systems. (748)

Opportunity cost. The amount of income that would result from the best available alternative to a proposed use of cash or its equivalent. (660, 933)

Organizing. The process by which management assigns responsibility to individuals for achieving enterprise goals. (649)

Other expense. An expense that cannot be associated definitely with operations. (164)

Other income. Revenue from sources other than the principal activity of a business. (164)

Overapplied factory overhead. The amount of factory overhead applied in excess of the actual factory overhead costs incurred for production during a period. (699)

Owner's equity. The rights of the owners in a business enterprise. (20)

P-Q

Paid-in capital. The capital acquired from stockholders. (459)

Par. The arbitrary monetary figure printed on a stock certificate. (423)

Parent company. The company owning all or a majority of the voting stock of another corporation. (545)

Participating preferred stock. Preferred stock that could receive dividends in excess of the specified amount granted by its preferential rights. (424)

Partnership. An unincorporated business owned by two or more individuals. (18)

Payroll. The total amount paid to employees for a certain period. (374)

Payroll register. A multi-column form used to assemble and summarize payroll data at the end of each payroll period. (380)

Percentage-of-completion method. The method of recognizing revenue from long-term contracts over the entire life of the contract. (310)

Period costs. Those costs that are used up in generating revenue during the current period and that are not involved in the manufacturing process. These costs are recognized as expenses on the current period's income statement. (663)

Periodic inventory system. A system of inventory accounting in which only the revenue from sales is recorded each time a sale is made; the cost of merchandise on hand at the end of a period is determined by a detailed listing (physical inventory) of the merchandise on hand. (156, 292)

Perpetual inventory system. A system of inventory accounting that employs records that continually disclose the amount of the inventory on hand. (156, 292)

Petty cash fund. A special cash fund used to pay relatively small amounts. (234)

Physical inventory. The detailed listing of merchandise on hand. (156, 292)

Planning. The process of setting goals for the use of an organization's resources and developing ways to achieve these goals. (648)

Plant asset. A tangible asset of a relatively fixed or permanent nature owned by a business enterprise. (105, 330)

Point of sale method. The method of recognizing revenue, whereby the revenue is determined to be realized at the time that title passes to the buyer. (268)

Pooling of interests method. A method of accounting for an affiliation of two corporations resulting from an exchange of voting stock of one corporation for substantially all of the voting stock of the other corporation. (546)

Post-closing trial balance. A trial balance prepared after all of the temporary accounts have been closed. (122)

Posting. The process of transferring debits and credits from a journal to the accounts. (56)

Predetermined factory overhead rate. The rate used to apply factory overhead costs to the goods manufactured. (698)

Preemptive right. The right of each shareholder to maintain the same fractional interest in the corporation by purchasing a proportionate number of shares of any additional issuances of stock. (423)

Preferred stock. A class of stock with preferential rights over common stock. (423)

Premium. (a) The excess of the sales price of stock over its par amount; (b) excess of the issue price of bonds over the face amount. (426, 508)

Prepaid expense. A purchased commodity or service that has not been consumed at the end of an accounting period. (21, 103)

Present value. The estimated present worth of an amount of cash to be received (or paid) in the future. (506, 982)

Present value index. An index computed by dividing the total present value of the net cash flow to be received from a proposed capital investment by the amount to be invested. (967)

Present value of an annuity. The sum of the present values of a series of equal cash flows to be received at fixed intervals. (969)

Price-earnings (P/E) ratio. The ratio of the market price per share of common stock, at a specific date, to the annual earnings per share. (1180)

Price-level index. The ratio of the total cost of a group of commodities prevailing at a particular time to the total cost of the same group of commodities at an earlier base time. (1190)

Price theory. A separate discipline in the area of microeconomics which studies the setting of product prices. (940)

Prime costs. The combination of direct materials and direct labor costs. (662)

Prior period adjustment. Correction of a material error related to a prior period or periods, excluded from the determination of net income. (468)

Private accounting. The profession whose members are accountants employed by a business firm or nonprofit organization. (5)

Proceeds. The net amount available from discounting a note. (259, 388)

Process cost system. A type of cost system that accumulates costs for each of the various departments or processes within a factory. (694)

Product cost concept. A concept used in applying the cost-plus approach to product pricing in which only the costs of manufacturing the product, termed the product cost, are included in the cost amount to which the markup is added. (937)

Product costing. The allocation of costs to products. (777)

Product costs. The three components of manufacturing cost: direct materials, direct labor, and factory overhead costs. (663)

Product life cycle. A concept that assumes that a product passes through various stages from the time that it is introduced until the time it disappears from the market. (942)

Product margin. A measure of the profitability of each product and its contribution to overall enterprise profits, determined by deducting the traceable fixed costs from the contribution margin of each product. (1015)

Profitability. The ability of a firm to earn income. (1176)

Profit center. A decentralized unit in which the manager has the responsibility and the authority to make decisions that affect both costs and revenues (and thus profits). (1117)

Profit margin. A component of the rate of return on investment, computed as the ratio of operating income to sales. (1131)

Profit-volume chart. A chart used to assist management in understanding the relationship between profit and volume. (867)

Promissory note. A written promise to pay a sum in money on demand or at a definite time. (254)

Public accounting. The profession whose members render accounting services on a fee basis. (5)

Purchase method. The accounting method employed when a parent company acquires a controlling share of the voting stock of a subsidiary other than by the exchange of voting common stock. (546)

Purchase order. The form issued by the purchasing department to suppliers, requesting the delivery of materials. (695)

Purchase requisition. The form used to inform the purchasing department that items are needed by a business. (695)

Purchases discounts. An available discount taken by the purchaser for early payment of an invoice; a contra account to Purchases. (149)

Purchases journal. The journal in which all items purchased on account are recorded. (F-3)

Purchases returns and allowances. Reduction in purchases, resulting from merchandise returned to the vendor or from the vendor's reduction in the original purchase price; a contra account to Purchases. (150)

Quality control chart. A chart, often developed using statistical methods, which shows desired operating conditions and limits within which production may vary. (1020)

Quick assets. The sum of cash, receivables, and marketable securities. (1172)

R

Rate earned on common stockholders' equity. A measure of profitability computed by dividing net income, reduced by preferred dividends requirement, by common stockholders' equity. (1178)

Rate earned on stockholders' equity. A measure of profitability computed by dividing net income by total stockholders' equity. (1177)

Rate earned on total assets. A measure of the profitability of assets, without regard to the equity of creditors and stockholders in the assets. (1177)

Rate of return on investment (ROI). A measure of managerial efficiency in the use of investments in assets. (1130)

Real account. A balance sheet account. (59)

Realization. The sale of assets when a partnership is being liquidated.

Realization principle. Recording sales when the title to the merchandise passes to the buyer in exchange for cash or claims to cash. (151)

Receiving report. The form used by the receiving department to indicate that materials have been received and inspected. (695)

Relevant range. The range of activity within which the enterprise is planning to operate. (817)

Report form of balance sheet. The form of balance sheet with the liability and owner's equity sections presented below the asset section. (27, 167)

Residual income. The excess of divisional operating income over a "minimum" amount of desired operating income. (1133)

Residual value. The estimated recoverable cost of a depreciable asset as of the time of its removal from service. (332)

Responsibility accounting. The process of measuring and reporting operating data by areas of responsibility. (1114)

Retail inventory method. A method of inventory costing based on the relationship of the cost and retail price of merchandise. (308)

Retained earnings. Net income retained in a corporation. (22, 422)

Retained earnings statement. A statement for a corporate enterprise, summarizing the changes in retained earnings during a specific period of time. (25)

Revenue. The gross increases in owner's equity as a result of business and professional activities entered into for the purpose of earning income. (22)

Revenue expenditure. An expenditure that benefits only the current period. (342)

Reversing entry. An entry that reverses a specific adjusting entry to facilitate the recording of routine transactions in the subsequent period. (124)

S

Safety stock. The amount of inventory that serves as a reserve for unforeseen circumstances, and therefore is not normally used in regular operations. (1007)

Sales discounts. An available discount granted by the seller for early payment of an invoice; a contra account to Sales. (153)

Sales journal. The journal in which all sales of merchandise on account are recorded. (F-10)

Sales mix. The relative distribution of sales among the various products available for sale. (871, 904)

Sales returns and allowances. Reductions in sales, resulting from merchandise returned by customers or from the seller's reduction in the original sales price; a contra account to Sales. (153)

Scattergraph method. A cost estimation method that uses a graph to estimate total cost and the fixed and variable cost components. (827)

Securities and Exchange Commission (SEC). The federal agency that exercises a dominant influence over the development of accounting principles for most companies whose securities are traded in interstate commerce. (15)

Selling expense. An expense incurred directly and entirely in connection with the sale of merchandise. (164)

Semivariable cost. A cost with both variable and fixed characteristics, sometimes referred to as a mixed or semifixed cost. (660, 837)

Service department. A factory department that does not process materials directly but renders services for the benefit of production departments. (736)

Simplex method. A mathematical equation approach to linear programming, which is often used more practically with a computer. (1010)

Single-step income statement. An income statement with the total of all expenses deducted from the total of all revenues. (166)

Sinking fund. Assets set side in a special fund to be used for a specific purpose. (514)

Slide. The erroneous movement of all digits in a number, one or more spaces to the right or the left, such as writing $542 as $5,420. (68)

Sole proprietorship. A business owned by one individual. (18)

Solvency. The ability of a firm to pay its debts as they come due. (1170)

Special journal. A journal designed to record a single type of transaction. (F-2)

Standard account form. A ledger account that contains debit and credit balance columns. Sometimes called a four-column account form. (60)

Standard costs. Detailed estimates of what a product should cost. (1085)

Standard cost system. An accounting system that uses standards for each element of manufacturing costs entering into the finished product. (1085)

Stated value. An amount assigned by the board of directors to each share of no-par stock. (423)

Statement of cash flows. A summary of the major cash receipts and cash payments for a period. (25, 592)

Statement of cost of goods manufactured. A separate statement for a manufacturer that reports the cost of goods manufactured during a period. (668)

Statement of owner's equity. A summary of the changes in the owner's equity of a business entity that have occurred during a specific period of time. (418)

Step method. A method of allocating service department costs. (775)

Step-wise fixed cost. A cost which varies in a step-wise fashion with changes in an activity base. Because of the long width of the range or production (steps) over which the total cost changes, the cost is classified as a fixed cost for managerial decision making. (819)

Step-wise variable cost. A cost which varies in a step-wise fashion with changes in an activity base. Because of the short width of the range or production (steps) over which the total cost changes, the cost is classified as a variable cost for managerial decision making. (815)

Stock dividend. Distribution of a company's own stock to its shareholders. (423, 475)

Stockholders. The owners of a corporation. (18, 421)

Stockholders' equity. The equity of the shareholders in a corporation. (28, 422)

Stock options. Rights given by a corporation to its employees to purchase shares of the corporation's stock at a stated price. (387)

Stock outstanding. The stock that has been issued to stockholders. (423)

Stock split. A reduction in the par or stated value of a share of common stock and the issuance of a proportionate number of additional shares. (477)

Straight-line depreciation method. A method of depreciation that provides for equal periodic charges to expense over the estimated life of an asset. (334)

Strategic planning. The development of a long-range course of action to achieve enterprise goals. (648, 1115)

Subsidiary company. The corporation that is controlled by a parent company. (545)

Subsidiary ledger. A ledger containing individual accounts with a common characteristic. (217)

Sum-of-the-years-digits depreciation method. A method of depreciation that provides for declining periodic depreciation charges to expense over the estimated life of an asset. (335)

Sunk cost. A cost that is not affected by subsequent decisions. (658, 928)

T

T account. A form of account resembling the letter T. (54)

Taxable income. The base on which the amount of income tax is determined. (461)

Temporary account. A revenue or expense account periodically closed to the income summary account; a nominal account. (59)

Temporary differences. Differences between income before income tax and taxable income created by items that are recognized in one period for income statement purposes and in another period for tax purposes. Such differences reverse or turn around in later years. (462)

Temporary investment. An investment in securities that can be readily sold when cash is needed. (268)

Theoretical standards. Standards that represent levels of performance that can be achieved only under perfect operating conditions, such as no idle time, no machine breakdowns, and no materials spoilage. (1087)

Throughput time. The time required to manufacture a product. Sometimes referred to as cycle time. (665, 1000)

Time tickets. The form on which the amount of time spent by each employee and the labor cost incurred for each individual job, or for factory overhead, are recorded. (697)

Total cost concept. A concept used in applying the cost-plus approach to product pricing in which all costs of manufacturing a product plus the selling and administrative expenses are included in the cost amount to which the markup is added. (935)

Total quality control. A quality control program that begins with product design and continues through production; it involves an ongoing commitment to improving product quality. (665, 1003)

Transfer price. The price charged one decentralized unit by another for the goods or services provided. (1134)

Transposition. The erroneous arrangement of digits in a number, such as writing $542 as $524. (68)

Treasury stock. A corporation's own outstanding stock that has been reacquired. (429)

Trial balance. A summary listing of the balances and the titles of the accounts. (67)

U

Underapplied factory overhead. The amount of actual factory overhead in excess of the factory overhead applied to production during a period. (699)

Unearned revenue. Revenue received in advance of its being earned. (159)

Unit contribution margin. The dollars available from each unit of product sold to cover fixed costs and provide operating profits. (859)

Units-of-production depreciation method. A method of depreciation that provides for depreciation expense based on the expected productive capacity of an asset. (334)

V

Value of perfect information. The maximum amount (cost) that will be paid to obtain perfect information concerning a decision. (1026)

Variable cost. A cost that varies in total dollar amount as the level of activity changes. (659, 814, 859)

Variable cost concept. A concept used in applying the cost-plus approach to product pricing in which only variable costs and expenses are included in the cost amount to which the markup is added. (937)

Variable costing. The concept that considers the cost of products manufactured to be composed only of those manufacturing costs that increase or decrease as the volume of production rise or falls (direct materials, direct labor, and variable factory overhead). (893)

Variance. Difference between standard cost and actual cost. (1085)

Vertical analysis. The percentage analysis of component parts in relation to the total of the parts in a single financial statement. (1167)

Voucher. A document that serves as evidence of authority to pay cash. (230)

Voucher system. Records, methods, and procedures employed in verifying and recording liabilities and paying and recording cash payments. (230)

W-Z

Working capital. The excess of total current assets over total current liabilities at some point in time. (1170)

Work in process inventory. The direct materials costs, the direct labor costs, and the factory overhead costs which have entered into the manufacturing process, but are associated with products that have not been finished. (310)

Work sheet. A working paper used to assist in the preparation of financial statements. (107)

Zero-base budgeting. A concept of budgeting that requires all levels of management to start from zero and estimate budget data as if there had been no previous activities in their unit. (1051)

INDEX

A

Absorption costing,
compared with variable costing, *illus., 894*
def., 893
income analysis under, 898
income statement, *illus.*, 895, 896, 897, 899
income statement under, 894
management's use of, 901
Accelerated Cost Recovery System (ACRS), 337
def., 978
Accelerated depreciation methods, *def.*, 336
Acceptance of business at a special price, 934
Account,
balance of, *illus.*, 55
capital, 418
controlling, *def.*, 217
credit side of, *illus.*, 55
debit side of, *illus.*, 55
def., 53
drawing, 418
four column, form, *def.*, 60
nature of, 54
standard, form, *def. and illus.*, 60
Account form of balance sheet,
def., 28, 167
illus., 168-169
Account in office equipment ledger, *illus., 340*
Account payable, *def.*, 21
Account receivable, *def.*, 22
Accounting,
as a provider of information to users, *illus.*, 13
as an information system, 12
def., 12
double entry, *def.*, 57
financial, 647
financial and managerial, 12; *illus.*, 14
for notes receivable, 258
hybrid cost systems, 748
managerial, 647; *def.*, 13
Accounting cycle,
def., 122
illus., 123
Accounting equation,
def., 20
transactions and the, 20
Accounting period, 99
Accounting principles, changes in, 466
Accounting rate of return, *def.*, 963
Accounting systems,
cost, 693
def., 217, 223
general, *def.*, 693
installation and revision, 219
principles of, 217
types of, 693
Accounts,
analysis for cash flows, 614
controlling and subsidiary compared, *illus.*, 707
doubtful, *def.*, 261
estimate of uncollectible, *illus.*, 266
ledger, 60
nominal, *def.*, 59
real, *def.*, 59
standard costs in, *illus.*, 1096
standards in, 1094
temporary, *def.*, 59
uncollectible, *def.*, 261
Accounts payable, 116
effect on cash flows statement, 601
Accounts receivable,
analysis of, 1172; *illus.*, 265
on the balance sheet, *illus.*, 263
turnover, *def.*, 1172
schedule of collections, *illus.*, 1058
Accrual basis, *def.*, 101
Accrued assets, *def.*, 158
Accrued expenses, *def.*, 106
Accrued liabilities,
adjustment for, *illus.*, 106
def., 106
Accrued revenues, *def.*, 158
Accumulated depreciation accounts, *def.*, 105
Accuracy, of managerial accounting reports, 655
Acid-test ratio, *def.*, 1172
Adequate disclosure, *def.*, 163
Adjusting entries, 167
def. and illus., 103
illus., 168
journalizing and posting, 116
Adjusting process, nature of, 102
Adjustment,
for accrued expense, *illus.*, 106
for depreciation, *illus.*, 105
for prepaid expense, *illus.*, 104
reversal for accrued salaries, *illus.*, 124-125
Adjustment columns on worksheet, *illus.*, 110-111
Administrative costs, *def.*, 663
Administrative expenses, *def.*, 164
Affiliated companies, *def.*, 545
Affiliations, accounting for parent-subsidiary, 546
Aging the receivables, *def.*, 265
Allocation of departmental charges to finished goods and inventory, *illus.*, 734
Allocation of joint costs, *illus.*, 738
Allowance account, write-offs to, 264
Allowance method,
def., 262
of accounting for uncollectibles, 262
Allowances,
purchases, *def.*, 150
sales, *def.*, 153
American Accounting Association (AAA), *def.*, 15
American Institute of Certified Public Accountants (AICPA), *def.*, 15
Amortization,
def., 349
of bond discount, 510; *illus.*, 511
of bond premium, 512; *illus.*, 513
Analysis,
accounts receivable, 1172
capital investment, 1017, *def.*, 962
current position, *def.*, 1170
differential, 1016; *def.*, 927
factors that complicate, 973
focus of financial statement, 1170
horizontal, *def.*, 1164
inventory, 1173
nature of, 962
profitability, 1176
qualitative considerations in, 971
solvency, *def.*, 1170
vertical, *def.*, 1167
Analytical measures, summary of, 1181
Annuity,
def., 508, 969
present value of, 508, *def.*, 969
present value of $1 at compound interest, *illus.*, 969
Appropriation of retained earnings, *def.*, 471
Appropriation,
for bonded indebtedness, 518
funded, *def.*, 518
Articles of incorporation, 421
Articles of partnership, 419
Assets,
accrued, *def.*, 158
current, *def.*, 115
def., 20
fixed, 105, 330
intangible, 349; *def.*, 330
plant, *def.*, 105, 330
rate earned on total, *def.*, 1177
ratio of net sales to assets, *def.*, 1176
Associated companies, *def.*, 545
Automated manufacturing processes, 1000
Automated perpetual inventory records, 304
Average cost method, 746
def., 297, 745
under perpetual system, 304
use of, 300
Average rate of return, *def.*, 963

B

Back-flush costing, 748
Bad debts, *def.*, 261
Balance, compensating, *def.*, 223
Balance sheet account, 55
expanded rules of debit and credit for, *illus.*, 58
Balance sheet, 115, 167
account form, *def.*, 28, 167; *illus., 168-169*
report form, *def.*, 167
budgeted, 1059
comparative, *illus.*, 597, 612
comparative--horizontal analysis, *illus., 1165*
consolidated, at date of acquisition, 548
consolidated, at date of affiliation, 555
consolidated, *illus.*, 555
consolidated, subsequent to acquisition, 551
consolidated, subsequent to affiliation, 557
consolidated, work sheet for, 553, 557; *illus.*, 554, 558
def., 25
illus., 26, 114
for manufacturing enterprises, 667
manufacturing enterprise, *illus.*, 709
of corporation, *illus.*, 560-561
premium on capital stock, 427
presentation of bonds payable, 519
report form, *def.*, 27
Bank reconciliation,
def., 226
format for, *illus.*, 227
illus., 228
Bank statement, 225
illus., 226
Basic analytical procedures, 1163
Basis,
accrual, *def.*, 101
cash, *def.*, 101
def., 269
Bearer bonds, *def.*, 506
Betterments, *def.*, 342
Bill, *def.*, 149
Board of directors, 421
Bond discount, *def.*, 508
Bond indenture, *def.*, 505
Bond investments,
accounting for, purchase, interest, amortization, 520
accounting for, sale, 521
Bond premium, *def.*, 508
Bond redemption, 518
Bond sinking fund, *def.*, 514
Bonded indebtedness, appropriation for, 518
Bonds,
bearer, *def.*, 506
callable, *def.*, 506
carrying amount of, *def.*, 511
characteristics of, 505
convertible, 506
coupon, 506
debenture, *def.*, 506
def., 269, 503
face value, 505
investments in, 519
issued at discount, 510
issued at face amount, 509
issued at premium, 512
registered, *def.*, 506
secured, *def.*, 506
serial, 506
term, 506
zero-coupon, 514
Bonds payable,
accounting for, 508
balance sheet presentation, 519
effect on cash flows statement, 603
present value concepts for, 506
Book inventories, 292
Book value, 511
def., 106
Book value per share, 431
Boot, *def.*, 346
Break-even chart, *def.*, 865
Break-even point, sales mix and, 871
Budget,
capital expenditures, 1057; *illus.*, 1057
cash, 1057; *illus.*, 1058
cost of goods sold, 1054; *illus.*, 1055
def., 860, 1049
direct labor cost, 1053; *illus.*, 1054
direct materials purchases, 1053; *illus.*, 1053
factory overhead cost, 1054; *illus.*, 1054
flexible, *def.*, 1060
master, *def.*, 1051
operating expenses, 1055; *illus.*, 1056
performance report, *def.*, 1060
production, 1052; *illus.*, 1052
sales, 1051; *illus.*, 1052
Budgeted balance sheet, 1059
Budgeted income statement, 1056; *illus.*, 1056
Budgeting,
and human behavior, 1062
computerized systems, 1062
continuous, *def.*, 1050
zero-base, *def.*, 1051
Budgeting systems, 1050
Budget performance report, *def.*, 1060

Building, effect on cash flows statement, 604
Business,
  segment of, 1188
  revenue by industry segment and classes of similar products or services, *illus.*, 1189
Business combinations, 544
  pooling of interests method of accounting, 546
  purchase method of accounting, 546
Business entity concept, *def.*, 17
Business transaction, *def.*, 19
Buy or make, 931
By-products,
  accounting for, 738
  def., 737

C

Callable bonds, *def.*, 506
Capital, paid-in, *def.*, 422
Capital account, 418
Capital and revenue expenditures, summary of, *illus.*, 343-344
Capital budgeting, *def.*, 962
Capital expenditures,
  budget, 1057; *illus.*, 976, 1057
  def., 342
Capital investment analysis, 1017
  def., 962
  factors that complicate, 973
  nature of, 962
  qualitative considerations in, 971
Capital investment,
  expenditures, planning and controlling, 976
  lease versus, 975
  proposals, methods of evaluating, 963
Capital leases, *def.*, 347
Capital rationing,
  decision process, *illus.*, 977
  def., 975
Capital stock,
  characteristics, 423
  def., 20, 423
  issuing, 426
Carrying amount,
  def., 269
  of bonds, *def.*, 511
Cash,
  bank account as a tool for controlling, 240
  control over, 223
  petty, *def.*, 234
  transactions and electronic funds transfer, 235
Cash basis, *def.*, 101
Cash budget, 1057,
  illus., 1058
Cash change funds, 230
Cash discount, *def.*, 149
Cash dividends, *def.*, 474
Cash flow activities, 614
Cash flow per share, 596
Cash flows,
  direct method of reporting, *def.*, 594
  for payment of dividends, 602
  from financing activities, *def.*, 593, 594
  from investing activities, *def.*, 593, 594
  from operating activities, 598; *def.*, 593
  indirect method of reporting, *def.*, 594
  preparation of statement, 619
  reporting, 593
  statement of, *def.*, 592; *illus.*, 606
Cash funds, other, 235
Cash payback period, *def.*, 965
Cash payments,
  for income taxes, *illus.*, 610
  for merchandise, 608, illus. 609
  for operating expenses, *illus.*,
  internal control over, 230
Cash receipts, internal control of, 229
Cash received from customers, *illus.*, 608
Cash short and over, 229
Centralized and decentralized operations, 1114
Certificate in Management Accounting (CMA), 653
Changes in price levels, 975
Characteristics of the new manufacturing environment, 999
Chart of accounts, *def. and illus.*, 54
Charter, of corporation, 421
Check,
  def., 224
  illus., 225
Clarity, of managerial accounting reports, 656
Classes of stock, 423
Clock cards, 697
Closing entries, 167
  def., 117
  flowchart, *illus.*, 118
  illus., 119, 169, 175
Closing process,
  flowchart, *illus.*, 118
  nature of, 117
Codes of professional conduct, *def.*, 16
Codes of professional ethics, *def.*, 16
Combined income and retained earnings statement,
  def., 166
  illus., 167
Common stock,
  def., 423
  earnings per share on, *def.*, 1179
  effect on cash flows statement, 602
Common-size income statement, *illus.*, 1169
Comparative balance sheet, *illus.*, 597, 612
Compensating balance, *def.*, 223
Completed-contract method, 310
Composite-rate depreciation method, *def. and illus.*, 341
Compound journal entry, 56
Computerized budgeting systems, 1062
Concept, managerial use of the expected value, 1023
Conciseness, of managerial accounting reports, 656
Consistency concept, *def.*, 466
Consolidated balance sheet,
  at date of acquisition, 548
  at date of affiliation, 555
  subsequent to acquisition, 551
  subsequent to affiliation, 557
Consolidated financial statements, with foreign subsidiaries, 563
Consolidated income statement, and other statements, 558
Consolidated statements,
  def., 547
  purchase method, 547
Consolidation,
  def., 545
  of financial statements, basic principles of, 547
Constant dollar,
  def., 1190
  equivalent, 1190
Contingent liabilities, 389
  def., 260, 374
Continuous budgeting, *def.*, 1050
Contra accounts, *def.*, 105
Contract rate of interest, *def.*, 508
Contributed capital, 422
Contribution margin,
  analyses, *def.*, 906
  analysis report, *illus.*, 907
  def., 858, 895
  ratio, *def.*, 858, 905
  unit, *def.*, 859
Contribution margin statement, sales territories, *illus.*, 905
  unit of product, *illus.*, 904
Contributory plan, 386
Control,
  over cash, 223
  over receivables, 255
  procedures, 221
Control environment, 221
Controllable costs, *def.*, 658, 901
Controller,
  def., 653
  department organization chart, *illus.*, 653
Controlling, 651; *def.*, 650
Controlling account, *def.*, 217
Controlling cash, the bank account as a tool for, 223
Conversion cost, *def.*, 662, 731
Convertible bonds, *def.*, 506
Copyright, *def.*, 350
Corporate annual reports, 1183
Corporate earnings and income taxes, 460
Corporations,
  accounting for, 422
  characteristics of, 420
  def., 18
  financial statements, 559
  financing, 503
  nonpublic, 421
  not-for-profit, 420
  parent and subsidiary, 545
  public, 421
  separate legal existence, 421
Cost accounting systems,
  hybrid, 748
  types of, 693
Cost allocation,
  def., 769
  in just-in-time manufacturing systems, 786
  in the new manufacturing environment, 1000
  objectives of, 769
  principles of, 771
  service department, 774
Cost behavior,
  def., 813
  summary of concepts, 823
Cost center,
  def., 1117
  responsibility accounting for, 1119
Cost concept,
  product, *def.*, 937
  target, *def.*, 939
  total, *def.*, 935
  variable, *def.*, 937
Cost control, 901
Cost driver, *def.*, 698, 771
Cost estimation, 824
  def., 813
  methods, comparison of, 832, 833
Costing,
  activity-based, 782, *def.*, 782
  back-flush, 748
  job order and process compared, 730
  operation, *def.*, 748
  variable, 1014
Costing products, 770
Cost ledger, *def.*, 701
Cost method, accounting for investment in stock, 542
Cost object, *def.*, 657, 769
Cost of goods manufactured, statement of, 668
Cost of goods sold, 668
  and finished goods, 703
  budget, 1054; *illus.*, 1055
  def., 164
Cost of merchandise purchased, *def.*, 157
Cost of merchandise sold, 668
  def. and illus., 157
Cost of production report, *def. and illus.*, 735, 742
Cost of sales, *def.*, 164
Cost-plus approach cost concept, choosing, 939
Cost price approach, *def.*, 1136
Cost principle, *def.*, 18
Costs, 940
  administrative, *def.*, 663
  budgeted and actual, *def.*, 772
  classification of, 660
  concepts and terminology, 656
  controllable, *def.*, 658, 901
  conversion, *def.*, 662, 731
  current, *def.*, 1189
  detection, 1021
  differential, *def.*, 658, 928
  direct, *def.*, 657
  direct labor, *def.*, 661
  direct materials, *def.*, 661
  discretionary, *def.*, 659
  external failure, 1021
  factory overhead, *def.*, 661
  fixed, *def.*, 659, 818, 858
  fixed and variable, 772
  flow in process cost system, 731
  flow through process cost accounts, *illus.*, 742
  indirect, *def.*, 657
  internal failure, 1021
  inventoriable, 663
  joint, *def.*, 737
  marginal, *def.*, 941
  manufacturing, 661
  mixed, 821; *def.*, 660, 858; *illus.*, 822
  noncontrollable, *def.*, 658, 901
  of interrupting production, 1004
  of investing in inventory, 1003
  opportunity, 1003, *def.*, 660, 933
  ordering, 1004
  period, *def.*, 662
  prevention, 1021
  prime, *def.*, 662
  processing, 731
  product, *def.*, 662
  quality control, summary of, 1021, *illus.*, 1021-2
  raw materials, 661
  selling, *def.*, 663
  semivariable, *def.*, 821
  service department charged to processing departments, *illus.*, 737
  standard, *def.*, 1085
  step-wise fixed, *def.*, 819, *illus.*, 882
  step-wise variable, *def.*, 815, *illus.*, 816
  storage, 1004
  sunk, *def.*, 658
  variable, *def.*, 659, 814, 858
  vs. benefits, of managerial accounting reports, 656
Cost-volume-profit analysis, 1014
  def., 857
  limitations of, 875
  use of computers in, 870
Cost-volume-profit chart, *def. and illus.*, 865, 866
Cost-volume-profit relationships, 857
  special, 873
Coupon bonds, 506
Coupon rate of interest, 508
Credit, *def.*, 55
Credit memorandum, *def.*, 150, *illus.*, 154
Credit period, *def.*, 149
Credit terms,
  def., 148
  illus, 149
Cumulative preferred stock, *def.*, 425
Current assets,
  def., 115
  effect on cash flows statement, 601
Current cost, *def.*, 1189
Current liabilities,
  def., 116
  effect on cash flows statement, 601
Current position analysis, *def.*, 1170
Current ratio, *def.*, 1171
Currently attainable standards, *def.*, 1087

Cycle time, *def.*, 665, 1000

D

Data base, *def.*, 217
Debenture bonds, *def.*, 506
Debit,
 def., 55
 diagram of posting, *illus.*, 61
Debit memorandum,
 def., 150
 illus., 151
Debt securities, *def.*, 519
Decentralization,
 advantages of, 1115
 def., 1114
Decision making, 651
 def., 650
 under uncertainty, 1023
Decision trees,
 def., 1025
 profit from sale of unimproved or improved land, *illus.*, 1025
 proposal, *illus.*, 1027
 with expected values, profit from sale of unimproved or improved land
Declining-balance method,
 def.,334
 illus., 335
Deductions, 377
 other, 378
Department costs, the reciprocal method of allocating service, 787
Departmental margin,
 def., 1121
 income statement departmentalized through, *illus.*, 1122
Depletion, *def.*, 348
Deposit tickets, *def.*, 224
Depreciation,
 accounting for, 332
 accumulated, accounts, 105
 adjustment for, *illus.*, 129
 composite-rate method, *def.*, 341
 def., 105, 331
 effect on cash flows statement, 600
 for federal income tax, 336
 nature of, 331
 periodic, revision of, 338
 plant assets of low unit cost, 341
 recording, 339
Depreciation methods,
 accelerated, *def.*, 336
 comparison of, 336
 comparison of, *illus.*, 337
 use of, *illus.*, 333
Detection costs, 1021
Differential analysis, 1016
 def., 927
 lease or sell, *illus.*, 928
Differential analysis report,
 discontinuance of unprofitable segment, *illus.*, 930
 equipment replacement, *illus.*, 932
 lease or sell, *illus.*, 928
 make or buy, *illus.*, 931
 process or sell, *illus.*, 933
 sale at special price, *illus.*, 934
Differential cost, *def.*, 658, 928
Differential revenue, *def.*, 927
Differentials, *def.*, 927
Direct charge-off method, *def.*, 262
Direct costing, 893, *def.*, 893
Direct costs, *def.*, 657
Directing, *def.*, 650
Direct labor, *def.*, 310
Direct labor cost, *def.*, 661
Direct labor cost budget, 1053; *illus.*, 1054
Direct labor cost variance, 1089; *illus.*, 1090
Direct labor rate variance,
 def., 1089
 illus., 1090
Direct labor time variance, *illus.*, 1090
Direct materials, *def.*, 310
Direct materials cost, *def.*, 661
Direct materials cost variance, *illus.*, 1088
Direct materials inventory, 667
Direct materials price variance, *illus.*, 1089
Direct materials purchases budget, *illus.*, 1053
Direct materials quantity variance,
 def., 1088,
 illus., 1089
Direct method, 774,
 def., 774
 of allocation, *illus.*, 775
 of reporting cash flows, *def.*, 594
 of reporting cash flows from operating activities, 607, *illus.*, 610
Direct write-off method,
 def., 262
 of accounting for uncollectibles, 267
Discarding plant assets, 344
Discontinuance of a segment or product, 929
Discontinued operations, *def.*, 465
Discount,
 amortization by interest method, *illus.*, 511
 amortization by straight-line method, 510
 def., 259, 388
 on bonds, *def.*, 508
 on stock, *def.*, 426
Discounted cash flow method, *def.*, 966
Discounted receivables, 390
Discounting,
 def., 388
 illus., 260
 notes receivable, 259
Discount rate, *def.*, 388
Discounts,
 purchases, 233, *def.*, 149
 sales, *def.*, 153
Discretionary cost, *def.*, 659
Dishonored,
 def., 261
 notes receivable, 261
Disposal of plant assets, 343
Dividend,
 and stock splits for treasury stock, 478
 cash flows for payment of, 602
 cash, *def.*, 474
 def., 23, 473
 liquidating, *def.*, 477
 nature of, 473
 stock, 475
 yield, *def.*, 1180
Double-entry accounting, *def.*, 57
Doubtful accounts, *def.*, 261
Drawee, *def.*, 224
Drawer, *def.*, 224
Drawing account, 418
Due date, 256
 determination of, a note, *illus.*, 257

E

Earnings per share, 469
 on common stock, *def.*, 1179
Economic order quantity (EOQ),
 def., 1006
 formula, *illus.*, 1007
 tabulation of, *illus.*, 1007
Economic theory of product pricing, 940
Economies of scale,
 def., 817, 941
 illus., 818
Effective rate of interest, *def.*, 508
Electronic funds transfer (EFT),
 and cash transactions, 235
 def., 235
Employee earnings,
 deductions from, 377
 determination, 375
 liability for, 375
Employee net pay, computation of, 378
Employee's earnings record,
 def., 382
 illus., 392-393
Employees' earnings, recording, 381
Employees' fringe benefits, liability for, 385
Employer's payroll taxes, liability for, 379
Engineering method, *def.*, 834
Entries,
 adjusting, def. and illus, 103
 closing, def, 117
Equipment replacement, 932
Equipment, effect on cash flows statement, 604
Equities, *def.*, 20
Equity method, accounting for investment in stock, 543
Equity per share, 431
Equity securities, *def.*, 541
Equivalent units of production,
 def., 733
 determination of, *illus.*, 733
Errors, discovery and correction of, 67
Estimate of uncollectible accounts, *illus.*, 266
Estimated total step-wise variable cost, *illus.*, 817
Estimating uncollectibles, 264
Ethics,
 def., 654
 for accountants, 16
Evaluating manufacturing processes, 770
Exchange gains and losses,
 realized, 560
 unrealized, 563
Exchange of plant assets, 346
 federal income tax requirements, 346
Exchange rate, *def.*, 560
Expanded rules of debit and credit,
 balance sheet accounts, *illus.*, 58
 income statement accounts, *illus.*, 58
Expected realizable value, *def.*, 263
Expected value, *def.*, 1023
Expenditures,
 capital budget, *illus.*, 976
 capital investment, planning and controlling, 976
Expenses,
 accrued, def. 106
 adjustment, prepaid, *illus.*, 104
 administrative, *def.*, 164
 advertising, 1124
 def., 22
 depreciation--store equipment, 1125
 direct, *def.*, 1121
 general, *def.*, 164
 heating and lighting, 1126
 indirect, *def.*, 1121
 insurance, 1126
 miscellaneous administrative, 1127
 miscellaneous selling, 1127
 nonoperating, *def.*, 164
 office salaries, 1126
 officers' salaries, 1126
 other, *def.*, 164
 prepaid, *def.*, 21, 103
 property tax, 1126
 rent, 1126
 sales salaries, 1124
 selling, *def.*, 164
 standards for nonmanufacturing, 1097
 uncollectible accounts, 1127
External failure costs, 1021
Extraordinary items,
 def., 466
 on income statement, 465
 repairs, *def.*, 343

F

Face value of bonds, 505
Factors that complicate capital investment analysis, 973
Factory burden, 661
Factory labor, 697
Factory overhead controllable variance,
 def., 1092,
 illus., 1093
Factory overhead cost,
 budget, *illus.*, 1054
 flexible budget for, *illus.*, 1061
Factory overhead cost budget indicating standard factory overhead rate, *illus.*, 1091
Factory overhead cost,
 def., 661
 variance, 1091, *illus.*, 1092
 variance report, *illus.*, 1094
Factory overhead, 697
 def., 310
 disposition of balance, 699
 predetermined rate, 698
 volume variance, *def. and illus.*, 1092
Federal income tax, 378
Federal unemployment compensation tax, 379
Fee, protest, 261
Feedback, *def.*, 650
FICA tax, 379; *def.*, 377
Fifo, perpetual inventory account, *illus.*, 303
Fifo cost method, *def.*, 745
Fifo method,
 def., 295
 under perpetual system, 302
 use of, 298
Financial Accounting Standards Board (FASB), *def.*, 15
Financial accounting,
 and managerial, 12
 concepts and principles, 17
 def., 12, 647
 development of concepts and principles, 14
Financial Executives Institute (FEI), *def.*, 16
Financial highlights, 1183
 section, *illus.*, 1184
Financial statement, 113
 basic principles of consolidation, 547
 consolidated, with foreign subsidiaries, 563
 corporation, 559
 def., 24
 for manufacturing enterprises, 666
 for merchandising enterprises, 163
 for process cost system, 743 *illus.*, 744-745
 manufacturing enterprise, *illus.*, 709
 reporting depreciation expense, plant assets, and intangible assets, 351
 reporting unusual items, 465
 worksheet for, 107
Financing activities,
 cash flows from, *def.*, 593, 594
 noncash, 596
Finished goods
 allocation of departmental charges, *illus.*, 734
 def., 309-310
 inventory, 667
 ledger, *def.*, 703
 ledger account, *illus.*, 703
First-in, first-out (fifo) cost method,
 def., 745, 295
 under perpetual system, 302
 use of, 298
Fiscal year, *def.*, 100
Fixed assets, 105, 330
Fixed costs,
 activity base for, 819
 def., 659, 818, 858

relevant range for, 820, illus. 821
step-wise, *def.*, 819, *illus.*, 820
total, graph, *illus.*, 819
Flexible budget,
def., 1060
for factory overhead cost, *illus.*, 1061
Flexible flow manufacturing systems, 664
def., 1001
Flow of business transaction data, *illus.*, 59
Flowchart, closing process, *illus.*, 118
FOB destination, *def.*, 155, 293
FOB shipping point, *def.*, 154, 293
Foreign companies, accounting for transactions with, 559
Foreign subsidiaries, consolidated financial statements, 563
Four-column account form, *def.*, 60
Fringe benefits, liability for, 385
Funded, *def.*, 472
Funded appropriation, *def.*, 518
Funded plan, 386
Future value,
def., 514
of $1 at compound interest, *illus.*, 515
of annuity, at compound interest, *illus.*, 516

G

Gains,
nonrecognition of, 346
on sale of investments, effect on cash flows statement, 601
Gains and losses,
realized currency exchange, 560
unrealized currency exchange, 563
General accounting system, *def.*, 693
General expenses, *def.*, 164
General ledger, *def.*, 217
General rules of debit and credit, *illus.*, 57
Generally accepted accounting principles (GAAP), *def.*, 12
Going concern, 332
Going concern concept, *def.*, 99
Goodwill, *def.*, 350
Governmental Accounting Standards Board (GASB), *def.*, 15
Gross margin, *def.*, 164
Gross pay, *def.*, 377
Gross profit,
by departments, 1123
def., 164
income statement departmentalized through, *illus.*, 1124
on sales, *def.*, 164
Gross profit method, *def.*, 309
Guarantees, 390

H

High-low method,
def., 824
estimated total cost for 200,000 units of production, *illus.*, 827
estimated total cost line, *illus.*, 826
Historical summary section, *illus.*, 1188
Horizontal analysis,
comparative income statement, *illus.*, 1166
comparative retained earnings statement, *illus.*, 1167
comparative schedule of current assets, *illus.*, 1166
def., 1164
Human behavior and budgeting, 1062

I

Ideal standards, *def.*, 1087
In-and-out-cards, 697
Income,
net, *def.*, 166
nonoperating, *def.*, 164
operating, *def.*, 164
other, *def.*, 164
Income analysis,
under absorption costing, 898
under variable costing, 898
Income from operations, *def.*, 164
Income statement accounts, 58
expanded rules of debit and credit for, *illus.*, 58
Income statement, 115, 163
absorption costing, *illus.*, 895, 896, 897, 899
budgeted, 1056; *illus.*, 1056
columns, 112-113
common-size, *illus.*, 1169
comparing current operations with Product A discontinued, *illus.*, 930
condensed, *illus.*, 936
consolidated, and other statements, 558
current operations, *illus.*, 930
def., 25
departmentalized through departmental margin, *illus.*, 1122
departmentalized through gross profit, *illus.*, 1124
departmentalized through income from operations, *illus.*, 1128
for manufacturing enterprise, 668
illus., 26, 114, 608
manufacturing enterprise, *illus.*, 669, 709
merchandising enterprise, *illus.*, 668
multiple-step, *def.*, 163, *illus.*, 165
presentation of unusual items, 467
single-step, *def. and illus.*, 166
under variable and absorption costing, 894
variable costing, illus. 895, 896, 898
variances from standards in, *illus.*, 1097
Income summary,
def., 117
Income Summary account, *illus.*, 170
Income taxes, 973
allocation between periods, 461
allocation to unusual items, 467
effect on cash flows statement, 601
Incremental cost, 658
Independent auditors' report,
def., 1184
section, *illus.*, 1186
Indirect costs, *def.*, 657
Indirect method, of reporting cash flows, *def.*, 594
Inflation,
def., 975
Information, value of, 1026
Installment method, *def. and illus.*, 268
Installment sales, receivables from, 267
Institute of Management Accountants (IMA), *def.*, 16
Intangible assets, 349
def., 330
Interest method,
amortization of bond discount, *illus.*, 510
amortization of bond premium, *illus.*, 513
Interest, 257
contract rate, *def.*, 508
effective rate, *def.*, 508
Interest-bearing note,
def., 257,
receivable, 259
Interim financial reports, 1191
Internal control,
and perpetual inventory systems, 304
def., 218
of cash payments, 230
of cash receipts, 229
structure, 220
Internal failure costs, 1021
Internal rate of return method, *def.*, 968
Internal Revenue Service (IRS), *def.*, 16
International operations, accounting for, 559
Inventoriable costs, 663
Inventories,
effect on cash flows statement, 601
of manufacturing enterprises, 309
of partially processed units, 732
Inventory, 289
allocation of departmental charges, *illus.*, 734
book, 292
comparison of periodic and perpetual systems, *illus.*, 301
determining actual quantities in, 292
determining cost of, 293
direct materials, 667
effect on current period's statements, *illus.*, 289
effect on following period's statements, *illus.*, 291
estimate by gross profit method, *illus.*, 309
finished goods, 667
importance of, 289
merchandise, *def.*, 289
number of days' sales in, *def.*, 1174
periodic system, *def.*, 156
perpetual system, *def.*, 156
physical, *def.*, 156, 292
turnover, *def.*, 1173
under perpetual system, accounting for and reporting, 300
valuation at lower of cost or market, 305, *illus.*, 305
valuation at net realizable value, 307
valuation at other than cost, 305
work in process, 667
Inventory accounts, controlling and subsidiary accounts compared, *illus.*, 707
Inventory cost, estimating, 307
Inventory costing methods, 745
and just-in-time manufacturing, 747
comparison of, 297
selection of, 300
under periodic system, 294
under perpetual system, 302
Inventory ledger, 302
Inventory management
in a just-in-time manufacturing system, 1005
in a traditional manufacturing system, 1006
Inventory reorder point, *def.*, 1007
Inventory systems, 292
periodic, *def.*, 292
perpetual, *def.*, 292
Investing activities,
cash flows from, *def.*, 593, 594
noncash, 596
Investment center, *def.*, 1118
Investment turnover, *def.*, 1131
Investments,
effect on cash flows statement, 605
gain on sale of, effect on cash flows statement, 601
in bonds, 519
in stocks, 541
long-term, 542
sale of, 544
long-term, *def.*, 519
temporary, *def.*, 268
Invoice, *def.*, 149; *illus.*, 150

J

Job cost sheet, *def.*, 701, *illus.*, 702
Job order cost accounting,
and process costing compared, 730
flow of costs through accounts, *illus.*, 706
illustration of, 704
Job order cost systems,
def., 693
for manufacturing enterprises, 695
for service enterprises, 708
Joint costs,
allocation of, *illus.*, 738
def., 737
Joint products,
accounting for, 737
def., 737
Journal entry,
compound, 56
def. and illus., 56
Journal, 55,
def. and illus., 60
Journalizing
adjusting entries, 116
def., 56
illus., 62
Judgmental method, *def.*, 833
Just-in-time (JIT) manufacturing systems,
and inventory costing methods, 747
def., 664, 1001
production line, furniture manufacturer, *illus.*, 1002

L

Labor, direct, *def.*, 310
Land, effect on cash flows statement, 605
Last-in, first-out (lifo) method,
def., 296
under perpetual system, 303
use of, 298
Lead time, *def.*, 1007
Lease or sell, 928
Leases,
def., 347
capital, 347
operating, *def.*, 348
Lease versus capital investment, 975
Leasing, acquisition of plant assets, 347
Least squares method,
def., 830
estimated total cost line, *illus.*, 832
Ledger accounts, 60
Ledger,
account in office equipment, *illus.*, 340
after accounts adjusted, closed, *illus.*, 119-122
cost, *def.*, 701
def., 53
finished goods, 703
general, *def.*, 217,
illus., 65-67
inventory, 302
materials, *def.*, 695
stockholders, 426
subsidiary, *def.*, 217
subsidiary, for plant assets, 339
Legal capital, 423
Lessee, *def.*, 347
Lessor, *def.*, 347
Leverage, *def.*, 1178
Liabilities, 115
accrued, 106
contingent, 389; *def.*, 260
current, 116
def., 20
fixed, 116
long-term, 116
product warranty, 388

ratio of plant assets to long-term, *def.*, 1174
ratio of stockholders' equity to, 1175
unlimited, 418
Lifo, perpetual inventory account, *illus.*, 303
Lifo method,
def., 296
under perpetual system, 303
use of, 298
Limited liability, 421
Limited life, 418
Linear programming,
def., 1009
for purchasing decisions, 1009
graph, alternative purchase plans, *illus.*, 1011
Liquidating dividend, *def.*, 477
Litigation, 389
Long-term construction contracts, 310
Long-term investments, *def.*, 519
Long-term investments in stock,
accounting for, cost method, 542
accounting for, equity method, 543
sale of, 544
Long-term liabilities, *def.*, 116
Loss,
from operations, *def.*, 164
net, *def.*, 166
recognition of, 347
Lower of cost or market,
def., 305
determination of, *illus.*, 306

M

Make or buy, 931
Maker, *def.*, 256
Management,
by exception, *def.*, 650
def., 647
use of absorption costing, 901
use of variable costing, 901
Management process,
def., 647
diagram, *illus.*, 648
role of managerial accounting in, 650
Management report,
def., 1187
section, *illus.*, 1187
Managerial accounting,
and quality control, 1022
as profession, 653
def., 13, 647
organization of function, 651
reports, characteristics of, 654
role in management process, 650
Managerial use of the expected value concept, 1023
Manufacturing cells, *def.*, 1002
Manufacturing, just-in-time systems, 664
Manufacturing costs, 661
to balance sheet, flow of, *illus.*, 667
Manufacturing enterprise,
balance sheet for, 667
financial statements for, 666; *illus.*, 709
income statement, 668; *illus.*, 669
job order cost systems for, 695
trends in, 664
Manufacturing margin, 895
Manufacturing operations, costs and terminology, 660
Manufacturing overhead cost, 661
Margin,
departmental, *def.*, 1121
product, *def.*, 1015
Marginal cost, *def.*, 941
Marginal revenue, *def.*, 940
Margin of safety, 873; *def.*, 873
Marketable securities, *def.*, 268
Market price, 432
approach, *def.*, 1135
Market rate of interest, 508
Market value method, cost allocation, *def.*, 738
Markup, *def.*, 935
Master budget, *def.*, 1051
Matching, *def.*, 27
Matching principle, *def.*, 101
Materiality, 69
Materials, 695
cost, raw, 661
def., 309-310
direct, *def.*, 310
flow of, 732
Materials ledger, *def.*, 695
Materials ledger account, *illus.*, 695
Materials requisitions, *illus.*, 696
Maturity value, *def.*, 258
Maximization of profits, 940
Memorandum, credit,
def., 150,
illus., 154
Memorandum, debit,
def., 150,
illus., 151
Merchandise available for sale, *def.*, 157
Merchandise inventory,
def., 289
on balance sheet, *illus.*, 307
Merchandise inventory systems, 156
Merchandising enterprise, income statement, *illus.*, 668
Merger, *def.*, 545
Methods of evaluating capital investment proposals, 963
that ignore present value, 963
Minority interests, *def.*, 551
Mixed cost,
def., 660, 821, 858
illus., 822
Modified Accelerated Cost Recovery System (MACRS),
def., 978
depreciation rate schedule, *illus.*, 978
Modified ACRS (MACRS), 337
depreciation rate schedule, *illus.*, 337
Motivating managers, 771
Moving average, *def.*, 304
Multiple-step income statement,
def., 163
illus., 165
Mutual agency, 419

N

Natural business year, *def.*, 100
Nature of an account, 54
Negotiated price approach, *def.*, 1135
Net cash flow, *def.*, 965
Net income, *def.*, 25, 166
Net loss, *def.*, 25, 166
Net pay,
computation of, 378
def., 377
Net present value analysis, *illus.*, 967
Net present value method, *def.*, 966
Net profit, *def.*, 25
Net purchases, *def.*, 157
Net realizable value, *def.*, 307
No-par stock, 423, 428
issuing, journal entries, *illus.*, 429
Nominal accounts, *def.*, 59
Non-interest-bearing note, *def.*, 257
Noncontributory plan, 386
Noncontrollable costs, *def.*, 658, 901
Noncumulative preferred stock, 425
Nonoperating, expense,
def., 164
income, *def.*, 164
Nonparticipating preferred stock, 424
Nonpublic corporations, 421
Nonrecognition of gain, 346
Nontaxable entity, 419
Normal balances of accounts, *illus.*, 59
Normal standards, *def.*, 1087
Not-for-profit corporation, 420
Note,
def., 254
interest-bearing, *def.*, 257
non-interest-bearing, *def.*, 257
promissory, *def.*, 254, *illus.*, 256
receivable, *def.*, 254
Note payable, *def.*, 56
Note receivable,
def., 254
characteristics of, 256
diagram of discounting, *illus.*, 260
Notes payable, 116
short-term, 387
Notes receivable,
accounting for, 258
characteristics of, 256
diagram of discounting, *illus.*, 260
discounting, 259
dishonored, 261
interest-bearing, 259
Number of days' sales in inventory, *def.*, 1174
Number of days' sales in receivables, *def.*, 1173

O

Objectivity, *def.*, 19
Operating activities,
assembling data for cash flows from, 607
cash flows from, *def.*, 593
direct method of reporting cash flows from, 607, 610
Operating expenses budget, 1055
Operating income, 1129
by departments, 1123
def., 164, 348
Operating leverage, 874,
def., 874
Operation costing, *def.*, 748
Operational planning, *def.*, 648
Operations,
centralized and decentralized, 1114
income from, *def.*, 164
loss from, *def.*, 164
Opportunity cost, 1003
def., 660, 933
Ordering costs, 1004
Organization, of managerial accounting function, 651
Organization chart, 651
controller's department, *illus.*, 653
depicting management responsibility for production, *illus.*, 1119
illus., 652
partial, for department store with profit centers, *illus.*, 1117
partial, for diversified company with investment centers, *illus.*, 1118
Organizational structure, of corporation, *illus.*, 421
Organization costs, 432
Organizing, 650
def., 649
Other analytical measures, 1170
Other cash funds, 235
Other expense, *def.*, 164
Other income, *def.*, 164
Overapplied overhead, *def.*, 699
Overhead rates,
departmental, 778
plant-wide, 777
predetermined, and product costing, 777
Owner's equity, *def.*, 20

P

Paid-in capital, 459
def., 422
Par, *def.*, 423
Parent company, *def.*, 545
Parent-subsidiary affiliations, accounting for, 546
Partially owned subsidiary, acquired at cost above or below book equity, 550
Participating preferred stock, *def.*, 424
Partner,
admission of, 435
admission of, by contribution of assets, 436
admission of, by purchase of an interest, 436
death of, 437
withdrawal of, 437
Partnership accounting, 433
Partnership agreement, 419
Partnership dissolution, 435
Partnership formation, 433
Partnership,
accounting for, 420
articles of, 419
characteristics of, 418
def., 18
income, participation in, 419
liquidation, 438
net income, division of, 434
property, co-ownership of, 419
Patents, 349
Payable,
accounts, 116
def., 21
notes, 116
Payee, *def.*, 224, 256
Payroll,
and payroll taxes, accounting systems for, 380
checks, 382
def., 374, 380
distribution, 391
illus., 391
register, 390
Payroll taxes, 374
employer's, liability for, 379
recording and paying, 381
Payroll system,
diagram, 383
flow diagram, *illus.*, 384
internal controls for, 384
Pension cost, net periodic, 386
Pensions, liability for, 386
Percentage-of-completion method, 310
Period costs,
and product costs distinguished, *illus.*, 663
def., 662
Periodic inventory system,
and perpetual systems, comparison of, *illus.*, 301
def., 156, 292
Periodic reporting for merchandise enterprises, 157
Periodic system, inventory costing methods under, 294
Perpetual inventory, automated records, 304
Perpetual inventory accounts
(fifo), *illus.*, 303
flow of costs through, *illus.*, 694
(lifo), *illus.*, 303
Perpetual inventory procedures, 694
Perpetual inventory system,
accounting for and reporting inventory under, 300
and internal control, 304
def., 156, 292
end-of-period procedures, 173
inventory costing methods under, 302
recording merchandise transactions in, 171
Petty cash, *def.*, 234
Physical inventory, *def.*, 156, 292
Planning, 650
def., 648

Planning and controlling capital investment expenditures, 976
Plant assets,
acquisition of, 330
acquisition through leasing, 347
additions to, 342
and intangible assets in balance sheet, *illus.*, 351
def., 105, 330
depreciation of, low unit cost, 341
discarding, 344
disposal of, 343
exchange of, 346
exchange of, federal income tax requirements, 346
replacement cost of, 351
sale of, 345
subsidiary ledgers for, 339
Point of sale method, *def. and illus.*, 268
Pooling of interests method,
accounting for business combinations, *def.*, 546
consolidation of financial statements, 555
Post-closing trial balance, *def. and illus.*, 122
Posting,
def., 56,
diagram of, a debit, *illus.*, 61
illus., 62
Posting adjusting entries, 116
Predetermined factory overhead rate, *def.*, 698
Preemptive right, 423
Preferential rights, other, 425
Preferred stock,
cumulative and noncumulative, 425
def., 423
effect on cash flows statement, 603
nonparticipating, 424
participating, 424
Premium,
amortization by interest method, *illus.*, 513
amortization by straight-line method, 512
on bonds, *def.*, 508
Premium on stock,
def., 426
on balance sheet, 427
Prepaid expense,
adjustment for, *illus.*, 104
def., 21, 103
effect on cash flows statement, 601
Present value methods, 966
Present value,
def., 506, 966
of $1 at compound interest, *illus.*, 507, 966
of annuity, *def.*, 969
of annuity of $1 at compound interest, *illus.*, 508, 969, 970
Present value concepts, 506
for bonds payable, 506
Present value index, *def.*, 967
President's letter, 1184, section, *illus.*, 1185
Prevention costs, 1021
Price, transfer, *def.*, 1134
Price approach,
cost price, *def.*, 1136
market, *def.*, 1135
negotiated, *def.*, 1135
Price-earnings (P/E) ratio, *def.*, 1180
Price-level changes, supplemental data on the effects of, 1189
Price-level index, *def.*, 1190
Price theory, *def.*, 940
Price variance,
def., 1088
direct materials, 1089
Prime costs, *def.*, 662
Principle,
cost, *def.*, 18
matching, *def.*, 101
realization, *def.*, 151
Prior period adjustments, *def.*, 468
Proceeds, *def.*, 259, 388
Process cost accounting,
and job order costing compared, 730
illustration of, 739-745
Process costs, and service departments, 736
Process cost system,
def., 694
financial statements for, 743, *illus.*, 744-745
flow of costs through accounts, 731, *illus.*, 742
Process or sell, 933
Processes, automated manufacturing, 1000
Processing cost, 731
Processing departments, service department costs charged to, *illus.*, 737
Product, discontinuance of segment or, 929
Product cost concept, *def.*, 937
Product costing, manufacturing overhead in, 777
Product costs,
def., 662
distortions of, 780
usefulness of, 692
Product life cycle, *illus.*, 943
Product margin, *def.*, 1015
Product price determination, 941
Product pricing, 902
economic theory of, 940
Product selling prices, setting normal, 934
Product warranty liability, 388
Production budget, *illus.*, 1052
Production planning, 903
Professional ethics for accountants, 16
Profit center,
def., 1117
responsibility accounting for, 1121
Profit margin, *def.*, 1131
Profit-making businesses, *illus.*, 18
Profit-sharing bonuses,
determination of, 375
illus., 376
Profit-volume chart, 866
def. 867
illus., 867-869
Profit-volume ratio, *def.*, 858
Profitability,
analysis, 1176
def., 1176
Promissory note,
def., 254
illus., 256
Property, plant, equipment, 330
Protest fee, *def.*, 261
Public corporations, 421
Purchase cost, 1004
Purchase method,
consolidation of financial statements, 547
of accounting for business combinations, *def.*, 546
Purchase orders, *def.*, 695
Purchase requisitions, *def.*, 695
Purchases,
accounting for, 148
allowances, *def.*, 150
discounts, *def.*, 149, 148
net, *def.*, 157
returns, *def.*, 150
Purchases discounts, 233

Q

Qualified plan, 386
Qualitative considerations in capital investment analysis, 971
Quality control,
and managerial accounting, 1022
chart, *illus.*, 1020
total costs, *illus.*, 1022
Quality control costs, 1021,
illus., 1021-2
summary of, 1021
Quantity variance,
def., 1088
direct materials, 1089
Quick assets, *def.*, 1172

R

Rate earned on common stockholders' equity, *def.*, 1178
Rate earned on stockholders' equity, *def.*, 1177
Rate earned on total assets, *def.*, 1177
Rate of return on assets, *def.*, 1130
Rate of return on investment, *def.*, 1130
Rate variance, *def.*, 1089
Ratio of net sales to assets, *def.*, 1176
Ratio of plant assets to long-term liabilities, *def.*, 1174
Ratio,
acid-test, *def.*, 1172
bankers', 1171
current, *def.*, 1171
price-earnings (P/E), *def.*, 1180
quick, *def.*, 1172
working capital, *def.*, 1171
Rationing,
capital, *def.*, 975
decision process, *illus.*, 977
Raw materials cost, 661
Real account, *def.*, 59
Realization principle, *def.*, 151
Realized currency exchange gains and losses, 560
Receivables,
account, 22
aging, *def.*, 265
and temporary investments in the balance sheet, *illus.*, 270
classification of, 254
control over, 255
def., 254
discounted, 390
from installment sales, 267
number of days' sales in, *def.*, 1173
trade, *def.*, 254
uncollectible, 261
Receiving report, *def.*, 695
Reciprocal method, *def.*, 787
Recognition of loss, 347
Registered bonds, *def.*, 506
Regression line, *def.*, 831
Relevance, of managerial accounting reports, 654
Relevant range,
def., 817
for fixed costs, *illus.*, 821
for variable costs, *illus.*, 818
Remittance advice,
def., 224
illus., 225
Replacement cost of plant assets, 351
Replacement of equipment, 932
Report form balance sheet, *def.*, 27, 167
Reports,
budget performance, *def.*, 1060
corporate annual, 1183
independent auditors' section, *def.*, 1184; *illus.*, 1186
interim financial, 1191
management section, *def.*, 1187; *illus.*, 1187
other information, 1190
responsibility accounting, *illus.*, 1120
scrap, *illus.*, 1121
Reported income,
when units manufactured are less than units sold, 897
when units manufactured equal units sold, 896
when units manufactured exceed units sold, 896
Research and development costs, 350
Reserve method, *def.*, 262
Residual income,
by division, 1133
def., 1133
Residual value, *def.*, 332
Responsibility accounting,
def., 1114
for cost centers, 1119
for investment centers, 1128; *illus.*, 1129
for profit centers, 1121
reports, *illus.*, 1120
Responsibility centers, types of, 1116
Retail inventory method,
def., 308
determination of inventory, *illus.*, 308
Retained earnings, 598
appropriation of, 471
def., 22, 422
Retained earnings statement, 115
def., 25
def. and illus., 166
illus., 26, 27, 114, 473
manufacturing enterprise, *illus.*, 709
unusual items, 467
Returns,
purchases, *def.*, 150
sales, *def.*, 153
Revenue expenditures, 343
def., 342
Revenues, 940
accrued, *def.*, 158
def., 22
differential, *def.*, 927
marginal, *def.*, 940
Reversing entry, def. 124
Revision of standards, 1097

S

Safety stock, *def.*, 1007
Salary, *def.*, 375
Sale of plant assets, 345
Sales, 703
Sales allowances, *def.*, 153
Sales analysis, 903
Sales budget, 1051, *illus.*, 1052
Sales discounts, *def.*, 153
Sales mix,
break-even point and, 871
considerations, 871
def., 871, 904
desired profit and, 872
Sales returns, *def.*, 153
Sales taxes, 153
Sales value method, cost allocation, *def.*, 738
Salespersons' analysis, *illus.*, 905
Salvage value, 332
Scattergraph method,
def., 827
estimated total cost for 250,000 units of production, *illus.*, 829
estimated total cost line, *illus.*, 828
Scattergraph, estimated total cost line, *illus.*, 832
Schedule of collections of accounts receivable, *illus.*, 1058
Scrap report, *illus.*, 1121
Scrap value, 332
Secured bonds, *def.*, 506
Securities and Exchange Commission (SEC), *def.*, 15
Securities,
debt, *def.*, 519
equity, *def.*, 541
Segment,
discontinuance of product or, 929
of a business, 1188

revenue by industry, and classes of similar products or services, *illus.*, 1189
Sell,
or lease, 928
or process, 933
Selling costs, *def.*, 663
Selling expenses, *def.*, 164
Semifixed costs, 660; *def.*, 821, 858
Semivariable costs, 660 *def.*, 821, 858
Sequential method, *def.*, 775
Serial bonds, *def.*, 506
Service departments,
and process costs, 736
costs charged to processing departments, *illus.*, 737
def., 736
Service enterprises,
flow of costs through, *illus.*, 708
job order cost systems for, 708
trends in, 664
Setting normal product selling prices, 934
Setting standards, 1086
Shareholders, *def.*, 18
Shipping terms, *illus.*, 155
Short-term notes payable, 387
Signature card, *def.*, 224
Single-step income statement, *def. and illus.*, 166
Sinking fund, bond, *def.*, 514
Slide, *def.*, 68
Sole proprietorship,
accounting for, 418
characteristics of, 417
def., 18
Solvency, *def.*, 1170
Specific identification, 294
Staff department, *def.*, 652
Standard account form, *def. and illus.*, 60
Standard costs,
def., 1085
in accounts, 1096
systems, *def.*, 1085
Standards,
currently attainable, *def.*, 1087
def., 1085
for nonmanufacturing expenses, 1097
ideal, *def.*, 1087
in accounts, 1094
nature and objectives of, 1085
normal, *def.*, 1087
revision of, 1097
setting, 1086
theoretical, *def.*, 1087
types of, 1087
variances from, 1087
variances from, in income statements, *illus.*, 1097
Standards for nonmanufacturing expenses, 1097
Stated value, *def.*, 423
Statement of cash flows,
assembling data and preparing, 596
def., 25, 592
direct method, *illus.*, 595
illus., 26, 29, 606
indirect method, *illus.*, 595
nature of, 591
preparation of, 606, 619
work sheet for, *illus.*, 613
work sheet procedures for, 611
Statement of cost of goods manufactured, 668
illus., 669
Statement of stockholders' equity, 559
Statement,
common-size, *def.*, 1169
financial, 113
income, *def.*, 25, 115, *illus.*, 114
retained earnings, 115; *def.*, 25, 166; *illus.*, 114, 166
State unemployment compensation tax, 380
Step method,
def., 775
of allocation, *illus.*, 776
Step-wise fixed costs,
def., 819,
illus., 820
Step-wise variable costs,
def., 815
illus., 816
Stock certificate, 423
Stock dividends, *def.*, 475
Stock ledger, 703
Stock options, *def.*, 387
Stock outstanding, *def.*, 423
Stock splits,
def., 477
for treasury stock, 478
Stock,
classes of, 423
common, earnings per share on, *def.*, 1179
discount, 426
issuing for assets other than cash, 428
no-par, 428
premium, 426
Stockholders, *def.*, 18, 421
Stockholder's equity, 116
chart of rate earned on, and total assets, *illus.*, 1178
def., 28, 422
rate earned on, *def.*, 1177
rate earned on common, *def.*, 1178
statement of, 559
Stockholders ledger, 426
Stocks,
def., 269
investments in, 541
sale of, 544
Storage costs, 1004
Straight-line method,
amortization of bond discount, 510
amortization of bond premium, 512
def., and *illus.*, 334
Strategic planning, *def.*, 648, 1115
Subsidiary company, *def.*, 545
Subsidiary ledger,
def., 217
plant assets, 339
Sum-of-the-years-digits method,
def., 335
illus., 336
Summary of quality control costs, 1021
Sunk costs, *def.*, 658
Supplemental data on the effects of price-level changes, 1189
Systems,
accounting, 217, types of, 693
design, 219
for payroll and payroll taxes, 380
implementation, 220
inventory, 292
job order cost, *def.*, 693
job order cost, for manufacturing enterprises, 695
principles of accounting, 217
process cost, *def.*, 694
voucher, *def.*, 230
Systems analysis, *def.*, 219

T

T account, *def. and illus.*, 54
Tabulation of economic order quantity, *illus.*, 1007
Tactical planning, 648
Target cost concept, *def.*, 939
Taxable income, *def.*, 461
Temporary account, *def.*, 59
Temporary differences, *def.*, 462
Temporary investments,
and receivables in the balance sheet, *illus.*, 270
def., 268
Term bonds, *def.*, 506
Theoretical standards, *def.*, 1087
Throughput time, *def.*, 1000
Time ticket, *def.*, and *illus.*, 697
Time variance, *def.*, 1089
Time-adjusted rate of return method, *def.*, 968
Timeliness, of managerial accounting reports, 655
Total cost concept, *def.*, 935
Total fixed cost graph, *illus.*, 819
Total quality control (TQC),
costs, *illus.*, 1022
def., 665, 1003
Total step-wise variable cost, *illus.*, 816
Total variable cost graph, *illus.*, 814
Trade-in value, 332
Trade receivables,
def., 254
effect on cash flows statement, 601, 608
Traditional production line, furniture manufacturer, *illus.*, 1001
Transactions,
and the accounting equation, 20
flow of business, data, *illus.*, 59
with foreign companies, accounting for, 559
Transfer pricing, 1134
Transportation costs, 154
Transposition, *def.*, 68
Treasury stock,
cost basis, 430
def., 429
dividends and stock splits for, 478
Trial balance,
columns on work sheet, *illus.*, 108-109
def. and illus., 67
post-closing, *def. and illus.*, 122
Trust indenture, 505
Turnover,
accounts receivable, *def.*, 1172
inventory, *def.*, 1173

U

Uncertainty, 975
Uncollectible accounts,
def., 261
estimate of, *illus.*, 266
Uncollectible receivables, 261
allowance method of accounting for, 284
direct write-off method of accounting for, 167
estimating, 264
Underapplied overhead, *def.*, 699
Unearned revenue, *def.*, 159
Unequal proposal lives, 973
Unfunded plan, 386
Unit contribution margin, *def.*, 859
Unit variable cost graph, *illus.*, 814
Units-of-production method, *def.*, and *illus.*, 334
Unrealized currency exchange gains and losses, 563
Unusual items,
allocation of income tax, 467
presentation in income statement, 467
reporting in financial statements, 465
that affect income statement, 465
that affect retained earnings statement, 467

V

Vacation pay, liability for, 385
Value,
book, *def.*, 106
expected realizable, *def.*, 263
maturity, *def.*, 258
Value of information, 1026
Valuing inventories, 771
Variable cost concept, *def.*, 937
Variable costing, 1014
compared with absorption costing, *illus.*, 894
def., 893
income analysis under, 898
income statement, 894, *illus.*, 895, 896, 898, 900
management's use of, 901
Variable costing income statement, *illus.*, 895, 896, 897, 900
Variable costs,
activity base for, 815
def., 659, 814, 858
estimated total step-wise, *illus.*, 817
relevant range for, 816, *illus.*, 818
step-wise, *def.*, 815
total step-wise, *illus.*, 816
total, graph, *illus.*, 814
unit, graph, *illus.*, 814
Variances,
def., 1085, 1087
direct labor cost, 1089, *illus.*, 1089
direct materials cost, 1088
direct materials price, 1089, illus. 1089
direct materials quantity, *def.*, 1088; *illus.*, 1089
factory overhead controllable, *def.*, 1092; illus. 1093
factory overhead cost, 1091, *illus.*, 1092
factory overhead cost report, *illus.*, 1094
factory overhead volume, *def. and illus.*, 1092
from standards, 1087
from standards in income statement, *illus.*, 1097
illus., 1088
price, *def.*, 1088
quantity, *def.*, 1088
rate, *def.*, 1089
time, *def.*, 1089
Vertical analysis,
comparative balance sheet, *illus.*, 1168
comparative income statement, *illus.*, 1168
def., 1167
Voucher,
def., 230
illus., 231
Voucher system, *def.*, 230

W

Wage and tax statement, *illus.*, 393
Wages, *def.*, 375
Wholly owned subsidiary,
acquired at cost above book equity, 548
acquired at cost below book equity, 550
acquired at cost equal to book equity, 548
Work centers, *def.*, 1002
Work in process, 700
def., 309-310
Work in process inventory, 667
Work sheet,
completed, *illus.*, 112-113
completing, 162, 618
def. 107
for consolidated balance sheet, 553, 557, *illus.*, 554, 558
for financial statements, 107, 166
for merchandising enterprises, 158
for statement of cash flows, *illus.*, 613
illus., 108-109, 160-161, 174
procedures for statement of cash flows, 611
Working capital,
def., 1170
ratio, *def.*, 1171
Working papers, *def.*, 107
Write-offs to the allowance account, 264

Z

Zero-base budgeting, *def.*, 1051
Zero-coupon bonds, *def.*, 514

INDEX OF REAL COMPANIES

Alcoa, 464
Allegis Corp., 505
American Airlines, Inc., 943
Amerock Corp., 700
Amoco Co., 152
Anheuser-Busch, Inc., 464
Apple Computer, Inc., 624
Arvin Industries, Inc., 17
Bethlehem Steel Corp., 425
The Boeing Co., 464
Boston Metal Products Corp., 985
Briggs & Stratton Corp., 390
Campbell Soup Company Ltd., 474
Chrysler Corp., 950
Circus Circus Enterprises, Inc., 464
The Coca-Cola Company, 353
Colgate-Palmolive Co., 559
Colt Industries Inc., 376
Concrete Pipe & Products Co. Inc., 1102
Crazy Eddie Inc., 291
Crusader, 572
Deere & Company, 390
Deloitte & Touche, 1187
Dutch Pantry Inc., 1086
Exxon Corporation, 152
Fay's Incorporated, 1198
Federated Department Stores, Inc., 133
FMC Corporation, 353
Ford Motor Co., 950, 1033
General Mills, Inc., 477, 885
General Motors Corp., 651, 732, 753, 950, 1033
Gruntal & Co., Incorporated, 592
Harris Trust and Savings Bank, 477
H. J. Heinz Company, 870
Hewlett-Packard Co., 714, 1116
Hilton Hotels Corp., 276
Humana Corporation, 377
International Business Machines (IBM) Corp., 464, 505, 972, 1116, 1189
ITT Corporation, 901
J.C. Penney Co., 133, 1185, 1186
K Mart Corp., 133, 187-88
Korn/Ferry International, 1118
KPMG Peat Marwick, 1186
Kraft General Foods, Inc., 549
La-Z-Boy Chair Co., 360
Laventhol & Horwath, 256, 419, 445
Kenneth Leventhal & Co., 353
The Limited, Inc., 133
Forstmann Little & Co., 901
Long Island Lighting Co., 425
McKinsey & Co., 1116
Merck & Co., Inc., 300
Minnesota Mining & Manufacturing (3M) Co., 652
Mobil Oil Corp., 152, 187
Morgan Stanley & Co., 901
Morrison Cohen Singer & Weinstein, 419
Motor Convoy Inc., 870
Munsingwear, Inc., 100
National Cash Register Co. (NCR), 1116
Owens-Corning Fiberglass Corp., 505
Parker Hannifin Corp., 972
Peat, Marwick, Mitchell & Co., 255
PepsiCo, Inc., 464, 1066
Perini Corp., 242
Philip Morris Companies, Inc., 549
Pillsbury Co., 471
The Price Club, 187-88
Proctor & Gamble Co., 134, 915
PTL, 420
Quaker Oats Co., 464
Reebok International Ltd., 376
Remington Aluminum, 1008
Sears, Roebuck and Co., 505, 1187
Seidman & Seidman, 464
Sohio Pipe Line Co., 152
Sperry, 1116
Tandy Corp., 79, 134, 389, 464, 1143
Texaco Inc., 187
Toys "R" Us Inc., 133, 627
Trico Products Inc., 676
Triton Energy Corp., 572
Walgreen Co., 317, 348, 464
Whirpool Corporation, 464
Wm. Wrigley Jr. Co., 1201
Wyatt Company, 377
Xerox Corp., 527
Zenith Electronics Corp., 399

CHECK FIGURES

Agreement between the following "check" figures and those obtained in solving the problems is an indication that a significant portion of the solution is basically correct, aside from matters of form and procedure.

Problem	Check Figure
1-41	Retained earnings balance, $1,920
1-42	Net income, $1,970
1-43	Net income, $2,475
1-44	Net income, $2,105
1-45	Net income, $74,300
1-46	Retained earnings, Oct. 31, $35,215
1-47	Retained earnings, Aug. 31, $7,800
1-41A	Retained earnings balance, $770
1-42A	Net income, $1,550
1-43A	Net income, $3,625
1-44A	Net income, $1,930
1-45A	Net income, $33,450
1-46A	Retained earnings, July 31, $151,265
1-47A	Retained earnings, Aug. 31, $5,930
2-33	Trial balance totals, $19,150
2-34	Trial balance totals, $66,350
2-35	Trial balance totals, $22,265
2-36	Trial balance totals, $103,015
2-37	Trial balance totals, $177,325
2-38	Trial balance totals, $311,450
2-39	Trial balance totals, $33,138.10
2-40	Trial balance totals, $122,380
2-33A	Trial balance totals, $23,210
2-34A	Trial balance totals, $63,400
2-35A	Trial balance totals, $29,100
2-36A	Trial balance totals, $103,265
2-37A	Trial balance totals, $293,670
2-38A	Trial balance totals, $311,350
2-39A	Trial balance totals, $33,138.10
2-40A	Trial balance totals, $109,940
3-43	Net income, $16,435
3-44	Retained earnings, Dec. 31, $65,020
3-45	Net income $1,775.34
3-46	Net income $22,590
3-47	Net income $42,130
3-43A	Net income $23,850
3-44A	Retained earnings, June 30, $26,335
3-45A	Net income $2,870.24
3-46A	Net income $22,424
3-47A	Net income $40,370

Problem	Check Figure
Comprehensive Problem 1	Total assets, Sep. 30, $23,700
4-49	Trial balance totals, $219,590
4-50	Net income, $76,400
4-51	Net income, $54,490
4-52	Retained earnings, Dec. 31, $167,700
4-53	Total assets, $638,250
4-54	Net income, $117,850
4-56	Net income, $139,955
4-58	Net income, $11,960
4-59	Net income, $111,800
4-49A	Trial balance totals, $208,140
4-50A	Net income, $106,050
4-51A	Net income, $84,000
4-52A	Retained earnings, Mar. 31, $187,250
4-53A	Total assets, $677,100
4-54A	Net income, $117,850
4-56A	Net income, $152,150
4-58A	Net income, $50,420
4-59A	Net income, $106,050
Comprehensive Problem 2	Total assets, May 31, $236,820
5-45	Adjusted balance, $16,341
5-46	Adjusted balance, $11,619.88
5-47	Adjusted balance, $12,986.09
5-45A	Adjusted balance, $22,627.55
5-46A	Adjusted balance, $14,879.87
5-47A	Adjusted balance, $9,398.02
6-38	Allowance for doubtful accounts, Dec. 31, $12,500
6-39	Allowance for doubtful accounts, end of 4th year, $12,800
6-40	Income from operations, 3rd year, $66,450
6-41	Gain on repossession, $34
6-42	Total assets, $521,300
6-38A	Allowance for doubtful accounts, Dec. 31, $31,250
6-39A	Allowance for doubtful account, end of 4th year, $11,850
6-40A	Income from operations, 3rd year, $53,240
6-41A	Loss on repossession, $30
6-42A	Total assets, $524,400

Problem	Check Figure
7-37	Net income, $85,000
7-38	Inventory (2), $12,767
7-39	Inventory (4), $2,900
7-40	Total inventory, lower of C or M, $49,710
7-41	Inventory (1), $299,520; (2) $422,750
7-42	Income from contracts, 1993, $655,000
7-37A	Net income, $98,000
7-38A	Inventory, (2), $7,870
7-39A	Inventory, (4), $150,250
7-40A	Total inventory, lower of C or M, $49,855
7-41A	Inventory (1) $213,500; (2) $627,500
7-42A	Income from contracts, 1993, $375,000
8-53	Accumulated depreciation, June 30, 1994, $2,250
8-54	Accumulated depreciation, Sept. 30, 1992, $266,250
8-53A	Accumulated depreciation, Dec. 31, 1993, $1,525
8-54A	Accumulated depreciation, Mar. 31, 1992, $269,700
8-55	Net income, $96,344
8-55A	Net income, $102,900
9-42	Total payroll tax expense, $19,853.10
9-42A	Total payroll tax expense, $19,904.50
Comprehensive Problem 3	Total assets, $997,390
10-49	Total common dividends per share, $15
10-50	Total stockholders' equity, $3,305,000
10-51	Total stockholders' equity, $1,572,875
10-52	Total stockholders' equity, $470,900
10-53	Total stockholders' equity, $426,900
10-49A	Total common dividends per share, $18.60
10-50A	Total stockholders' equity, $2,875,000
10-51A	Total stockholders' equity, $6,711,000
10-52A	Total stockholders' equity, $357,200
10-53A	Total stockholders' equity, $431,700
11-36	Deferred income tax payable, end of 4th year, $17,800
11-37	Net income, $139,000

Problem	Check Figure
11-38	Total retained earnings, $1,640,000
11-39	Total stockholders' equity, $2,202,000
11-40	Total stockholders' equity, $2,588,000
11-41	Net income, $130,200
11-35A	Deferred income tax payable, end of 4th year, $37,200
11-37A	Net income, $93,000
11-38A	Total retained earnings, $1,338,500
11-39A	Total stockholders' equity, $1,180,100
11-40A	Total stockholders' equity, $2,025,000
11-41A	Net income, $105,600
12-40	Earnings per share on common stock, Plan 3 (2), $.40
12-43	Premiums on bonds, end of 1993, $1,100,000
12-44	Carrying amount of bonds, Dec. 31, 1993, $4,436,355
12-40A	Earnings per share on common stock, Plan 3 (2), $.80
12-43A	Discount on bonds, end of 1993, $227,200
12-44A	Carrying amount of bonds, Dec. 31, 1993, $22,095,305
Comprehensive Problem 4	Net income, $400,950
13-34	Total assets, $2,297,000
13-35	Total assets: (1), $2,210,000; (2), $2,160,000; (3), $2,160,000
13-36	Total assets, $2,002,000; net income, $435,800
13-37	Total assets, $4,437,000
13-38	Total assets, $1,202,200
13-39	Total assets, $3,095,000
13-34A	Total assets, $1,610,400
13-35A	Total assets: (1), $1,800,000; (2), $1,740,000 (3), $1,740,000
13-36A	Total assets, $1,938,150; net income, $258,000
13-37A	Total assets, $4,009,000
13-38A	Total assets, $1,017,200
13-39A	Total assets, $3,190,000
14-42	Net cash flow from operating activities, $103,700
14-43	Net cash flow from operating activities, $137,100
14-44	Net cash flow from operating activities, $66,950
14-45	Net cash flow from operating activities, $60,500
14-46	Net cash flow from operating activities, $87,360

Problem	Check Figure
14-42A	Net cash flow from operating activities, $96,800
14-43A	Net cash flow from operating activities, $181,400
14-44A	Net cash flow from operating activities, $73,100
14-45A	Net cash flow from operating activities, $(800)
14-46A	Net cash flow from operating activities, $87,360
16-31	Finished goods, $17,805 (2) f
16-33	Total assets, $765,991 (5)
16-34	Trial balance totals, $1,725,860 (3)
16-31A	Finished goods, $56,425 (4)
16-33A	Total assets, $815,225 (5)
16-34A	Trial balance totals, $1,637,704 (3)
17-32	Work in process, May 31, $15,300 (2) d
17-33	Equivalent units of production, 35,500 (1) a
17-35	Equivalent units of production, 12,000
17-37	Total assets, $746,380 (3)
17-38	Equivalent units of production, 17,500 (1) b
17-32A	Work in process, October 31, $25,415 (2) d
17-33A	Equivalent units of production, 12,500 (1) a
17-35A	Equivalent units of production, 23,870
17-37A	Total assets, $982,640 (3)
17-38A	Equivalent units of production, 29,500 (1) b
18-34	Total costs, Cutting, $1,929,000 (2)
18-35	Total costs, Cutting, $1,913,520 (2)
18-36	Total overhead costs, (6), Product S, $48,000
18-37	Total overhead costs, (2), Product A, $460,000
18-38	Selling price, (5), Product E, $39.36
18-34A	Total costs, Cutting, $917,000 (2)
18-35A	Total costs, Cutting, $916,775 (2)
18-36A	Total overhead costs, (6) Product Q, $95,000
18-37A	Total overhead costs, (2) Product W, $61,700
18-38A	Selling price, (5), Product H, $31.00
20-46	Present breakeven sales (units), 13,750 (3)

Problem	Check Figure
20-47	Anticipated break-even sales (units), 3,000 (1)
20-48	Maximum operating profit: (2), $160,000; (b)(4), $120,000 (b)
20-50	Break-even point, $600,000 (3) b
20-46A	Present break-even sales (units), 40,000 (3)
20-47A	Anticipated break-even sales (units), 10,000 (1)
20-48A	Maximum operating profit: (2), $135,000; (b)(4) $90,000 (b)
20-50A	Break-even point, $1,500,000 (3) b
21-27	Income from operations (2), $37,500 (2)
21-28	Operating loss, $53,600 (2)
21-29	Income from operations for June (2b), $298,000
21-30	Contribution margin ratio, Thom, 17.7 (1)
21-31	Total contribution margin (1), $1,027,200; (3), $1,122,000
21-32	Decrease in contribution margin, $63,000 (1)
21-27A	Income from operations (2), $1,946,000
21-28A	Operating loss, $47,000 (1) & (2)
21-29A	Income from operations for August (2B), $148,000
21-30A	Contribution margin ratio, Thom, 15.0
21-31A	Total contribution margin (1), $466,300 (3), $511,280
21-32A	Decrease in contribution margin, $81,000 (1)
22-35	Gain from operating warehouse, $280,000 (1)
22-36	Net cost reduction, $450,000 (1)
22-37	Gain from promotion campaign, Product F, $90,000 (1)
22-38	Net advantage, $3,000 (1)
22-39	Net advantage, $9,000 (1)
22-40	Selling price, $19.20 (2)
22-35A	Loss from operating warehouse, $70,000 (1)
22-36A	Net cost reduction, $500,000 (1)
22-37A	Gain from promotion campaign, Product A, $105,000 (1)
22-38A	Net advantage, $900 (1)
22-39A	Net advantage, $7,500 (1)
22-40A	Selling price, $21.60 (2) c
23-29	Net present value Project W, $41,420 (1) b
23-30	Net present value Project N, $39,005 (1) b

Problem	Check Figure
23-31	Present value index, Proposal L, .94 (2)
23-32	Internal rate of return, Proposal E, 20% (2) b
23-33	Net present value, (2) Project II $6,360
23-34	Net present value Proposal E, $19,673 (4)
23-29A	Net present value Project K, $3,545
23-30A	Net present value Project R, $21,450 (1) b
23-31A	Present value index, Proposal V, 1.06 (2)
23-32A	Internal rate of return, Proposal J, 10% (2) b
23-33A	Net present value, (2) Project B, $7,080 (1)
23-34A	Net present value, Proposal E, $19,673 (4)
24-50	EOQ, 540 units (3)
24-51	EOQ, (3), 180 units
24-52	Most economical plan (4), Plan 2
24-53	Break-even sales, (2), 10,500
24-54	Total product margin, $55,500 (1)
24-55	Net present value (1), $5,901 (1)
24-50A	EOQ, 1,200 units (3)
24-51A	EOQ, (3), 300 units
24-52A	Most economic plan (4), Plan 3
24-53A	Break-even sales, (2), 10,250
24-54A	Total product margin, $85,800 (1)
24-55A	Net present value (1), $21,530
25-28	Total sales for 1993, $2,559,860 (3)
25-29	Total production, Product E, 41,600 units (2)
25-30	Net income, $857,070 (8)
25-31	Defiency, June, $16,900 (1)
25-32	Net income, $236,500; cash, $39,500 (2) a
25-28A	Total sales for 1993, $6,021,400 (3)
25-29A	Total production, Product E, 13,500 units (2)
25-30A	Net income, $670,170 (8)
25-31A	Excess, August, $3,200 (1)
25-32A	Net income, $175,500; (1) cash, $54,500 (2) a
26-27	Total factory overhead cost variance - unfavorable, $10,900 c
26-28	Total factory overhead cost variance - unfavorable, $3,650

Problem	Check Figure
26-29	Total factory overhead cost variance - favorable $2,020
26-30	Work in process, $4,950 (credit) (2)
26-31	Income before income tax, $49,000
26-27A	Total factory overhead cost variance - unfavorable, $8,800c
26-28A	Total factory overhead cost variance - unfavorable, $3,160
26-29A	Total factory overhead cost variance - unfavorable, $42,150(2)
26-30A	Work in process, $11,590 (2)
26-31A	Income before income tax, $29,990
27-44	Income before income tax, $43,750 (1)
27-45	Total departmental margin, $153,956 (1)
27-46	Total departmental margin, $377,900 (1)
27-47	Net income, $138,600
27-48	ROI, Division R, 16.8% (2)
27-49	ROI, Proposal 3, 18.5% (3)
27-50	Division V is most profitable (3)
27-51	ROI, Division C 19.5% (2)
27-44A	Income before income tax, $60,900 (1)
27-45A	Total departmental margin, $219,610 (1)
27-46A	Total departmental margin, $162,800
27-47A	Net income, $53,600
27-48A	ROI, Division Z, 18% (2)
27-49A	ROI, Proposal 3, 17.4% (3)
27-51A	ROI, Division W, 19% (2)
28-44	Working Capital, Dec. 31, 1992, $112,500 (4)
28-44A	Working Capital, Dec. 31, 1992, $199,500 (4)
F-2	Accounts payable, May 31, $51,681.35
F-3	Accounts payable, Mar. 31, $12,727
F-4	Accounts receivable, May 31, $14,570
F-5	Accounts receivable, July 31, $10,860
F-6	Accounts receivable, June 30, $19,950
F-7	Trial balance totals, $171,760

ABBREVIATIONS & ACRONYMS

ABBREVIATIONS AND ACRONYMS
Commonly Used in Business and Accounting

AAA	American Accounting Association
ABC	Activity-based costing
ACRS	Accelerated Cost Recovery System
AICPA	American Institute of Certified Public Accountants
CIA	Certified Internal Auditor
CIM	Computer-integrated manufacturing
CMA	Certified Management Accountant
CPA	Certified Public Accountant
Cr.	Credit
Dr.	Debit
EFT	Electronic funds transfer
EOQ	Economic order quantity
EPS	Earnings per share
FAF	Financial Accounting Foundation
FASB	Financial Accounting Standards Board
FEI	Financial Executives Institute
FICA tax	Federal Insurance Contributions Act tax
FIFO	First-in, first-out
FOB	Free on board
GAAP	Generally accepted accounting principles
GASB	Governmental Accounting Standards Board
GNP	Gross National Product
IRC	Internal Revenue Code
IRS	Internal Revenue Service
JIT	Just-in-time
LIFO	Last-in, first-out
Lower of C or M	Lower of cost or market
MACRS	Modified Accelerated Cost Recovery System
MRP	Materials requirements planning
NAA	National Association of Accountants
n/30	Net 30
n/eom	Net, end-of-month
P/E Ratio	Price-earnings ratio
POS	Point of sale
ROI	Return on investment
SEC	Securities and Exchange Commission
TQC	Total quality control

CLASSIFICATION OF ACCOUNTS

Account Title	Account Classification	Normal Balance	Financial Statement
Accounts Payable	Current liability	Credit	Balance sheet
Accounts Receivable	Current asset	Debit	Balance sheet
Accumulated Depreciation	Plant asset	Credit	Balance sheet
Accumulated Depletion	Plant asset	Credit	Balance sheet
Advertising Expense	Operating expense	Debit	Income statement
Allowance for Doubtful Accounts	Current asset	Credit	Balance sheet
Amortization Expense	Operating expense	Debit	Income statement
Appropriation for ________	Stockholders' equity	Credit	Retained earnings statement/ Balance sheet
Bonds Payable	Long-term liability	Credit	Balance sheet
Building	Plant asset	Debit	Balance sheet
________ Capital	Owners' equity	Credit	Statement of owner's equity/ Balance sheet
Capital Stock	Stockholders' equity	Credit	Balance sheet
Cash	Current asset	Debit	Balance sheet
Cash Dividends	Stockholders' equity	Debit	Retained earnings statement
Cash Dividends Payable	Current liability	Credit	Balance sheet
Common Stock	Stockholders' equity	Credit	Balance sheet
Cost of Merchandise (Goods) Sold	Cost of merchandise (goods sold)	Debit	Income statement
Deferred Income Tax	Current liability/Long-term liability	Credit	Balance sheet
Depletion Expense	Operating expense	Debit	Income statement
Discount on Bonds Payable	Long-term liability	Debit	Balance sheet
Discounts Lost	Other expense	Debit	Income statement
Dividend Income	Other income	Credit	Income statement
Dividends	Stockholders' equity	Debit	Retained earnings statement
Donated Capital	Stockholders' equity	Credit	Balance sheet
Employees Federal Income Tax Payable	Current liability	Credit	Balance sheet
Equipment	Plant asset	Debit	Balance sheet
Exchange Gain	Other income	Credit	Income statement
Exchange Loss	Other expense	Debit	Income statement
Factory Overhead (Overapplied)	Deferred credit	Credit	Balance sheet (interim)
Factory Overhead (Underapplied)	Deferred debit	Debit	Balance sheet (interim)
Federal Income Tax Payable	Current liability	Credit	Balance sheet
Federal Unemployment Tax Payable	Current liability	Credit	Balance sheet
FICA Tax Payable	Current liability	Credit	Balance sheet
Finished Goods	Current asset	Debit	Balance sheet
Gain on Disposal of Plant Assets	Other income	Credit	Income statement
Gain on Redemption of Bonds	Extraordinary item	Credit	Income statement
Gain on Sale of Investments	Other income	Credit	Income statement
Goodwill	Intangible asset	Debit	Balance sheet
Income Tax	Income tax	Debit	Income statement
Income Tax Payable	Current liability	Credit	Balance sheet
Insurance Expense	Operating expense	Debit	Income statement
Interest Expense	Other expense	Debit	Income statement
Interest Income	Other income	Credit	Income statement
Interest Receivable	Current asset	Debit	Balance sheet
Investment in Bonds	Investment	Debit	Balance sheet
Investment in Stocks	Investment	Debit	Balance sheet
Investment in Subsidiary	Investment	Debit	Balance sheet